AF479004

BRITISH VISION

Observation and Imagination in British Art 1750-1950

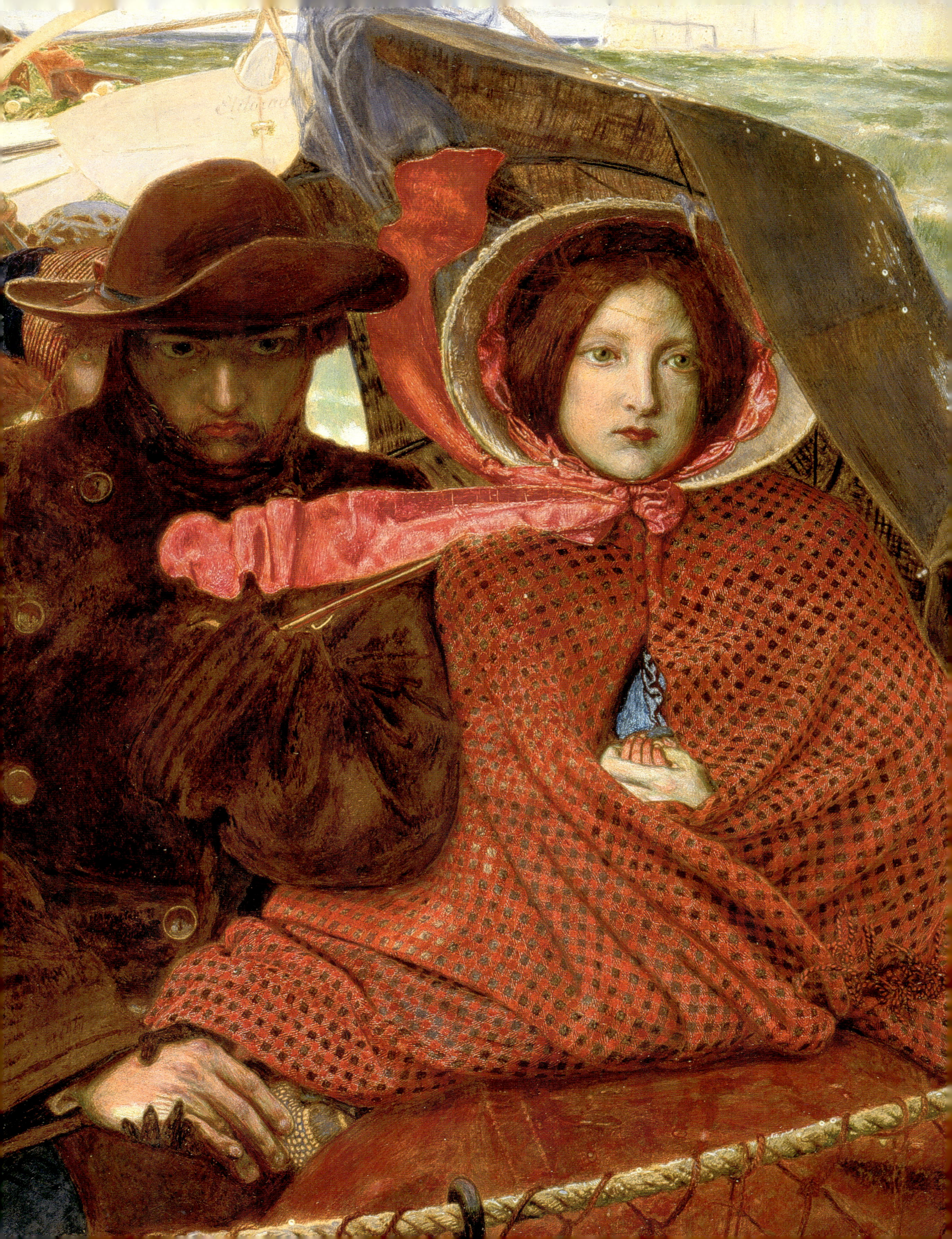

ACKNOWLEDGEMENTS

As this book goes to press the Museum voor Schone Kunsten Ghent would like to thank everyone who contributed to 'British Vision'.

Government of Flanders

Kris Peeters, Prime Minister
Yves Leterme, former Prime Minister
Fientje Moerman, Deputy Prime Minister
Bert Anciaux, Flemish Minister responsible for Culture
Geert Bourgeois, Flemish Minister responsible for Tourism

Federal Government

Guy Verhofstadt, outgoing First Minister
Freya Van den Bossche, Deputy First Minister
Bruno Tuybens, State Secretary for Public Sector Enterprises

Province of Oost-Vlaanderen

André Denys, Governor

City of Ghent

Daniël Termont, Mayor
Lieven Decaluwe, Alderman for Culture

The Friends of the Museum voor Schone Kunsten
Dany Vandenbossche, Chairman

The exhibition was supported by

His Excellency Mr Richard Kinchen, MVO
Ambassador of the United Kingdom

The British Council
Andrea Rose, Director of Visual Arts, London
Stephan Roman, Regional Director for Western Europe and North America, Brussels

---

The exhibition project benefited from the close collaboration of the Tate and Victoria and Albert Museum, London, and the Yale Center for British Art, New Haven.

The organisers of the exhibition thank the following artists, estates, private collectors and institutions:

Mr and Mrs David Dallas, Mr Andrew Edmunds, Mr and Mrs Thomas Gibson, Richard Hamilton, the Earl and Countess of Harewood, the estate of Barbara Hepworth, Leon Kossoff, the Henry Moore Family Collection, the Robertson Collection and the Peter Simon Family Trust.

And the private collectors who wish to remain anonymous.

Lending Institutions

Aberdeen Art Gallery & Museums Collections: Jennifer Melville, Christine Rew, Sally McIntosh, Emily Thomson

Aberystwyth, National Library of Wales: Andrew Green, Jamie Thomas, Camway McDonald

Amsterdam, Stedelijk Museum: Gijs van Tuyl, Ron Ruyzendael, Ankie van den Berg

Bath, Holburne Museum: Amina Wright

Bedburg Hau, Stiftung Museum Schloss Moyland: Barbara Strieder

Bedford, Cecil Higgins Art Gallery: Caroline Bacon

Belfast, Ulster Museum: Martyn Anglesea, Anne Stewart, Anne Orr

Birkenhead, Williamson Art Gallery and Museum: Colin Simpson

Birmingham, Barber Institute of Fine Arts, University of Birmingham: Richard Verdi, Paul Spencer-Longhurst, Yvonne Locke

Birmingham Museum & Art Gallery: Brendan Flynn, Varshali Patel, Alicia Bradley

Bradford, National Media Museum: Colin Philpott, Toni Booth, Paul Goodman, Brian Liddy

Brighton, Royal Pavilion, Libraries & Museum: Pauline Scott-Garrett, David Beevers

Brussels, Koninklijke Sterrenwacht van België: Pierre Alexander, Roger Van de Linden

Cambridge, Fitzwilliam Museum: David Scrase, Jane Munro, Thyrza Smith, Liz Woods

Cambridge, Kettle's Yard, University of Cambridge: Michael Harrison, Sebastiano Barassi, Maree Allitt

Cardiff, Amgueddfa Cymru – National Museum Wales: Michael Tooby, Oliver Fairclough, Tim Egan, Kay Kays

Carlisle, Tullie House Museum & Art Gallery: David Clarke, Melanie Gardner

Cookham, Stanley Spencer Gallery: Richard Hurley, Diana Benson

Derby Museums and Art Gallery: Jonathan Wallis, Sarah Allard, Diana Peake

Edinburgh, City of Edinburgh Museums and Galleries: Ian O'Riordan, David Patterson

Edinburgh, National Gallery of Scotland: Michael Clarke, Janice Slater, Anne Steinberg, Shona Corner, Rachel Travers

Edinburgh, Scottish National Gallery of Modern Art: Patrick Elliott, Keith Hartley

Edinburgh, Scottish National Portrait Gallery: James Holloway, Sara Stevenson

Ghent, Stedelijk Museum voor Actuele Kunst: Philippe Van Cauteren, Rom Bohez

The Hague, Gemeentemuseum: Wim van Krimpen, Hans Janssen, Peter Loorij

Hamburg, Departmentbibliothek Physik, Universität Hamburg / MIN-Facultät: Sabine Hilger

Ipswich Borough Council Museums & Galleries: Peter Berridge, Robert Entwhistle, Joan Lyall

Kendal, Abbot Hall Art Gallery: Edward King, Hannah Neale

Leeds, Harewood House Trust: Heather Griffiths, David Stockdale, Melissa Gallimore

Leeds Museums & Galleries (City Art Gallery): Layla Bloom, Jen Kaines, Jim Bright, Rebecca Grant, Sheel Bharj

Leicester, Arts & Museums Service: Nick Gordon, Simon Lake

Leuven, K.U. Leuven, Centrale Bibliotheek: Christiaan Coppens, Katherina Smeyers

Lille, Palais des Beaux-Arts: Alain Tapié, Annie Scottez-De Wambrechies

Liverpool, National Museums Liverpool, Walker Art Gallery and Lady Lever Art Gallery: Alex Kidson, Godfrey Burke

London, Arts Council Collection, South Bank Centre: Caroline Douglas, Jill Constantine, Christie Countin, Marianne Mulvey

London, Ben Uri Art Gallery, The London Jewish Museum of Art: David Aronowitz-Mercer, David Glasser, Suzanne Lewis, Julia Weiner

London, British Council: Andrea Rose, Diana Eccles, Richard Riley, Nansi O'Connor, Antony Watson

London, British Library: Sally Brown, Andrea Clarke, Barbara O'Connor, Robert Davies, John Falconer

London, British Museum: Neil McGregor, Antony Griffiths, Kim Sloan, Janice Reading, Philippa Kirkham

London, The Samuel Courtauld Trust, Courtauld Institute of Art Gallery: Deborah Swallow, Ernst Vegelin, Julia Blanks

London, Guildhall Art Gallery, City of London: Vivien Knight, Jeremy Johnson

London, Imperial War Museum: Robert Crawford, Roger Tolson, Jenny Wood, Pauline Alwright

London, Museum of London: Mark Bills, Alex Werner, Nickos Gogolos

London, National Portrait Gallery: Sandy Nairne, Paul Moorhouse, David McNeff

London, The National Trust: Alistair Laing, Chezzey Brownen

London, Palestine Exploration Fund: Felicity Cobbing

London, Royal Academy of Arts: Mary Anne Stevens, Edwina Mulvaney, Miranda Bennion

London, Royal College of Art Collection: Christopher Frayling, Juliet Thorp

London, Royal Society of Arts: Penny Egan, Rob Baker

London, Science Museum: Martin Earwicker, Alison Boyle, Maria Rollo

London, Tate: Nicholas Serota, Stephen Deuchar, Alex Beard, Caroline Collier, Anne Lyles, Nicola Moorby, Alison Smith, Robert Upstone, Ian Warrell, Rosie Bass, Susan Breen, Catherine Clement, Nicole Samõez da Silva, Marcus Leith, Marcella Leith

London, University College London: Emma Chambers, Andrea Fredericksen

London, Victoria and Albert Museum: Mark Jones, Mark Evans, Martin Barnes, Julius Bryant, Stephen Calloway, Ruth Hibbard, Juliet Creosole, Rebecca Wallace, Peter Ellis, Roxanne Peters

London, William Morris Gallery: Peter McCormack, Amy Gaimster

Manchester Art Gallery: Virgina Tandy, Sandra Martin, Phillipa Wood

Manchester, Whitworth Art Gallery, University of Manchester: Maria Balshaw, Heather Birchall, Jacqui Fortnum, Gillian Smithson

Much Hadham, Henry Moore Foundation: Richard Calvocoressi, Anita Feldman-Bennett, Charlotte Booth

New Haven, Yale Center for British Art, Paul Mellon Collection: Amy Meyers, Scott Wilcox, Angus Trumble, Elisabeth Fairman, Timothy Goodhue, Melissa Gold-Fournier

New York, New York Public Library: Roberta Waddell, Nicole Simpson, Sonia Dingilian

Newcastle-upon-Tyne, Laing Art Gallery: Julie Milne, Sarah Richardson, Lesley Richardson

Newmarket, Stewards of the Jockey Club: Julian Richmond-Watson, William Gittus

Norwich, Norfolk Museums & Archaeology Service: Vanessa Trevelyan, Caroline Ellis

Nottingham City Museum & Galleries: Michael Williams, Sarah Skinner

Nottingham, University of Nottingham Library, Manuscripts and Special Collections: Dorothy Johnson, Corinne Fawcett

Oldham, Gallery Oldham: Stephan Whittle, Dinah Winch

Oxford, Ashmolean Museum: Christopher Brown, Colin Harrison, Geraldine Glynn, Aisha Gibbons

Paris, Musée d'Orsay: Serge Lemoine, Delphine Pechard, Odile Michel

Paris, Museé du Louvre: Henri Loyrette, Vincent Pomarède, Olivier Meslay, Carel van Tuyll van Serooskerken, Aurélie Merle

Preston, Harris Museum & Art Gallery: Alexandra Walker, Amanda Draper

Rotterdam, Museum Boijmans Van Beuningen: Sjarel Ex, Jaap Guldemond

Salford, The L.S. Lowry Collection: Mark Doyle, Rosie Grieve

Southampton City Art Gallery: Tim Craven, Esta Mion-Jones, Clare Mitchell, John Lawrence, Peter Jones

Southport, Atkinson Art Gallery: Joanna Jones

Stuttgart, Staatsgalerie: Christian von Holst, Christofer Conrad, Peter Frei

Sudbury, Gainsborough's House: Diane Perkins, Linda Theophilus

Swansea, Glynn Vivian Art Gallery: Jenni Spencer-Davies

York, National Railway Museum: Andrew Scott, Helen Ashby, Helen Batchelor

Zurich, Kunsthaus: Christian Klemm, Karin Marti

Additional Thanks

Andrea Addison, Bente Arnild, Anne-Louise Ballis, Tim Barringer, Nancy Behaegel, Kim Beirnaert, Nigel Bellingham, David Bindman, Patrick Bourne, Sophie Bowness, Alan Bowness, Rachel Boyd, Ivor Braka, Lindsay Brooks, Dorothee Capelle, Jos Casier, Roger Claeys, Gordon Cooke, David Peters Corbett, Alexander Corcoran, Alan Cristea, David Dallas, Kristin Van Damme, Jan Debbaut, Helena De Brabandere, Alan Doig, Bart Doucet, Hannelore Duflou, Sally Dummer, Mark Graham Dunn, Xanthe Edmunds, Pascal Ennaert, Urs Fischer, Thomas Gibson, Dana Gildenhorn, William Gittus, Anne Goodchild, Peter Goulds, Richard Green, Roland Gulliver, Petra Gunst, Emmeline Hallmark, John Hayes, Sophie Hayles, Kaat Heirbrant, Michiel Hendryckx, Anthony Hyne, David Fraser Jenkins, John Paul Kernot, John A. Kim, Catherine Lampert, Katrien Laporte, Jerry Losty, Anne Low, Carol Ann Lowry, Anne Luyckx, Hans Martens, Thérèse Meier, Ann Mestdag, Corinne Miller, Cheska Moon, Mary Moore, Christopher Newall, Charles Nugent, Jenny Page, John Pasmore, Nic Peeters, Ivan Pittevils, Martin Postle, Rudy Van Quaquebeke, Penny Rae, Judith Ravenscroft, James Rawlin, Diana Rawstron, Julian Richmond-Watson, Alex Robertson, Duncan Robinson, Nigel Semmens, Emma Simpson, Peyton Skipwith, Iain Slessor, Alistair Smith, Lennie Stevens, Bill Stevenson, Koen Van Synghel, Nancy Thomson, Lisa Tickner, Julian Treuherz, Wim Vandendriessche, Joris Verdoodt, Raymonda Verdyck, Jodie Waldron, Anna Warrilow, Helen Waters, Angela Weight, Henry Wemyss, Johan Van de Wiele

Museum of Fine Arts Personnel

René Albani, Liliane De Backer, Pascale De Backer, Jos De Baeck, Cinderella Blomme, Achiel Bonne, Carine Van Bruwaene, Michel Burez, Sofie Corneillie, Ronny De Corte, Marie Decoodt, Bruno Fornari, Lieven Gerard, Patrick Gerard, Isabelle Heytens, Anne Marie Jacobs, Pierre De Keuckeleire, Senta Kochanek, Ilker Kurtulus, Helke Lauwaert, Pascale Van Lent, Carine Lievens, Jan Van Looveren, Pascale De Meyer, Ruth Monteyne, Lucien Mussche, Annick De Muynck, Rita De Muynck, Moniek Nagels, Hassan Norouzi, Tine Van Poucke, Marleen Schermie, Johan De Smet, Monique Tahon-Vanroose, Corinne Trop, Nathalie Verbeken, Veerle Verhasselt, Nora Verhoeyen, Cathérine Verleysen, Norbert Verschoore, Brigitte De Vos, Marhilde Wiels

Special thanks to

The Courtauld Institute of Art Library, London, the City Services of Ghent, Museum Dr Guislain, Museum voor Industriële Archeologie en Textiel (MIAT), Design Museum, Kunstencentrum Vooruit, Stedelijke Openbare Bibliotheek Ghent, Handelsbeurs, De Bijloke Muziekcentrum, Festival van Vlaanderen

I speak of spiritual things, not of natural;
of things known only to myself and to spirits of good and evil,
but not known to men on earth.

WILLIAM BLAKE

In such an age as this, painting should be *understood*,
not looked at with blind wonder, nor considered only as a poetic aspiration,
but as a pursuit, *legitimate*, *scientific* and *mechanical*.

JOHN CONSTABLE

PREFACE

'British Vision' is the first major exhibition in the renovated Museum voor Schone Kunsten, which reopened in the spring. The museum was closed for four years for a thorough renovation during which the building was restored inside and out and equipped with modern technical facilities. It is exactly ten years since the museum last staged a project of this magnitude. In 1997 the museum mounted the 'Paris-Bruxelles/Brussel-Parijs' exhibition, an exhibition about Franco-Belgian artistic relationships in the nineteenth century, in association with the Musée d'Orsay.

In 'British Vision' we are literally looking the other way in an introduction to an artistic tradition which was often an alternative to the artistic life of Paris in the period from around 1750 to 1950.

British culture has often been an inspiring factor in Europe since the eighteenth century, when Great Britain became a global economic power, and the Anglo-Saxon influence has been predominant in several European countries since the 1960s. Against this background it is surprising that British art, surely an essential component of this engaging culture, is so rarely seen in exhibitions in Europe. The major figures are sometimes represented in retrospectives, as were Constable and Hogarth in Paris recently, but it has been decades since there was a retrospective of British art.

'British Vision' is therefore a long-awaited opportunity to discover or rediscover British art. And, for the first time, this exhibition forges a link between earlier British art and the developments in the twentieth century. The organizers believe that there are constants – aspects of a British Vision – that unite the British 'Golden Age' and modern art.

Although the Museum voor Schone Kunsten has a tradition in international cooperation and in organizing international exhibitions, 'British Vision' was still a special challenge. Therefore it was decided to collaborate on different government levels in order to realise this important project. The City of Ghent and the Flemish Government took the initiative and were supported in this by the Federal Government and the Province of Oost-Vlaanderen. In London and in Brussels we received the support of the British Council. The Kredietbank and the Nationale Loterij of Belgium, together with several project sponsors, provided more financial support. We thank the many museums, private collectors and specialists who have contributed to the success of this exhibition. Thanks to all these forms of collaboration it has been possible to mount an exhibition with more than three hundred items, loaned by no fewer than seventy-nine museums and several private collections. This unique overview of two centuries of British art is an important moment in the history of the Museum voor Schone Kunsten, and of the entire European community.

Kris Peeters
Prime Minister
of the Flemish Government

Bert Anciaux
Flemish Minister
responsible for Culture

Lieven Decaluwe
Alderman for Culture
of the City of Ghent

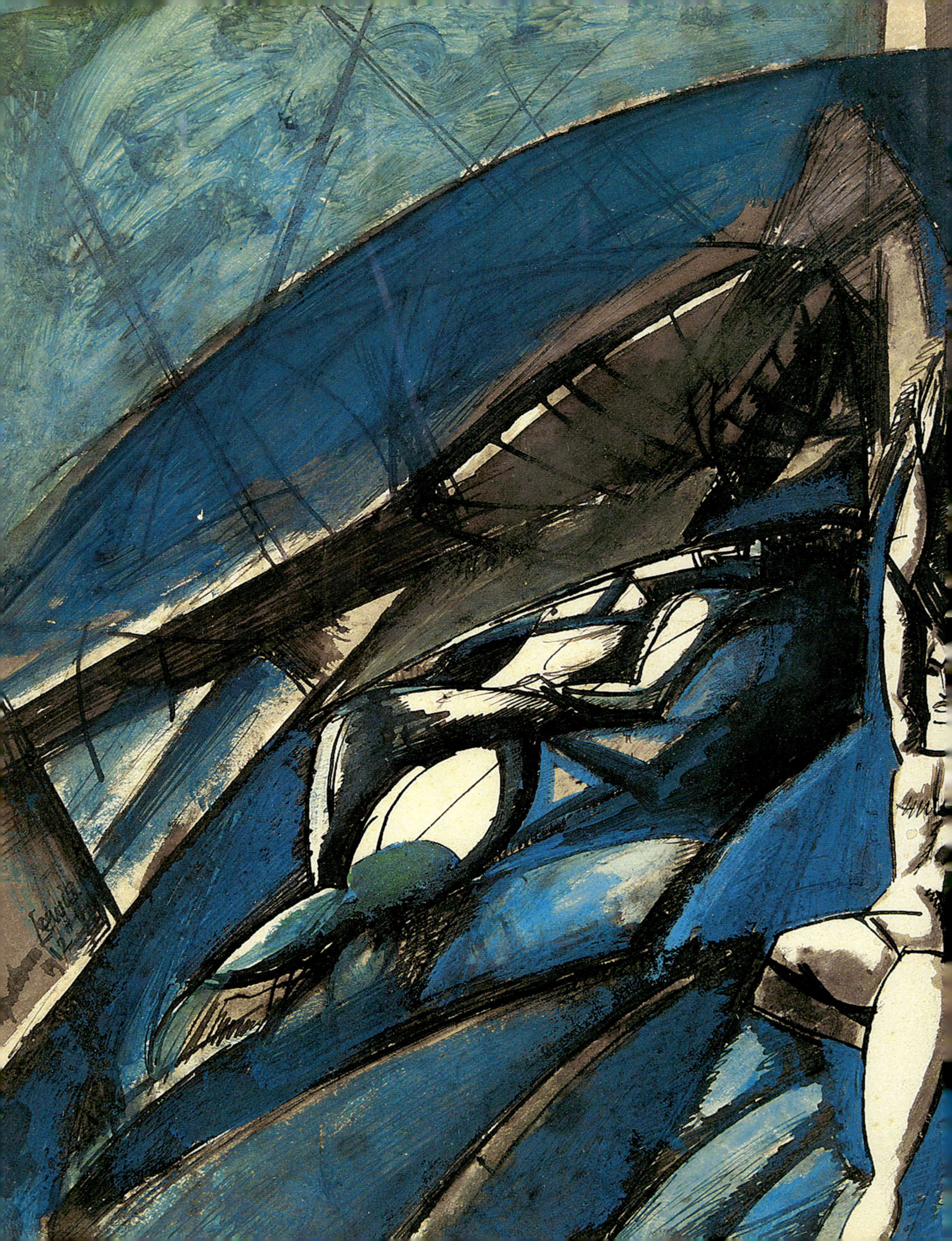

INTRODUCTION

ROBERT HOOZEE

From the Industrial Revolution onward – that is, from around the middle of the eighteenth century – Great Britain has played a prominent role in western art. At the risk of some oversimplification, one could say that the visual arts in Britain before that time were determined by art and artists imported from the Continent. Although *émigrés* and foreign influences would continue to play a significant role, a recognizably British tradition began to evolve from around 1750. This development coincided with the formation of what has been called the 'first modern society'. Guided by a fervent liberalism and influenced by an upcoming class of entrepreneurs and tradesmen, this modern society implied a new relationship with the arts. As has often been pointed out, a new public for the arts arose during this period, a new context in which artists found more possibilities for reaching an audience.

At the beginning of the eighteenth century, Voltaire was already full of praise for the climate of freedom he encountered in England. With respect to religion, he wrote in 1726 that 'England is properly the country of sectarists, ... An Englishman, as one to whom liberty is natural, may go to heaven his own way.'[1] Until well into the nineteenth century, artists and critics were fascinated by the specific circumstances under which art in Great Britain was able to thrive. One of these, Théophile Thoré, wrote in 1863:

> Self-government is complete in English art, just as it is in all the institutions and all the customs of this proud people, where individuality asserts itself. It is this that is lacking in French artists, who almost always obey some higher authority, tradition or prejudice.[2]

Many comments from this period and later can be reduced to an opposition between the canon of western art, on the one hand, and a British alternative on the other. Of course, this is a crude simplification, because other alternatives appeared elsewhere in Europe as well – the German Nazarenes, for example, or Gustave Courbet. Nevertheless, it has some basis in truth, and one is forced to acknowledge that a succession of alternative moments occurred in Great Britain that is sufficiently homogeneous to be identified as a kind of marginal tradition. In the present exhibition, we are concerned with this margin, alongside the mainstream of art history (if that idea can still be accepted). As the subtitle of the exhibition implies, it is possible to distinguish between two characteristics or attitudes that link these scattered moments in time: the empirical stance, or observation, on the one hand, and the imaginative approach, or inclination towards the visionary, on the other.

Before proceeding further, we should take a moment to consider another aspect of our concept – namely, the fact that we are taking a national school as a point of departure. It will be generally agreed that the nationalist art history of the past is a historically determined, outmoded way to approach art. Nevertheless, studies continue to be written and exhibitions organized in which the art of a given country is isolated or put in the context of international developments. The most obvious reason for this is that art frequently *did* develop within national boundaries – something that only really began to change in the 1960s. In our case, the national model was a natural choice as a point of departure, and our decision was reinforced because we were not so much interested in what was being played out within national boundaries but wanted to get a feeling for what it was that made it so typically British or English. However, it must be understood that we do not mean national in the nationalist sense, but rather in the sense proposed in an interview by the Italian artist Luciano Fabro: 'Nationality is an address, not a consciousness. A lot of things happen at that address.'[3] We have deliberately used the word 'British' in the title of the exhibition, because artists from all parts of Britain and Ireland are included. But we are aware that our exhibition necessarily focuses on England, with London as the main artistic centre where artists from all over the country, from Europe and America, generally worked and exhibited.

Percy Wyndham Lewis, ***Study in Blue*** (detail), cat. 289

From the eighteenth century onwards, England has been a location, an environment where a specific artistic approach was possible. An analysis of this environment in socio-cultural terms would take us too far, but the many studies devoted to the subject point to a number of regularly recurring factors, such as new technologies, urbanization, the rise of a new middle class, the climate, isolation, Protestantism and the limited impact of institutions like the Academy. Let us just say that it was above all a combination of these circumstances that produced the British artistic character, rather than any inherent national characteristics.

In British artistic life from the eighteenth to the twentieth century, there was no shortage of attempts to establish a national school along Continental lines through the creation of official institutions and the publication of theoretical works. The founding of the Royal Academy and the writings of Joshua Reynolds are the best-known examples. What interests us in the present exhibition, however, is what took place alongside, or in spite of, this academic life. Academicism stands for universal rules and discipline. The other side chooses the particular, which is perhaps the key word. Something of this division is found in Blake's well-known protest against Reynolds: 'To Generalize is to be an Idiot. To Particularize is the Alone Distinction of Merit.'[4] In focusing on observation and imagination as components of this alternative tradition we are not attempting a complete overview of British art.[5] Nor can Britishness be reduced to these two components only – although we find them important enough to serve as red threads running throughout our story.

'Observation' implies a methodical and empirical approach, which is strongly present at certain moments. It is an adherence to details, a systematic registration of observed facts, a consideration of nature as if for the first time. This manner of observation is very strong in the work of William Hogarth and John Constable. It also determined the methods of the Pre-Raphaelites, who, furthermore, provided a detailed picture of their systematic, dedicated manner of working in their letters and diaries. After the Pre-Raphaelites, this accuracy vanished in the face of French Naturalism, Impressionism and Fauvism, but it returned in the work of a number of modern artists – particularly Stanley Spencer, who once again rejected fluidity and facility in favour of setting to work with a searching gaze and patient craftsmanship. There are also contemporary artists active in Great Britain today who share the same sense of social observation as Hogarth or the humble depiction of nature so characteristic of Constable. When William Blake saw a study of a tree by Constable, he cried out, 'Why, this is not drawing, but inspiration,' to which Constable answered, 'I never knew it before; I meant it for drawing.'[6] This well-known anecdote, which is also cited elsewhere in the catalogue (p. 46), illustrates an artistic 'no nonsense' approach. The same approach, which places the process of painting and drawing above the conceptual, characterizes the work of important contemporary artists such as Lucian Freud, Frank Auerbach and Leon Kossoff.

The meaning of 'visionary' is more difficult to define. In fact, this term really applies only to William Blake – 'inspiration and vision are my element'[7] – but the tradition that he founded of extremely individual and eccentric allegorical narratives is particularly strong in British art, even today. Here, too, we encounter the Pre-Raphaelites, with their literary and moralizing subjects. The tendency towards the symbolic and the unusual, the inspiration of literature and the interest in early English history occur again after the turn of the century in the work of a number of modern artists, among them Stanley Spencer, who worked in the margins of a modernism that had spilled over from its French origins into the contemporary London art world. The emphasis on content and the use of expressive form are also characteristic of the work of Francis Bacon and Graham Sutherland. The transcendental approach to nature, as it can be seen in the work of John Martin, J.M.W. Turner, Samuel Palmer and the Pre-Raphaelites, returns in the work of Paul Nash and the so-called Neo-Romantics of the 1930s. In more recent art, the line continues to Henry Moore and the British exponents of Land Art, such as Richard Long and Hamish Fulton.

Our two red threads – observation and imagination – tend to converge rather than develop separately alongside one another. This is true even of Constable, who viewed art as a branch of the natural sciences but also emphasized that art was 'to make something out of nothing, in attempting which [the artist] must almost of necessity become poetical.'[8] With some artists, such as Turner or Nash, the observation of nature is absorbed in the representation of the cosmic. For others, landscape artists as well as figure painters, accurate observation becomes so concentrated that it gives rise to something poetic, sometimes alienating, even hallucinatory. The transcendental and the empirical often appear to stand in each other's way in British art, or at least to coexist in an uneasy relationship. Even with the self-proclaimed visionary William Blake the physical element is strongly present. William Holman Hunt's *Scapegoat* – a central work in the present exhibition (cat. 264) – is, in spite of its moralizing, biblical content, inseparable from tangible reality. The unwillingness (or inability) to sublimate can also be found in the work of Francis Bacon, where the figures sometimes appear to engage in ritual behaviour while at the same time emphasizing the fact that they are flesh and blood.[9] Stanley Spencer seemed to express this dualism when he said: 'I am on the side of angels and dirt.'[10]

Whether the method adopted here produces a convincing picture of two centuries of British art will have to be answered by the exhibition itself. It was not conceived

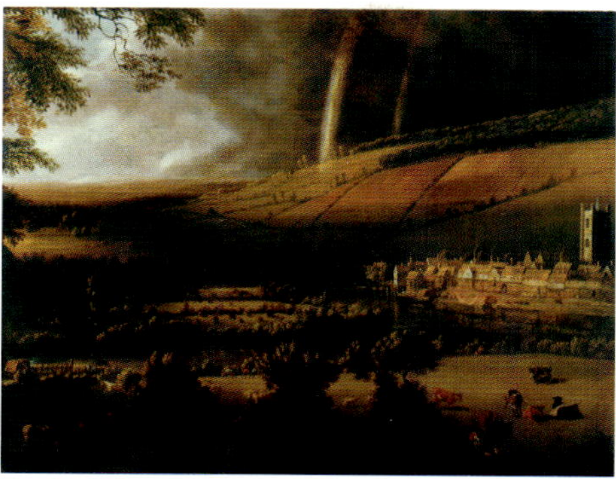

fig. 1
Jan Siberechts
Landscape with Rainbow, Henley-on-Thames, c. 1690
Oil on canvas, 81.9 x 102.9 cm
Tate, London

within a determinist historical framework, like so many contemporary studies of British art; rather, it has been assembled intuitively with an eye toward the intrinsic meaning and the representative quality of specific works of art. With hindsight, we must admit that the progression of our story is not continuous, because neither observation nor the visionary is always present in equal measure. In most cases, our survey is limited to the beginnings of a specific tendency or category. British humour, for example, is primarily important in the eighteenth century and at the beginning of the nineteenth. The satirical tradition continues, of course, but no attempt has been made here to cover the whole tradition. Its initial intensity is enough, together with examples by later artists who also explored this amalgam of humour and bitterness. Another example is British watercolour painting. The early development and the highlights of this tradition in the first half of the nineteenth century are the primary points of interest. Its subsequent development, though valuable in itself, falls outside the scope of the present exhibition. Finally, it should be noted that we have not tried to give equal representation to different media. After oil paintings, works on paper are given special attention, because drawings, watercolours and prints occupied a central position in British art, particularly in the two areas we are focusing on. Sculpture, with a few significant exceptions, hardly appears in this survey, but photography is well represented because of the powerful early development of the medium in Britain, and because it exemplifies the themes of the exhibition.

This catalogue follows the structure of the exhibition, which is divided into three main sections - observation of society, observation of the landscape, and the visionary - preceded by two longer essays. The individual sections begin with a brief introduction explaining the selection of the exhibited works, and this is followed by focused essays dealing with important individual works or series of works that are in some sense representative of the whole. All the works in the exhibition are then discussed in individual catalogue entries.

The strong focus of the exhibition means that the overview it provides is fragmentary and that there are significant gaps in its chronology. One particular hiatus coincides with the latter years of the nineteenth century and the start of the twentieth, when British artists took part in international stylistic developments, which - thanks to a lively exhibition circuit and art market - created a kind of international style. This period produced a number of interesting artistic currents, such as British Impressionism, the Aesthetic Movement, the Arts and Crafts Movement and the Bloomsbury Group. If we pass over or just touch upon these important episodes, it is because they are not essential to our narrative of typically British observation and imagination. In many studies, the 'golden age' of British art stops before this gap and 'resumes' with some delay after the European avant-gardes have been assimilated. However, in this exhibition an effort has been made to avoid seeing these two periods as separate entities, not so much by introducing transitional figures, but rather by seeking continuity in the qualities of observation and imagination that can be traced from the eighteenth century onwards.

As far as imagination is concerned, it is easy to compare modern artists with earlier masters: everyone will understand that figures like Stanley Spencer, Jacob Epstein, Paul Nash, Graham Sutherland and Francis Bacon have a natural kinship with William Blake, Samuel Palmer, J.M.W. Turner and John Martin. In contrast to this, the chapters on the observation of modern society and on modern landscape painting are conceived more as hypotheses. They pose questions: how did social observation continue in the twentieth century? Do the great landscape painters of the eighteenth and nineteenth centuries have their modern equivalents?

British Vision makes its appearance at the Museum of Fine Arts in Ghent ten years after *Paris-Bruxelles/Brussel-Parijs*, organized in 1997 together with the Musée d'Orsay.[11] In that exhibition it was possible to see how artistic exchange arose between two neighbouring countries bound together by history. The present exhibition has a

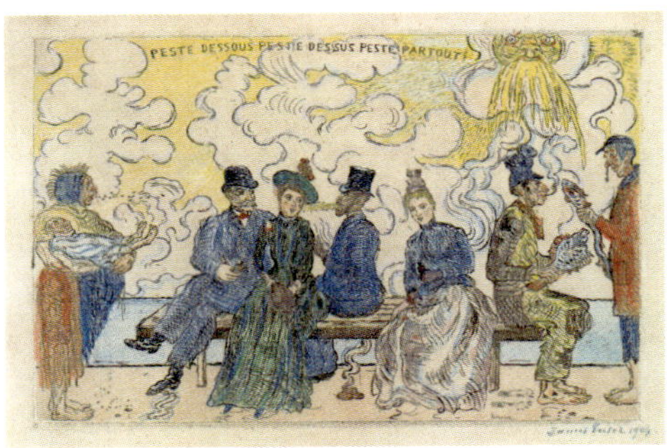

fig. 2
James Ensor
Plague here, Plague there, Plague everywhere!, 1904
Coloured etching
19.7 x 27.1 cm
Museum voor Schone Kunsten, Ghent

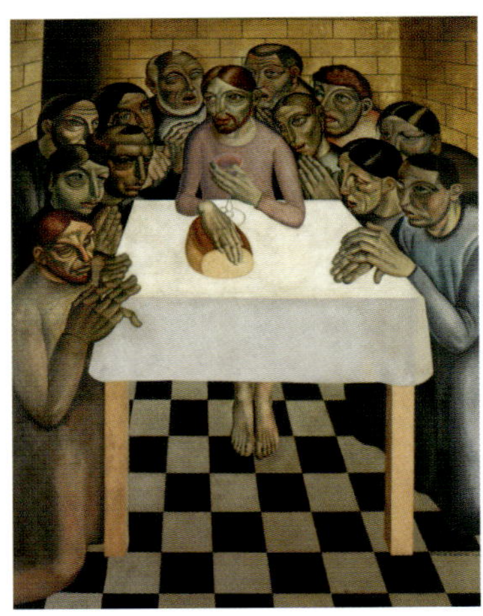

fig. 3
Gustave Van de Woestyne
The Last Supper, 1927
Oil on canvas
395 x 300 cm
Groeningemuseum, Bruges

different approach, and the main aim of *British Vision* is to acquaint the visitor with British art, which is still a well-kept secret on the European mainland. Numerous relationships have existed between the art of Great Britain and this part of the Continent, but they do not really form as homogeneous a narrative as the exchange between Belgium and France. Nevertheless, there are artistic ties that go back to the Middle Ages, when Flemish artists and craftsmen were active in England. In the sixteenth and seventeenth centuries Flemish and Dutch artists were drawn to London. The significance of Anthony van Dyck for the development of British portraiture is widely known, but less familiar is the fact that important stimuli for the development of group portraiture, genre subjects and landscape painting also came from Flanders and the Netherlands. The Antwerp artist Jan Siberechts was one of the most important topographical painters in England at the end of the seventeenth century (fig. 1). The landscapes of Peter Paul Rubens ended up in English collections and exercised considerable influence on English landscape painters like Thomas Gainsborough and John Constable.[12]

In the present exhibition, which investigates the British talent for observation, we often encounter the influence of Flemish realism. The detailed realism of the Flemish Primitives inspired the Pre-Raphaelites; the popular types of Pieter Brueghel the Elder and David Teniers the Younger influenced the great British observers of human behaviour like William Hogarth and David Wilkie.

On the occasion of the 1824 Paris Salon, where a delegation of British artists was present for the first time, Eugène Delacroix wrote that, 'These are no longer the times in which one asks if there are painters in England.'[13] Beginning with that Salon, French critics and artists continued to be fascinated by British art, and the influence of British art and literature on Romanticism and French landscape painting also reached Belgium. Later in the century, anglophilia played an essential role in Belgian Symbolism, particularly in the art of Jean Delville, Léon Frédéric and Fernand Khnopff. The latter, as a correspondent for *The Studio*, was an important link between British and Belgian Symbolism around 1900. In the same period, the British Arts and Crafts Movement was an important stimulus for the development of Belgian Art Nouveau.

The grotesque is an important feature of British art that appears frequently in the present exhibition. Here too there are parallels with the work of Belgian artists like Félicien Rops or Antoine Wiertz. The satire that characterizes the art of William Hogarth and James Gillray, who were themselves to some degree indebted to Flemish predecessors, reached a peak in Belgian art with the work of the Ostend painter James Ensor (fig. 2), significantly, perhaps, the son of a British father and a Flemish mother.

Figurative modernism from the first half of the twentieth century also receives a great deal of attention in this exhibition. This aspect of British art is scarcely known outside the United Kingdom, and it is difficult to understand how so important an artist as Stanley Spencer, a central figure in the exhibition, has not received attention sooner. Stanley Spencer's humane and troubled art was one of the inspirations for the conception of this exhibition and for the decision to extend our survey into the twentieth century. It is to be hoped that this exhibition will help to re-establish this artist as one of the most original modern British artists. Interest from the Flemish side comes as no surprise. After all, there are striking similarities between the social expressionism of various British artists and Flemish Expressionism between the two World Wars. By this is meant not so much the rustic power of Constant Permeke (who influenced the little known British artist Josef Herman), as the mixture of humour, observation and imagination in the work of Frits Van den Berghe and Gustave Van de Woestyne (fig. 3) – the latter sought refuge in England, along with many other Flemish artists, during the First World War.[14] Van de Woestyne's 'religious realism' of the 1920s shows striking parallels with that of Spencer. It is just one aspect of the relationship between British and Flemish figurative modernism that merits further investigation.

British Vision has been a collaborative effort, benefiting enormously from discussions with our specialist British advisers John Gage and Timothy Hyman, each of whom has provided a major essay to this catalogue. Andrew Dempsey has been with the exhibition from the outset in his role as coordinator in the UK and has also made important contributions to the content, form and catalogue of the exhibition. Our team has been completed by Helen Simpson, who has contributed to our discussions and has undertaken the very considerable task, in collaboration with our Museum staff, of realizing such a complex exhibition and catalogue. I am very grateful to them for their friendship and professional assistance. I should also like to thank the British Council, particularly Andrea Rose, for making our collaboration possible. Mark Haworth-Booth is to be thanked for selecting the photos, guided by his years of experience as head of the photography department of the Victoria and Albert Museum.

The concept developed by this group was favourably received by a great many museums, and in many cases we received concrete support and suggestions from our colleagues. I hope I am not doing an injustice to others when I acknowledge the special collaboration that sprang up with our colleagues at Tate Britain and at the Yale Center for British Art. Most of the authors who worked on the catalogue emerged from these stimulating contacts. I would like to thank all the authors of the essays and catalogue entries for their professional contributions.

Numerous museums and private collections have supported this project with loans, and several major museums with special collections of British art have loaned us important groups of works. However, the generosity of the private collectors and smaller collections has been equally vital for the exhibition's success.

For the practical realization of this project, I would like to thank the Federal and Flemish governments as well as the city of Ghent, The British Council in London and Brussels, and our partners in media and business. *British Vision* is the first major exhibition to take place in the renovated Museum voor Schone Kunsten in Ghent. My thanks go out to all the museum personnel who have helped to bring the exhibition to realization during the difficult period of renovation.

1. 'Letter V. On the Church England', in *Letters concerning the English Nation by Mr. de Voltaire*, Dublin (George Faulkner) 1733, p. 34
2. Thoré-Bürger, 'Salon de 1863', in *Les Salons. Etudes de critique et d'esthétique, avant propos par Emile Leclerq*, part 1, Brussels (H. Lamertin) 1893, p. 421.
3. Interview by Jan Braet in *Knack*, 28 July 2004, p. 72.
4. Annotations to Sir Joshua Reynolds' *Discourses*, c. 1808; cit. Eitner 1971, p. 121.
5. Nikolaus Pevsner found this opposition essential for English art: 'On the one hand there are moderation, reasonableness, rationalism, observation and conservatism, on the other there are imagination, fantasy, irrationalism.' Pevsner 1956, p. 186.
6. Leslie 1951, p. 280.
7. Annotations to Sir Joshua Reynolds's *Discourses*, c. 1808; cit. Eitner 1971, p. 125.
8. Beckett 1962-68, vol. 7, p. 6.
9. In this connection, see 'Types of ambiguity' in Hammer 2005, pp. 132-142.
10. Cit. Hyman and Wright 2001, p. 10.
11. *Paris-Bruxelles/Bruxelles-Paris. Réalisme, impressionnisme, symbolisme, art nouveau. Les relations artistiques entre la France et la Belgique, 1848-1914*, under the direction of Anne Pingeot and Robert Hoozee, Paris (Galeries nationales du Grand Palais) & Ghent (Museum voor Schone Kunsten) 1997.
12. See Brown 1996.
13. 'Thomas Lawrence', in *Revue de Paris*, 1829; cit. Eugène Delacroix, *Ecrits II. Essais sur les artistes*, Paris (Éditions du Sandre) 2006, p. 145.
14. *Art in Exile, Flanders, Wales and the First World War*, under the direction of Oliver Fairclough, Robert Hoozee and Caterina Verdickt, Ghent (Museum voor Schone Kunsten), Heino/Wijhe (Hannema de Stuers Fundatie) & Cardiff (National Museum and Gallery of Wales) 2002.

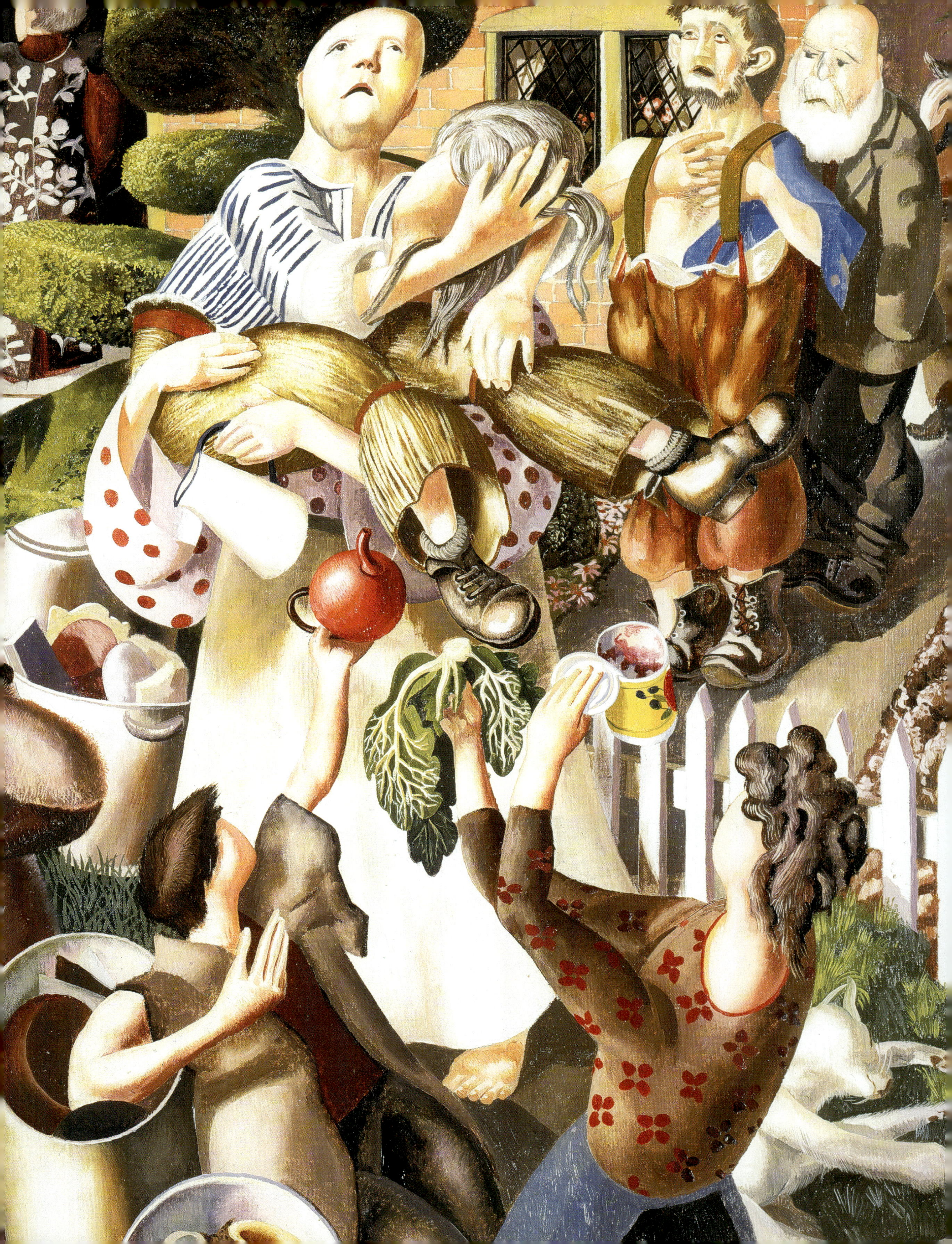

BETWEEN THE METICULOUS AND THE MAD

TIMOTHY HYMAN

Where British art is most rewarding, it often aspires to transcend the too limited local genres of portrait and landscape, and to create a richer, more complex kind of imagery – whether we name it 'history painting' or 'narrative' or 'figure composition'; although, in practice, the strange insular hybrids that result are misfits in any of European art's usual categories. And so, what we might call a 'tradition of the thwarted history painting' takes shape, which links Hogarth's *Rake's Progress* (cat. 36) to the grand Enlightenment altarpiece of Wright's *A Philosopher Lecturing on the Orrery* (cat. 6), and connects the encompassing moral microcosm of Ford Madox Brown's *Work* (cat. 22) to the astonishing twentieth-century self-explorations of Stanley Spencer (cat. 87).

Assembled here together, such public-scale projects offer just one of the several perspectives through which we might view this exhibition. But in British art, the most ambitious quests have sometimes been enacted on quite small sheets of paper. Whenever I encounter William Blake's majestic watercolour *The Sea of Time and Space* (cat. 247), I am surprised at its restricted scale; while in his 'Prophetic books' (another home-grown, one-off species) Blake's cosmic figures threaten to burst the pages of *Urizen* (cat. 236-238) or *Jerusalem* (cat. 239-242). His comic counterpart, James Gillray, brings a new convoluted energy to the London genre of the caricature print (cat. 42-44), but his thwarted ambition is inherent in these mock-history-paintings-in-miniature.

Whether large or small, whether famous or hidden in their own time, all the images I want to single out shared a difficulty: that their ambition was at odds with the prevailing visual culture. This problem went deeper than any local failure of patronage, or of 'the market'. In the words of the most frustrated history painter of them all, James Barry (fig. 1), it was the residue of 'our former religious bigotry, which kept out art of all kinds, except mere servile face-painting and a little landscape.'[1] Fifty years before our exhibition opens, almost all complex imagery had disappeared from British public life. In repeated campaigns, from the first 'stripping of the altars' in the 1540s, to the long aftermath of Cromwell's revolution, Protestant iconoclasm had transformed one of the most visually rich cultures of Europe into one of the most visually barren. Mutilation and maladjustment will be part of the legacy of British artists. Yet from that awkward misrelation will emerge a sequence of extraordinary pictures, a succession of singularities, which together build a fascinating extension to the main palace of European art.

BEYOND THE SILENCE OF THE ENGLISH PORTRAIT

When the *émigré* art historian Nikolaus Pevsner sought for the essence of 'Englishness', he registered *reticence* and *taciturnity*: 'Thus the English portrait keeps long silences and when it speaks, speaks in a low voice.'[2] One hesitates to categorize Joseph Highmore's *Mr Oldham and his Guests* (cat. 3) as a conversation piece, since there is none; his trio of English curmudgeons seem content to sit, glaring and staring, evening after evening, over their tobacco and punch. Yet when painted together, they witness – as a single figure would not – a specific social atmosphere: proud of their plainness, refusing all elegance, rejoicing in the solid comfort of their buttoned brown broadcloth. Whether he is visiting in prison the triple murderess *Sarah Malcolm* (cat. 1), awaiting execution in 1733, or painting his profound and moving *Heads of his Six Servants* (fig. 2) in the 1750s, William Hogarth sometimes portrays with such a sober directness the ordinary common people that he brings to British art a newly democratic brand of realism; in which George Stubbs also participates when in 1800, at the end of his painting life, he depicts the gamekeeper *Freeman* (cat. 5). A Liverpudlian and largely self-taught, Stubbs had kept his distance from the world of the Academy and the connoisseurs. Now, at seventy-six, he encounters this torchlit apparition against the encroaching darkness – emblematic of Freeman's nightly

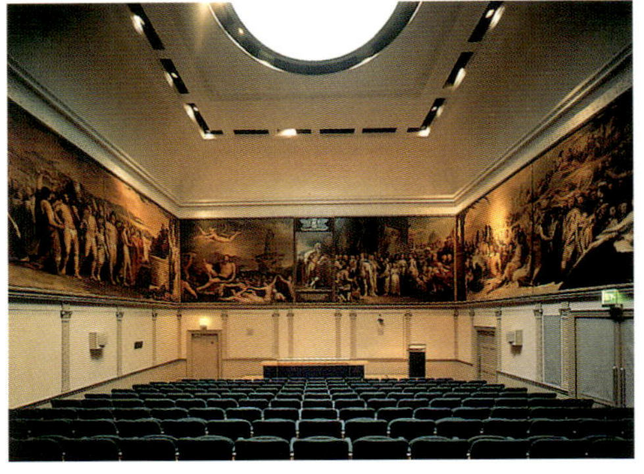

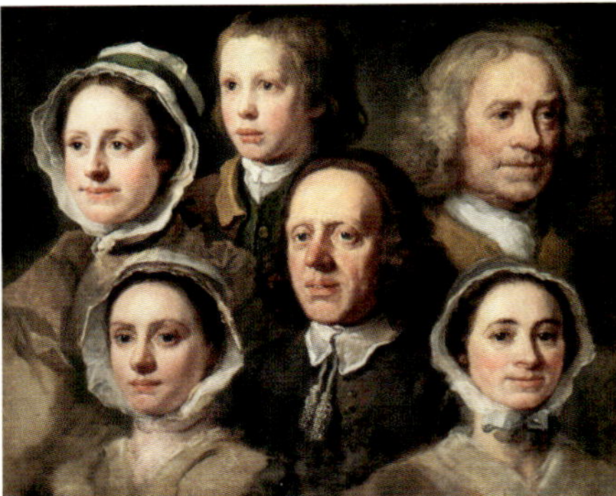

fig. 1
James Barry
The Progress of Human Culture, 1777-83
Six panels, oil on canvas,
in the Great Room
at the Society of Arts, London

fig. 2
William Hogarth
Heads of his Six Servants, 1750-55
Oil on canvas, 63 x 75.5 cm
Tate, London

patrols in the forest, but also (as the American critic Sanford Schwartz has intimated) of frailty and mortality:

> The animals connect like dancers stepping towards one another – their crossed legs are balletic – but then we can see that the dog stands upright on the ground and that the deer is lying back against Freeman's legs. The painter, you believe, wants this confusion ... We are to see that the dog is no villain, and that the dog, the gamekeeper and the doe – this linking triangular shape – are one. All of life and death are tied together in this image, which expands as we think about it.[3]

The unidentified 'philosopher' who dominates Joseph Wright's *Lecture on the Orrery* (cat. 6) of 1776 seems nearer to magus than to rational demonstrator; a benign Prospero whose red-sleeved splendour dwarfs all his grey encircling audience. Through his 'orrery' he becomes master of the cosmos, inducing first the sun's eclipse, then its arising. Wright of Derby has been associated with a group of experimenters, the 'Lunar Society', who from 1775 would meet in Birmingham on the Sunday nearest to each full moon.[4] They included Wright's doctor, Erasmus Darwin (who treated him for depression), as well as the inventor James Watt, the potter Josiah Wedgwood, and the chemist and apostle of 'rational dissent' Dr Joseph Priestley. Together these men were already fast transforming the Midlands into Europe's first industrial heartland, opening the dales to the sun of a rational Enlightenment. Yet, for this milieu, as Benedict Nicolson has pointed out, 'reason, because new, is steeped in romance'.[5] And Wright's nocturnal art is a kind of shadow-magic that embodies this romance – a firelight that equates experimenter with alchemist; or throws up the deep-scored lines on the face of a blacksmith-metaphysician. Fifteen years after *The Orrery*, Wright would celebrate the glamour of Sir Richard Arkwright's vast new-built cotton mills, windows still ablaze with the night shift, under the full moon (cat. 7). The dark silhouette of the solitary carter is painted with a visceral rawness, nearer to Daumier than to any of Wright's Academician contemporaries.

Many eighteenth-century English portrait groups are miniaturized, doll-like, with Arthur Devis the most consistent of these puppet-masters (cat. 2). But his son, A.W. Devis, has gradually re-emerged as a more complex artist, and *The Palmer Family* (cat. 4) is his unfinished masterpiece, opening a fascinating window onto the still fluid Anglo-Indian encounter. Formerly attributed to Zoffany, the picture was thought to be set in the 'native' court of Lucknow; but Devis must have painted the Palmers in colonial Calcutta. The tragic history of the Palmer dynasty has recently been told by William Dalrymple in *White Mughals*;[6] how the 'gentle, thoughtful and highly intelligent' Major Palmer embarked on a lifelong marriage to a Delhi noblewoman, Faiz Baksh. In Devis's atmospheric nocturne, the redcoat has been transplanted to a shadowy, 'feminized' realm of statuesque ayahs and mantled princesses. The intensity of Faiz's gaze outwards and the tenderness of Palmer's towards her and towards their children create an exceptionally moving interaction – an image suggestive of a lost phase of our history. British rule would harden, intermarriage become a stigma; Palmer would be an early victim of this imperial racism, dying neglected and disgraced.

'ABSOLUTE, UNCOMPROMISING TRUTH'

We call it a society ... it is a mutual hostility.
Thomas Carlyle in *Past and Present*, 1843.

In many British artists, from Blake and Dadd to the Pre-Raphaelites and Stanley Spencer, a tight, minutely detailed execution is strangely mingled with wildness, exuberance – suspended between repression and the irrepressible. This British pursuit of detail may have moralizing overtones (painting as penitential discipline); or it

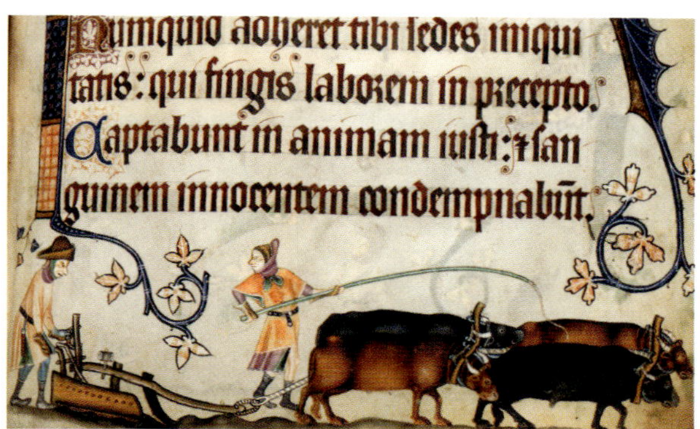

fig. 3
Winter ploughing;
detail of miniature on page (Psalm 91, f. 170)
from ***The Luttrell Psalter***, English, c. 1330
British Library, London

may become obsessional, linked to some eccentric personal mythology. It will often be difficult in this exhibition to separate observational from visionary.

A history of English meticulousness might begin with Holbein and the Elizabethan miniaturists; or perhaps, with the vivid scenes of everyday working lives illuminated into the margins of fourteenth-century manuscripts such as the Luttrell Psalter, c. 1330 (fig. 3).[7] (According to Pevsner, 'no continental country has anything like these riches of observed life in medieval art.'[8]) But it is above all in the mid-nineteenth century that meticulous observation would become the basis of an entire British School. As early as 1843 Ruskin outlined a programme: 'Go to Nature ... rejecting nothing, selecting nothing and scorning nothing'; and this was fulfilled in the earliest works of the Pre-Raphaelite Brotherhood, as well as in their close associates William Dyce and Ford Madox Brown. Brown emerges in this exhibition as a central linking figure. His early formation was European, not English, including a year at sixteen training in Antwerp, and, in 1845, a visit to the Nazarenes in Rome.[9] Established in London, he gave Rossetti his first painting lessons in 1848 and also influenced the future photographer Roger Fenton. Later he would join Morris and Burne-Jones in 'The Firm', becoming an influential designer himself and remaining all his life a fiery libertarian. He saw himself as the heir to Hogarth; his early ambition was to paint 'what I called, a Holbein of the nineteenth-century'.

Brown's climacteric occurred in his early thirties, when he was living in Hampstead 'most of the time intensely miserable, very hard up and a little mad'.[10] In the space of eighteen months he began the three iconic images for which he is best known: *The Last of England* (cat. 23), *An English Autumn Afternoon* (cat. 196), and his masterpiece, *Work* (see cat. 22), which would take another ten years to complete. The origins of *Work* lie partly in Carlyle's *Past and Present*; Carlyle smiles out as a kind of authorial presence and 'brainworker' on the margins of Brown's own state-of-the-nation microcosm. His fellow observer is F.D. Maurice, founder of the Working Men's College, where Brown, along with Rossetti and Morris, taught unpaid. This young man's maddened vision of social injustice was also fed by Henry Mayhew's articles of 1849-50, which would eventually be published as *London Labour and the London Poor* (cat. 18). *Work*'s immense ambition was reflected in its monumental scale as well as in its complexity.[11] The construction of so lucid a continuum of space and tone, sustained in tiny marks across so large a surface, is an astonishing achievement.

Brown intended through this 'minuteness' to 'bring the pathos of the subject more home to the beholder'.[12] His art shared in the Pre-Raphaelite pursuit of (in Ruskin's formulation) 'absolute uncompromising truth, down to the most minute detail, from nature and *from nature alone*'.[13] But when in 1856 Brown began a strange new picture (it would eventually take the Hogarthian title, *Stages of Cruelty*), his diary entries show him divided. After many hours painting leaves *from nature alone*, he 'scraped the leaves with a razor and set them to right *from feeling* indoors'.[14] (The terms correspond to the Old Flemish distinction between 'naer het leven' – from the life; and 'uyt den gheest' – from imagination, from spirit.) When finally completed after thirty-six years,[15] *Stages of Cruelty* (cat. 21) would become one of the creepiest of all Victorian paintings. It is the precision with which each element is rendered – not only the obdurate little girl who so steadily whips her dog, and the demonic woman she grows up into, delighting in her lover's drowning torment, but also the wall, leaves, steps, dress – all conjure an 'overexposed' intensity, nearer to dream than to any natural truth. This hyperreality breaks down all distinction between 'observation' and 'vision', and brings to mind another meticulous obsessional at work in 1850s London: the murderer Richard Dadd, confined to the asylum of 'Bedlam', where we will encounter him later in this essay.

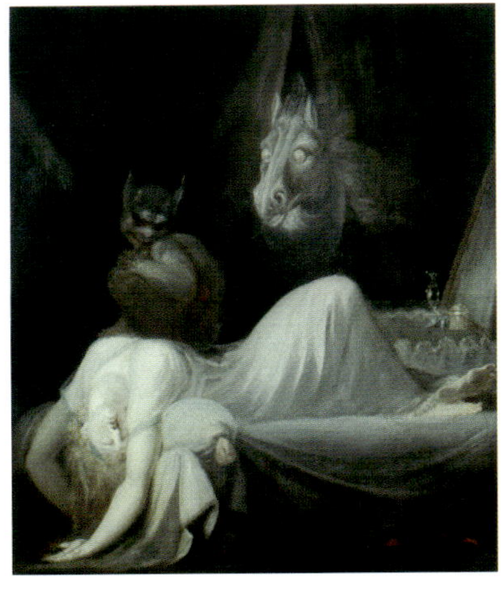

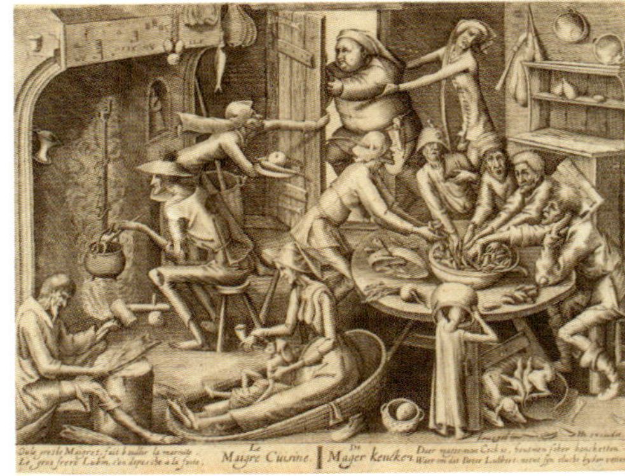

fig. 4
Henry Fuseli
The Nightmare, 1790-91
Oil on canvas, 75.5 x 64 cm
Goethe Museum, Frankfurt am Main

fig. 5
Pieter Bruegel
The Thin Kitchen, 1563
Engraving, 22 x 29 cm
Museum Plantin-Moretus
(Collectie Prentenkabinet), Antwerp

HOGARTH: 'THE LUDICROUS WITH THE TERRIBLE'

For there is one strange but quite essential character in us … a delight in the forms of burlesque which are connected in some degree with the foulness of evil … You find that whenever Englishmen are wholly without this instinct, their genius is comparatively weak and restricted.
John Ruskin, in *Lectures on Art*, 1870

'Bedlam' is Bethlem Hospital, the London madhouse where Hogarth's naked Rake is dying at the end of his downhill Progress. In creating his new genre of 'Modern Moral Subjects' ('a field … unbroken upon in any country or age') Hogarth brings art close to the territory of the newly emergent novel: the narrative of disenchantment. 'A comic history painter' is how his friend Henry Fielding, both novelist and Covent Garden magistrate, would identify Hogarth in the preface to *Joseph Andrews*. When the artist himself looked back, he saw his life work as a witness, 'descriptive of the peculiar manners and characters of the English nation'.

Or, more specifically, of London. No subsequent artist has mapped the capital so substantially. A miser's son inherits a fortune in the 'City' (the old mercantile centre) but loses it in the aristocratic 'West End', where he is arrested for debt in Piccadilly, at the top of fashionable St James's Street. Between City and West End lies the 'Town' – the socially fluid area centred on Covent Garden – where, one freezing morning at five to eight, a priggish old maid minces churchwards past overnight revellers and whores, her ill-treated servant boy shivering behind her (cat. 39a). And on the cold night of 29 March, in a piss-reeking alley near Charing Cross composed of bathhouses ('bagnios') and brothels, the 'Salisbury Flying Coach' has collapsed, trapping its passengers dangerously close to a roaring fire: the smoke of a distant conflagration rises behind them (cat. 39b).

Both *Night* and *Morning* are staged within far more compelling and complex urban spaces than the primitive doll's house perspectives of the *Rake's Progress* (cat. 36). He sets the addicts of *Gin Lane* (cat. 38) in the notorious back slums and boozing 'kens' of St Giles ('The Holy Land'), where a falling façade echoes the falling child, and a suicide dangles above a burial. The darkness of Hogarth's comic vision has led admirers to make comparison with Shakespeare's 'very tragical mirth', that characteristically English mingling of genres: 'the ludicrous with the terrible'.[16] The idea of the Hogarthian crowd inspired several great Europeans, from Domenico Tiepolo and Goya to the socially critical artists of Weimar Germany. Max Beckmann, in 1918, defined his artistic lineage: 'Brueghel, Hogarth, Goya. All three have the metaphysical in the objective. That is also my goal.'[17] Yet such company also defines Hogarth's limitations: his decorum and restraint, a certain coldness and literal-mindedness in his essentially prosaic idiom.

LONDON AS A 'CITY OF LAUGHTER'

Could it have gone another way? That punchbowl and tobacco we encountered as guests of *Mr Oldham* presides also over Hogarth's large early canvas, *A Midnight Modern Conversation*, c. 1732 (cat. 37) which enacts a kind of panorama of all the ways in which eleven men might be drunk: roaring-and-groaning drunk; tottering-and-blind drunk; tipping-a-chair drunk; all dominated by the central red sprawling figure on the floor – dead drunk. This frieze of folly seems more celebration than moral indictment. The scene is St John's Coffee House, off the Strand, and the clock tells us it is way past midnight, almost four in the morning. As an engraving, it would become his most pirated, until Hogarth, in 1735, established the first printmaker's copyright law, laying the commercial foundation for the great second flowering of English graphic humour later in the century.

Between 1780 and 1820 well over 15,000 separate comic images were published in London, often in editions of hundreds, occasionally of thousands. Engraved or etched, sometimes hand-coloured, they sold for about four shillings each (in 2007 values, perhaps equivalent to £50). They were luxury goods, purchased mainly from West End specialist shops (of the kind shown here in Dighton's print, cat. 41) and in front of these window displays, large crowds would gather. Some collections were enormous; that of George IV comprised almost ten thousand.[18] But a portfolio could be hired out for an evening's entertainment. (And however grossly masculine much of this imagery might appear, a significant portion of its clientele was female.) Quite large numbers of prints were also exported – hence Gillray's pan-European influence, on contemporaries as various as David and Goya.

James Gillray is both the product of this 'low' culture of political and social satire, hacking out on average a print each week for twenty years, and the very exceptional artist who raised English caricature to a level never surpassed. Already in the early 1770s, William Austin, an accomplished drawing master in the polite mode, had published some surprisingly monumental grotesques, his big figures filling the page with a kind of infantile majesty (cat. 40). And from 1780 onwards the presence in London of Henry Fuseli as the leader of a visual culture of gothick fantasy, of dreams and excess (as in *The Nightmare*, fig. 4), had opened new vistas. (Gillray would come to understand the comic potential also in Fuseli's high-camp heroics.) At forty-seven, Fuseli married an English model of eighteen and developed a semi-private, sometimes pornographic, archetype of her as dominatrix or cruel courtesan. The ink drawing here of a doubled Sophia, exhibiting herself at a draped box as she takes tea (cat. 48), dates from two years into the marriage; Fuseli's misogynist satire carries over into the simpering, whorish fairies of his *Midsummer Night's Dream*.

When Gillray published *A March to the Bank* (cat. 42) anonymously in 1787, he was several years out of the Royal Academy Schools, but still hoped for recognition as a 'straight' engraver of historical compositions. Only a draughtsman of immense ambition could negotiate each twist of this heap, as the wasp-waisted martinet and his somnambulistic soldiery shatter the market, exposing coarse thighs alongside beautiful breasts, and, sickeningly, the snapped leg-bone of the foreground victim – all of them enclosed within a perfect contour. (The beauty of Gillray's bitten line is most evident in the uncoloured versions.) By contrast, the bare-bottomed cannibal sansculottes of *Un petit souper á la Parisienne* (cat. 43) are drawn with an expressive violence, nearer to the primitive graffiti they have scrawled on their own walls than to any academic correctness. The composition – both a rapid response to the 1792 September Massacres, and a satirical exaggeration of the horror stories spread by the anti-revolutionary press – is based on Bruegel's *The Thin Kitchen* (fig. 5), indicative of Gillray's joyous regression to the grotesque and the anti-Classical.

In a letter of 1800, he affirms his interest in Fuseli, and 'ye use to be made of him. *I am convinced how very necessary his mock-sublime mad taste*.'[19] The mock-sublime is everywhere in *Confederated Coalition – or – The Giants Storming Heaven* (cat. 44) – every cliché of the Michelangelesque nude, parodied in the pot-bellied reality of middle-aged politicians. Gillray's exuberant invention outdoes any academic history painter, his convoluted copiousness a wonderful antidote to Neo-Classicism's programme of visual cleansing. His 'mad taste' is a vision of mania that goes beyond aesthetic strategy: it is the eruption of a national carnivalesque, nourished by the insanity of Britain's reigning monarch, George III, as well as by the revolutionary overturnings in France. And for a child of Scottish parentage, brought up a strict Calvinist, it is as if Gillray's pictorial appetite needed to make up for centuries of image-starvation.

Although Thomas Rowlandson is often coupled with Gillray (they were friends, and had overlapped at Royal Academy Schools), his art is in many respects opposed. In its charm and elegant facility, Rowlandson's *The Prize Fight* (cat. 51) is a masterpiece, owing much to two early years he had spent in Paris. The essential serenity of the scene, unified by his tinted watercolour washes, is never really threatened by the slapstick comic incident; its light-filled sky and compositional grandeur (with echoes of Calvary, even of Rembrandt's *Three Crosses*) confer an unexpected permanence on the ephemeral sporting crowd.

In his fine recent book, *City of Laughter*, the social historian Vic Gatrell identifies a drastic shift in English graphic humour around 1820 – the 'taming', the 'silencing'. Gillray died insane in 1815 (I write about his late drawings in a separate essay, pp. 101-3), while both Rowlandson and Cruikshank lost their satiric edge. Gatrell traces a sequence of 'debauchery prints', beginning with Hogarth's *Midnight Modern Conversation* (cat. 37), to which Rowlandson's watercolour *Serving Punch* (cat. 52) is obviously related. Suddenly this imagery of roistering and libertinage, of vomiting and farting, becomes unimaginable, with 1821 as 'the last occasion in art when low conviviality is represented as a source of pleasure and happiness'.[20]

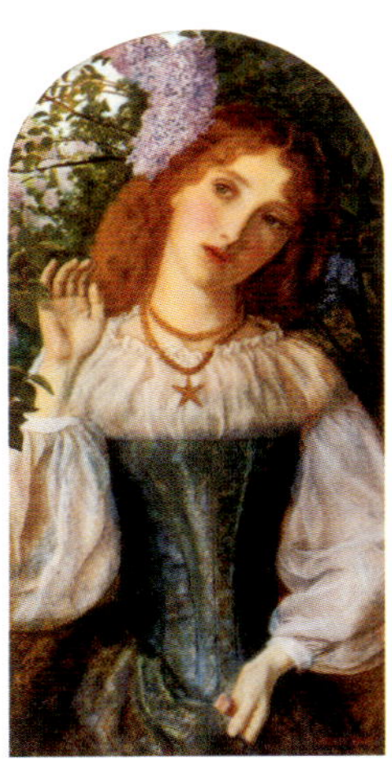

fig. 6
Arthur Hughes
The Lady of the Lilacs, 1836
Oil on panel, 44.5 x 22.5 cm
Art Gallery of Ontario, Toronto

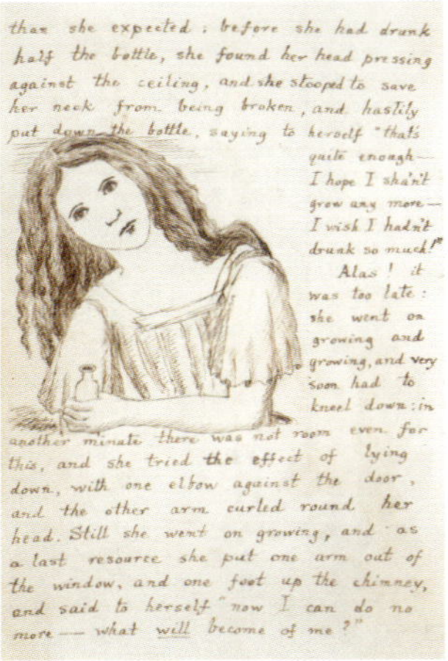

than she expected: before she had drunk half the bottle, she found her head pressing against the ceiling, and she stooped to save her neck from being broken, and hastily put down the bottle, saying to herself "that's quite enough — I hope I shan't grow any more — I wish I hadn't drunk so much!"

Alas! it was too late: she went on growing and growing, and very soon had to kneel down: in another minute there was not room even for this, and she tried the effect of lying down, with one elbow against the door, and the other arm curled round her head. Still she went on growing, and as a last resource she put one arm out of the window, and one foot up the chimney, and said to herself "now I can do no more — what will become of me?"

fig. 7
Lewis Carroll
Alice Puts Down the Bottle, from the autograph manuscript of ***Alice's Adventures Under Ground***, 1862-64
Pen and ink on paper, 19 x 12.3 cm
British Library, London

NURSERY TRUTHS

... *'and what is the use of a book' thought Alice 'without pictures?'*...
Lewis Carroll, *Alice's Adventures in Wonderland*, 1865

Fusing image and word beyond 'illustration', the children's classic is essential to our national visual culture: countless millions of English psyches have been built upon the foundation of *Nonsense* and *Wonderland*. Edward Lear was a lifelong epileptic, wandering alone through southern Europe and the East, and his greatest creations were melancholy outsiders, singularities such as Mister, or 'The', Yonghy-Bonghy-Bo. He was largely self-taught (though in his late thirties he became a disciple of the young Holman Hunt, adopting his punishing procedures for his own landscapes); by then he had already published, in 1846, his first *Book of Nonsense* (cat. 57), to become a nursery staple only in the 1860s. The pen drawings that accompany his rhymes are powerful and primitive – frightening and strange in just the way that children love. His freakish obsessionals, badly behaved, huge-nosed, are trapped in a wilfully disproportionate line that conjures hysteria, extremity.

The creator of 'Nonsense' claims the license to be 'silly', to turn away from adult concerns; and this freedom, allied to a parodic intelligence, is part of the appeal of the two great *Alice* books by 'Lewis Carroll', pen name of a solitary Oxford mathematics don and photographer of little girls, the Rev. C.L. Dodgson. We have placed his original illustrated manuscript, *Alice's Adventures Underground* (cat. 274), in the visionary category; when Alice goes 'Underground', she is entering the territory of nightmare, and Dodgson's own drawings have a strangeness about them that is scarcely 'funny' at all. He admired the Pre-Raphaelites (he had purchased in 1863 *The Lady of the Lilacs*, from Arthur Hughes – the surprising source for his own 'growing and growing', huge-headed girl), and his Alice fits best among their feminine archetypes (fig. 6-7).

John Tenniel, Dodgson's eventual collaborator, was a leading Punch cartoonist, who in his youth had visited the Nazarenes[21] in Munich and learnt from them a hard, cross-hatched pencil line, perfect for transcription into wood engravings. His drawing (cat. 58) for *The Walrus and The Carpenter* (the sad poem recited by Tweedledum and Tweedledee in *Through the Looking-Glass*) stands here for a great tradition, extending through *Winnie-the-Pooh* and Kathleen Hale's *Orlando* to Edward Ardizzone and the *Molesworth* drawings of Ronald Searle.[22]

'SOMERSET HOUSE / TRIUMPH OF YE ARTS POLITE'

Portrait with them is everything.
Their taste and feelings all go to realities ...
matter of fact they may encourage
Henry Fuseli to Joseph Farington, 24 July 1805

The foundation of the Royal Academy in 1768, with Joshua Reynolds as its first President, was in some respects a catastrophe for any emergent British culture of visual art. In his influential *Discourses*, Reynolds played down Hogarthian realism and discouraged close observation of 'common nature'. Yet Reynolds's idealizing ethos (unmasked by Blake in his savage *Annotations*) was a lie since his own practice was dominated by – to quote Barry again – 'mere servile face-painting'. Gainsborough's response, in 1772, was that of a hard-headed portrait professional: 'Sir Joshua either forgets or does not chuse see, that his Instruction is all adapted to form the History Painter, which he must know there is no call for in this country.'

Long before, Hogarth had scorned the new nexus of the 'Polite' in the hangers-on who surround the Heir in plate II of his Rake's Progress (cat. 36b): landscape gardeners, dance masters and fencing teachers, all surmounted by the worthless *Judgement of Paris* behind.

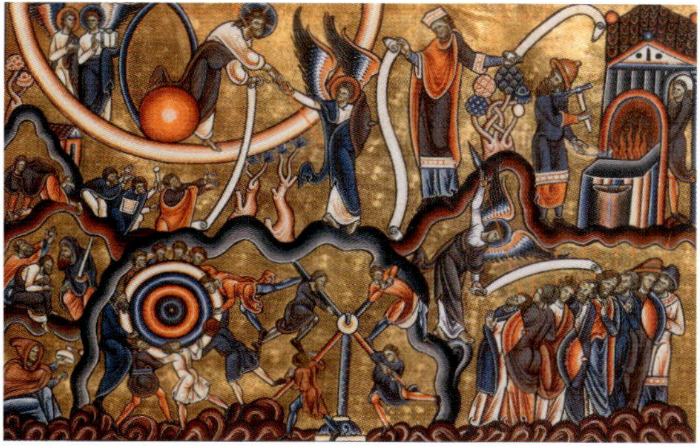

fig. 8
Miniature illustrating Psalm 11
(*'Save me Lord'* – beseeching for help
against the wicked, f. 20),
from the ***Canterbury Psalter***
English, c. 1200
Bibliothèque nationale de France, Paris

By the 1800s, the Academy's Annual Exhibition at Somerset House was set mostly in the society portrait mould. Gillray, below his own 'List of Subjects' (p. 103, fig. 2), scrawls bitterly: 'Somerset House / Triumph of ye arts polite'.[23] In a lighter vein, Rowlandson mocks the elegantly Italianate, but notoriously dangerous, stairs ascending to the Academy (they lead today to the Courtauld Institute Galleries); except that the 'exhibition' on Rowlandson's 'stare-case' (cat. 53) is of Neo-Classical beauties tumbling knickerless down, with gnarled connoisseurs making their appraisal.

Our own exhibition represents the exceptional, rather than the mainstream in British art. But one weakness in our nineteenth-century exceptionals is that – unlike their Parisian counterparts – they were never able to construct a counterculture, a London 'Bohemia' that would provide some respite from the polite norm. Many were dissenters, in both religion and politics, but that only isolated them still further; or else, like Edward Burne-Jones, the lifelong comrade of William Morris, they ended by succumbing to a baronetcy. (This was the same republican Ned who, at the time of Queen Victoria's Jubilee, observed: 'All this enthusiasm spent over one unimportant old lady is the one effort of imagination of the English race.'[24])

Only quite recently has the academic canon of British art been challenged; Stubbs and Wright, Blake and Palmer, Ford Madox Brown and Richard Dadd are essentially twentieth-century rediscoveries; the reappraisal of Fuseli dates mostly since 1940, and of Gillray since 1960. At the beginning of the twenty-first century, it does not seem a mere provocation if one encounters in a newspaper the pronouncement: 'The two greatest of British artists are Blake and Stubbs.'[25] But when money and attention goes to landscape and portrait, the kinds of imagery of which Blake is our greatest exponent, will suffer neglect. Here is his first-person testament: 'Having spent the vigour of my Youth and Genius under the Oppression of Sir Joshua and his Gang of Cunning Hired Knaves, Without Employment and as much as could possibly be, Without Bread, the reader must expect ... nothing but Indignation and Resentment. While Sir Joshua was rolling in Riches, Barry was poor and unemployed except by his own energy ... and only portrait painting applauded and rewarded by the Rich and Great. ... Fuseli, indignant, almost hid himself. I am hid.'[26]

CIRCLING BLAKE'S VOID

There are States in which
all Visionary Men are accounted Mad Men.
William Blake, *Laocoon*, 1826-7

Several of the key voices in this exhibition – Blake and Palmer, Ruskin and the Pre-Raphaelites, Morris and Spencer – were acutely conscious of the English medieval world. It came to assume for them something like a prelapsarian or Edenic state, a childhood of the image to which their own art yearned. Among the few surviving remnants were English illuminated manuscripts. Although it is most unlikely that Blake ever saw these particular pages, I want to associate his imagery here with a Canterbury psalm-book of around 1200; compartmented worlds upon worlds, the earth's crust opening as a living being (fig. 8).[27] *Songs of Innocence* (1789) is, among much else, a children's book and an illuminated text (cat. 231-235); as in all Blake's subsequent Prophetic books, the image not only expands and enriches, but also *redeems* the word. Split ever since adolescence between poet and engraver, he would find only in his thirties this composite form, to render word and image, line and colour, intellect and sense, indissoluble.

Infant Joy (cat. 235) is a kind of lullaby, sung by (as well as to) a newborn baby, and the accompanying emblem sets a fairy-nativity within the petals of a crimson flower. Yet this *Innocence* is not sickly-sweet: with a radical and almost shaming vulnerability, we are made to confront the beginnings of consciousness. It is a shock, five years on, to shift into the hellish darkness of *Urizen* (1794): a

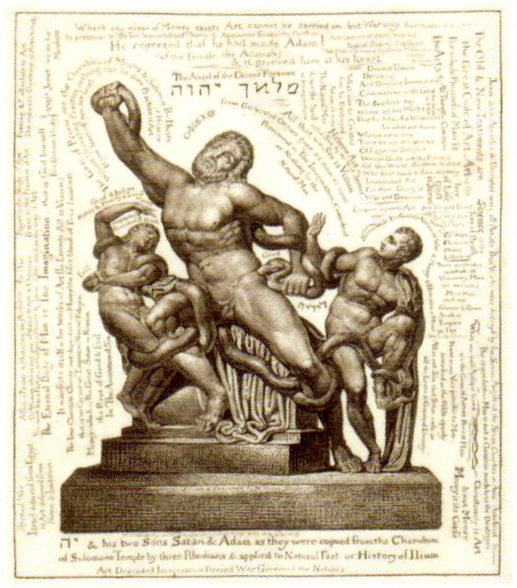

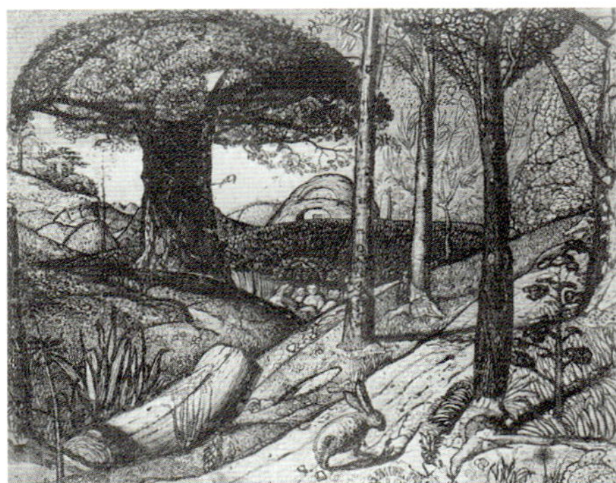

fig. 9
William Blake
Laocoön, 1818
Engraving with inscriptions, 27.4 x 22.7 cm
Fitzwilliam Museum, Cambridge

fig. 10
Samuel Palmer
Early Morning, 1825
Pen and brush in brown ink, mixed with gum, on paper, varnished, 18.8 x 23.2 cm
Ashmolean Museum, Oxford

figure writhing in flames, chained to a skeleton; a bursting head from which emanates a fiery globe. In its groaning violence and its weird mottled surface (the colour here printed, not brushed) the *Urizen* plates are magnificent (cat. 236-238). But they show Blake at his most isolated, his revolutionary hopes collapsed – the ravings of a prophet, barely containable within the book format.

Only seven copies are known of Urizen; and only one complete coloured Jerusalem. (Four of those unique sheets are exhibited here; cat. 239-242). The poem is a plate-by-plate account of his inner state, across some fifteen years (c.1804-20) with text and image often out of sync, so that the archetypal figures seems to haunt the pages almost at random. Its hundred plates enact vast cycles of mental disintegration and reintegration, the psychological processes by which inward experience unfolds in time: 'There is a void outside of Existence, which, if entered into, englobes itself and becomes a womb.'[28] To turn the page is to watch experience being turned inside out. As a book, Jerusalem is in every way a culmination. Within the larger format, Blake's imagery grows more fantastic and takes on a new authority. No one since the romanesque had created pages of such splendour: Blake remains incomparably the supreme master of the book in modern times.

Jerusalem was Blake's last poem; his greatest watercolours would be made in his final seven years, when he was exclusively a painter. Every part of *The Sea of Time and Space* (cat. 247) is fully realized: the marvellous living ocean, the complex but weirdly convincing space (with its sudden breathtaking glimpse of the temple on the shore) and the beautiful circling rhythms as the thread of life is passed upward on the spindles of the Fates. Its alternative title, *The Circle of Man's Destiny*, emphasizes those cyclic energies so often encountered in Blake: the serpentine 'primitive British' temple, whose winding menhir-stones appear in plate 100 of *Jerusalem* (cat. 242); or, most amazingly, that *Whirlwind of Lovers* (cat. 246) from which the fainting Dante hears the testimony of Paolo and Francesca. Journeying through the *Inferno*'s circles, Blake becomes less linear, more tender and sensuous; nothing is forced, a line or a hue may remain tentative; and the pencil-drawing *An Angel Striding Among the Stars* (cat. 243) has a similar intimacy. The large-headed, stumpy, late figure-types no longer attempt a classical suavity but seem closer to the Trecento. In his watercolour of a retold *Laocoön* – a struggling Urizen raising both arms in a tragic gesture akin to a crucifixion – the nudes of the antique have become gowned figures of magnificent amplitude and pathos (cat. 244/fig. 9).

In 1973 the historian E.P. Thompson declared: 'If I devised my own pantheon I would without hesitation place within it the Christian antinomian William Blake and I would place him beside Marx.'[29] I give this as just one example of Blake's living voice in contemporary British and American culture. Among European painters, there is no parallel for Blake's role as a prophetic artist.[30]

EXTOLLAGERS OF THE MOON

If Mr. Blake had a crack,
it was a crack that let the light through.
Samuel Palmer

In the autumn of 1824, the landscape painter John Linnell introduced his nineteen-year-old protégé, Samuel Palmer, to William Blake, already sixty-seven. Blake had begun work on the Dante watercolours (commissioned by Linnell); but the Blakes that most inspired Palmer were a series of tiny wood engravings for an edition of Virgil's pastorals (cat. 248). Forty years later, Palmer would recall his youthful response to Blake's nocturnes, 'models of the exquisitest pitch of intense poetry'; their 'intense depth, solemnity and vivid brilliancy', their 'mystic and dreamy glimmer'.[31] Two motifs especially, the winding stream and the sickle moon above the fields, fed into Palmer's art. He developed a consciously primitive, almost childlike idiom, learning both from the separateness of the marks in early northern engravings, and from fresh observation. 'Sometimes the rising moon seems to stand tiptoe on a green hill to see if the day be going,' he notes in the 1824 sketchbook, from which two related sheets are exhibited here (cat. 251-252). The hill that doubles as a thatched cottage appears also in *Early Morning* (fig. 10), one of the 1825 'sepias' that are Palmer's defining achievement – a very young man's return into the landscape of Eden.

By 1830, the group of young men that called themselves the 'Ancients', centred on Palmer's house in Shoreham, had established a pattern of night expeditions into 'this Valley of Vision'.[32] The locals, seeing the enthusiasts pass, loud in praises of the moon and stars, coined the word 'extollagers'.[33] *Cornfield by Moonlight* (cat. 255) is such an extolling, with its huge celestial body so close to the hill, sending out visible rays into the warm night. Much later, Palmer recorded 'Thoughts On Rising Moon, with raving-mad splendour of orange twilight glow on landscape. I saw that at Shoreham'[34]. His fellow-Ancient, Edward Calvert, had travelled in Greece before encountering Blake and Palmer; his own version of Virgilian pastoral eroticized by the nude *Bride* from the biblical *Song of Songs* (cat. 249). Calvert's miniscule but astonishingly intense wood engravings culminate in his *Chamber Idyll* – the primitive hut, where the shepherdess is stripping as she stands between her lover's thighs (cat. 250).

The early imagery of Palmer would have an enormous influence on Spencer and Nash, and later, on the 'Neo-Romantic' generation of Sutherland and Piper. But Palmer has subsequently been condemned as infantile or escapist – notably by John Berger, writing of 'his landscapes like furnished wombs'; while William Vaughan has recently documented the decline of Palmer's reputation in 'modish critical and academic circles' over the past thirty years.[35]

'FAERY LANDS FORLORN'

We are soaked in Puritanism and it will never
be out of us and I hate it and it makes us
the most cautious hypocritical race on earth.
Edward Burne-Jones, 1893[36]

If others can see it as I have seen it,
then it may be called a vision rather than a dream.
William Morris, *News from Nowhere*, 1892

In 1842, when Richard Dadd returned from a voyage to the East, he was already manifesting insanity. He had started out the central figure of the 'Clique' in 1830s London (a group that included W.P. Frith and Augustus Egg). But now, in his mid-twenties, he slaughtered his father with knife and razor one night in a Kentish park, was captured in France and confined in Bethlem Hospital. Timelessness, utter stillness, comes to pervade all the best works of his confinement – accreted very slowly in tiny concentrated marks. The unpeopled rocky landscape on Rhodes (cat. 140) is re-imagined with the same hallucinatory intensity as the portrait he paints under the funereal gaze of his 'alienist', Sir Alexander Morrison (cat. 258). (The dark figure is then dropped like a phantom into its incongruous 'Scottish' setting.) Dadd records how he began *The Fairy Feller's Masterstroke* (fig. 11) by staring at random smears of paint until, over a ten-year span, the microscopic fairy world took shape; in his own phrase, 'displayed as in a trance',[37] half-hidden behind tangled grasses, many of the faces weirdly 'morphed'. Fuseli and Blake had already shown how the Shakespearean faery-lore – our indigenous mythology, free of all classical or Christian baggage – could be employed for explorations inward, or into the archetypal world of childhood. Even in the second version exhibited here (cat. 261), carried out in watercolour and in a lighter key, Dadd's microcosm is of a fantastic intricacy.

Literature and landscape meet in William Dyce's quiet masterpiece *George Herbert at Bemerton* (cat. 193). Twenty years older that the Pre-Raphaelites, Dyce had emerged in the 1840s as the 'British Nazarene'.[38] His early theological training at Aberdeen made him exceptionally susceptible to the Oxford Movement.[39] Herbert's house at Bemerton, within sight of the spire of Salisbury Cathedral, had become something of an Anglican shrine; and to appreciate Dyce's picture fully, we may need some sense of that great seventeenth-century devotional poet. Dyce shows him at the moment of receiving an epiphany in nature (perhaps the latent subject in all the best Victorian landscapes); and this fine tribute delicately embodies something of Herbert's calm rapture.[40]

A great question hangs over the early Pre-Raphaelite painters, not in their landscape and naturalistic, but in their Arthurian and Christian mode; and then, even more insistently, over the medievalizing of Burne-Jones and Morris: is this a true and convinced vision or a mere aesthetic dream? Morris, like Ruskin, had loved the medieval world, as an alternative to present-day society, as a past that might provide some model for a better future. Together with Burne-Jones, he had pioneered what we now call the Arts and Crafts Movement; the wallpapers and stained glass of the 'Firm' defined the medievalizing taste of a generation. 'We were born into a dull time,' wrote Morris, 'oppressed with bourgeoisdom and philistinism so sorely that we were forced to turn back on ourselves, and only in ourselves and the world of art and literature was there any hope.'[41] The airlessness of Burne-Jones, even in his impressive *Perseus* series (cat. 278-279), comes partly out of that 'turning back'. Morris would shift much of his energy away from 'beauty' to

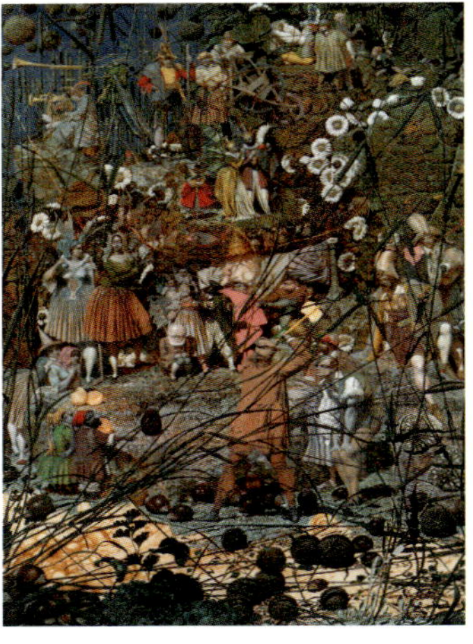

fig. 11
Richard Dadd
The Fairy Feller's Masterstroke, 1855-64
Oil on canvas, 54 x 39.4 cm
Tate, London

libertarian socialism, to become the greatest public speaker of his time; among his final works were his utopian novel, *News from Nowhere*, as well as the Kelmscott edition of *Chaucer*, exhibited here (cat. 280). Burne-Jones remained in thrall to his muses. Soon, Aubrey Beardsley, who had begun as an imitator of the Burne-Jones Kelmscott idiom, was explaining to his erstwhile mentor that he now hated King Arthur 'and all medieval things'.[42] By 1914, Sickert could write conclusively, 'The Burne-Jones attitude is almost intolerable to the present generation.'[43]

OBSERVATION AS DISILLUSIONMENT

Stick to the French School – il n'y a que cela in modern art. We are good only in as much as we derive from them.
Walter Sickert, Letter to Sir William Eden, 1901

Modernism in British art became associated with Parisian values - with a rejection not only of Pre-Raphaelite medievalism, of the literary and narrative aspirations that had fed the very concept of history painting, but an embargo also on detailed observational painting. Roger Fry, the dominant early twentieth-century critical voice in Britain, set out 'to bring the English into touch with European art'.[44] He believed content was overstressed in painting, 'that all the essential quality had to do with pure form'.[45] His canon was classicizing. But the most distinctive British painting had always been anti-classical - and the mismatch was often bitter and recriminatory. Sickert himself was both very 'French' and very 'English'. Long before he painted the silted-up misery of *Ennui* (cat. 62), Parisian critics had recognized a distinctive note in his dinginess, 'steeped in London winters, in the foul flow of the Thames'.[46] His long bedroom series showing naked prostitute alongside clothed client (as in cat. 61) remained ambiguous, poised between lowlife genre-scene and - as they were after interpreted - the narrative depiction of a famous London sex murder. Only in the photo-derived paintings of his seventies, such as the 1934 portrait of Beaverbrook exhibited here (cat. 86), does Sickert convert emotional vacancy into an unexpected and exhilarating modernity.

His often brilliant critical writing - increasingly in opposition to Fry - privileged the factual, the banal. That version of realism, close to miserabilism, was Sickert's legacy to the Camden Town painters; to Coldstream and the Euston Road School; to one aspect of Bacon, and even, as our own exhibition ends, to Frank Auerbach. Coldstream's generation had reacted against all aestheticism; as he explained, 'the 1930s slump affected us very considerably,'[47] turning them towards a culture of documentary and 'Mass-Observation'. But Coldstream developed an extreme English empiricism, art stripped of all metaphor and metaphysic - what Lawrence Gowing once called 'representation-as-such' - so that his *St Pancras Station* (cat. 94) quietly challenges with a new 'absolute uncompromising truth' all the consolations of the English Romantic tradition.

Seen through European eyes, British painting often appears 'colourless'. Of all our monochrome visionaries, L.S. Lowry is the most distinctive. Out of the industrial wastelands of Manchester (those once glamorous mills of the Lunar men, now fallen into decay) Lowry creates a new, polluted poetry. He joins his sophisticated painting-culture (his long training under a French master, Adolphe Vallette) to a defiantly localized and populist concern. *Family Group* (cat. 103) is both a homage to Bruegel and a plea for the estranged - but rescued from sentiment by Lowry's hard, acerbic pencil line. Since his death, we have also become aware of such images as the clamped girl (cat. 104) - his compelling metamorphoses of *Alice*, and of the Victorian fixations implicit in the Rossetti drawings of 'stunners' that Lowry admired and collected.

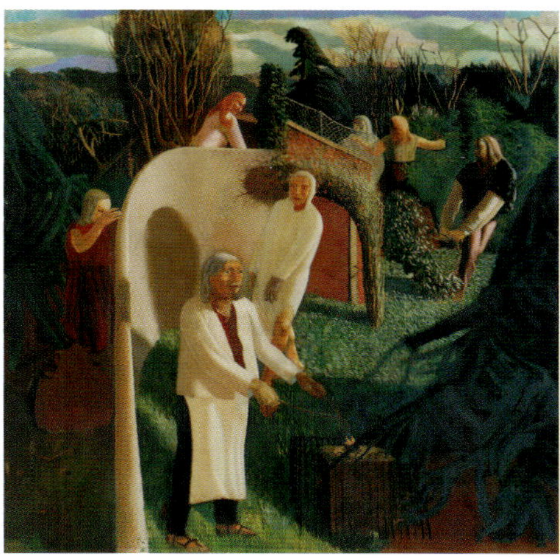

fig. 12
Stanley Spencer
Zacharias and Elizabeth, 1913-14
Oil and pencil on canvas, 142.6 x 142.8 cm
Tate, London, and Sheffield Galleries & Museums Trust

The painter-critic Merlin James has recently hailed Lowry as 'one of the alternative heroes of modern art'.[48] The next two sections put forward a cast of other twentieth-century 'alternatives', still little known in Europe, but whose robust imagery stands against the bleaker and greyer aspects of our 'British vision'.

THE MOMENT OF NEO-PRIMITIVISM

This new conception of art, in which
the decorative elements preponderate
at the expense of the representative,
is not the outcome of any conscious archaistic
endeavour, such as made, and perhaps inevitably
marred, our own Pre-Raphaelite movement.[49]
Roger Fry, 1910

The eighteen-year-old Stanley Spencer attended Fry's 1909 lectures at the Slade, and his excited reception of that gospel of Giotto-and-Gauguin is still evident in his terse, beautiful little canvas *John Donne Arriving in Heaven* (cat. 285) – recruited by Fry for his second Post-Impressionist show in 1912. Spencer's fellow students included William Roberts, Mark Gertler and C.R.W. Nevinson, all sharing in this synthesis of Parisian modernity with Florentine Trecento and sometimes collectively grouped as the 'Neo-Primitives'. The Slade (though almost exclusively a school of figure drawing) gave its annual prize to a large 'Composition' – that is, in our terms, a history painting – to be completed in the summer vacation. The 1912 winner was Spencer's *Nativity* (cat. 286), set in his childhood Eden, Cookham; the sense of place seeming to generate the embracing couples, extensions of the enfolding trellis and palings. The ink study (cat. 284) for *Zacharias and Elizabeth* (fig. 12) suggests that Spencer was already identifying with Palmer;[50] the mood is of trance and ritual, of landscape conceived as sacred narrative.

At nineteen, Gertler explored his own East End Jewish immigrant community in *The Rabbi and his Grandchild* (cat. 65), still in the Neo-Primitive idiom: flattened, half-naive but very solid. A much older painter, Henry Lamb, back in London after stints in Paris and Pont-Aven, also came under Spencer's spell, and was able at last to realize his huge icon of *Lytton Strachey* (cat. 63), begun two years before: the comical archetype of the drooping, boneless intellectual, extended almost life-size above Hampstead Heath. Spencer himself went out into the Cookham fields and painted '*from nature alone*', with the sharp-focused hallucinatory intensity of a Pre-Raphaelite (cat. 207). Roberts had visited Spencer in Cookham while still a teenager but now drew nearer to David Bomberg; they worked together at Wyndham Lewis's *Rebel Art Centre*, transposing Pollaiuolo into hard, quasi-mechanized compositions and both moving rapidly towards abstraction. Until, into this ferment of very young artists, broke the war.

BETWEEN WARS: TOWARDS A BRITISH *NEUE SACHLICHKEIT*

England is just as unkind and inimical to Art
as the Arctic Zone is to life.
This is the Siberia of the Mind.
Wyndham Lewis, *BLAST*, 1914

England still stands outside Europe.
Europe's voiceless tremors do not reach her.
Europe is apart and England is not
of her flesh and body.
John Maynard Keynes,
The Economic Consequences of the Peace, 1919

In the years immediately after the First World War, a group of as many as ten like-minded painters might sometimes meet in Hampstead;[51] among them, Lamb, Roberts, Gertler and Nevinson, as well as Spencer and

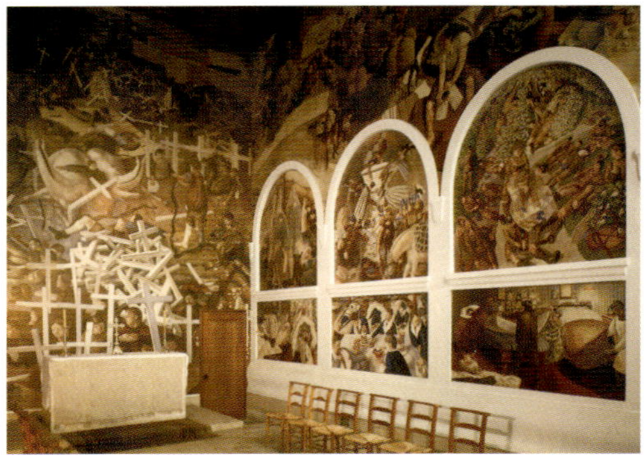

fig. 13
Stanley Spencer
Sandham Memorial Chapel, Burghclere, Hampshire, showing ***The Resurrection of the Soldiers***, 1927-32
National Trust

Paul Nash. Most had seen active service and had painted extraordinary pictures under the 'Official War Artists' scheme. Nash's *The Ypres Salient at Night* (cat. 73) is one of his earliest oil paintings, begun after his return from the trenches, jolted out of his late-Romantic dreamscapes by shells exploding above mud and chaos. 'I have seen the most frightful nightmare of a country,' he wrote. 'I am no longer an artist interested and curious. I am a messenger...'[52] In *The Menin Road* (cat. 294), Nash's characteristically dry matte paint and formalized design – the slant of searchlights and shadows against the verticals of blasted trees – reinforces the impact of its monumental three-metre scale. The tiny figures barely register within the vast apocalypse.

All these artists would have considered themselves as 'modernists', yet also (like so many of their European contemporaries) as *reconstructors*. After the smash-up of war, after the fragmentations of Cubism, the wholeness of the image must again be retrieved. Their shared idiom was never as verist as that of the *Neue Sachlichkeit* ('return to objectivity') painters in Germany, nor as classicizing as the '*rappel à l'ordre*' ('call to order') of Picasso and Léger, Carrà and Rivera; but it does convey a similarly renewed belief in the object. Roberts shed his abstraction to become a painter of everyday London life (as in his 1920 *The Cinema*, cat. 76), setting his androids to work, cogs in his compositional machines. Yet this willed stylization proves surprisingly flexible when he depicts his odd couple, big Keynes and little Lopokova, who told him they 'wanted to be done together' – economist and dancer, flourishing their reciprocal cigarettes (cat. 85); among the most humorously sympathetic of all modern portraits.

Edward Burra was the great comic addition to this already strong cast of figurative masters. The title of *Marriage à la Mode* (cat. 79) pays homage to Hogarth, though Burra's sophisticated eclecticism has also assimilated Juan Gris, George Grosz, the Mexicans, to bring the English satirical tradition into the era of international modernism. The scene could be paralleled in such novels as Henry Green's *Party Going* and Evelyn Waugh's *Vile Bodies*, where clever, fashionable young people pursue heartless entanglements. The weeping mother-in-law, surmounted by an entire nest-and-hen; the camp vicar and his knowing choirboys; the aerial putti with perfume-spray and watering can – all create a vision of British hypocrisy, fuelled by (in Burra's own phrase) his 'impotent venom'. A lifelong invalid, his staid existence in Rye was punctuated by wild lowlife breakouts – to Toulon, Barcelona, New York; source material for his sailors' bars, drug haunts, burlesque theatres. In 1933 he lived in Harlem for two months, and the recently rediscovered *Savoy Ballroom* (cat. 81) is a triumph of black-and-brown watercolour; the purple eyeballs and white smiling lips of the huge female head, vertiginously juxtaposed to the tiny smoker, catching our eye from the lower corner.

More elusive is David Jones, the poet-painter-calligrapher of Welsh descent, who in 1937 published *In Parenthesis*, the verse-narrative of his front-line experiences some twenty years before. His watercolour frontispiece (cat. 303) has the same tangled, dense but unexpectedly *light* tonality as his poem; we only slowly register the vulnerability of the boy-soldier's nakedness, so close to the barbed wire. A decade later, after another war and another breakdown, and perhaps in response to the Blake rediscovered at Arlington Court that same year (cat. 247) Jones made his emblematic *Vexilla Regis* (cat. 304): the Blakeian world-tree that is also the cross, reaching upwards from the midst of a collapsed Romano-British world.

Paul Nash had floundered in the twenties, calling himself 'a war-artist without a war'. Only at the end of his life, in the sequence that includes *The Landscape of the Vernal Equinox* (cat. 214), would he retrieve his earliest dreamscape vein, but now seen by the clear light of a daytime intelligence.

Spencer's case was the most complex. Images such as *The Betrayal* (cat. 296), for all their qualities, failed to ignite the pre-war Cookham rapture, though the commissioning of his anti-heroic war chapel at Burghclere[53]

– the most remarkable mural-scheme of modern Europe (fig. 13) – gave him respite; until, in the 1930s, the previously harmonized realist and visionary strands pulled violently apart. He found himself painting 'meticulous' local landscapes direct from life simultaneously with 'mad' compositions of grotesque invented figures, such as *The Dustman* (cat. 298) of 1934. 'This is the glorifying and magnifying of a dustman ... Nothing I love is rubbish, and so I resurrect the tea-pot and the empty jam tin and cabbage stalk and, as there is a mystery in the Trinity, so there is in these three objects and in many others of no consequence.'[54] Spencer's new figure-types, a race of rag-dolls, bring him closer to Edward Lear than to the Trecento. For his new imaginary chapel-of-love, his '*Church of Me*', he now has need of the comic genres of childhood, jettisoning all authority and dignity, along with current dogmas of 'significant form'.[55] To render sacred all that is most 'ordinary', Spencer enacts a passionate espousal of *insignificant* form; and then vindicates his 'dogged' landscape procedures in the new genre of the 'naked portrait', where he likens the slow movement of his brush to the ant 'crawling over every inch of the skin'. In the culminating *Leg of Mutton Nude* (cat. 87), he squats bespectacled and bared before the altar of an uncaring Patricia Preece; the intensity of detail makes both raw meat and unidealized human flesh shockingly present. (Perhaps it is a tribute to the power of this extraordinary self-image that Spencer's daughters have now forbidden its reproduction.) And again, in *Hilda, Unity and Dolls* (cat. 88), an apparently 'straight' or 'objective' depiction yields up a startling psychological disclosure.[56]

After years of personal obsession, the Second World War returned Spencer to engagement with the public world. Commissioned in 1940 to draw in a Clyde shipyard, he then returned to his small bedroom above a Gloucestershire pub, where he painted his five-and-a-half-metre triptych *Burners* (cat. 98). Format and scale endow the humdrum industrial process with a sacramental significance. The composition of the central canvas, with each worker so separate in his metal island, carries allegorical overtones: the childlike self-figure removes his goggles to survey the flame-lit inferno that stretches to either side, as a kind of witness.

Each of these painters, long marginalized as 'insular' or 'eccentric', now seems to me more engaging than such overtly universalizing artists as Ben Nicholson or Henry Moore. British art criticism has often been dominated by formalist criteria, but we no longer equate abstraction with modernity, nor judge all descriptive painting as 'reactionary'. In 1919 we may have had reason, as Keynes implies, to be ashamed at the separateness of 'England' from the experience of war-torn Europe. But today, in their ambition and humour, in their sharpness of observed life and in their visionary intensity, artists such as Burra and Spencer offer an evident continuity with our 'thwarted history painting' vein in British art.[57]

CONFRONTATIONS

So many apologies have been made
for English art ... an English artist would seem
to be almost a contradiction in terms. ...
Paul Nash, 1934

This exploration ends with Francis Bacon's 1955 *Study (after the Life Mask of William Blake)* (cat. 310). An obituary hailed Bacon in 1992 as 'the greatest British painter since Turner',[58] yet he felt little connection to British art and remains hard to place within any account of it, let alone in the terms of our exhibition. The sheer economy of his *Man in Blue* of 1954 (cat. 90) – stripes of a business suit migrating into an elegantly imprisoning space-frame – renders it very 'un-English'. Bacon rejected all meticulous depiction as 'illustration'; he cared only for painting where 'the brushstroke creates the form and does not fill it in. That is why *real painting* is a mysterious and continuous struggle with chance.'[59] Himself a singularity, Bacon chose nearly always to confront the solitary figure, rejecting narrative: 'the moment the story enters, the boredom sets in.'[60] (His triptych of 1962, fig. 14, is, however, one of the most memorable narratives in all modern British painting.[61]) He denied any homage to Blake; yet in his best decade, between 1952 and 1962, Bacon can be reckoned a true 'visionary' (even if his subject is nothingness) and the heir to Blake's radical fire-and-brimstone. Unlike any of the other painters here, he became an international culture-hero, whose images stood as signposts – as in the opening shots of Bertolucci's *Last Tango in Paris*, and at the centre of Pasolini's *Teorema* – confirming his resonance beyond Britain, and beyond painting.

When David Hockney stencilled BEDLAM onto the last of his *Rake's Progress* etchings (cat. 111), he was joining his art to a British tradition of seriocomic storytelling that had often been lost to sight in the culture wars of the twentieth century. He did so under the protection of the useful avant-garde umbrella of 'Pop', but in the subsequent decades many painters would more openly align themselves as 'narrative' or 'visionary'. (For me, the most convincing have been R.B. Kitaj's collaged history paintings, Peter de Francia's monumental charcoal compositions and Ken Kiff's visionary *Sequence*.)

The very notion of some indigenous 'English' tradition of painting was repugnant to me as a student at the Slade in the mid-1960s (just after this exhibition ends); we were a post-imperialist, anti-nationalist generation, and we looked far more at European and American than

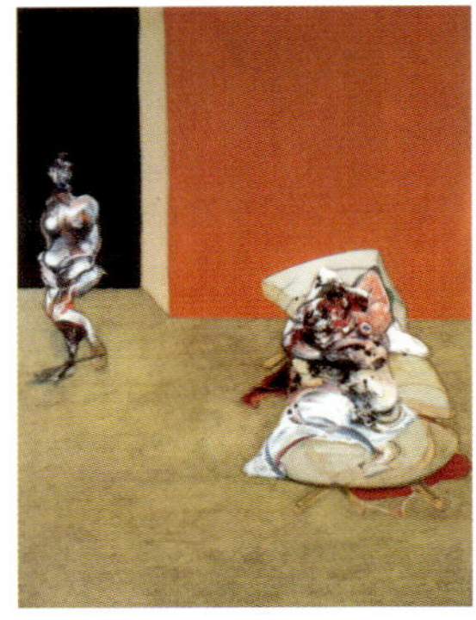
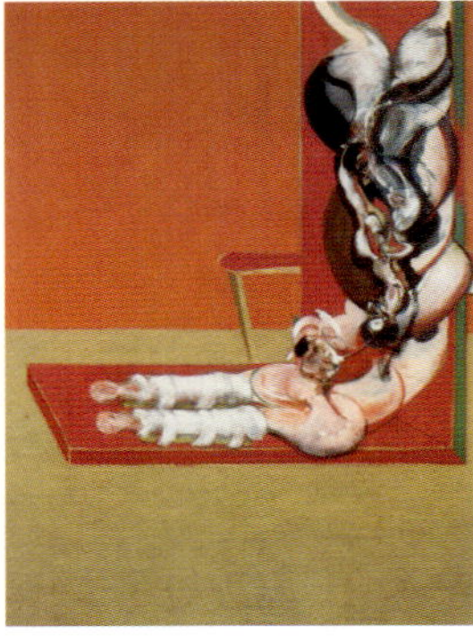
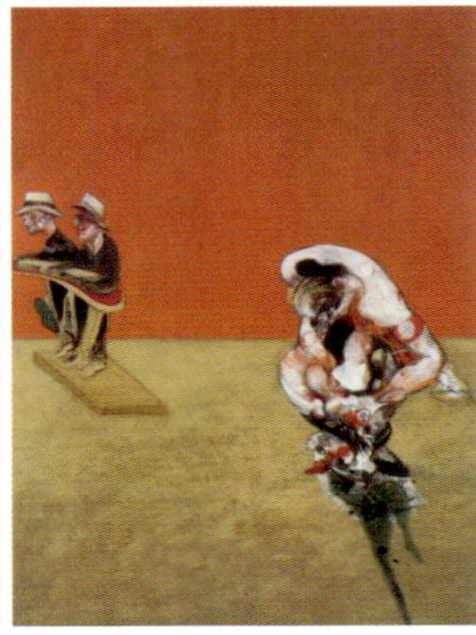

fig. 14
Francis Bacon
Triptych (Three Studies for a Crucifixion), 1962
Oil with sand on canvas, each panel 198.2 x 144.8 cm
Solomon R. Guggenheim Museum, New York

at any British art. Only much later was I made to recognize, through the eyes of foreign friends (and through reading such *émigré* historians as Pevsner, Antal, Pächt), that 'British Art' was after all an identifiable category; and that I was formed by it, whether I wished it or not. My hope is that European audiences will share some of the excitement and sense of discovery I have felt while wandering about in what is still the least explored wing of the European treasure house.

This essay is dedicated to the memory of the painter Ken Kiff (1935-2000). It owes much to my co-curators, Robert Hoozee and John Gage; among the many others who have helped in numerous ways, I want especially to acknowledge: David Bindman, Andrew Dempsey, Vic Gatrell, David Goodway, Merlin James, David Fraser Jenkins, Judith Ravenscroft, Will Vaughan, Francis West and Trevor Winkfield.

1. James Barry, *An Inquiry into the Real and Imaginary/OBSTRUCTIONS/to the/Acquisition of the Arts/in England*, London (T. Becket) 1775. Two years later, Barry would embark on a six-year project: to paint *The Progress of Human Culture* on the walls of The Society for the Encouragement of Arts, Manufactures and Commerce in the Adelphi (see fig. 1).
2. Pevsner 1956 (broadcast as Reith lectures, 1955), p. 59.
3. Schwartz 1990, pp. 171-72.
4. See Uglow 2002. The lunar theme will overlap with William Blake's delightful early nonsense narrative *An Island in the Moon*, where farcical experiments are carried out by Priestley under the name 'Inflammable Laughing Gass'. The manuscript was owned by Samuel Palmer.
5. Nicolson 1968, p. 2.
6. Dalrymple 2002.
7. See Backhouse 1989.
8. Pevsner 1956, p. 27.
9. The German 'Nazarenes' were important to several British artists around 1850, including Millais, William Dyce, Ford Madox Brown and John Tenniel. Based in Rome and Munich, the two best known masters were Overbeck and Cornelius. As early as 1848, the youthful Brown wrote in *The Builder* (4 November) of the Nazarenes' reversion to Raphael's predecessors - i.e. to the so-called 'Italian Primitives' - 'because in their less sophisticated works they found a powerful antidote to the false taste and pseudo-classical style then everywhere prevalent.'
10. Surtees 1981, p. 78.
11. The reduced-scale replica of *Work* in our exhibition is inevitably misleading.
12. *The Exhibition of Work and other Paintings by Ford Madox Brown at the Gallery, 191, Piccadilly*, London 1865; reprinted in Bendiner 1998, p. 136.
13. John Ruskin, *Pre-Raphaelitism*, Lecture (1853) (my italics).
14. Surtees 1981, pp. 180-82, 191.
15. Throughout much of the 1880s, Brown was living in Manchester, devoting himself to a vast mural scheme in the Town Hall. The most ambitious history paintings since Barry, they confront issues of industry and society: for example, the introduction of weights and measures; the social unrest triggered by new machines; or *Dalton Collecting Marsh-Fire Gas* (see fig. 15). Brown had also intended to represent the Peterloo Massacre. What results is an idiom that lies somewhere between the illustrations in Victorian children's History books, and the murals made in the 1930s under Soviet or WPA programmes.
16. Lamb 1811.

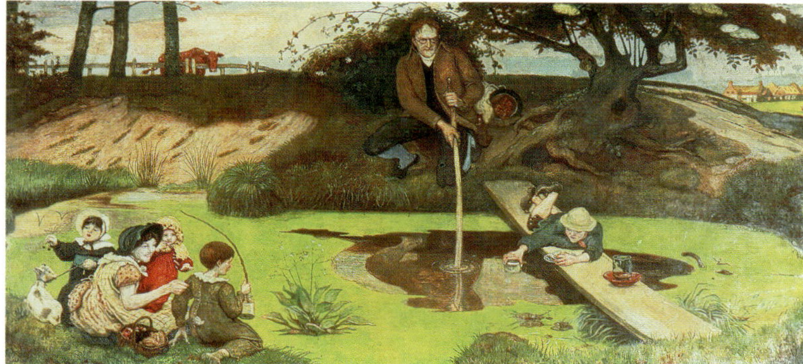

fig. 15
Ford Madox Brown
***Dalton Collecting Marsh-Fire Gas*, 1887**
Oil on canvas glued to plaster wall,
143.3 x 317.5 cm
Town Hall, Manchester

17. Max Beckmann, Letter to his publisher Reinhard Piper; in Schneede 1979, p. 73.
18. They were sold in 1921 to the Library of Congress, Washington, in order to pay for the expansion of George V's postage-stamp collection; an indication of how little such caricatures were then valued as art. See Gatrell 2006, p. 239.
19. Underlined in Gillray's letter to Sneyd, quoted in Hill 1965, p. 90. In 1791 Gillray inscribed above his print *Wierd Sisters*: 'To H. Fuzelli Esqr. this attempt in the Caricatura-Sublime, is respectfully dedicated.'
20. The context is Cruikshank's illustrations for *Life in London*. See Gatrell 2006, *passim*.
21. See note 9 on the Nazarenes.
22. For their European reach, see for example the young Balthus's superb *Alice*-haunted pen drawings to the childhood episodes of *Wuthering Heights*.
23. For Gillray's '*List of Subjects*' see fig. 2 in my essay on *The Faro Table*, p. 103.
24. Fitzgerald 1975, p. 274.
25. Tom Lubbock in *The Independent*, 16 August 2005.
26. Blake, *Annotations to Reynolds' Discourses* (Blake 1966, p. 445).
27. The psalm-book is now in the Bibliothèque nationale de France, Paris, and is usually referred to by its pressmark, '8846'.
28. The opening lines on the frontispiece of *Jerusalem* – later erased, but occurring also in Blake's poem *Milton*.
29. E.P. Thompson; cit. Goodway 2006, p. 28.
30. There is, however, no single location where much of Blake's art is constantly on show – a function the Tate has notably failed to fulfil in London.
31. Palmer 1892, pp. 15-16.
32. 'This Valley of Vision', Palmer's letter to George Richmond, 14 November 1827.
33. I came across this episode in one of the excellent captions by Stephen Calloway in the Victoria and Albert Museum's small Samuel Palmer centenary exhibition, 2005.
34. Quoted in Grigson 1947, p. 26.
35. William Vaughan in London & New York 2005, p. 16.
36. Fitzgerald 1975, p. 127.
37. Allderidge 1974, p. 125.
38. For 'Nazarenes' see note 9.
39. Dyce appears as the high-minded painter 'Mr. Shene' in Charlotte Yonge's tractarian novel of 1853, *The Heir of Redclyffe*, who in Munich asks the young 'Sir Guy' to pose as Sir Galahad.
40. Rose 1977, p. 37, has linked Dyce's picture to George Herbert's lines from *The Flower*: 'Who would have thought my shrivelled heart/ Could have recovered greenness?'.
41. William Morris, letter to Fred Henderson (1885); cit. Thompson 1977, p. 14.
42. Fitzgerald 1975, p. 249.
43. Sickert in *The New Age*, 28 May 1914.
44. Woolf 1940, pp. 165-66.
45. Ibid.
46. Félix Monod, in *Art et Décoration*, July 1909; cit. Robins and Thomson 2005-6, p. 180.
47. Coldstream, writing in 1937 in *The Listener*.
48. Brooks and James 2000, p. 16.
49. Roger Fry, *Burlington Magazine*, no. 16, Jan.-Feb. 1910. Fry is introducing Maurice Denis's writing on Cézanne.
50. Palmer's early sepias had been shown, and admired, at the Fine Art Society in 1882, and in 1893 at Burlington House; but the decisive 'rediscovery' began when several of Palmer's earliest works were included in the Tate's *Blake* exhibition in 1913. See also London & New York 2005, pp. 55, 87.
51. At the house of Spencer's future in-laws, the Carlines, in Downshire Hill.
52. Nash, letter to his wife Margaret, autumn 1917.
53. The Sandham Memorial Chapel, Burghclere, is now open to the public as part of the National Trust. In 1923 Spencer had made detailed designs for an imaginary fresco scheme, a chapel that would incorporate his war experiences both as a hospital orderly in Bristol, and on the Salonica campaign. Promptly – almost miraculously – patrons appeared. (The agreement was sealed with Spencer's famous cry, 'What-ho, Giotto!'.) From 1926 to 1932 Burghclere was Spencer's almost exclusive occupation.
54. Spencer, Tate Archive (733.3.75). See Hyman and Wright 2001, p. 31.
55. Fry's hostility towards Spencer's work can be documented. A 1932 diary entry of Patricia Preece (Spencer's future nemesis) records Fry's outburst: 'I am sick of his muck'. In the same year, Gwen Raverat writes: 'Dear Cookham, I'm afraid I do know that Roger Fry is against you ... The only good thing you ever did was *John Donne* ...'. See Hyman and Wright 2001, pp. 26, 32.
56. See catalogue entry, p. 156.
57. In grouping these disparate artists, I have played down their mutual dissensions. For example, Nash writes of Spencer in 1922, 'I used to pin my faith to him, but it would be better for him and for us if he hadn't been born behind his time.' See London 2001, p. 23.
58. Grey Gowrie in *The Guardian*, 29 April 1992.
59. Bacon was writing in 1953, in tribute to the painter Matthew Smith.
60. Sylvester 1975, p. 22.
61. Peppiatt 2006 suggests a specific narrative for the triptych.

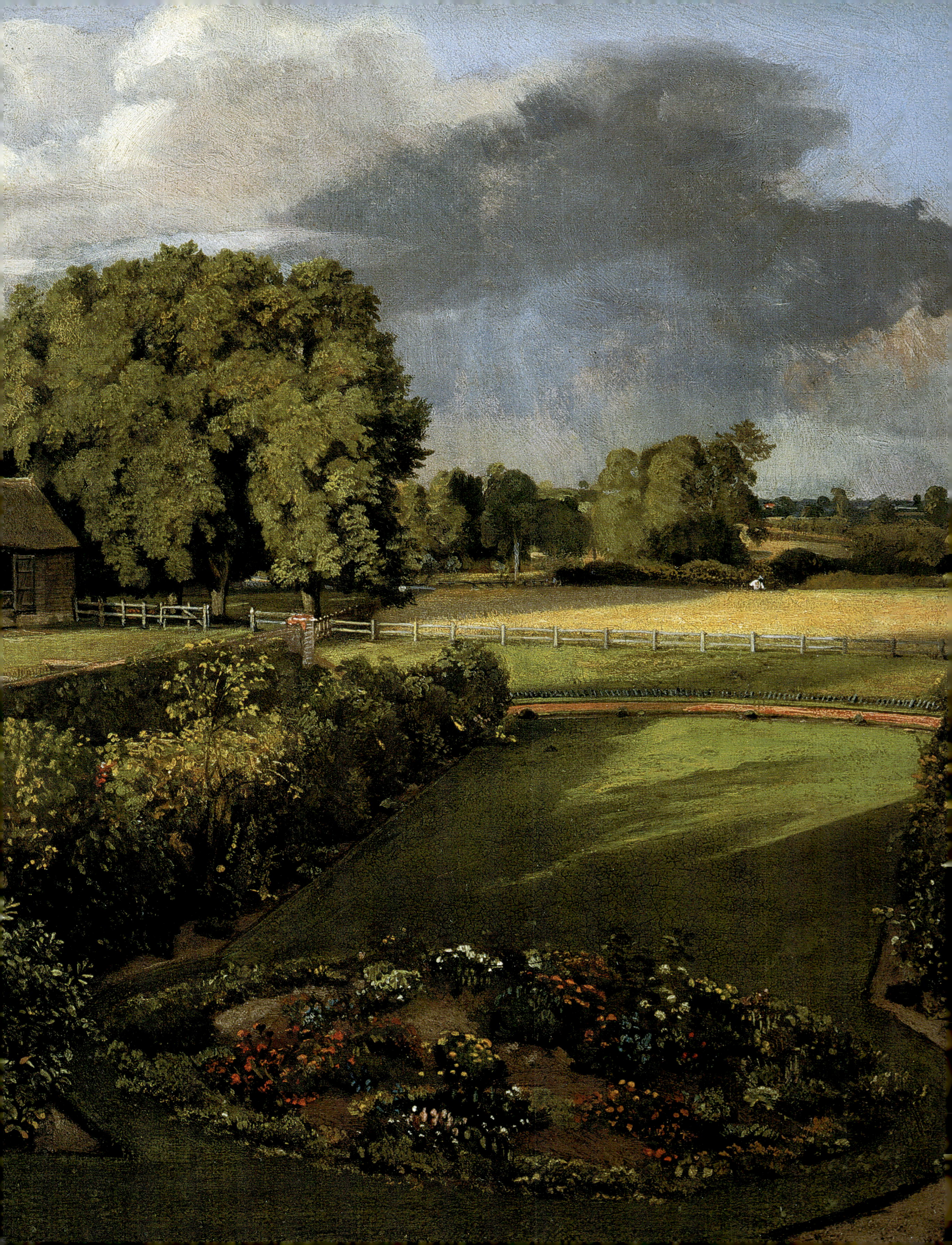

VISIONS OF LANDSCAPE

JOHN GAGE

IN SEARCH OF ENGLISHNESS

Writing from Rome in May 1762, the figure painter and portraitist Matthew William Peters confessed:

> It is true, in regard to the country, there is more fair weather here than in England; the air is certainly much purer; you see objects more distinctly at a distance, and the distant mountains are tinged with a clearer azure. But then has the best colourist here, who is thought to be Claude de Lorrain, made a more transparent glow of colours than we see on a fine evening from Hampstead Heath or the terrace at Windsor or is it possible for colours to make such? If not, why do we leave so great a field of science to follow chimaeras ...?[1]

Peters was articulating the feelings of many British Grand Tourists, for Britain was already thought to offer subjects as striking as Italy's, even though – and this was a running complaint through the literature of landscape into the twentieth century – available materials and techniques might be inadequate to represent them. British landscape was crucially implicated in the mid-eighteenth-century campaign to establish a national school of painting. Until then it had been represented very largely by foreigners, such as the Antwerp painter Jan Siberechts or the Haarlem artist Leonhard Knyff, but now a generation of ambitious native landscapists such as Richard Wilson (cat. 112-114) and Thomas Gainsborough (cat. 147-148) were exploring their own countryside in regional Britain.

Twenty years after Peters made his observations in Rome, a young Cambridge graduate, Joseph Holden Pott, published a treatise on landscape painting, in which he claimed:

> Hitherto few attempts have been made towards forming an English School ... [but] In this country, the merely copying from nature would of itself give a character to the landscapes of our painters, which would be peculiar, and would sufficiently establish the taste of an English School ... Every foreigner is immediately and powerfully struck with the beautiful verdure that prevails here through the year ... Nothing is to be found in any country at all resembling an English park; nature no where appears in so luxuriant a dress, so uncontrolled in her forms, and so lively in her tints ... The English park and forest afford an infinite variety of character in its trees, an endless choice of foliage. We have also a great advantage over Italy itself, in the great variety and beauty of our northern skies, the forms of which are often so lovely and magnificent, where so much action is seen in the rolling of the clouds: all this is nearly unknown to the placid southern hemisphere ...[2]

Pott pointed to the variety of the English and Welsh castles, so much more 'noble and interesting' than Poussin's monotonous buildings; the mountains and waterfalls of Wales, Derbyshire and the West of England and the 'effects of nature' in the English Lakes. A few years later the writer who did most to promote these landscape features, Rev. William Gilpin (see cat. 119), published his view that, 'From whatever cause it proceeds, certain I believe it is, that this country exceeds most countries in the *variety* of its picturesque beauties.'[3]

Although it was Gilpin more than anyone who popularized the notion of the Picturesque – nature viewed as a series of pictures – he was remarkably unenthusiastic about the painting of Claude, the most influential of the Old Masters of landscape, for he felt that in Claude's work 'we rarely find an instance of good composition in any of his pictures, and still more rarely an exhibition of any grand scene or appearance of Nature.'[4] We shall find that this was a view entirely at odds with that of painters in the Romantic period. Wilson, who had studied for several years in Rome, was notorious for flooding his British scenery with Italian light, and even Gainsborough, who had not travelled

John Constable, ***Golding Constable's Flower Garden*** (detail), cat. 153

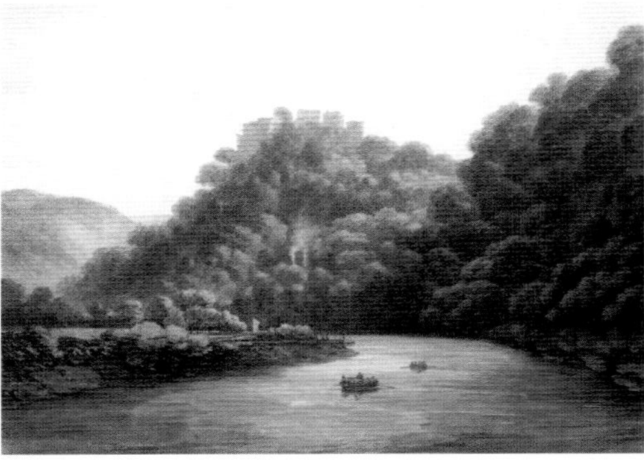

fig. 1
Thomas Hearne
Goodrich Castle on the Wye, c. 1785
Watercolour, pen and black ink, touches of white chalk, over graphite on paper, 22.5 x 31.3 cm
Yale Center for British Art, Paul Mellon Collection, New Haven

abroad, wrote in the 1760s that he had never found an English scene that 'affords a Subject equal to the poorest imitations of Gaspar or Claude'.[5]

A generation later, when landscape painting had established itself firmly in the repertory of British art, J.M.W. Turner, who, unlike Pott or Gilpin, had some experience of continental travel, pointed to the changeability of the British weather as giving a particular impetus to landscape art in his own country:

> [In] our variable climate, where [all] the seasons are recognizable in one day, where all the vapoury turbulence involves the face of things, where nature seems to sport in all her dignity and dispensing incidents for the artist's study and deep revealing more than any other ... how happily is the landscape painter situated, how roused by every change of nature in every moment that allows no languor even in her effects which she places before him, and demands most peremptorily every moment his admiration and investigation, to store his mind with every change of time and place...[6]

But of course the vagaries of weather were far from peculiar to the British Isles, and later in the same passage Turner argued that some of the weather effects in works by Nicolas Poussin and Gaspar Dughet were 'indebted to clouds of a northern atmosphere' – presumably over France.

There were other, more decisive, factors that encouraged a specifically British approach to landscape. One was the tradition of landscape gardening, which, from the earliest years of the eighteenth century, had promoted the idea of a 'natural' garden as opposed to the formal garden developed on the Continent, although some of the ingredients of this style of gardening, which came to be known as 'English', were French in origin, for example the *ha-ha* or sunken fence.[7] The English landscape garden, whether in the style of Lancelot 'Capability' Brown, with its extensive vistas across well-mown meadows (see cat. 113), or the more intimate wooded walks of William Kent's Rousham or Henry Hoare's Stourhead, was always fashioned under the banner of 'nature'. One of the last designers of extensive gardens, Humphrey Repton, gave among his 'Rules of Gardening':

> *First,* it must display the natural beauties, and hide the natural defects of every situation.
> *Secondly,* it should give the appearance of extent and freedom, by carefully disguising or hiding the boundary.
> *Thirdly,* it must studiously conceal every interference of art, however expensive, by which the natural scenery is improved, making the whole appear the production of nature only...[8]

Repton came to specialize in modest, middle-class gardens, but the landscape garden movement had originally flourished on the expansive estates of the aristocracy. The rise of British landscape art could not depend upon such a limited patronage, and the very widespread support it enjoyed had been created by far more accessible factors. One was landscape poetry, notably the Scottish poet James Thomson's *The Seasons,* first published in 1730 and with more than three hundred editions over the following century. As an early commentator, Joseph Warton, wrote:

> The *Seasons* of Thomson have been very instrumental in diffusing a general taste for the beauties of *nature* and *landscape.* It is only within a few years that the picturesque scenes of our own country, our lakes, mountains, cascades, caverns and castles, have been visited and described...[9]

Landscape painters such as Turner and Constable had frequent recourse to quotations – and misquotations – from Thomson, to enrich their catalogue titles for public exhibitions by reference to a sister art; and the *Seasons* was often cited in the new literature of landscape.

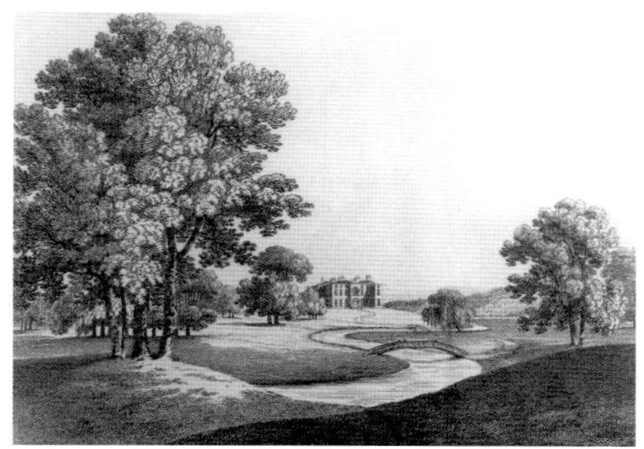
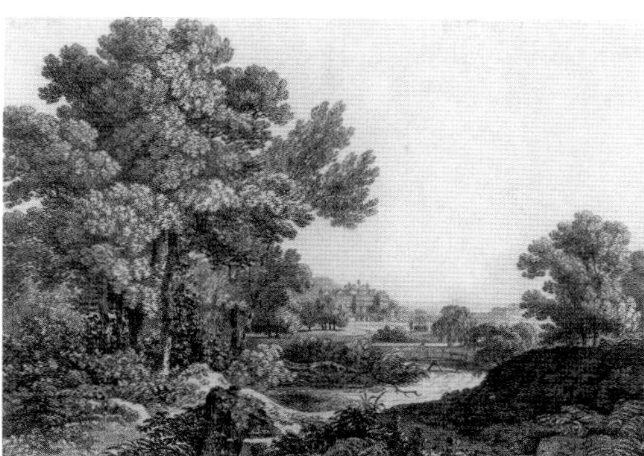

fig. 2, 3
Benjamin Pouncey after **Thomas Hearne**
A Brownian Landscape and ***A Picturesque View of the Same Landscape Park***,
from Richard Payne Knight,
The Landscape: A Didactic Poem in three books addressed to Uvedale Price, 1794
Etchings, 27.4 x 30 cm
Yale Center for British Art,
Paul Mellon Collection, New Haven

Warton's 'picturesque' signals what was probably the most decisive factor in encouraging the spread of British landscape art. The word had migrated from Italian *pittoresco* early in the eighteenth century, but it later became a heavily loaded aesthetic term, the focus of a debate on the relationship of art to nature, which not only stimulated a good deal of theoretical writing, but also – and more importantly – led to the publication of many guidebooks to the 'picturesque' regions of Britain, guidebooks which, in turn, encouraged tourism itself. The chief promoter of the picturesque tour was Gilpin, who began his career as a writer, significantly, with a short book on the landscape garden at Stowe in Buckinghamshire (1748).

Gilpin's first published Tour was *Observations on the River Wye, and Several Parts of South Wales, etc., relative chiefly to Picturesque Beauty; Made in the Summer of the Year, 1770* (1782); and he had been able to travel in the tour-boats which were already plying on this river (fig. 1).[10] In 1786 Gilpin published his guide to the English Lakes, where, a decade earlier, Thomas West, author of another very popular guide, had established 'stations', directing tourists to the most 'picturesque' views. Gilpin's Scottish Highlands guide followed in 1789.

In all these guidebooks Gilpin was leading his readers through the grand, mountainous country, which in earlier discussions would have been called 'sublime'. He had little time for the agricultural landscape, which came to occupy many painters in the years around 1800. His posthumous guide to the flatlands of East Anglia was not published until 1809; and apropos of the Isle of Wight, in the English Channel off Portsmouth, a few years earlier, he had written:

> *Picturesque beauty* is a phrase but little understood. We precisely mean by it that kind of beauty which *would look well in a picture*. Neither grounds laid out by art [i.e. landscape gardens], nor improved by agriculture, are of this kind. The Isle of Wight is, in fact, a large garden, or, rather, a field, which in every part has been disfigured by the spade, the coulter and the harrow. It abounds much more in tillage than in pasturage; and of all species of cultivation, cornlands are the most unpicturesque. The regularity of corn-fields disgusts; and the colour of corn, especially near harvest, is out of tune with every thing else...[11]

It was left to other writers to distinguish between 'sublime', 'beautiful' and 'picturesque'; but all of them agreed that picturesqueness implied irregularity, roughness and variety; and one of them, Richard Payne Knight, illustrated this idea graphically in his poem *The Landscape* (1794), where a bare Brownian park, with its occasional clumps of trees (fig. 2), very similar to Wilson's *Tabley House* (cat. 113), is contrasted with the rich plantings and undergrowth around a mansion close in style to Knight's own Downton Castle (fig. 3). The vocabulary of viewing real landscape was indeed confused: when the novelist Ann Radcliffe visited Derwentwater in the Lake District in 1794, she found that:

> the beauty of its banks contending with the wildness of its rocks, gives opposite impressions to the mind, and the force of each is, perhaps, destroyed by the admission of the other. Sublimity can scarcely exist without simplicity; and even grandeur loses much of its elevating effect when united with a considerable portion of beauty; then descending to become magnificence.[12]

The Lake poet William Wordsworth sought for many years to bring some order into these notions, and in an unpublished essay on the sublime and the beautiful of around 1811, he rejected the Gilpinesque methods of visual analysis out of hand:

> ...I cannot pass from the sublime without guarding the ingenuous reader against those caprices of vanity & presumption derived from false teachers in the philosophy of the fine arts & of taste, which Painters, connesieurs [*sic*] , & amateurs are perpetually interposing between the light of nature & their own minds

> ... 'Oh,' says one of these tutored spectators, 'what a scene should we have before us here upon the shores of Windermere, if we could but strike out those pikes of Langdale by which it is terminated; they are so intensely *picturesque* that their presence excludes from the mind all sense of the sublime.' Extravagant as such an ejaculation is, it has been heard from the mouths of Persons who pass for intelligent men of cultivated mind.[13]

The understanding of the 'picturesque' was vastly extended in the nineteenth century, and ambitious and innovative landscape artists of a later generation had no inhibitions about using the term in the loosest way. The young Turner had recourse to the older vocabulary on trips to Wales, Scotland and Switzerland around 1800, but in his maturity he was happy to entitle a thoroughly heterogeneous collection of landscape engravings *Picturesque Views in England and Wales*.[14] Constable, too, referred to his characteristic scenes of agricultural country, the bane of Gilpin, as 'picturesque'.[15] Even the promoters of the new 'scientific' aesthetic of the mid-century (p. 41) still used this by now almost meaningless term: Prof. D.T. Ansted entitled one of his editorials for *The Art Journal* in 1863, 'Clouds, Air and Atmospheric Meteors, in their Relation to the Picturesque'. But the Picturesque movement had nevertheless done a great service to British art.

THE ROLE OF THE ACADEMY

Towards the close of the 1760s Lord Shelburne commissioned a number of painters to execute landscapes for the decoration of the drawing-room at Bowood, his country seat in Wiltshire, and three of them – it is assumed that they were Wilson, Gainsborough and the Irish artist George Barret – were exhorted to produce a *chef d'oeuvre*, 'as they were intended to lay the *foundation of a school of British landscapes,* the want of which has been often lamented.'[16] What is striking about the singling out of these three artists is not simply that they were the then most distinguished British landscapists, but that they were all foundation members of the Royal Academy, established in these years precisely to raise the profile of British art. For the Royal Academy, modelled as it was on the art academies of Continental Europe, did not rank landscape very highly: it never formed part of its teaching; and even within the genre of landscape itself it distinguished a hierarchy of prestige. When Gilpin showed his essay, 'On Picturesque Beauty' (cat. 119) to Sir Joshua Reynolds, first President of the new Academy, Reynolds retorted that 'picturesque' could only be applied to nature, not fine art, and he later stated that it was a term appropriate only to the 'inferior schools' of art, the Venetians and Rubens: 'variety of tints and forms is picturesque; but ... the reverse of this – (uniformity of colour and a long continuation of lines) produces grandeur', the basis of the 'grand stile'.[17]

Although even the most ambitious landscape painters, Wilson and Gainsborough, sometimes represented particular places (cat. 112-114, 147), topography was shunned in the Academy as the province of humble specialists, who usually worked in watercolour: when Gainsborough rejected Lord Hardwicke's commission to paint topography, he referred to the watercolourist Paul Sandby R.A, as 'the only Man of Genius' in this line.[18] Constable, whose devotion to particular places was fundamental, and who manipulated them far less than, say, Wilson or Turner, rarely gave specific topographical titles to his exhibited works. Thus the large view of his father's mill at Flatford in Suffolk (cat. 162) was exhibited at the Academy as *Scene on a Navigable River,* and Flatford Lock (cat. 163) at the British Institution as *Landscape and Lock.* As a young man, Constable had rejected teaching topographical drawing at the Royal Military Academy, since 'it would have been a death blow to all my prospects of perfection in the Art I love'.[19]

The Picturesque movement had often sought to disarm criticism that British scenery was unworthy of serious attention by relating it to admired Old Master styles: here, for example, from a guide to the Lake District of 1774:

> The paintings of Poussin describe the nobleness of Hulls-water; the works of Salvator Rosa express the romantic and rocky scenes of Keswick; and the tender and elegant touches of Claude Lorraine and Smith [probably Thomas Smith of Derby] pencil forth the rich variety of Windermere.[20]

Similarly, Gilpin had scattered untranslated quotations from Latin poets in his first excursion into picturesque publishing, the *Wye Tour* of 1782 (although they were translated in the second edition),[21] just as Constable dignified his landscape manifesto, *English Landscape Scenery,* of 1830, with a Latin inscription captioning an image of his childhood home (fig. 4).[22]

Reynolds (who had occasionally painted landscapes, one of which was owned by Constable) especially condemned those fleeting effects of light or weather which 'the Painters call "Accidents of Nature"';[23] yet he was not followed by all the teachers at the Academy. The Irish history painter James Barry, for example, Professor of Painting in the late 1780s and 1790s, introduced into a lecture on chiaroscuro a vivid evocation of the lighting of some scenery around London:

> There are times when the scenes about Hyde Park, Richmond, Windsor and Blackheath appear very little interesting. The differences between a meridian and

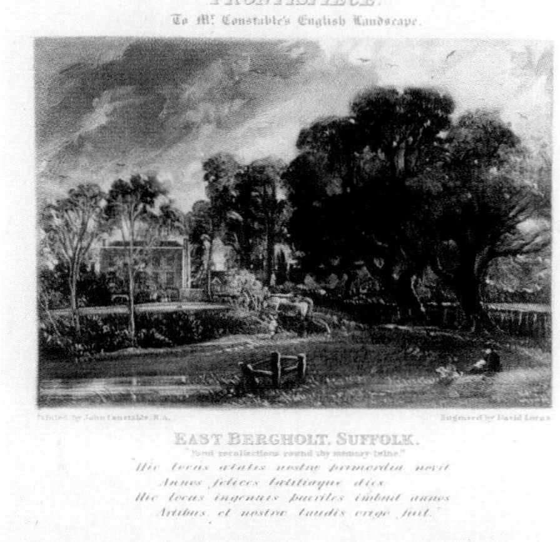

fig. 4
David Lucas
Frontispiece to Constable's
English Landscape Scenery, 1830
Mezzotint, 13.9 x 18.7 cm
Private Collection

> evening light, the reposes of extensive shadow, the half-lights and catching splendours that those scenes sometimes exhibit, compared with their ordinary appearance, do abundantly show how much is gained by seizing upon those transitory moments of fascination, when nature appears with such accumulated advantage ...[24]

Landscape painters, including Turner and Constable, may well have heard these words as Academy students; and Barry's remarks will have chimed with their own developing attitudes.

But probably much more influential than the lectures by the professors at the Academy was the exchange of ideas among the students themselves;[25] and it is clear that around 1800 there was a very active interest in outdoor landscape painting in the circle of the Scottish student Andrew Robertson, including Constable, who was to take sketching from nature to an unprecedented level of subtlety. In a letter of 1802, Robertson outlined a programme of sketching outdoor motifs, including, significantly, the study of moving clouds; but most far-sighted of all was his proposal to finish landscape paintings outdoors, a practice that Constable was not able to follow until many years later, although he had long talked about it.[26] Working from nature was now axiomatic for most British landscapists.

British landscape art is especially remarkable for the inventive use of watercolour, which was regarded in the early nineteenth century as a peculiarly British medium as a Scottish artist wrote from Rome in 1816: '... in the beautiful art of painting in watercolours, Britain stands supreme, or rather, she may be said to have appropriated it exclusively.'[27] Yet the Royal Academy was officially even more prejudiced against watercolour than it was against landscape. Watercolourists, if they aspired to membership, were obliged to exhibit work in oils; and towards the end of the eighteenth century, an Associate of the Academy, Joseph Wright of Derby, sneered, 'Paper and camel hair pencils [i.e.watercolour brushes] are better adapted for the amusement of ladies than the pursuit of an artist.'[28] Nonetheless, Wright's unusual oil technique (cat. 7, 115), using a monochrome underpainting and very thin glazes over a pure white ground, was closely related to contemporary watercolour procedures, just as Turner and Constable developed a supremely fluent handling of oils from their earlier watercolour practice.[29]

The many specialists in the medium who emerged during this period soon formed themselves into societies, to combat the indifference and even open hostility of the Academy; and yet it was the exhibiting arrangements of this body that gave them the courage to do so. Thomas Uwins, a member of the Watercolour Society, which had been established in 1804, recalled that the Council Room at the Academy around 1800 was devoted, during the Summer Exhibition, to works in this medium, and it was there that the public could view

> the beautiful landscapes of Girtin ... and the splendid creations of Turner – the mightiest enchanter who has ever wielded the magic power of art in any age or country. At this time the council room ... was itself the great point of attraction. Here crowds first collected, and here they lingered longest, because it was here the imagination was addressed through the means of an art which added the charm of novelty to excellence. It was the fascination of this room that first led to the idea of forming an exhibition entirely of pictures in water-colours.[30]

From this time the Academic prejudice against the medium began to be relaxed, and Reynolds's successor as President, the American Benjamin West, who was also something of a devotee of naturalistic landscape, proposed in 1810 that the law which prohibited membership to watercolour specialists should be rescinded: 'The law ... was made against inferior works done on paper, but the works now produced are of a quality not then [in 1769] known.'[31]

Thus the Royal Academy was deeply implicated in the rise of landscape in Britain, and ambitious artists

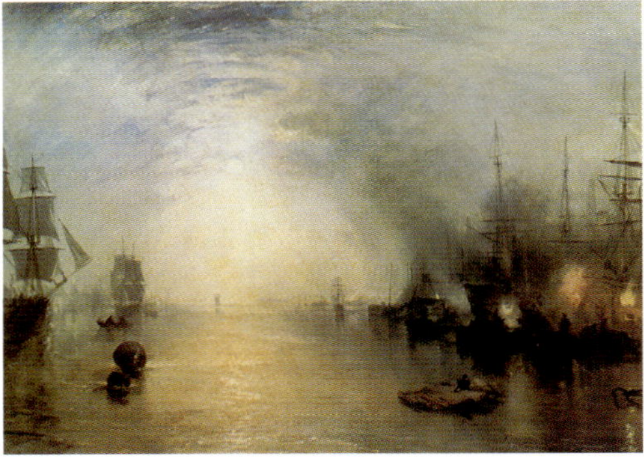

fig. 5
J.M.W. Turner
Keelmen Heaving in Coals by Night, 1835
Oil on canvas, 90.2 x 121.9 cm
National Gallery of Art, Washington,
Widener Collection

such as Turner and Constable made its Exhibition a platform for their most ambitious works. Yet in the course of the nineteenth century, it was the growing number of rival exhibiting societies which attracted most landscape work. In 1865 the *Cornhill Magazine* noted that in the previous quarter century only two landscape painters had been elected to the Academy, and landscapes were being skied in its Exhibitions, 'so ... as to render them invisible'.[32]

Although landscapists outside the Academy, such as John Linnell (cat. 181), continued to make a very substantial living, prominent Academicians such as Leighton and Watts, who were gifted landscape sketchers, never made landscape a central preoccupation. The Pre-Raphaelite Brotherhood did put landscape in the forefront of their studies, as we shall see below, but even they were more concerned to use it in the elaboration of figure subjects than in its own right.

THE INDUSTRIAL SCENE

The eighteenth and nineteenth centuries in Britain witnessed an unprecedented wave of industrial development, aided successively by steam power, gas lighting and electricity. These technological developments for the most part refashioned the towns and cities of the Midlands and the North, yet the landscape, too, was often transformed and offered a range of novel motifs, which continued to fascinate artists well into the twentieth century.

At first, the appearance of mills, mines and furnaces in often mountainous areas of the British Isles could easily be accommodated within the familiar concept of the Sublime. Thus Sir William Chambers in his fantasy of landscape design, *A Dissertation on Oriental Gardening* (1772) imagined that the Chinese 'conceal in cavities, on the summits of the highest mountains, foundries, lime-kilns, and glass-works, which send forth large volumes of flame, and continued columns of thick smoke, that give these mountains the appearance of volcanoes.'[33] The many tourists who turned aside from gorges and waterfalls to undergo the considerable discomforts of a visit to a furnace or a mine, were often sustained by recollections of some snatch of ancient or modern mythology. Here, for example, an account of an iron works in Staffordshire around 1811:

> ... I was not only astonished by the works of art, but Nature had also contributed to add terror to the scene, by the earth smoking at different places; in consequence of the burning coal-pits ... The roaring of the furnaces, the clanking of iron chains and machinery, reminded the traveller of the poetical descriptions given us of the infernal regions ... The awfulness of the scene reminded me of the description of the Cyclops forging thunder for Jupiter. [Nevertheless,] ... sight of this concussion of wind, fire and water, exceeds all ancient or modern descriptions I have heretofore read of as much as reality does imagination.[34]

Artists also dressed the industrial scene in the conventional trappings of Sublimity. Thus Wright of Derby's view of Arkwright's cotton mill is a moonlight picture (cat. 7), just as Turner later showed colliers being loaded at night near an industrialized Newcastle upon Tyne, a subject which allowed him to make an exciting contrast between moonlight and firelight (fig. 5).[35] But night scenes of industry also conveyed the serious and novel message that the new economics of mechanization demanded that plant be operative round the clock.

One of the most visible consequences of industrialization was atmospheric pollution, to which many tourists in the early nineteenth century drew particular attention. In 1802, for example, Rev. Richard Warner visited Coalbrookdale in Shropshire, one of the most visited industrial sites and the subject of many pictures, notably those by the Alsatian artist Philippe Jacques de Loutherbourg (cat. 8). The valley, said Warner,

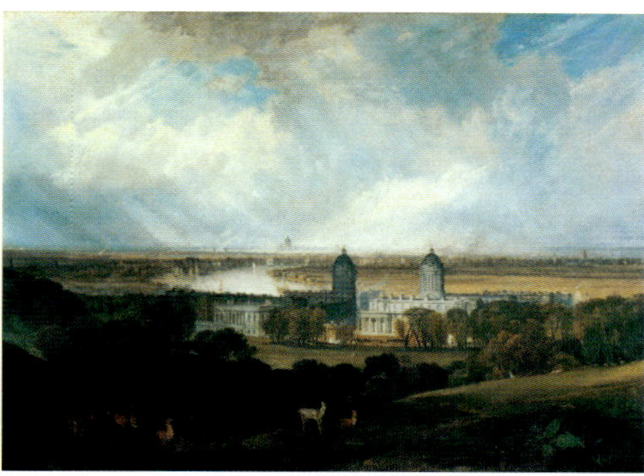

fig. 6
J.M.W. Turner
***London from Greenwich Park*, 1809**
Oil on canvas, 90 x 120 cm
Tate, London

> ... would be exceedingly picturesque, were it not for the huge foundries, which, volcanolike, send up volumes of smoke ... discolouring nature, and robbing the trees of their beauty; and the vast heaps of red-hot iron ore and coke, that give the bottom ever burning with solid fire more the appearance of Milton's hell, than that of paradise.[36]

Similarly, nearly thirty years later, the more down-to-earth Scottish engineer James Nasmyth surveyed the Black Country in Worcestershire, 'with its blazing furnaces, the smoke of which blackened the country as far as the eye could reach ... We pay a heavy price for it [industrial supremacy] in the loss of picturesqueness and beauty.'[37]

Most of the more ambitious landscapists agreed, and they rarely represented these subjects, although one of them, the Norwich painter John Sell Cotman, showed precisely this Black Country devastation (cat. 9). On the other hand, with aerial pollution Turner was in his element, and he often depicted industrial towns, with their dense haze of smoke and steam (cat. 11). Where his early friend Thomas Girtin might take a distant view of the smoke-plume from a lone lime kiln on a Yorkshire river (cat. 127), Turner allowed polluted atmosphere to suffuse the whole picture, softening the outlines of distant objects, whether factory chimneys or steamboats on river, lake or ocean. As Constable noted in the 1830s, Turner 'seems to paint with tinted steam, so evanescent and so airy'.[38]

Yet Turner's attitude to industrial developments has remained ambiguous. That he was not entirely happy with them is suggested by a poem, drafted about 1808, on some large town, in which the 'high raised smoke' is 'no prototype of Rest', but rather part of the 'World of Care'.[39] The idea crystallized in the caption to a distant view of *London from Greenwich,* shown at the Academy in 1809 (fig. 6):

> Where burthen'd Thames reflects the crowded sail,
> Commercial care and busy toil prevail,
> Whose murky veil, aspiring to the skies,
> Obscures thy beauty, and thy form denies,
> Save where thy spires pierce the doubtful air,
> As gleams of hope amidst a world of care.[40]

The difficulty of identifying a clear-cut attitude towards the modern industrial world in Turner[41] is compounded in our reading of his rural landscapes, where he was one of the first British artists to highlight aspects of the modern agricultural economy, which also transformed the appearance of many parts of the country. *Frosty Morning* of c. 1813 (cat. 152) was the culmination of a series of landscapes that represented hard and unpleasant work by the rural workforce. But without the aid of specific titles or captions, the subject is problematic: modern commentators have identified the labouring figures as digging turnips, excavating gravel or sand to repair the road, and even killing bees in order to harvest the honey.[42] Turner, however, seems to have been interested primarily in an effect of weather: his caption in the Academy catalogue was from Thomson's *Winter* - 'The rigid hoar frost melts before his beam' - and this was certainly the message picked up by the reviewers.[43]

In 1811 a Major Cartwright complained that 'English gentlemen are perpetually travelling. Some go to see Lakes and mountains. Were it not allowable to travel for seeing the actual conditions of a starving society?'[44] Although there was some talk in the late eighteenth century of the morality of landscape,[45] there is little indication that landscape painters, working as they did for a wealthy market, were much concerned with the acute deprivation suffered by industrial or agricultural workers. It was not until the social reform movements of the Victorian period that artists began to look with greater sympathy at the humble inhabitants of their scenes. The heroism of gamekeepers (cat. 5) was supplemented by the heroism of labourers (cat. 22), fisherfolk (cat. 16-17) and even poachers (cat. 35).

In *Hereford from Haywood Lodge* (cat. 157) G.R. Lewis presents a picture of untroubled rural work. The time is 1815, at the close of the Napoleonic wars, when agricul-

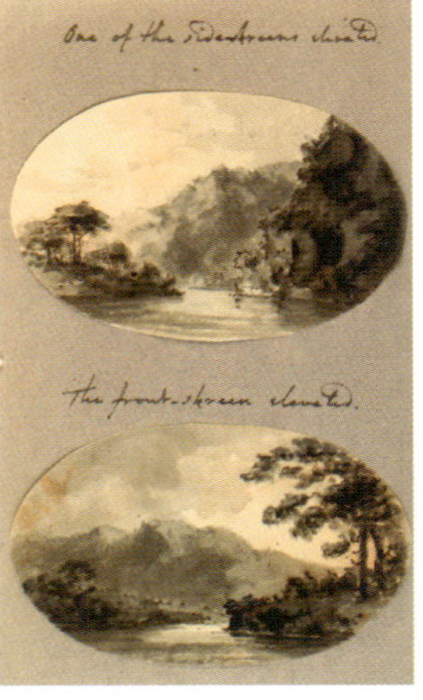

fig. 7
William Gilpin
Sketches of River Scenery for
Observations on the River Wye, 1782
Pen and ink and wash drawings, 13.5 cm x 22.5 cm,
2 oval drawings on page, each measuring 12.5 cm x 8 cm
Llyfrgell Genedlaethol Cymru –
National Library of Wales, Aberystwyth

tural prices were still high; the place, the Wye Valley in Herefordshire, a region where the naturally fertile soil permitted entirely traditional agricultural practices, and where, in the words of a contemporary agricultural analyst, 'Health, peace and plenty smile in the countenance of its very peasantry.'[46] Lewis's peasants are not smiling, but neither are they downtrodden, or merely picturesque accessories to a supremely naturalistic landscape. The Picturesque movement was now fully in retreat, but the agricultural countryside, before it could be represented, had already been fashioned to serve human needs.

The landscape of East Anglia was also shaped by industry, as we see already in the chain of reservoirs servicing Cobbold's Suffolk brewery in Gainsborough's *Holywells Park*. (cat. 147). Constable's Suffolk, too, was profoundly marked by the rural economy. His father's large mill at Flatford was the subject of many studies and several exhibited paintings (cat. 159-160, 162), and Constable also painted a second mill managed by his father at nearby Dedham. A windmill owned by the family can be seen in the distance in the view over the kitchen garden of their house in East Bergholt (cat. 154). Constable senior was a shipper of the grain he milled as well as of coal; and the river Stour, which had been partly canalized in the eighteenth century, was essential to this traffic. The painter made two of the thirteen locks, for whose upkeep his father was partly responsible, the subjects of major paintings (cat. 163).[47] So this was an industrialized landscape: Constable's 'nature' was very far from the wild 'nature' of the Picturesque tourists, but it was a nature which, in the nineteenth century, was increasingly the subject of art.

CLOSE ENCOUNTERS

In 1803 Constable wrote to a friend about the then novel branch of painting, the Panorama, which, in its attempt at absolute realism, was the ancestor of IMAX cinema and 'virtual reality'. It was, said Constable, 'all the rage', and his former friend, the landscape and portrait painter Ramsay Richard Reinagle (1775-1862), was much occupied with it; yet 'great principles are neither expected nor looked for in this mode of describing nature.' Reinagle 'views Nature minutely and *cunningly* , but with no greatness or breadth ... it is not to be considered as a whole ...'[48] Constable himself always considered his landscapes as wholes, as compositions, which was one reason for his close study of Old Master painting, and this was a common idea in eighteenth-century Britain. Alexander Cozens, whose generalizing approach to landscape 'species' was fascinating to Constable as late as the 1820s,[49] also emphasized composition in his landscape teaching (cat. 116, 166); and Gilpin, whose style of sketching was in this tradition (fig. 7), insisted in his theoretical writing (cat. 119), that the sketcher must 'remove little objects, which in nature push themselves too much in sight, and serve only to introduce too many parts into your *composition* ... No beauty of light, colouring or execution, can atone for the want of *composition*.'[50]

Yet, even in the eighteenth century some landscapists were clear that there were other values to be cultivated. Gainsborough wrote at the end of his life of one of his early imitations of Ruisdael (fig. 8), 'though there is very little idea of composition in the picture, the touch and closeness to nature in the study of the parts and *minutiae* are equal to any of my latter productions.'[51] His mid-nineteenth-century biographer, G.W. Fulcher, also described some studies of trees (now lost), 'drawn and coloured in the open air', one of which, a young oak, 'is painted leaf for leaf, whilst ferns and grasses are portrayed with microscopic fidelity.'[52]

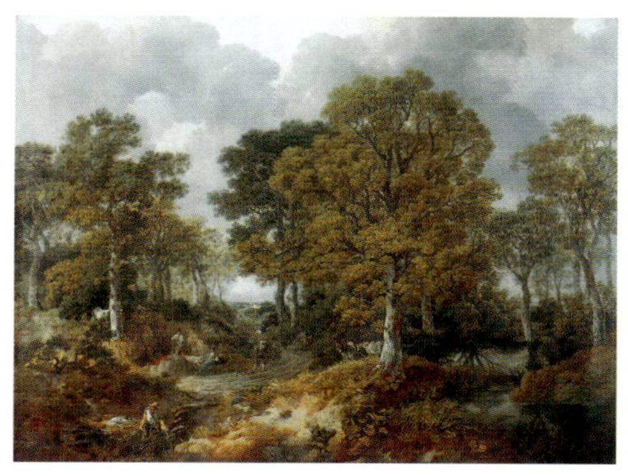

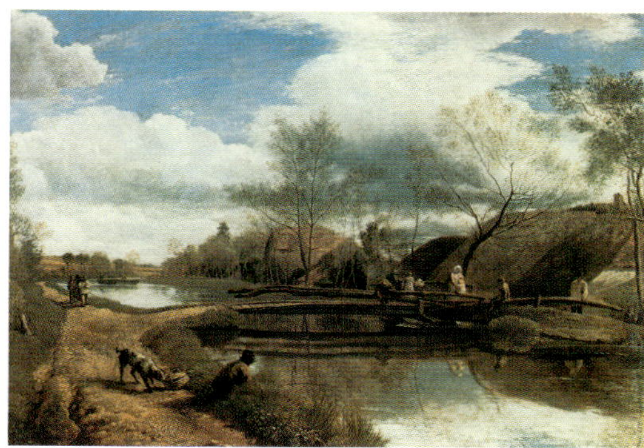

fig. 8
Thomas Gainsborough
Gainsborough's Forest, c. 1746-48
Oil on canvas, 121.9 x 154.9 cm
National Gallery, London

fig. 9
John Linnell
The River Kennet near Newbury, 1815
Oil on canvas on wood,
45.1 x 65.2 cm
Fitzwilliam Museum, Cambridge

The minute study of the particulars of nature had, of course, a very long history in Europe, going back at least to Dürer, and it was a very active landscape practice in England during the Romantic period. Constable sometimes made highly detailed sketches of plants, trees and clouds, and in the 1830s he began to study the natural sciences, botany, geology and, especially, meteorology with great enthusiasm. This was the decade when he proclaimed to an audience at a scientific institution that 'painting is a science, and should be pursued as an enquiry into the laws of nature.'[53] Yet Constable was reluctant to treat his exhibited paintings in this particularizing fashion, and, with the exception of a short period in the mid-1810s (when he was responding to academic criticisms of his technique),[54] he never did so. Nor, in general, did his contemporaries, although there are occasional examples in John Linnell (fig. 9) and, more importantly, in the early period of the career of Linnell's protégé Samuel Palmer (cat. 253-255). Yet Palmer's finished drawings of the 1820s, with their densely worked all-over surfaces, were in no sense out-of-door images; their style is closest to Blake's illustrations to Virgil (cat. 248), and in a letter to Linnell of 1828 Palmer maintained that, 'The thousand repetitions of little forms [in nature] ... seem hard to be reconciled with the unwinning severity, the awfulness, the ponderous globosity of art ...'[55] Palmer conveyed this 'ponderous globosity' at this time by means of a broad, blot-like technique (cat. 254).

Palmer's visionary style was stimulated by access, through Blake and Linnell, to Old Master prints, especially those by Dürer and Lucas van Leyden. This taste for what had hitherto been spurned as 'primitive' was taken up again in the mid-nineteenth century with greater rigour and consistency by the group of artists who signed their works 'PRB': the Pre-Raphaelite Brotherhood. Linnell, who, like his friend Blake, was familiar with a London collection of early German and Netherlandish art and reproduced a copy of part of Van Eyck's *Ghent Altarpiece* there, became one of the earliest supporters of this emerging group.[56]

The 1840s was the crucial decade, when there was an active public interest in early art (Van Eyck's *Arnolfini Portrait* entered the National Gallery in 1843), and when, in 1848, the British Institution mounted a major exhibition of early Italian, German and Netherlandish painting, including attributions to Van Eyck, Van der Goes, Lucas van Leyden , Memlinc and Massys. This interest in more 'natural' Old Masters coincided with the belief that landscape art should above all reveal truths about the nature of nature, exemplified in the 1842 edition of Wordsworth's *Guide to the Lakes*, which, for the first time, included supplements on botany and geology, this last by a leading Cambridge geologist, Adam Sedgwick.[57]

There is no doubt that the PRB saw itself, and was seen, as a wholly new breed of landscape artists. In 1850 one of the Brothers, F.G. Stephens, spoke of their 'entire seeking after originality in a more humble manner than has been practised since the decline of Italian Art in the Middle Ages'. This was clearest in landscape: they had founded 'an entirely new school of natural painting ... the simple attention to nature in detail as well as in generalities. By this they have succeeded in earning for themselves the reputation of being the finest landscape painters in Europe.' Stephens concluded, significantly:

> The sciences have become almost exact within the present century. Geology and chemistry are almost re-instituted ... If this adherence to fact, to experiment and not theory – to begin at the beginning and not fly to the end – has added so much to the knowledge of man in science, why may it not greatly assist the moral purposes of the Arts?[58]

The reference to 'generalities' here was over-optimistic, for, from the outset, the Pre-Raphaelites cultivated a laborious outdoor method which worked against the holistic approach to picture-making advocated by the earlier generation. John Ruskin, their most eloquent advocate, had been taught by a number of older landscapists, and during the early 1840s had been the warmest supporter of Turner; but from about 1845 he began in his own art to focus on closely-observed fragments (cat. 189), turning against the whole notion of 'composition', so that his father (who supported him financially) deplored his 'now constant habit of making little patches and scratches of the sections and fractions of things in a notebook ... instead of the former Proutesque or Robertsonian outlines of grand buildings and sublime scenes.'[59] In *The Elements of Drawing* (1857), Ruskin advocated the isolation of sections of the view through a small window cut in a card, in order to study the 'true' colour-relationships.[60] Lack of 'composition' continued to be held against, for example, Collins (cat. 194) and Boyce (cat. 192), into the 1860s.

This piecemeal approach to outdoor landscape painting was particularly burdensome to the Belgian-trained Ford Madox Brown, who often mentioned it in his diary. Brown's *An English Autumn Afternoon, Hampstead – Scenery in 1853* (cat. 196) had the advantage of being a view from a window, like Constable's garden scenes (cat. 153-154), but after four months' work it was abandoned, because 'the leafage began to play such fantastic tricks', and the room with the view was temporarily unavailable.[61] Brown took the painting up again in September of the following year, working on it for another month. His later claim that it was 'a literal transcript', at 3 p.m. late in October, is thus hard to sustain, not least because of the several active figures and the foreground knoll invented to accommodate the largest two.

The original, 1852-55 version of *The Last of England* (cat. 23) was, similarly, begun outdoors, but 'in the most inhuman weather': 'This work representing an outdoor scene without sunlight, I painted it chiefly out of doors when the snow was lieing [*sic*] on the ground. The madder ribbons of the bonnet took me 4 weeks to paint.'[62] Brown continued to work on it from September to November 1854, not always *en plein air*, for 'to have painted it all out of doors would have taken six weeks of intense cold & suffering & perhaps have failed.'[63] He was still engaged on it through the summer of 1855; nevertheless in 1865 he wrote simply:

> To insure the peculiar look of *light all round,* which objects have on a dull day at sea, it was painted for the most part in the open air on dull days, and when the flesh was being painted, on cold days. Absolutely without regard to the art of any period or country, I have tried to render this scene as it would appear. The minuteness of detail which would be visible under such conditions of broad day-light, I have thought necessary to imitate, as bringing the pathos of the subject more home to the beholder.[64]

Yet Brown's acute discomforts while painting *The Last of England* were nothing compared to Holman Hunt's dangerous and frustrating work at the Dead Sea, executing *The Scapegoat* (cat. 264) in 1854 and 1855. Hunt confessed to D.G. Rossetti that it was 'the opportunity of painting this extraordinary spot from Nature' which made him fix on this subject, but, quite apart from the death of the original white goat (a rare type that had been particularly hard to find) transported from Jerusalem, and the danger of attacks by thieves (Hunt was always armed), he was unable to complete the landscape *in situ* and, as he wrote to Thomas Seddon from Jerusalem in December 1854, 'humbled ... in having to do my Dead Sea work almost entirely without Nature'. Much of the foreground and the sky – as well as the goat – had to be painted in Jerusalem, 'or otherwise I must throw the picture away.' It was substantially finished by April 1855, but the final touches were not made until Hunt was back in London in the spring of the following year. Although he had been happy enough with it on the spot, Hunt now found the shrill colour of the painting 'rather absurd'.[65]

In spite of everything, Hunt believed that it was the job of landscapists to be 'merchants of nature', with 'something like the spirit of the Apostles fearing nothing. going amongst robbers. and in deserts with impunity as men without anything to lose. and every thing must be painted even the pebbles of the foreground from the place itself. unless on trial this prove *impossible* ... I think this must be the next stage of PRB indoctrination and it has been this conviction which brought me out there [to the Holy Land]. and which keeps me away in patience until the experiment has been fairly tried.'[66]

Quite apart from these temporary contingencies, Brown and Hunt thought nothing of gathering details of nature painted in different places at different times into the same 'outdoor' composition, and it is clear that for them 'nature' meant something quite different from the 'nature' of the Romantics. For Constable and Turner the paradigm of the natural world was the wind and the movement of clouds and water: a dynamism that they conveyed in their works with swift and emphatic brushwork. For the PRB, on the other hand, this paradigm was geology, with its slow accretion of forms, matched by their laborious technique; for, as a writer in the *Art Journal* declared in 1855, 'the beauties of landscape' are dependent 'on great geological phenomena.'[67]

By the 1870s, Pre-Raphaelitism was seen to be all but extinct, and although Stanley Spencer re-introduced some of its preoccupations with detail and informality (cat. 209-210), British landscape in the twentieth century, notably in Bomberg and Hitchens (cat. 216, 219) followed the more gestural course of the Romantics.

THE DIVINE PRESENCE

What most of the Pre-Raphaelites shared with most of the Romantics was a sense of the immanence of God in nature. At least one early tourist in the English Lakes regarded a visit there as 'a religious act',[68] and Wordsworth, too, in his unpublished tour of the region (c. 1812) asserted that 'The Soul of objects [of nature] must be communicated with, & that intercourse can only be realized by some degree of the divine influence of a religious imagination.'[69] The poet, on a walk with Constable one spring, applied to the new blossom the words of Christ, 'I am the resurrection and the life' (John 11: 25), an idea appropriated by the painter – a devout Anglican, whose closest friend, John Fisher, was a cleric – and retold to his wife, Maria, in a letter of 1819.[70] Constable's ordering of the landscape can be seen in the light of his reading of the *Natural Theology* of William Paley and the related ideas of the French zoologist and biologist Georges Leopold Cuvier, whose *Animal Kingdom* (1817) spoke of 'that harmony of nature irresistibly regulated by Providence'.[71] But this was common currency in eighteenth- and early nineteenth-century British culture, and was implied, rather that proclaimed, in landscape art. To find the effects of religious beliefs in landscape painting – apart from subject-pictures, such as John Martin's *Deluge* (cat. 256) – we must turn first of all to the most important provincial group of artists in the period: the Norwich School.

Visiting Norwich in 1812, Constable's friend Andrew Robertson observed:

> Painting and Drawing are as much esteemed [as music], and many are nearly as great proficients. There are some very wealthy families of Quakers, bankers etc. People of fashion and great style too, as far as is consistent with their principles. They excel very much in drawing, and some ladies here have studied anatomy very closely ... The studies of landscape about the town are infinitely beautiful and inexhaustible. The buildings, cottages etc. are charming, and have invited people to the general practice of drawing, or rather painting in water colours from nature, assisted by a man of considerable abilities as a teacher and landscape painter, who follows the art in the true way, and quite an enthusiast, as all the people here seem to be in everything ...[72]

The able artist in question was almost certainly John Crome, who, although better known as an oil painter (cat. 158), also taught watercolour, notably to a family of Quakers, the Gurneys of Earlham Hall, on the outskirts of the city. Robertson's reference to the principles of Quakerism, austere and unworldly as they usually were, hints at a very contentious issue of the time: when Linnell, an extreme Nonconformist, was considering joining the Quaker Society of Friends around 1830, the Quaker poet Bernard Barton advised him that being a Quaker painter would involve 'much difficulty and perplexity'. Barton saw himself as unusual in having a collection of art, but he noted that most affluent members of the Friends were happy to have their children taught drawing, although 'pictures are barely tolerated amongst us ... and a painter of any eminence amongst us is unknown ...'[73] Barton, who lived in neighbouring Suffolk, was supported by the Gurneys from time to time and was a great admirer of Crome, a number of whose landscapes he owned. As he wrote to the painter's biographer in 1843, contemplating his 'great Crome' was 'like looking out abroad on the unsophisticated face of Nature ...'[74] So at least the study of nature was entirely acceptable to Quakers, and drawing *en plein air* was a good means of access to it.

Catherine Gurney, drawing up a programme of study for her children in 1788, included 'a knowledge of the most approved branches of natural history, and a capacity for drawing from nature in order to promote that knowledge and facilitate the pursuit of it.'[75] Catherine's son, John Joseph, was an avid sketcher, and he in turn passed on his interest to his children, including the daughter who became the penal reformer, Elizabeth Fry. One of Catherine Gurney's favourite quotations was a famous tag from Alexander Pope's poem *An Essay on Man* (*Epistle* IV, 331):

> I love to 'look through Nature up to Nature's God'. I have no more religion than that, and in the little I have I am not the least devotional, but when I admire the beauties of Nature, I cannot help thinking of the source from whence such beauties flow.[76]

Crome was employed to teach the Gurney daughters from January 1798 and frequently took them outside to work in Earlham Park[77], but it is clear that he was not dogmatic about drawing out of doors when the weather was poor, as it was in the Lake District (where the Gurneys had a house) in October 1802, when a two- or three-hour session indoors was completed before the family and the artist set off on walking or riding excursions.[78]

Thus Norwich patronage put a premium on teaching drawing, and it was a source of wonder to a later generation of Gurneys that, although the family still had large numbers of sketches by his pupils, it owned no paintings by Crome himself.[79] This was indeed the norm in Norwich at large: at the first Norwich Society exhibition in 1805, most landscapists advertised themselves as drawing masters, offering very few oil paintings for sale; and in 1809 John Sell Cotman, a Norwich-born artist trained in London, who had returned to his native

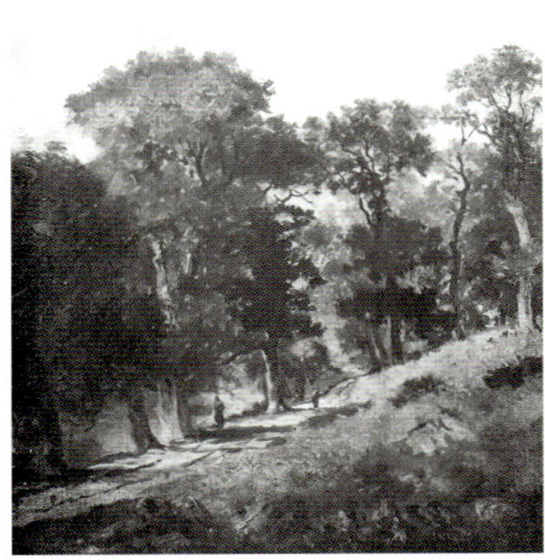

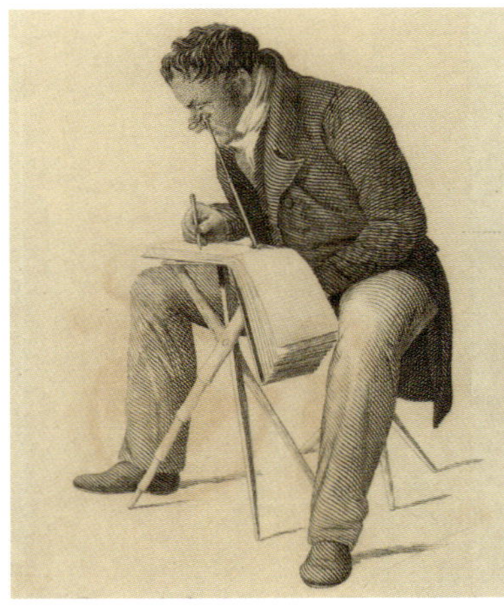

fig. 10
John Crome
Postwick Grove, 1816
Oil on millboard, 48 x 32.5 cm
Norfolk Museums and Archaeology Service, Norwich

fig. 11
Cornelius Varley
Artist sketching with a Camera Lucida, c. 1830
Engraving (detail)
Gernsheim Collection, Harry Ransom Humanities Research Center, The University of Texas at Austin

city a few year earlier, advertised in the exhibition catalogue his Circulating Library of drawings for copying. By the 1810s Norwich painters left for London to make a living, as Cotman was eventually to do. One of them, George Vincent, complained, 'I had nearly given up the hope of ever selling a picture in Norwich.' Norwich artists had far greater success in other centres, with new exhibitions beginning to be set up in Edinburgh, Leeds, Liverpool, Manchester, Newcastle and Carlisle, as well as London.[80]

The styles of both Crome and Cotman, and that of their families and pupils, are notable for breadth, rather than for precision of detail, but Crome had some experience of painting directly from nature (fig. 10), and Cotman, at least when making outdoor studies of architectural subjects in 1817, used a *camera lucida*, a recently invented device for obtaining an exact outline (fig. 11).[81] But their commitment to working out of doors was no match for Constable's or the Pre-Raphaelites', and it was probably only in their teaching practice that they worked in this way at all.

This approach to the Divine presence in Nature, no doubt more common among patrons than among artists themselves, was at the opposite pole to that of another religious extremist in this period, the High Anglican Samuel Palmer. Palmer's love of nature is clear from the sketchbook from his early teens, which shows considerable verbal and visual precocity, to the note of the mid-forties, with its proto-PRB dislike of broad, sloppy handling when painting 'a gray stem with lichens and mosses, rich as a cabinet of gems ...'[82] But in the late 1820s, under the powerful influence of Blake, Palmer rejected the difficult task of representing nature out of hand; and when Linnell, hoping that his future son-in-law would at last earn money, persuaded him to make saleable studies from nature, Palmer confessed to his friend George Richmond, 'I will, God help me, never be a naturalist by profession.'[83]

In a note from the mid-twenties, when his visionary primitivism was at its height, Palmer stated his antipathy to nature in the clearest terms, although it is characteristic that his idealism was anchored to a specific place, in this case the south London suburb of Dulwich:

> Nature is not at all the standard of Art, but art is the standard of nature. The visions of the soul, being perfect, are the only true standard by which nature must be tried ... In proportion as we enjoy and improve in imaginative art we shall love the material works of God more and more. Sometimes landscape is seen as a vision, and then seems as fine as art; but this is seldom, and bits of nature are generally much improved by being received into he soul ... Often, and I think generally, at Dulwich, the distant hills seem the most powerful objects in colour, and clear force of line: we are not troubled with aerial perspective in the valley of vision ...[84]

Such intensity could hardly be sustained for long, and when, in Italy in the late 1830s, Blake's presence was finally superseded by that of Giorgione and Titian, Palmer recognized that he could 'never paint in my old style again – even though I may paint worse ...'[85] In the event his late style, brilliant though it was, moved closer to the florid manner of his father-in-law Linnell, to whom these words had been written. Neither nature nor interior vision could any longer supply Palmer, nor any artist before Spencer, with a convincing image of the landscape divine.

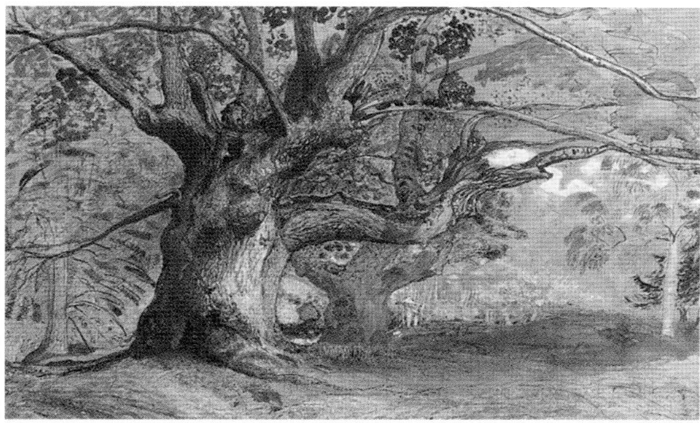

fig. 12
Samuel Palmer
Oaks Trees, Lullingstone Park, 1828
Pen and brown ink and pencil, with watercolour and bodycolour, heightened with gum on paper, 29.5 x 46.8 cm
National Gallery of Canada, Ottawa

THE LANGUAGE OF TREES

William Dyce's *George Herbert at Bemerton* (cat. 193) presents the early seventeenth-century cleric and devotional poet at his country living in Wiltshire towards the end of his life. True to his Pre-Raphaelite convictions, Dyce painted the scene at Bemerton itself, where Herbert's successor as rector was a friend.[86] But the screen of ivy-clad oaks flanking the river is not simply true to the place; it recalls the 'dark and shadie grove' in Herbert's poem 'Baptism', where the poet 'looks beyond it on the skie' [i.e. to Heaven]. Perhaps he is declaiming this very poem in Dyce's picture. Herbert was much read by High Anglicans in the nineteenth century, and Samuel Palmer was one of his most devoted admirers: on the recommendation of Linnell, he named his son Herbert, after the poet.[87] Both the poet and the painter associated trees with humanity: 'We are trees,' declared Herbert in 'Affliction', 'whom shaking fastens more,' and Herbert Palmer quoted a visionary saying of his father's that, 'Sometimes trees are seen as men. I saw one, a princess, walking stately with majestic train ...'[88] Among the nature studies which Linnell encouraged Palmer to make in 1828 are a number of brilliantly observed watercolours of oaks in Lullingstone Park in Kent (fig. 12). Palmer's embarrassed confession of failure emphasized the anthropomorphic vitality of these massive specimens:

> Milton, by one epithet, draws an oak of the largest girth I ever saw; 'Pine and *Monumental* oak' [*Il Penseroso* l.135]: I have just been trying to draw a large one in Lullingstone, but the Poet's tree is huger than any in the park: there the moss, and rifts, and barky furrows, and the mouldering grey, tho' that adds majesty to the lord of the forests; mostly catch the eye before the grasp and grapple of the roots; the muscular belly and shoulders; the twisted sinews ...[89]

Lucian Freud in our own time has made an etching of Constable's *Study of the Trunk of an Elm Tree* (cat. 185 and fig. 15), whose human quality he sensed and made the stimulus for his *Naked Portrait Standing*.[90] Constable characterized a favourite elm at Hampstead as a young lady and was distressed when it was largely destroyed by being pierced with the nails attaching a warning notice against vagrancy.[91]

One very characteristic type of British landscape subject in this period was indeed the 'portrait' of an individual tree. Gainsborough made around 1760 a portrait of a large beech tree on the estate of his friend, the theorist of the Picturesque, Uvedale Price (fig. 13), centring this prime specimen and raising it, as it were, on a pedestal. Images of single trees had long formed a part of pagan and Christian nature symbolism,[92] and in the eighteenth century they also served as political propaganda (fig. 14), but now an interest in particular trees seems to have become part of a new approach to landscape, and by the close of the century they entered the repertory of many artists.[93] In this they were helped by Gilpin's efforts to release trees from the literature of arboriculture and place them firmly in the orbit of the Picturesque. As he wrote in *Remarks on Forest Scenery* (1791), 'Perhaps of all species of landscape, there is none, which so universally captivates mankind, as forest-scenery ...'[94] The present exhibition includes many 'tree-portraits' in painting, drawing and photography, and this was a landscape motif that continued to be treated imaginatively well into the middle of the twentieth century (cat. 186-187, 209, 304).

But an anthropomorphic apprehension of the forest world was not for everyone. It is paradoxical that Blake, who condemned the 'vegetated mortality' of material existence in favour of the world of the imagination, and who in his enigmatic watercolour *The Sea of Time and Space* (cat. 247) placed the trees firmly on the side of nature and the material world,[95] should have introduced vigorous plant and tree imagery so frequently in his designs (cat. 231-232). Blake wrote in an early letter that the sight of a tree might move some spectators to 'tears of joy', while to

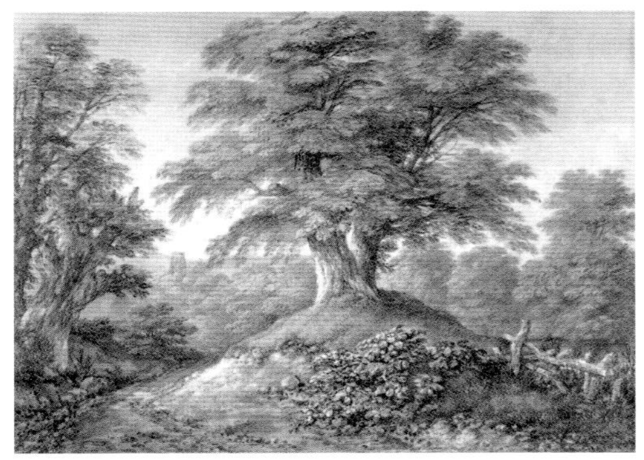

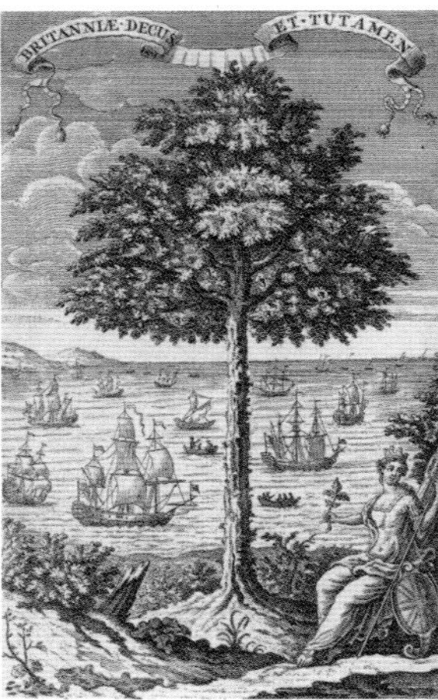

fig. 13
Thomas Gainsborough
Study of Beech Trees at Foxley, 1760
Chalk, watercolour and bodycolour,
28.7 x 38.9 cm
Whitworth Art Gallery, University of Manchester

fig. 14
Joshua Kirby
Frontispiece to James Wheeler,
The Modern Druid, 1747
British Library, London
The motto reads: 'The glory and defence of Britain'

others it might be 'only a Green thing that stands in the way'.[96] When Constable, his neighbour at Hampstead, showed Blake a drawing of firs on the Heath, Blake exclaimed, 'This is not drawing, but *inspiration*.' Constable retorted that he never knew it: 'I meant it for drawing.'[97]

Trees were vital to Britain as a mercantile island nation. Kirby's emblematic frontispiece (fig. 14) demonstrates that English oak was essential to shipbuilding and thus to defence as well as to commerce: oaks were 'the wooden walls of England'. As the agricultural writer William Marshall put it at the end of the eighteenth century, 'our existence as a nation depends upon the oak.'[98] So war and commerce provoked a spate of reforestation in a country whose woodlands had long been the least extensive in Europe. Planting campaigns were sponsored by the Society for the Encouragement of Arts, Manufactures and Commerce (founded in 1754 and also the first British public institution to mount regular exhibitions of art); one of the most frequent winners of awards was Thomas Johnes of Hafod, in North Wales, who, by the late 1790s, claimed to have planted more than two million trees and raised 922,000 oaks. Johnes had also laid out his estate specifically to attract Picturesque tourists, among whom were many artists.[99] The slow-growing native hardwoods, oak, elm and beech, were set against the 'foreign' softwoods, pine, larch and spruce, in a debate not only about the integrity of the British nation, but also about Picturesque propriety.[100] Wordsworth, for example, devoted several pages of his *Guide to the Lakes* to condemning the introduction of plantations of the exotic and spiky larch, since, he felt, they were incapable of harmonizing with the surrounding country.[101]

The urgent need for timber during the French wars, up to 1815, fostered a new appreciation of the British woodlands, just as the agricultural landscape, so despised by the Picturesque movement, was revalued in the light of the needs of a wartime economy. Certainly the Sublime landscape of the older Picturesque tradition continued to enjoy a vigorous life in the United States, Australia and New Zealand, with the development of National Parks and mass tourism, and was even revived in Britain in the early years of the twentieth century (cat. 202-203, 205). But it was the more novel aspects of the British landscape vision around 1800 – the woods, the open ploughland and pasture – which were exported, largely via the Barbizon School,[102] into the landscape repertory of Europe.

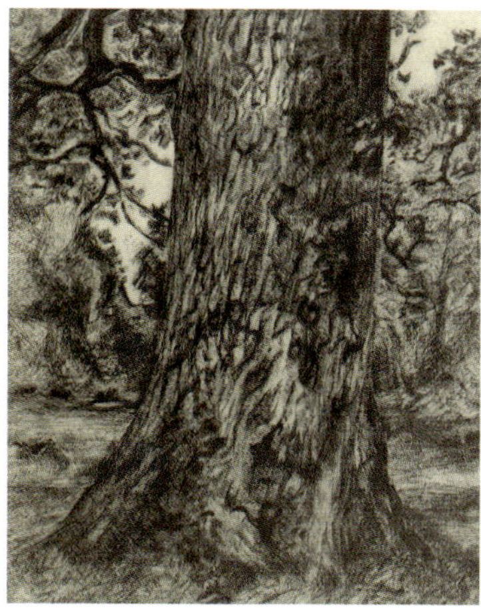

fig. 15
Lucian Freud
Elm Tree after Constable, 2003
Etching, 31 x 23.9 cm
Private Collection

---

1. William Oram, Precepts and Observations on the Art of Colouring in Landscape Painting, ed. C. Clarke, London (C. Clarke) 1810, p. 82. But Italy did not always live up to its landscape reputation. In the 1820s another English figure painter, William Hilton, was disappointed to find that, although the 'light and shadow of Italy is greatly more vivid than in England,' he was not able to 'discover the blueness in the distance which we sometimes see represented in the best masters.' Pointon 1972, p. 348.
2. [Joseph Holden Pott], *An Essay on Landscape Painting*, London 1782, pp. 53-56, 61-63.
3. William Gilpin, *Observations, relative chiefly to Picturesque Beauty, made in the Year 1772, on several parts of England; particularly the Mountains and Lakes of Cumberland and Westmoreland*, 2 vols., London (R. Blamire) 1786, vol. 1, p. 5.
4. William Gilpin, *Observations on the Western parts of England,... to which are added a few remarks on the picturesque beauties of the Isle of Wight*, London (T. Cadell and W. Davies) 1798, p. 75.
5. Gainsborough to Lord Hardwicke, in Woodall 1963, p. 87.
6. J. M. W. Turner, in British Library, Add MS 46151 CC (c. 1810): Gage 1969a, p. 213.
7. Gage 1979.
8. Humphry Repton, *An Enquiry into the changes of taste in Landscape Gardening*, London 1806, p. 23.
9. Joseph Warton, *An Essay on the Genius and Writings of Pope* (1756), 4th ed., 2 vols., London (J. Dodsley) 1782, vol. 2, p. 185 n.; cit. Andrews 1989, p. 9.
10. The fullest study of the major tours is in Andrews 1989. See also Moir 1964.
11. Gilpin, *Observations on the Western parts of England*, p. 32.
12. Ann Radcliffe, *A Journey made in the Summer of 1794... Observations during a Tour to the Lakes...*, Dublin (P. Wogan) 1795, pp. 450-51; cit. Moir 1964, pp.151-2.
13. William Wordsworth, '[The Sublime and the Beautiful]' in Wordsworth 1974, vol. 2, p. 360.
14. For Turner's early tours, see Gage 1965. The 1792 'Diary of a Tour in Wales', which I published as Turner's in Turner 1980 and which has been cited by Andrews 1989, is now known to be by another writer. For the engraved series, see Shanes 1979.
15. See Reynolds 1996, nos. 06.204, 06.209, 06.219. For Constable's later comments, Beckett 1962-68, vol. 3, p. 111. Constable owned a number of Gilpin's guides and theoretical writings: see Parris, Shields and Fleming-Williams 1975, p. 31.
16. [John Britton], *The Beauties of Wiltshire*, 2 vols., London (Vernor and Hood), 1801, vol. 2, p. 218; cit. Hayes 1982, vol. 1, p. 17. Only the Gainsborough has been traced so far: *Wooded Landscape with Mounted Peasants and Pack Horse returning from Market, and Cows at a Pool*, c.1767-8 (Toledo, Ohio, Museum of Art; Hayes 1982, no. 89). This painting is close in style to *The Harvest Wagon* (cat. 148 in the present exhibition).
17. Ingamells and Edgcumbe 2000, no. 221, pp. 221-22. This was one of the few points on which Blake was entirely in agreement with Reynolds, whom he quoted in a letter of 1802 (W. Blake to Thomas Butts, 22 November 1802; Keynes 1980, p. 41).
18. Woodall 1963, p. 87. Sandby had secured his election through the influence of the King, who employed him at Windsor. He accompanied Sir Watkin Williams-Wynn on the first Picturesque tour of Wales in 1771 (Andrews 1989, pp. 112-13).
19. J. Constable to J .Dunthorne, 29 May 1802. Beckett 1962-68, vol. 2, p. 31. Constable had been advised to reject this post by two Royal Academicians, Benjamin West and Joseph Farington.
20. W[illiam] H[utchinson], *An Excursion to the Lakes in Westmoreland and Cumberland, August, 1773*, 1774; cit. Reynolds 1909, pp. 323-24, with further examples. For Thomas Smith of Derby in the Lakes, see Andrews 1989, pp. 184-85.
21. Andrews 1989, p. 11.
22. The caption, printed on the frontipiece: *East Bergholt, Suffolk* (first published state) reads: *Hic locus aetatis nostrae primordia novit / Annos felices laetitiaeque dies: / Hic locus ingenuis pueriles imbuit annos / Artibus et nostrae laudis origo fuit*. If it is not an original composition – unlikely but possible: *ingenuis pueriles* recalls the famous phrase 'careless boyhood' used in a letter of 1821 – its source is still untraced. Constable's friend John Fisher wrote an English version in one of the painter's sketchbooks, now in the Louvre (no. 08701): *This spot saw the day spring of my life, / Years of Happiness and days of Joy. / This place first tinged my boyish fancy / with a love of the art, / This place was the origin of my fame* (Beckett 1962-68, vol. 6, p. 54; a slightly different reading in Beckett 1970, p. 14). The verse is here dated August 1820 at Salisbury, where Constable was staying with Fisher. He had been elected Associate of the Royal Academy in 1819 and may have already been thinking of his *English Landscape Scenery*, which was not executed until after his election to full membership ten years later.
23. Rubens, who animated 'his otherwise uninteresting views, by introducing a rainbow, storm, or some particular accidental effect of light' is contrasted with Claude, who 'seldom, if ever, availed himself of those accidents'. *Discourse IV* (1771) in Reynolds 1975, p. 70.
24. J. Barry, *Lecture V*, in Wornum 1848, pp. 178-79. See also Barry's remarks on Italian scenery in 1762 (Barry 1809, vol. 1, pp. 16, 59).
25. Thus Reynolds in his first address to the Academy students, noted that 'it is generally found, that a youth more easily receives instruction from the companions of his studies, whose minds are nearly on a level with his own, than from those who are much his superiors; and it is from his equals only that he catches the fire of emulation ...' *Discourse I* (1769), in Reynolds 1975, p. 16.
26. Robertson 1897, p. 84. For Constable on finishing from nature, J. Constable to J. Dunthorne, 22 February 1814 (Beckett 1962-68, vol. 1, p. 101). For his friendship with Robertson, Beckett 1962-68, vol. 4, pp. 307-8.
27. Hugh William Williams, *Travels in Italy, Greece and the Ionian Islands*, 2 vols., Edinburgh (Constable) 1820, vol. 1, p. 333; cit. Gage 1996, p. 106. What follows is based substantially on this essay.
28. Bemrose 1885, p. 95. For the widespread practice of watercolour among often female amateurs, see Clarke 1981.
29. For Wright's methods, see Jones 1990, pp. 263, 267, 269-70. Constable exhibited very few watercolours, and Turner, although

he made his earliest reputation as a watercolourist, and continued to be a prolific producer in this medium, exhibited very few after he became a full Academician in 1802.

30. Uwins 1978, vol. 1, pp. 30-31. Uwins's recollection is supported by the unprecedentedly high attendance figures at the Summer Exhibitions in 1800 (59,110) and 1802 (56,480): Hoock 2003, p. 64.
31. Joseph Farington, *Diary*, 23 August 1810 (Farington 1978-84, vol. 10, p. 3715). For West's advice to Constable, see Leslie 1951, p. 14. For West's landscapes including 'accidents of light', see Erffa and Staley 1986, nos. 470, 478.
32. *Cornhill Magazine*, vol. 11 (1865), p. 291; cit. Bermingham 1986, p. 157.
33. William Chambers, *A Dissertation on Oriental Gardening*, London (W. Griffin) 1772, p. 37; cit. Wagner 1979, p. 132 n. 71.
34. Daniel Carless Webb, *Observations and Remarks during Four Excursions made to various parts of Great Britain in the years 1810 and 1811*, London 1812, pp. 186-90, cit. Moir 1964, p. 99. For similar observations, Wagner 1979, pp. 74-76.
35. For Turner's industrial scenes at Newcastle, see Rodner 1997, pp. 96-103.
36. Richard Warner, *A Tour through the Northern Counties of England and the Borders of Scotland*, 2 vols., Bath 1802, vol. 2, p. 186; cit. Wagner 1979, p. 76. For the pictorial history of Coalbrookdale, see Daniels 1992.
37. Nasmyth 1885, pp. 159-60; cit. Rodner 1997, p. 110.
38. Letter of 12 May 1836 in Beckett 1962-68, vol. 5, pp. 32-33.
39. Lindsay 1966, p. 99.
40. Butlin and Joll 1984, no. 69.
41. Polarized interpretations have accumulated, particularly around Turner's railway painting *Rain, Steam and Speed* (Butlin and Joll 1984, no. 409). In my monograph *Turner: Rain Steam and Speed*, London (Allen Lane) 1972, I took the view that it was essentially celebratory, and this has been largely endorsed by Rodner 1997, ch. 6. The opposite view, that Turner was, like Wordsworth and Ruskin, highly critical of railway development, has been proposed by McCoubrey 1986, pp. 33-39, and Finley 1988, pp. 19-30.
42. These various interpretations have been listed in Miller 1995, p. 576 n. 13. Miller inclines to the first reading and presents a lengthy discussion of turnips as a symbol of the 'farmer' King George III and as the food of the poverty-stricken peasantry, ousted from the land by modern farming practices (pp. 576-81).
43. Cit. Moir 1964, p. 117.
44. See, for example, William Gilpin, *Two Essays: One on the author's method of executing rough sketches; the other on the principles on which they are composed*, London 1804, p. 25 and Farington, *Diary*, 30 November 1794 (Farington 1978-84, vol. 1, p. 266).
45. Butlin and Joll 1984, no. 127.
46. John Clark, *General view of the agriculture of the county of Hereford*, London 1794, p. 32; cit. Prince 1988, pp. 113-14. Prince gives an extended analysis of this painting's context.
47. For Constable senior's activities, see Rosenthal 1983, p. 7.
48. John Constable to John Dunthorne, 23 May 1803 (Beckett 1962-68, vol. 2, p. 34). For the Panorama, see Altick 1978, pp. 128-210.
49. For Constable's many copies from Alexander Cozens' didactic works, see Gage 2006, p. 25.
50. William Gilpin, *Three Essays: -on Picturesque Beauty; -on Picturesque Travel; -and, on sketching Landscape*, London (R. Blamire) 1792, p. 70. See also the watercolourist Edward Dayes, 'An Essay to Illustrate the Principles of Composition, as Connected with Landscape Painting', *Universal Magazine* 108 (1801), pp. 112-13.
51. Gainsborough to Henry Bate, 11 March 1788 (Woodall 1963, p. 35).
52. Fulcher 1856, p. 171. Bermingham 1986, p. 63, points to the fact that Fulcher was writing at the time of high Pre-Raphaelitism and may not be reliable, but she perhaps underestimates Gainsborough's stylistic variousness.
53. Beckett 1970, p. 69 (1836). For Constable's scientific interests, see Gage 2002-3, pp. 38-39; and Gage 2006, pp. 34-35.
54. See the important essay, Lyles 2006.
55. Lister 1974a, p. 47 (1828, 11).
56. For Linnell's engraving after Van Eyck's *Righteous Judges* (1826), see London & New York 2005, no. 23. For Linnell's support of the PRB, see Story 1892, vol. 2, pp. 26, 37, 40; and Hueffer 1896, p. 77.
57. See Wordsworth 1974, vol. 2, p. 134.
58. 'John Seward' (F. G. Stephens), 'The Purpose and Tendency of Early Italian Art', *The Germ*, no. 2 (February 1850), pp. 58, 61. For Stephens, see London 1984, p. 39.
59. Cook and Wedderburn 1903-12, vol. 35, p. 419. The references are to Samuel Prout (1783-1852) and David Roberts (1796-1864). Ruskin also dissuaded a beginner from attending the private art school of J. M. Leigh (1808-1860), which focused on composition (see Oppé 1934, p. 146n.), although Leigh's pupils included D. G. Rossetti and Holman Hunt.
60. Cook and Wedderburn 1903-12, vol. 15, p. 143; Staley 1973, p. 128.
61. Allen Staley in Staley and Newall 2004, no. 29.
62. Surtees 1981, p. 80 (16 August 1854).
63. Ibid. p. 107 (30 November 1854); M. Bennett in London 1984, no. 62.
64. *The Exhibition of Work and other Paintings by Ford Madox Brown at the Gallery, 191, Piccadilly*, London 1865
65. For these details, see Bronkhurst 2006, vol. 1 no. 88; and Bronkhurst 1984, p. 122.
66. Hunt to W. M. Rossetti, 12 August 1855, in Bronkhurst 1984, p. 123.
67. 'Geology in its Relation to the Picturesque', *Art Journal*, 1855, pp. 275-76; cit. Newall 2004a, p. 134. For meteorology, see Lyles 2000.
68. Dr John Brown, *Description of the Vale of Keswick*, c. 1753; cit. Andrews 1989, p. 177.
69. Wordsworth 1974, vol. 2, p. 306.
70. Constable to Maria Constable, 9 May 1819 (Beckett 1962-68, vol. 2, p. 246); for the origin of the idea with Wordsworth, see Parris, Shields and Fleming-Williams 1975, pp. 56-57. The metaphor was something of a commonplace of natural theology: see, for example, Christoph Christian Sturm, *Betrachtungen über die Werke Gottes im Reiche der Natur und der Vorsehung auf alle Tage des Jahres* (1772), a new English edition of which was published in Constable's Suffolk in 1813: *Reflections for Every Day of the Year, on the Works of God in Nature and Providence,*

2 vols., Bungay 1813, vol. 1, pp. 300-2 (25 May). The English edition went through more than fourteen editions by 1855.

71. Cuvier 1827-35, vol. 1, p. xvi. For Constable's reading of him (cf. Parris, Shields and Fleming-Williams 1975, p. 44), see Vaughan 1996, p. 25. For Paley, see Gage 2006, p. 37.
72. Robertson 1897, p. 173.
73. Barton to Linnell, 15 June 1830; cit. Story 1892, vol. 1, pp. 179-80.
74. Barton to J. Wodderspoon, 22 December 1843 (British Library, Add. MS 37032, f.11v).
75. Fry and Creswell 1847, vol. 1, p. 6.
76. Elizabeth Gurney, *Journal*, 16 May 1797; cit. Fry and Creswell 1847, vol. 1, p. 18. Cf. also 6 April 1825 (p. 484). Also Joseph John Gurney, *Observations on the Religious Peculiarities of the Society of Friends*, London 1824, pp. 341-42.
77. Hare 1895, vol. 1, pp. 74, 249 (1813).
78. Hannah to Elizabeth Gurney, Ambleside 1802; cit. Hare 1895, vol. 1, p. 116.
79. Clifford and Clifford 1968, p. 77. For modern studies of the exiguous patronage in Norwich, see Hemingway 2000, p. 20; Blayney Brown 2000, pp. 24-25; Gage 1969b.
80. Cotman to Dawson Turner, 2 July 1827; cit. Oppé 1942, p. 170.
81. For the *camera lucida*, see Pidgley 1972, ills. 55-57.
82. Palmer 1892, p. 83. The 1819 sketchbook is in the British Museum (1966-2-12-11; see especially f. 4).
83. Lister 1974a, vol. 1, p. 36 (1828, 9).
84. Grigson 1960, p. 19 (1825).
85. Lister 1974a, vol. 1, p. 385 (14 December 1839, 22).
86. Pointon 1979, pp. 175-76.
87. Lister 1974b, p. 194.
88. Ibid., p. 50.
89. Samuel Palmer to John Linnell, 21 December 1828 (11), Lister 1974a, vol. 1, pp. 47-48.
90. Freud 2003, p. 35.
91. Beckett 1970, p.71. Anne Lyles, in her entry for a related drawing in Paris 2002 (no.122), p. 189, has suggested that the painter was hinting at a Crucifixion here.
92. There is an extensive literature on tree symbolism: see, for example, Schama 1995, pp. 214-26.
93. See, for example, Turner's particular love of beeches, which had been disparaged by Picturesque theorists (Gage 1965, p. 75).
94. William Gilpin, *Remarks on Forest Scenery*, 2 vols., London (R. Blamire) 1791, vol. 1, p. 269.
95. In his essay on the iconographical complexities in this watercolour (pp. 315-17), David Bindman, following Kathleen Raine, identifies the standing female as Athena, and relates her to Blake's goddess of Nature, Vala, so it is appropriate that she gestures towards the woody grove in this image. Blake spoke of 'vegetated mortality' in a letter to the sculptor John Flaxman on 21 September 1800 (Keynes 1980, p. 23); and on pl. 77 of *Jerusalem* (cf. cat. 239-242) he wrote: 'Imagination, the real & eternal World of which this Vegetable Universe is but a faint shadow, & in which we shall live in our Eternal or Imaginative Bodies, when these Vegetable Mortal Bodies are no more.' (Erdman 1965, p. 229).
96. Blake to Dr Trusler, 23 August 1799, Keynes 1980, p. 9.
97. Leslie 1951, p. 280.
98. William Marshall, *Planting and Ornamental Gardening*, London (J. Dodsley) 1785; cit. Short 2000, p. 149.
99. Schama 1995, p. 168. For the Hafod estate, see Andrews 1989, pp. 145-50.
100. For the political dimension, see Daniels 1988, especially pp. 65-66.
101. Wordsworth 1974, vol. 2, pp. 217-23.
102. For the opening-up of Barbizon and the Forest of Fontainebleau to tourism in the nineteenth century, see Green 1990, pp. 84-120.

CHAPTER ONE

SOCIETY

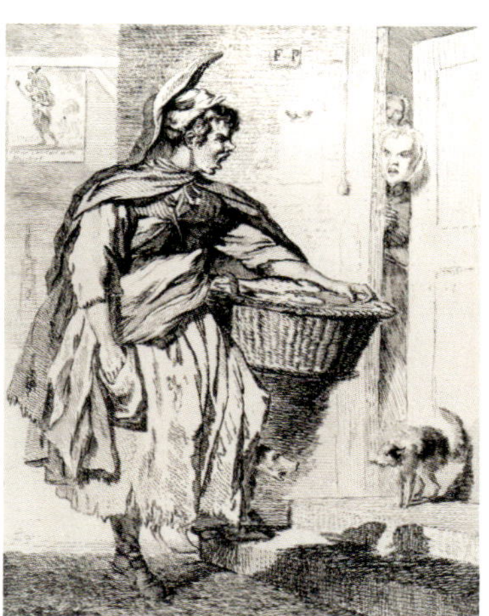

OBSERVATION OF SOCIETY

ROBERT HOOZEE

Ever since the eighteenth century, British artists have been unusually zealous in recording social situations. In general, they were responding to the demands of an increasingly large public of patrons and purchasers from the growing middle class. In British art – particularly in the eighteenth century – there are numerous portraits of individuals, often depicted in the midst of their possessions or with the attributes of their profession, as well as topographical portraits of country houses, parks and agricultural estates, as if this self-confident society had an insatiable need for visual self-confirmation. The status portrait (cat. 2) was nothing new in western art. It is a type of burgher portrait, like that of the Dutch Golden Age, developed and adapted to suit modern times.

But new points of view emerged from this hunger for representation. A number of artists invested classic genres like the group portrait or the hunt scene with fresh significance. George Stubbs often portrayed the 'subcategory' of servants, who were respected as specialists in fields such as hunting or equestrian sport (cat. 5). Joseph Highmore, who usually painted classic conversation pieces, depicted a middle-class social gathering in an everyday context in *Mr Oldham and His Guests* (cat. 3). Just as informal is the Anglo-Indian family scene, formerly attributed to Johann Zoffany and now assigned to Arthur William Devis (cat. 4). Joseph Wright of Derby alludes to the popularization of modern science by depicting a scientific demonstration in a domestic context (cat. 6). William Hogarth's portrait of a common woman (cat. 1), in itself a classic theme, acquires the aspect of modern reportage when we learn that the artist visited this condemned woman in her cell in order to make a portrait that he could afterwards publish as a print.

Landscape painters were also employed in the portrayal of modern society. In the albums of 'picturesque tours', about which more in a later chapter (p. 180), industrial images became increasingly common, recording the developments that profoundly changed the British landscape (cat. 7-11). The modernization of agriculture and industrialization brought about the transformation from city to metropolis in many places, particularly in the Midlands. But it was London that caught the contemporary imagination as exhibiting a new form of society, through which artists roamed around as observers.

This phenomenon had international reverberations that also attracted foreigners to the modern laboratory. One of them was the Frenchman Théodore Géricault, who came to London in 1820 to exhibit his epic depiction of a modern catastrophe, the *Wreck of the Medusa*, and who found themes for his socially motivated art in the streets of London. Géricault published a series of lithographs depicting street scenes in 1821 entitled *Various Subjects Drawn from Life and on Stone* (fig. 1). These prints form part of a British tradition of social observation in the form of albums and illustrated books featuring characters from the lower classes and marginal trades, such as *The Cries of London* (cat. 13), which itself continues, and indeed updates a long European tradition.[1] Such illustrations range from familiar portraits to detached inventories of types, such as those found in the books of Henry Mayhew,

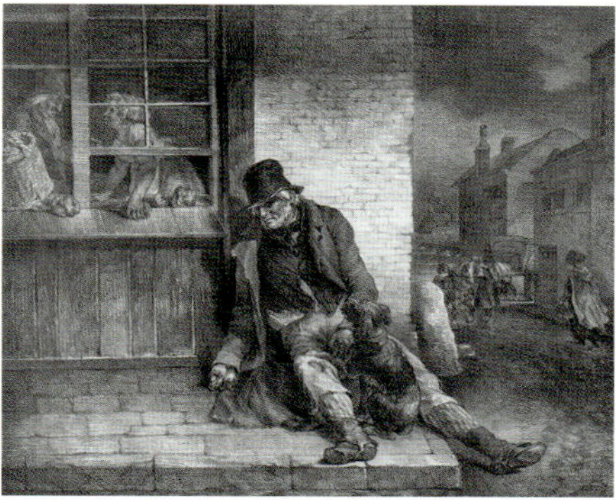

fig. 1
Théodore Géricault
Pity the Sorrows of a Poor Old Man, from
Various Subjects Drawn from Life and on Stone, 1821
Lithograph, 31.7 x 37.6 cm
Bibliothèque nationale de France, Paris

who described the physical appearance of various representatives of the lower classes in his *London Labour and the London Poor* (cat. 18), giving them an opportunity to speak for themselves, and finally giving a summary of their financial circumstances. This topography, as it were, of the British people received an important new impetus from the developing technique of photography (cat. 25-30). Observation of society also made its way into literature, in the social novels of Elizabeth Gaskell and Charles Dickens, for example.

London as a modern Babylon quickly became a cliché, and writers and illustrators were happy to exploit its extremes of misery – as Gustave Doré did in his *London Pilgrimage*.[2] As against such dramatic representations of life in the city, Whistler's studies of the banks of the Thames offer a more positive image.[3] Here we see more of the bustling activity that made London the capital of an industrial and commercial world power (cat. 32). These aspects of modern times – industry and the far-reaching changes that took place in the large cities, particularly London – appear sporadically in literature, photography and painting.

William Hogarth is rightly considered to be one of the most important social observers and commentators among British artists (cat. 36-39). He worked as a painter and graphic artist within a long European tradition of moralizing subjects (the memory of Bruegel is never far away in his crowded scenes), but he used his art to record observations of modern English society. Hogarth targeted the masses as well as the individual, and recognizable people and places regularly appear in his work. As the artistic counterpart of the empirical scientist and modern novelist, he realized that art was a form of instantaneous recording. He provided some of his prints with written explanations so that they would also be understood at a later date, 'when the customs manners fashions Characters and humours of the present age in this country may be alter'd'.[4] From Hogarth's time onwards, satire has been an important constant in British visual culture; it shows, as it were, the reverse side of modern social life. Although Hogarth and many later anonymous satirical illustrators sought primarily to comment and offer a moral message, their medium was of course based on the critical observation of the physical appearance, behaviour and background of the various representatives of British society.

The extent and intensity of British satire in the eighteenth century and at the beginning of the nineteenth reflects the climate of an age that can only be described as particularly intense itself, a time of great events, great changes and great consequences. This intensity was dissipated during the nineteenth century, which – after all the great revolutions – was essentially a period of consolidation. During this period British satire lost its bite, its extreme character – apart from a few exceptions such as Aubrey Beardsley (cat. 59-60), who was considered subversive by the British bourgeoisie at the end of the nineteenth century because of the grotesque character of his drawings. Industrialization and urbanization, with their familiar social consequences, had now become an international phenomenon, and corresponding artistic genres and styles appeared in practically every other country in Europe. The many socially concerned scenes of the late Victorian period lack the experimental and empirical power of earlier observations; they belong to an internationally accepted naturalistic canon, although this is really a contradiction in terms.

Within this broader development, the Pre-Raphaelites provide an interesting episode. The Pre-Raphaelite Brotherhood was established in 1848 by several talented artists who believed that English art had sunk to an all-time low.[5] With their religious, literary and historical subjects and their precise style, which is related to that of the Italian and Flemish Primitives as well as the German Nazarenes, they might not appear to be observers of modern life – at least not at first glance. Nevertheless, these were socially committed artists whose depictions of the past are filled with references to problems of their own day. Moreover, they also painted contemporary subjects, which reveal their modernity with the same precision and theatricality. Hogarth's critical view of human relations returns in a new guise in works like *The Woodman's Daughter* by John Everett Millais (cat. 19) or *Stages of Cruelty* by Ford Madox Brown (cat. 21). Brown, who did not belong to the Brotherhood but did form part of the movement, proved just how much he had his finger on the pulse of the times with *Work* (see cat. 22) and *The Last of England* (see cat. 23). The former is an allegory of labour in a modern urban context, the latter an apparently random image of a group of emigrants, with all the power of a world press photograph *avant la lettre*.

The figure of Walter Sickert appears rather abruptly in this exhibition with works painted after he had returned to England in 1905, having spent several years in France (cat. 61-62). Sickert was trained in the elegant manner of Whistler and Impressionism, but he is much more than an 'English Impressionist' and was in fact opposed to any attempt to fashion modern English art after the example of the French. With Sickert we witness the return of the powerful combination of craftsmanship and objective observation established by Hogarth. Like Hogarth, Sickert wanted to bear witness to the modern urban environment, and he systematically studied the banal reality of the average city-dweller. He believed that art should leave the drawing-room and concentrate on the kitchen: 'The plastic arts are gross arts, dealing joyously with gross material facts.'[6] Sickert was a pivotal figure, who not only looked back to predecessors like Hogarth and Brown, but also set the tone for the objective and sometimes confrontational realism that characterizes later developments in British art.

Sickert was the key figure in the Camden Town Group, which consisted of artists who, from around 1911, took the everyday aspects of London city life as the point of departure for their art (cat. 64, 68-71). When compared with Sickert's unvarnished accounts of everyday life in urban interiors, the neatly painted observations of the members of the Camden Town Group seem rather neutral. Moreover, the human figure is less dominant in their work than in Sickert's, although Harold Gilman's *Mrs Mounter* (cat. 64) is one of the great characters in English art. By contrast, there is a much more direct link between Sickert and the face-to-face realism of Stanley Spencer's *Leg of Mutton Nude* (cat. 87), *Hilda, Unity and Dolls* (cat. 88), or the later portraits and figures of Francis Bacon (cat. 90) and Lucian Freud (cat. 89). Spencer, Bacon and Freud, however, go a step further and expose themselves or the human figure literally and symbolically to an almost penitential analysis, while at the same time, like Sickert, they clothe the revealing in a rich pictorial form.

Sickert and the Camden Town Group formed a counterbalance to the more formalistic and even decorative interpretations of Impressionism and Post-Impressionism produced by many British modernists. They gave the narrative and the specific locality a greater presence than was customary in the more generalizing aesthetics of the modernists. In the end, Blake's emphasis on the 'particularizing' (cf. p. 12) returns as opposed to the generalizations of academicism – whether in its old or modern form.

This realism also turns up among artists who had attempted to join the European avant-garde before and at the beginning of the First World War, the so-called Vorticists. This short-lived movement consisted of artists who, encouraged by Wyndham Lewis, experimented with abstract 'mechanical' forms inspired by Cubism and Futurism (cat. 286, 288-290). After several years of experimentation under the influence of Vorticism, William Roberts and David Bomberg painted realistic scenes from everyday life (cat. 76-77) in the years following the First World War. Their forceful, schematic style shows striking similarities to the Expressionist schools encountered during the inter-war period in Flanders, and indeed throughout Europe.

In the 1930s, the more detached, narrative style of the Camden Town painters found a successor in the Euston Road School, named after the independent 'School of Painting and Drawing' on Euston Road established by several artists who had turned against abstract art, preferring realistic representation. The school itself was a response to a widespread social awareness, which found expression among writers like George Orwell, painters like William Coldstream (cat. 94-95), and photographers like Bill Brandt (cat. 82-84) and Humphrey Jennings (cat. 91-93). This interest was channelled by 'Mass-Observation', a movement joined by various artists, which had as its goal the objective depiction of the circumstances in which the people lived. The movement should be seen in the context of the many discussions among British art critics in the 1930s, in which realistic art, accessible to a broad public, was seen as an alternative to elitist modernism.[7] The seemingly naive representation of the masses in industrial cities by L.S. Lowry (cat. 101) and the urban satires of Edward Burra (cat. 79-80) can also be associated with this social awareness.

Similar documentary goals were pursued in British wartime art, a unique phenomenon in the history of European art. During the First and Second World Wars, numerous artists worked for the Government, 'to preserve a pictorial record as complete as possible of the various sites and stages of the war'.[8] Some artists showed images of wartime industry or (in the Second World War) the consequences on the home front. Some, like Sickert, painted war scenes from photographs. During the First World War, several artists served at the front, and their first-hand experience of the miseries of war often left no room for detached representation, so that the observed facts acquired an apocalyptic dimension. The most important wartime artist was Paul Nash, who gave expression to his experiences on the Flemish front in letters and paintings. His paintings were made from drawings, and in both one feels the power of direct observation beneath the expressionistic effects (cat. 73-74, 294).

The case of Stanley Spencer is different. During the First World War he served both in the Medical Corps and as an infantryman in Macedonia, and in 1927-32 he created a personal war memorial by filling an entire chapel, the Sandham Memorial Chapel in Burghclere, with murals based on his war experience (p.28, fig.13). During the Second World War, he was commissioned to depict shipbuilding in Glasgow. He did this in the form of four triptychs, in which the way that the workers submit to and become one with their materials is elevated to an ode to collective labour (cat. 98), comparable with the work of the Mexican muralists. These works are documentary, but their pathos ranks them alongside art of a more visionary nature.

British art of the first half of the twentieth century offers sufficient examples of realistic observation of the urban milieu and the human figure to allow us to speak of a revival of the empirical tradition. In turn, this revival forms the background to the realism in British art from the 1950s to the present day. It is perhaps in this strong empirical tradition that we can find an explanation for the fact that figurative painting and humanist subject matter have remained valid in the hands of British artists, through a time in which the art world has been ruled by more abstract and conceptual experiment. Nor has the dissemination of mass communication in Pop Art prevented important British artists from continuing to use figurative drawing and painting to render penetrating images of their personal surroundings. In this exhibition, only a few works by Francis Bacon (cat. 90), Lucian Freud (cat. 89), Frank Auerbach (cat. 224) and Leon Kossoff (cat. 223) illustrate the beginning of this important strand in contemporary British art.

With the revival of social observation in the twentieth century, British satire also regained its former strength. When Wyndham Lewis, the central figure of the English avant-garde, settled accounts both with the inheritance of the Victorian age and with the imported aesthetics of modernism, he assumed an attitude of inflexible irony. In the satirical mordancy and grotesque exaggerations of the characters he created both before and after the war (cat. 78), we feel the return of the mockery that was lost in the gentle humour of the nineteenth century. In 1914 and 1915 Lewis published the manifesto-like periodical *Blast* (cat. 75), a journal filled with barbed and socially critical texts that dared 'to show modernity its face in an honest glass'.[9] In the period between the two World Wars, the satirical and the grotesque in the work of Edward Burra (cat. 79-81), L.S. Lowry (cat. 103) and Stanley Spencer (cat. 298) alluded to the heritage of Hogarth and Gillray. In subsequent generations, satire and irony return again in the work of Pop artists like Richard Hamilton (cat. 105-109) and David Hockney (cat. 110-111), who in their different ways opened a new chapter in the unending development of British humour. Thanks to the Pop artists of the sixties, social satire and absurd humour would again become a lasting trademark of British culture.

1. See Shesgreen 2001.
2. William Blanchard Jerrold, *London: A Pilgrimage*, with illustrations by Gustave Doré, London 1872.
3. See Spencer 1987, pp. 49-69.
4. Donald 2001, p. 172.
5. Alan Bowness, in London 1984, p. 11.
6. 'Idealism,' in *The Art News*, 12 May 1910; cit. Baron 1998, p. 246.
7. Harrison 1994, p. 338.
8. Cit. Harrison 1994, p. 120.
9. *Blast* 2, War Number, July 1915, p. 85.

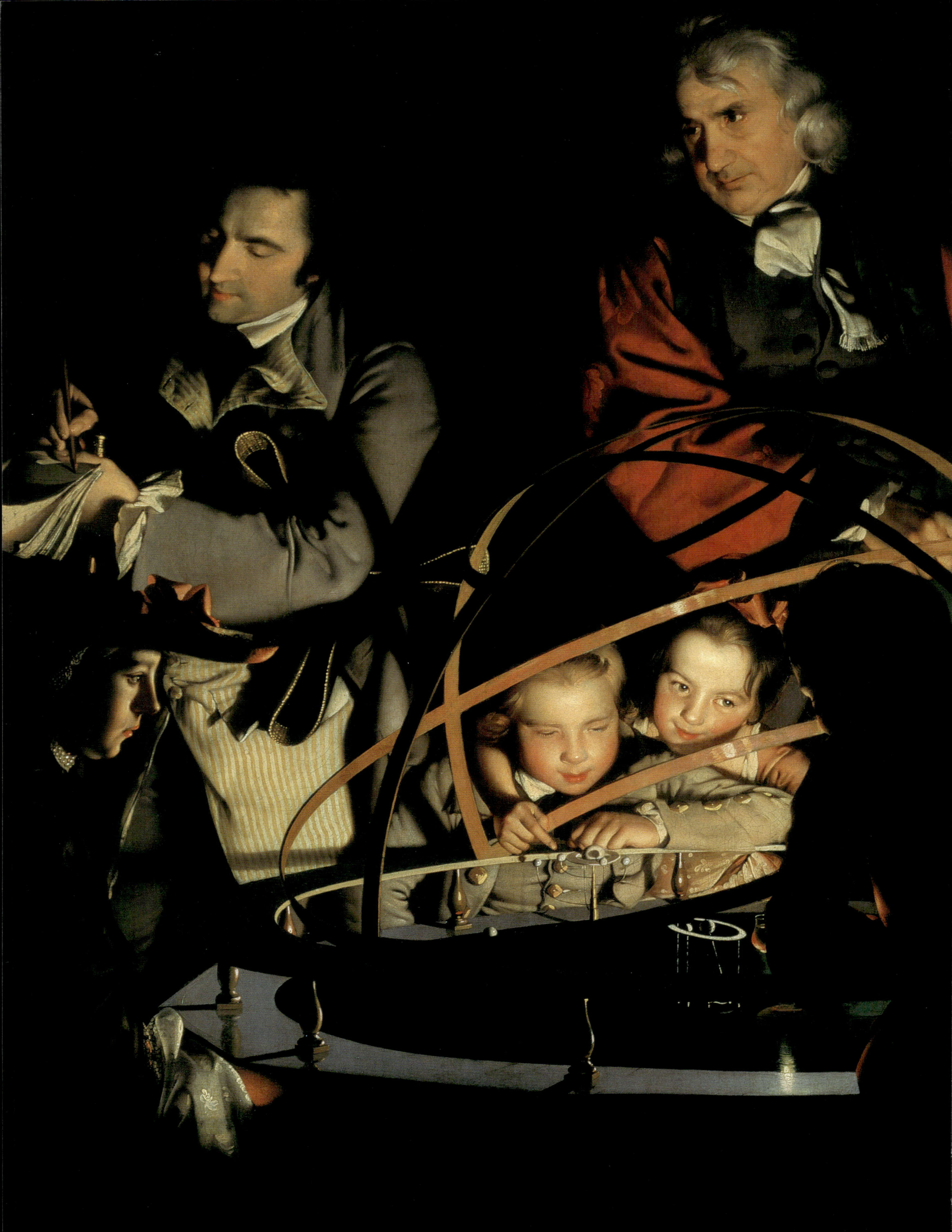

CHANGING SOCIETY

JOSEPH WRIGHT OF DERBY

A Philosopher Lecturing on the Orrery, in which a Lamp is put in Place of the Sun, c. 1766

JOHN GAGE

This was the first of Wright's paintings on a scientific theme, and the second of the artificial light subjects with which he made his reputation as a painter. The first to be exhibited had been *Three Persons Viewing the Gladiator by Candle-Light* (Private Collection),[1] shown at the Society of Artists the previous year and his first work in a public exhibition. But that was a far more traditional artistic subject, connoisseurs studying ancient art, a theme going back to the sixteenth century, while *The Orrery* was unique, not only in British but also in European art, for earlier representations of philosopher-scientists at work had invariably been satirical and painted on a cabinet scale.

So it is not surprising that most commentators on this beautiful painting have focused on its subject matter and have sought to unravel its meaning in the context of Enlightenment culture in provincial England. It has seemed to some, in fact, to be almost the embodiment of Enlightenment itself. One clue to its significance is in the title given to the picture in the catalogue of the Society of Artists' London exhibition in 1766, which refers to 'that Lecture on the Orrery', suggesting that lectures on such topics were common knowledge; and David Fraser has shown that demonstrations of eclipses involving the replacement of the central sun-ball in the apparatus with a burning lamp, were indeed well known.[2] Wright had almost certainly witnessed such a demonstration, since the Scottish astronomer James Ferguson, a maker of scientific instruments including an orrery, had lectured using it in the painter's home town of Derby in 1762. Ferguson's lecture courses in these years included one designed 'To explain the Laws by which the Deity Regulates and Governs all the Motions of the Planets and the Comets by Machinery: to show the Courses of the Different Seasons, the Motions and Phases of the Moon, the Harvest Moon, the Tides, and all the Eclipses of the Sun and Moon, by means of an Orrery.'[3]

The orrery was a typical product of Enlightenment science, devised in the early eighteenth century to demonstrate the laws of celestial mechanics as expounded by Sir Isaac Newton; and Judy Egerton has noticed some similarity between the features of this English mathematician, who had died in 1727, and the gowned lecturer in Wright's painting. What is clear is that this is a private, not a public, lecture: it is set in a small room, possibly the lecturer's study, with a shelf of his books behind a curtain to the right, or perhaps in the house of some patron, such as Washington Shirley, 5th Earl of Ferrers, an amateur astronomer who had made his own orrery and had a paper on the transit of the planet Venus published by the Royal Society in 1762. Ferrers's country seat was at Staunton Harold, not far from Derby, and this was also the home of Wright's close friend Peter Perez Burdett, a surveyor who knew Ferrers and who has been plausibly identified as the man taking notes to the left in *The Orrery*.[4] Lord Ferrers was the first owner of Wright's painting, and it may well have been a commission from him.

In the most important study of Wright, Benedict Nicolson has shown that the apparatus in *The Orrery* is exactly the same model as that illustrated in John Warltire's *Analysis of a Course of Lectures in Experimental Philosophy,* published about the same time as the picture was painted, although the arrangement of the planets is not quite the same, and Warltire's sun is not in the form of an oil lamp.[5] Warltire had strong Midlands connections and was later to teach chemistry to the children of the scientific poet Erasmus Darwin, who was Wright's doctor and was portrayed by him in 1770 and again in the 1790s, and to those of the pottery entrepreneur Josiah Wedgwood, for whom

Joseph Wright of Derby, ***A Philosopher Lecturing on the Orrery, in which a Lamp is put in Place of the Sun*** (detail), cat. 6

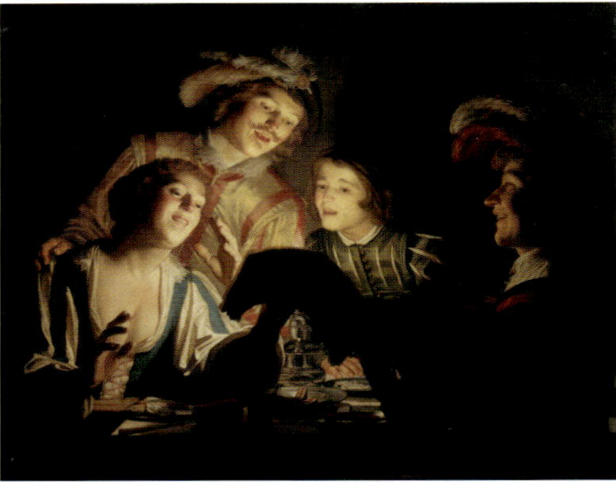

fig. 1
Gerrit van Honthorst
***Musical Group by Candlelight*, 1623**
Oil on canvas, 117 x 146.5 cm
Statens Museum for Kunst, Copenhagen

Wright also worked in the 1780s. So many strands of eighteenth-century Midlands scientific culture are woven into the subject matter of Wright's *Orrery,* and he was to go on to paint other scientific subjects in the following decades.

Yet it would be misleading to focus exclusively on the thematic content of this masterpiece, and to regard it as essentially an illustration of the popular science in action in Wright's time and place. Wright has here had the brilliant idea of using the lamp/sun as a pretext for painting an artificial light-piece very much in the tradition of the Utrecht School of painters, beginning as far back as the 1620s. Nicolson, also a distinguished student of this School, has been unable to identify direct links between Wright and, in particular, Gerrit van Honthorst and Hendrick ter Brugghen, whose works were apparently rare in England at this time and not engraved; but the analogies, especially with Honthorst, are surely too close to be purely coincidental. The scale of the figures, and particularly the device of occluding the light source, so that those facing the spectator are illuminated with a sharp but mysterious light with much of their bodies and features thrown into shadow, are all characteristics frequently found in Honthorst and his companions and followers. A notably striking comparison is with Honthorst's *Musical Group by Candlelight* of 1623, now in Copenhagen (fig. 1), where a group of men and a woman, of various ages, focus on the musical score, which, together with the arm of the woman and the lute of her companion, hides the source of light.[6] Wright had already experimented with this type of effect on a minor scale in his first *Girl Reading a Letter by Candlelight* (c.1762),[7] a subject more directly related to Dutch precedents, but purged of lubriciousness; and he continued to work in this vein into the 1790s. It was these candlelight paintings, rather than his many portraits and landscapes, which made his high reputation among contemporaries.

But *The Orrery* is in quite a different vein. The company is not merry – although the small boy (traditionally identified as Ferrers's nephew Laurence Shirley) and his smiling sister (?) seem about to have fun with the toy-like apparatus while the lecturer is not looking – and there is a contemplative gravity about the painting, which is entirely appropriate to its awe-inspiring subject. Nicolson has emphasized the rather religious quiet of the treatment and has introduced a comparison with a *Christ at Emmaus* in Hull by a Honthorst follower, Crijn Hendricksz. Volmarijn. But here, in the Dutch tradition of religious narrative, the expressions of the actors are far more animated; and Nicolson has also pointed to the grave sculpturesque face of the woman on the left of Wright's painting, which has even led him to reach for a comparison with Piero della Francesca.

Wright's subject-pictures, of which *The Orrery* is the first, astonishing, example, give the lie to a widespread modern belief that he was the epitome of middle-class culture in the Midlands. *The Orrery* was, as we have seen, acquired by an aristocrat (and the apparatus itself derived its name from Charles Boyle, 4th Earl of Orrery, for whom an early version was made around 1712), and many of Wright's other subject-pictures were destined for noble collections. Scientific culture embraced all social classes.

Nor can Wright be properly understood as a provincial painter: he was trained in London and made his reputation there, although it is true that Sir Joshua Reynolds, President of the Royal Academy, of which Wright had become an Associate in 1781, justified his being passed over as a full Academician two years later on the grounds that the Academy needed someone London-based and able to handle Academy business at that moment.[8] Wright had in fact already been elected, and this slight caused him to refuse the appointment, although he continued to exhibit at the Academy's summer exhibitions. He was seen in his time to be in the highest class of artistic achievement: a pupil of Reynolds, James Northcote, reported with pardonable exaggeration in 1772 of some of Wright's exhibited candlelights, that he was, 'in this way the greatest in the world'.[9]

---

1. Nicolson 1968, no.188.
2. Fraser 1990, p. 16.
3. Ibid.
4. Ibid. p. 17.
5. Nicolson 1968, vol. 1, pp. 115-16, fig. 119.
6. See Spicer and Orr 1997, no. 35.
7. Nicolson 1998, no. 207.
8. Reported by Joseph Farington on 20 October 1796; Garlick and Macintyre 1978-84, vol. 3, p. 679.
9. Whitley 1968, vol. 2, p. 291.

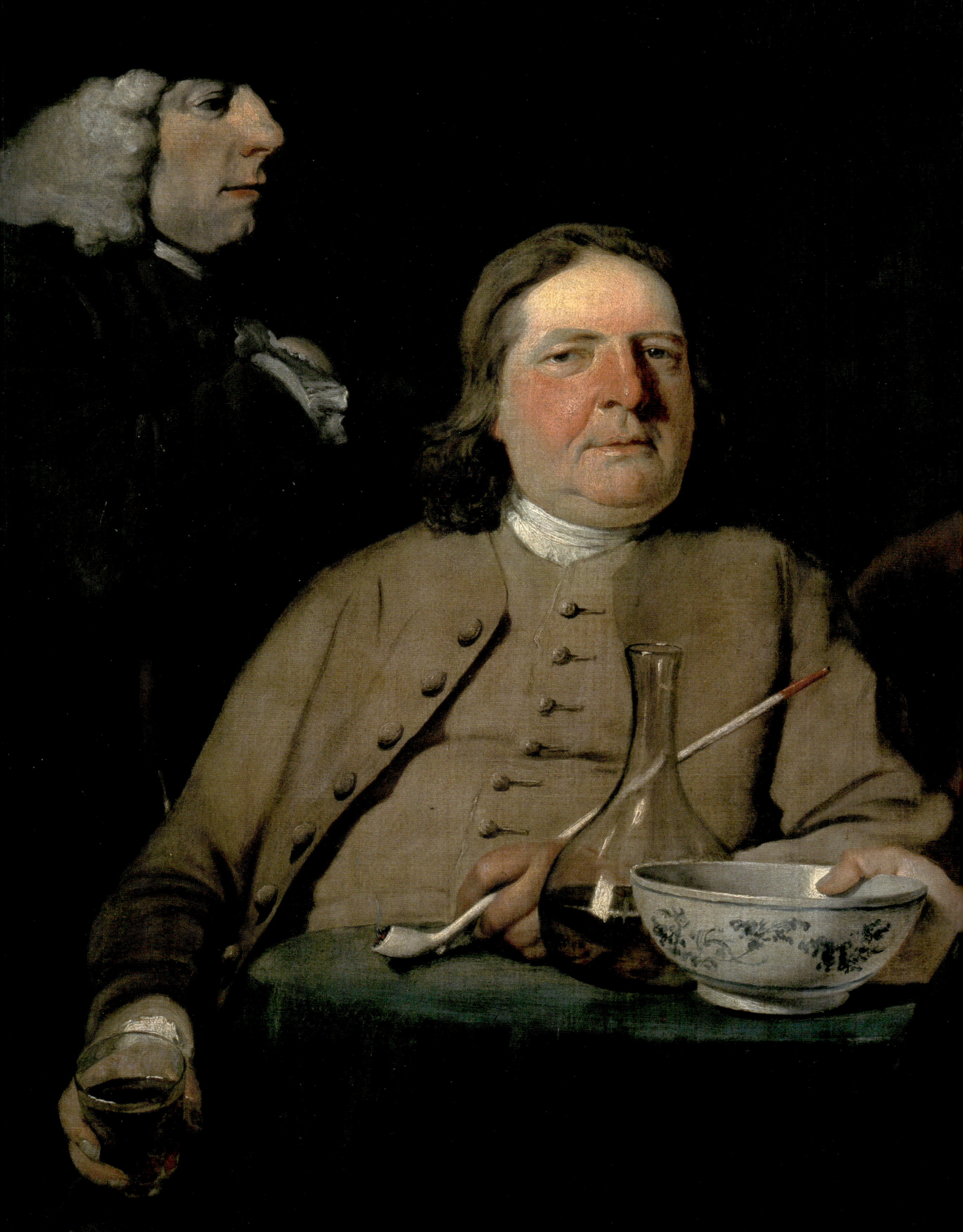

CHANGING SOCIETY

JOSEPH HIGHMORE

Mr Oldham and his Guests, c. 1732-45

MARTIN POSTLE

Mr Oldham and his Guests is among the most idiosyncratic works to have been produced in England in the first half of the eighteenth century. Highmore painted it at the specific request of the eccentric collector Nathaniel Oldham, to commemorate a dinner party held at his home, to which he had arrived belatedly.[1] The story of the picture's creation was first told by the artist and antiquarian John Thomas Smith, who heard it from his father. The fact that Smith senior had at one time owned the picture and was the godson of Mr Oldham makes the account entirely credible: 'Mr Oldham had invited three friends to dine with him at his house at Ealing; but being a famous and constant sportsman he did not arrive till they had dined; and then he found them so comfortably seated with their pipes over a bowl of negus, that he commissioned Highmore to paint the scene and desired that he might be introduced in it just as he then appeared.'[2] Nathaniel Oldham owned Ealing House, Middlesex, a fine two-storey brick villa set in forty acres of parkland, from 1728 to 1735.[3] It may be assumed, therefore, that Oldham's Ealing residence was the location of the dinner party commemorated in Highmore's picture.

On a superficial level, *Mr Oldham and his Guests* can be related to the 'conversation piece', a newly fashionable genre in British portraiture in which sitters and their friends and family were depicted informally in a domestic environment. However, the painting does not evince any interest in Oldham's material wealth or social status, a *desideratum* of the conversation piece. Instead, it focuses in detail, and with remarkable acuity, on the characterization of the individuals portrayed.

Mr Oldham stands at the extreme left of the painting, his arms folded over the top of the chair. He wears a tricorn hat, indicating that he has just entered the house. Beside him, a large, red-faced man, apparently a neighbouring farmer, sits comfortably, in one hand his clay pipe and in the other a glass of negus tilted artfully towards the viewer. To the right, dressed in black and clutching a porcelain punch-bowl, is the ample figure of the local schoolmaster. Depicted in profile, he seems to be lost in thought, although his impassive posture and expression would appear to relate more to the bibulous nature of the evening than to serious contemplation. Between these two figures, peering over his wineglass, is the artist, Joseph Highmore. Considered as a whole, one of the curious aspects of this group is the manner in which Oldham and Highmore take on the role of spectators, scrutinizing their companions – stalwart members of Britain's yeoman stock. Indeed, while Highmore was responsible for the picture, Mr Oldham, who was himself an unconventional character, may also have played a formative role in its creation.

Nathaniel Oldham, who had served in his youth with the British army in India, inherited a considerable fortune, which enabled him to indulge his love of field sports and fine art. Oldham owned a townhouse in Southampton Row, Bloomsbury, and was also a close friend of several noted collectors, including Dr Richard Mead and Sir Hans Sloane, the scientist and physician, whose celebrated collection of natural history objects and antiquities was housed in nearby Bloomsbury Place. Bitten by the collecting bug, Oldham assembled his own extensive cabinet of curiosities, including a 'choice collection of butterflies'. He also collected art, his taste in this sphere presumably being influenced by his friendship with Highmore. Unfortunately, exactly

Joseph Highmore, ***Mr Oldham and his Guests*** (detail), cat. 3

what kind of art he owned is unknown, since, despite his considerable income, Oldham eventually ran up huge debts. These compelled him to sell his entire collection, which was auctioned off in February 1747. Oldham managed to evade his creditors by seeking sanctuary in the court of St James, where he entertained onlookers with his eccentric mode of dress and impromptu musical performances. However, he was eventually bankrupted and imprisoned for debt in the King's Bench prison, where he is said to have died.[4]

Oldham and Highmore were close friends, one contemporary describing them as 'very intimate'.[5] And, as well as the present picture, Highmore also painted a full-length portrait of Oldham as a huntsman, although this picture is now known only from an engraving.[6] From the visual evidence of the present picture, Joseph Highmore, who was born in 1692, appears to have been about the same age as Nathaniel Oldham. A versatile artist, Highmore was adept at both full-scale portraiture, conversation pieces and genre subjects. He was a friend of William Hogarth, and in 1743-44 made twelve Hogarthian paintings to illustrate Samuel Richardson's *Pamela: or, Virtue rewarded* (fig. 1), the celebrated novel which traces the trials and tribulations of a lady's maid as she continually evades seduction and moral turpitude.[7] And yet, while he shared many of Hogarth's traits, Highmore was never a mere follower. His career as a portraitist was already well established before that of Hogarth, during the 1720s. Indeed, in a poem of 1723 Highmore was even compared favourably to Sir Godfrey Kneller, England's most fashionable and successful society portrait painter:

> No more let Britain for Her Kneller greive;
> In Highmore see a rising Kneller live,
> Whose happy Pencil claims as high a Name
> If equal Merit challenge equal Fame.[8]

The poem centred upon Highmore's skill in female portraiture. Yet, while Highmore was capable of painting glamorous images of society beauties, his portrait style was also commented upon by another contemporary for its 'extream likeness'.[9]

Highmore was a cultivated individual, having studied law and, in addition to his artistic practice, taking a keen interest in art theory. He had also travelled in Europe and is known to have visited the Low Countries in 1732 and Paris in 1734. It is not therefore surprising that he was able to produce in *Mr Oldham and his Guests* a work which was in essence more closely allied to the traditions of seventeenth-century European art than to contemporary British practice. In terms of its relative scale and its concentration upon a small group of figures engaged in a popular pastime – in this case drinking – the painting recalls the type of genre piece made popular in the Low Countries by the so-called Utrecht Caravaggisti; Dirck van Baburen, Gerrit van Honthorst and Hendrick ter Brugghen. Although Highmore's picture is not as dramatically lit as some of those made by his Dutch predecessors, the compact composition, the unidealized characterization and the starkness of the setting provide a common bond. In Dutch art, genre pictures involving carousing, gambling and prostitution have traditionally been associated with moral paradigms. Yet, while they may have served ostensibly to provide a warning against immodest behaviour, at heart they relished the vitality of earthly pleasures. In a similar way, *Mr Oldham and his Guests* celebrates unpretentiously the pleasurable bodily sensations associated with a boozy evening. There is, as has been observed, 'an almost rude directness about the picture that reminds us that Highmore had ... travelled in the Low Countries in 1732'.[10] It may be that Highmore was inspired to paint this portrait in the way that he did because of particular works that he had recently seen in the Dutch republic and that may also have appealed to Oldham's taste in art.

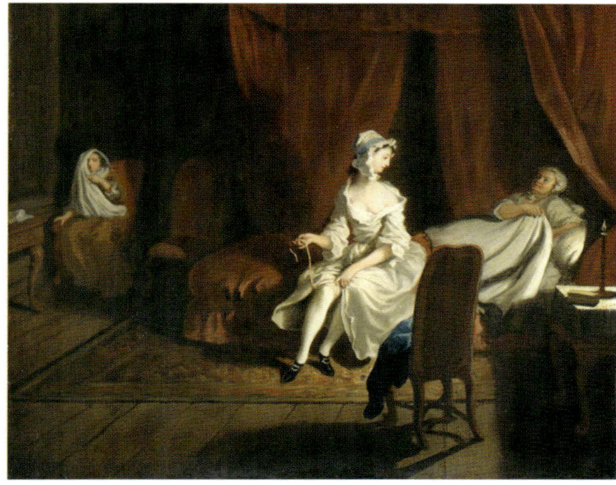

fig. 1
Joseph Highmore
Pamela in the Bedroom with Mrs Jewkes and Mr B.
Scene VII from Samuel Richardson's ***Pamela***, 1743-44
Oil on canvas, 62.7 x 75.7 cm
Tate, London

Partly because of the unusual format of this picture and the way in which it differs from Highmore's other work, *Mr Oldham and his Guests* is difficult to date precisely on stylistic grounds. Although Highmore's exact age in the picture cannot be determined, he would appear to be between forty and fifty years old. If that were so, the picture could have been painted as early as 1732 – at the time when Oldham still had his house in Ealing. Certainly, it must have been painted well before 1747, when Oldham's collection was put up for sale.

Whenever it was made, the most compelling aspect of the picture is its arresting air of reality, as it appears to capture a spontaneous moment in time. However, it must be remembered that *Mr Oldham and his Guests* is the re-creation and distillation of a particular social occasion, crafted with considerable artifice in the artist's studio. To be sure, the picture's main protagonists, the farmer and the schoolmaster, sat to Highmore for their portraits, but the extent of their complicity in the tableau is unknown. On one level, the picture can be regarded as the portrayal of a 'genial company', a group of friends relaxing over a drink. And yet, the group remains oddly dislocated, each man remaining in his own reverie. Regarded in this light, Mr Oldham's guests are transmuted from individuals to types, formed through the artist's vision and the collector's taxonomic obsession into specimens for scrutiny in a cabinet of curiosities.

---

1. See Antal 1949; Einberg and Egerton 1988, pp.47-50.
2. Smith 1828, vol. 2, p. 219.
3. Baker 1982, pp.128-31.
4. See Martin Postle, 'Nathaniel Oldham', in *Oxford Dictionary of National Biography*, Oxford (Oxford University Press) 2004 (electronic edition).
5. Einberg and Egerton 1988, pp.48.
6. The painting dates to around 1740. Although it is untraced, it is known by a mezzotint after it by John. Faber Jr (1684-1756).
7. See Einberg and Egerton 1988, pp. 50-59.
8. William (or John) Bunce, 'To Mr Higmore [sic] a painter' (Leeds University Library, Brotherton Collection MS Lt q 26).
9. 'he intirely sett him self to imitate Nature. In its just appearance. in the portrait way and soon with great success, & extream likeness'.
George Vertue (1683-1756), Vertue Note Books, vol. 3, *The Walpole Society*, vol. 22, 1933-34, p. 29.
10. Allen 1991, chapter 2, 'The Age of Hogarth 1720-1760', pp. 153-57.

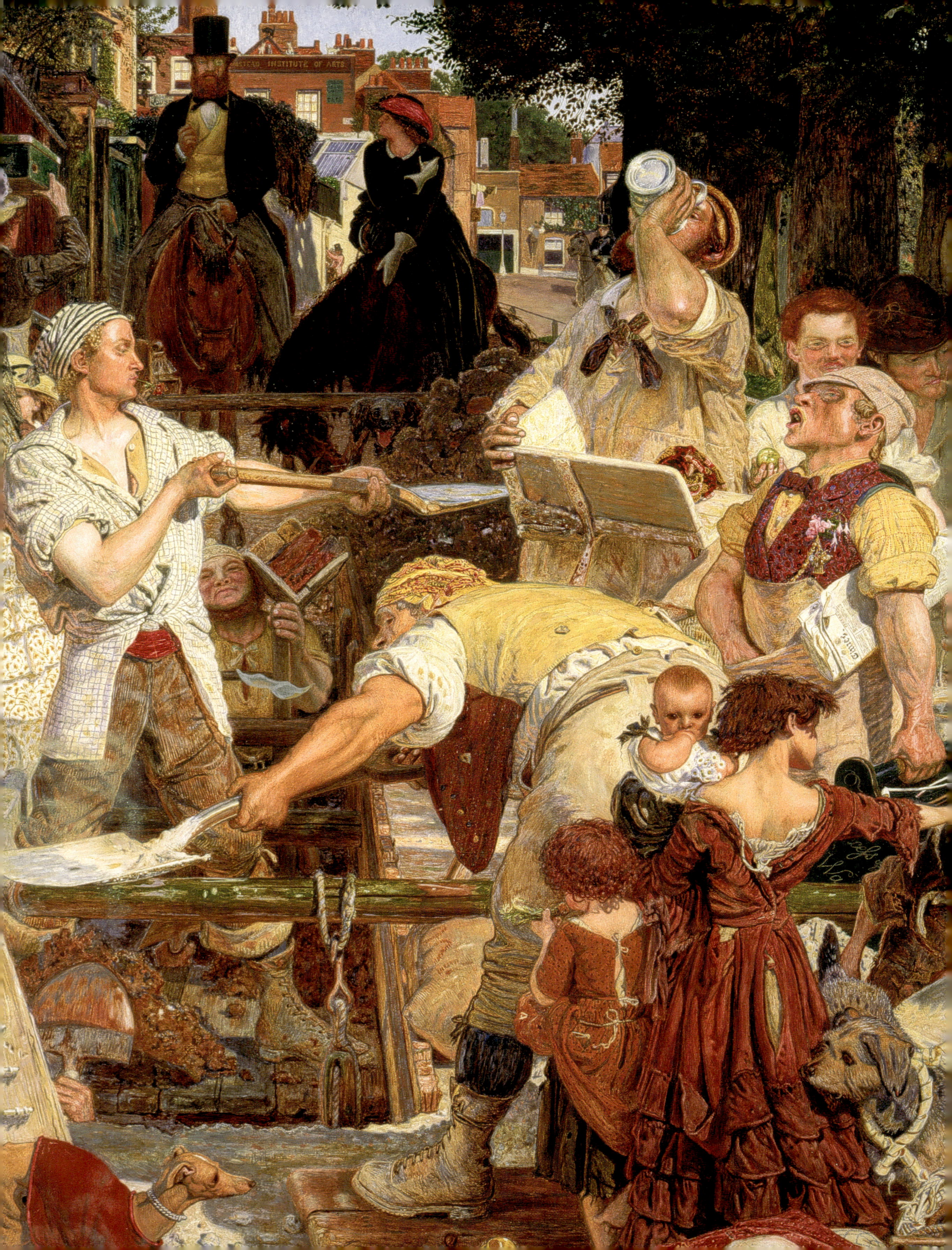
INSTITUTE OF ARTS

CHANGING SOCIETY

FORD MADOX BROWN

Work, 1860-63

TIMOTHY BARRINGER

Work the curse of Adam; a manly duty; the expression of moral rectitude; the essence of modern capitalism; or the route to artistic achievement? Ford Madox Brown's Pre-Raphaelite panorama of Victorian city life explores, in turn, all of these aspects of the mysterious set of practices collectively known as work, which give lives structure and meaning in the modern world.[1] In creating this painting over a period of eleven years, Madox Brown attempted to fashion a new artistic genre, a history painting of modern life both scientific in its exactitude and probing in its moral and allegorical interrogation of the world it depicts. The painting's fanatical level of detail is testimony to the artist's own massive expenditure of labour and is also revelatory of his profound analytical insights. He provides a comprehensive taxonomy of Victorian society, deliberately encapsulating the gamut of social types, from the leisured aristocrat, in the form of a mounted gentleman at the rear of the composition, to the manual labourer, in the form of the navvies in the foreground, heroes around whom the composition is built. Brown uses the painting's dramatic chiaroscuro and its complex deployment of figures to emphasize the merits of honest manual labour and to push other forms of work to the margins. Most significantly, he locates in the body of the mysterious and shifty-looking flower-seller to the extreme left the tragedy of the 'ragged wretch who has never been taught how to work'.[2]

Work has achieved an unassailable place among canonical representations of Victorian society. Constantly on public display and widely reproduced commercially, Madox Brown's composition with its central group of manual workers has been incorporated into modern culture as an all-purpose sign of the Victorian working-class male hero and as a visual equivalent of the sententious voice of the Victorian novelist.[3] The fact that *Work* is widely known and reproduced signifies the ultimate fulfilment of Madox Brown's aspirations for it. Conceiving of the painting as a major public statement – 'my *magnum opus*'[4] – he laboured on it for over a decade: when it was completed in August 1863,[5] he devised an elaborate strategy for launching the image into the public domain. Following the precedent of Benjamin Haydon, John Martin[6] and, more recently, William Holman Hunt,[7] he organized a privately funded, one-man-exhibition, which was held at the Piccadilly Gallery in 1865 with *Work* at its centre. The exhibition was, however, only a qualified success, and the failure of a plan to produce an engraving of *Work*[8] precluded the hoped-for spreading of its gospel into homes and institutions across the world.

Key to the work's interpretation is the lengthy catalogue published by Madox Brown in 1865, in which he offers ruminations about the identity of the various characters depicted, allotting to them past and future life-histories and presenting a tendentious account of their significance.[9] Madox Brown's painting was meant not only to represent the entirety of modern life but also to analyze it. The process of labour serves as the refiner's fire, sorting out the good from the bad, the wheat from the chaff of humanity. It strives to be the equivalent both of a work of supposedly impartial social analysis, such as Henry Mayhew's *London Labour and the London Poor* (see cat. 18), and of a sermon on social and moral questions, like those delivered by the Christian Socialist divine, the Rev. Frederic Denison Maurice. A portrait of him, a diminutive,

Ford Madox Brown, ***Work*** (detail), cat. 22

grey-haired man carrying a Bible, can be seen in the front right hand corner of *Work*. But what gospel was Brown preaching and why? Undoubtedly, the artist's understanding of work was deeply conditioned by religion. Inscribed on the frame are biblical texts, forming the first of several verbal commentaries provided by Brown himself, which offer the germ of an exegesis of the world contained within:

> *'In the sweat of thy face shalt thou eat bread'* (Genesis 3:19)
> *'Neither did we eat any man's bread for naught but wrought with labour and travail night and day'* (2 Thess. 3.8)
> *'I must work while it is day for night cometh, when no man can work'* (John 9:4)
> *'Seest thou a man diligent in his business? He shall stand before Kings'* (Proverbs 22:29)

In the first of these inscriptions, work is presented, conventionally, as the curse of Adam from the Book of Genesis, the wages of sin; its performance is man's punitive destiny. These ideas provided the theological underpinnings of political economy.[10] Yet Brown's painting – and his related sonnet – also celebrates the redemptive qualities of labour: the man of labour shall stand before kings. Deeply embedded in Protestant theology was the notion that work in an earthly calling tests and displays the moral fibre of the individual, by which each can earn a place for himself not only on earth but also thereafter. These ideas owe much to the writings of the social commentator, philosopher and all-purpose Victorian sage Thomas Carlyle, who is represented as the second man from the right. For Carlyle, work was perhaps the sole means of access to the grace of God: 'Blessed is he who has found his work: let him ask no other blessedness. He has a work, a life-purpose.'[11] Visual scrutiny – the work of looking – and artistic interpretation – the work of art – will together reveal underlying truths about society, just as Carlyle did in carefully observed but also wildly judgemental texts such as *Sartor Resartus* and *Past and Present.* The revelation of truth through visual scrutiny and the hard work of artistic representation is the project of Madox Brown's painting. The labour of painting is both an intellectual and a manual pursuit and stands as a summation of all the forms of labour seen within the composition, from the philosopher to the excavator of holes in the road.

Work is, in fact, not merely a single painting, but a cluster of objects and texts produced over a period of more than a decade of hard labour, between 1852 and 1863. The large version, now in Manchester, exhibited at the one-man show in 1865, must be understood alongside a number of pencil sketches, a specially commissioned photograph of Thomas Carlyle and a watercolour which captures the composition at an earlier stage.[12] The smaller oil version, exhibited here, was painted concurrently with the large painting and probably completed first, although its status is technically that of a 'replica'. Specially commissioned in 1859 by the Newcastle lead manufacturer James Leathart, it is an astonishingly careful replication of one of the greatest of all feats of realist painting. Leathart wrote to Brown on 17 November 1859 to commission 'a copy in oil of your large picture of "Work" of the size mentioned viz 3ft 4in by 2ft 3in at the price of 300 guineas', noting carefully that: 'Of course I would expect if you paint me this picture that you would make it equal, so far as the size will permit, to the large one. In short that you will do your best to make it a credit to yourself & satisfactory to me.'[13] Brown certainly achieved this goal, even subtly altering the composition to include a portrait of Leathart's wife as the figure of a young middle-class lady with a red dress and blue parasol. There may be a playful irony in this choice, since this young woman stood for a rather thoughtless and idle form of life, emblematized by her fancy little dog (also wearing a red garment), which is wantonly disturbing a (useful) pile of sand needed for the making of cement. The artist and the labourers are united in their seriousness of purpose – a manly endeavour, according to Madox Brown, in contrast to the trivial concerns of women. The proper sphere of woman's work is represented – though not without irony – by the slightly older woman behind the 'beauteous tripping dame with bell-like skirts' whom Brown teasingly criticizes. This more serious woman is distributing tracts to the labourers, trying to convert them to teetotalism, but as Brown points out, she neglects the proper object of her attentions, her small daughter with a yellow hat, who can be seen at her left side. Brown, radical in political matters, here represented conventional Victorian views on the role of women in society.

In the end, what is on display in *Work* is not merely a painting as a reified form of labour - a work of art, frozen in time - but the process of labour itself. The image celebrates the heroic endeavour of the manual labourers, the brave and original thought of the brainworkers - Carlyle and Maurice - and most of all, the artistic labour of Madox Brown himself. The painting demands labour, too, in the form of close looking and thinking. Its detailed iconography demands, and repays, intensive study. But ultimately, Brown's painting is blissfully ambivalent. One of the most sophisticated and fully worked-out statements of nineteenth-century bourgeois ideology, it also contains the germs of a critique of capitalism parallel to the one being formulated in the same years and in the same city by Karl Marx. A supreme attempt to efface the personality of the artist and present the world as it actually is, *Work* draws attention most of all to the artist's own spectacular labours. It offers a philosophical analysis while simultaneously articulating a critique of bourgeois labour and brainwork as feeble compared with the real sweat of earthmoving. Ultimately, Brown's canvas, private testimonial and public icon, brings the nineteenth-century city sharply into focus, triumphantly registering, and humorously critiquing, its many contradictions.

---

1. For a full discussion of the painting, see Barringer 2005, pp. 19-81. The massive literature on this painting is acknowledged in the footnotes to that chapter. I would like to acknowledge the work of Mary Bennett as fundamental to all other studies of Brown. Her catalogue raisonné of the artist is forthcoming from Yale University Press.
2. [Ford Madox Brown], *An Exhibition of WORK and other Paintings by Ford Madox Brown at the Gallery, 191 Piccadilly (opposite Sackville Street)*, London: McCorquodale, 1865; almost all of the text is reproduced in Bendiner 1998, p. 156.
3. See, for example, details of *Work* reproduced on the covers of the Penguin Classics edition of George Eliot's *Felix Holt the Radical*, (1982) and the Oxford University Press World's Classics edition of Charles Kingsley's *Alton Locke* (paperback, 1983).
4. Brown to George Rae, c. 1864 (Lady Lever Art Gallery, Port Sunlight). See Bennett 1984, pp. 148-50.
5. Hueffer 1896, p. 189.
6. Feaver 1975, p. 72; Taylor 1853, vol. 1, pp. 279-83.
7. Holman Hunt's *The Finding of the Saviour in the Temple* was exhibited alone at the German Gallery in April 1860, attracting 800-1,000 visitors per day. See Leeds etc. 1978, p. 46; Hunt 1905, vol. 2, pp. 193-94.
8. See James Leathart to Ford Madox Brown, 17 November 1859 (Victoria and Albert Museum, MSL/1995/14/55/6). See also Bennett 1984, pp. 143-52, esp. pp. 151-52; Bennett quotes a letter from James Leathart, the Newcastle patron, to Ford Madox Brown, dated 13 August 1863, in which Leathart quotes the art dealer Ernest Gambart as saying 'that he expected the engraving would be a success'; see also Maas 1975, esp. pp. 119-21.
9. Brown, *An Exhibition of WORK*, in Bendiner 1998, p. 156.
10. Hilton 1988, *passim*.
11. Carlyle 1912, p. 189.
12. *Work*, oil on canvas, frame with arch top; inscriptions underneath spandrels [see photographs, Manchester City Art Gallery, hereafter MCAG], 137 x 197.3 cm, signed and dated 1852-65 (MCAG); *Heath Street, Hampstead*, oil on canvas, 22.8 x 30.8 cm, begun 1852, retouched 1855 (MCAG); *Work*, watercolour, 19.7 x 28 cm, signed with monogram FMB (MCAG); *Rough Compositional Sketch for 'Work'*, pencil, 27.8 x 39.7 cm (MCAG), *Study of Rev. F.D. Maurice and Thomas Carlyle for 'Work'*, 1858, pencil, 83 x 45.3 cm (MCAG); *Study of Emma for 'Work'*, pencil, 17.5 x 12.5 cm (Walker Art Gallery, Liverpool); *Study of the Rev. F.D. Maurice and Thomas Carlyle*, pencil, 32.75 x 17.25 cm (MCAG); *Slight Sketch for the Old Woman Carrying Sandwich Boards*, pencil, 12.6 x 27.8 cm, signed dated and inscribed 'F.M.B. 1855 for Work' (Tate, London); *Study of a Greyhound*, pencil 15 x 48.5 cm (Private Collection); *Study of Baby for Centre Group*, pencil, 12 x 8.9 cm (Private Collection).
13. James Leathart to Ford Madox Brown 17 November 1859 (Victoria and Albert Museum, MSL/1995/14/55/6).

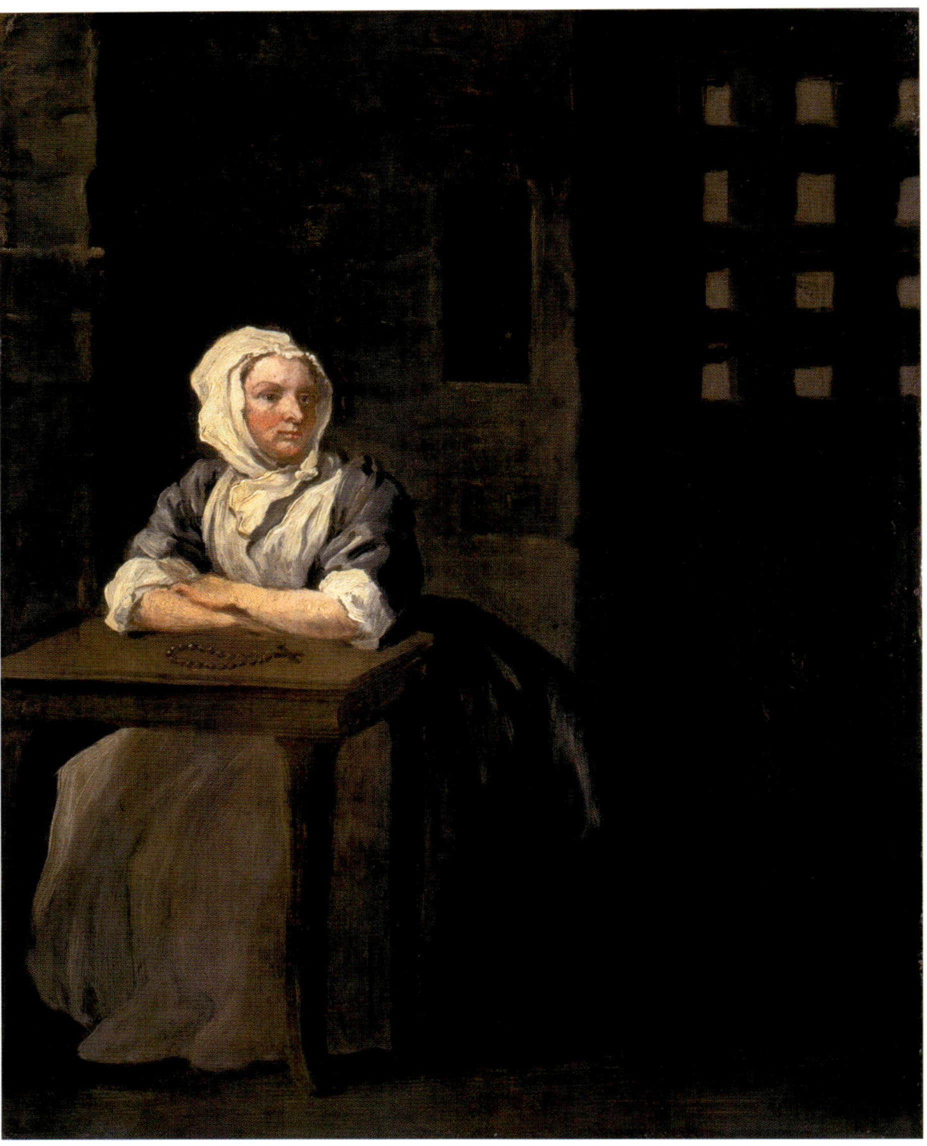

1

1. **William Hogarth**
London, 1697 - London, 1764
Sarah Malcolm in Prison, 1733
Oil on canvas, 47 x 37 cm
National Gallery of Scotland, Edinburgh

In February 1733, twenty-two-year-old Sarah Malcolm was the focus of a sensational murder trial, where she was accused of stabbing and strangling to death an old woman and her two servants in the course of a robbery at chambers in London's Inns of Court. Two days before she was executed, Hogarth visited Malcolm in her prison cell with his father-in-law, Sir James Thornhill. There he sketched her portrait in oils; a work which may well have formed the basis of the finished painting. On the table Hogarth included prominently a set of rosary beads, an indication of Malcolm's professed Roman Catholic faith. On Wednesday 7 March 1733, Malcolm was hanged close to the scene of her crime, still protesting her innocence. The following day Hogarth took out a newspaper advertisement announcing the imminent publication of his engraving of Sarah Malcolm, price six pence, which duly appeared the following Saturday. (MP)

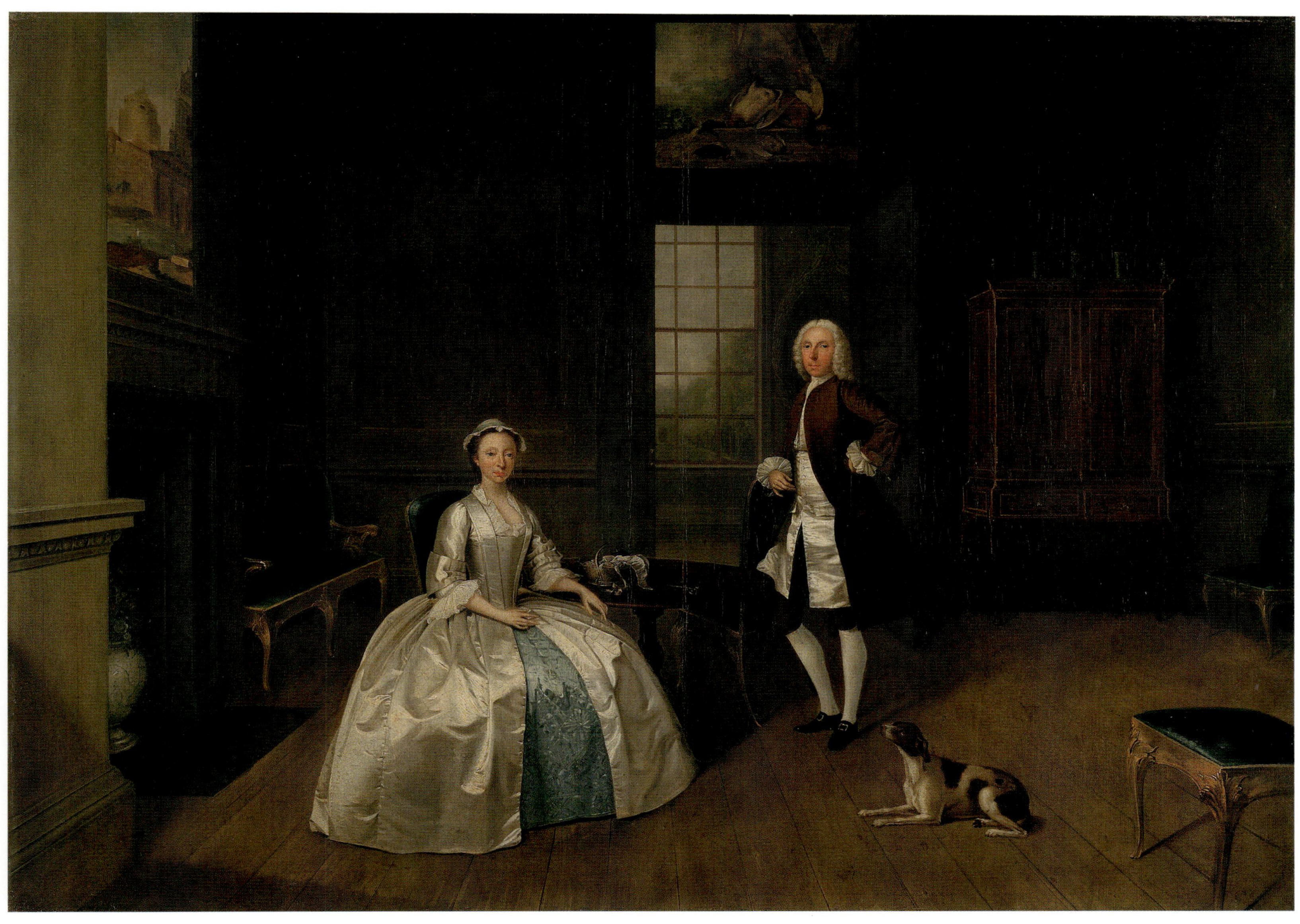

2

2. **Arthur Devis**
Preston, Lancashire, 1711 – Brighton, 1787
Mr and Mrs William Atherton, c. 1743
Oil on canvas, 92 x 127 cm
National Museums Liverpool, Walker Art Gallery

Arthur Devis trained as an artist under the Flemish-born painter Peter Tillemans, from whom he derived a penchant for detailed precision. He based his portrait practice in the Lancashire area, where he was born, as well as in London, specializing in neat, small-scale depictions of families in finely furnished interiors and rolling parkland; works which exemplified the portrait genre known as the 'conversation piece'. The majority of Devis's clientele were affluent middle-class families, whose conspicuous material wealth was an integral part of their public image. The present picture portrays William Atherton, an alderman and Mayor of Preston, and a friend of Devis's father. In 1730 Atherton had married, taking up residence in the market-place in Preston. Among the couple's prize possessions featured here are a large cabinet, a still life of dead game and a painting of Castel Sant'Angelo, Rome – presumably an indication of their cosmopolitan taste. (MP)

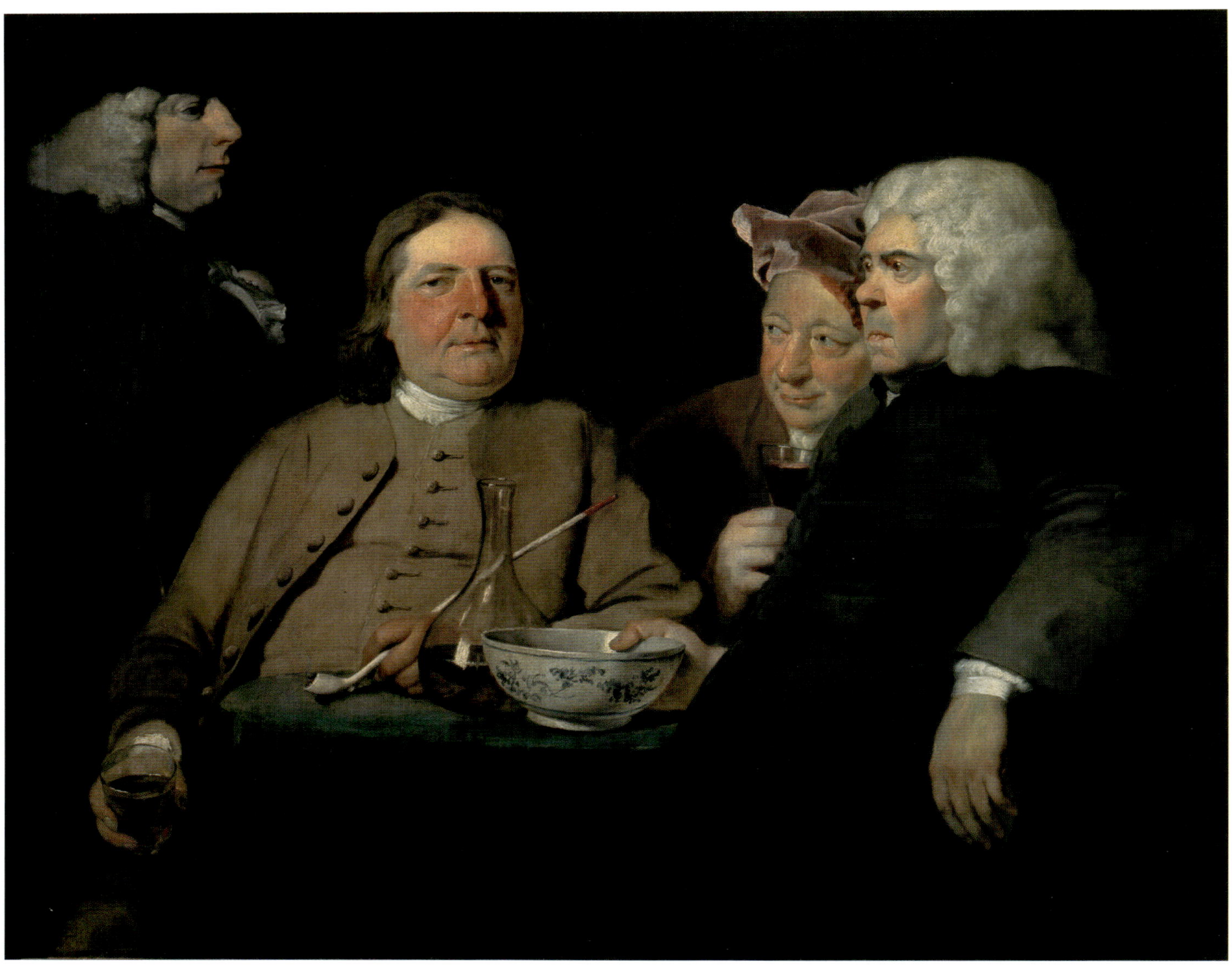

3

3. **Joseph Highmore**
London, 1692 - Canterbury, 1780
Mr Oldham and his Guests, c. 1732-45
Oil on canvas, 105.5 x 129.5 cm
Tate, London

Joseph Highmore's quirky group portrait was apparently an impromptu commission by the eccentric art collector Nathaniel Oldham, who upon returning late home for dinner, found that his guests had already dined well in his absence. Oldham, the standing figure to the left (who has just entered the room), observes his three companions, a local farmer, Highmore, and a schoolmaster - whose serious expression relates to the quantity of punch he has consumed rather than any philosophical ruminations. Highmore's picture, which is unusual for its large-scale format and air of snug intimacy, was evidently inspired as much by the Utrecht 'Caravaggisti' of Dutch seventeenth-century genre painting as by the current vogue in Britain for the 'conversation piece', or informal group portrait. The precise date of the picture is unknown, although it could have been painted as early as 1732, when Oldham lived in Ealing, than a village west of London, where the event commemorated took place. (MP)

See essay pp. 63-65.

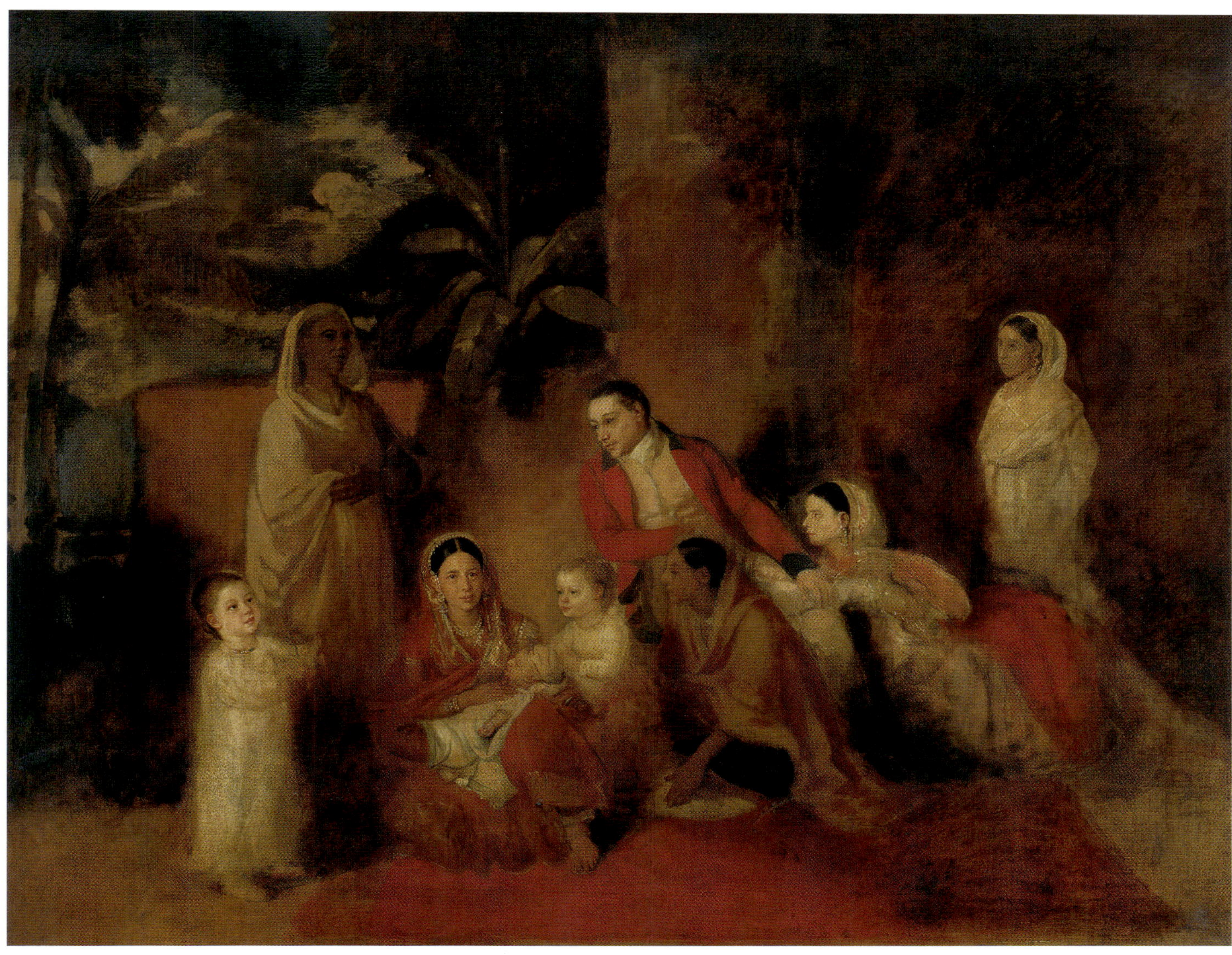

4

4. **Arthur William Devis**
London, 1762 – London, 1822
The Palmer Family, 1786
Oil on canvas, 104 x 128 cm
British Library, London

This unfinished painting portrays the British soldier Major William Palmer with his Indian wife and family. Palmer, who came to India in 1766, pursued a successful career with the East India Company, acting as military secretary to the Governor-General, Warren Hastings. Around 1779 he formed an attachment to a high-born Indian woman, Faiz Baksh, with whom he had six children. Palmer's wife (whom he is supposed to have married in a Muslim ceremony) is seated left of centre holding the couple's baby, Hastings, who was christened in Calcutta in December 1785. The couple's eldest son, William, stands at the extreme left, and his sister, Mary, to the right of the mother and baby. Other adult members of the Indian family stand in attendance. The painting has been attributed to several European artists then working in India, including Francesco Renaldi and Johann Zoffany. However, stylistically it approximates most closely to Arthur William Devis, who was then in Calcutta, where the portrait was presumably painted. (MP)

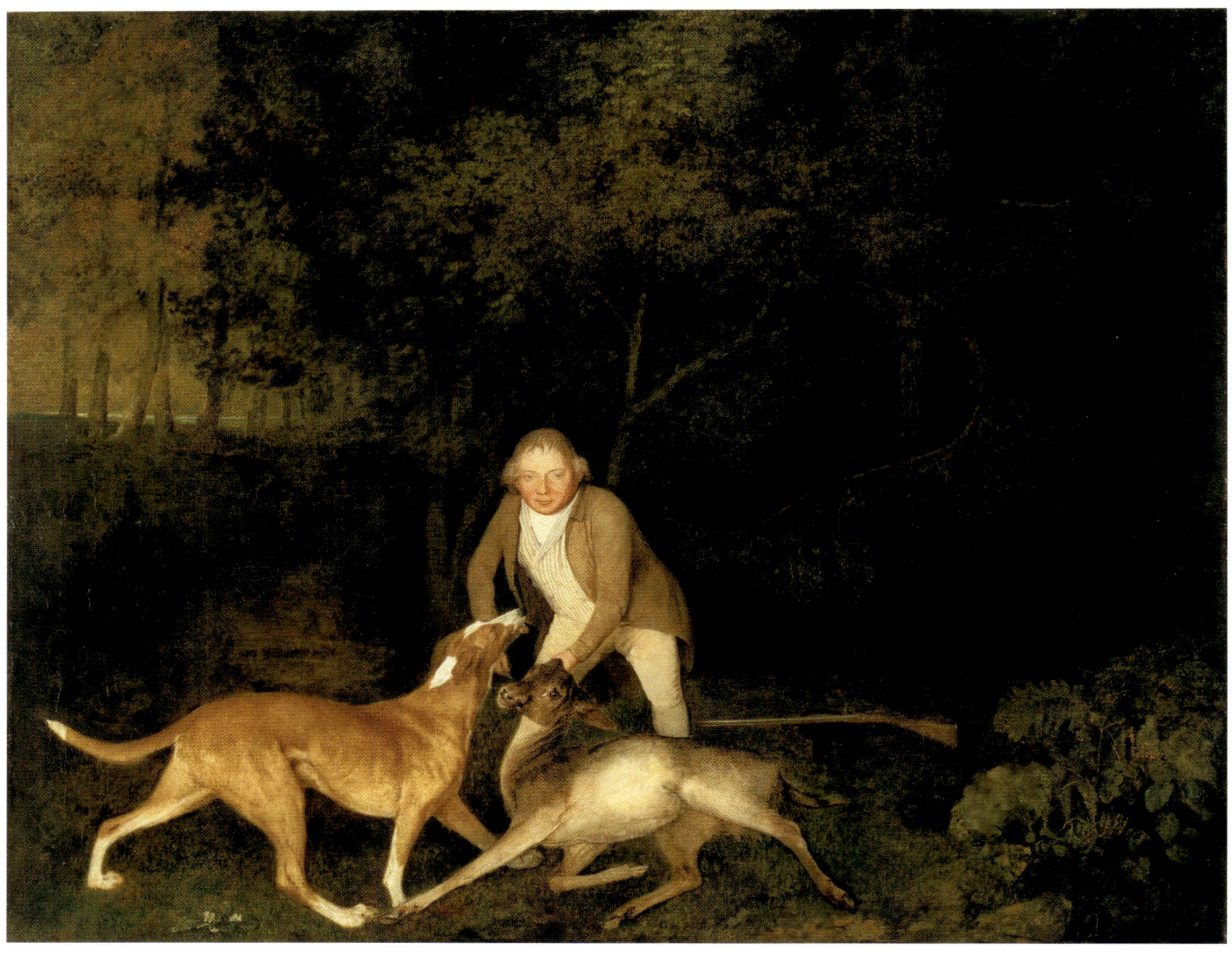

5

5. **George Stubbs**
Liverpool, 1724 – London, 1806
Freeman, the Earl of Clarendon's Gamekeeper, with a Dying Doe and a Stag-Hound, 1800
Oil on canvas, 101.6 x 127 cm
Bottom right: Geo:Stubbs pinxit / 1800
Yale Center for British Art, Paul Mellon Collection, New Haven

The subject is the killing at dusk of a wounded doe at The Grove at Watford in Hertfordshire, the wooded estate of Thomas Villiers, 2nd Earl of Clarendon, one of Stubbs's most important late patrons. Taking hold of the ear of the stricken animal, forcing her eye into plaintive contact with the spectator, Thomas Freeman, the bachelor earl's trusted gamekeeper, stoops to administer the *coup de grâce*. A bleeding bullet wound in the doe's back aligns suggestively with the gun that may be seen a little way distant, lying across the stout brim of Freeman's upturned high hat. Meanwhile the well-trained stag-hound on the left refrains from goring the doe and concentrates instead on licking a button on Freeman's coat. The symmetry Stubbs creates from the lines of the two animals thrust into the shallow foreground space; the careful transition from the major key of busy paws to the minor of prone, expiring hooves; above all, the manner in which Freeman's gaze is directed squarely toward the spectator, underlining his unique legal authority to cull game (the first Night Poaching Bill was enacted by Parliament in 1800): all of these qualities are consistent with Stubbs's finest portraits of the trusted servants of his aristocratic patrons. Stubbs did much to elevate this novel subgenre, in which the servant, tenant or estate worker is viewed through the maybe affectionate, always socially distant eyes of the grandee. At the same time, he characterized the figure with superb detachment. The hair on Freeman's head, for example, demonstrates Stubbs's complete understanding of the way in which, after prolonged exertion, sweat builds up under a high hat – that emblem of gentlemen's attire which increasingly set the gamekeeper apart from other estate workers (Deuchar 1988, pp. 122-26). While the picture was first exhibited at the Royal Academy in 1801 with the title *A Park Scene at The Grove, Watford, Herts., the Seat of the Earl of*

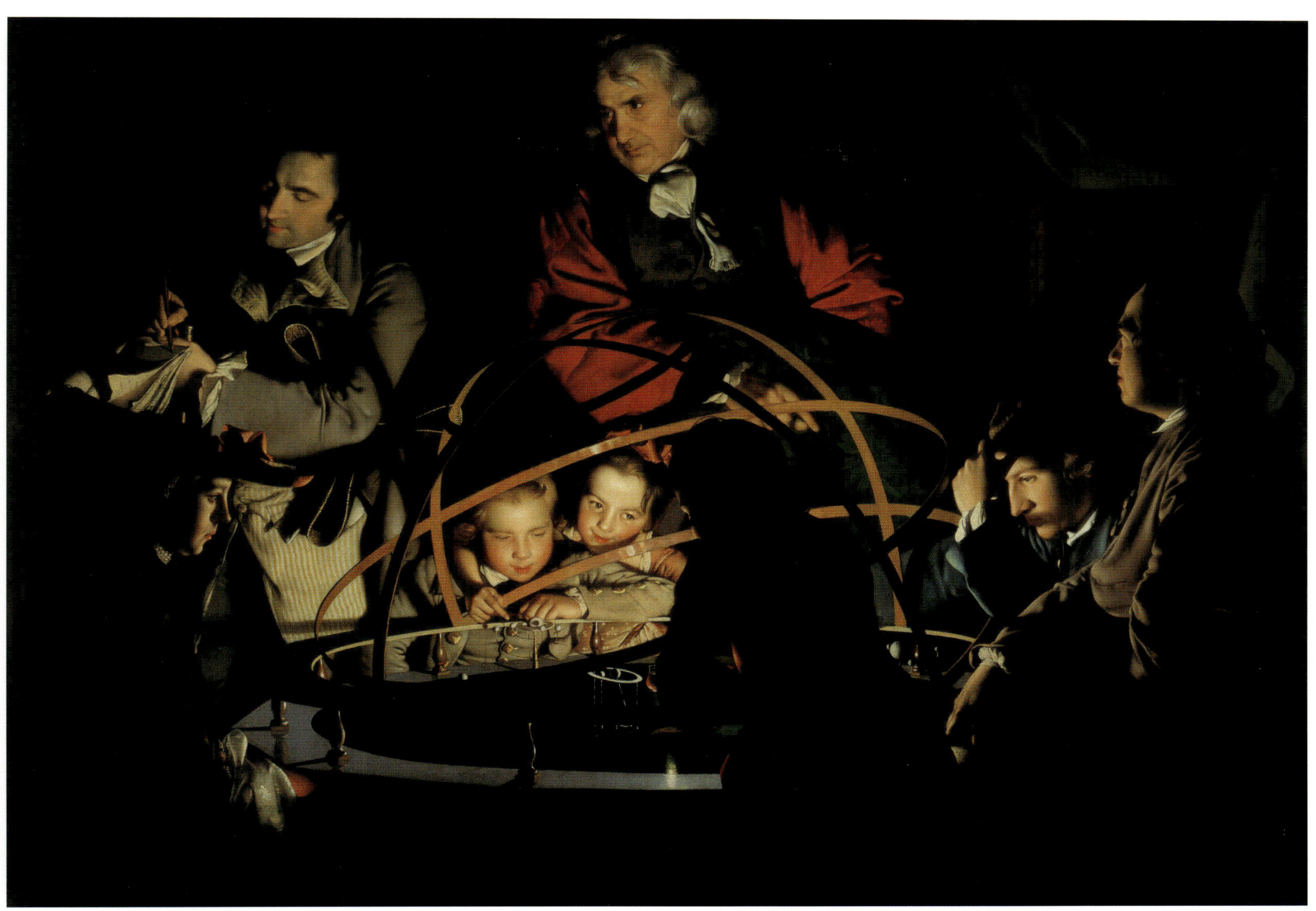

6

Clarendon, it was engraved in mezzotint in 1804, either by Stubbs himself or his son George Townly Stubbs, and in due course sold under the more generic title *The Death of the Doe* (Egerton 1984, p. 241). (AT)

6. **Joseph Wright of Derby**
Derby, 1734 - Derby, 1797
A Philosopher Lecturing on the Orrery, in which a Lamp is put in Place of the Sun, c. 1766
Oil on canvas, 147.3 x 203.2 cm
Derby Museums & Art Gallery

This painting (Nicolson 1968, no. 190), Wright's first on a scientific theme, was exhibited at the Society of Artists, London, in 1766, and it was engraved by William Pether two years later. The orrery, a mechanical device for demonstrating the motions of the planets in the solar system, was invented in the early eighteenth century for the Earl of Orrery and was much used by public lecturers, one of whom, the Scottish astronomer James Ferguson, FRS, was active in Derby in 1762. But here Wright shows a private lecture, which may evoke occasions at the house of Washington Shirley, 5th Earl Ferrers, an amateur astronomer who constructed his own orrery and was the first owner of this painting. The religious underpinning of these scientific demonstrations was made clear not only in Ferguson's lectures but also in a later (1789-92) didactic poem by Wright's friend Erasmus Darwin:

> Let there be light! proclaim'd the Almighty Lord...
> Through all his realms the kindling ether runs
> And the mass starts into a million suns...
> Orbs wheel in orbs, round centres centres roll,
> And form, self-balanced, one revolving whole...
> (*The Botanic Garden*, canto I, 107-118). (JG)

See essay pp. 59-61.

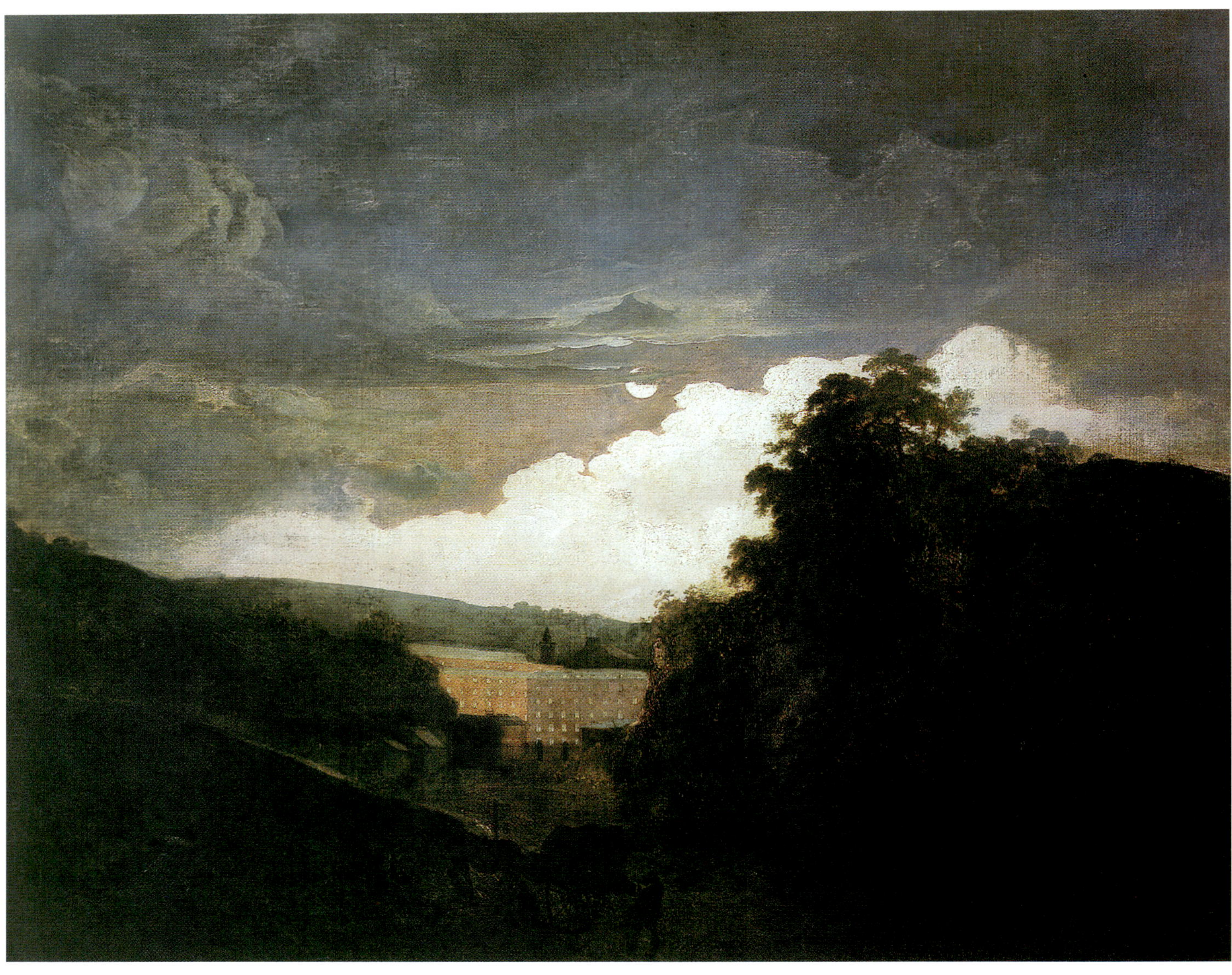

7

7. **Joseph Wright of Derby**
Derby, 1734 - Derby, 1797
Arkwright's Cotton Mills by Night, c. 1782-83
Oil on canvas, 99.7 x 125.7 cm
Private Collection

Richard Arkwright built the mill in the foreground of this painting (Nicolson 1968, no. 311) in 1771, to produce cotton thread on his new, water-powered spinning frame. The seven-storey building set the pattern for factories throughout the eighteenth and nineteenth centuries. Wright painted a smaller view of the scene by day (untraced; Nicolson 1968, no. 312), but the night-scene here was crucial, for moonlight was one of Wright's specialities, and it also underlined the economics of industrialized spinning, which was conducted on the night shift, whereas by day the thread was carded and finished. The painting shows a second mill beyond the first, erected in 1776.

The Picturesque theorist Uvedale Price felt that nothing could touch these cotton mills 'for the purpose of dis-beautifying an enchanting piece of scenery ... they contaminate the most interesting views...' (Price 1810, p. 198). Another tourist, Hon. John Byng, agreed but felt that the mills became beautiful precisely when illuminated at night. (JG)

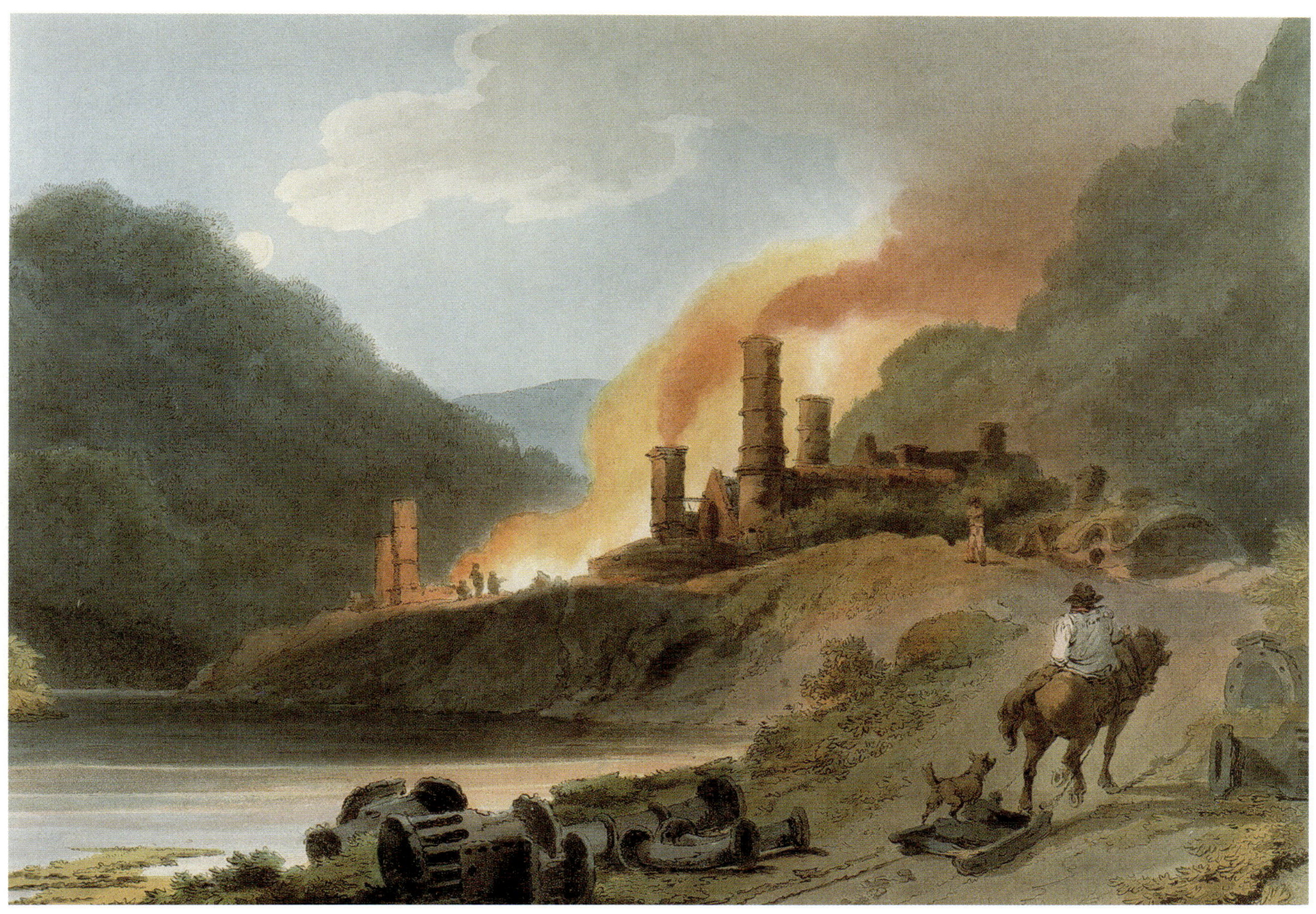

8

8. **Philippe Jacques de Loutherbourg**
Strasbourg, 1740 – London, 1812
Iron Works, Coalbrook Dale, from ***The Romantic and Picturesque Scenery of England and Wales, from Drawings made Expressly for this Undertaking by P.J. de Loutherbourg ... with Historical and Descriptive Accounts of the Several Places of which Views are Given***, 1805
Hand-coloured aquatint
Engraved by W. Pickett, coloured by John Clark
Book published by Robert Bowyer, London, 50.7 x 35.7 cm
Yale Center for British Art, Paul Mellon Collection, New Haven

The French painter of landscapes and seascapes Philippe Jacques de Loutherbourg settled in London in 1771. He was primarily active as a designer of theatre sets, and in 1781 he opened a miniature theatre featuring moving scenery, known as the Eidophusikon. In 1805 he published an album with eighteen hand-coloured prints after his own drawings, *The Romantic and Picturesque Scenery of England and Wales*, which was a typical collection of dramatic landscapes with lonely mountain peaks and waterfalls, catering to the taste of the public. Since the Industrial Revolution, the new factories that had risen along the riverbanks had also become tourist attractions, and the ironworks at Coalbrookdale, near the border between England and Wales, was an important and spectacular industrial site (it now forms part of a museum of industrial archaeology). With his experience of set design, de Loutherbourg contrasted the varied aspects of the landscape and the factory buildings with the glowing fires of the foundries. The same theatrical effects also characterize his well-known painting *Coalbrook Dale by Night* (1801), now in the Science Museum, London. (RH)

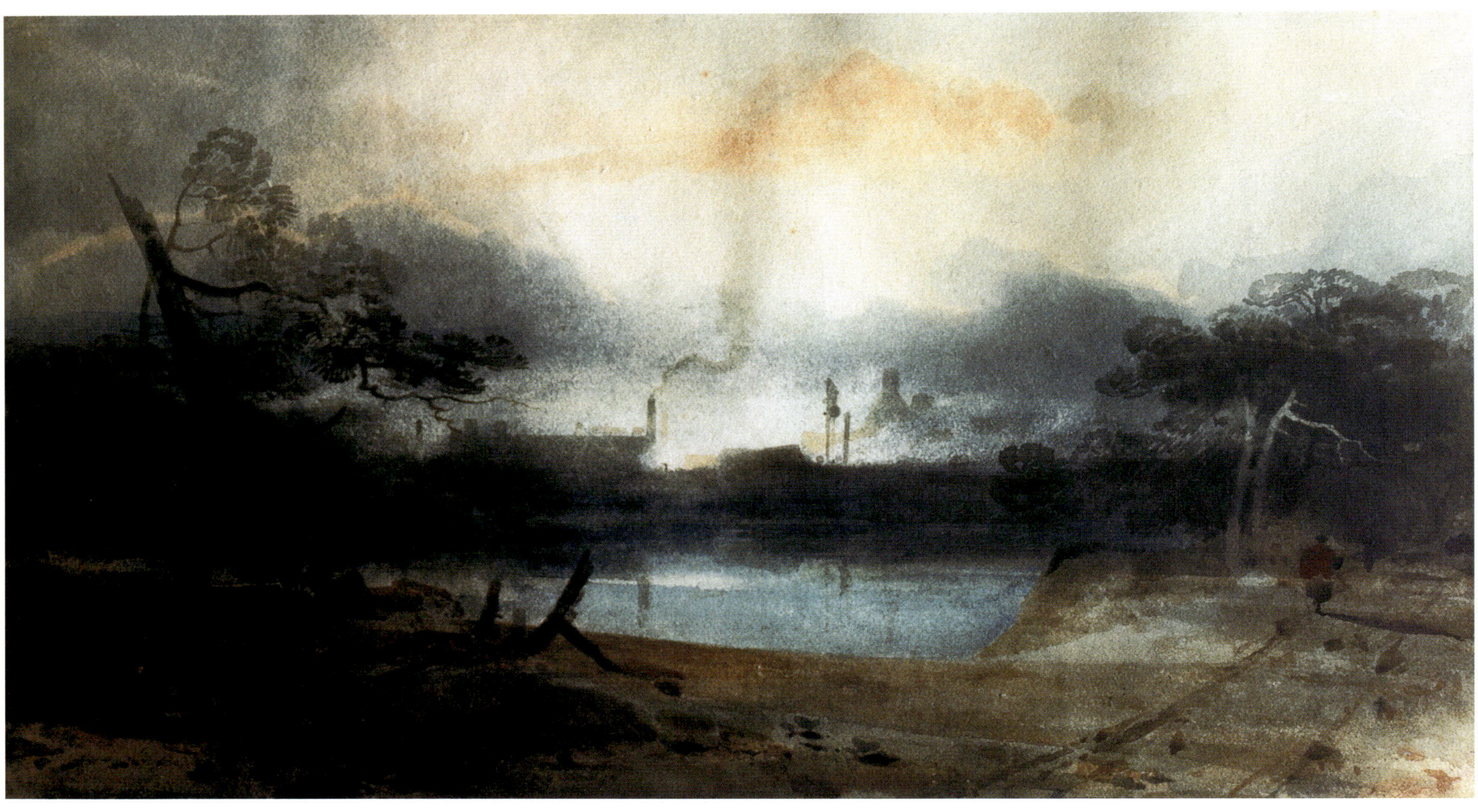

9

9. **John Sell Cotman**
Norwich, 1782 - London, 1842
Scene in the Black Country: Bedlam Furnace near Ironbridge, Shropshire, c. 1802-03
Watercolour on paper, 25.4 x 45.7 cm
Private Collection

Cotman passed through Coalbrookdale in the Severn Gorge when travelling to Wales in 1802 in company with his artist friend Paul Sandby Munn. Although the heavily wooded gorge was itself an object of great natural beauty, by this date the area had become better known as the cradle of the Industrial Revolution. For it was here that Abraham Darby had first pioneered a method of smelting iron using coke rather than charcoal, which enabled him, in 1779, to erect the world's first cast-iron bridge in the vicinity.

Visitors to the area at the turn of the century were especially attracted to the contrast between the natural beauty of the landscape and the sublime horror of industry, and Cotman and Munn - who made his own watercolour of Bedlam Furnace in 1803 from a different angle (*Bedlam Furnace, Madeley Dale, Shropshire*; Tate, London) - were apparently no exception. The key to the dramatic mood of Cotman's watercolour lies in the sky, pierced by the silhouettes of blast furnaces belching out trails of black smoke, which mingle with the livid red tones of a lingering heat haze above. Not for nothing were these furnaces named after the infamous lunatic asylum in London (Bethlem or Bedlam hospital), as if the frenzy and uproar of industry were directly comparable with the noise and confusion associated with a madhouse. (AL)

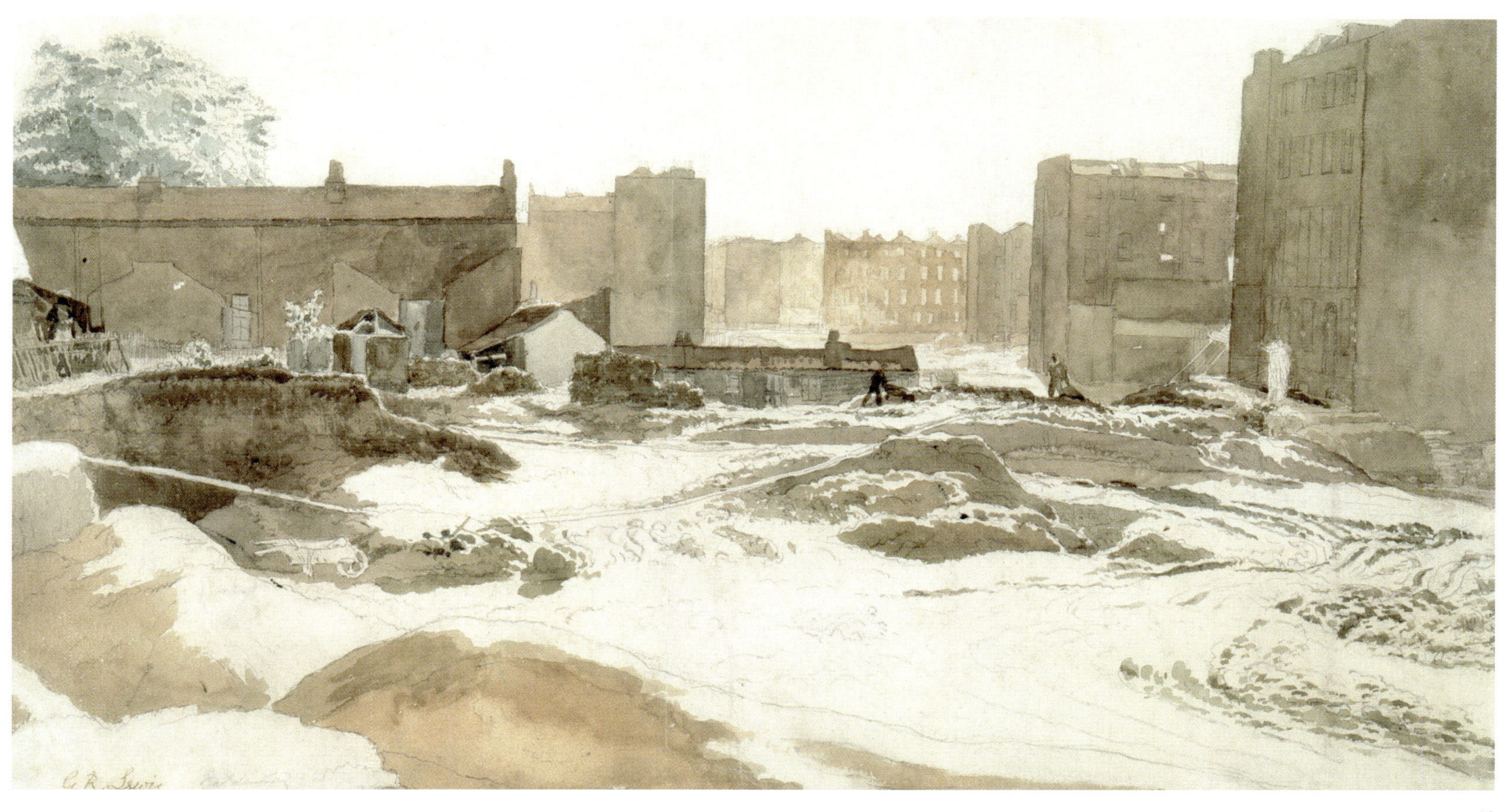

10

10. **George Robert Lewis**
London, 1782 - London, 1871
Clearing a Site in Paddington for Development, c. 1815-23
Pencil and watercolour on paper, 26.7 x 49.5 cm
Bottom left: G. R. Lewis / Paddington
Tate, London

George Robert Lewis belonged to a group of artists in London that included the brothers John and Cornelius Varley as well as John Linnell, all of whom experimented with studies of everyday subjects from their own environment in the first decades of the nineteenth century (cat. 181-182). In 1816, Lewis exhibited a series of works on agricultural themes, which were painted from life (see cat. 157). From c.1815 to c.1823 he lived in Paddington, a village which was then being engulfed by the expanding metropolis, and in this unfinished watercolour, undoubtedly painted in the immediate vicinity of his home, we see the ground being prepared for the construction of a new neighbourhood. (RH)

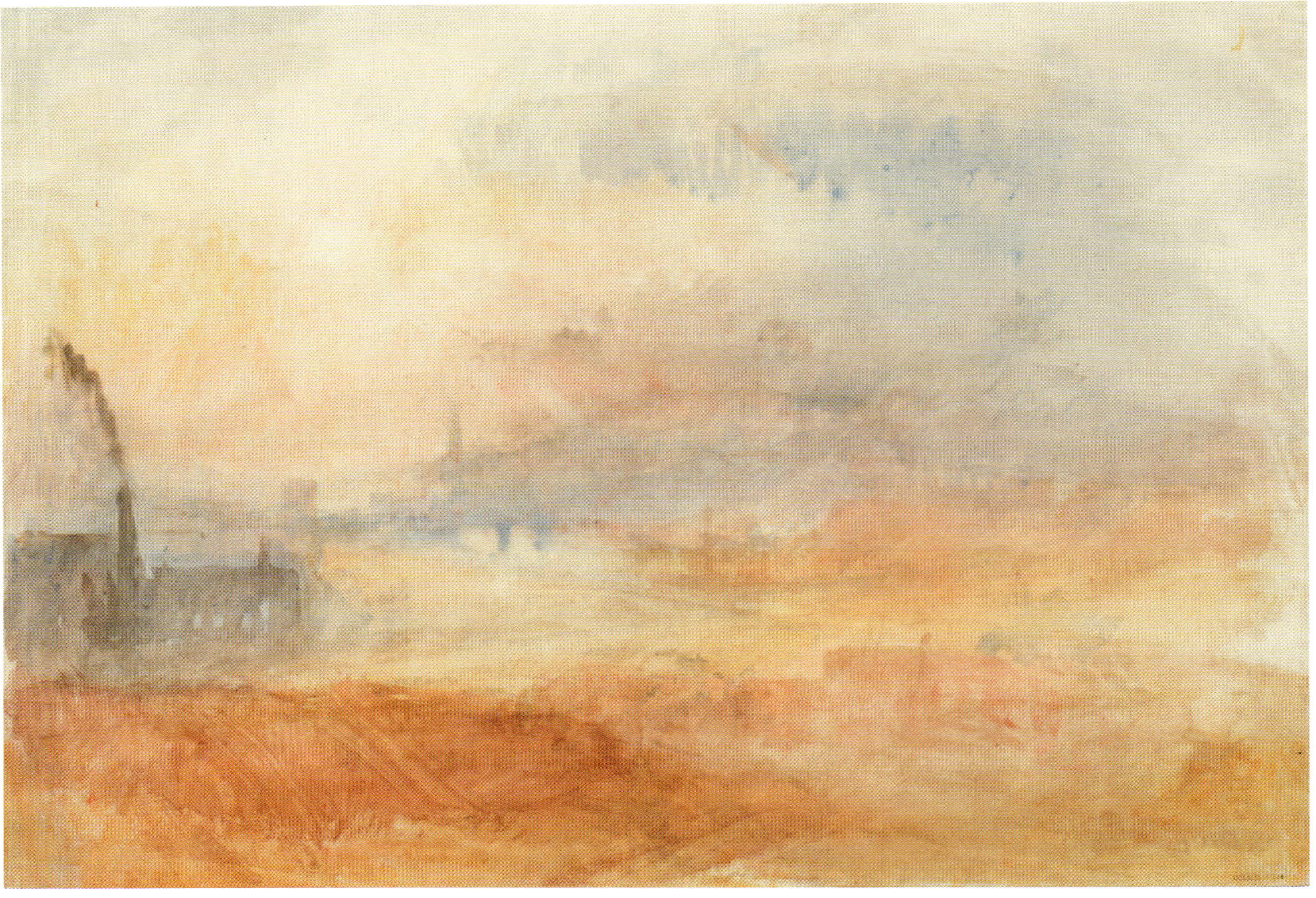

11

11. **Joseph Mallord William Turner**
London, 1775 – London, 1851
An Industrial Town, probably Birmingham, at Sunset; Colour study, c. 1830-32
Watercolour on paper, 34.8 x 48.2 cm
Tate, London, Bequeathed by the artist 1856

Throughout his career Turner demonstrated a profound fascination for scientific and industrial innovation. Numerous paintings and sketches reveal that he was attentive to the mechanisms of change, especially relishing the improvements they brought to all forms of transport, and thereby to the national economy.

The set of *Picturesque Views in England and Wales* he created as an engraved part-work during the 1820s and 1830s incorporated a striking view of the canal and factories at Dudley (Lady Lever Art Gallery, Port Sunlight), in which the glare from the furnaces competes unnaturally with the moonlight. The present colour study (Turner Bequest CCLXIII 128) has sometimes been linked with the Dudley watercolour but seems more likely to be a distant view of Birmingham, which lies at the heart of the 'Black Country', the region that was so completely transformed during the Industrial Revolution. Turner was there in 1830, sketching in and around the city (see the 'Kenilworth' Sketchbook, TB CCXXXVIII ff.14v, 16v, 26v; Tate, London). This study is typical of Turner's numerous 'colour beginnings', in which he tested ideas for compositions in bold blocks of colour. (IW)

12. **Paul Sandby**
Nottingham, 1731 – London, 1809
Rare Mackerel, Three a Groat Or Four for Sixpence, from ***Twelve London Cries done from the Life***, c. 1759
Etching with roulette work, 27.8 x 21.3 cm
Museum of London

This pungent image is one of a series of twelve etchings made by Paul Sandby devoted to the street cries of London trades-

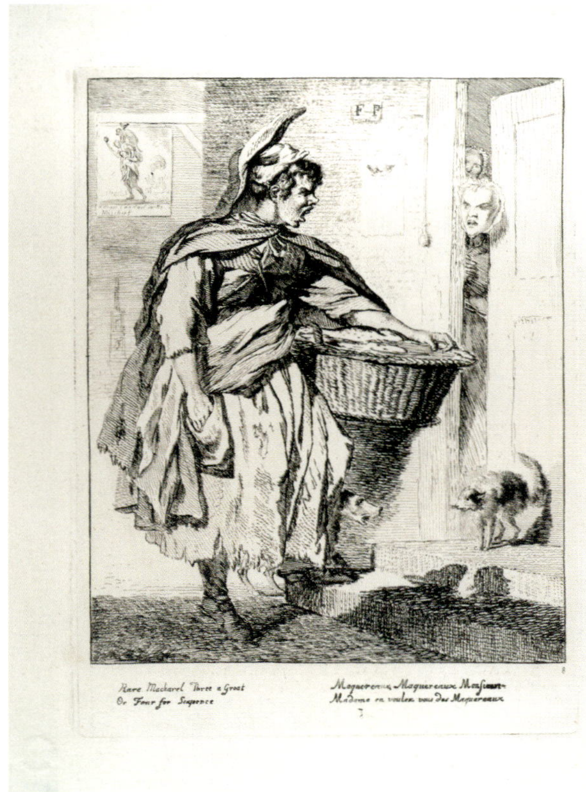

12

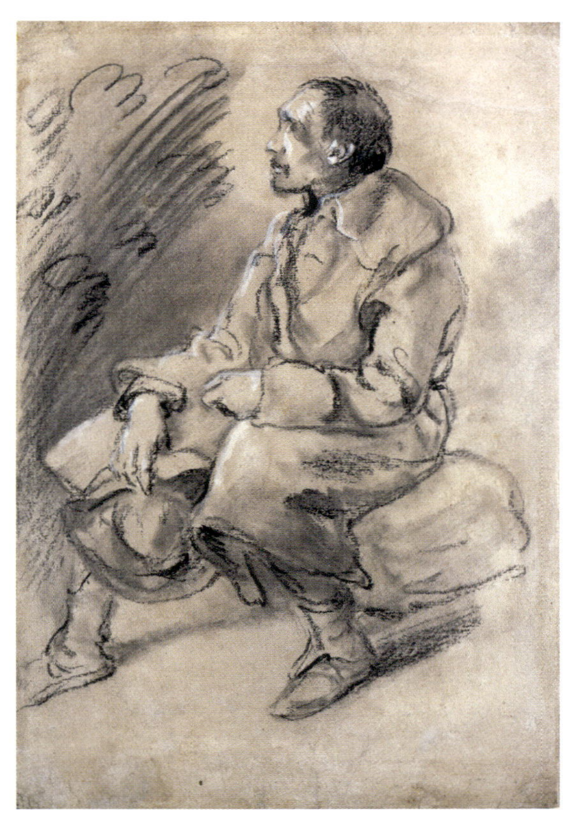

13

people. In England, the tradition of portraying street vendors in print form had been pioneered by Marcellus Laroon's *Cryes of the City of London Drawne after the Life*, published in 1687, although by this time 'Cries' were already a popular art form throughout Europe in broadsheets and popular ballads. Paul Sandby's *Twelve London Cries done from the Life* formed part of an ambitious project featuring some one hundred illustrations of street vendors. In his 'Cries', Sandby sought to produce a more naturalistic image of London's lower orders, depicting his inelegant subjects in discordant or confrontational situations. In adopting this approach, Sandby set out deliberately to undermine the sanitized, picturesque tradition of 'Cries' adopted by Laroon and his followers. The public, however, did not respond positively to Sandby's more earthy 'Cries', and he was forced to abandon plans for further engravings in the series. (MP)

13. **Thomas Gainsborough**
Sudbury, Suffolk, 1727 - London, 1788
Study of a Woodman, c. 1787
Black and white chalk on paper, 48.2 x 32 cm
Gainsborough's House Society, Sudbury

Gainsborough had always populated his landscapes with appropriate figures, and at the end of his life, in the 1780s, he turned to making large-scale paintings of country people. These paintings, reminiscent of the genre subjects of the Spanish seventeenth-century painter Murillo, much admired and copied by Gainsborough, are often sentimental, but the drawings associated with them, of which this is a recently discovered example, are much more robust. None of the drawings of woodmen relate directly to the large painting of 1787, which was destroyed in 1810 and is now known only from the engraving by Peter Simon (1790) and a copy (see Hayes 1970, nos. 850-852; Rosenthal and Myrone 2002, no. 127); and they all convey a sense of fatigue that is rare in eighteenth-century British art. (JG)

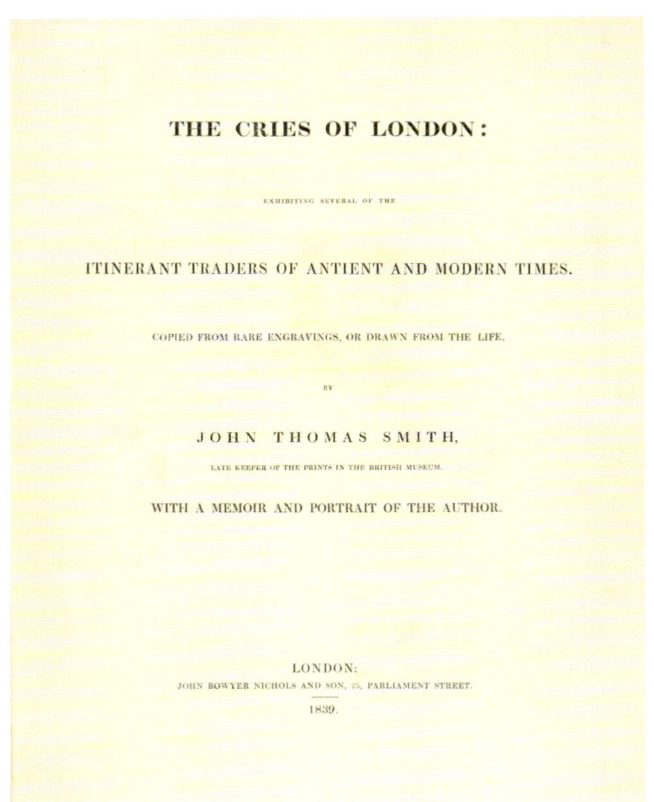

THE CRIES OF LONDON:

EXHIBITING SEVERAL OF THE

ITINERANT TRADERS OF ANTIENT AND MODERN TIMES.

COPIED FROM RARE ENGRAVINGS, OR DRAWN FROM THE LIFE.

BY

JOHN THOMAS SMITH,

LATE KEEPER OF THE PRINTS IN THE BRITISH MUSEUM.

WITH A MEMOIR AND PORTRAIT OF THE AUTHOR.

LONDON:
JOHN BOWYER NICHOLS AND SON, 25, PARLIAMENT STREET.
1839.

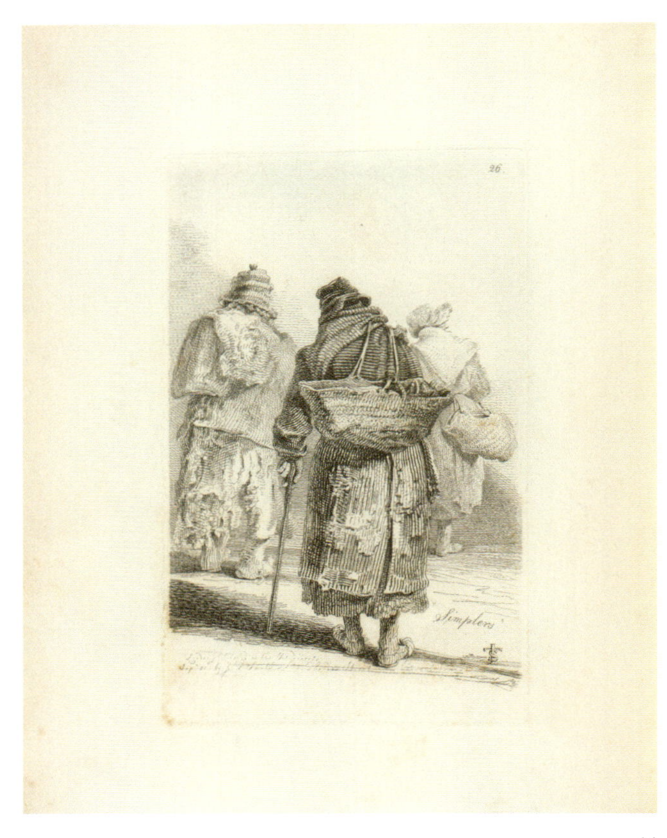

14

14. **John Thomas Smith**
London, 1766 - London, 1833
Simplers, from ***The Cries of London: Exhibiting Several of the Itinerant Traders of Antient and Modern Times***, 1839
Etching
Monogram bottom right: JTS
Book published by J.B. Nichols & Son, London, 46.5 x 28.7 cm
Yale Center for British Art, Paul Mellon Collection, New Haven

John Thomas Smith, an engraver and topographical draughtsman by trade, was also one of London's leading antiquarians, with a fascination for London's history and its people. A pupil of the sculptor, Joseph Nollekens, Smith also became his biographer, with the publication in 1828 of *Nollekens and his Times*. Smith's abiding interest in the capital's underclass emerged in several publications, notably *Vagabondia: Or, anecdotes of Mendicant Wanderers through the Streets of London* of 1817, in which he combined engravings of celebrated beggars with an explanatory text. Smith's obsession with London's street culture emerged in the posthumously published *Cries of London* of 1839, a valediction to a rapidly disappearing world. The subjects of the present plate, 'Simplers', were vendors of herbs and medicinal plants, sold in London's street markets at Newgate, Fleet and Covent Garden. Equipped with large baskets, they garnered a variety of plants from the surrounding countryside, including watercress, nettles and dandelions. (MP)

15. **David Wilkie**
Cults, Fife, 1785 - off Malta, 1841
The Greenwich Pensioner, 1823
Black chalk and watercolour on paper, 36.4 x 25.1 cm
Bottom right: D Wilkie 1823.
National Gallery of Scotland, Edinburgh

This brilliant study by the most celebrated genre painter of his day was one of the very few drawings Wilkie exhibited at the Royal Academy (1824; no. 445: *A Study for Commodore Trunnion, made at Greenwich Hospital*) and had reproduced in aquatint (engraved by F.C. Lewis, 1826). Allan Cunningham stated that

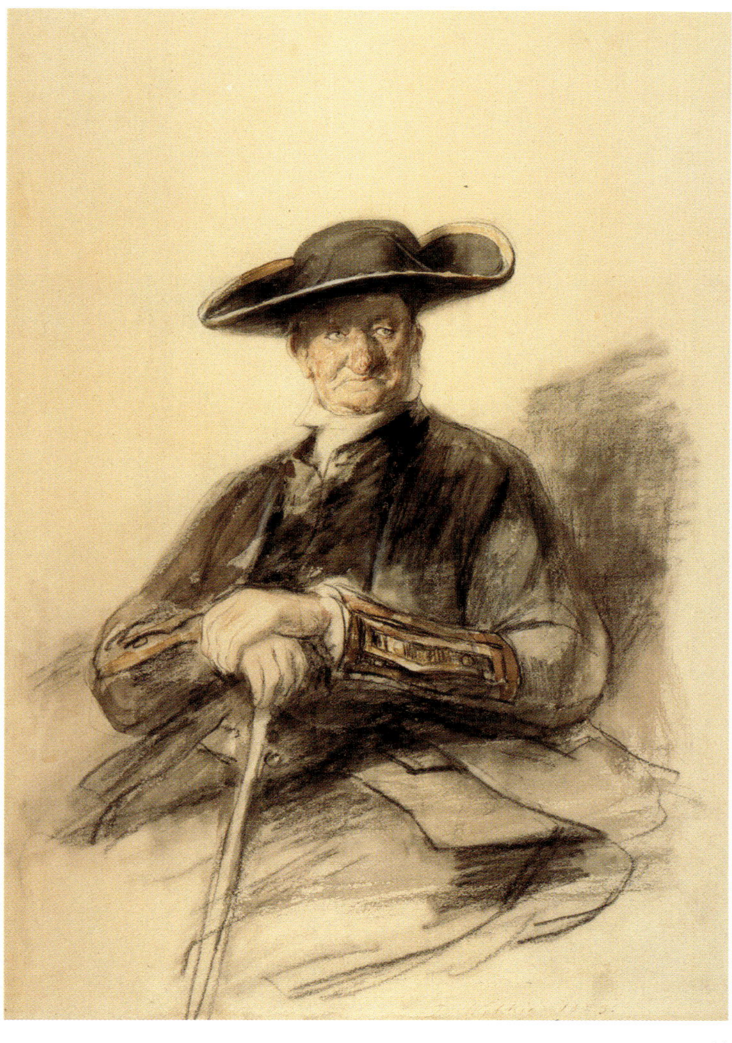

15

the painter's visit to Greenwich Hospital on the Thames, where this study of an elderly naval pensioner was made, was casual (Cunningham 1843, vol. 2, pp. 106-7); but it seems likely that Wilkie was thinking of capitalizing on the sensation aroused by his 1822 *Chelsea Pensioners Reading the Gazette of the Battle of Waterloo* (Apsley House, London) by painting a companion picture for his patron, the Duke of Wellington. In the event, this companion was supplied by Wilkie's Scottish friend, the painter and engraver John Burnet, with the mediocre canvas *Greenwich Pensioners Commemorating the Anniversary of the Battle Trafalgar* (Apsley House). The reference in Wilkie's title to Hawser Trunnion, the eccentric naval uncle of the hero in Tobias Smollett's picaresque novel *The Adventures of Peregrine Pickle* (1751), may mean no more than that the painter found his subject as garrulous as Smollett's commodore, but Cunningham noted, and the wording of the title suggests, that he was contemplating a painting illustrating the novel, a plan that does not seem to have been developed any further. (JG)

16. **David Octavius Hill**
Perth, 1802 - Edinburgh, 1870
and **Robert Adamson**
St Andrews, 1821 - St Andrews 1848
Mrs Elizabeth (Johnstone) Hall, A Newhaven Beauty, c. 1845
Salted paper print from calotype negative, 19.5 x 14.5 cm
Scottish National Photography Collection,
National Galleries of Scotland, Edinburgh

The partnership of Hill, a painter, and Adamson, a chemist, flourished from 1843 to 1847, when it was terminated by the latter's early death. Hill and Adamson were introduced to each other by the scientist Sir David Brewster, a friend of Henry Talbot. The studio produced memorable portraits of a Scottish elite that included artists, barristers, the clergy, musicians and writers - but also of the fishing community at Newhaven on the Firth of Forth just outside Edinburgh. The success of this portrait resides not only in the sitter's beauty, which later captivated Walter Benjamin, but in the careful posing of the figure, the interplay of chiaroscuro and carefully observed texture, and the visual contrast and rhyming between the striped skirt and the wicker basket. In an album of calotypes given to James Wilson, this photograph is annotated with a quotation from Sir Walter Scott's novel *The Antiquary* (1816): 'It's no' fish ye're buying, it's men's lives'. (MHB)

17. **David Octavius Hill**
Perth, 1802 - Edinburgh, 1870
and **Robert Adamson**
St Andrews, 1821 - St Andrews, 1848
Sandy (or James) Linton, His Boat and Bairns, 1843/45
Salted paper print from calotype negative, 19.5 x 14.5 cm
Scottish National Photography Collection,
National Galleries of Scotland, Edinburgh

Hill and Adamson created what is arguably the first social documentary project in the history of photography. Their projected volume on *The Fishermen and Women of the Firth of Forth*, based on the fishing community of Newhaven, was announced in 1844 but never appeared, although many photographs were taken, which addressed the subject from a variety of points of view. There was no obvious model for such a study, and the major influences were, Dr Sara Stevenson argues, the poetry of Robert Burns, the paintings of Sir David Wilkie and the writings of Sir Walter Scott (Stevenson 1991, *passim*). In the album referred to in the preceding entry, the brawny fisherman in this photograph is identified as 'Sanders Mucklebackit of Musselcrag', a character in *The Antiquary*. (MHB)

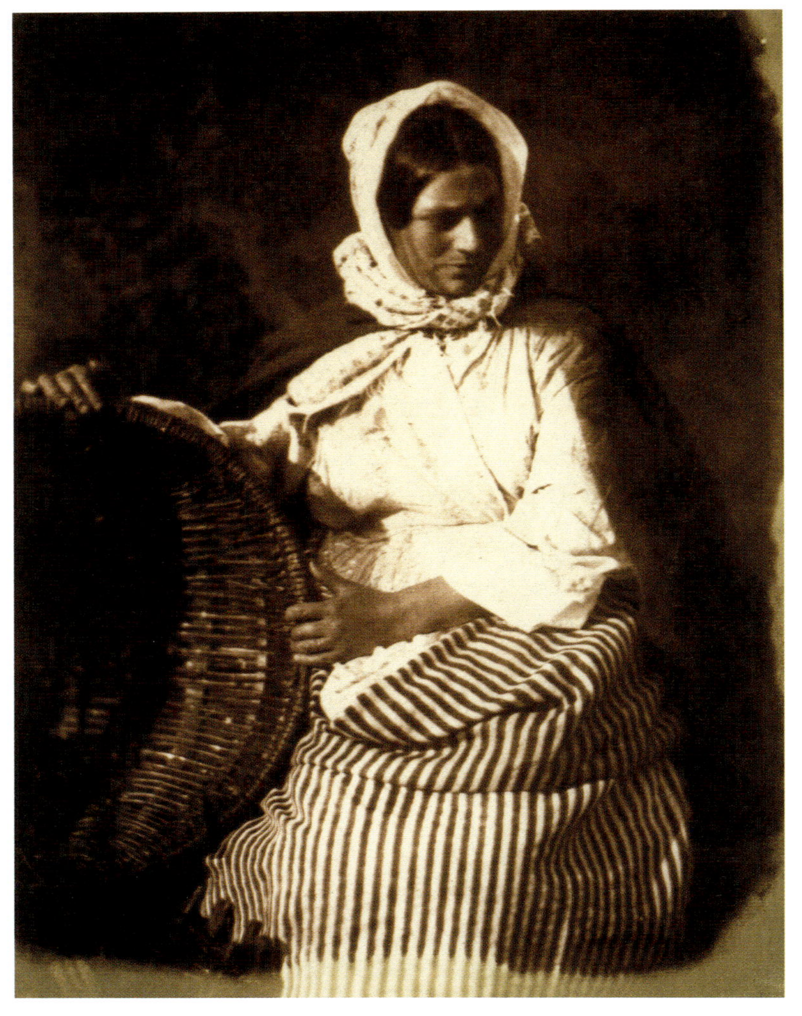

16

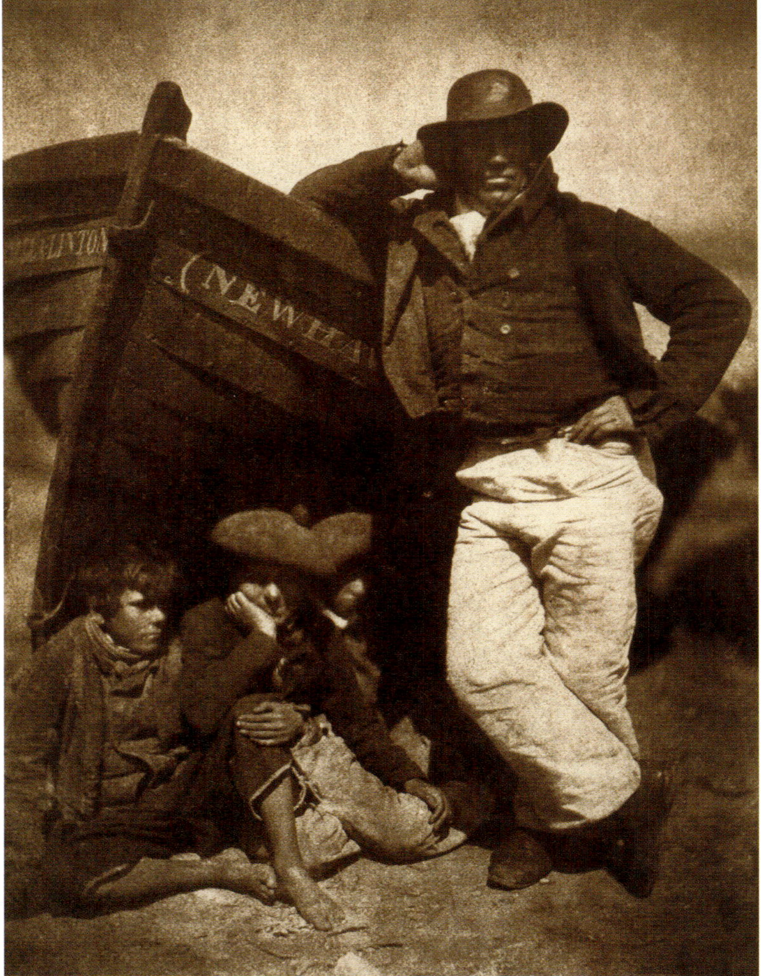

17

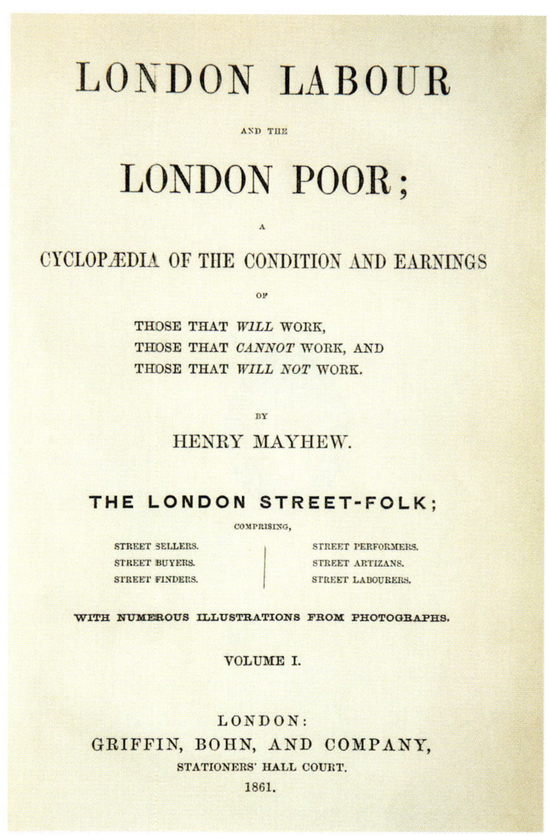

LONDON LABOUR

AND THE

LONDON POOR;

A

CYCLOPÆDIA OF THE CONDITION AND EARNINGS

OF

THOSE THAT *WILL* WORK,
THOSE THAT *CANNOT* WORK, AND
THOSE THAT *WILL NOT* WORK.

BY

HENRY MAYHEW.

THE LONDON STREET-FOLK;

COMPRISING,

STREET SELLERS.	STREET PERFORMERS.
STREET BUYERS.	STREET ARTIZANS.
STREET FINDERS.	STREET LABOURERS.

WITH NUMEROUS ILLUSTRATIONS FROM PHOTOGRAPHS.

VOLUME I.

LONDON:
GRIFFIN, BOHN, AND COMPANY,
STATIONERS' HALL COURT.
1861.

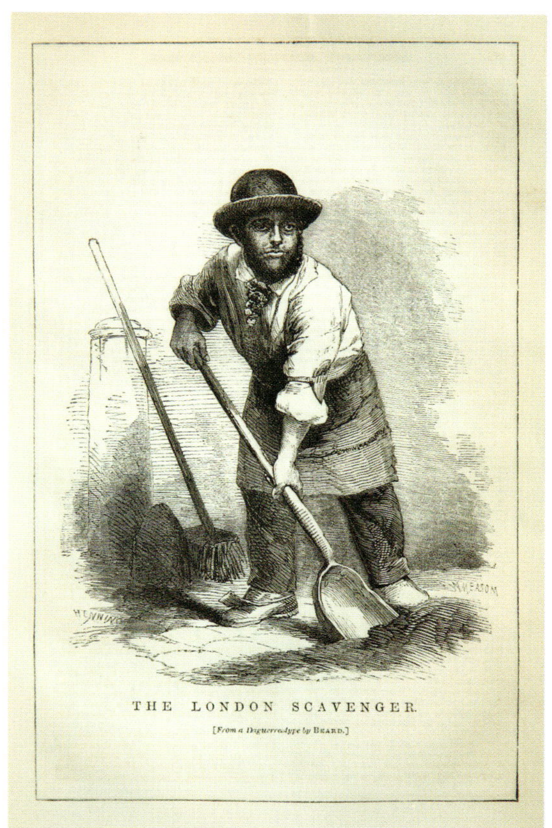

18

18. **Henry Mayhew**
London, 1812 - London, 1887
London Labour and the London Poor; A cyclopaedia of the condition and earnings of those that* will *work, those that* cannot *work, and those that* will not *work, 1861-62
Book published by Griffin, Bohn and Company, London, 23.5 x 15.2 cm
K.U.Leuven, Centrale Bibliotheek

Henry Mayhew wrote novels and plays, but he was best known as a socially committed journalist. In 1841 he was one of the founders of *Punch*, and for two years he acted as its publisher. In 1849, Mayhew and two other journalists began to write columns for the *Morning Chronicle*, in which a 'full and detailed description of the moral, intellectual, material and physical condition of the industrial poor' would be given (Mayhew 1985, p. xix). Mayhew was to cover London, while his two colleagues took the Continent and the industrial centres of northern England. The collaboration with the *Morning Chronicle* lasted only a year, after which Mayhew published his articles himself in separate instalments. These were ultimately collected in *London Labour and the London Poor*, which first appeared in two volumes in 1852 and was later enlarged and published in four volumes. In his articles Mayhew tried to describe the living conditions of the lowest classes in a way that was as objective as possible without succumbing to sentimentality, basing his observations on interviews. Mayhew opposed the paternalism of the middle classes and believed that the poor should be given the opportunity for self-improvement. (RH)

19. **John Everett Millais**
Southampton, 1829 - London, 1896
The Woodman's Daughter, 1850-51 (retouched in 1886)
Oil on canvas, 88.9 x 64.8 cm
Bottom right: JMillais 1851 [initials in monogram]
Guildhall Art Gallery, City of London

The painting's subject comes from Coventry Patmore's poem of the same title, which tells the sad story of a country girl and a young squire. They had first met as children, which is how we see them. Patmore described how the boy, 'with sullen tone, / would offer fruits, and she, / always received his gifts with an air so unreserved and free.' Later they became lovers but could not marry because of the social difference between them. She falls pregnant but then drowns her baby and descends into madness. The body language and styles of dress of the two children indicate the future. She wears a peasant smock and stands with hands outstretched to receive the fruit; he leans casually against a tree in a manner that might appear relaxed but which in fact betrays intense nervous tension and even restrained aggression. In his left hand he holds a crop, alluding to the cruelty with which he

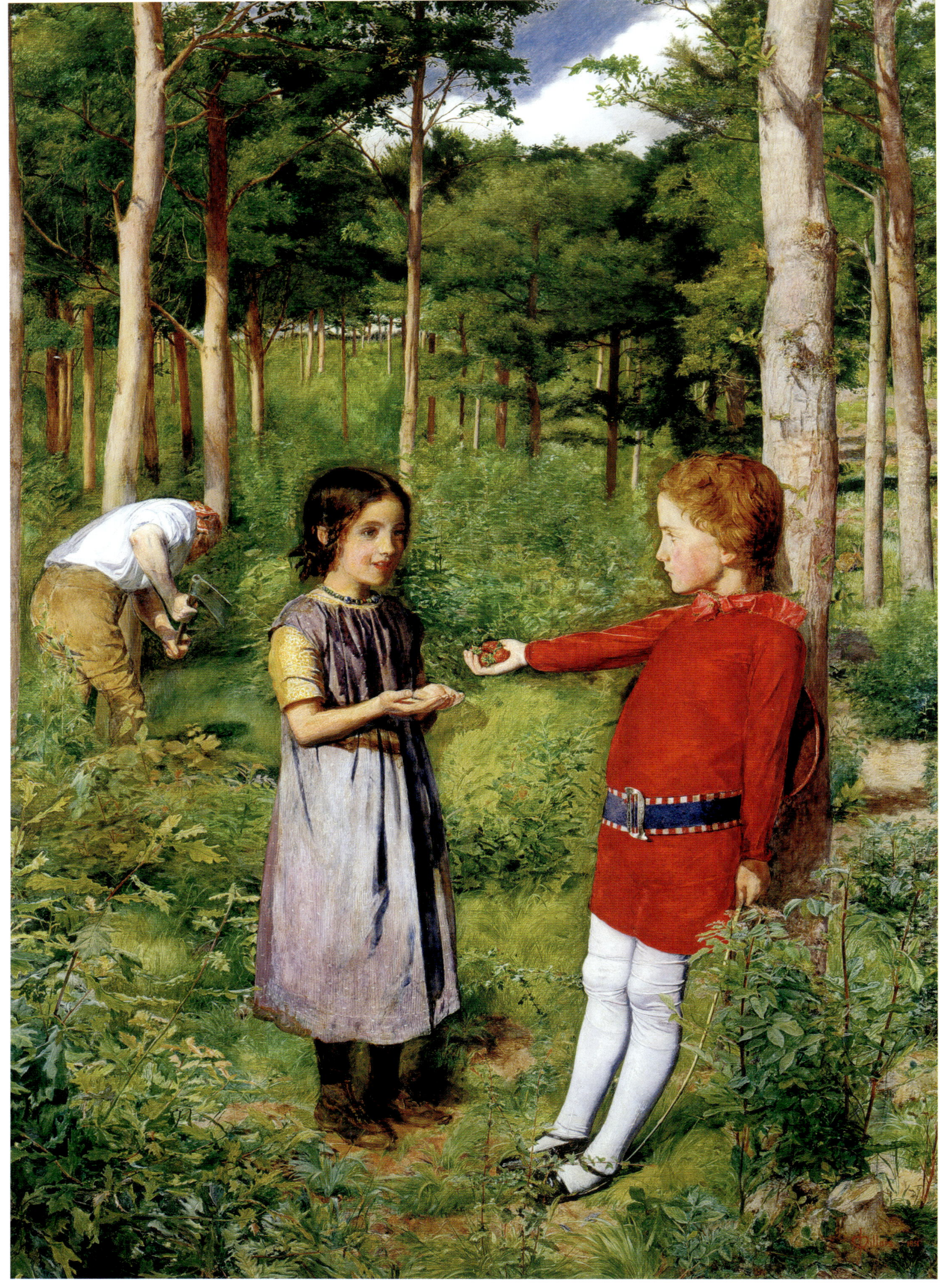

19

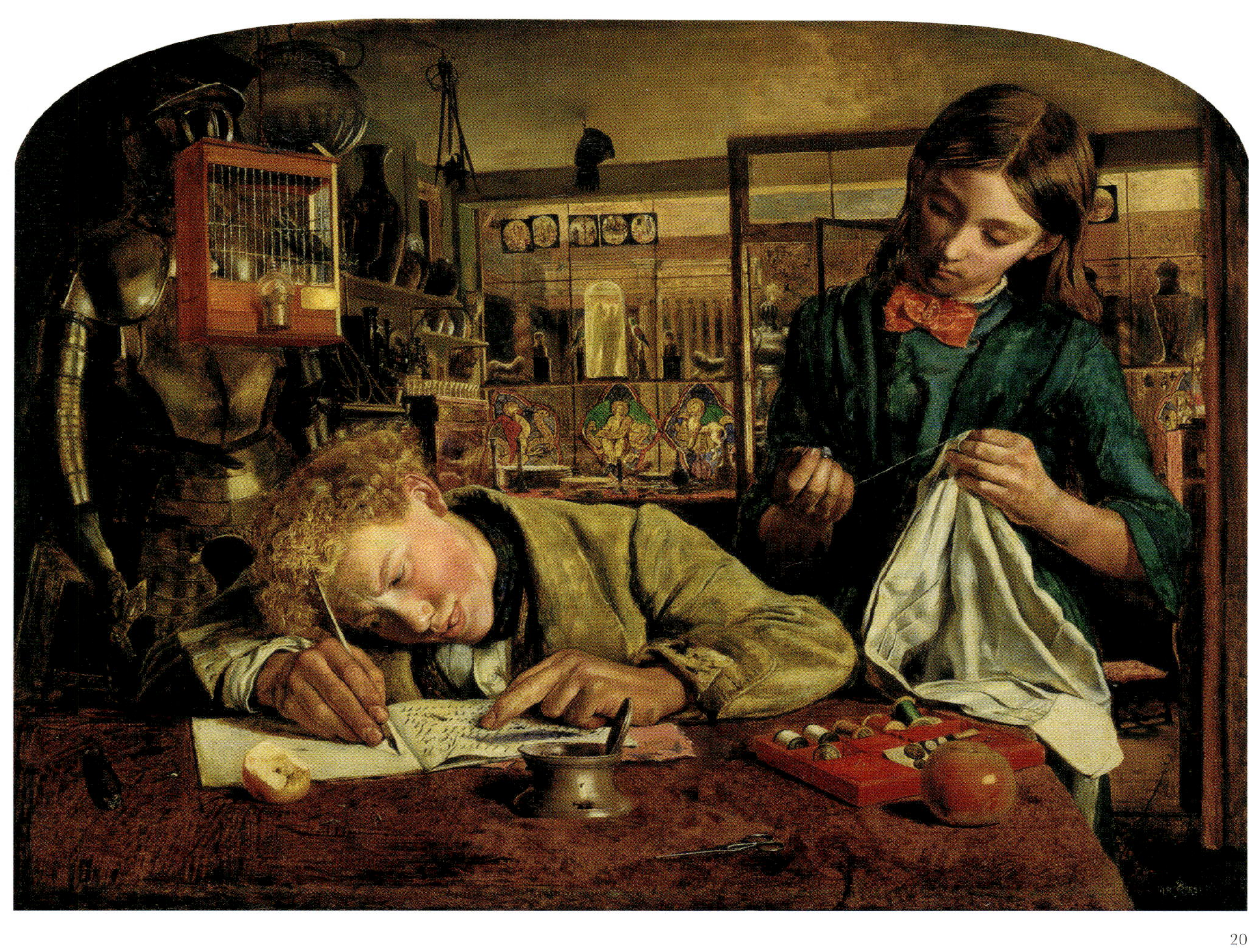

20

will treat the girl in years to come. As first seen, the improbability of friendship between these two children of different social rank was even more emphatic. Patmore explained that Millais had painted the girl as 'a vulgar little slut' (quoted in London 1984, p. 86). The fact that the painting did not sell at the Royal Academy in 1851 was put down to the girl's physical appearance. In 1886, at the request of the painting's then owner, Millais repainted the face, in doing so spoiling the painting - not least because he could not, nor attempted to, match the painstaking Pre-Raphaelite technique with which the rest of the composition is treated.

The landscape setting is particularly beautiful and represents one of the earliest treatments of woodland glades, tree stems and leafy canopies in Pre-Raphaelite art. It was painted directly from the motif in Wytham Wood near Oxford. Millais then used a studio in Oxford to set the two figures, working slowly and with the utmost conscientiousness, as was reported by a friend who described how 'three hairs on the workman's little girl's head or two freckles on her face' would occupy him for an entire day (London 1984, p. 86). (CSN)

20. **Robert Braithwaite Martineau**
London, 1826 - London, 1869
Kit's Writing Lesson, 1852
Oil on canvas, 52.1 x 70.5 cm
Bottom right: RBM [monogram] / 1852
Tate, London, Presented by Mrs Phyllis Tillyard 1955

In about 1851 R.B. Martineau, who had previously followed a career in the law, met and applied for painting lessons from William Holman Hunt. Martineau's father, who was himself a successful lawyer, was prepared to support his son, and therefore, as Hunt put it, 'the lucrativeness of the pursuit was not at first a vital question'. Thus were overcome 'the scruples [Hunt] had against encouraging any one native born needing to live by his profession from becoming a painter in this country' (Hunt 1905, vol. 1, p. 302).

Kit's Writing Lesson is Martineau's first recorded painting and was done under Hunt's supervision. Its subject comes from Charles Dickens's novel *The Old Curiosity Shop* (1841), where at the end of chapter 3 Little Nell attempts to teach her

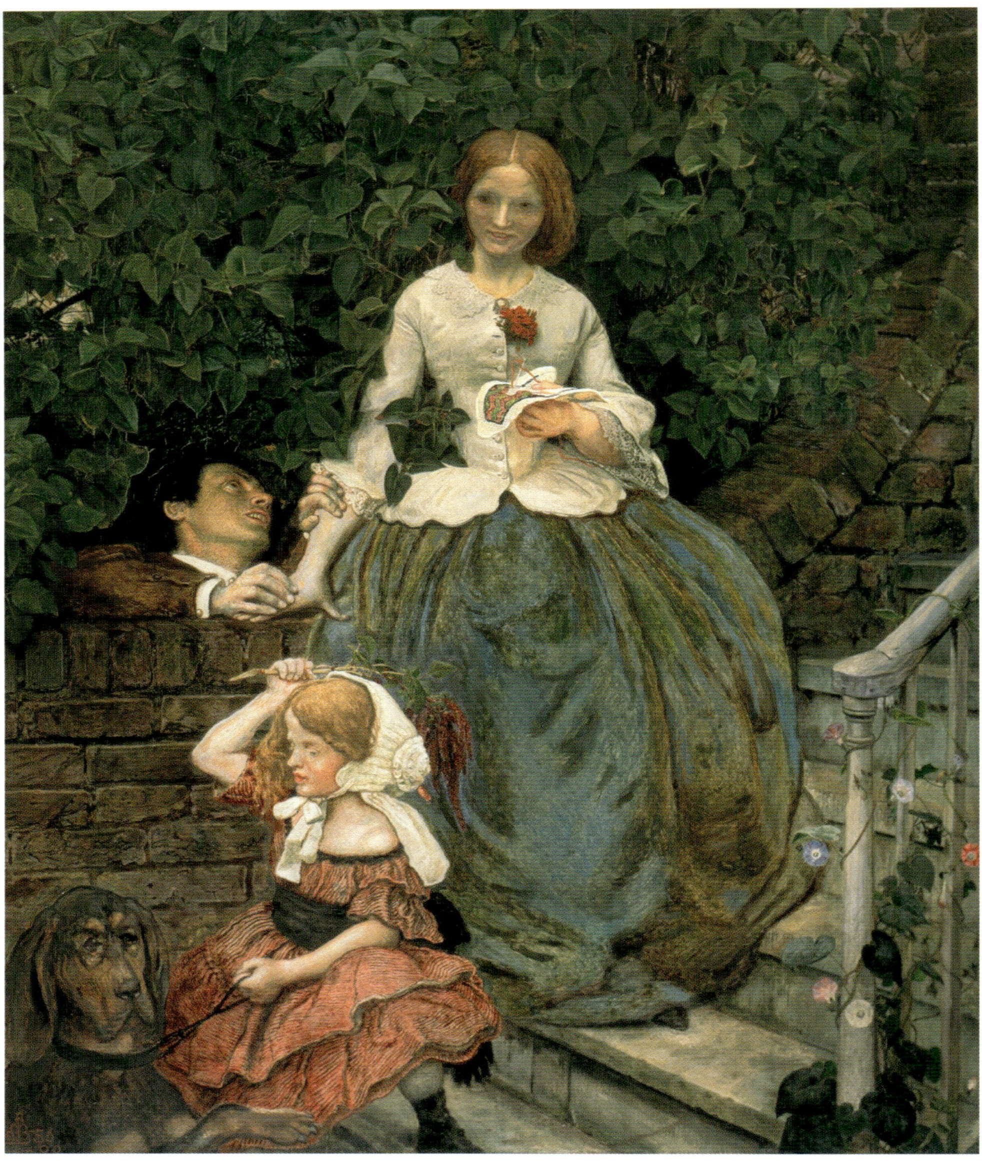

21

friend Kit Nubbles to write. In his early career Martineau seems to have been uncertain as to how to convey a sense of a three-dimensional space. The figures appear to be crowded into a foreground plane, with the peripheral areas flattened and densely filled with meticulously represented props such as the inkwell and cotton reels, apple and clasp knife. In a critical account of *Kit's Writing Lesson*, William Michael Rossetti expressed the view that 'some of the background objects are too prominent; their multiplicity and minuteness easily leading to this error' (*Spectator*, 5 June 1852, p. 543), an intuition prompted by a certain naive quality, which is consistent in Martineau's work.

Martineau followed *Kit's Writing Lesson* in 1856 with *The Spelling Lesson* (Musée d'Orsay, Paris), a work which has no literary pretext and which further demonstrates the painter's interest in the issue of education and his support for the cause of literacy for all. (CSN)

21. **Ford Madox Brown**
Calais, 1821 - London, 1893
Stages of Cruelty, 1856-57 (retouched in 1890)
Oil on canvas, 73.3 x 59.9 cm
Bottom left: fmB [monogram] - 56 / - 90
Manchester Art Gallery

Even though Brown's fortunes were somewhat improved by the time he undertook *Stages of Cruelty*, it seems that his first intention with it was to paint an unchallenging and even sentimental subject which might have been readily saleable. In the event, something much more sinister emerged, with complex if ambiguous allegorical implications, which remain as disconcerting now as they were in the 1850s. When it was finished, Brown offered it to a succession of clients but only eventually got it off his hands in 1890.

A young woman in a flowing skirt and tight-waisted jacket rests on a wall that presumably forms the boundary to her father's house. In her left hand is a piece of embroidery, while

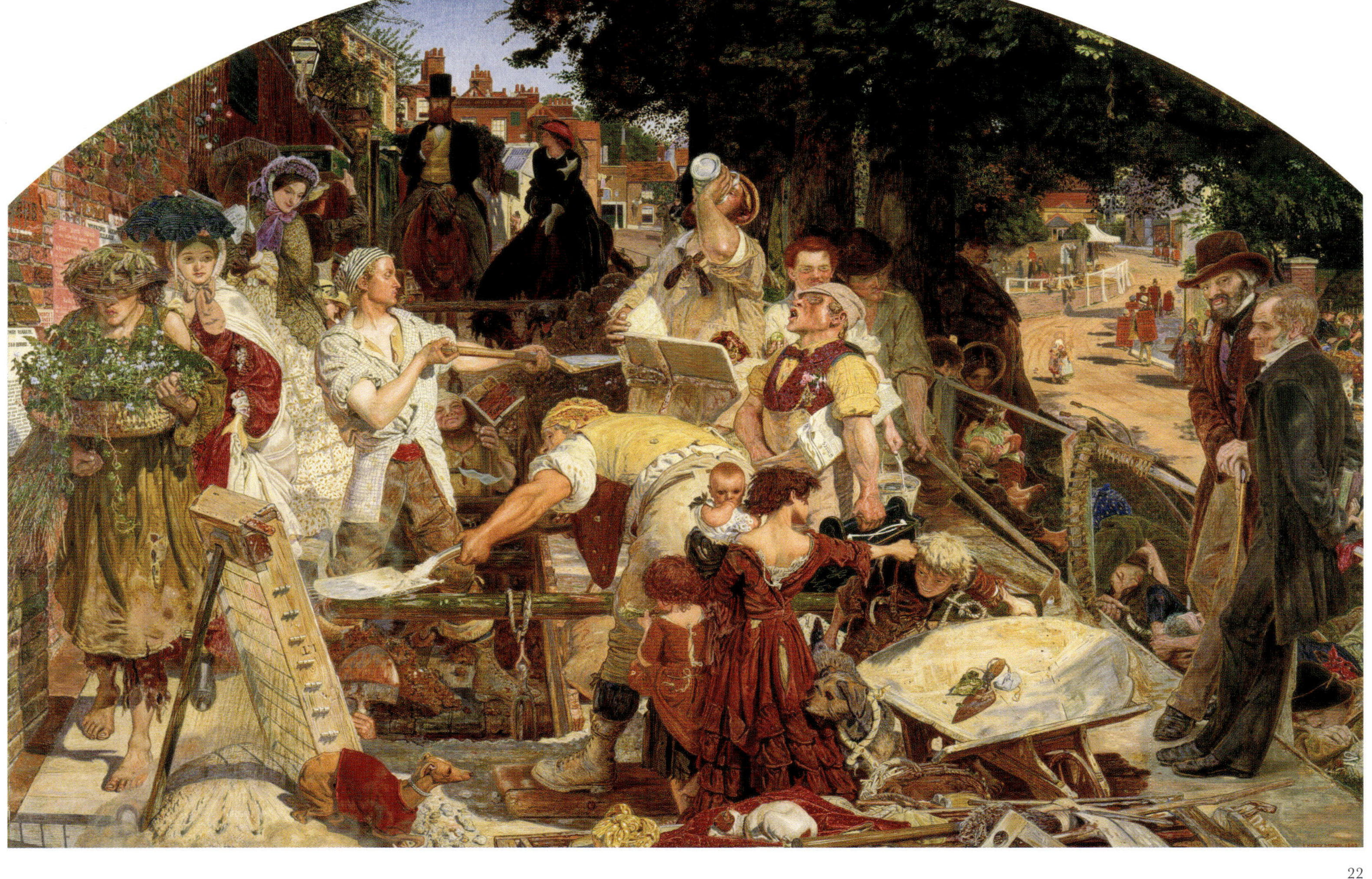

22

her right arm is clutched at by a young man, her suitor, who emerges from the garden beyond. There appears to be something illicit about this meeting, and the relationship between the two would seem to be one of foolish infatuation on his part and callous indifference, although without any positive disavowal, on hers. A parallel text, supporting the theme of the painting as an essay about the war of the sexes, is provided by the figure of the female child, likewise elaborately dressed and perhaps the younger sister of the other, who flogs a sad old hound with a switch of wild flowers (identified as 'Love-lies-Bleeding') (Mary Bennett, in London 1984, p. 147).

Brown painted in the open air so as to capture the scene with the utmost realism and authentic quality of light. To do this, he improvised some kind of awning, 'for I find one thing very necessary when painting out of doors & that is to shade off the too great light that falls on ones work, otherwise when brought in doors it looks flat & colorless, the colors showing more bright in the open air' (Surtees 1981, p. 178). (CSN)

22. **Ford Madox Brown**
Calais, 1821 - London, 1893
Work (small version), 1860-63
Oil on canvas with arched top, 68.4 x 99 cm
Bottom right: F. MADOX BROWN 1863
Birmingham Museum & Art Gallery

This version of *Work* is a half-size 'replica', commissioned in 1859, of the painting that Brown had began in 1852 but was not to finish until 1863 (Manchester Art Gallery). This version, also completed in 1863, was commissioned by the Newcastle manufacturer James Leathart. It is extremely close to the larger painting, but Brown made slight alterations to the composition so as to include a portrait of Leathart's wife (the figure second from left wearing a red dress and carrying a blue parasol). (TB)

See essay pp. 67-69.

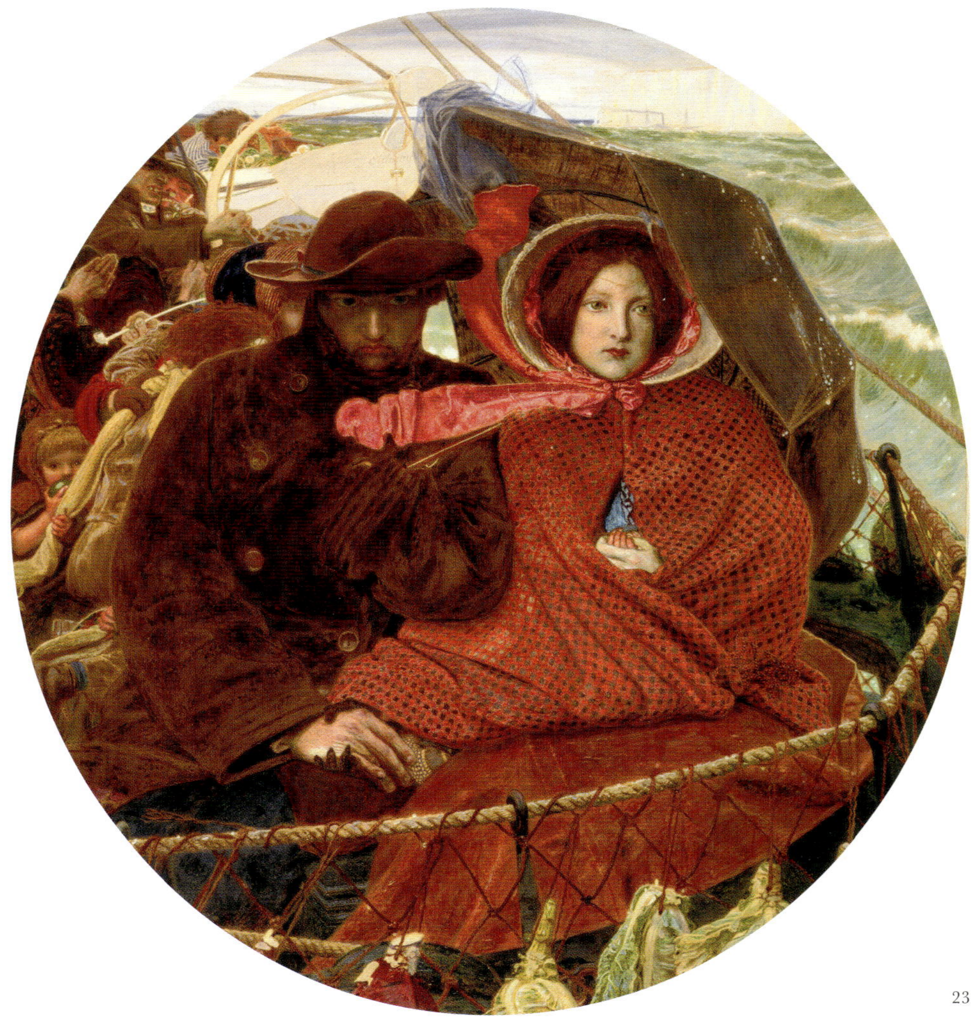

23

23. **Ford Madox Brown**
Calais, 1821 - London, 1893
The Last of England (small version), 1860
Oil on canvas, oval, 47.7 x 43.9 cm
Bottom right: F. MADOX BROWN 1860
Lent by the Syndics of the Fitzwilliam Museum, Cambridge

One of the most enduring and iconic images of the nineteenth century, Brown's *The Last of England* documents the anxieties and financial insecurity that people endured in Britain in the mid-century, despite the country's great wealth, but also the stalwart resolution of men and women of all backgrounds. The couple, who form the subject of this near-tondo, and their child, whose hand appears from the fold of the mother's shawl, have been forced by economic circumstances to emigrate and are seen on shipboard, presumably bound for Australia. The chalk cliffs of Dover are glimpsed in the background, although neither one looks back at the place of their departure. In the upper left part, men, women and children are crowded together - with a black-toothed rake shaking a fist in farewell to the land of his misdemeanours.

The Last of England is a self-portrait and a portrait of the artist's wife Emma. In 1852 Brown was himself close to desperation, 'most of the time intensely miserable, very hard up & a little mad' (Surtees 1981, p. 78), as he recalled, and he was contemplating emigration to India. In the painting Brown sought 'the particular look of *light all round*, which objects have on a dull day at sea'. To achieve this, he worked 'for the most part in the open air on dull days, and when the flesh was being painted on cold days'. The radical modernity of this approach is underlined by Brown's simple statement of intent: 'Absolutely without regard to the art of any period or country, I have tried to render this scene as it would appear' (quoted in London 1984, p. 124).

The original version of *The Last of England* was completed in 1855 and is now in Birmingham Museum & Art Gallery. The present reduced replica was made in 1860 for William James Gillum, a retired army officer (he had lost a leg in the Crimea) and generous philanthropist who had taken painting lessons from Brown and who persuaded Brown to teach in the Destitute Boys' Home that he had established in London's Euston Road. The social and political implications of the subject were presumably of particular interest to Gillum. (CSN)

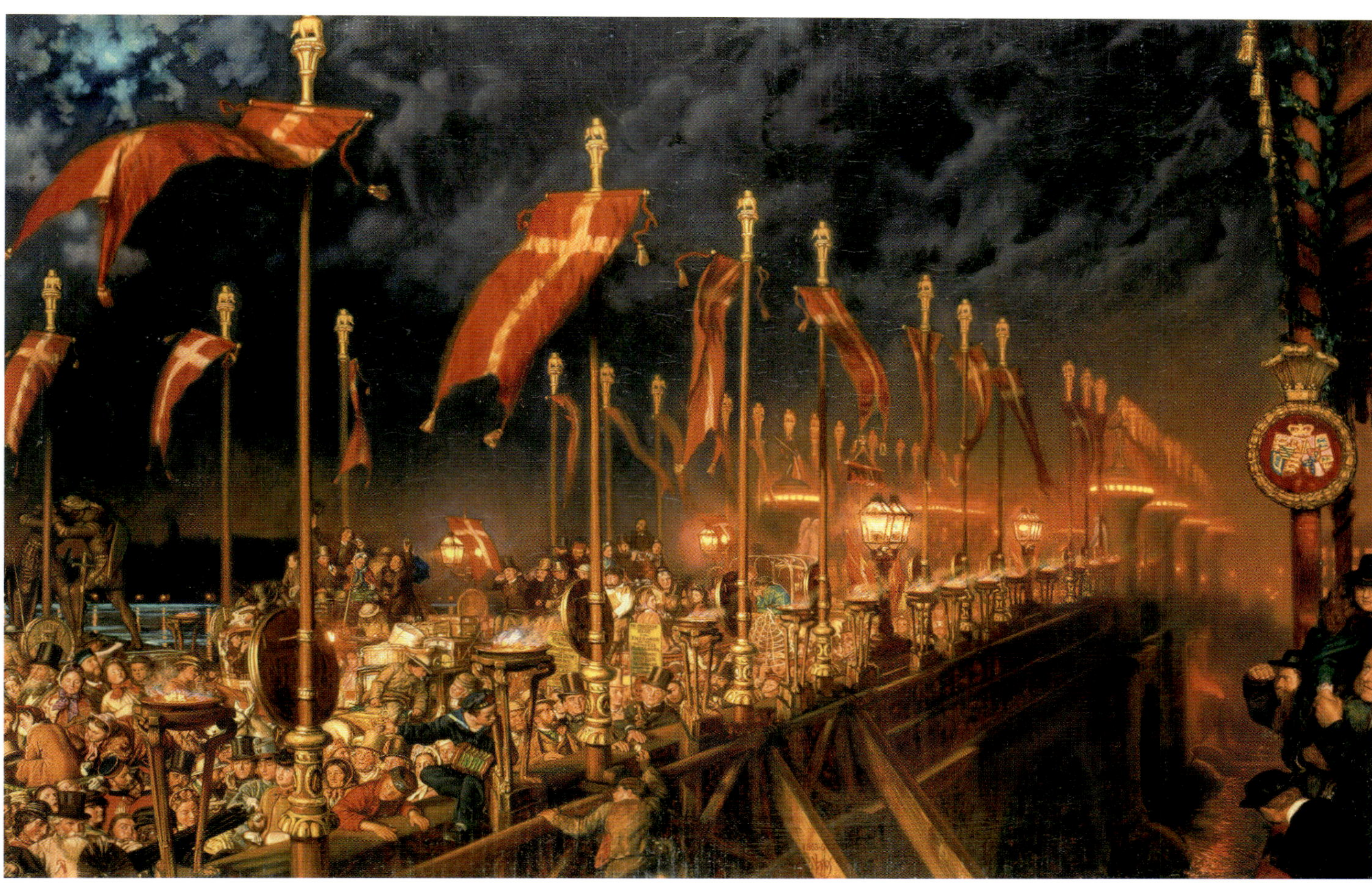

24

24. **William Holman Hunt**
London, 1827 - London, 1910
London Bridge on the Night of the Marriage of the Prince and Princess of Wales (The Sea-King's Peaceful Triumph on London Bridge, 10th of March, 1863),
1863-64 (retouched in 1866 and 1868)
Oil on canvas, 65 x 98 cm
Bottom edge right of centre: 1863.6 / Whh [monogram]
Ashmolean Museum, Oxford, Combe Bequest, 1893

Hunt was in London on the night of 10 March 1863 and witnessed the scenes of festivity that marked the wedding of the Prince of Wales to Princess Alexandra of Denmark. London Bridge was decorated for the occasion with standards bearing the Danish pennant, and with carved and gilded elephants on top and portraits of the kings of Denmark at their bases. Between the standards were placed tripods supporting braziers of burning incense. Hunt made sketches of the bridge, but he also depended for his subject on photographs taken by the London Stereoscopic Company and engraved views which appeared in the Illustrated London News. The painting's original title, *The Sea-King's Peaceful Triumph on London Bridge, 10th of March, 1863*, explains the significance of the setting; an earlier London Bridge had apparently been burnt by Danish raiders in the tenth century, so the royal wedding was celebrated as a reconciliation and a declaration of peacefulness between the two nations.

The painting shows the figures of hundreds of revellers weirdly illuminated within what a commentator called 'a lane of brilliant fantastic colour, ... full of eager struggling human beings' (Hudson 1972, p. 153), as the commentator Arthur Munby described it, and with the glow of artificial light being dispersed into the inky darkness of the night. Hunt himself related that it was the 'Hogarthian humour' of the thronging crowd that attracted him, and that the painting was intended as a celebration of the lives of the people of London, joined together in good-hearted excitement and patriotic feeling. All sorts of incidental events are incorporated into the subject, to be read anecdotally and in close detail. In addition, Hunt included portraits of various friends among the crowd.

London crowd subjects enjoyed something of a vogue in the mid-century. George Elgar Hicks had commenced a series of metropolitan subjects with *Dividend Day at the Bank* (Bank of England collection) in 1859, while William Powell

Frith's *The Railway Station* (Royal Holloway College) was exhibited in 1862. Hunt was accused by some of attempting to exploit this market, by appealing as P.G. Hamerton wrote, 'to the London crowd by giving it a picture of itself'. The critic high-mindedly continued: 'For such a subject to be chosen by one of the chiefs of an intellectual school of painting is an exceedingly bad symptom' (quoted in London 1984, p. 202). (CSN)

25. **Benjamin Brecknell Turner**
London, 1815 - London, 1894
The Nave, Crystal Palace, Hyde Park, 1852
Albumen silver print from calotype negative, 47 x 57.2 cm
Victoria and Albert Museum, London

Turner was an amateur who took up the new medium of photography in the late 1840s. He acquired a very large camera - which could expose negatives the size of this print - in time to make two extraordinary exposures of the interior of the Crystal Palace in 1852. The Crystal Palace, designed by Joseph Paxton to house the Great Exhibition of the Industrial Arts of All Nations in 1851, provided sufficient illumination in an interior space for photography to be practicable. The Great Exhibition included photographs and photographic equipment. Turner's photograph, made when the exhibits had been removed, thrillingly captured a new kind of architectural space with a new kind of composition. It is one of a number of key works by Turner and his contemporaries which suggest that the contemplation of phenomena on the rectangular ground glass of a camera encouraged a remarkable new geometry of composition. (MHB)

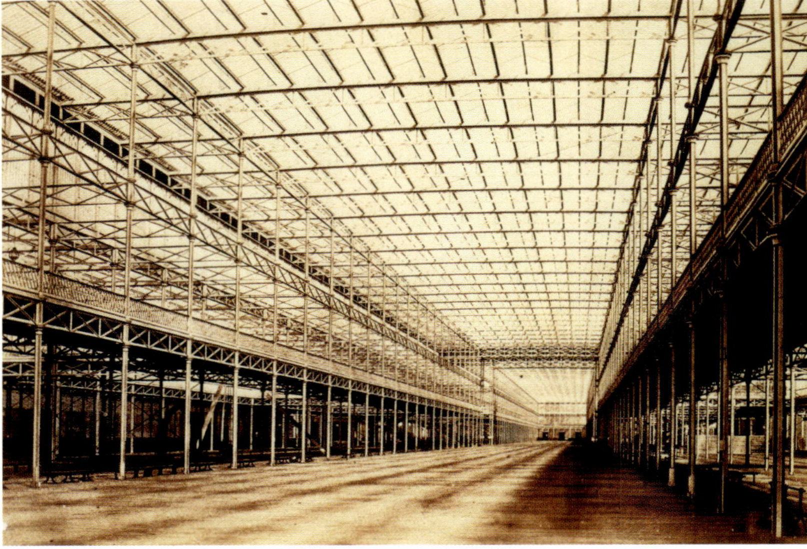

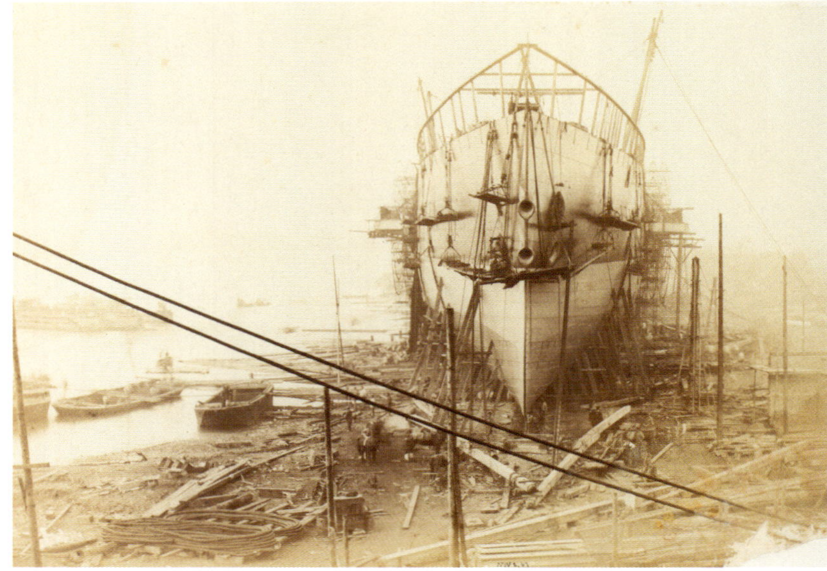

25 – 26

26. **Robert Howlett**
1830/31 - London, 1858
The Great Eastern: Bow-on-View, 1857
Albumen silver print from wet collodion negative, 28.7 x 36.4 cm
Bottom Centre: Nov 2, 57
Victoria and Albert Museum, London

Nine engravings based on Howlett's photographs of *The Great Eastern* and its charismatic engineer were published in *The Illustrated Times* on 16 June 1858. They may well have been commissioned from Howlett by the magazine. If so, we are looking at an early and highly impressive form of photojournalism. This photograph shows the construction of the ship at Millwall, on the southern tip of the Isle of Dogs. Its great size required that *The Great Eastern* - whose name honoured the place of its construction in the East End of London - should be launched sideways into the Thames from the mud-bank on which it was built. This unusual launching method explains the massive size of the chains seen in the portrait of Brunel (cat. 27). This iron steamship was begun in 1853 and launched on 31 January 1858. Howlett's photograph captures the swarming activity out of which it was produced. (MHB)

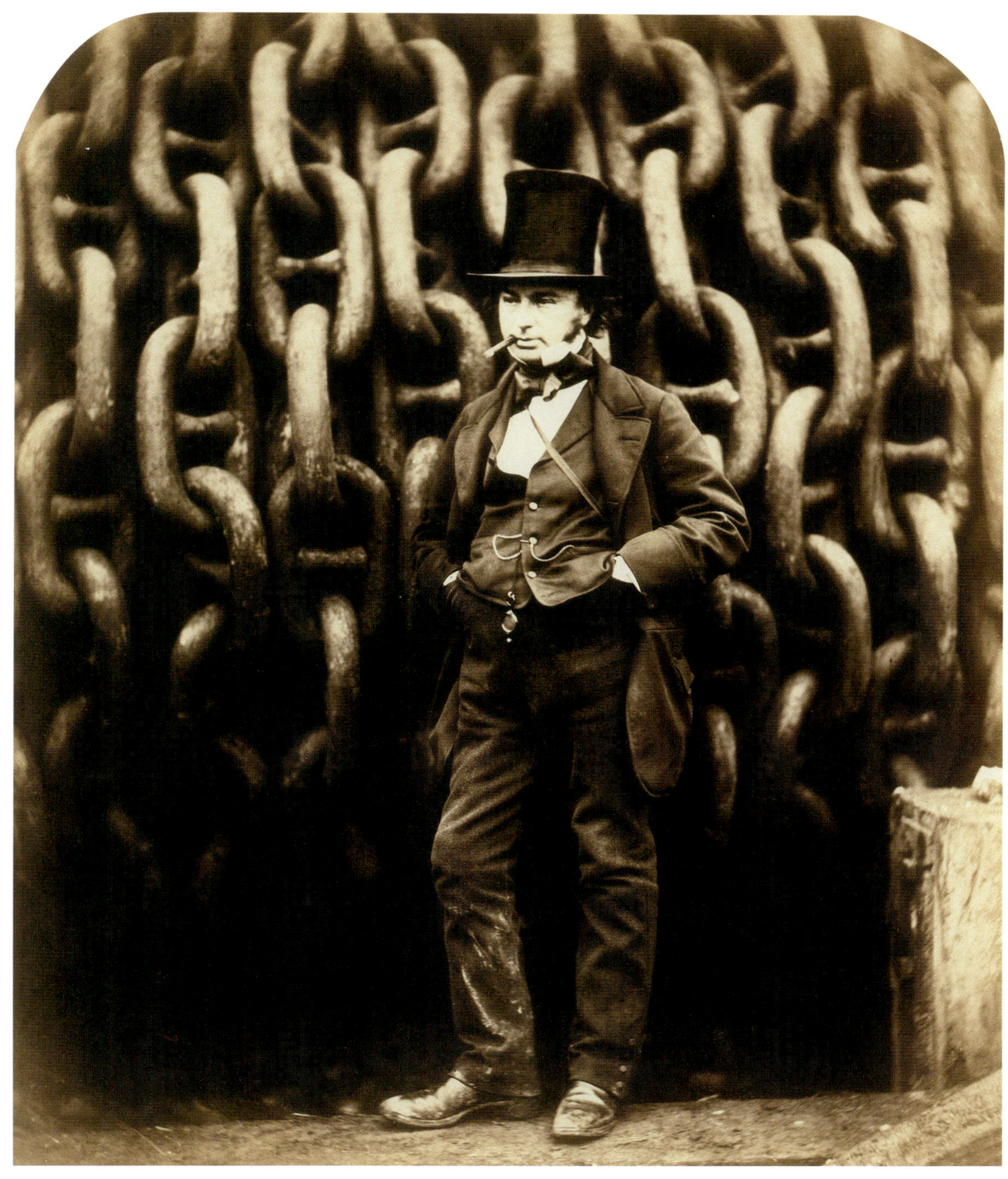

27

27. **Robert Howlett**
1830/31 - London, 1858
Portrait of Isambard Kingdom Brunel and Launching Chains of 'The Great Eastern', 1857
Albumen silver print from wet collodion negative, 28.7 x 23.2 cm
Victoria and Albert Museum, London

This early example of 'environmental' portraiture shows Brunel, engineer of the largest ship afloat in the nineteenth century, in control of the power implicit in its huge launching chains. He is shown in his daily professional clothes, which appear rather unkempt - in fact, Brunel often slept in his clothes at his office on site, during the crises which often occurred over the long period of its construction. This heroic enterprise ranked among Brunel's finest - which included the Clifton Suspension Bridge, the Great Western Railway and the Royal Albert Bridge at Saltash, Cornwall. The engineer presents a jaunty demeanour, complete with cheroot (did Churchill model himself on this heroic prototype?), and his 'hands-on' approach is indicated by his mud-spattered trousers. The gold-toning of the print was surely intended not only to preserve it from tarnishing but to remind us of the colour and qualities of iron. (MHB)

28. **Thomas Annan**
Dairsie, Fife, 1829/1830 - Lenzie, Lanarkshire, 1887
Close no 193, High Street, from the portfolio
Old Closes and Streets, a Series of Photogravures, 1868
(photogravure of 1900)
Photogravure, 22.2 cm x 18.1 cm
Victoria and Albert Museum, London

Britain was the first country in which a historic shift occurred in the 1850s: in that decade the balance of its population swung from rural to urban. The Glasgow City Improvement Act of 1866 was the first massive municipal intervention designed to sweep away central slum areas. The trustees of this Act commissioned Thomas Annan's photographs in 1866. His starkly frontal photographs were taken in the narrow 'wynds' and passageways of the city. These poorly illuminated spaces required long exposures, in which the carefully posed children have inevitably moved (as shown by the way they are retouched) and by the hazy outlines of the washing hanging in the dim alleys. The photographs were presented to the authorities in 1868 and reissued with some later photographs (taken after Annan's death) in the volume *Old Closes and Streets, a Series of Photogravures 1868-1899* (1900). (MHB)

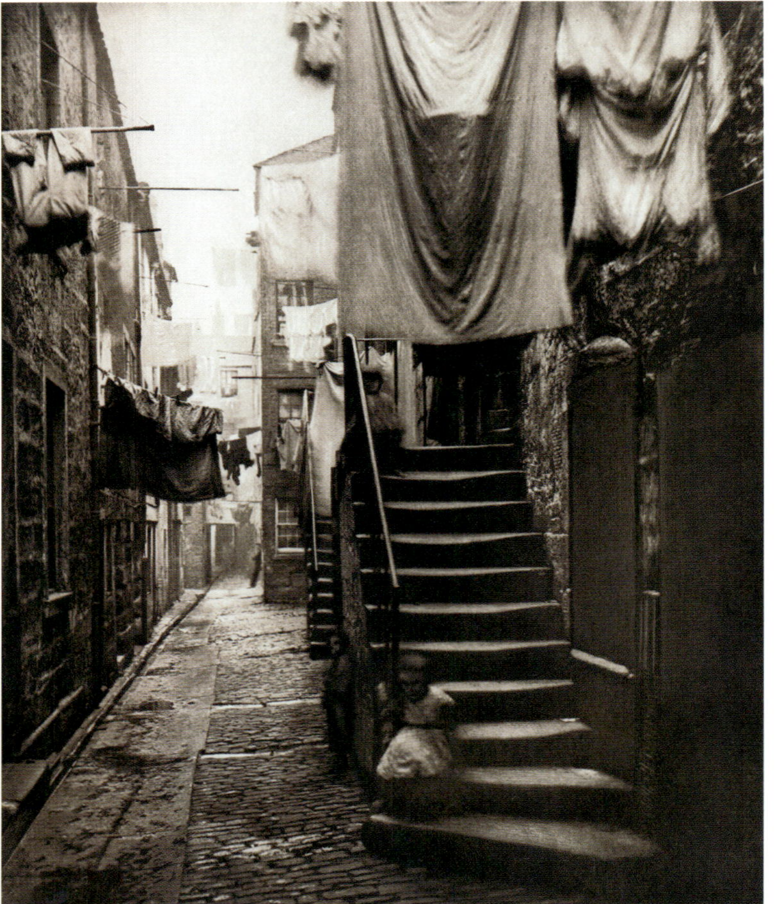

28

29. **John Thomson**
Edinburgh, 1837 - London, 1921
The Crawlers, from ***Street Life in London***, 1877-78
Woodbury type, 11.6 x 8.8 cm
Victoria and Albert Museum, London

This is arguably the most memorable close-up photograph of street beggars made in the nineteenth century. It was accompanied when first issued as part of a serial publication, and a little later when gathered into a book, by a long text by the reforming journalist Adolphe Smith. The location was steps leading up to St Giles's workhouse in Short's Gardens, Covent Garden, in central London. Smith described the plight of the woman in the same close-up detail as the photograph, recounting the story of her blameless descent into destitution and her occupation as child-minder for another 'crawler' who had found work in a nearby coffee house. The woman cared for the baby eight hours a day and received in payment a cup of tea and a little bread: 'Even this modest remuneration is not always forthcoming, and the crawler has often to content herself with bread without tea, or tea without bread...' (MHB)

30. **John Thomson**
Edinburgh, 1837 - London, 1921
Hookey Alf of Whitechapel,
from ***Street Life in London***, 1877-78
Woodbury type, 11.3 x 8.7 cm
Victoria and Albert Museum, London

The writings of Mayhew and Dickens resonate in the prose style of Smith and in the choice of tableaux arranged before his camera by Thomson. Here the setting is a seventeenth-century tavern (later demolished) in the Whitechapel Road in the working-class East End of London. A young girl, whose fair hair is lit by strong sunlight from the left, has 'penetrated boldly into the group, as if about to reclaim some relation in danger and drag him away from evil companionship'. However, this scenario is at odds with what we learn by continuing to read Smith's text. The awkwardly posed man the girl appears to address, 'Hookey Alf', so named because of the hook which replaced a hand amputated after an industrial accident, was an epileptic who lived a blameless life. Smith compared him to the good-hearted 'Captain Cuttle' in Dickens's *Dombey and Son*, a man of 'transparent simplicity'. (MHB)

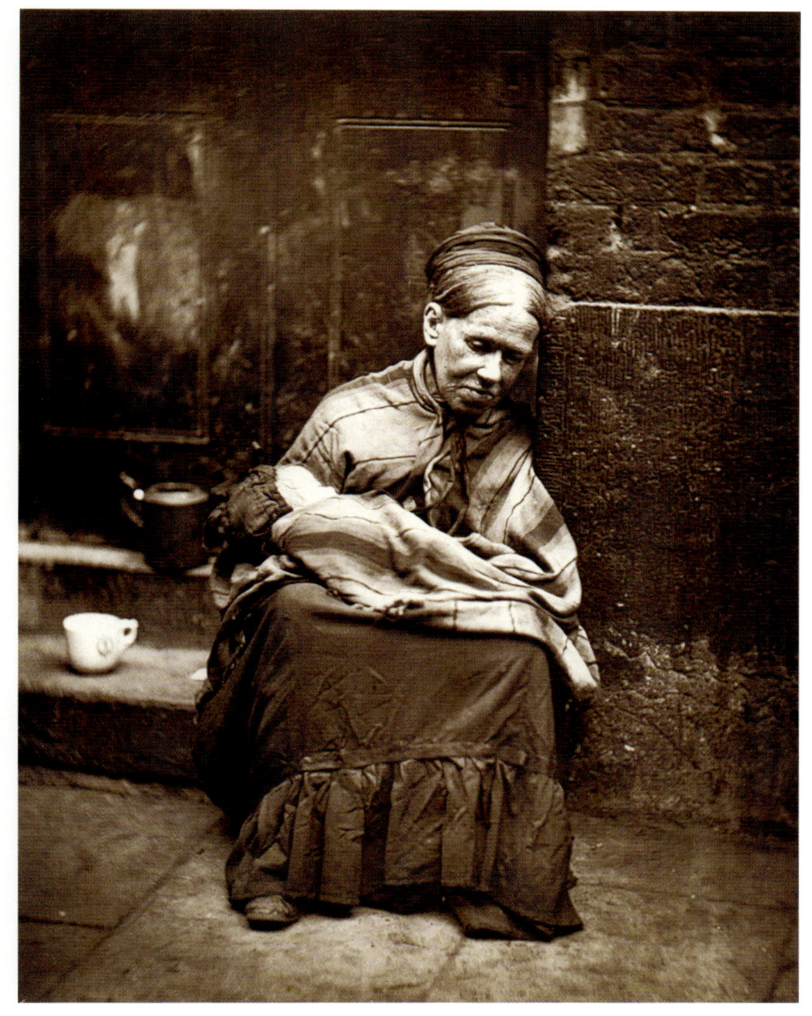

29

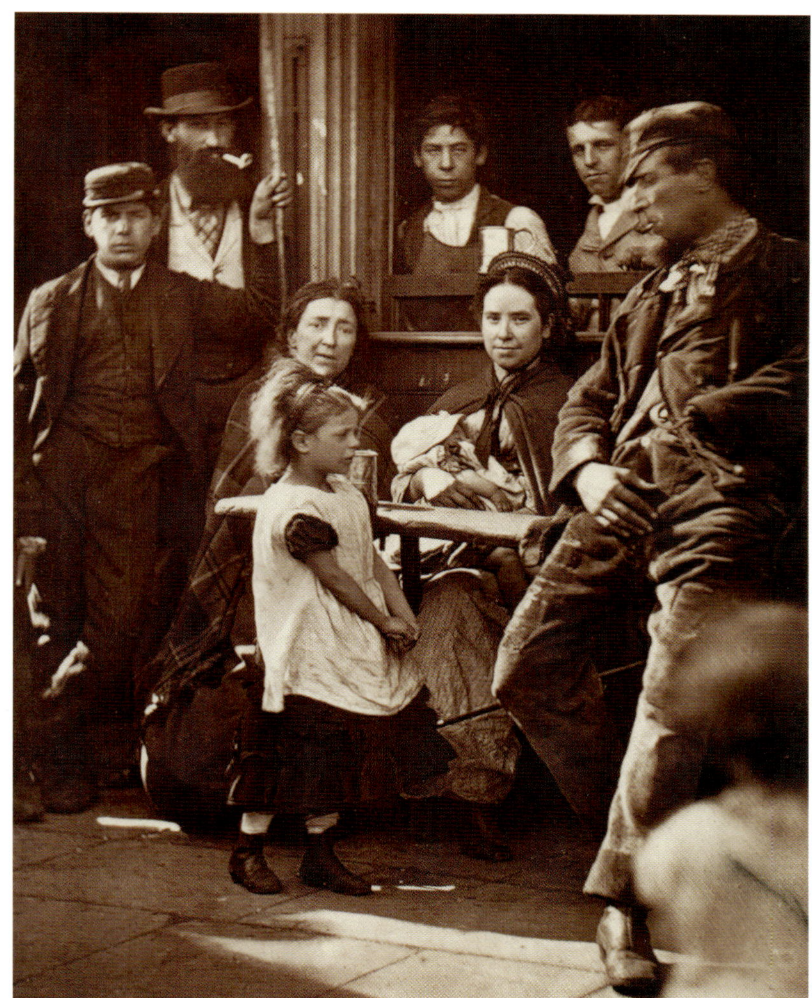

30

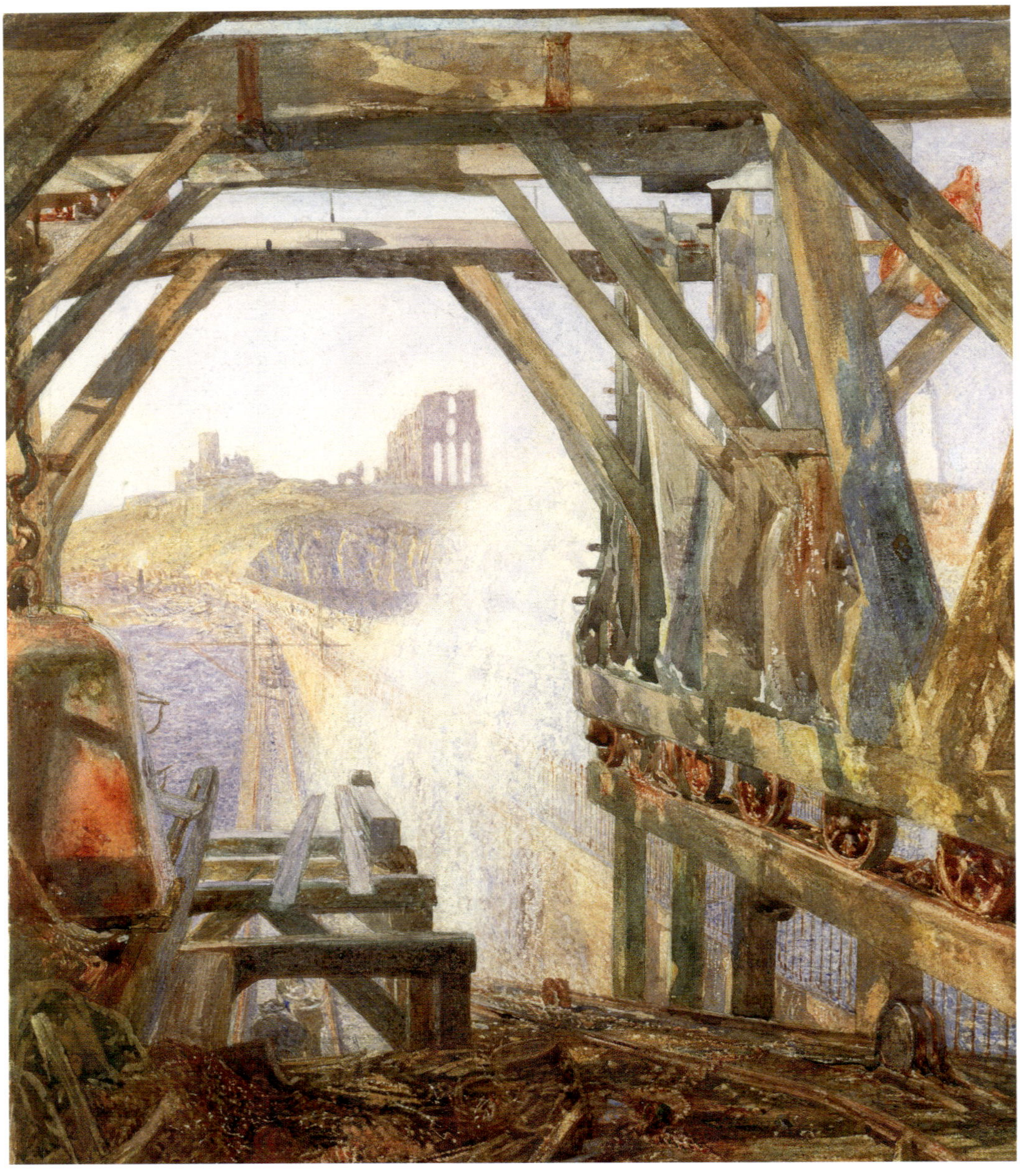

31

31. **Alfred William Hunt**
Liverpool, 1830 - London, 1896
Travelling Cranes, Diving Bells & etc. at the Extremity of Tynemouth Pier, c. 1867
Watercolour on paper, 31.8 x 26.7 cm
Private Collection

Hunt's watercolour shows one of the massive wheeled cranes, known as 'Goliaths', which were used to transport materials out into the mouth of the River Tyne, on the North Sea coast to the east of Newcastle, during the construction of two piers intended to give protection for shipping at the notoriously dangerous entrance to the river. The view is from the most seaward point on the north pier, on the Tyne's Northumberland shore, which had by 1867 reached approximately 500 metres out to sea - about two-thirds of its eventual length. Through a rising cloud of spray, is seen the pier itself, with a lower part on the left with tramlines, and a raised walkway enclosed with railings on the right. This was a stupendous feat of engineering, and one that suffered many setbacks and in which a number of men lost their lives. In November 1867, shortly after the present watercolour was first exhibited, devastating gales struck the construction site, destroying six of the eleven sets of cranes.

Hunt adopted a professional career as a painter in 1861, after he had given up a fellowship at Oxford University so that he might marry. He and his wife settled in Durham, which allowed Hunt to familiarize himself with the landscape and ancient buildings of the north-east. In the distance, through the crane's timber frame, is seen Tynemouth Priory, mostly built from around 1190 on the site where St Oswin was buried in 651, with the east wall of the Early English presbytery standing virtually to its original height. Hunt's highly original and abstract composition therefore combines references to the industrial and economic expansion of Newcastle and its region in the nineteenth century and to the ancient history of Northumberland. (CSN)

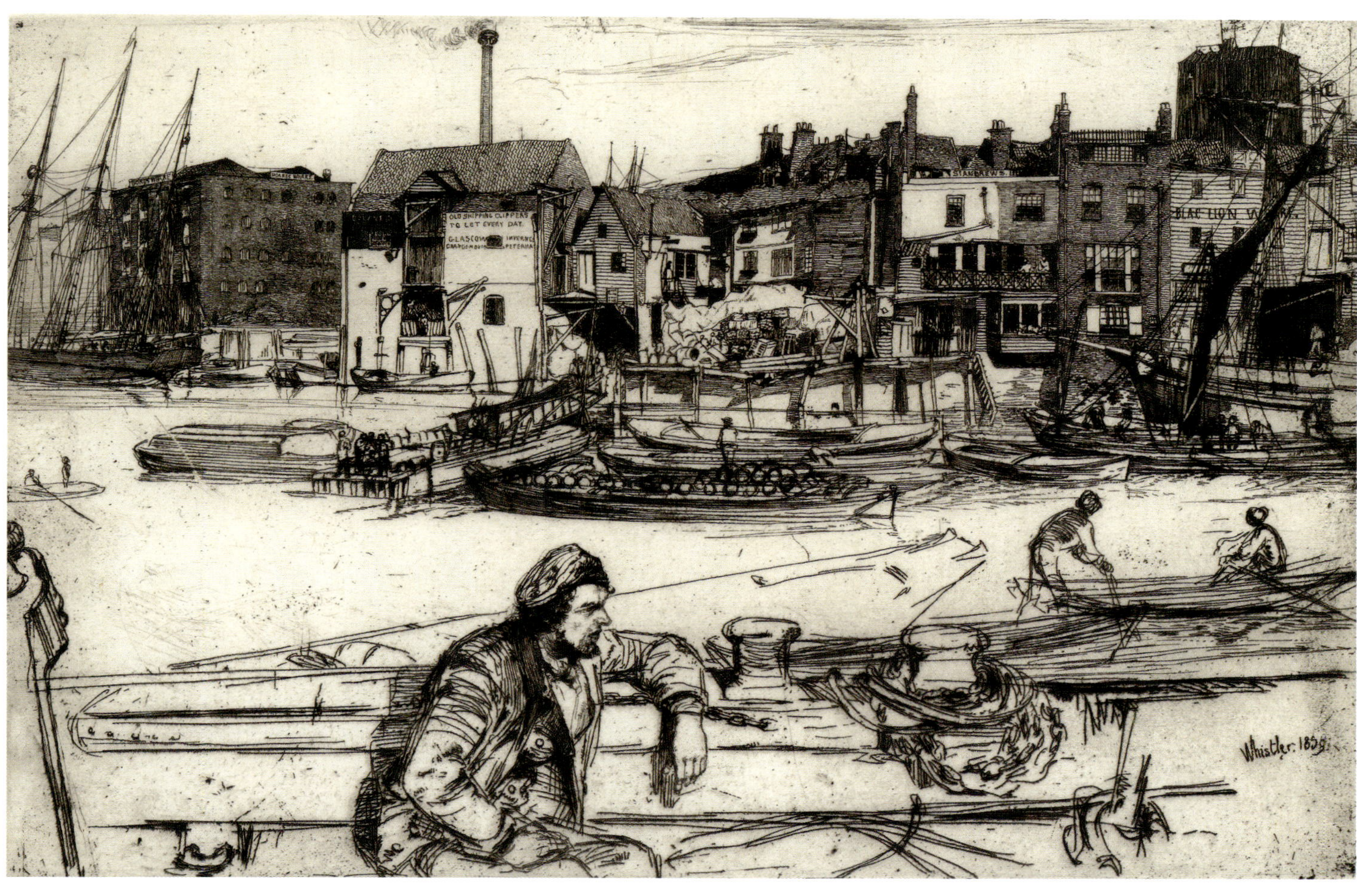

32

32. **James McNeill Whistler**
Lowell, Massachusetts, 1834 - London 1903
Black Lion Wharf, from ***Sixteen Etchings of Scenes on the Thames and Other Subjects (Thames Set)***, designed in 1859, printed in 1871 [?]
Etching, 15.1 x 26.8 cm
Bottom right: Whistler. 1859
Stiftung Museum Schloss Moyland, Bedburg Hau, Germany

33. **James McNeill Whistler**
Lowell, Massachusetts, 1834 - London 1903
Nocturne: the River at Battersea, designed in 1878, printed in 1887
Lithograph, 17.2 x 26 cm
Printed by Thomas Way, published by Boussod, Valadon & Co.
Victoria and Albert Museum, London

Whistler was an American who lived in France and England. He was interested - certainly as a young artist - in the underbelly of large cities like London and often found inspiration along the banks of the Thames. *Black Lion Wharf* belongs to a collection of etchings known as the *Thames Set*, which he worked on while living above a tavern in Wapping, close to the river, between August and October 1859. Thanks to his acute sense of observation, Whistler was able to preserve the life of the bustling, gritty docklands, with their ships from all parts of the British Empire, their warehouses and their slums, where the poorest inhabitants of the metropolis huddled together. In the foreground of *Black Lion Wharf* we see one of the dockworkers described by journalist Henry Mayhew in his *London Labour and the London Poor* (1851; see cat. 18) as 'a striking instance of mere brute force with brute appetites' (Mayhew 1968, vol.3, p. 301). The quality of Whistler's etchings shows in the manner in which they are able to grasp the typical poetry of this rough theme.

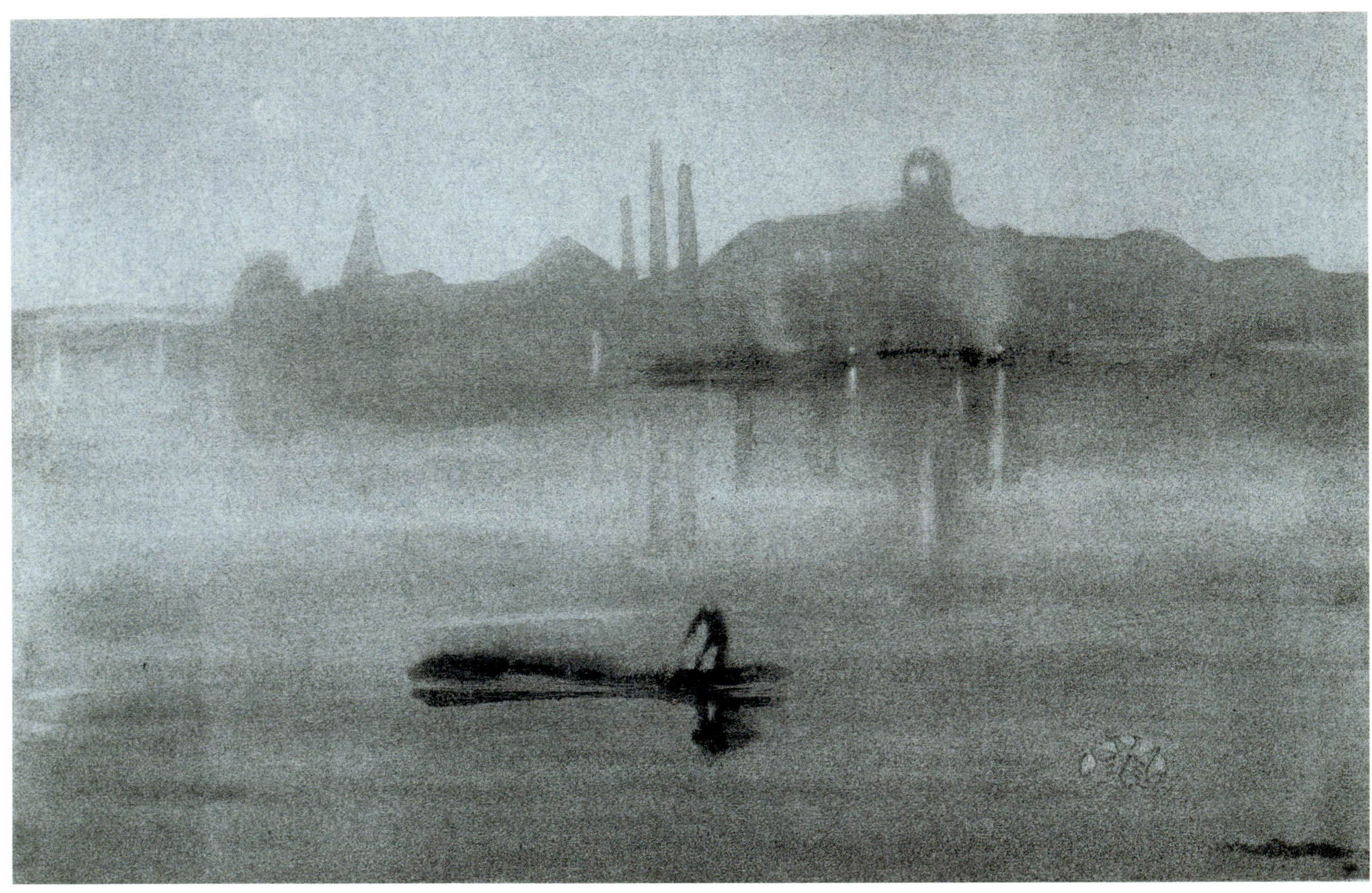

33

Nocturne: The River at Battersea, which Whistler made nearly twenty years later, is much more freely executed than the etchings of the *Thames Set*. By that time, the artist had become one of the leading figures in the Aesthetic Movement. Here, rather than accurately describing, the artist seeks to produce a direct sensation in the viewer by means of forms and colours. Nevertheless, the working-class environment is still recognizable: from the Chelsea shore of the Thames we can make out Battersea Church, the illuminated tower of the Morgan Crucible Company, the rubbish heap of the graphite factory, warehouses, smokestacks and a river barge. In later works like *Nocturne: The River at Battersea*, Whistler continued to depict subjects from everyday reality, but in a more visionary way. (NP)

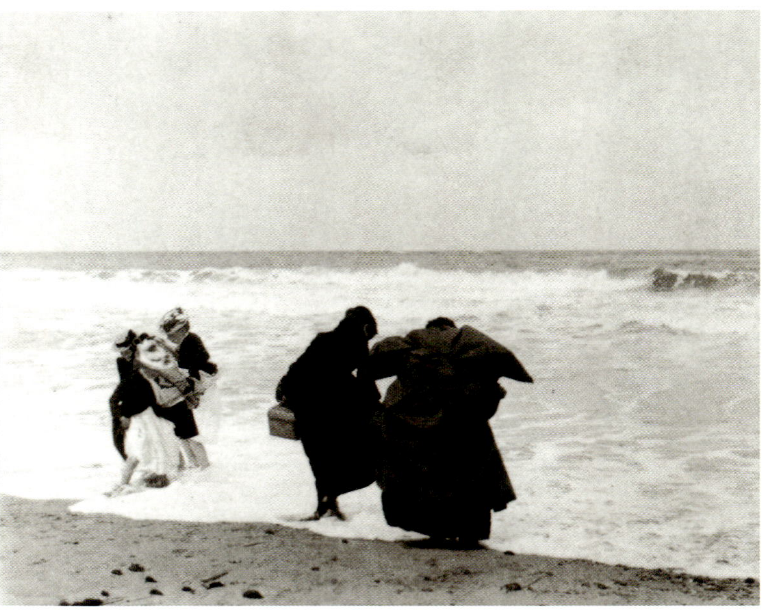

34

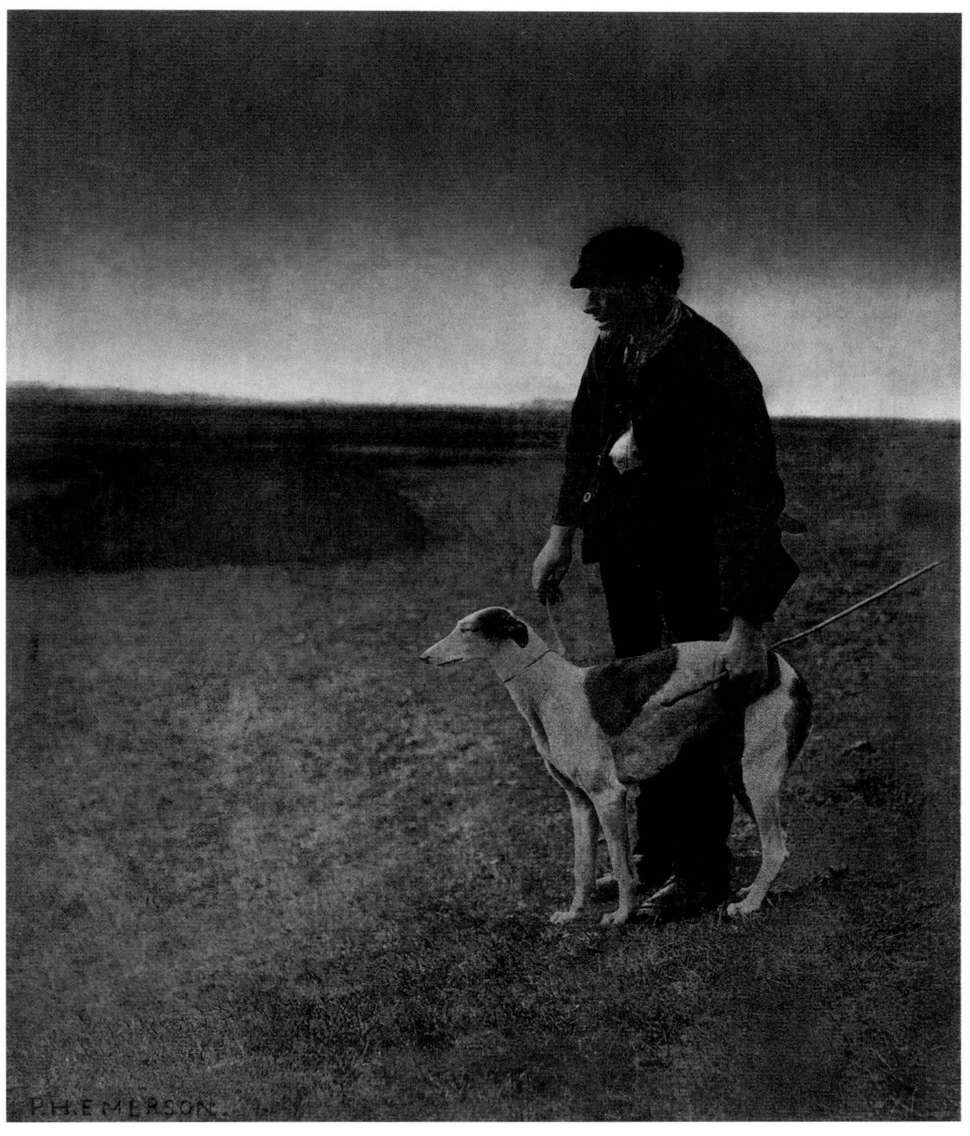

35

34. **Paul Martin**
Herbeuville, Alsace-Lorraine, 1864 - London, 1944
Trippers at Cromer, 1892
Platinum print, 8 x 9.5 cm
Victoria and Albert Museum, London

Paul Martin served an apprenticeship as a wood-engraver but realized that this trade was doomed to extinction and moved into photography. He brought to the medium an eye trained to see tonal patterns and active silhouettes. He used one of the new 'Facile' or 'Detective' hand-cameras popular at the time. These were relatively small cameras, which could easily be disguised. Their battery of glass negatives allowed trial-and-error shooting. Martin's most successful use of the camera occurred on a holiday in Norfolk in 1892. Martin captured the pleasant comedy of women and girls paddling in the North Sea. As usual the sea breeze is bracing. Martin evidently enjoyed the contrast between the heavier silhouettes of the mature figures on the right and the skittish girls at the left, and relished the way the froth chimes with their lacy petticoats and the jaunty millinery of their hats. (MHB)

35. **Peter Henry Emerson**
Cuba, 1856 - Falmouth, Cornwall, 1936
The Poacher - A Hare in View, Suffolk, 1888
Photogravure, 28.8 x 23.8 cm
Bottom left on the photograph: P.H. Emerson
Victoria and Albert Museum, London, Given by the photographer

This innovative study of a poacher and his lurcher at dusk is part of Emerson's thorough study of *The Life and Landscape on the Norfolk Broads,* to use the title of the major volume of his writings and photographs published in 1886. This image comes from his portfolio *Pictures of East Anglian Life* (1888). Emerson made full use of the gelatino-bromide dry-plate negatives introduced in 1879. These made possible the studies of the apparently spontaneous photographs of figures in landscapes that were his forte. He was also a theorist, with a strong interest in naturalistic painting. He believed that human vision did not see with overall sharpness but focused only on major points of interest. Here he focuses on the poacher and his exquisitely outlined lurcher. The rest of the scene is relatively unfocused and is, in fact, a daylight photograph manipulated by Emerson to convey the onset of dusk. (MHB)

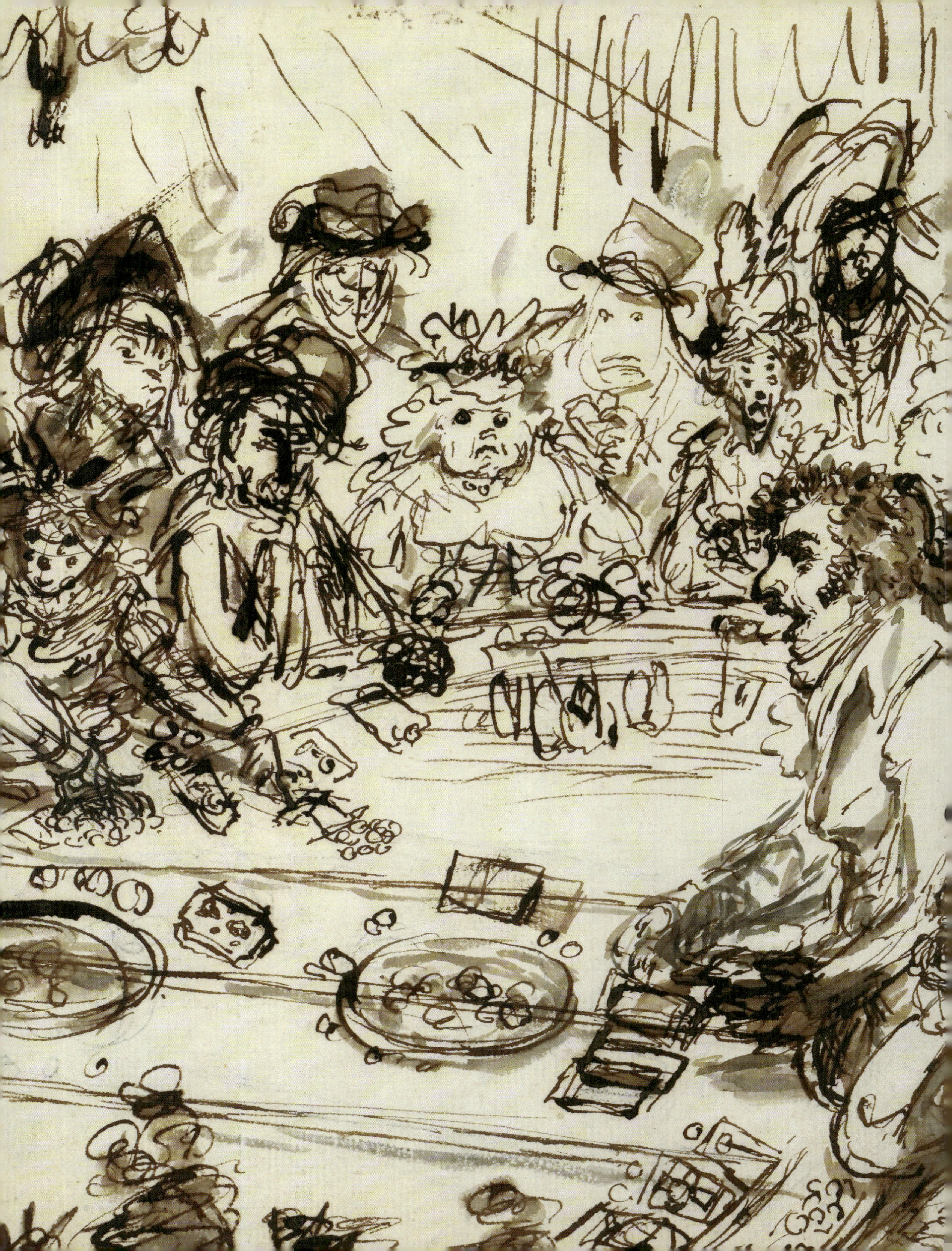

BRITISH HUMOUR

JAMES GILLRAY

The Faro Table, *c.* 1800

TIMOTHY HYMAN

The study of Gillray's drawings is still at an early stage. Over four hundred sheets are now known, most of them from his later years. Taken together, they are some of the boldest and most original graphic works in the whole of British art, and they deserve to be much more widely reproduced. In many of these late drawings, Gillray's mark has become extraordinarily wild and broken, in striking contrast to the relatively firm engraved line of his prints. To conjure the crowd of *The Faro Table*, he proceeded in three steps: first, a light and tentative pencil; then, taking a brush, loose swirls of sepia wash, indicating the oval arena of the gaming-table and the punters around; finally, with pen or quill, a blacker ink-scribble – more linear, but still astonishingly mobile. In the left margin, the zigzags can perhaps be read as feathers, from the female headdress below, but they take on a life of their own, like the dots and curlicues alongside. Elsewhere, a flurry of short stabs might stand for ribcage or cravat, from which a calligraphic flourish emerges as a head; or an abrupt pen-stroke shoots up to become an arm raised high. Most extreme of all, running as a kind of frieze along this sheet's lower edge, are the squiggles that resolve themselves into fragments of hairy heads seen from the back, together with a pair of spiky hands. Yet these separate signs and marks do improvise into existence a surprisingly coherent scene: a chandelier-lit room, filled with vividly individuated characters, dominated by the pug-faced croupier, raking in coins with both arms; opposite him, in profile, the young gambler, standing up and shouting; and between them – vicious, rapacious, stupid, helpless – an entire society at play.

One comparison within the present exhibition allows us to view *The Faro Table* alongside a more 'public' and saleable drawing from the same decade, and to recognize just how extreme Gillray's handling is. Rowlandson improvises his masterly *Exhibition Stare-Case* (cat. 53) in the same three steps: pencil, brush, pen. On the staircase up to the Royal Academy's annual exhibition, the British artworld is being turned upside-down. Yet Rowlandson himself never loses control; as in all his other drawings, he homogenizes every figure into the same roly-poly type,[1] and they tumble down the stairs like clockwork. Gillray, by contrast, possesses no ready-made language for 'how to make a person': the breakdown of order is inherent in his risky, unpredictable, exclamatory marks.

The wildness of Gillray's later art may owe as much to personal circumstance as to contemporary aesthetics. All that we know of his own disorderly, heavy-drinking bachelor existence suggests a breaking out from the Calvinist austerity of his childhood.[2] His father, a Scottish soldier who lost his right arm in battle and became a Chelsea Pensioner, had joined the Moravian Brethren; Gillray was probably sent away at four to the sect's grim boarding school (where his elder brother would die two years later). In a parallel aesthetic reversal, Gillray would throw off his classical indoctrination at the Royal Academy Schools. After his unsuccessful two-and-a-half years as a stipple engraver of portraits and historical compositions, and his return to caricature in 1786, he had developed a much more extravagant burlesque idiom. In many of his later prints (such as *Confederate Coalition*, cat. 44), the generosity of the Baroque (outmoded, discredited) is employed by Gillray as a weapon – a slapstick – with which to mock the moralizing sparseness of doctrinaire Neo-Classicism. His atmospheric little oil-sketch of 1800, *Voltaire Instructing the Infant Jacobinism* (cat. 47), confirms that he might have been a considerable painter. The scene is set

James Gillray, ***The Faro Table*** (detail), cat. 46

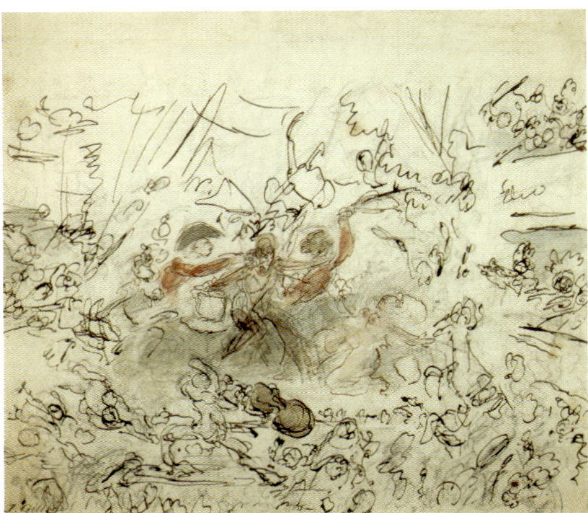

fig. 1 (cat. 45, recto)
James Gillray
Theatre of the World: The Revolutionary Wars, 1805
Pencil, ink and watercolour on paper, 29 x 32 cm
Private Collection

in Hell, with the ever-smiling *philosophe* enthroned, surrounded by murky ghouls, and schooling his latest demon-of-radicalism for his mission upwards into contemporary Britain. As in much of late Gillray, the message may be conservative, but the medium is anti-authoritarian, disorderly, anarchic.

Diana Donald sees Gillray's art as expressing, through burlesque, 'something of the mania and extremism of post-revolutionary politics'.[3] He had inherited also a tradition by which contemporary events were experienced as theatre: 'The farce now acting upon all the stages in Great Britain is *The World in Uproar*,'[4] wrote Josiah Wedgwood at the time of the Gordon Riots, when the mob burnt and looted central London over several days (probably witnessed by the young Gillray). Twenty-five years later, the Europe-wide 'Uproar' of the renewed Napoleonic Wars was presented by Gillray as a *Theatre of the World* (fig. 1). The audience for this melodrama is not passive: from the boxes on either side, spectators are brandishing, gesticulating, hurling; even the orchestra has risen up, and a great brown cello threatens to invade the stage. On the verso (fig. 2) Gillray has jotted down a long list, at the same breakneck speed.[5] (His words hardly able to keep pace with his images and ideas.) The heading reads: '*This sketch for a British Institution of arts is offered as containing a series of subjects in ye year 1805, quite new and never attempted by ye antients – worthy of ye talents of British artists*'. A year later the 'British Institution' would open at 52 Pall Mall; it was a connoisseur powerbase, in contrast to the artist-led Royal Academy, and its bias towards imported continental art was widely distrusted by contemporary British painters. (Constable warned, 'there will be no genuine painting in England in thirty years.') When Gillray lists his own 'subjects', he is mocking the limitations of subject matter imposed by such polite institutions. As we scan the four columns, we find references to specific London activities (*Taking Refreshment in Piccadilly, Going to Christie's on a Frosty Morn*) as well as to theatre and artworld, politics and scandal. At the top of one column we read *Devil on Two Sticks* – the title of Le Sage's once famous novel, in which the crippled devil Asmodeus lifts the roofs off the city, to reveal its true life. Cumulatively, Gillray's list might be seen as a disclosure of this kind, an unmasking of the false view of contemporary society perpetrated by the Academy; hence, at lower right, '*Somerset house/~~humbugdom~~/triumph of ye arts polite*'.

In 1807 Gillray suffered a physical and mental collapse, from which he may never have fully recovered. There are no prints after 1810, and the large ink drawing of his publisher's nephew, *George Humphrey* (cat. 230), is inscribed 'Drawn by James Gillray on the 1st July 1811. he being at that time Insane.' When shown in the Tate's superb Gillray retrospective in 2001, the curator, Richard Godfrey, pronounced this drawing 'incoherent', and 'in which not a trace of the artist's skill remains'.[6] Yet it is an image of extraordinary, confrontational power. We are brought very near-in to this wild-haired, aslant, possibly angry and shouting figure – a close encounter of the most alarming kind. Crooked arm and huge turned hand are brought to life in a weird wobbly line, while the curved form that pokes up into the empty space to the right could read as another figure; or else as a separate, detached (paternal?) arm.

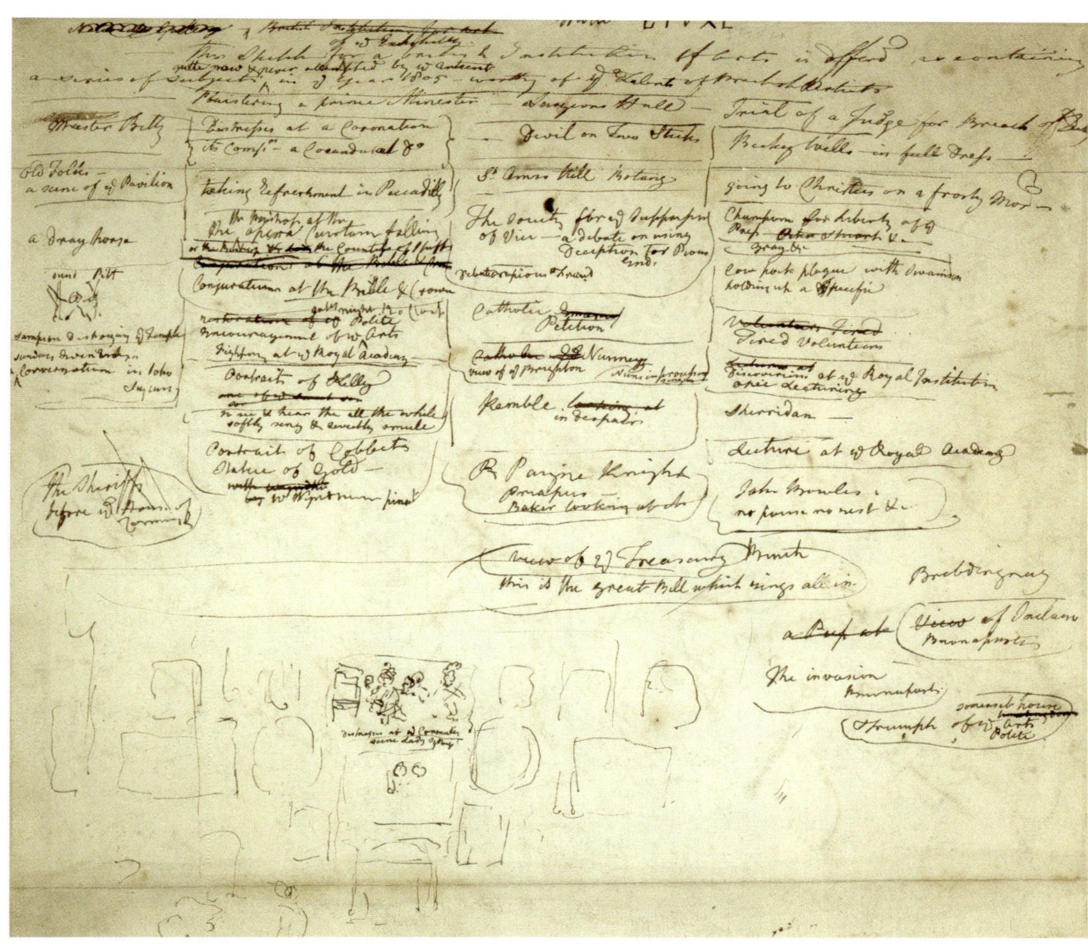

fig. 2 (cat. 45, verso), **James Gillray**, ***A List of Subjects 'worthy of ye talents of British Artists'***, 1805

Three weeks later it was reported in *The Examiner*: 'On Wednesday afternoon Mr. Gillray the caricaturist who resides at Mrs. Humphrey's in St James's Street, attempted to throw himself out of the window of the attic story. There being iron bars his head got jammed and being perceived by one of the [sedan] chairmen who attends at White's and who instantly went up to give assistance, the unfortunate man was extricated, and proper persons appointed to take care of him.'[7] This blackly absurd episode was Gillray's final appearance, since his eventual death in 1815 went almost unnoticed in the excitement of the Hundred Days leading up to Waterloo. Although *The Faro Table* and other late drawings did slowly trickle into public collections, the rediscovery of Gillray as a draughtsman had to wait at least one hundred and fifty years. It coincided with a new appreciation, among both English and Scottish painters, for northern European art. His extreme autonomy of mark brings to mind much later draughtsmen; Gillray's real affinities are with such hard-to-classify individualists as James Ensor or Asger Jorn.

---

1. The Rowlandson formula derives, I believe, from the little staffage-figures in Canaletto drawings.
2. Hill 1965, pp. 8-12.
3. Donald 1996, p. 73. The context is Horace's *Ars Poetica*, with its opening line, 'If some mad painter, by his fancy led …'.
4. Uglow 2002, p. 339.
5. In elucidating this list, I want to acknowledge the assistance of Simon Turner. I have also benefited from conversations with David Bindman and Richard Maxwell.
6. Godfrey 2001, p. 233.
7. Quoted from Hill 1965, p. 146.

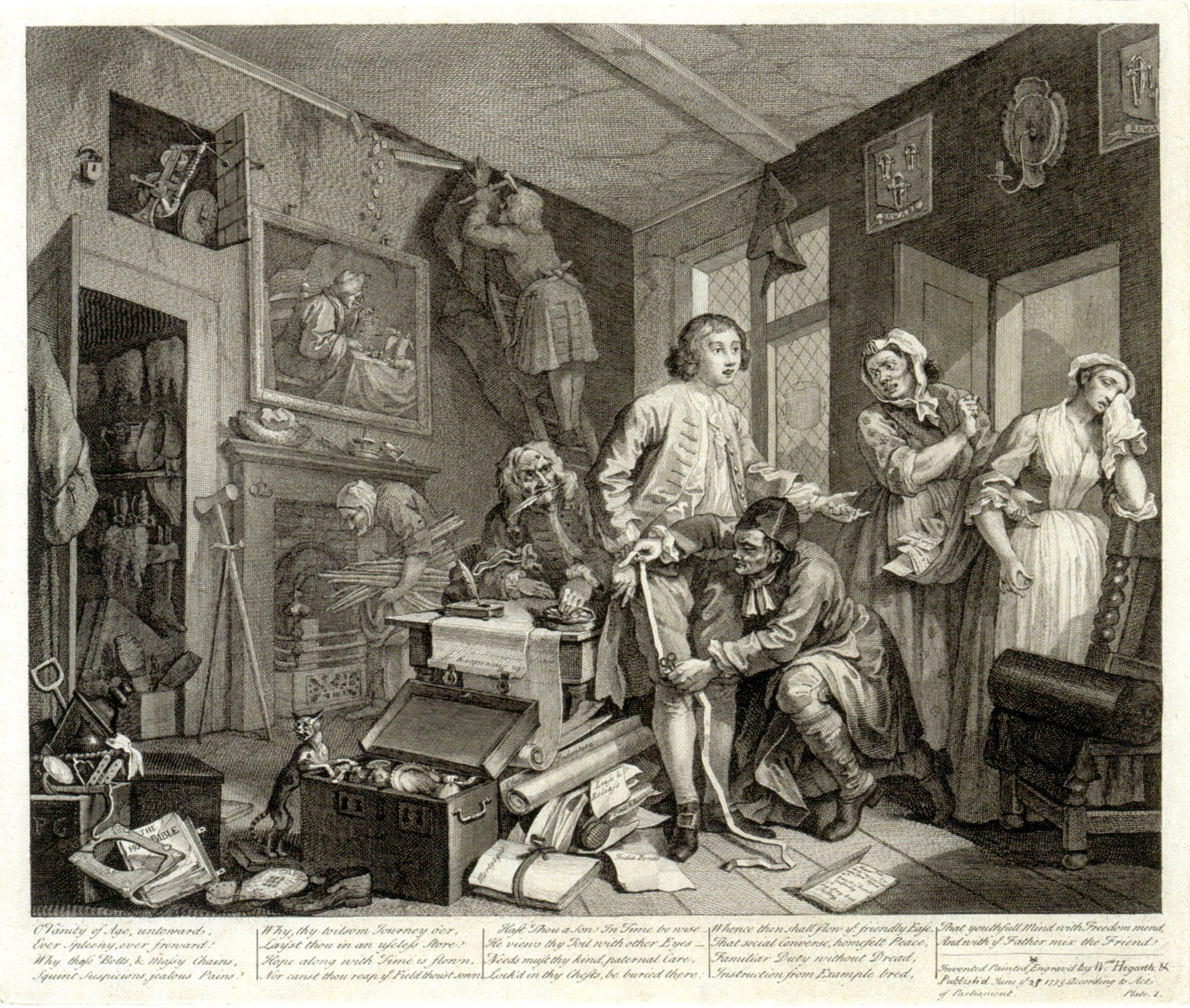

36a

36. **William Hogarth**
London, 1697 - London, 1764
assisted by Louis Gérard Scotin
(born 1690)
A Rake's Progress (8 plates), first published 1735,
lifetime edition 1750s

a. ***The Rake Taking Possession of his Estate***
b. ***The Rake's Levée***
c. ***The Rake at the Rose Tavern***
d. ***The Rake Arrested, Going to Court***
e. ***The Rake Marrying an Old Woman***
f. ***The Rake at the Gaming House***
g. ***The Rake in Prison***
h. ***The Rake in Bedlam***

Etching and engraving, each approx. 35.7 x 40.9 cm
Published by William Hogarth
Andrew Edmunds, London

Hogarth announced the subscription for the engraved series *A Rake's Progress* in 1733, although he delayed its publication until 1735, when he had successfully established a copyright Act (subsequently known as 'Hogarth's Act'), which he hoped would protect his work from piracy. The eight scenes that made up the present series, which have since become some of his most acclaimed works, chart the rise and fall of a profligate young man who inherits a fortune and ends up in a madhouse. Collectively, the engravings, which were based upon original paintings (now in Sir John Soane's Museum, London), focus on the moral degradation endemic in all sectors of society. Indeed, Hogarth himself referred to these series, in which he both invented and executed the narrative scenes, as 'modern moral subjects'. As an art form this was, as he claimed with some justification, entirely new - although its close parallels to recent developments in the English novel and the stage would not have been lost upon his viewers.

The protagonist in *A Rake's Progress* is Tom Rakewell, who in the first scene uses his newly acquired fortune, amongst other things, to pay off his pregnant girlfriend, Sarah Young. In the second scene the rake has entered fashionable society

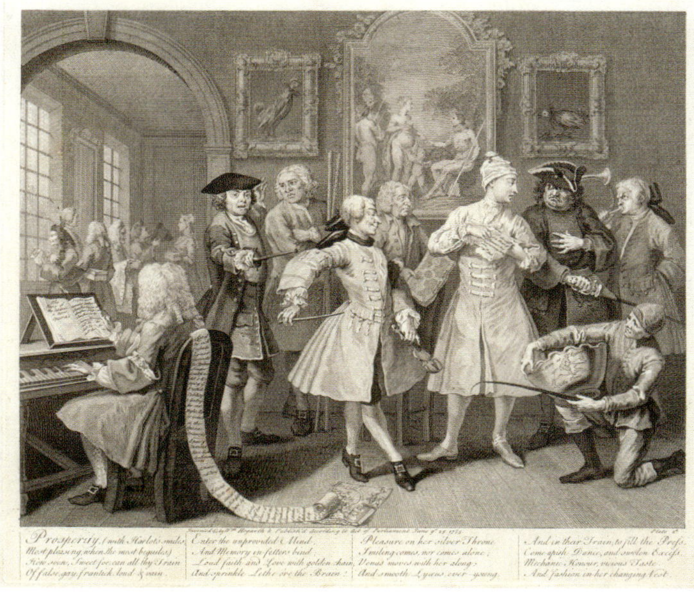

36b

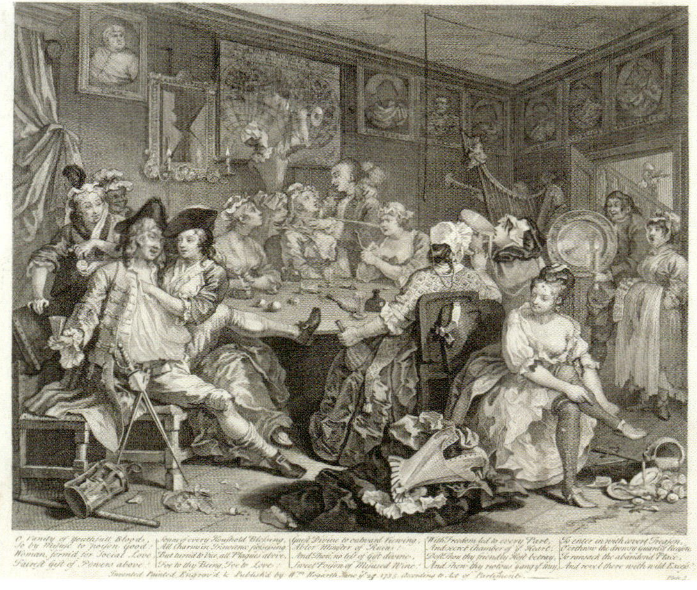

36c

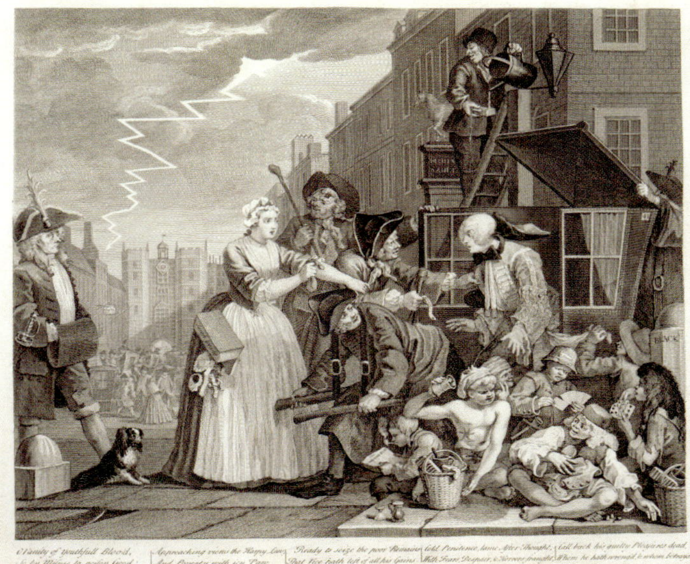

36d

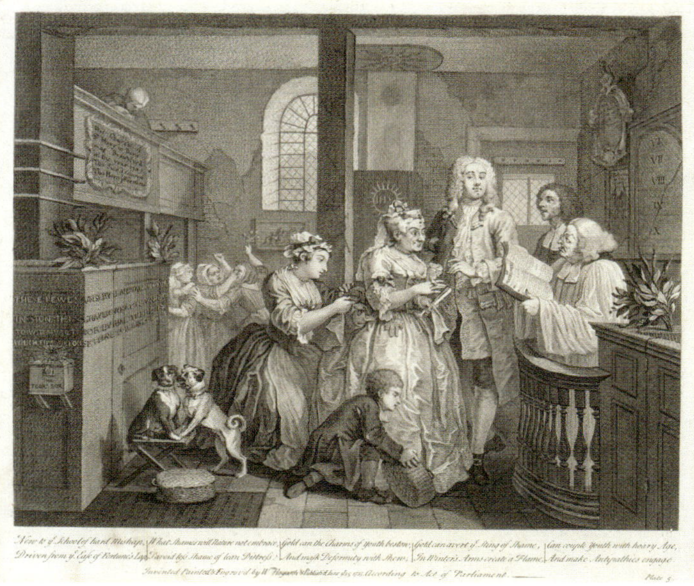

36e

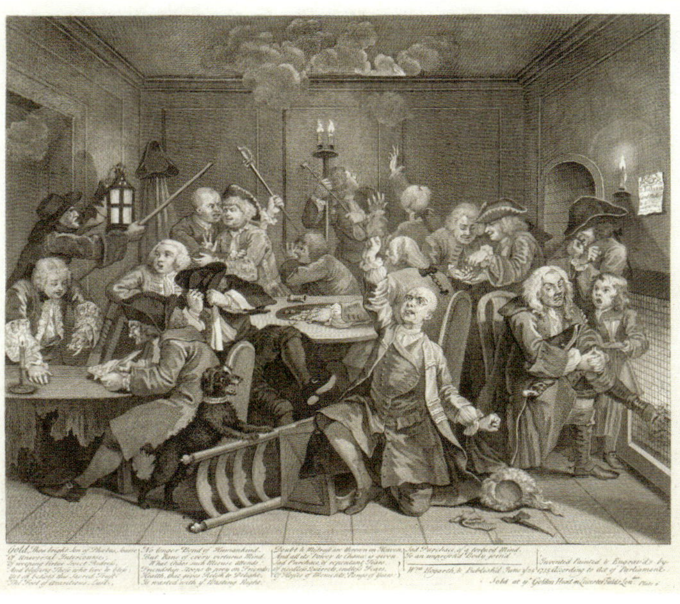

36f

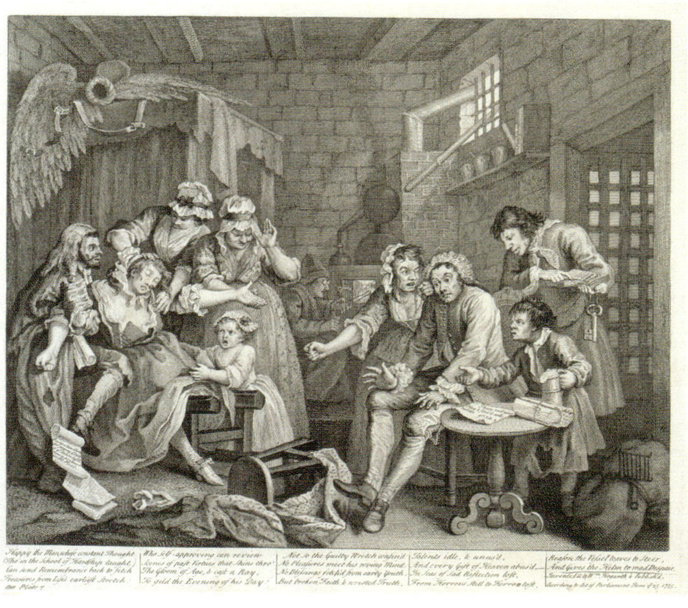

36g

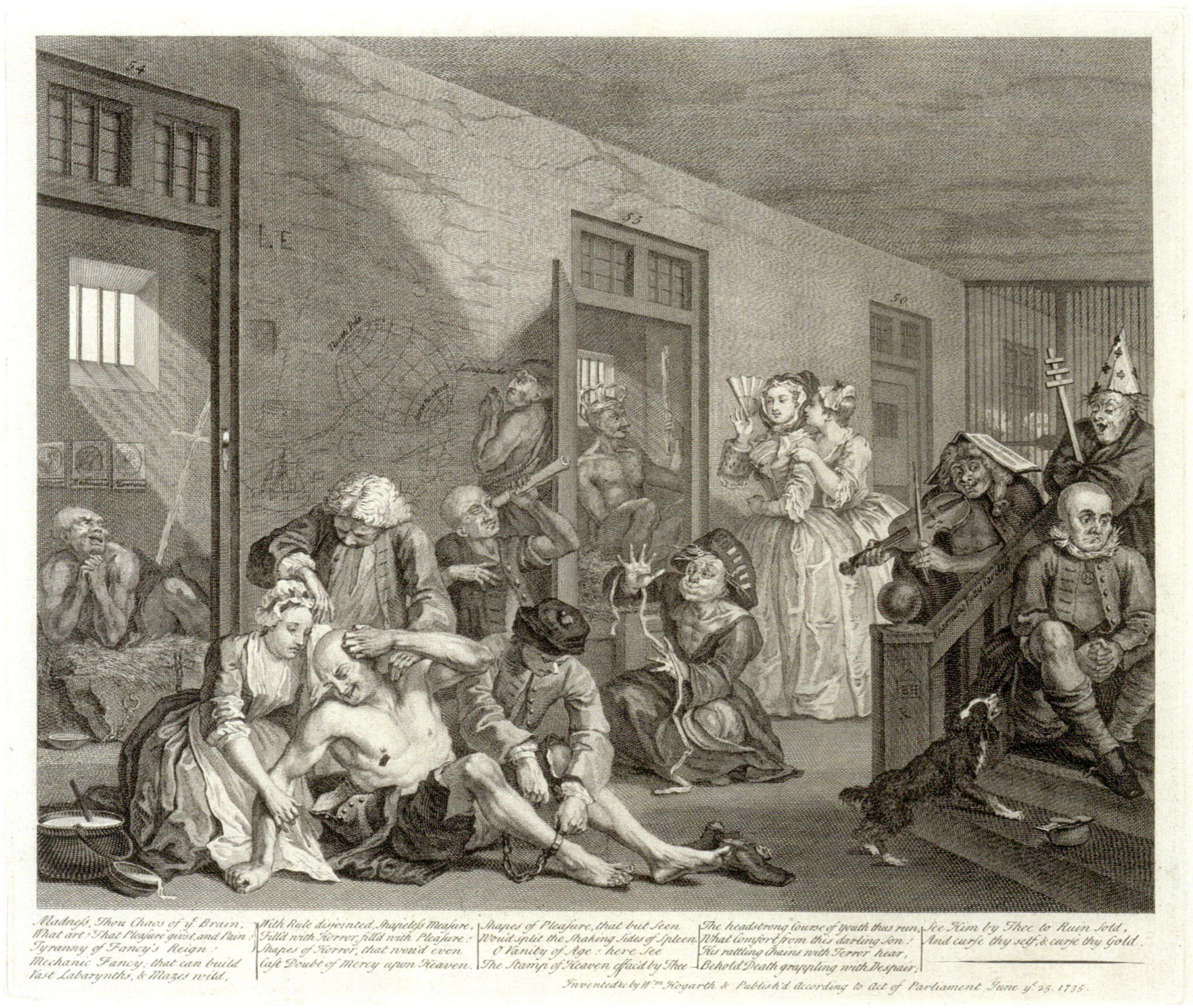

36h

and is surrounded by various flunkeys, including fencing and dancing masters, a jockey and a composer, who serenades him with his latest opera, *The Rape of the Sabines*. This print is followed by the famous tavern scene, set in a Covent Garden brothel, where the rake is about to enjoy an act performed by a stripper, or 'posture woman'. In the fourth scene the rake is arrested for debt in the environs of St James's Palace, only to be saved by his erstwhile sweetheart with money saved from her honest trade in trinkets. Following his marriage to a rich old crone in the fifth scene, the rake proceeds to gamble away his new fortune; which leads in the penultimate scene to his incarceration in a debtor's prison. The final scene takes place in Bethlem Royal Hospital, a lunatic asylum, more popularly known as Bedlam. Here the weeping Sarah comforts the rake, now deprived of his mind as well as his clothing, as in the background two ladies enjoy eyeing the inmates, then a popular form of recreation in fashionable society. (MP)

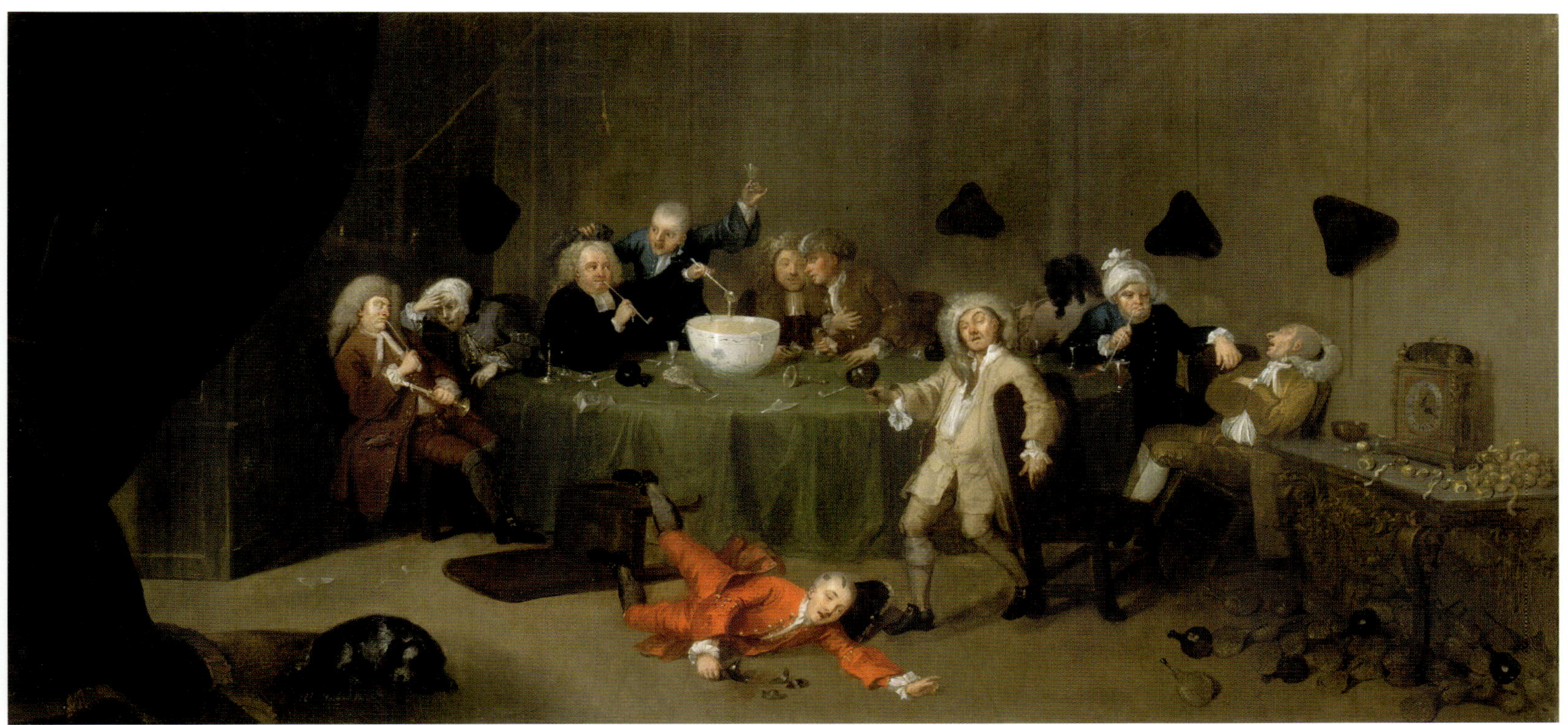

37

37. **William Hogarth**
London, 1697 - London, 1764
A Midnight Modern Conversation, c. 1732
Oil on canvas, 76.2 x 163,8 cm
Bottom left: W. Hogarth Pinx
Yale Center for British Art, Paul Mellon Collection, New Haven

One of several known versions of the subject, which was in due course widely disseminated through an engraving published in March 1733, Hogarth's satire upon a party of otherwise respectable gentlemen is a grotesque contortion of the conversation piece, with its polite dramatis personae arranged indoors or out. Despite the reference in the title to midnight, the clock on the side table clearly shows that this scene of debauchery in fact takes place at four o'clock in the morning, and that between them the gentlemen drinkers have ploughed through well over two dozen bottles of claret and have now embarked on a large bowl of punch, the principal ingredient of which is gin flavoured with lemon rind - a mound of discarded lemons is accumulating beside the clock. The gentlemen are in various, carefully differentiated states of intoxication, ranging from the still-functioning parson who, ladling punch, presides, to the sleepy gentleman on the left who lights his sleeve, not his downturned pipe; his next-door neighbour who is about to be sick; the standing figure on the far side of the table who idiotically thrusts his wig on top of the parson's; and the well-dressed man in the foreground, perhaps a successful prizefighter, who, wigless, collapses onto the floor amid broken glass. In later printed versions of the subject the dog, who sleeps through the chaos, is vulgarly replaced by a chamber pot. In the caption to the engraving, Hogarth issued the stern warning

> ...Think not to find one *meant Resemblance* there;
> We lash the *Vices* but the *Persons* spare...

But this disclaimer did little to discourage the circulation of rumours in London as to the identity of the various drinkers. On the contrary (see Hallett and Riding 2006). In the early eighteenth century the word *modern* could refer to dates as far distant as two hundred years earlier (Trumble 2006). (AT)

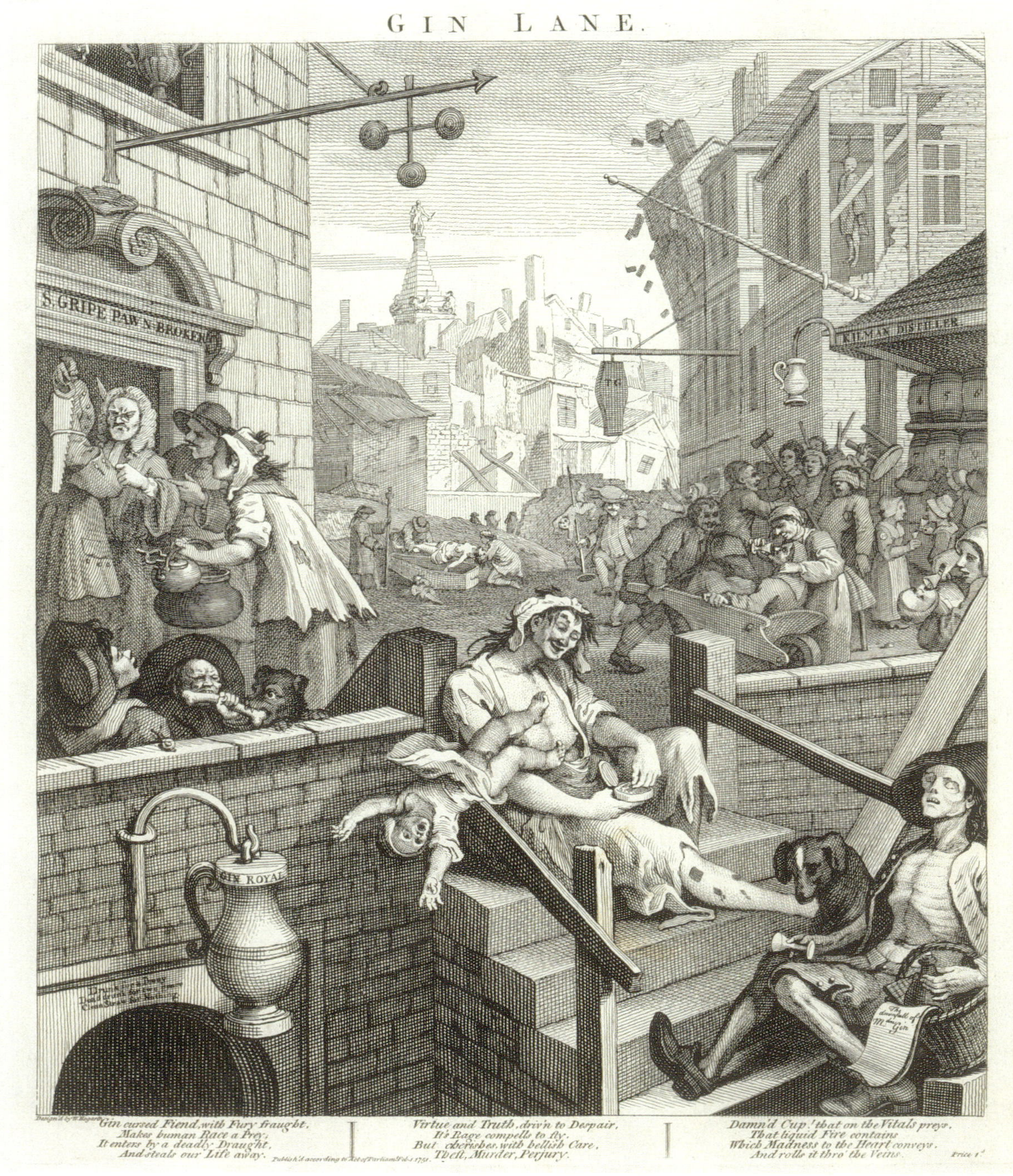

38

38. **William Hogarth**
London, 1697 - London, 1764
Gin Lane, 1751
Etching and engraving, 35.7 x 32.2 cm
Published by William Hogarth
Andrew Edmunds, London

Hogarth's popular print *Gin Lane*, together with its pendant print, *Beer Street*, formed a trenchant commentary on the behaviour of London's ordinary citizens, and was, as he himself stated, part of a calculated attempt 'to reform some reigning Vices peculiar to the lower class of People'. In the late 1740s there had been a marked upsurge in the consumption of cheap gin, which, as the iconography of *Gin Lane* indicates, led to an increase in poverty, malnutrition and mortality rates. As a response, in 1751 the Government passed the Gin Act, increasing the duties on gin with the aim of putting the distillers out of business. Hogarth's print can be seen as party to the official campaign, portraying in graphic detail the ruination of a populace in thrall to gin shop owners and pawnbrokers. Typically, in order to stress the relevance of his print to real life, Hogarth locates the scene in a readily recognizable location; in this case the slums around the parish of St Giles. (MP)

39. **William Hogarth**
London, 1697 - London, 1764
Morning and ***Night*** from ***The Four Times of Day***, 1738
Etching and engraving, each approx. 48.7 x 40.3 cm
Published 25 March 1738 by William Hogarth
Andrew Edmunds, London

The *Four Times of the Day* was conceived by Hogarth as a series of independent yet related vignettes featuring incidents from London life, its origin lying in the allegorical traditions of north European art, where seasonal changes are linked to moral paradigms. Unlike Hogarth's previous series, such as *A Rake's Progress*, there is no attempt here to provide a unified narrative, but rather the artist juxtaposes in a comic vein the manners and morals of various city dwellers as they go about their daily business. The first scene, *Morning*, is set in Covent Garden Piazza, outside Tom King's Coffee House, which forms a 'profane' contrast to the sacred environs of St Paul's church. Here, on an icy winter morning a couple of rakes indulge in a groping session with two wenches, observed in fascinated silence by a pious old maid, who shields her interest with a suitable look of contempt. Her air of moral superiority is undercut further by the presence of the snivelling boy who carries her prayer book.

Night, the fourth and final engraving of this series, is located in an alleyway in Westminster. The oak branches decorating the barber's shop indicate that the scene is set specifically on 29 May, 'Restoration Day', which marked the anniversary of Charles II's triumphal entry into London as king in 1660. In the background is Hubert Le Sueur's statue of Charles I, then situated in nearby Charing Cross. A celebratory bonfire burns in the street, its flames fanned by the wreckage of a stagecoach. On the left of the street, as indicated by the signboard, is the Rummer and Grapes tavern, a recognized rendezvous of the Freemasons in the early decades of the eighteenth century. Outside on the street a pair of drunken Masons stagger home, depicted by Hogarth, quite literally, as brothers in arms. In a typical Hogarthian gesture, the contents of a chamber pot are emptied unceremoniously onto their heads from an upstairs window. (MP)

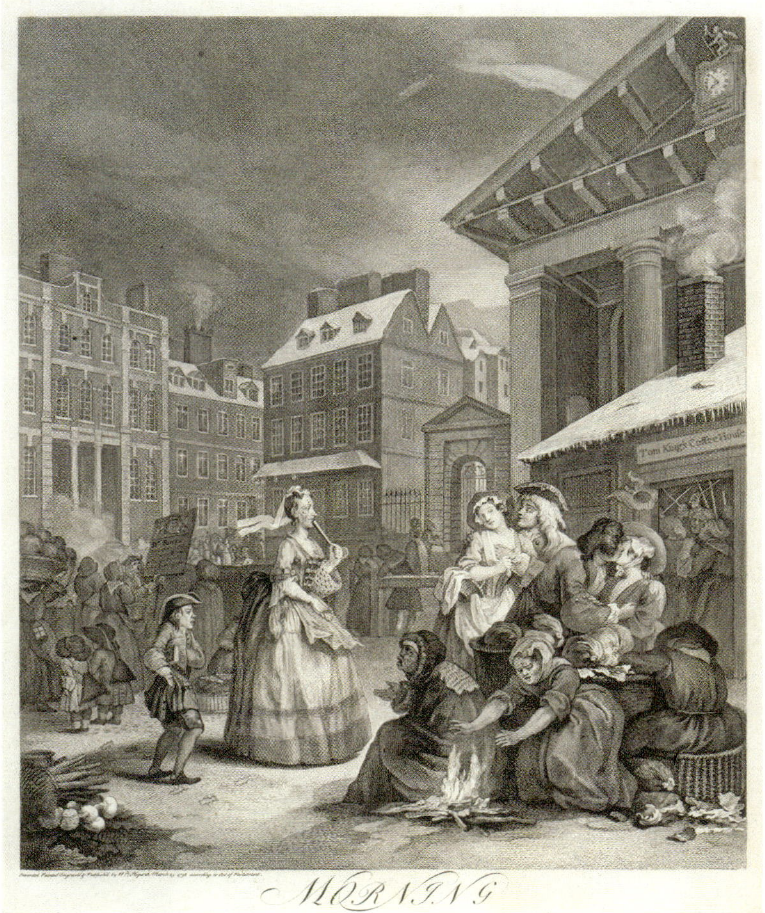

39a

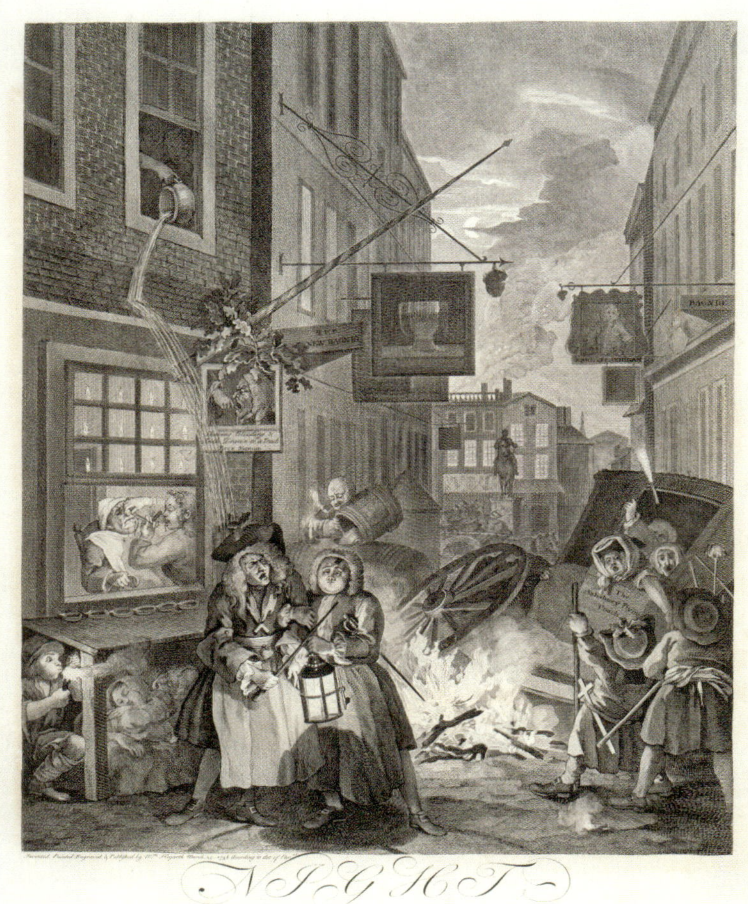

39b

40. **William Austin**

London, 1721 - Brighton, 1820

The Anatomist Overtaken by the Watch ... Carrying off Miss W- in a Hamper, 1773

Etching, 27 x 36 cm

Published 1 May 1773

Private Collection

A night scene, but exhibited here in its uncoloured state. The famous physician Dr William Hunter (one of the founding figures of the British Medical Establishment) is unmasked in his secret life as a body-snatcher, exhuming corpses for his dissections. He has dropped his hamper, spilling out the pallid, doll-like or larval corpse of the very recently buried 'Miss Watts'. Austin himself, like many caricature masters from Guercino and the Tiepolos onwards, had a double identity: the 'serious' academic drawing teacher who was capable of a kind of willed regression into a 'childish' art of ugly monsters. His etched line remains however very pure, and oddly 'elegant' in its repeated tonal strokes. Austin's best prints, with their exceptionally large-scale figures, are among the few significant images of English humour between Hogarth and Gillray. (TH)

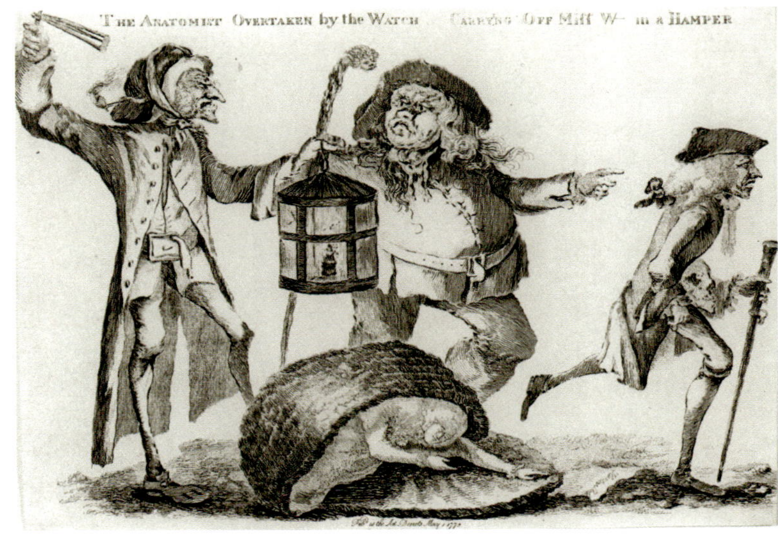

40

41. **Robert Dighton**

London [?], 1752 [?] - London, 1814

A Real Scene in St Paul's Church Yard, on a Windy Day, c. 1783

Watercolour on paper, 32.5 x 25 cm

Victoria and Albert Museum, London

This celebrated print shop image was published as a mezzotint engraving by Carington Bowles, who published many of Dighton's satirical prints. Bowles's print shop was situated at 69 St Paul's Churchyard, the setting for the present watercolour. In the shop window are displayed popular genre subjects of love and courtship, while, in sharp contrast, the top tier consists of noted clerics and preachers, including (third from the right) the founder of the Methodist movement, John Wesley, in a print after Nathaniel Hone. Robert Dighton, the son of a printseller, was among the most versatile artists and printmakers of the later Georgian period. Equally adept in portraiture and caricature, Dighton also performed as an actor and singer. In later life, when in financial straits, he supplemented his income by stealing prints from the British Museum, which curtailed his professional career in London, forcing him to flee to the provinces. (MP)

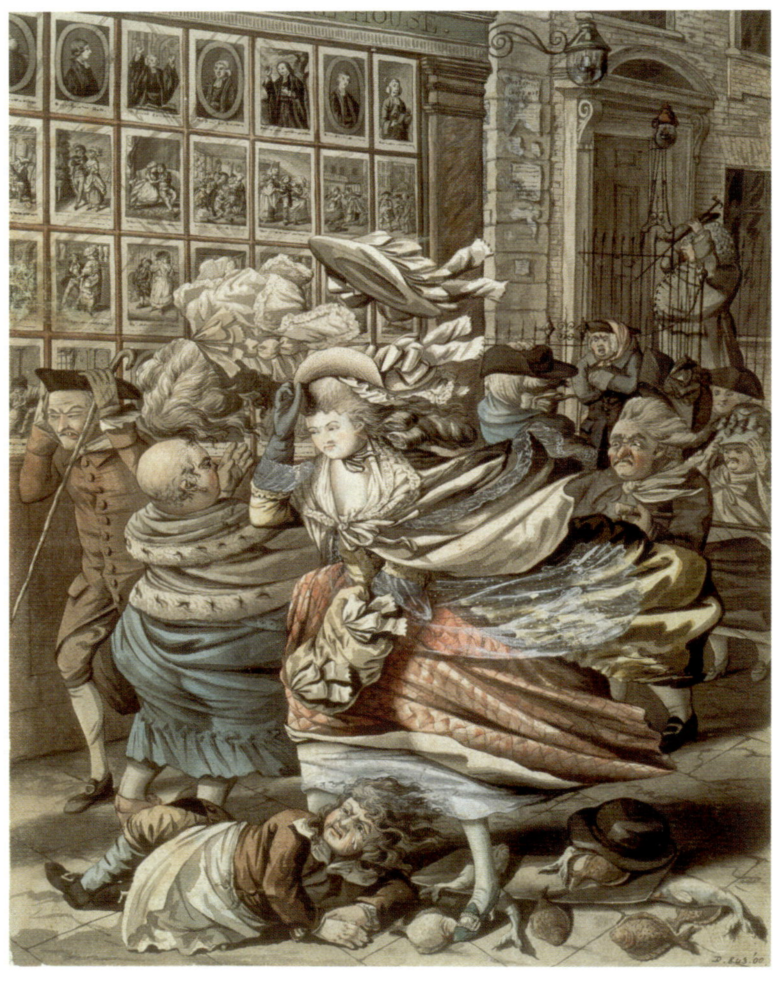

41

42. **James Gillray**
London, 1756 – London, 1815
A March to the Bank, 1787
Etching and engraving, with publisher's or artist's watercolour, 42.1 x 54.5 cm
Published 22 August 1787 by S.W. Fores, London
Andrew Edmunds, London

The three prints by Gillray in *British Vision* give only an indication of his thematic and stylistic range. The underlying subject of *A March to the Bank* is the arrogance of Government authority, trampling over the populace it should be serving. Ever since the Gordon Riots had threatened London in 1780, a troop of guardsmen had been marched in formation twice daily from their barracks through the Strand to the Bank of England, causing appalling disruption in the crowded streets. Gillray sets the scene close to Billingsgate Fish Market; the central mock-Baroque group has a captain pirouetting triumphantly on the belly of an upended fishwife. In the foreground, her fishy thigh encloses the shocked-rigid visage of another victim, whose leg has been horrifically snapped below the calf. Elsewhere, a baby's head is crushed, strings of onions are falling off a wagon, and a French hairdresser is taking the opportunity to grasp the beautiful costermaid's crotch. Virtuoso figure groups and elaborate tonal hatching display Gillray's unrivalled technical accomplishment. In 1786, after a bruising two-and-a-half years of failure as a 'serious' engraver of historical compositions, he had reluctantly stooped again to the lowly genre of the satirical print. But *A March*, like his earlier caricatures, remained unsigned, and he probably still hoped to evade the taint of professional caricaturist. (TH)

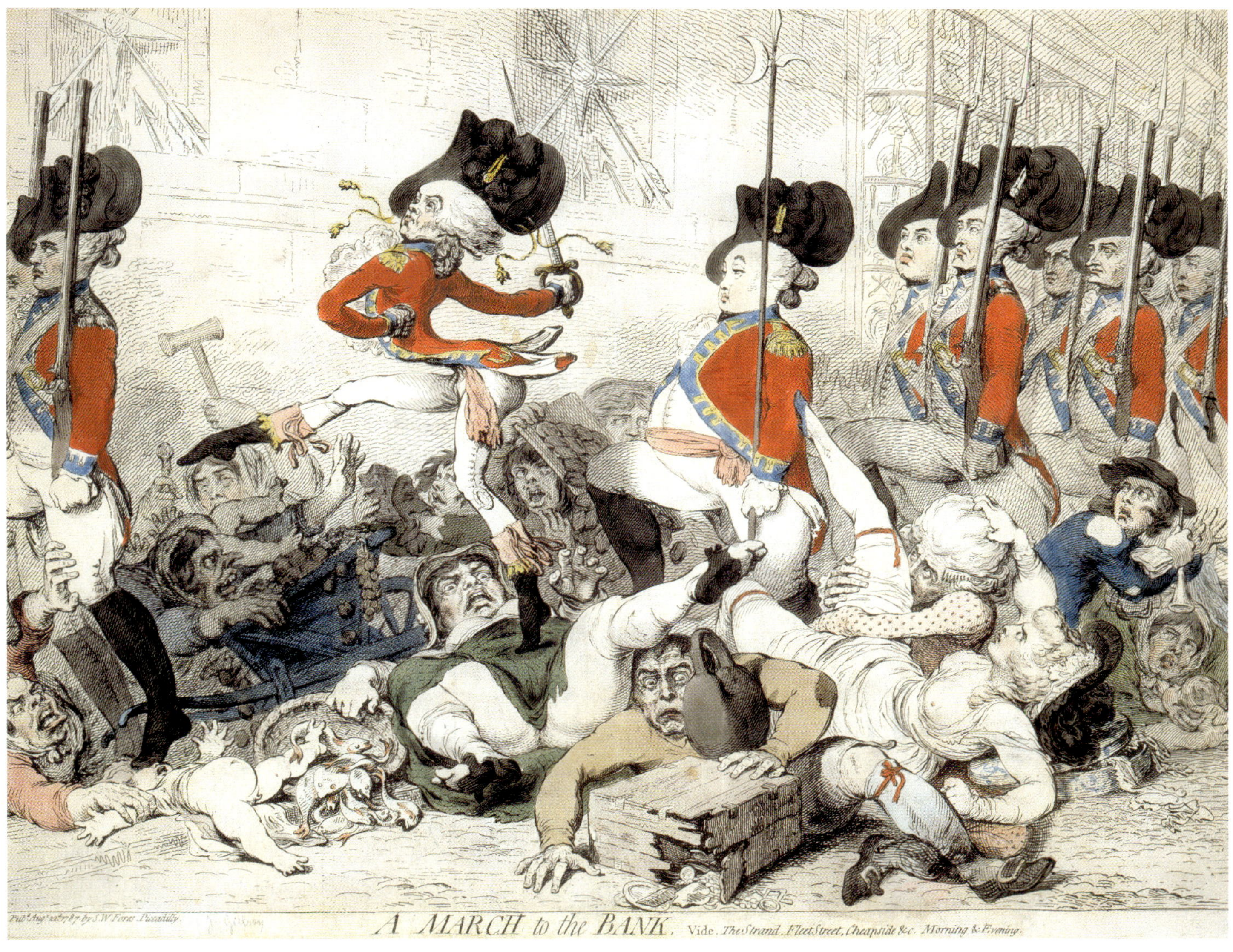

42

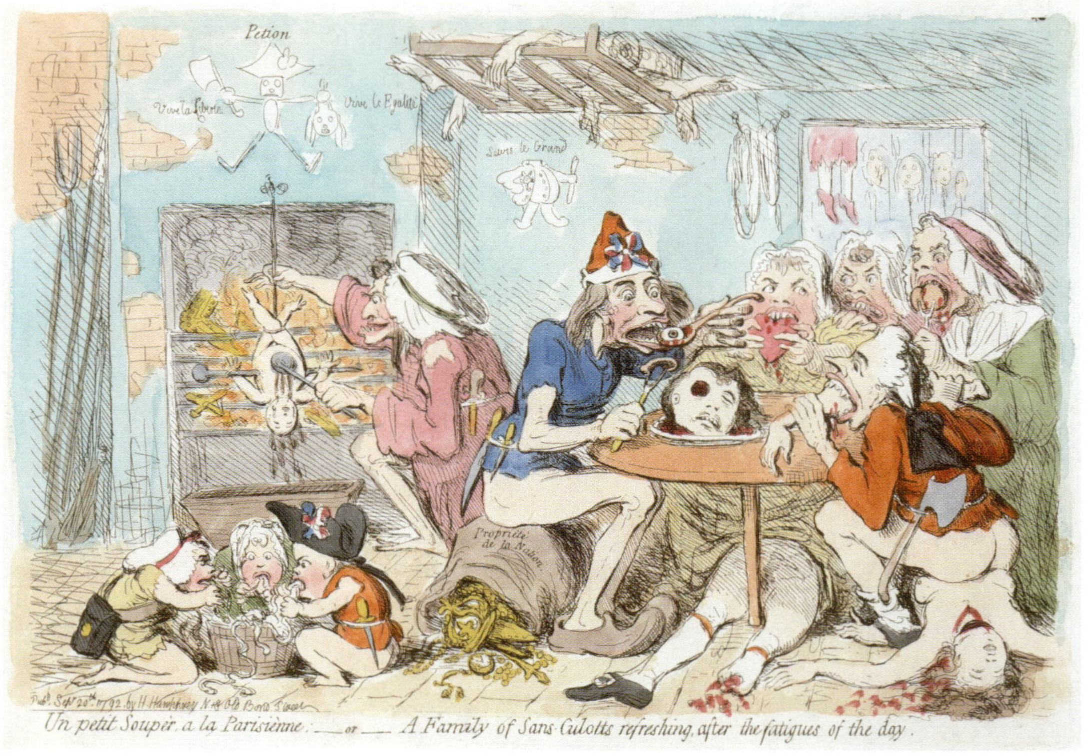

43

43. **James Gillray**
London, 1756 - London, 1815
Un petit souper à la Parisienne - or A Family of Sans-Culottes refreshing, after the fatigues of the day, 1792
Etching with engraving, with publisher's watercolour, 25.2 x 35.3 cm
Published 20 September 1792 by H. Humphrey, London
Andrew Edmunds, London

The 'September Massacres' - random executions of all kinds of prisoners, priests and politicos, along with prostitutes and thieves - shocked even the most ardent revolutionary sympathizers; although the London newspaper reports were so lurid as to be scarcely believable. Gillray goes one better, and, characteristically, has it both ways. Taking as his model Bruegel's grotesque engraving of 1563, *The Thin Kitchen* (see p. 20), he creates a fantasy of cannibal feasting, drawn in a deliberately 'primitive' mode, and including on the walls some infantile revolutionary graffiti. We can work our way around the room, from the murderous little children gobbling human intestines, to the pistol-packing old granny basting a trussed infant at the fire. The larder behind is hung with fresh victims, the shelf laden with chopped-off limbs. Hearts and eyeballs are relished. As Richard Godfrey has pointed out, only six days earlier Gillray had completed one of his most refined and sophisticated prints: 'it must have been a relief that his next work was to gouge out this brutal subject and plunge the plate into the acid.' (Godfrey 2001, p. 94) (TH)

44. **James Gillray**
London, 1756 - London, 1815
Confederated Coalition; - or - The Giants Storming Heaven, 1804
Etching and engraving, with some aquatint, with publisher's watercolour, impression in brown ink, 46.7 x 33.6 cm
Published 1 May 1804 by H. Humphrey, London
Andrew Edmunds, London

This large late print is a sustained parody of the Grand Manner, as applied to the sordid realities of contemporary power struggles. The cloudy Treasury ('Heaven') is under assault from a motley alliance of nude, but hideously unidealized, politicians. Addington, squeezing an enema down at them, gets one in the eye from the blunderbuss fired by Charles James Fox - the fat, hairy Silenus-figure, held aloft by big-tummied, bespectacled Buckingham. Pitt (the ever-scrawny 'bottomless' Pitt) is at the apex of Mount Olympus, about to hurl a bundle inscribed 'Knockdown Arguments'. At the right, red-nosed Sheridan and his cohorts are climbing a siege-ladder. Elsewhere, a dog is pissing on official papers, and a nude midget carrying a book entitled *The Duty of Man* is directing his urine-jet upwards. Some of these characters - especially Fox and Pitt - had by now been mocked by Gillray for upwards of fifteen years. The day before the print's publication, the Government had already fallen, with the old enemies Pitt and Fox forming the new coalition administration. (TH)

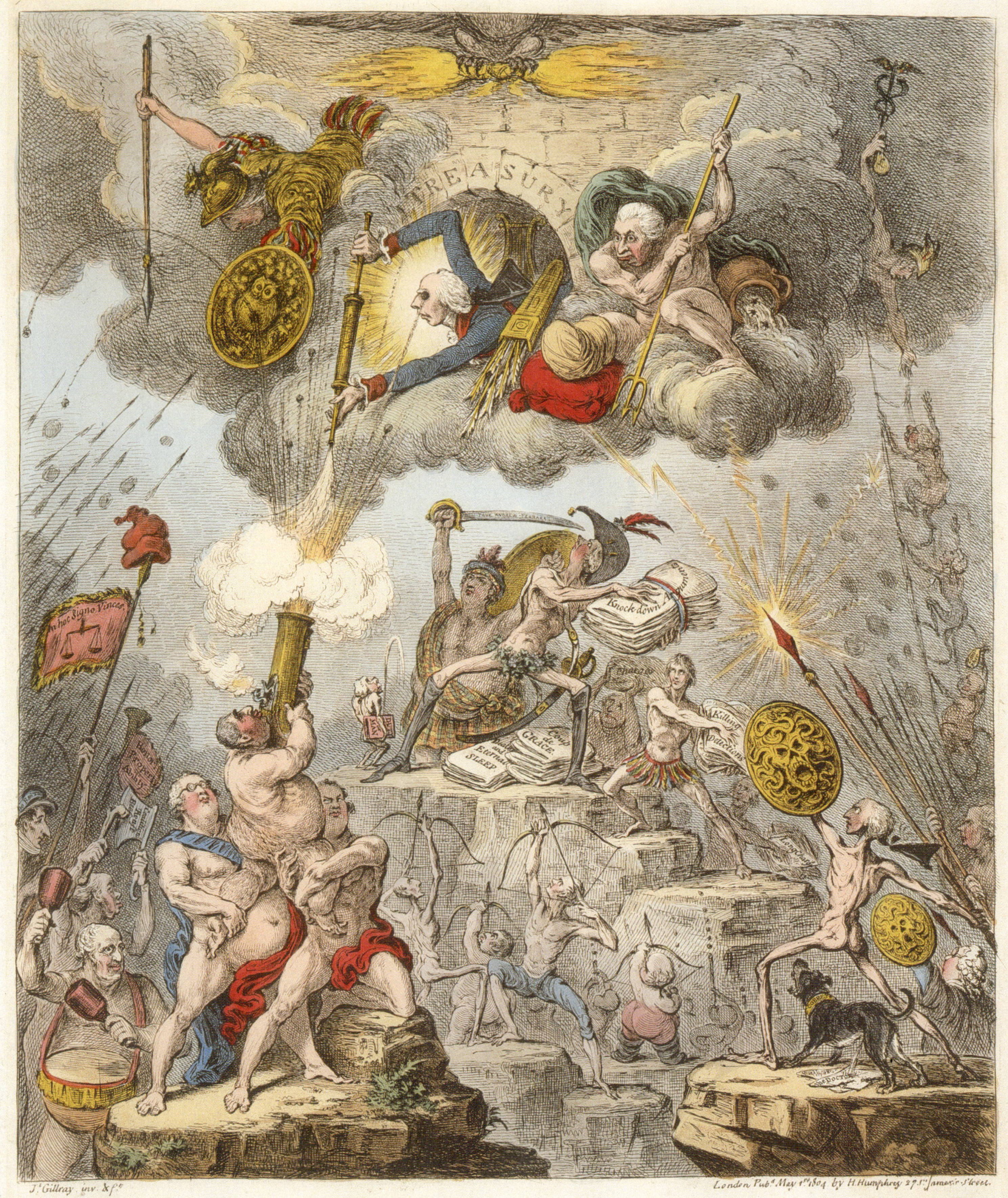

Confederated-Coalition; —or —The Giants storming Heaven; —with, the Gods alarmed for their everlasting-abodes.
—"They never complain'd of Fatigue, but like Giants refreshed, were ready to enter immediately upon the attack!"
Vide. Lord Ch—c—llor's Speech 24th April 1804.
—"Not to destroy! but root them out of Heaven". Milton.

44

45. **James Gillray**
London, 1756 - London, 1815
Theatre of the World: The Revolutionary Wars (recto)
A List of Subjects 'worthy of ye talents of British Artists' (verso), 1805
Pencil, ink and watercolour on paper, 29 x 32 cm
Bottom left: J. Gillray.
Private Collection

The only published print that approximates to this theatre scene is Gillray's *Pacific Overtures* of 5 April 1806, where Napleon attempts to dictate peace terms to a scornful George III. The drawn drama is far more animated: on stage, the redcoat allies are clobbering a brown France (the Phrygian-capped 'Marianne', or possibly 'Little Boney' himself), while a fat nude female spreads her arms in supplication. All around them is mayhem, as the proscenium is overwhelmed by audience and orchestra in a calligraphy of chaos. Pierre Schneider has observed (Schneider 2002, p. 129): 'The comical is expressed in art by caricature, which has something in common with both script and image ... it is speed which turns an image into character; a sign is a lightened simplified form, condensed by the swiftness of the draughtsman's hand.' Many of Gillray's late drawings are made up of 'signs' of this kind and spattered with writing (trial captions and snatches of dialogue). In this case we find the words on the reverse (p. 103, fig.2): a list of 'subjects' that vividly conjures up the London scene of 1805, including the theatre of 'Kemble in Despair' and 'Master Betty'. (TH)

46. **James Gillray**
London, 1756 - London, 1815
The Faro Table, c. 1800
Pen, brown ink and grey wash on paper, 22.5 x 34.4 cm
British Museum, London

Faro (or 'Pharaoh') was among the most widely played of all card games in the illicit gambling-hells of eighteenth-century London. The clientele was often aristocratic; in 1797 Lady Buckinghamshire was fined for running a notorious Faro bank (see Gatrell 2006, especially pp. 152-53). That was the year Gillray moved to 27 St James's Street, living above the print shop of his publisher, Hannah Humphrey; and in the same street stood - and still stand - two of the most legendary of London's licensed gaming-clubs, Brooks's and White's; one or other may well provide the setting for *The Faro Table*. Gillray must have started out with a print in mind, since, unlike his contemporary Thomas Rowlandson, he appears never to have made drawings for sale as independent works of art. But no published print corresponds to this preliminary design. (TH)

See essay pp. 101-3.

47. **James Gillray**
London, 1756 - London, 1815
Voltaire Instructing the Infant Jacobinism, c. 1800
Oil on paper, 27.3 x 20.3 cm
Print Collection, Miriam and Ira D. Wallach Division of Art, Prints and Photographs, The New York Public Library, Astor, Lenox and Tilden Foundations

In its command of tone and its Rembrandtesque impasto, this beautifully handled small masterpiece suggests the oil painter that Gillray might have become. Voltaire, as prophet of atheism and inspirer of revolution, reigns enthroned within an excremental underworld, crowded with smirking demons; he gives his infernal book into the hand of the ragged 'Infant Jacobinism', who stands on another big volume. From 1797 onwards, Gillray succumbed to intimidation and bribery, accepting a secret grant from the Tory administration of two hundred pounds a year. The artistically ambitious, but politically reactionary, allegories that Gillray designed for George Canning's de luxe publication, *The Poetry of the Anti-Jacobin*, promised to be the culminating works of his career. But the project foundered; and, as Gillray wrote in 1800, this collapse of all his hopes and expectations 'hurts me beyond anything I met with, during a life made up of hardships and disappointments ... I believe that, was I to reflect much upon it ... it would drive me mad.' (see Hill 1965, p. 95) (TH)

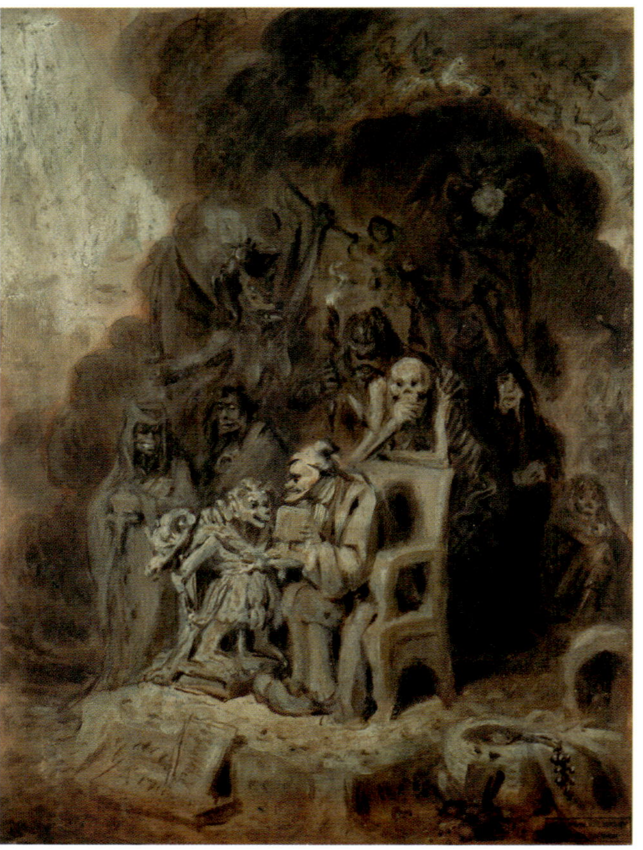

47

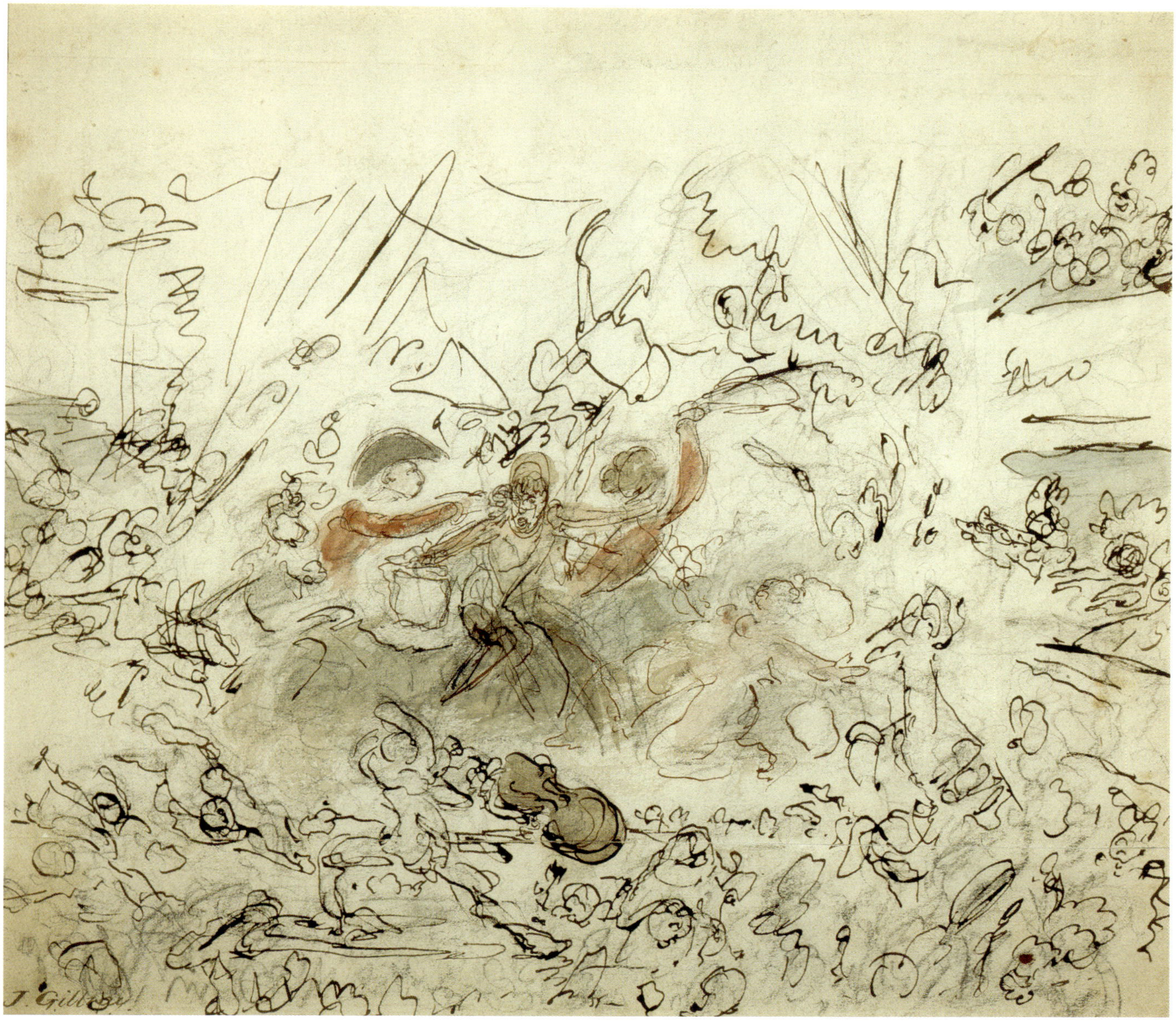

45

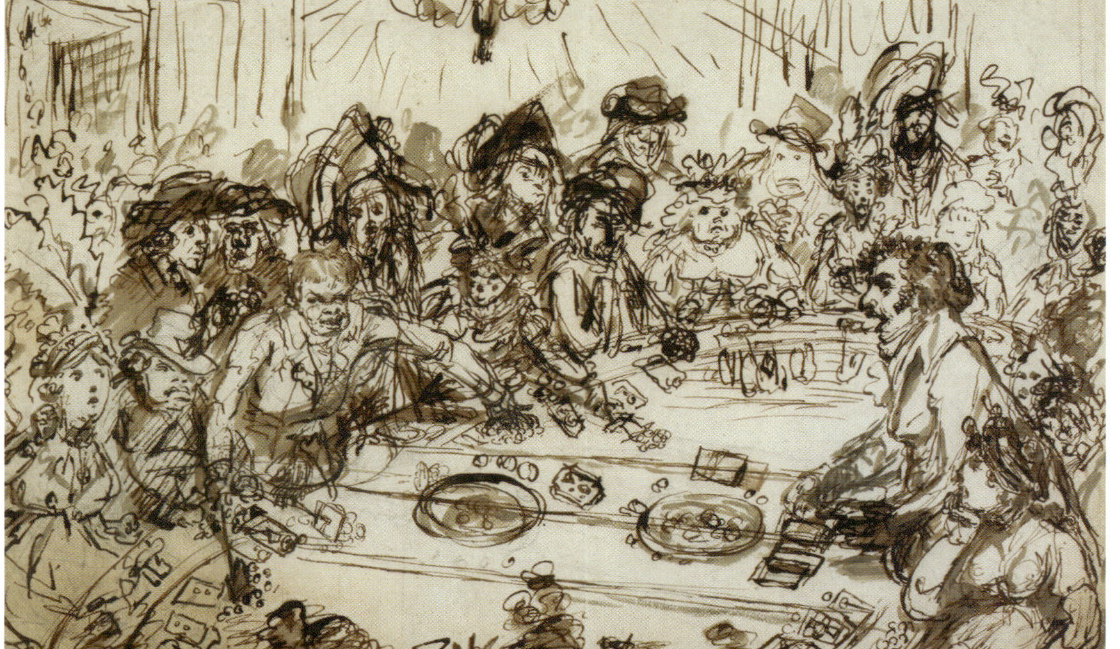

46

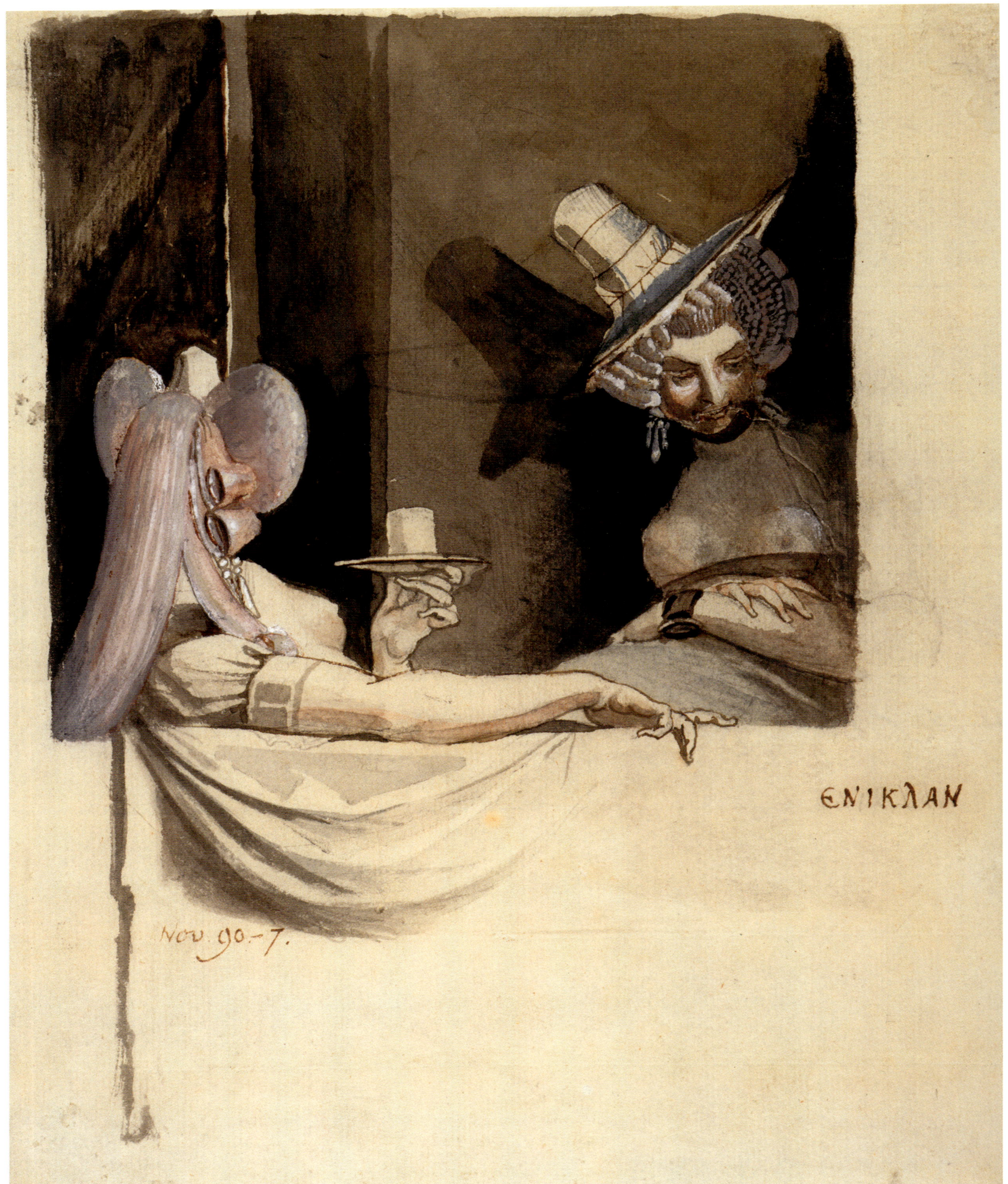

48

48. **John Henry Fuseli**
Zurich, 1741 - Putney Hill, near London, 1825
Two Courtesans at a Window (recto)
Three-quarter-length Figure and Head of Mrs Fuseli (verso), 1790
Pen, sepia, grey washes and watercolour, heightened with white, on paper, 22.2 x 17.8 cm
Bottom left: Nov 90-7.
Bottom right: ENIKλAN
Ulster Museum, Belfast

Aside from his public art, which was occupied with grand themes taken from classical mythology, northern legends and epic literature, Henry Fuseli produced work of a more private nature, often involving the erotic depiction of powerful women. Some of Fuseli's drawings are explicitly sexual; others, like the present one, derive from the artist's obsessive interest in exotic costume and elaborate coiffure. During the later eighteenth century many fashionable women, including Fuseli's own wife, lavished enormous attention on their appearance, including ingenious hairstyles and headpieces, lurid face paint and increasingly low-cut gowns. The two women in the present drawing are seated by a window, taking tea with their breasts exposed. Their revealing attire, which features in other similar drawings by Fuseli, suggests that they are prostitutes, or more precisely fashionable 'courtesans'; products, perhaps of Fuseli's vivid imagination rather than women of his personal acquaintance. (MP)

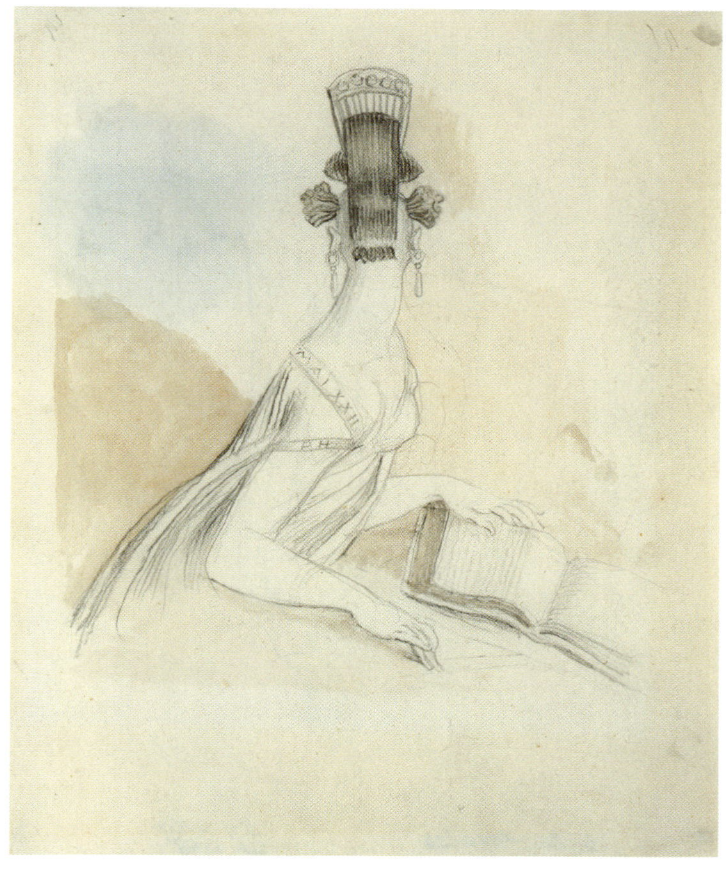

49

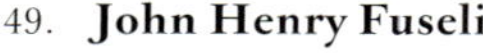

49. **John Henry Fuseli**
Zurich, 1741 - Putney Hill, near London, 1825
Seated Woman with eccentric Haircut (recto)
Sketch of Sleeping Figure (verso), 1822
Pencil and sepia on paper, 22.5 x 18.4 cm
On the shoulder strap: MAI XXII/ P H [Putney Hill]
Kunsthaus, Zurich

Since his youth Henry Fuseli had formed a fetish for women's hair, incorporating the figures of dominant women with exotic hairstyles into his mythological and literary works. In 1788, the forty-seven-year-old Fuseli married a young woman, Sophia Rawlins, who had previously modelled for him. In the many portrait studies he made of her Fuseli conceived a fascination for her complex coiffure, twisted, tied, beribboned and plaited into a bewildering range of styles. In these portraits, as in his other studies of women, the image reveals a physically powerful and sexually dominant presence. Fuseli continued to make studies of women's hair for the remainder of his life, the present study being produced when he was over eighty years old. Here, the woman's hair, constricted into an extreme classical style, takes on an almost abstract quality with a life of its own, akin to a decorative capital. (MP)

50. **Thomas Rowlandson**
London, 1756 or 1757 – London, 1827
The Gibbet, c. 1790
Pen, ink and watercolour over pencil on paper, 35.9 x 27.5 cm
Yale Center for British Art, Paul Mellon Collection, New Haven

Rowlandson's macabre sense of humour, which emerged in various satirical depictions of skeletons, cadavers and dissected bodies, is at its bleakest in this drawing of two highwaymen encountering the partly decayed corpse of an executed criminal suspended in an iron gibbet cage – a common deterrent to would-be murderers and highwaymen in eighteenth-century England. Rowlandson himself came from a respectable background and trained as a student at the Royal Academy schools, before establishing a successful career as a social and political satirist. Despite his ability to portray refined subjects, he was instinctively drawn to the underbelly of society. In 1789, having been left a substantial legacy by his aunt (with whom he lodged), Rowlandson squandered his fortune on gambling, which led to his impoverishment in the 1790s. None the less, despite his straightened circumstances, his ingrained work ethic ensured that Rowlandson continued to produce a steady stream of drawings and book illustrations until the early 1820s. (MP)

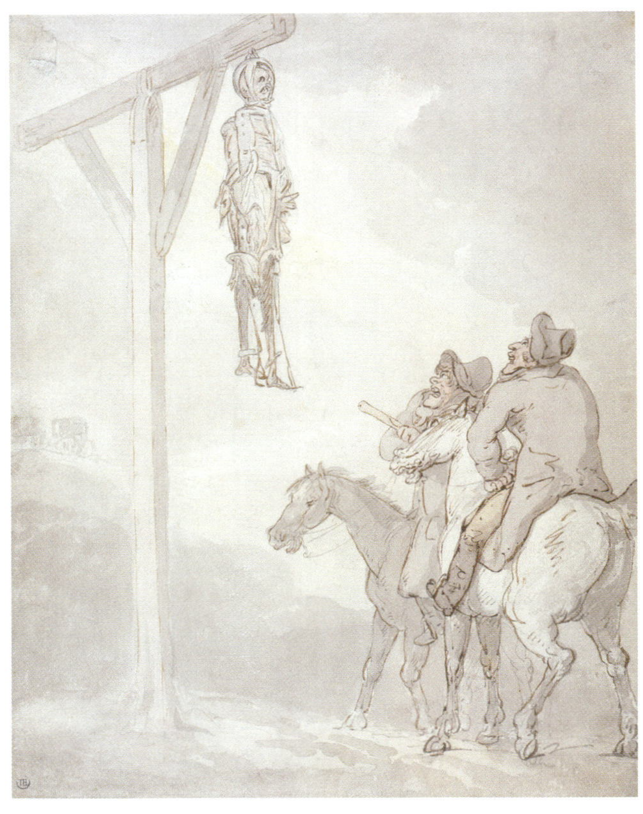

50

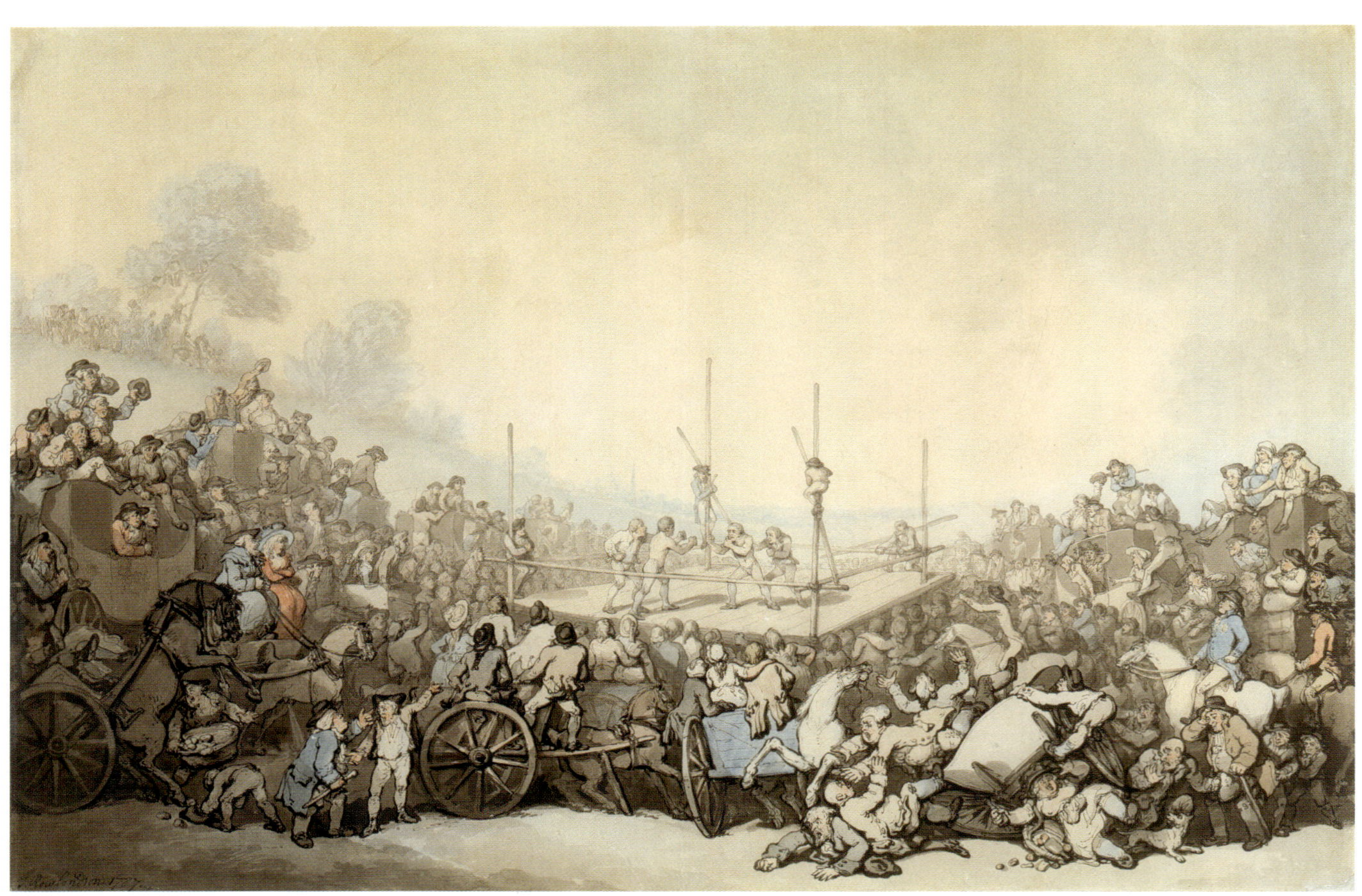

51

51. **Thomas Rowlandson**
London, 1756 or 1757 - London, 1827
The Prize Fight, 1787
Pen, ink and watercolour over pencil on paper, 46.4 x 69.5 cm
Bottom left: T. Rowlandson. 1787
Yale Center for British Art, Paul Mellon Collection, New Haven

This is among Rowlandson's most pictorially sophisticated works, based upon a subject ideally suited to his satirical powers and his eye for details drawn from everyday life. Signed and dated 1787, the scene represents a celebrated boxing match, possibly that fought between Richard Humphries, the 'Gentleman Boxer', and Samuel Martin, the 'Bath Butcher', which took place near Newmarket on 3 May 1786, or perhaps another bout which took place the following April in Barnet, north of London, between Martin and the celebrated pugilist Daniel Mendoza. According to contemporary newspaper reports, these matches could last for as long as an hour and a half and involved thousands of pounds worth of wagers. They were witnessed by a broad spectrum of society, including the Prince of Wales, who is seen here on horseback, to the right, dressed in blue. However, if the drawing does depict the Humphries-Martin bout, the Prince was in fact absent, having returned from Newmarket the previous evening 'indisposed'. (MP)

52. **Thomas Rowlandson**
London, 1756 or 1757 - London, 1827
Serving Punch, c. 1815-20
Pen, ink and watercolour over pencil on paper, 24.4 x 35.2 cm
Yale Center for British Art, Paul Mellon Collection, New Haven

This grotesque caricature is among Rowlandson's most savage satires on the social rituals that surrounded the avid consumption of alcohol in male Georgian society. The figures, their features ravaged by disease and deformed by the effects of relentless bingeing, possess an animal energy, not least the central figure who jealously guards the precious contents of the punch bowl. While the drawing relates to Rowlandson's personal observations, it is may also have been influenced by earlier depictions of drunken debauchery, notably Hogarth's print, *A Midnight Modern Conversation* (see cat. 37), of the early 1730s, the popularity of which led to its replication on cups and punch bowls. Rowlandson may have recalled also Hogarth's etching *Characters and Caricaturas* of 1743, with its tightly packed scrum of bewigged male heads. (MP)

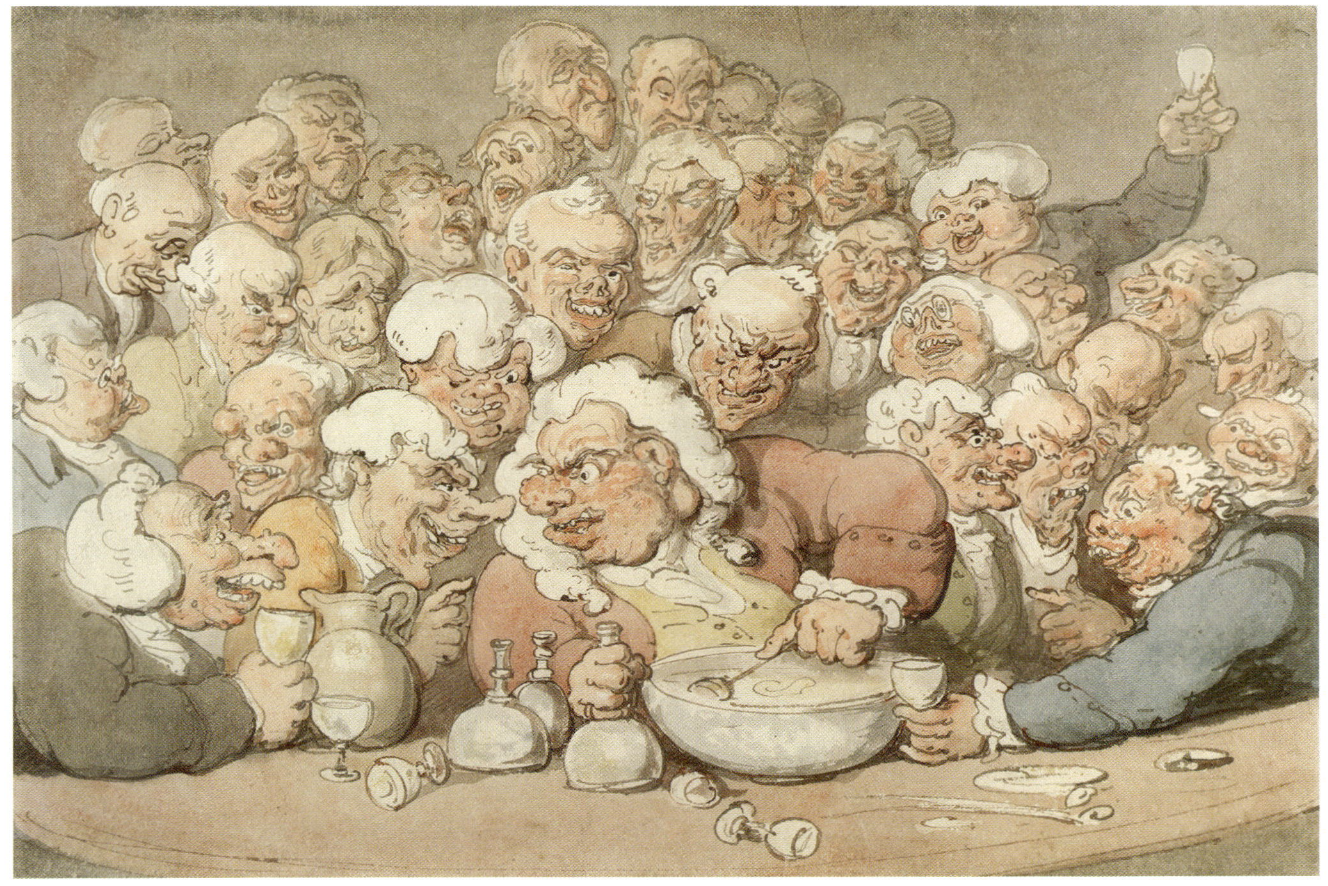

52

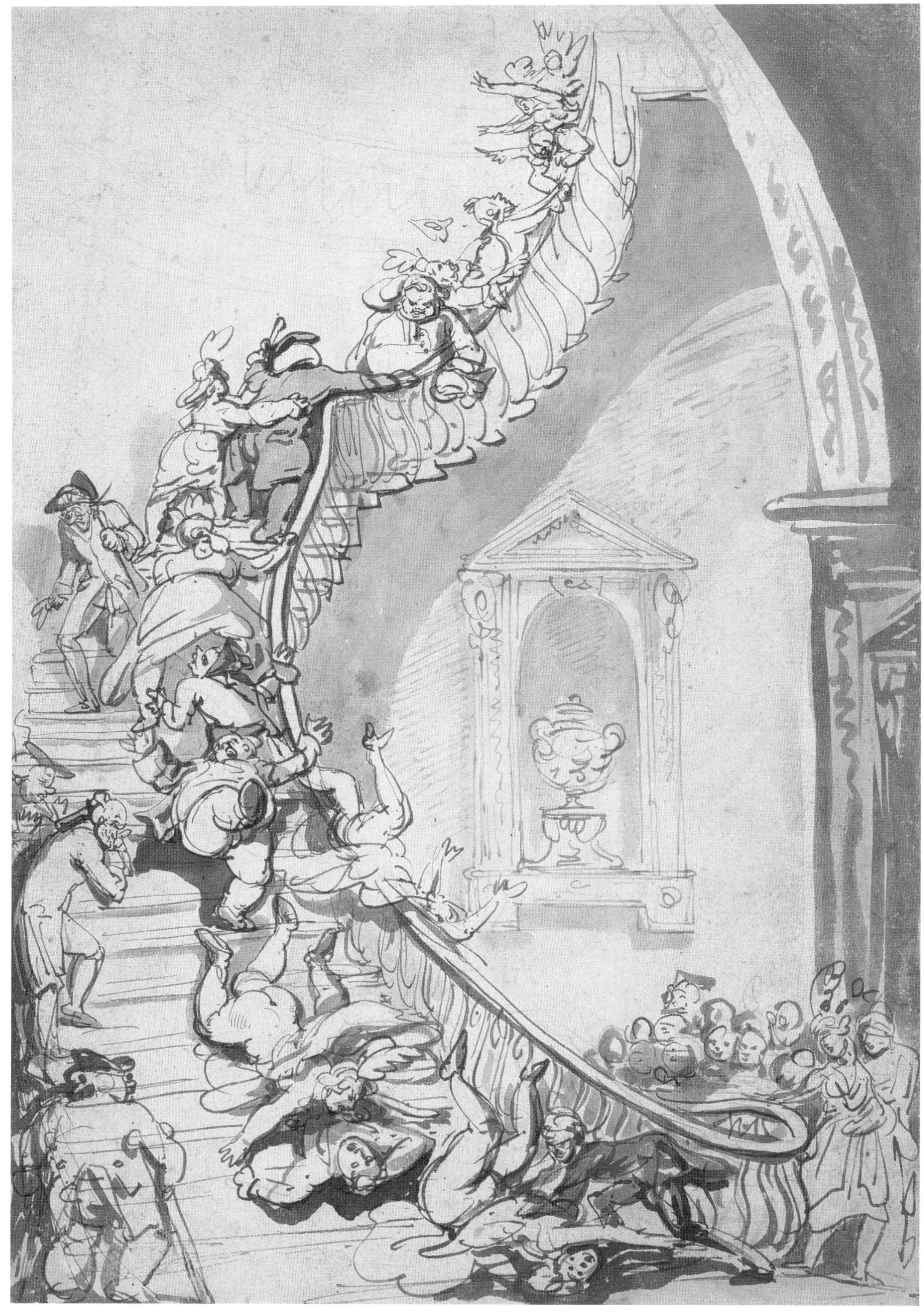

53

53. **Thomas Rowlandson**
London, 1756 or 1757 – London, 1827
The Exhibition 'Stare' Case, Somerset House, c. 1800
Watercolour, pen and ink on paper, 44.5 x 29.7 cm
UCL Art Collections, University College London

The location for Rowlandson's ambiguously titled drawing was the grand staircase of New Somerset House, designed in 1780 by Sir William Chambers as the headquarters of the Royal Academy of Arts and as the venue for the Academy's annual exhibition. The exhibitions proved to be great crowd-pullers, attracting thousands of visitors each spring to their congested displays in the Great Room on the building's top floor. Here, however, Rowlandson has concentrated upon a mêlée of ungainly exhibition-goers who tumble head over heels, exposing in the process acres of bare flesh. In the present drawing the niche is occupied by an urn, although in a later version (Yale Center for British Art, New Haven) Rowlandson replaced it with a statue of the Callipygian Venus, a classical figure renowned for the manner in which she admired her own buttocks. (MP)

55. **George Cruikshank**
London, 1792 – London, 1878
Ostend Packet – in a Squall, 1824
Etching, engraving and aquatint, with publisher's watercolour, 26.2 x 39.5 cm
Published 15 June 1824 by G. Humphrey, London
Andrew Edmunds, London

Ostend Packet – in a Squall is one of several prints in which Cruikshank parodied the perils of overseas travel, in this case the journey from Dover to Ostend by packet-boat. As Charles Dickens, later a friend of Cruikshank, wrote, it was a notoriously difficult passage: 'The storm was most magnificent at Dover… The sea came in like a great sky of immense clouds, forever breaking suddenly into furious rain… The unhappy Ostend packet unable to get in or go back, beat about the Channel all Tuesday night and until noon yesterday, when I saw her come in, with five men at the wheel, a picture of misery inconceivable.' (House, Storey and Tillotson 1997, p. 497) In Cruikshank's print the misery of the hapless cabin passengers is graphically portrayed as they are tossed from their bunks, while food, drink and the contents of a chamber pot fly through the air. (MP)

54. **George Cruikshank**
London, 1792 – London, 1878
Monstrosities of 1825-26
Etching, with publisher's watercolour, 24.7 x 40.3 cm
Published 10 February 1826 by G. Humphrey, London
Andrew Edmunds, London

George Cruikshank was among the most inventive graphic artists in nineteenth-century Britain. The son of the London caricaturist Isaac Cruikshank, George carried on the family tradition of making satirical images based upon metropolitan street life, politics, court scandals and popular books and novels. Among his most celebrated targets in the earlier part of his career were Napoleon Bonaparte and George, Prince of Wales. Indeed, such was the power of Cruikshank's propagandist images that George, upon succeeding his father to the throne in 1820, paid him £100 'not to caricature His Majesty in any immoral situation'. In 1816, influenced by James Gillray's *Monstrosities* of 1799, Cruikshank began to make a series of his own *Monstrosities*, which poked fun at contemporary fashion, such as the present print depicting overdressed women and dandies promenading on a blustery day in a London park. Cruikshank's *Monstrosities* were published by George Humphrey, for whom the artist worked intensively at the time. (MP)

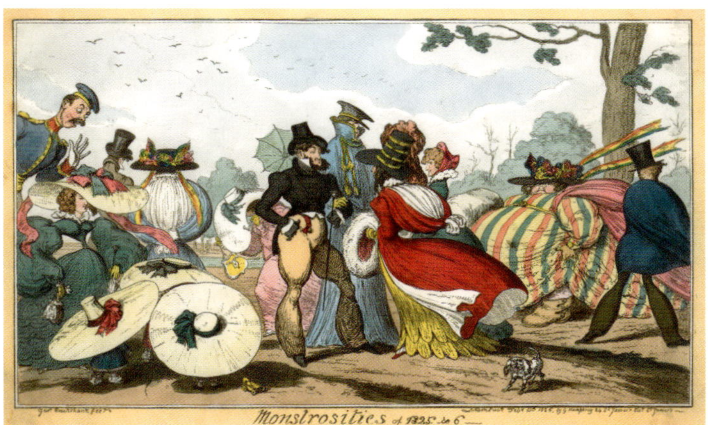

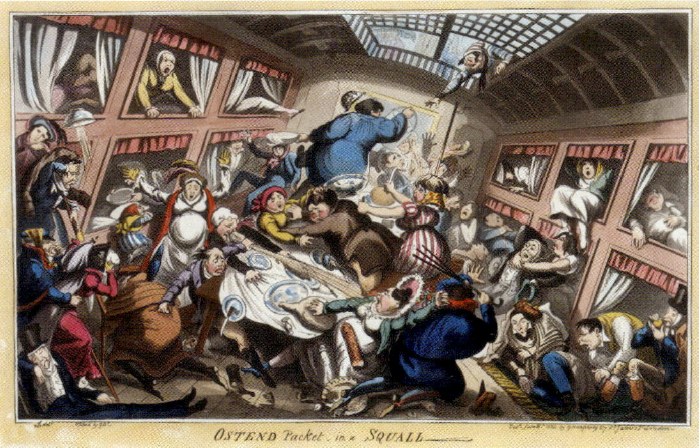

54 – 55

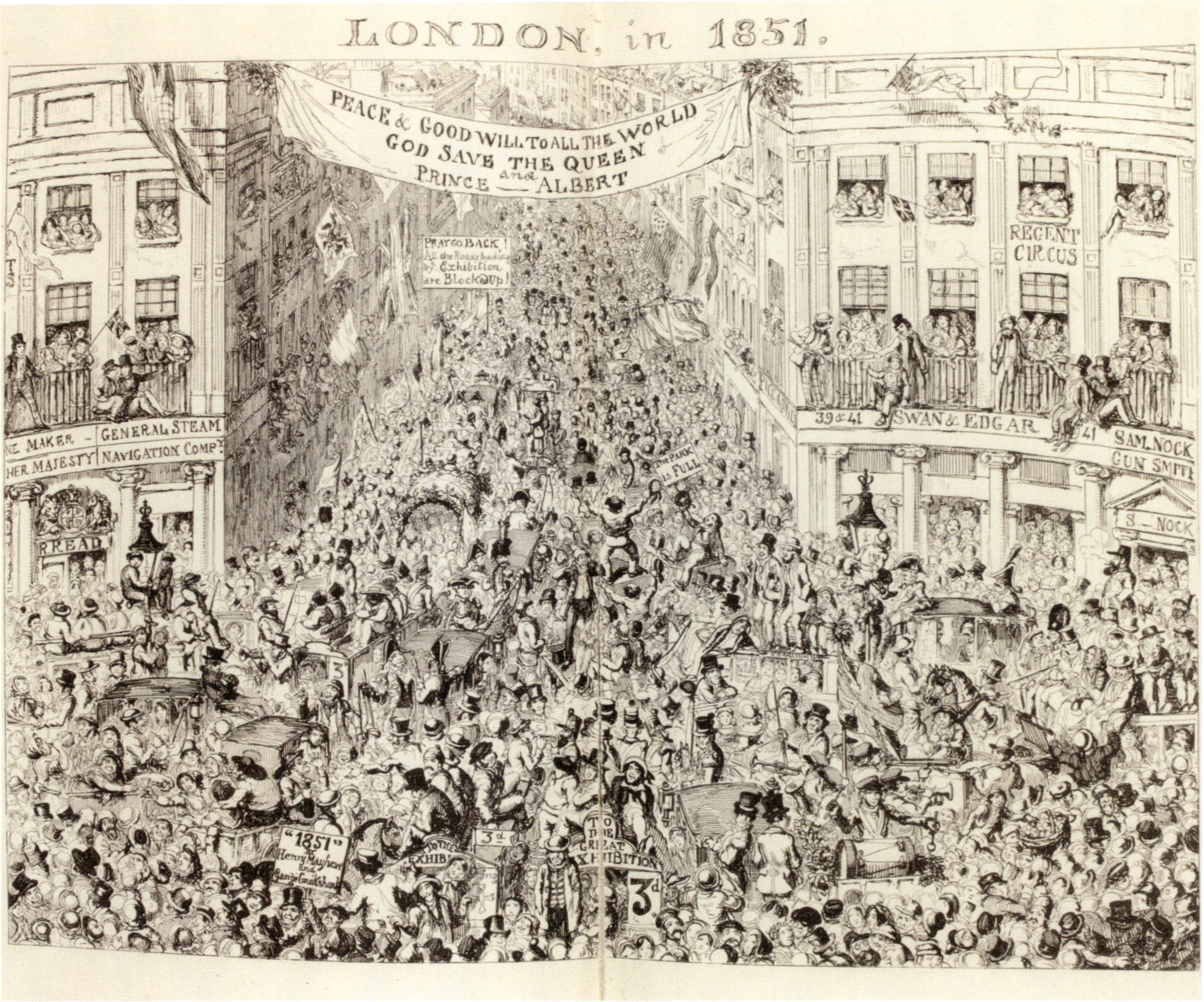

56

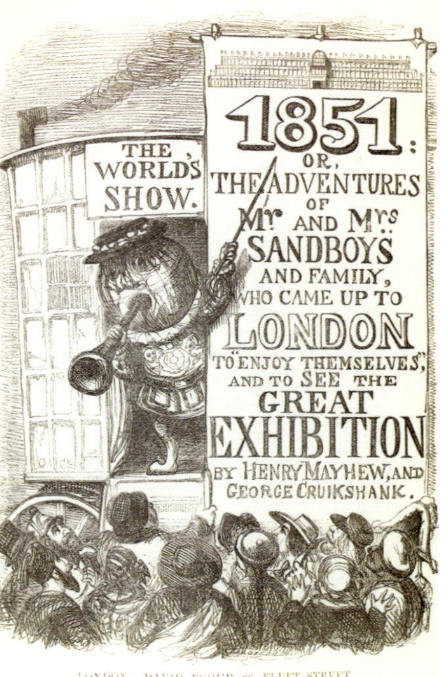

56. **George Cruikshank**
London, 1792 - London, 1878
and **Henry Mayhew**
London, 1812 - London, 1887
The World's Show. 1851: or, The Adventures of Mr and Mrs Sandboys and family who came up to London to "enjoy themselves", and to see the Great Exhibition, c. 1851
Book published by David Bogue, London, 23 x 15 cm
Victoria and Albert Museum, London

The Great Exhibition of 1851, held in London's Hyde Park, prompted George Cruikshank to embark upon a book illustration project, similar to the comic narratives he had been producing over the previous two decades, notably with Charles Dickens. The present narrative, made in partnership with the journalist Henry Mayhew, concerned a family from Cumberland who travel to London to visit the Great Exhibition and was entitled *1851: or, The Adventures of Mr and Mrs Sandboys*. In the present illustration the Sandboys family are swept up in a traffic jam in Regent Circus, Oxford Street. Despite the vexations occasioned by modern urban congestion, the large banner overhead proclaims a positive message of national unity:

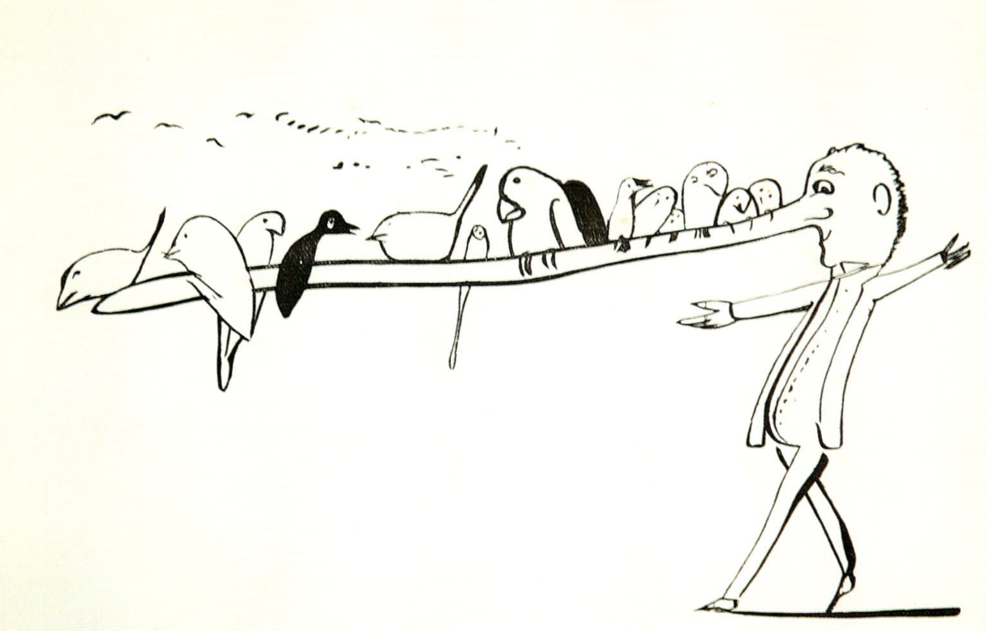

57

'Peace & Good Will to All the World / God Save the Queen and Prince Albert'. The Great Exhibition was a phenomenal success. However, Cruikshank's and Mayhew's venture proved to be a commercial failure. (MP)

57. **Edward Lear**
London, 1812 – San Remo, 1888
There was an Old Man on whose nose, most birds of the air could repose; But they all flew away at the closing of day, Which relieved that Old Man and his nose, from ***The Book of Nonsense***, 1846 (exhibited: Twenty-seventh edition, 1889)
Engraved by the Dalziel Brothers
Book published by Frederick Warne and Co., London and New York, 21.5 x 25.4 cm
Private Collection

Lear's vehement and exuberant line is best appreciated in the large-format editions: infantile, yet masterful, it has the marginal and anarchic character of the finest British humour. His freakish figures and accompanying rhymes began to be composed in 1845-46, when the thirty-three-year-old had returned to England after several years in Italy as a self-taught landscape painter. Always short of money, he had accepted an informal role as tutor to the children of the Earl of Derby – his initial audience. He soon returned to his landscapes, working with Holman Hunt in the early 1850s. Based in San Remo, Lear ventured all over southern Europe and the Near East; meanwhile, the fame of his *Nonsense* grew. In 1867 he published *The Owl and the Pussycat*; in 1870, *The Yonghy-Bonghy-Bo*. By 1886 – two years before Lear's death – Ruskin could write: 'I really don't know any author to whom I am half so grateful … I shall put him first of my hundred authors' (*Pall Mall Gazette*, 15 February 1886). (TH)

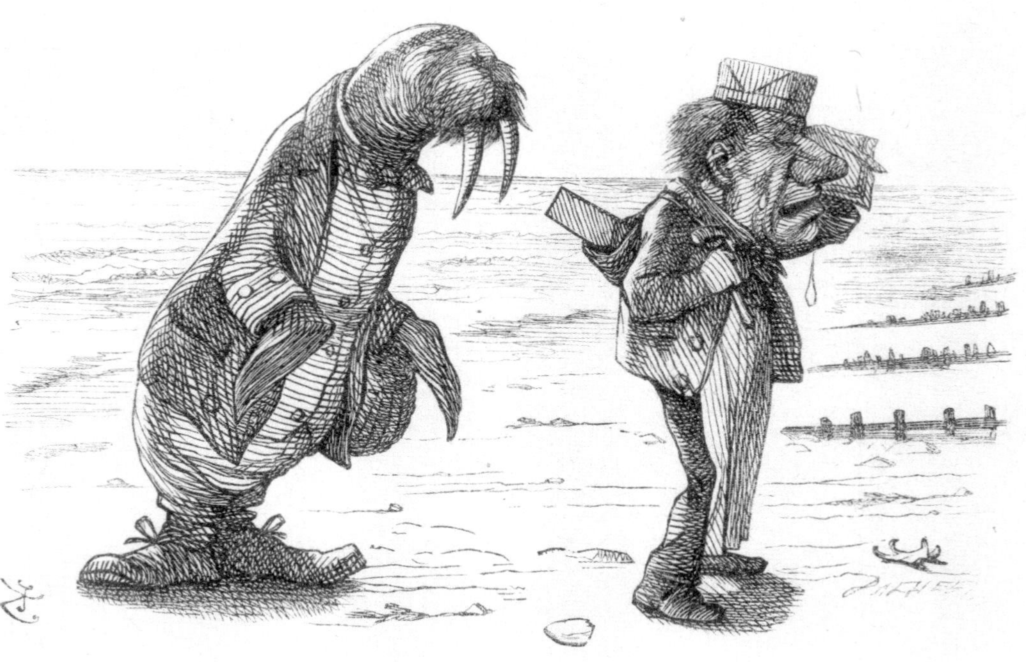

58

58. **John Tenniel**
London, 1820 - London, 1914
The Walrus and the Carpenter, illustration for
Through the Looking-Glass, and What Alice Found There
by Lewis Carroll, 1871
Engraving (by the Dalziel Brothers), proof, 7.6 x 10.8 cm
Bottom left: JT [monogram]
Bottom right: Dalziel
Victoria and Albert Museum, London

Tenniel was essentially self-taught, although (like Dyce and Ford Madox Brown) he came under the influence of the Nazarenes as a young man, visiting them in Munich and deriving from them a 'primitive' purity of line, well suited to reproduction by wood engraving. His *Alice* drawings also owe much to Grandville's comic animal imagery of the 1830s. In his second collaboration with Carroll, *Through the Looking Glass,* Tenniel no longer had the author's own illustrations to contend with (see cat. 274), and the book includes many of his most memorable inventions, including *Humpty Dumpty* and *Jabberwocky*, as well as those sentimental, tearful monsters, the Walrus and the Carpenter. They lure the 'little oysters' along the beach, and sermonize them:

> The time has come, the Walrus said,
> To talk of many things:
> Of shoes – and ships – and sealing-wax
> of cabbages – and kings –

By the end of the poem all the oysters have been eaten. Interpreted sometimes as a political parable (Tenniel was chief cartoonist for *Punch*), this nonsense masterpiece would eventually generate one of The Beatles' finest songs. (TH)

59. **Aubrey Beardsley**
Brighton, 1872 - Menton, 1898
Education sentimentale from ***The Yellow Book, An Illustrated Quarterly***
(volume 1, April 1894)
Half-tone and line-block reproductions
Book published by Elkin Mathews and John Lane, London, and Copeland and Day, Boston, 20.9 x 16.5 cm
Museum voor Schone Kunsten, Ghent

60. **Aubrey Beardsley**
Brighton, 1872 - Menton, 1898
Lysistrata Defending the Acropolis from ***The Lysistrata of Aristophanes; now first wholly translated into English and illustrated with eight full-page drawings by Aubrey Beardsley***, 1896
Line-block engraving
Bottom left: Aubrey/Beardsley
Book published by Leonard Smithers, London, 30.2 x 23.8 cm
Victoria and Albert Museum, London

During his short life, Aubrey Beardsley played a prominent role in the London art world of the 1890s. Apart from his graphic work, he was known for his refinement and witty remarks, which were a match for those of Oscar Wilde. He enjoyed shocking the prudish Victorians with his drawings, but he was frequently required to eliminate details that were considered too erotic before his work could be published. Beardsley served as art editor of the first four issues of *The Yellow Book* (1894), a periodical that sought to draw attention to the stylish new literature and art of the *fin de siècle*, which more often than not offered a challenge to established morality. Beardsley's illustrations for *The Yellow Book* attracted particular notice

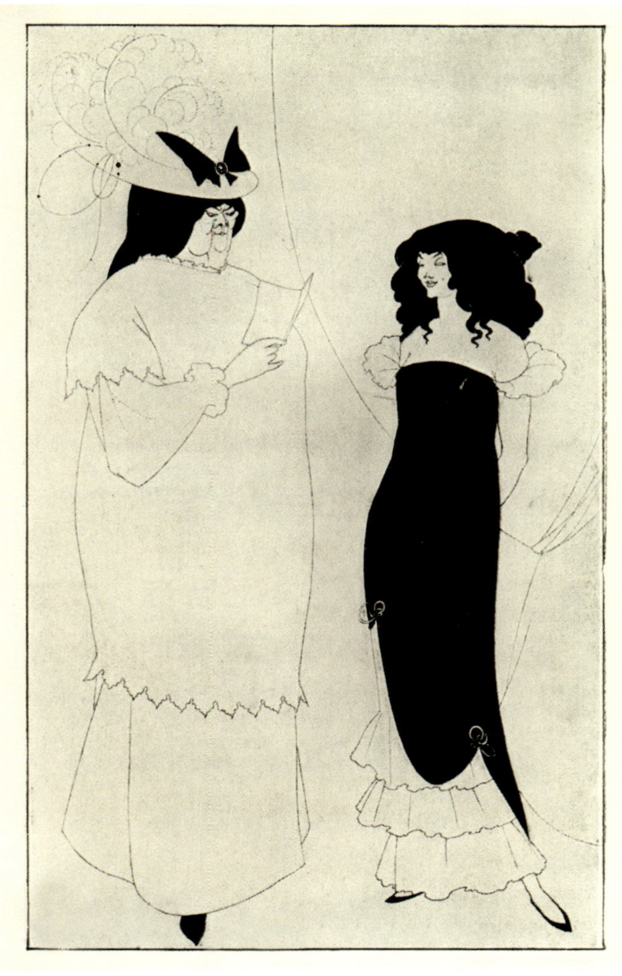

59

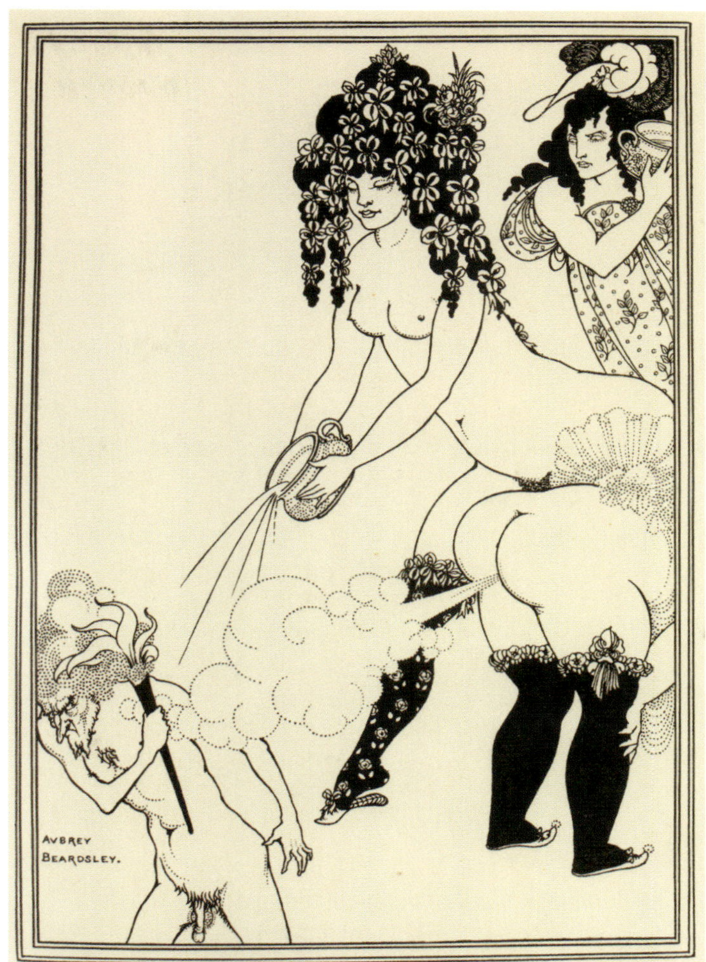

60

and in the eyes of the public it established him as one of the 'Decadents'. This successful period came to an end with the trial of Oscar Wilde in 1895. Publisher John Lane dismissed Beardsley because his name evoked too many associations with Wilde; after all, Beardsley had illustrated the English translation of Wilde's play *Salomé* in 1893 (see cat. 281).

The Lysistrata of Aristophanes was a private edition (with a very limited run) of Aristophanes' Greek comedy of manners with erotic illustrations by Beardsley. His satirical drawings were probably influenced by his study of light-hearted Greek vase paintings in the British Museum. According to Brian Reade, the impact of the Belgian artist Félicien Rops may also be present in a couple of illustrations (Reade 1987, note to pl. 466). These are the most frankly explicit drawings in Beardsley's oeuvre and could only be published uncensored in 1966. (NP)

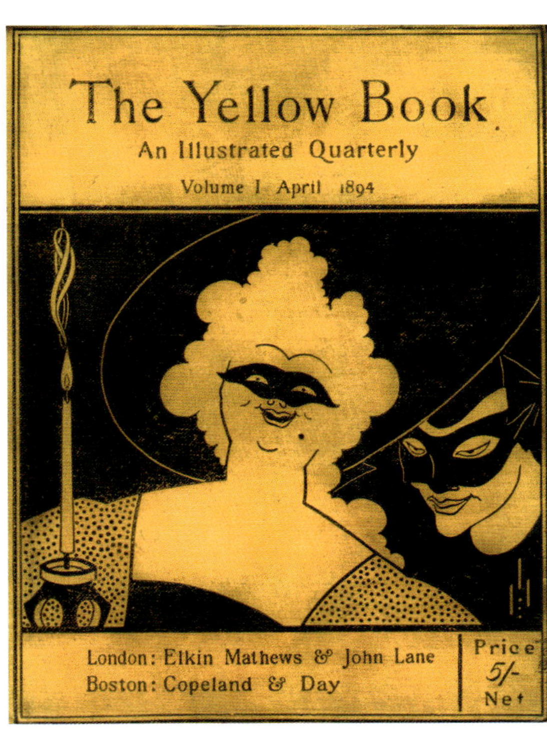

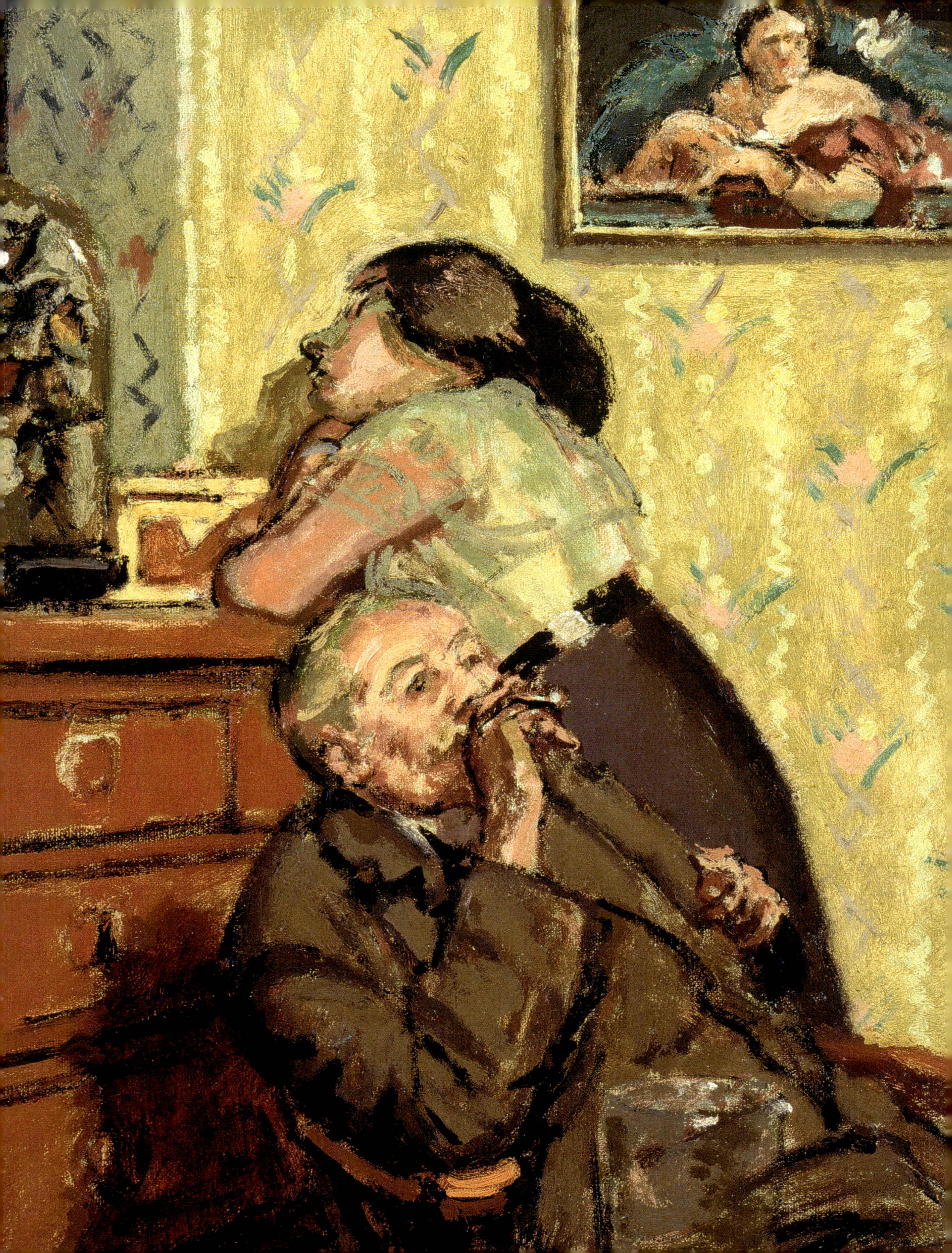

MODERN LIFE

WALTER SICKERT

Ennui, 1917-18

DAVID PETERS CORBETT

'Sickert is among the best of biographers,' wrote Virginia Woolf in 1934, placing these words in the mouth of one of the conversationalists she set talking in her short pamphlet on the artist published in that year.[1] His skills, we learn, are not those of the biographer as historian, having to do with 'those miserable impediments called facts' (p. 12). Rather they are those of the painter, and they communicate the painter's particular insight into the world: 'Sickert takes his brush, squeezes his tube, looks at the face; and then ...he paints - lies, paltriness, splendour, depravity, endurance, beauty' (p. 13). According to this speaker, Sickert is a champion, a monarch of 'the silent kingdom of paint', that place where the visual arts triumph in their grasp of reality over the 'impure medium' of words (p. 13).

But this vision of the artist as denizen of 'the silent land ... out of reach of the human voice' (p. 11) is not the only way of looking at Sickert. Another speaker in Woolf's conversation takes a different tack: 'To me Sickert always seems more of a novelist than a biographer,' says this person, 'he likes to set his characters in motion, to watch them in action' (p. 13). Once they are seen, 'it is difficult to look at them and not to invent a plot, to hear what they are saying: You remember the picture of the old publican, with his glass on the table before him and a cigar gone cold at his lips, looking out of his shrewd little pig's eyes at the intolerable waste of desolation in front of him? A fat woman lounges, her arm on a cheap yellow chest of drawers, behind him. It is all over with them, one feels. The accumulated weariness of innumerable days has discharged its burden on them. They are buried under an avalanche of rubbish. In the street beneath, the trams are squeaking, children are shrieking. Even now somebody is tapping his glass impatiently on the bar counter. She will have to bestir herself; to pull her heavy, indolent body together and go and serve him. The grimness of that situation lies in the fact that there is no crisis; dull minutes are mounting, old matches are accumulating and dirty glasses and dead cigars; still on they must go, up they must get' (pp. 13-14).

There can be no doubt that Woolf is thinking of *Ennui* here. She had seen the painting in this version at Sickert's 1933 exhibition held at Agnew's gallery. It is presented in this dramatized debate as a leading piece of evidence for the idea of Sickert as literary painter, as master of content and narrative meaning, a chronicler of 'the life of the lower middle class ... innkeepers, shopkeepers, music-hall actors and actresses' (p. 17), a 'realist' like those masters of words, 'Dickens ... Balzac, Gissing ... Arnold Bennett' (p. 17).

Such an opposition expresses something fundamental about Sickert's art. On the one hand, Sickert had a deep commitment to the technical possibilities and expressiveness of the visual arts. He was in love with painting (and, at certain moments, with etching) for its capacity to describe the world in a medium utterly different from language, and Wendy Baron has shown how preoccupied with the technical exigencies of painting Sickert was at the time he made the various versions of *Ennui*.[2] Certainly, the audacious use of perspective, which, although entirely accurate, produces the almost shocking scale of the beer glass on the table, reflects Sickert's refinement and sophistication in exploring the technical aspects of his art. This is Sickert at home in the 'silent kingdom', celebrating the capacity of the visual arts to penetrate the realities of the world around us and manifesting as he does so an almost dandyish preoccupation with his own sophisticated technique.[3]

Walter Sickert, *Ennui* (detail), cat. 62

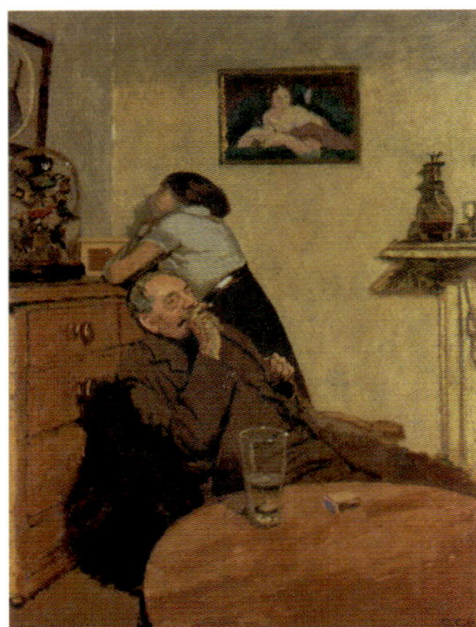

fig. 1
Walter Richard Sickert
Ennui, c. 1914
Oil on canvas, 152.4 x 112.4 cm
Tate, London

On the other hand, Baron is just as correct in viewing the painting as a strong example of what Woolf calls Sickert the 'novelist'. Baron suggests that *Ennui* can be seen as 'the climax of the long series of drawings and paintings done in 1912 and 1913 in which Sickert explored the compositional and psychological relationships of two figures, man and woman, in a domestic setting'.[4] Like *Jack Ashore* (1912-13; Pallant House Gallery, Chichester, fig. 2), or *Sunday Afternoon* (1912-13; The Beaverbrook Foundation, Fredericton, New Brunswick, fig. 3), it offers us a silent but telling moment in a relationship. The world of the 'lower middle class', as Woolf's speaker has it, is given a concrete realization through the depiction of an instant that provokes us to consider event and psychology, even to elaborate an explanatory plot, rather than to focus on the technique. A critic of the *Morning Post* summed up this interest in psychological reality as Sickert's 'brooding on the ironies and the satiated joys of unfortunate people', and it is what Woolf means by her image of the desolate accumulation of 'old matches ... and dirty glasses and cigars'.[5] It is an aspect of the painting that harks back to Sickert's many depictions of modern London from the 1880s onwards and that is central to his art throughout his life.

The Agnew's show had provoked Woolf to write a letter to Sickert praising his paintings.[6] Provoked in his turn by this renewed contact with an old acquaintance, the hard-up seventy-three-year-old Sickert replied asking her if she would do 'a serious service' for him by writing something on his work for public consumption. The emphasis he suggested is significant, dismissing 'all paint-box technical twaddle about art' as certain 'to bore everybody stiff', and recommending instead that she concentrate on 'the humour & drama you find in it'. 'You would be the first to do so,' he wrote, 'I have always been a literary painter, thank goodness, like all decent painters. Do be the first to say so.'[7] This was disingenuous of course, typical of the teasing, ironic Sickert, who, chameleon-like, could as easily espouse a role as denounce it. Sickert, who certainly felt that 'technical' matters were of paramount importance to the artist, is perhaps proposing merely what he thinks Woolf the novelist will find most congenial. We should not be surprised to find that Woolf was too curious and clear-sighted about the work to take this suggestion entirely at its face value. *Walter Sickert: A Conversation* sets the two elements of Sickert's art in tension with each other, and gives voices to them both.

Ennui is a complicated painting, then, but it is so for other reasons as well as these. The version presented here is one of five in total and, along with the painting now in Tate, London (fig. 1), one of only two that show the whole composition. There are, in addition, a number of graphic versions.[8] It is probably the latest of the series, being painted some four or five years after the subject was first broached; the Tate version having been exhibited at the New English Art Club as early as 1914. Woolf's discussion has made *Ennui* the best known of Sickert's paintings, to the frequent exasperation of his interpreters, who are disappointed that the differences between the various versions are smoothed away in the popular imagination. The differences are important. Sickert, preoccupied in 1913-14 with technical innovation and discovery and clearly in a mood to push these things hard in *Ennui*, produced at first what Baron rightly calls 'a perplexing picture'.[9] After two preparatory studies had been painted, the Tate version, Baron argues, 'represents a climatic achievement, in which Sickert expressed his current solution to all sorts of problems of handling

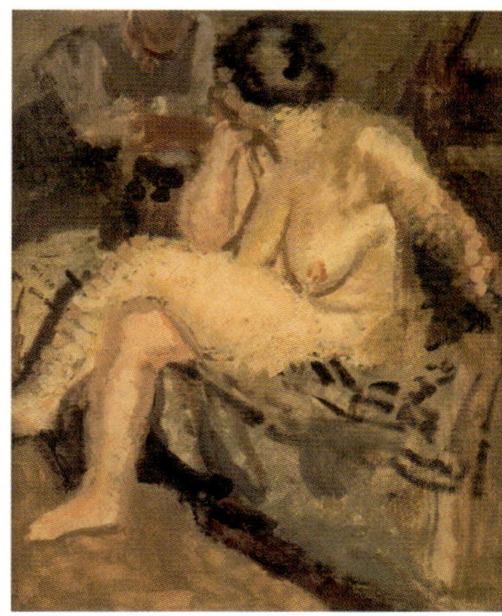

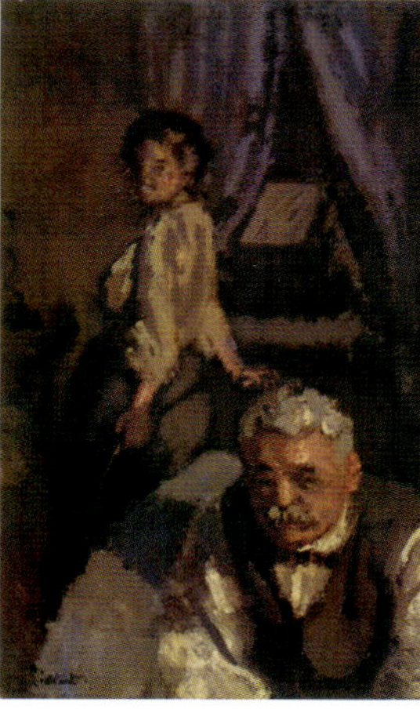

fig. 2
Walter Richard Sickert
Jack Ashore, 1912-1913
Oil on canvas, 36.8 x 29.8 cm
Pallant House Gallery, Chichester

fig. 3
Walter Richard Sickert
Sunday Afternoon, 1912-1913
Oil on canvas, 50.8 x 30.5 cm
Beaverbrook Foundation,
Fredericton, New Brunswick

and composition' that were then at the forefront of his mind.[10] Scaling up from his drawings, Sickert produced an almost mechanical surface in his quest to make a large painting that could successfully maintain the ratios between the objects depicted in smaller versions (the Tate *Ennui* measures 152 x 112 cm). Baron describes the result of this technical experiment as a mechanical desert of 'individual patches of uniform tone and colour stretched almost beyond endurance' and suggests that it may well have been Sickert's realization of this effect that led him to paint the Ashmolean version, which halves the scale (76 x 56 cm) and does away with the greater part of the smooth areas of colour by introducing the highly patterned wallpaper, tablecloth and blouse we see here.[11]

It is worth noting that this interest in scale was partly driven by Sickert's desire to maintain psychologically resonant spatial relationships in differently sized versions of the same composition. Baron concludes that *Ennui* succeeds in this, thus meshing together the abstrusely technical and the novelistically meaningful. Sickert's friend, the French painter Jacques-Emile Blanche, said of him that his characteristic gift was the capacity 'to suggest situations guessed at rather than seen', so that 'all relations with Sickert have an extraordinary, a mysterious character'.[12] Sickert himself asserted that '*mastery ... is avid of complications*', making that comment in a context that suggests a largely but not exclusively technical sense.[13] Complication for Sickert resides in the 'novelist's' description of relationship, emotion and 'the human voice', as well as in the artist's 'silent', powerful, currents of understanding. *Ennui* presents us with an image of both these aspects of his art. As Virginia Woolf put it, the painter takes up his brushes and tubes and describes all things for us, 'lies, paltriness, splendour, depravity, endurance, beauty'.

1. Woolf 1934, p. 12.
2. Baron 1973, pp. 142-44.
3. There is a very detailed composition drawing for *Ennui* in the Ashmolean collection, which gives a sense of the preparatory work Sickert undertook. See Hull, Glasgow & Plymouth 1977, pp. 43-44. See also the comments in Shone 1988, p. 110.
4. Baron 1973, p. 143.
5. 'Three Remarkable Works', *Morning Post*, 2 December 1914.
6. In 1934 Woolf places her conversation in the context of 'a show of Sickert's pictures at Agnew's' (p. 9), although Wendy Baron believes she is also drawing on her experience of viewing the version now in Tate Britain and in the Tate from 1924. See Baron 1973, p. 148, n. 51. For the letter, see Sturgis 2005, p. 590.
7. This letter from Sickert to Woolf is cited in Sturgis 2005, p. 590.
8. See, for reproductions and detailed discussion, Bromberg 2000, pp. 181-87.
9. Baron 1973, p. 142. The discussion on pp. 142-44 of Baron's book is an essential point of reference for understanding the painting.
10. Ibid., p. 143.
11. Ibid.
12. Blanche 1939, p. 117.
13. Cited in Corbett 2001, p. 13.

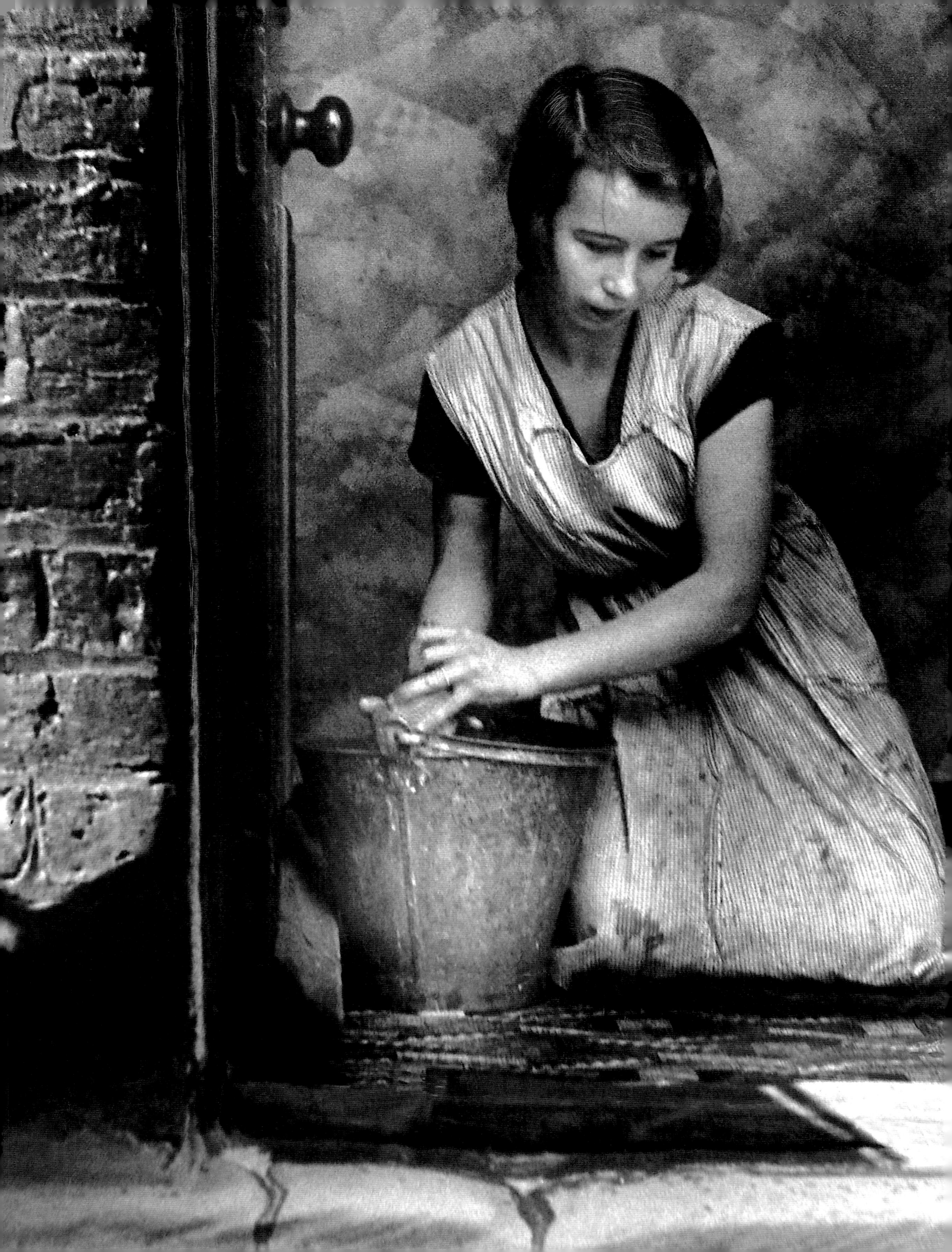

MODERN LIFE

BILL BRANDT

Young Housewife, Bethnal Green, 1937

MARK HAWORTH-BOOTH

The photograph introduces the viewer to a young working-class woman who is washing the front step of her house. The camera position is low, as if on a level with the housewife, and apparently close to her. We see a beautiful face, a side parting in the dark hair, a slim figure and arms, a wedding ring, a stained apron and a much-used galvanized iron bucket. Beyond the woman we can make out Art Deco wallpaper in the hall and patterned lino on the floor. It is an intimate, respectful portrait of a woman at work, defining her domestic territory in a street of typical working-class terraced housing. At the left edge of the photograph we see a fragment of an object and a shadow below it. Perhaps this fragment is part of the push-bar of a pram, to which the shadow also belongs in which case the housewife has put her baby outside to have an 'airing' while she works.

The first publication of this photograph appears to have been in the pages of *Lilliput* magazine in September 1941, with this caption: 'IF ONLY I COULD HAVE GONE ON THE STAGE'.[1] On the facing, right-hand, page, a second Brandt photograph was printed. This one, in which a blonde young ballet-dancer in a black slip and leg warmers kneels on a wooden floor, is captioned: 'HOUSEWORK WOULD BE A REST CURE COMPARED WITH THIS'. Also, in smaller type: 'Tatiana Riabouchbinska from the Russian Ballet'. The young women are compared, contrasted, linked and separated by the layout and the captions. Such juxtapositions were a favourite editorial ploy of the editor of *Lilliput*, Stefan Lorant. Lorant had pioneered the new art of photographic picture-editing at the *Münchner Illustrierte Presse* from 1928. Following the Nazi takeover, he left Germany for England in 1933, where he founded and edited *Weekly Illustrated*. Brandt visited Lorant at the magazine soon after it began publication in 1934, and he returned in 1936 for a stay of several weeks to study the way the magazine was put together.[2] Lorant went on to found the illustrated pocket magazine *Lilliput* in 1937. Brandt himself might have proposed the pairing of his photographs of the kneeling young women to the editors (Lorant had emigrated to the USA in 1940 and had been replaced by Tom Hopkinson, assisted by Kaye Webb). The captions unite the women, across the gutter of the magazine, in the physical activity of labour and the mental activity of day-dreaming. The contrast is made more poignant by the beauty of the housewife.

In the 1930s the documentary impulse touched many media – photography and film, but also literary reporting. The greatest English exponent of the latter was George Orwell, most notably, perhaps, in *The Road to Wigan Pier* (1937). It is curious that Orwell's book was published in the year of Brandt's photograph. Brandt was naturally very well aware of Orwell's book. We spoke of it in our conversations between 1974 and 1983, and I recall Brandt's critical view of the photographs used to illustrate *The Road to Wigan Pier* – which he attributed disdainfully to a 'Fleet Street photographer' or photographers. One of the photographs shows a woman cleaning the area around the coal-hole beside her front door. The kneeling woman is seen through railings and is looking away from the camera. There is none of the visual clarity and psychological connection of Brandt's version of the subject. Perhaps he was consciously improving upon the cruder rendition of the subject reproduced in Orwell's book. *The Road to Wigan Pier* was published in March 1937 and Brandt took *Young Housewife, Bethnal Green* in September that year: the dating is unusually precise for reasons that will shortly appear. The photographs in Orwell's book were selected by the

Bill Brandt, ***Young Housewife, Bethnal Green*** (detail), cat. 84

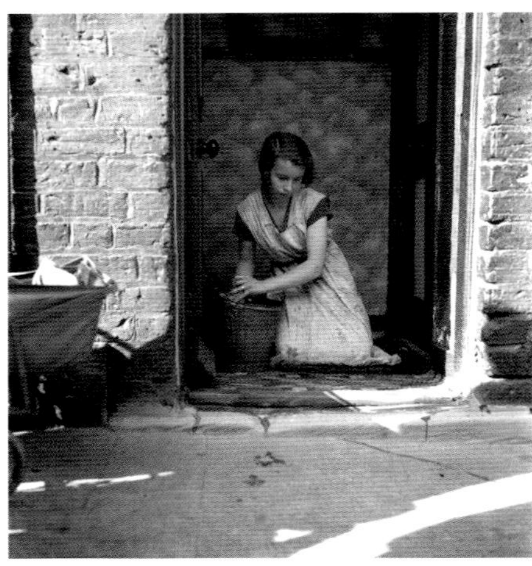

fig. 1
Bill Brandt
Young Housewife, Bethnal Green, 1937
Gelatin silver print (full frame)
Bill Brandt Archive, London

publisher, Victor Gollancz, who had turned down Brandt's first book, *The English at Home* (1934), so possibly Brandt felt a certain personal animus against Gollancz and his expertise in picture selection.

The second publication of *Young Housewife, Bethnal Green* appears to be in Brandt's third book, *Camera in London*, published by Focal Press in London and New York in 1948. It was reproduced on page 48 as 'East End morning', contrasted with 'Mayfair morning' on the facing page, which shows a smartly dressed domestic servant polishing tall sash windows in a brightly illuminated interior. Brandt's technical notes at the back of the book included a column headed 'Lighting Conditions': there he provided the information that *Young Housewife, Bethnal Green* was photographed on a 'Morning in September' (thus six months after the appearance of Orwell's book). The cropping is different from that in *Lilliput*: now the housewife is seen from a greater distance, with more of the pavement, of the pram at the left, and more of a piece of furniture, a hall-stand perhaps, at the right, and more of the wallpaper visible above the woman's head. The scale of the housewife is diminished by the inclusion of more of her surroundings, with a loss of psychological connection. However, the reason for Brandt's re-cropping of the image can be deduced: he wished to give the figure a similar scale to the maid in the facing photograph, the better to contrast and compare their roles. This is the same cropping strategy as we saw in the pages of *Lilliput*.

Edward Steichen, director of the Department of Photography at The Museum of Modern Art, New York, exhibited Brandt's photographs in 1948. Brandt was part of a four-person show, alongside Lisette Model, Ted Croner and Harry Callahan. 'East end [sic] of London' – the photograph we are discussing – was among the twelve Brandt photographs selected by Steichen for the exhibition. Steichen commented in the press release that Brandt 'translates into the modern idiom of the camera the atmosphere and mood of person, moment and place, often with nostalgic suggestions of other periods and influences. He creates an emotional impression through the atmosphere within the photograph...'[13] These remarks are derived from Brandt's own declaration in *Camera in London*, which Steichen quoted in the exhibition checklist: 'When I have seen or sensed – I do not know which it is – the atmosphere of my subject, I try to convey that atmosphere by intensifying the elements that compose it...' The word 'atmosphere' – German *Stimmung* – refers to the signature tonality of Brandt's street photography, in which his subjects emerge mysteriously from a kind of twilight, generally created by Brandt during his long hours of printing. Interestingly, the cropping of *Young Housewife, Bethnal Green* in the exhibition print Brandt sent to MoMA differs from the book plate: the version in the exhibition print is very close to the one in *British Vision* – Brandt's final version of the photograph.

The next important publication of *Young Housewife, Bethnal Green* occurred in Steichen's celebrated exhibition *The Family of Man* (1955). The composition is again very close to the final version. The chief differences are these: *The Family of Man* version crops away the fold of the housewife's striped overall at the right – and it is a lighter, brighter, less mysterious rendering of the subject. Brandt's 1948 exhibition print and all later versions are darker, as if the young housewife is emerging from apparent dusk. It is known that Steichen rejected Brandt's first offering of prints for *The Family of Man*. Perhaps he persuaded Brandt to send lighter prints. The plate is captioned simply 'England – Bill Brandt'. It appeared at the base of a page which illustrated seven photographs of women engaged in various kinds of domestic labour. Full page, opposite, Steichen illustrated an Elliot Erwitt photograph of a street filled with lines of washing. This juxtaposition appears to have left a trace on later presentations of Brandt's photograph.

Young Housewife, Bethnal Green appeared in its now classic form in Brandt's great summing-up of his life work, *Shadow of Light* (1966). Cyril Connolly, who had published Brandt's wartime studies of London by night in his magazine *Horizon*, wrote of the photograph in his elegant introduction to the book. He referred to it with this phrase: 'the beauty of some East End faces'.[4] Perhaps influenced by the layout in *The Family of Man*, with the endless lines of washing, Brandt inflected the photograph in this and the next edition of *Shadow of Light* (1976) by facing it with a photograph of endlessly repeated suburban houses. This juxtaposition suggests that the Bethnal Green housewife is occupied less in an assertion of domestic pride than in a routine of grim and unending toil. However, the crushing uniformity of the houses is at least partially relieved by a line of freshly laundered clothes, like unexpected notes of music, in the midst of the gloom.

The history of this photograph shows that Brandt cropped it differently for different magazine contexts, although he chose its preferred appearance as an exhibition print from at least 1948 onwards. It also shows how the meaning of the photograph was inflected by its companion photographs in publications and exhibitions.

There is another twist to this tale of one photograph. In 2004 Christie's included a version of *Young Housewife, Bethnal Green* in a sale in London on 19 May. It was lot 171, one of three Brandt photographs with the provenance 'The Property of a Descendant of A.L. Lloyd'. From 1939 onwards, A.L. ('Bert') Lloyd worked as a journalist at *Picture Post* magazine, to which Brandt was a prolific contributor during the Second World War. The photograph of the Bethnal Green housewife is virtually the same as the one reproduced in *Camera in London*. However, it is titled on the reverse, in what looks like Brandt's hand, with one word: Jarrow. This print is now in the Wilson Photography Centre, London. An identical print is with the Edwynn Houk Gallery, New York. It too is titled 'Jarrow' on the reverse (in a hand identified by the gallery as Brandt's). It was not unknown for Brandt to use the same photograph under quite different titles. However, Vince Rea, a local historian in Jarrow, asserted unequivocally in a letter to the present writer in October 2006: 'This photo is not Jarrow. Everything about it seems to be the East End of London. [The housewife] is not a Geordie woman, the wood frame of the door is not of this area, the step and the short pavement are not Tyneside.' For the moment, the inscription 'Jarrow' remains a mystery.

Thanks to the kind courtesy of John-Paul Kernot, director of the Bill Brandt Archive, we can look at the scene as captured on Brandt's original Rolleiflex negative (fig. 1). The full frame shows that Brandt was several paces away from the young woman – very respectfully keeping his distance from her. This means that the full frame includes more of the pavement, the pram and the space above the woman's head. The parallax seen in the converging verticals of the door frame shows that Brandt angled his camera downwards. By cropping the photograph so dramatically, Brandt managed not only to bring the subject into psychological connection with the viewer but to disguise any sense that the viewer is looking down (optically and psychologically) on the subject: this was very typical not only of Brandt's skill as a photographer and of his broad political sympathies, but also of his delicacy of feeling and his humanity.

1. *Lilliput* 9, no. 3 (Sept. 1941), p. 220.
2. Delany 2004, pp. 99-100, 120-21.
3. My warm thanks are due to Peter Galassi, Chief Curator of Photography at The Museum of Modern Art, and to Sarah Hermanson Meister, Associate Curator, Department of Photography, for very kindly copying and making available to me the Brandt documents in their exhibition files.
4. Brandt 1966, p. 7.

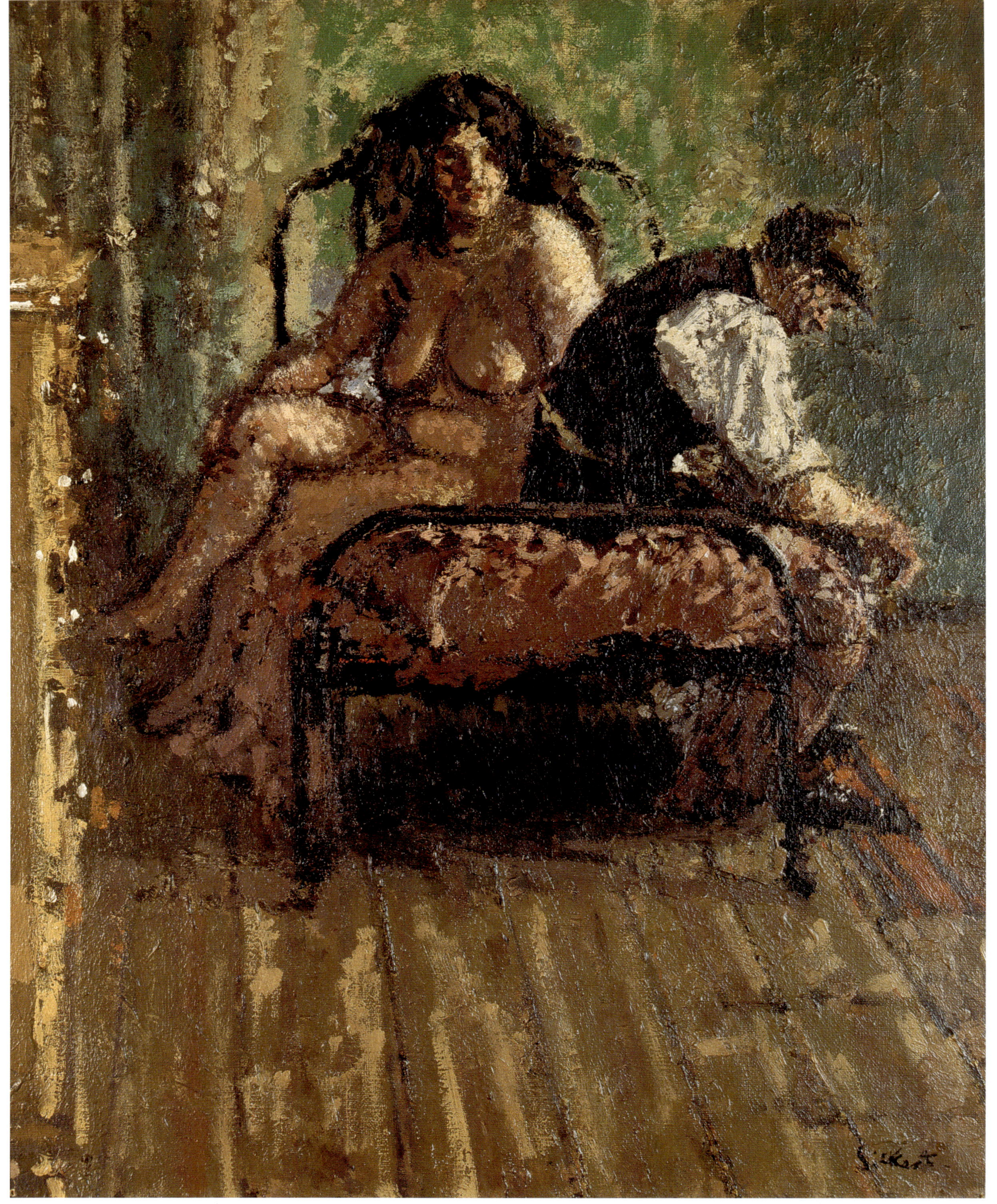

61

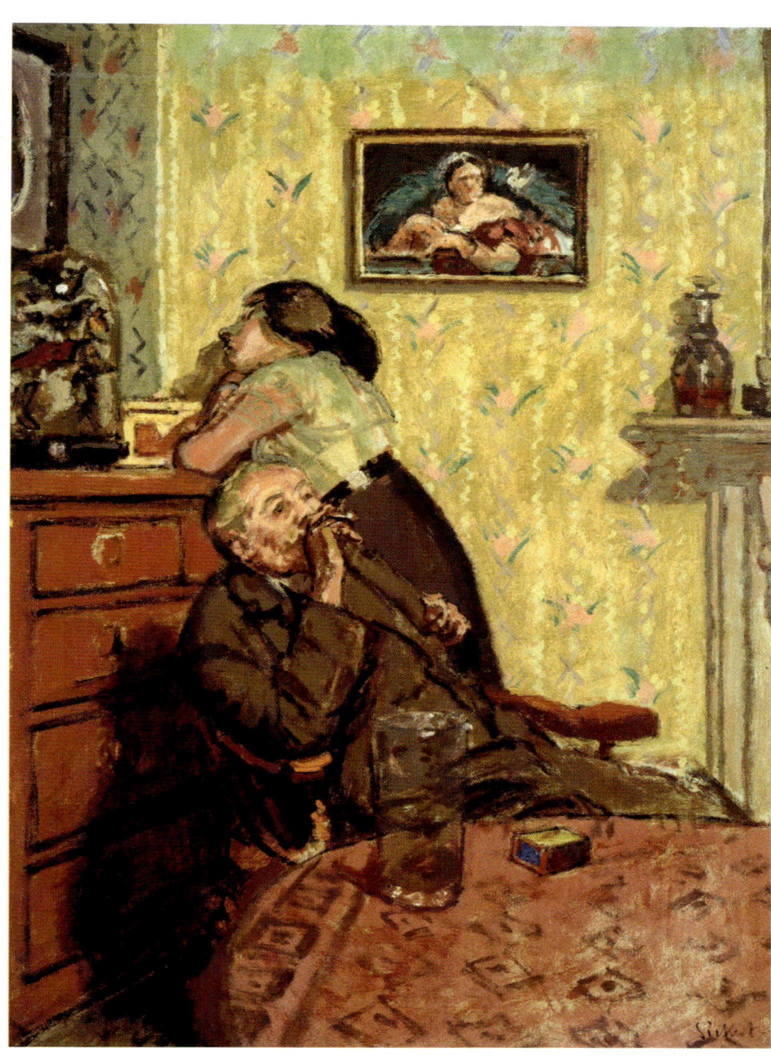

62

61. **Walter Richard Sickert**
Munich, 1860 - Bathampton, Somerset, 1942
Dawn, Camden Town, c. 1909
Oil on canvas, 51 x 40 cm
Bottom right: Sickert
The Earl and Countess of Harewood
and the Trustees of the Harewood House Trust

Sickert often used cleverly evocative or enigmatic titles to lend an added dimension of interpretation to the picture itself. He also commonly changed titles; when it was first exhibited in 1912 this picture was originally called, somewhat improbably, 'Summer in Naples'. Its combination of twin figures in a bedroom relates it closely to Sickert's sequence of 'Camden Town Murder' pictures, and its present title, given by the artist in the 1930s confirms this link. Sickert deliberately intended to provoke; exaggerating the woman's nudity by showing her with a fully dressed male companion would have scandalized an Edwardian audience, and so too would the indication from the setting in a grimy bedroom that this was a scene of a prostitute and her client. The newspaper reviews in 1912 condemned it, highlighting the physical dirtiness of the scene as an analogy of its moral degradation, although the *Daily Telegraph* complimented Sickert on the picture's 'masterly, sordid, unemotional study'. (RU)

62. **Walter Richard Sickert**
Munich, 1860 - Bathampton, Somerset, 1942
Ennui, 1917-18
Oil on canvas, 76 x 56 cm
Bottom right: Sickert.
Ashmolean Museum, Oxford

Himself an ex-actor, Walter Sickert liked to arrange the figures in his pictures like people on a stage. In *Ennui* the couple silently stares into space, utterly stifled by the boredom of their marriage. There are no words left for them to say to each other. Witnessing such private moments in these paintings forces the viewer into the role of voyeur, searching for meaning or reflections of their own lives. Sickert's new hunger for naturalism might be linked to a more widespread enthusiasm for the plays of August Strindberg when they were shown for the first time in London. Instead of simple action and dialogue, Strindberg utilized silence, stillness and atmosphere to create dramatic tension. Along with other painters such as Gwen John and William Orpen, Sickert realized the potential to adapt this approach for his art. (RU)

See essay pp. 127-29.

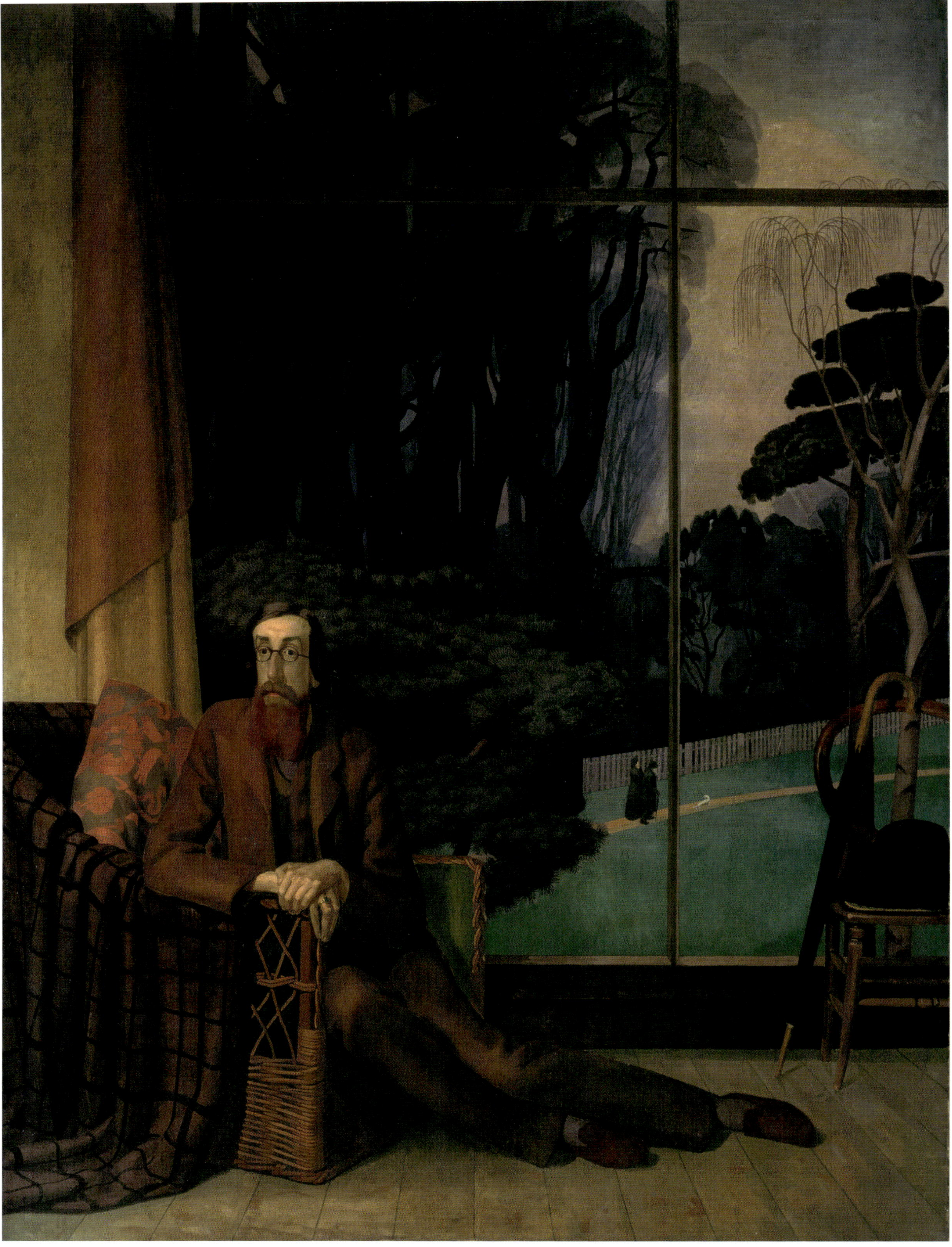

63. **Henry Lamb**
Adelaide, Australia, 1883 - London, 1960
Lytton Strachey, 1914
Oil on canvas, 244.5 x 178.4 cm
Tate, London, Presented by the Trustees of the Chantrey Bequest 1957

Giles Lytton Strachey was a critic and biographer, who established an immediate reputation when his book *Eminent Victorians* was published in 1918. He was one of the members of the Bloomsbury Group, which included the writer Virginia Woolf, the painters Vanessa Bell and Duncan Grant, and the painter and critic Roger Fry. Henry Lamb painted a small portrait of Strachey in his studio in the Vale of Health Hotel, Hampstead, in 1912, and then subsequently painted this grander, much larger version. Strachey once said that he was unable to lift a match before breakfast, and Lamb's portrait shows him in a typically languid pose, his eyebrows raised in perpetual question. Lamb combines empathy and respect for the somewhat camp Strachey with a suppressed irony and a sense that he is an exotic specimen cut off from the Rousseau-like landscape behind him. Such ambivalence arose from the artist's complicated relationship with the sitter. Close friends, Strachey constantly and publicly voiced his sexual longing for Lamb, who repeatedly rebuffed him. (RU)

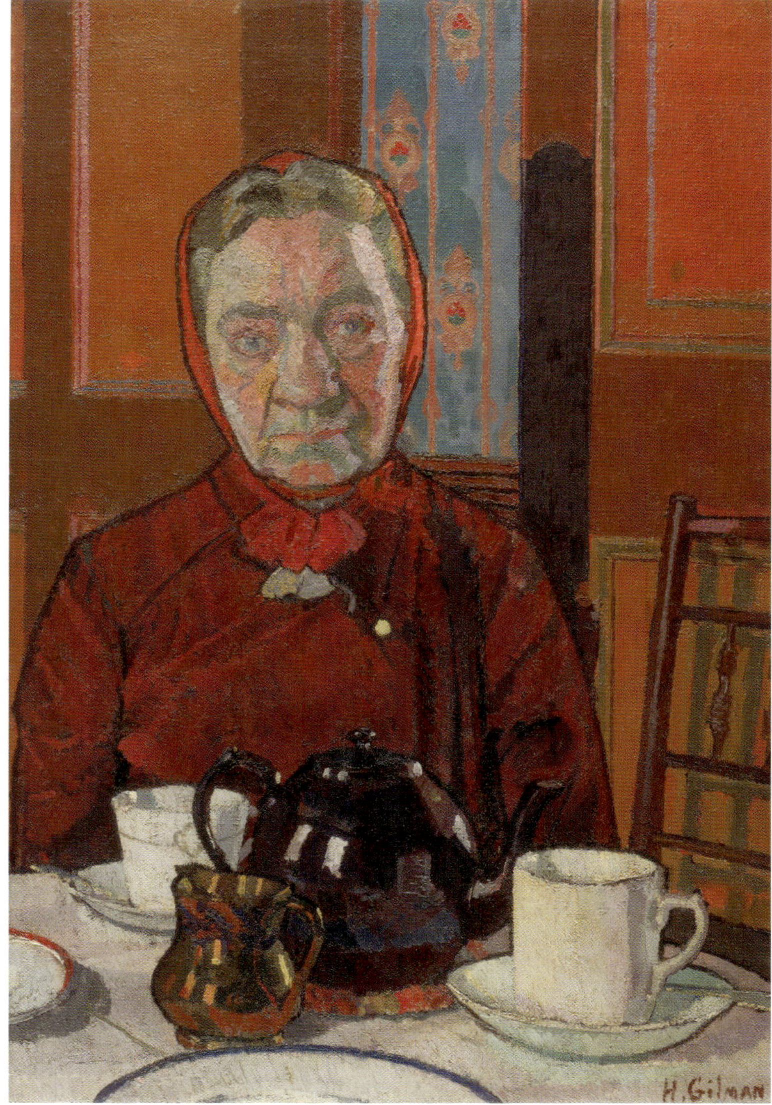

64

64. **Harold Gilman**
Rode, Somerset, 1876 - London, 1919
Mrs Mounter, 1916-17
Oil on canvas, 91.8 x 61.5 cm
Bottom right: H. Gilman
National Museums Liverpool, Walker Art Gallery

Gilman uses a psychologically sophisticated composition to draw us into Mrs Mounter's space. The foreground consists only of the tea table, cutting the nearest plate in half, and it is as if we are sitting opposite her. She is placed against wooden doors, so that the lack of background recession further reinforces this personal proximity. Mrs Mounter looks straight at us, her face enigmatic, neither questioning nor emotive, but her eyes show fierce intensity. It is a study of a face that has aged, its deep lines and sags testifying to a life of work and probable hardship. This is a working-class London woman, elderly, but still strong and full of native character. Gilman had always painted those around him, mostly his family, and sometimes servants. But here there seems to be a more naturalist and deliberate commemoration or investigation of a social type. Gilman's sympathy with ordinary people found expression in socialist beliefs, which reputedly irritated Sickert on occasion. Gilman offers something more intimate and direct with Mrs Mounter; this is someone with whom he is on close terms. There are two cups on the table, and it is clear that Mrs Mounter has come to join him for breakfast in his rooms. Her exact status as housekeeper, cleaner or landlady at Maple Street remains unclear, but it is evident the picture records two people from very different social backgrounds and classes meeting as equals. Painted at the height of the submarine blockade in the First World War, food supplies were extremely short. It is against this background of dwindling food that Mrs Mounter at the breakfast table might partly be viewed. It makes the sharing of breakfast a poignant connection between the artist and his landlady. Tea in particular was hard to come by. Although never rationed, it was extremely difficult to obtain because it was imported from India and the Far East. (RU)

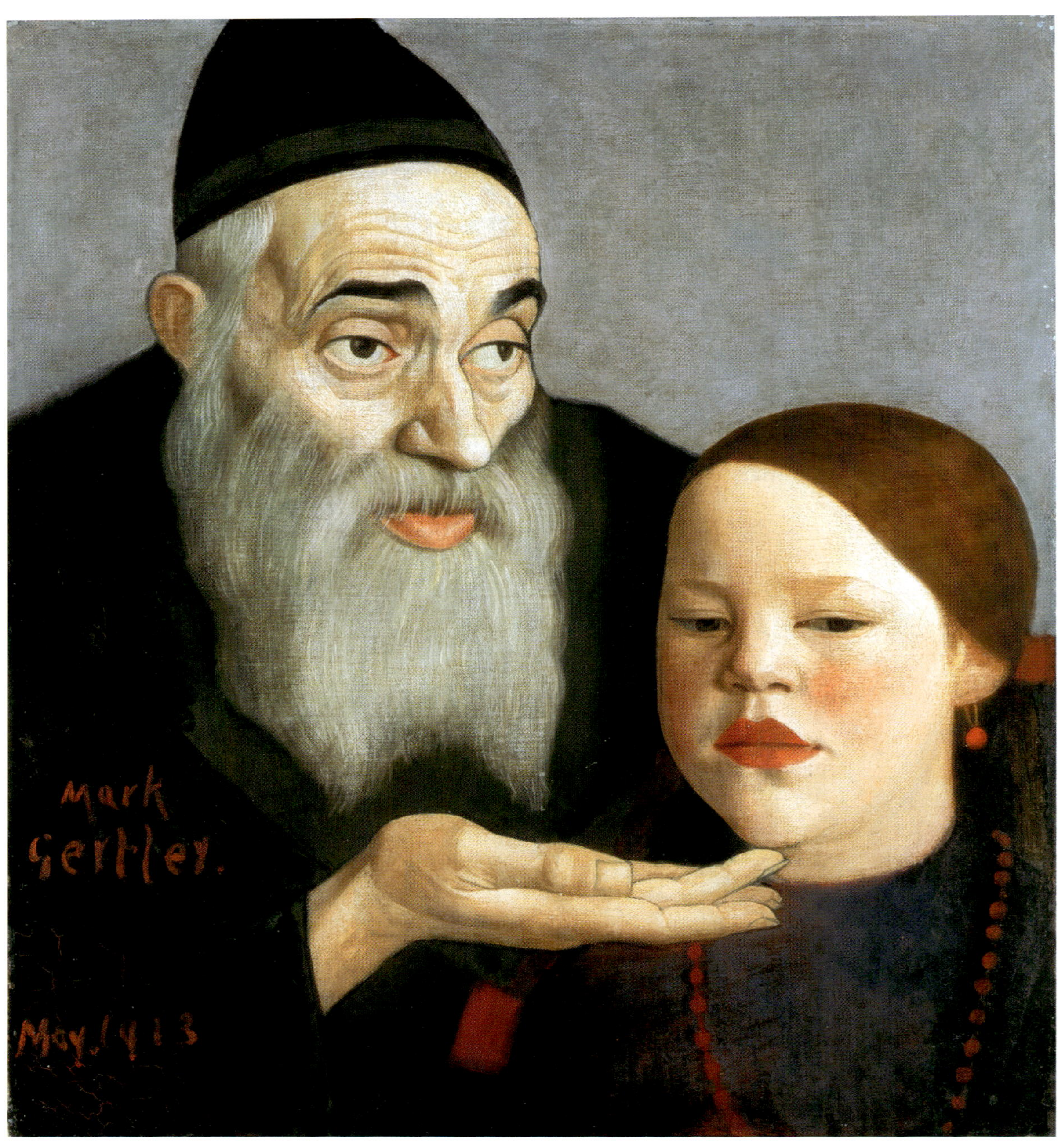

65

65. **Mark Gertler**
London, 1891 - London, 1939
The Rabbi and his Grandchild, 1913
Oil on canvas, 50.8 x 45.9 cm
Bottom left: Mark / Gertler. / May. 1913
Southampton City Art Gallery

The example of the Camden Town Group encouraged a new generation of younger artists to find inspiration in modern, urban life. The son of Jewish immigrants, Mark Gertler was born and raised in London's East End and described himself as 'a child of the ghetto'. His early work focused on intimate portraits and studies of life within the community in which he had grown up and combines the insight of familiarity with the objectivity of a detached observer. The two sitters for this painting were both local Spitalfields residents, whom Gertler sketched separately over the course of many sittings. He suddenly seems to have conceived the idea of combining them as a double portrait contrasting the elderly man's 'very old, pale and wrinkled head near that healthy, fresh, young face of my little girl'. He exhibited the painting at the summer exhibition of the New English Art Club, where his modernist stylization of facial features provoked consternation amongst some of the viewers. A rich Jewish woman wrote a courteous letter to him suggesting he consult an optometrist to address his evident sight problems. (NM)

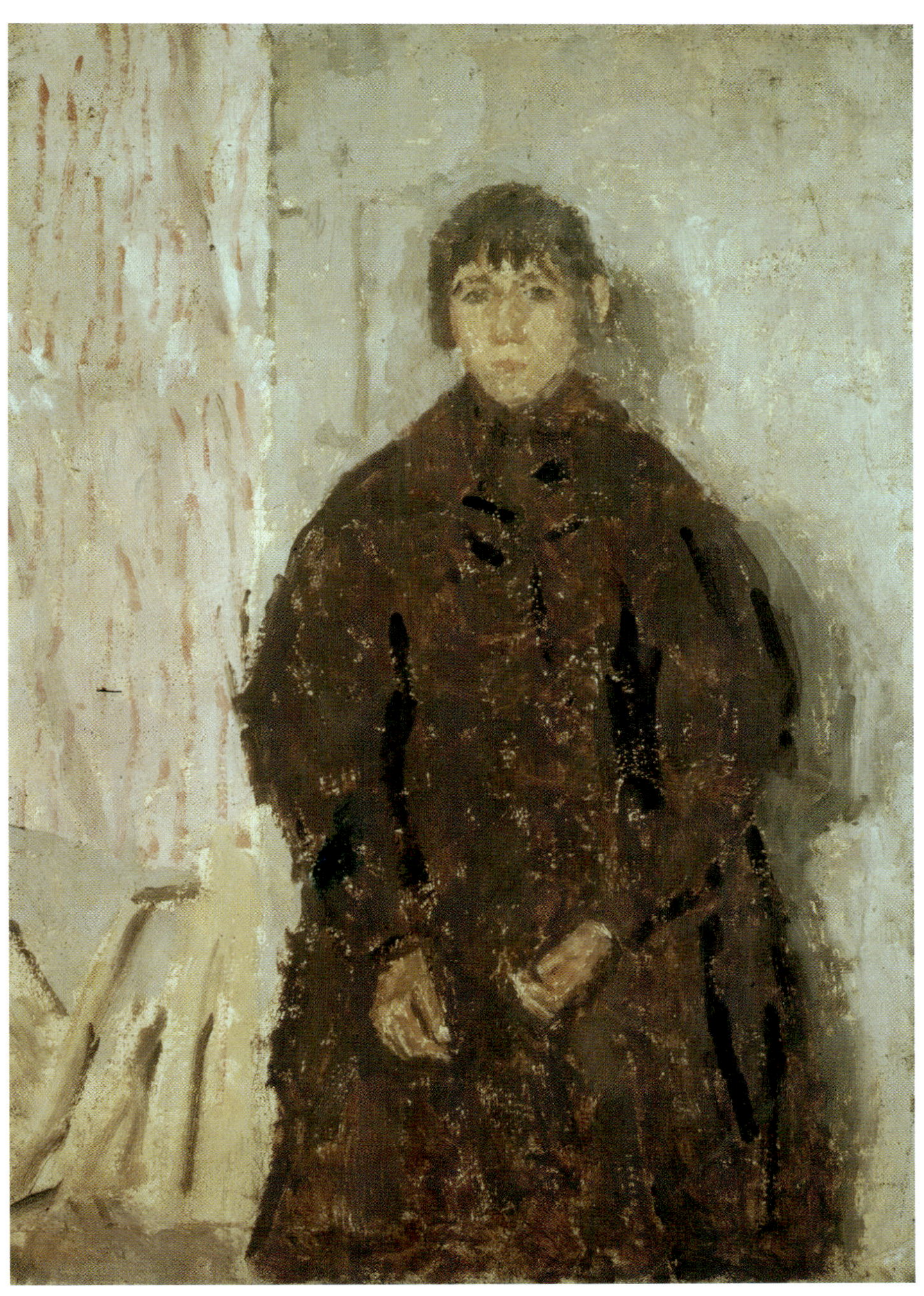

66

66. **Gwen John**
Haverfordwest, Pembrokeshire, 1876 – Dieppe, 1939
Girl in Mulberry Dress, c. 1923-24
Oil on canvas, mounted on panel, 54 x 37.5 cm
Southampton City Art Gallery

A woman in a career still largely dominated by men – including her more worldly brother Augustus – Gwen John trained at the Slade School of Art in London before settling in 1904 in Paris, where she initially supported herself by working as a model. She is the figure in Rodin's unfinished monument to Whistler. Her relationship with Rodin, as sometime lover and confidante, was of central importance to her. She was to spend the rest of her life in Paris, in self-imposed seclusion, though she exhibited on both sides of the Channel. The portrait shown here is one of nine studies of an unidentified sitter. Its harmonious, subdued colouring, short foreground and the model's direct gaze create a deeply intense atmosphere. By placing the figure against the wall, and allowing no foreground for the composition, John forces the figure forward to capture our attention. Narrative or commentary has been wholly abandoned, to be replaced by a subtle invocation of mood or atmosphere. Gwen John's contemplative studies of lone women in the calm surroundings of their home suggest intimacy and peace, but also a simultaneous sadness. (RU)

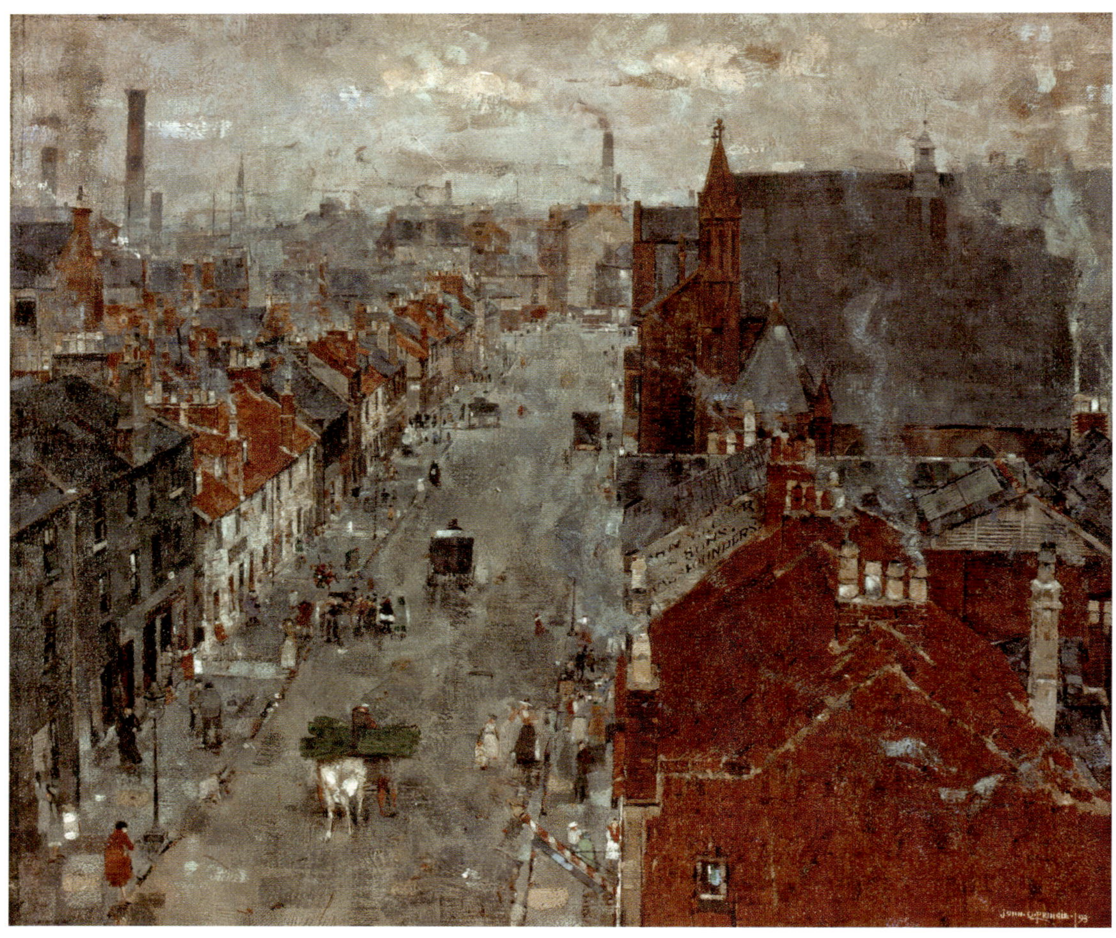

67

67. **John Quinton Pringle**
Glasgow, 1865 - East Kilbride, South Lanarkshire, 1925
Muslin Street, Bridgeton, 1895-96
Oil on canvas, 35.9 x 41.2 cm
Bottom right: John. Q. Pringle. / 93 [inaccurate date, added in 1923]
City of Edinburgh Museums and Galleries

J.Q. Pringle was an optician by trade and a painter by vocation. After apprenticeship he went into business on his own, running an opticians and general repairs shop near Glasgow Cross from 1896 until ill health forced him into retirement in 1923. The shop was under a railway bridge and consequently dark and lit by gas jets. After hours he would use it as a studio. Apparently he never felt any conflict between his art and his business. He did not marry and he never took on any employees. His interest in painting is said to have begun when his father was station-master in the early 1870s at Langbank on the Glasgow to Greenock railway line, a favourite place for local artists. In 1885, with an evening school bursary, he began attending classes at the Glasgow School of Art. He was to continue these classes for ten years. In 1891 he won a gold medal in the 'South Kensington National Competition for Life Drawing'. Among his fellow students at the art school was the architect and designer Charles Rennie Mackintosh, and it is thought that Mackintosh might have been responsible for Pringle exhibiting in the XV Secession in Vienna in 1902 (Pringle exhibited seldom in his life, and his complete oeuvre is not much more than 100 works). Both were encouraged by the progressive head of the Glasgow art school, Francis H. Newbury. Newbury bought work and commissioned miniatures of his children (Pringle made a number of exquisite miniatures in which one is tempted to see something of the optician). In 1914 Pringle exhibited in the Whitechapel Art Gallery in London in the exhibition 'Twentieth Century Art: A Review of Modern Movements'. *Muslin Street, Bridgeton* was painted from the roof of his brother's house. There are few precedents for a city view such as this. Other Glasgow artists left the city to find their motifs. The painting might be said to look forward to the townscapes of the Camden Town Group in London some years later. It was apparently Pringle's favourite amongst his works. He refused to sell it and in 1922 it became the first of his paintings to enter a public collection. (AD)

68. **Robert Polhill Bevan**
Hove, Sussex, 1865 – London, 1925
Cab Yard, Night, c. 1910
Oil on canvas, 63.5 x 69.7 cm
Bottom right: Robert Bevan
Royal Pavilion, Libraries and Museum, Brighton and Hove

Bevan was one of the members of the Camden Town Group. Sickert advised him to paint what interested him in London, and Bevan, who was a lifelong horseman, began a series of pictures portraying the working horses of the metropolis. An important sequence showed cab horses, at that moment a dying trade, as they were within a very short time superseded by motor taxis. The present picture was the first work by Bevan to enter a public collection: it was bought by Brighton Art Gallery in 1913. A vibrating harmony of colours, Bevan's picture is emphatically a scene from working-class life and a commemoration of a working horse rather than the sleek thoroughbred of traditional equestrian painting. Bevan made studies for the painting at the cab yard in Ormonde Terrace, London NW8, overlooking Primrose Hill, and just a few minutes' walk from his house in Adamson Road, Swiss Cottage. (RU)

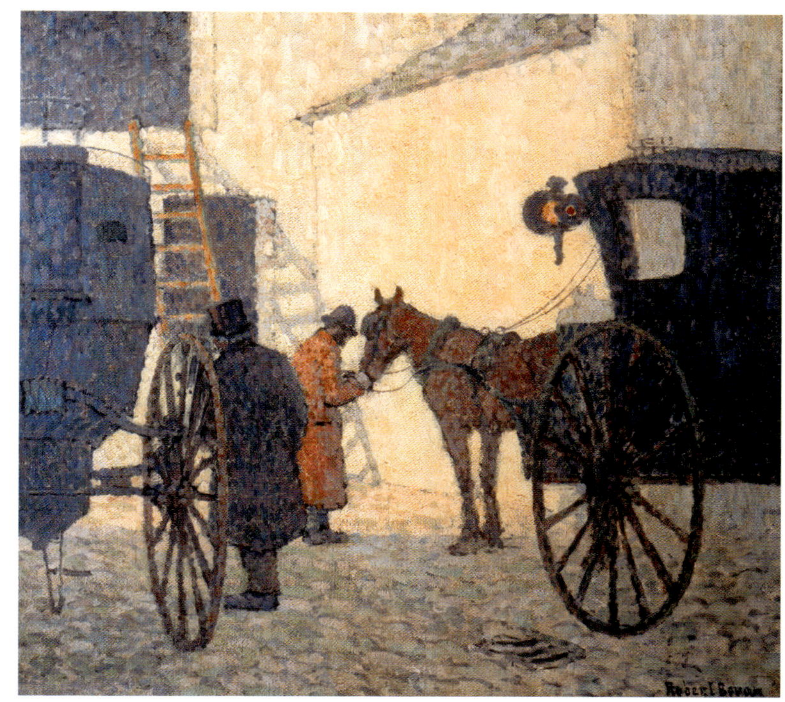

68

69. **Spencer Frederick Gore**
Epsom, Surrey, 1878 – Richmond, Surrey, 1914
Letchworth Station, 1912
Oil on canvas, 63.1 x 76.2 cm
National Railway Museum, York

Spencer Gore was one of the leaders of the Camden Town Group, formed in 1910 and dedicated to painting urban scenes in a Post-Impressionist style. In August 1912 Gore moved his family to Letchworth for some months, taking over the house of his fellow Camden Town painter Harold Gilman. Letchworth was an adventurous and idealistic experiment in modern living, a purpose-built 'Garden Suburb' north of London, which sought to mix town and countryside, fresh air and contemporary design. Many of its businesses were run as co-operatives, and the town pub was teetotal. Gore shows the scene as people leave the railway station, probably returning from their commute to London. The station and railway lines cut across the picture diagonally, truncating the landscape. Stylizing the forms into angular patterns and employing vibrant colour harmonies, Gore produced a picture that was startlingly original both in its design and modern subject matter. (RU)

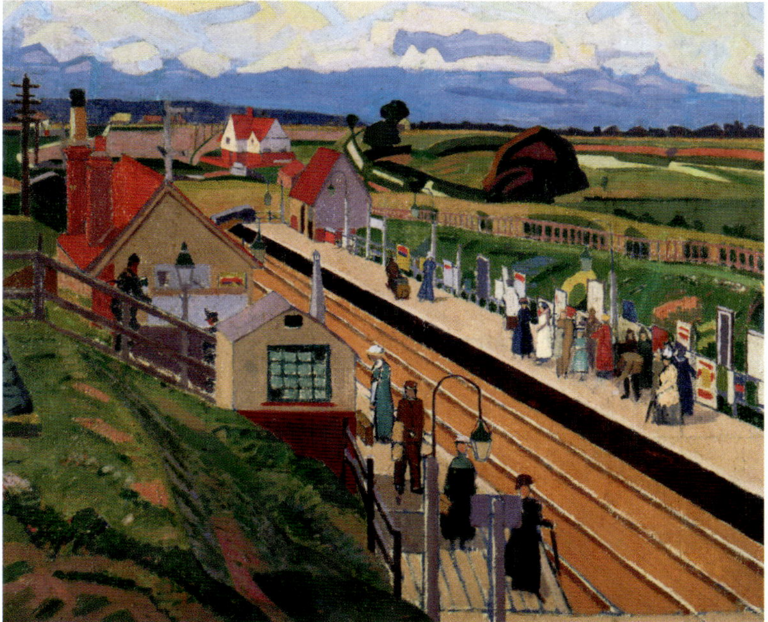

69

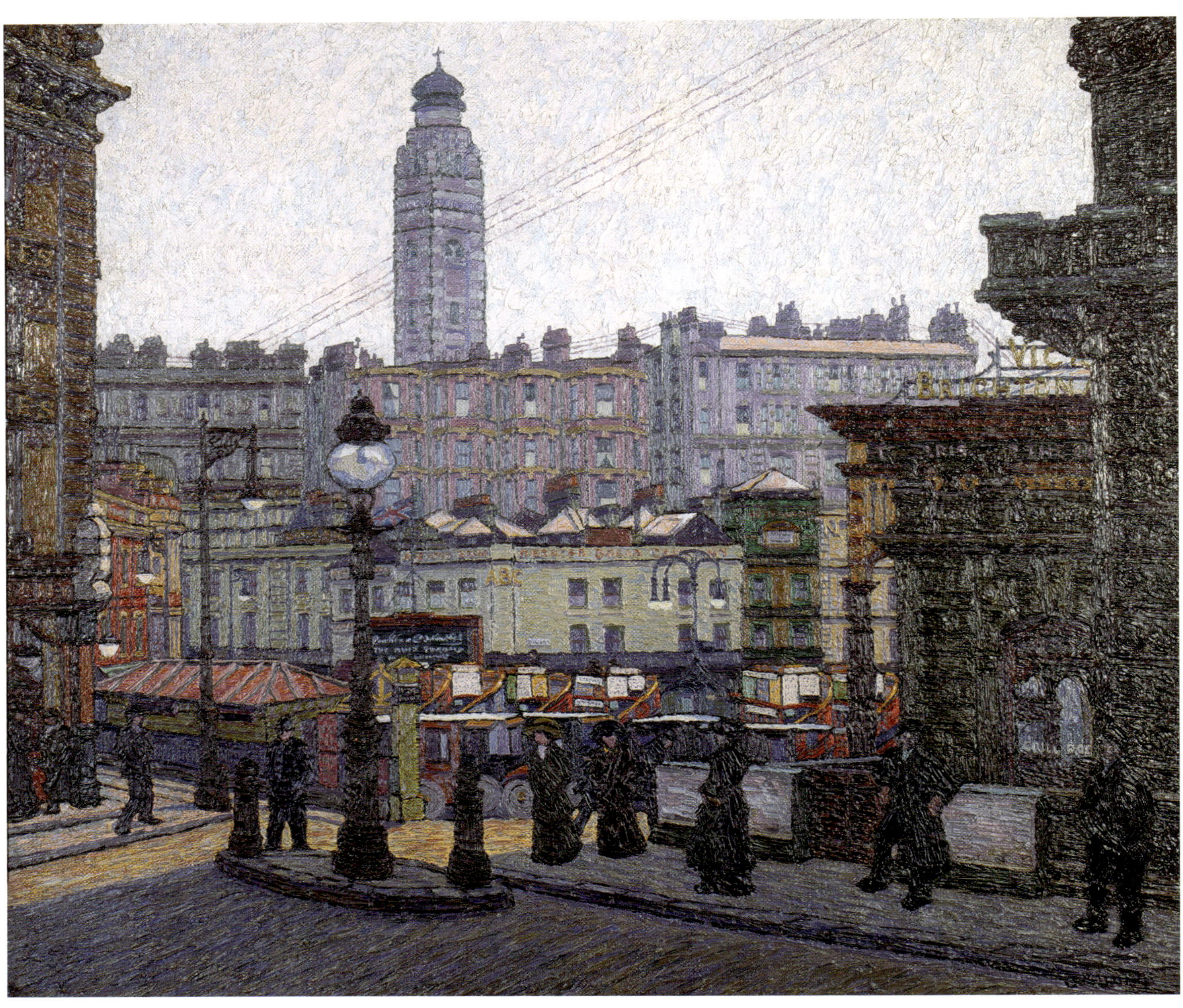

70

70. **Isaac Charles Ginner**
Cannes, 1878 – London, 1952
Victoria Station. The Sunlit Square, 1913
Oil on canvas, 76.2 x 88.3 cm
Bottom right: C. Ginner
Atkinson Art Gallery, Southport

Ginner was born in France, of Anglo-Scottish parents, but settled in London in 1909. With Sickert, Gilman and Gore, in 1910 he was a founder member of the Camden Town Group, committed to painting images of life in the modern metropolis. Here Ginner shows the forecourt of Victoria Station looking towards the campanile of Westminster Cathedral. Its title might be read as ironic, but is perhaps more likely testimony to Ginner's belief in the potential beauty of the urban landscape. Victoria was the point of arrival for boat-train visitors to London from France, and perhaps this was Ginner's own first view of the imperial British capital. Ginner was notable for the extremely thick, mosaic-like impasto of his painting, along with a deep devotion to a vivid Post-Impressionist palette. (RU)

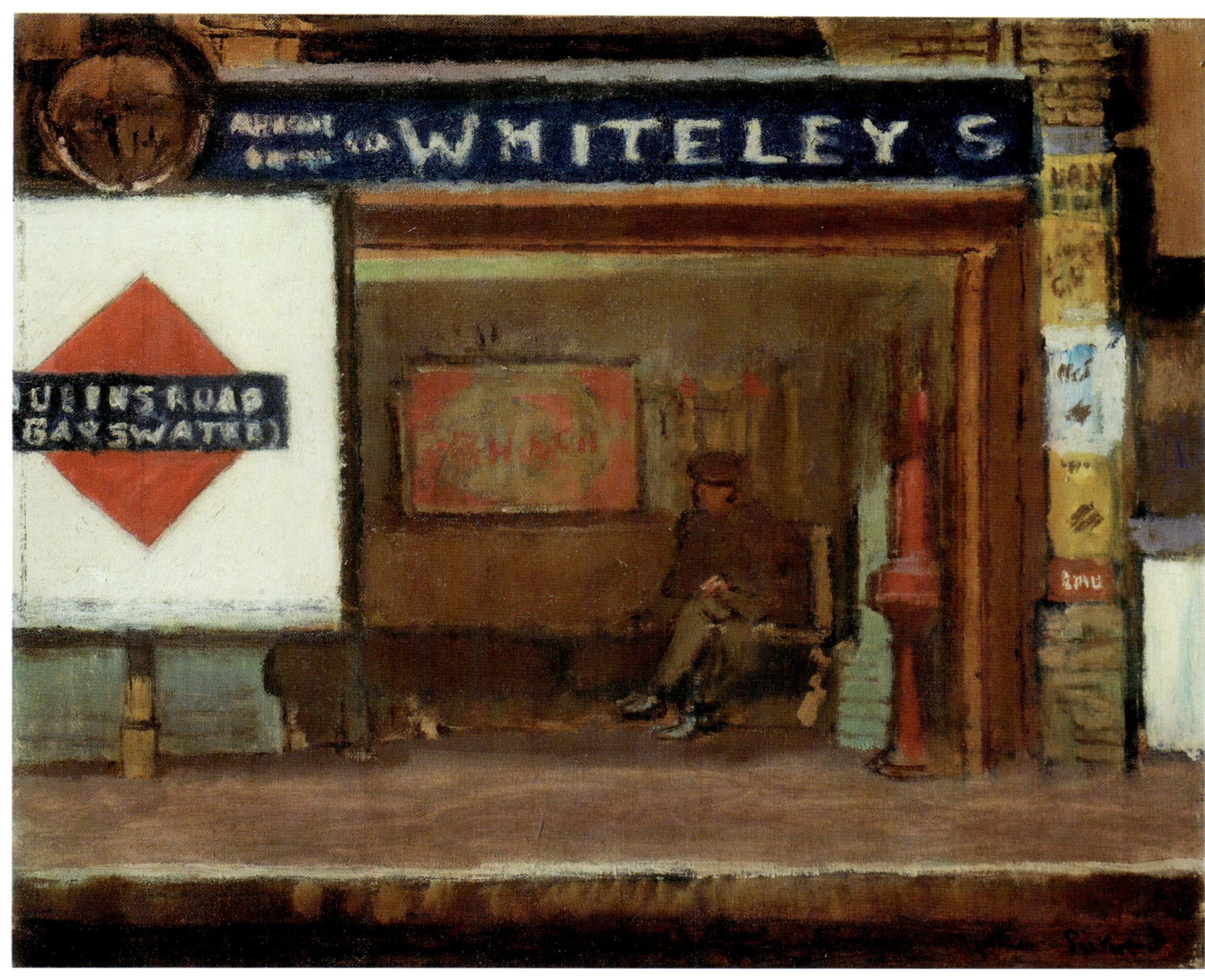

71

71. **Walter Richard Sickert**
Munich, 1860 - Bathampton, Somerset, 1942
Queens Road, Bayswater, c. 1916
Oil on canvas, 63.5 x 76.2 cm
Bottom right: Sickert.
Samuel Courtauld Trust,
Courtauld Institute of Art Gallery, London

Sickert has been quoted elsewhere in this catalogue on the plastic arts being 'gross arts, dealing joyously with gross material facts' (p. 54). Well, here is a scene of gross material fact, the platform of Sickert's local underground station when he was living in Bayswater, west London. The arrangement of shapes, the overlapping rectangles and diamonds and circles, has been read as a nod in the direction of Cubism, but the painting's originality, and modernity, lies more in its matter-of-factness. Although it is full of explicit references, such as the name of the station and the reference to Whiteley's (the department store served by the station), the scene is nondescript, a slice of life brought into art. Its focus is closer than the city views painted about this time by members of the Camden Town Group (cat. 68, 70). The painting formerly belonged to the painter, writer and promoter of modern artists Roger Fry. (AD)

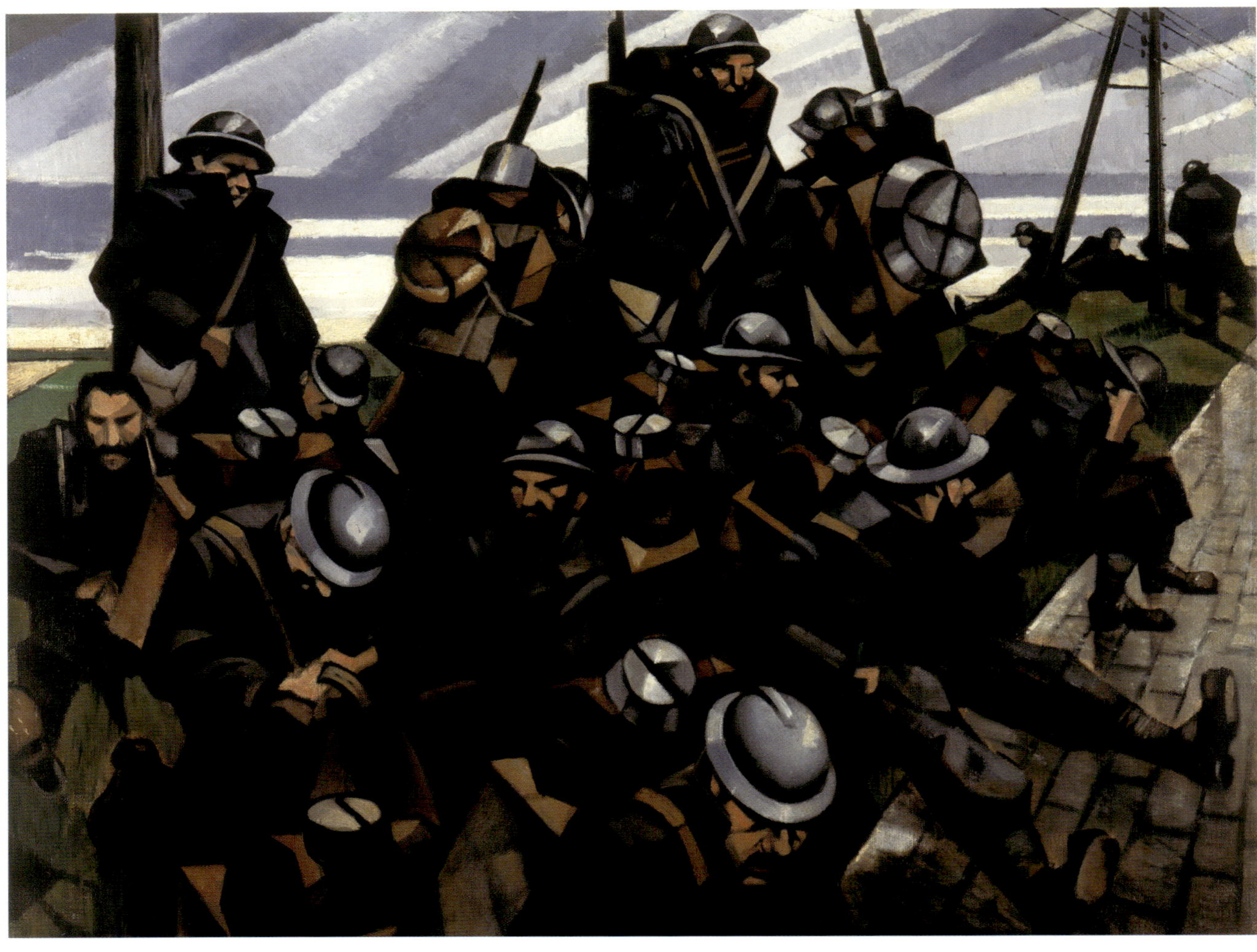

72

72. **Christopher Nevinson**
London, 1889 - London, 1946
French Troops Resting, 1916
Oil on canvas, 71.1 x 91.4 cm
Bottom centre: C. R. W. NEVINSON.
Imperial War Museum, London

C. R. W. Nevinson's strong and public association with F. T. Marinetti, leader of the dynamic and aggressive Futurist movement, before the First World War probably compelled him into military service in spite of his poor health (Black 1999, p. 28). His brief experiences with the Friends Ambulance Unit in northern France and Flanders in 1914 quickly led him to reject Futurism's acclaim for war. However, he did continue to argue that only its visual language could reflect the 'apparent ugliness and dullness of modern warfare' (*Daily Express*, 25 February 1915). Nevinson's images of soldiers were immediately received with critical and public acclaim. They are usually tightly framed, and the soldiers, *en masse*, crudely formed and readily dispensable, are unwitting components of a larger, uncontrollable machine, singularly unaware of its wider purpose. The tension between exhausted individuals with no final destination in sight and compelling force, represented in the driving lines of the landscape, make this one of the most powerful images of the War. (RT)

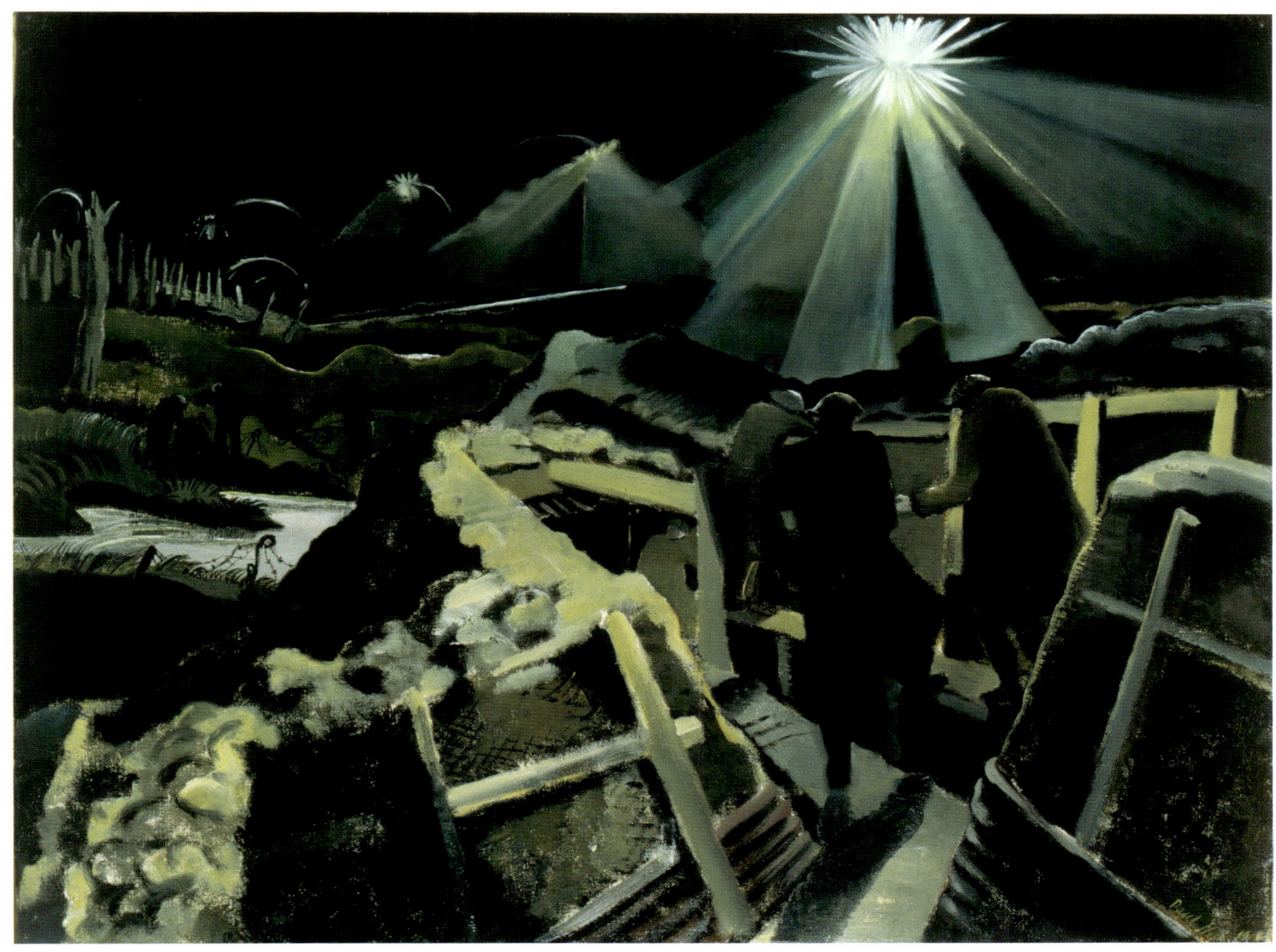

73

73. **Paul Nash**
London, 1889 - Boscombe, Hampshire, 1946
The Ypres Salient at Night, 1918
Oil on canvas, 71.4 x 92 cm
Bottom right: Paul Nash / 1918
Imperial War Museum, London

74. **Paul Nash**
London, 1889 - Boscombe, Hampshire, 1946
The Landscape, Hill 60, 1918
Ink, pencil and watercolour on paper, 40.5 x 50.5 cm
Bottom right: Paul Nash 1918 [covered by the frame]
Imperial War Museum, London

Paul Nash had served at the Ypres Salient with the Hampshire Regiment but was discharged shortly before most of his company was killed at Hill 60. Returning as an official war artist for the British Government, he wrote, 'I have seen the most frightful nightmare of a country more conceived by Dante or Poe than by nature, unspeakable, utterly indescribable. In the fifteen drawings I have made I may give you some idea of its horror, but only being in it and of it can ever make you sensible of its dreadful nature and of what our men in France have to face' (letter to Margaret Nash, 16 November 1917, London, Tate Archive). A peculiar feature of the Salient was the disorientation, caused by the changes in direction of the line, experienced by the defenders; this was often exacerbated at

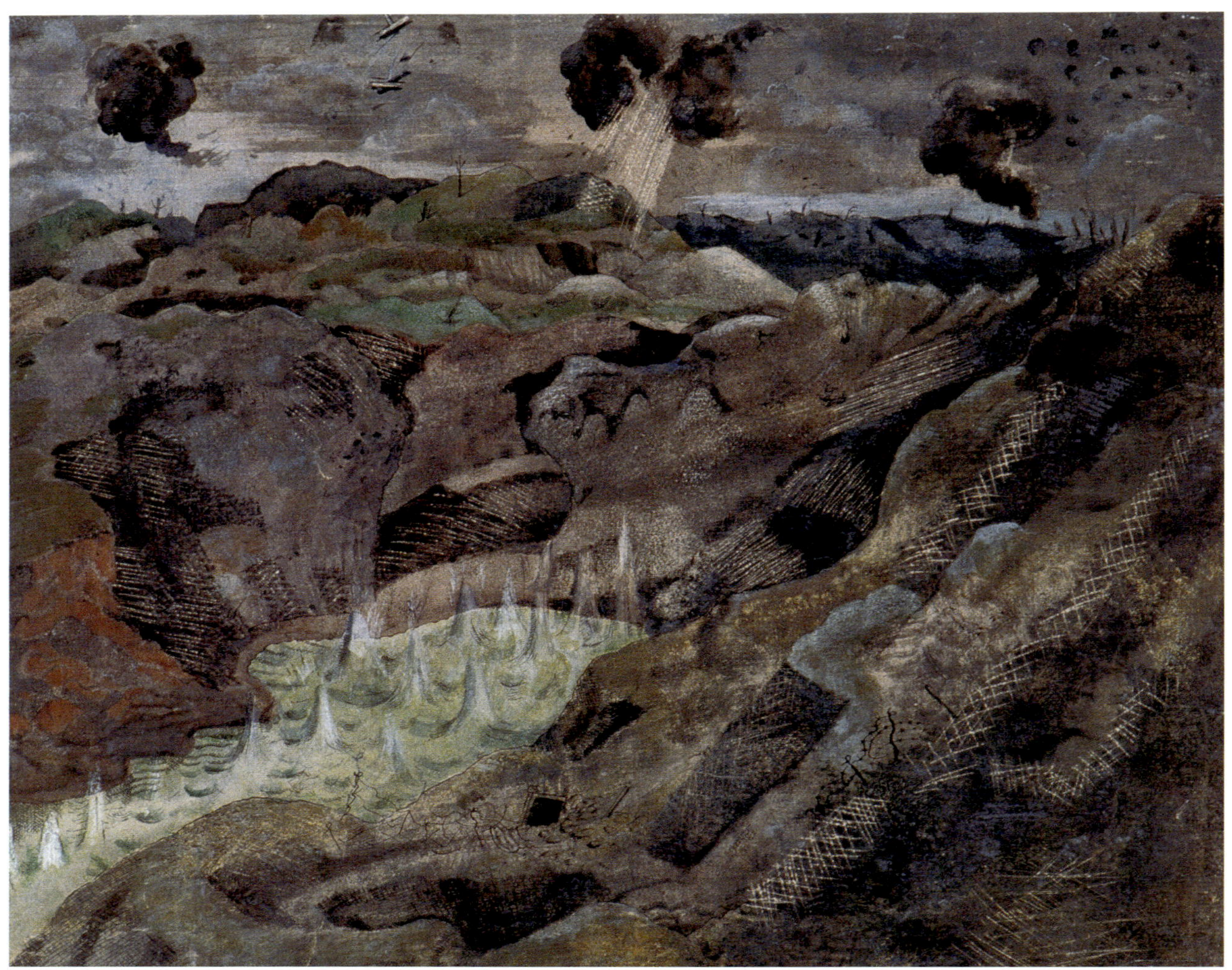

74

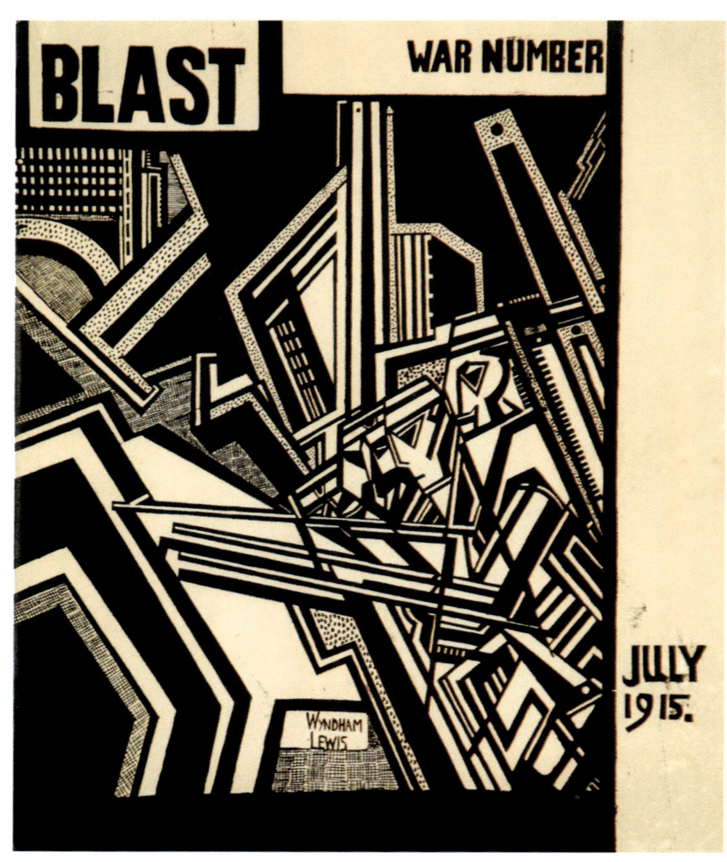

75

night by the almost constant discharge of shells, signal rockets and observation flares by both sides. Like an earthquake or boats caught in a storm, the shifting ground hints at this disorientation and deeper disturbances. Andrew Causey notes, 'Nash found the expressive forms of Vorticism an equivalent for the sense of death in whose shadow he was constantly living' (Causey 1980, pp. 61-62), and that the disorder embodies Blakeian notations of the void and its chaotic annihilation (ibid., pp. 76-77). The British Government war artist schemes in both the First and Second World Wars employed and commissioned many of the leading artists of the day (Nash was employed in both wars). The schemes were propagandist in that they sought to demonstrate the Government's liberal values to audiences both at home and overseas through the commissioning, purchasing and exhibiting of high-quality, eyewitness and frequently critical imagery. They also served as a record of a nation and empire at war, and a memorial to their sacrifices. (RT)

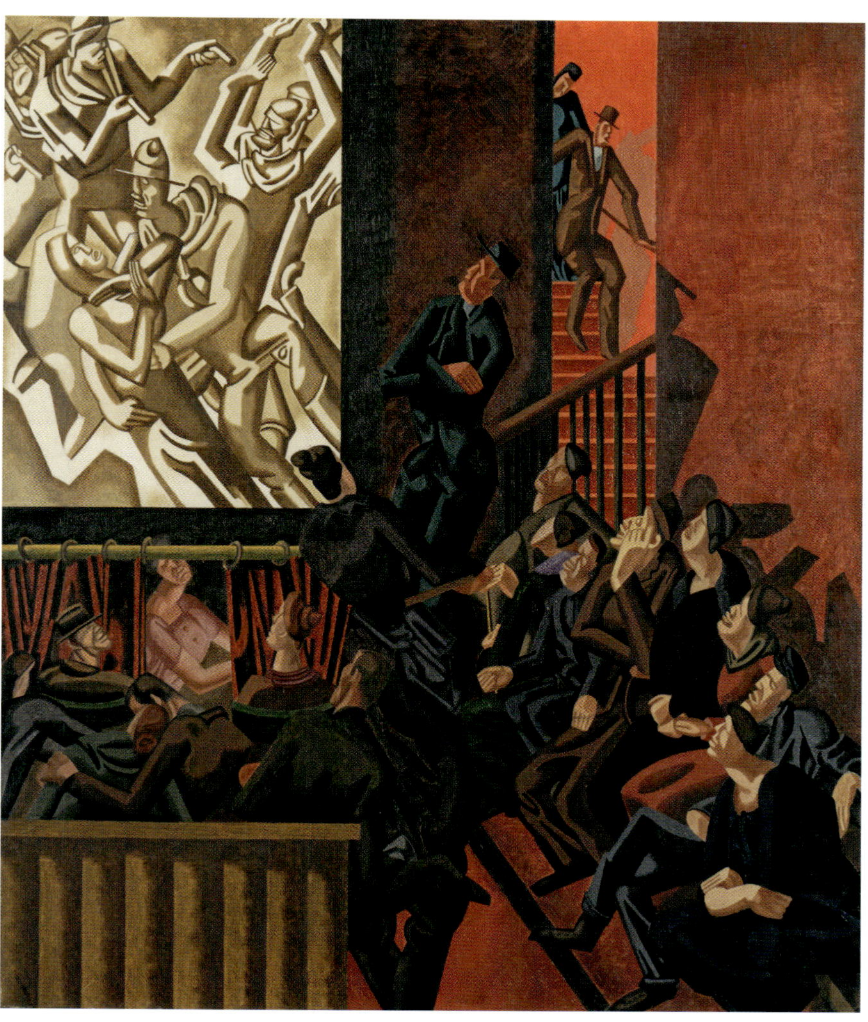

76

75. **Percy Wyndham Lewis**
Amherst, Nova Scotia, 1882 - London, 1957
Cover for ***Blast,*** no 2 (War Number), July 1915
Journal edited by P. W. Lewis, published by John Lane, London, 30 x 24,5 cm
Museum voor Schone Kunsten, Ghent

Blast was the journal of the Vorticists, the English modernist movement led by Percy Wyndham Lewis. Lewis's cover design for the second and final edition interplays text and image around the double meaning of the word 'Blast' as curse and explosion. The fractured surface, like shattered glass, is an aesthetic rejection of the Victorian values and aspirations that are cursed, 'blasted', within the journal, while the construction, like typography, distils the values of urbanity and mechanization that are equally 'blessed'. The movement's aesthetic and philosophy were influenced by both Futurism and Cubism, but they rejected the cinematic movement of the former and the latter's fragmentation, to develop a visual language of hard abstraction and human form caught in flux and on the edge of chaotic void. The soldiers and their rifles, absorbed into the staccato architecture, enshrined Lewis's disillusioned belief that war was embedded into the culture and society of modernity: 'Everything will be arranged for convenience of War. Murder and Destruction is man's fundamental occupation.' (Wyndham Lewis 1915, p. 16) (RT)

76. **William Roberts**
London, 1895 - London, 1980
The Cinema, 1920
Oil on canvas, 91.4 x 76.2 cm
Bottom centre: Roberts
Tate, London

Before the First World War, Roberts made abstract paintings like Wyndham Lewis and his fellow Vorticists. After the war, he produced a series of scenes of urban popular entertainment, such as this view of the inside of a cinema. Originally titled 'The Silent Screen', it is like an updated version of the views of music hall performances painted by Degas or by British artists such as Sickert. There is, perhaps, something significant in the contrast between the rich colouring of the audience and the monochrome, silent action on the screen that seems to hold them enthralled. Roberts himself later described his reaction against abstract art in terms of the artist's moral responsibility to record the world around him. As he put it, 'the artist who tells no more of his life and times, than a collection of abstract designs might as well never have been born' (Roberts, 1976). Despite his later misgivings about abstraction, Roberts was not a straightforward realist. In this work, for example, he combined naturalistic figure painting with skewed, cubist perspectives, which distorted viewpoints and confounded the sense of distance between objects. (RU)

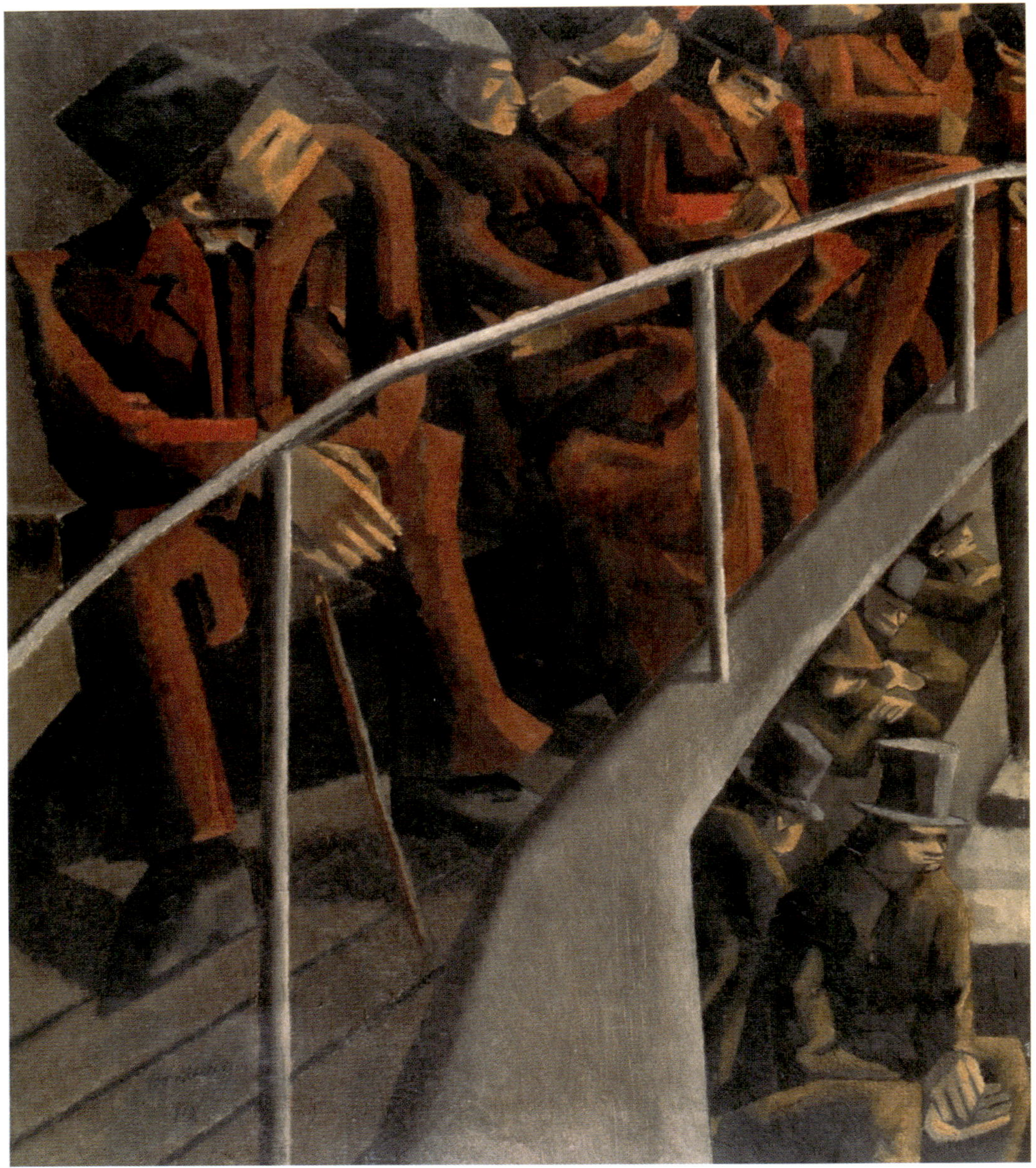

77

77. **David Bomberg**
Birmingham, 1890 - London, 1957
Ghetto Theatre, 1920
Oil on canvas, 75 x 62.5 cm
Bottom left: Bomberg / 1920
Ben Uri Gallery, London Jewish Museum of Art

The Jewish district in London nurtured so many artists that the exhibition 'Twentieth Century Art: A Review of Modern Movements' held at the Whitechapel Art Gallery in 1914 devoted an entire room to 'The Jewish Section'. Another 'child of the ghetto', David Bomberg depicted the grim reality of life for the working classes after the First World War. This painting depicts the Pavilion Theatre in Whitechapel, an establishment which staged plays for the local community in Yiddish. The theatre was particularly famous for the boisterous and noisy appreciation of its patrons, a marked contrast to the audience in Bomberg's picture, who are decidedly lacking in *joie de vivre*. These figures are more humanistic than the mechanized forms of his earlier war paintings, but they do not have the same vitality and dynamism. Sombrely hunched behind the rail of the auditorium, they stare gloomily at the stage ahead, devoid of animation and character. (NM)

78. **Percy Wyndham Lewis**
Amherst, Nova Scotia, 1882 - London, 1957
A Reading of Ovid - Tyros, c. 1920
Oil on canvas, 165.2 x 90.2 cm
Scottish National Gallery of Modern Art, Edinburgh

'Art today needs waking up,' declared Wyndham Lewis in 1921 ('Dean Swift with a Brush: The Tyroist Explains his Art', *Daily Express*, 11 April 1921). Rather than existing solely for 'art's sake' it should be socially engaged and actively reflect the experience of the world. To this end Lewis created the character of the 'tyro', a satirical critique of the aesthetics promoted by the

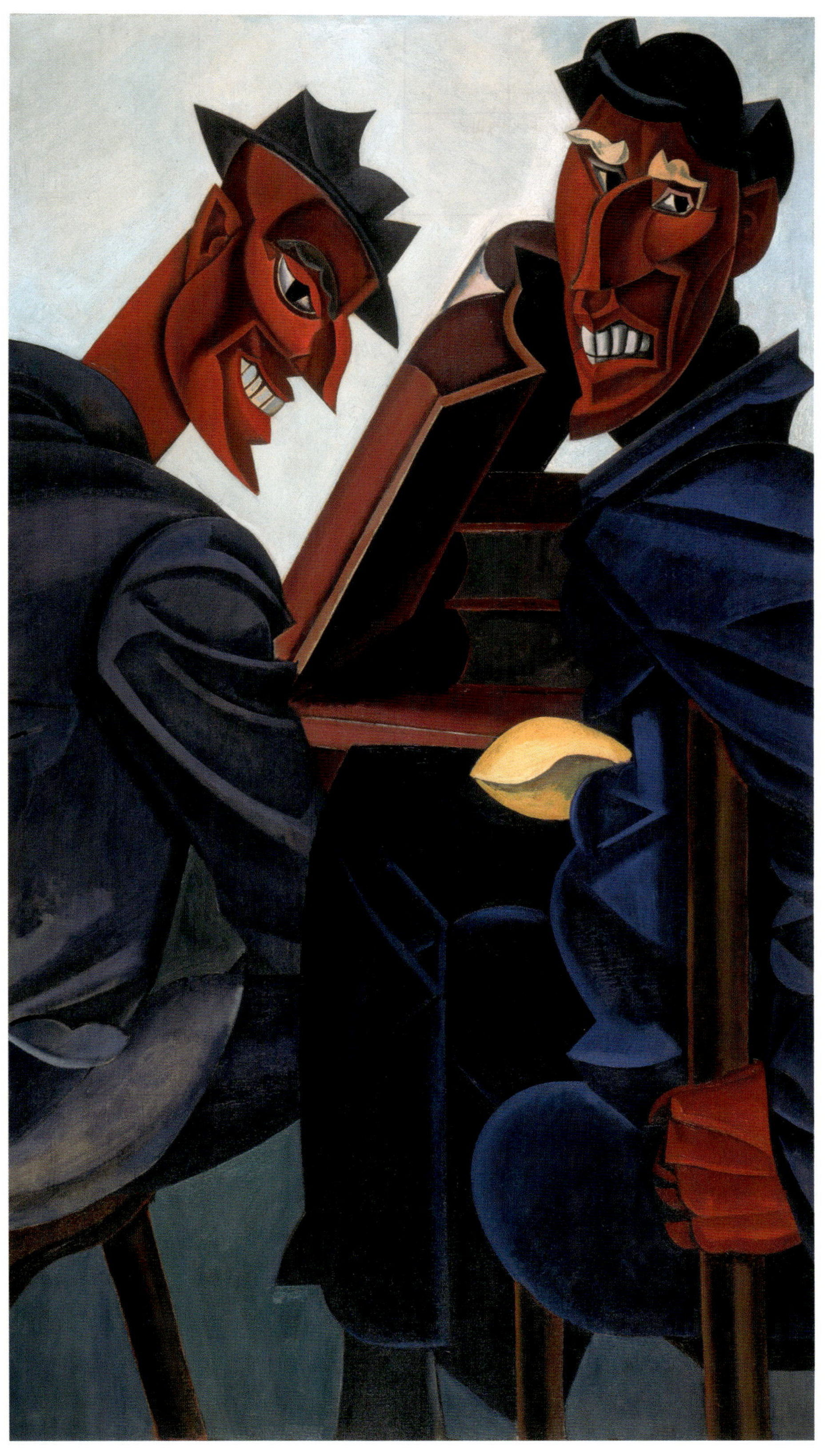

78

Bloomsbury Group, which he believed dominated post-war British culture.

Lewis described the tyro as 'an animated but artificial puppet', with a 'screaming voice underneath', the embodiment of post-war denial (ibid. and London 1921). The maniacal, vacuous grin displayed by the figures is an extreme manifestation of the ubiquitous British stiff upper lip. A semblance of normality is preserved, but severely disrupted by repressed trauma, suggested by the tyros' mechanistic features and lurid coloured skin. In this painting two tyros read Ovid. Their response is enthusiastic but ultimately limited by their stunted intellectual and emotional capacity. Contemporary art, Lewis is suggesting, had suffered a similar fate. (NM)

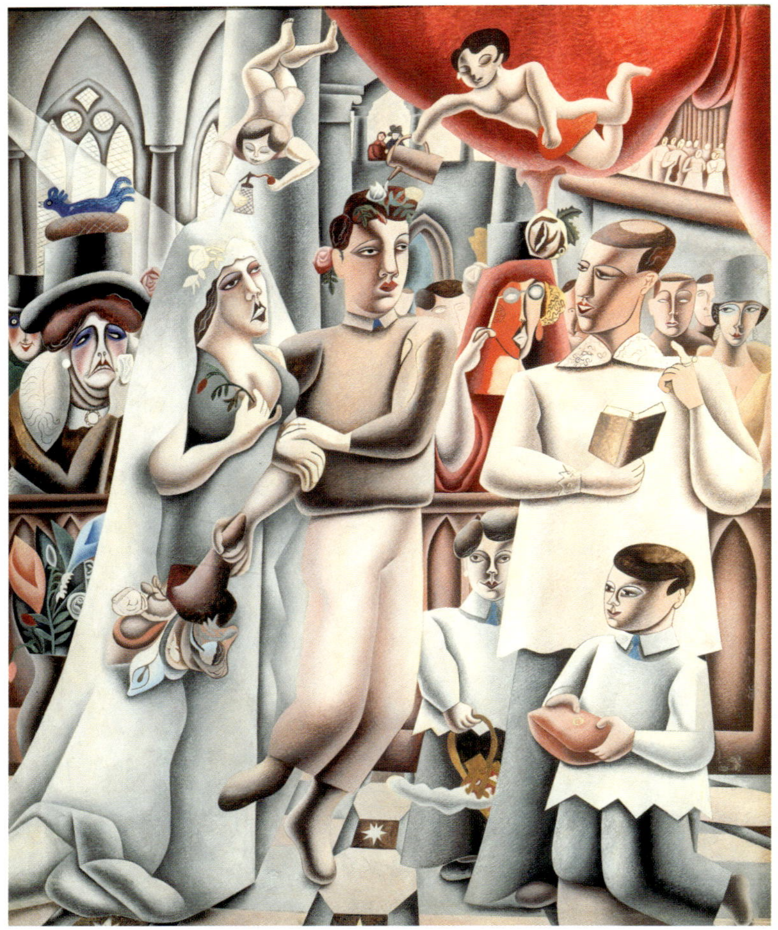

79

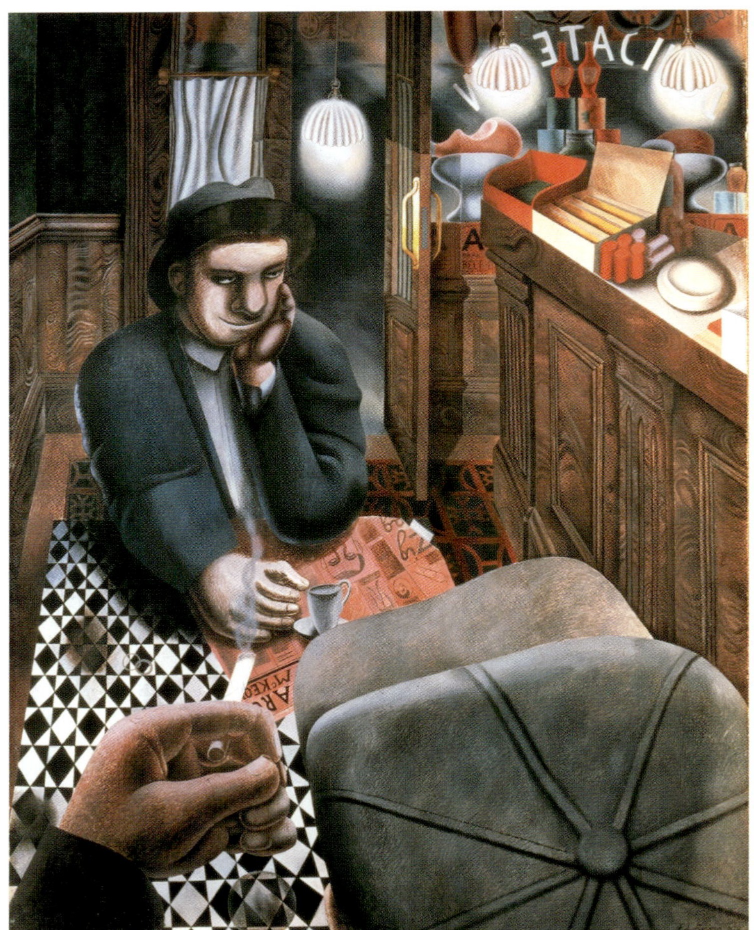

80

79. **Edward Burra**
London, 1905 – Hastings, Sussex, 1976
Marriage à la Mode, 1928-29
Watercolour on paper, 62.2 x 50.8 cm
Private Collection, courtesy of Lefevre Fine Art, London

Burra was stricken by rheumatic fever as a schoolboy, and by his mid-twenties he had settled into a double life: painting as an invalid at the family home near Rye, but nourished by rash sorties to London, Paris, Marseilles or further afield, in the company of an exceptionally smart circle of camp, cosmopolitan friends. *Marriage à la Mode* takes its title from Hogarth and recreates English satire as Art Deco high style. Limbs and faces, clothes and objects, are all crisply reprocessed – even the altar-boy's solidified incense-cloud – to re-emerge as though out of the same plastic mould, smoothed out, bright-sprayed. Arthritis and anaemia restricted Burra mainly to watercolour ('I must sit most of the time; if I could work lying down, I'd do so'). But he employs gouache almost as tempera, in minute cross-hatched touches. Sexual innuendo is everywhere – in the bride's suggestive handling of her bouquet, in the red vaginal drapes from which the nude cupid flies out with watering-can to freshen the roses blooming in the hair of the epicene groom. This is a vision of marriage fed by malice and spite; as Burra admitted, 'I get in such paroxysms of impotent venom I feel I must poison the atmosphere.' (TH)

80. **Edward Burra**
London, 1905 – Hastings, Sussex, 1976
The Café, 1930
Watercolour on paper, 66 x 50.5 cm
Bottom right: Ed.Burra 1930 / June July
Southampton City Art Gallery

Although his imagery was often fantastical, Burra emerged around 1930 as one of the twentieth century's finest 'painters of modern life'. As an eighteen-year-old at the Royal College of Art, he had learnt much from an exhibition of William Roberts's London scenes (such as *The Cinema*, cat. 76), with their celebration of popular pleasures. The *Café* is also a loving inventory of a specific interior – the detail of engraved glass and wood grain, the clutter of a gas-lit counter – realized with some of the formal artifice of a Juan Gris. Burra enjoys the play of scale: the tiny coffee-cup juxtaposed with the huge hand and lighted cigarette, and the flat cap that fills half the foreground, to make of each us a participant. (TH)

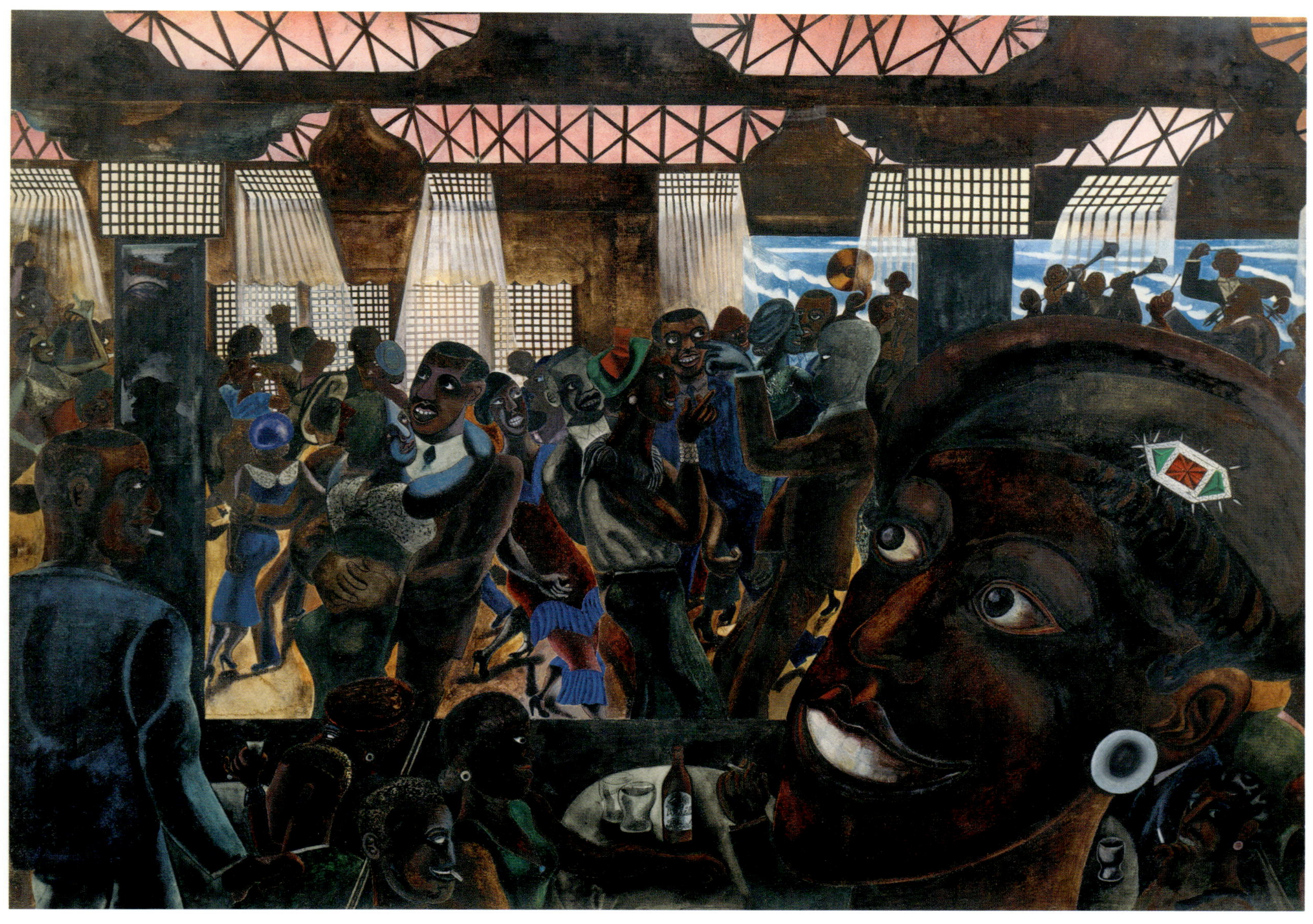

81

81. **Edward Burra**
London, 1905 - Hastings, Sussex, 1976
Savoy Ballroom, Harlem, 1934
Gouache and watercolour on paper, 54.3 x 76.2 cm
Bottom centre: Ed Burra 1934
Courtesy of Lefevre Fine Art, London, on behalf of the Edward Burra Estate

The six months Burra stayed in New York (October 1933 to March 1934) were arguably the climax of his life work. The Savoy had opened in 1926, with a dance floor two hundred feet long, and it remained one of the centres of the black jazz culture, even after the 1929 slump that shut down so much of the 'Harlem Renaissance'. In 1933 Burra wrote to the photographer Barbara Ker-Seymer: 'We went to the Savoy dance hall the other night my dear you would go mad ... I've never seen such wonderful dancing ...' In the later 1920s Burra was taken up by Paul Nash, sixteen years his senior, who wrote in *The Listener* (July 27, 1932) of 'Burra's extraordinary fantasies, perhaps the most original of any contemporary English artist.' It was through Nash that he met the American poet Conrad Aiken, and, in turn, the novelist Malcolm Lowry: they would become his travel companions in Spain and in Mexico.

The big features of the foreground girl recall the frescoed heads of Diego Rivera, her warm expanses of brown-and-black flesh surmounted by the ruby-and-emerald hatpin. Suddenly, behind her enormous ear, we catch the eye of a tiny smoker far below. Everyone is smiling. There isn't a white in sight. We are a long way from Rye. (TH)

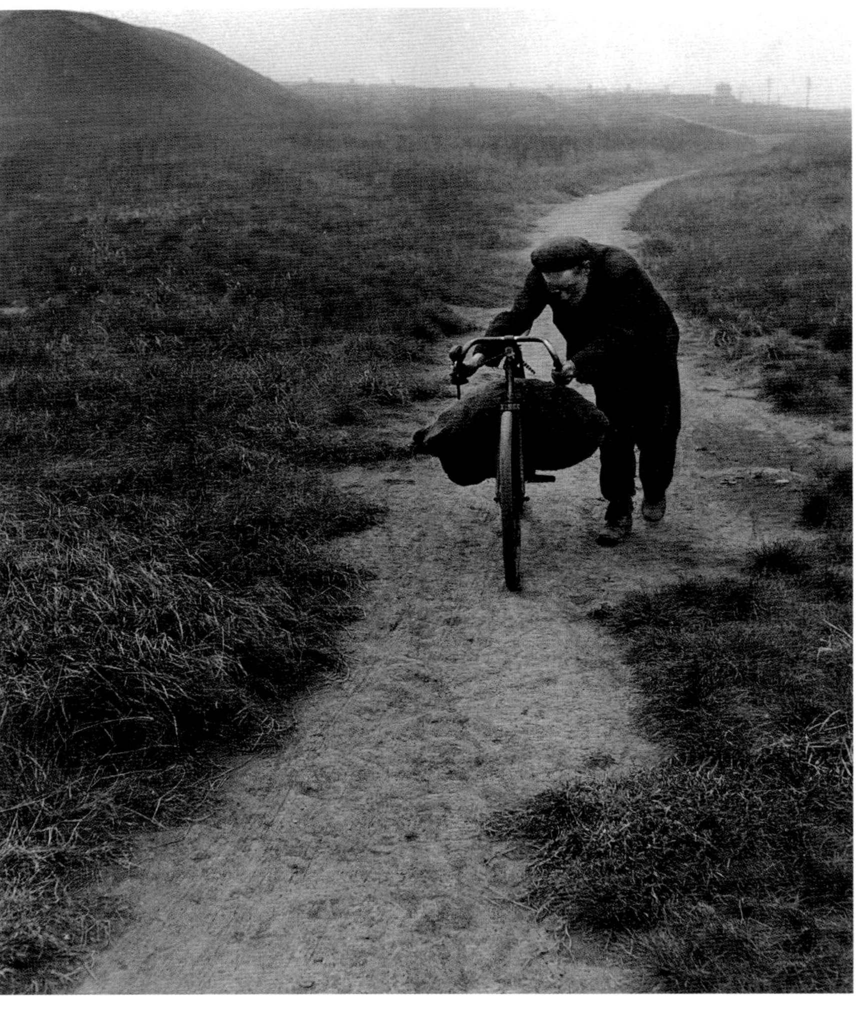

82

82. **Bill Brandt**
Hamburg, 1904 - London, 1983
Coal-Searcher Going Home to Jarrow, 1937 (printed in 1976)
Gelatin silver print, 34 x 29.5 cm
Bottom right: Bill Brandt
Victoria and Albert Museum, London

When the novelist J.B. Priestley visited Jarrow in the north-east of England for his book *An English Journey* (1934), unemployment stood at 80 per cent. Priestley wrote that the 'whole town looked as if it had entered a perpetual penniless bleak Sabbath' (Priestley 1934, p. 34). Brandt was moved by the book and by the 'Jarrow Crusade', a march from the town to London by workers drawing attention to their plight, in 1936. Brandt wrote of meeting this coal-searcher with his sack filled with scraps of coal from a spoil heap. He was 'leaning over his bicycle; the man's clothes were black and the grass beside the path was black, as it is near pitheads. The scene was dreary in the extreme, yet moving by its very atmosphere of drabness. A dark print of the photograph added to the effect of darkness associated with the miner's life.' ('A Photographer's London' in Brandt 1948, p. 141). (MHB)

83. **Bill Brandt**
Hamburg, 1904 - London, 1983
Parlourmaid and Under-Parlourmaid Ready to Serve Dinner, 1932-35 [?] (first published in 1938, printed in 1976)
Gelatin silver print, 33.8 x 29.1 cm
Bottom right: Bill Brandt
Victoria and Albert Museum, London

Like many other notable British photographers, including Cameron, Martin and Emerson, Brandt spent his early years elsewhere: he was born in Hamburg of an English-born father and German mother, trained as a photographer in Vienna and Paris, and settled in London in 1934. His eye, trained by Surrealist Paris, found an extraordinary novelty in English social ritual. His first two books, *The English at Home* (1936) and *A Night in London* (1938) are documentary classics. This photograph of the maids in the house of one of his banker uncles captures the Edwardian uniforms, already out of date in 1938, and the pride in service of the senior parlourmaid, whom Brandt greatly admired. The younger maid seems less identified with her occupation. The photograph looks back to England's assured, imperial past - and forward to 1945, when the era of domestic service ended and a new social dispensation began. (MHB)

84. **Bill Brandt**
Hamburg, 1904 - London, 1983
Young Housewife, Bethnal Green, 1937 (printed in 1976)
Gelatin silver print, 33.1 x 28.9 cm
Bottom right: Bill Brandt
Victoria and Albert Museum, London

Brandt's photograph of a young working-class woman washing the front step of her house was published or exhibited several times in different contexts. On its first publication, in *Lilliput* in September 1941, the subject was contrasted with a Russian ballet dancer, while in Brandt's own *Camera in London* (1948) it appeared as 'East End morning', with a 'Mayfair morning' on the facing page. It was also twice included by Edward Steichen in exhibitions at the Museum of Modern Art, New York, and the changing environments, as well as variation in the cropping, make subtle alterations to its significance. The print here is very close to the one Brandt sent for exhibition in New York in 1948. (MHB)

See essay pp. 131-33.

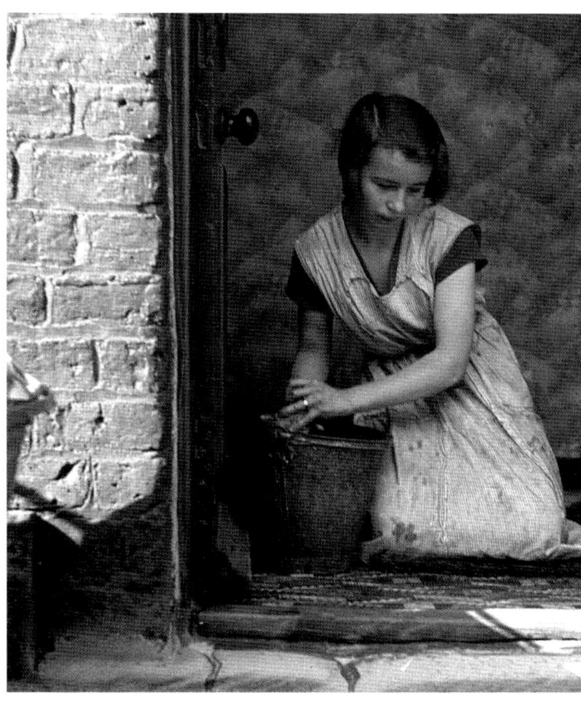

84

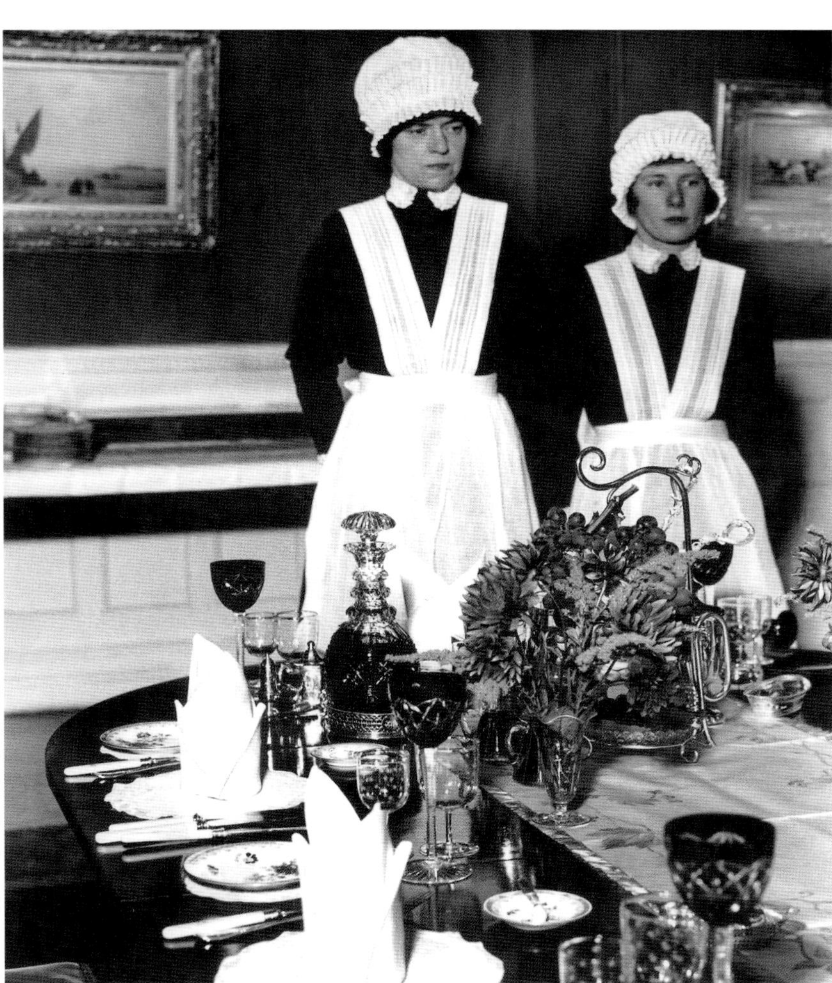

83

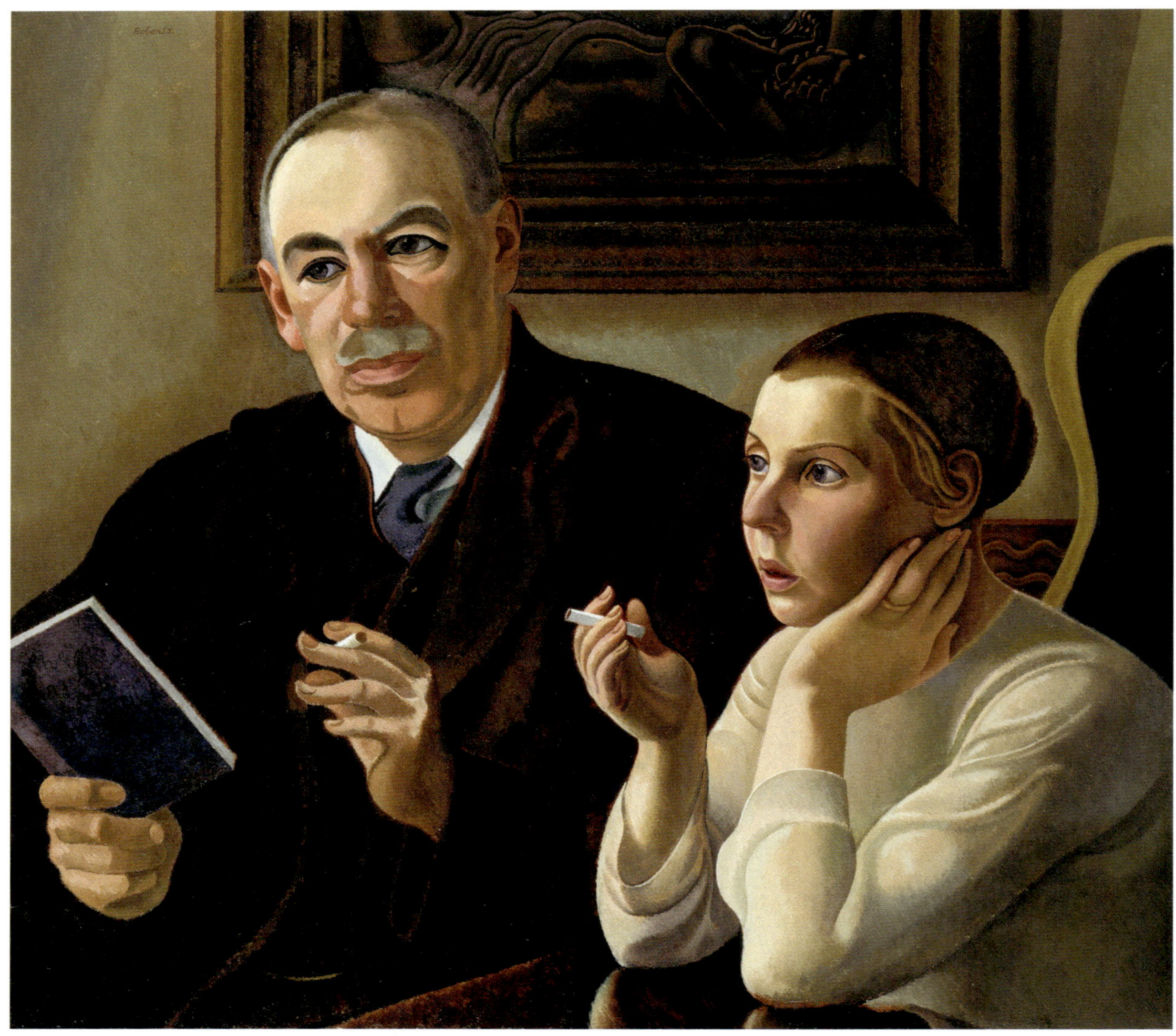

85

85. **William Roberts**
London, 1895 – London, 1980
John Maynard Keynes, Baron Keynes and his Wife Lydia Lopokova, c. 1932
Oil on canvas, 72.4 x 81.6 cm
Top left: Roberts.
National Portrait Gallery, London

The world of the London intelligentsia during the early twentieth century was a close-knit network of perpetually evolving, interconnected cliques and circles. The famous economist John Maynard Keynes was a key member of the Bloomsbury Group, close friend of Lytton Strachey (see cat. 63) and former lover of the painter Duncan Grant. Keynes's wife, the Russian ballerina Lydia Lopokova, came to London in 1918 with Diaghilev's Ballets Russes and met her future husband at a party given by the Sitwell siblings, Osbert, Edith and Sacheverell.

Keynes combined his economic theories with an appreciation of modern art. In 1925 he was the prime instigator behind the London Artist's Association, an enterprise that provided contemporary artists with a measure of financial security. One of the artists who most benefited from the scheme was William Roberts, a painter whom Keynes particularly admired. This double portrait, commissioned and exhibited in 1932, combines Roberts's characteristic rounded and stylized forms with a sensitive portrayal of his patron. (NM)

86. **Walter Richard Sickert**
Munich, 1860 – Bathampton, Somerset, 1942
William Maxwell Aitken, 1st Baron Beaverbrook, 1934-35
Oil on canvas, 176.2 x 107.3 cm
Bottom right: Sickert. / 1935
National Portrait Gallery, London

Max Beaverbrook was a press baron, who famously acquired the *Daily Express* newspaper and used it as a campaigning vehicle. It was one of the first papers to carry gossip, sports and women's features, and the first newspaper in Britain to have a

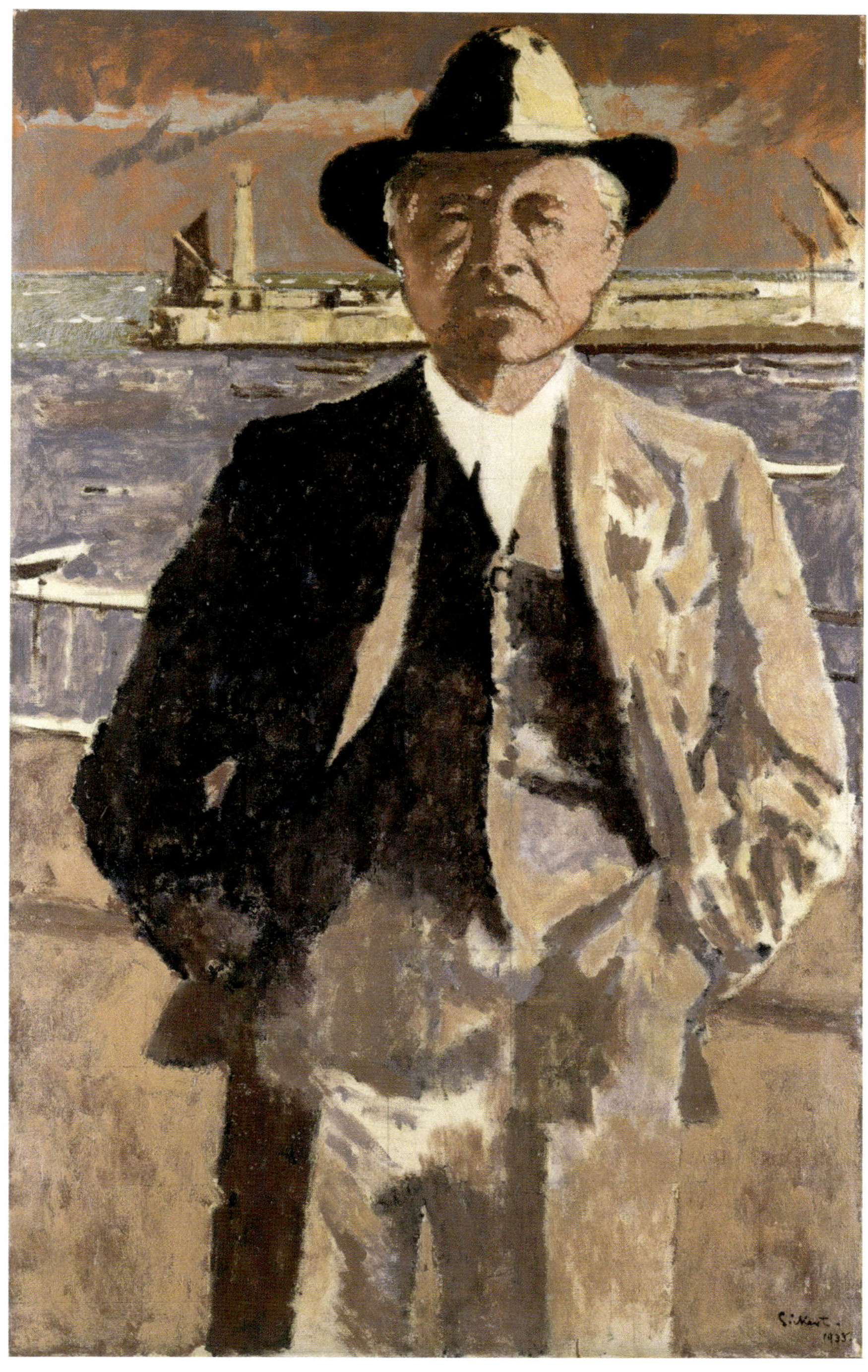

86

crossword. It moved in 1931 to 133 Fleet Street, a specially commissioned Art Deco building, which strengthened its image as a modernizing force in British society. Under Beaverbrook the newspaper achieved a phenomenally high circulation, setting new records for newspaper sales several times throughout the 1930s.

By the early 1930s, Sickert was enjoying a new-found celebrity and success. He freely used press images clipped from newspapers and magazines to produce paintings of celebrities or events of the day, such as Amelia Earhart's arrival in England. Sickert was delighted to acknowledge this source for his art and claimed it as a modern artist's tool for the pursuit of naturalism. His portrait of Beaverbrook was based on a photograph he spotted after receiving the commission, although he decided to change the background from Beaverbrook's home to the unlikely setting of Margate harbour. Its large scale consciously harked back to Grand Manner portraits of the eighteenth century by Reynolds and Gainsborough, but updated to a contemporary idiom. Notoriously, the portrait was rejected at the Royal Academy annual exhibition, most probably on political grounds. Beaverbrook had crossed swords with Baldwin's Government over British Empire trade protectionism and was involved in a variety of campaigns. Sickert acknowledged the political aspect of his painting, writing to Beaverbrook that it 'is and remains a political portrait in the grand manner by a painter who appreciates and admires your policy' (Baron and Shone 1992, p. 320). (RU)

87. **Stanley Spencer**
Cookham, Berkshire, 1891 – Cliveden, Buckinghamshire, 1959
Double Nude Portrait: The Artist and his Second Wife (The Leg of Mutton Nude), 1937
Oil on canvas, 83.8 x 93.7 cm
Tate, London
Not reproduced due to copyright restrictions

Two months before his marriage to Patricia Preece, Spencer completed the most compelling of his 'Naked Portraits', in which his procedure seems to have followed that of his landscapes: working steadily across the surface, patch by patch, with small brushes. The result is a confrontation with fleshly fact, a kind of numbness that becomes in itself expressive and meaningful. Looking back in 1955, Spencer commented: 'There is in it male, female and animal flesh ... It was done with zest and any direct painting capacity I had.' (Hyman and Wright 2001, p. 150) The uneaten flesh has variously been seen as referring to their unconsummated relationship or to the sacramental lamb. Preece was already in her forties (though Spencer believed her to be six years younger), and since 1918 her partner had been Dorothy Hepworth, her fellow-student at the Slade.

Publicly exhibited only once in his lifetime, *The Leg of Mutton Nude* entered the Tate in 1974 and was instrumental in reviving Spencer's reputation among young artists. (TH)

88. **Stanley Spencer**
Cookham, Berkshire, 1891 – Cliveden, Buckinghamshire, 1959
Hilda, Unity and Dolls, 1937
Oil on canvas, 76.2 x 50.8 cm
Leeds Museums and Galleries (City Art Gallery)

One of Spencer's supreme achievements in 'straight painting', this apparently objective depiction, showing his first wife Hilda Carline and their daughter Unity, turns out to be as complex in its psychological narrative as *The Leg of Mutton Nude* (cat. 87) of five months earlier. It was completed in a ten-day visit to Hampstead; Spencer was now living alone in Cookham following the fiasco of his second marriage (with Preece returned forever to Dorothy Hepworth). In late August he journeyed up to 17 Pond Street, where his first wife and younger daughter were living with the Carline family. Each element must have been painted in separate sessions, then spliced together: the adult turning wearily away, the child gazing intently, the dolls providing a kind of grotesque chorus. Embodied in the totality of the composition is Hilda's refusal to renew their marriage. (TH)

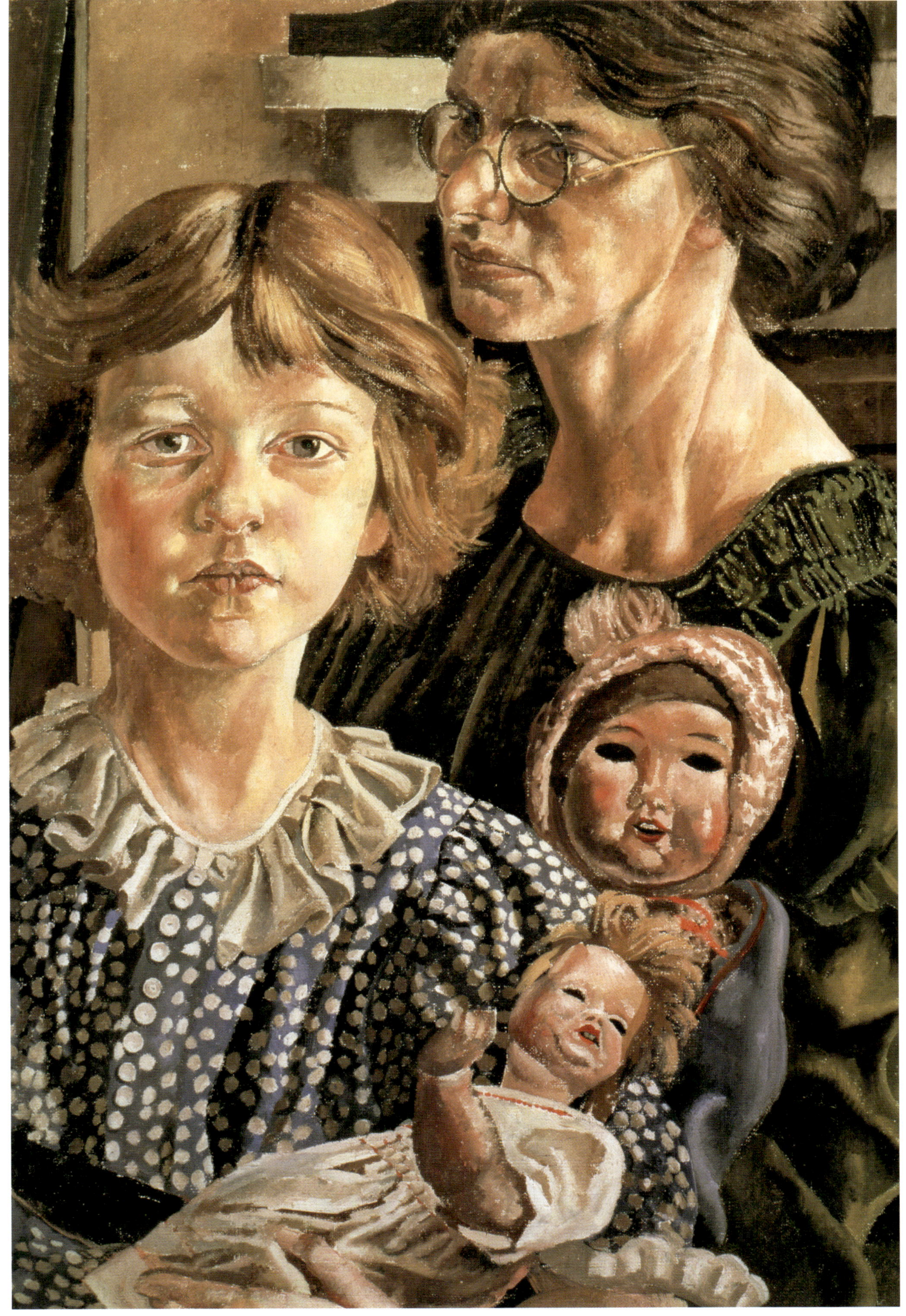

88

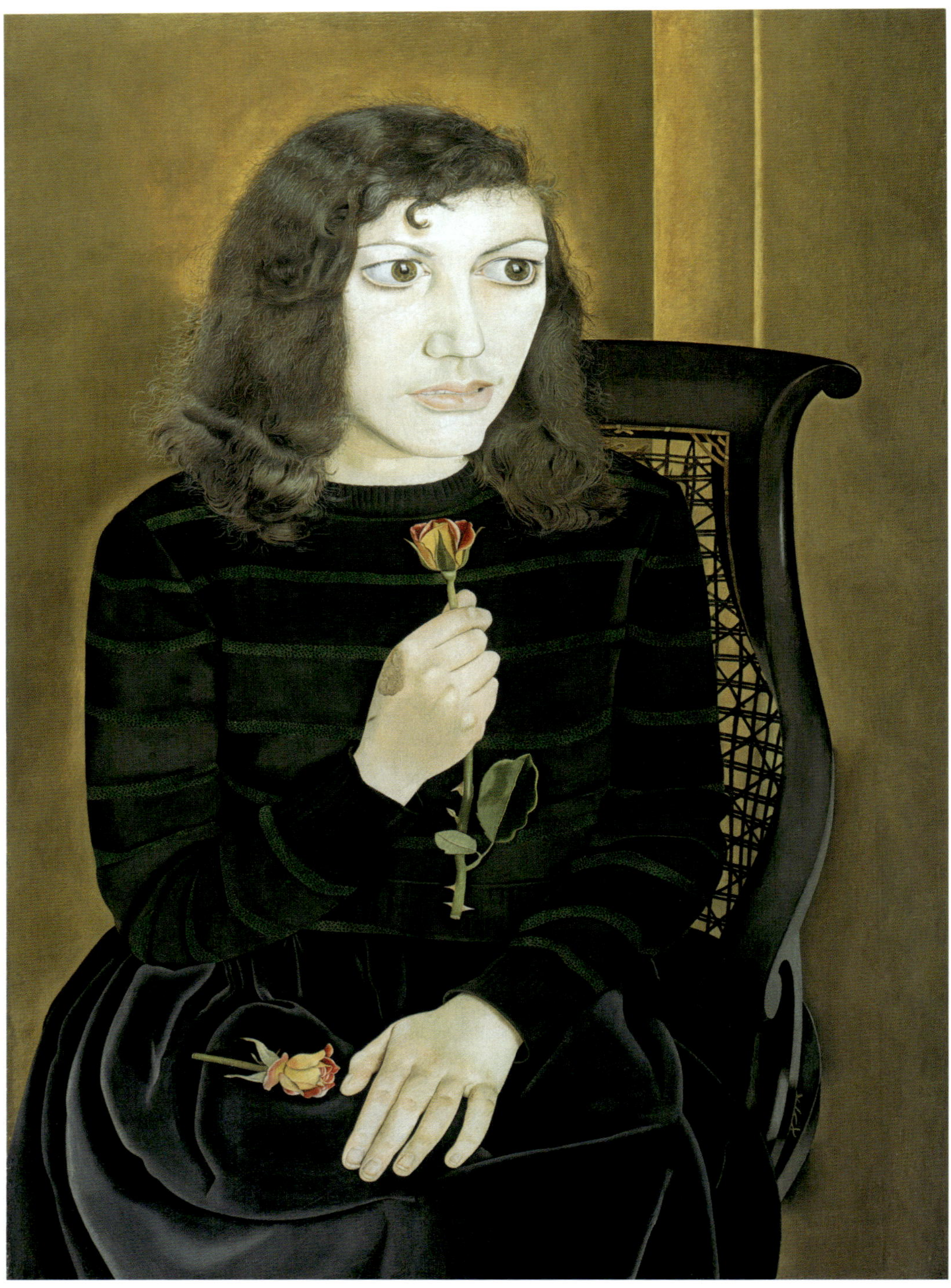

89

89. **Lucian Freud**
Berlin, 1922
Girl with Roses, 1947-48
Oil on canvas, 106 x 75.6 cm
British Council, London

The model for this and a number of other major early works by Freud was his first wife, Kitty Garman, daughter of the sculptor Jacob Epstein. The leading British figure painter of his generation, Freud made this tender portrait while he was still in his twenties. It is extremely detailed – every strand of Kitty's hair is visible, the petals of the rose and the frayed cane of the chair she sits on are carefully delineated, and Freud even paints reflections in her exaggeratedly large eyes. Such detail seems to encapsulate his love for her and, perhaps, a search to try to understand her. It is a uniquely intense portrait. Every aspect of his lover is enumerated ardently but also obsessively. Stylistically, Freud looks to the crisp drawing and precision of the northern Renaissance, and the rose that Kitty holds is a traditional Renaissance emblem of love. But Kitty's uncertain, almost fearful, expression lends Freud's love portrait a sense of dislocation, an unease at the heart of such strong feelings. (RU)

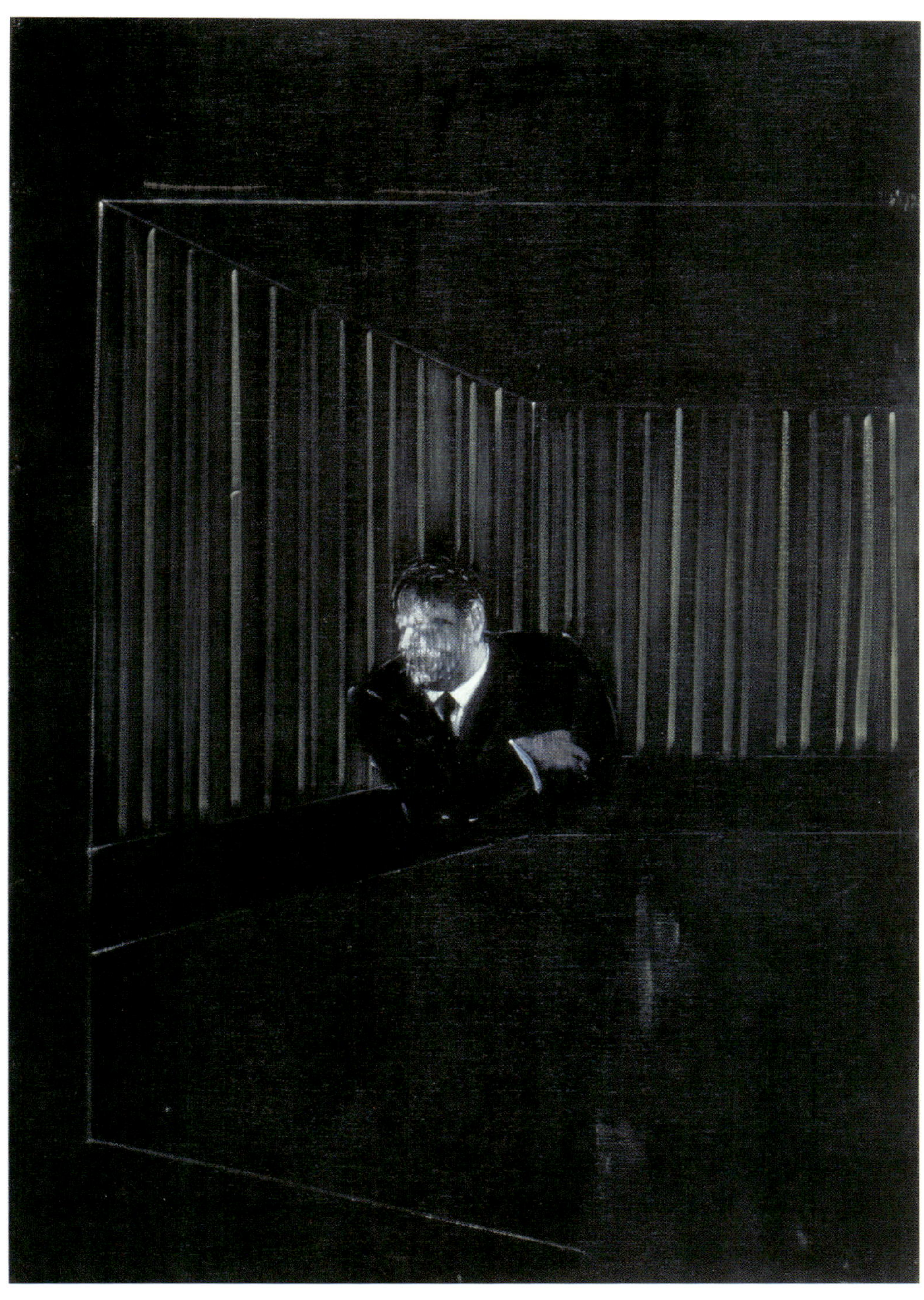

90

90. **Francis Bacon**
Dublin, 1909 - Madrid, 1992
Man in Blue I, 1954
Oil on canvas, 198 x 137 cm
Museum Boijmans Van Beuningen, Rotterdam
(on long term loan to the Gemeentemuseum, The Hague)

Bacon is the 'British' artist who is both most acknowledged as a modern master in Europe and most typifies, in our time, the imaginative or visionary focus of the present exhibition. (This has nothing to do with invention and fantasy, but is another and extreme way of representing reality.) To what extent he is British might be disputed, but he was certainly London-based and a crucial figure in post-war British culture. This painting was the first in a series depicting a 'city-suited' man. Ronald Alley, author of the 1964 catalogue raisonné, referred to this character as recalling Senator McCarthy, and indeed it has the feeling of a figure haranguing or menacing from a tribunal. With his tie and his suit his only attributes, Bacon's character is akin to those of fellow-Irishman Samuel Beckett, both specific to that period and timeless in their power to move us. The *Man in Blue* series was begun in the unlikely location of the Imperial Hotel in Henley-on-Thames. The model was someone Bacon had met in the hotel, and unusually, as Alley records, 'to some extent they were painted from life' (Alley 1964, no. 81). 1954, the date of this painting, was the year when Bacon, Freud and Nicholson were shown together in the British Pavilion at the Venice Biennale. (AD)

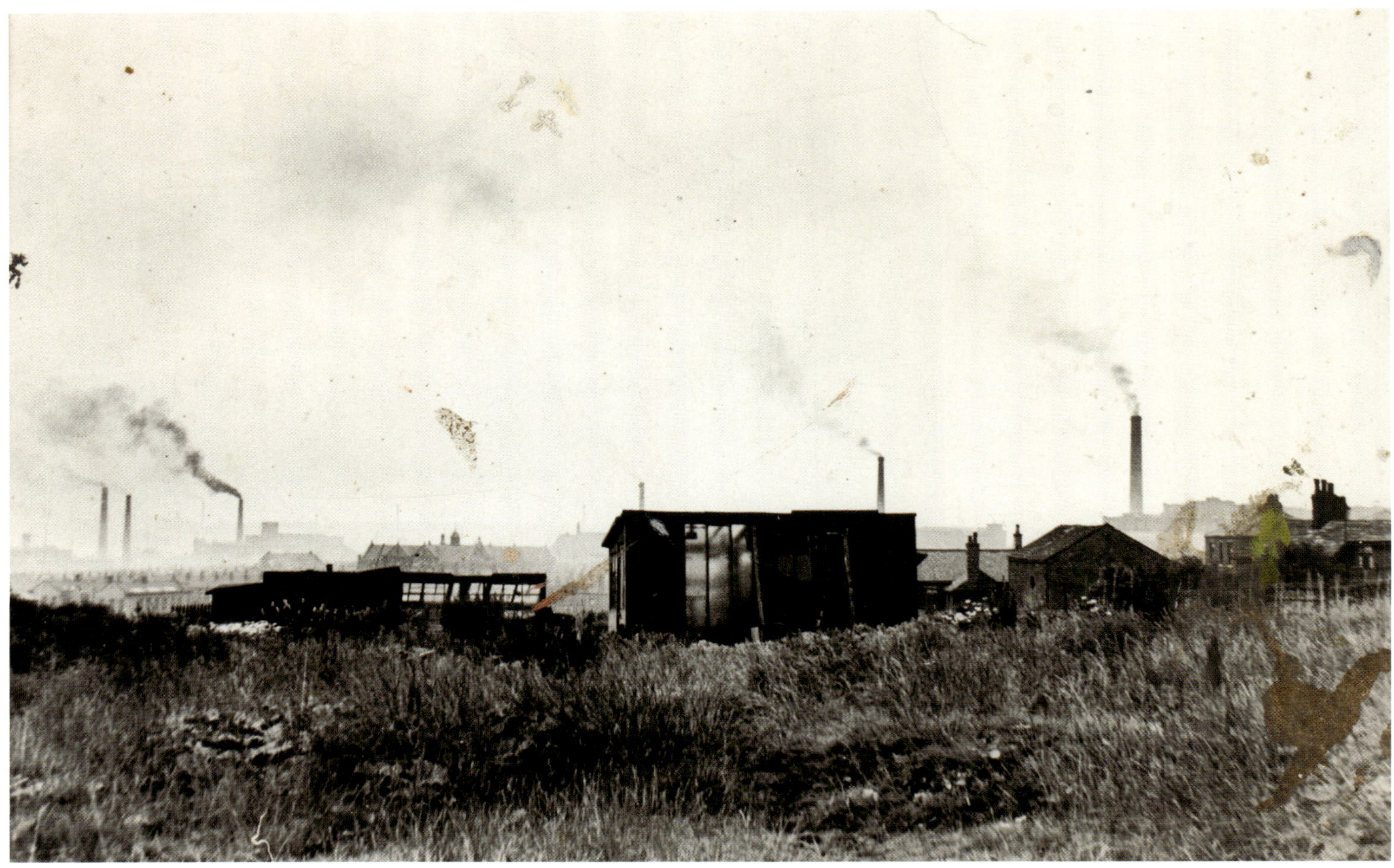

91

91. **Humphrey Jennings**
Walberswick, Suffolk, 1907 – Poros, Greece, 1950
Pigeon Lofts, 1937-38
Gelatin silver print, 19.5 x 30 cm
Victoria and Albert Museum, London

92. **Humphrey Jennings**
Walberswick, Suffolk, 1907 – Poros, Greece, 1950
Factory, 1937-38
Gelatin silver print, 25.5 x 43 cm
Victoria and Albert Museum, London

93. **Humphrey Jennings**
Walberswick, Suffolk, 1907 – Poros, Greece, 1950
Gasometer, 1937-38
Gelatin silver print, 24.5 x 37.5 cm
Victoria and Albert Museum, London

Jennings was one of the most extraordinary British creative talents of his time, admired as a painter and draughtsman, a promoter of the Surrealist movement, an intellectual historian with a special expertise in the Industrial Revolution, a poet, critic, photographer and (most impressively) film-maker. These photographs were taken as part of Jennings's involvement with Mass-Observation – a kind of anthropological analysis of British social mores by an army of voluntary 'observers' – of which he was a co-founder in 1937. The project attracted a number of artists, including the photographer Humphrey Spender and the painters Graham Bell, William Coldstream and Julian Trevelyan. The innovative poet and literary scholar William Empson 'was assigned to take notes on the contents of sweetshop windows' (Jackson 2004, p. 186).

The photographs here are probably all from Bolton, in the north-west of England, which was known in Mass-Observation writings and slang as 'Worktown' (Dickens's 'Coketown' in *Hard Times* was based on nearby Preston). According to a 1944 profile of Jennings by Allen Hutt, 'At 5 a.m. on a summer day in the middle nineteen-thirties, a young man, with a Leica ... over his shoulder, stepped out of the station at Bolton and took his first look at that typical Lancashire manufacturing town.' He saw something completely new to him: 'the land of industry, of the factory and of the working class' (quoted ibid., p. 187). Jennings's view of the interlocking functional buildings and apparatus of a factory is unlike the typical photography of his time: unusually, Jennings found the forms and materials interesting in themselves without seeking dramatic angles of view or lighting effects. The matter-of-factness of this factory view links interestingly with Jennings's quick appreciation of Walker Evans, on whose seminal book *American Photographs* (1938) he based a poem in May 1939 (Jennings 1982, p. 18). The photograph of pigeon lofts, in the setting of allotment gardens, demonstrated Jennings's interest in working-class pastimes and served as the basis for a painting. (The splashes of paint on this print suggest that it was the one Jennings worked from.) It was the poetic, rather than purely anthropological or political side of Mass-Observation that appealed to Jennings, as is seen in his view of a gasometer. This made the most of his access to the top of the structure, from which he could photograph its dramatically streaked cover. The journal *Contemporary Poetry and Prose* announced publication of *Reports and Photographs* by Jennings, but this never appeared, presumably because of the paper shortages of the Second World War. (MHB)

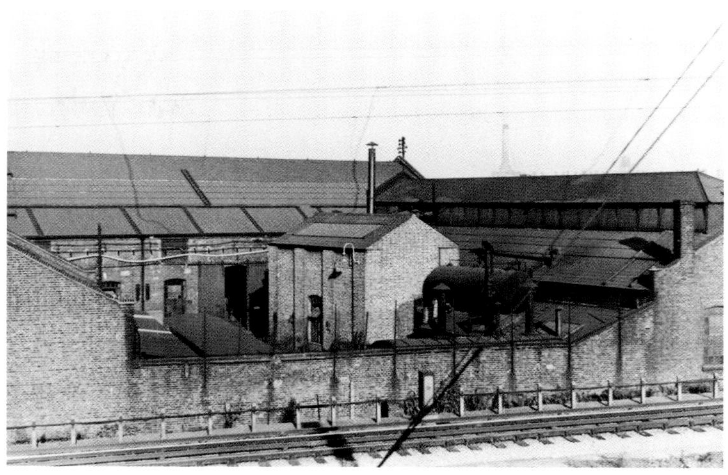

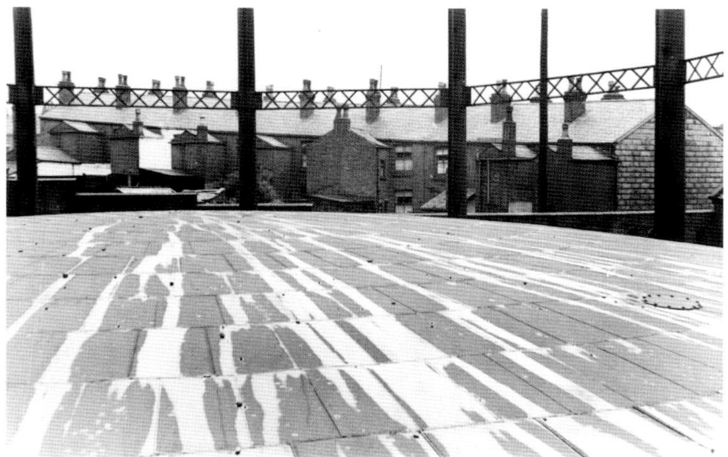

92 – 93

94. **William Coldstream**
Belford, Northumberland, 1908 – London, 1987
St Pancras Station, 1938
Oil on canvas, 71.1 x 91.4 cm
Private Collection

95. **William Coldstream**
Belford, Northumberland, 1908 – London, 1987
St Giles, Cripplegate, 1946-48
Oil on canvas, 78.7 x 91.4 cm
Arts Council Collection, South Bank Centre, London

Coldstream studied at the Slade School in London. He began exhibiting in the 1930s but worked for the documentary film unit of the GPO (General Post Office) in the middle of the decade, uncertain of his direction or of the value of painting. He returned to full-time painting in 1937 with a belief in the need for an objective way of making art. With Victor Pasmore and Claude Rogers, he established the Euston Road School. During the Second World War he was an official war artist in Egypt and Italy. He continued painting after the war (mainly painting portraits and nudes from life) and also entered British cultural public life, as Slade Professor, Chairman of the Art Panel of the Arts Council, Chairman of the British Film Institute and, most notably, as Chairman of the National Advisory Council on Art Education, in which position he transformed art education in Britain.

St Pancras Station was begun after Coldstream returned in May 1938 from Bolton in Lancashire, where he had painted the dark terraces of the industrial town from the roof of the Art Gallery as part of a Mass-Observation study (see cat. 91-93). The Bolton painting (National Gallery of Canada, Ottawa), was criticized for not including people, and the carefully placed figures on the platform in St Pancras were a response to this. Both paintings suggest the inherent difficulty of recording the social scene in such a painstaking manner, a problem that is evident also in Coldstream's war paintings. But, equally, both paintings – they are on a similarly ambitious scale – are amongst the most memorable British paintings of that troubled decade.

Bomb-damaged post-war London provided Coldstream with equally resonant subjects. He wrote in a letter of finding 'some wonderful views. One in particular, Cripplegate Church standing alone on a devastated plain and part of the old wall of London exposed' (letter to John Rake, 9 October 1946, Tate Archive). *Cripplegate* was painted from a window overlooking the site and completed during forty-three sessions over a period of two years. Another work, on a smaller scale, of bomb damage in London, *St Nicholas Cole Abbey* (British Council), was completed at this time. Such subjects were eventually to lead to Coldstream's late paintings of Westminster Abbey, in which the history and meaning of this building is expressed through the careful recording of its visual reality. (AD)

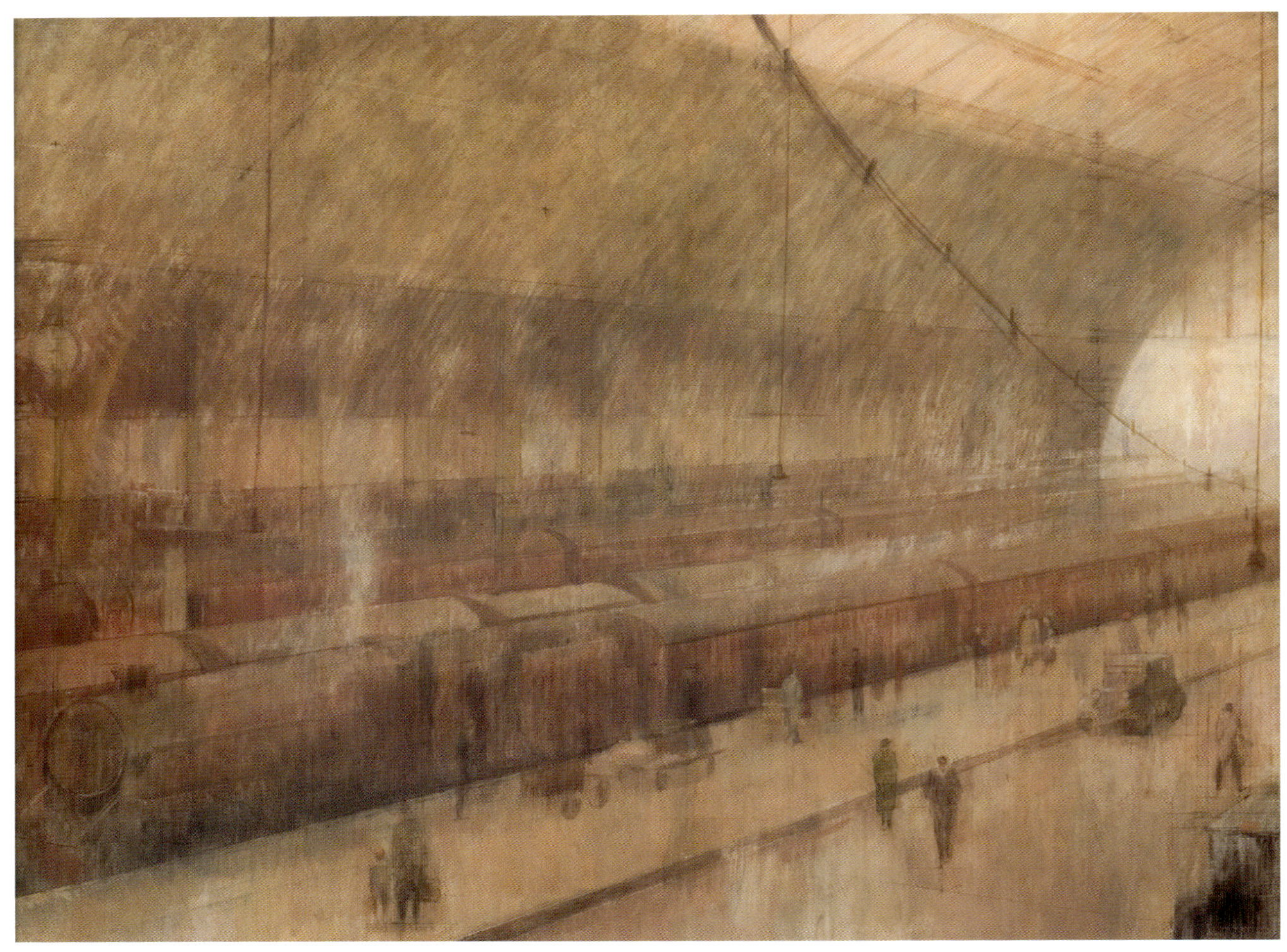

94

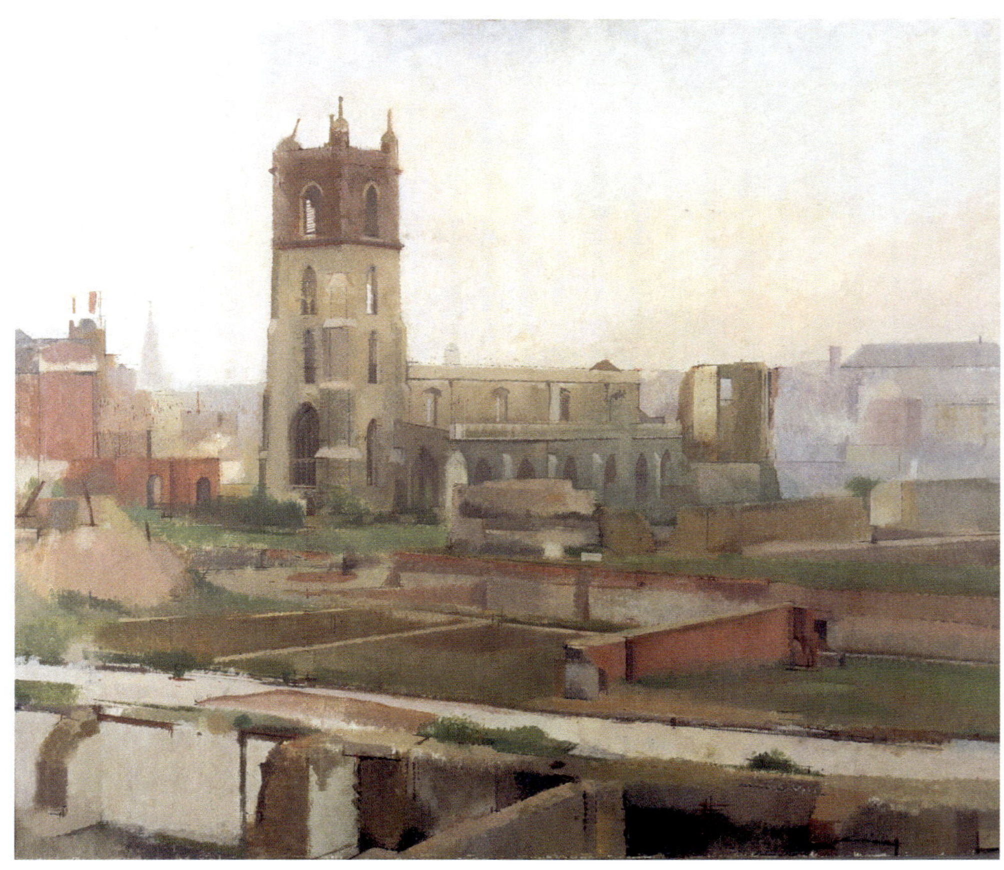

95

96. **Bill Brandt**
Hamburg, 1904 – London, 1983
People Sheltering in the Tube, Elephant and Castle Tube Station, 1940
Gelatin silver print, 25 x 19.5 cm
Victoria and Albert Museum, London

In autumn 1940 Brandt was commissioned by the British Government's Ministry of Information to photograph London's improvised air-raid shelters. A complete set of the photographs was sent to President Roosevelt. Two underground stations were selected. Brandt later recalled the eerie silence of the shelters in contrast to the noisy bombardment of the Blitz overhead. He remembered 'the long alley of intermingled bodies, with the hot, smelly air and continual murmur of snores' (Haworth-Booth and Mellor 1985, p. 37). Cyril Connolly published Brandt's photographs in *Horizon* (February 1942) and wrote that Brandt's photograph of Elephant and Castle Station at 3:45 a.m. 'eternalizes for me the dreamlike monotony of wartime London'. *Lilliput* magazine published the photographs alongside Henry Moore's shelter drawings in December 1942. This is a vintage print; in the 1970s Brandt retouched his prints to remove the alert man in the right foreground, the better to evoke a Surrealist scene of silence and sleep. (MHB)

97. **Henry Moore**
Castleford, West Yorkshire, 1898 – Perry Green, Much Hadham, Hertfordshire, 1986
Row of Sleepers, 1941
Watercolour and ink on paper, 54.5 x 32 cm
Bottom right: Moore/41
British Council, London

Henry Moore's sketchbooks from the start of the Second World War are rich in complexity and allusion as he sought both subject and form to respond to the London Blitz. His encounter with shelterers on Belsize Park underground station opened a deeply rewarding seam, inspiring drawing for its own sake and not simply as preparation for sculpture. (Moore produced no sculpture from October 1940 until the end of 1942.) The lines of figures echoed his own pre-war sculptural forms, and he empathized deeply with their plight. In Moore's work, sleep becomes a metaphor both for death raining from the sky – many of the figures are covered in ash like bodies excavated from Pompeii – and for the possibility of escape from the nightmare of daily life (Andrews 2002, p. 48; and Eric Newton, commentary to *Out of Chaos*, directed by Jill Craigie, produced by Two Cities, 1944: Newton refers specifically to how Moore captures the disturbed rhythms of sleep.) Prompted by Kenneth Clark, Moore completed a number of finished drawings for purchase by the British war artist scheme. (RT)

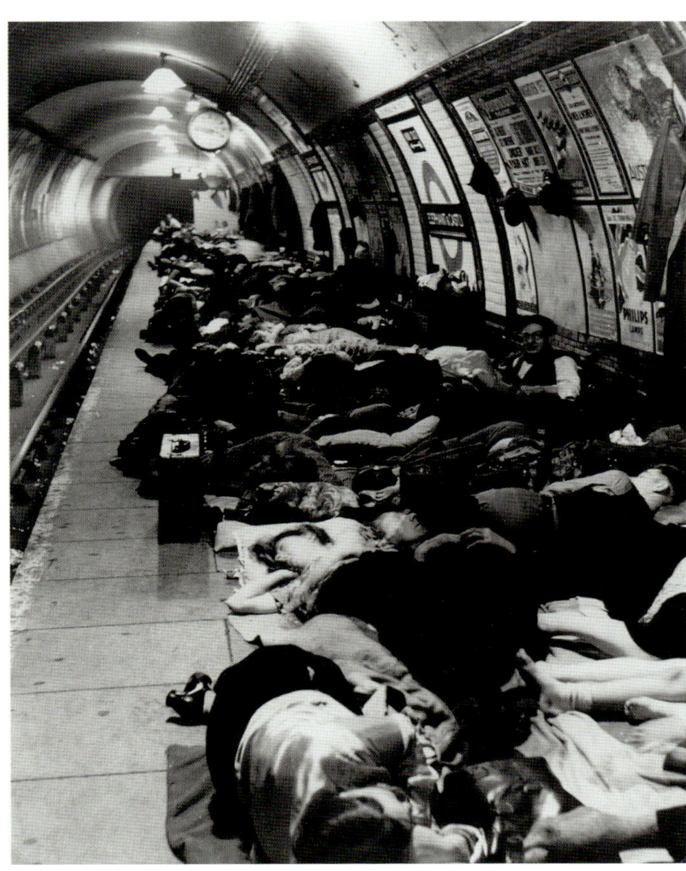
96

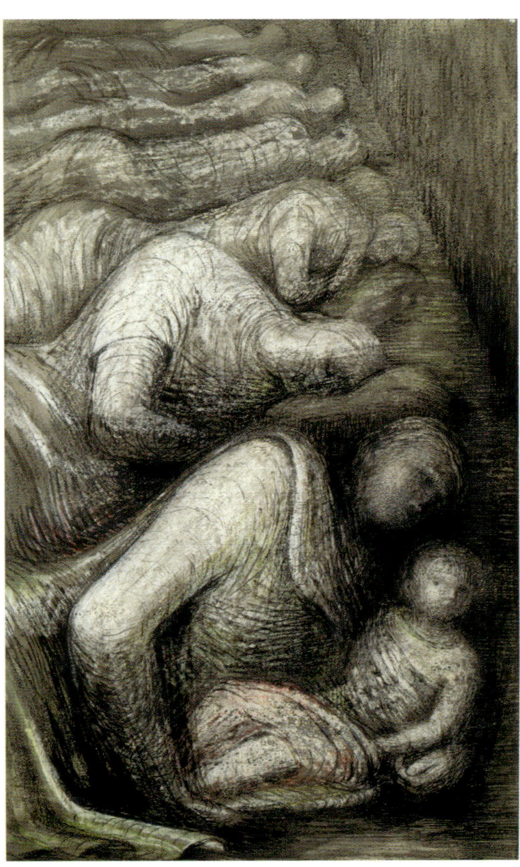
97

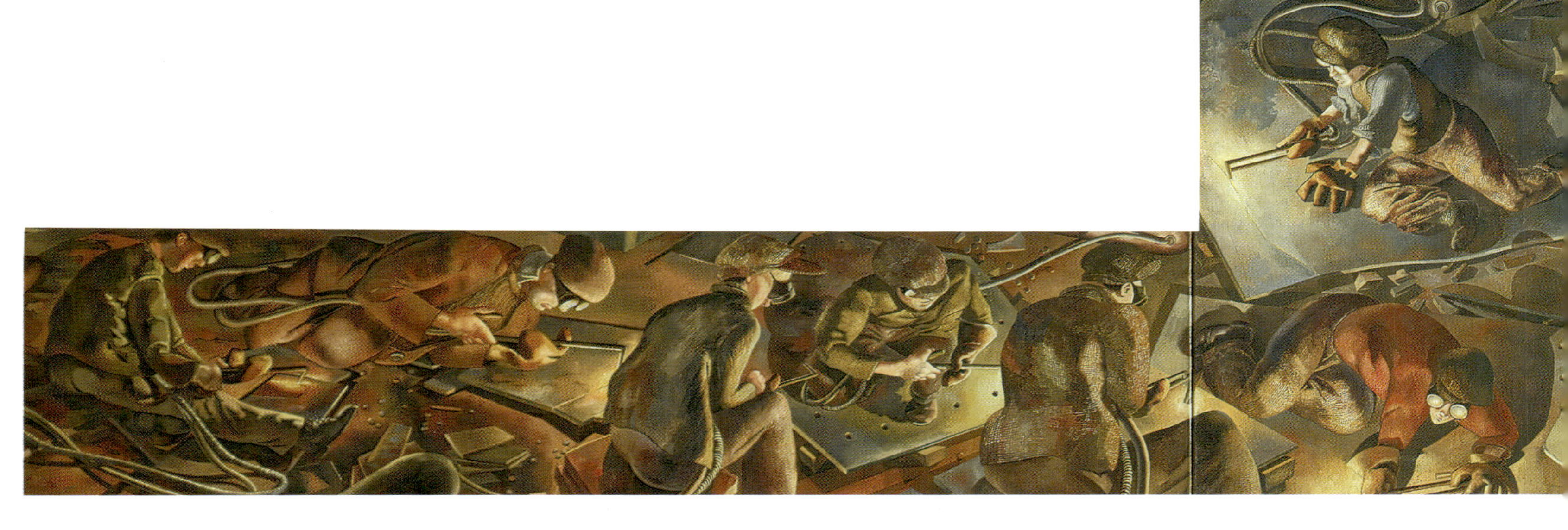

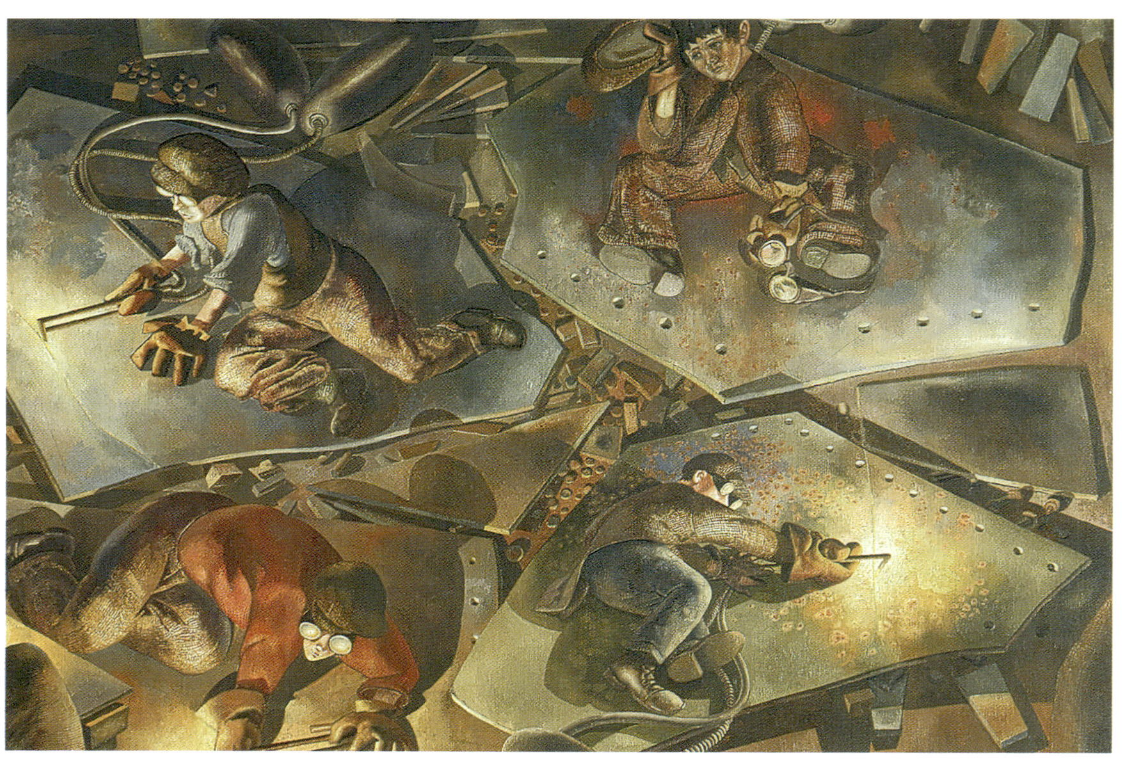

98, central panel

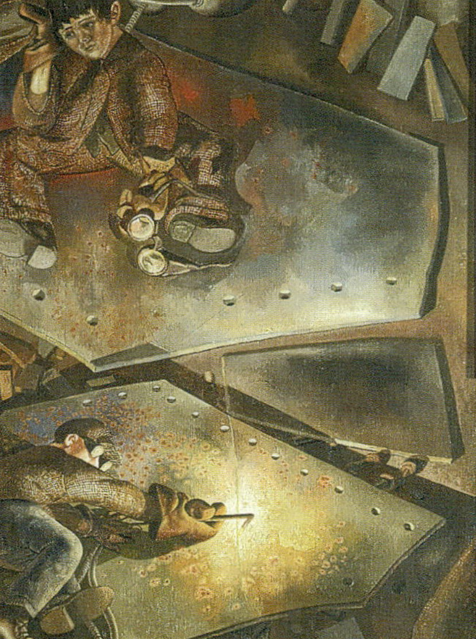
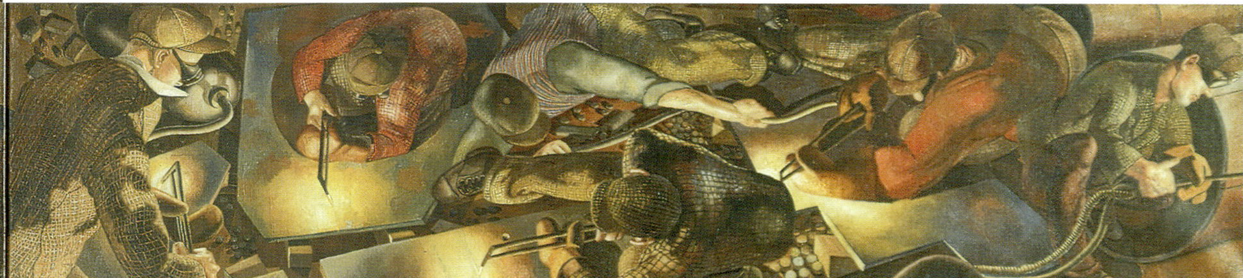

98

98. **Stanley Spencer**
Cookham, Berkshire, 1891 – Cliveden, Buckinghamshire, 1959
Shipbuilding on the Clyde: Burners (triptych), 1940
Oil on canvas, left to right: 50.8 x 203.2 cm,
106.7 x 153.4 cm, 50.8 x 203.2 cm
Imperial War Museum, London

Painted very rapidly between July and August 1940, *Burners* eschews all those grotesque elements that had so alienated Spencer's patrons from *The Dustman* (cat. 298) onwards. In May, commissioned by the War Artists' Advisory Committee, he had travelled up to Port Glasgow, drawing for several days in the Lithgow shipyard. Then he returned to his small bedroom-cum-studio above a pub in the Gloucestershire village of Leonard Stanley, where the fifteen-foot picture could be completed in three sections. As at Burghclere Chapel (p.28, fig. 13), Spencer exalts everyday activity to visionary altarpiece. He would have been aware of the Detroit murals of Diego Rivera (with their similar aesthetic of crowding); and he would also have seen photographs of some of the American WPA imagery. *Burners* was well-received, and exhibited in October at the National Gallery. (TH)

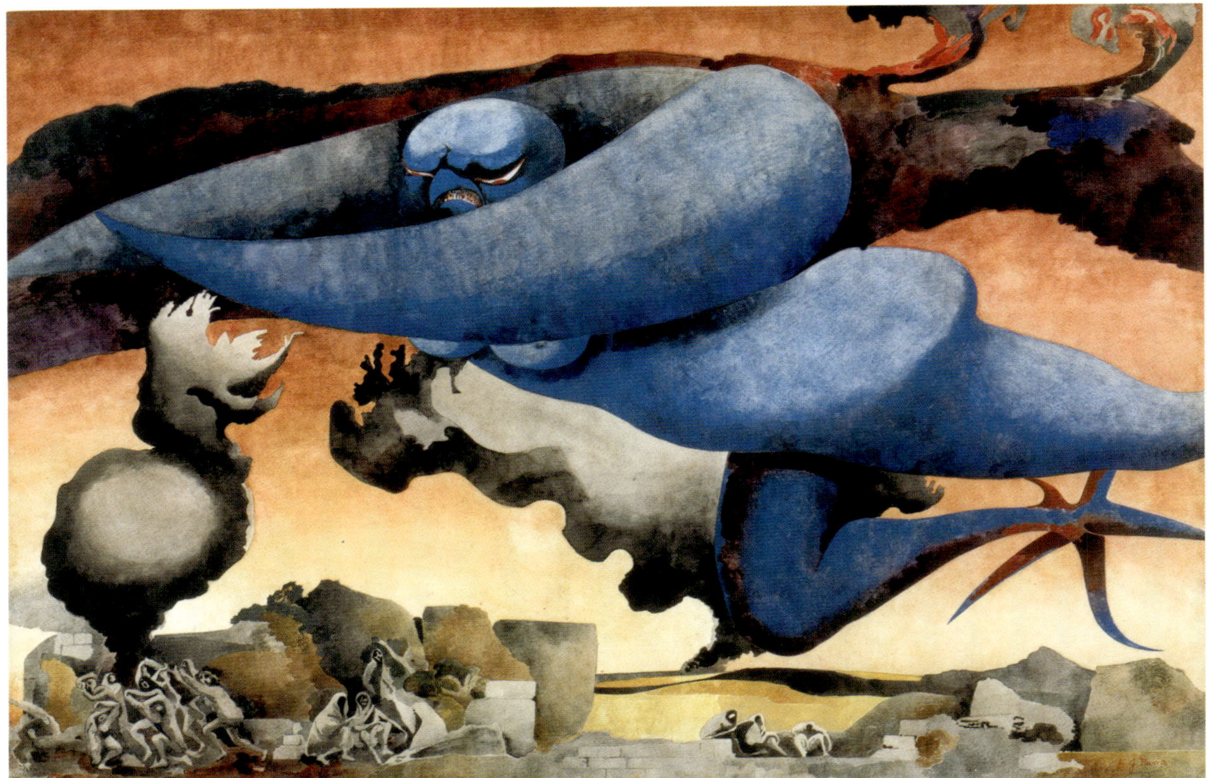

99

99. **Edward Burra**
London, 1905 – Hastings, Sussex, 1976
Blue Baby, Blitz over Britain, 1941
Watercolour and gouache on paper, 67.5 x 100.5 cm
Bottom right: E.J. Burra
Imperial War Museum, London

Surreal images of menace had appeared in Edward Burra's paintings during the 1930s, and in *Blue Baby* the menace is personified into a monstrous harpy, constructed from aircraft parts, dispensing punishment and retribution. With the outbreak of war, Burra had returned to Rye on the South Coast and lived through the Luftwaffe's attempts to destroy the chain of radar stations during the winter of 1940-41. He described the impact of the bombing both with despair and with a certain relish, as patterns of ordered urban life were radically changed. One incident. when 'a bomb or so fell round the cinema suddenly turned into one of its own newsreels', and he stumbled on 'a crowd of picturesquely dressed figurants poking about in the yellowish dust' (letter to unnamed recipient, 1 October 1942; cited in Rothenstein 1973, p. 30), seems relevant to this image, where a cartoon-like, cinematic fantasy-character gloats over the defenceless, terrified population, reduced to a primitive existence amongst the rubble. (RT)

100. **Edward Burra**
London, 1905 – Hastings, Sussex, 1976
Rye Landscape with Figure, 1947
Pencil and watercolour on paper, 88.3 x 110.2 cm
Trustees of the Cecil Higgins Art Gallery, Bedford

Burra spent the war years in Rye, in his family's home. His lifelong friend the American poet Conrad Aiken returned to Rye in 1946, and they travelled to the Lake District together. The following year he visited Dublin and Galway, but it was not until a few years later that he resumed his continental and American trips. Generally, the work of the post-war years was to be more centred in Britain and Ireland. At the end of his life landscape was the predominant subject but his work of the 1940s and 1950s was as varied as ever: religious subjects, still lifes, designs for the stage, and the bar scenes which include so much human life. Burra apparently never sketched directly, and his landscapes are the result of deep knowledge of the subject, as is clearly the case with this Rye landscape, or of a phenomenal memory for place – or at least the atmosphere of place, for they are rarely topographically accurate. The half-sinister and half-comic figure was based on someone who worked for the Burra family. He is free of the masks and devices of some more menacing Burra figures and perhaps for that reason has a stronger presence in the landscape. (AD)

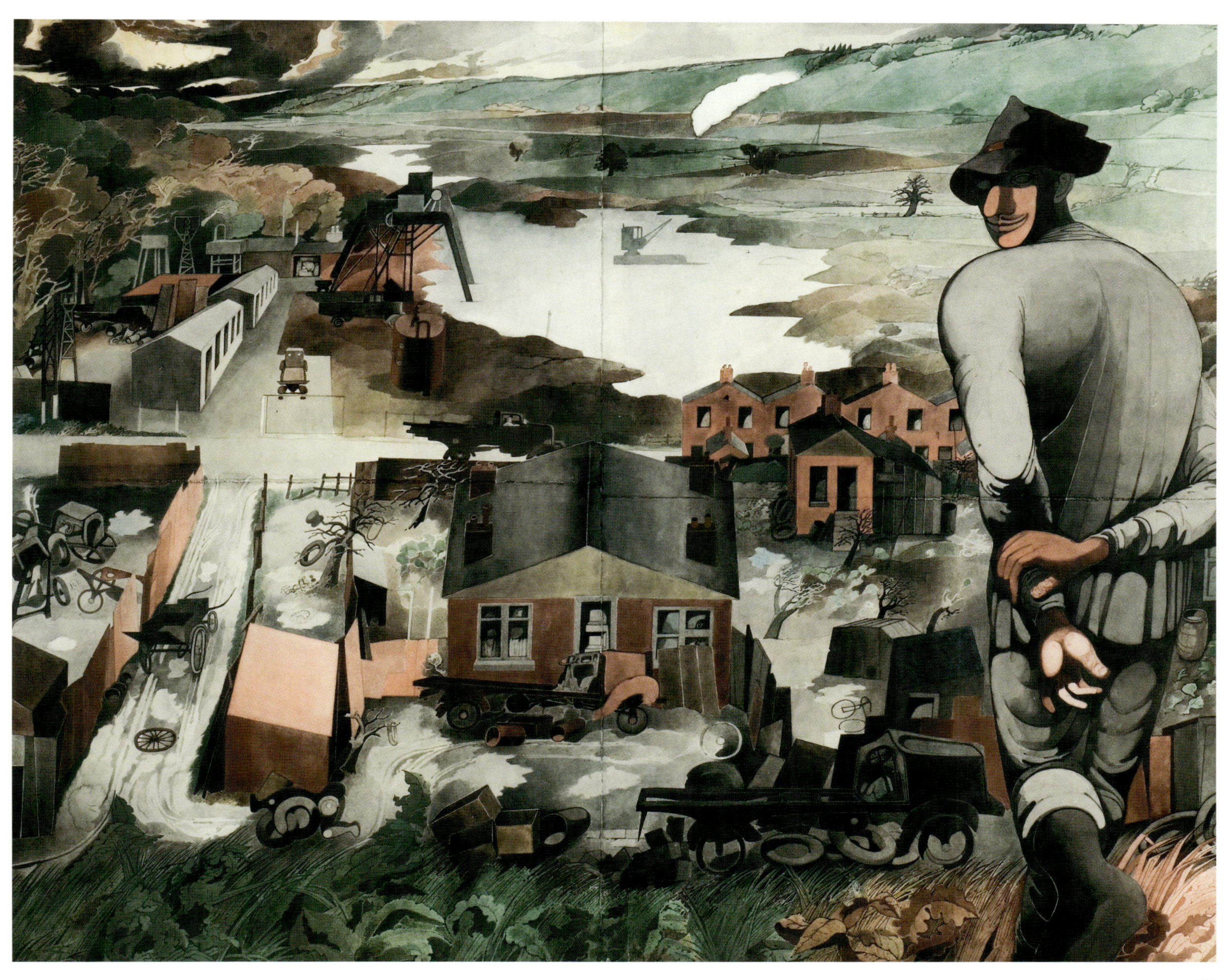

100

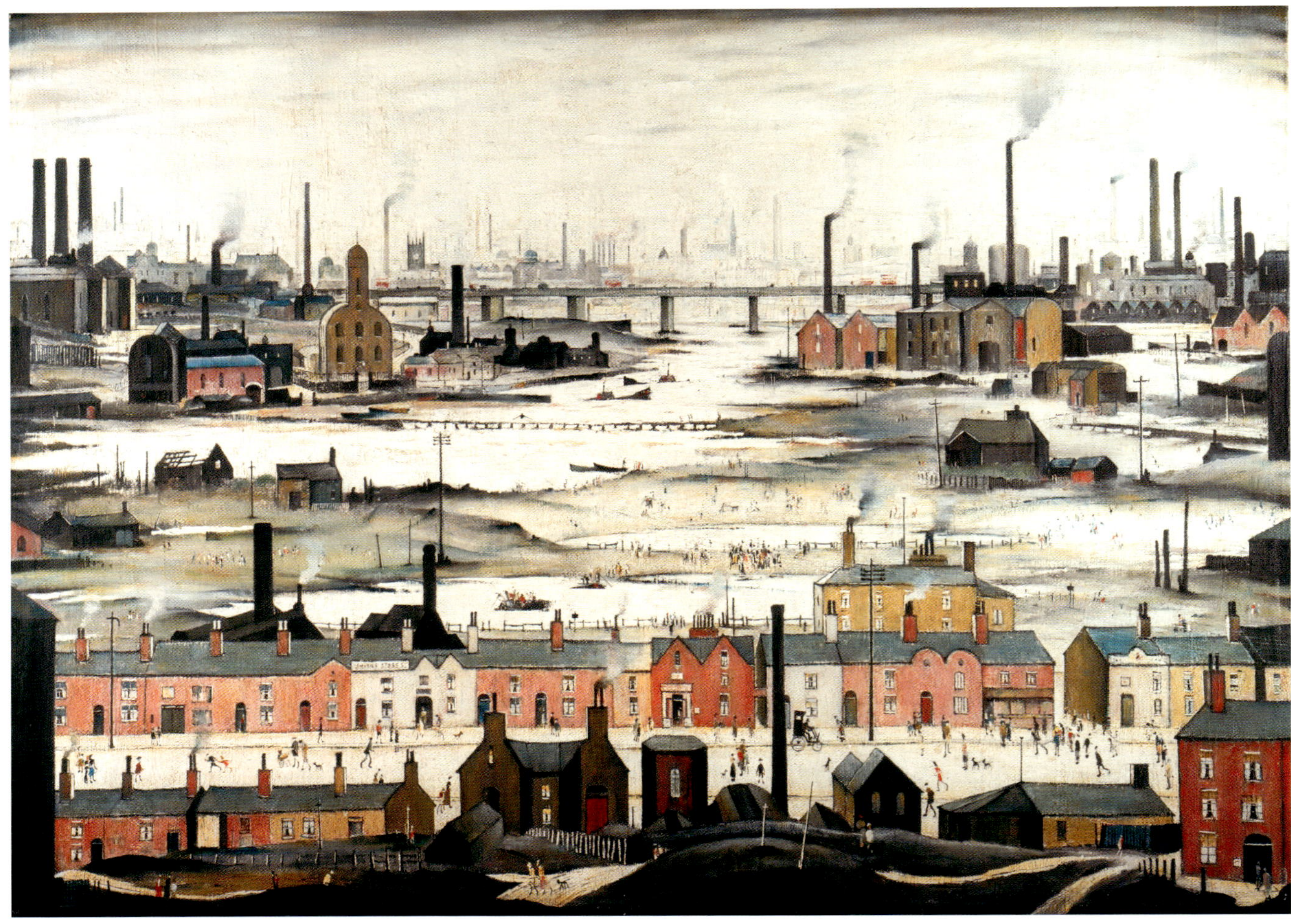

101

101. **Laurence Stephen Lowry**
Stretford, near Manchester, 1887 – Glossop, Derbyshire, 1976
Industrial Landscape, 1950
Oil on canvas, 110.2 x 148.3 cm
Bottom left: L.S. Lowry 1950
Leicester Arts and Museums Service

Industrial Landscape is typical of the urban panoramas which Lowry painted throughout his life, an alternative outlook to England's famous 'green and pleasant lands'. Although based upon his own first-hand perambulations through the streets of northern towns such as Salford and Pendlebury, Lowry's paintings evoke a generic, rather than specific sense of place. His landscapes were as much a creation of his imagination as the product of observation. He evolved a pictorial vocabulary of smoking chimneys, terraced housing, telegraph poles and railway bridges, which conjured up the quintessential experience of the industrial north. Lowry frequently referred to his pictures as 'dreamscapes'. In addition to the simplicity of his forms and colouring, his work is characterized by a sense of detachment. Although replete with physical objects and local details, *Industrial Landscape* is markedly devoid of emotion. The tiny, gestural figures mill about the blank streets without interaction or awareness of each other. (NM)

102. **Laurence Stephen Lowry**
Stretford, near Manchester, 1887 – Glossop, Derbyshire, 1976
Pendlebury Scene, 1931
Pencil on paper, 28.3 x 37.8 cm
Bottom right: LS Lowry 1931
LS Lowry Collection, Salford, Manchester

'At first I detested it', wrote Lowry of Pendlebury, the industrial town where he lived from 1908 to 1947. Walking the Manchester region in his full-time job as a rent collector, he came to internalize this unique topography. 'As I got to the top of the station steps, I saw the Acme Mill, a great dark-red block with the low streets of mill-cottages running right up to it – and suddenly I knew what I had to paint.' Lowry's long academic training had given him a sophisticated awareness of urban masters such as Meryon and Daumier, but he developed a work-process, based mainly on drawings made from memory: scenes peopled by 'matchstick-men', often mistakenly categorized as 'naïve'. 'I wanted to paint myself into what absorbed me,' Lowry wrote later. 'Natural figures would have broken the spell of it, so I made my figures half unreal ... They are part of a private beauty that haunted me. I loved them and the houses in the same way: as part of a vision.' (Howard 2000, p. 123) (TH)

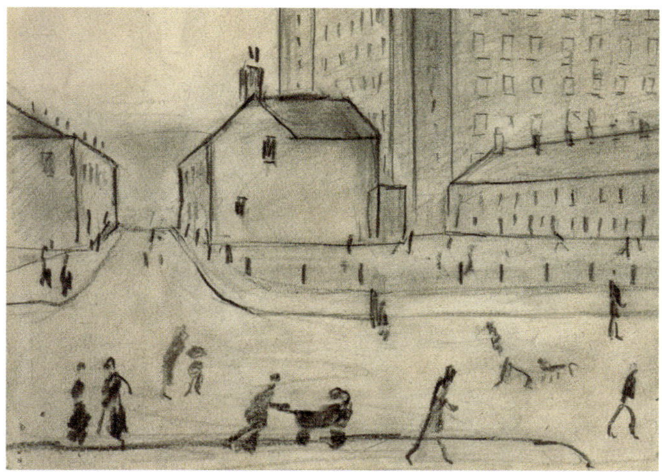

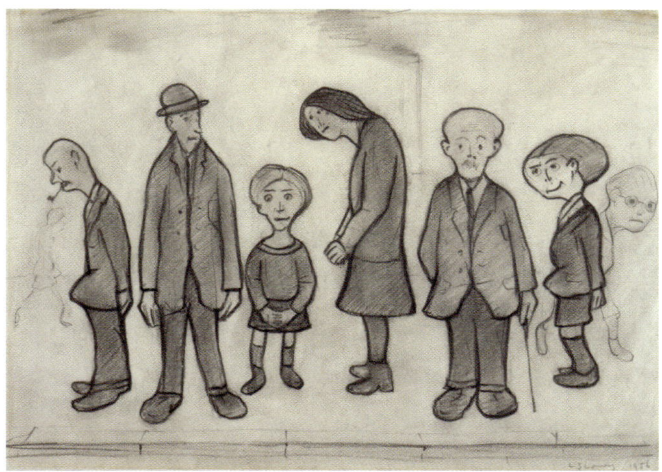

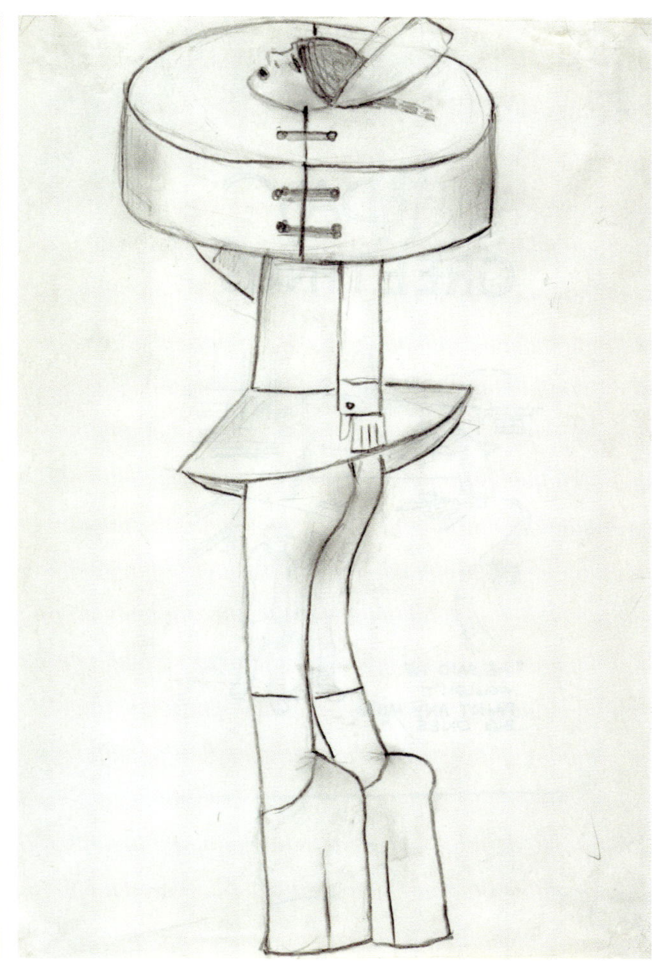

102 – 103

104

103. **Laurence Stephen Lowry**
Stretford, near Manchester, 1887 – Glossop, Derbyshire, 1976
Family Group, 1956
Pencil on paper, 25.5 x 35.5 cm
Bottom right: LS Lowry 1956
LS Lowry Collection, Salford, Manchester

In parallel to his industrial landscapes, Lowry developed an imagery of near-caricatural 'street-types', ranging from the Chaplinesque or clown-like (Stan Laurel was also a Lancashire man) to the misshapen, the crippled, the mad. The frieze of *Family Group* is essentially in the English comic tradition – each of them a descendant of Edward Lear's freakish solitaries. (Lowry figures have also often been related to the grotesques of Stanley Spencer in the 1930s; see *The Dustman*, cat. 298.) But Lowry learnt much from Bruegel and Daumier, and these drab dysfunctionals can be interpreted in class terms – as working-class victims of the depression era. Almost twenty years after this drawing, Lowry would be mesmerized by Pirandello's *Six Characters in Search of an Author*; returning again and again to Ralph Richardson's production, Lowry registered an intense recognition as the tragic family stepped forward together to the edge of the stage. (TH)

104. **Laurence Stephen Lowry**
Stretford, near Manchester, 1887 – Glossop, Derbyshire, 1976
Girl with Bow, c. 1960-70
Pencil on paper, 33 x 21.5 cm
LS Lowry Collection, Salford, Manchester

After his death in 1976, Lowry's executors discovered a large cache of unexhibited obsessional imagery. Living alone (having retired on full pension in 1952), he began to depict an imaginary young girl, 'Ann', as a kind of automaton or fetish-doll (Lowry's favourite ballet was *Coppélia*). In *Girl with Bow*, the clamped ruff is akin to a surgical collar, or a garrotte, while her rising miniskirt, together with her platform shoes, may date this fantasy to the 'dolly bird' fashions of the sixties. Born in 1887, Lowry always described himself as a 'Victorian', and he surrounded himself at home with Rossetti's drawings of *femmes fatales* ('like snakes', he said). Eventually he was able to purchase major late Rossetti paintings, such as *Proserpine*. But although on one level Lowry's erotic drawings are a last echo of the repressed English sexuality that produced Lewis Carroll's *Alice*, they also bring him close to the armoured sexual warriors of Richard Lindner in New York, and even to the imagery of 'outsiders' such as Henry Darger. (TH)

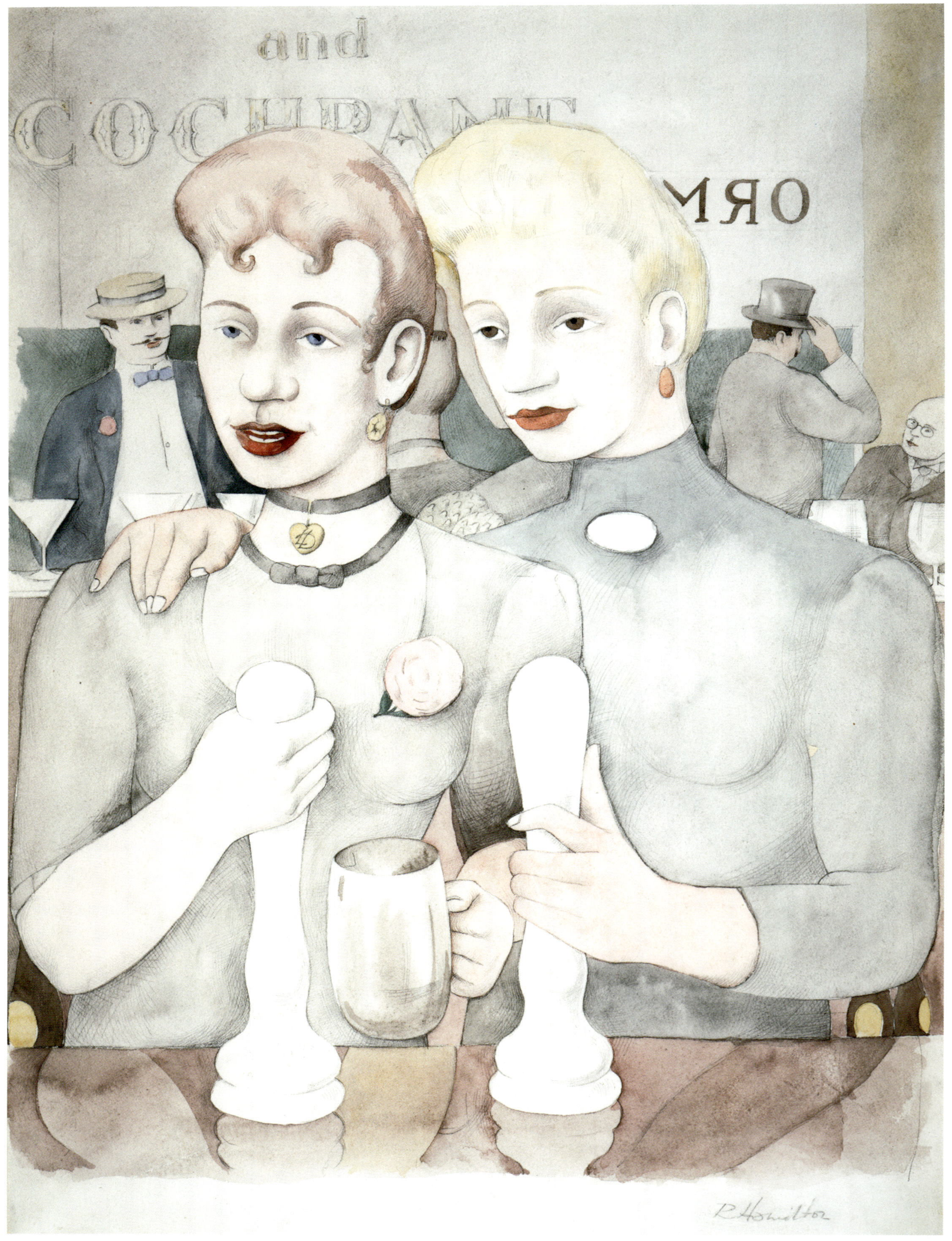

109

105. **Richard Hamilton**
London, 1922
Stately Plump Buck Mulligan, 1948
Ink and watercolour on paper, 57.8 x 39.7 cm
Collection of the artist

106. **Richard Hamilton**
London, 1922
He Foresaw His Pale Body, 1948
Pencil and watercolour on paper, 57 x 39.5 cm
Collection of the artist

107. **Richard Hamilton**
London, 1922
The Transmogrifications of Bloom, 1949
Pencil on paper, 55 x 39.5 cm
Collection of the artist

108. **Richard Hamilton**
London, 1922
Going to Dark Bed, 1949
Ink and wash on paper, 39 x 57 cm
Bottom right: RHamilton
Collection of the artist

109. **Richard Hamilton**
London, 1922
Bronze by Gold, 1949
Pencil and watercolour on paper, 57 x 38.5 cm
Bottom right: RHamilton
Ulster Museum, Belfast

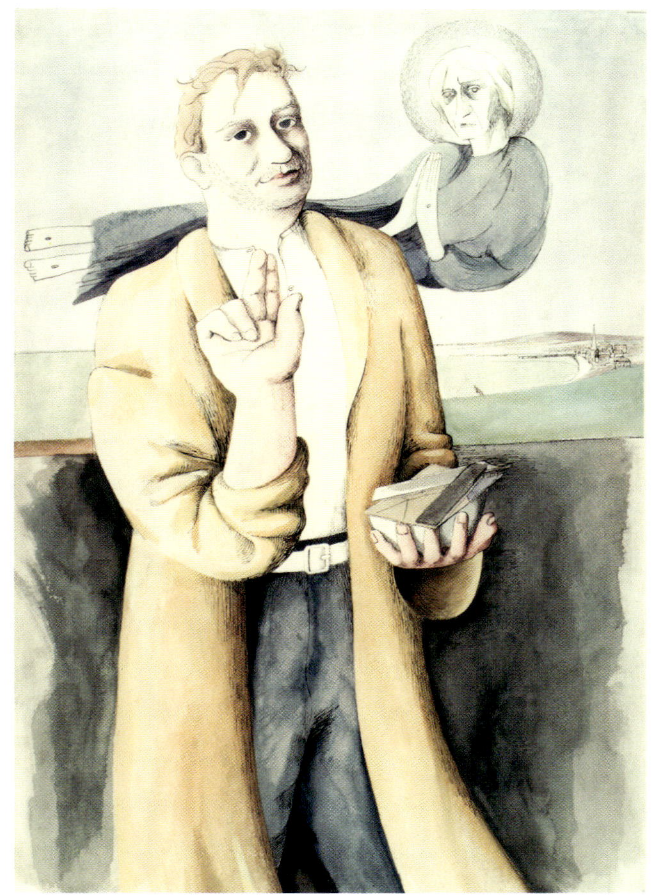

105

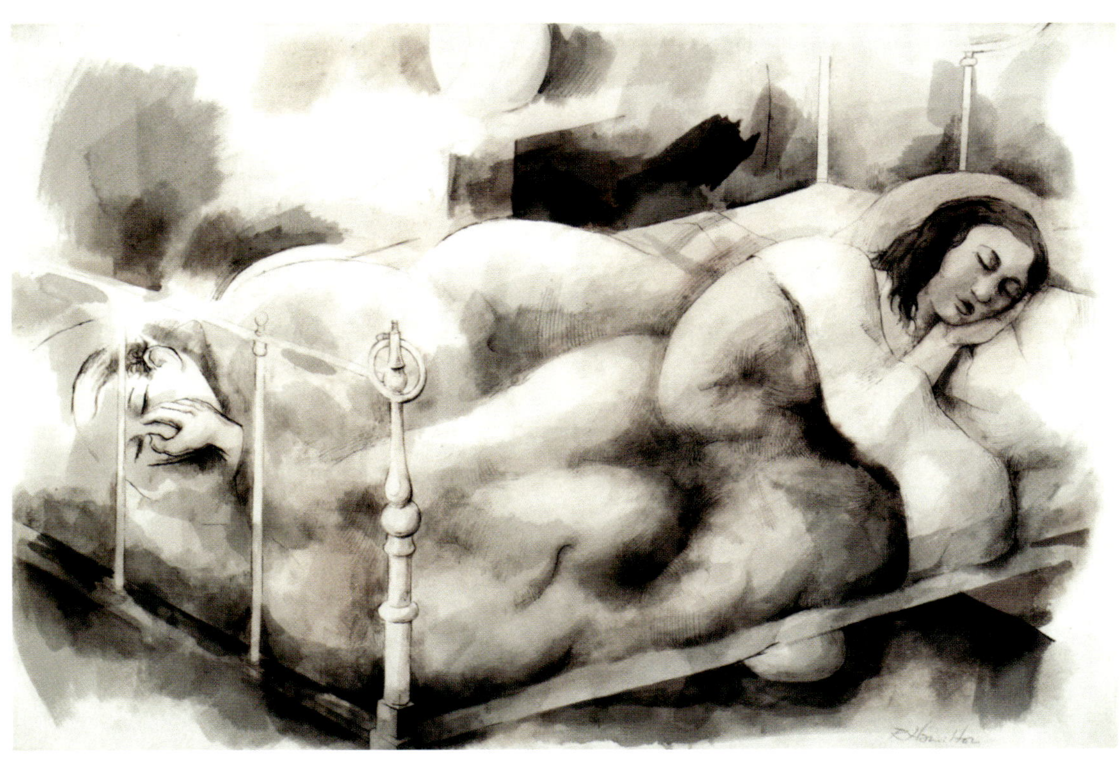

108

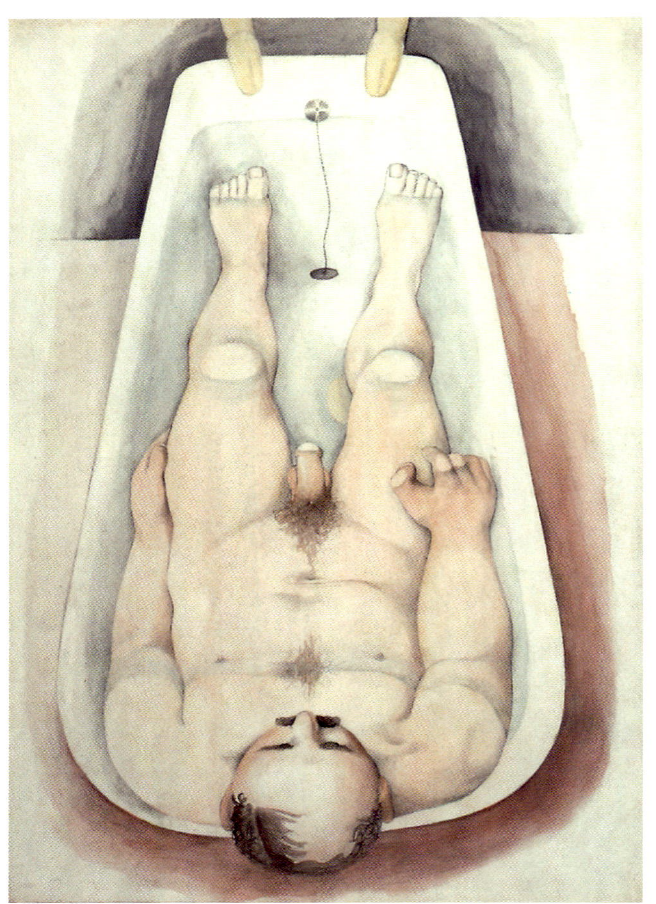

106

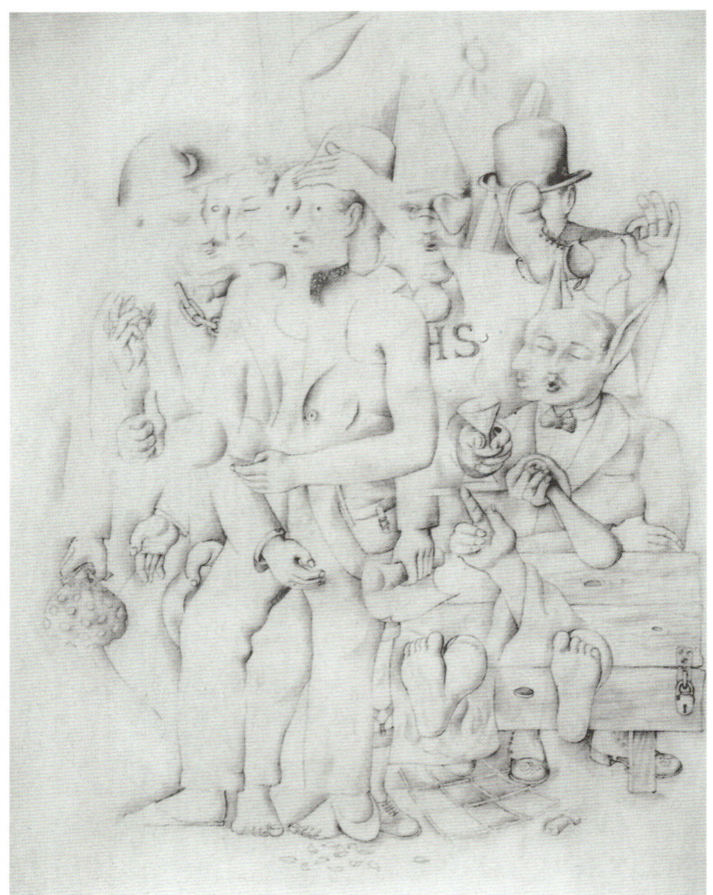

107

Richard Hamilton is one of the initiators of British Pop and a hugely influential figure in recent British art. He has been described (by David Sylvester) as having a 'consuming obsession with the modern – modern living, modern technology, modern equipment, modern communications, modern materials, modern processes, modern attitudes' (Sylvester 1991, p. 9). At the same time he is also, in his words, 'an old-fashioned artist' (public interview with Michael Craig-Martin, Institute of Contemporary Arts, London 1990). His subjects and his techniques are both new and traditional. In this exhibition his interest in new technology might be compared with Wright of Derby, his satire and his irony with James Gillray, and his engagement with modern life with Hogarth and Ford Madox Brown. Hamilton's full achievements lie outside the time-frame of the present exhibition, but they are already evident in his early work, in his lifelong project to illustrate Joyce's great modern novel. The project took shape during military service at the end of the 1940s: 'The only benefit I gained from eighteen months of enforced detention in our post-war army was time to read … With illustration in mind my examination of *Ulysses* was more intensive than that of any book I had read. The process of studying Joyce did more than provide me with subject matter. It made me aware of a stylistic and technical freedom that might be applied to painting in general' (Hamilton 2002, p. 89). Anne Seymour has written that the Joyce illustrations represent 'Hamilton's first concerted exploration of a subject in multiple ways' (Seymour 1979). In this small selection from the beginning of the project, *The Transmogrifications of Bloom* suggests the range of approaches he was to introduce as the work developed, but all show the originality of his visualization of Joyce, his barmaids so wonderfully evoked with their hands on 'the smooth jutting beerpull'. A variety of fine prints, mostly made in the Paris studio of Aldo Crommelynck, were published in the 1980s, but the actual project of producing an illustrated version of the novel was abandoned early when T.S. Eliot explained to the young Hamilton the likely cost involved in just setting the type for such a *livre d'artiste*. (AD)

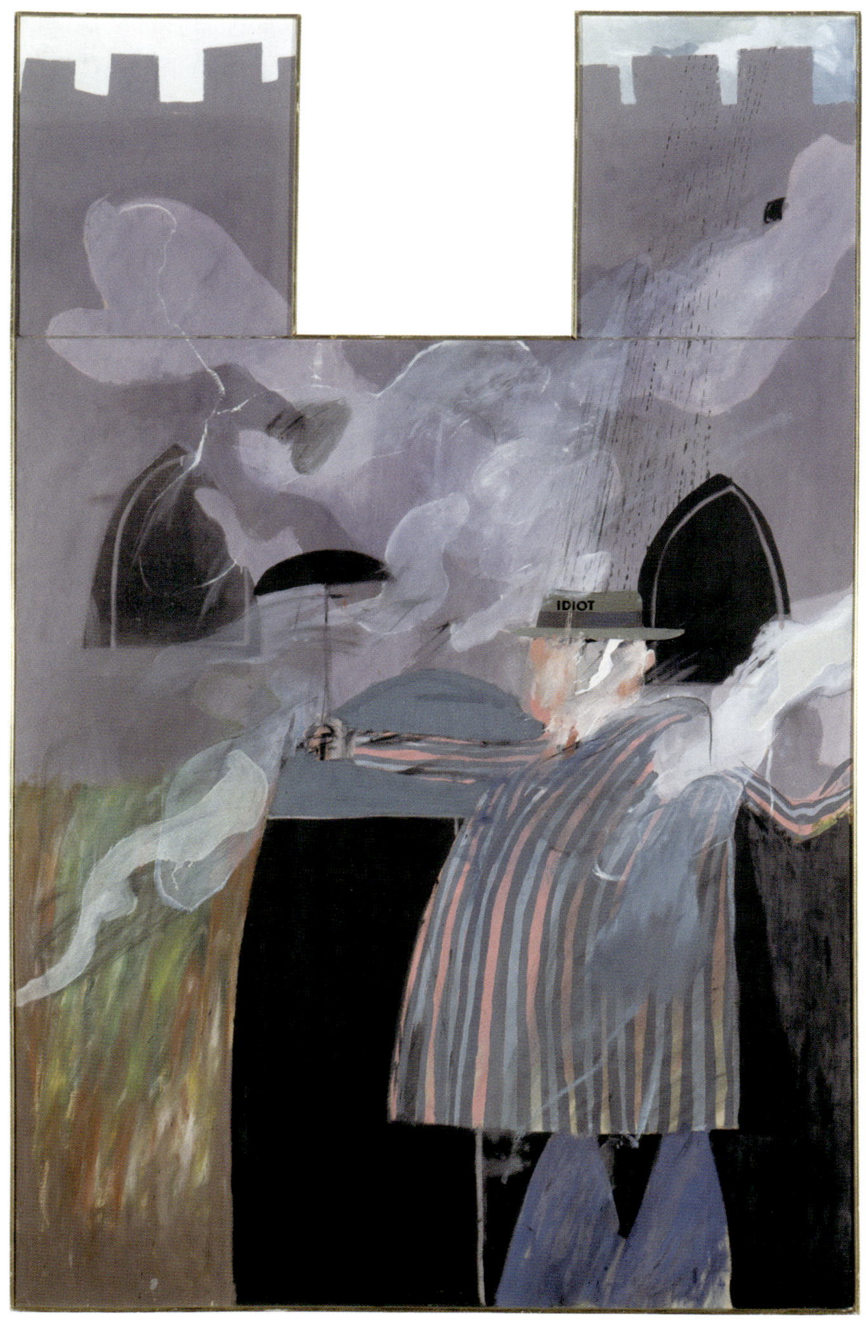

110

110. **David Hockney**
Bradford, West Yorkshire, 1937
Man Stood in Front of his House with Rain Descending (The Idiot), 1962
Oil on canvas, 243 x 152.5 cm
Stedelijk Museum voor Actuele Kunst, Ghent

The titles of Hockney's early paintings are almost as original as the way in which they are painted, and this is surely one of the funniest renderings of idiocy in the long British tradition of social satire. The rain falls on the character's hat (printed with the word 'idiot') while he holds his umbrella at a distance. The crenellated castle towers, added to the top of the canvas, may allude to the popular expression 'an Englishman's home is his castle', not a sentiment with which the young Hockney had much sympathy. Such humour was characteristic of Hockney. In the same year he painted *Picture Emphasising Stillness* (private collection), in which a leaping leopard is about to land on the two protagonists, though we are reassured by an inscription that: 'They are perfectly safe. This is a Still'. These paintings use pictorial devices drawn both from modern art and children's art. They are characteristic of the Pop Art movement on both sides of the Atlantic but also owe something to the interest in naive or untutored art of the French painter Jean Dubuffet. (AD)

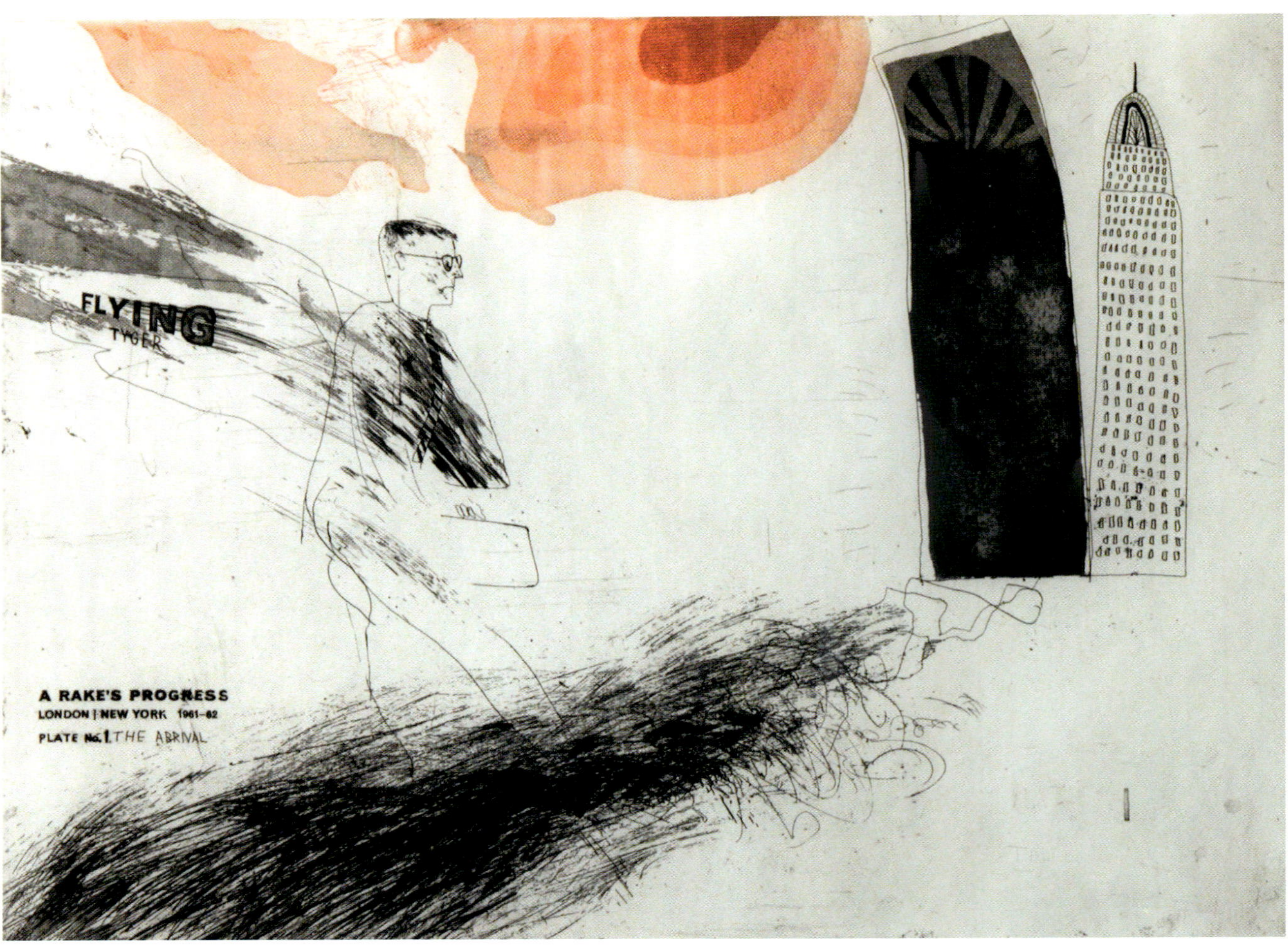

111a

111. **David Hockney**
Bradford, West Yorkshire, 1937
A Rake's Progress (16 plates), 1961-63

a. ***The Arrival***
b. ***Receiving the Inheritance***
c. ***Meeting the Good People***
d. ***The Gospel Singing (Good People) (Madison Sq Garden)***
e. ***The Start of the Spending Spree and the Door Opening for a Blonde***
f. ***The 7-Stone Weakling*** (facsimile)
g. ***The Drinking Scene*** (facsimile)
h. ***Marries an Old Maid***
i. ***The Election Campaign (with Dark Messages)***
j. ***Viewing a Prison Scene***
k. ***Death in Harlem***
l. ***The Wallet Begins to Empty***
m. ***Disintigration***
n. ***Cast Aside***
o. ***Meeting the Other People***
p. ***Bedlam***

Etchings, each approx. 30.5 x 41 cm
Inscribed on each print [apart from facsimiles]:
Bottom left: Artist's Proof
Bottom right: David Hockney
Royal College of Art Collection, London

David Hockney is the youngest of the artists in this exhibition. Whilst still at college he began a novel and refreshing contribution to our theme of social observation. He has recounted how he was not taken seriously at the Royal College of Art until Richard Hamilton, a visiting artist, awarded him a prize, an incident that provides an appropriate link between the two artists with whom the social observation line of our exhibition ends. In these etchings, prepared and proofed at the Royal College of Art (and increased, it should be said, beyond the originally intended eight plates at the behest of the College authorities), Hockney takes Hogarth's idea, does it over again in a modern setting, in a completely contemporary style and with a modern story line. In this case the story is autobiographical and recounts the artist's experience of America, and New York in particular. Our hero's 'Inheritance' comes from selling an etching (*'Myself and My Heroes'*,

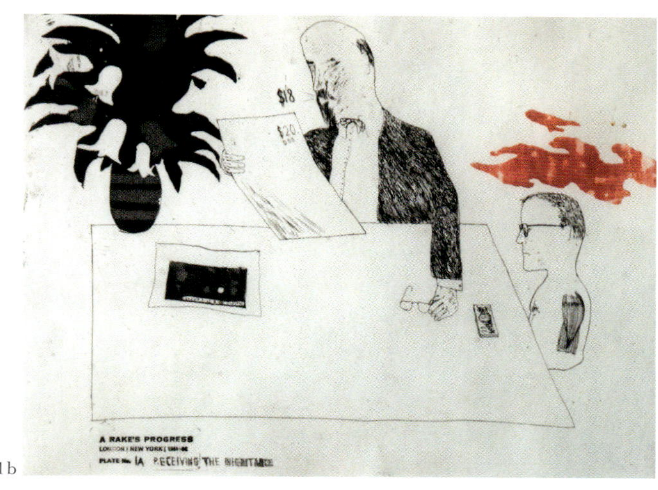

111b

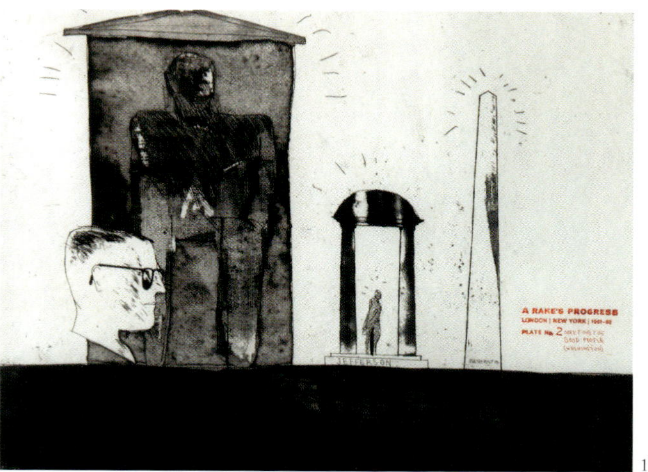

111c

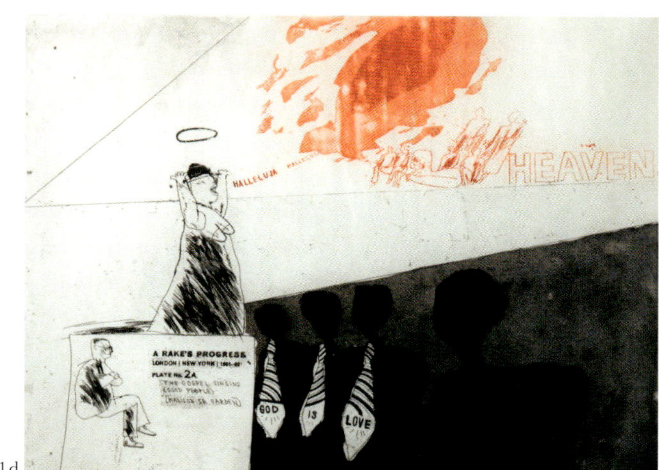

111d

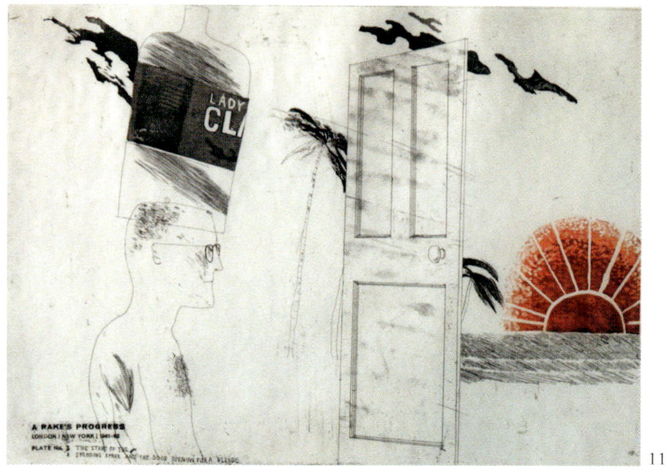

111e

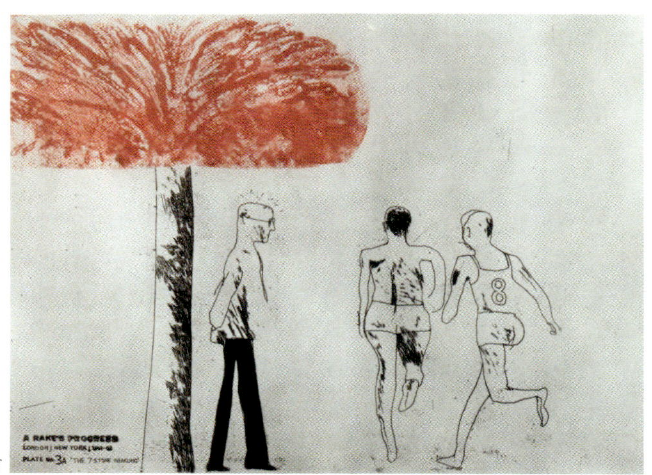

111f

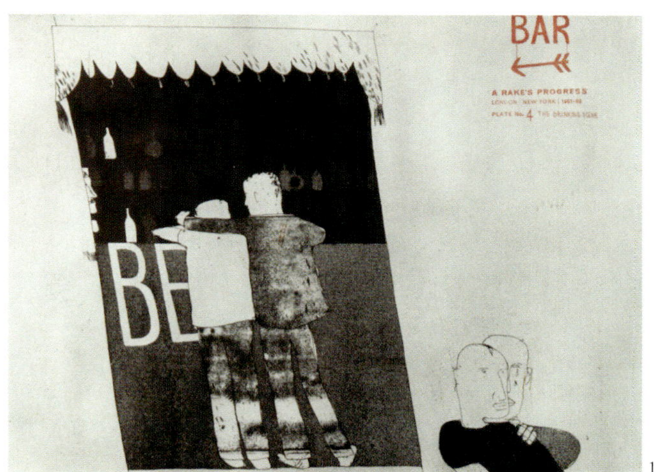

111g

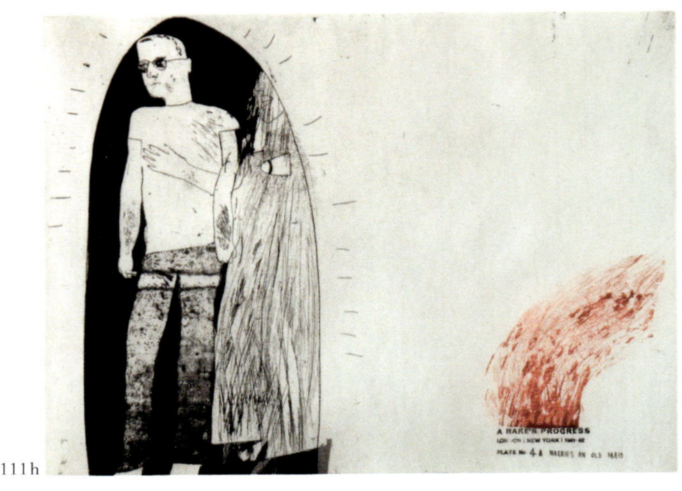

111h

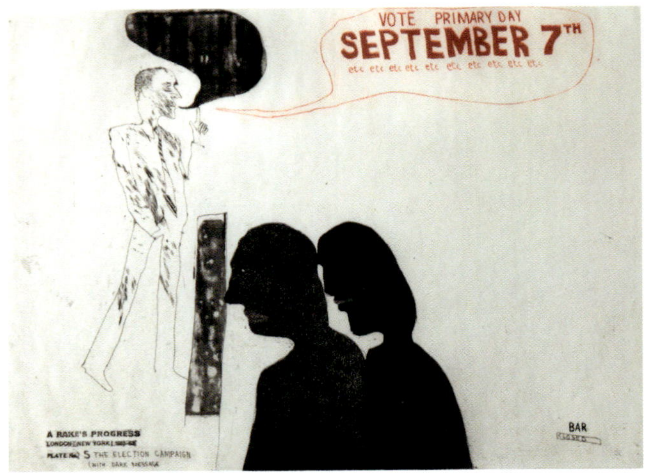

111i

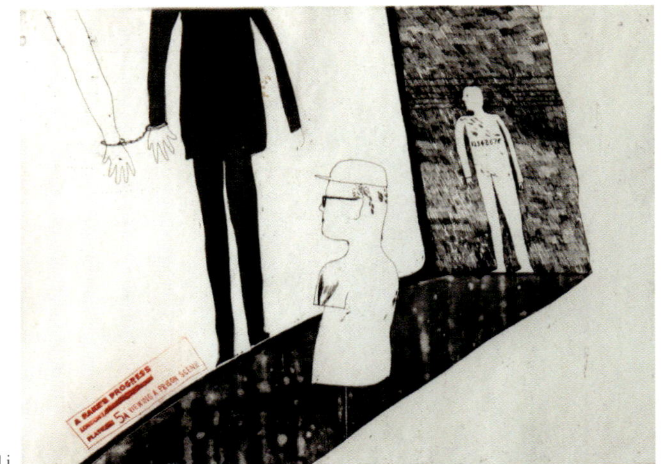

111j

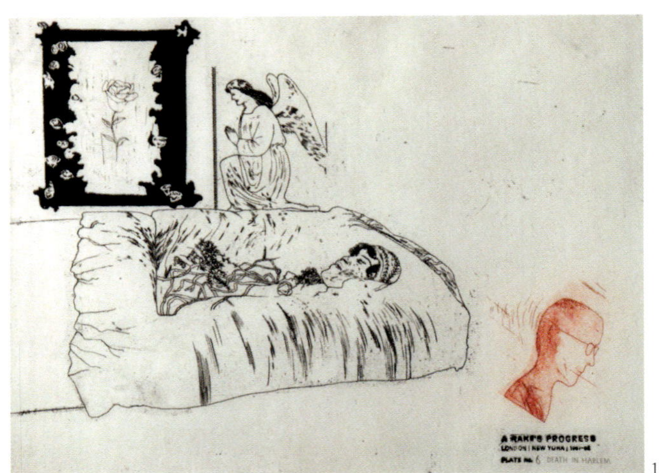

111k

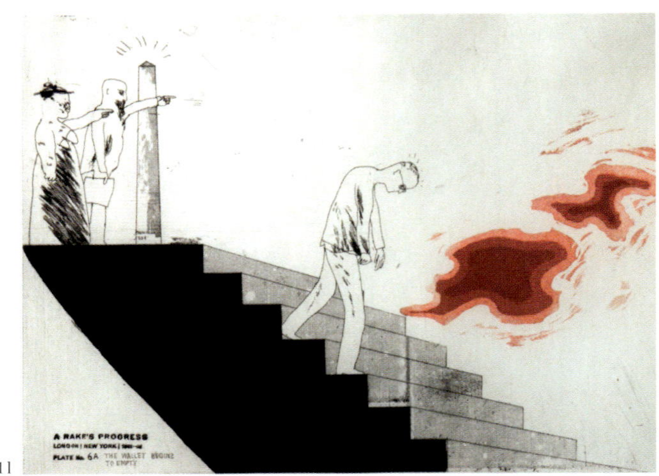

111l

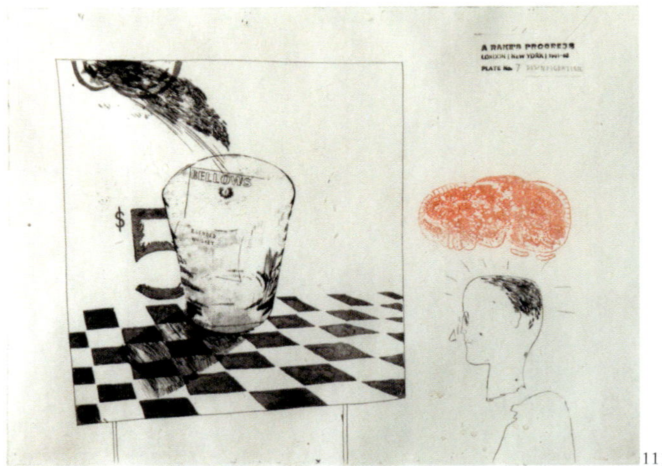

111m

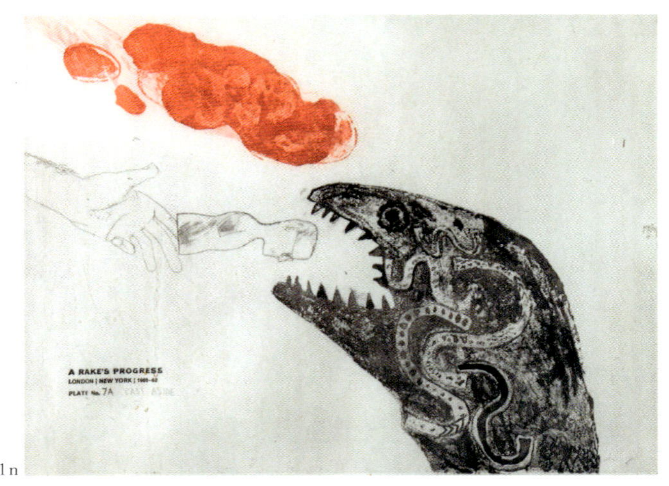

111n

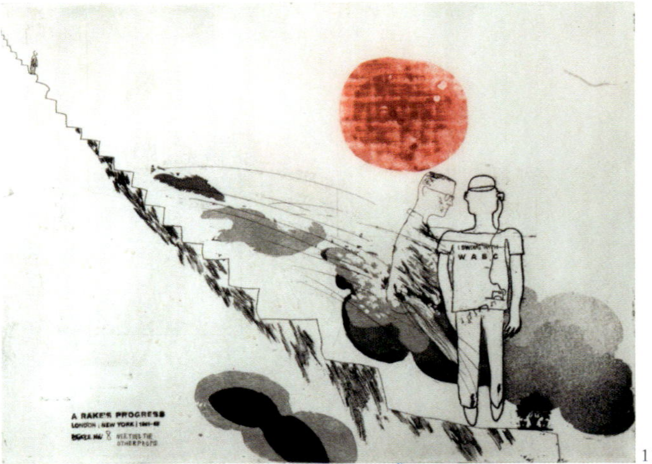

111o

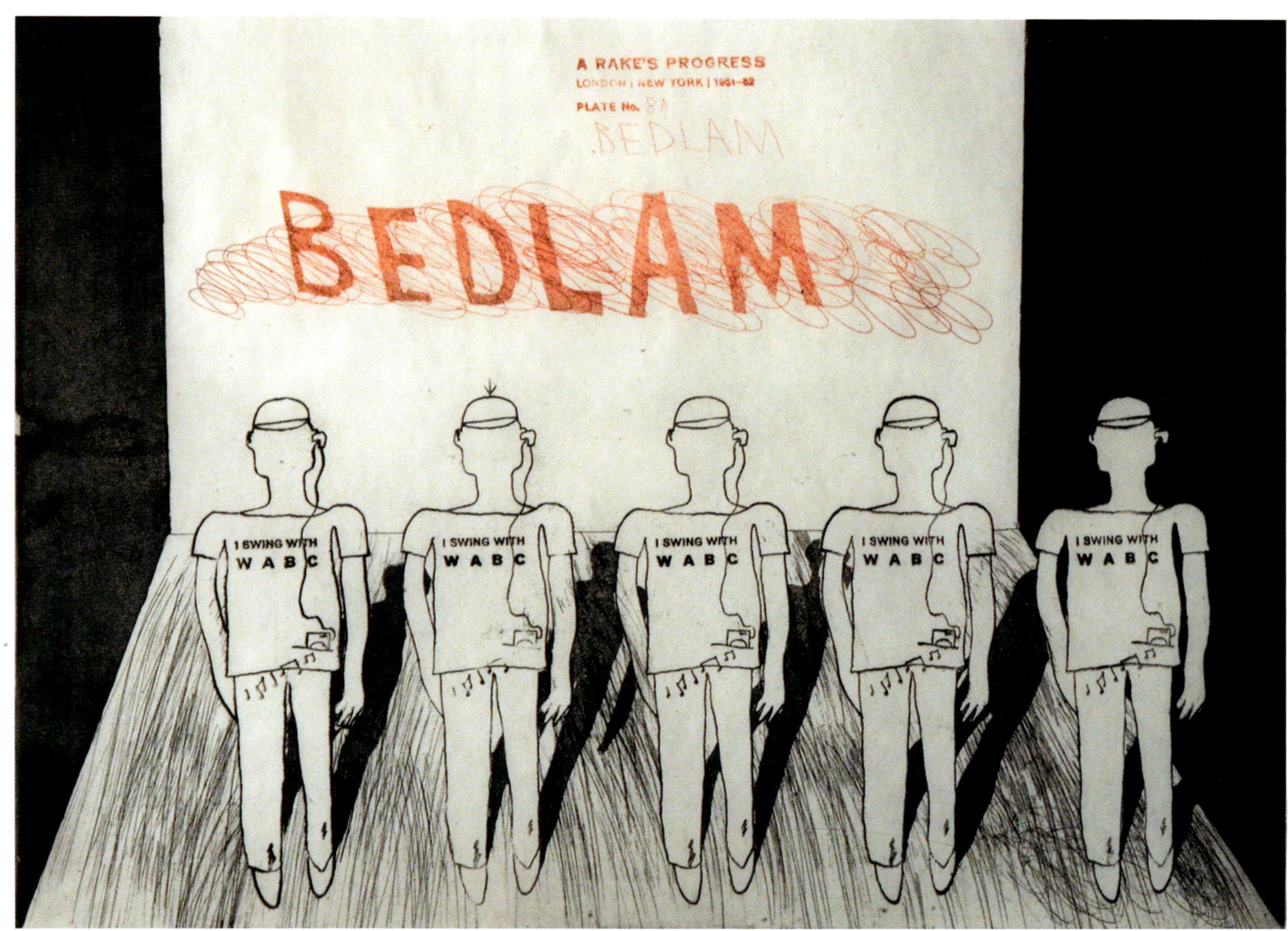

111p

one of Hockney's earliest prints) to a dealer or museum curator who knocks off 10%; he has his hair dyed blonde (*Door Opening for a Blonde*) and goes on a spending spree; but his 'Wallet Begins to Empty' and he ends up in Bedlam, though this is a Bedlam that does not appear to be so terminal. This was the first of a number of sets of etchings – illustrations to the poems of Cavafy in 1966; the *Fairy Tales of the Brothers Grimm* in 1969; and Wallace Stevens's *The Blue Guitar* in 1976-77 – in which Hockney has shown a special responsiveness to literature and tradition. Re-interpreting tradition began early with Hockney. Apart from *A Rake's Progress*, there is a painting from 1961 (private collection) in which he gives a modern rendering of Ford Madox Brown's *Last of England* (cat. 23). (AD)

CHAPTER TWO

LANDSCAPE

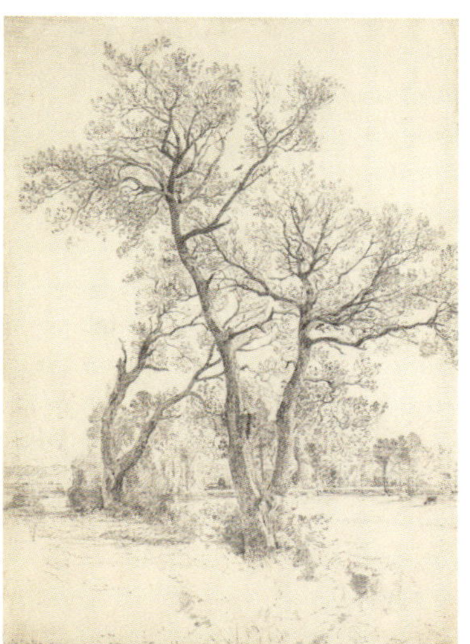

OBSERVATION OF LANDSCAPE

ROBERT HOOZEE

The empirical approach in British art is at its most evident in the development of landscape painting. For artists who were interested in observation – as for scientists – nature was the obvious starting point. The British landscape boom of the eighteenth and nineteenth centuries is also related to a number of social factors, as has been abundantly shown in the literature of recent decades.[1] Thanks to these studies, we now have a better insight into the public for which landscape painters worked, as well as the influence of industrialization, urbanization and the development of land ownership, agriculture and tourism. Nevertheless, it is not for these reasons that certain artists, such as Richard Wilson and John Constable, are considered so innovative even today, but because they achieved an exceptional level of quality within their socially and historically determined 'role'. And this has to do with the place that observation occupied in their practice.

In landscape painting, direct observation must lead to a break with artistic conventions and academic formulae – at least in principle. Observation is, after all, fragmentary, as is demonstrated by Constable's studies and by the development of later landscape painting, from Realism to Impressionism. Academic tradition, by contrast, relies on general concepts. However, for all the precedence that British artists accorded to fidelity to nature, they continued to cling to conventions that they tested only gradually against observable reality. These conventions were implicit in the Continental traditions both of classical landscape and the realistic landscapes of Holland and Flanders. British landscape painters were for a long time judged by contemporaries who used these traditions as the norm, because the importation of works and painters from the Continent initially stood in the way of native talent – much as it had in the case of portraiture.

It is therefore no accident that our survey begins with Richard Wilson (cat. 112-114). Like his British contemporaries, this artist worked entirely within the Continental tradition, following the example of Claude Lorrain and Gaspard Dughet. He painted Italianate landscapes and views of castles and country houses, as well as noteworthy landscapes in England and Wales. Within the limitations of academic tradition, he stands out for two qualities: the taste and inventiveness with which he was able to vary classical compositional schemes, and the 'air' he introduced into these schemes through his subtle depiction of atmospheric effects. Wilson's significance was already understood soon after his death both by collectors and by artists like Constable, who contrasted his work with the dull and artificial landscapes of his contemporaries.[2] After a visit to a collection in 1823, he was immensely struck by a 'large, solemn, bright, warm, fresh landscape by Wilson, which still swims in my brain like a delicious dream'.[3]

This convergence of formula and direct observation typifies most of the eighteenth- and nineteenth-century landscapes brought together here. Supported by theoretical writings on landscape and literary descriptions of natural beauty in Britain and abroad, numerous artists answered the demand for magnificent, characteristic landscapes in the form of paintings, watercolours and prints. Landscape painters were also engaged as topographical artists for scientific expeditions. In general, the British speciality in watercolours was able to develop in the context of topography and travel art. Watercolour had been used as a medium for studies from nature by artists as early as Albrecht Dürer, but the British developed the medium into something more than just an expedient, and the technique was used not only for studies but also for autonomous works of art made for exhibition. The luminosity specific to the medium made watercolours particularly suited to reproducing effects of light, and the sketching technique gave occasion for genuine virtuosity and lively interpretations among the great watercolourists such as the Cozenses, father and son (cat. 117-118, 122-123), and Francis Towne (cat. 124). Thomas Girtin, who died young, enriched the formal language of watercolours with monumental and sharply observed landscapes (cat. 125-128), while J.M.W. Turner went a step further by taking to an extreme the capacity of watercolours to capture or suggest effects of light and colour in his almost abstract 'colour beginnings' (cat. 138). The same period that watercolours began to come into their own also saw the development of the oil study, and the typical studio technique of painting in oils was now adapted to working in a small format directly before the motif. Oil studies were popular with artists who worked in Italy, such as the Frenchman Pierre-Henri de Valenciennes and the Welshman Thomas Jones (cat. 120-121), both of whom painted modern, almost photographic landscapes and cityscapes that have little to do with the conventional work that they executed in their studios.[4]

Until well into the nineteenth century, travelling in order to document extraordinary landscapes remained a constant practice among British artists. Although this development later became somewhat stereotyped, topography experienced an interesting revival around the middle of the century, stimulated by the Pre-Raphaelite ideal of fidelity to nature. During this period, artists were joined by the photographers, who – thanks to the rapid development of photographic techniques – had at their disposal the medium *par excellence* for working outside the studio and making lifelike images. In 1855, William Holman Hunt was of the opinion that 'Providence' had sent photography to show painters their shortcomings.[5] He considered it the task of painters to depart as 'merchants of nature' and 'bring home precious merchandise in faithful pictures of scenes interesting from historical considerations or from the strangeness of the subject itself'.[6] The Holy Land was a popular destination in this regard (cat. 142, 144). There, painters and photographers alike found striking landscapes filled with religious significance.

The recording of varied and stimulating impressions from nature was only one aspect of British landscape art. One could also view the entire phenomenon of travel art as a modern form of idealistic landscape painting, where the ideal that is sought lies beyond what is nearby and ordinary. The other tradition, which from the point of view of observation is of even greater interest to us, sought precisely the opposite. Its goal was the nature of the familiar environment – not spectacular or refined, nor even varied. This nature is discovered not by travelling, but in ordinary surroundings or within a reasonable distance, the landscape where activities that affect the daily life of the townsman take place – primarily agriculture, but also rest and relaxation.

This more everyday view of nature can already be found in the eighteenth century among painters both in oils and watercolours, and it should come as no surprise that this kind of landscape is more closely related to Dutch and Flemish tradition than to the idealizing Italian style. Aelbrecht Cuyp, Jacob van Ruisdael and Peter Paul Rubens had already depicted familiar nature with its seasonal human activities, and in the course of the eighteenth century a form of rustic, decorative landscape painting developed that was able to compete with ideal landscape. An artist like John Constable, however, takes us a step further. Constable also painted traditional views of country houses, just as Wilson had done, but his primary activity was devoted to the systematic exploration of nature in Suffolk, the region in which he was born. This type of observation received its most radical expression in the views taken from his parents' house, with his father's flower and kitchen gardens in the foreground (cat. 153-154). These two paintings demonstrate a degree of objectivity and spontaneity that had previously appeared only sporadically in British art. Thomas Gainsborough painted a few objective landscapes in his youth, but his later work strikes a balance between observation and the rustic tradition referred to above (cat. 147-148). As a portraitist and animal painter, George Stubbs was perhaps the most objective artist in British history. An apparently dispassionate matter-of-factness colours his entire oeuvre, including the only two surviving landscape studies for the backgrounds of several portraits of horses and jockeys (cat. 149-150). Constable's studies and paintings reveal a more emotional response to nature than those of his eighteenth-century predecessors. Nevertheless, the 'pure and unaffected' depiction of nature was for him both a principle and an end in itself.[7] He felt that a painter should look at nature with a humble spirit, and he compared landscapes to scientific experiments.[8] His vision resulted in repeated studies in oil and pencil of landscapes that reappear again and again in varying conditions, depending on the time of day and the season (cat. 155-156, 159-161, 183-184).

Everyday landscape and labour in the countryside also inspired a number of Constable's contemporaries, including J.M.W. Turner (cat. 151-152), George Robert Lewis (cat. 157), John Linnell (cat. 181. p. 41, fig. 9) and John Crome (cat. 158). In the urbanized society of the nineteenth century, the depiction of rural life – whether idealized or realistic – would become popular throughout Europe. Turner's *Frosty Morning* (cat. 152) is in some ways the forerunner of this tradition. Its grey tonality signals the advent of the many 'grey schools' of the nineteenth century, and its emphasis on hardship looks ahead to social realism. This work by Turner is an example of the type of landscape in which labour on the land is the principal motif. The so-called 'working landscape', with its frequently moralizing undertones, became a staple of the Victorian period. By contrast, the more objective, almost documentary, depiction – the likes of which are found in works by Constable (cat. 153-154, 162) and Lewis (cat. 157) in the present exhibition – was a characteristic phenomenon limited to the first few decades of the nineteenth century.[9]

The observation from which painters of both grand and more everyday landscapes drew their strength and originality involved great attention to detail and to natural phenomena, which kept pace with the empirical sciences. Making sketches directly from nature was in this sense more than just an occasional activity – it was exercised as a method and goal in itself. Some artists used scientific procedures and instruments and worked alongside astronomers, anatomists and meteorologists (cat. 164-165, 168-170). The isolation of landscape details was a direct way of approaching the motif and studying it as an autonomous fact, outside the usual classic formulae. Sketching details from the surrounding landscape had already been practised as a method of study as early as 1806 by artists associated with the brothers John and Cornelius Varley, including the young John Linnell (cat. 181).[10] The nature studies that Constable painted in Hampstead around 1820 are equally focused on fragments of nature. Figures rarely make an appearance in these landscapes. Constable concentrated instead on pure landscape elements such as trees, shrubbery, a house among the trees, a distant view (with tiny figures) under the changing light of the sky, rows of trees against the clouds, and finally the cloudy sky itself (cat. 174, 176, 183-185). Constable's cloud studies are not unique in the history of art, but their number, systematic approach and quality make them quite extraordinary and a high point of observation in British art. Turner also concentrated on specific phenomena, as in the series of nature studies painted on the Thames and the Wey in 1805 (cat. 173), or the studies he made from a boat while staying on the Isle of Wight in 1827 (cat. 178-179). It is well known that Turner usually made his sketches from life using a pencil and continued to elaborate his impressions in the studio. Many of Turner's compositions are romantic interpretations of classical themes, but colour, light and atmosphere – in other words, visual observation – nevertheless constitute a fundamental theme in his work. They are, moreover, the principal theme of several masterpieces such as *Rain, Steam and Speed* (Tate, London), and they form the essence of the numerous 'colour beginnings' and unfinished paintings that remained in his studio and were eventually bequeathed to the nation (cat. 11, 137-138, 180).

The scientifically inspired approach to nature taken by Constable, Turner and several of their contemporaries acquired a sequel in the middle of the nineteenth century in the work of the Pre-Raphaelites and associated artists, whose vision of nature was put into words and to a certain extent also directed by the critic John Ruskin. Ruskin studied meteorological, geological and botanical phenomena himself (cat. 189). He was an advocate of analytical and extremely detailed transcription, and his statement that art is founded in truth and consists in imagination is a fine summary of the art of the Pre-Raphaelites, with whom he was associated.[11] The result of this aesthetic was that painters – now joined by photographers like William Henry Fox Talbot (cat. 186-187) and Roger Fenton (cat. 188) – armed, as it were, with magnifying glasses, began to depict with extreme patience a frozen nature.[12] Fine execution, emphasis on detail, pure colours and the effect of light and shadow captured 'as it exists at any one moment, instead of approximately, or in generalised style' give these works a bright, static effect.[13] The sometimes hyperrealistic landscapes of the

Pre-Raphaelites (cat. 19, 191-200) stand in direct contrast to the Pre-Impressionist landscape painting that was appearing elsewhere in Europe around the same time, which was directed more towards the expression of mood and the depiction of movement. However, the concentration and careful painterly technique of the Pre-Raphaelites produced a poetic strength that counterbalances the landscapes – sometimes produced with too much facility – of many of their contemporaries.

The model of French landscape painting, which inspired the practice of most European landscape painters from the rise of the Barbizon School to Post-Impressionism, also generated interesting landscapes in Great Britain, but there were no masterpieces in the observation of nature such as one encounters in the age of Constable, Turner or the Pre-Raphaelites. The painstaking copying of a specific landscape, which can be associated with Pre-Raphaelite aesthetics, was only sustained for around a decade; from the 1860s onward, a more relaxed style evolved, which was directed towards generalized effects.[14] James McNeill Whistler's *Nocturnes* (cat. 33) and views of the Thames are the most original expressions of this new approach to nature, which the British would now follow, with its orientation more towards suggestion than definition.

In the twentieth century, landscape was a remarkably important subject and a vital factor in modern British art. Contact with European – particularly French – avant-garde trends forced the British to define their own position, and the heritage of the empirical landscape tradition played a major role in that process.

For some, like Paul Nash (cat. 214) and Graham Sutherland (cat. 213), the observation of nature and the exploration of specific exceptional landscapes gave rise to symbolist and surrealist interpretations. With others, the approach to nature that characterized the eighteenth- and nineteenth-century travel artists was revived, as was the case with the group of artists working in Wales around 1910 in a region where Wilson and Turner had preceded them (cat. 202-203, 205). David Bomberg's Spanish mountain landscapes (cat. 215) are also reminiscent of examples from the nineteenth century, such as those by Turner or the richly detailed panoramas of the Holy Land by the Pre-Raphaelites. Other artists, like William Nicholson (cat. 206) and the young Ben Nicholson (cat. 212), immersed themselves in the study of a limited environment, effectively reliving the humble explorations of Constable. The work of Stanley Spencer (cat. 207, 209-210), who also restricted himself to the depiction of familiar landscapes, brings to mind the objectivity of Constable's generation as well as the realistic detail, workmanlike handling and, at times, strange focus of the Pre-Raphaelites.

While landscape painting occupied a secondary place in European modernism, it remained important in the work of British modernists, who increasingly sought points of contact with international developments – particularly abstract art – after the Second World War. This is true of David Bomberg (cat. 216) and Ben Nicholson (cat. 212) in their later years, of Victor Pasmore (cat. 217-218) and Ivon Hitchens (cat. 219), and also of the sculptors Henry Moore (cat. 221-222) and Barbara Hepworth (cat. 220). For these two, working in nature and the use of forms encountered in nature formed the point of departure for abstract and anthropomorphic sculptures that can be approached as fragments of landscape.

The observation of nature continues to be a noteworthy feature in contemporary British art – Land Art is a prime example. Among the post-war artists who continue to practise figurative painting, both Frank Auerbach (cat. 224) and Leon Kossoff (cat. 223) rely on the observation of the familiar landscape or cityscape in at least some of their work. With them, however, it is not a detached form of observation, but rather a form of response to the visual sensation, conveyed with expressive materiality, a process that recalls the sketches of Turner and Constable. There is nothing traditional about the work of Auerbach and Kossoff, but it does form a convincing synthesis between the concepts of British landscape tradition and a contemporary, concrete experience of reality.

1. See Barrell 1980; Rosenthal 1982; Solkin 1982; Bermingham 1986; Payne 1993.
2. See Leslie 1951, p. 321.
3. Leslie 1951, p. 101.
4. Galassi 1981, pp. 21-22.
5. Letter to William Michael Rossetti, Jerusalem, 1855; cit. Allen Staley, in Staley and Newall 2004, p. 99.
6. Ibid.
7. Letter to John Dunthorne, 1802. Beckett 1962-68, vol. 2, p. 32.
8. Beckett 1970, pp. 71, 69.
9. Charlotte Klonk speaks of a phenomenalist depiction in this regard. Klonk 1996, p. 149.
10. See Parris 1973, pp. 100-103; Gage 1969c, pp. 11-12; Klonk 1996, pp. 101ff.
11. *The Eagle's Nest: Ten Lectures on the Relation of Natural Science to Art given before the University of Oxford in Lent Term 1872*, London 1872; cit. Klonk 1996, p. 150.
12. Geoffrey Grigson, *The Harp of Aeolus*, 1947; cit. Alan Bowness, in London 1984, p. 12, n.
13. Ford Madox Brown in 1865; cit. Mary Bennett, in London 1984, p. 53.
14. See Newall 2004b.

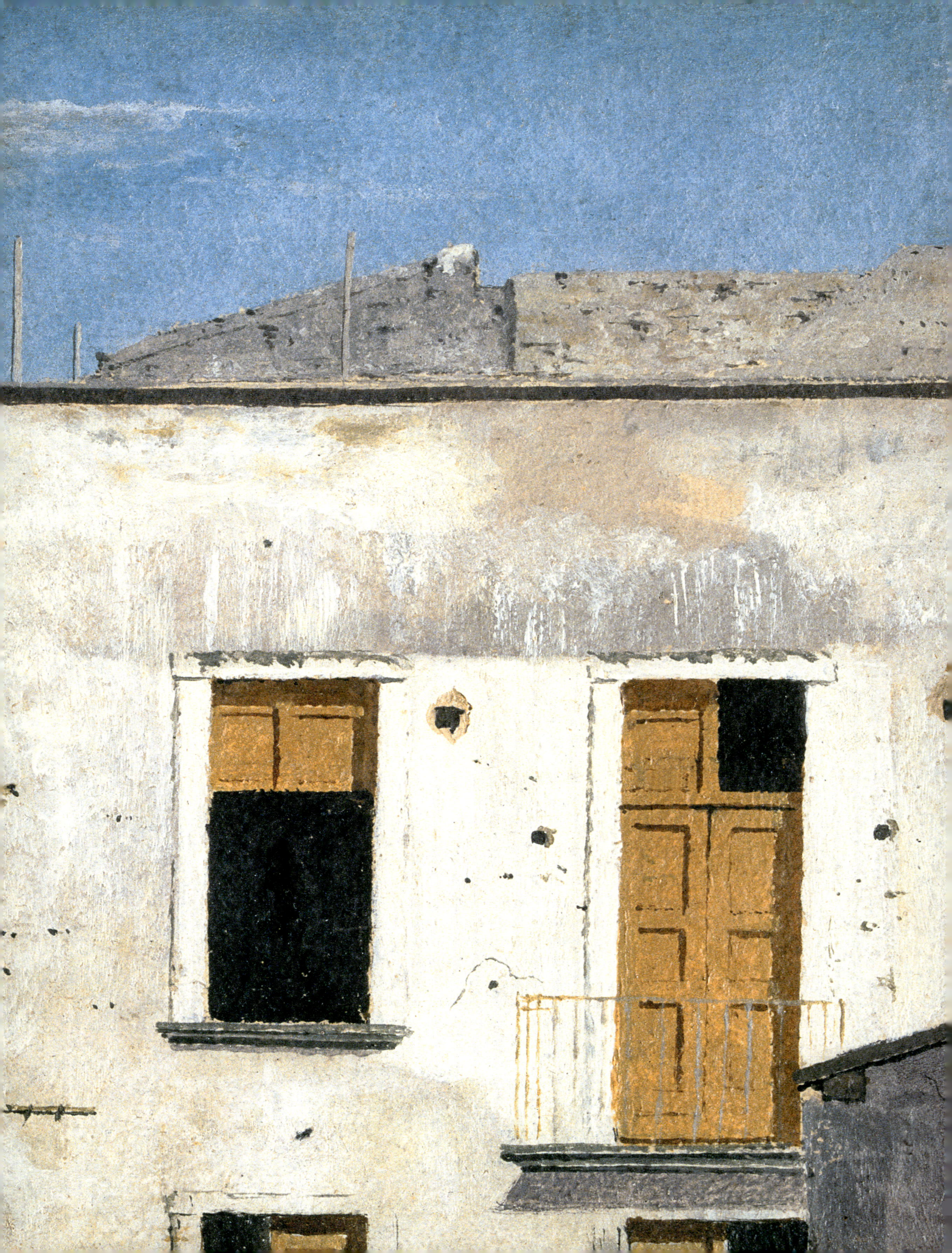

POINTS OF VIEW

THOMAS JONES

Buildings in Naples, 1782

MARK EVANS

Lawrence Gowing's appreciation of Thomas Jones's *Buildings in Naples* is unsurpassed: 'The simplicity of the thing in itself is rendered with unaccustomed, measured sharpness. It is just a white façade with a window and a door, which penetrate the radiant stucco with a clarity of other times. We notice a mathematical precision. The unshuttered window is four/sixths full of shadow ... The recesses are cut a shallow, yet measurable depth into the white and the cavernous shadow is hollowed deeply back behind them. In the urban scene which fills the remainder, the rooftops are graduated steps in space, which make the building, voids and all, an urgent presence.'[1]

As a painter, professor and curator, Gowing was an influential champion of modernism, and his formal analysis of Jones's oil sketch reflects his fascination with Cézanne.[2] Gowing was supportive of the exhibition *Before Photography*, which argued that the 'fundamentally modern pictorial syntax' of such works provided 'the critical shift in artistic norms that led to the invention of photography'.[3] In this context, Jones seems a prophet of the *plein air* paintings of Corot and the Barbizon School. This apparent modernity was all the greater as his oil sketches had been unknown prior to their rediscovery in 1954-55. Previously, he had been regarded as a minor follower of Richard Wilson and a commentator on the Grand Tour in his *Memoirs*, published in 1951.[4]

Jones was born in Radnorshire in mid-Wales, the second son of a squire. He studied at Oxford with the intention of becoming a clergyman but left without a degree, and in 1763-65 he studied with Wilson. Initially he was 'confined entirely to making Drawings with black and White Chalks on paper of a Middle Tint ... to ground me in the Principles of Light & Shade, without being dazzled and mislead by the flutter of Colours', and 'copied so many Studies of that great man, & my old Master, Richard Wilson ... that I insensibly became familiarized with Italian Scenes, and enamoured of Italian forms.'[5] Jones departed for Rome in October 1776 and moved to Naples in May 1780. In Italy he made numerous crisp pencil landscape studies, and oil paintings and watercolours of celebrated views, arranged according to the principles of Claude. Returning home in 1783, Jones exhibited at the Royal Academy, but found that 'the prospect of Employment ... was dark and gloomy'.[6] Inheriting his family estate, he settled into the comfortable life of a country squire, painting only for his own amusement.

Ironically, Jones did not regard his oil sketches on paper as finished works. Around fifty in number, these principally comprise landscapes near his home at Pencerrig dated 1772 and 1776, views of caverns and excavations in Rome made in 1777-78, and depictions of buildings and rooftops at Naples dating from 1782-83. The Welsh sketches mostly measure around 22 x 31 cm, while those produced in Italy vary from as little as 11.2 x 15.8 cm to as large as 38 x 55.5 cm. Technical analysis shows that they were painted over careful underdrawing, and their characteristic luminosity is caused by the absorbency of their priming and supports and the absence of varnish.[7]

Thomas Jones, ***Buildings in Naples*** (detail), cat. 121

In his *Memoirs* Jones mentions making 'Studies in Oil on thick primed paper – after Nature' in August-October 1770, August 1772, and between February and September 1776.[8] Outside Rome in June 1778 he 'made some Studies in Oil of the surrounding Scenery' and near Naples in April 1781 was similarly 'employed in rambling about the Country still finding something new – I like wise made several Studies upon paper in oil.'[9] He describes working from a studio in Naples in May 1782; 'The Room which I was in possession of ... was large and commodious ... and as it was on a ground floor and vaulted above, very cool and pleasant at this Season ... The only window it had, looked into a Small Garden, and over a part of the Suburbs ... all of which Objects, I did not omit making finished Studies of in Oil upon primed paper.'[10]

Jones's reputation rests principally upon a dozen oil studies made in 1782, such as *Buildings in Naples*, which are devoid of figures or incident. Their understated force is anticipated by two watercolours by a pair of British painters who made the Grand Tour together in 1773-75. These are *View of Roof Tops, Nice* (fig. 1) by the Welsh artist John Downman and *House Built on Top of a Wall* (fig. 2) by Joseph Wright of Derby.[11] At Rome in the 1750s, Claude-Joseph Vernet had painted in oils from nature; a practice praised by Sir Joshua Reynolds, who valued 'the truth which those works only have which are produced while the impression is warm from Nature'.[12] Wilson was in Rome at this time, and seems to have recommended the technique to his students.[13] The surviving *plein air* oil sketches which most closely resemble those by Jones were made at Rome in 1782-84 by the French artist Pierre-Henri de Valenciennes.[14] Although both artists were in Italy at the same time, there is no evidence that they were acquainted, which is hardly surprising, as Jones found the French of 'a Character ... as distinct from the rest of mankind as the Chinese'.[15] The similarities between their work probably reflect a mutual debt to the precepts of Vernet, whose international reputation validated a practice recommended by the amateur Roger De Piles as early as 1708.[16] The English painter Jonathan Skelton associated painting out of doors with the landscape of Tivoli and the practice of Claude Lorrain. Writing from there to a friend in April 1758, he remarked, 'This antient City of Tivole I planly see has been ye only school where our two most celebrated Landscape Painters Claude and Gasper [Gaspard Dughet] studied,' and the following October he continued, 'The Picture I have been painting in Oil after Nature is almost done, it is a strange mixture altogether, tho' I have learn'd many things in the painting of it.'[17] One of a pair of views of Tivoli by Wilson dated 1752 includes a painter in the open air working at a canvas on an easel, while its companion piece depicts his servant labouring under the burden of this studio apparatus.[18] These instances bring to mind Joachim von Sandrart's account of Claude's discovery of painting from nature, published in 1675: 'He tried by every means to penetrate nature, lying in the fields before the break of day and until night in order to learn to represent very exactly the red morningsky, sunrise and sunset and the evening hours.... He finally met me, with the brush in my hands, in Tivoli, in the wild rocks at the famous cascade, where he found me painting from life ...; this pleased him so much that he applied himself eagerly to adopting the same method.'[19]

Whether Claude actually painted *en plein air* (or was introduced to it by Sandrart) is hardly relevant; it was the belief that he had done so which invested this practice with immense prestige for Jones and, a generation later, John Constable.[20] In 1811 J.M.W. Turner, who did not himself utilize this technique, drily characterized Claude's practice: 'We must consider how he could have attained such powers but by a continual study of parts of nature. Parts, for, had he not so studied, we should have found him sooner pleased with simple subjects of nature, and [would] not [have], as we now have, pictures made up of bits, but pictures of bits.'[21]

While Constable wrought the great exhibition paintings he called 'six footers' from such painstaking oil studies, Jones's 'pictures of bits' remain autonomous. As unconnected fragments of experience, they recall the diary entries in his *Memoirs*. The latter includes self-deprecating comic episodes reminiscent of Laurence Sterne's *A Sentimental Journey through France and Italy* (1768), as well as lyrical passages such as this description of the landscape at Tivoli: 'Where the

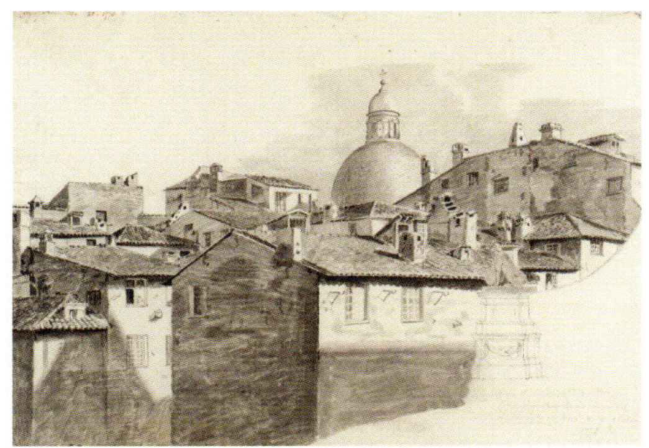

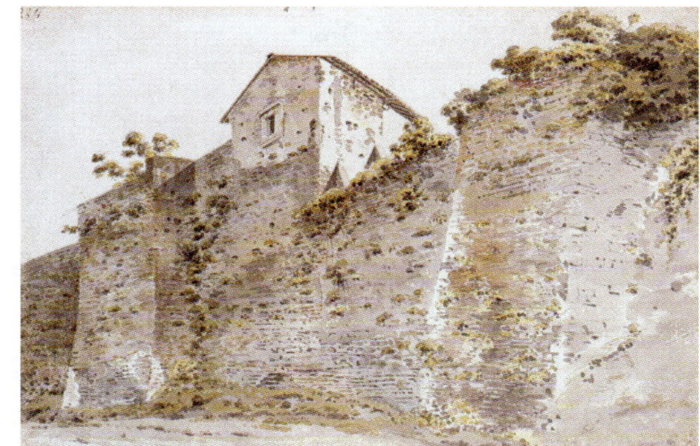

fig. 1
John Downman
***View of Roof Tops, Nice*, 1773**
Pencil, watercolour, pen and ink on paper, 26.5 x 36.7 cm
Tate, London

fig. 2
Joseph Wright of Derby
***House Built on Top of a Wall*, c. 1774-75**
Pencil and watercolour on paper, 26.9 x 41.6 cm
Royal Collection

perpendicular & hanging Sides admit of no vegetation & you discover the naked Rock - the Eye is charmed with the most beautiful variegated Tints - White, Grey, Red & Yellow - opposing, or blending their different Dyes together.'[22] Jones may have been familiar with the revolutionary 'word-painting' of the Welsh poet and clergyman John Dyer, best known today for his topographical poem on the beauties of the Tywi valley, *Grongar Hill* (1726).[23] After studying with the painter Jonathan Richardson, Dyer spent 1724-25 sketching in Italy, where his experiences inspired the descriptive poem *The Ruins of Rome* (1740), which includes the following:

> Of Maro's humble tenement; a low
> Plain wall remains; a little sun-gilt heap,
> Grotesque and wild: the gourd and olive brown
> Weave the light roof; the gourd and olive fan
> Their amorous foliage, mingling with the vine,
> Who drops her purple clusters through the green.[24]

Conditioned by respect for Antiquity, the timeless objectivity of Jones's oil sketches transcends the mutability of *plein air* vision and continues to address our pressing needs.

---

1. Gowing 1985, p. 44.
2. Stephen Bury, 'Sir Lawrence Burnett Gowing (1918-1991)', *Oxford Dictionary of National Biography*, Oxford 2004, article 49755, accessed 14 December 2006. *www.oxforddnb.com*.
3. Galassi 1981, pp. 22, 34, 128-29, end-cover.
4. Oppé 1951.
5. Ibid., pp. 9, 55.
6. Ibid., p. 141.
7. Lowry 2003, pp. 97-98.
8. Oppé 1951, pp. 22, 27, 38.
9. Ibid., pp. 73, 103
10. Ibid., p. 111.
11. The former in the Tate Gallery and the latter in the Royal Collection; Lyles and Hamlyn 1997, pp. 144-45; Nicolson 1968, vol. 1, p. 75; vol. 2, pl. 147.
12. Cited in Galassi 1991, p. 18.
13. Smith 1983, pp. 144-45.
14. This was initially pointed out by John Gere in 1959; Sumner 2003, pp. 11-12, 15-17; and Riopelle 2003, pp. 58-59.
15. Oppé 1951, p. 53.
16. Conisbee 1979, pp. 422-25; Galassi 1991, pp. 16-20.
17. Ford 1960, pp. 42, 60; cit. Howard 1969, pp. 728, 731.
18. Conisbee 1979, p. 425; Smith 1983, p. 144.
19. Trans. in Röthlisberger 1961, vol. 1, pp. 47-48; cit. Conisbee 1979, p. 416.
20. Oppé 1951, pp.10, 29; Evans 2002, p. 46.
21. Cit. Stainton 2003, p. 43.
22. Oppé 1951, pp. 66-67.
23. Stainton 2003, p. 26; Belinda Humfrey, 'John Dyer (1699-1757)', *Oxford Dictionary of National Biography*, Oxford 2004, article 8350, accessed 12 December 2006. *www.oxforddnb.com*.
24. Gilfillan 1858, p. 215.

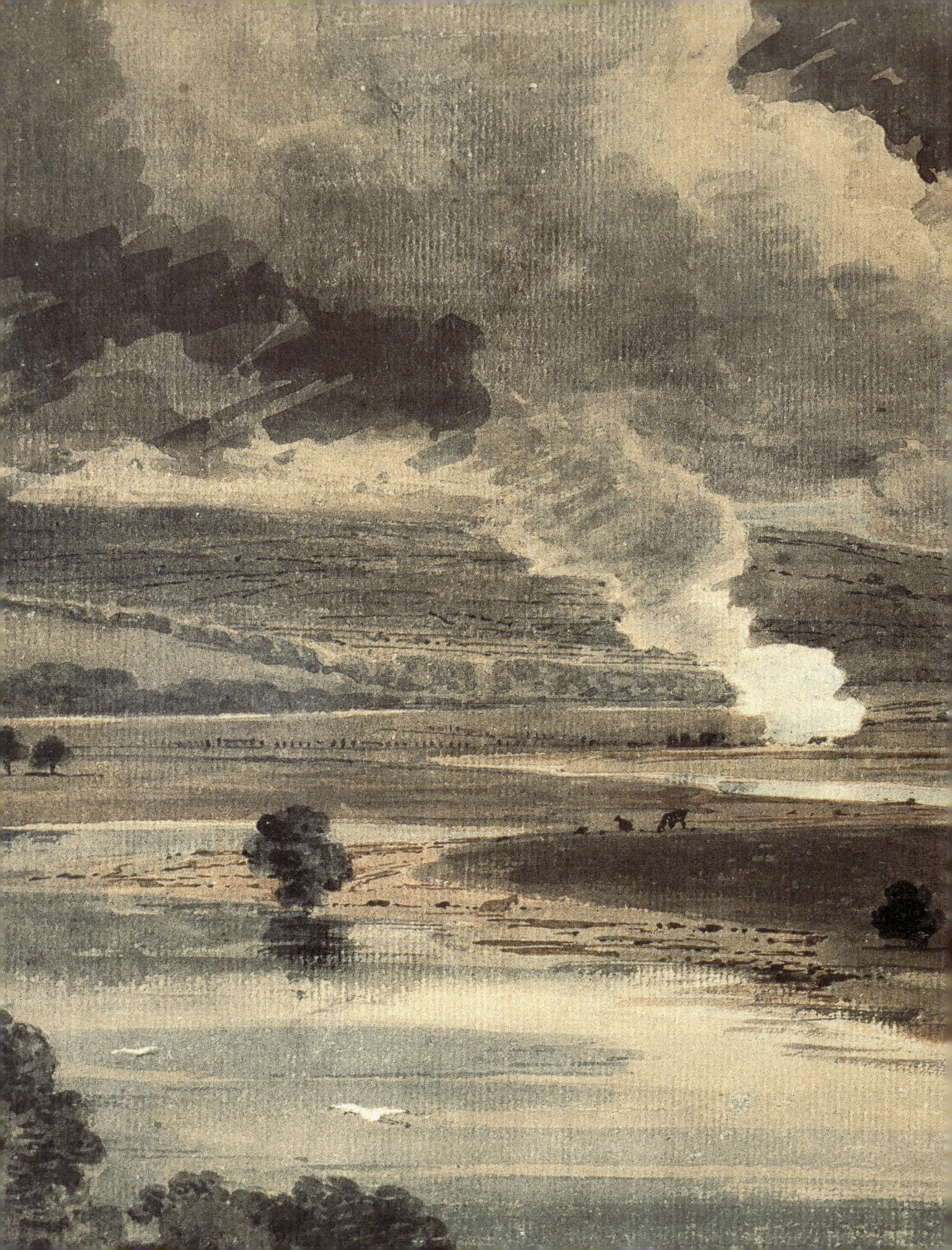

POINTS OF VIEW

THOMAS GIRTIN

View on the River Wharfe, Yorkshire, c. 1800

ANNE LYLES

Like J.M.W. Turner, Thomas Girtin is recognized as one of the greatest masters of British watercolour painting. Together the two artists led the revolution in watercolour technique around the turn of the nineteenth century, helping to extend the medium's expressive range as well as its perceived status. It is a reflection of Turner's admiration for Girtin's extraordinary skills as a watercolourist that he is reported to have said that, had Girtin's life not been brought to such an untimely end, in 1802 at the age of twenty-seven, he himself (Turner) would have starved.[1] *View on the River Wharfe, Yorkshire* is just the sort of atmospheric and highly eloquent landscape subject that Turner would have been thinking about when he made this remark, and as it happens he shared with Girtin a particular affection for this stretch of Yorkshire countryside. However, as was the case with Turner himself, it was to take Girtin a number of years before he arrived at the point where he was able to make such powerful statements.

Born only two months before Turner in Southwark in London, the son of a brush-maker, Girtin became an apprentice to the topographical draughtsman Edward Dayes in 1788. Thus he was trained (again, like Turner) in the tradition of topographical view-making. The art of topography – that is to say, the making of detailed and accurate representations of a particular place, city or town – was very popular at this date, and nowhere more than in the field of watercolour painting, thanks to its close links in the late eighteenth century with the market for engraved antiquarian views.

Girtin was taught by Dayes first to make a careful pencil drawing of his chosen subject – perhaps a medieval church or cathedral, a ruined castle, or a city with buildings rich in historical associations – so as to represent accurately its various architectural forms. To this intricate outline he would then add what Dayes himself called the 'dead coloring', that is to say layers of underpainting in grey or brown washes to indicate light and shade.[2] Finally Girtin would add delicate finishing layers of restrained and carefully applied watercolour washes; indeed, works painted in this manner were generally referred to not as watercolours at all but as 'stained' or 'tinted' drawings. Girtin's first exhibited work, a view of *Ely Cathedral from the South-East* (Ashmolean Museum, Oxford), shown at the Royal Academy in 1794, was an exercise in this manner and is executed in a very Dayes-like palette of blues, greens and greys.[3] The emphasis in all his early topographical works was on detail and precision, rather than breadth or freedom of artistic expression, especially as they were often designed to be handed over to the printmaker to be engraved.

By the middle of the 1790s, however, Girtin's art began to move in new directions. In 1795, for example, he joined an informal drawing 'academy' established by the medical doctor and art enthusiast, Dr Thomas Monro. At Monro's house in London, often alongside J.M.W. Turner, Girtin would be set to copying examples of the remarkable landscape watercolours made by John Robert Cozens, one of the first artists to use watercolour consistently for its own sake as a purely expressive medium (see cat. 122-123). Thanks to Cozens's example, Girtin now began to learn to express form through tone rather than through outline – that is actually to paint rather than to draw in watercolour – and gradually he abandoned the 'underpainting' of his earlier years. He also began to learn how to use atmospheric recession in landscape, and thus how to suggest great distances and broad vistas. These lessons were to prove especially valuable to Girtin in

Thomas Girtin, ***View on the River Wharfe, Yorkshire*** (detail), cat. 127

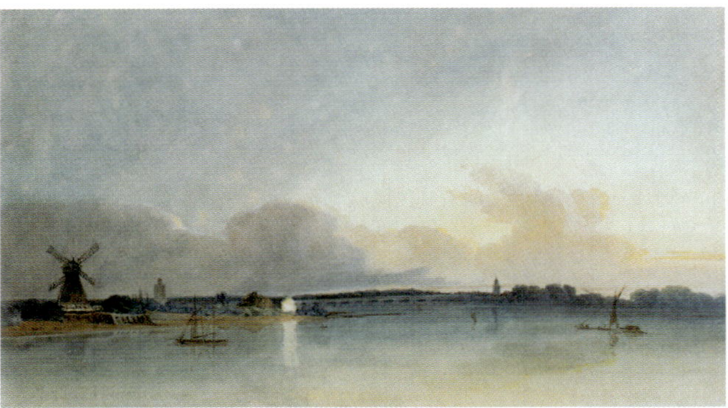

fig. 1
Thomas Girtin
***The White House at Chelsea*, 1800**
Pencil and watercolour on paper, 29.8 x 51.5 cm
Tate, London

subsequent years, especially when – between 1796 and 1798 in particular – he found himself coming into contact with different types of landscape, which were to provoke a new and more intense response in his art.

In 1796, for example, Girtin toured Yorkshire, the north of England and the Scottish lowlands, developing a sympathy for wide, open spaces, especially for broad stretches of moorland, barren hills and atmospheric skies, perhaps punctuated by flowing water as in *View on the River Wharfe, Yorkshire*. It was, in particular, the scenery of the Yorkshire Dales as shown in this watercolour that was to inspire some of Girtin's most memorable images, not only *View on the River Wharfe, Yorkshire* itself, but also for example *Stepping Stones on the Wharfe, Yorkshire*, c.1800 (National Gallery of Scotland, Edinburgh), *Storiths Heights, near Bolton Abbey, Yorkshire*, c.1800 (Fitzwilliam Museum, Cambridge) and *Ilkley, Yorkshire, from the River Wharfe*, c.1801 (Leeds City Art Gallery).[4]

Painted around 1800 to 1801, when Girtin was at the height of his artistic powers, these Yorkshire subjects reveal how he had now put behind him the rather prosaic and literal topographical records of his youth in favour of more generalized landscapes, where broad and simplified effects prevailed over small details.[5] In *View on the River Wharfe, Yorkshire*, for example, he has pared down details to an absolute minimum, which contributes a sense of melancholy to the composition, even a sense of austerity, though fading may have made the watercolour appear more severe than it might have been when first painted.[6] Even subjects Girtin took from his northern tour that had a more inherently topographical basis, such as *Jedburgh* (cat. 125), were to evolve over the years to take on a less antiquarian and more expressive character.

In terms of composition, *View on the River Wharfe, Yorkshire* contains many of the features of Girtin's new approach to landscape that marks him out as thoroughly modern for his time. He had learned (especially from Dutch art) how to place the main subject of the landscape – however minimal this might now be – in the middle distance and parallel to the picture plane, often, as here, beyond an expanse of water in the foreground. This allowed the viewer's eye to move rapidly across an uncluttered foreground and to proceed into the depth of the landscape beyond. He also dispensed with conventional framing devices, so beloved by classical artists such as Claude, the better to open up these broad vistas with their extensive skies.[7] In this example, Girtin also employs a favourite motif, a coil of billowing smoke – drifting up from the far side of the river and blending almost imperceptibly with the rolling clouds above – to remarkably powerful effect.

Meanwhile, a trip in 1797 to the West Country, an area noted for its striking coastal scenery, encouraged Girtin to experiment with more panoramic formats, so as to capture a sense of these wide, extensive landscape views (for example, *Lyme Regis, Dorset*, c.1797; Yale Center for British Art; and *Appledore, North Devon*, c.1798; Courtauld Institute Gallery). This more elongated format was to find its ultimate expression in the huge Panorama of London Girtin painted in oils around 1801 and exhibited at Spring Gardens in August 1802, some atmospheric studies for which survive in the British Museum.[8] The panoramic format is also evident in Girtin's famous watercolour of the *The White House at Chelsea*, 1800 (fig. 1), whose pronounced horizontal emphasis and lack of carefully articulated planes of recession again fly in the face of conventional notions of landscape composition. Like the remarkable watercolour of *St Vincent's Rocks, Clifton, Bristol* (cat. 126), probably painted by Girtin in the same year, *The White House* is seen in the fading light of evening. The long stretch of the river bank forms a low horizon that is gently punctuated by a few vertical accents such as the windmill to the left, two towers, a few clumps of trees and the white house itself, which forms a bold and effective accent in the composition, as well as producing a dramatic reflection in the glassy water. It is masterful in its understatement and was to prove one of the most influential of all Girtin's landscapes on the watercolour artists of the next generation.

However, Girtin's reputation had now been rising for some time. A tour in 1798 to north Wales, noted for its dramatic mountainous scenery, had prompted him to make landscapes of a grander, more monumental and brooding character, such as the powerful large watercolour of a *View near Beddgelert, North Wales*, c.1799 (National Museums and Galleries of Wales, Cardiff). When he exhibited this watercolour at the Royal Academy in 1799, it drew a great deal of praise from the critics, prompting the *Morning Chronicle*, for example, to comment on the extent to which it had enhanced the artist's 'professional reputation', to the point indeed where he was now one of the 'most promising talents in this line of the Arts'.[9]

Interestingly, this large watercolour is based on a small watercolour sketch of the scene that Girtin had almost certainly made – and coloured – on the spot during his tour of north Wales the previous year.[10] For Girtin's habit of sketching from nature in all weathers was noted by his early biographers, and the practice made a powerful impression on, for example, the young Cornelius Varley, who produced many similar plein-air sketches in his early career (see, for example, cat. 172).[11] In this way, Girtin's example contributed to an emerging Romantic appreciation for more naturalistic modes of representation in the early nineteenth century. Although most of the watercolours by Girtin in this exhibition are likely to be studio works, made from watercolour or pencil studies executed on earlier sketching tours, it is possible that the striking study of *La Rue St Denis, Paris*, c. 1802 (cat. 128) was one of the large sketches he referred to in a letter written to his brother from Paris as having been coloured on the spot.[12]

La Rue St Denis, Paris is probably a design for a theatrical backdrop for a London pantomime, which was not to open to the public until December 1802, a month after Girtin's untimely death.[13] In its obituary published shortly afterwards, the *Morning Herald* wrote of the artist's death as constituting nothing less than a 'national loss' of an 'extraordinary and celebrated young artist'.[14] In similarly eulogistic terms, eleven years later, the artist and engraver John Hassell was to state that Girtin had burst 'like a meteor upon the public', and could 'be said to have been the projector of the new school of water-colour painters'. Indeed, Hassell even believed that it was thanks to Girtin's 'example' that 'we are now indebted for the works of the ingenious J.M.W. Turner'.[15]

1. Thornbury 1877, p. 71.
2. Dayes 1805, p. 301 ('Drawing and Coloring Landcapes').
3. Smith 2002, no. 1.
4. Ibid., nos. 129, 128, 171 and 165.
5. Ibid., p. 143.
6. Hill 1999, p. 38.
7. Smith 2002, pp. 143-44.
8. The Panorama itself no longer survives, having been destroyed in a warehouse fire containing the entire stock of the entrepreneur James Thayer in the early years of the nineteenth century shortly after being exhibited in Paris, Amsterdam and Lyon (Smith 2002, p. 193). For the colour studies, and other studies in pen and ink, see also Smith 2002, nos. 149-158.
9. Ibid., p. 153 (no. 116).
10. Ibid, no. 115.
11. For Girtin and colouring on the spot, see a reference from *The Gentleman's Magazine* cited by Roget 1891, vol. 1, p. 95.
12. See Smith 2002, no. 178.
13. Ibid.
14. Ibid., p. 263.
15. Ibid., p. 235.

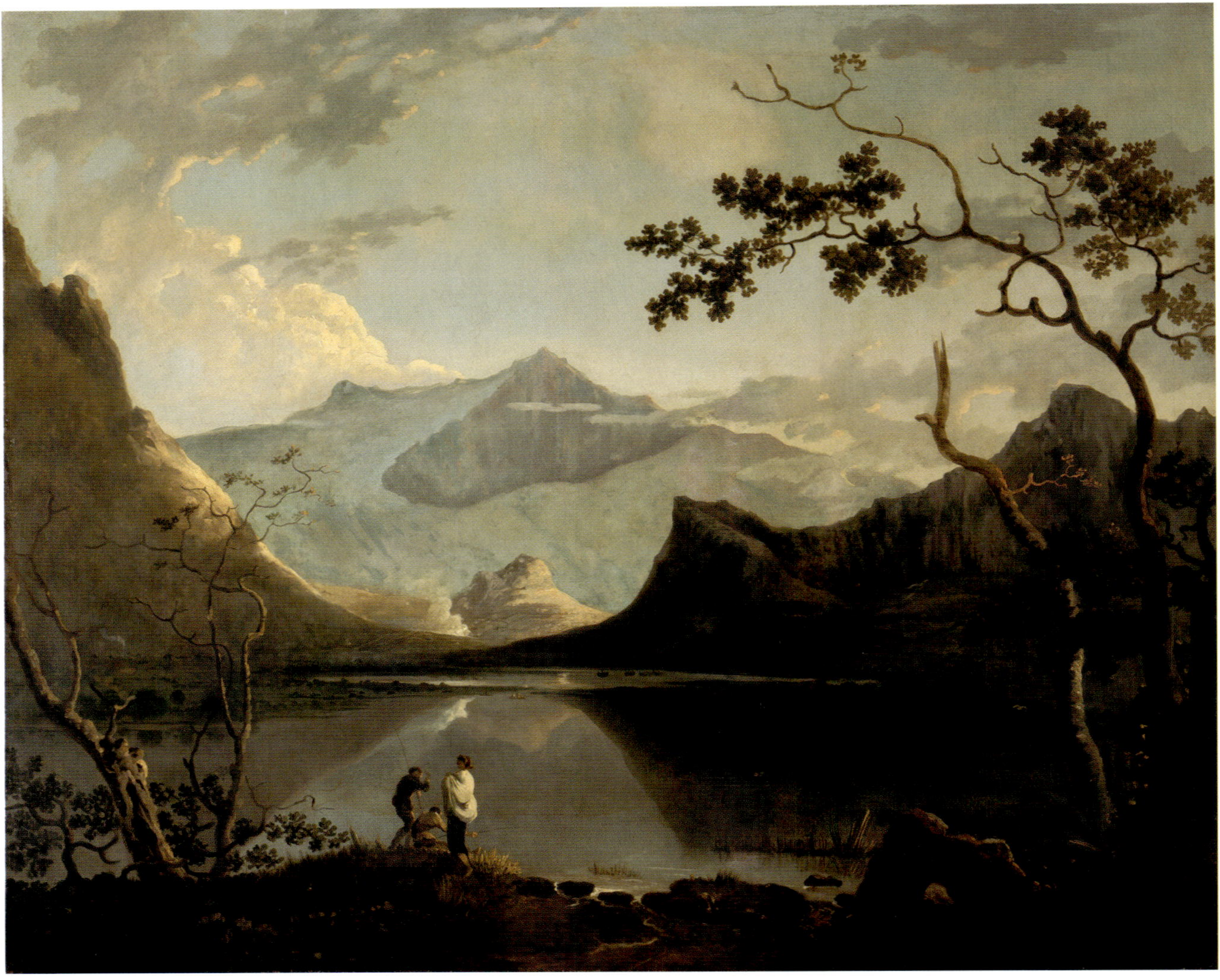

112

112. **Richard Wilson**
Penegoes, Powys, 1713 or 1714 - Colomendy, Clwyd, 1782
Snowdon from Llyn Nantlle, c. 1765-67
Oil on canvas, 104.1 x 127 cm
Nottingham City Museums & Galleries

Wilson's view is taken from the upper end of Llyn Nantlle, a glaciated valley in north-west Wales, looking east across the lake towards Mount Snowdon. In order to achieve the required sense of monumentality, Wilson altered the topography, exaggerating the sharpness of the summit of Snowdon, and reducing in height the scale of the peaks on the right. Known in Welsh as Yr Wyddfa, 'The Tomb', Snowdon was a forbidding sight and a suitable focus for a pictorial meditation upon the Sublime. At the time Wilson painted this view, the area was still largely a wilderness, with little trace of human habitation other than the remains of Iron Age settlements and small-scale slate quarries and copper mines. The figures of the anglers in the foreground may not, however, have simply been inserted as picturesque motifs, since the lake was, and continues to be, one of the region's finest fishing grounds. (MP)

113. **Richard Wilson**
Penegoes, Powys, 1713 or 1714 - Colomendy, Clwyd, 1782
Tabley House, Cheshire, c. 1764-66
Oil on canvas, 100.3 x 125.7 cm
Private Collection

Richard Wilson turned his attention exclusively to landscape painting during his formative years in Italy, from 1750 to around 1757. During this time he developed a formula for painting classical landscape that combined close observation of nature with lessons learnt from the renowned seventeenth-century masters Gaspard Dughet and Claude Lorrain. On his return to Britain, Wilson continued to frame his native subject matter within the classical tradition, evoking the same Arcadian atmosphere that was then being pursued by his wealthy patrons in their building and emparkment schemes. Typical of such schemes was Tabley House, Cheshire, the Palladian mansion designed by John Carr for Sir Peter Leicester. The house was completed around 1767, at which time the grounds were also developed. It was also probably in the mid-1760s that Wilson painted the present work, although it was not exhibited at the Royal Academy until 1780. (MP)

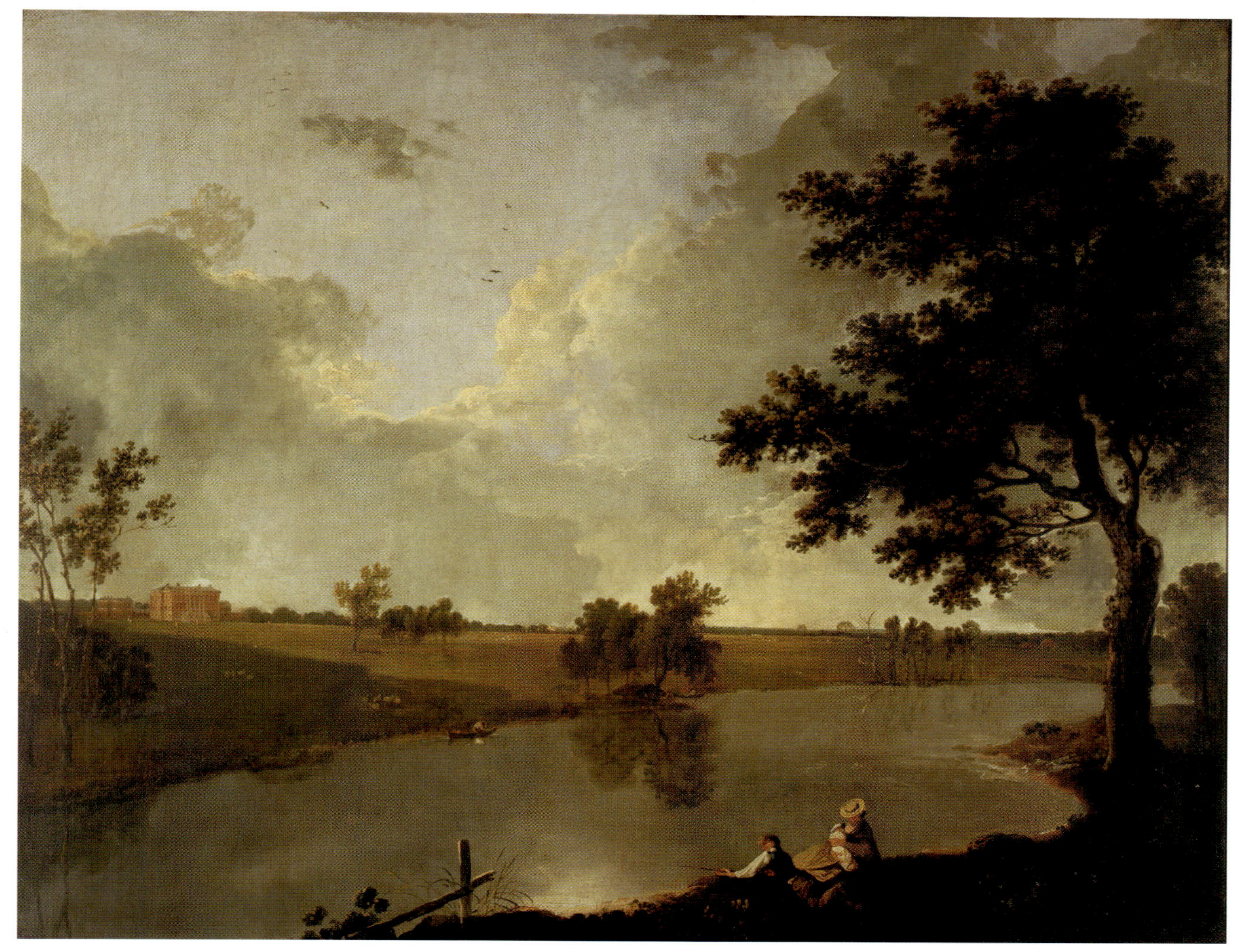

113

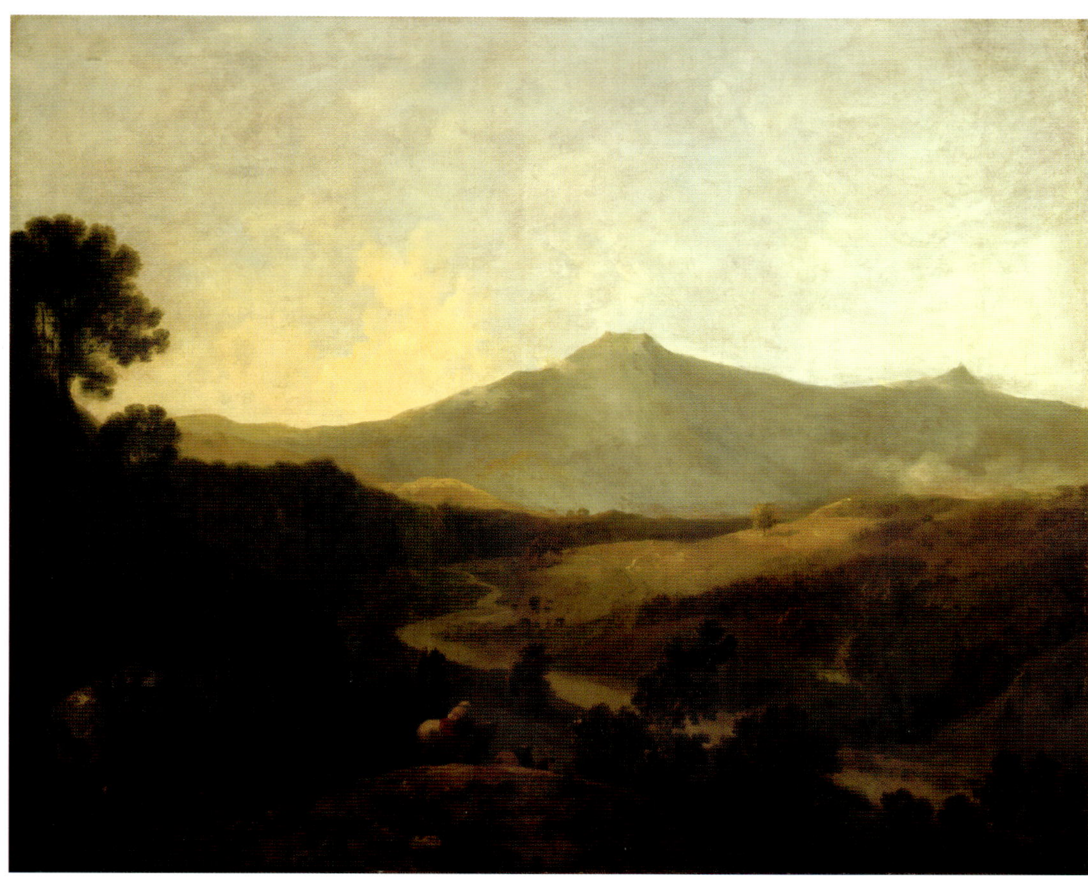

114

114. **Richard Wilson**

Penegoes, Powys, 1713 or 1714 - Colomendy, Clwyd, 1782

The Valley of the Mawddach, with Cader Idris beyond, early 1770s

Oil on canvas, 92 x 110 cm

National Museums Liverpool, Walker Art Gallery

The present picture is one of several similar views that Wilson painted from this particular location and that he exhibited at the Royal Academy in 1774. Wilson, who came from nearby Penegoes, in north Wales, would have been familiar since his youth with the countryside of the Mawddach valley. Here, the most imposing landmark is the mountain Cader Idris, which, as Wilson had depicted in an earlier picture (Tate, London), contains the volcanic lake Lyn-y-Cau. Cader Idris was, not surprisingly, the focus of countless legends: supposedly the home of a monstrous giant and a Welsh seat of King Arthur. Indeed, one of the factors that prompted Wilson to paint this countryside, aside from its rugged beauty, was its association with ancient legends, stories that compared with the classical myths of Italy. Even so, as has been suggested, this landscape may have been intended to cater not only to intellectual tastes but to the burgeoning tourist market, as the Welsh landscape was absorbed into the Picturesque aesthetic. (MP)

115. **Joseph Wright of Derby**

Derby, 1734 - Derby, 1797

Landscape with Figures and a Tilted Cart: Matlock High Tor in the Distance, c. 1790

Oil on canvas, 101.5 x 128.5 cm

Southampton City Art Gallery

Judy Egerton has identified this painting with one offered for sale at Christie's on 6 May 1801 (lot 28), and its title serves to identify the subject as one of Wright's many views of the Derbyshire peak of Matlock. Following his Italian tour of 1773-75 Wright turned increasingly to landscape and often, as here, bathed it in a warm Italianate atmosphere. The striking motif of powerful sunlight bursting through foliage had been a favourite of Rubens and was revived by several painters in Romantic England: by the American Benjamin West about 1799, by Peter de Wint about 1810, and in 1823 by Constable (Gage 2002, p. 40). Here it establishes Wright's abiding fascination with light. (JG)

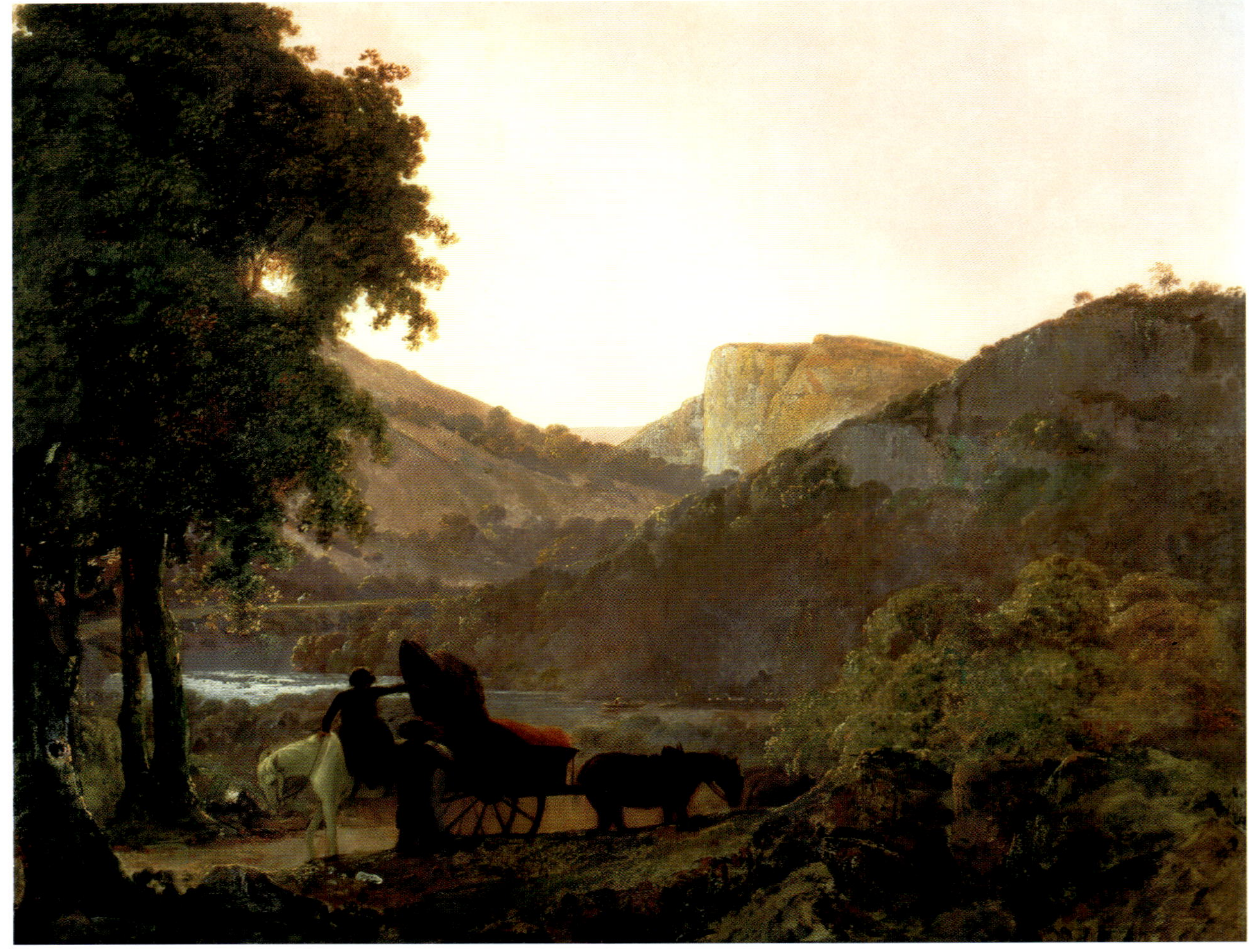

115

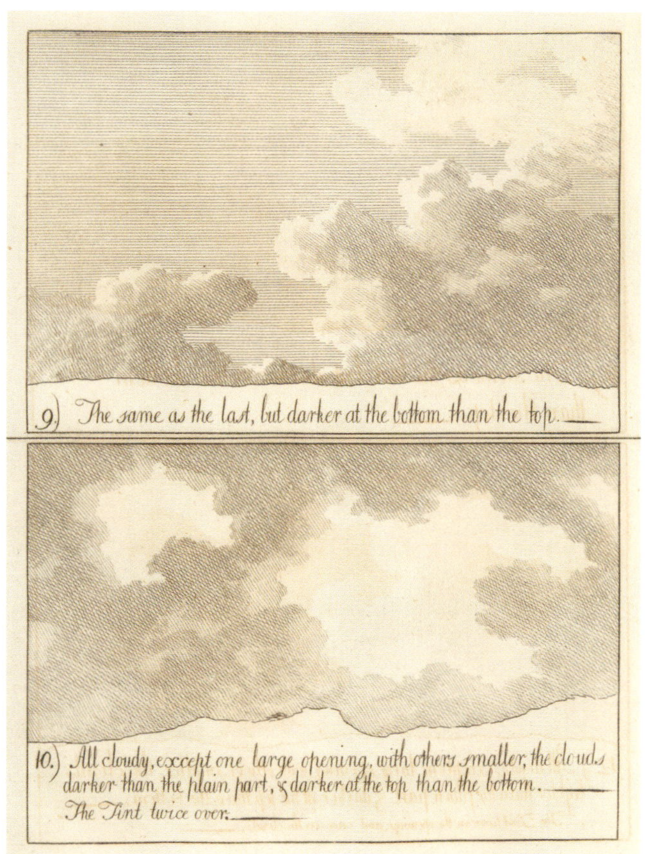

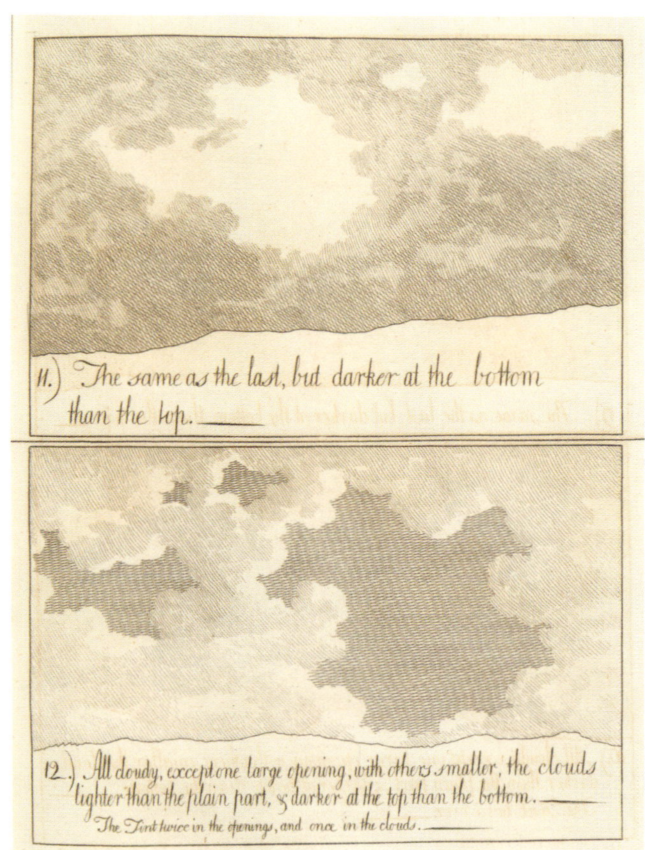

116

116. **Alexander Cozens**
St Petersburg [?], 1717 – London, 1786
A New Method of Assisting the Invention in Drawing Original Compositions of Landscape, 1786
Book, 27 x 20 [text volume], 32 x 26 cm [cloud plates volume]
Published by J. Dixwell, London
University of Nottingham, Manuscripts and Special Collections

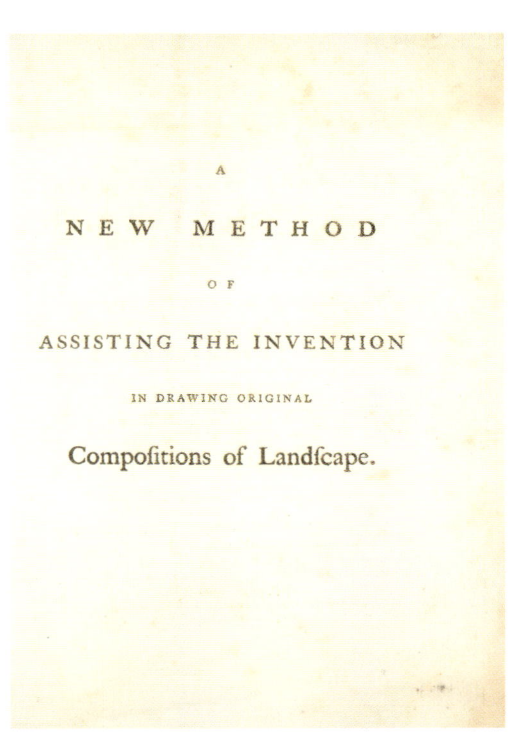
A

NEW METHOD

OF

ASSISTING THE INVENTION

IN DRAWING ORIGINAL

Compofitions of Landfcape.

The Russian-born artist Alexander Cozens was educated in London before returning to St Petersburg in 1737. From there, in 1746, he travelled to Italy, residing principally in Rome before moving back to London. In the 1750s he was employed as a drawing master at Christ's Hospital school, and later at Eton College. An avid theorist, Cozens published a number of artistic treatises, including, in 1759, *An Essay to Facilitate the Inventing of Landskips, Intended for Students in the Art*, and, in 1785/6, *A New Method of Assisting the Invention in Drawing Original Compositions of Landscape*, Cozens's final treatise on art, published the year before his death. Sadly, due to a very restricted print run, its impact upon Cozens's contemporaries was limited. A slim volume, it consists of 33 pages of text and 27 engraved plates, including 16 full-page reproductions of

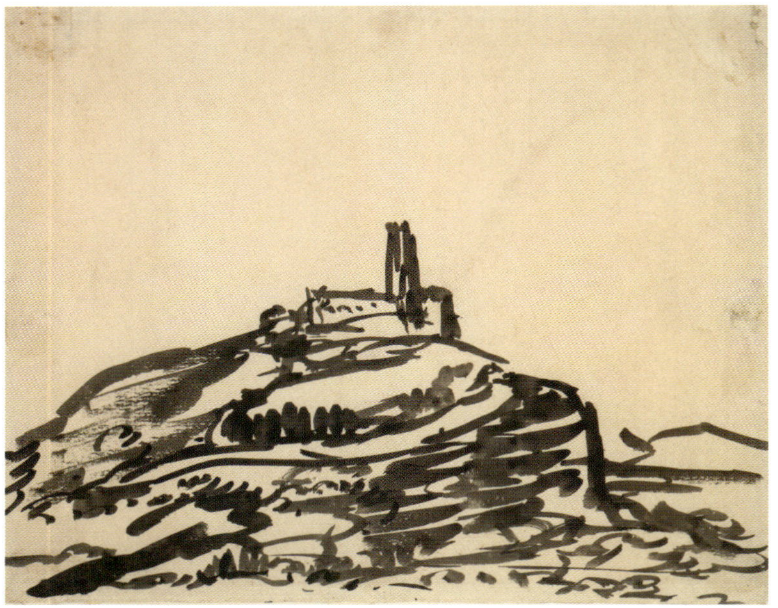

117

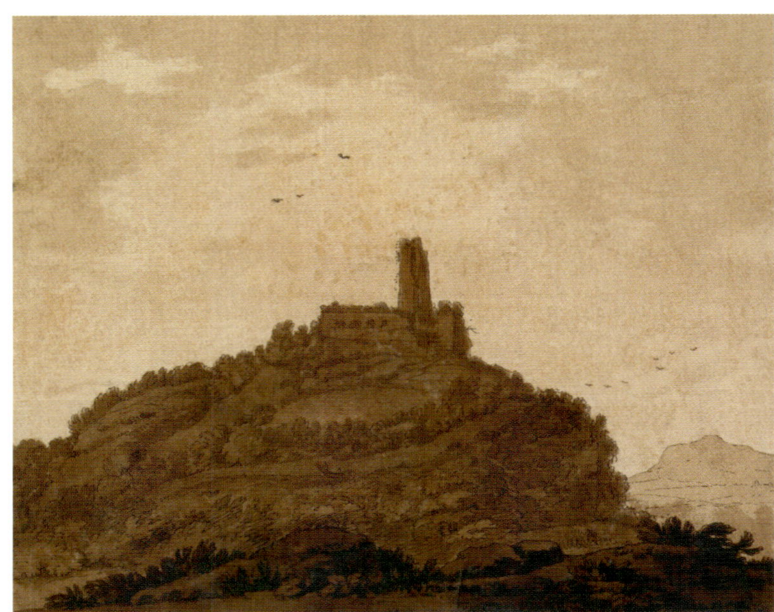

118

aquatint ink 'blots', which he believed could serve as the basis for the formation of spontaneous landscape drawings. The reproductions correspond approximately to the sixteen kinds of composition included in Cozens's earlier treatise, *The Various Species of Composition of Landscape, in Nature*. The illustrations of *A New Method* also include twenty different cloud formations which Cozens provides to help build a landscape composition. John Constable made copies of these compositions (Courtauld Institute, London), including Cozens' comments, presumably in the early 1820s, when he himself was deeply involved in the study of skies.

As Cozens explained in his accompanying text, his 'method' was designed to promote more original and spontaneous ways of approaching landscape, and to counter the prevalent academic trend of copying the works of other artists, 'which tends to weaken the powers of invention'. The origin of his 'blot' technique, stated Cozens, derived from an exercise he had carried out with a pupil, in which the two artists had improvised a landscape composition using as its basis the stains on a piece of paper. 'The blot,' as Cozens noted, 'is not a drawing, but an assemblage of accidental shapes, from which a drawing may be made.' (MP)

117. **Alexander Cozens**
St Petersburg [?], 1717 – London, 1786
'Blot' Landscape, with a tower on a hill
Brush drawing in grey wash on paper, 15.7 x 19.3 cm
British Museum, London

118. **Alexander Cozens**
St Petersburg [?], 1717 – London, 1786
Landscape from a 'blot' drawing, with a tower on a hill
Pen and black ink with brown wash, slightly varnished, on paper, 15.9 x 19.6 cm
British Museum, London

These drawings demonstrate the way in which Cozens used one of his 'blot' drawings to form the basis of a finished landscape composition. In *A New Method of Assisting the Invention in Drawing Original Compositions of Landscape*, Cozens set out five rules concerning the making of blot drawings and the ways in which they can be transformed into finished drawings. In Rule IV, Cozens explains that once the blot drawing is complete, a sheet of semi-transparent paper is laid over it. On this sheet the artist refines the composition, studying 'every individual form with attention till you produce some proper meaning, such as the blot suggests'. The composition is built up in a series of layers, using thin washes, so that the unity of the composition and the general effect is maintained. (MP)

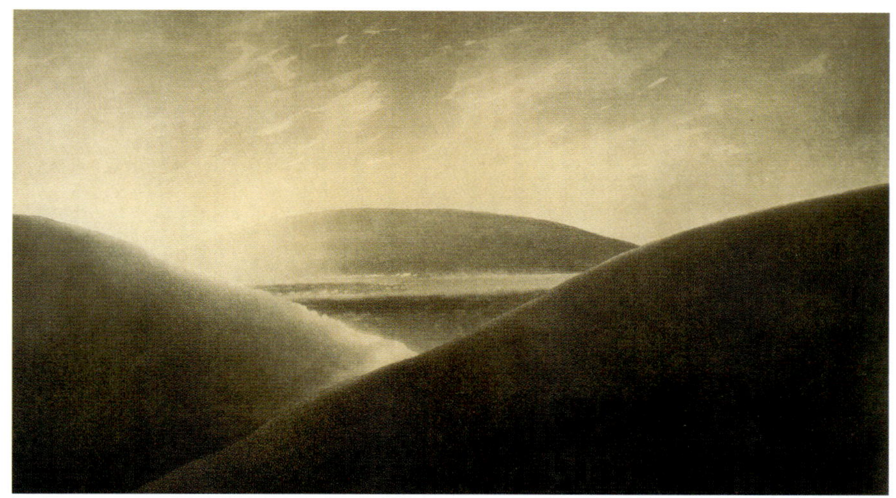

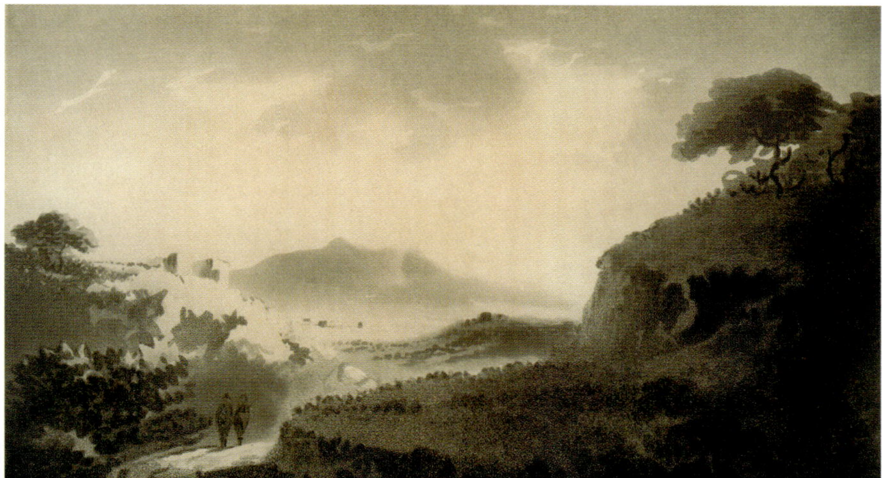

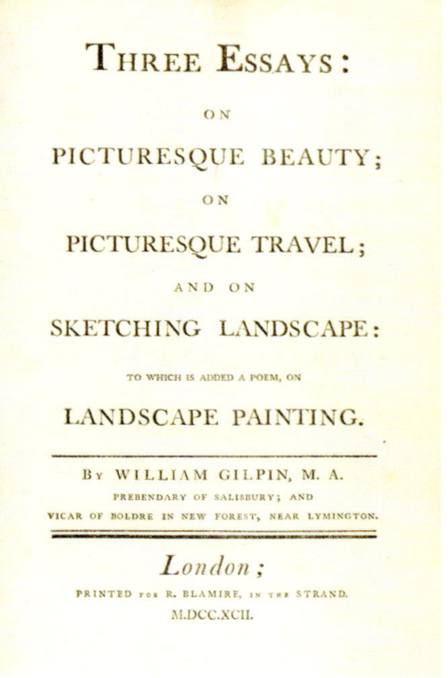

THREE ESSAYS:
ON
PICTURESQUE BEAUTY;
ON
PICTURESQUE TRAVEL;
AND ON
SKETCHING LANDSCAPE:
TO WHICH IS ADDED A POEM, ON
LANDSCAPE PAINTING.

BY WILLIAM GILPIN, M. A.
PREBENDARY OF SALISBURY; AND
VICAR OF BOLDRE IN NEW FOREST, NEAR LYMINGTON.

London;
PRINTED FOR R. BLAMIRE, IN THE STRAND.
M.DCC.XCII.

119

119. **William Gilpin**
Scaleby, Cumbria, 1724 – Boldre, Hampshire, 1804
Three Essays: On Picturesque Beauty; On Picturesque Travel; and On Sketching Landscape: To which Is Added a Poem, On Landscape Painting, 1792
Book published by R. Blamire, 30.6 x 22.3 cm
Yale Center for British Art, Paul Mellon Collection, New Haven

At the end of the eighteenth century, several authors provided a theoretical framework for the increasing interest in nature that was expressed both in painting and through the dissemination of prints in albums and travel literature. William Gilpin illustrated this group of essays on 'picturesque beauty' with views in which he contrasts a flat, uninteresting composition with a landscape filled with rough and broken forms that 'look good in a painting'. According to Gilpin, an artist can find the necessary wealth of textures and chiaroscuro effects in a picturesque landscape to inspire him to a lively interpretation of nature. It is interesting that Gilpin made a connection between picturesque nature and a free, sketch-like technique, which would become increasingly important in landscape painting: 'It is not merely for the sake of his execution, that the painter prefers rough objects to smooth. The very essence of his art requires it.' (cit. Hipple 1957, p. 194; see also essay, p. 35) (RH)

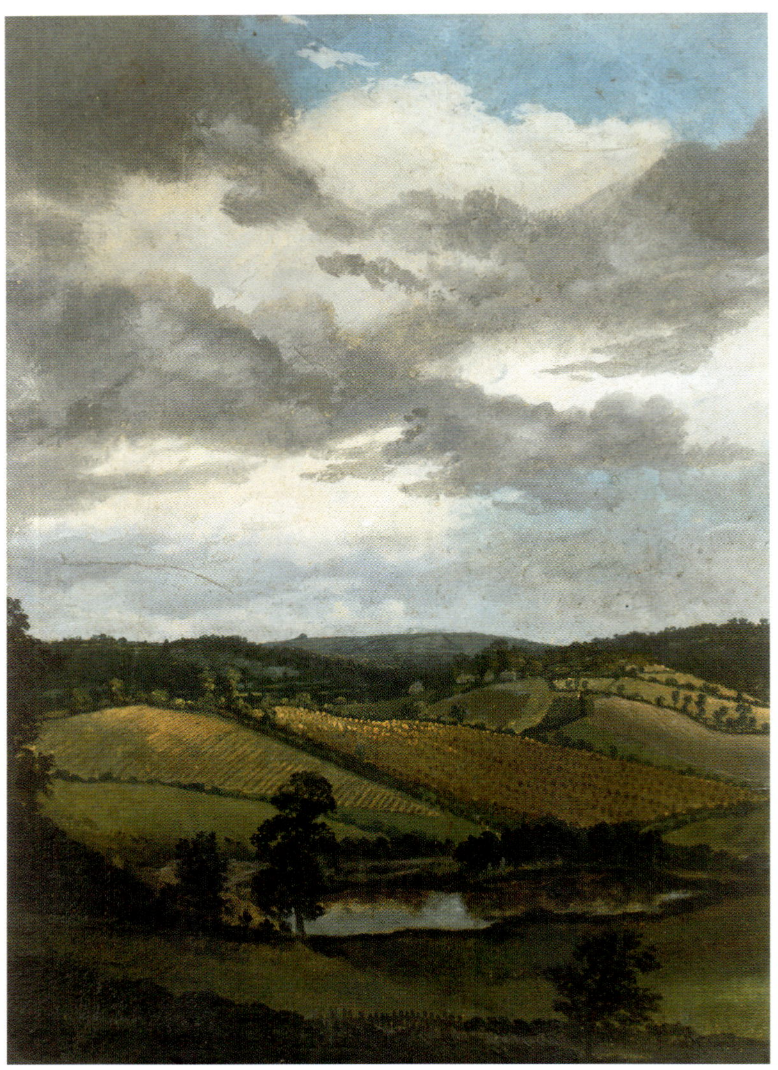

120. **Thomas Jones**

Trevonen, Powys, 1742 - Pencerrig, Powys, 1803

Pencerrig, 1772

Oil on paper, 31.8 x 22.2 cm

Verso: ptd in 1772

Tate, London, Purchased as part of the Oppé Collection with assistance from the National Lottery through the Heritage Lottery Fund 1996

In 1750 Jones's family took up residence at Pencerrig, an estate near the spa town of Builth Wells in the mountainous county of Radnorshire, part of Powys in mid-Wales. After moving to London, he visited his parental home on several occasions, and he eventually retired there in 1789. This view northwards from a vantage point to the east of the house is one of 'a good many Studies in Oil on paper' made there between July and December 1772. The harvested corn suggests a date in the late summer. There is considerable underdrawing beneath the landscape, and the foreground trees were probably added as compositional devices. The unusual vertical format provides space for the towering cloudscape, which fills over half the composition, anticipating Constable's cloud studies of the 1820s. Gowing described this sketch as 'a glimpse of the future' for its 'sense of visual experience as constituting a whole' (Gowing, 1985, p. 12). (ME)

120

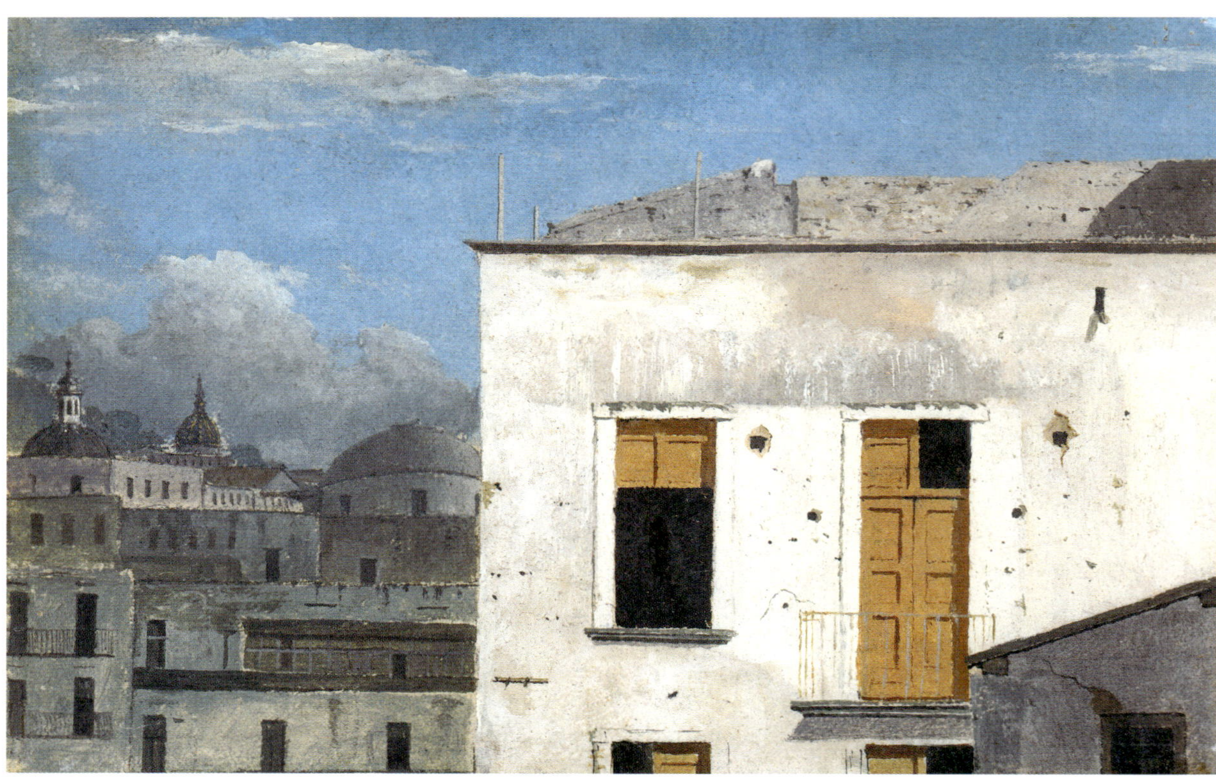

121

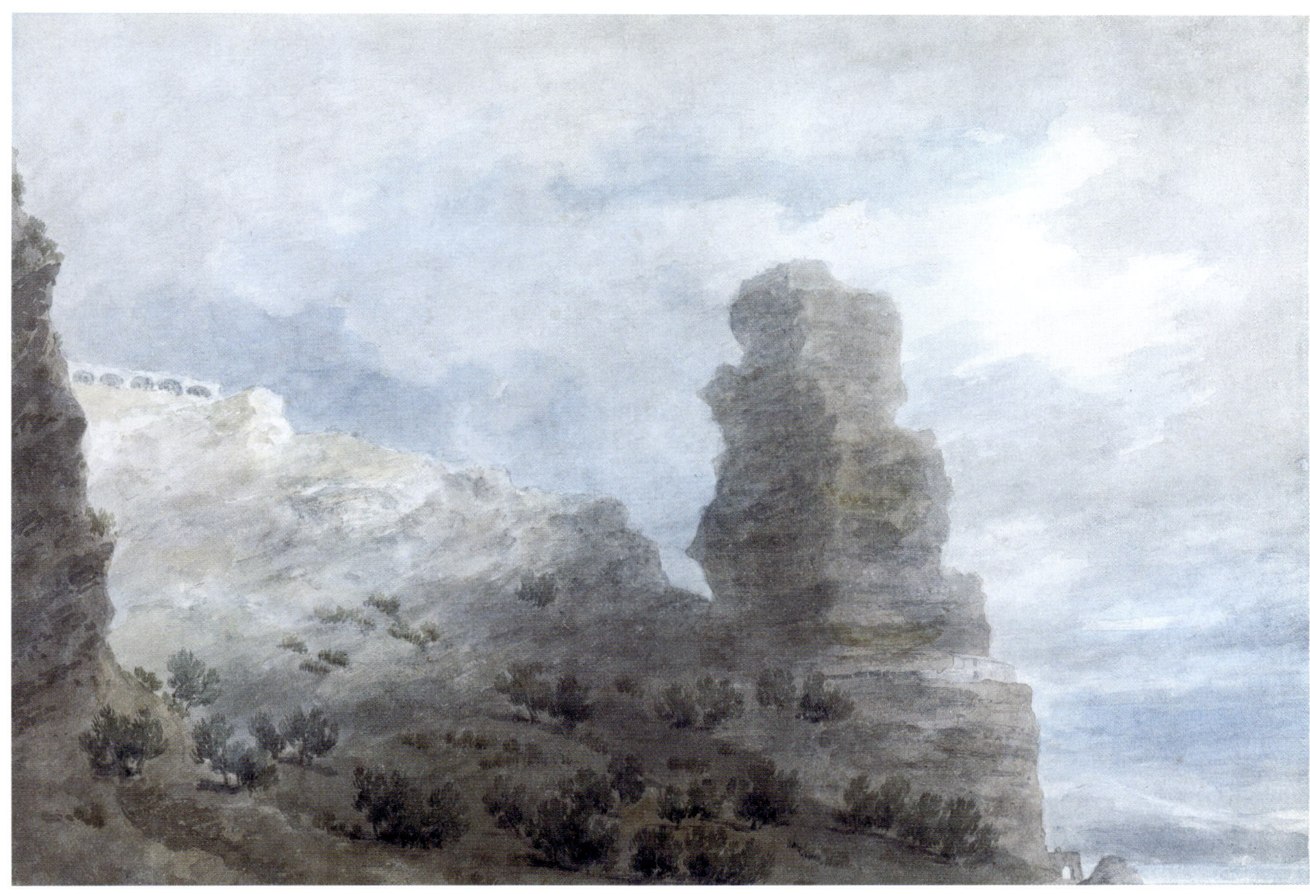

122

121. **Thomas Jones**
Trevonen, Powys, 1742 - Pencerrig, Powys, 1803
Buildings in Naples, 1782
Oil on paper, 14.2 x 21.6 cm
Verso: Thos Jones. Naples Aprile 1782
Amgueddfa Cymru - National Museum Wales, Cardiff

At the time of Jones's stay, Naples was the most populous city in Italy and the residence of the Bourbon court. He lodged near the harbour in a 'large new built house or Palace ... with the use of the *Lastrica* or Terras Roof', and subsequently in a house 'with the exclusive use of the Lastrica ... where I spent many a happy hour in painting from Nature'. From these viewpoints Jones painted a remarkable series of oil studies of the neighbouring buildings. Characteristically, these portray, exactly parallel to the picture plane, a pitted masonry wall bathed in sunlight and punctuated by dark apertures against a bright blue sky. His enthusiasm for such views may have been fed by his friendship with the watercolourist Giovanni Battista Lusieri (d. 1821), who specialized in panoramic townscapes. Gowing observed that Jones's 'Naples sketches achieved an enveloping unity... They are gentle and precise and they illustrate nothing. They simply *are*.' (Gowing, 1985, p. 52) (ME)

See essay pp. 187-89.

122. **John Robert Cozens**
London, 1752 - London, 1797
View from the Inn at Terracina, towards the Rock Pillar of Pesco Montano, 1783 [?]
Pencil and watercolour on paper, 26.2 x 36.4 cm
Yale Center for British Art, Paul Mellon Collection, New Haven

John Robert Cozens made his first visit to Italy, via the Swiss Alps, in 1776 with the Grand Tourist and collector Richard Payne Knight. He remained there until 1779, making drawings and watercolours notably of Rome and the Campagna. In May 1782 Cozens returned to Italy, this time as a draughtsman for William Beckford, who was a friend of his father. On both visits Cozens stayed at the inn at Terracina, in October 1777 and July 1782, and made a number of sketches and related finished watercolours. Terracina, a coastal hilltop town south of Rome, had been strategically important since ancient times. The Pisco Montano, a promontory of rock to the east of the town, was celebrated not just as a natural landmark but as the site of a remarkable Roman road, incised into the cliff-face by the Emperor Trajan as a short cut for the Appian Way. Shown in Cozens's watercolour, to the left and above the rock, are the ancient vaults made to support the, now destroyed, temple complex. (MP)

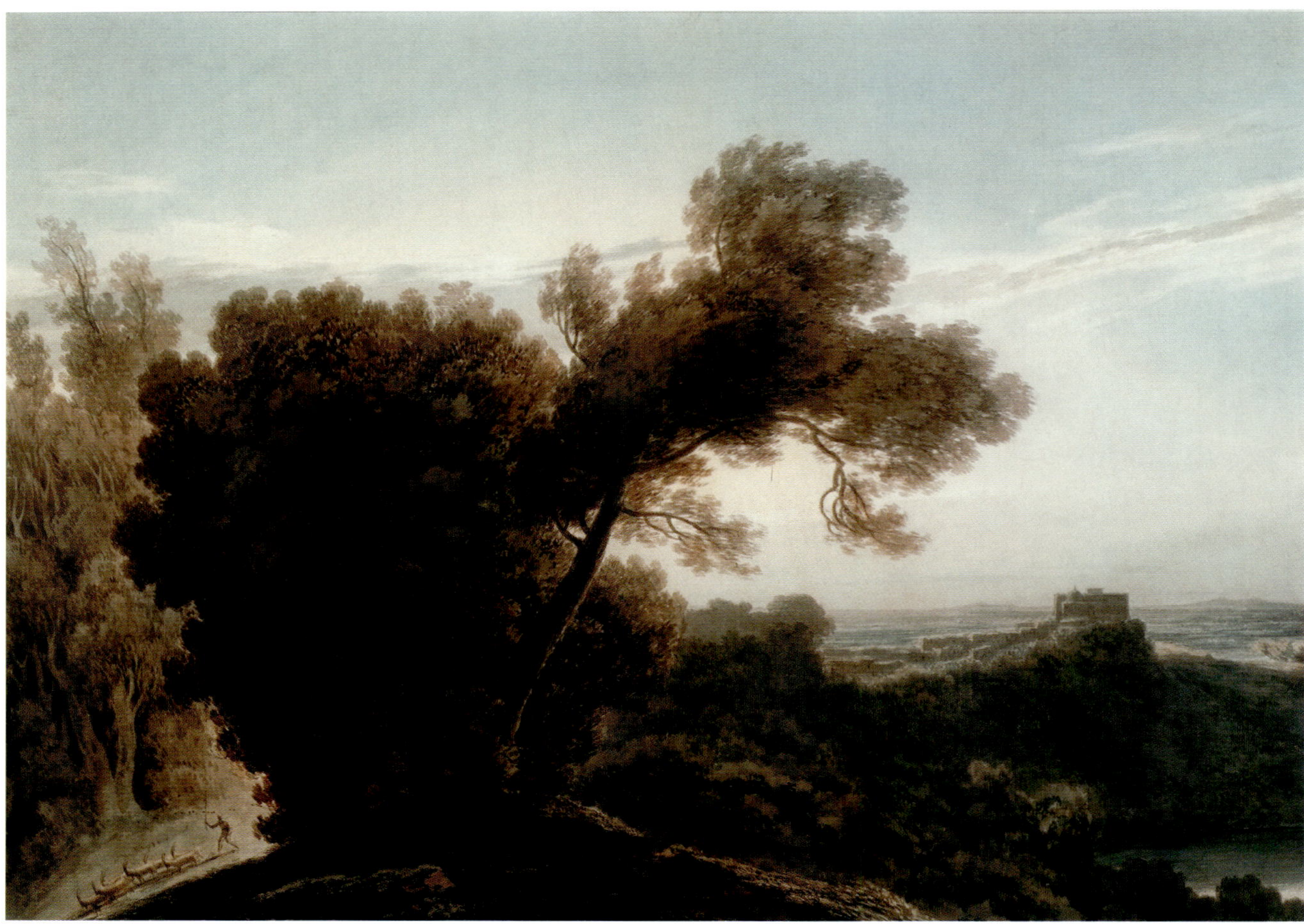

123

123. **John Robert Cozens**
London, 1752 - London, 1797
The Lake of Albano and Castel Gandolfo, c. 1783-88
Pencil and watercolour on paper, 48.9 x 67.9 cm
Tate, London, Presented by A.E. Anderson in memory of his brother Frank through The Art Fund 1928

A solitary soul, John Robert Cozens sought in his Italian watercolours to endow an elegiac quality to his subjects, notably those based upon the countryside around Rome. Employing a restricted range of colours, and muted tones, Cozens's subtle watercolours drew inspiration not only from the immediate landscape but the Ideal pastoral paintings of the Roman *campagna* by the seventeenth-century master Gaspard Dughet. Lake Albano, glimpsed at the extreme right of Cozens's composition, was a popular site among artists and Grand Tourists. Situated in the Colli Albini, the lake was formed in the crater of two fused volcanoes, fed by underground springs. Beyond the lake, on a promontory, is the papal palace at Castel Gandolfo. Cozens probably made this haunting watercolour following his second Italian sojourn from 1782 to 1783. Plagued increasingly by mental illness, he was by 1794 confined in an asylum, although his work continued to have a tremendous influence upon a younger generation of British landscape painters, in particular J.M.W. Turner. (MP)

124. **Francis Towne**
Exeter [?], 1739/40 - Exeter, 1816
The Source of the Arveiron: Mont Blanc in the Background, 1781
Pen, ink and watercolour on paper, 42.5 x 31.1 cm
Bottom right: F. Towne delt. / 1781 / N°. 53
Victoria and Albert Museum, London

Francis Towne spent a year in Italy from September 1780 to the end of the following summer. By the time he made his visit he was already a well established landscape artist in oils and watercolour, and, like many men of his profession, also a drawing master. His distinctive style, employing flat planes of colour, bounded by tight, well defined, lines was remarked upon in Italy, a contemporary noting that his was 'one of the strangest genius's I have ever seen'. The present watercolour is one of several that Towne made of the source of the river Arveiron, in the Mer de Glace, which he encountered on his way back from Italy in September 1781. The subject was increasingly popular among artists, as travellers were drawn to the Sublime aspect of Alpine scenery. However, in Towne's watercolour the icefield takes on an abstract quality, as the artist's concern with pure form eclipses any potential interest in topography or climate. (MP)

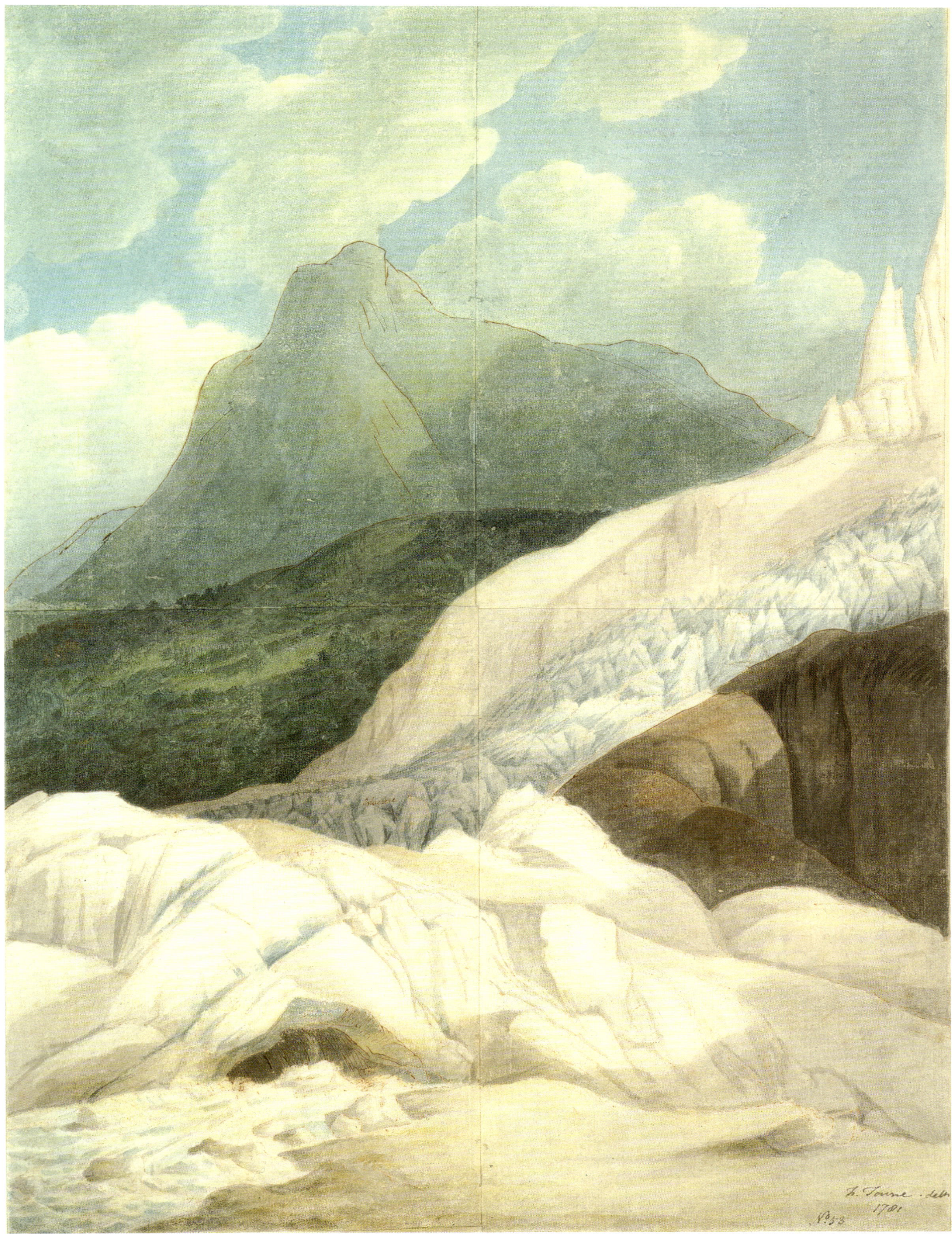

124

125

125. **Thomas Girtin**
London, 1775 – London, 1802
The Village of Jedburgh, Scotland, 1800
Watercolour on paper, 30.1 x 51.1 cm
Bottom left: Girtin 1800
National Gallery of Scotland, Edinburgh

Girtin visited the Scottish borders when on a tour to the north of England in 1796. During that trip he made a careful panoramic drawing in pencil of the village of Jedburgh, which included, as well as the main street shown here, the ruined abbey beyond it to the right (British Museum, London). That pencil drawing, and a related watercolour made the following year (Private Collection), thus preserve the essential elements of the original scene as observed by Girtin on the spot.

Significantly, when he made this version of the subject three years later, Girtin decided to crop part of the original composition severely on the right, thus omitting the key antiquarian element – the abbey itself – and concentrating instead on the village and the encircling hills. In this way he transformed a topographical record into a landscape of much greater drama and expressive force, also making more of a feature of the drifts of smoke emanating from chimneys on the high street to help create atmosphere and mood.

This watercolour was sold through the engraver S.W. Reynolds – who acted as an agent, finding buyers for Girtin's paintings – to Elizabeth Weddell, widow of William Weddell of Newby Hall, Yorkshire. In later life, Weddell was affiliated to a circle of enthusiasts for Girtin's work who lived in Kent. (AL)

126. **Thomas Girtin**
London, 1775 – London, 1802
St Vincent's Rocks, Clifton, Bristol, c. 1800
Pencil and watercolour on paper, 32.1 x 52.7 cm
Whitworth Art Gallery, University of Manchester

Although Girtin made other watercolours of Bristol, such as *Bristol Harbour and St Mary Redcliffe Church*, 1800 (City Art Gallery, Bristol) and is thus assumed to have visited the city, perhaps in connection with his tour to the West County in 1797, it is not known for certain whether he actually visited the dramatic gorge at Clifton to the north-west of Bristol.

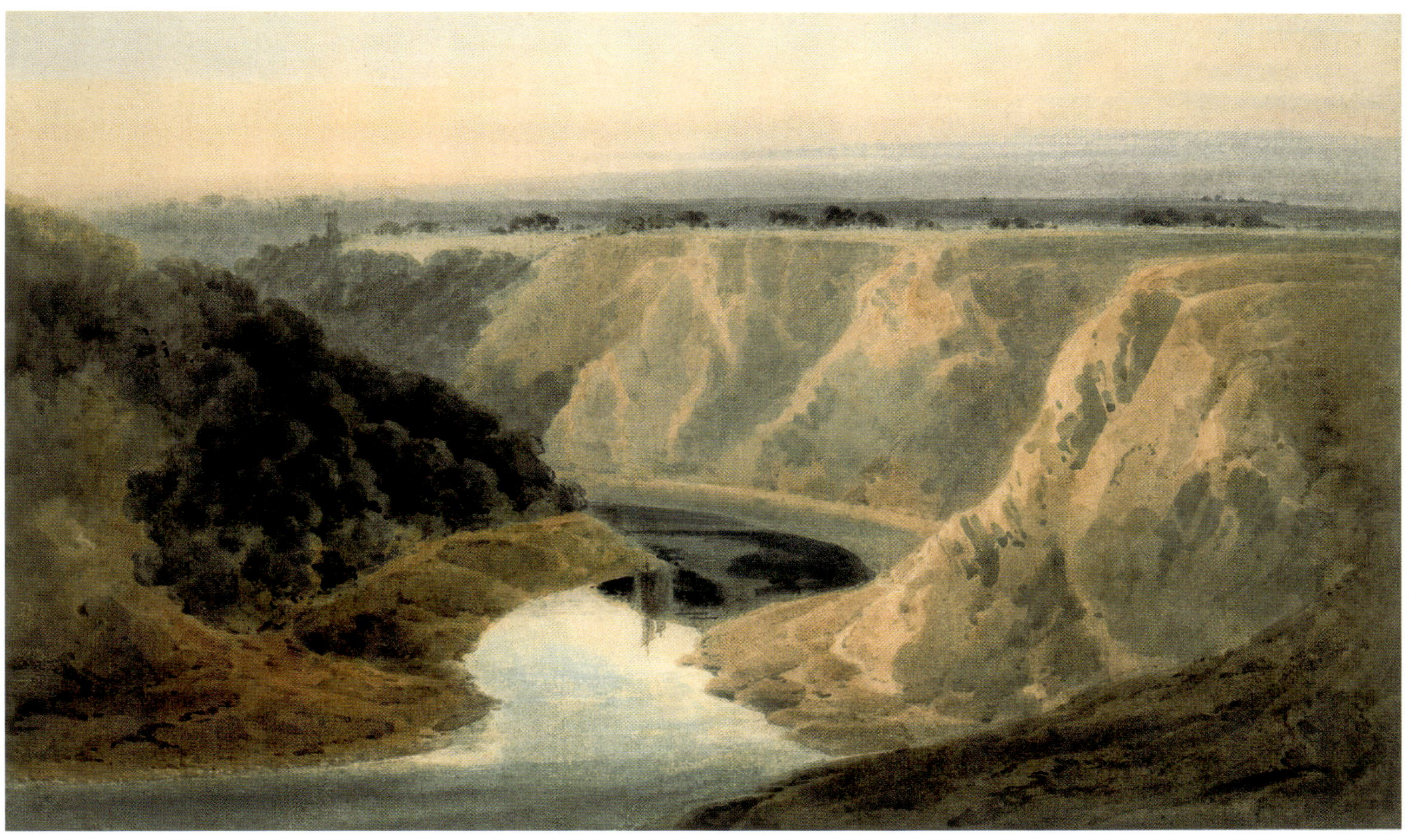

126

The Avon Gorge was a celebrated beauty spot - and was later to become a favourite subject with artists of the Bristol School such as Francis Danby (see cat. 134-135) - so it is likely that Girtin would have been attracted to the site. However, it is conceivable that he actually based this watercolour on an earlier engraving made after another artist's representation of the Gorge.

Whatever the origin of the image, however, in this watercolour Girtin has produced one of his most powerful and evocative landscapes. The features of the landscape are pared down to their most simplified form, and little detracts from the striking effect of the sun's sinking rays catching the edges of the cliffs on the right and enveloping the gorge in the rich and mellow light of evening. So intense is the mood which Girtin creates in this watercolour that it was once interpreted as the very last he painted - romantically believed to have been produced in a final flourish of creative energy when he was in the throes of severely declining health. Such an idea is no longer accepted, and indeed this watercolour is now thought to date from some two years before Girtin's death in 1802. (AL)

127. **Thomas Girtin**
London, 1775 - London, 1802
View on the River Wharfe, Yorkshire, c. 1800
Pencil and watercolour on paper, 31.7 x 52.8 cm
Private Collection

The River Wharfe runs through part of the county of Yorkshire in the North of England. It rises in the heart of the Yorkshire Dales, a scenic upland area of limestone hills and pastoral valleys which forms part of the Pennines, and then joins the River Ouse just south of the historic Roman city of York. The stretch of the river that Girtin shows here was previously identified as a view on the Wharfe at Farnley, not far from Harewood House, the home of his (and Turner's) great patron, Edward Lascelles, where Girtin in particular seems to have been a frequent guest. However, it is now thought more likely that it shows a scene on the Wharfe between Ilkley and Bolton Abbey, and thus close to the site of another of Girtin's most famous watercolours, *Stepping Stones on the Wharfe, Yorkshire* c.1800 (National Gallery of Scotland, Edinburgh). Indeed, the difficulty of arriving at an exact location for the scene is to some extent indicative

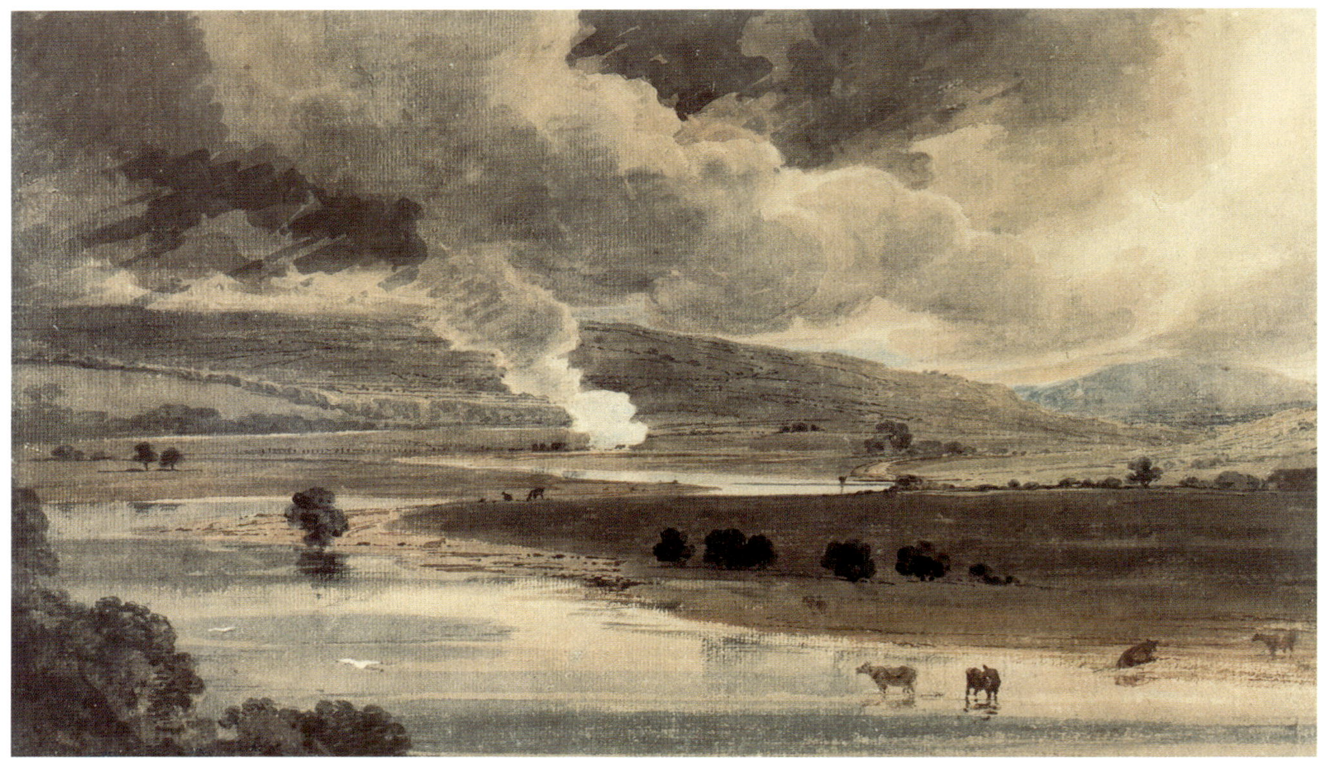

127

of the degree to which Girtin had now moved away from landscapes with obvious topographical features that help to identify the view and in the direction of pure landscape. (AL)

See essay pp. 191-93.

128. **Thomas Girtin**
London, 1775 - London, 1802
La Rue St Denis, Paris, c. 1802
Pencil and watercolour on paper, 39.3 x 48.3 cm
Private Collection

Girtin lived in Paris between November 1801 and May 1802, taking lodgings close to the rue St Denis. Indeed, the seventeenth-century gateway on the street (Porte St Denis) formed the entry point for most British visitors travelling to Paris at this date.

Girtin seems originally to have come to Paris with the intention of finding an exhibition venue for a large Panorama of London he was painting in oils around that time, known as the *Eidometropolis*. He may also have contemplated painting a Panorama of Paris as well, only to abandon the idea when he discovered a rival. Instead, he decided to publish a series of prints of the city, *Selection of Twenty of the Most Picturesque Views in Paris and its Environs* (1803).

The *Views in Paris* actually include a print of the rue St Denis very similar to the view shown in this striking watercolour, and this would tend to suggest that the watercolour itself was made in connection with that publication. However, it seems more likely that the watercolour was originally painted as a design for a theatrical backdrop for an English pantomime set in Paris, Thomas Dibdin's *Harlequin Habeas*. The production opened in London, at the Theatre Royal, Covent Garden, in December 1802, a month after Girtin's death, and attracted many favourable reviews - especially for its sets. (AL)

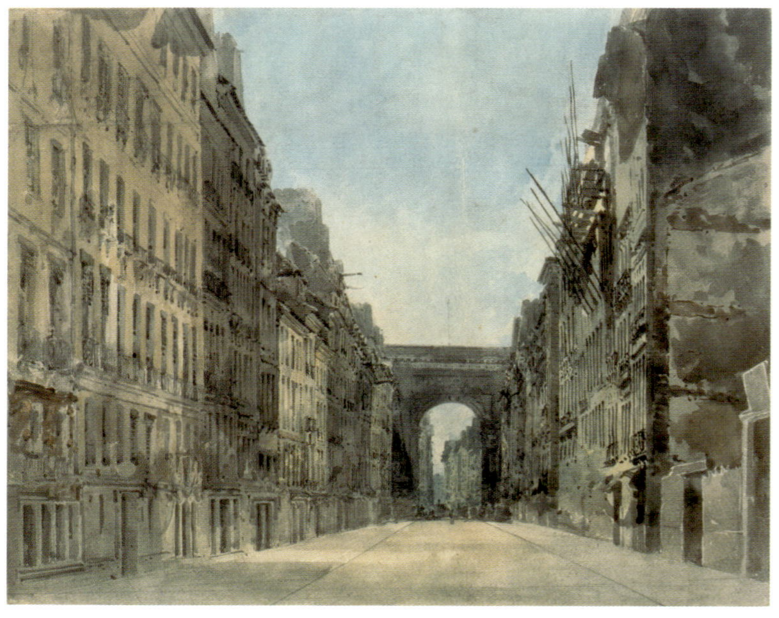

128

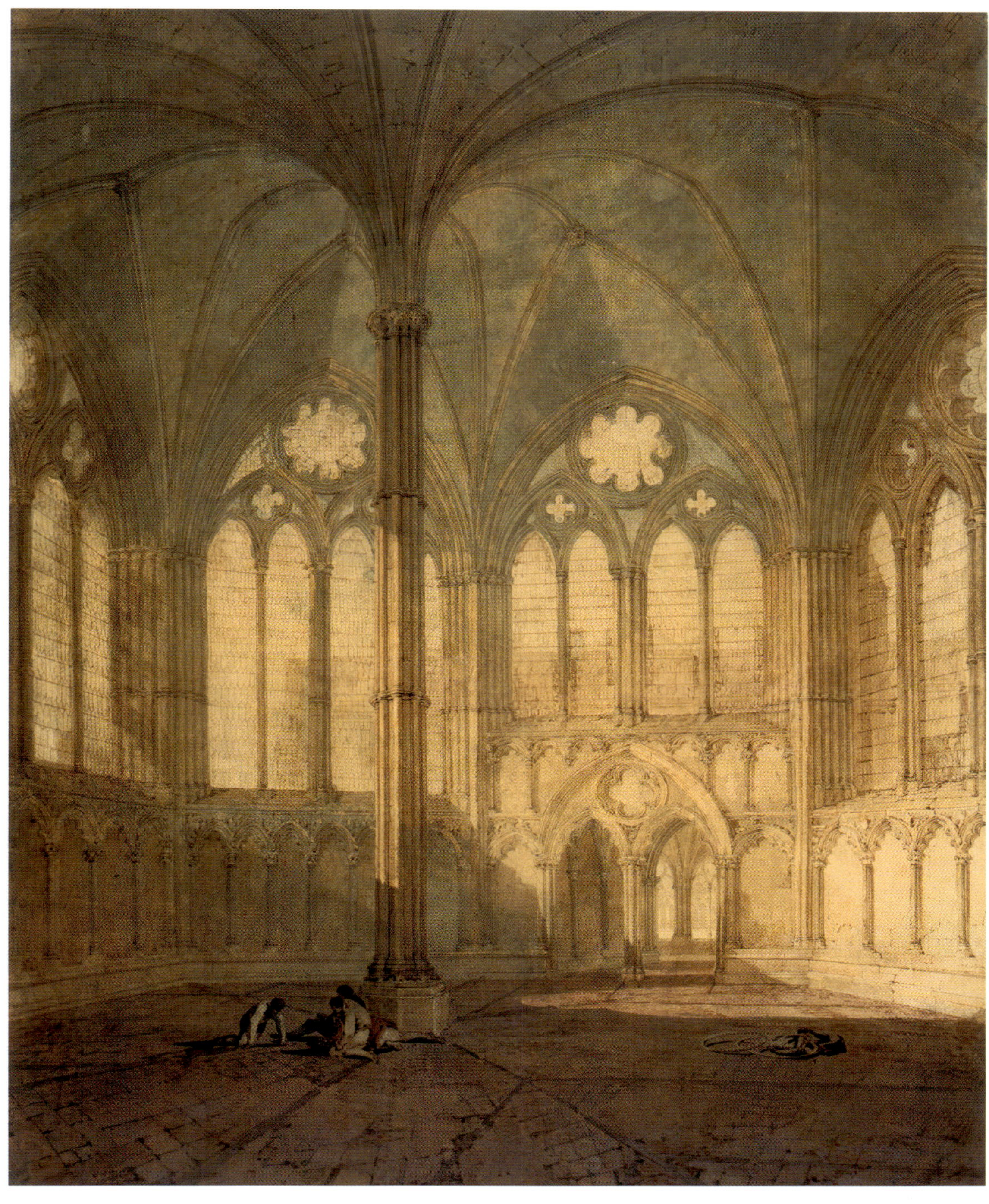

129

129. **Joseph Mallord William Turner**
London, 1775 – London, 1851
The Chapter House, Salisbury Cathedral, c. 1799
Pencil, brown ink, watercolour, on paper, 64.5 x 51.2 cm
Whitworth Art Gallery, University of Manchester

Turner generally undertook finished watercolours for one of three reasons: for exhibition at the Royal Academy; for the purpose of being engraved as topographical landscape prints; or as commissions for wealthy patrons. One of his most important early supporters was Sir Richard Colt Hoare, a wealthy antiquarian and amateur artist who charged Turner with painting a suite of vistas of Salisbury Cathedral. This view of the chapter house was one of eight watercolours completed by the artist and hung in Colt Hoare's family seat of Stourhead in Wiltshire.

The turn of the century was a period of transition for Turner, and this watercolour is a fusion of two phases of his art. The narrow tonal range, exquisitely defined architectural details and inclusion of human interest in the foreground are characteristic of his early Picturesque views. The extreme shafts of light, however, streaming through the windows and illuminating the otherwise dim interior, belies his developing interest in the Sublime. (NM)

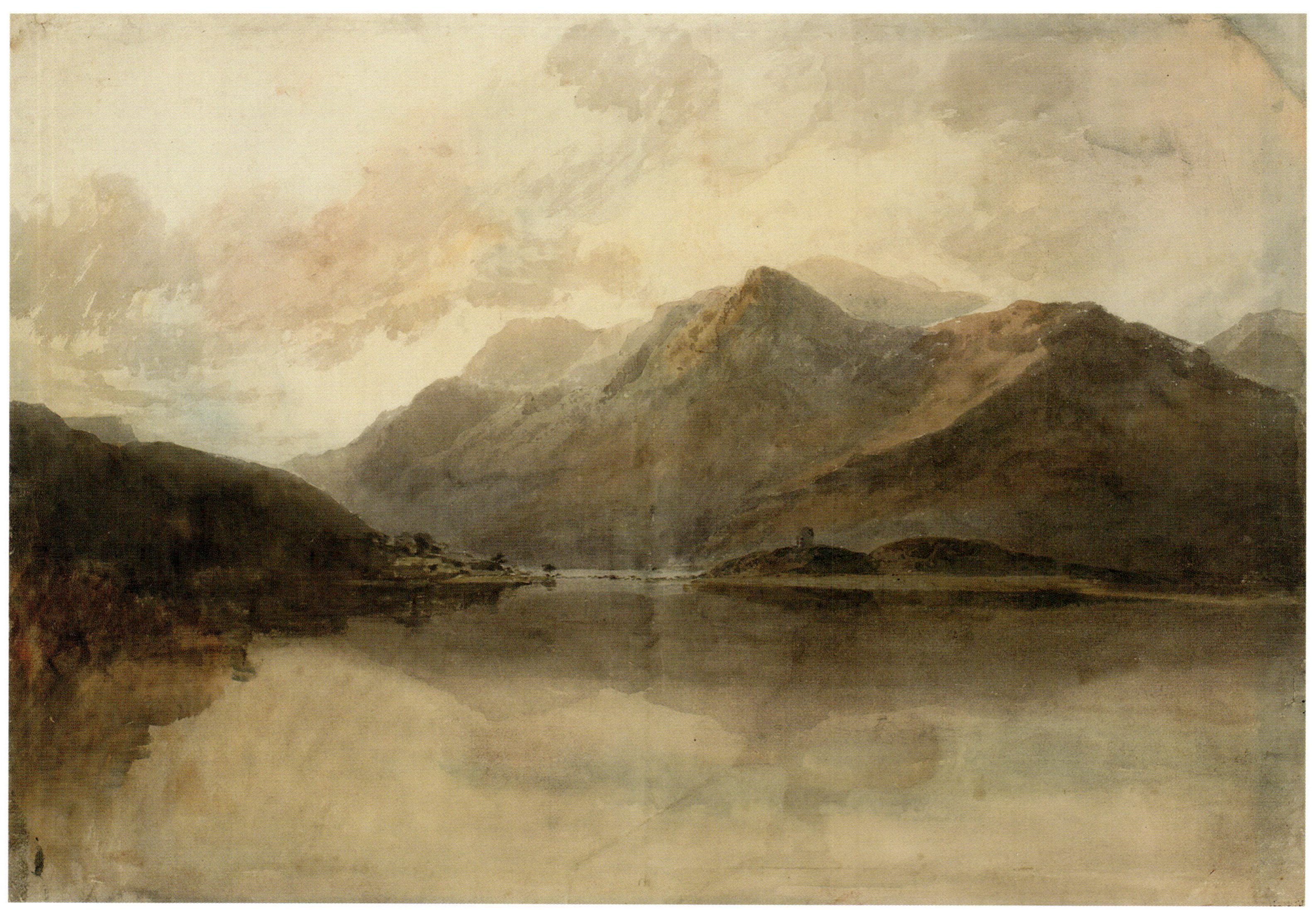

130

130. **Joseph Mallord William Turner**
London, 1775 - London, 1851
Llanberis Lake and Dolbadarn Castle, 1799/1800
Pencil and watercolour on paper
55.7 x 76.4 cm
Tate, London, Bequeathed by the artist 1856

Wales offered London-born Turner his first experience of dramatic mountainous scenery. A sketching trip to Snowdonia in 1799 resulted in a number of watercolours in which the artist demonstrated his pre-eminence and originality in the medium. By choosing to work on large-scale sheets of paper with densely worked-up areas of paint, Turner was seeking to create Sublime effects more usually found within oil paintings. In this view, the soaring peaks of Snowdon overshadow and dwarf the distinctive round slate tower of Dolbadarn Castle, a thirteenth-century fortress on the banks of Llyn Peris. The lowering mountains are reflected in the glass-like lake beneath. The castle was already a popular landmark for eighteenth-century artists, most famously for Welsh landscape painter Richard Wilson. It subsequently became one of Turner's favourite early motifs. In 1802 he presented an oil painting of the subject to the Royal Academy on the occasion of his election to full Academician. (NM)

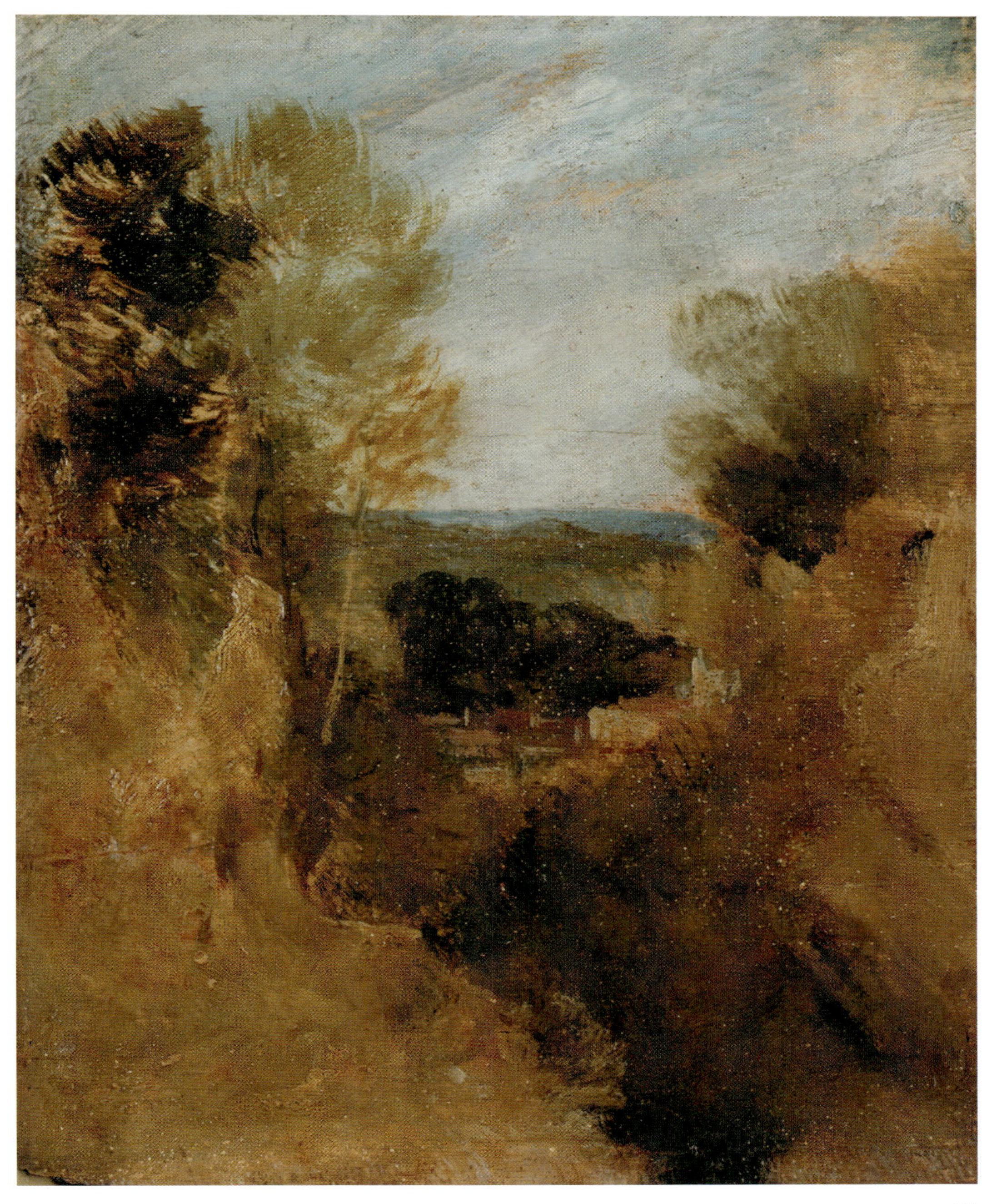

131

131. **Joseph Mallord William Turner**
London, 1775 - London, 1851
A Narrow Valley, 1805
Oil on mahogany veneer
20.6 x 16.5 cm
Tate, London, Bequeathed by the artist 1856

At the beginning of the nineteenth century, Turner sought to create a modern form of landscape art that could rival the achievements of the Old Masters. His art therefore took a new direction as he resolved to combine the tradition of topographical landscape with the poetry and spirit of classicism. During the summer of 1805, in search of suitably inspiring countryside, he spent several weeks sketching in pencil, watercolour and oil from his base at Isleworth on the Thames. The visual material he gathered provided the basis for several finished works for sale and exhibition later in the year. The view in *A Narrow Valley* probably shows Guildford, Surrey, and is one of a number of freely handled oil sketches on mahogany panel painted out of doors. Despite the unfinished informality of the view and its execution, Turner's structuring of the composition reveals his interest in the elements of Italianate, Claudian landscape. (NM)

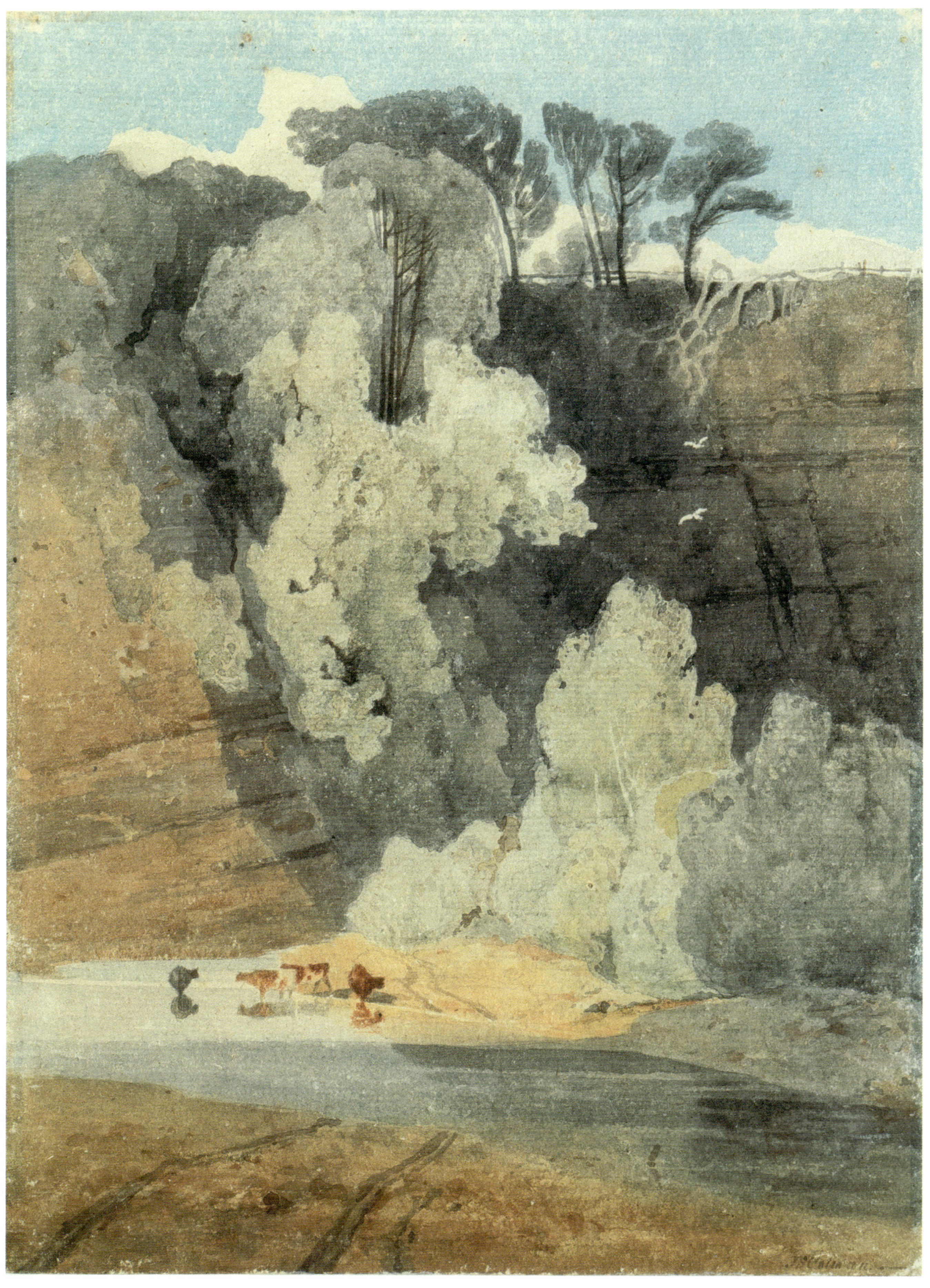

132

132. **John Sell Cotman**
Norwich, 1782 – London, 1842
On the River Greta, Yorkshire, c. 1806-07
Pencil and watercolour on paper, 32.6 x 22.9 cm
Bottom right: J S Cotman.
Verso: No 68 / On the River Greta / Yorkshire / J. Cotman
Norfolk Museums and Archaeology Service, Norwich

The scenery of Yorkshire in the north of England was to serve as a powerful inspiration for Cotman, just it had done for Girtin a few years before (see cat. 127). Cotman visited Yorkshire on three occasions in his early career. However, it was the watercolours he made of scenes on the banks of the River Greta near Rokeby Hall, which he visited in 1805 on his third visit, that were to prove the finest of all his Yorkshire subjects. They were described by the English poet and art historian Laurence Binyon as 'the most perfect examples of pure watercolour ever painted in Europe (Binyon 1931, p. 132).

By 1805 Cotman had begun to develop a new style of painting in watercolour, using pure, translucent wash layers, which he would carefully apply one over the other – without any evidence of blotting – to build form. At the same time, he would tend to reduce natural forms to simple, flat shapes, and to keep shadow to a minimum. In this way, whilst carefully avoiding any sense of movement, Cotman succeeded in creating images that are often semi-abstract in appearance, if always compelling in their combination of shape and pattern. Although a soft and understated palette sometimes contributes to a sense of austerity in these watercolours, this is offset by a decorative quality, which derives from their inherent pictorial rhythms. Indeed, one author has tellingly described Cotman's work in this period as a 'compound of logic and poetry' (Hardie 1966-68, vol. 2, p. 81).

The site shown in this watercolour is traditionally identified as one in the grounds of Rokeby Park known as 'Devil's Elbow'. However, it seems more likely that the location is one beyond the boundaries of the park, upstream of Greta Bridge, close to a point where the River Greta is bounded by cliffs and high, steep banks similar to those shown here. (AL)

133. **John Sell Cotman**
Norwich, 1782 – London, 1842
A Beached Barge near Battersea Bridge, c. 1809
Watercolour on paper, 33 x 28.8 cm
Private Collection

Born in Norwich in East Anglia and, like Turner, the son of a barber, Cotman spent his formative artistic years in London. In 1806, however, discouraged by fellow artists from joining their recently founded Society of Painters in Water-Colour in London, he returned to Norwich, where he was to become a leading member of the Norwich Society of Artists.

The attribution to Cotman of this watercolour has sometimes been doubted. However, any reservations about its authenticity can no longer be sustained thanks to the recent discovery of some autograph backing sheets on the verso (Shanes 2001, p. 76) and, furthermore, because Timothy Wilcox points out (verbal communication) that it is surely the work exhibited by Cotman at the Norwich Society of Artists in 1810 as *North End of Battersea Bridge* (as suggested by Rajnai and Allthorpe-Guyton 1979, p. 81). Indeed, following his move back to Norwich, Cotman did sometimes return to London, as for example in 1809, when he made sketches of Cheyne Walk, Chelsea, very close to the location shown here.

Cotman would have associated this spot with the memory of Thomas Girtin, whose watercolour of *The White House at Chelsea* (p. 192, fig. 1) made such a powerful impression on artists of Cotman's generation. However, whilst Girtin's panoramic watercolour showed the full span of old Battersea Bridge at dusk as if viewed from a point on the river itself, Cotman's watercolour – on an upright format – shows just a small section of the wooden bridge from the north bank, viewed in full daylight and from close to. Characteristically, Cotman makes a feature of the contrast between its elegant, structured silhouette and the heavier, rounded forms of the hull of a beached boat on the riverbank nearby. (AL)

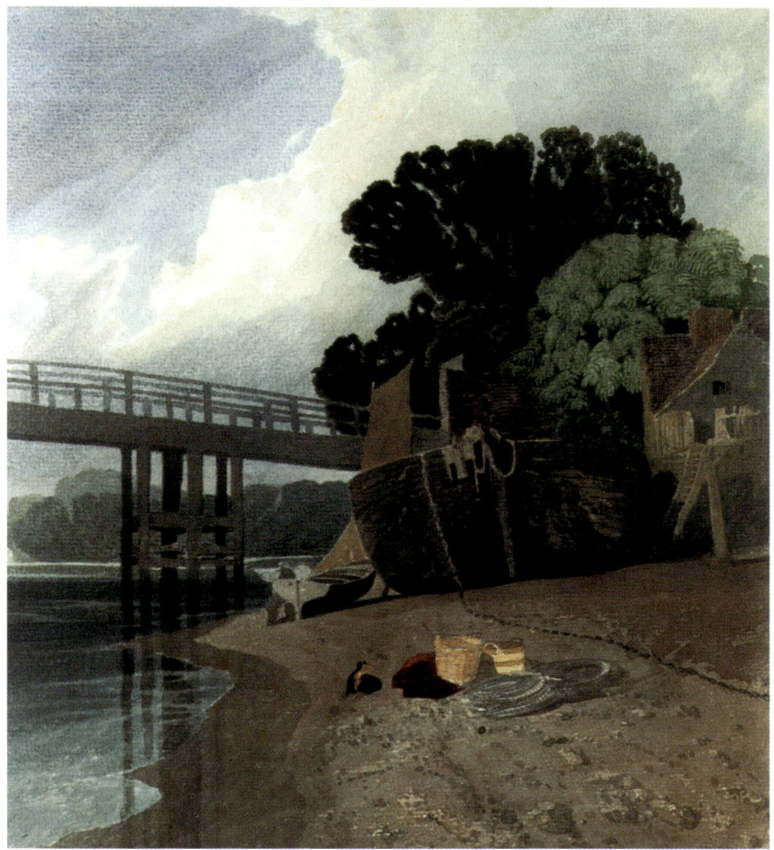
133

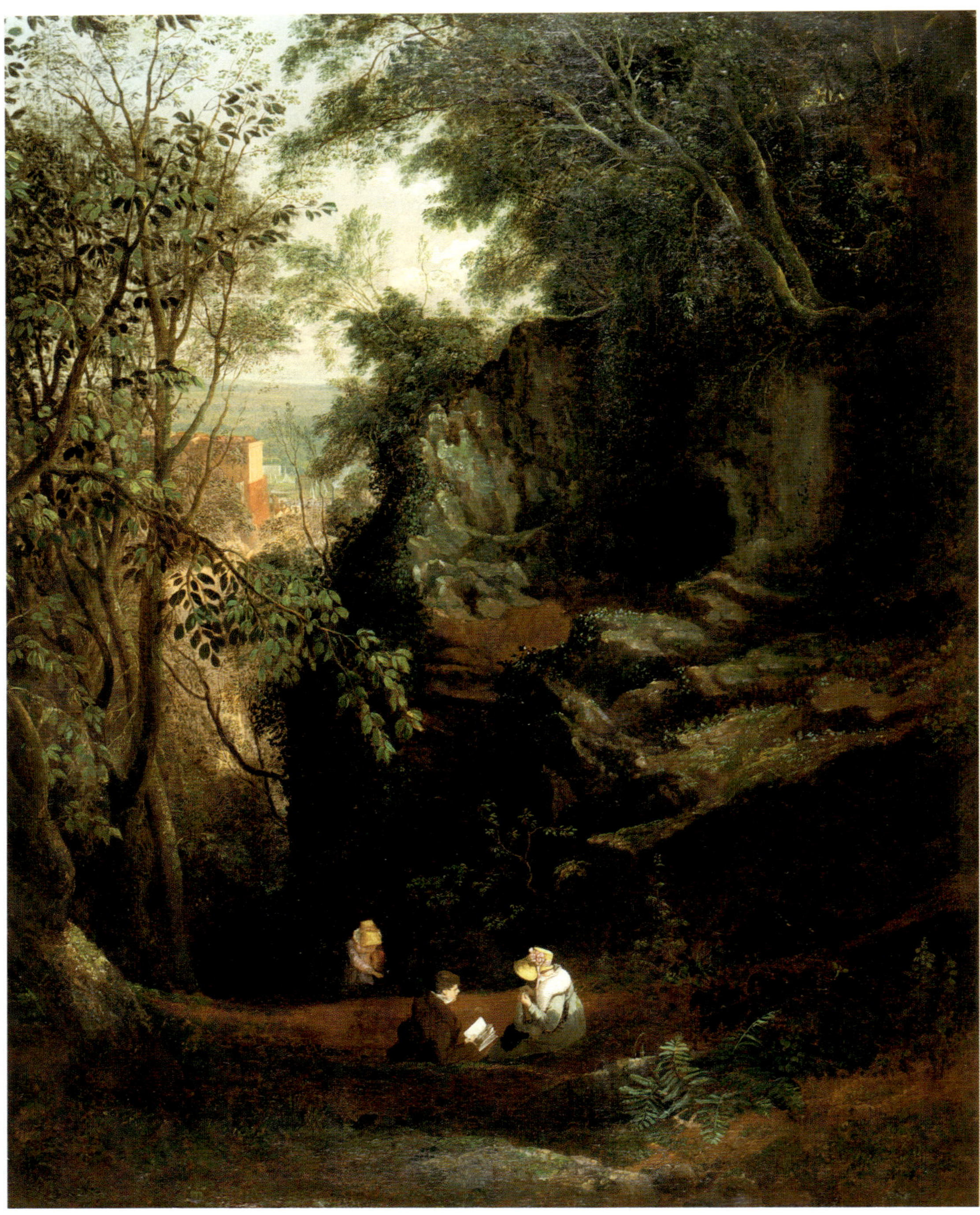

134

134. **Francis Danby**
Wexford, Ireland, 1793 - Exmouth, Devon, 1861
Landscape near Clifton, c. 1822-23
Oil on canvas, 91.4 x 71.1 cm
Yale Center for British Art, Paul Mellon Collection, New Haven

Dating from towards the end of Danby's prolonged residence in the industrial city of Bristol (1813-25), this view is taken from a spot in Leigh Woods high above the south bank of the River Avon, looking towards Windsor Terrace in Clifton on the far bank. In the distance, a glimpse of sails and a smoking funnel suggest river traffic near the mouth of Cumberland basin. When Danby knew them, Leigh Woods were a pretty and popular destination for sketchers, and it has been argued - perhaps more forcefully than is justified, for the figures in the foreground are unapologetically modern and obviously at leisure - that this and related paintings of the locality were Danby's tribute to the art of Gaspard Dughet, a figure much lionized by the artist's friend the Reverend John Eagles, who was inclined to see the dramatic topography of the woods as a kind of Elysium comparable with Dughet's views of Tivoli (Greenacre 2005, p. 71; London 1980, pp. 28, 92-93). (AT)

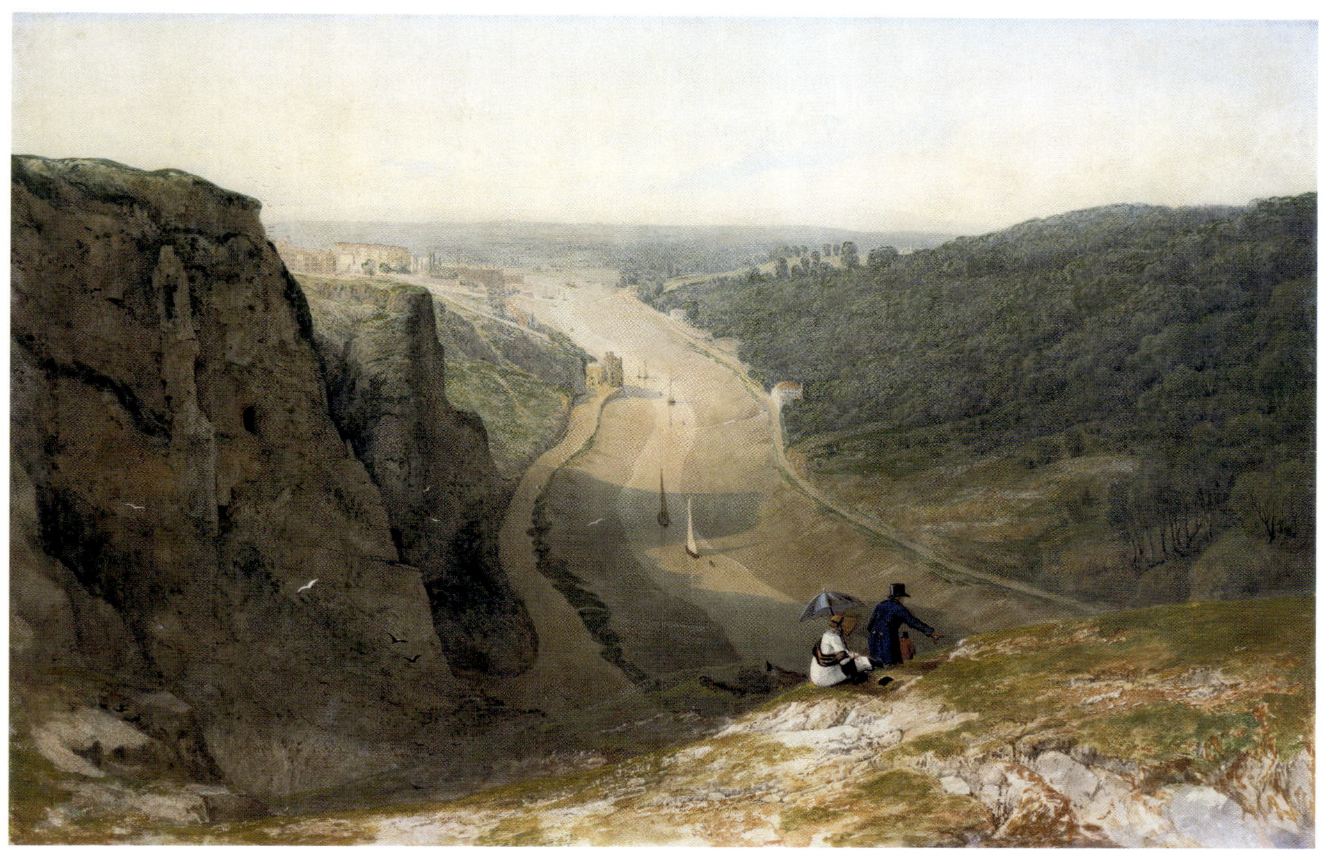

135

135. **Francis Danby**
Wexford, Ireland, 1793 - Exmouth, Devon, 1861
The Avon Gorge Looking Towards Clifton, c. 1820-21
Watercolour and bodycolour over pencil,
on paper, 48.9 x 73.7cm
Yale Center for British Art, Paul Mellon Collection, New Haven

Francis Danby, who came from Ireland, lived for a while in Bristol and belonged to a local group of landscape painters there. His ambitions lay more in the direction of the Sublime, as in the work of John Martin (cat. 256), but in the vicinity of Bristol he painted landscapes that are striking for their simplicity. On several occasions Danby painted distant views across the Avon, the river that winds its way between the cliffs to create a ravine that was a favourite of both artists and tourists. In this watercolour, the river is depicted at low tide, lying partly in the shadow of St Vincent's Rocks (Greenacre 1988, p. 136). For another view of St Vincent's Rocks, by Thomas Girtin, see cat. 126. (RH)

136. **Joseph Mallord William Turner**
London, 1775 - London, 1851
Warwick Castle, Warwickshire, 1830-31
Watercolour and bodycolour on paper, 29.7 x 45.1 cm
Whitworth Art Gallery, University of Manchester

Many of Turner's great, finished watercolours were produced in relation to topographical engraving projects, the most extensive and ambitious of which was *Picturesque Views in England and Wales*, commissioned in 1824 by the publisher Charles Heath. By 1838 Turner had painted over one hundred watercolours, ninety-six of which had been engraved and published in two volumes. As a commercial venture the scheme was ultimately a failure, but the artistic achievements of both Turner and his engravers were undisputed. Few people today would take issue with the critic of the *Athenaeum*, who wrote in 1833, 'these drawings are of a beauty for which we can find no parallels'.

The *England and Wales* series depict a breadth of national landscape: coastal, urban, industrial, pastoral and architectural. Turner drew upon the hundreds of pencil studies he had amassed over the years, but he also undertook one new sketching campaign in the Midlands in 1830. *Warwick Castle, Warwickshire* is based upon several on-the-spot pencil studies in the *Kenilworth* sketchbook, used during this tour. It shows the magnificent vista of the medieval castle seen from a bridge spanning the River Avon. The delicacy of the colouring and subtlety of the atmospheric effects are a typical example of Turner at the height of his powers as a watercolour painter. (NM)

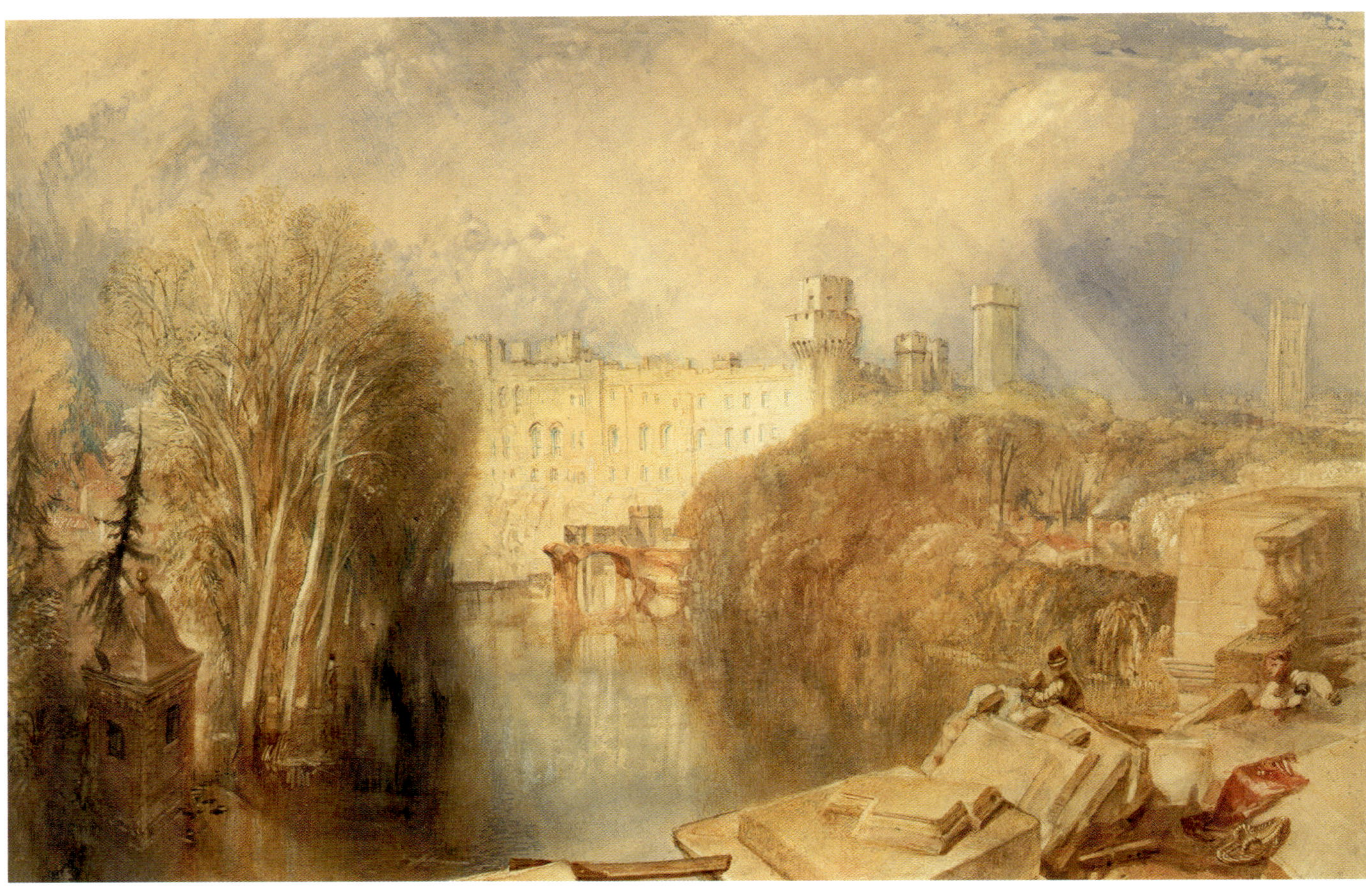

136

137. **Joseph Mallord William Turner**
London, 1775 - London, 1851
Burg Rheinfels on the Rhine, c. 1841
Pencil and watercolour on paper, 18.5 x 24.1 cm
Private Collection

Turner's notebooks reveal that his method of finding the best view of a subject was often akin to a hunter stalking his prey. In sketches spilling over several pages, he circles his motif, varying his distance, before finally deciding on the ideal arrangement of forms. This view shows Burg Rheinfels, above the left bank of the Rhine to the south of Koblenz, and it is a sheet from a now dismembered and widely dispersed sketchbook, which also contained a view of the castle from the opposite direction (National Museum Wales, Cardiff).

Turner had already recorded Burg Rheinfels on four earlier journeys on the Rhine and was consequently very familiar with the details of its architecture and the impact it had on its setting. Despite this, as at other sites that he revisited, he continued to make studies of the castle. Here he adds colour washes to his preliminary outline, working the paint very freely and also scratching the surface of the paper. (IW)

138. **Joseph Mallord William Turner**
London, 1775 - London, 1851
Tivoli, A Colour Beginning, 1827-29
Watercolour on paper, 30.3 x 43.6 cm
Whitworth Art Gallery, University of Manchester

Turner painted numerous preparatory studies where he laid out landscape in broad chromatic washes. Known as 'colour beginnings', these watercolours generally lack finish and detail and would not have been seen during the artist's lifetime, since they were intended for private use, a necessary component of a larger process, rather than individual images in their own right. Nevertheless, they have an inherent aesthetic appeal for the modern viewer due to their use of simplified forms and vibrant colour. They also provide a wonderful insight into the range of Turner's painting techniques. In this colour beginning, for example, we see the use of wet-in-wet and diffused washes as well as watercolour applied with a dry brush. Many of the studies bear no identifiable relation to known finished works and are therefore informal experiments in technique and composition. This 'beginning', however, bears similarities to other sketches of Tivoli and is therefore possibly evidence of a design Turner intended to paint for a topographical project, *Picturesque Views in Italy*. In this instance, neither the watercolour nor the engraved series came to fruition. (NM)

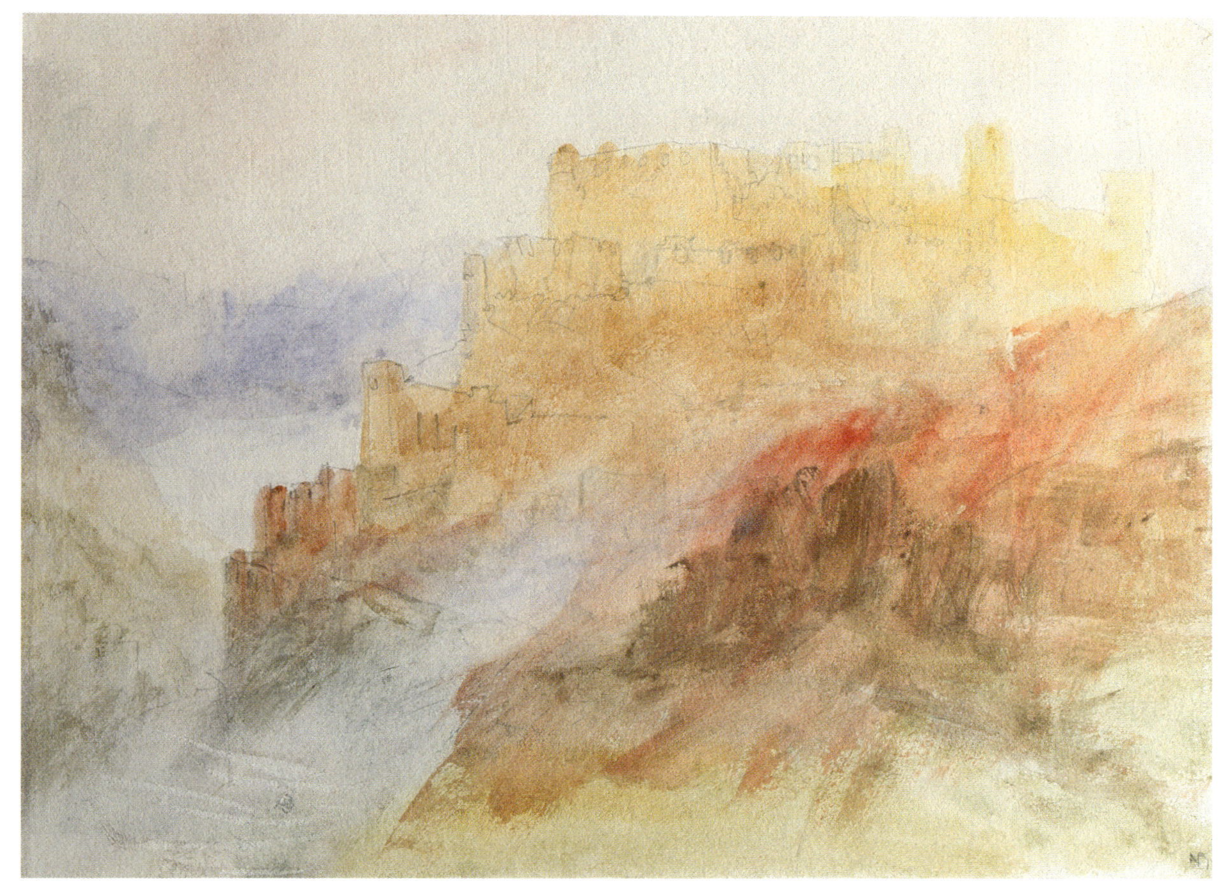

137

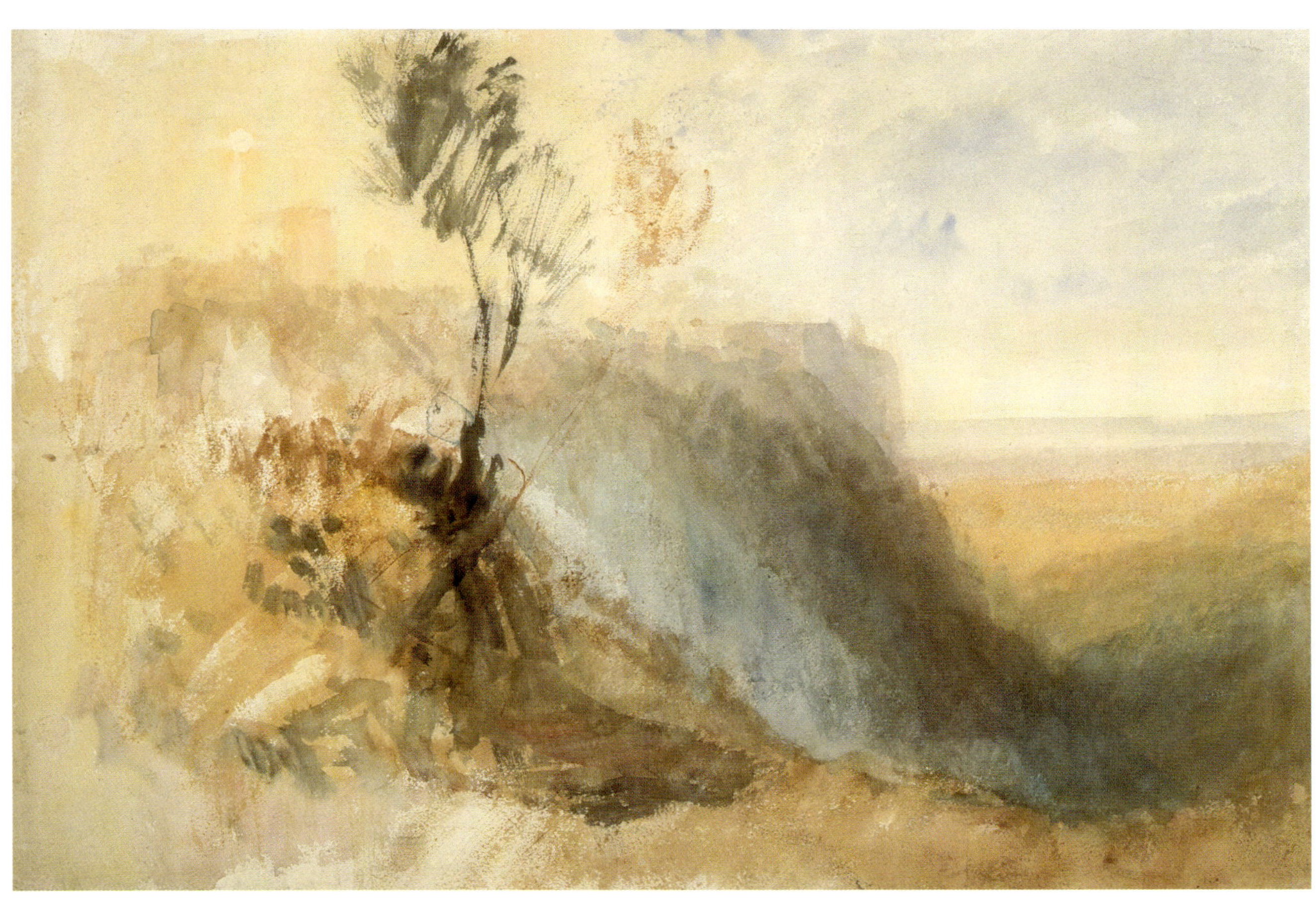

138

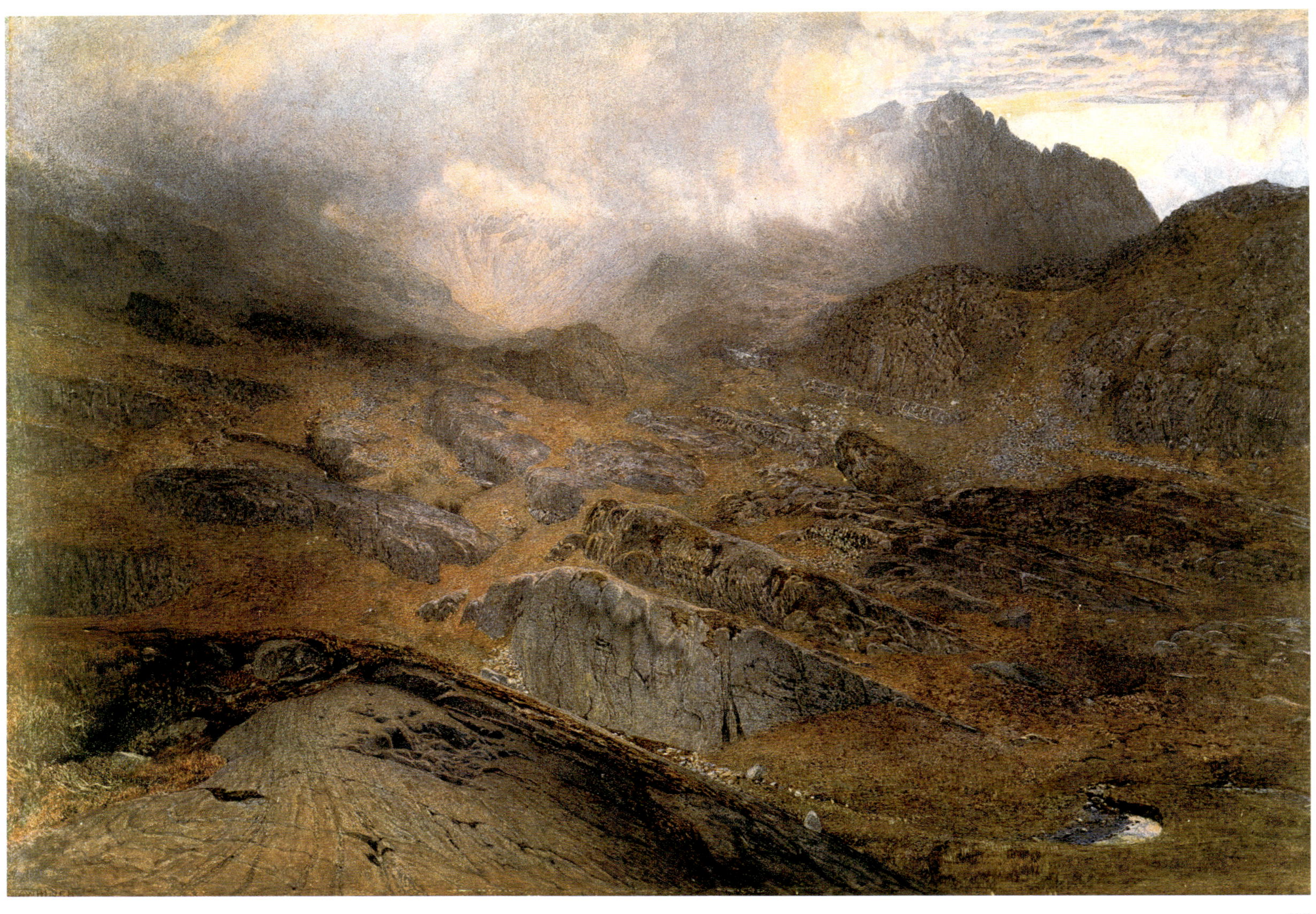

139

139. **Alfred William Hunt**
Liverpool, 1830 – London, 1896
Mountain Landscape – Cwm Trifaen, 1856
Watercolour and bodycolour on paper, 26.7 x 38.7 cm
Bottom left: AHW [monogram] 1856
Robertson Collection, Orkney

April 1856 saw the publication of the fourth volume of *Modern Painters*, which bore the sub-title 'Of Mountain Beauty'. In it Ruskin insisted that the representation of mountains was meaningless without a comprehension of how such landscapes were formed. This book prompted many artists to travel to the Alps and the upland ranges of the British Isles to represent mountains on the basis of an understanding of past and ongoing geological mechanisms.

Alfred Hunt's family home was in Liverpool, and from a young age he had made painting expeditions both to north Wales and to the English Lakes. *Cwm Trifaen* shows the desolate bowl-shaped north-eastern flank of a mountain named Glyder Fach, in the Snowdon range, with Tryfan rising out of view to the right. This is a landscape which clearly reveals the impact of past eras of glaciation – the sheet of granite seen in the left foreground has been smoothed by the flow of ice and is marked with long grooves, known as striations, which have been cut by sharp boulders lodged within the masses of ice. These features are described by an artist well informed about and himself fascinated by the processes of physical geography. (CSN)

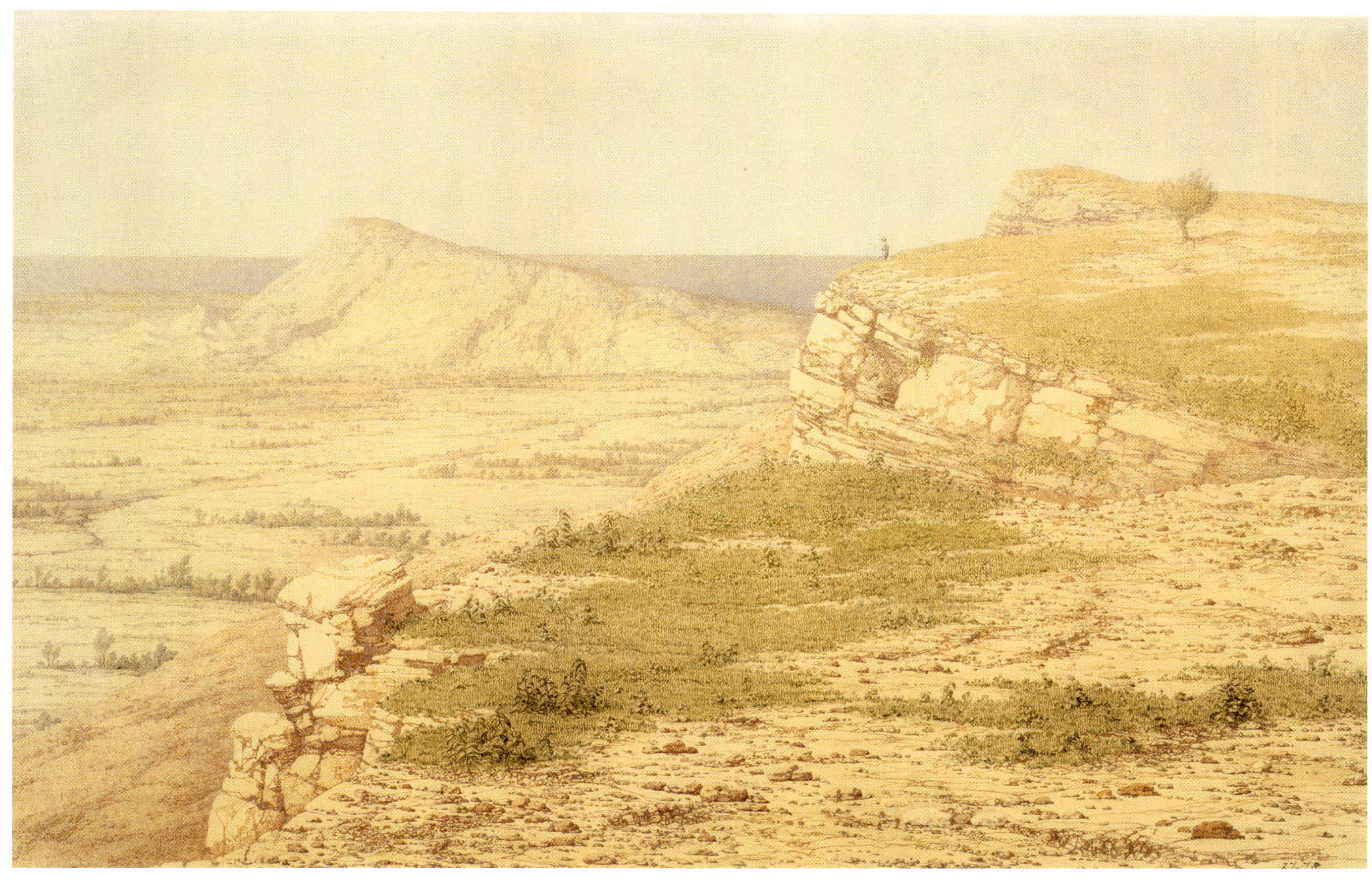

140

140. **Richard Dadd**
Chatham, Kent, 1817 – Broadmoor Hospital, Berkshire, 1886
View in the Islands of Rhodes, c. 1842-43
Verso: Vieuw in the Island of Rhodes. / near the site of a castle of the Knights of S[t]. John. / a part of which still remains in ruins.
Watercolour on paper, 24.5 x 37.2 cm
Victoria and Albert Museum, London

In 1842-43 the young Richard Dadd, already considered a talented and promising painter, made an extended tour of Europe and the eastern Mediterranean, accompanying his eccentric patron Sir Thomas Phillips. Phillips was a voracious sightseer and kept up a relentless pace, travelling by any means available, from steamship and train to mule. Dadd was allowed little time to make the drawings that were the reason for his presence and mostly managed only to fill sketchbooks with rapid, but often beautifully detailed, pencil drawings. Occasionally during stops he completed a few watercolours.

It was in Egypt that Dadd was said to have contracted the severe sunstroke which unleashed an inherent mental disorder. On his return to England, in a fit of insanity, Dadd murdered his father and was subsequently confined for the rest of his life. In the old Bethlem Asylum he was allowed and encouraged to paint. Some of his earlier paintings, such as the present work, are worked up from travel sketches and display an accomplished topographical technique but also the incipient obsession with minute detail that would characterize the artist's later, ever more fanciful, subjects.

Purchased by the Victoria and Albert Museum in 1878 as 'an Eastern Scene', the drawing was discovered to have a precise location when the old inscription on the reverse was uncovered. Phillips and Dadd spent four days on Rhodes, 21-25 October 1842 waiting for a boat to take them on to Beirut. (SC)

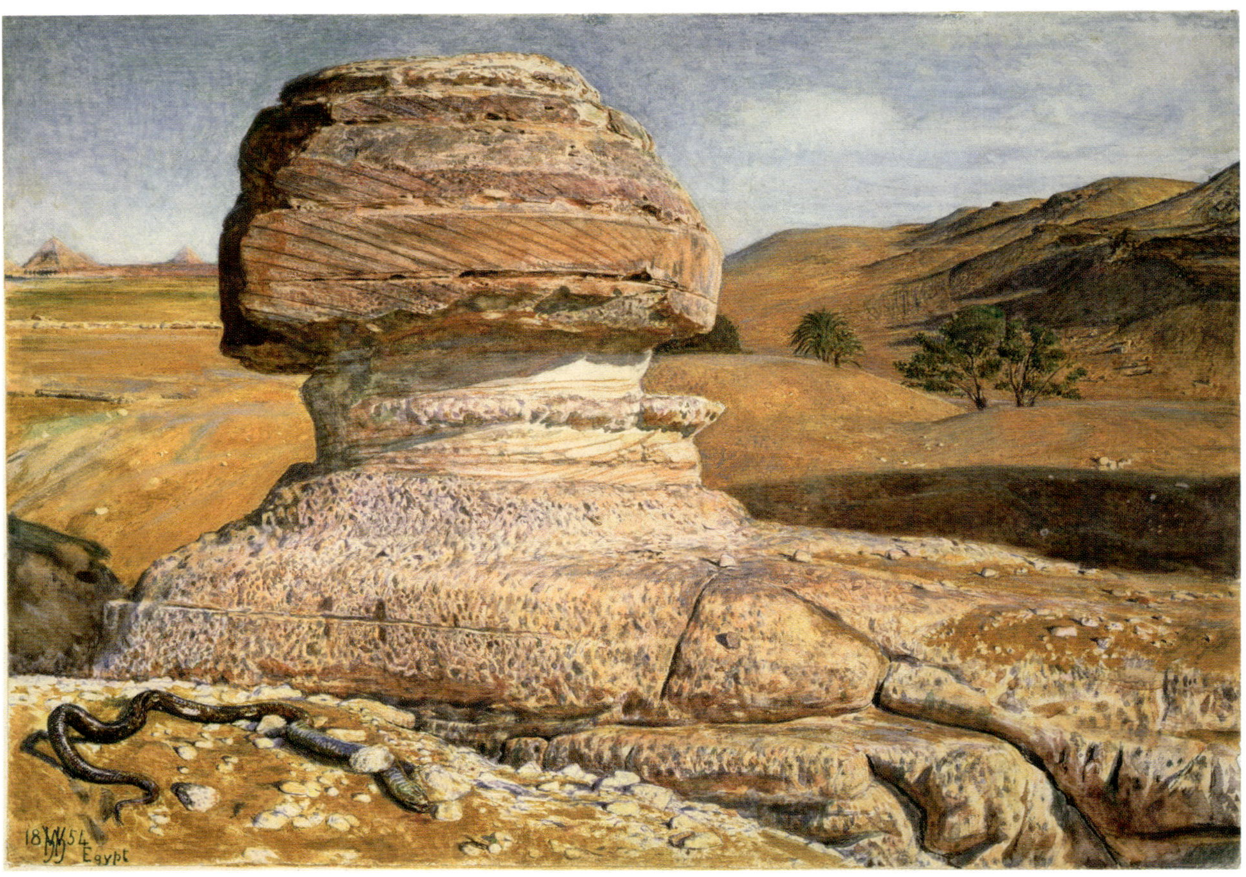

141

141. **William Holman Hunt**
London, 1827 – London, 1910
The Sphinx, Giza, Looking Towards the Pyramids of Saqqara, 1854
Watercolour and bodycolour on paper, 25.2 x 35.2 cm
Bottom left: 18 Whh [monogram] 54 / Egypt
Harris Museum and Art Gallery, Preston

When Hunt went to the Middle East in January 1854, he joined Thomas Seddon in Cairo. The two decided to move out of the city to Giza, where they stayed in February and March; after some weeks back in Cairo, Hunt returned to Giza in late April, remaining until early May. The present drawing was begun during Hunt's first stay but abandoned because of 'the wind which disturbed the sand so much as to make sketching in colours a task of too much time for the result' (Bronkhurst 2006, vol. 2, p. 50), and was then completed during the second desert sojourn.

Hunt looked for vantage points that allowed him to simplify and dramatize the extraordinary scenery. In his drawing of the Sphinx, he positioned himself to observe the back of the head so as to observe the horizontal strata of the limestone outcrop from which the figure is carved, with only a glimpse offered of the Sphinx's profile and inscrutable smile. At the time that Hunt was there the French archaeologist Auguste Mariette was excavating the site. Seddon, in his watercolour of the Sphinx (Ashmolean Museum, Oxford; see London 2004, p. 109), shows figures at work, but Hunt omits any human presence. In this sense, geology superseded antiquarianism as the artist's principal motivation in making the drawing, linked to a purely aesthetic response to the strangeness of the landscape in terms of texture and colour.

In the left foreground lies the contorted body of a huge snake, stoned to death. This serves as a reminder of the dangers that lurked in the desert landscape; on one occasion during Hunt's second visit to Giza he himself had been menaced by an 'enormous serpent … between six and seven feet long, [and] of the most deadly kind' (Ibid., p. 51). In addition, the motif of the dead snake is presumably intended as an eschatological symbol, one that draws on Hunt's intense interest in the Old Testament and relates specifically to the prophecy that the serpent's temptation of Eve should be revenged through the generations. (CSN)

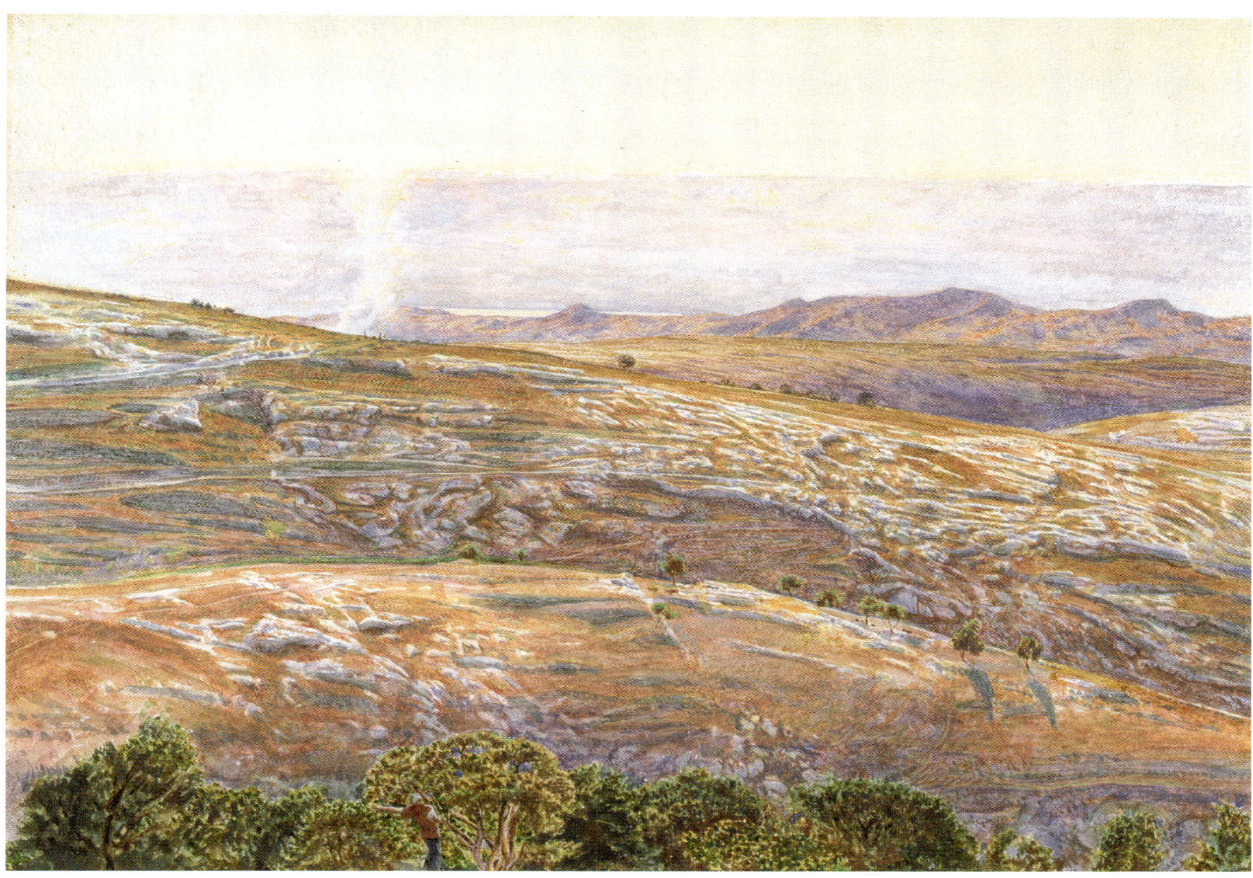

142

142. **William Holman Hunt**
London, 1827 - London, 1910
View from the Mount of Offence, Looking Towards the Dead Sea and the Mountains of Moab, morning, otherwise known as ***The Dead Sea, from Siloam***, 1854, 1855, 1861[?]
Watercolour and bodycolour over pencil on paper, 25.1 x 35.2 cm
Birmingham Museum & Art Gallery

The Mount of Offence stands on the eastern side of Jerusalem and is part of the range of hills of which the Mount of Olives is the highest part. In the far distance, about twenty kilometres away and showing as a thin bar of white, is the Dead Sea, and beyond, forming the eastern horizon, the Mountains of Moab. The view was taken in the early morning - hence the indefinite quality of the distant elements and the long shadows, while the particular effect of light on the distant landscape, of 'mysterious cloud-land and a vaporous unreality, which make you doubt whether they can be solid earth like the nearer hills' (Seddon 1858, p. 125) was apparently only to be observed in the later months of the year. For this reason, Hunt waited a year to complete the subject that he had commenced in the autumn of 1854.

Although the artist may seem to have been principally interested in how such optical effects might be conveyed in the medium of watercolour, he was also seeking to provide a reliable record of the place where Christ had lived and where he had carried out his ministry. Hunt wrote that 'the smoke rising behind the second ridge, which is the spur of the Mount of Olives, marks the site of Bethany'. This was where Jesus visited Simon the Leper and where his head was anointed with ointments by an unknown woman, the event that commences the sequence of events which lead to his Passion and death on earth. It was also where he raised Lazarus from the dead, foreshadowing his own death and resurrection. According to the Gospel of Luke (24:50), Bethany was also the place from which Jesus ascended to heaven.

The watercolour's alternative title, *The Dead Sea, from Siloam*, is topographically consistent, because the Pool of Siloam, where Jesus restored sight to the Blind Man (John, 9:1-41), is to the south-east of Jerusalem and just outside the old city walls. Siloam may have been particularly meaningful to Hunt because of the value that he personally placed upon the faculty of sight. Furthermore, he had previously meditated upon Christ's words to his disciples spoken at Siloam, 'I must work the works of him that sent me, while it is day: the night cometh when no man can work. As long as I am in the world, I am the light of the world' (John, 9:4-5), and he drew the title of his painting of Jesus Christ at the door of man's soul, *The Light of the World* (Keble College, Oxford), from them (see Bronkhurst 2006, vol. 1, no. 74, pp. 150-54). (CSN)

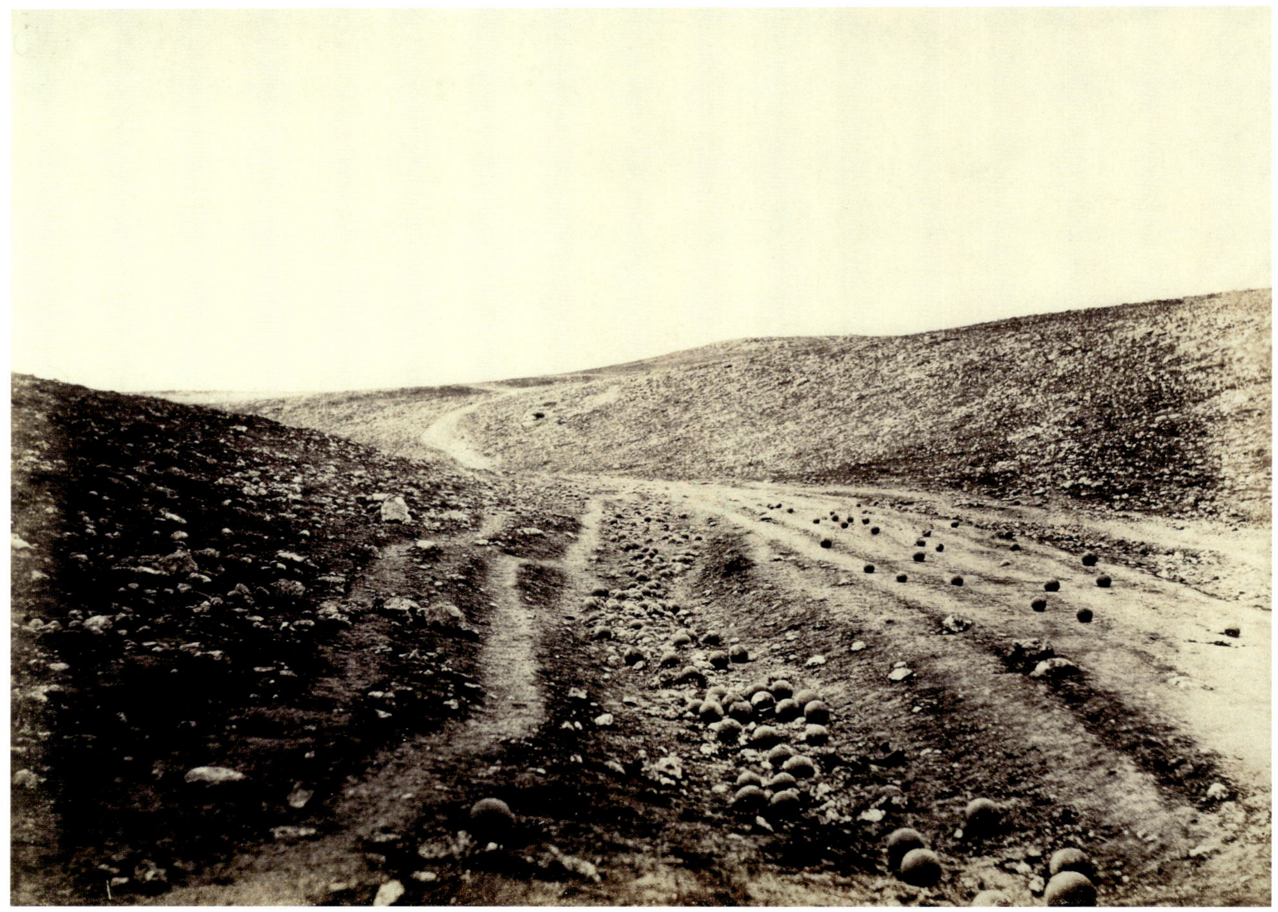

143

143. **Roger Fenton**
Bury, Lancashire, 1819 – London, 1869
The Valley of the Shadow of Death, 1855
Albumen on salted paper print, from wet collodion negative, 27.1 x 36.2 cm
Royal Photographic Society at the National Media Museum, Bradford

Fenton travelled to the Crimean War under royal patronage and with a commission from the print publisher Thomas Agnew. The power of the photograph lies, perhaps, in the simplicity of its means: an empty, battle-scarred terrain that anticipates Flanders in World War I, with spent cannon balls strewn across the scene. In another version of the photograph, all the cannon balls are clustered in the rut at the left. It has been suggested that Fenton may have manipulated the scene by sprinkling the balls artistically across the terrain as if just fired from the Russian cannons. However, Gordon Baldwin has proposed that the reason why one version has fewer balls is that it was common practice for British soldiers to harvest the enemy cannon balls, which were then fired back (Baldwin 2006, p. 30). (MHB)

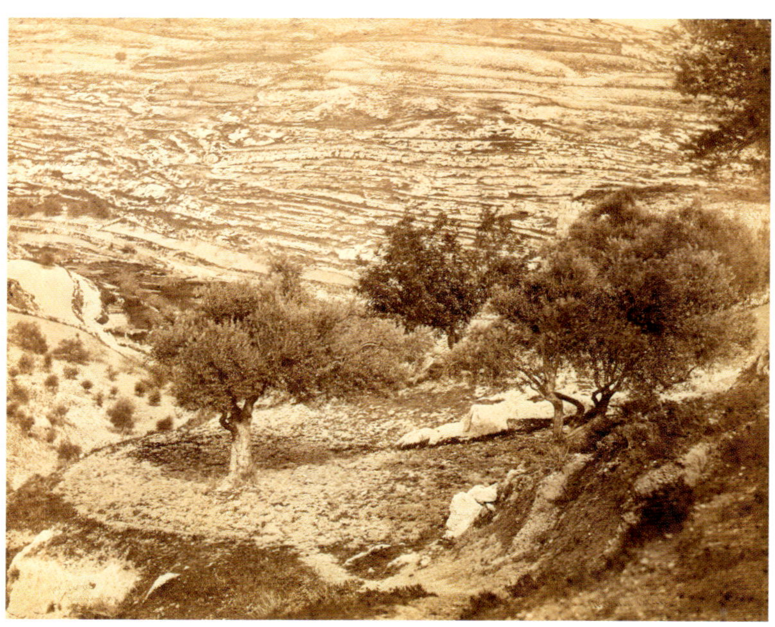

144

144. **James Robertson**
Middlesex, c. 1813 – Yokohama, 1888
and **Felice A Beato**
The Veneto [?], c. 1830 – Mandalay, after 1904
The Aceldama, Jerusalem, 1857
Albumen print from wet collodion on glass negative, 26.3 x 31.5 cm
Palestine Exploration Fund, London

Robertson was in partnership with Beato from 1853 to 1860. They photographed the Crimean War in 1855-56 and afterwards travelled to India to photograph the aftermath of the Mutiny, or Great Rebellion, in 1857. They photographed in Palestine in the same year. Aceldama is the 'Field of Blood', bought with Judas Iscariot's '30 pieces of silver'. The lithographer and photographer William Lake Price wrote of the attraction of such photographs in *A Manual of Photographic Manipulation* (1858): 'The traces of those generations long ages since passed from [the earth's] surface, who, with the inherent feeling of our kind have striven to leave a dim posterity, by their gigantic but decaying efforts, some relic and memento of their passage: all have been or will be brought in intense reality to our very hearths.' (MHB)

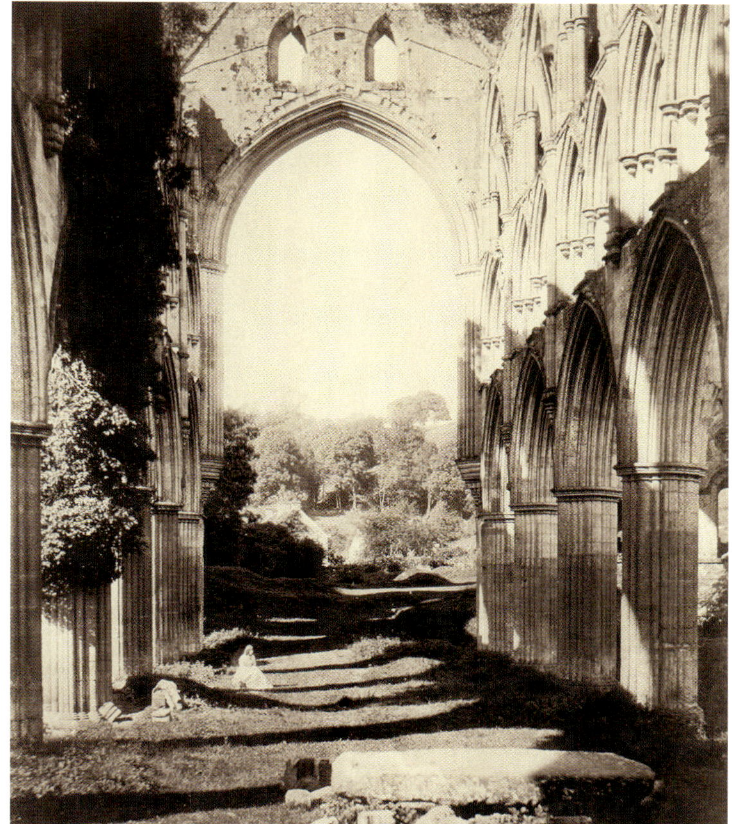

145

145. **Roger Fenton**
Bury, Lancashire, 1819 – London, 1869
Rievaulx Abbey, 1854
Albumen print from a wet collodion negative, 34.4 x 28.9 cm
Victoria and Albert Museum, London

The first generation of professional photographers, of which Fenton was a leading member, was drawn from a variety of earlier occupations – including the natural sciences, printmaking, architecture and painting. Fenton was well versed in the cult of the Picturesque which informed the English watercolour tradition of the late eighteenth and early nineteenth centuries. At Rievaulx he set up his camera close to the position earlier chosen to take a watercolour view by J.M.W. Turner. The new medium of photography began to find itself by using the codes of the earlier media it was eventually to supplant. The wet collodion on glass negative that Fenton used allowed him to make meticulously detailed, exhibition-scale prints. They were widely exhibited, reviewed, admired and collected. (MHB)

146. **Mary Dillwyn**
Swansea, 1816 – Arthog, Gwynedd, 1906
The Reverend Davis and Family in Three Cliffs Bay,
from ***The Llewelyn Album***, August 1854
Salted paper print from a glass negative, 14.8 x 12.7 cm
Victoria and Albert Museum, London

This is a unique photograph from one of the finest Victorian albums. The album was begun by Bessie Llewelyn in 1853 and included photographs by John Dillwyn Llewelyn, his wife Emma, sister Mary and members of their circle. The Dillwyn Llewelyns were related to Henry Talbot and received early news, and specimens, of his invention of positive/negative photography. They photographed many things for the first time – including the motion of the sea and the steam from a paddleboat: John Dillwyn Llewelyn received a gold medal for his 'Motion Studies' at the Paris Exhibition of 1855. The family also probably achieved such photographic firsts as a picnic, and (as in this example) a seaside excursion. The presence of a telescope in this scene suggests the world of 'rational entertainments', often making use of optical 'philosophical instruments', to which – at least among the privileged classes – early photography belonged. (MHB)

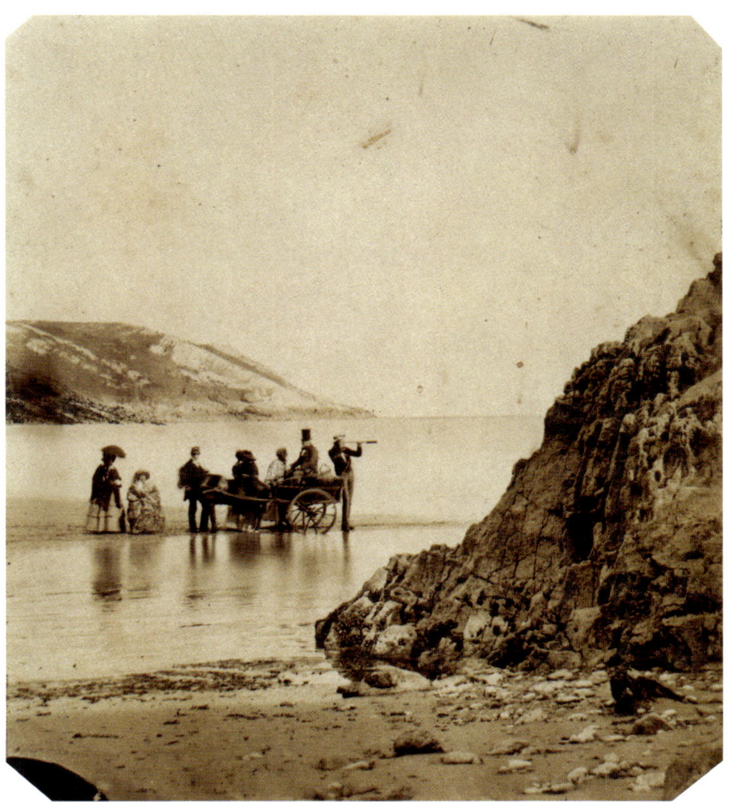

146

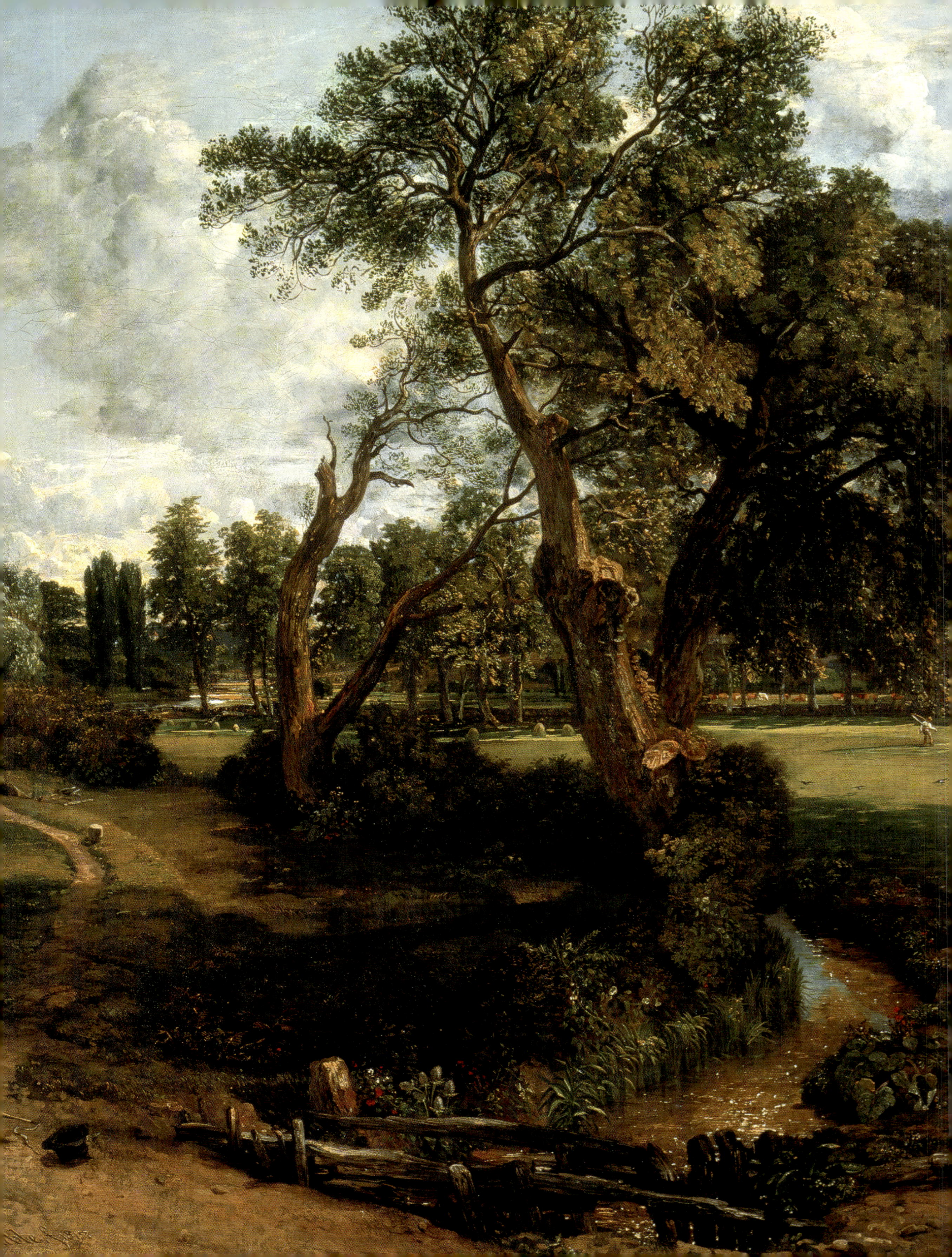

EVERYDAY LANDSCAPE

JOHN CONSTABLE

Flatford Mill, 1817

ROBERT HOOZEE

To support himself as a painter in London at the beginning of his career, Constable took on various portrait commissions and tried to find his way with various kinds of landscape, ranging from picturesque scenes to more grandiose mountain views in the Lake District. Gradually, the familiar surroundings of the village in which he was born, East Bergholt in Suffolk, began to come to the fore. He returned there regularly – particularly during the summer months – and from around 1810 it was clear that Constable wanted his art to be created in this environment. The decision-making process can be followed in his correspondence and in a number of surviving drawings and oil sketches.[1] *Flatford Mill* forms the conclusion of this process, in which Constable sums up and demonstrates his vision as a painter of nature on a large scale. It is one of the most important works in Constable's oeuvre and in the history of landscape painting.

As far as we know, *Flatford Mill* is the only large finished painting by Constable which is directly based on studies from nature – it was, in fact, almost entirely painted in front of the motif. Later, Constable regularly painted landscapes from the same district, but these were usually compositions developed in the studio from material recorded in sketches. *Flatford Mill*, by contrast, contains little or nothing in the way of studio additions and could almost be called a study from nature on a large scale.

From around 1810, Constable used the time he spent in East Bergholt to explore the area surrounding the village in drawings and paintings. Two sketchbooks from the period have been preserved, which give a vivid image of his exploration of this relatively limited region (fig. 2-3). They contain studies of details as well as a striking number of complete landscapes, which Constable focused on while surveying the area for suitable compositions. He worked in the open air with a single goal in mind: to produce exemplary paintings for which he could find both buyers and a public in London.

Constable enjoyed painting distant views of his home county, in which he depicted the softly glowing agricultural region on the east coast of England near Ipswich under varying atmospheric conditions (cat. 155-156). However, he was most often found on the banks of the Stour, a partly canalized river, which flowed past East Bergholt and on which his father owned two mills. Even later, when he lived in London, he cherished the memory of these surroundings in his work and correspondence. In a letter of 1821, he wrote his friend John Fisher: 'As long as I do paint I shall never cease to paint such Places. … I should paint my own places best – Painting is but another word for feeling, I associate my "careless boyhood" to all that lies on the banks of the Stour. They made me a painter (& I am grateful) that is I had often thought of pictures of them before I had ever touched a pencil.'[2]

The centre of this region was Flatford Mill, owned by Constable's father and located near a small island and lock in the Stour. These surroundings made up a complex scene that consisted of water enclosed by trees and shrubs, between which the fields could be seen in the distance, punctuated occasionally by buildings, bridges and locks – a scene in which some activity or another was always taking place. As the son of a miller, Constable was quite familiar with transportation by boat, which might sometimes be powered by the wind but was more frequently drawn by horses or manoeuvred with poles. In 1815, he even exhibited a work in which he depicted a barge of this kind under construction with all the necessary details (Victoria and Albert Museum, London).

John Constable, ***Flatford Mill*** (detail), cat. 162

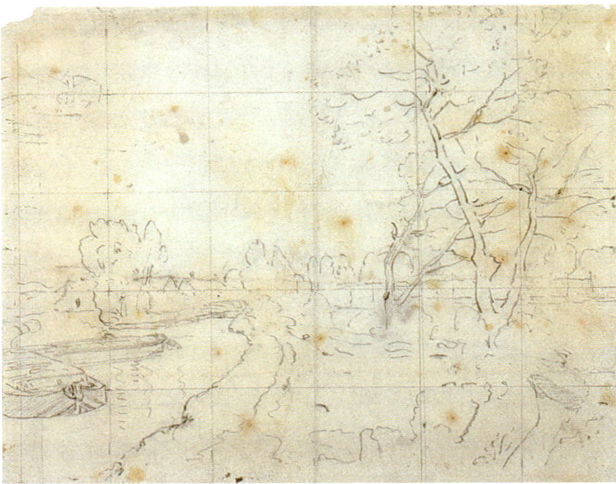

fig. 1
John Constable
Study for 'Flatford Mill', c. 1814-1816
Pencil on tracing on paper,
25.5 x 31.2 cm
Tate, London

Each of the oil sketches that Constable painted in this region shows a different interpretation of the landscape. Some of the studies are directed towards the recording of visual information; but in many cases they are dramatic compositions, in which the components of the landscape acquire monumental proportions, accented by a dynamic play of light and shadow. The mill, seen from the lock, is the subject of no less than six oil sketches, the most dramatic of which is shown here (cat. 159).[3] In this instance, Constable builds his composition with powerful brushstrokes, between which the reddish-brown ground is visible throughout: a dense landscape in which he assembles a multitude of textures and forms under an intense atmospheric effect - he himself spoke of the 'chiaroscuro of nature'. There are also several studies of the view along the water in the direction of the lock, taken from Flatford Bridge further upstream, which feature the mill in the distance - the actual subject of *Flatford Mill* - and interpret the landscape in a similarly dense and dramatic way (cat. 160).[4] On the basis of studies like these, Constable painted a number of finished landscapes in small format. The composition of the *Study for Flatford Mill from the Lock* (cat. 159) was developed into a finished version measuring about 60 x 90 cm, which he exhibited in 1814.[5] For *Flatford Mill* itself, however, Constable used a canvas that was twice as large. Apparently he had reached the point at which he could work out the subject that had occupied him for so long - and which he had already explored in numerous variants, both drawings and paintings - on an ambitious scale.

From his correspondence we know that Constable was still working on this painting on location in September 1816. At that time the artist had decided to marry Maria Bicknell, to whom he had been engaged since 1809. They were planning to settle in London, which would bring to an end the long periods he spent every year in Suffolk. For this reason, *Flatford Mill* has also been taken to mark the conclusion, as it were, of the artist's youth and formative years, even though he was already forty-one years old at the time.[6]

The precise working methods by which Constable managed to transfer the landscape of *Flatford Mill* to a large canvas with all its proportions intact are not entirely clear.[7] He probably used a drawing with a grid transferred from a sketch on glass made directly from the motif (fig. 1).[8] Overpainted areas in the sky and the large group of trees at the right indicate that the artist corrected his original work in these areas.[9] The repainting in the group of trees corresponds for the most part to the extremely detailed tree study that Constable drew on 17 October 1817, probably with these changes in view (cat. 161).

The two-part composition of *Flatford Mill*, which features a large group of trees on the right throwing a shadow onto the foreground and a view into the distance on the left, recalls traditional compositional schemes. Comparison with the drawings and studies, however, reveals that the composition is not imaginary but taken from reality. Here, in contrast to traditional landscapes, in which the gaze usually comes to rest in the distance, we are confronted at the end of a steep perspective with a closed frieze of trees and buildings offering only an occasional glimpse into the distance. In the middle of this frieze we notice the vertical accent of the trees that are seen from another angle in the oil sketch taken from the lock (cat. 159). Both foreground and background are filled with a large quantity of information about the landscape and the activities that take place there. The sharp focus and wealth of detail found in this work seem to continue even in the diversity of the clouds of the sky.

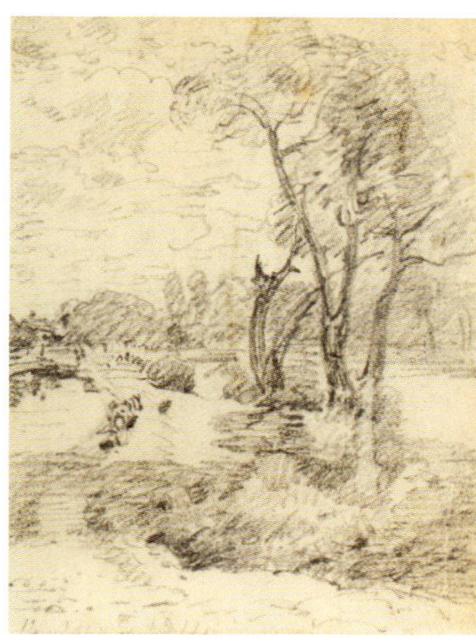

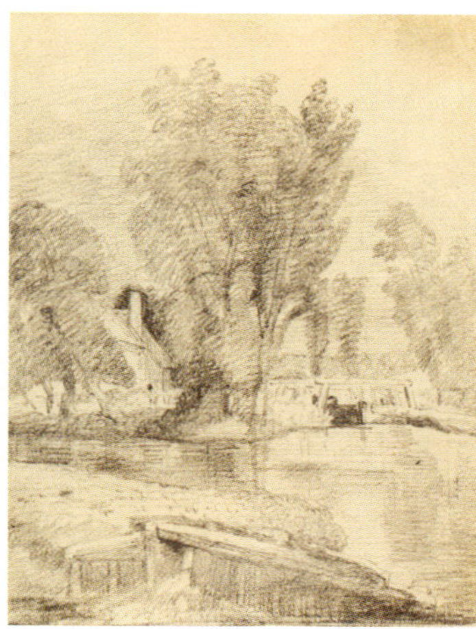

fig. 2
John Constable
***Flatford Mill from the Towpath*, 1814**
Page from a sketchbook, pencil,
10.8 x 8 cm
Victoria and Albert Museum, London

fig. 3
John Constable
***Flatford Mill*, 1814**
Page from a sketchbook, pencil,
10.8 x 8 cm
Victoria and Albert Museum, London

Flatford Mill is not the only British landscape of the period in which human labour, in harmony with nature, is depicted in such detail – although it is probably the most ambitious. Some of Constable's contemporaries painted comparable scenes, odes, as it were, to the productivity of agriculture (cat. 157). Although a work of this kind presented a certain moral message to the London public and offered a real alternative to the traditional rustic landscape, *Flatford Mill* remained unsold after the artist showed it at the exhibitions of 1817 and 1818. The work was still in his possession at his death in 1837.

Constable continued to paint the Suffolk landscape after 1817, as has been noted, although his contact with the region was no longer so regular. He pursued his study of nature in Hampstead, a village to the north of London, where he spent his summers and where he lived from 1827 onward. The studies he painted there increasingly took on the aspect of small autonomous paintings, and in contrast to his earlier studies they were seldom used in the making of finished paintings. While on the one hand he penetrated deeper into nature – for example, in his revolutionary cloud studies (cat. 174) – he also returned to old subjects in his studio in order to make large paintings for the annual exhibitions. From 1819 onward, he used an even larger format for such works, a canvas six foot wide, and he also developed the practice of making preliminary sketches on the same scale as the final work, the so called 'full scale sketches'.[10] He no longer attempted to make detailed 'transcriptions' of landscapes with the depth and complexity of *Flatford Mill* but limited himself to simple subjects, such as the famous *Haywain*.[11] After a time he even introduced dramatic motifs into his landscapes, such as the leap of a tow horse or the opening of a lock (cat. 163), in which the lock serves as a sort of stage in the middle of the landscape; in *Flatford Mill*, the same lock was only one detail among many.[12] In his later large-scale works, Constable would also resort to strengthening compositions by shifting or exaggerating certain elements in the landscape. Seen in light of this evolution, *Flatford Mill* was Constable's most thoroughgoing attempt to maintain on a large scale the power of observation found in his drawings and oil studies.

1. See 'Chronology' in London 1991, pp. 19-38; Rhyne 1990.
2. Beckett 1962-68, vol. 6, pp. 77-78.
3. Reynolds 1996, cat. 12.5-10.
4. See also Reynolds 1996, cat. 16.102.
5. Reynolds 1996, cat. 12.1.
6. London 1991, p. 181.
7. The realization of the painting was discussed in detail in London, 1976, p. 101; London 1991, pp. 179-81; London, Washington & San Marino 2006, pp. 110-13.
8. Constable placed a glass on his easel and drew the outlines of the landscape that he saw through the glass. Afterwards he traced a drawing onto a sheet of paper that he laid over the glass and held against the light. This procedure is described by Arthur Parsey in his book *The Science of Vision* (1840); see Fleming-Williams 1990, p. 119; and by Lyles in London, Washington & San Marino 2006, p. 111.
9. London 1991, p. 181.
10. This procedure is discussed extensively in London, Washington & San Marino 2006.
11. Exhibited in 1821, oil on canvas, 130.5 x 185.5 cm; National Gallery, London.
12. *The Leaping Horse*, exhibited in 1825, oil on canvas, 142.2 x 187.3 cm; Royal Academy, London.

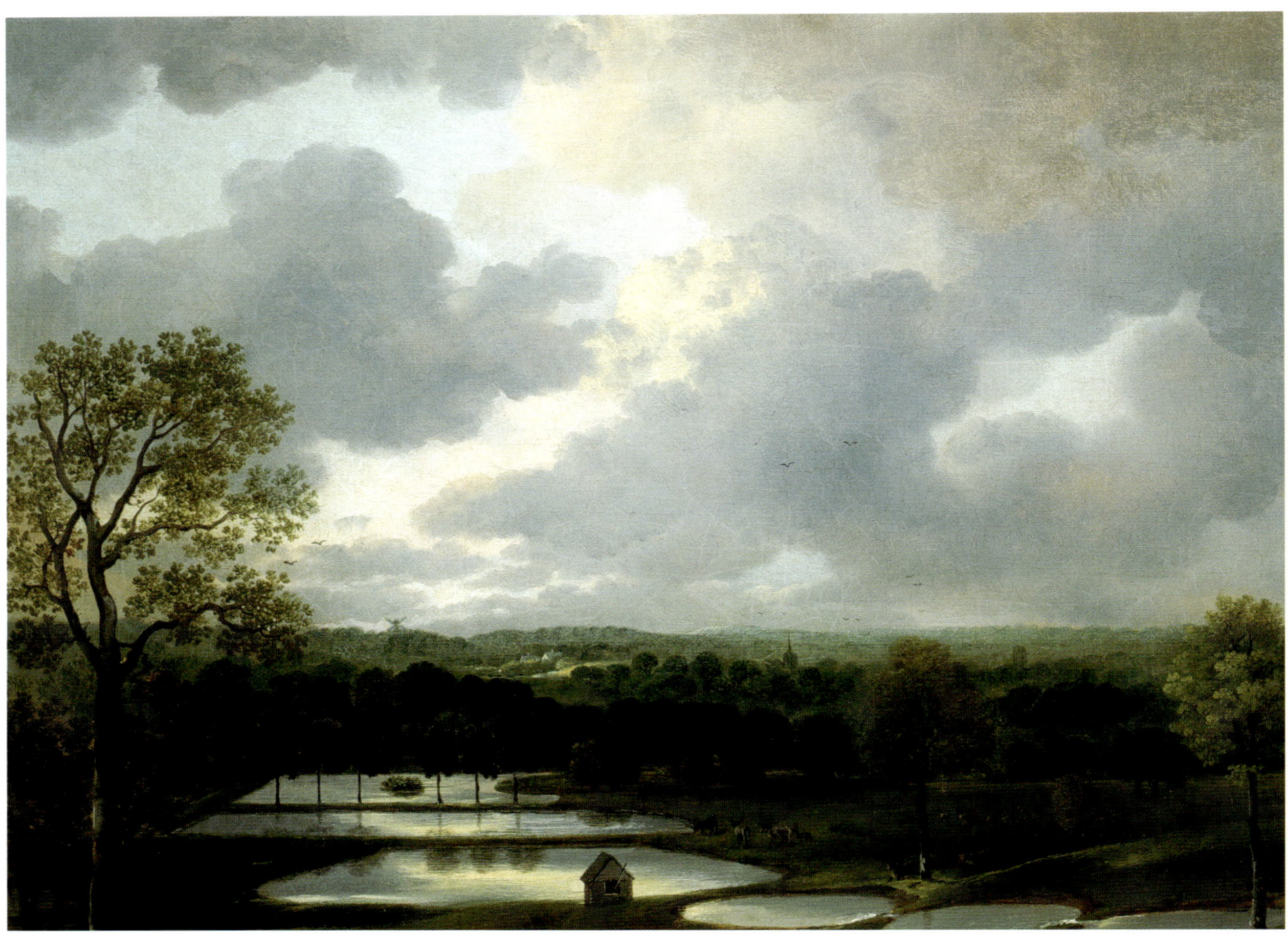

147

147. **Thomas Gainsborough**
Sudbury, Suffolk, 1727 - London, 1788
Holywells Park, Ipswich, c. 1748-50
Oil on canvas, 48.5 x 65 cm
Ipswich Borough Council Museums & Galleries,
Acquired through the National Art Collections Fund

During the 1740s the young Thomas Gainsborough was highly influenced by the example of Dutch seventeenth-century landscape painters, notably Ruisdael, Wijnants and Hobbema. Aside from emulating their style and painting technique, he is known to have repaired Dutch landscapes and even added figures to them. Gainsborough's interest in these artists was no doubt prompted by the physical similarities between his native Suffolk and the lowland regions of the Netherlands, as well as by the collecting habits of his British aristocratic patrons. The present landscape, despite its reliance upon Dutch models, features a specific Suffolk location: a series of man-made ponds constructed by Thomas Cobbold on his own estate at Holy Wells, to supply pure spring water to the brewery he had recently established at nearby Cliff Lane, Ipswich. Thus, while it may appear to be, on the surface, a picturesque country landscape, this painting, commissioned no doubt by Cobbold, is closely allied to contemporary local industrial concerns. (MP)

148. **Thomas Gainsborough**
Sudbury, Suffolk, 1727 - London, 1788
The Harvest Wagon, c. 1767 [?]
Oil on canvas, 120.7 x 144.8 cm
Trustees of the Henry Barber Trust,
University of Birmingham

The subject of the harvest wagon was among a series of pictures by Gainsborough in which he idealized the lives and the occupations of the English peasantry, drawing upon both the pastoral and georgic traditions of art and literature. Gainsborough's peasants inhabit a bucolic world, where they toil and yet have time to enjoy the fruits of their labour. At the time he painted the present picture Gainsborough was living in Bath, although the surrounding countryside bore only a general resemblance to his landscape art. The wagon, which is the focal point of the present picture, became at this time a prominent feature in a number of his paintings, suggesting that it had a symbolic meaning relating to the passage of human life. Here the wagon is the site of rural courtship, as a young woman is hauled up to join a group of lusty haymakers; although the pictorial source for Gainsborough's composition is incongruously Rubens's *Descent from the Cross*. (MP)

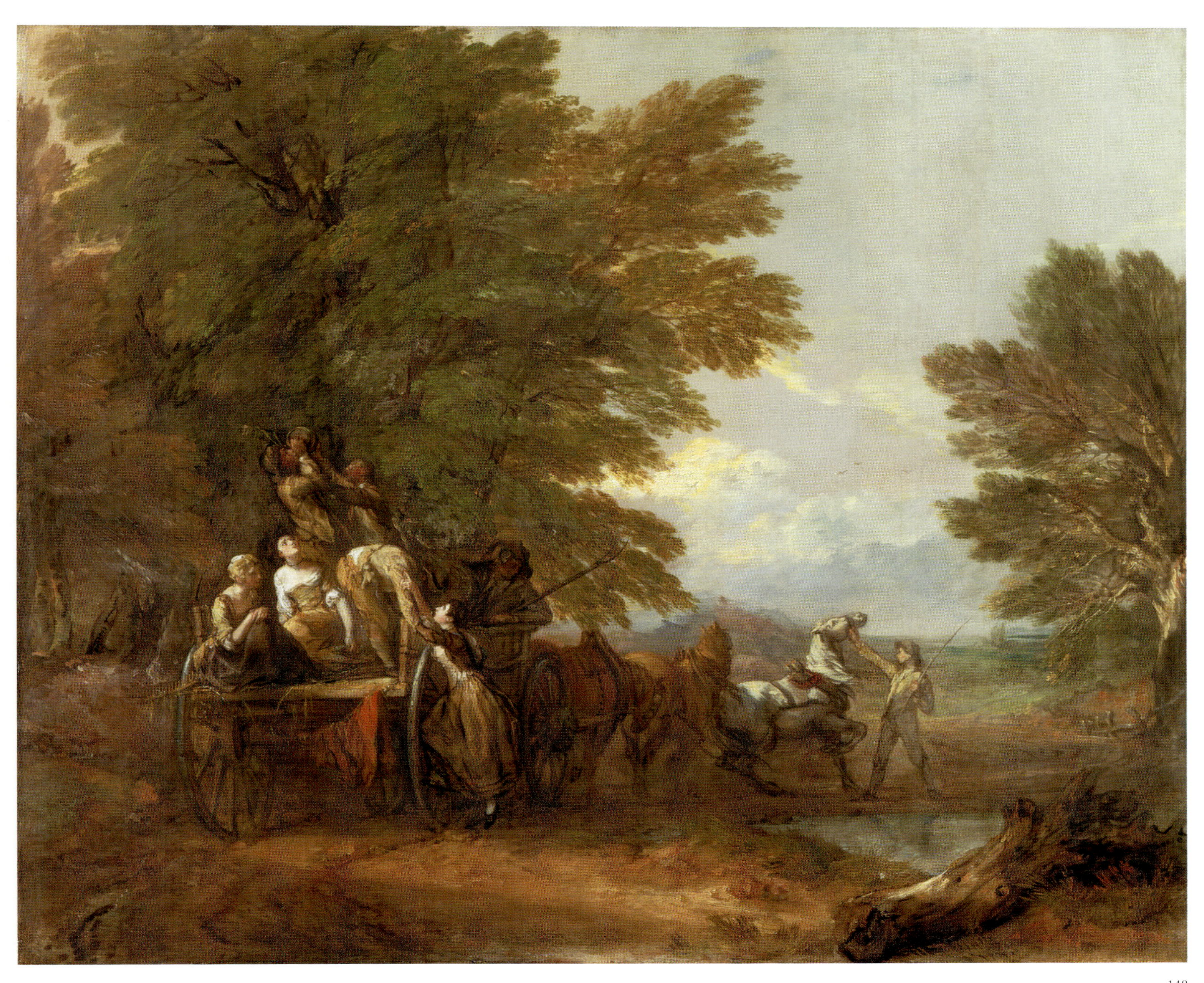

148

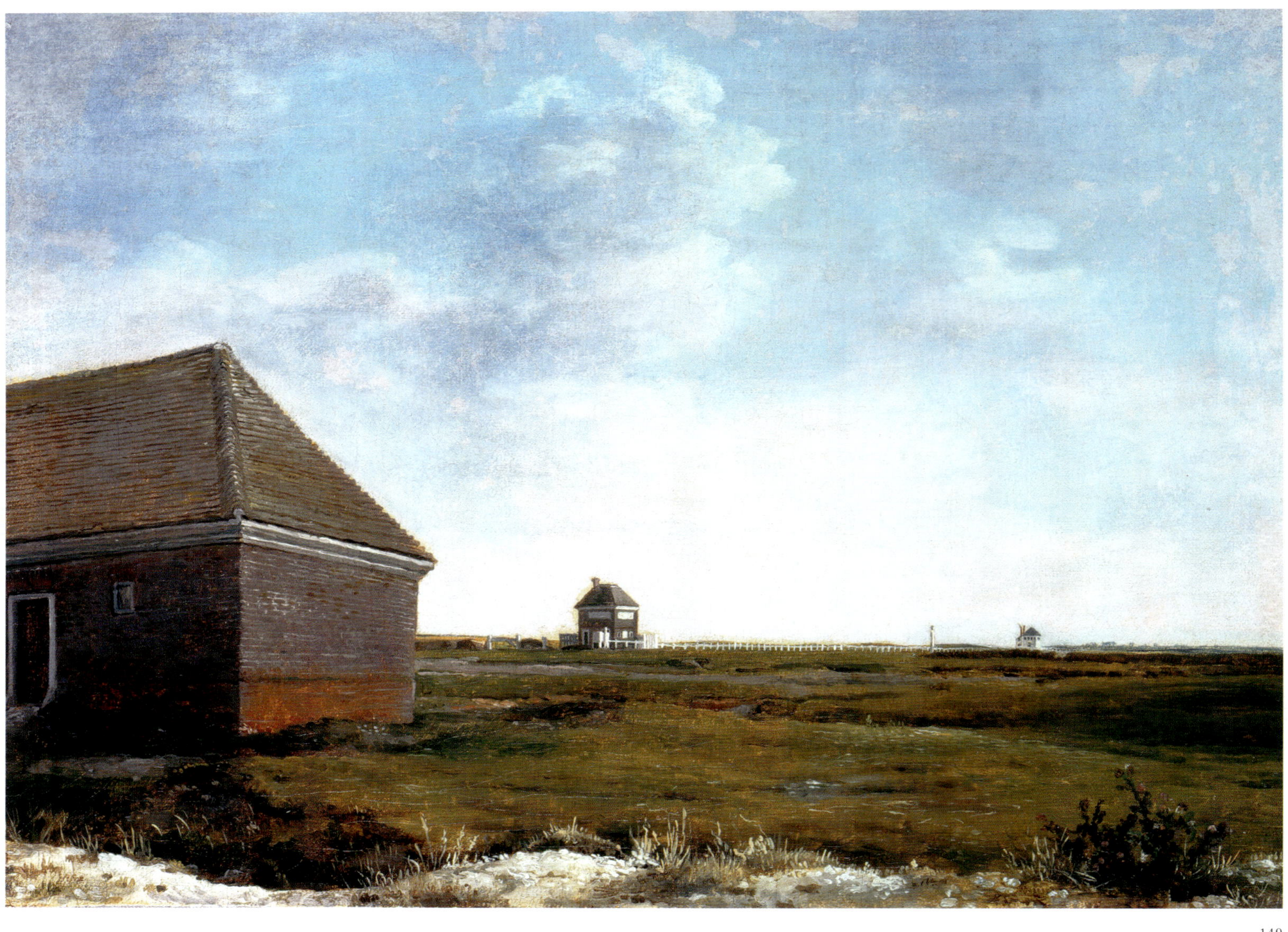

149

149. **George Stubbs**
Liverpool, 1724 – London, 1806
Newmarket Heath, with a Rubbing-Down House, c. 1765
Oil on canvas, 30.2 x 41.9 cm
Tate, London

George Stubbs, the son of a Liverpool currier and leather seller, from the early 1760s found patronage among the aristocratic racing fraternity, who commissioned him to paint their horses and jockeys, both in training and on the racecourse. The present work, although it closely relates to such commissions, is unusual in the artist's oeuvre in that it features a 'racing' landscape devoid of any human or equine presence. In the foreground, to the left, is a plain brick building, one of four such structures at Newmarket used to rub down horses after exercise and racing. On the horizon, at the centre, is a spectators' stand, with a second on the skyline to the right. This modest-sized painting, and another similar work, which shows the rubbing-down house from a different angle, served as the bases for several racing pictures, notably that featuring the famous horse Gimcrack, with his trainer, stable-lad and jockey (Private Collection). (MP)

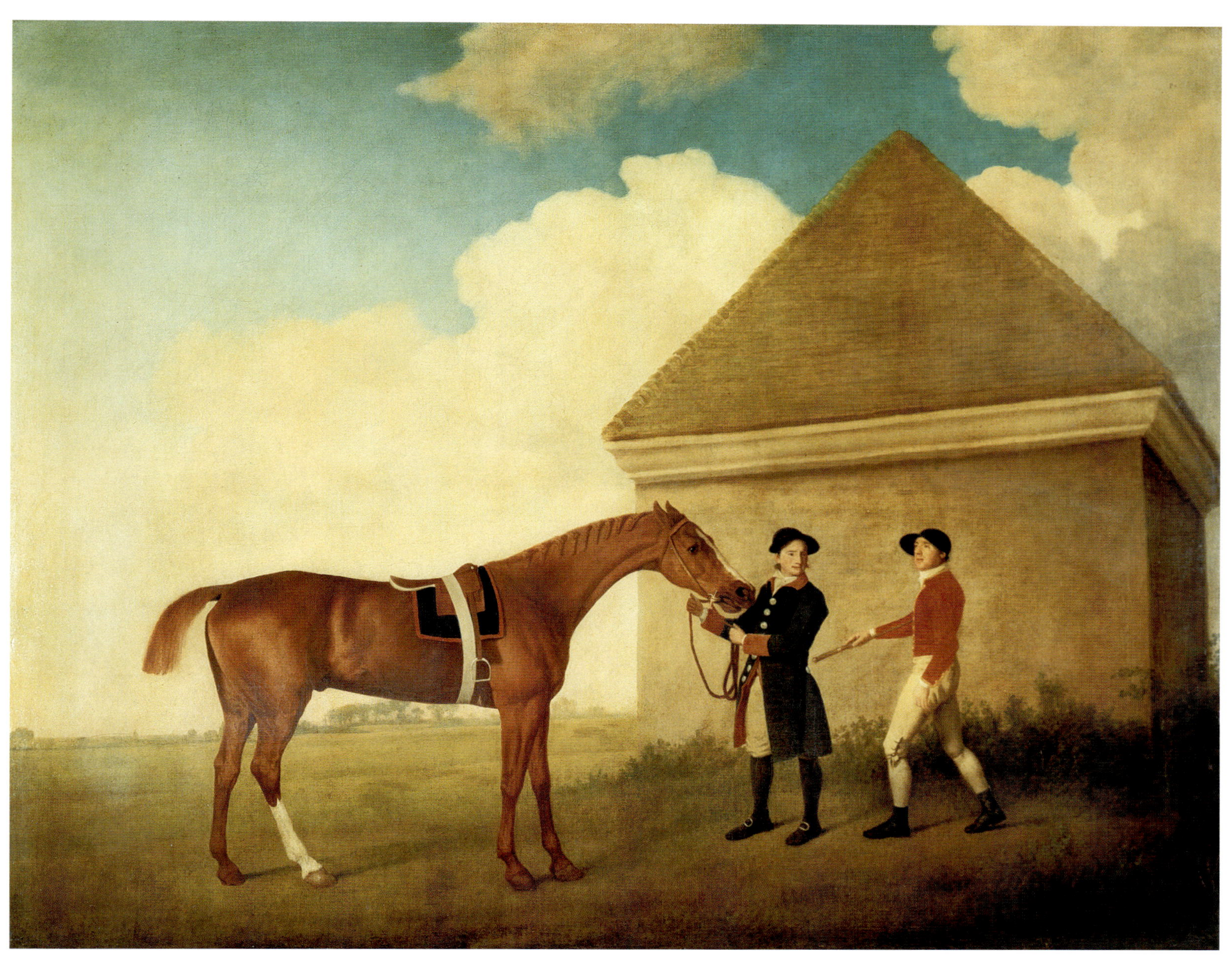

150

150. **George Stubbs**
Liverpool, 1724 - London, 1806
Eclipse at Newmarket with a Groom and Jockey, 1770, replica c. 1793
Oil on canvas, 100.3 x 131.5 cm
Bottom right: Geo Stubbs pinxit / 1770
Jockey Club Estates Limited, Newmarket, Suffolk

Stubbs began painting racehorses in the early 1760s, including famous winners such as Lustre, Whistlejacket and Gimcrack. These works were commissioned by the elite corps of owners and breeders who prized their horses' pedigree, and who wagered vast sums on their performance at the track. Many of these horses were portrayed by Stubbs at Newmarket, where they had secured their victories; often in the company of their groom and jockey and - as here - standing before the rubbing-down house. At the time Stubbs painted the first version of this picture in 1770, Eclipse belonged to William Wildman, whose racing colours the jockey wears. Shortly afterwards, however, the horse was purchased from Wildman by Colonel Dennis O'Kelly, who also acquired Stubbs's painting. The present replica, also made by Stubbs, was painted around 1793 for the *Turf Review*, an ambitious - and ultimately failed - project which aspired to reproduce images of the most famous race-horses 'from the Godolphin Arabian to the most distinguished Race Horse of the present time'. It was exhibited, alongside fifteen other works by Stubbs, the following year at the Turf Gallery in Conduit Street, London, and reproduced as a popular engraving by Stubbs's son, George Townly Stubbs. (MP)

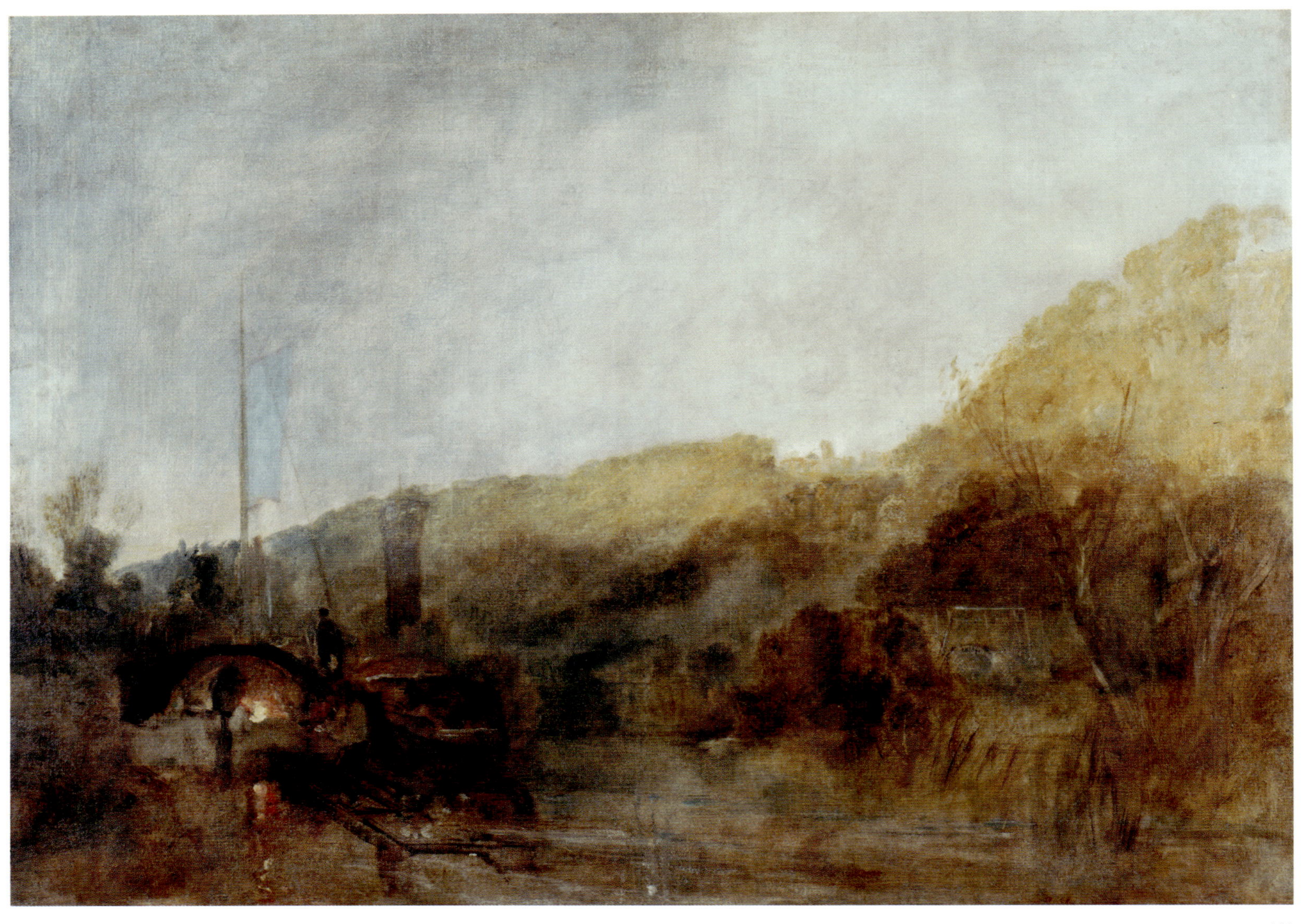

151

151. **Joseph Mallord William Turner**
London, 1775 – London, 1851
Barge on the River, Sunset, c. 1806-07
Oil on canvas, 85.1 x 116.2 cm
Tate, London, Bequeathed by the artist 1856

The location of *Barge on the River, Sunset* has been identified as the view from the Thames looking up towards the ruins of Cliveden House in Buckinghamshire. In the bottom left hand corner, two bargemen have moored their boats for the evening and are huddled around a small camp fire. Turner was always an interested observer of contemporary life and frequently sketched details of everyday human activity, which he included in his landscapes. He himself came from lowly beginnings and his sympathies often lay with the daily lot of the working man.

The painting recalls John Ruskin's description of Turner's art as 'what the mind sees when it looks for poetry in humble actual life'. (NM)

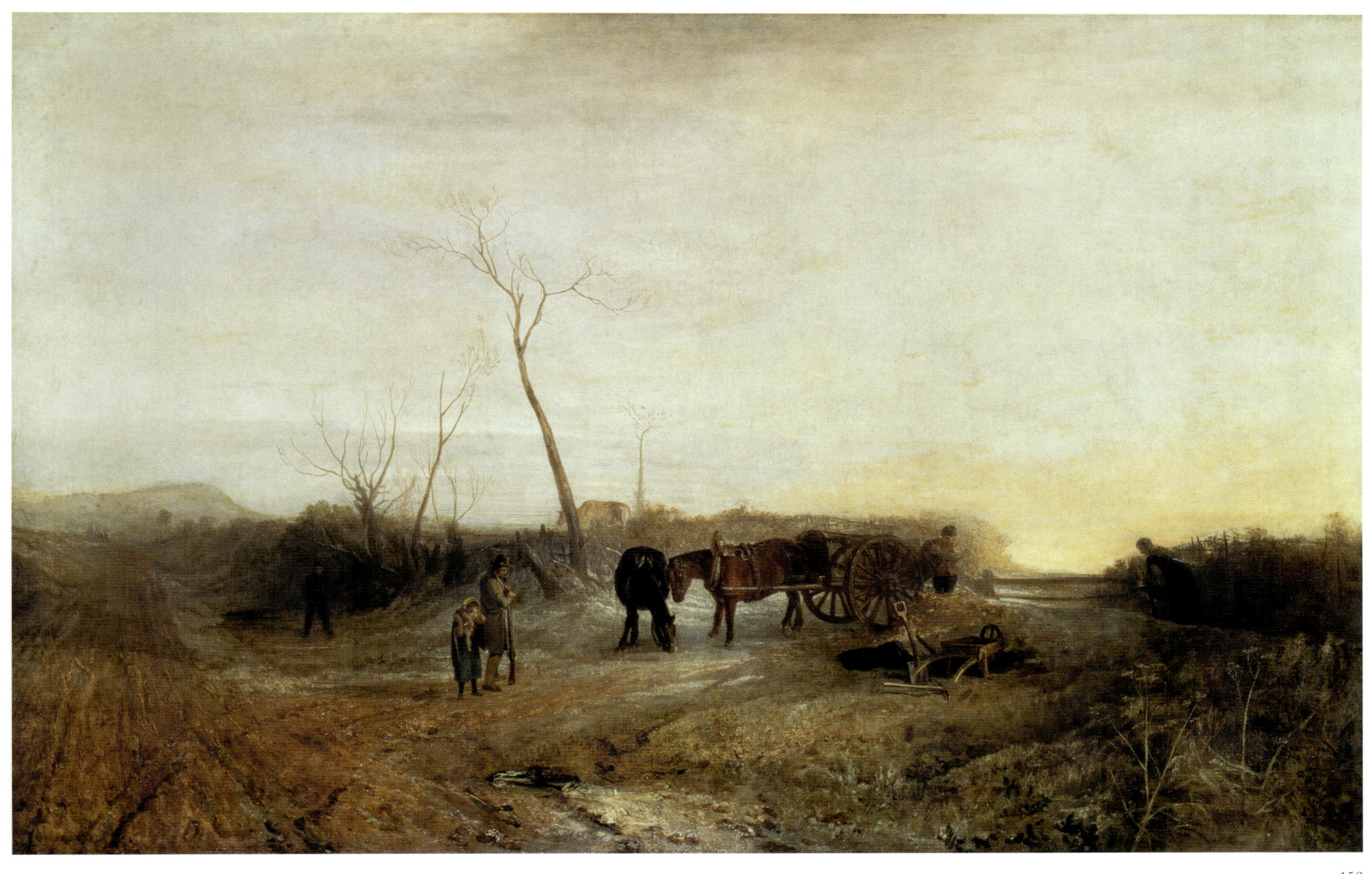

152

152. **Joseph Mallord William Turner**
London, 1775 - London, 1851
Frosty Morning, c. 1813
Oil on canvas, 113.7 x 174.6 cm
Tate, London, Bequeathed by the artist 1856

This painting perfectly expresses Turner's understanding of the paradox of nature. The beauty of the natural world is apparent in the pale dawn light suffusing the sky and the delicate, fragile-looking forms of the bare, leafless trees. Yet this landscape is no rural idyll, and Turner lends the scene a critical edge with the uncompromising reality of his observation. The dirt road is painted with attentive detail to the rutted tracks of countless carts. The gaze of the viewer is drawn from the weak golden glimpse of sun to the stocky working farm ponies and the dark figures of the labourers struggling to work the frozen land.

According to contemporary reports, the model for the girl in the blue dress with the hare slung across one shoulder was Turner's eldest daughter, Evelina, whilst the horse pulling the cart was the artist's own 'crop-eared bay'. (NM)

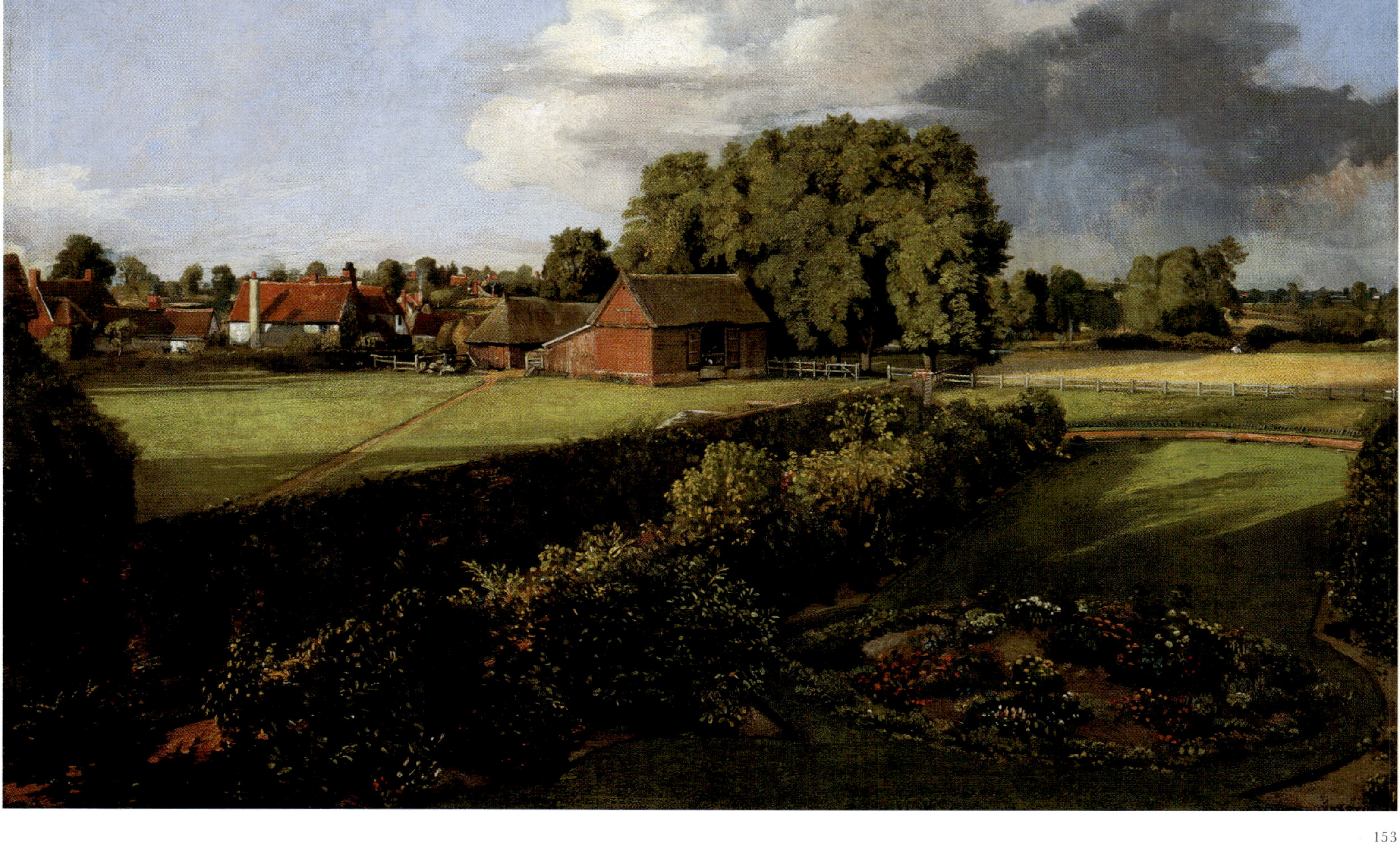

153

153. **John Constable**
East Bergholt, Suffolk, 1776 - London, 1837
Golding Constable's Flower Garden, 1815
Oil on canvas, 33.1 x 50.8 cm
Ipswich Borough Council Museums & Galleries
Acquired through the National Art Collections Fund

154. **John Constable**
East Bergholt, Suffolk, 1776 - London, 1837
Golding Constable's Vegetable Garden, 1815
Oil on canvas, 33 x 50.8 cm
Ipswich Borough Council Museums & Galleries
Acquired through the National Art Collections Fund

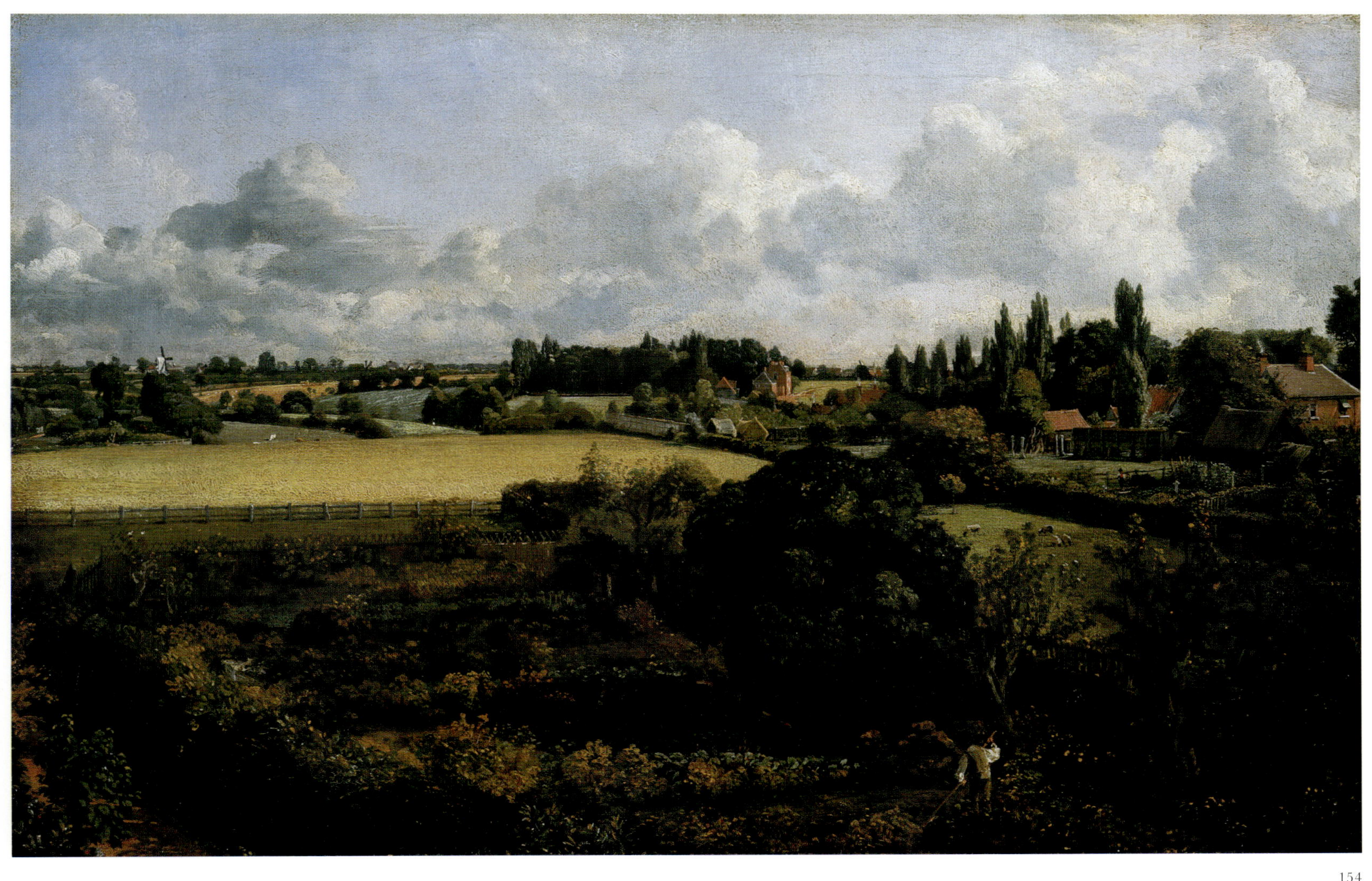

154

These two panoramas were viewed from the house in East Bergholt where Constable was born and spent his youth. From his room on the upper floor he looked out over his father's garden and fields, and he made various drawings and oil studies of this landscape or parts of it. The garden of the rectory, visible in the distance at the centre of cat. 154, appears in a number of studies. The artist was particularly interested in the sculptural aspect of the park, closed off at the right by the shape of the rectory.

The panoramas shown here are a pair, with the family's flower garden on the left and the vegetable garden on the right. However, the two landscapes are depicted under different atmospheric conditions: the flower garden appears in evening light with a threatening rain cloud on the right, the vegetable garden in morning light with a calm cloudy sky. The artist depicted both the gardens in the foreground and the landscapes in the background with an extraordinary attention to detail. There is also a detailed drawing of the same view (Victoria and Albert Museum, London), which Constable exhibited at the Royal Academy in 1815 (Fleming-Williams 1990, p. 127). Around 1815, Constable was very much taken up with the detailed finish of his paintings, a number of which were taken directly from nature. The two panoramas seen from his parents' house are extreme examples of this very exact form of observation. (RH)

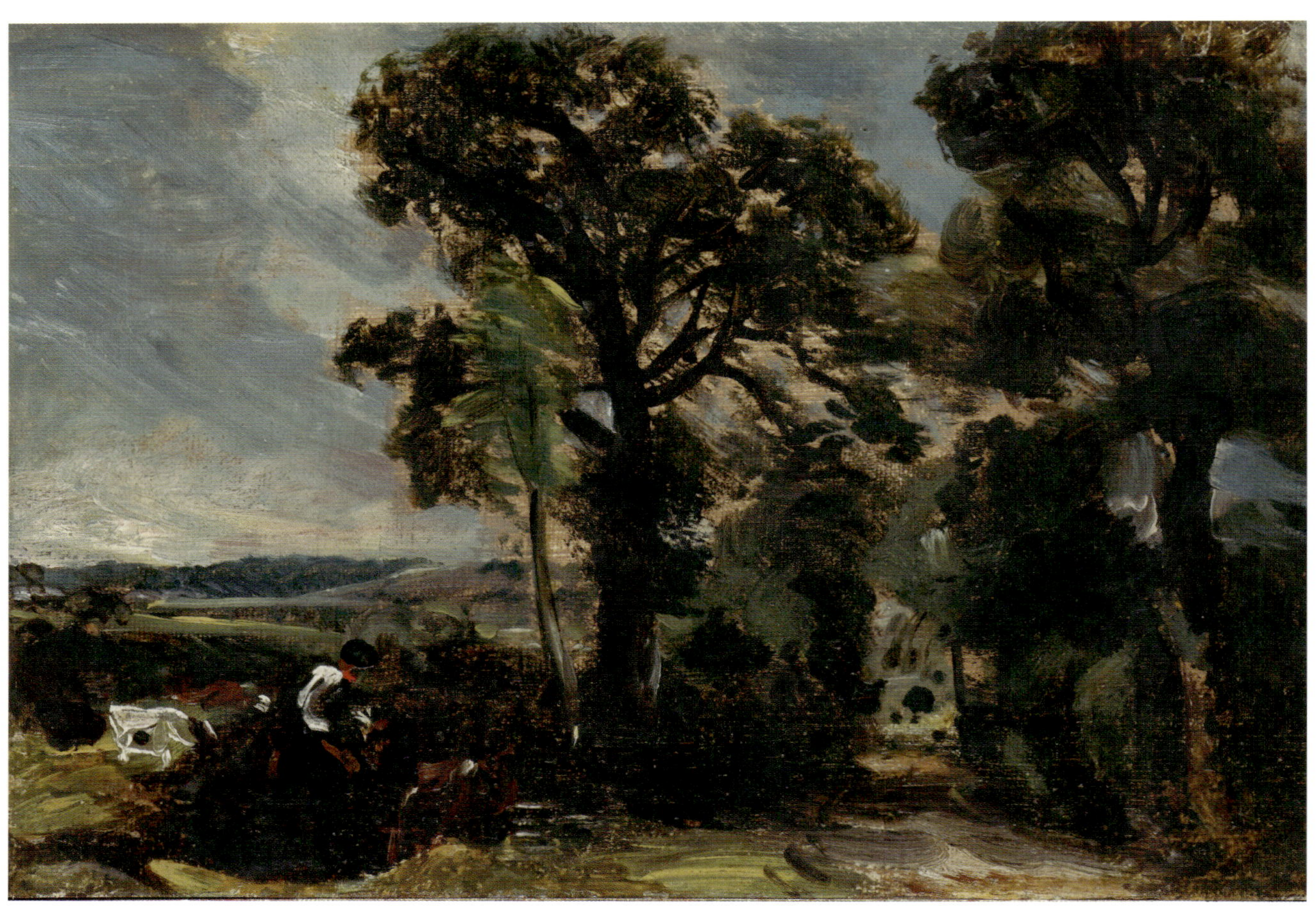

155

155. **John Constable**
East Bergholt, Suffolk, 1776 – London, 1837
A Lane at East Bergholt, c. 1811-12
Oil on canvas, mounted on panel, 14.9 x 21.6 cm
Palais des Beaux-Arts, Lille

156. **John Constable**
East Bergholt, Suffolk, 1776 – London, 1837
Dedham from Langham, c. 1811-12
Oil on canvas, 21.6 x 30.5 cm
Victoria and Albert Museum, London,
Given by Isabel Constable, daughter of the artist

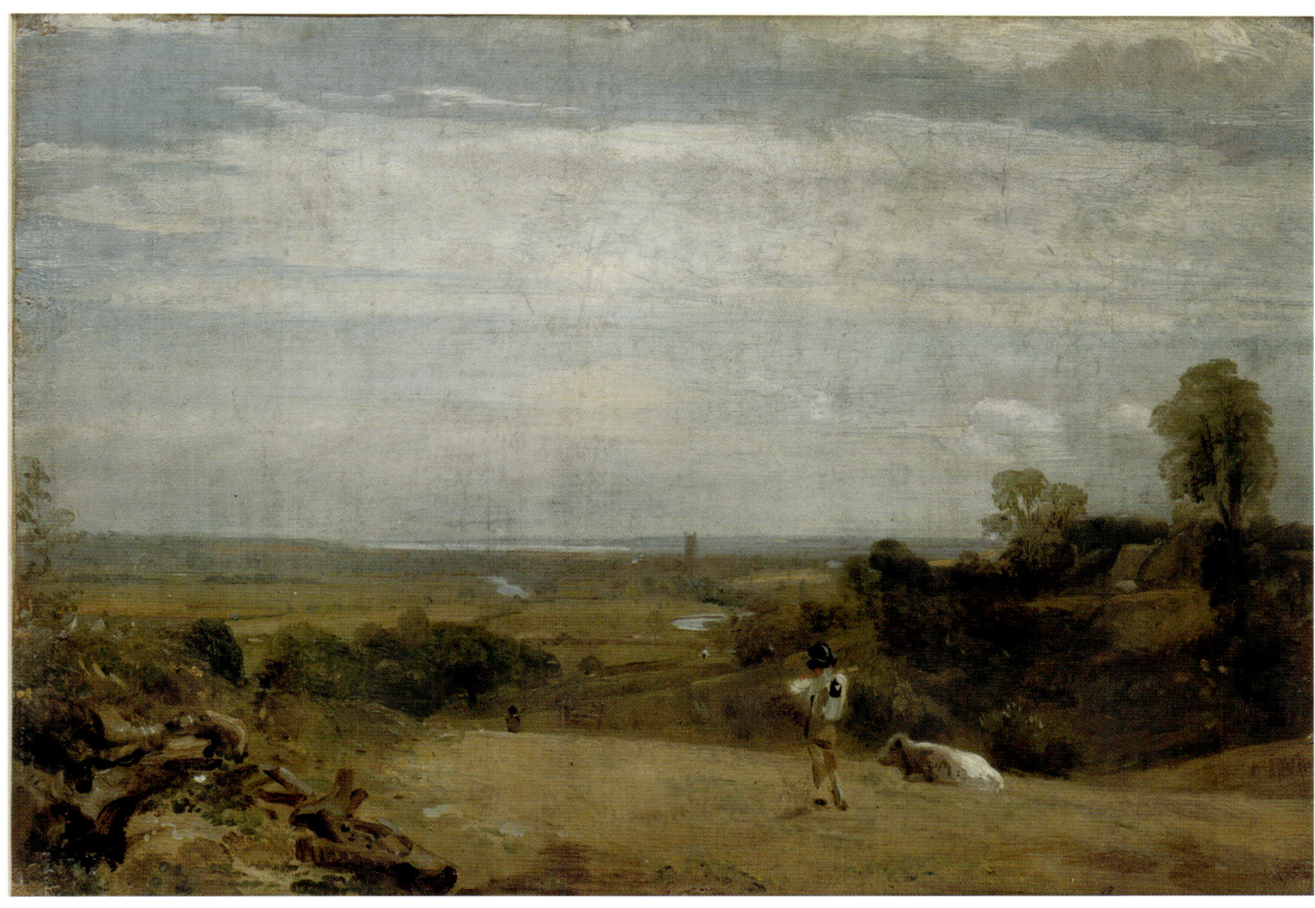

156

East Bergholt, the village from which Constable usually set out to sketch the surrounding area, is situated on high ground with a view of the valley formed by the river Stour. To judge by the countless times he drew and painted there, the Dedham Vale, named after the village on the other side of the river, was one of Constable's favourite places to work.

In his painted studies, it is striking how the artist's manner of painting and use of colour alter according to his mood and the particular observation made. Some studies – of which cat. 155 is a good example – are painted dynamically, with intense contrasts and colour accents. Here we see a lane between trees in the vicinity of East Bergholt, with a view of the glowing landscape to the left – a two-part composition of a kind that often recurs in Constable's studies. Cat. 156 shows Dedham Vale seen from Langham. The landscape is carefully balanced, with the gently accentuated church tower of Dedham beside the clear strip of light that represents the river-mouth, the curve of the winding river in the centre, intersecting slopes and the accents in the foreground. Constable repeated this composition in several drawings and oil sketches. The most accomplished of these, cat. 156, is built up with carefully juxtaposed tones, which produce a subtle coherence between the clear cloudy sky and the softly lit landscape. (RH)

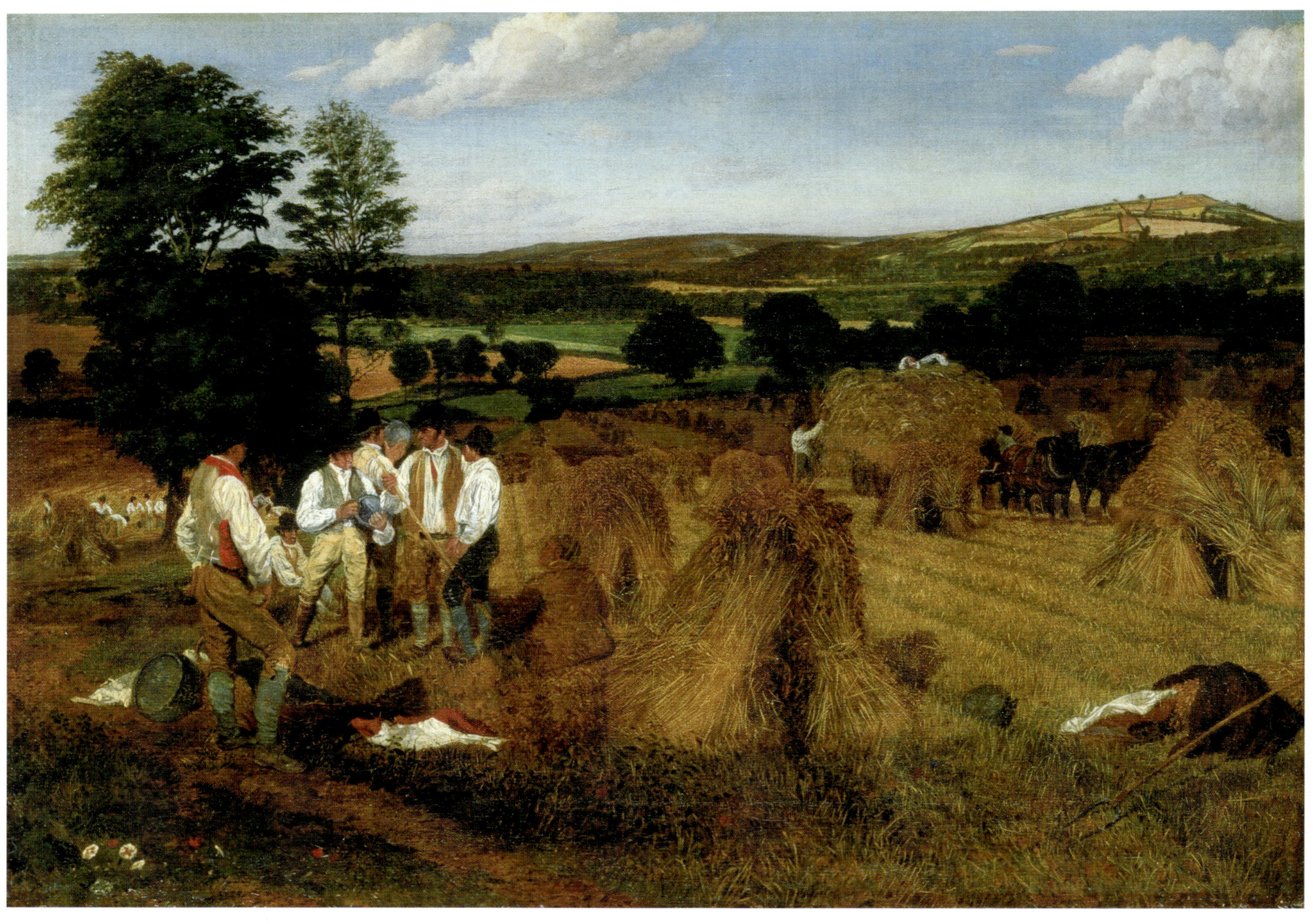

157

157. **George Robert Lewis**
London, 1782 – London, 1871
Hereford, Dynedor and the Malvern Hills from the Haywood Lodge, Harvest Scene, Afternoon, c. 1815
Oil on canvas, 41.6 x 59.7 cm
Tate, London, presented by the Reverend Stopford Brooke 1904

When exhibited at the Society of Painters in Oil & Water Colours in London in 1816 (no. 139), this remarkable landscape, together with eleven other views of the same area, was said to have been 'painted on the spot', a rare practice at this time, but one that was being (briefly) followed by Constable, who also exhibited a rather larger harvesting scene the same year. So this was an advanced painting for the period, but its subject shows entirely traditional agricultural methods in a part of the west of England well known for its conservative farmers and almost untouched by the agrarian distress which was common in these years. The direct characterization of the labourers and their easy, upright stances – in Barrell's words, 'everything about them speaks of ... manly dignity' – suggests that they may even have posed for Lewis in this very field, although, as Christiana Payne has shown (Payne 1993, p. 96), a jacketed 'bailiff' has been painted out, which suggests studio work on the figure composition. (JG)

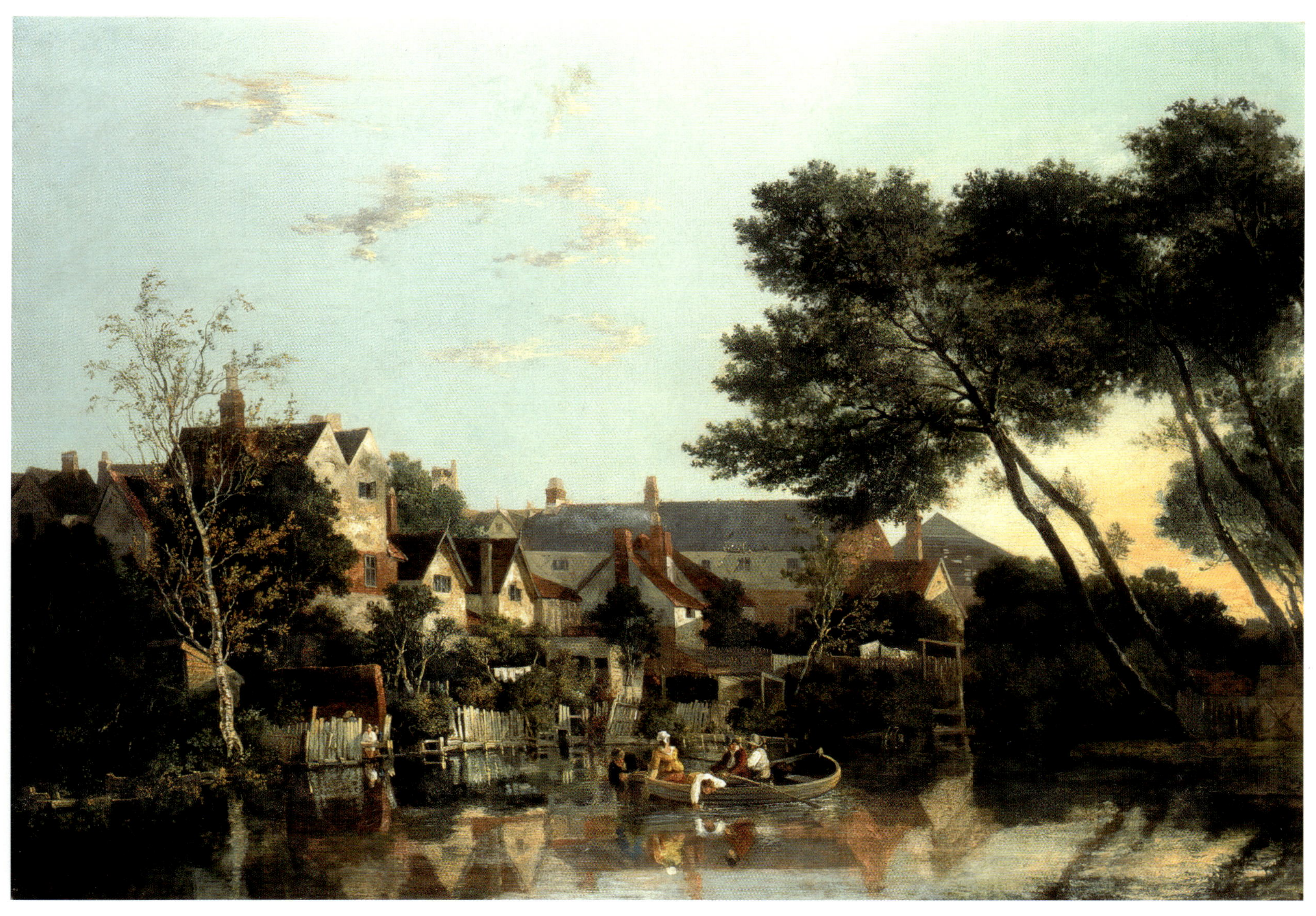

158

158. **John Crome**
Norwich, 1768 - Norwich, 1821
Norwich River: Afternoon, c. 1819
Oil on canvas, 71.1 x 100.3 cm
Norfolk Museums and Archaeology Service, Norwich

John Crome was the leading landscapist in Norwich until his death in 1821. Although the motif here recalls Dutch seventeenth-century townscape painters, such as Jan van der Heyden, the large scale, the broad technique and, above all, the handling of the soft afternoon light are fully Romantic. Crome's Yarmouth patron, Dawson Turner, spoke indeed of the painter's bringing J.M.W. Turner's 'magic light' into his late work; and, as David Blayney Brown has noted (Blayney Brown 2000, p. 31), the patron went on to recall Crome's enthusiasm for the London painter's 'effects of light and shade and brilliant colour, and poetical feeling, and grandeur of composition' in work at the 1818 Royal Academy Exhibition. J.M.W. Turner's chief exhibit there had been *Dort or Dordrecht, the Dort Packet-Boat from Rotterdam Becalmed* (Yale Center for British Art, New Haven), and Crome's *Norwich River* may well owe a good deal to that masterpiece. In one telling detail, Crome has made a figure in his boat lean out to ruffle the glassy calm of the River Wensum , as one of Turner's passengers does in *Dort,* although there it is a mallard duck (Turner's 'signature'), rising from the dead calm of the surface, which creates the almost audible ripple. (JG)

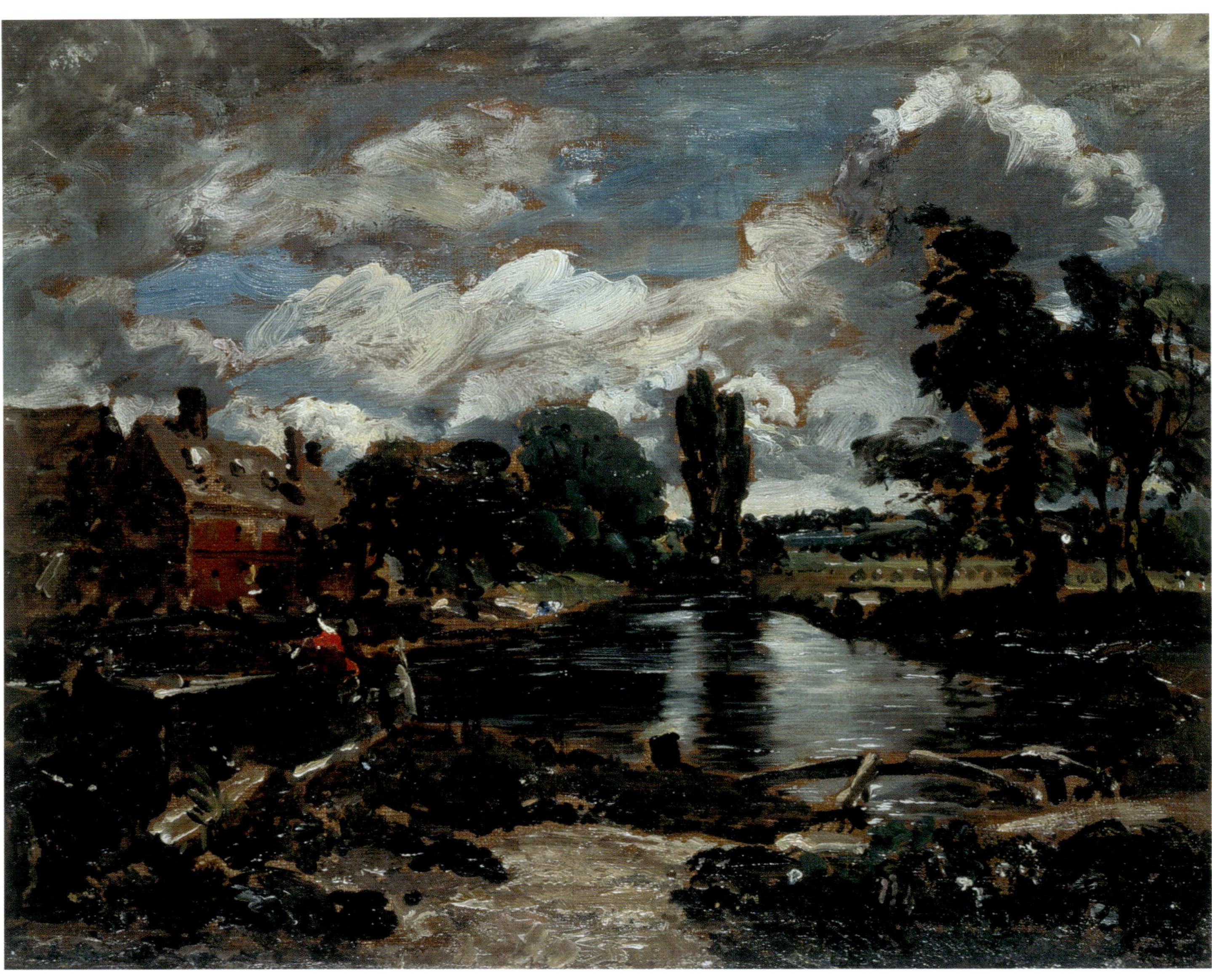

159

159. **John Constable**
East Bergholt, Suffolk, 1776 - London, 1837
Study for Flatford Mill from the Lock, c. 1811
Oil on canvas, 24.8 x 29.8 cm
Victoria and Albert Museum, London,
Given by Isabel Constable, daughter of the artist

Flatford Mill, which was owned by Constable's father, is visible here at the left behind one of the many locks that made the river Stour navigable. Here we are in the heart of the area that Constable explored intensely from around 1810 to 1816. This striking view across the triangular surface of the water in the direction of the two poplars in the centre was the subject of six known oil studies by Constable (Reynolds 1996, nos. 12.5-12.10). The one shown here most closely resembles a finished painting exhibited by the artist in 1812 (ibid., no. 12.1). It has been suggested that the present work - unlike the other studies - is actually a compositional sketch made in the studio (London 1991, pp. 525-26), but there is no reason to suppose that this is the case. Like the other studies of this landscape, the work illustrates the manner in which Constable sought out interesting compositions in his early studies from nature. In each of the six studies a lock-keeper adopts a different pose, and these and other compositional elements may have come from the artist's imagination. However, this does not change the fact that the essence of these studies is the recording of momentary atmospheric impressions and the creation of a powerful - in this case even dramatic - composition on the basis of observation and first-hand experience. (RH)

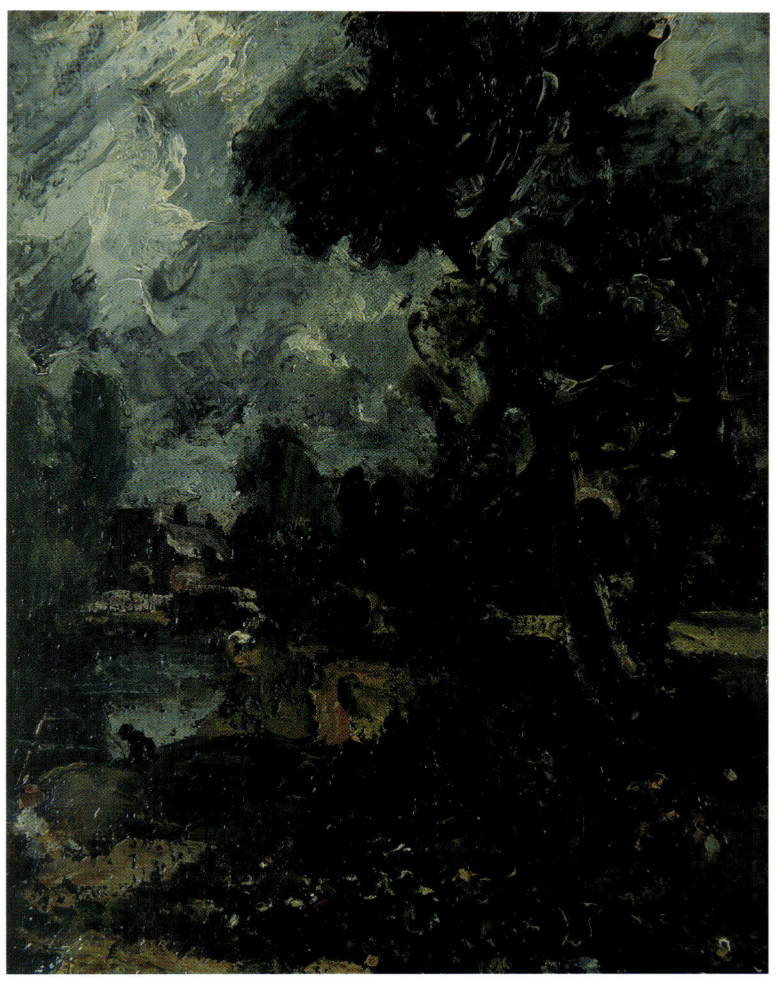

160

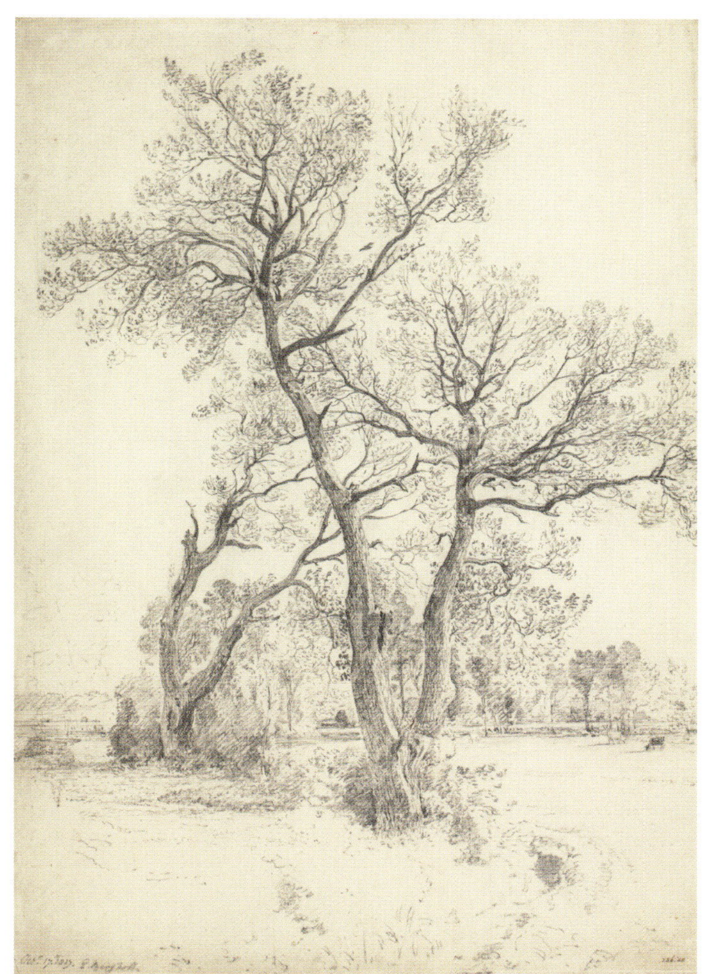

161

160. **John Constable**
East Bergholt, Suffolk, 1776 - London, 1837
Flatford Mill from the Tow Path, c. 1814-16
Oil on canvas, 23 x 18 cm
Private Collection, long-term loan
to the Holburne Museum of Art, Bath

This study has roughly the same perspective as that found in the finished painting *Flatford Mill* (cat. 162). The framing of the landscape is almost identical to a drawing in a sketchbook dated 14 August 1814 (p. 225, fig. 2), but in the drawing the tree at the front has three heavy branches, while in the oil study the middle branch has been reduced to a stub. This suggests that it was probably painted after August 1814 and certainly before 1816, the year in which Constable synthesized his studies of Flatford in a large-scale painting (cat. 162). The landscape is correctly depicted, but in comparison with the finished painting, and even with the small drawing mentioned above, the entire composition is compressed, as if Constable wanted to draw all the elements in his field of vision as tangibly as possible and in close up. With its limited palette and impetuously applied paint, this is an excellent example of the direct sketching technique that Constable used to explore his surroundings. (RH)

161. **John Constable**
East Bergholt, Suffolk, 1776 - London, 1837
Trees at East Bergholt, 1817
Pencil on paper, 53.3 x 38.1 cm
Bottom left: Octr. 17th 1817. E. Bergholt
Victoria and Albert Museum, London,
Given by Isabel Constable, daughter of the artist

This drawing, one of the most detailed in Constable's oeuvre, was created in conjunction with the painting *Flatford Mill* (cat. 162), in which the clouds and trees were repainted by the artist after the work was finished (see essay, p. 223). Constable made this drawing on the spot in October 1817 and probably reworked the painting before he exhibited it for the second time at the annual exhibition of the British Institution in January 1818. The group of black poplars was one of the distinctive features of the area around Flatford Mill (London, Washington & San Marino 2006, p. 106), and it appears several times in the artist's early sketchbooks and oil studies. (RH)

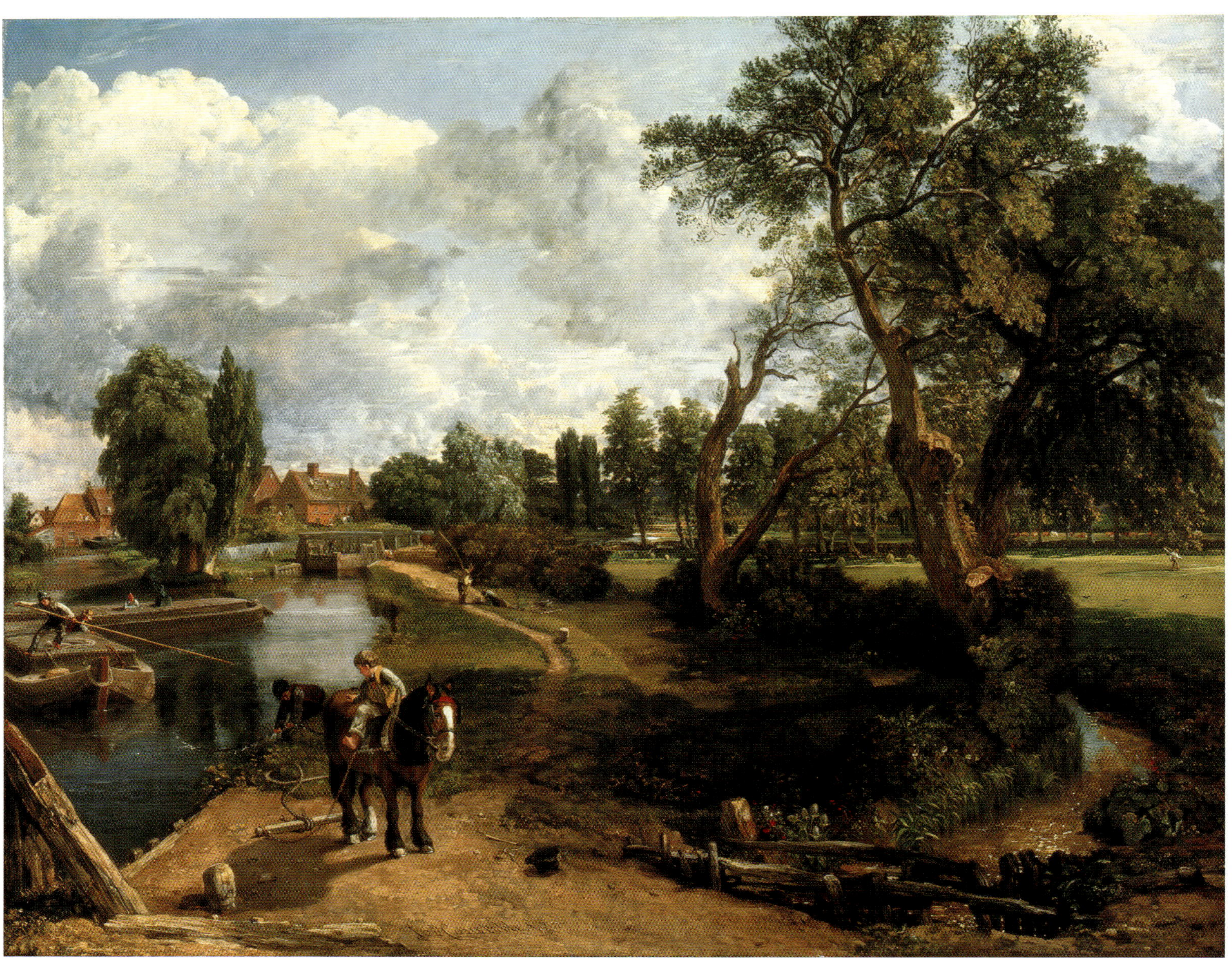

162

162. **John Constable**
East Bergholt, Suffolk, 1776 - London, 1837
Flatford Mill (Scene on a Navigable River), 1817
Oil on canvas, 101.6 x 127 cm
Bottom centre: Jo^{n} Constable. f: 1817.
Tate, London, Bequeathed by Isabel Constable as the gift of Maria Louisa, Isabel and Lionel Bicknell Constable 1888

Constable exhibited this painting at the Royal Academy in 1817. It was his ultimate attempt at transposing the wealth of observation contained in his numerous early drawings and oil studies to a large-scale canvas. The work is presumed to have been painted from nature. It depicts his father's mill seen from a point near Flatford Bridge, part of the structure of which is visible at the lower left. The scene shows a draught horse being unhitched so that the two boats can be manoeuvred under the bridge with poles. Originally there was a second horse further up, which Constable later painted over and replaced with the two boys (London 1991, p. 181). The activity in the foreground and the studied placement of various details helped the artist fill in the large space at the front and draw the viewer's eye further into the landscape. (RH)

See essay pp. 223-25.

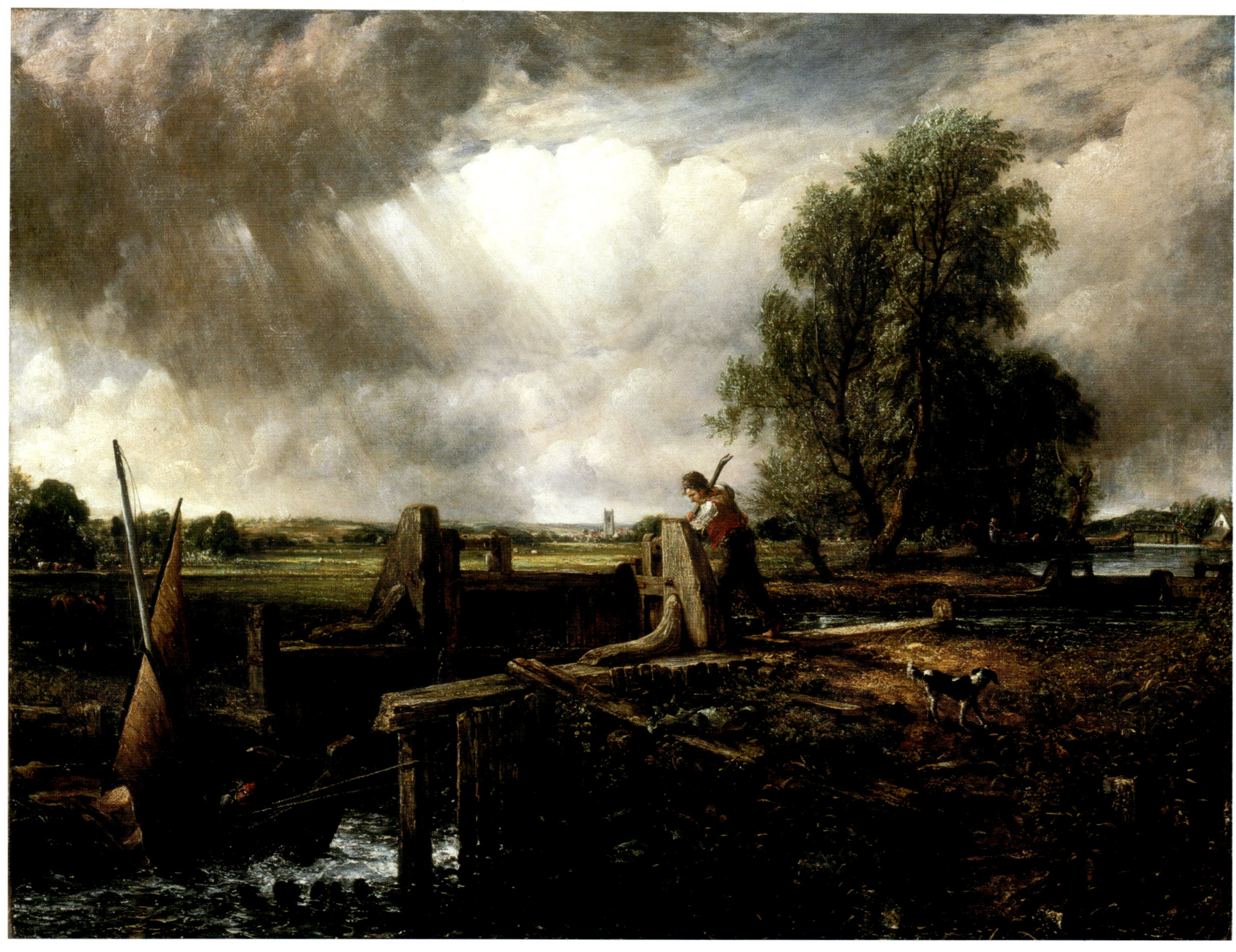

163

163. **John Constable**
East Bergholt, Suffolk, 1776 – London, 1837
A Boat Passing a Lock, 1826
Oil on canvas, 101.6 x 127 cm
Bottom left: John Constable. f. 1826
Royal Academy of Arts, London

Although smaller than the six-foot canvases that Constable used for his most important works from 1819 onward, this work also belongs to the series of large-format views of the Stour with which he established his reputation. In these large compositions, he constantly returned to motifs from the region where he was born, which had featured in numerous studies he made before settling in London in 1816. In contrast to Flatford Mill (cat. 162), this composition was probably not made directly from nature, but was, rather, put together in the studio, incorporating elements from individual studies. Constable first painted the subject in 1824 in a vertical format (Philadelphia Museum of Art and Thyssen-Bornemisza Museum, Madrid), with a monumental group of trees behind the lock-keeper filling almost a quarter of the whole composition. In the present horizontal version, the group of trees is depicted on a more modest scale, closer to its actual appearance, to judge by several related drawings (London 1991, p. 290, and nos. 305 and 315). Nevertheless, we are still looking at an invented composition: we know that Constable changed the construction of the lock by omitting a crossbeam in the centre that connected the two vertical beams at the left and right. *A Boat Passing a Lock* illustrates a phase in Constable's work in which he sought to lend his landscapes a certain monumentality and drama. The lock is strikingly placed in the middle of the landscape with a church tower in the distance, and although the lock-keeper is not given heroic stature, he is nevertheless emphatically present. The grandeur and complexity of the cloudy sky reveals the extraordinary mastery that Constable's repeated studies (cat. 174) had enabled him to achieve in the depiction of clouds. (RH)

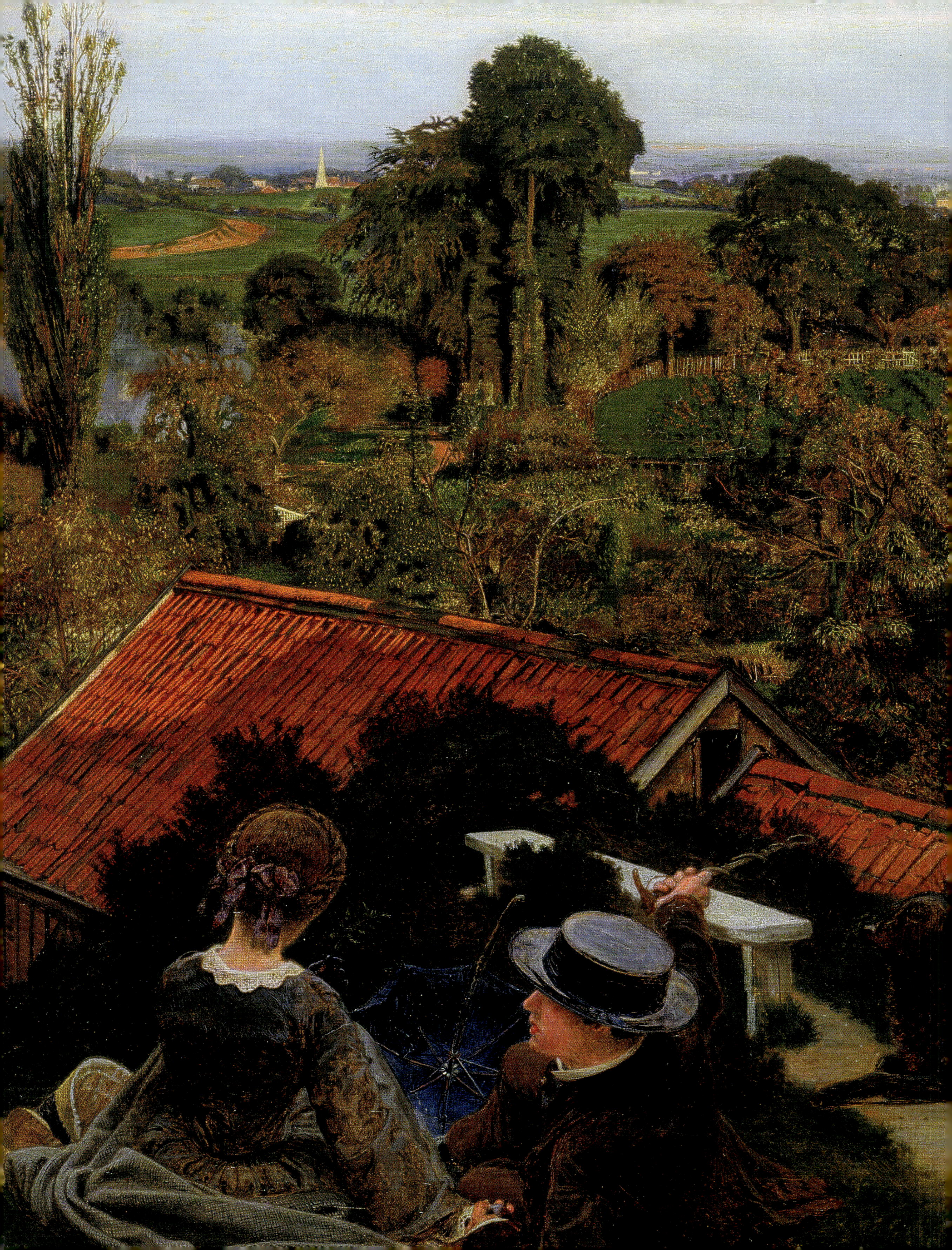

ATMOSPHERE AND DETAIL

FORD MADOX BROWN

An English Autumn Afternoon, 1852-1853, 1855

JULIAN TREUHERZ

Painted from the window of his lodgings in Hampstead, north of London, Ford Madox Brown's *An English Autumn Afternoon* depicts a young couple seated in front of a landscape of rooftops and gardens looking across Hampstead Heath. Brown has lovingly captured the exact effect of warm autumn sunlight, the foliage turning from green to gold, and the crisp clarity of the distant view of the Heath; prominent amongst the tiny white highlights of sunlit buildings scattered across the horizon is the spire of the newly built St Anne's Church, Highgate, at the upper left.

Brown's concern to depict a particular place and time in specific atmospheric conditions is shown in the way he later described the painting as 'a literal transcript of the scenery round London, as looked at from Hampstead. The smoke of London is seen rising half way above the fantastic shaped, small distant cumuli, which accompany particularly fine weather. The upper portion of the sky would be blue as reflected in the youth's hat; the grey mist of autumn only rising a certain height. The time is 3 p.m., when late in October the shadows already lie long, and the sun's rays (coming from behind us in this work) are preternaturally glowing, as in rivalry of the foliage.'[1]

As with other Pre-Raphaelite paintings that pin down a momentary effect, it took him a great deal of trouble and time, in this case about six months, necessitating return visits to the scene at particular times. We know this from entries in his diary, which show that although he started the painting in the autumn of 1852, he had to stop after a month because the upper room from which he was looking out at the view was required by his landlady. He then waited until the next autumn, by which time he had moved to Finchley. He worked at it for another month in September and October 1853, and then again several times the following year.[2] In 1847 he was still adhering to the traditional practice of making a study out of doors (see cat. 195) and later copying it into the final painting; in *An English Autumn Afternoon*, as in the large version of *Work,* also begun whilst Brown was lodging at Hampstead (see cat. 22), he painted onto the full-sized canvas direct from the scene in front of him.[3] Unable to sell the picture privately, he put it into an auction, where it fetched nine guineas, the frame having cost him four.[4] No wonder he described himself at this period as 'most of the time intensely miserable very hard up & a little mad.'[5]

On 14 July 1855 the painting was the subject of an altercation between Brown and the art critic John Ruskin, recorded by Brown in his diary. They met by chance in the studio of Brown's friend the painter Dante Gabriel Rossetti. Just as Brown was preparing to leave, Ruskin suddenly said to him 'Mr. Brown will you tell me why you chose such a very ugly subject for your last picture.' Dumbfounded at this unexpected opening, Brown asked which one, to which Ruskin answered 'Your picture at the British Exhibition. What made you take such a very ugly subject? It was a pity for there was some *nice* painting in it.' Brown, 'satisfied that he intended impertinence', replied contemptuously 'Because it lay out of a back window' and left the room.[6]

Leaving aside the antipathy that existed between the two men, we might still reasonably suppose that the painting would have pleased Ruskin, for it appears to be a faithful example of what he had in mind when he wrote the famous passage in *Modern Painters* advising artists to 'go to Nature in all singleness of heart, and walk with her trustingly, having no other thoughts but how best to penetrate her meaning, and remember her instruction, rejecting nothing, selecting nothing, and scorning nothing, believing all things to be right and good, and rejoicing always in the

Ford Madox Brown, ***An English Autumn Afternoon*** (detail), cat. 196

truth.'[7] Yet Ruskin, whilst condescending to admire some of the 'nice' painting in it, dismissed the subject as ugly. Why?

Although Ruskin's writings, and indeed his watercolours, are much concerned with questions of naturalistic accuracy, he demanded more than this from a finished painting. Indeed, the passage quoted above continues, 'Then, when their memories are stored, and their imaginations fed, and their hands firm, let them take up the scarlet and gold, give the reins to their fancy, and show us what their heads are made of.' For Ruskin, the imaginative or intellectual faculty had to be evident in landscape painting: he had no room for mechanical reproduction of natural effects, dismissing a painting by John Brett as 'Mirror's work, not Man's'.[8] In a later volume of *Modern Painters,* Ruskin described the modern landscape he most admired as 'contemplative' or 'theoretical': 'Directed principally to the observance of the powers of Nature, and record of the historical associations connected with landscape, illustrated by, or contrasted with, existing states of human life.'[9]

Brown's approach to landscape was very different. Just as with reference to *The Last of England* (cat. 23) he wrote that, 'Absolutely without regard to the art of any period or county, I have tried to render this scene as it would appear,'[10] here he was self-consciously trying to look with fresh eyes to create a picture free not only from art-historical precedent but also from the extraneous associations demanded by Ruskin.

In *An English Autumn Afternoon* Brown discarded the visual means used by most artists to give their landscapes sentiment, grandeur or decorative appeal. The horizon is high, so that there is no opportunity to include an expansive sky. The view is not depicted through a rectangular 'window' nor is it framed by trees or buildings; there is no central focus and no sequence of receding planes to lead the eye into the distance. Instead, there are horizontal banks of trees, similar to the composition of Collins's *May in the Regent's Park* (cat. 194). The wide oval shape, although previously used by printmakers and decorative painters, was unusual for a major painting; it corresponds to the binocular field of human vision and enhances the sense of our being part of the scene rather than detached spectators. Brown did put into the picture one invented element, the raised viewing point in the foreground with its handrail, steps and the bench from which to admire the view, something perhaps that he had seen on another part of the Heath.[11] There is nothing like this outside the upper window from which Brown painted his view, but the raised viewing point serves the same purpose as the window, to give a sense of elevation. This device has many antecedents in earlier art and is Brown's only concession to traditional ways of depicting landscape.[12]

On this viewing point, Brown has placed a man and a woman in modern dress, with a dog, quite different from the rustic figures in generalized peasant dress with which artists often populated traditional landscapes. Their clothing identifies them as middle-class. Brown's description of the couple is puzzling: 'The figures are peculiarly English – they are hardly lovers – more boy and girl, neighbours and friends. In no other country would they be so allowed out together, save in America, where (if report says true) the young ladies all carry latch-keys.'[13] Brown suggests that that they are not lovers, but if they were merely neighbours or friends, surely there would be no objection in any country to their being out together unchaperoned. The fact that they are holding hands suggests that they are indeed lovers. Brown often included a self-portrait, sometimes with his wife, looking on in the foreground of his landscape paintings. The couple here do not resemble Brown and his wife, but the two figures may still allude to Brown's personal circumstances, for Brown was married in the spring of 1853 between the first and the second periods of painting *An English Autumn Afternoon*.

The figures seem to have been out for a walk with their dog and are seated on the ground enjoying the view and the autumn sunshine, the woman having discarded her parasol, the man gesticulating over the landscape with his stick. They may be an oblique reference to the contemporary debate about the future of Hampstead Heath, which at this time was threatened by development, involving the building of villas, which would have prevented Londoners from walking there.[14] But more immediately, the figures make it clear that this is a modern landscape painting.

Brown's painting celebrates the ordinary.[15] Where Ruskin demanded natural grandeur or historical interest, Brown depicted what happened to be visible from his window, an unpretentious scene of back gardens, orchards, the roofs of sheds and humble workshops, and incidental details such as the blue smoke from a bonfire and the wooden pigeon-house stained with bird droppings. Amongst the trees are glimpses of people engaged in everyday activities, such as a woman feeding chickens and a man on a ladder picking fruit from a tree. This type of landscape was a fairly recent development. Lying between town and country, neither picturesquely rustic nor aggressively urban, it was shaped by mundane domestic events rather than the forces of history or the power of nature. For an artist to make it the subject not of a sketch but of a major picture intended for exhibition was entirely new.

Despite the highly particular nature of his subject, Brown entitled his painting of an ordinary, modern landscape with the middle-class couple and their dog freely enjoying their leisure time in the October sunshine, not a *Hampstead* autumn afternoon but *An English Autumn Afternoon*. The title gives the painting a modern, informal equivalent to the generalized or 'contemplative' meaning Ruskin wished for in a landscape – an image of ordinary, understated Englishness.

1. *The Exhibition of Work and other Paintings by Ford Madox Brown at the Gallery, 191, Piccadilly*, London 1865, reprinted in Bendiner 1998, p. 136.
2. Surtees 1981, pp. 78, 80, 82. Brown also retouched the landscape in 1855: London 1984, pp. 110-11 (entry by Mary Bennett).
3. Hueffer 1896, p. 91.
4. Surtees 1981, p. 82.
5. Ibid., p. 78.
6. Ibid., p. 144.
7. Cook and Wedderburn 1903-12, vol. 3, p. 623.
8. Ibid., vol. 14, p. 237.
9. Ibid., vol. 7, p. 254.
10. Bendiner 1998, p. 137.
11. Bryant 1997, p. 41 and fig. 2, a photograph of the view from the same window that Brown painted from.
12. Staley 2001, p. 41.
13. Bendiner 1998, p. 136.
14. Bryant 1997, p. 42; and Wright 1997, p. 189.
15. London 1984, pp. 110-11 (entry by Mary Bennett).

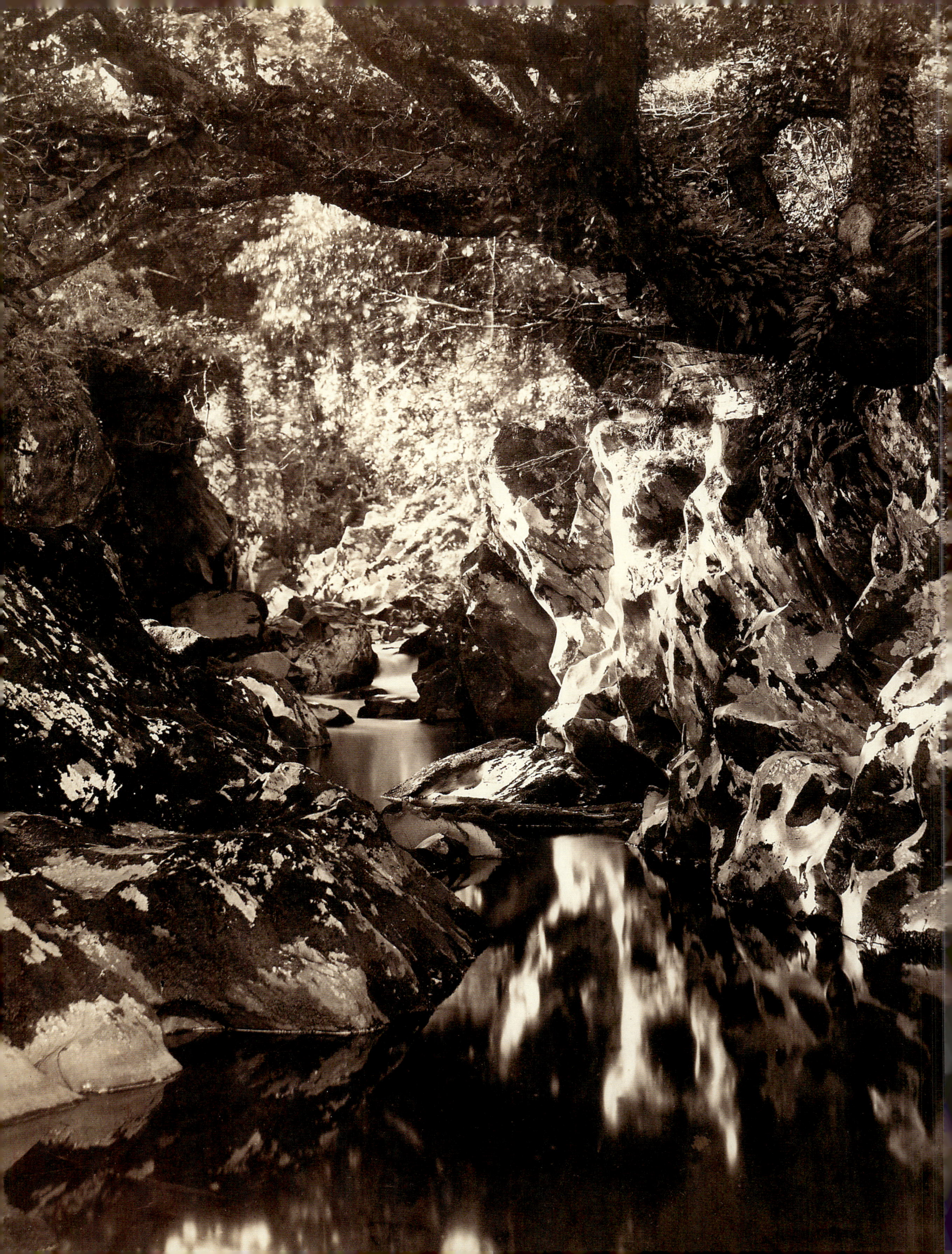

ATMOSPHERE AND DETAIL

ROGER FENTON

Double Bridge on the Machno, 1857

MARK HAWORTH-BOOTH

Fenton, like many of the leading figures in early photographic history, was well off and well educated. He trained as a painter in Paris in 1844-46 and afterwards continued his studies in London under the painter Charles Lucy. He exhibited at the Royal Academy in 1849, 1850 and 1851, while also training as a lawyer. As with many others, a major catalyst for his career was probably the large display of photography at the Great Exhibition of 1851. Fenton threw himself full-bloodedly into practising and promoting photography in 1852. In that year he contributed forty-one photographs, plus an introductory text offering an overview of photography in the catalogue, to the world's first exhibition devoted exclusively to photographs. This was *Recent Specimens of Photography,* organized by the Society of Arts in London and later toured around the country.

The title of the present photograph is at once misleading and revealing. It is misleading because the photograph does not show us the 'double bridge' – two narrow spans across the River Machno, a famous beauty spot in North Wales. However, it is illuminating in that the presence of the double bridge indicates a road or track. This is important, as access for his mobile darkroom was essential for Roger Fenton's practice as a landscape photographer in the 1850s. He was a pioneer of the wet collodion process (introduced in 1851), which required on-site processing of the glass negative. Many of Fenton's Welsh photographs feature bridges or were executed close to them. The demands of the wet collodion process – involving coating the negative shortly prior to exposure and developing it immediately afterwards – caused photographers to choose their motifs with a high degree of deliberation. As enlargement was, although feasible, impractical for the creation of high-quality, sharp and tonally rich exhibition prints, the camera itself was built on a grand scale, sufficient to house glass negatives of the same impressive size as this print.

The Machno valley is close to those of the Conwy and the Lledr. All are served by the resort town of Betws-y-Coed in what is now the Snowdonia National Park. The district provided a host of treasured motifs for watercolour artists in the first half of the nineteenth century. Among the most prominent are Samuel Palmer and David Cox. The former, as Malcolm Daniel has felicitously observed, executed *A Cascade in Shadow, Drawn on the Spot, near the Junction of the Machno and the Conway, North Wales* (1835-36; Malcolm Wiener Collection) (fig. 1).[1] This watercolour is close in composition as well as location to *Double Bridge on the Machno* and to another Fenton landscape from 1857, *Gorge of the Foss Nevin*, on the Conwy (National Media Museum, Bradford). It is well established that photographers placed their tripods on the sites previously occupied by painters' easels. Both sets of practitioners would have consulted the same guidebook to the area – Thomas Roscoe's *Wanderings and Excursions in North Wales*. Whereas the 1836 edition would have guided painters, the 1853 edition had a new clientele among photographers. Both editions carried engravings after drawings by George Cattermole, David Cox and Thomas Creswick. However, Fenton's image of the Machno is of another order. His photograph is remarkable for the intensity and vigour of its tonal structure. Where the sun illuminates the river bank in the upper part of the photograph, the foliage is a blaze of light. The sun's rays also burn out areas of the dramatically craggy rocks at the centre of the picture.

Roger Fenton, ***Double Bridge on the Machno*** (detail), cat. 188

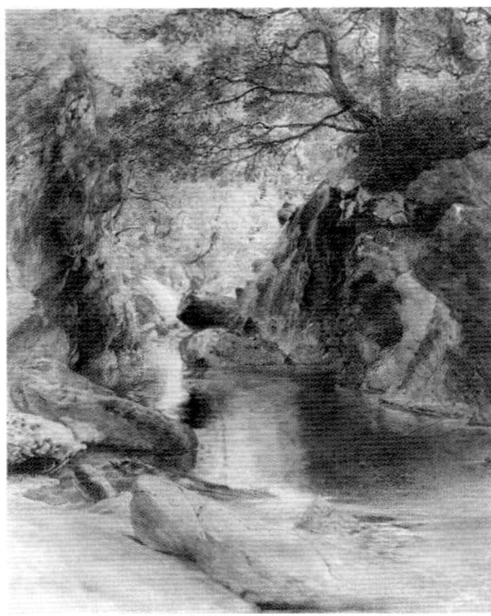

fig. 1
Samuel Palmer
A Cascade in Shadow, Drawn on the Spot, near the Junction of the Machno and Conway, North Wales, 1835 or 1836
Pencil, pen and brown ink, and watercolour, 46.4 x 37.5 cm
Private Collection, USA

There is a glittering ambiguity to much of the photograph. The dappled, lichen-patched rocks are at first solid, then dissolve into shapes impossible to read with exactness – and they also reappear in counterpoint as blurred reflections in the moving waters of the Machno. A black band of water across the base is echoed in the upper part of the composition by lunging tree branches, which cantilever from the right bank. Such vigorous tonal effects, plus emphatic abstract patterning, are characteristic of Fenton.

The photographs from Fenton's Welsh campaign met with critical acclaim when they were exhibited in 1858 at the annual exhibition of the Photographic Society of London at the South Kensington Museum (later renamed the Victoria and Albert). This was the first photographic exhibition presented in any museum in the world, and its layout was considered to have offered a new model of clarity. Nevertheless, the praise of the critics may have seemed hollow to such an ambitious and innovative photographic artist. For example, the *Journal of the Photographic Society* wrote that 'There is such an artistic feeling about the whole of these pictures ... that they cannot fail to strike the beholder as being something more than mere photographs,' while the *Photographic News* stated that Fenton 'has succeeded in giving such breadth to his landscape pictures, that one is at first almost inclined to look upon them as copies of pictures.'[2]

Fenton gave up photography and returned to law in 1862. It is hard not to read this as a sign that his high hopes for the new art of photography had finally been reduced to disappointment. The reassessment of his work by later generations parallels the fate of the most innovative – and in his time obscure – of Victorian poets, Gerard Manley Hopkins. Hopkins's poem *Pied Beauty*, which reconfigured the traditional sonnet form, was written in North Wales twenty years after Fenton's visit. Like the photograph, *Pied Beauty* celebrates 'dappled things' and 'All things counter, original, spare, strange'.

1. Daniel 2004, p. 44
2. Ibid., p. 46

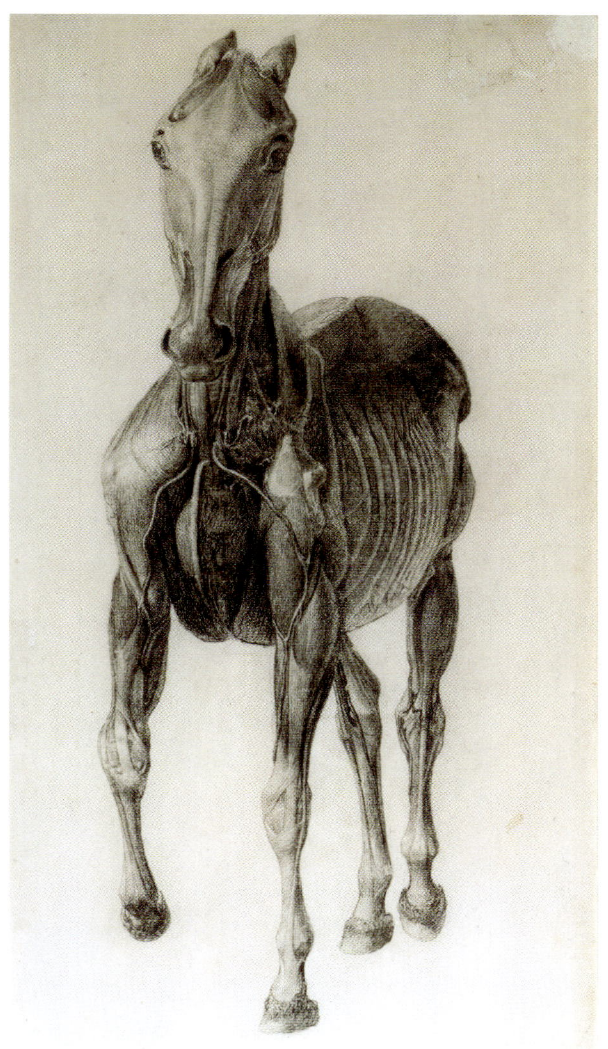

164

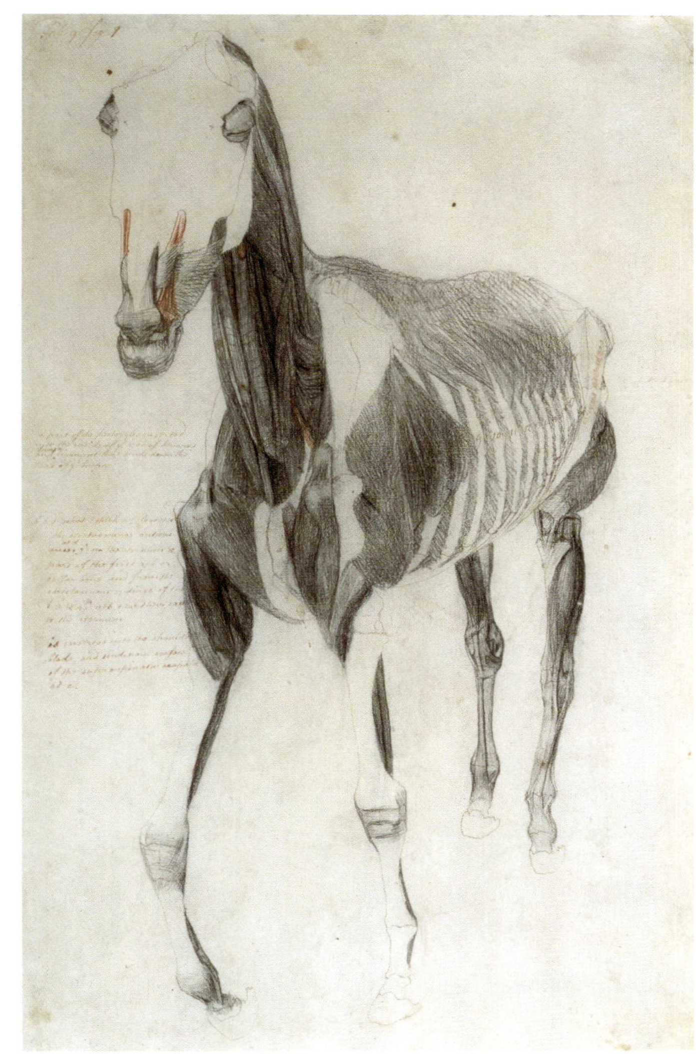

165

164. **George Stubbs**
Liverpool, 1724 - London, 1806
Finished study for 'The Eighth Anatomical Table of the Muscles ... of the Horse', 1756-58
Pencil and black chalk on paper, 35.5 x 18.4 cm
Royal Academy of Arts, London

165. **George Stubbs**
Liverpool, 1724 - London, 1806
Working drawing for 'The Ninth Anatomical Table of the Muscles ... of the Horse', 1756-58
Pencil, black and red chalk, [faded] red-brown ink on paper, 48 x 30.5 cm
Royal Academy of Arts, London

These are two of the forty-two surviving drawings made by Stubbs in preparation for his monumental treatise on equine anatomy, *The Anatomy of the Horse*, published in March 1766. Stubbs's intensive investigation of the equine form had been carried out over ten years earlier, from 1756 to 1758, in a remote farmhouse in the village of Horkstow, Lincolnshire. Over a period of eighteen months he personally dissected and drew the carcasses of horses, assisted by his companion, Mary Spencer. The task involved bleeding the horses to death, injecting their veins with melted wax and suspending the carcass from the ceiling with hooks. As Stubbs's obituarist recalled, 'He very frequently braved those dangers from putridity, &c. which would have appalled the most experienced practitioner.' (William Upcott, *Gentleman's Magazine*, no. 76 (October 1806), p. 979, cit. Warner and Blake 2006 pp. 2-3) The resulting drawings consisted of working studies and finished compositions, which were reproduced as etchings in his book, alongside a series of eighteen tables of the skeleton and muscles, and a 50,000 word commentary. Although Stubbs had hoped to employ others to engrave the illustrations for *The Anatomy of the Horse*, he was compelled to undertake them himself, underwriting the cost of the work through subscriptions. In addition to its appeal to artists and veterinarians, Stubbs stated in his preface that he hoped the book would be 'by no means unacceptable to those gentlemen who delight in horses, and who either breed or keep any considerable number of them'. The book proved to be a considerable critical success, and the drawings, even before its publication, helped to promote Stubbs's credentials as the leading equine artist of the period. (MP)

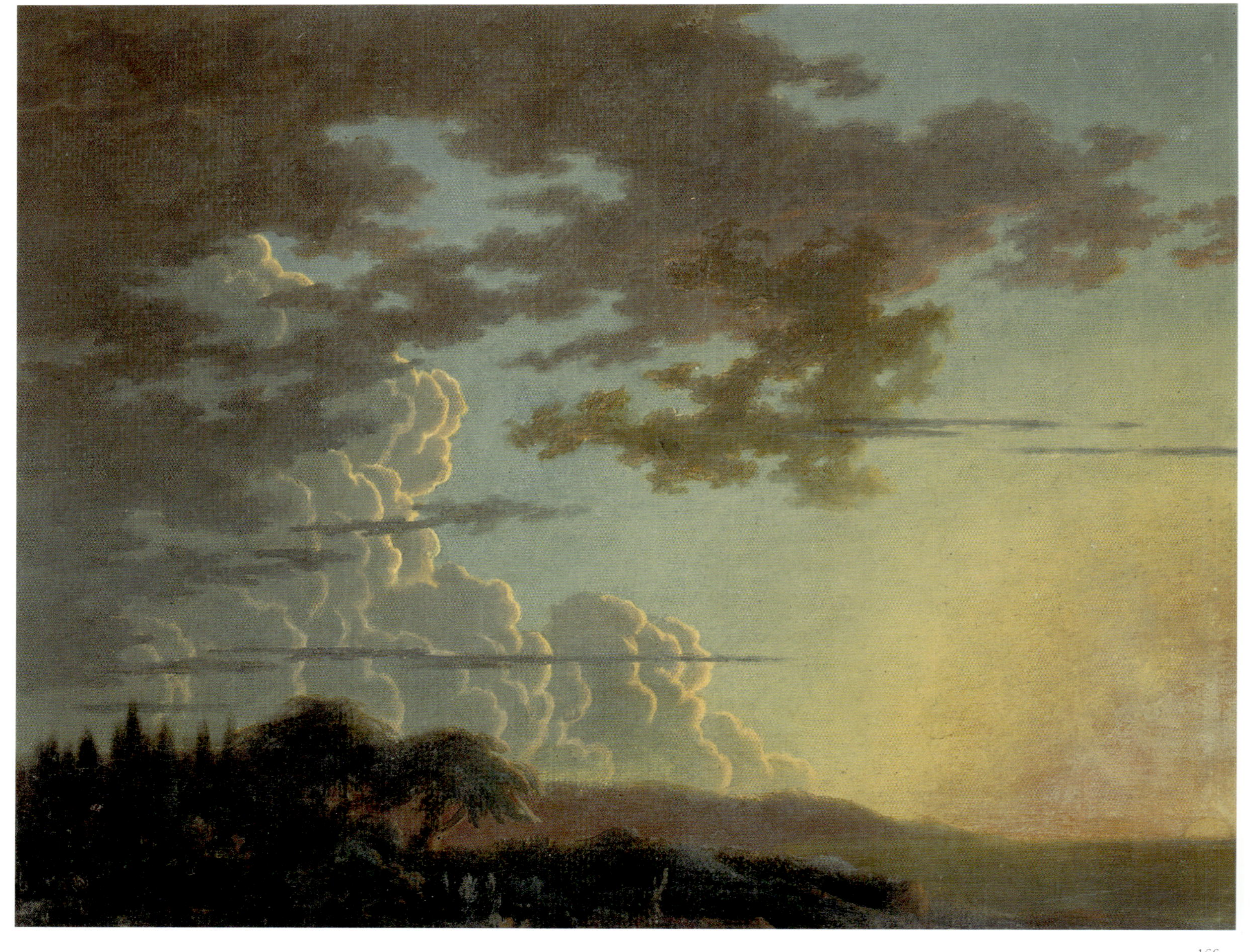

166

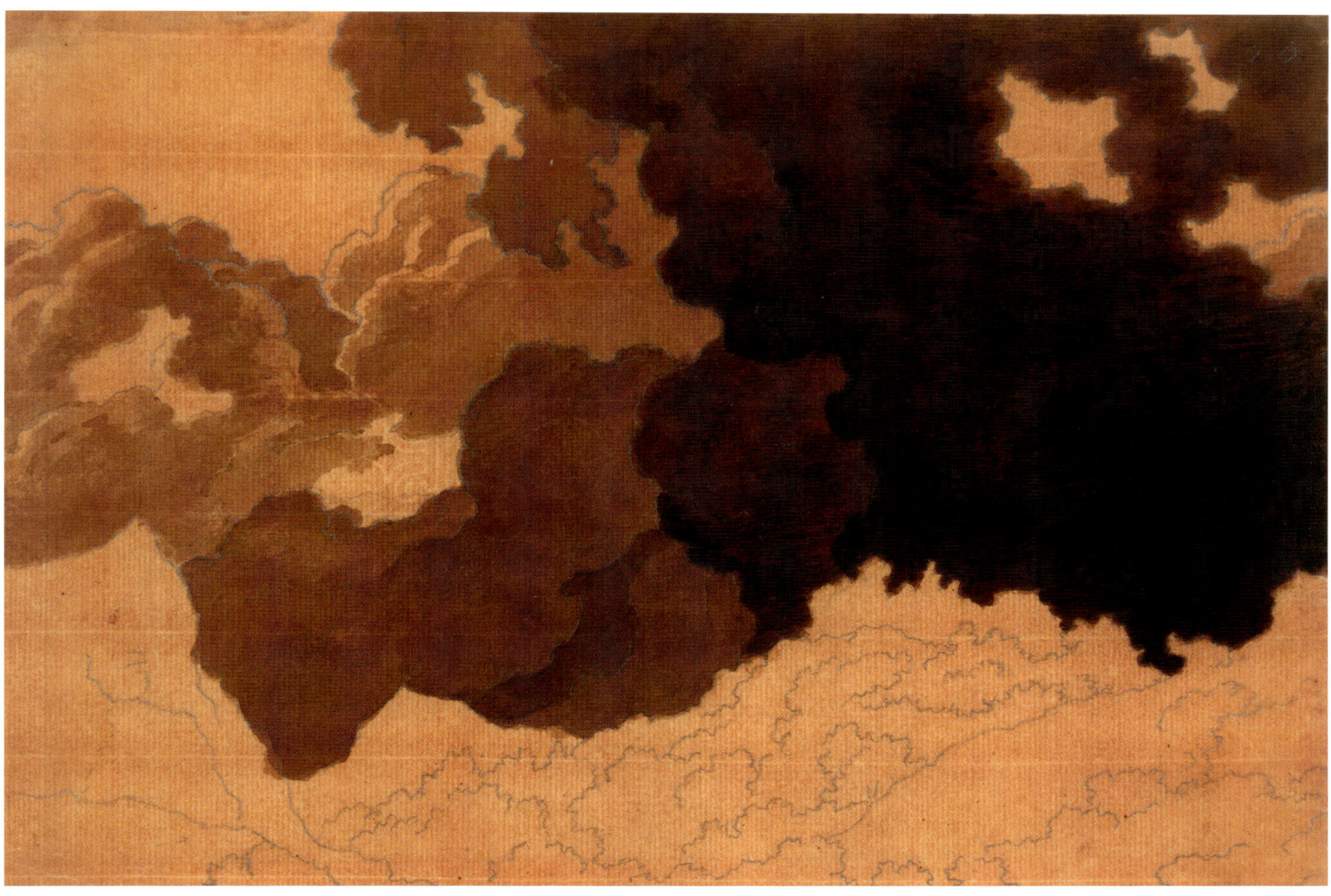

167

166. **Alexander Cozens**
St Petersburg [?], 1717 - London, 1786
Study of Sky No. 4 with Landscape,
from the ***Mackworth Praed Album***
Pencil and watercolour on paper, 22 x 31.5 cm
Tate, London, Purchased as part of the Oppé Collection
with assistance from the National Lottery through
the Heritage Lottery Fund 1996

167. **Alexander Cozens**
St Petersburg [?], 1717 - London, 1786
Setting Sun, c. 1770-73
Oil on paper, 24.2 x 30.8 cm
Whitworth Art Gallery, University of Manchester

These two studies relate to an innovative landscape system that Alexander Cozens was evolving during the 1760s and 1770s, entitled *The Various Species of Composition of Landscape, in Nature*. One of Cozens's most original contributions to British art, the treatise included a focus upon skies and cloud formations as a distinct category in their own right. More generally, Cozens also stressed his desire to arouse through the images a series of emotions, including silence, peace and even a sense of liberty, which could generate 'moral' landscapes. Never apparently published in its complete form, *The Various Species* consisted of 16 compositions, which Cozens reproduced as etchings. They included *The tops of hills, or mountains*, *A waterfall*, and *A spacious, or extensive landscape*. In addition, the system included 14 'Objects', such as 'Water', 'Ground, earth, or dry land', and 27 'Circumstances', including 'Dawn, 'sun rising', 'noon', and 'setting sun'. *Study of Sky No. 4 with Landscape* is one of a sequence of annotated pencil and monochrome wash studies of skies and clouds in the Mackworth Praed album at the Tate, relating to the various 'Circumstances' in Cozens's treatise - possibly number 25: 'The intermixture of the sky, or clouds, with the landscape'. *Setting Sun*, is one of a small series of finished oil-on-paper studies which also relate to *The Various Species*, and it may also possibly be the work entitled 'A Setting Sun' that Cozens exhibited at the Royal Academy in 1775. In the treatise it would appear to illustrate Composition 1, 'The Edge of a hill or Mountain near the Eye'; Object 3, 'Woodland or shrubby'; and Circumstance 7, 'Setting sun'. Despite its fragmentary nature, *The Various Species* influenced a number of later landscape artists, including John Constable, who made pen, ink and wash copies of Cozens's sixteen 'Composition' etchings complete with captions (Tate, London). (MP)

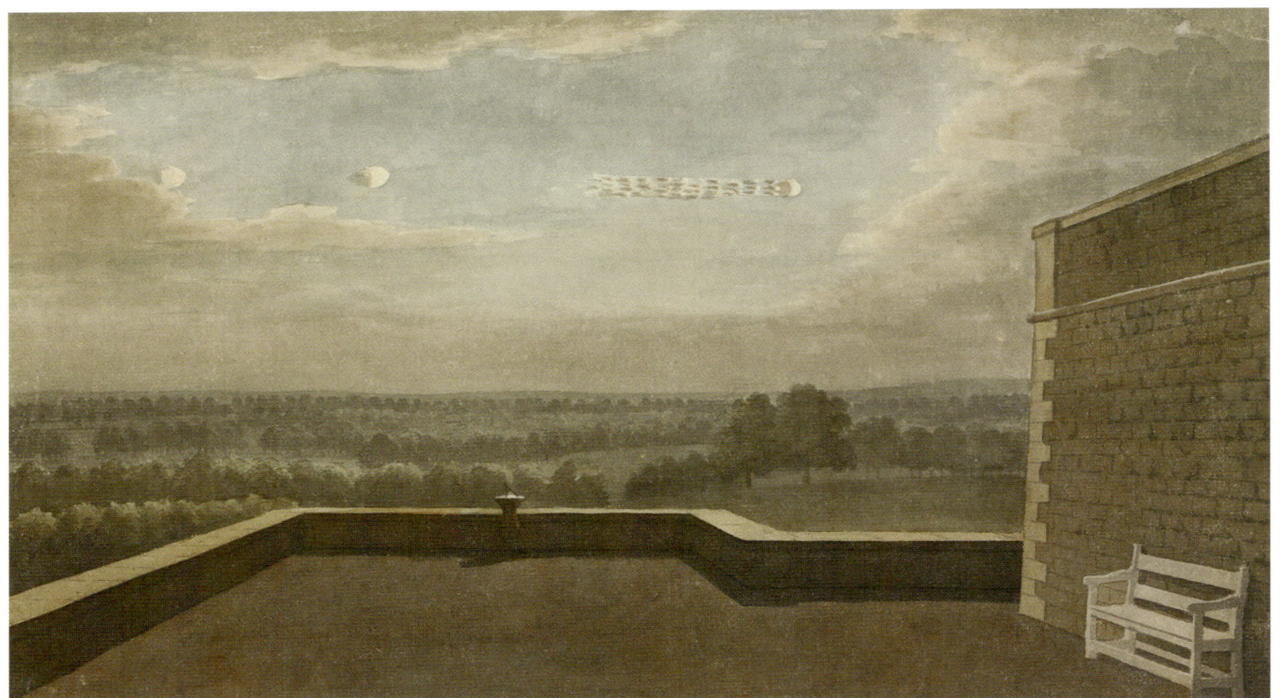

168

168. **Thomas Sandby**
Nottingham, 1723 - Windsor, 1798
and **Paul Sandby**
Nottingham, 1731 - London, 1809
The Meteor of 18 August 1783 from the East Angle of the North Terrace at Windsor Castle, 1783
Watercolour on paper, 28.5 x 46 cm
Bottom centre: Windsor Terrace
Bottom right: by Paul Sandby [inscribed by William Sandby]
British Museum, London

This is one of four watercolours made by Thomas Sandby, in collaboration with his brother. Paul, for an aquatint print published in October 1783 and dedicated to Sir Joseph Banks, President of the Royal Society. The watercolour (inscribed 'by Paul Sandby') is based upon first-hand observation of a spectacular meteor on the evening of 18 August 1783 by Thomas Sandby, together with the scientist Dr Tiberius Cavallo, Dr James Lind, and several others on the terrace of Windsor Castle. The sighting of the meteor, which took place at around 9:30 pm and lasted some twenty seconds, was recorded meticulously by Cavallo. His description of the three stages of the meteor is reflected in the watercolour, where it appears first at the left, as it emerged from cloud cover; at the centre, when it became elongated; and to the right, when it began to disintegrate. Other watercolours in the series, as well as the published aquatint, also include the group of observers on the terrace of Windsor Castle. (MP)

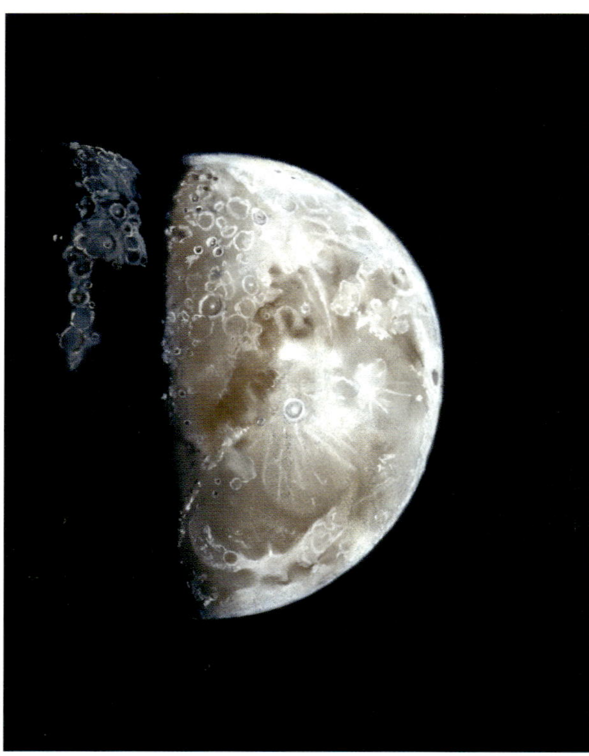

169

169. **John Russell**
Guildford, Surrey, 1745 - Kingston-upon-Hull, Humberside, 1806
Telescopic Study of the Moon, 1796
Pastel on paper, mounted on cardboard, 46 x 61 cm
Science Museum, London

John Russell, who earned his living as a professional society portrait painter, was also a pioneer of modern lunar mapping. Around 1764, Russell first observed the moon through a telescope in the garden of the sculptor John Bacon. In 1785, using his own telescopes, he began to make a series of accurate lunar observations, which culminated in 1795 in a large pastel drawing of the moon (Museum of the History of Science, Oxford). Interest in the drawing led Russell to produce a lunar globe, or 'Selenographia'. Although his role in the evolution of astronomical studies remains undervalued, during his lifetime

Russell was encouraged by leading scientists, including the President of the Royal Society, Sir Joseph Banks, Sir William Herschel and Nevil Maskelyne. Following Russell's death in 1806, two engraved moon maps, the 'Lunar Planispheres', were printed by his son. Although, Russell's portrait career brought him considerable financial success, his lunar observations - which earned him no income - were, arguably, his most significant contribution to British visual culture. (MP)

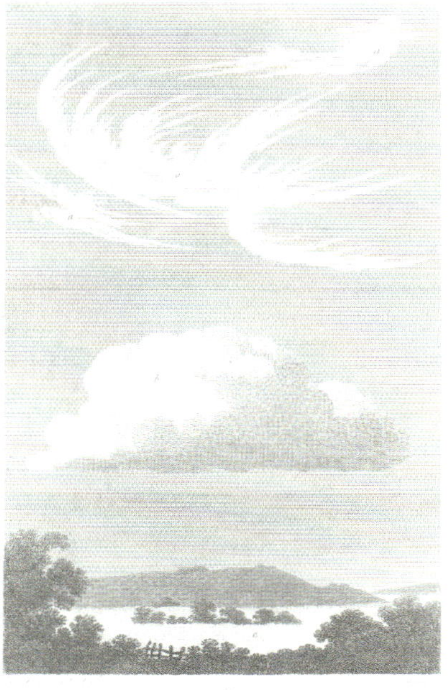

170

170. **Luke Howard**
London, 1772 - London, 1864
On the Modification of Clouds,
in ***Philosophical Magazine*** (vol. XVI), London 1803
Book, 22 x 14 cm
Departmentbibliothek Physik,
Universität Hamburg / MIN-Fakultät

171. **Thomas Forster**
London, 1789 - Brussels, 1860
Researches About Atmospheric Phaenomena
(third edition), 1823
Book published by Harding, Mavor and Lepard, London,
29 x 13.7 cm
a. Yale Center for British Art, Paul Mellon Collection, New Haven
b. Koninklijke Sterrenwacht van België, Brussels

In the eighteenth and nineteenth centuries meteorology was the perfect ground for a meeting of minds between scientists and artists - both engaged in the observation of nature. The cloud types of Alexander Cozens (cat. 116) were conceived from the perspective of art, but they are nevertheless evidence of an interest in the variety of cloud formations. In 1803 Luke Howard published a classification of cloud types, the names of which are still in use. Howard presented his meteorological observations to the scientific association in London to which he belonged, and his lecture was published in the *Philosophical Magazine*, in which Cornelius Varley (see cat. 172) also published meteorological studies (Klonk 1996, pp. 126-27). In 1818 Howard wrote a second book, *The Climate of London*. Howard's first study also appeared in German and inspired Goethe, who not only dedicated a poem to Howard but also applied his system to his own scientific observations.

Forster's book was partly based on Howard's classifications and was aimed at a broad public with an interest in climatological conditions (entry by John Thornes in Morris 2000, p. 123). John Constable, who had also copied Cozens's cloud types, owned a copy of Forster's book. (RH)

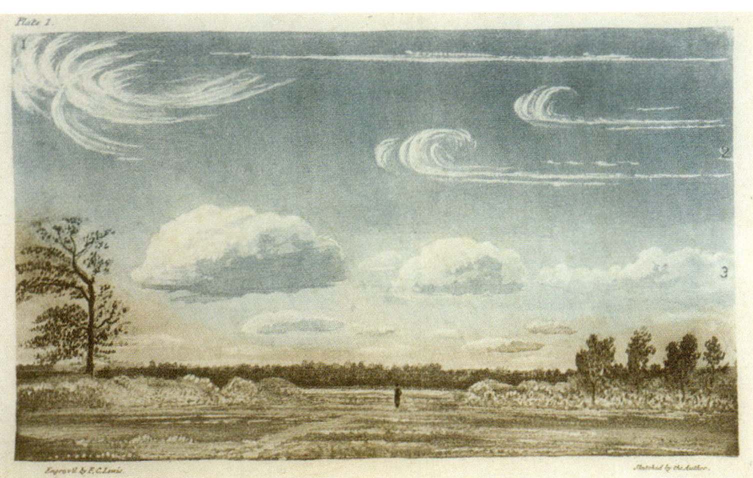

171

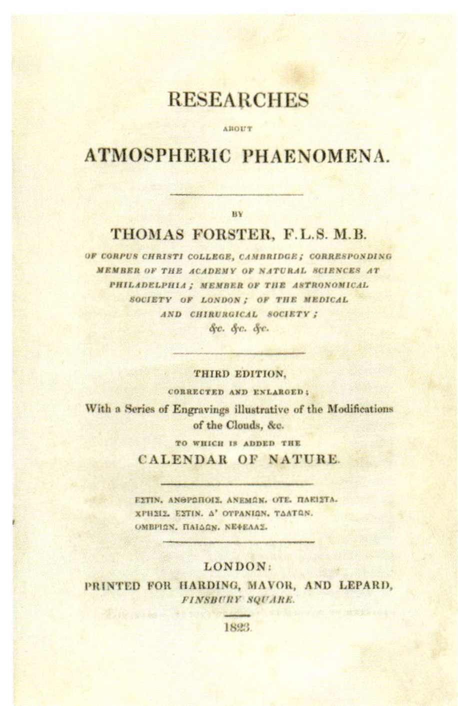

RESEARCHES
ABOUT
ATMOSPHERIC PHAENOMENA.

BY
THOMAS FORSTER, F.L.S. M.B.
OF CORPUS CHRISTI COLLEGE, CAMBRIDGE; CORRESPONDING MEMBER OF THE ACADEMY OF NATURAL SCIENCES AT PHILADELPHIA; MEMBER OF THE ASTRONOMICAL SOCIETY OF LONDON; OF THE MEDICAL AND CHIRURGICAL SOCIETY;
&c. &c. &c.

THIRD EDITION,
CORRECTED AND ENLARGED;
With a Series of Engravings illustrative of the Modifications of the Clouds, &c.
TO WHICH IS ADDED THE
CALENDAR OF NATURE.

ΕΣΤΙΝ. ΑΝΘΡΩΠΟΙΣ. ΑΝΕΜΩΝ. ΟΤΕ. ΠΛΕΙΣΤΑ.
ΧΡΗΣΙΣ. ΕΣΤΙΝ. Δ' ΟΥΡΑΝΙΩΝ. ΥΔΑΤΩΝ.
ΟΜΒΡΙΩΝ. ΠΑΙΔΩΝ. ΝΕΦΕΛΑΣ.

LONDON:
PRINTED FOR HARDING, MAVOR, AND LEPARD,
FINSBURY SQUARE.
1823.

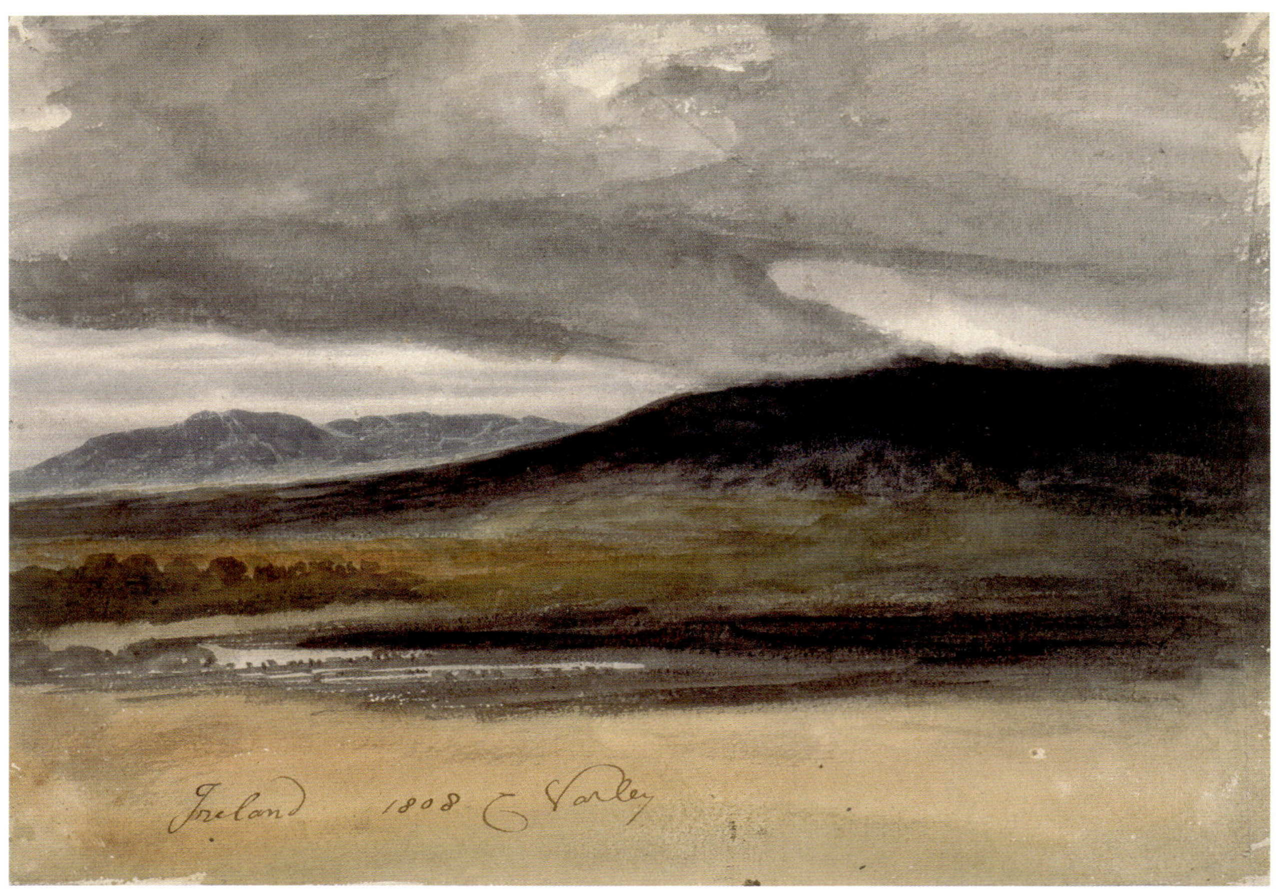

172

172. **Cornelius Varley**
London, 1781 - London, 1873
Mountainous Landscape, Ireland, 1808
Watercolour on paper, 19.3 x 26.9 cm
Bottom left to center: Ireland 1808 C Varley
Whitworth Art Gallery, University of Manchester

Together with his better-known brother John, Cornelius Varley was a founder member of the Society of Painters in Water-Colour in 1805. However, Cornelius was a less prolific contributor to the Society's annual exhibitions in London than John, and he was also to prove less interested than his brother in pursuing an artistic career. In fact, in later years Cornelius Varley was to develop a significant professional reputation as a scientist and inventor.

Varley's most prolific period as a watercolourist was in the years 1800-25. During this time, most of his fellow members of the Water-Colour Society, including his brother John, were tending to produce rather elaborate, ambitious watercolours for exhibition as part of their shared mission to raise the status of watercolour so that it could be seen to compete with oil painting. By contrast, most of the work that Cornelius produced during these years was in the form of freely executed, unfinished watercolour sketches or pencil drawings that combine a sense of careful observation with intensity of feeling.

Indeed, especially in his early career, Cornelius Varley seems to have been strongly influenced by Thomas Girtin's habit of sketching outdoors in all weathers, often for hours at a time, so that - as Varley himself recorded of Girtin's practice - he could 'observe the effect of storms and clouds upon the atmosphere' (Pidgley 1972, p. 781 n. 4). He himself made many sketches of cloud formations and rapidly changing weather effects, especially when travelling in the mountainous regions of Wales in 1802, 1803 and 1805. This atmospheric watercolour was made in 1808, when Varley visited Ireland at the invitation of Lady Olivia Sparrow. As well as spending about six months in the vicinity of Armagh in the north of the country, he also travelled extensively in southern Ireland. The exact location of this view is not known. (AL)

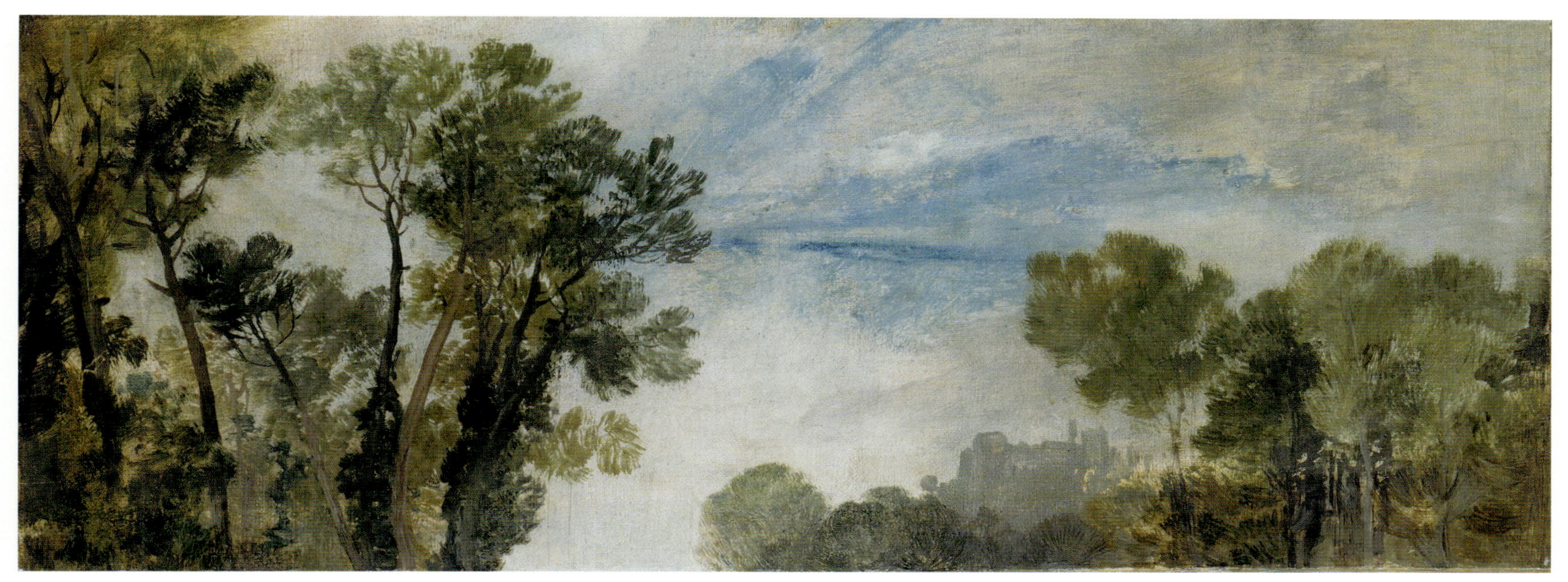

173

173. **Joseph Mallord William Turner**
London, 1775 - London, 1851
Tree Tops and Sky, Guildford Castle [?], Evening, 1805
Oil on mahogany veneer, 27.6 x 73.7 cm
Tate, London, Bequeathed by the artist 1856

The Barbizon School and the Impressionists are often credited with being the first to work out of doors directly from nature, although in fact many other artists had painted *en plein air* across the centuries. Turner's preferred method of work was to sketch on the spot and refer back to his drawings when painting in the studio. On several occasions, however, he is known to ventured outside with his oil paints. In 1805 he undertook a sketching campaign along the course of the River Thames and its tributary, the River Wey, working from a boat and painting directly onto mahogany panels. He focused on the lush, green landscape of his native countryside and the changeable weather effects of a typical English summer. In this bravura study from the series, Turner has outlined the distant silhouette of Guildford Castle [?], but the main focus is undoubtedly the panoramic stretch of sky with its brilliant patch of blue clearing amidst the clouds. (NM)

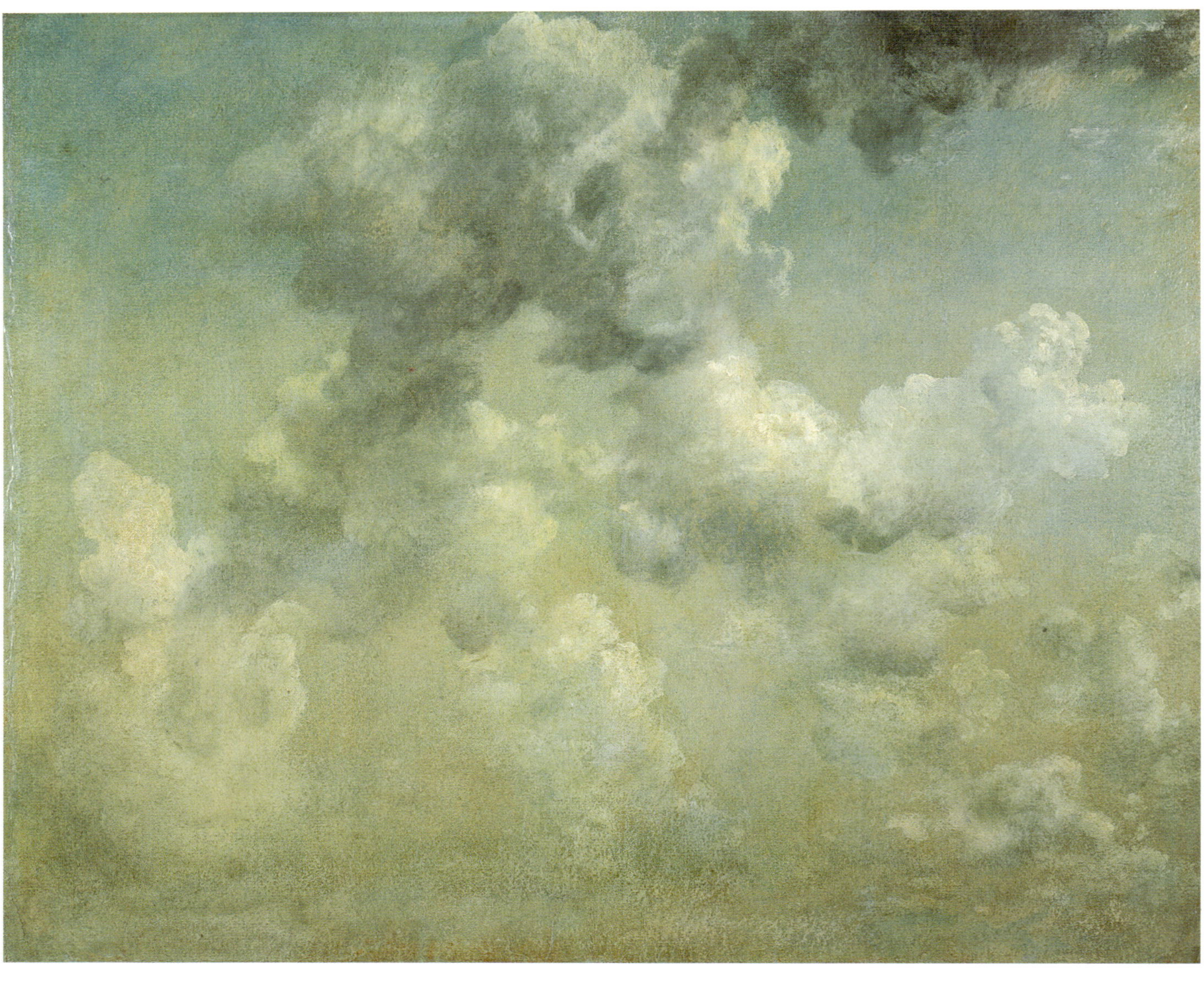

174

174. **John Constable**
East Bergholt, Suffolk, 1776 - London, 1837
Cloud study, 1822
Oil on paper, mounted on canvas, 48 x 59 cm
Verso: 31st Sepr 10-11 o'clock morning looking
Eastward a gentle wind to East
Ashmolean Museum, Oxford, presented by
Sir E. Farquhar Buzzard, Bt, 1933

Constable's cloud studies are perhaps the best illustration of his scientific view of nature, which he formulated in a lecture as follows: 'Painting is a science, and should be pursued as an inquiry into the laws of nature. Why, then, may not landscape be considered as a branch of natural philosophy, of which the pictures are but the experiments?' (Beckett 1970, p. 69). Many of Constable's early oil sketches contain cloud studies, but it was only from around 1820 that the artist began to study clouds systematically. From the elevated vantage point of the Heath in Hampstead, the village to the north of London where he spent his summers, he sketched dozens of cloudy skies above the distant horizon, or above the tops of shrubs and trees (cat. 176, 183). In addition, he sketched a series of independent cloud studies in 1820-22. On the reverse of these studies he often noted detailed information concerning the time and weather conditions under which the work was painted. Although these studies for the most part capture fleeting appearances, most of them are carefully executed and some, like this study, have the presence of a finished painting.

Constable's interest in clouds can be associated with the developing science of meteorology (see cat. 170-171). For the painter, however, the cloudy sky was also a means of expression, a part of the composition that he found particularly important: 'Certainly if the Sky is *obtrusive* - (as mine are) it is bad, but if they are *evaded* (as mine are not) it is worse, they must and always shall with me make an effectual part of the composition. It will be difficult to name a class of Landscape, in which the sky is not the *"key note"*, the *standard of "Scale"*, and the chief *"Organ of sentiment"*.' (Beckett 1962-68, vol. 6, p. 77) (RH)

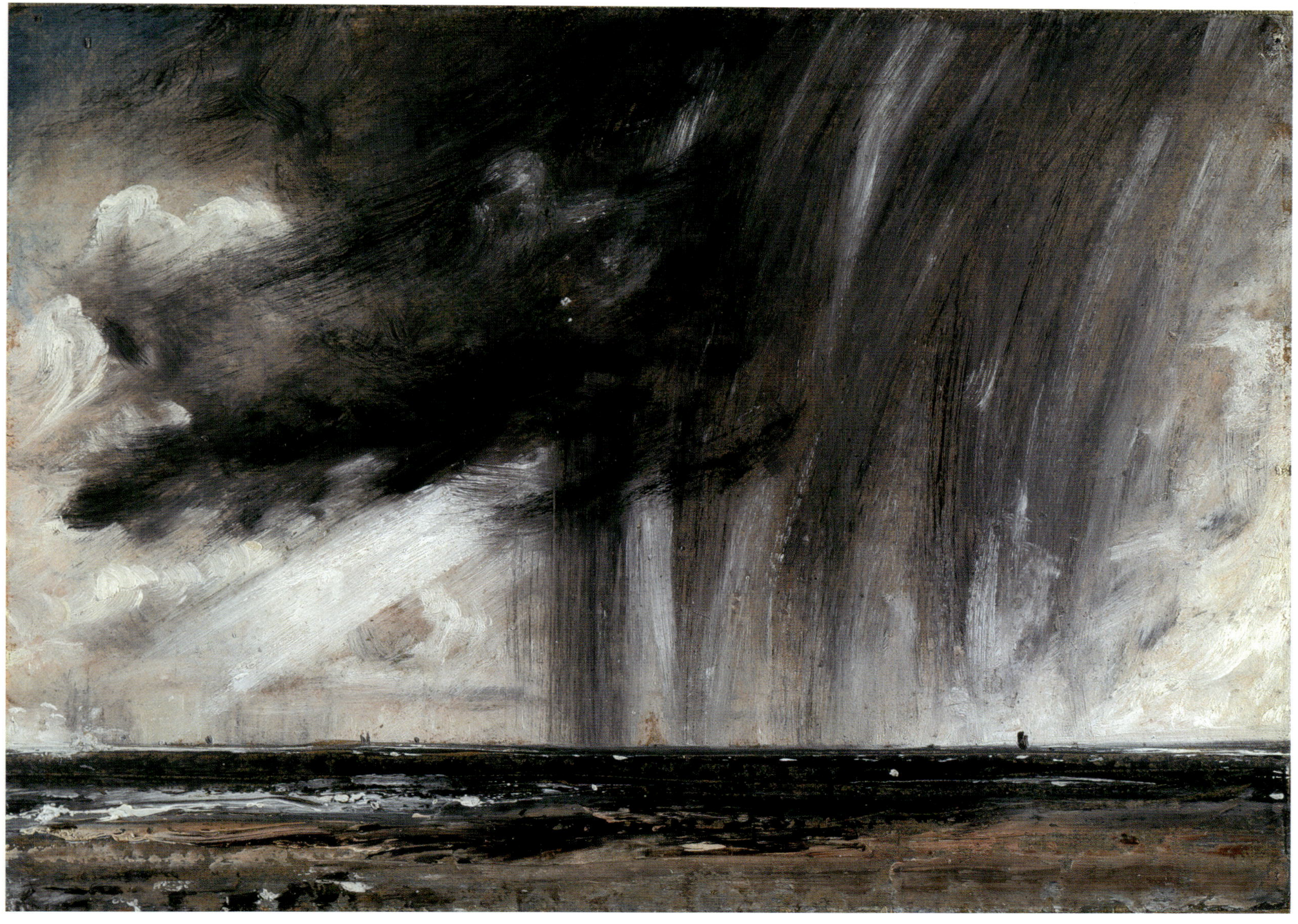

175

175. **John Constable**
East Bergholt, Suffolk, 1776 - London, 1837
Rainstorm over the Sea, c. 1824-28
Oil on paper, mounted on canvas, 23.5 x 32.6 cm
Royal Academy of Arts, London

From 1824 onwards Constable stayed in Brighton on several occasions for the sake of his wife's health (she was to die in 1828 of tuberculosis). This bustling seaside resort did not really interest him, although it did inspire him to make one large painting (Tate, London), exhibited in 1827. He painted several oil studies of the beach, sea and, especially, the cloudy sky, which are among his best works. Some are particularly subtle in their depiction of static effects of colour and light above a calm sea. Others, like this work, are impetuously drawn observations of sombre atmospheric effects.

Like the studies Constable painted in Hampstead in the 1820s (cat. 183-184), these sketches have little to do with the artist's studio production. Each one is an independent painting on a small scale. The emotional quality of *Rainstorm over the Sea* is characteristic of Constable's later work, in which the romantic experience of nature is tinged with pessimism. (RH)

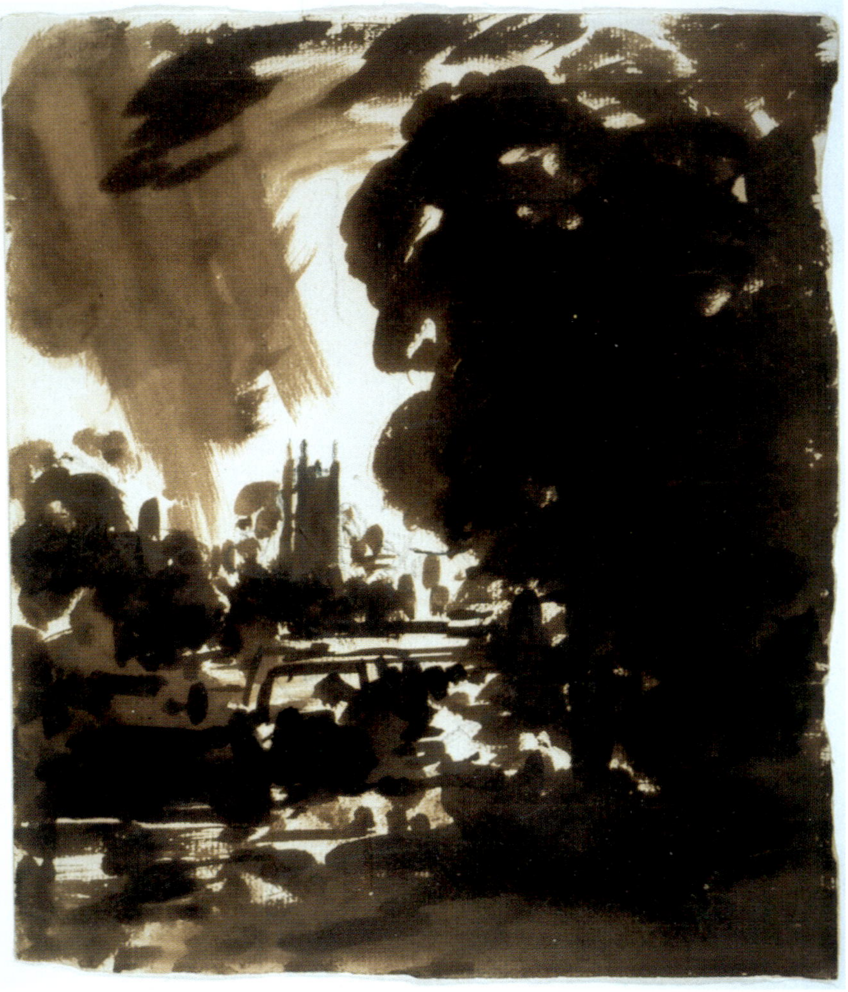

177

176. **John Constable**
East Bergholt, Suffolk, 1776 - London, 1837
Trees, Sky and a Red House (page from a sketchbook), c. 1821
Pencil and watercolour on paper, 15.2 x 25.4 cm
Victoria and Albert Museum, London,
Given by Isabel Constable, daughter of the artist

Constable used the medium of watercolour principally at the beginning of his career. Later, he employed it sporadically, but in the 1830s he painted with watercolours more and more frequently. This work belongs to the group of tree and cloud studies made in Hampstead around 1820-22, most of which were executed in oil (cat. 183). The study was originally part of a sketchbook. (RH)

177. **John Constable**
East Bergholt, Suffolk, 1776 - London, 1837
View on the Stour: the Church of Dedham in the Distance, c. 1836
Pencil and sepia wash on paper, 20.3 x 16.9 cm
Victoria and Albert Museum, London,
Given by Isabel Constable, daughter of the artist

Constable's later work often has a dramatic and informal character, and some of his drawings of the 1830s are made up of improvisational lines. In his late oil sketches, Constable sometimes used paint in an extremely sketchy, chaotic manner, usually applying it with a palette knife. His later work also includes several sketches in brown ink, like the present work, in which Constable gives the suggestion of a landscape near the Stour with the church of Dedham in the background. These monochrome sketches recall the blot drawings of Alexander Cozens (cat. 117), and they are certainly also related to the fact that the artist was engaged in the translation of his work into graphic techniques at the time. In 1830-32, he had twenty-two works made into an album of mezzotints by an assistant, David Lucas. There are also several expressive pen-and-ink sketches for a print in a Shakespeare album (Fleming-Williams 1990, pp. 276-309). In all of these later drawings, sketches and paintings, Constable is more concerned with the expression of feeling than with observation. This work shows his instinctive approach, in which the 'chiaroscuro of nature', as Constable often called it, has become the main subject. In the final analysis, these works are not far removed from the poetic black-and-white landscapes of Samuel Palmer (see cat. 254). (RH)

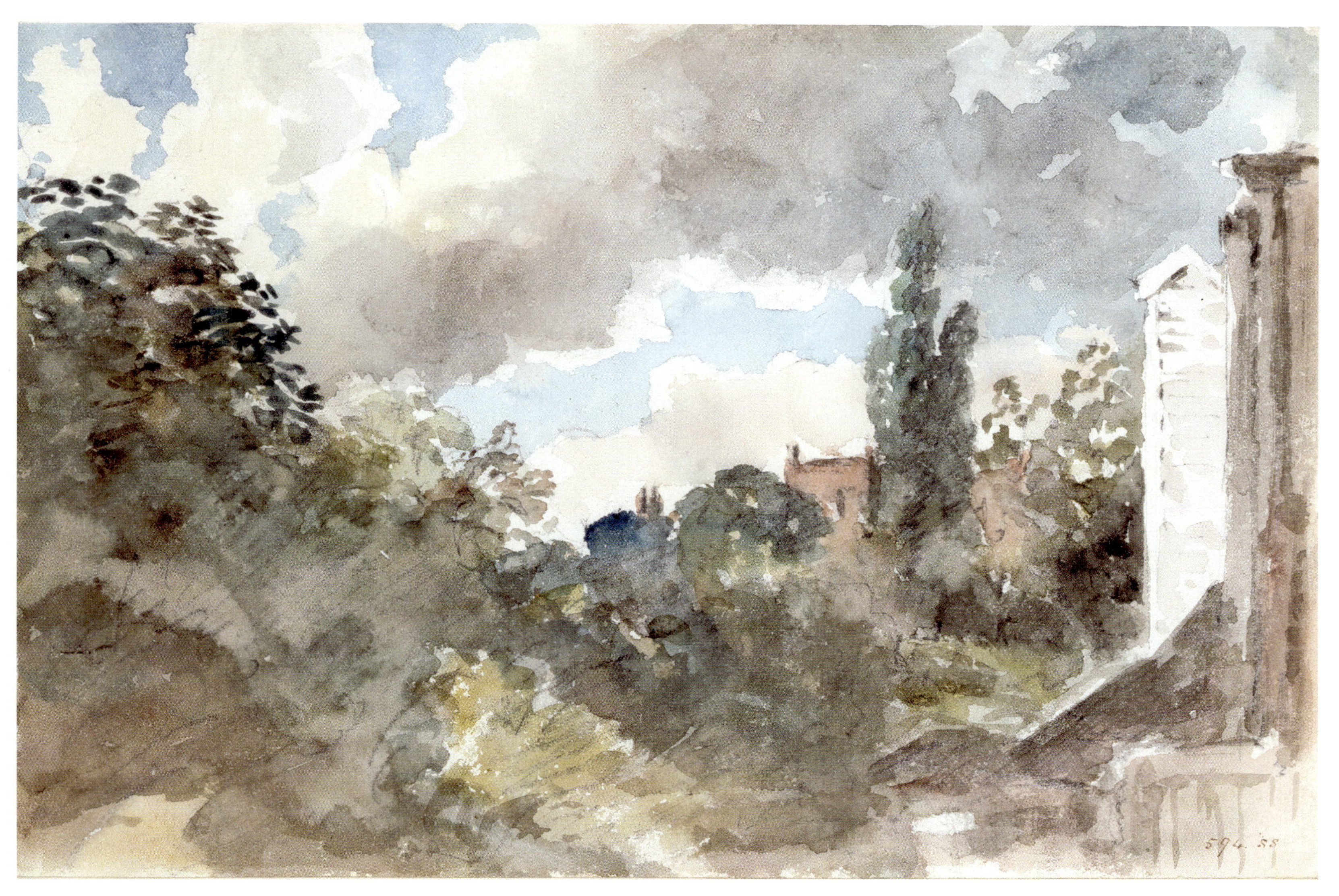

176

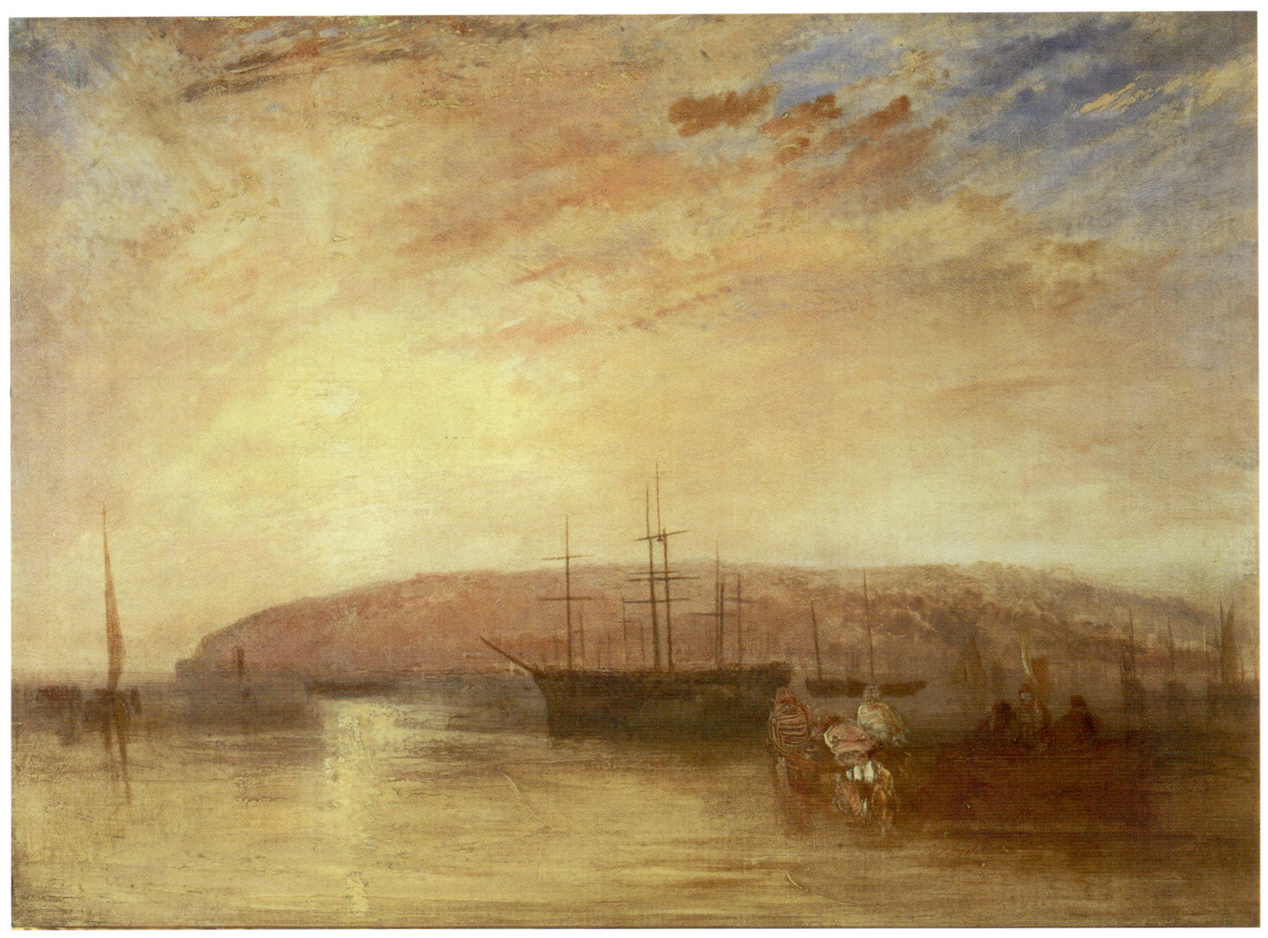

178

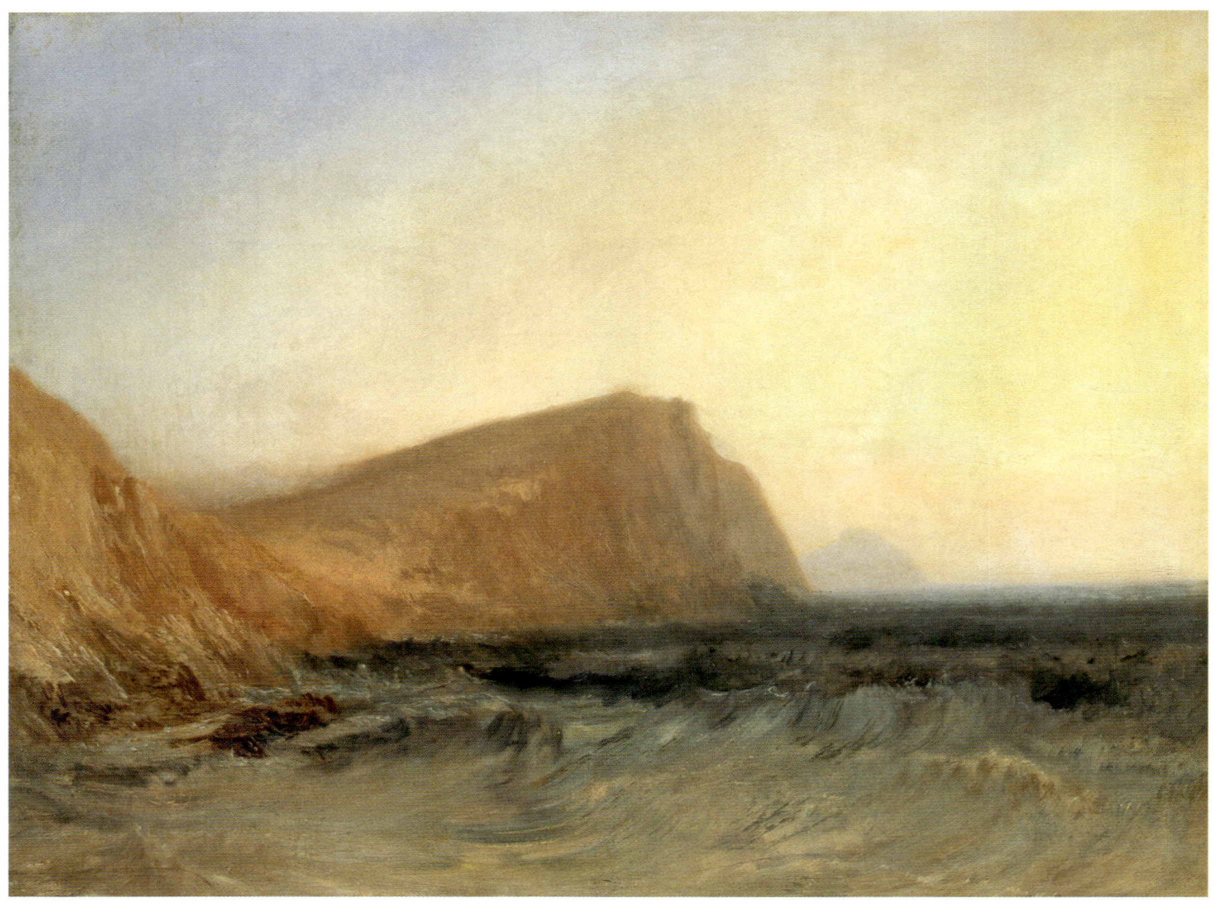

179

178. **Joseph Mallord William Turner**
London, 1775 - London, 1851
Shipping off East Cowes Headland (Isle of Wight), 1827
Oil on canvas, 46 x 60.3 cm
Tate, London, Bequeathed by the artist 1856

179. **Joseph Mallord William Turner**
London, 1775 - London, 1851
Rocky Coast, c. 1825-30
Oil on canvas, 50.2 x 65.7 cm
Tate, London, Bequeathed by the artist 1856

Unlike Constable and several of his peers, Turner only rarely worked in oils *en plein air*, preferring instead to digest his chosen subjects in a more omnivorous way through making multiple pencil sketches. He famously said that he was able to record fifteen or sixteen outlines in the time it would take to produce a coloured sketch.

One of the few instances of him working in colour directly from nature relates to the visit he made to the Isle of Wight in the summer of 1827. He was then the guest of the architect John Nash, whose Neo-Gothic home, East Cowes Castle, appears incidentally in the two oil paintings Turner exhibited at the Royal Academy the following year (Indianapolis Museum of Art; Victoria and Albert Museum; see cat. 257 and essay pp. 317-21). Those pictures were developed from a series of preliminary studies that Turner apparently painted across some large pieces of canvas while actually on board a ship anchored off the island during the Cowes Regatta. The canvases were only rediscovered and cut into individual images at the beginning of the twentieth century.

Shipping off East Cowes Headland was among this cache of works, revealed to the public for the first time in 1906. The essence of the topographical setting is readily identifiable, but Turner was far more intent on recording the glowing radiance of the rising sun, its reflection forming a path across the water below. The similar dimensions of the *Rocky Coast* canvas suggest it is possibly its pendant, and was prepared during the same visit. It seems likely to be another sunrise study, showing the cliffs on the southern coast of the Isle of Wight. (IW)

180. **Joseph Mallord William Turner**
London, 1775 - London, 1851
Junction of the Severn and the Wye (also known as ***Landscape with a River and a Bay in the Distance***), c. 1845
Oil on canvas, 94 x 124 cm
Musée du Louvre, Département des Peintures, Paris

This picture was among the first of Turner's unfinished canvases to be shown in a public exhibition. Unlike the majority of works of this type, which remained in the Turner Bequest, unseen in Britain until 1906, it had entered the collection of Camille Groult in Paris by 1890, where it was admired by Symbolists and Post-Impressionists alike. An entry in Goncourt's *Journal* even claimed that it surpassed 'the originality of Monet'.

It is significant, however, that the painting's initial viewers did not necessarily recognize that it was an incomplete work, arrested at an intermediate stage. The design is based on one of the *Liber Studiorum* mezzotints, dating from 1811, showing the celebrated Picturesque view over the Severn Estuary. In the mid-1840s Turner reworked ten images from this series, as if emphasizing the enduring significance for him of the Claudian prototype that underlies so many of his mature paintings. Had the picture been exhibited in his lifetime, he would probably have added detail and introduced contrasts to his broad atmospheric areas of colour. (IW)

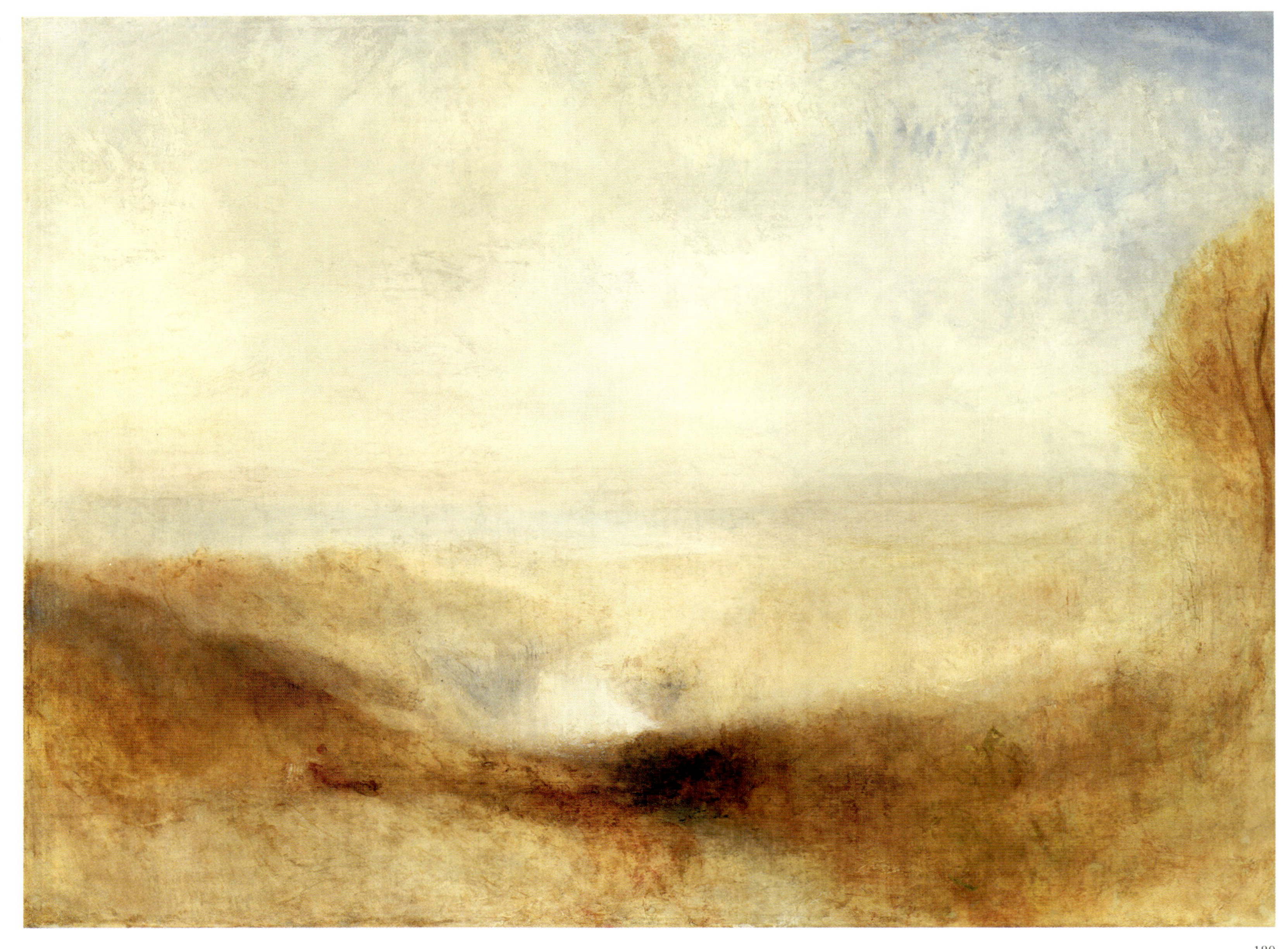

180

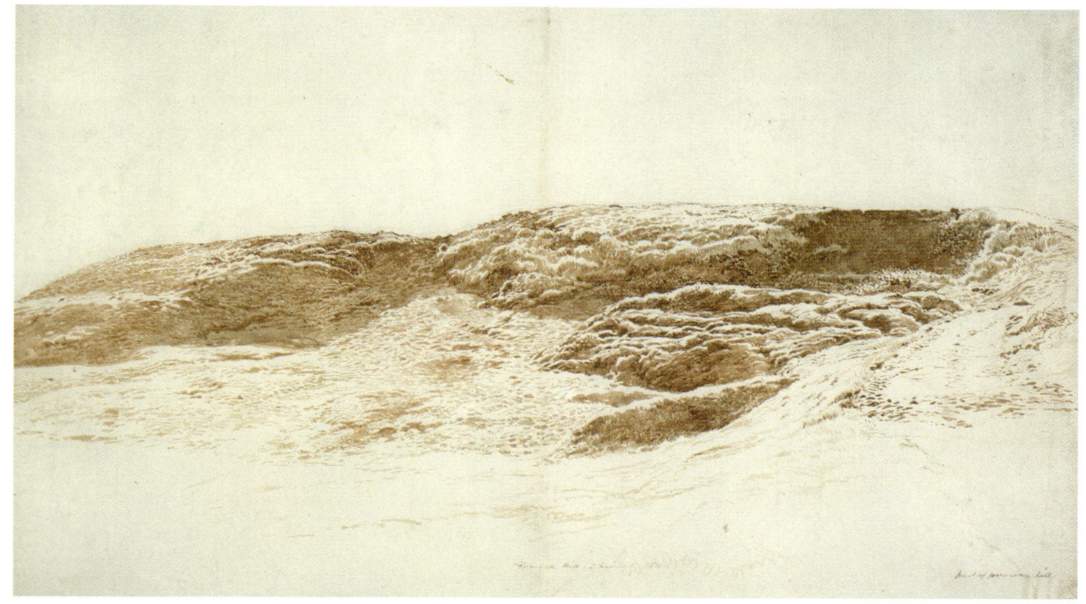

181

181. ***John Linnell***
London, 1792 - Redhill, Surrey, 1882
Primrose Hill, 1811
Watercolour with pen and brown ink and white chalk on paper, 39.7 x 66.7 cm
Bottom centre: Primrose Hill . J Linnell 1811 .
Bottom right: part of primrose hill
Lent by the Syndics of the Fitzwilliam Museum, Cambridge

Apart from Turner, John Linnell was the most successful British landscapist of the nineteenth century. His career began early, and this precocious drawing was done while he was still a student at the Royal Academy. Yet he was never elected to that institution, and his closest friendships were with the radically anti-establishment artists William Blake and Samuel Palmer, the second of whom became his son-in-law (see Linnell 1994). This abbreviated but intensely observed study of a stretch of heathland in London (still a park) exemplifies his idea of 'carefully copying all the beautiful varieties of tint and texture' in nature (J. Linnell, *Autobiographical Notes,* cit. Crouan 1982), and indicates why, forty years later, he became an early supporter of the Pre-Raphaelite Brotherhood. (JG)

182. **Cornelius Varley**
London, 1781 - London, 1873
Study of a Barge on a Shore, c. 1811-23
Pencil and watercolour on paper, 17.6 x 32.5 cm
Top left: 6 / Patent Graphic Telescope [partially trimmed]
British Museum, London

From the age of twelve, Varley was brought up by his uncle, Samuel Varley, a watch and instrument maker and amateur scientist. Cornelius himself became an inventor of lenses, microscopes and other scientific instruments, the best known of these being the Graphic Telescope, which he patented in 1811.

The 'Patent Graphic Telescope' was a drawing aid which, like the camera lucida, could be used in the open air. By means of a simple inverting telescope and a series of reflecting mirrors, it enabled the user to project onto paper an erect reduced image of an object or scene that could then be traced by hand. Varley used the telescope for drawing landscapes, portraits, buildings and other objects such as shipping and plants. Drawings made by Varley with the telescope are usually inscribed, as in this example, with the words 'Patent Graphic Telescope' (or 'PGT'), and sometimes they also carry a number (in this case '6'), which indicates the power of magnification he used to make that particular drawing (Pidgley 1972, pp. 782-85).

Varley made studies of boats and shipping throughout his life. Some of them were drawn on the edge of the River Thames, which may well be the location shown here. In 1809, together with his brother John, Cornelius published a series of etchings and lithographs of *Shipping, Barges, Fishing Boats*, which were influential on John Sell Cotman (cat. 133). (AL)

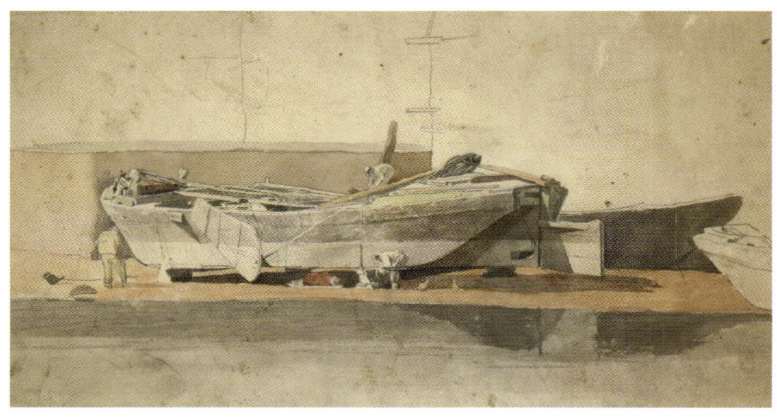

182

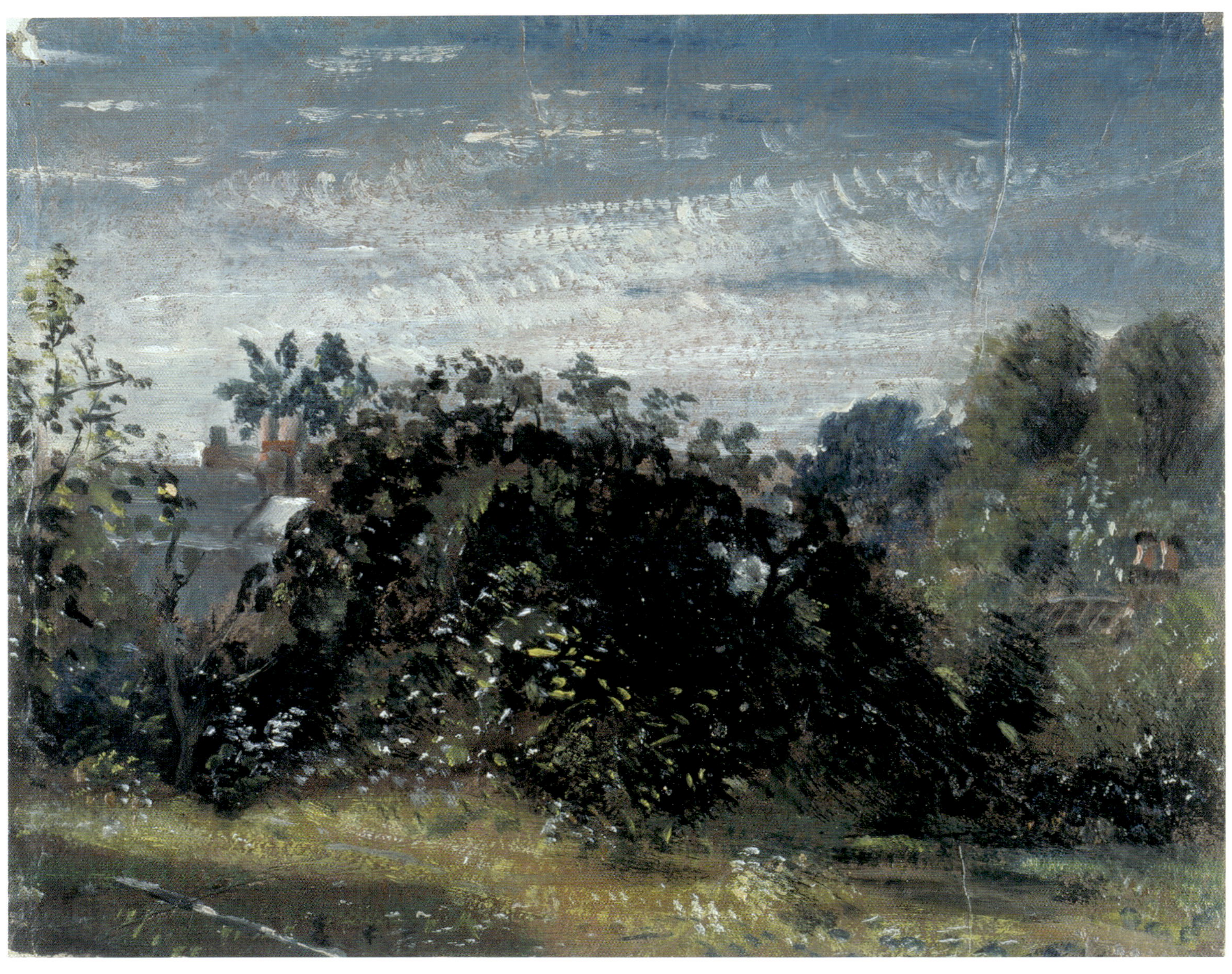

183

183. **John Constable**
East Bergholt, Suffolk, 1776 – London, 1837
Study of Sky and Trees at Hampstead, 1821
Oil on paper, 22.9 x 27.9 cm
Verso: Ocr. 2d. 1821. 8. to 9. very fine still morning. turned out a may day. Rode with Revd. Dr. White. round by Highgate. Muswell Hill. Coney Hatch. Finchley. by Hendon Home
Verso: JC [monogram]
Victoria and Albert Museum, London,
Given by Isabel Constable, daughter of the artist

184. **John Constable**
East Bergholt, Suffolk, 1776 – London, 1837
Study of a Tree, with 'The Grove' or Grove House in the Distance, 1822
Oil on paper, mounted on canvas, 30.8 x 26 cm
Verso on a label: 29 July 1822 looking east 10 in the morning – silvery clouds [probably a copy of an original inscription by John Constable]
Royal Academy of Arts, London

Constable's studies from nature acquired a fragmentary character in the 1820s. He used them not so much as a means of finding suitable compositions, but as studies in their own right. In this way, he could isolate particular details of the

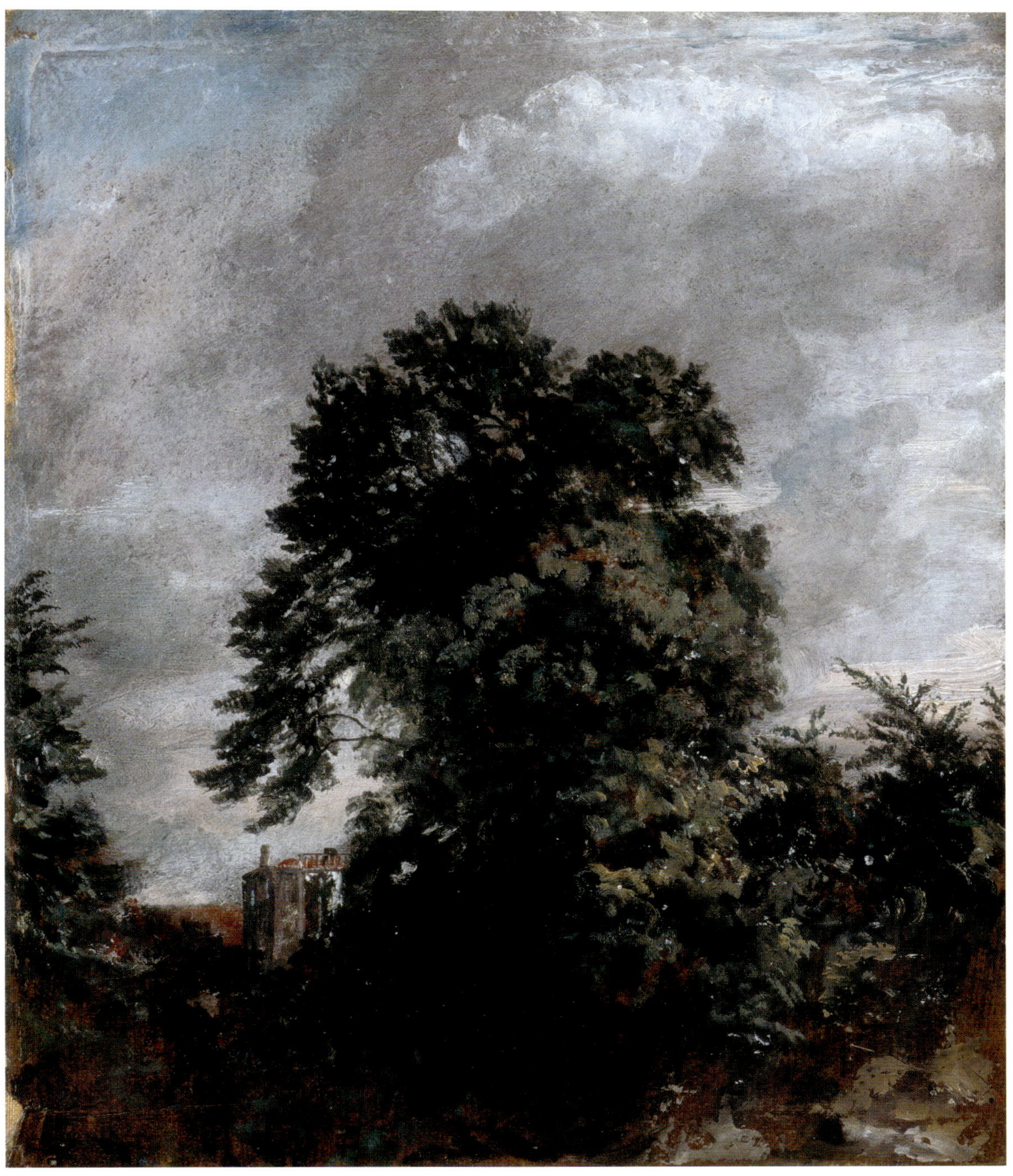

184

landscape at will, such as the clouds in the sky, a lone tree-trunk, the silhouette of a tree or simply a cluster of bushes. Works like these represent Constable's landscape painting in its least academic and most progressive form.

Constable usually worked in the vicinity of Hampstead, north of London. It offered a rolling terrain with grassy meadows, sandy hills, shrubs and trees. Here and there were houses, which Constable often depicted between the trees as pictorial accents.

Hampstead lies on a hill, and Constable often painted panoramas from there, some of which show London in the distance. The studies exhibited here illustrate how the artist penetrated the landscape to focus on specific details. Cat. 183, which could have been painted from Constable's garden (Reynolds 1984, p. 84), belongs to a group of cloud studies above bushes and treetops realized in 1820-22. Here, the sky and the foliage interested the artist in equal measure. Cat. 184 shows a house in Hampstead at the lower left, a small detail in a study of a monumental treetop.

Constable once wrote that 'the trees and the clouds seem to ask me to do something like them,' (Beckett 1962-68, vol. 3, p. 107) and on another occasion he commented on 'the vivid pencil that nature requires' (ibid., vol. 2, p. 84). In studies such as this we see the artist working with extraordinary confidence and versatility in the handling of paint and colour, the elements through which the delight he felt in nature, which he often described in words, could achieve its perfect expression. (RH)

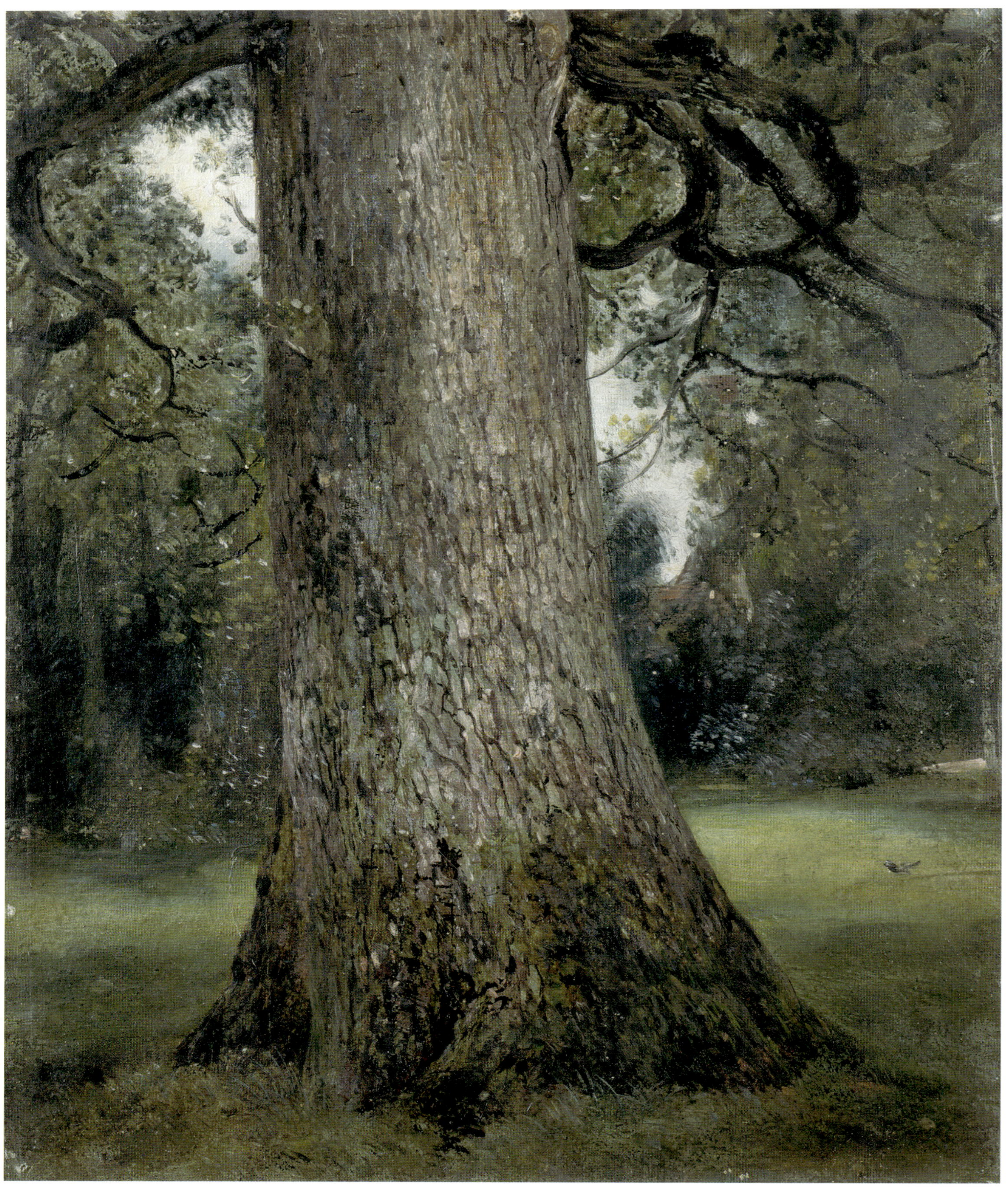

185

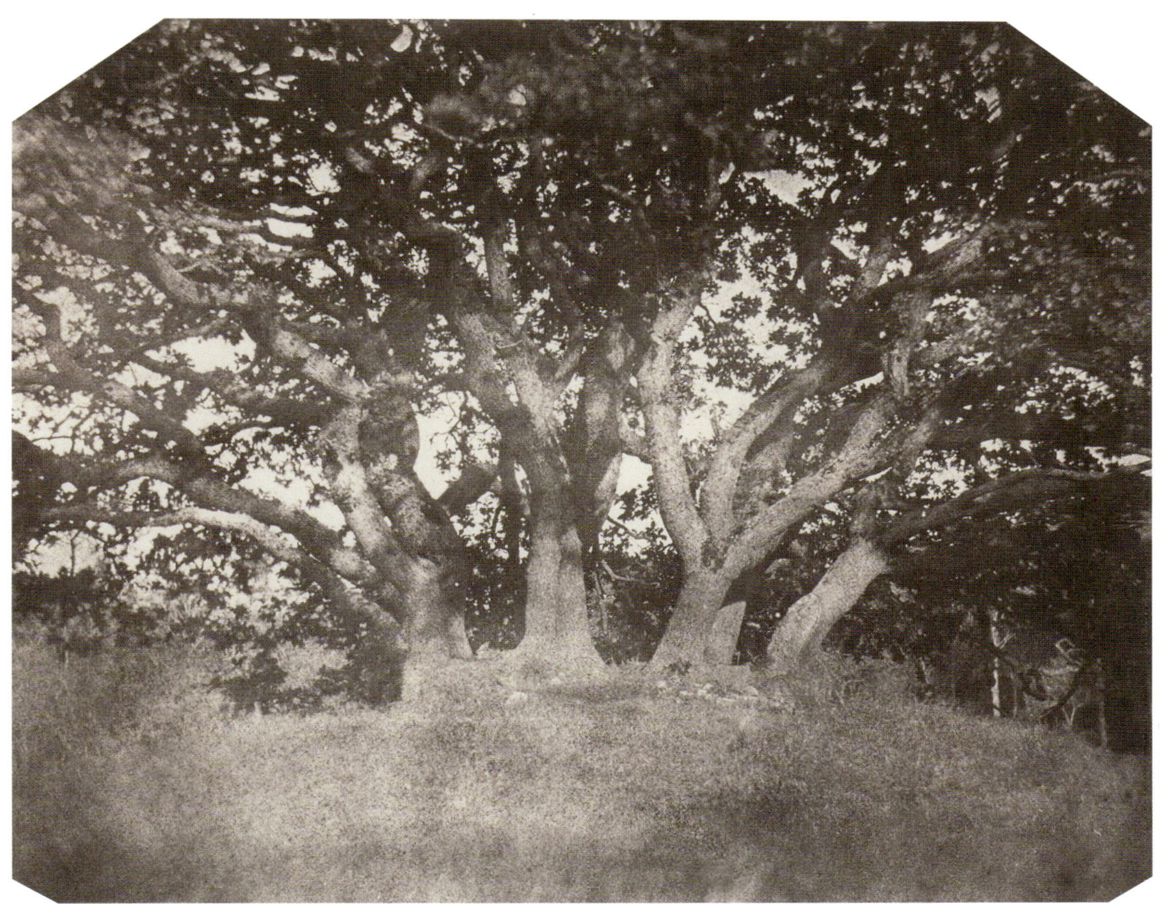

186

185. **John Constable**
East Bergholt, Suffolk, 1776 - London, 1837
Study of the Trunk of an Elm Tree, c. 1820-23
Oil on paper, 30.6 x 24.8 cm
Verso: JC [monogram]
Victoria and Albert Museum, London,
Given by Isabel Constable, daughter of the artist, 1888

Of Constable, his friend and biographer C.R. Leslie observed: 'I have seen him admire a fine tree with an ecstasy of delight like that with which he would catch up a beautiful child in his arms.' (Leslie 1951, p. 282) The artist made many studies of trees in the early 1820s, principally in Hampstead. This *plein air* oil sketch is remarkable for what Graham Reynolds called its 'first impression … of uncompromising and "photographic" naturalism' (Reynolds 1973, p. 146). Compositionally, it resembles a similarly truncated wash drawing of an oak tree by Claude Lorrain from Richard Payne Knight's major bequest of his drawings to the British Museum. Although Constable castigated these in a letter of January 1824 as resembling 'papers used and otherwise mauled, & purloined from a Water Closet' whose 'mere charm was their age' (Beckett 1962-68, vol.6, pp. 149-50), this oil study probably reflects his knowledge of such a work by Claude, whom he revered as a tireless student of nature. Lucian Freud has admired Constable's sketch, and in 2003 made an etching after it (see p. 47, fig. 15). (ME)

186. **William Henry Fox Talbot**
Melbury, Dorset, 1800 - Lacock Abbey, Wiltshire, 1877
Oak Tree, Carlclew Park, Cornwall, 1841
Salted paper print from calotype negative, 16.2 x 20.8 cm
National Media Museum, Bradford

If Talbot had not been one of the two principal inventors of photography - the other being Daguerre - perhaps his achievements as a photographer would have become apparent much earlier. However, in the past generation his virtues as a camera artist have attracted considerable commentary, most notably by Larry J. Schaaf. Schaaf points out that Talbot used a low camera angle for this photograph, taken in the grounds of his uncle, Sir Charles Lemon, which contained many unusual and exotic trees (Schaaf 2000, p. 120). The viewpoint invites the viewer to see grandeur in the powerful forms of the extraordinary, many-trunked, tree - writhing like an arboreal Laocoön. Schaaf adds that 'this image was so popular that Nicolaas Henneman (who managed Talbot's photographic sales) had a printed title made up to attach to the mounts of copies offered for sale'. (MHB)

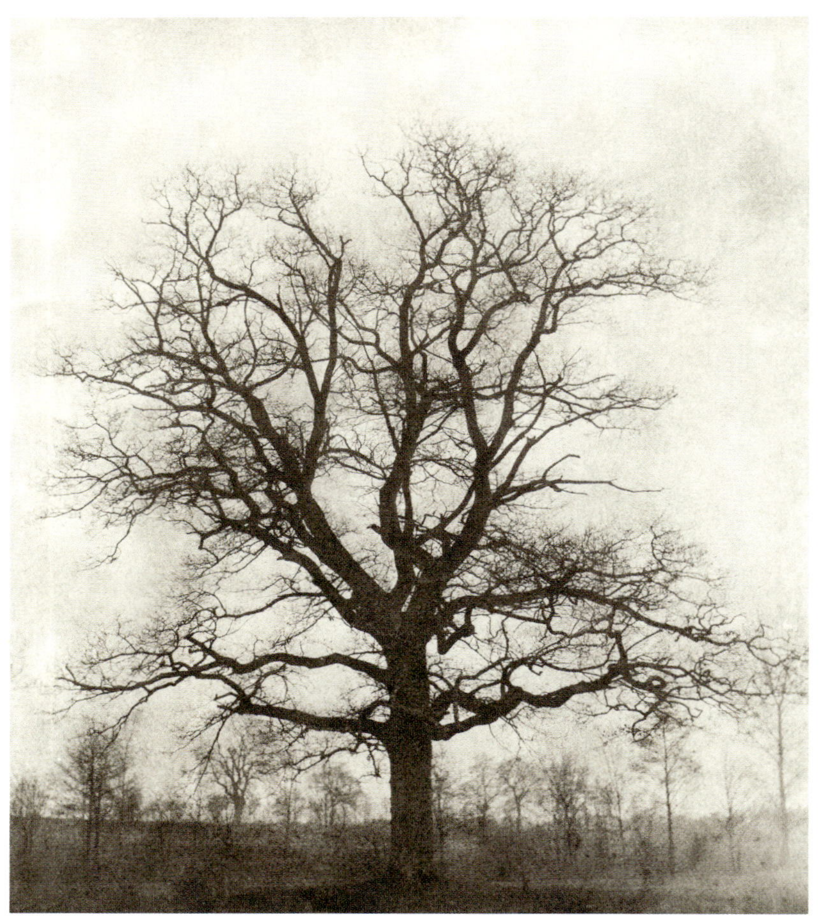

187

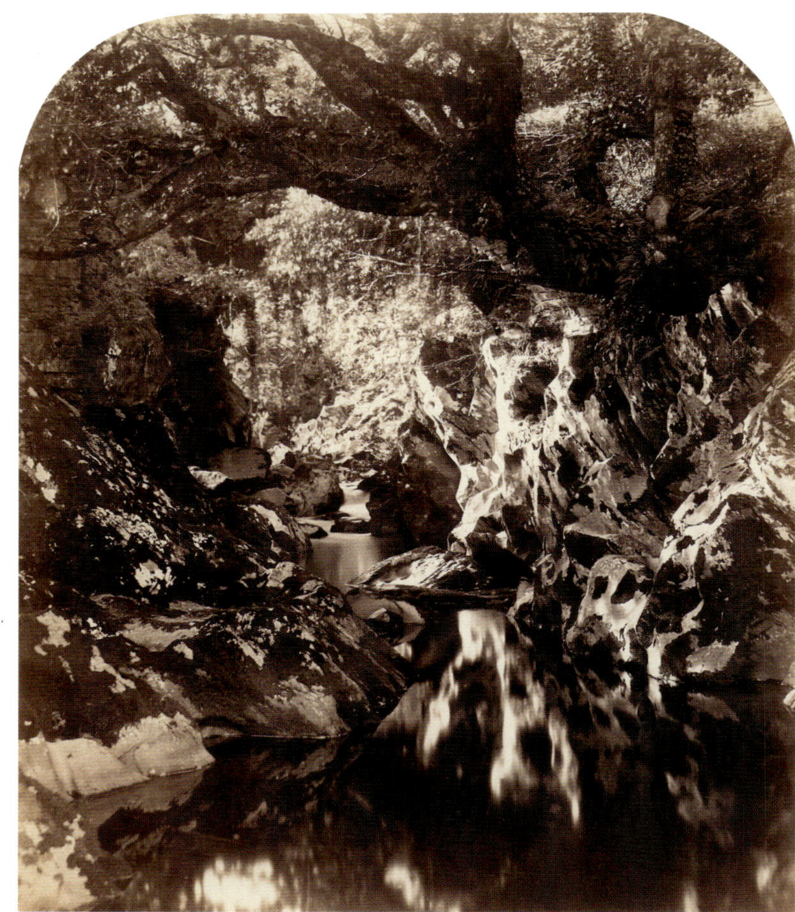

188

187. **William Henry Fox Talbot**
Melbury, Dorset, 1800 – Lacock Abbey, Wiltshire, 1877
Oak Tree in Winter, c. 1842-43
Salted paper print from calotype negative, 19.6 x 16 cm
National Media Museum, Bradford

Talbot's prints vary considerably in colour. They were created when photographic materials were handmade or hand-mixed – prior to the advent of factory suppliers during the 1850s – and when procedures were still experimental. Trees were one of Talbot's fortes and for good reason. The complexity of foliage and bark encouraged draughtsmen and painters to establish formulaic methods of description. Photography, on the other hand, excelled in rapid, unconventionalized, denotation of every singular characteristic of a tree. This handsome oak grew on Talbot's estate, Lacock Abbey. Such studies as this one were seen as models for artists. Talbot's friend and mentor, Dr George Butler, urged him in 1841 to photograph trees: 'This would be the greatest stride towards effective drawing & painting that has been made for a Century' (Schaaf 2000, p. 150). (MHB)

188. **Roger Fenton**
Bury, Lancashire, 1819 – London, 1869
Double Bridge on the Machno, 1857
Albumen print from wet collodion negative, 40.3 x 33.6 cm
Royal Photographic Society at the National
Media Museum, Bradford

Double Bridge on the Machno belongs to the pinnacle of Fenton's ambition for the art of photography. The site, in the Machno valley, was one that had already attracted watercolour artists, including Samuel Palmer and David Cox, but Fenton's photograph attempts to use photography to provide a quite new range of visual and tonal effects. It was first exhibited in 1858, with twenty-one other photographs from Fenton's Welsh campaign, at the annual exhibition of the Photographic Society of London at the South Kensington Museum, where Fenton escorted Queen Victoria and Prince Albert, Patrons of the society, around the exhibition at the opening. (MHB)

See essay p. 247-48.

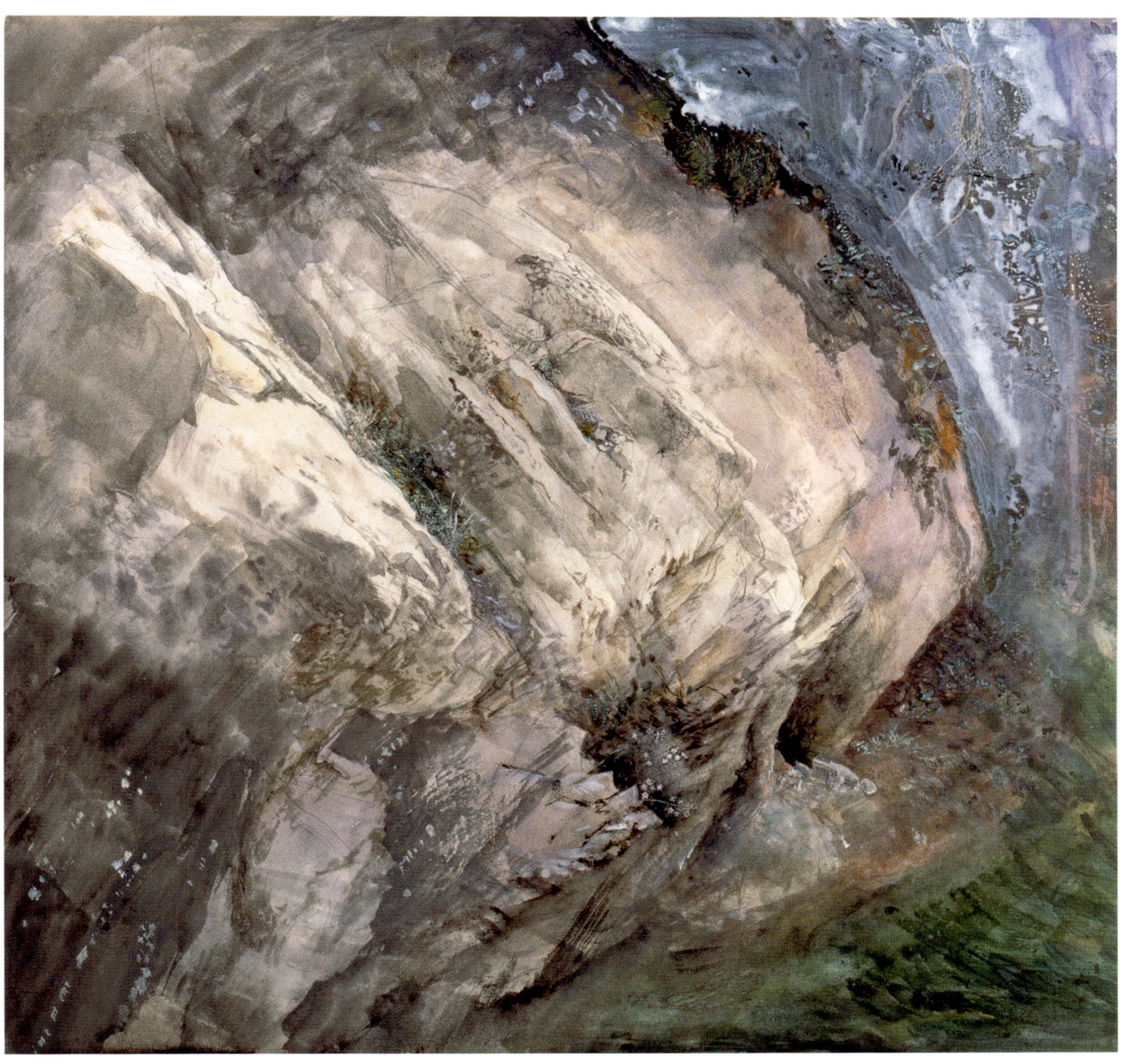

189

189. **John Ruskin**
London, 1819 – Brantwood, Cumbria, 1900
Chamonix: Rocks and Vegetation, c. 1854
Watercolour, bodycolour and pencil on paper, 25 x 26.7 cm
Abbot Hall Art Gallery, Kendal, Cumbria

This fascinating and beautiful drawing of an eroded rock surface, with some allusion to a wider landscape in the glimpse of sky and foreground grass, may be associated with Ruskin's 1854 visit to Chamonix. It is possibly identical with the study that he exhibited in 1878 as *Old Sketch of Gneiss, with its weeds in colour (Chamouni)*.

Whereas Ruskin besought artists to represent mountains and geological subjects with such careful attention to the physical mechanisms that had operated upon those landscapes that their work might be regarded as a reliable source of information about such places, his own drawings often depart from such a documentary purpose. The present watercolour is so confusing to look at that there have even been different opinions as to which way up it should be placed (in my view, the area of blue bodycolour which stands for the sky should be at the upper right, implying that we are looking at a piece of glacially eroded rock in the form known to geologists as *roche moutonnée*, i.e. with an upper surface smoothed by the flow of ice and a rougher undercut flank made irregular by the plucking action of the ice flow). As it is not obvious at what range we are seeing the landscape forms, we are reminded of Ruskin's admonition in volume 4 of *Modern Painters* that 'a stone, when it is examined, will be found a mountain in miniature', because Nature 'can compress as many changes of form and structure, on a small scale, as she needs for her mountains on a large one' (Cook and Wedderburn 1903-12, vol. 6, p. 368).

While on the one hand Ruskin believed that the purpose of drawing was simply to convey what was seen, and by drawing to learn to see more clearly, on other occasions he explored the appearance of the physical world in an instinctive and emotional way, departing from the mimetic function towards a representation that is visceral, urgent and ecstatic. (CSN)

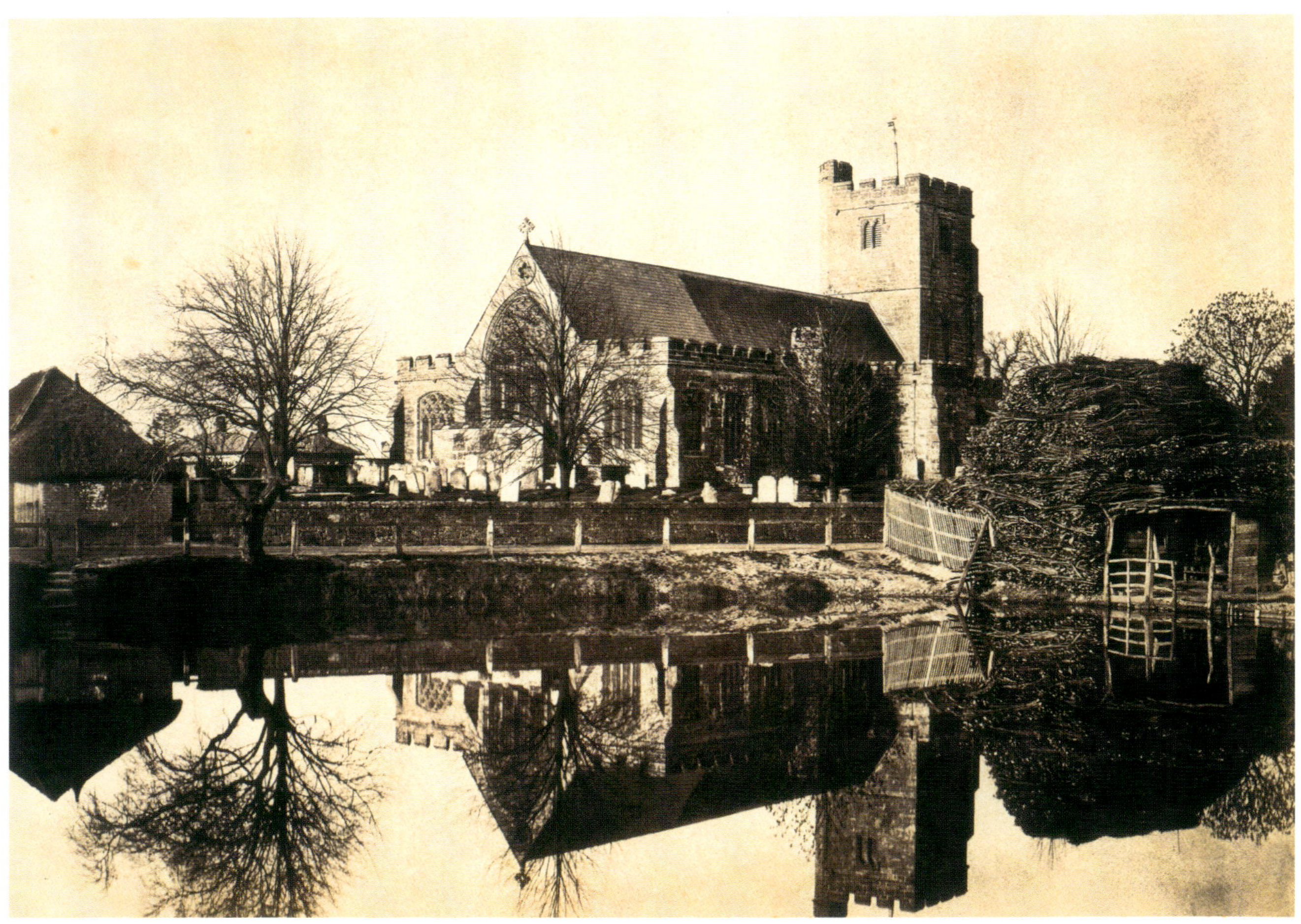

190

190. **Benjamin Brecknell Turner**
London, 1815 - London, 1894
A Photographic Truth or ***Hawkhurst Church, Kent***, 1852
Albumen print from calotype negative, 26.1 x 36.2 cm
Victoria and Albert Museum, London

This photograph was shown in *Recent Specimens of Photography*, the first-ever purely photographic exhibition, which was organized by the Society of Arts in London and subsequently toured throughout Britain. The title *A Photographic Truth* surely refers to the likeness between a reflection in water and the way, thanks to the special characteristics of the new medium of photography, nature drew its own portrait on light-sensitive paper or glass. Perhaps Roger Fenton was thinking of this photograph when he wrote in his introduction to the same catalogue of 'the still lake, so still that you must drop a stone into its surface before you can tell which is the real village on its margin, and which the reflection.' In these early years photographs - then often called 'Sun prints' - had links with the Romantic idea that a soul could be impressed by the benevolent spirit of nature. (MHB)

191. **Rosa Brett**
Camberwell, Surrey, 1829 - Caterham, Surrey, 1882
The Artist's Garden, c. 1859
Oil on board, 16.5 x 14.2 cm
Bottom right: RB [monogram]
Collection of Mr and Mrs Dallas

Rosa Brett's inspection of the variety of colours and textures to be observed within the restricted scope offered by a walled garden seems to have been made in about 1859: in May of that year she describes herself in a letter painting the flowers of a horse-chestnut tree (Marsh and Nunn 1997, p. 106). At that time, Rosa was living with her parents in the village of Detling, near Maidstone in Kent.

The artist had commenced painting nature subjects by applying minute touches of colour so as to gain the utmost veracity of detail as long before as 1852, according to her brother John Brett (himself a painter), who wrote of her at that time: 'Rosa has lately made a few - first-rate - sketches on Preraffaelite principles' (Marsh and Nunn 1989, p. 53). The two of them had previously collaborated on a series of studies, grouped under the headings of 'blight' and 'fungus', which seem likely to have been works of conscientious botanical

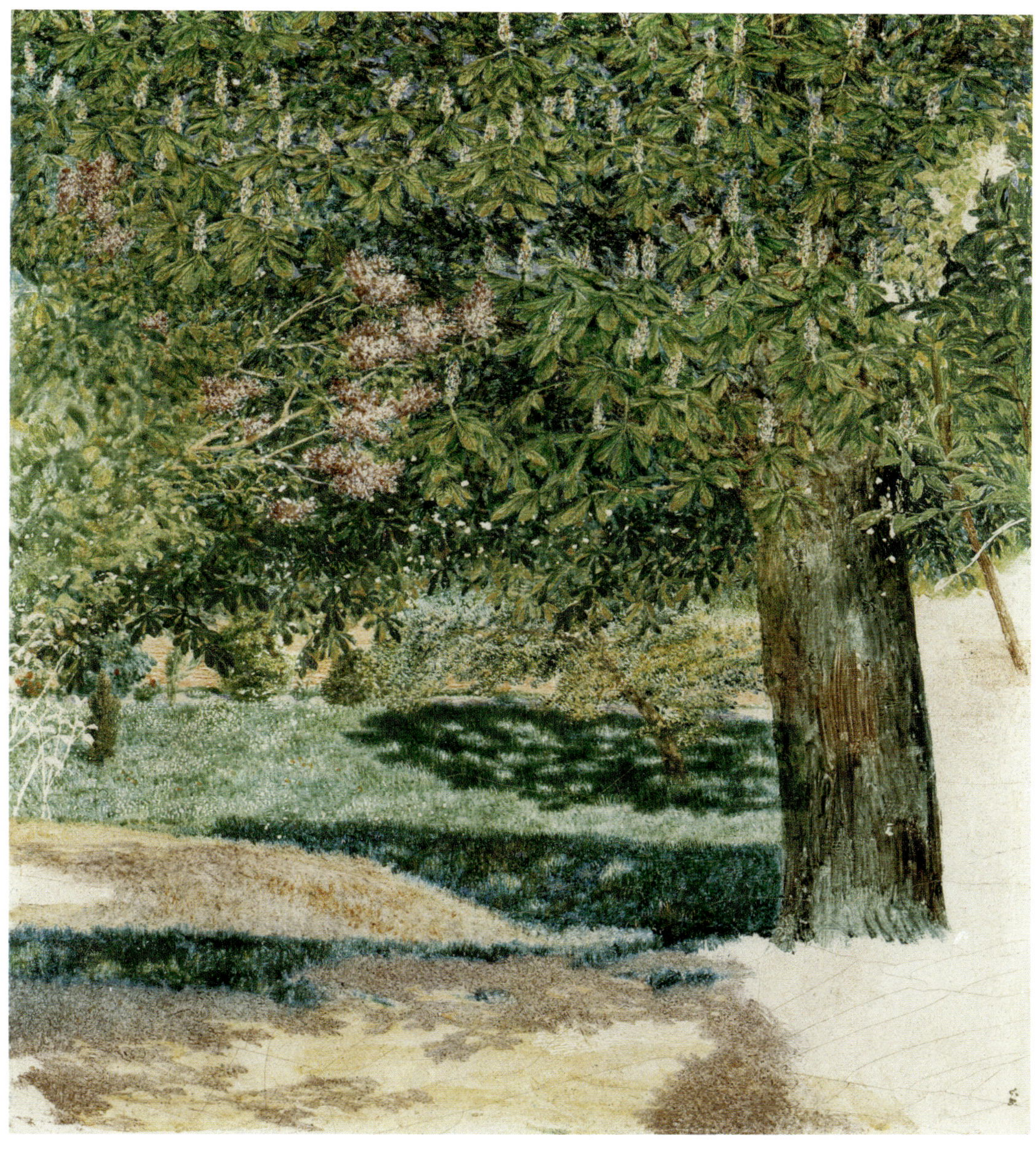

191

observation. In the course of the 1850s, both Rosa and John Brett adopted the technique of preparing their canvases with layers of gesso, onto which translucent areas of colour were applied, and which gained a brightness and intensity from the whiteness of the gesso below. In *The Artist's Garden* an area on the right side and in the foreground remains untouched.

This is a most personal and unselfconscious type of work. All documentary purposes are subordinated to the delight in looking into the secluded space, which one may imagine is a familiar view glimpsed from the artist's room. Dispensing with the conventions of perspective in favour of semi-abstract registers of dark and light, and likewise avoiding the usual tendency towards an identifiable principal subject, so that one has the sense that the zones of grass, leaves and gravel continue unbrokenly beyond the pictorial format, the very simplicity of the painting is challenging, even subversive, in the context of mid-century landscape painting.

Rosa Brett seems to have occupied a position on the fringes of the art world. and she undoubtedly suffered the disadvantage that was placed upon women who wanted to follow careers as painters. She seems to have been someone who was quite detached from the larger world, and was perhaps content to live at home and care for her parents. In addition, there is evidence that she did not enjoy good health. On the other hand, distinct professional ambitions are indicated by her having resorted to a masculine pseudonym – 'Rosarius' – under which name she sent paintings to the exhibitions of the Royal Academy from 1858 to 1862. The first work to be so exhibited, a painting of a sleeping cat in a hayloft, caused excitement in the Pre-Raphaelite circle and speculation as to who the unknown (and, it was probably assumed, male) author might have been. (CSN)

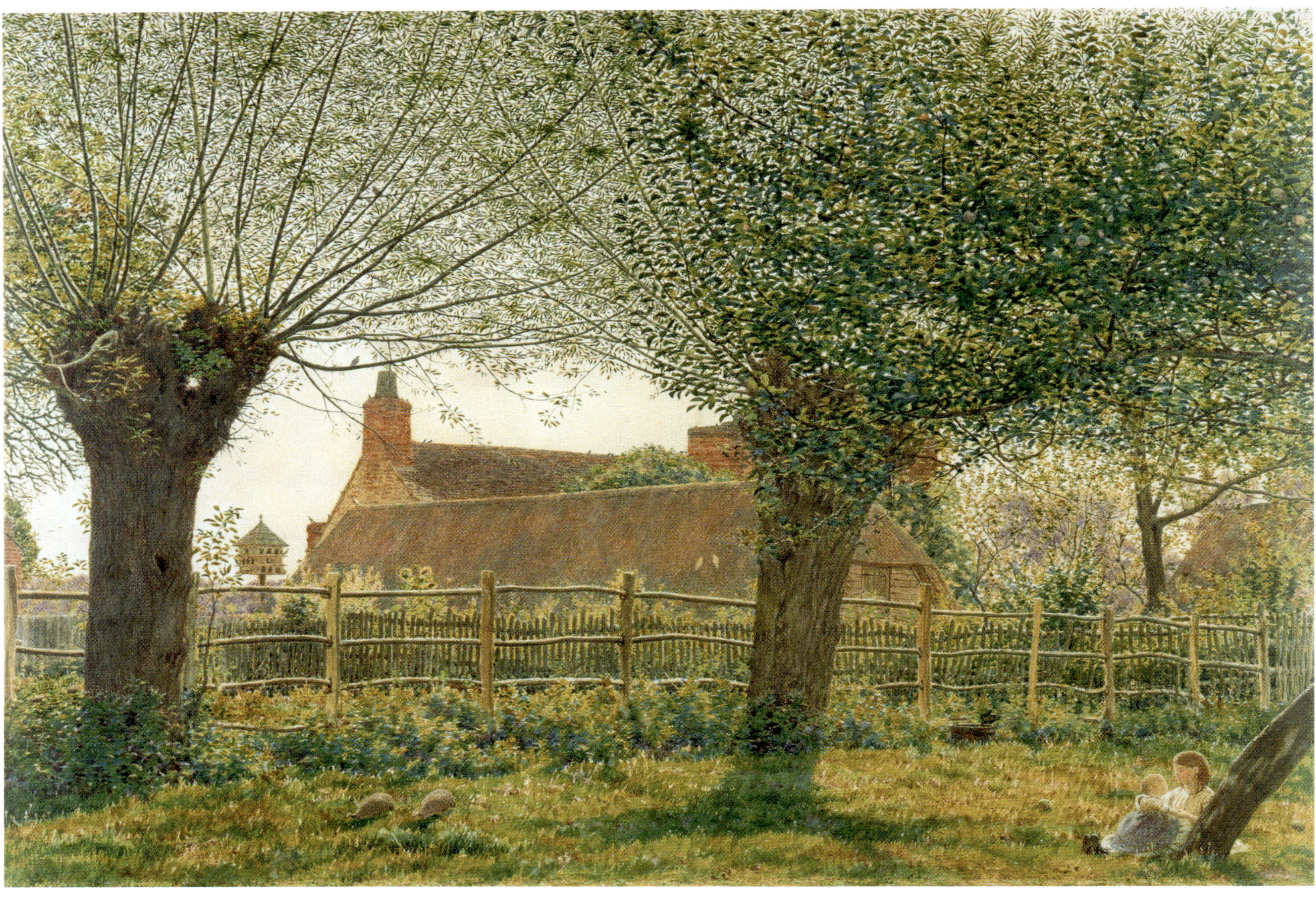

192

192. **George Price Boyce**
London, 1826 – London, 1897
At Binsey, near Oxford, 1862
Watercolour and ink on paper, 31.1 x 53.7 cm
Bottom right: G. P. Boyce Sepr. 1862
Trustees of the Cecil Higgins Art Gallery, Bedford

At Binsey is one of the immensely detailed and brightly coloured watercolours of English rural subjects that Boyce painted in the early 1860s. What might seem an almost spontaneous and unconsidered response to a glimpsed corner of the countryside emerges as something enormously complex and of great aesthetic sophistication. Trees and fences forming a series of superimposed screens are placed across the width of the composition, framing, masking or obscuring what lies behind. The farmhouse and buildings that are seen beyond are themselves observed from a vantage point which causes one to block the view of the other. Although the artist was congratulated for his 'single eye for simple nature, which, in the reverence of deep feeling, he ventures not to alter, or even to compose' (*Art Journal*, 1864, p. 171), this is in fact a most careful and even contrived way of seeing, and one which plays elaborate games with the spectator – causing one to want to know more about a place for which only a modicum of geographical data is provided. (CSN)

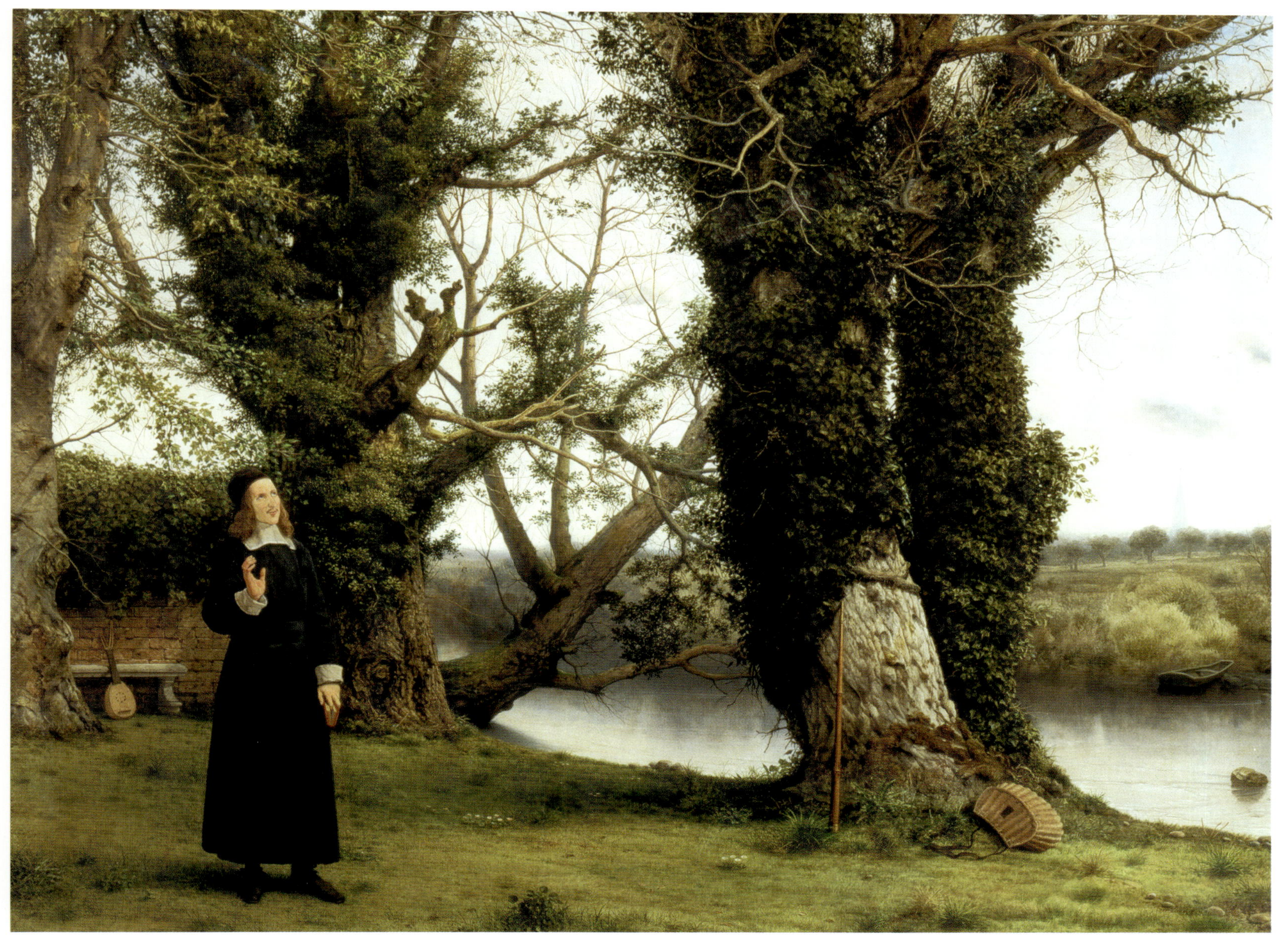

193

193. **William Dyce**
Aberdeen, 1806 - London, 1864
George Herbert at Bemerton, c. 1861
Oil on canvas, 86.3 x 117.7 cm
Guildhall Art Gallery, City of London

Dyce shows the seventeenth-century clergyman and poet George Herbert standing in the garden of his rectory at Bemerton in Wiltshire. The River Nadder flows past peacefully, while in the distance over water meadows may be seen the spire of Salisbury Cathedral. There was a revival of interest in Herbert's poetry in the early nineteenth century, and a particular admiration was felt for the way in which he found moral significance in everyday objects in support of a simple and trusting Protestant faith. Likewise, the retiring and devout life that Herbert led at Bemerton, avoiding as he did all sophistication and worldliness so that he might devotedly serve his parishioners, appealed to Victorians who were nostalgic for a time when it seemed that the patterns of existence were less fraught. Two of Herbert's particular enthusiasms are alluded to: his love of music, in the lute which rests against the stone bench on the left side, and angling, in the rod and basket leaning against the oak tree closest to the spectator.

William Dyce only occasionally painted pure landscapes, doing so for the most part while on holiday. He may have taken the present subject as a means of recuperation from the strain of work on the frescoes for the Queen's Robing Room at the Palace of Westminster, which he was then engaged on. He had clearly visited the rectory at Bemerton, where in fact his friend and occasional model the Rev. Cyril Page was then living, because the setting as represented corresponds closely to the actual landscape, even as it exists today. (CSN)

194

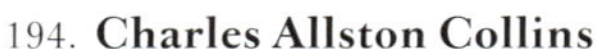

194. **Charles Allston Collins**
London, 1828 - London, 1873
May, in the Regent's Park, 1851
Oil on mahogany veneer, 44.5 x 69.2 cm
Bottom right: CACollins / 1851 [monogram]
Tate, London

Pre-Raphaelite landscape painting frequently celebrates the habitual setting of an artist's life, on the understanding that even scenery that is dulled by familiarity offers beauties of colour and light, pattern and texture. Because the technique was exacting and time-consuming, but also because - at least in the early 1850s - it was considered a necessity to have the landscape subject before one as one worked, many artists painted from bedroom windows. If Brown's *An English Autumn Afternoon* (cat. 196) is the most famous example of a landscape subject taken simply 'because it lay out of a back window', Collins's view from a first- or second-floor window at the front of his parents' house in Hanover Terrace, a mile or two further to the south and overlooking London's Regent's Park, likewise makes a virtue of the rectilinear shapes and downward perspective which is the consequence of such a vantage point.

Using a painterly technique, the artist has relished the effulgent greens of the trees and grass of the park and of the garden at the front of the terrace where he lived. These two zones are separated by a bar of creamy-yellow colour, standing for the sunlit surface of the road and pavement of the Outer Circle. The title of the painting, under which it was exhibited for the first time in 1852, refers both to the month of the year when it was painted, and the blossom on the left side, which is a variety of pink hawthorn usually called 'may'.

Collins was not a member of the Pre-Raphaelite Brotherhood but was on friendly terms with members of the group; his most famous painting, *Convent Thoughts* (Ashmolean Museum, Oxford), is one of the enduring images of the 1850s, admired by John Ruskin for its careful painting of water-lily leaves (as stated in a letter of support for the Pre-Raphaelites, published in *The Times*, 13 May 1851; see *Cook and Wedderburn* 1903-12, vol. 12, p. 321). (CSN)

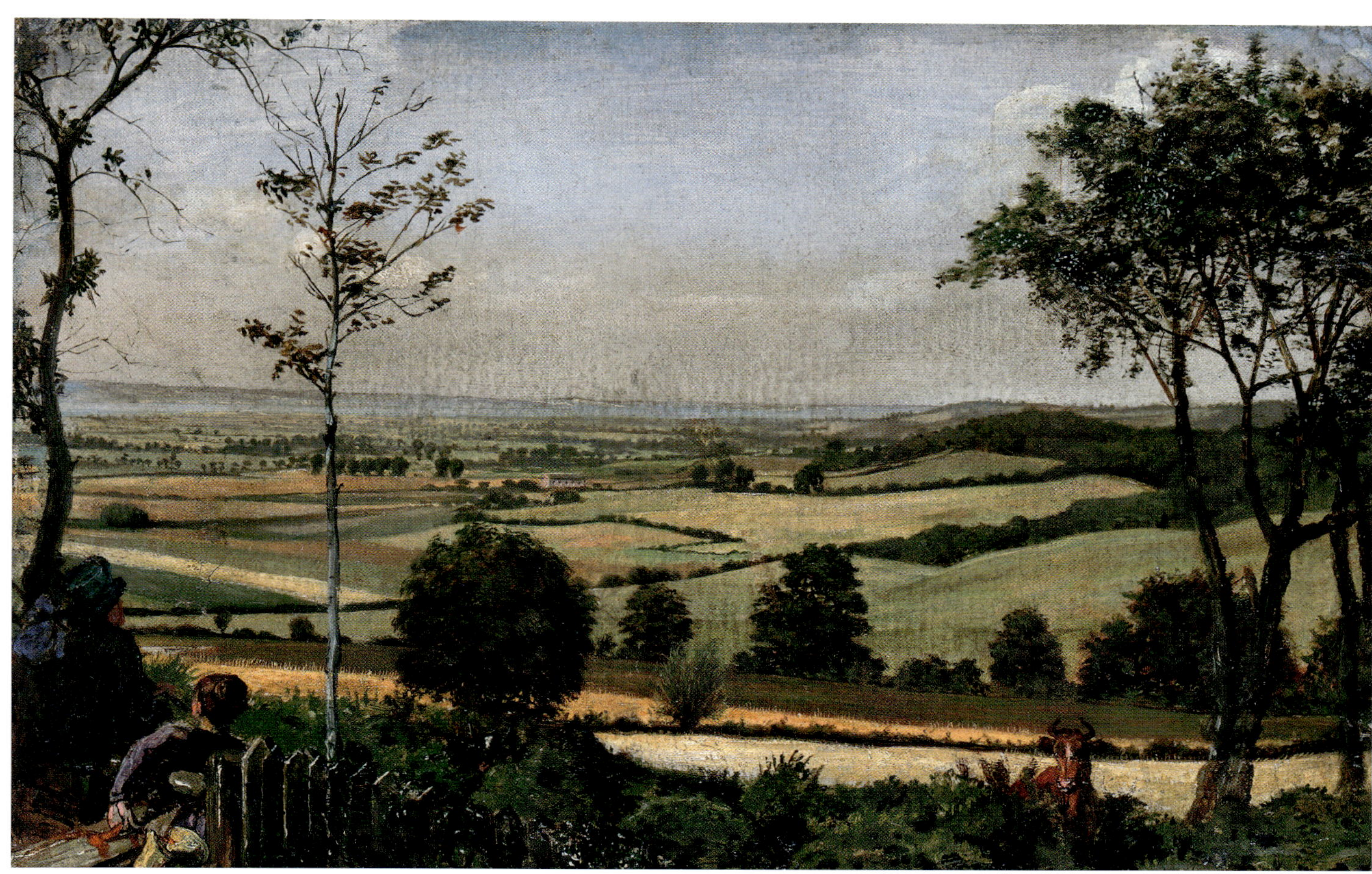

195

195. **Ford Madox Brown**
Calais, 1821 - London, 1893
The Medway Seen from Shorne Ridgeway, Kent, 1849
(retouched in 1873)
Oil on board, 21 x 31 cm
Verso: F.M.B. 49-73
Amgueddfa Cymru - National Museum Wales, Cardiff

Brown visited the village of Shorne Ridgeway, near Gravesend, in July 1849. Here he painted this view of fields with clumps of horse-chestnut trees looking towards the distant River Thames. The painting was not intended to be a finished work. It was a study for the background of *Geoffrey Chaucer Reading the 'Legend of Custance' to Edward III and his Court* (1849-51; Art Gallery of New South Wales, Sydney). This enormous historical composition with many figures was Brown's first attempt to treat light and shade as it existed at one moment, instead of painting a generalized effect. The study must have been undertaken in a similar naturalistic spirit, but in the large painting truth to nature was compromised: Brown reversed the view and enlarged the fields seen in the foreground of the study in order to include a scene of medieval ploughing. In 1873, Brown repainted the foreground of the study, adding the figures in the left-hand corner to make the sketch more saleable. (JT)

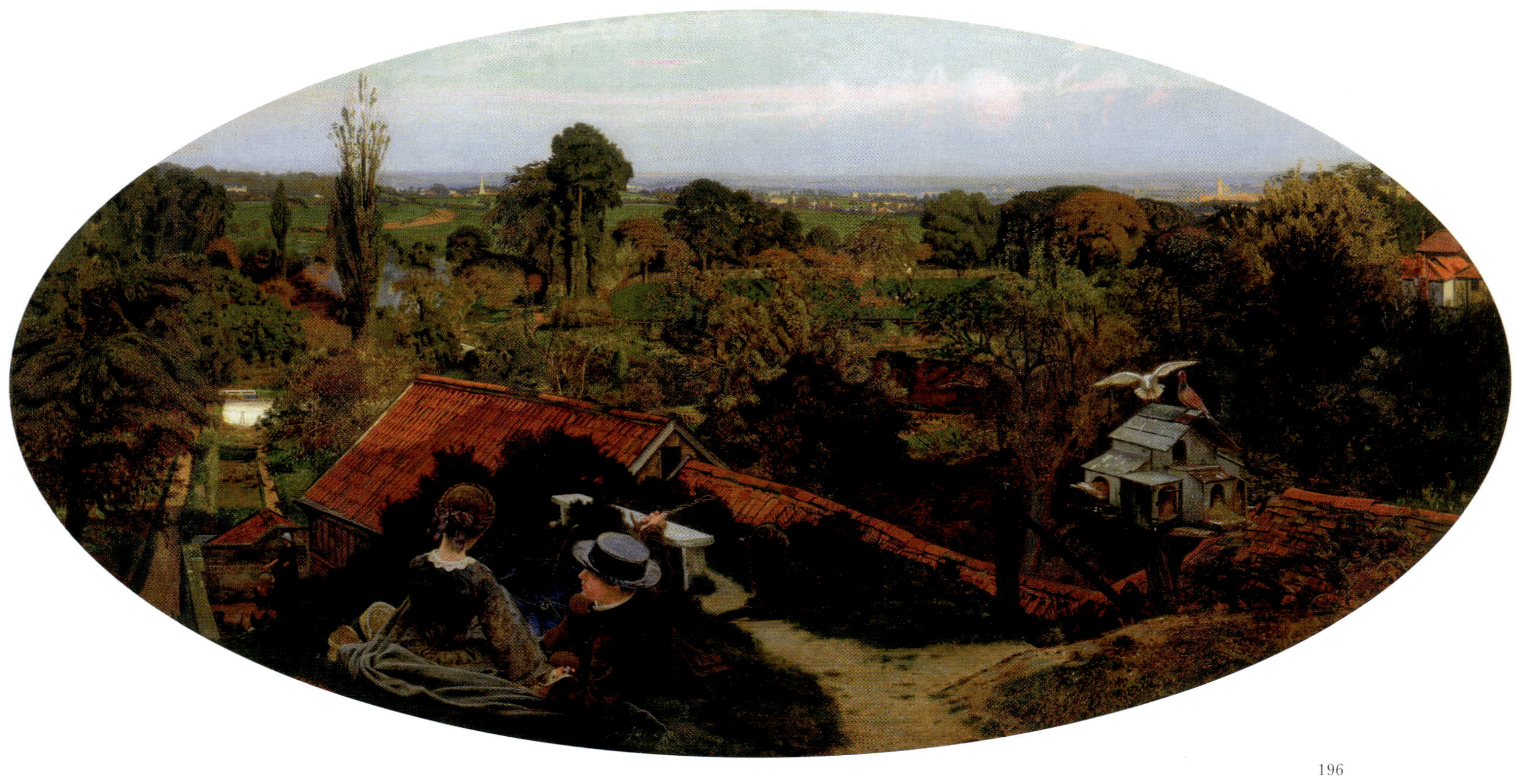

196

196. **Ford Madox Brown**
Calais, 1821 – London, 1893
An English Autumn Afternoon, Hampstead (Scenery in 1853), 1852-53, 1855
Oil on canvas, 71.2 x 134.8 cm
Bottom to left: F. Madox Brown.
Birmingham Museum & Art Gallery

Brown painted this view of Hampstead Heath, north of London, from the upper window of his lodgings. In accordance with Pre-Raphaelite ideas of truth to nature, it is a literal transcription of a particular place and effect of light at a precise time, 3 p.m. in late October: Brown has carefully observed the lengthening shadows, and the glowing colours of the autumn foliage. The unusual shape and the lack of conventional compositional devices to frame the view also attest to Brown's determination to see things anew, but the painting's originality lies in its celebration of the ordinary: an unpretentious mixture of back gardens, orchards and rooftops, with glimpses of everyday activities such as fruit picking and feeding chickens. The sole artifice is in the raised foreground, added to give a sense of elevation, and in the inclusion of the two figures enjoying the autumn sunshine, whose contemporary dress emphasizes that this is a modern landscape painting. (JT)

See essay pp. 243-45.

197. **Daniel Alexander Williamson**
Liverpool, 1823 – Broughton-in-Furness, Cumbria, 1903
The Startled Rabbit, c. 1862
Oil on panel, 26.5 x 39 cm
Williamson Art Gallery and Museum, Wirral Museums Service, Birkenhead

This is one of the series of paintings that Williamson made at Warton Crag in north Lancashire (see cat. 198). The artist has paid close attention to the limestone pavements (horizontal strata of carboniferous rock, divided into blocks by fissures cut by moisture seeping through the permeable and water-soluble material), which are such a distinctive feature of the landscape. Unusually for Williamson, he has here introduced a human element: the young man and girl who pause momentarily to watch a rabbit bound out of their path.

The painting was exhibited in Liverpool in 1863. A year later, Williamson moved from Warton to Broughton-in-Furness in the English Lakes. In 1865 he largely abandoned oil painting, taking instead to watercolour and devising a technique that involved placing patches of colour onto moistened paper so that hues would blend together and coalesce. In this highly personal and experimental method he looked for artistic freedom and spontaneity. (CSN)

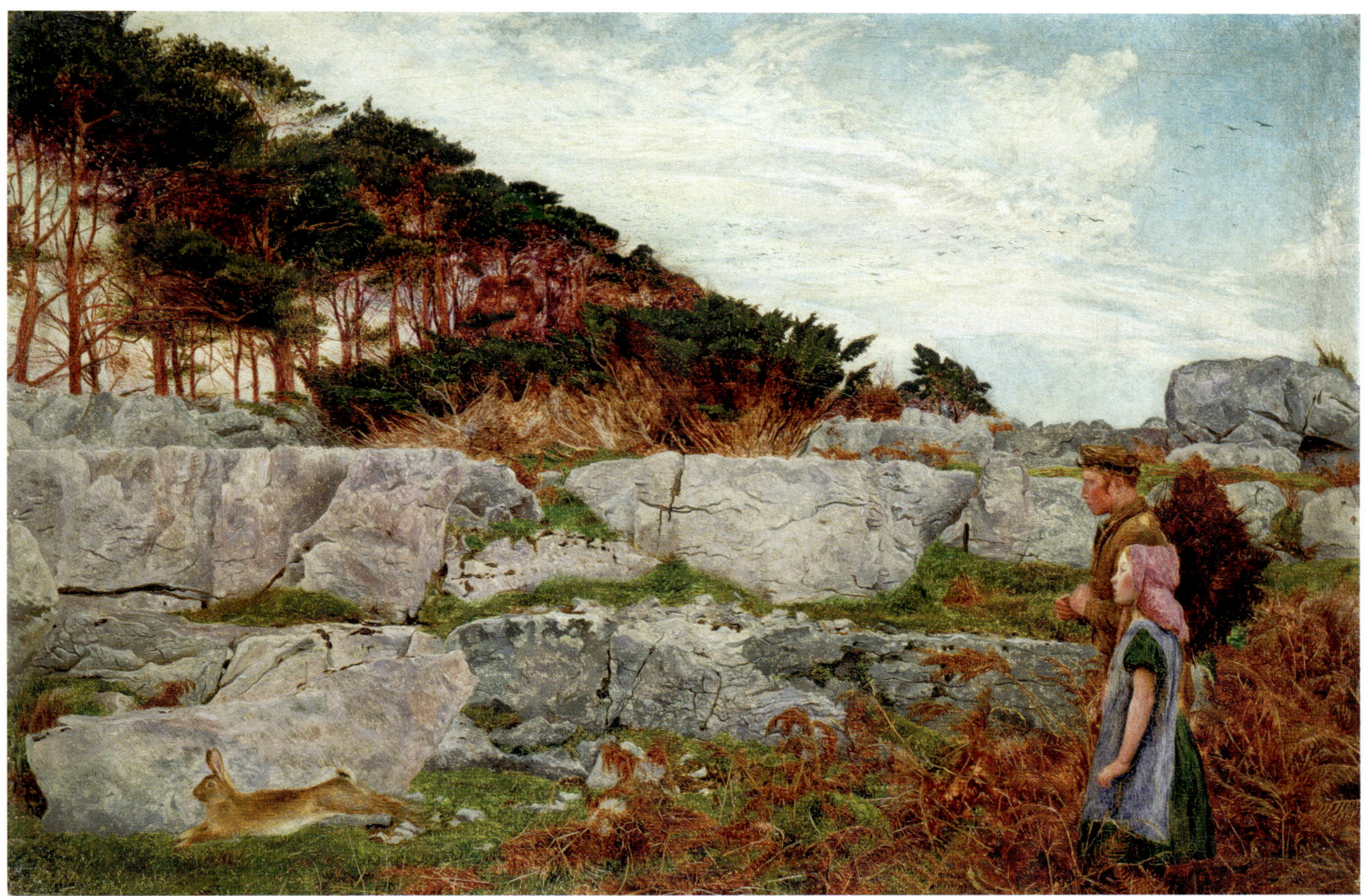

197

198. **Daniel Alexander Williamson**
Liverpool, 1823 – Broughton-in-Furness, Cumbria, 1903
Spring: Arnside Knot and Coniston Range of Hills from Warton Crag, c. 1863
Oil on canvas, 27 x 40.6 cm
National Museums Liverpool, Walker Art Gallery

Williamson was born in Liverpool and, after a period in London in the 1850s, returned to the north-west, living at Warton in north Lancashire and later in the English Lakes. In the early 1860s he painted a series of views of the carboniferous hillsides which rise close to the coast at Morecambe Bay. *Spring* is one of these, showing in the left foreground pieces of broken limestone; Arnside Knot itself is the wooded ridge in the middle distance, viewed at a range of about four kilometres, while on the far horizon may be seen the higher mountains of the Coniston Fells. The artist adopted a meticulous technique, which allowed the distinctive textures and colours of the landscape to be seen and relished: the limestone is a pale grey colour, while the flowers of the gorse are a brilliant yellow; fresh grass is sprigging through, but the ravages of winter are seen in the masses of dead bracken, which shows as a foxy red. The sky is a neutral grey, except on the right where rain clouds sweep across.

This is a work of utter simplicity and one that was perhaps intended to be seen in conjunction with others in the series of Williamson's views of and from Warton Crag. Together they form an exercise in the description of a particular and immediate locality, which was clearly dear to the artist, and this stands as a single-minded enterprise in mountain portraiture. (CSN)

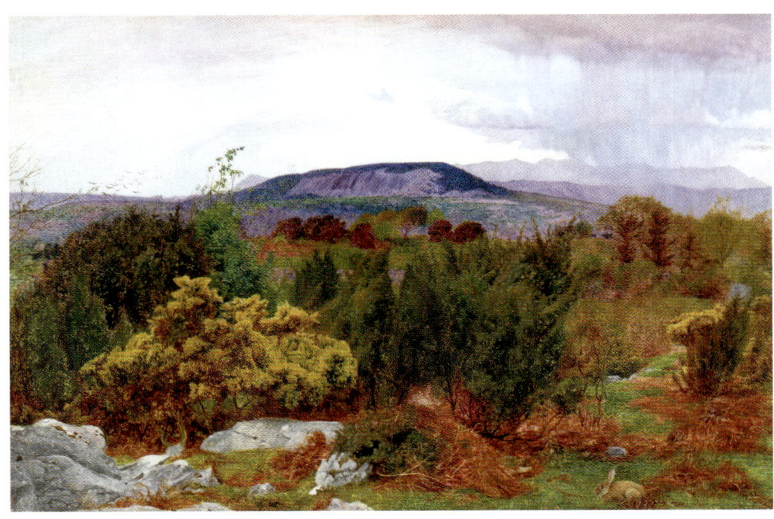

198

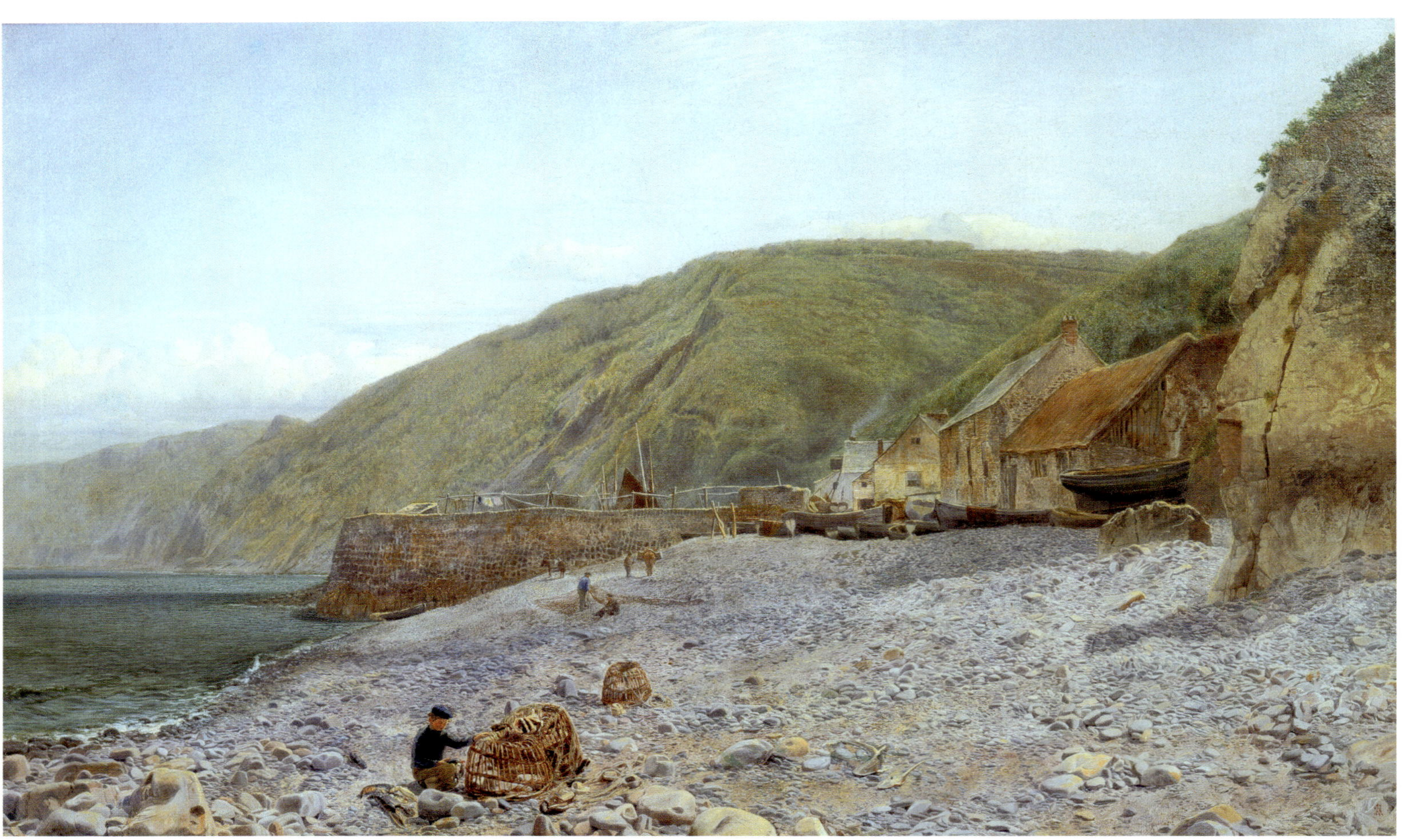

199

199. **Charles Napier Hemy**
Newcastle upon Tyne, 1841 – Falmouth, Cornwall, 1917
Among the Shingle at Clovelly, 1864
Oil on canvas, 43.5 x 72.1 cm
Bottom right: CNH [monogram] / 1864
Laing Art Gallery (Tyne and Wear Museums), Newcastle upon Tyne

Hemy's view shows the shingle beach and jetty at Clovelly in north Devon. Fishermen's cottages and a pub are clustered together in the middle distance (the main body of the village, with its precipitous streets, picturesque architecture and donkeys, is out of view on the hillside to the right); in the foreground a boy mends lobster-pots. The place remains almost exactly as Hemy represented it 143 years ago: the Red Lion is still there, and the village is otherwise carefully preserved, although serving holiday-makers rather than depending, as it had historically done, on mackerel and herring fishing. In terms of physical geography, the sloping sandstone spur at the right side of the view still stands, but the wedge of stone that may be seen in the painting to be detached from the living stone by a long vertical fracture has gone.

Hemy was about ten years younger than the principal members of the Pre-Raphaelite Brotherhood and had no immediate contact with them. Therefore, a certain caution should be used in describing him as 'Pre-Raphaelite', even when he paints with such painstaking attention to detail as is seen here. By the mid-1860s, the meticulous representation of the actuality of landscape was beginning to be regarded as a redundant artistic purpose, while the faculty of memory and impression gradually superseded that of observation. (CSN)

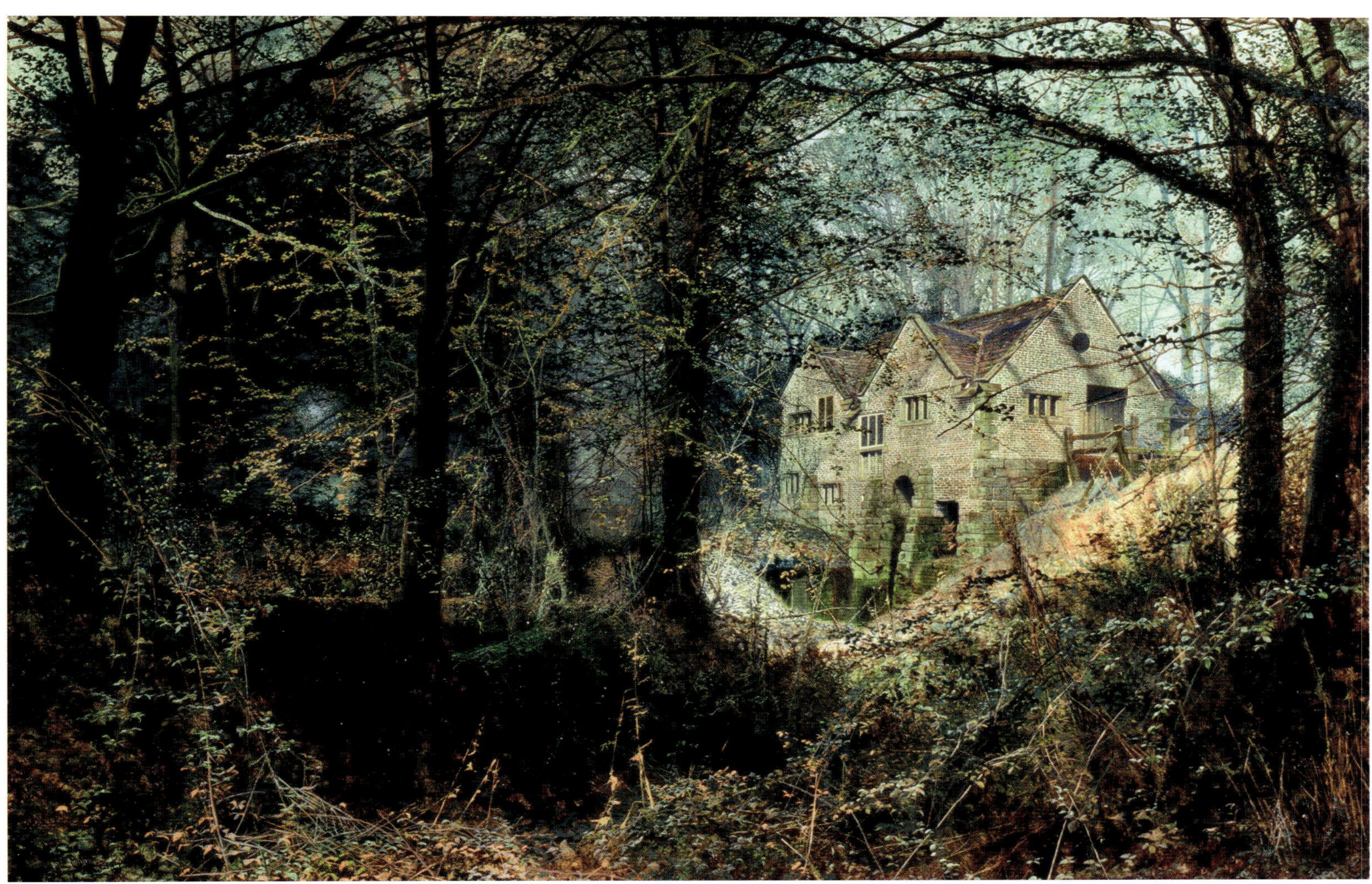

200

200. **John Atkinson Grimshaw**
Leeds, 1836 – Leeds, 1893
Autumn Glory: The Old Mill, 1869
Oil on canvas, 62.2 x 87.6 cm
Bottom left: Atkinson Grimshaw / 1869
Leeds Museums and Galleries (City Art Gallery)

Atkinson Grimshaw, the son of a Leeds policeman, was self-taught as an artist. He was only able to devote himself to painting full time from 1861, having begun his working life as a clerk with the railways. He exhibited locally and in London with Thomas Agnew's and at the Royal Academy (from 1874) with considerable success. But he remained a Leeds artist and developed an instantly recognizable style, a little like L.S. Lowry in the following century, depicting the urban scene, city streets and docks, often under moonlight. Like Lowry, his range was greater than the typical example and included interiors, figure paintings, and some striking images of fairies. The present painting is apparently a moonlight scene and represents a 'most painstaking rendering of a woodland scene, painted in minute detail from foreground to distance' (Bromfield and Robertson 1979, p. 26). This is a relatively early painting and may show the influence of another Leeds painter whose works are characterized by precision, J.W. Inchbold, who had trained at the Royal Academy Schools and became a member of the Pre-Raphaelite Brotherhood. (AD)

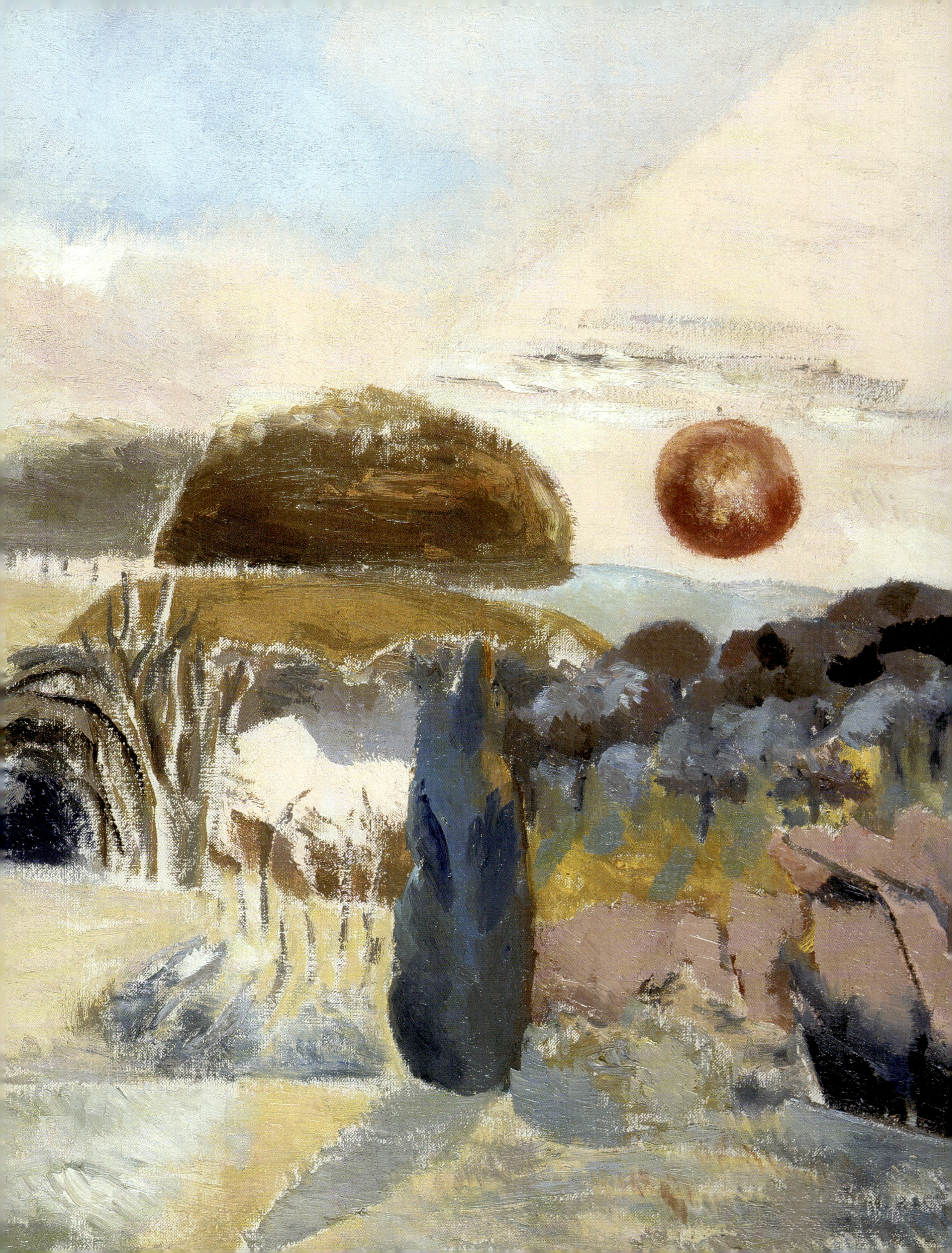

MODERN LANDSCAPE

PAUL NASH

Landscape of the Vernal Equinox (III), 1944

DAVID FRASER JENKINS

The vernal equinox is the time of year in the spring when day and night are of equal duration, which occurs usually on either March 21 or 22. It is often taken to be the first day of spring, just as the autumn equinox on about September 22 or 23 is the first day of autumn. These are the opposite quarters of the year to the summer and winter solstices, which mark the longest and shortest days. These basic astronomical matters quickly become, if pursued, extremely complicated, despite referring to such everyday routines as the changing seasons. In effect, for most people they mark one of the frontiers between our conventional lives and an aspect of science that is evidently wholly relevant but is mysterious. It was just this link, however, that appealed to Nash as one of the access points between the ordinary and the strange. This threshold was the more fascinating since the details of astronomy were closed also to Nash, who was in no way a mathematician or scientist. Furthermore, since astronomy is such an ancient interest, it still used terms that have embedded in them distant echoes of the manner of understanding things from before modern science, which also appealed to Nash as a gateway between the most ancient and the most modern.

A landscape presumably looks much the same a few days before or after the equinoxes. However, Paul Nash's career as a landscape painter was devoted not to the topography that he also practised, but to a search for more or less natural visual symbols. He wanted to be able to place these in drawings or paintings, to be able to re-enact his particular experiences of southern England, where he grew up and always lived, and where he had discovered that nature could sometimes offer an access point to some hidden significance. His career had begun properly only after the First World War, but as a youth, rather precious and naive, he already wrote poetry and drew Rossetti-like landscapes and figures, which indicated this experience of transcendence. He shed from year to year the more extraneous or contrived aspects of these inventions, and at the same time became more convincing in fashioning their suggestiveness. This progress was not straightforward, and rather went in fits and starts, but in the last four years of his life his work culminated in a series of large landscape paintings of Oxfordshire.

In *Landscape of the Vernal Equinox*, one of the best of his last paintings, Nash brought together topics that had often concerned him. He had been obsessed by the Wittenham Clumps, which he could reach from his cousin's house, since childhood. His early watercolour *The Wanderer*, 1911 (cat. 291), shows a figure, perhaps the young artist, setting off through farmland to make his own path into a wood. This myth of access into primitive landscape is repeated in his earliest pictures, which borrowed from William Blake's Virgil woodcuts and Samuel Palmer's rhapsodies about rural religion. Nash also linked this pathway to a search for love, sometimes embedding a figure of a young woman or naked bather within his hills and lakes, with a sense of secrecy equivalent to Calvert's tiny intimacies. But Nash had no Christian belief and became a modern artist. His late landscapes also carry forward skills of design and colour from his more abstract paintings, and from his more overtly surreal landscapes the freedom both to place together things that were not there and to insist in his title on the force of ancient astronomy. There is no usual sense in the English language of a landscape '*of*' an equinox:

Paul Nash, ***Landscape of the Vernal Equinox (III)*** (detail), cat. 214

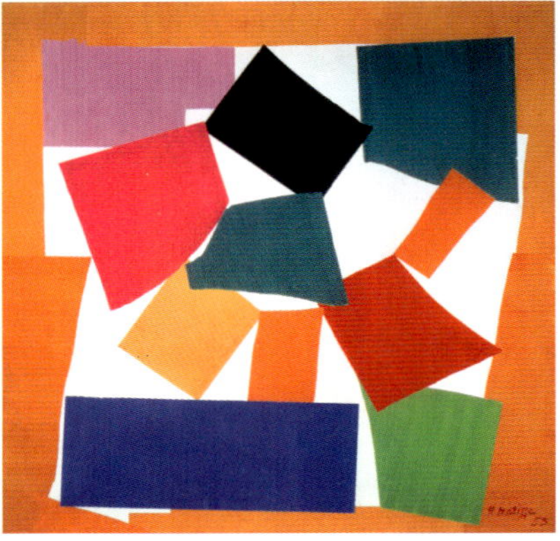

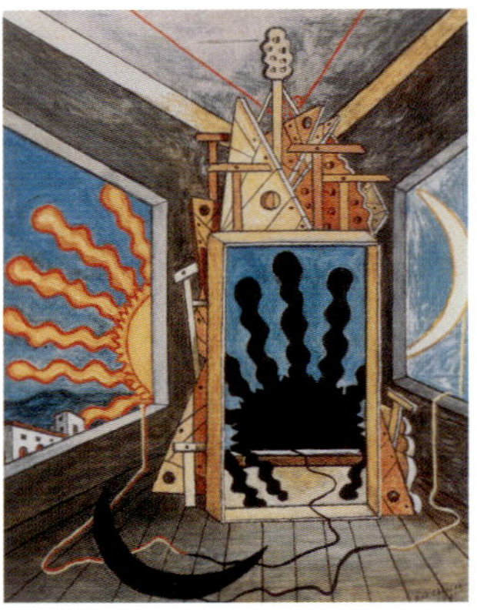

fig. 1
Henri Matisse
The Snail, 1953
Gouache on paper, cut and pasted on paper, mounted on canvas, 286.4 x 287 cm
Tate, London

fig. 2
Giorgio De Chirico
Metaphysical Interior with Extinguished Sun, 1971
Oil on canvas, 80 x 60 cm
Fondazione Giorgio e Isa de Chirico, Rome

there might be a landscape of some quality such as 'beauty', but Nash used these relational kind of titles often, as in his *Landscape of Ancient Country* (1945) or the *Landscape of the Megaliths* (1934). This was an attitude that shifted the sense from the eyes to the mind.

It was unusual that Nash made three versions of this painting. It was of the first that he left a written account, for future critics.[1] Here he intermingled the different aspects of the painting so as to mutually reinforce them, particularly through the colouring, which he called 'ghostly tints': 'Red and deep yellows, with a range of fading and dying rose and pink, and blue from its palest cold tints, deepening to the tones of night.' He concluded that this 'place has a compelling image which makes it a sympathetic setting for the occasion of the Equinox'. It is this active colouring that binds the separate topics. This is the third version of the painting, which he made specifically for his wife Margaret and at first titled 'The Marriage', leaving unknowable quite how to read these conjunctions and harmonies within his private life. There is no reference to politics in these works, but Margaret Nash wrote after his death that 'The progress of the war ... and all the various heroic deeds whose Elizabethan atmosphere appealed to the poetic imagination, produced in Paul an astonishing mental vitality and a clarity of vision which enabled him to work unceasingly.' Although they both knew that he was dying, he felt, she wrote, that he 'was not at the end of his personal existence. It seemed to me as if we lived in two worlds, a restricted, drab, cruel world of war, and the lovely other world which was quite clearly on the other side of life, in which he and I were quite free in our minds ... Certainly I entered that world through his mind.'

The painting shows a relation between earth and sky, and the changes brought across the earth by night following day. At the right, the slightly smaller half of the painting is illuminated by the setting sun. Everything is focused just off centre by a perspective that leads to the two Clumps and to the entrance to a central black tunnel into the wood beneath them. At the left, advancing across a diagonal divide in the colour, is the rising moon, showing the larger section of the landscape under moonlight. The title indicates that a period of longer night time will be followed by summer. The crux of the painting is a tenuous but compelling visual analogy to a body within the landscape, and with it to the recurring generations of birth and death that echo the recurring seasons. The analogy is nowhere at all explicit, but is a part of the entire tradition that began with the Roman landscapes of Claude Lorrain and were developed so effectively by Richard Wilson, J.M.W. Turner, John Ruskin (in writing), Ford Madox Brown, and on to Michael Andrews. Each of these artists made play with edgy counterpoised forces within what used to be called 'nature', seen as a potential allegory implicit within real observation. This applies as much to photographs as to drawing and painting, and Bill Brandt's *Barbary Castle Marlborough Downs, Wiltshire* (cat. 306) is directly comparable and perhaps was referring to Nash's Wittenham Clumps. This tradition is not restricted to British artists, and it also fits well within the modern canon. Nash's last landscapes may be compared to the compelling reality of De Chirico's illogical rooms and landscapes, where his protagonists encounter challenges to sense and personality and, at times at the end of his life, also between sun and moon (fig. 2). Equally, the Symbolist mode that recurs in Matisse's finest paintings took on more geometric form towards the end of his life in the series of studies of lovers in a

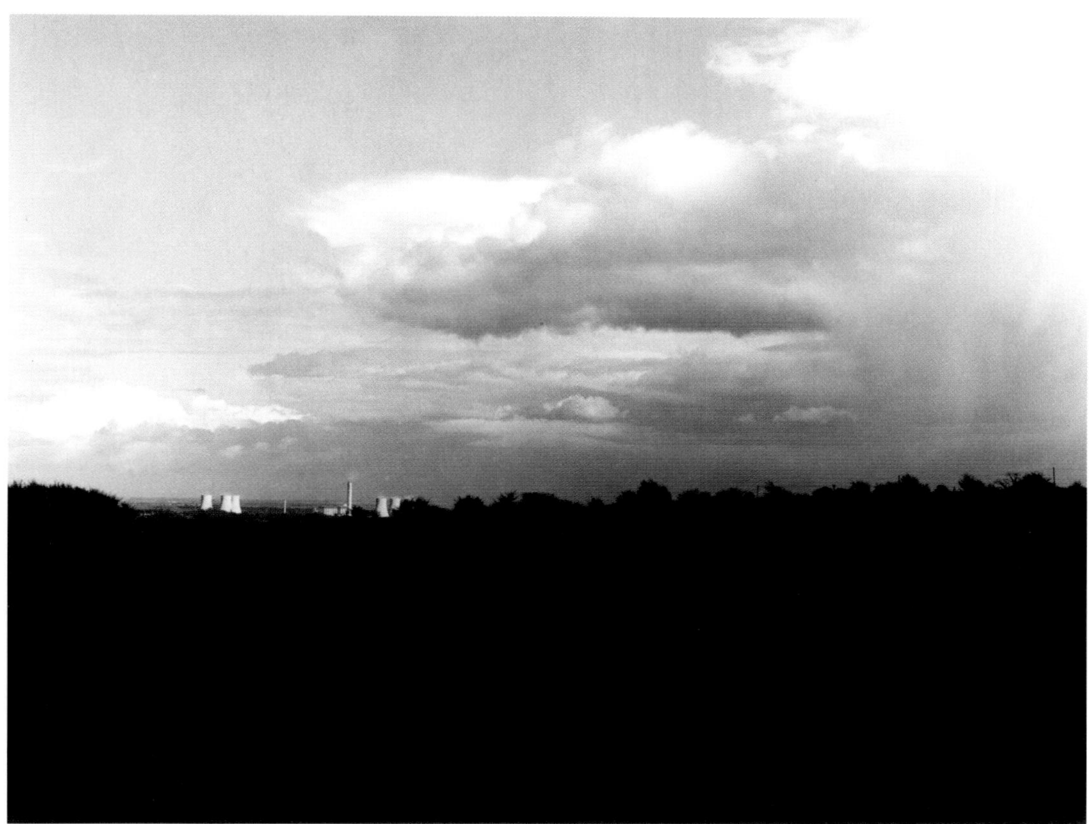

fig. 3
Fay Godwin; ***Didcot Power Station from Segsbury Fort***, c. 1975; Gelatin silver print, 28.8 x 37.8 cm; British Library, London

landscape that lead to *The Snail* (fig. 1). This huge paper cut-out conceals his young lovers within a pattern of abstract shapes that spirals endlessly around lively colours and a deathly black.

Nash's view from Boar's Hill no longer exists, as the Wittenham Clumps now share their dominance with the huge cooling towers of Didcot Power Station (fig. 3). They are likely soon to be joined by a third element, a vast water reservoir that is probably to be built nearby. Such a combination of fire and water, land and sky, with new technology and ancient history, all of it set in geometrical shapes, might have appealed to him.

1. Tate Archive, Nash papers, TGA 769.1.35

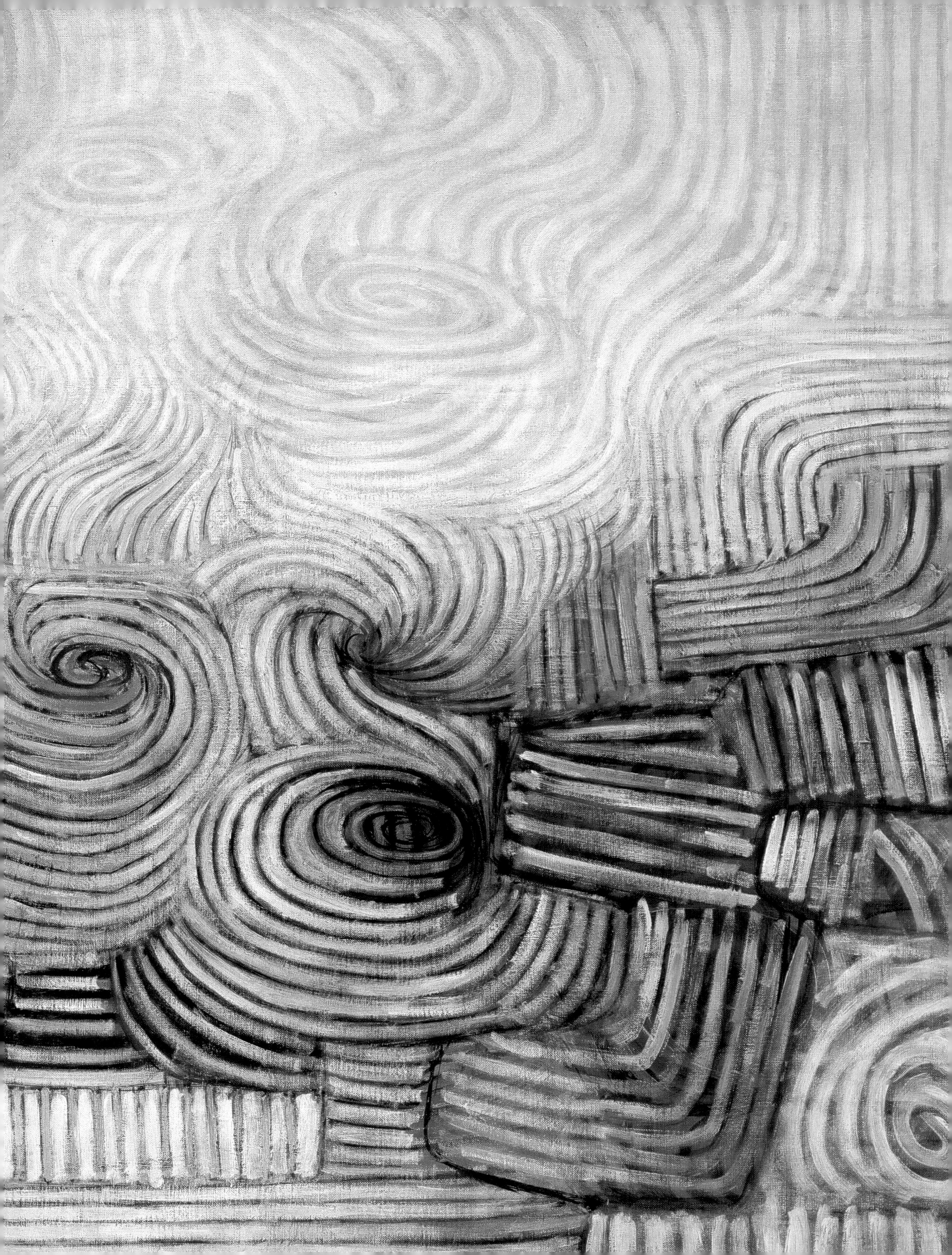

MODERN LANDSCAPE

VICTOR PASMORE

The Snowstorm: Spiral Motif in Black and White, 1950-51

ANDREW DEMPSEY

When Victor Pasmore's painting *The Snowstorm: Spiral Motif in Black and White* was exhibited in the Hayward Gallery, London, in the autumn of 2006 in the exhibition 'How to Improve the World: 60 Years of British Art', the label bore the following quotation from Pasmore himself: 'That snowstorm's not a snowstorm, never was; I put that title on afterwards to please the Arts Council.' This might lead one to wonder what the painting is doing in the landscape section of an exhibition devoted to observation and imagination as continuities in British art. The comment comes from an interview published in 1991 on the occasion of a Pasmore retrospective at the Serpentine Gallery and is both true and also a little tongue-in-cheek.[1] It is characteristic of Pasmore, who was often proselytizing but also had what his lifelong friend William Coldstream referred to as a 'sublime disregard in practice for all rules'.[2]

The *Snowstorm*, as it has certainly become known, was the result of a commission from The Arts Council of Great Britain in the context of the national celebration of the Festival of Britain in 1951. The Council's idea was that the commissioning of large paintings (a minimum of 45 x 60 inches, 114 x 152 cm) might lead to the purchase of contemporary paintings for public buildings; for schools, hospitals, health centres and town halls. Sixty artists were commissioned, and the results formed an exhibition, ' 60 Paintings for '51 ', which was shown at Manchester City Art Gallery and eleven other venues, including the RBA Galleries in London. ('British Vision' includes another work resulting from the commission, L. S. Lowry's *Industrial Landscape*, 1950, cat. 101). The exhibition did not quite reflect the 'brave new world' of the Festival. Out of the fifty-four paintings (there were six non-starters from amongst those originally commissioned) only three were non-representational: Pasmore, Ben Nicholson and William Gear, whose *Autumn Landscape* aroused the most controversy. However, the exhibition and commission proved far-sighted, though not quite in the way intended. Pasmore's painting is one of the masterpieces of the Arts Council Collection, as is another of the commissioned works, *Interior in Paddington* by Lucian Freud. Both paintings were purchased by the Council, the Freud being given subsequently to the Walker Art Gallery in Liverpool. The Pasmore combines abstraction and realism in a fine balance, and it carries into the new art a quality in the actual painting which is part of a long tradition.

The spirit of the 1951 Festival was optimistic, utopian, modern. Pasmore was in many ways the artist of the moment. His conversion to abstraction had been high-profile. He was included in the three exhibitions the Arts Council created to coincide with the event, and he was also commissioned to make a mural for the Regatta Restaurant at the entrance to the Festival site, a work that used the same spiral motifs as the painting (it was titled *The Waterfall*) and captured just the new spirit of the Festival. Unfortunately it did not survive; restaurant, garden and mural were all temporary.

Pasmore was born in 1908. He was fortunate to attend a school that encouraged an interest in the arts, and he carried off prizes for his drawings and paintings. After school he worked for the London County Council, London's city government, and attended art classes at the Central School. He was early in the company of painters, exhibiting with Rodrigo Moynihan, Geoffrey Tibble and others in 'Objective Abstractions' at Zwemmer's Gallery, London, in 1934.

Victor Pasmore, ***The Snowstorm: Spiral Motif in Black and White*** (detail), cat. 218

In 1938 he was able to quit his full-time work at the LCC thanks to the patronage of Kenneth Clark, who was then Director of the National Gallery. At different times Clark owned 'at least twenty' of Pasmore's early paintings.[3] Clive Bell, in the Penguin Modern Painters book on Pasmore (1945), referred to him as 'that fairy godfather of young artists'.[4]

In 1937 Pasmore was one of the initiators of the Euston Road School. Pasmore's main companions in this venture were fellow painters William Coldstream (see cat. 94-95) and Claude Rogers. The purpose of the new academy, first in Fitzroy Street and then, when the studios there became too small for the growing number of pupils, on Euston Road ('the long, unlovely street') is described by Clive Bell as a 'call to order and an antidote to the sensationalism and amateurishness of the school of Paris [by which Bell meant the hordes of international artists who descended on Montparnasse in the inter-war years] ... the Eustonians had no confidence in abstractions, thus parting company at once with Cubism, Neo-Constructivism and all that; also they abhorred literature in painting, which meant that they had no use for Surrealism'.[5] This is a little sweeping, as it is clear that Cézanne and Cubism were important for both Coldstream and Pasmore. In answer to the question of what the new school was for, Pasmore has suggested that each of the four originators - he included Graham Bell amongst those involved 'in the direction' of the school - would have given a different answer but that they were 'united about its main theme - a return to an objective process of visual representation in painting'.[6]

Coldstream may indeed have been the 'animator' (Bell's word) of the new school, and his biographer, Bruce Laughton, acknowledges that 'for years afterwards his [Coldstream's] personal style was considered to be synonymous with the term Euston Road'. But he also points out that amongst the artists early associated with the school were Vanessa Bell and Duncan Grant, who might be thought to represent precisely that 'School of Paris' in its English variant.[7] The new school was no place of dogma, and its parties were famous. The real spirit underlying its belief in objectivity was identification with society and the world in the 1930s. In this sense both Euston Road and Coldstream have a strong relevance to the 'Observation' that is one of the two arteries of the present exhibition. Pasmore's position remained less engaged. He appeared more concerned with the role of painting, though at this time and into the war years he was influenced by Coldstream's odd combination of rigour and doubt.

The school closed shortly after the outbreak of war. Pasmore registered as a conscientious objector, he was imprisoned for a short period and spent the later war years painting in the west of London. The paintings of these years, scenes of the river near Chiswick, the gardens of Hammersmith and nude paintings of his newly married wife Wendy Blood, are amongst the most engaging in modern English art. In the landscapes the journey towards abstraction is evident. The motif of the spiral develops before one's eyes from a detail in the railings of the gardens in Hammersmith (fig. 1, 2). (The nudes are more robust, more French, more Sickertian.) The antecedents of these Chiswick and Hammersmith paintings are clear. They are on that edge of representation and abstraction that characterizes Whistler's *Nocturnes*, and behind them, the paintings of Turner in which the subject is not place but atmosphere.

Lawrence Gowing recalls meeting Kenneth Clark in the newly reopened National Gallery about 1950. He had 'just returned from a visit to Pasmore, who was at the time largely dependent on him. Honest puzzlement shone from his eyes. He said, "Victor is really extraordinary. Do you know he is scrawling spirals all over his pictures. Really, he is the most eccentric man. Great rampant curlicues like nothing on earth".'[8] But Clark regarded Pasmore as 'one of the two or three most talented English painters of this century',[9] and there was general consternation when, after the moment of *The Snowstorm*, Pasmore ceased painting and turned towards the constructed relief, to the work of art occupying real space as an independent object. This was the moment when he turned his back on the illusionism of even non-representational painting, sometimes expressed as Pasmore's 'going abstract', although in reality he left painting.

Lawrence Gowing, painter and one of the finest of recent writers in English on art and artists, had been a friend of Pasmore's since the thirties (and a student at the Euston Road School), and they were to be colleagues at the University in Newcastle in the early fifties. Richard Hamilton (see cat. 105-109) was also there, and Gowing describes the 'roaring' of these three heavyweights as part of the education of the students. For Gowing, Pasmore was 'an enchanting friend and an incomparable painter'. He shared the regret when Pasmore set aside

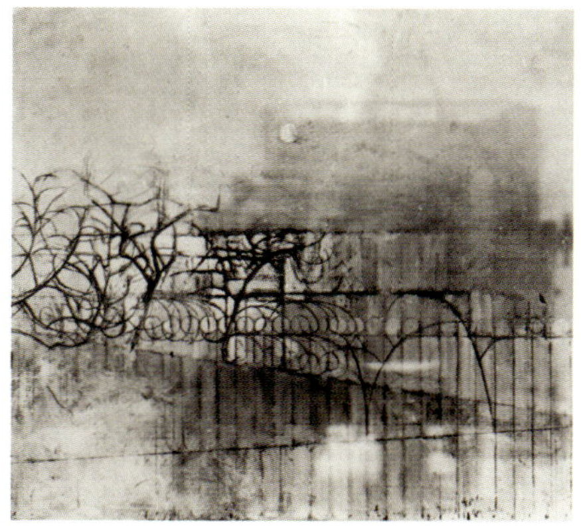

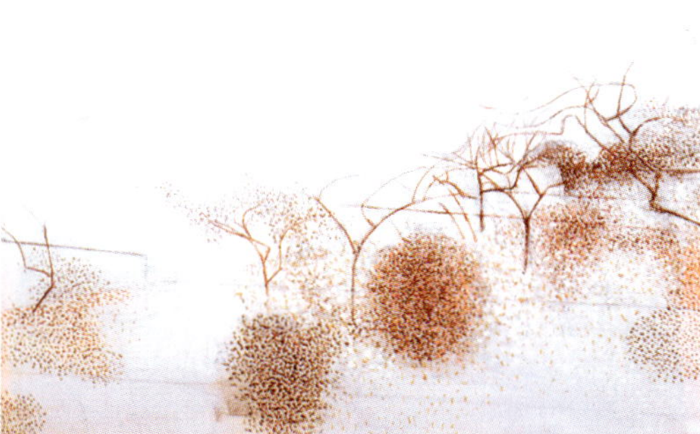

fig. 1
Victor Pasmore
The Hanging Gardens of Hammersmith, no 3, 1947-49
Oil on canvas, 76 x 80 cm
Private Collection

fig. 2
Victor Pasmore
The Hanging Gardens of Hammersmith, no 1, 1944-47
Oil on canvas, 76 x 101.5 cm
Private Collection

his easel: 'The anxiety remained unspoken through the 1950s, through all one's admiration for his constructed work, the question of when and how Victor would paint again.'[10] And he recounts with humour and affection the way he used to leave attractive painting supports lying around the Newcastle studio and would watch Pasmore run his hands over them, but all to no avail.

Pasmore did not return to painting, at least not to the kind of painting that he left at the beginning of the fifties. He was to become a major figure in the history of modernism in Britain, and the key works are the constructed reliefs of the fifties and sixties. The kind of abstract painting represented by *The Snowstorm*, in which a sense of touch (*facture*) is an important element, was taken up Kenneth Martin, a colleague both at Camberwell and in what Alastair Grieve calls the 'neglected avant-garde' of constructed abstract art in post-war England.[11]

I hope it will be clear that the place of Pasmore's *Snowstorm* in this exhibition on observation and imagination in British art is not an anomaly, indeed that this remarkable painting can be placed at the fulcrum of British art in the mid-twentieth century.

1. 'Victor Pasmore in conversation with Mel Gooding and Peter Townsend', *Art Monthly*, no. 146, London, 1991, p. 13.
2. Laughton 2004, p. 29.
3. Clark 1974, p. 220.
4. Bell 1945, p. 5. Sir Kenneth Clark was the General Editor of 'The Penguin Modern Painters' series. He was also Chairman of the War Artists' Advisory Committee in the Second World War and, in the 1950s, Chairman of the Arts Council of Great Britain.
5. Ibid. p. 14.
6. In a memorial tribute included in the pamphlet privately printed by University College London, 1988: *William Coldstream Memorial Meeting*, 24 April 1987, pp. 31-32.
7. Laughton 2004, pp. 47-49.
8. Pasmore 1988, p. 6.
9. Clark 1974, p. 220.
10. Pasmore 1988. p. 9.
11. Grieve 2005. The book gives an authoritative account of the development of Pasmore's art from the paintings of the 1940s to the constructed reliefs of the 1950s and beyond, as well as of his engagement with teaching and architecture.

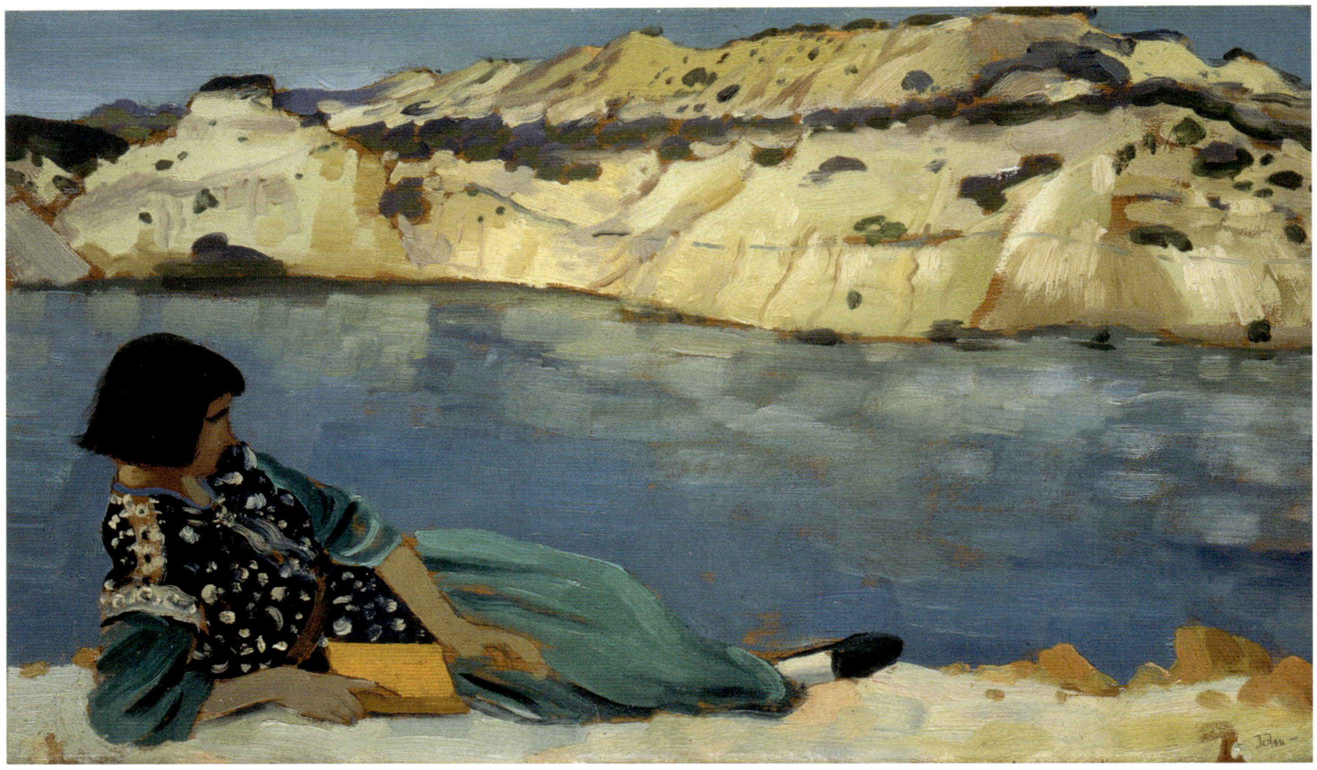

201

201. **Augustus John**
Tenby, Pembrokeshire, 1878 – Fordingbridge, Hampshire, 1961
The Blue Pool, 1911
Oil on panel, 30.2 x 50.5 cm
Bottom right: John
Aberdeen Art Gallery & Museums Collections

The legendary bohemian life of Augustus John, the *enfant terrible* of the British art world during the early twentieth century, has somewhat eclipsed the significance of his achievements as one of the protagonists of modernism in the years preceding the First World War. Strong, vibrant colour began to appear in his work in response to the bright, hot countryside of Provence, where he retreated in January 1910 with his itinerant and ever-burgeoning family. The following year he moved to Alderney Manor in Dorset, but the rich simplicity of his Provençal vision of landscape remained with him. This painting from the summer of 1911 depicts the artist's model and second wife, Dorelia, reclining beside the Blue Pool, a lake in Wareham Heath, near Poole in Dorset. The pool, a former claypit, contained light-diffracting particles which gave the water its intense turquoise colour. The liquid fluidity of the paint on wood panel complements the chromatic force of the scene. (NM)

202. **Augustus John**
Tenby, Pembrokeshire, 1878 – Fordingbridge, Hampshire, 1961
Arenig, 1911-13
Oil on canvas, 45.2 x 76 cm
Bottom left: John
City & County of Swansea: Glynn Vivian Art Gallery Collection

203. **James Dickson Innes**
Llanelli, Carmarthenshire, 1887 – Swanley, Kent, 1914
Arenig Mountain, 1911-12
Oil on canvas, 25.5 x 35.4 cm
City & County of Swansea: Glynn Vivian Art Gallery Collection

Although short lived, the small artistic community of John, Lees and Innes produced a significant number of paintings of the landscape of Merionethshire (Gwynedd) during the years 1910-13. In particular, the artists returned again and again to the motif of the mountain of Arenig, the Welsh equivalent of Cézanne's Mont Sainte-Victoire. They repeatedly painted the distinctive profile in all weathers and at different times of the day. The spectacle of the mountain was most inspiring for Innes, who had 'discovered' it and described it as 'the nearest place to Heaven'. He produced

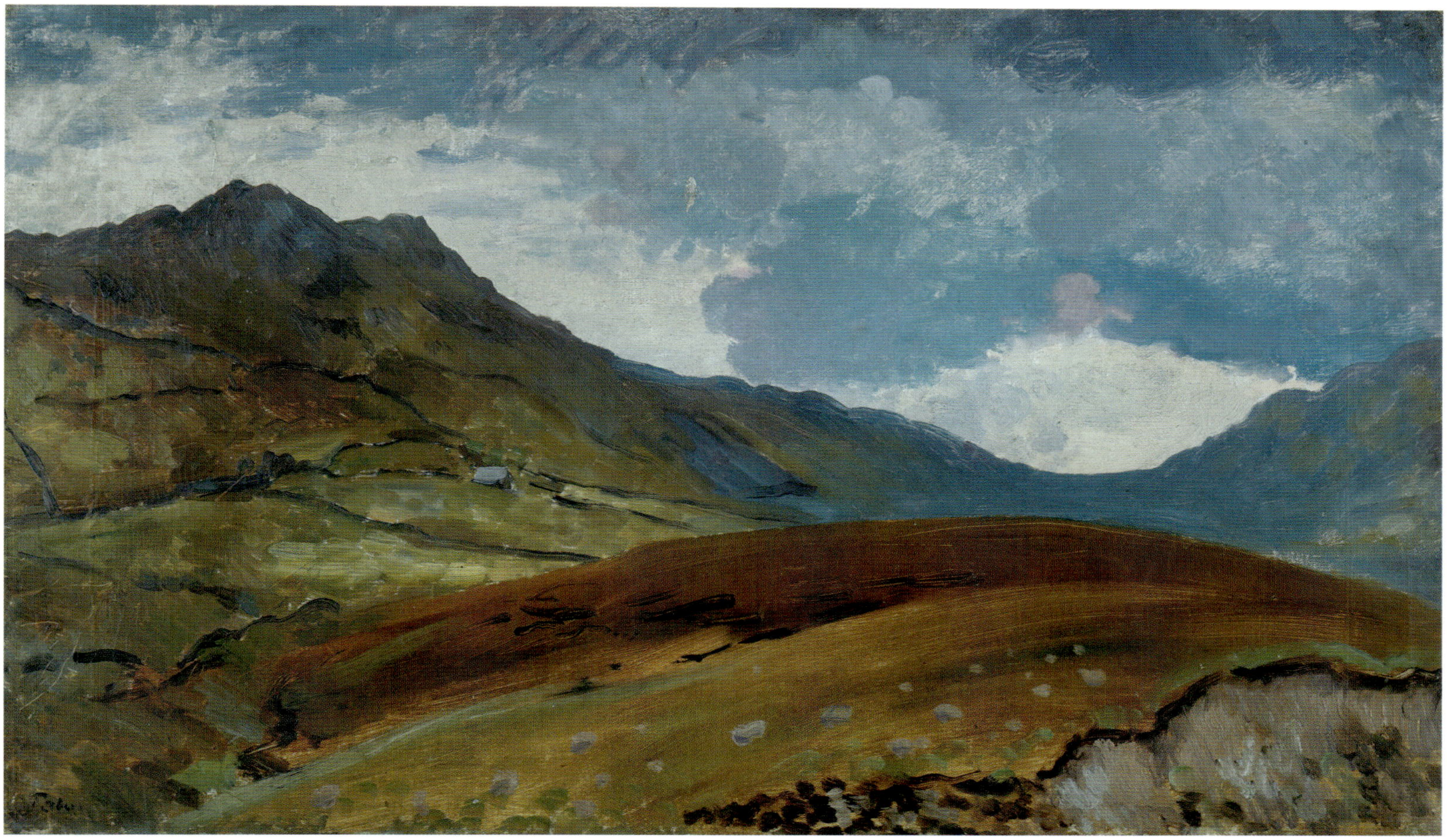

202

small, intense, jewel-like scenes with glowing colours and bold, free forms. By the end of 1913, Innes was too ill to paint, and he died the following year. In the introduction to the catalogue of the memorial exhibition, Augustus John described the significance of Mount Arenig for his friend, explaining that, 'On and around it he did his finest and most inspired work.' (exh. cat. *Memorial Exhibition of Watercolour Drawings and Paintings by the late James Dickson Innes*, London (Chenil Galleries) 1923) (NM)

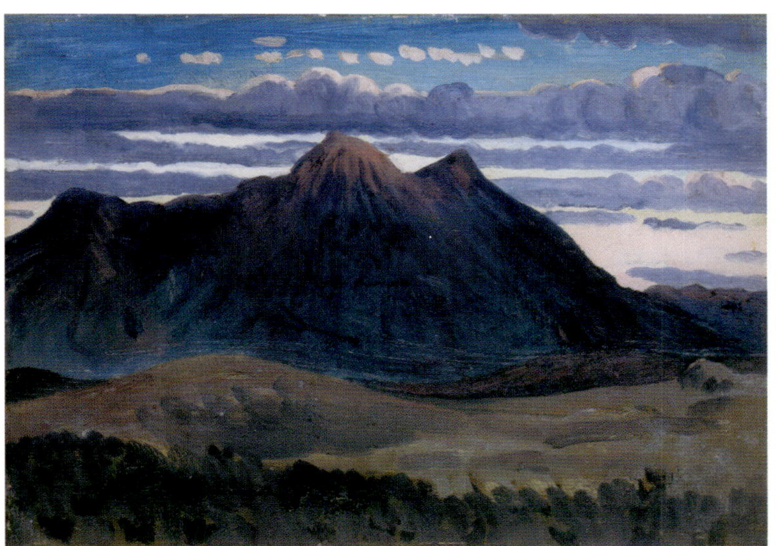

203

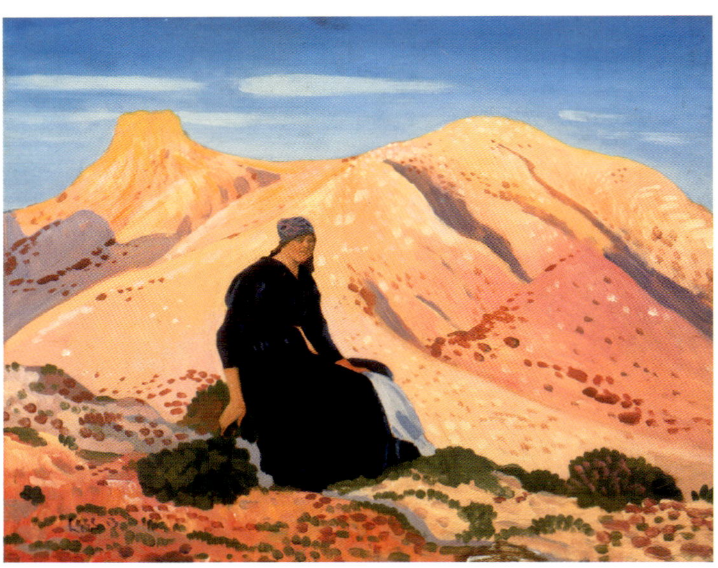

204

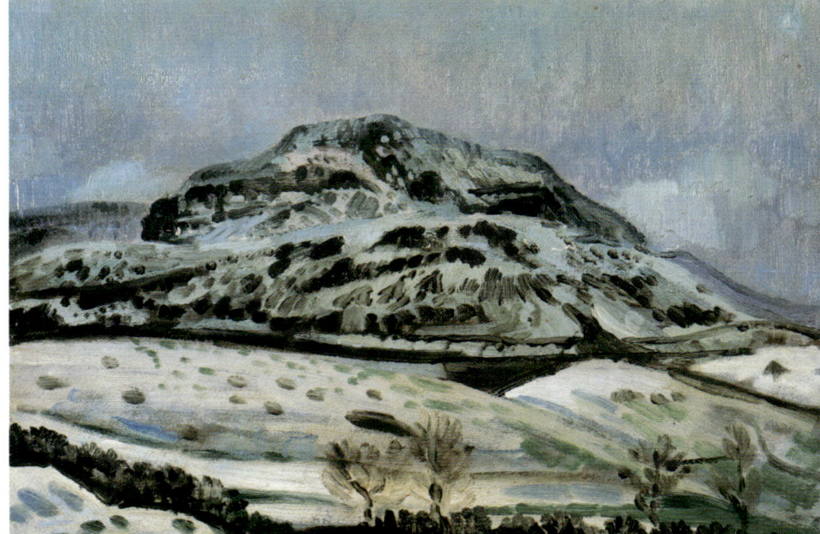

205

204. **Derwent Lees**
Melbourne, Australia, 1885 – London, 1931
Lyndra in the Pyrenees, 1913
Oil on panel, 41.7 x 52 cm
Bottom left: LEES'13
Aberdeen Art Gallery & Museums Collections

Derwent Lees had met Augustus John at the Slade School in London, where he enrolled as a student and later taught drawing. His teaching duties left him little scope for his own work in term time, but during the holidays he travelled widely in Britain and Europe, often in the company of Augustus John or J.D. Innes, painting small oil panels or watercolours. In 1913 he married one of John's models, Lyndra, and produced a number of pictures of her as a solitary female figure standing within a remote and uncultivated landscape. The style of painting was a far remove from the polished, virtuouso draughtsmanship advocated by the Slade for drawings of the human figure but was reminiscent of John's paintings of his wife, Dorelia. The image of the pensive Lyndra in unconventional dress and headscarf, seated against the backdrop of the French Pyrenees was designed to emphasize the wild and meaningful nature of the landscape. (NM)

205. **Derwent Lees**
Melbourne, Australia, 1885 – London, 1931
Welsh Landscape in Winter, 1912-13
Oil on panel, 23 x 33.6 cm
City & County of Swansea: Glynn Vivian Art Gallery Collection

Between 1911 and 1913, native Welshman James Dickson Innes persuaded his fellow-countryman Augustus John and their Slade colleague Derwent Lees to join him on a painting campaign in the mountains of north Wales. The three artists made a colourful and chaotic trio: the eccentric and flamboyant John, the consumptive and romantic Innes and Derwent Lees, the Australian-born *émigré* with a wooden leg. They all responded to the wild, remote landscape in different ways. This atmospheric oil painting of the Arenig Mountain in the snow replicates the delicacy of Lees's work in watercolour.

Throughout his life Lees suffered from a mental health problem. The wife of one of John's patrons, Lady Howard de Walden, recalled that, 'he did paint rather well but was as mad as a hatter.' (quoted in Rowan 1982, p. 19) His illness would eventually curtail his artistic career. In 1918 he was committed to an asylum, where he remained for the rest of his life. (NM)

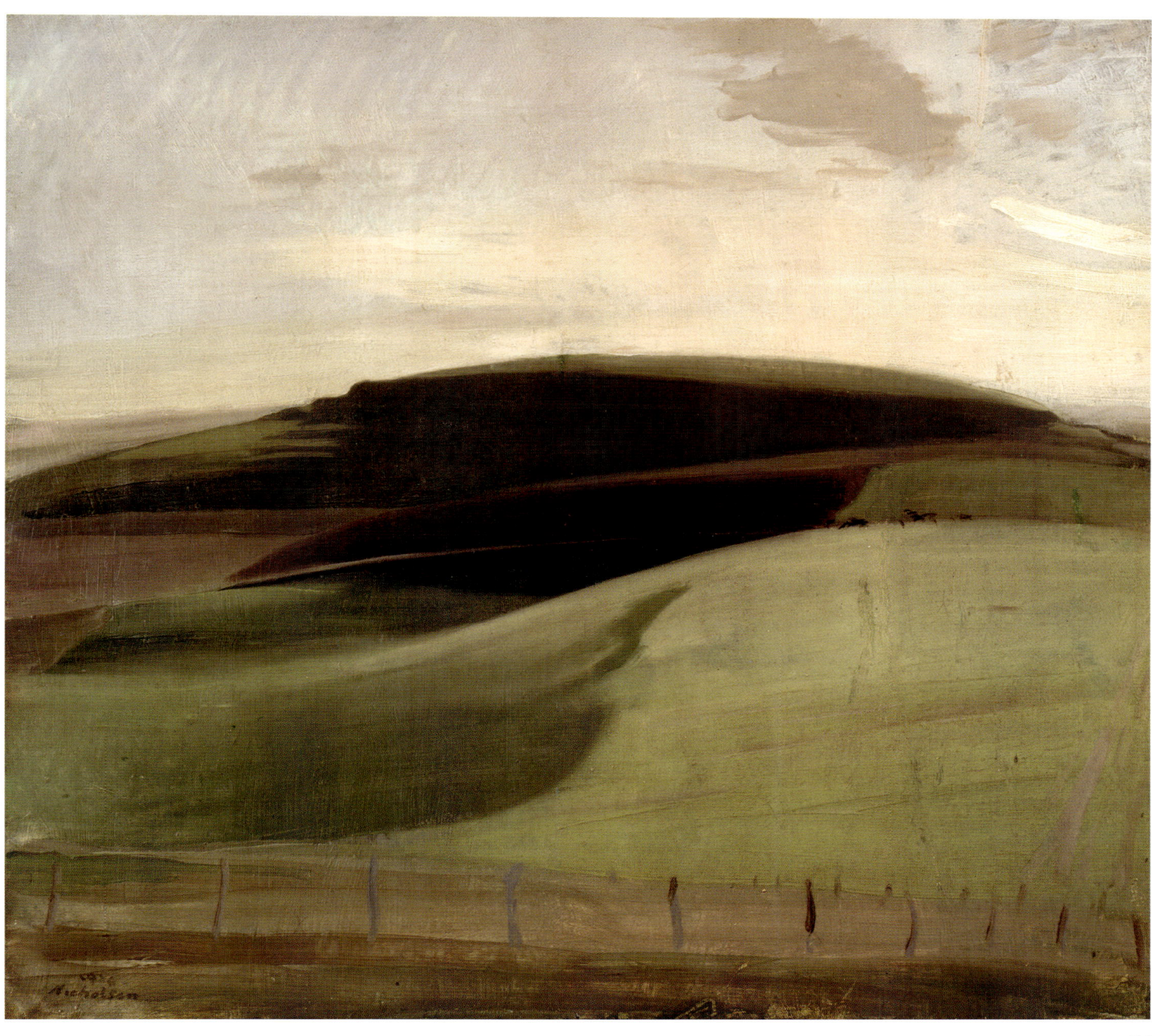

206

206. **William Nicholson**
Newark-on-Trent, Nottinghamshire, 1872 - Blewbury, Berkshire, 1949
On the Downs (Wiltshire Landscape), 1924
Oil on canvas, 53.2 x 59.8 cm
Bottom left: 1924 / Nicholson
Leeds Museums and Galleries (City Art Gallery)

Best known for his distinctive black and tan woodcut illustrations, William Nicholson was also a painter of portraits, still lifes and landscapes. In 1923 he moved to Sutton Veny in Wiltshire, where, as in his earlier paintings of Sussex, he was drawn to the area's wide valleys and rolling downland. Nicholson's landscapes are modern evocations of space and light. He was fond of painting *contre jour*, looking towards the sun, so that the gentle luminosity of the sky is offset against the dark smoothness of the silhouetted horizon. A sense of depth and scale is achieved by the inclusion in the foreground of a line of fencing, the only sign of human intervention within the scene. This incidental detail serves to heighten the emptiness and flatness of the picture plane and create a mood of contemplative isolation. (NM)

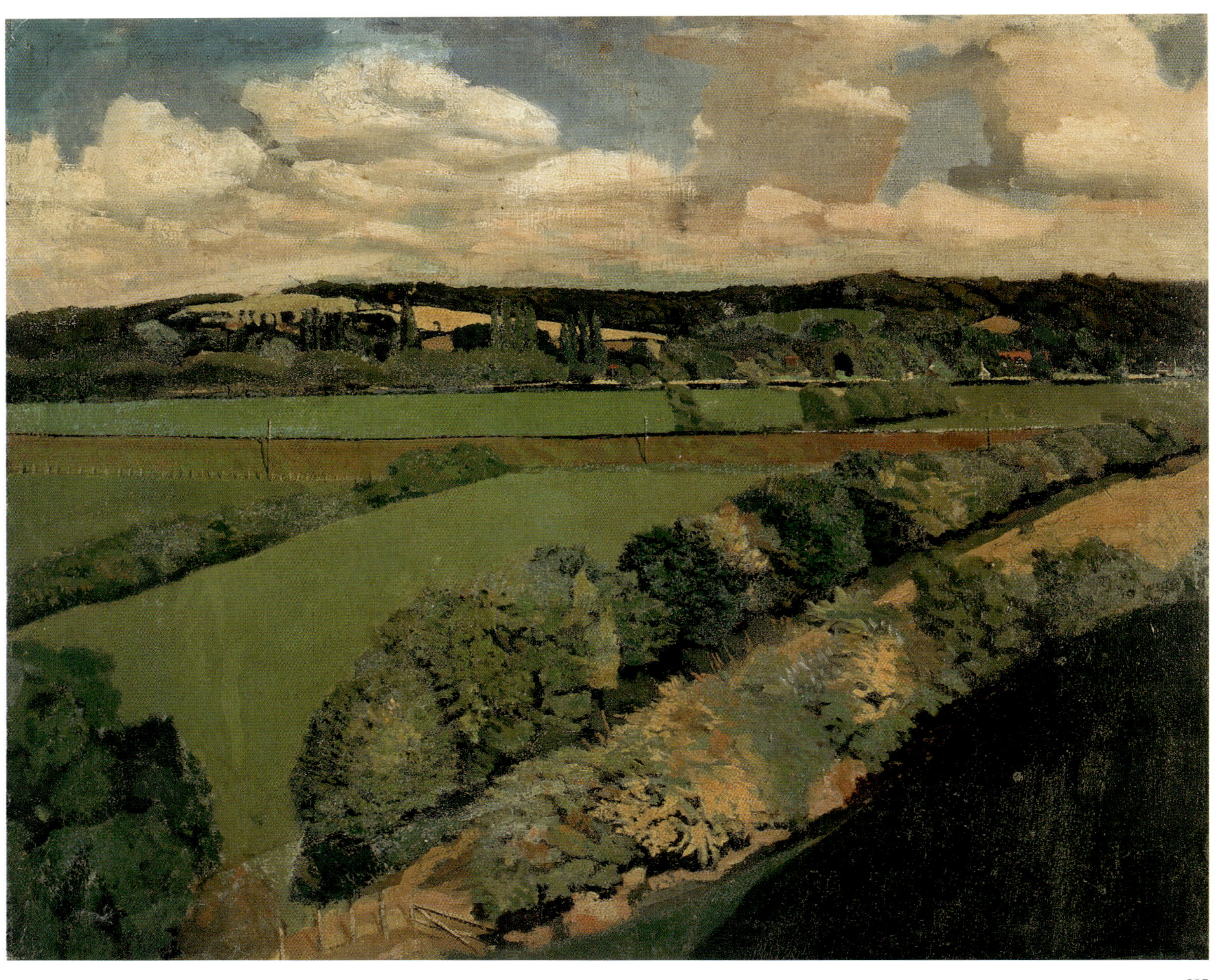

207

207. **Stanley Spencer**
Cookham, Berkshire, 1891 – Cliveden, Buckinghamshire, 1959
Cookham, 1914
Oil on canvas, 44.8 x 54.5 cm
Tullie House Museum & Art Gallery, Carlisle

By the summer of 1914, Spencer, still living in the parental home, had brought off two of his most compelling imaginative compositions, *Zacharias and Elizabeth* (see cat. 284) and *The Centurion's Servant* (Tate, London). But he had also painted an impressive *Self-Portrait* directly from life; and from *The Nativity* (cat. 286) onwards, several elements were painted outdoors from close natural observation. England is – as this exhibition demonstrates – centrally a landscape culture; and, despite his theoretical resistance, in this first 'pure' landscape Spencer achieved a masterpiece of transcendent naturalism, hedgerow and foliage rendered with such a sharp-focused intensity that they become strange, 'uncanny'. The gulf of darkness at bottom right is telling and powerful. He had looked closely at the landscapes of Ford Madox Brown and other Pre-Raphaelites; his father is known to have visited Holman Hunt. Something of the PRB fascination with minutely observed forms would persist throughout his work. (TH)

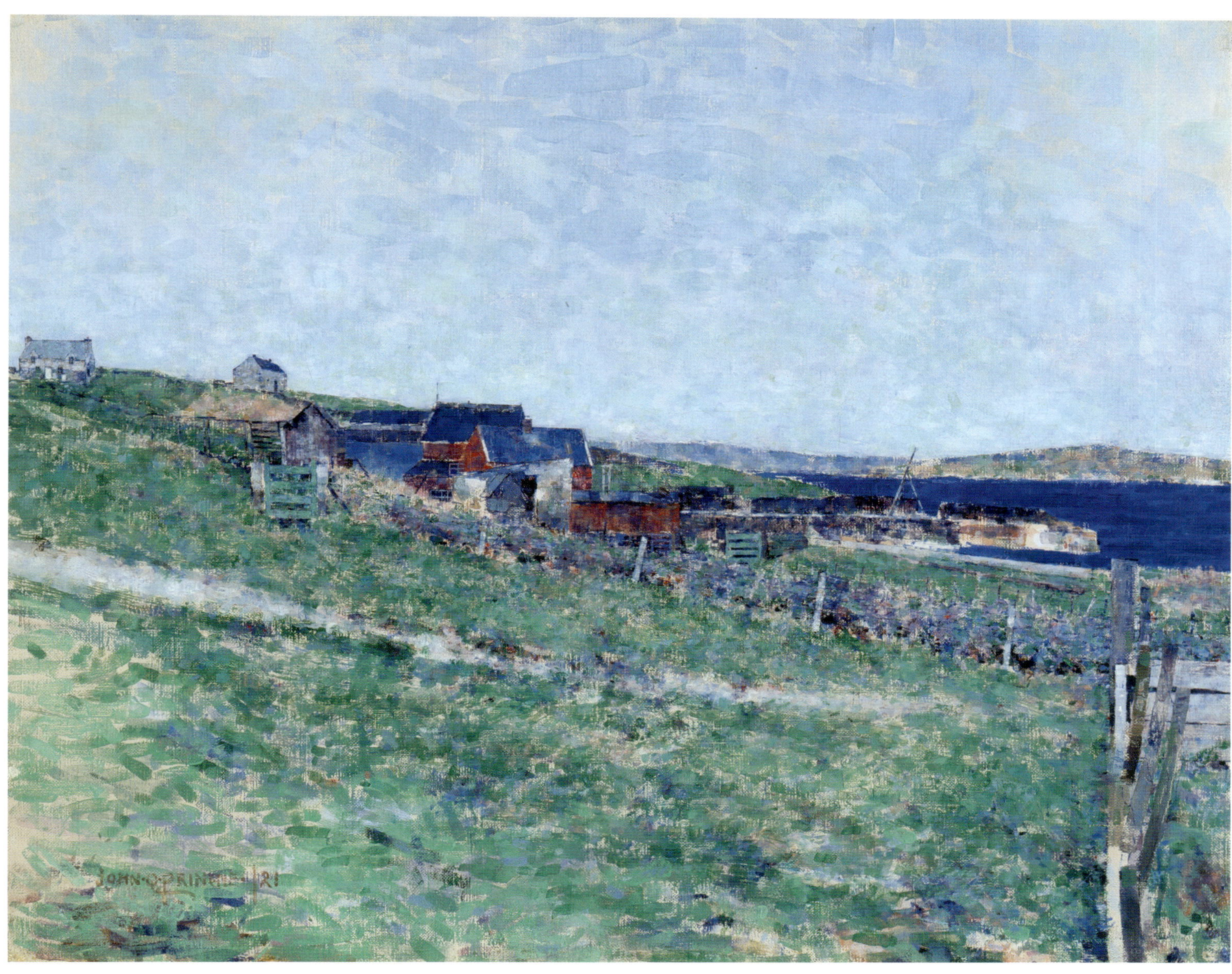

208

208. **John Quinton Pringle**
Glasgow, 1864 - Glasgow, 1925
Curing Station Whalsay, Shetland, 1921
Oil on canvas, 50 x 60.5 cm
Bottom left: JOHN Q. PRINGLE. / 21
Aberdeen Art Gallery & Museum Collections

In 1910 during the Glasgow Fair Fortnight Pringle closed his shop and went to Caudebec in Normandy on a painting holiday. This was his only known trip abroad, though he would have been familiar with modern French painting through the early appreciation of Glasgow collectors. This coruscating view of a fish-curing station in Whalsay, Shetland, was painted while Pringle was staying with a doctor friend. It was on a similar visit to Whalsay in 1921 that he had resumed painting in oils after about ten years of working only in watercolours (presumably because of ill health and the pressure of his business life). Pringle's characteristic square brush mark derives from the French painter Jules Bastien-Lepage, who was hugely influential north of the border, but Pringle developed it into a decorative variation of *pointillisme* that was entirely his own, thinning his paint so that it appears almost like watercolour. Impressionism, or rather Post-Impressionism, in the British Isles gets no better than *Curing Station, Whalsay*. (AD)

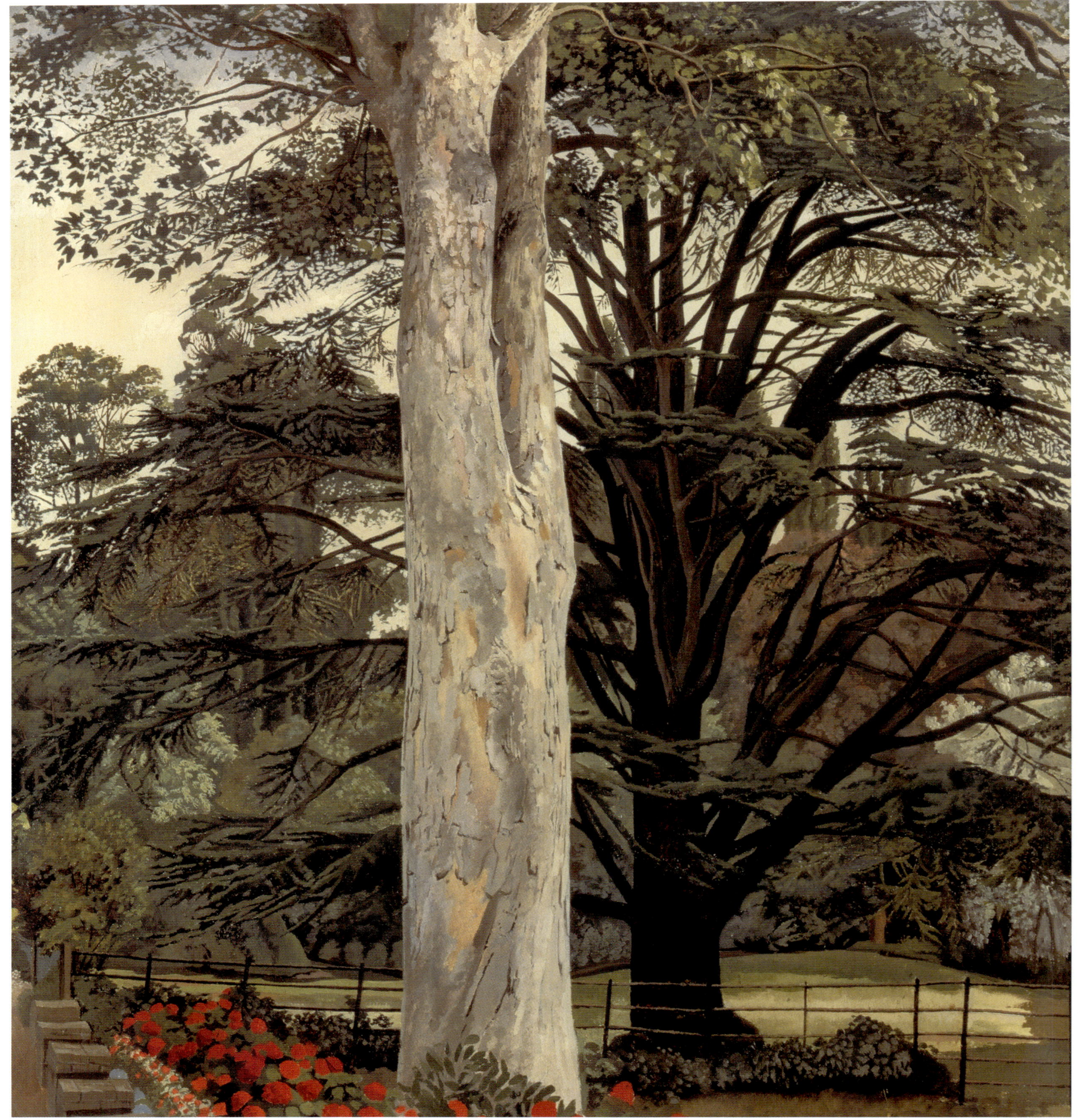

209

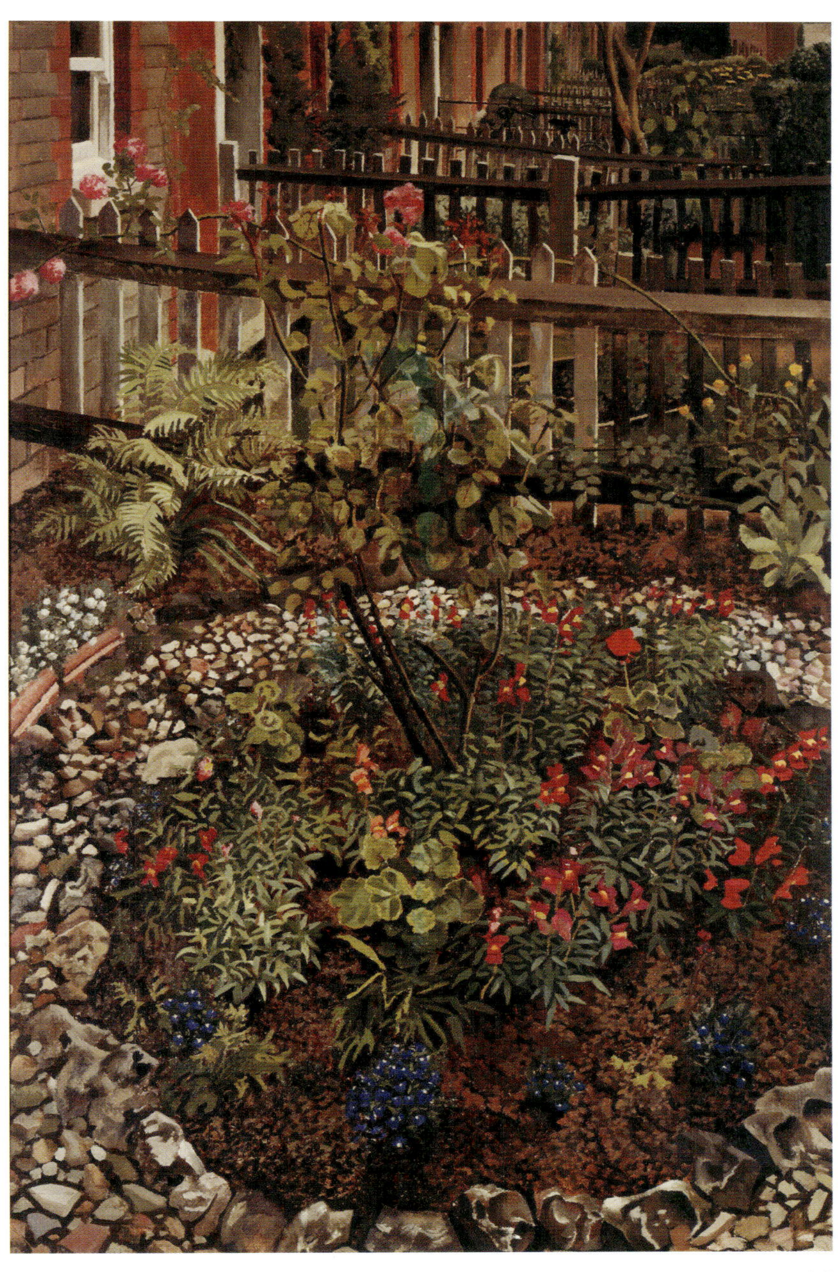

210

209. **Stanley Spencer**
Cookham, Berkshire, 1891 - Cliveden, Buckinghamshire, 1959
The Cedar Tree, Cookham, 1935
Oil on canvas, 76.2 x 71.1 cm
Private Collection

210. **Stanley Spencer**
Cookham, Berkshire, 1891 - Cliveden, Buckinghamshire, 1959
Cookham Rise Cottages, c. 1935-36
Oil on canvas, 75.6 x 49.5 cm
Private Collection

Spencer's landscapes of the 1930s come out of a complex history. By 1926, he already experienced a split: 'I feel really that everything in one that is not vision is mainly vulgarity. It has always puzzled me the way people have always preferred my landscapes. I can sell them but not my Joachims. This fact of recent years has had a wearing effect on me ...' (Hyman and Wright 2001, p. 24). When he returned to Cookham in 1932, after almost a decade away (first in Hampstead, then at Burghclere chapel), he was in a difficult situation. With his war memorial chapel completed, he dreamt of a new kind of painted interior, both domestic and sacramental -a 'Church House' dedicated to love, partly inspired by the temples of Khajuraho. Beginning with pictures such as *The Dustman* (cat. 298), this would occupy him much of the next ten years. In addition, his marriage to Hilda was in trouble, and he soon fell prey to a local woman, Patricia Preece, to whom he made large gifts of jewellery that put him into debt. Hence what he called 'this complacent stream of landscapes ... Money need ...

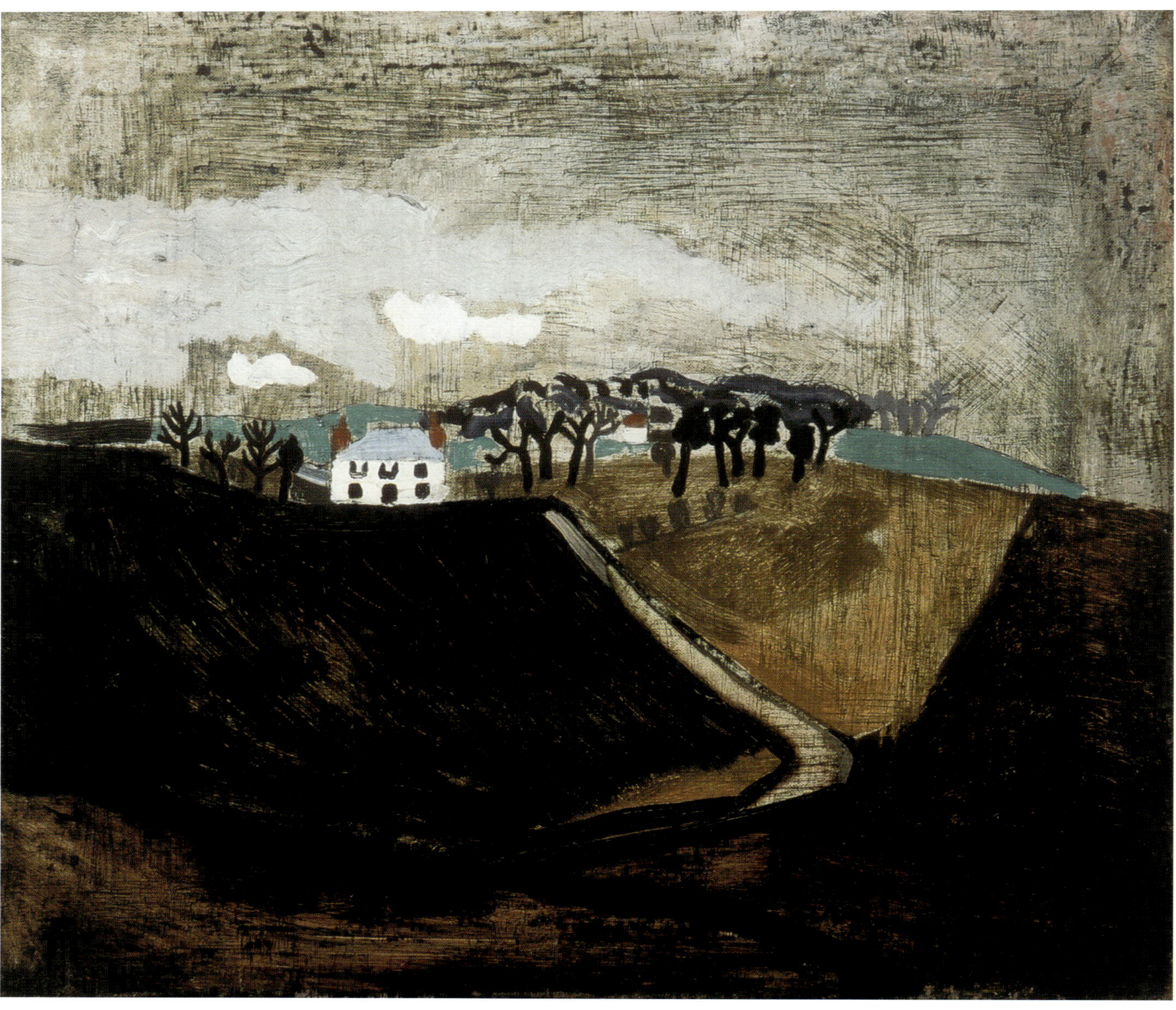

211

Doggedness' (ibid.). But Spencer did have a genuine feeling for the minutiae of nature; while some landscapes may appear heartless and mechanical, others are works of the highest quality, which vigorously take up the landscape traditions discussed in this catalogue. As the cultural historian Patrick Wright has shown, Spencer's choice of motif – humdrum, 'lower-middle-class', or downright 'ugly' – often distances him from his more conservative Ruralist contemporaries, those 'morbid elegists of English country life' (ibid., p. 70). Spencer was challenged and excited by close study of anything, be it plant or brick wall or portrait: 'I want to see John Donnes and Joachims in the shape of people's noses and mouths.' His landscape practice developed his extraordinary talent for highly controlled sharp-focused detail, which would feed directly into his 'Naked Portraits' (see cat. 87). (TH)

211. **Ben Nicholson**
Denham, Buckinghamshire, 1894 – London, 1982
Cumberland Farm, 1930
Oil and pencil on canvas, 38.5 x 43 cm
Verso: Ben Nicholson 1930 / Kit from Ben
Royal Pavilion, Libraries and Museum, Brighton and Hove

212. **Ben Nicholson**
Denham, Buckinghamshire, 1894 – London, 1982
Mousehole, 1947
Oil and pencil on canvas, mounted on board, 46.5 x 58.5 cm
British Council, London

In the immediate post-war period, Ben Nicholson, son of William Nicholson, became one of three instantly identifiable modern masters of twentieth-century British art. The others are Henry Moore and Barbara Hepworth. They are the artists whose reputations were both national and international. Of

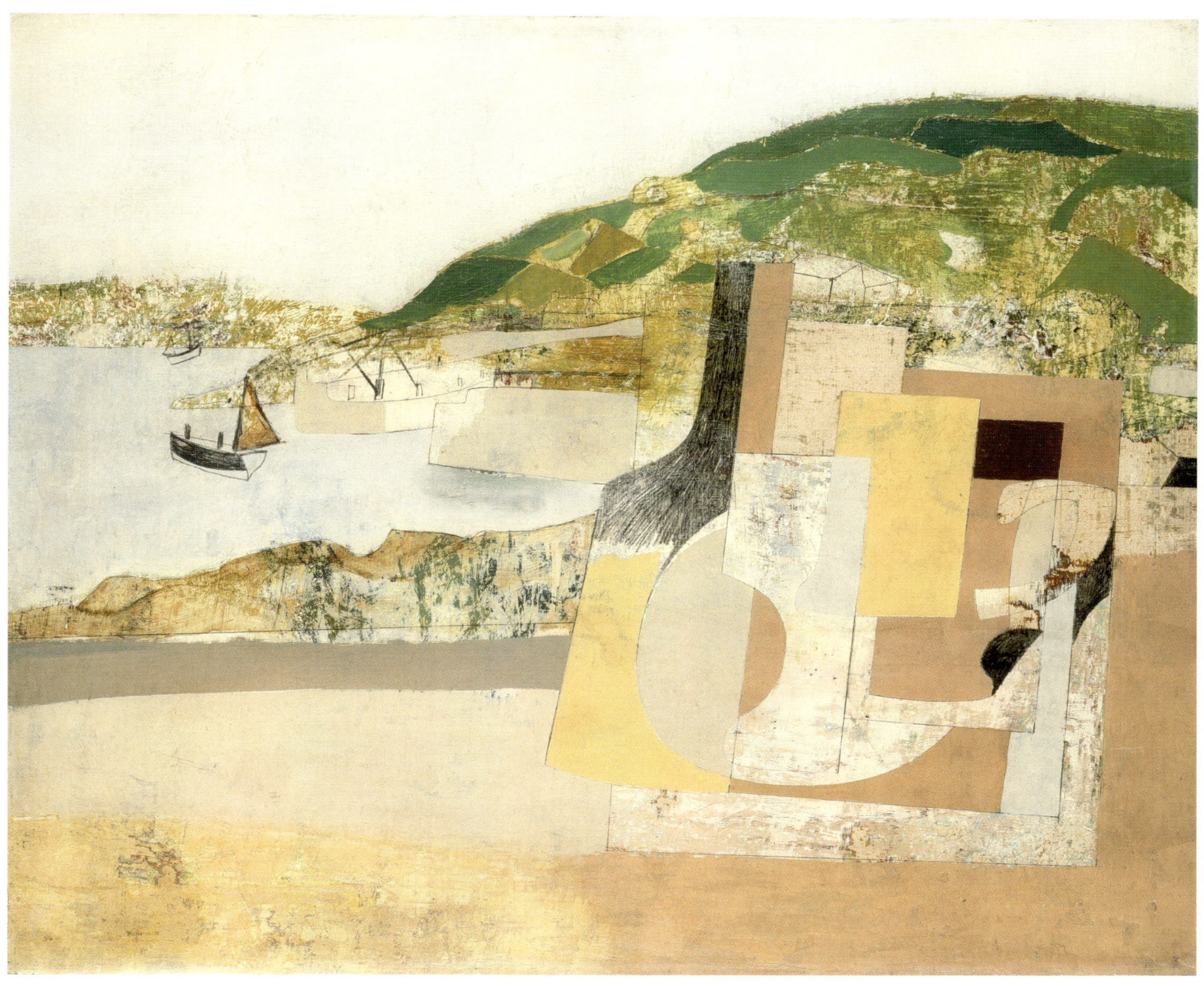

212

the three, Nicholson's range is perhaps the greatest. Herbert Read writes of his 'extremes of realism and abstraction' ('Notes on Abstract Art' in Nicholson 1948, p. 17), though Nicholson's realism was a far cry from his father's. One extreme to which Read was referring was that of the monochromatic abstract reliefs of the 1930s, which remain amongst the finest works of British 'modernism', but which are outside the scope of the present exhibition. Nicholson wrote that 'the kind of painting which I find exciting is not necessarily representational or non-representational, but it is both musical and architectural, where the architectural construction is used to express a "musical" relationship between form, tone and colour and whether this visual "musical" relationship is slightly more or slightly less abstract is for me beside the point' (ibid., p. 27).

The Cumberland landscape dates from the period of Nicholson's first marriage to the painter Winifred Nicholson (née Roberts) and shows Nicholson's supreme ability to synthesize and simplify. His combination of representation and non-representation led him to make some strange hybrids, such as this landscape of the Cornish fishing village of Mousehole, in which the hills are depicted in the greens that were to become so characteristic of the St Ives School but in which a cubist still life of overlapping planes is inserted into the painted view. Nicholson called this kind of image 'still life-landscape', its combination of inside and outside deriving from painting a scene from a window. (AD)

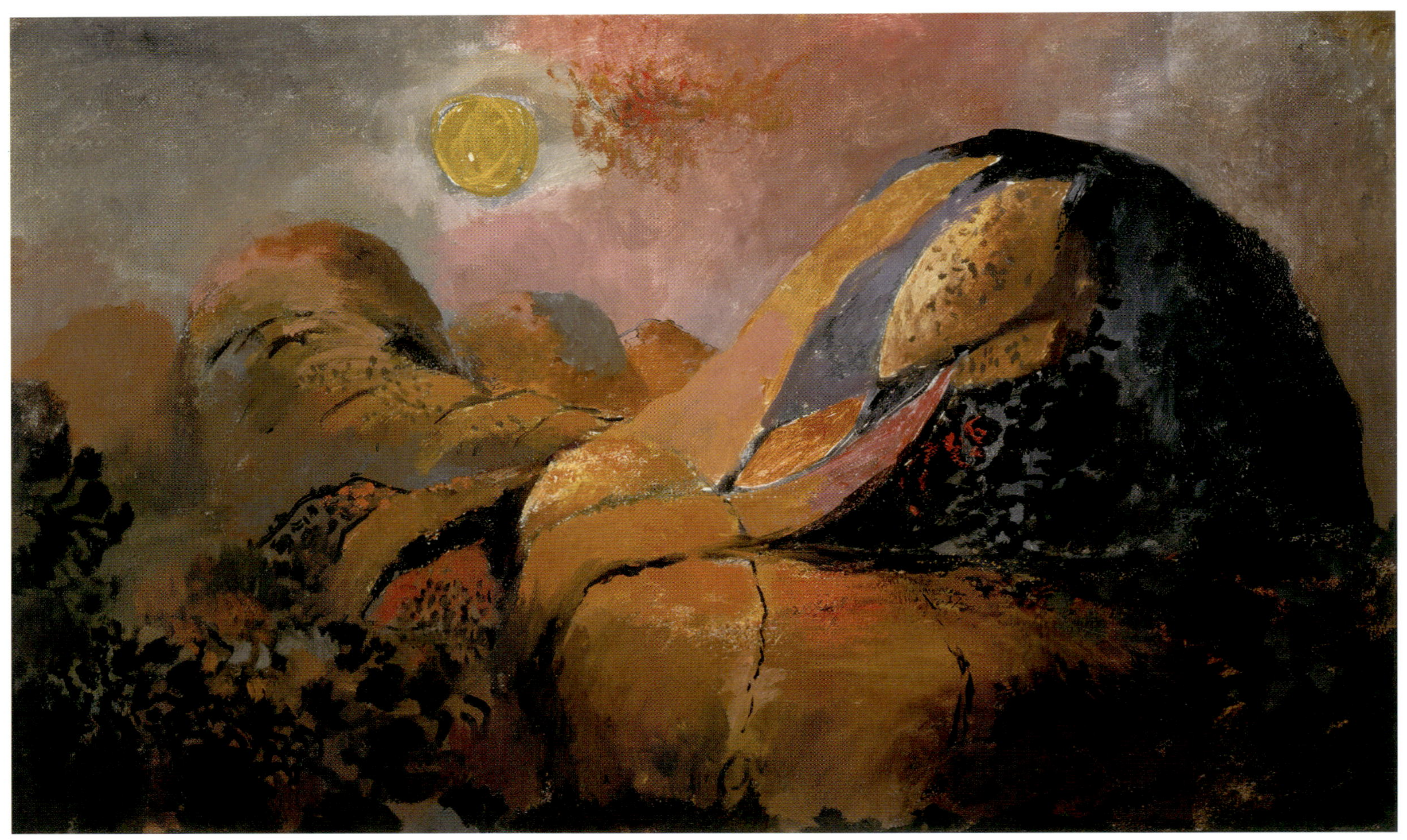

213

213. **Graham Sutherland**
London, 1903 - London, 1980
Western Hills, 1938-41
Oil on canvas, 55.5 x 90.5 cm
Scottish National Gallery of Modern Art, Edinburgh

Graham Sutherland started his artistic career as a printmaker but was inspired to begin oil painting during the 1930s after visiting the wild Pembrokeshire coastline. He experienced a deeply personal response to the Welsh landscape and consequently returned to the area every summer for six years. From these trips he developed a dramatic and subjective method of painting from memory, aided by sketches paraphrasing the elements of the landscape. He later wrote to a friend 'I did not feel that my imagination was in conflict with the real, but that reality was a dispersed and disintegrated form of imagination' (Sutherland 1942, p. 235). The overlap between what is real and what is imagined is evident in the contrast between the vibrant patches of textured earth, illuminated by the yellow disc of sun, and the intense black linearity of the Clegyr Boia, the rocky outcrop Sutherland depicted in a number of works of this period. (NM)

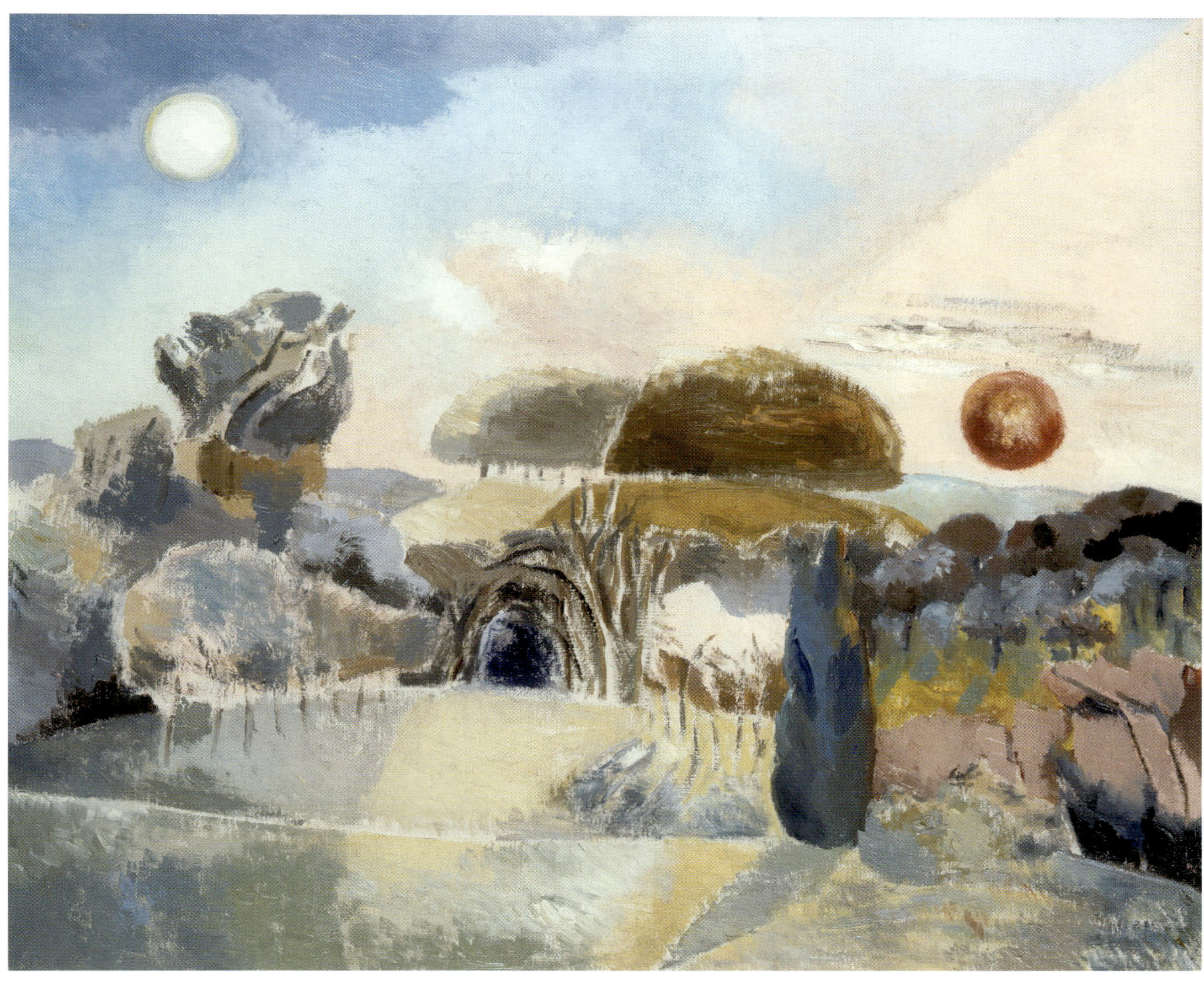

214

214. **Paul Nash**
London, 1889 - Boscombe, Hampshire, 1946
Landscape of the Vernal Equinox (III), 1944
Oil on canvas, 63.5 x 76.2 cm
Scottish National Gallery of Modern Art, Edinburgh

The *Landscape of the Vernal Equinox* is one of a series of large landscape paintings done at the end of Nash's life. Characteristically, what he shows was more or less there but is changed in arrangement, scale and colouring. He was then thoroughly ill and painted mostly in his Oxford house on the Banbury Road, but he saw this scene often from a friend's house at Sandlands on Boar's Hill, a few miles to the west of the city. The view is about due south, showing in middle ground a garden in early spring, looking towards the entrance to a small wood. In the centre ground, painted out of scale and large, are the pair of hills called the Wittenham Clumps, each with a cluster of beeches on top. At either side, brought in from their real places further apart, are a rising full moon at the left and a setting sun at right. The picture has an overt geometrical structure in the shape of an X and partly abstract colouring. Nash had in fact stared at the Wittenham Clumps from Sandlands through binoculars, and perhaps he used a mirror to see the sun and moon at the same time. It was important to him that everything was actually there, as an observed fact, and yet also that it could be slightly manipulated to reveal something more serious. (DFJ)

See essay pp. 281-83.

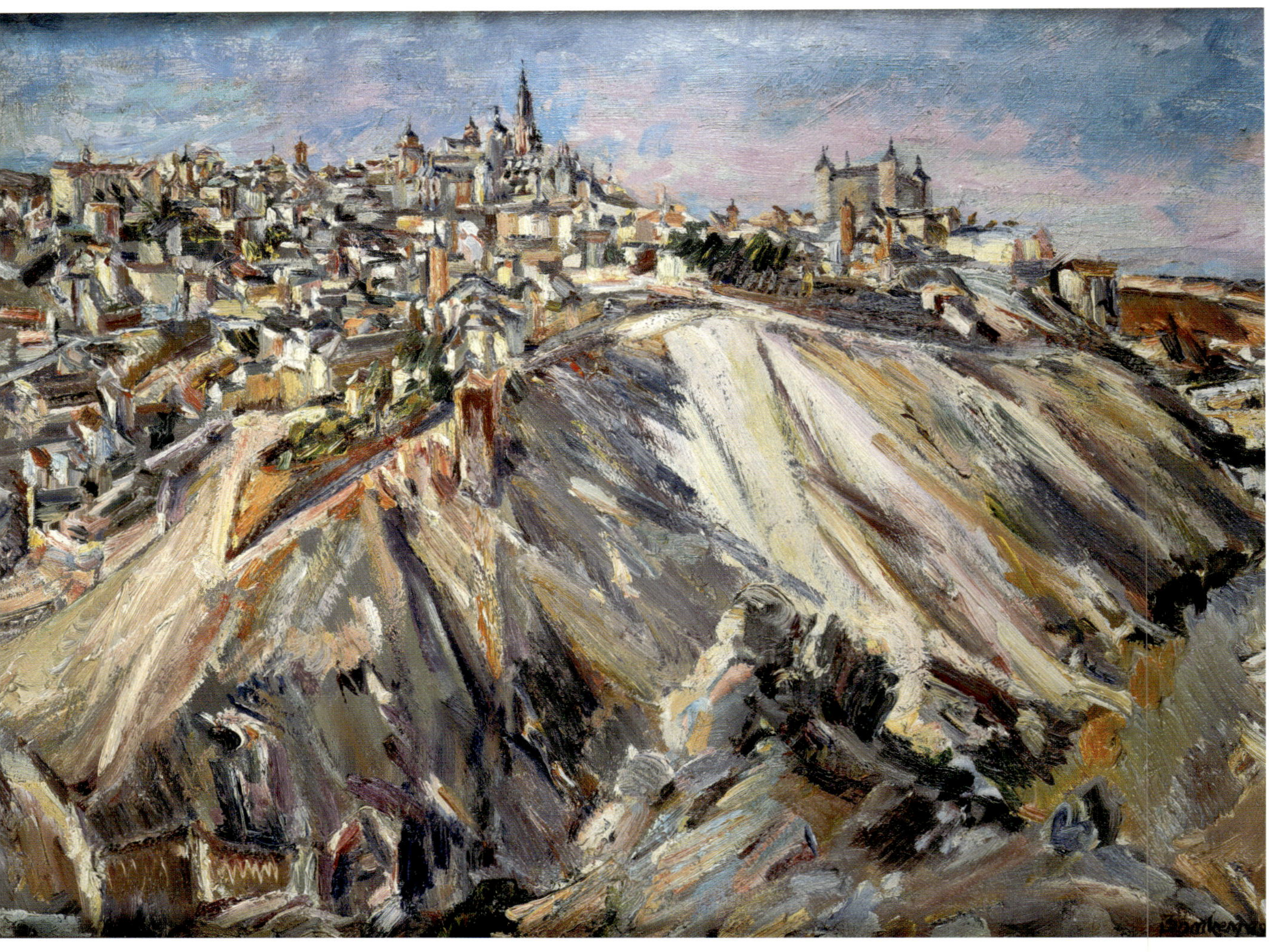

215

215. **David Bomberg**
Birmingham, 1890 - London, 1957
Toledo and River Tajo, 1929
Oil on canvas, 58.4 x 76.2 cm
Bottom right: Bomberg 29
Gallery Oldham

It is arguable that Bomberg's mature style was forged in Toledo in the six months he spent there in 1929. It was his first visit to a country that was to provide a rich subject for his landscape paintings (he returned for eighteen months in 1934-35 and again, to live in the south near Ronda, in the 1950s). In Toledo the literalism and clear structure of the Jerusalem paintings (1923-27) gives way to a more expressive handling. A quality of the Toledo paintings is that the energy and breadth of the painting still permits a remarkable precision of detail. Churches, streets, houses, vegetation, hillsides, mountains are all rendered (shaped would be a better word) so that they are instantly legible; and the elements, the light and the wind, are almost tangible. None of the paintings were sold when exhibited in London in 1932. (AD)

216. **David Bomberg**
Birmingham, 1890 - London, 1957
Trendrine, Cornwall, 1947
Oil on canvas, 81.3 x 106.7 cm
Bottom right: Bomberg / 47
Arts Council Collection, South Bank Centre, London

Bomberg spent the war years in London. He obtained only one commission from the War Artists' Advisory Committee and began teaching drawing, not in the art schools which were closed to him, but in Evening Institutes and architectural schools. After the war he taught at the Borough Polytechnic, where a group of students receptive to his approach to form, his search for 'the spirit in the mass', formed themselves around him. The landscapes made on painting expeditions to Devon and Cornwall in these years and in Cyprus on a summer visit in 1948 have come to be regarded as the summation of his work. They have a lyrical abstraction that is in marked contrast to art in England in the immediate post-war period. The example of Bomberg was important for younger painters such as Leon Kossoff and Frank Auerbach. (AD)

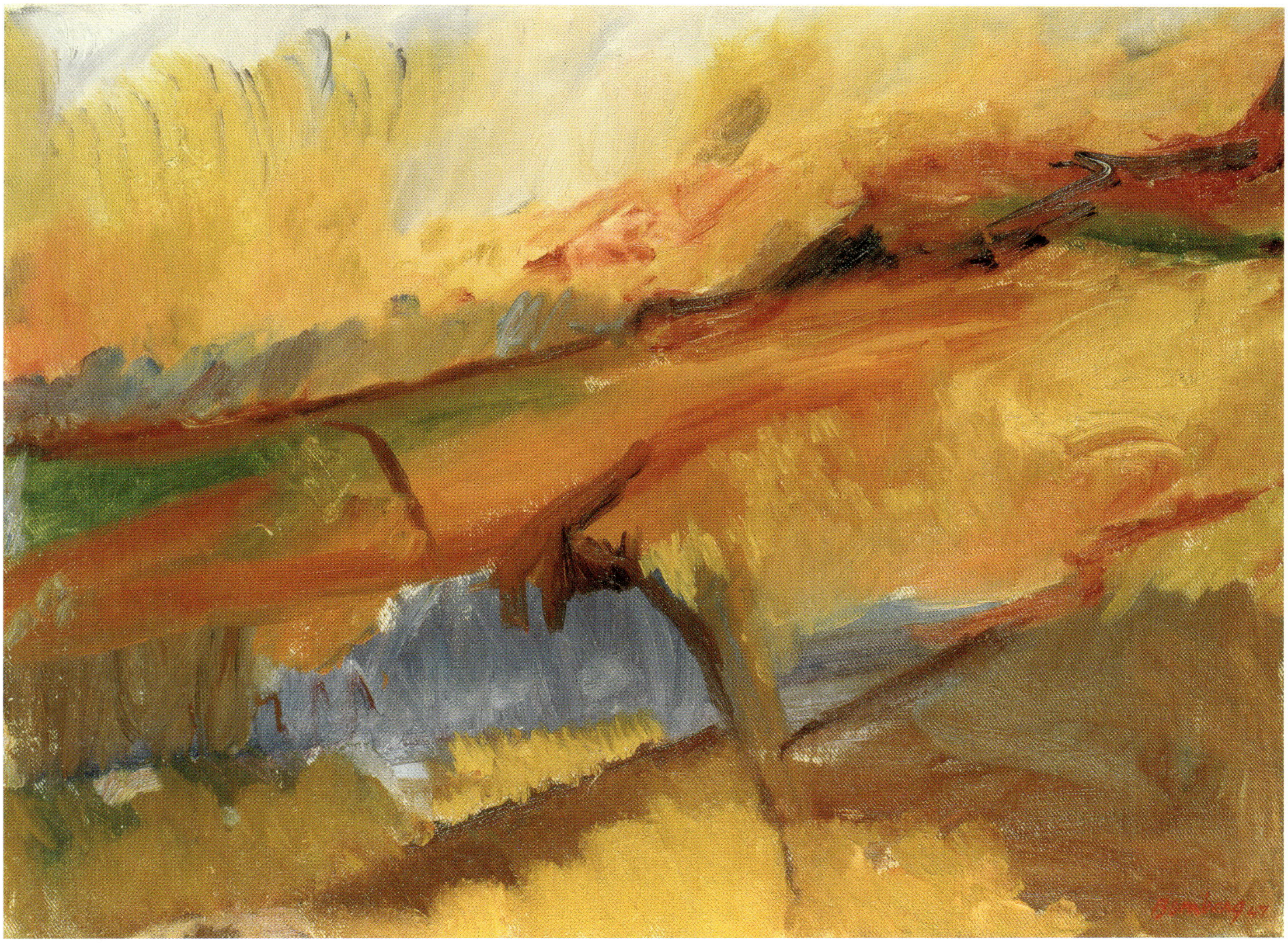

216

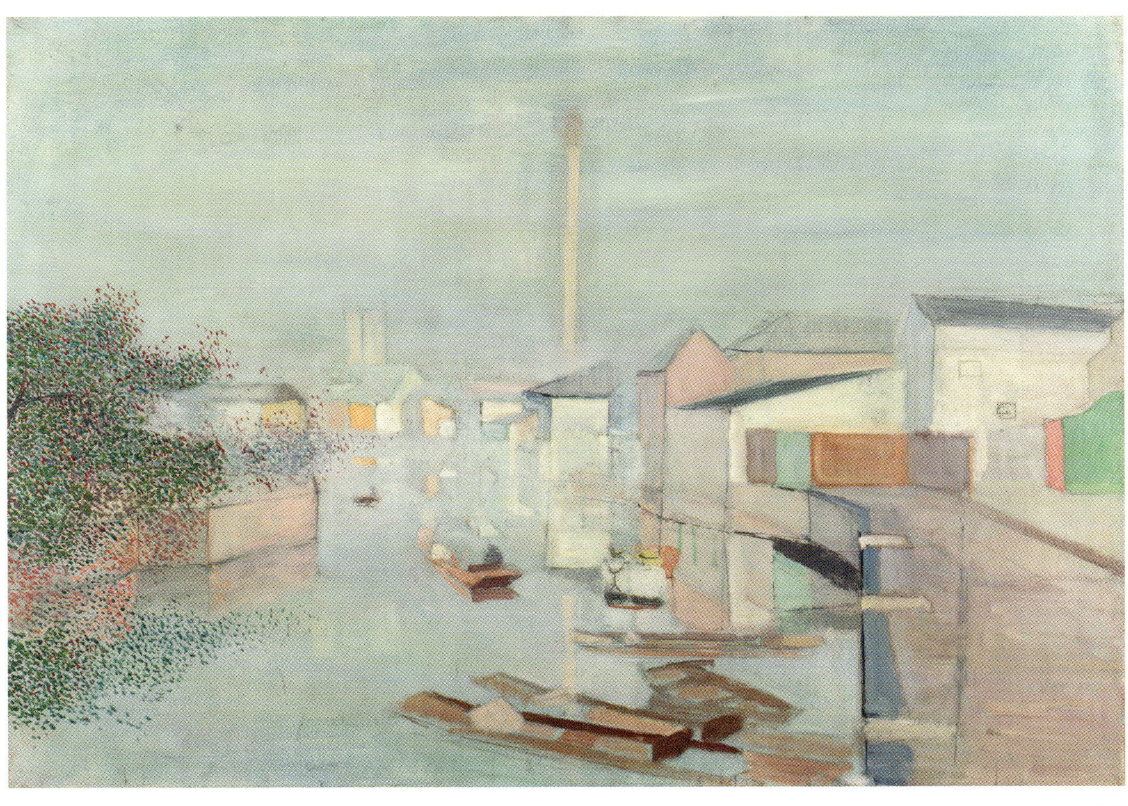

217

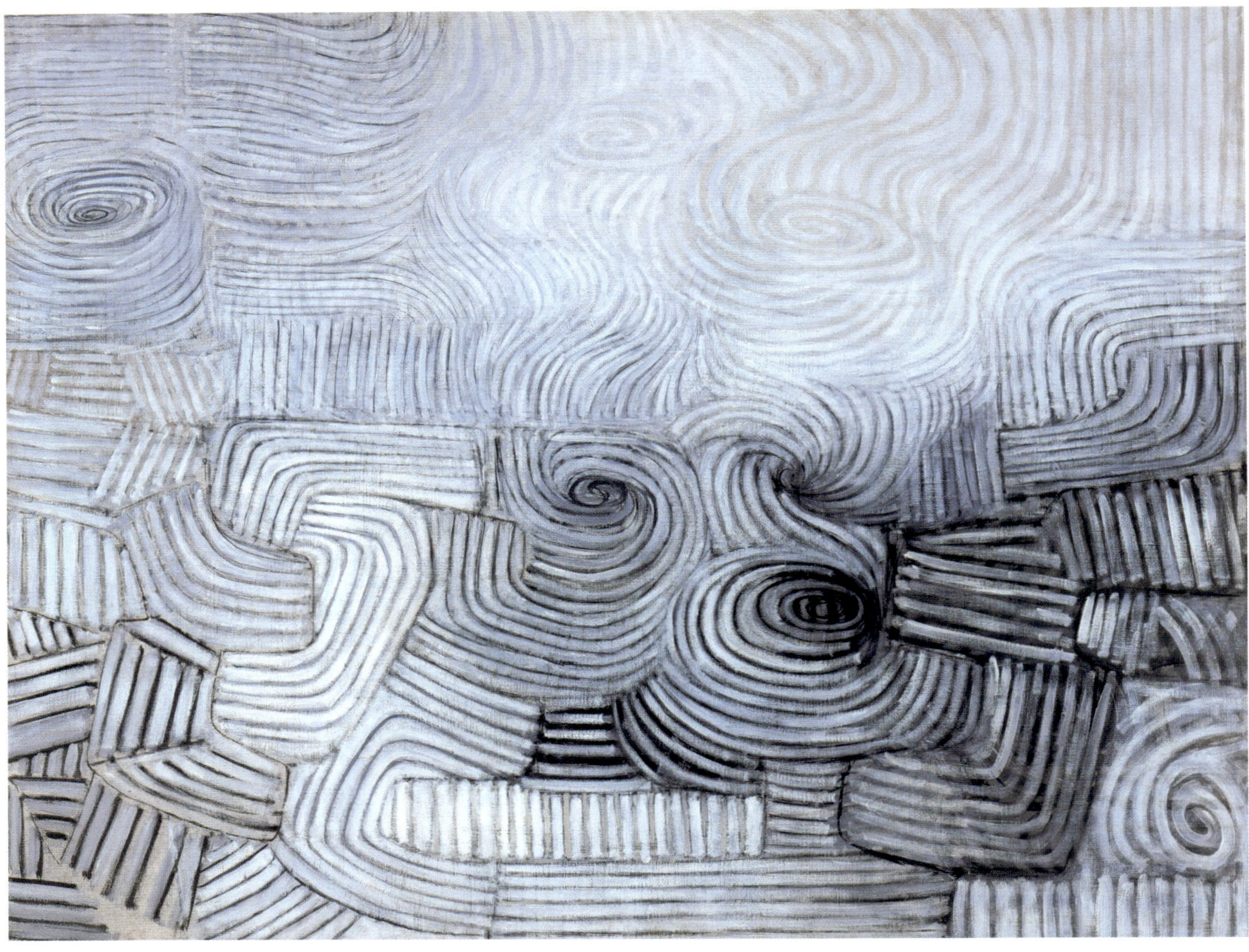

218

217. **Victor Pasmore**
Chelsham, Surrey, 1908 - Malta, 1998
View on the Cam from Magdalene Bridge, Cambridge no. 1, 1940, 1947
Oil on canvas, 56 x 81 cm
Private Collection

218. **Victor Pasmore**
Chelsham, Surrey, 1908 - Malta, 1998
The Snowstorm: Spiral Motif in Black and White, 1950-51
Oil on canvas, 119.4 x 152.4 cm
Arts Council Collection, South Bank Centre, London

After the trials of the early war years, when he was imprisoned as a conscientious objector, Pasmore and his young wife, the painter Wendy Blood, moved to west London, where he made a series of paintings of the River Thames at Chiswick and of the gardens of Hammersmith, as well as a number of nude and figure compositions. The mood of these paintings suggests this was a period of personal happiness. The view on the Cam, which was apparently a favourite of Pasmore's, is related in style to these Thames paintings, though the shades of Whistler and Turner are less evident and it directly acknowledges the influence of French painting, so that Cambridge appears to have factories like those in Seurat's *Bathers at Asnières* (National Gallery, London).

At the end of the decade the spiral motif, which derived from details in the Hammersmith paintings, was developed in increasingly abstract works, which also use the rectangle, the triangle and the circle, creating an 'abstract language of great strength, character and distinction' (Bowness 1975, p. 12). These paintings were shown at the Redfern Gallery, London, in 1950 and immediately precede *The Snowstorm*, which is generally regarded as their culmination and the platform from which Pasmore passed on to the constructed relief. Pasmore talked about his new paintings at the Institute of Contemporary Arts in London on 9 January 1951: 'I have tried to compose as music is composed, with formal elements which, in themselves, have no descriptive qualities .... As these elements combine with each other on the canvas, so are emotions and ideas evoked - the act of drawing a spiral in a variety of ways will evoke emotions similar to those associated with the spiral movements of nature. When this takes place, I proceed to select and, by organization and analogy, unite what I have done into a single form' (Pasmore 1951). (AD)

See essay pp. 285-87.

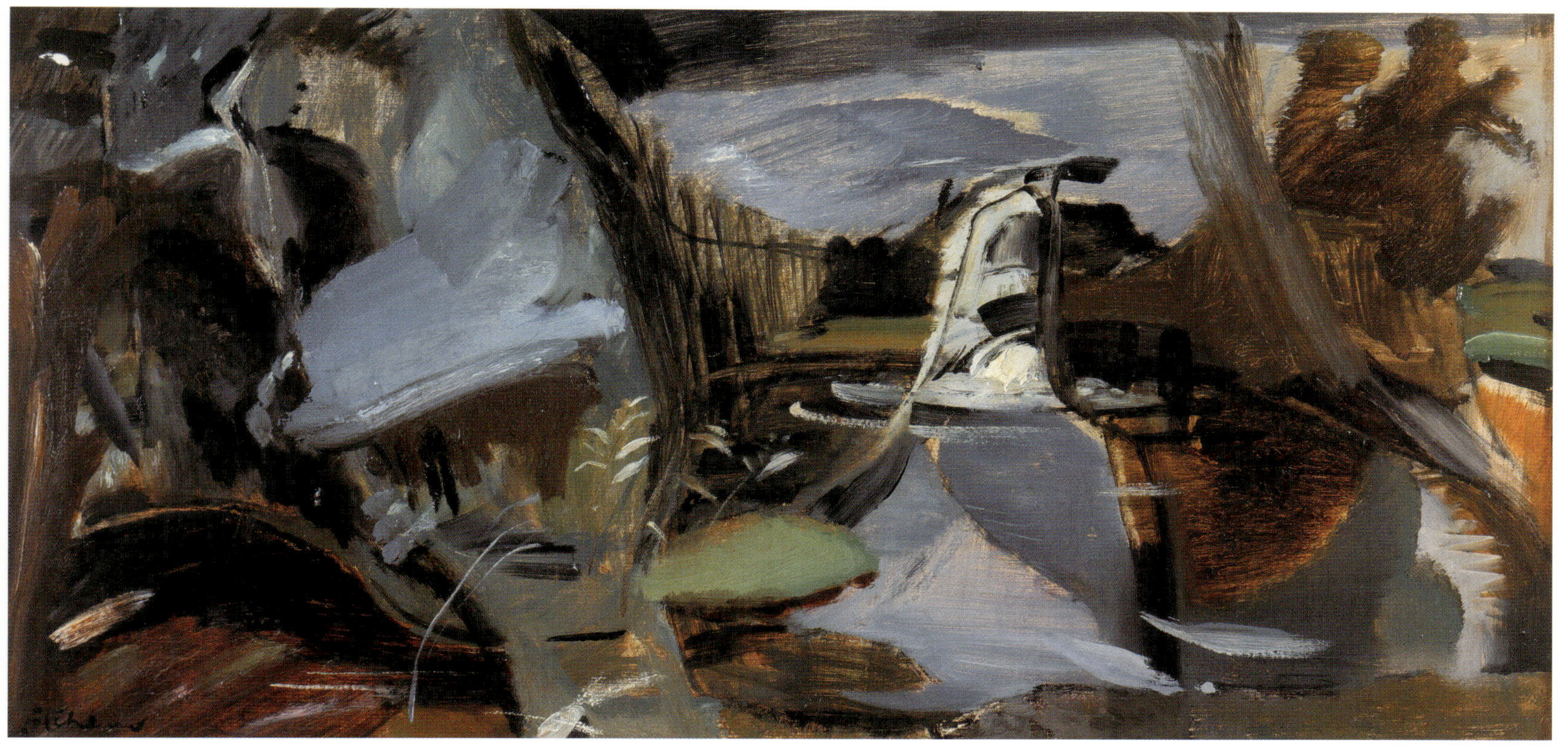

219

219. **Ivon Hitchens**
London, 1893 – Lavington Common, Sussex, 1979
Terwick Mill No 7 Splashing Fall, 1944
Oil on canvas, 52 x 105.8 cm
Bottom left: Hitchens
Laing Art Gallery (Tyne and Wear Museums), Newcastle upon Tyne

Ivon Hitchens was associated with 'advanced' artists in the 1930s, with the Seven and Five Society and with Nicholson and Moore, but he is best known for the landscapes he made in Sussex after the Second World War. This painting is part of a series of about twenty made from the same motif over a period of a year and a half soon after Hitchens and his family left the London of the Blitz for a caravan in land he owned near Petworth, where he and his wife built a house that was to be both home and studio for the rest of his life. Hitchens has been seen as representing tradition and continuity (which he does), but his landscapes, still lifes and nudes show that he learned from the modern European masters, particularly Matisse and Braque. Hitchens was extraordinarily productive, and few artists have had as many one-person exhibitions (which included retrospectives at the Tate Gallery and the Royal Academy in 1963 and 1979). In his best work he achieves an almost miraculous precision, in his words, of 'things falling into place with so clear a notation...' (Khoroche 1990, p. 18). He described the Terwick Mill paintings as 'a complicated subject needing to combine the romance of foaming water pouring from the upper mill pool with an indication of the mill itself and the tree-hung mill pool on a splashing windy day' (London etc. 1979, p. 18). The painting is in Hitchens's characteristic format of the double square, which allowed him to paint directly in a landscape format with space receding and returning across the surface of the canvas. (AD)

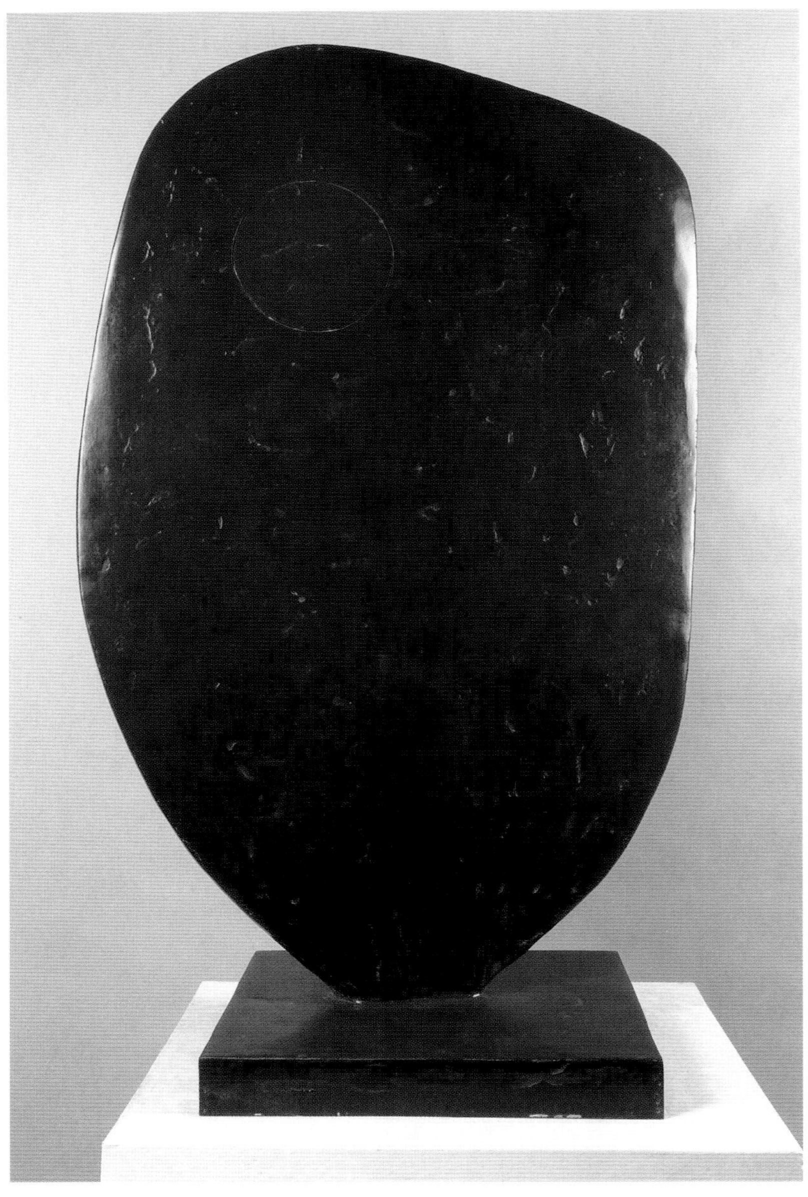

220

220. **Barbara Hepworth**
Wakefield, West Yorkshire, 1903 – St Ives, Cornwall, 1975
Single Form (Chûn Quoit), 1961
Bronze, 105 x 67.5 x 11 cm
On the base: 1/7
Estate of Barbara Hepworth

Landscape was part of Barbara Hepworth's life, from the West Riding of Yorkshire, where she was born, to the coast of Cornwall, where she lived from 1939, having moved to St Ives (where Naum Gabo and his wife had also taken up residence) following the outbreak of war. Landscape and light and the sea are elements in her work. The title of this work refers to a specific prehistoric stone structure in Cornwall. At the time it was made Hepworth was turning increasingly to bronze, although her international renown was as a carver, in both wood and stone. The single standing form occurs throughout Hepworth's oeuvre, of great purity, even austerity, in her radical work of the 1930s. 1961, the date of this sculpture, was the year in which the Secretary General of the United Nations, Dag Hammarskjöld, was killed in a plane crash. In 1964, a six-metre high standing form was placed outside the United Nations building in New York as a tribute to Hammarskjöld. It is one of the greatest of modern public sculptures. *Standing Form (Chûn Quoit)* is part of a sequence leading to the United Nations work: 'Dag Hammarskjöld wanted me to do a scheme for the United Nations building in New York ... We talked about the nature of the site, and about the kind of shapes he liked. I also made *Chûn Quoit* and the small walnut carving *Single Form (September)* with Dag in mind – we discussed an idea together but hadn't reached any conclusion.... Then, when I heard of his death, in a kind of despair, I made the ten foot high *Single Form (Memorial)*' (interview in Bowness 1971, p. 10). (AD)

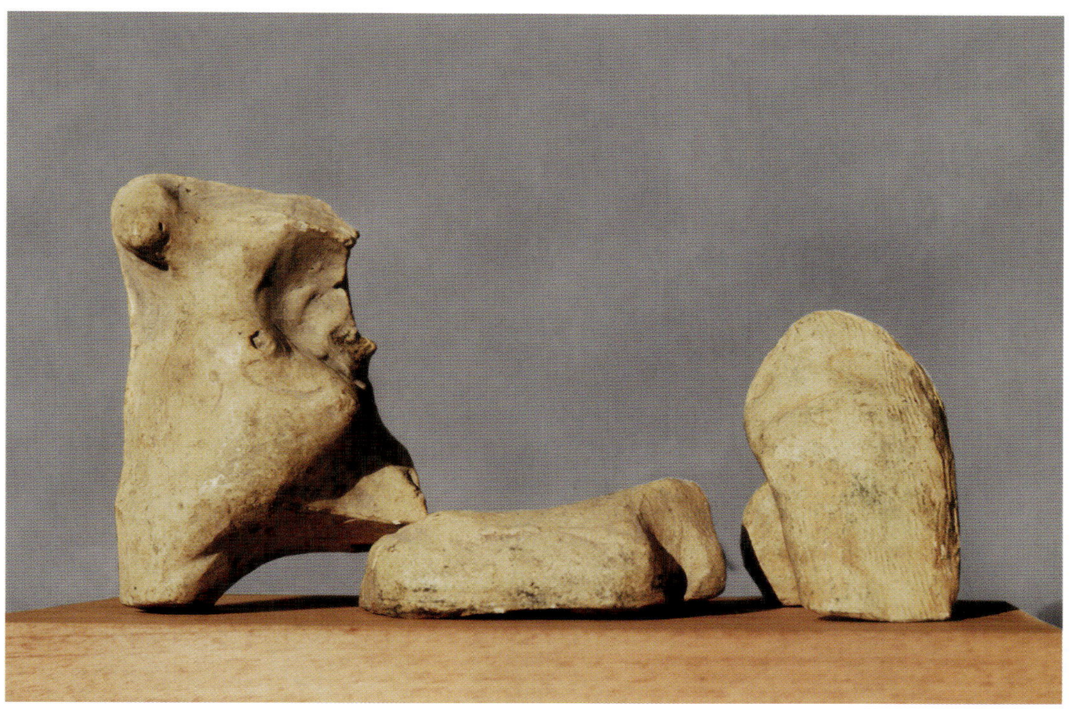

221

221. **Henry Moore**
Castleford, West Yorkshire, 1898 – Perry Green, Much Hadham, Hertfordshire, 1986
Three Piece Reclining Figure: Maquette No.1, 1961
Plaster, length 19.5 cm
Henry Moore Foundation, Much Hadham, Hertfordshire

222. **Henry Moore**
Castleford, West Yorkshire, 1898 – Perry Green, Much Hadham, Hertfordshire, 1986
Two Piece Reclining Figure: Maquette No.4, 1961
Bronze, length 21 cm
On the back: Moore / 0 / 6
Henry Moore Foundation, Much Hadham, Hertfordshire

Exhibitions, prizes, honours: Moore's prestige was quite exceptional in the years after the Second World War. He was awarded the International Prize for sculpture at the Venice Biennale in 1948 and at the São Paulo Bienal in 1953. A retrospective was held at the Museum of Modern Art in New York in 1946, the first of over one hundred such exhibitions outside Britain in his lifetime. There were continual commissions for public sculptures, in urban and landscape settings, in bronze and in stone. He now had the resources to work on many sculptures simultaneously and these, his middle years were remarkably productive, although, while working from a small scale, he maintained a personal touch even in considerable enlargements.

The reclining figure, almost invariably female, had been a constant in Moore's work from the late 1920s. In the post-war years the gender of the figure is less evident; it is often divided into parts and suggests landscape or earth references. Herbert Read quotes Erich Neumann: '...the feminine archetype in modern man signifies at the same time the development of human relatedness, of his social capacity, and the growing consciousness of the unity of mankind on earth' (introduction to Bowness 1965). These two small sculptures are really try-outs for larger sculpture and eventually led to a series of monumental two- and three-piece reclining figures, which have very strong landscape references. (AD)

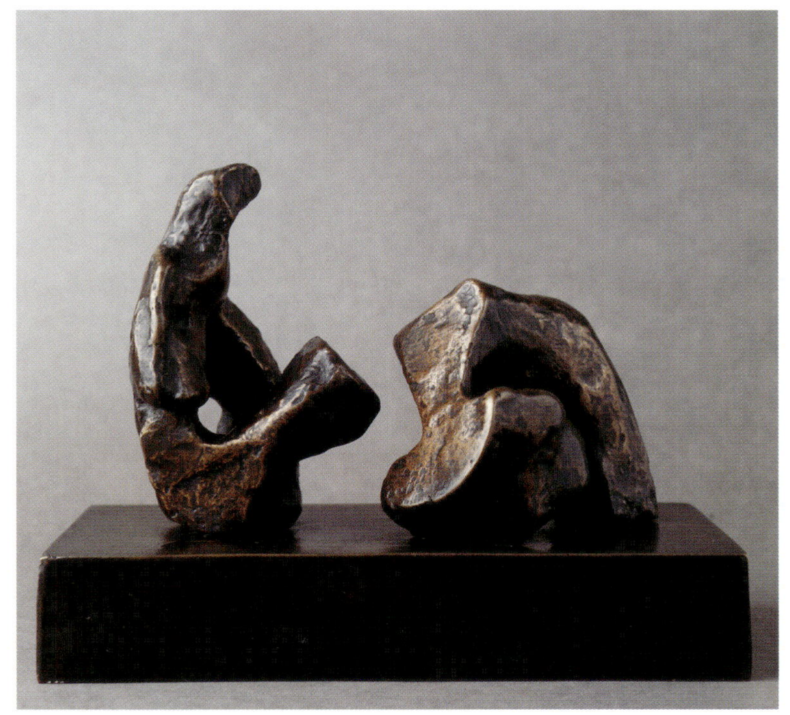

222

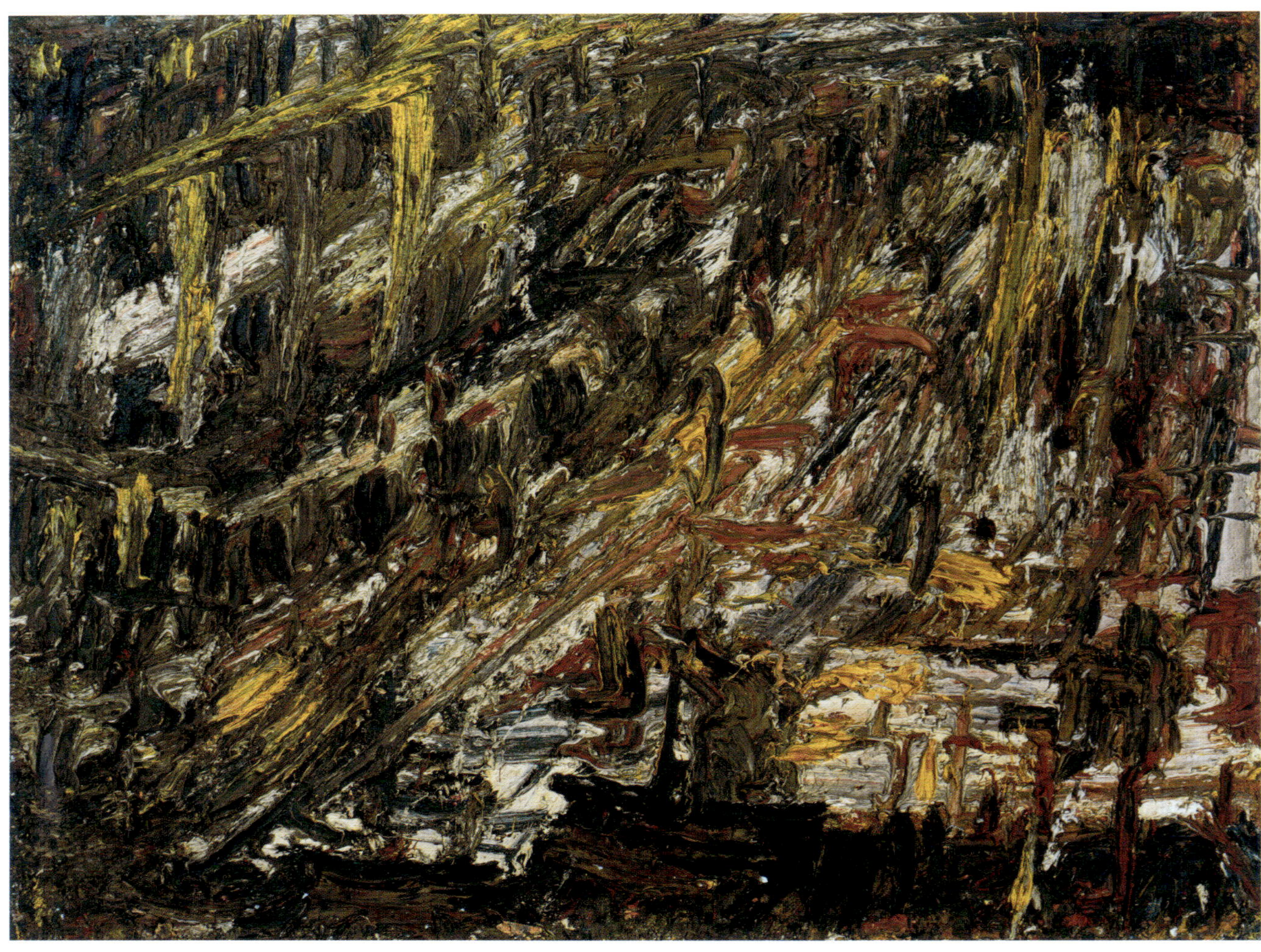

223

223. **Leon Kossoff**
London, 1926
City Building Site, 1961
Oil on canvas, 121.9 x 157.5 cm
Collection of the artist, Courtesy of LA Louver, Venice, California

Leon Kossoff was born and brought up in the East End of London; his family came originally from the Ukraine. He did military service from 1945 to 1948 before studying at St Martin's School of Art, where he met Frank Auerbach; both attended the evening classes of David Bomberg at the Borough Polytechnic. Building sites, resulting from reconstruction in post-war London, were the subjects of Kossoff's landscapes in the 1950s and 1960s, while he also developed figure paintings, from life, in parallel. The range of Kossoff's London subjects has expanded over the years to take in the animated scene of his local swimming pool (1970s), the railways junctions of north-west London (late 1980s), Hawksmoor's Christchurch Spitalfields (late 1980s and early 1990s), amongst other subjects. This has become a formidable picture of London in the second half of the twentieth century, in paintings that are expressive yet contain a wealth of detail and incident, are densely worked yet full of light. Although they are quite specific in time and place, there is always a sense that these paintings are part of a long tradition. Their facture has, for example, been likened to Constable's (Gowing 1988). Indeed, Kossoff has always made drawings from the paintings of old masters he admires, such as Titian and Poussin. (AD)

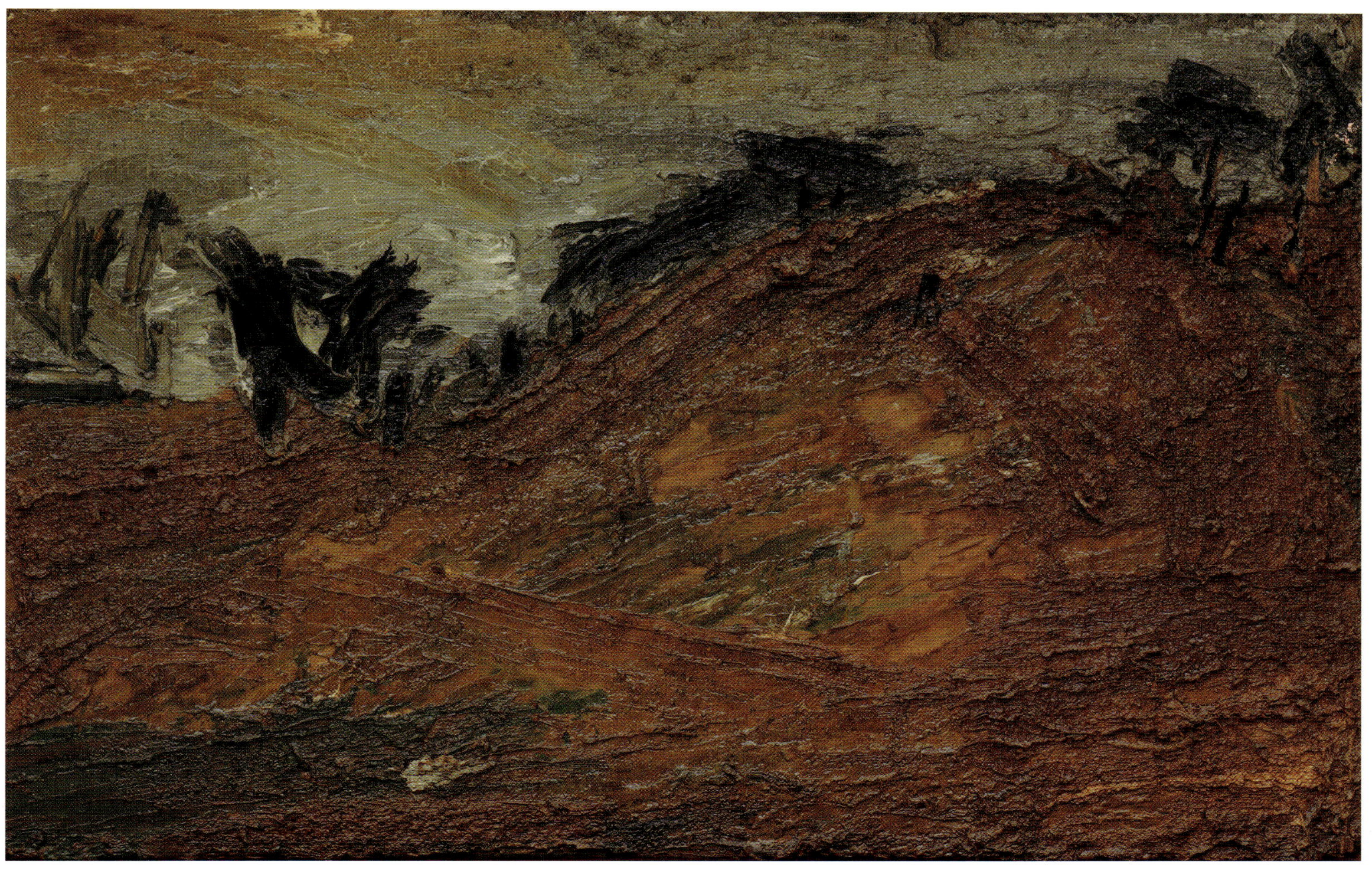

224

224. ***Frank Auerbach***
Berlin, 1931
Primrose Hill, Winter, 1961
Oil on canvas, 91.4 x 137.2 cm
Private Collection

Frank Auerbach came to Britain as a refugee, alone, in April 1939. He attended Bomberg's drawing classes at the Borough Polytechnic at the same time as Leon Kossoff, while studying at St Martin's School and the Royal College of Art. In his landscapes of the city Auerbach has taken as his subject an area of north London within walking distance of his studio in Camden Town. These are expressive paintings, which retain a strong sense of place and time and the elements. They are developed from drawings made on site each day before returning to the studio. Primrose Hill, one of London's parks, marking a rise of the land to the north, was an important early subject. He painted the area in all seasons and this painting, unmistakeably wintry, was one of a number made in the early 1960s. His method or 'idiom' involves continually reworking: 'The way I work means putting up a whole image, and dismantling it and putting up another whole image, which is actually physically extremely strenuous, and I don't think I've ever finished a landscape without a six or seven hour bout of work' (Lampert 1978, p. 13). Landscape is only a part of his practice, as with Kossoff. He has devoted at least equal attention to painting from life. In paintings that are not exactly portraits (though nevertheless recognizable likenesses) but which are certainly fully achieved paintings, Auerbach has made an original contribution to the portrait genre. His presence in Sickert's Camden Town is no accident, and his championship of Sickert has been important in re-establishing Sickert's place in British painting. (AD)

CHAPTER THREE

THE VISIONARY

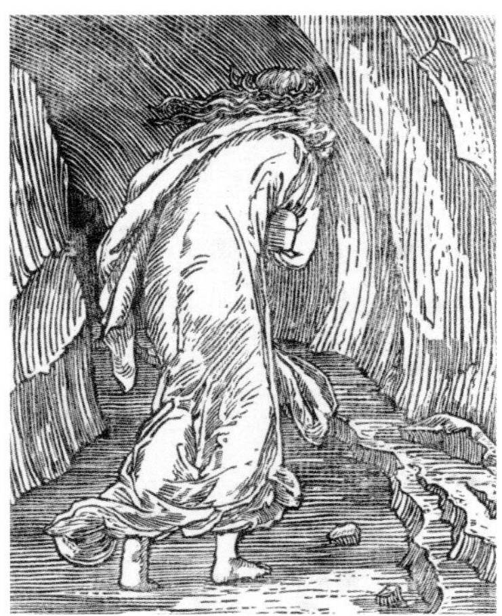

THE VISIONARY

ROBERT HOOZEE

Francis Bacon usually denied his relationship to earlier British art, but it is difficult not to see his concentrated portrait of William Blake's life-mask (cat. 310) as more than just a chance inspiration. In a sense, this work is a symbol of the degree to which British artists, even today, invest their work with important content, and of their natural alliance with their own artistic traditions. The content can be biblical or literary, purely psychological or drawn from a personal mythology. The self-evident and respectful manner in which so many British artists - from Blake to Bacon - refer to their literary and artistic background is an essential aspect of their 'Britishness'. Comparison with other countries, where by the beginning of the nineteenth century very few artists were preoccupied with this sort of content, and where it sometimes disappears entirely in modern times, is revealing in this connection. One cannot view this 'thinking with Milton or Shakespeare' or 'seeing with Blake or Rossetti' as a form of traditionalism; rather, it is a form of civilization and depth. This by way of introduction to a section devoted to art that puts a premium on the imaginary and the visionary, usually in opposition to - but sometimes in combination with - the sense of empirical observation that forms the subject of the two preceding sections.

That a visionary quality can also be sought in observation is evident in the confrontational portrait, which constitutes a timeless (and admittedly not exclusively British) phenomenon from the beginning to the end of our period. It may be an expressive self-portrait or psychological portrait-study. Even the apparently impassive portrait that Richard Dadd painted of his alienist, Alexander Morison (cat. 258), provokes a sense of spirituality through the stiff, mutual fixation between artist and model. Dadd achieved a similar effect with the help of an unusual setting in the mysterious child's portrait entitled *The Child's Problem* (cat. 259). The sense of alienation is almost tangible in the playing children spied on by Arthur Boyd Houghton (cat. 275) and the uneasy close-up of Alice drawn by the author of *Alice in Wonderland* (cat. 274).

The earliest manifestation of what we might call art with a visionary tendency occurred during a period of extraordinary scientific progress, a period in which political and religious structures were also being tested against new ideas. The artists with whom this chapter begins, Henry Fuseli, George Romney, John Martin, William Blake and J.M.W. Turner, all possessed a social awareness and reflected on the destiny of contemporary man in their work, however much it adopted the guise of classical mythology and biblical history. One associates Fuseli, Romney and Martin (cat. 225-227, 256) with the elevated iconography that characterized the period of Classicism and the Romantic, but the intensity of their work and their preference for extreme, even eccentric, interpretations is striking. Even Turner, in spite of his pictorial innovations, continued to work within the old iconographic concepts, although he was also the creator of several visionary reflections on industry and the fate of his country. In his work, the symbolism of subject, colour and light is just as essential as the power of his observations. Both achieve an almost abstract synthesis in the interior study, identified in this catalogue by Ian Warrell (pp. 325-29) as the

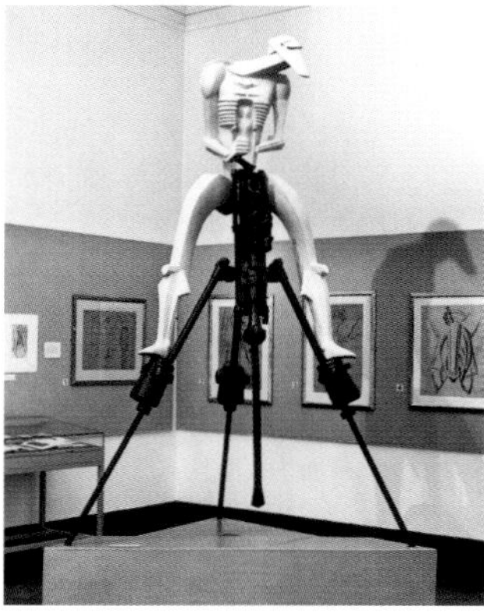

fig. 1
Jacob Epstein
Rock Drill, 1913-15 (reconstruction 1976)
Polyester resin (figure), metal and wood (drill),
205 x 141.5 cm
Birmingham Museum & Art Gallery

Drawing Room of East Cowes Castle (cat. 257). In this unfinished painting, the exact meaning of which is unclear, these components - imagination and observation - are condensed into a revolutionary form.

In the case of William Blake, one can use the term visionary - which today sounds rather hollow - in the fullest sense of the word. Blake, who earned his living as a graphic artist and illustrator (he illustrated the Wedgwood catalogue among other things), wrote a great deal of poetry and prophetic texts, which contain his personal account of the creation and his cultural philosophy. Like a medieval book illuminator, he translated his entire vision into narrative and decorative representations, which bear witness to an extraordinary imagination and power of expression (cat. 231-242). His books are total concepts: the artist even engraved the text, printed it all himself and coloured in everything by hand. Like the other Romantics, Blake started from the old artistic and literary traditions, but he parted company with the world of historical forms and images in order to tell his own stories, imagine his own constructions, and conjure up his own forms and beings. The artist himself referred repeatedly to the visionary meaning of his work. In a letter to the sculptor John Flaxman he wrote: 'In my brain are studies and chambers filled with books and pictures of old, which I wrote and painted in ages of eternity before my mortal life.'[1] He was 'under the direction of messengers from heaven, daily and nightly,'[2] and explained: 'Inspiration & Vision was then, & now is, & I hope will always Remain, my Element, my Eternal Dwelling place.'[3]

As much as one might be inclined to take Blake's pronouncements with a pinch of salt, and however much one can relate him to the poets and painters of the Romantic era, he remains an extreme case on account of his divine madness, and the originality and inspired nature of his work continue to command respect. During his lifetime he was known only to a select few, but even so he provided the initial impetus for the formation of a Blakeian tradition. He was admired by the young Samuel Palmer, who was himself in search of forms and subjects in order to express his feeling for nature and to interpret nature in a deeper, more visionary way.[4]

Blake's world of imagination and Palmer's spiritual landscapes continued to inspire individual British artists well into the twentieth century, establishing a tradition of which working on paper, writing texts and even the act of making books were important elements. For this reason, this exhibition includes a large selection of works on paper, which brings together work by artists who continued to explore the possibilities of Blake's visual language: among them Dante Gabriel Rossetti (cat. 267-268, 271), Edward Burne-Jones (cat. 276-277, 280) and Aubrey Beardsley (cat. 281). Richard Dadd occupies a special place in this context. After 1843 he was insane, and he made his drawings and watercolours in the isolation of the psychiatric institution in which he lived. His works are 'interior visions' in the literal sense, telling no comprehensible narrative and announcing no prophecies. Dadd's dreamlike images were executed with meticulous descriptive detail. (cat. 259-261).

Among the works on paper in this section are several by modern artists. The avant-garde artist Wyndham Lewis was, like Blake, a fervent cultural philosopher, and in drawings like *Study in Blue* (cat. 289) and *The Vorticist* (cat. 290) one recognizes a Blakeian dimension. In landscape, it was primarily Paul Nash and Graham Sutherland who were clearly influenced by the vision of Palmer in their early drawings (cat. 291-293), while with David Jones (cat. 302-304) we find recollections of both Palmer (in the landscapes) and Blake (in the abundant pictorial motifs and the relationship between image and text).

In the mid-nineteenth century, at a moment when materialistic realism was on the rise everywhere in Europe, a brotherhood was founded in England, in the spirit of the German Nazarenes, by artists who aspired to a spiritual art inspired by the Italian, German and Flemish Primitives. In some of their early work, these Pre-Raphaelites seemed to take on the very identity of their idealizedPrimitives, but in most of their work they achieved a synthesis between religious and symbolic vision, on the one hand, and an almost scientifically analytical, detailed realism on the other. This last was the result of their quest for true-to-life representation, led by the theoretician John Ruskin.

The Scapegoat by Holman Hunt (cat. 264), discussed in detail elsewhere in the catalogue (pp. 331-33), is an extreme example of the ideals just described. The prophetic tone, the dramatic presentation of the symbolic animal – from its attributes to the texts on the frame – and the unusual use of colour, all bring Blake to mind. The scientific precision of this allegorical representation, however, lends it a surreal dimension.

The Pre-Raphaelite Brotherhood only existed for a few years and the 'total identification of realism and symbolism' was only sustained with this intensity for a short while and in a limited circle.[5] The broader movement, consisting of the original members and associated artists, was aiming rather for a pure, symbolic art inspired by medieval history and literature. Out of this background, various iconographic types emerged which would become widespread in European Symbolism, but it was the notion of woman as an unfathomable being that dominated, in different poetic interpretations, the art of the Pre-Raphaelites and their circle (cat. 265-266).

In the later development of Pre-Raphaelitism in the orbit of the Aesthetic Movement, it was chiefly Edward Burne-Jones who continued to be a persuasive artist of the imagination. While many of his contemporaries produced repetitive compositions, which showed great virtuosity but were purely decorative, Burne-Jones brought his heroes on stage like a dramatist, allowing them to fall prey to their emotions and to tragic events. In some works, like the Perseus cycle (cat. 278-279), the intensity of Blake's visions is revived. Together with William Morris, Burne-Jones worked on a book in the best Blakeian tradition, *The Earthly Paradise*, which was never completed (cat. 276-277).

In the twentieth century, a number of modernists combined formal experimentation with themes and compositions from the repertory of Blake, Palmer and the Pre-Raphaelites in a quite striking way. With the Vorticists, William Roberts, David Bomberg and Percy Wyndham Lewis, these references are important, but they lasted for only a short time. For Stanley Spencer, the connection with the past was more fundamental. As a reaction against the more modish adaptations of the French avant-garde, which flooded the London art world during his years as a student, he cultivated a form of primitivism similar in spirit to that of artists like Paul Gauguin or the Nabis. For Spencer, this primitivism opened the way to a deep and lifelong kinship with the visionary tradition that Blake, Palmer and the Pre-Raphaelites had established. As with Palmer, and later with the Pre-Raphaelites, Spencer's religious subjects and biblical scenes appear as revelations in the reality of everyday life, and he visualized them with almost Franciscan caudour. *The Nativity* (cat. 286), *The Betrayal* (cat. 296) and *The Dustman* (cat. 298) illustrate various stages in Spencer's development: the first is a stylish allusion to the Nabis and the Italian Primitives, the second is a more turbulent biblical event in which, as it were, the artist himself becomes involved, and the third is an almost burlesque display of everyday reality, which, seen through the eyes of Spencer, acquires a sacred dimension.

The sacred was also essential for the sculptor Jacob Epstein, even when – under the influence of French Cubism and primitive art – he engaged in formal experiments that brought him into the ranks of the Vorticists. The *Rock Drill* (fig. 1), created in 1913-15, of which only a fragment still exists, was Epstein's interpretation of man involved in mechanical labour. The expression of a dynamic figure, however, was not sufficient for Epstein, as it would have been for a Futurist. Instead, the figure acquires a prophetic stature, and the artist even included a symbolic foetus within the harness of the 'machine-like robot, visored, menacing, and carrying within itself its progeny, protectively ensconced.'[6] In the 1930s he made monumental statues with biblical themes and a prophetic aspect (cat. 300-301), and the combination of barbaric forms with Christian themes shocked the public.[7] Nevertheless, a classical sense of calm emanates from these alabaster sculptures.

Modern British landscape painting is a more marginal phenomenon within European modernism, but even in this margin the work of Paul Nash and Graham Sutherland is exceptional. In their youth, as we have seen, they made drawings and prints in the tradition of Palmer (cat. 291-293). As more mature artists, they still found it meaningful to study particular scenery in the British landscape in search of a deeper truth than the merely visual (cat. 213-214). The history of a particular landscape, the associations evoked by striking natural formations and the influence of heavenly bodies were all factors that could give specific symbolic meaning to a view. In contrast to the Surrealists, to whom they are often linked, Nash and Sutherland usually kept a firm grip on visible reality.

The experience of war had a considerable influence on both artists. During the Second World War, Sutherland transformed landscape elements into expressive symbols (cat. 307). Nash interpreted his experiences on the battlefield of the First World War in stirring landscapes (cat. 74), which are related to the apocalyptic visions of John Martin (cat. 256). Nash's visions, however, are less theatrical, and there is no doubt that they must be acknowledged as the result of first-hand observation.

The spiritual climate after the Second World War is usually given as an explanation for the pessimism in the work realized in the fifties by Henry Moore and Francis Bacon. In British art history these artists are carefully kept apart, as if they belonged to different worlds. They were undoubtedly inspired differently and developed in different ways, but there is a similarity in their responses to human fate by the creation of tragically and theatrically distorted figures, and both speak the language of pathos that we encounter in the British visionary tradition beginning with Blake and Fuseli – the latter being one of the artists that Bacon most detested.[8]

1. Letter of 21 September 1800; cit. Russell 1906, p. 76.
2. Letter to Thomas Butts, 10 January 1802; cit. Russell 1906, p. 100.
3. Eitner 1987, vol. 1, p. 125.
4. See William Vaughan, in London & New York 2005.
5. Alan Bowness, in London 1984, p. 12.
6. Jacob Epstein, *Let there be Sculpture: An autobiography*, London (Michael Joseph) 1940; cit. Cork 1974, p. 73.
7. Evelyn Silber and Terry Friedman, in Leeds & London 1987, p. 233.
8. See Russell 1971, p. 90; and Sylvester 1975, p. 82.

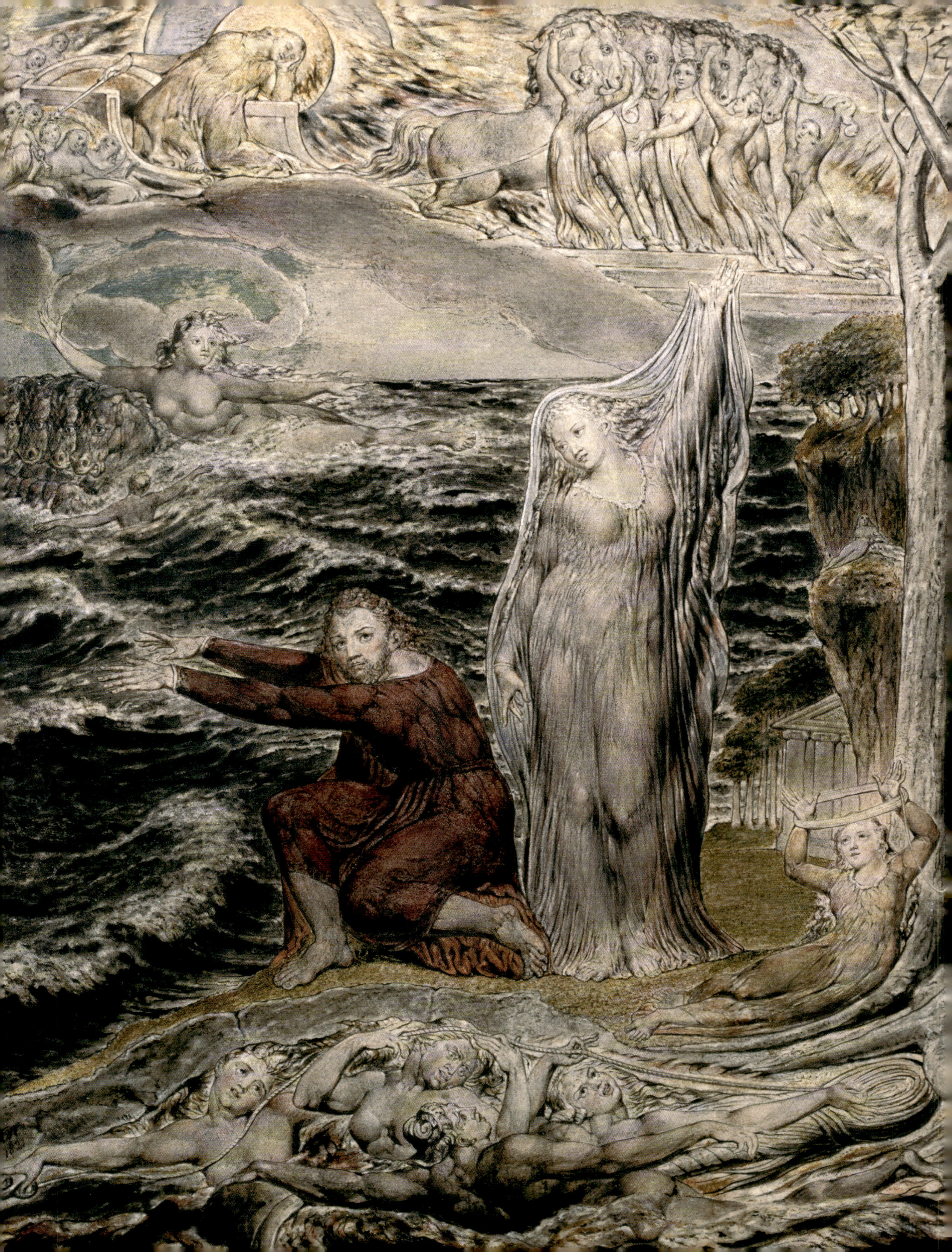

WILLIAM BLAKE

The Sea of Time and Space, 1821

DAVID BINDMAN

If the spectrum of British art runs from the close study of nature to the visionary, then Blake's art is at the furthest reach of the latter. Nothing could be further from his intention than to produce works dependent on observation, which he professed to despise; his work is about ideas, and the language he used to express these ideas is based on the human figure used expressively rather than naturalistically. In his most ambitious and complex series of works, like the illustrations to Milton and to Dante, he attempts to explain visually a whole system of ideas, and I will argue that this is also the case with the Arlington Court picture, though its actual source has long been a matter of dispute among scholars. I do not, however, claim to offer a comprehensive reading of the painting.

Blake's Arlington Court picture has remained a mystery since its discovery in 1947 in the country house of that name in Devon, where it was found discarded on top of a cupboard. Nothing has been yet discovered to connect the Chichester family to the art world, let alone to the circle of William Blake, though the painting was framed by the father of Blake's friend the landscape painter John Linnell.[1] Since its discovery its imagery has attracted the attention of many scholars, but no consensus has emerged about its subject, though Blake signed and dated it 1821, which puts it among the works of his last years. What has never been doubted is its richness of technique (it is in pen, watercolour and gouache on paper), the brilliant complexity of the composition and the beauty and elegance of the predominantly female figures. There has been disagreement over whether the work has its source in an outside text or is based directly on Blake's own mythology. The main figure, dressed in a red garment, has been identified variously as Christ, Blake himself, Albion, Isaiah or Odysseus, and the female figure next to him as Vala, Blake's goddess of nature, and/or Athena.[2]

In fact, all but a few of Blake's paintings, particularly of his later years, have as a starting point a text from the Bible or from literature. I believe that Kathleen Raine was right to identify the figure in red as Odysseus and his standing companion as Athena,[3] for the setting seems to correspond to the description of Ithaca in Homer's *Odyssey* book XIII, when Odysseus arrives back for the first time in his homeland: 'At the head of the harbour there is a long-leaved olive tree, and near it a lovely misty cave sacred to the nymphs who are called Naiads. In this cave there are stone mixing-bowls and stone jars, and bees store their honey there. And there are great tall looms of stone, where the nymphs weave their cloth of sea-purple wool, a wondrous sight: and in it too there are springs of ever-flowing water.'[4] Cave, jars, weaving nymphs and flowing water can all be seen, but most telling are the main figures, the man in a red garment apparently about to dive into the sea and the elegant woman next to him pointing to the heavens. According to Homer, Odysseus when he landed did not recognize his homeland, because Athena did not want him 'to be recognized by wife or family or people before the suitors had paid in full for their crimes'. Athena confronts him at first as a shepherd, but in the course of the conversation she took 'the form of a woman, tall and beautiful'. She fails at first to persuade him that he really is in Ithaca, noting the wiliness of his refusal, but urges on him vengeance against the suitors of his wife Penelope.[5]

What then is Odysseus doing? He appears to be contemplating a choice between the way of Athena and that represented by the female figure reclining on the back of four horses cleaving through the water. Raine suggests that she is Leucothea in *Odyssey* book V, who rescues Odysseus

William Blake, ***The Sea of Time and Space*** (detail), cat. 247

when he is in distress in the sea by giving him a magic shawl that protects him, enabling him to get to the shore. Raine argues that he is throwing the shawl back to Leucothea, but there is no trace of it in the painting; in any case Odyssey was naked at this point in the story. It is worth noting that the Phaiacian ship that brought him to Ithaca is described by Homer as moving like 'four stallions [who] are yoked together and race off over the plain', but I will argue later for another identification of the woman in the water.

The identification of the main figures as Odysseus and Athena would be compatible with the general agreement among Blake scholars that the painting is concerned with the Classical universe. There is the indisputable presence of Classical gods or powers: the Three Fates with the thread of human life, the chariot of Apollo in the sky, and there is a lack of any reference to Christian symbolism. Blake in his later years made many scathing comments on the Greeks and Romans as 'silly Greek & Latin Slaves of the sword', and on the great Greek and Roman authors: 'The Stolen and Perverted Writings of Homer & Ovid; of Plato & Cicero, which all men ought to contemn: are set up by artifice against the Sublime of the Bible.'[6] Their beliefs were in every respect the antithesis of Christian Revelation, and the great Greek sculptures were mere imitation of the Hebraic originals on the Temple of Solomon. Athena's call to vengeance on his wife's suitors is then directly in opposition to Blake's often repeated claim that forgiveness of sin was the essential distinction of Christianity.

It is worth looking at this point at a survey of Greek theology by Blake's contemporary, the radical scientist Joseph Priestley, entitled *The Doctrines of Heathen Philosophy*, 1804, which gives a more comprehensive view than can be gleaned from Blake's writings. An obvious objection to Greek religion that Blake and Priestley shared was to its polytheism. Priestley sees Socrates, for example, as a man of virtue but also an 'idolater, or a worshipper of a multiplicity of gods';[7] the Arlington Court painting contains at least two, Apollo and Athena, and lurking behind Odysseus' dilemma are the Fates and Zeus and Poseidon. Priestley also objected that in Greek religion the world had no beginning or an end: 'The world therefore remains as it was created by God, free from corruption or death.' Such a belief, Priestley claims, is 'contrary to our scriptures which hold out to us a far more pleasing prospect viz. a perpetual progress to a better state of things. Of this no heathen philosopher had the least idea.'[8]

In other words Christianity offers the prospect of spiritual rebirth and a heaven beyond this world; for the heathen 'a moderate and temperate life ... is in the way to true felicity'. This sense of a static and enclosed universe is perhaps addressed in the painting by the fact that either of Odysseus' choices end in the same place: both Athena and the woman in the sea lead him upwards to the realm of Apollo, and there is a sense of circularity in the composition, that human life is bounded by the physical elements of earth, air, fire and water in an endless round. Odysseus thus inhabits a moral universe in which there is no real moral choice that might lead to either damnation or redemption. Furthermore, this moral universe, because it has no sense of the liberation of a heaven beyond, is confined to what Blake often referred to as the prison of the senses. Therefore nature in Greek belief is the dominant force. She is represented in Blake's Prophetic books by the female figure of Vala, who may lie behind the representation of Athena. Blake was strongly opposed to pantheism or the worship of nature, which he saw as a kind of idolatry of materialism. Priestley connects this worship of nature also to the 'multiplicity of gods' in heathen mythology: 'In every part of the world, says Ocellus Lucanus, there are inhabitants of a nature proper to it, as gods in the heaven, men upon the earth, in the higher regions demons.'[9] Though Priestley attributes to Plato a form of monotheism, for Blake the Greek gods were reducible to spirits of nature, each associated with an element.

This is confirmed by the nearest painting in spirit by Blake to the Arlington Court picture, a watercolour from the series of illustrations to John Milton's early paired poems, *L'Allegro* and *Il Penseroso* (Pierpont Morgan Library, New York). Blake makes the poems into a continuous biographical account of Milton's poetic career, from his youthful brilliance represented by the two poems, through his descent into the melancholy world of experience, to the final synthesis in his late epic *Paradise Lost*. Blake, in a commentary on these illustrations, blames immersion in 'the Spirit of Plato', mentioned by Milton, for the latter's descent into experience: 'The Spirit of Plato unfolds his Worlds to Milton in Contemplation. The Three destinies [Fates] sit on the Circles of Platos Heavens weaving the Thread of Mortal Life these Heavens are Venus Jupiter & Mars.

Hermes [Milton in fact means not the god Hermes but the philosopher Hermes Trismegistus, or 'thrice great Hermes'] flies before as attending on the Heaven of Jupiter the Great Bear is seen in the Sky beneath Hermes & the Spirits of Fire. Air, Water & Earth Surround Miltons Chair.' In the watercolour, as Christopher Heppner has pointed out, the elements of fire and water are identified with Mars and Venus respectively.[10] This suggests that the female figure in the sea in the Arlington Court picture is in fact Venus, who rose originally from the waves. Like the Arlington Court picture, the *Spirit of Plato* watercolour refers to the baleful effect on the mind of the Greek vision of nature in a complex composition involving numbers of female nature sprites.

Nature for Blake was the seductive face of the material world. While for the Greeks and such pantheistic poets as Wordsworth the beauties of nature were an argument for the providential existence of the gods or God, for Blake they offered a path to idolatry and a limited material perception of the universe. The Arlington Court painting should be understood not simply as a condemnation of the Greek universe, but as a demonstration of how dangerously seductive the beauty of nature could be; hence the disconcerting combination in the painting of beautiful forms and an essentially negative message.[11]

---

1. Keynes 1971, pp. 196-97.
2. Heppner 1995, pp. 238-39.
3. Raine 1968, vol. 1, p. 75.
4. Homer, *The Odyssey*, trans. Martin Hammond, London 2000, p. 132.
5. Ibid., p. 138.
6. *Milton a Poem*, Blake Trust / Tate Gallery, 1995, pl. 2a.
7. Priestley 1804, p. 50.
8. Ibid., pp. 34-35.
9. Ibid., pp. 36-37.
10. Heppner 1995, pp. 246-47.
11. Robert Essick, although he does not see the man in red as Odysseus and sees him rejecting Classical civilization rather than trapped in it, comes to a broadly similar conclusion: 'The presence of the Fates and an Apollo-like sun god in this complex composition indicate Blake's deep involvement in classical art and mythology during his final years. Yet, his written references to classicism are harshly critical. For all its detailed beauty, The Sea of Time and Space would also seem to indicate a rejection of Greek and Roman civilization by the male (possibly Isaiah) at the center of the design' (in Eaves 2003, p. 265).

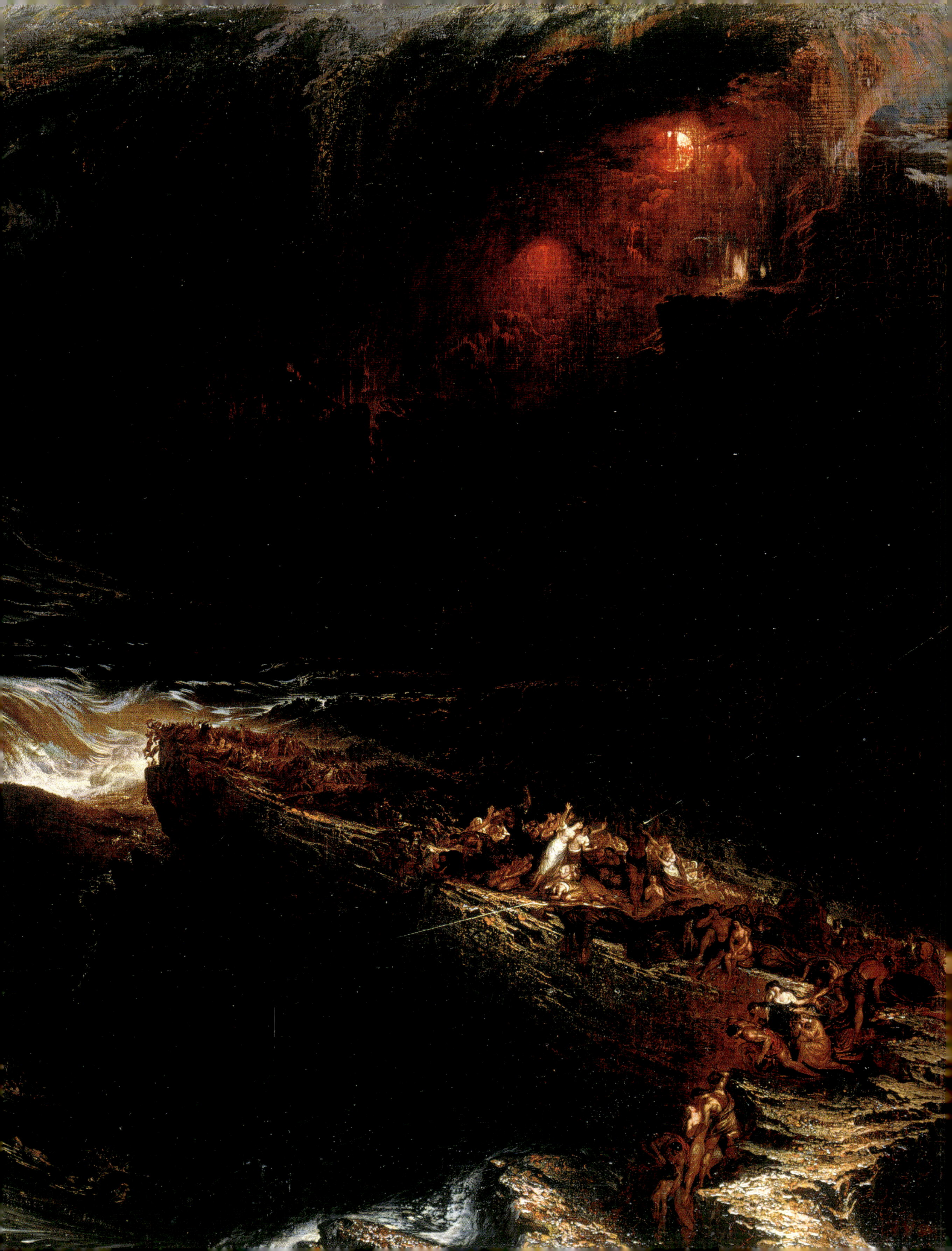

JOHN MARTIN

The Deluge, 1834

ANGUS TRUMBLE

In many respects the account of the flood in the Book of Genesis offered to the Romantic imagination an almost uncanny template of certain of Edmund Burke's ideas about the Sublime, particularly his entirely reasonable contention that 'No passion so effectually robs the mind of all its powers of acting and reasoning as fear!'[1] But, in a larger sense, the flood was the biblical prototype, the *ne plus ultra* of all cataclysms. Predictably, ahead of John Martin's lost composition of 1826 and the present painting, which was developed out of it in 1834, numerous artists, including Henry Fuseli, Francis Danby, Philippe Jacques de Loutherbourg, Jacob More and others, attempted full-scale renditions of the height of the destructive energies unleashed by the Mosaic deluge, but none, not even J.M.W. Turner (Tate), charged that primitive biblical subject with the excess of emotional and physical energy that animated Martin's evolving composition, the epitome of what Burke called 'greatness of dimension'.[2]

The scriptural framework is stark. Faced with the apparently irredeemable corruption, violence and wickedness of the generations following Adam and Eve, God despairs of His own work of creation and actually resolves to undo it: 'I will destroy man whom I have created from the face of the earth; both man, and beast, and the creeping thing, and the fowls of the air; for it repenteth me that I have made them.' (Genesis 6: 7) Even in the context of the Pentateuch, the language here is surprisingly strong, just as the bringing of the flood is paradoxical in a text that is in all other respects concerned with God's general commandment to 'be fruitful, and multiply, and replenish the earth' (1: 28).[3] Of antediluvian man, for example, it is said that 'every imagination of the thoughts of his heart was only evil continually' (6: 5), so the righteousness and grace of Noah – with whom God forges a covenant for the preservation and contingent posterity of life itself – are correspondingly acute.[4] After Noah builds the ark, he fills it with two of every species in obedience to the word of God and then: 'It came to pass after seven days, that the waters of the flood were upon the earth. In the six hundredth year of Noah's life, in the second month, the seventeenth day of the month, the same day were all the fountains of the deep broken up, and the windows of heaven were opened. And the rain was upon the earth forty days and forty nights...' (7: 10–12).

The subject of the commencement of the deluge of Genesis was in many ways perfectly suited to the temperament and interests of the northerner John Martin, who from the early 1820s onward achieved great success with history subjects of transformation, prophylaxis and destruction, many of which were disseminated through brilliantly executed and shrewdly marketed mezzotint engravings. The pictorial formula to which Martin adhered with remarkable consistency through the 1820s and 1830s relied upon landscape and architectural settings of vast scale, in which complex groups, sometimes scores of figures, were reduced to triviality, dwarfed by the immense natural or divine forces ominously arrayed against them. The effects of colour, cold light and ferocious theatricality that Martin poured into paintings such as the hugely successful *Belshazzar's Feast* of 1821 (Private Collection) stretched the boundaries of history painting almost to breaking point.

The first version of the present picture was exhibited at the British Institution in 1826, and was accompanied by an explanatory pamphlet that clearly focused the composition on Genesis

John Martin, ***The Deluge*** (detail), cat. 256

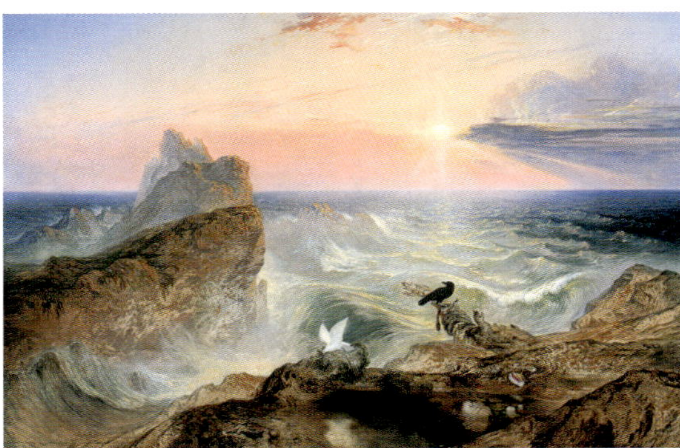

fig. 1
John Martin
The Eve of the Deluge, 1842
Oil on canvas, 142.8 x 218.4 cm
Royal Collection

7: 11 and 12, that is, the point at which God commenced His work of destruction. Just as the biblical account exploits for dramatic effect the date of the inundation (indexed against the great age of Noah in years, months and days), as well as the exact high watermark in cubits, so, too, Martin sought to underline in writing the exactness of the action and topography: 'This representation of the universal inundation of the earth comprehends that portion of time when the valleys are supposed to be completely overflowed, and the intermediate hills nearly overwhelmed, and the people who have escaped from drowning there are flying to the rocks and mountains for safety.'[5]

Martin was also at pains to introduce a supernatural and portentous convergence of heavenly bodies, a 'detailed computation that argued for Methuselah's presence at the time of the Flood'; a plausible explanation of scale, whereby 'the highest mountain in the picture will be found to be 15,000 feet, the next in height, 10,000 feet, and the middle-ground perpendicular rock 4,000 feet'; and concluded by further contextualizing the narrative by means of accompanying verses by Lord Byron, a robust truncation of several speeches in a dialogue between Noah's son Japheth and the 'chorus of mortals' in Byron's 'dramatic poem of antediluvian tragedy' *Heaven and Earth* (1822):

> [And where]
> Shall prayer ascend
> When the swoln clouds unto the mountains bend
> And burst,
> And gushing oceans every barrier rend,
> Until the very deserts know no thirst
> [Accursed...?]
> [...]
> Where shall we fly?
> Not to the mountains high;
> For now their torrents rush with double roar,
> To meet the ocean, which, advancing still,
> Already grasps each drowning hill,
> Nor leaves an unsearch'd cave.[6]

As Lynn R. Matteson remarks, 'One can only assume from so impassioned and intricate an exposition of scientific observation, biblical exegesis *[sic]*, and Byronic despair, that the subject of the Mosaic Deluge was of crucial importance to Martin,'[7] but what is more striking visually is the sheer doggedness with which, in his evolving composition, the artist sought to create an effective convergence of word and image: the unarguable word of God; the word of a nearly current poetic celebrity, and an awesomely commensurate visual extrapolation of both. Martin built from raw data, through tiny, cold details of rocks and waves and people, up to the barren hotness of geological, even celestial, drama, and thus aimed at a whole spectacle with far greater assurance than he assembled such minutiae (at least in the present picture) as the naked, implausibly buoyant,

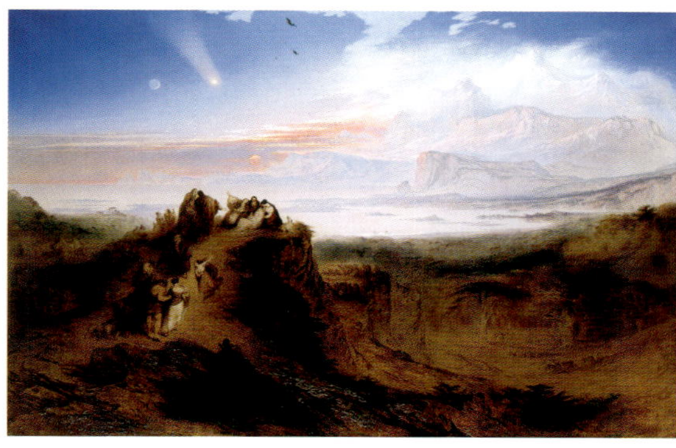

fig. 2
John Martin
The Assuaging of the Waters, 1840
Oil on canvas, 143.5 x 219.1 cm
Fine Arts Museums of San Francisco

drowning woman in the bottom left-hand corner, her arms raised heavenward, and the bolt of lightning which, contradicting the savage, cross-canvas diagonal it traces, in the end plops disappointingly into the water nearby, like a firecracker.

The first version of *The Deluge* formed the basis of Martin's mezzotint engraving, which was published two years later, in 1828, and advertised as being 'in the manner of "BELSHAZZAR'S FEAST", ... with the addition of superior Composition' (fig. 3).[8] This coincided with the showing of the painting at the Royal Scottish Academy in Edinburgh, and in a new pamphlet that accompanied the print the artist reiterated that he had here made 'improvements in the composition, giving it a degree of originality which could not attach to a mere copy of any picture'.[9]

Having in 1830 supplied a frontispiece to *The Last Days of the Antediluvian World*, a volume of poems by his brother Richard, and in 1833 collaborated with John Galt on an illustrated book, *The Ouranoulogos*, the subject of the first part of which was the Deluge,[10] Martin further developed his stupendous subject in the present, second version of *The Deluge* in 1834. Evidently he elongated the composition a good deal, and transformed its superstructure from an essentially tunnel-like, centrifugal concentration of volcanic energy (in the mezzotint) to a dramatic convergence of complementary diagonals (reinforced at the corners) - one of which is carried by that single, daring bolt of lightning - apparently diffusing somewhat the remarkable effects of light.

The 1834 picture was not shown at the Royal Academy in London and at the Salon in Paris until 1837. By this date Martin was inclined to see *The Deluge* as his favourite work,[11] and in 1839 the newly-married Prince Albert of Saxe-Coburg and Gotha, consort to the young Queen Victoria, visited the artist in his studio, saw the picture and commissioned him to produce a new one (on a smaller scale), that would take as its subject a slightly earlier stage of the flood narrative. That picture became *The Eve of the Deluge* (fig. 1). A third and final canvas, *The Assuaging of the Waters* (fig. 2), was commissioned by the ranking female courtier, Harriet, Duchess of Sutherland. Both new pictures, for which *The Deluge* was the conceptual keystone and centrepiece, were completed in 1840 and first exhibited with the present picture as a kind of triptych at that year's Royal Academy Summer Exhibition, a considerable amplification of the original idea, carrying forward the concept of a whole flood narrative, not merely its thunderous opening chords, *fortissimo*, in the minor key.

Long before the great controversy arising from Charles Darwin's *The Origin of Species* (1859), Martin's *The Deluge* and its slightly later pendants lay at the heart of as fundamental a tension as then existed between the proponents of new theories about the geological formation of the earth and more orthodox thinking enshrined in holy writ. On the orthodox side, despite the wide range of 'parties' that existed within and around the Church of England in the period between the death of John Wesley (1791) and the arrival of the Oxford Movement (1833), belief in the basic truth of Genesis was unanimously upheld, so it is worth noting that new scientific ideas were the more radical.[12] In 1795, the Scottish geologist James Hutton had argued in his *History of the Earth* that the immense forces that formed mountains, carved out valleys, rivers, lakes and other geophysical features of the planet must have taken millions of years longer to operate than the approximately 6,000 extrapolated from a close analytical reading of the Pentateuch. Hutton was followed in due course, and in greater and more persuasive detail, by Charles Lyell's *Principles of*

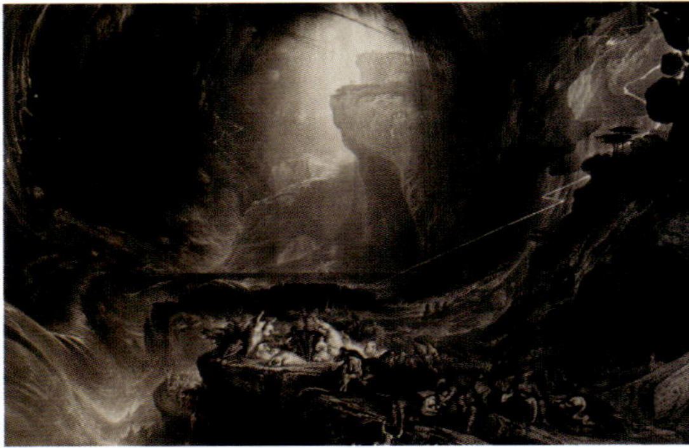

fig. 3
John Martin
The Deluge, 1828
Mezzotint with etching, 59.2 x 81.2 cm
British Museum, London

Geology (1830–33). In between, the proto-palaeontologist Georges Cuvier argued on the basis of rapidly accumulating scientific and historiographical data that the same processes required waves of catastrophic inundation, for which Genesis 6 and 7 stood as a reliable archetype, certainly, but wholly truncated in terms of the true, geologically realistic span of time actually needed. Byron had been familiar with Baron Cuvier's ideas, as was Martin himself. Indeed, Martin's son Leopold later recalled the red-letter day when, visiting the studio unfortunately when the artist himself was absent, Baron Cuvier sat in front of *The Deluge* for some time, then 'rose, with the exclamation "Mon Dieu!", at the same time taking a small bouquet from his buttonhole, placing it on his card, and depositing both on my father's palette.'[13]

Most intriguingly, in 1835 Martin experienced an incomparable opportunity to test what had necessarily been an imaginary rendition of the conjunction of sun, moon and comet when in October and November, a year after he finished this second version of *The Deluge*, he was able to observe at first hand Halley's Comet in the sky over England and, five years later, introduced the entirely different but no less remarkable astronomical effects into the portentous sky overhanging Prince Albert's *The Eve of the Deluge*.[14] In 1840, what must have seemed an eerily familiar sky in that later picture merely added to the sense of cataclysmic reordering and heavenly collapse represented by the entirely different heavenly bodies, which are brought to a sullen, blood-red standstill within *The Deluge* of 1834.

Two historical addenda suggest further contexts in which to place the evolution of Martin's great flood subject. In 1824 work began on the construction of a new bridge slightly upstream from Old London Bridge, which was finally torn down soon after the new one was finished. It had long been recognized that the medieval bridge had too many arches and therefore constricted the tidal flow of the River Thames. It acted as a kind of ford, sometimes perilous to river traffic. However, over the centuries, the bridge had actually served to control the tides, especially when the position of the sun and moon coincided with an easterly gale, forcing huge amounts of water upstream, so that when, in 1831, the new bridge opened, floods became an unexpected and costly problem in the City of London.[15] Martin himself had also become interested in the issue of the pollution of Thames water, publishing at his own expense no fewer than twelve pamphlets on the topic between 1827 and 1850.[16]

Meanwhile, it was observed that the whole of Britain was getting steadily wetter, especially since the dry decades of the mid-eighteenth century. Then, in August 1829, massive floods took place in Scotland, where Martin's first *Deluge* picture had been shown only a year earlier: 'The rainfall which caused the floods was of extraordinary intensity, great persistence, and fell over a wide area, and the total volume of water concerned … was enormous.'[17] In other words, comet, sun and moon – insofar as they were known to affect floods – as well as a real inundation on a scale rarely if ever witnessed in Britain, certainly not in living memory, these were all in the news, often sensationally, during the long period in which John Martin tackled successive versions and later extrapolations of *The Deluge*.

Finally, in the same period, notwithstanding the revulsion with which the Duke of Wellington and other reactionary statesmen greeted it, Reform: unstoppable, progressively renewable, but cautiously calibrated political and social reform, culminating in the Reform Act of 1832 – Reform was undoubtedly one of the most important foundations of intellectual and artistic life in the 1830s. Indeed it could be argued that Reform, with all its social and political consequences through the reign of King William IV, was the most precious asset, together with the throne of England, that was inherited in 1837 by his eighteen-year-old niece Princess Victoria Alexandrina of Kent.[18] As a result, the political earthquakes that in 1848 shook apart so many of the polities of continental Europe simply did not happen in England, where comparable tremors were greatly feared, but (if not entirely contained) certainly corralled – not unlike the giddy energy that reverberates powerfully throughout Martin's grand, nearly contemporaneous visions of the flood in Genesis.

Acknowledgments: I am grateful to Robert Hoozee for inviting me to write this necessarily brief essay, and to Amy Meyers, Director of the Yale Center for British Art in New Haven, Conn., Andrew Dempsey, Helen Simpson, Cassandra Albinson and Patrick McCaughey, for their generous assistance.

1. Burke 1757 (Penguin ed.) Part II, Section II, p. 101.
2. Matteson 1981. I have relied heavily on Matteson's important article, as will become clear, especially in respect of the material relating to the theories of Georges Cuvier and other early nineteenth-century pioneers of geology. See also Paley 1986, passim; and Sadrin 1995.
3. Alter and Kermode 1987, p. 42.
4. Rad 1956, pp. 112 ff.
5. Martin 1828; see also Pendered 1923, p. 131.
6. See also Byron 1848, p. 252.
7. Matteson 1981, p. 220.
8. 'PROPOSALS for publishing *The Print* of THE DELUGE', octavo pamphlet [1828], British Library, London (bound in Tracts 1602/293), incorrectly dated 1838 in the *British Library General Catalogue of Printed Books to 1975*, vol. 213, p. 71. 'Price to subscribers, Proofs before the Letters, Ten Guineas, Proofs Five Guineas; Prints Two Guineas and a Half each.'
9. Balston 1947, pp. 88–89.
10. Balston 1934, pp. 393–94, 411.
11. Martin to Edwin Athelstone, 12 November 1841, Somerset County Museum; cit. Feaver 1975, p. 92.
12. In an eighteen page pamphlet printed in Newcastle in 1834, Martin's eldest brother William placed himself firmly in the orthodox camp: *The Christian Philosopher's Explanation of the General Deluge, and the Proper Cause of all the different Strata: wherein it is clearly demonstrated, that One Deluge was the Cause of the Whole, which divinely proves that God is not a Liar, but that the Bible is strictly true.* See Balston 1934, p. 429.
13. Pendered 1923, p. 133; Feaver 1975, p. 94.
14. Olson and Pasachoff 1986, pp. 212–13.
15. Brooks and Glasspoole 1928, pp. 90–91.
16. Balston 1934, p. 403.
17. Brooks and Glasspoole 1928, p. 98.
18. Pearce 2003, *passim*.

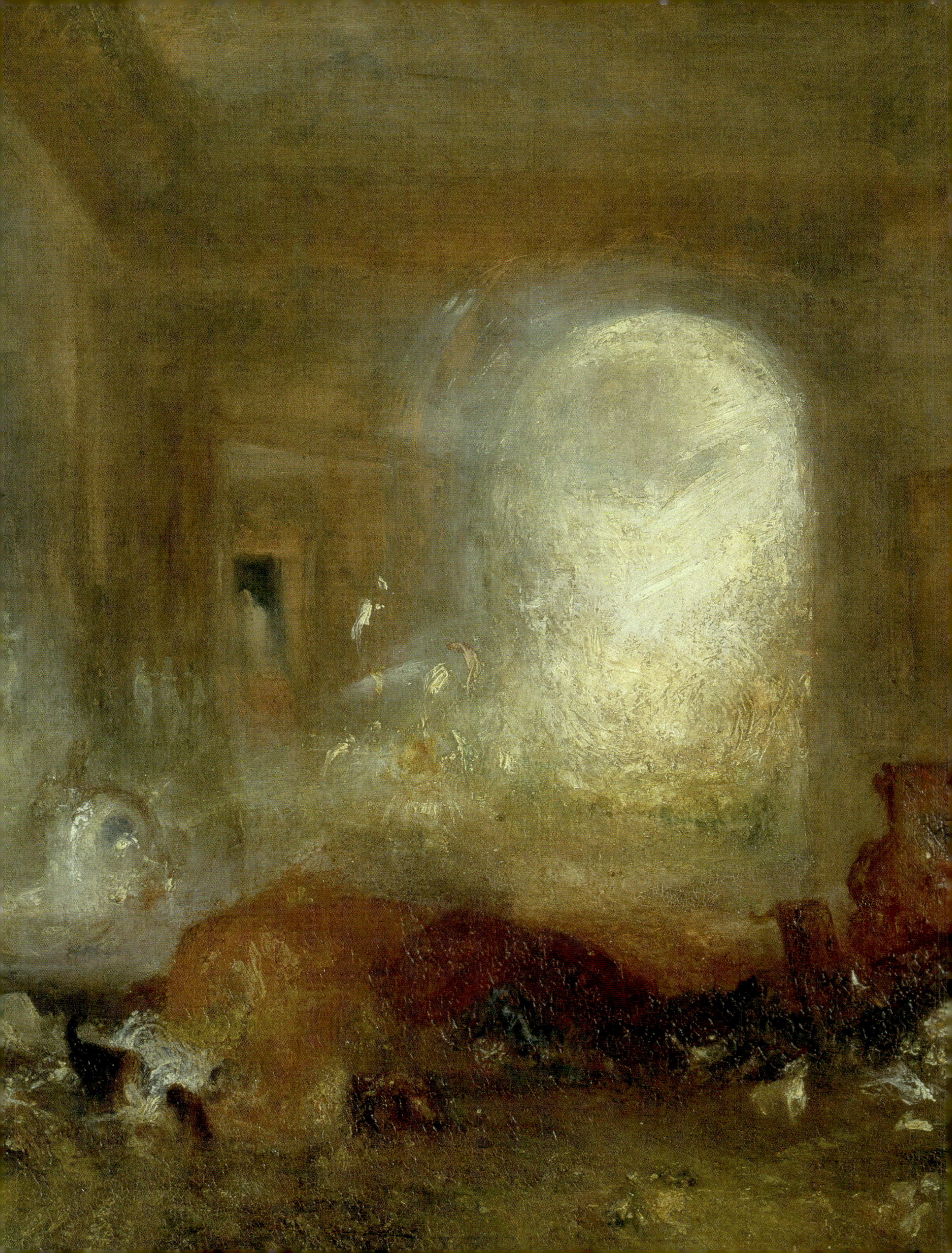

J.M.W. TURNER

Interior of a Great House: the Drawing Room, East Cowes Castle, c. 1830

IAN WARRELL

Writing about this unfinished canvas in 1910, just a few years after it was publicly displayed for the first time, Charles Lewis Hind declared that it was 'a puzzle to almost everybody', while another critic observed that 'the picture might just as well hang upside down'.[1] As the following summary will indicate, this state of intrigued bemusement has very largely continued to be the case, despite several bold and ingenious theories about Turner's image. During the last quarter of a century especially, scholars have speculated about the location depicted and the possible causes of the turmoil seen in the room, in which chairs are overturned and dogs howl. Yet, despite its lack of a fixed meaning, the picture has been widely acclaimed and seen as particularly exemplary of the characteristics generally associated with Turner's later, more indistinct style.

In its unresolved, interrupted state of development, the main appeal of the painting is the seemingly transcendent way Turner fills the space with light, powerfully suggesting a state of visionary flux. The abiding impression is that the paint itself has assumed the quality of light passing through air. This is skilfully laid in with brush and palette knife to filter horizontally across the room from the deep window opening on the right, while, through the arch directly ahead, the area of white impasto achieves an intense brilliance to dazzling effect. Turner adopts a low perspective, looking up sharply towards a mirror on the left. In the corners of the wall opposite the viewer there are two more oblong shapes, which may be further mirrors or openings into other rooms. That on the left features a white shape that could possibly be a reflected figure or sculpture.

Running across the image from left to right, there are a number of objects, each of which seems to offer tantalizing clues about what Turner intended. These begin on the mantelpiece in front of the mirror with a series of yellow verticals that resemble candlesticks. On the floor there is a hat decorated with a feather, redolent of the seventeenth century, or a costume party. Above this there is a white and gold object, which has been described as a cradle, but which could also be the back of a chair. Next to the hat there is a cornucopia, symbol of wealth and plenty. Then the eye lingers on a vibrant use of yellow, orange and red, although this swathe of paint does not seem to describe anything readily identifiable. At the centre of the image are several small dogs, including a barking spaniel, and behind it a fallen chair. The most significant form in the image, however, is the large dark red shape, which bears on its side the Royal Coat of Arms, the Lion and the Unicorn, a combined emblem that was introduced after James I assumed the throne in 1603. This has been seen as a sofa, an open coffin or a pianoforte, but Turner's realization is not sufficiently advanced to permit precise identification. In front of this, the summarily sketched white forms have been perceived as 'religious plate' and 'the silver Rimmon or Torah finial of Jewish ritual, with its tiers and bells'.[2] However, these, too, are difficult to interpret conclusively.

The painting is one of a group of atypical interior scenes and figure subjects that Turner painted in the late 1820s, for which he often redeployed and worked over earlier images.[3] In 1990 an X-radiograph revealed that the image we now see is painted over another composition that also shows an interior, but which included figures gathered round a piano-like object on

J.M.W. Turner, ***Interior of a Great House: the Drawing Room, East Cowes Castle*** (detail), cat. 257

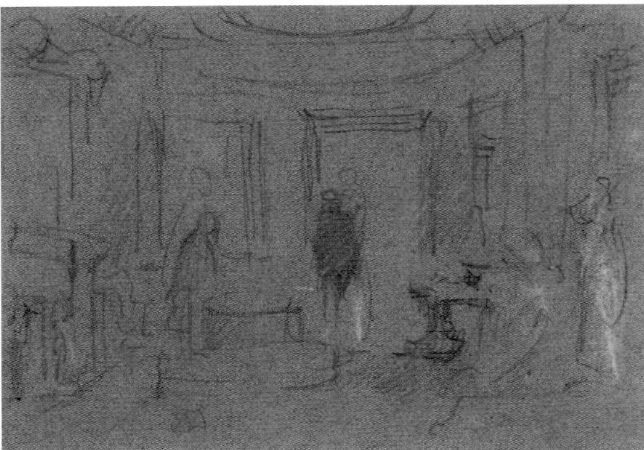

fig. 1
J.M.W. Turner
***East Cowes Castle: The Drawing Room, looking South-West into the Conservatory*, 1827**
Pencil and chalk on paper, 14.4 x 19.2 cm
Tate, London

the right, as well as a large round seat to the left of the arched opening, where Turner subsequently added the bright orange.[4] This resembles a round ottoman with a back support, an article that was the height of fashion in grand houses in the 1820s.[5] The essence of this earlier picture is preserved in a pencil and chalk study made in 1827, which also features this seat (fig. 1). In the oil painting, the use of a red ground and an emerald green (not generally found in Turner's work) have been used as a means of determining that the date when he is most likely to have reworked the canvas is the winter of 1829-30, when he was preparing *Pilate Washing his Hands* and *Jessica* for exhibition at the Royal Academy; both pictures feature these exceptional technical characteristics.[6]

For some reason, Turner abandoned the body of work that the *Interior* is part of, and the only public intimation he gave that he had conducted this kind of experimentation took the form of two small genre scenes that he exhibited in 1831.[7] When the work was eventually exhibited at the Tate Gallery in 1906, the curators related the composition to the informal gouache studies recording one of Turner's visits to the Sussex home of the 3rd Earl of Egremont, and as a result first listed it as 'Interior at Petworth Castle, a Study in Colour' (the word 'Castle' was later dropped and sometimes replaced by the more correct 'House').

There was an amazed response to the 'new Turner' that the *Interior* and its fellow canvases revealed. While recognizing that these were unfinished pictures, several zealously patriotic writers seized on them as evidence that Turner had anticipated the appearance of Impressionist painting. Some evidently believed that the picture was created in the Impressionist manner during a limited time period, the vibrancy of the brushwork supposedly being indicative of Turner's haste in capturing his effect. Laurence Housman in the *Manchester Guardian*, for example, claimed, 'here indeed we see "the very pulse of the machine"'.[8] And the painting continued to be viewed in this way, with later commentators making a link with the domestic subjects of Bonnard and Vuillard.[9]

Housman was also among the first to detect an element of art-for-art's-sake experimentation in the image, noting that, 'The colours lie about on the canvas often with no possible explanation save that there they are needed for balance, for harmony, or for movement.' This tack was explored at greater length in an article by Professor Josef Strzygowski, which perversely compared the earlier, factual style of Turner's *Frosty Morning* (cat. 152), with the unfinished *Interior*. Like many subsequent writers, he believed the later work marked a 'wonderful clarification', as Turner progressed from 'nature to art'. In effect, he was advancing Turner as a proto-Expressionist: 'He does not see a fragment of nature through the medium of his temperament; but gives us rather, on the contrary, his own temperament seen through a fragment of nature. Nature is wholly subordinated to his impetuous need for self-expression.'[10]

In the 1940s, in his influential volume *Landscape into Art*, Kenneth Clark also ignored the painting's unfinished character and announced that it was 'the first attempt to make light and colour alone the basis of a design', and he subsequently declared it 'the most liberated picture of the nineteenth century'.[11] Endorsed by such a powerful advocate, the *Interior*, not surprisingly, thereafter achieved an iconic status among Turner's later works. It was generally shown

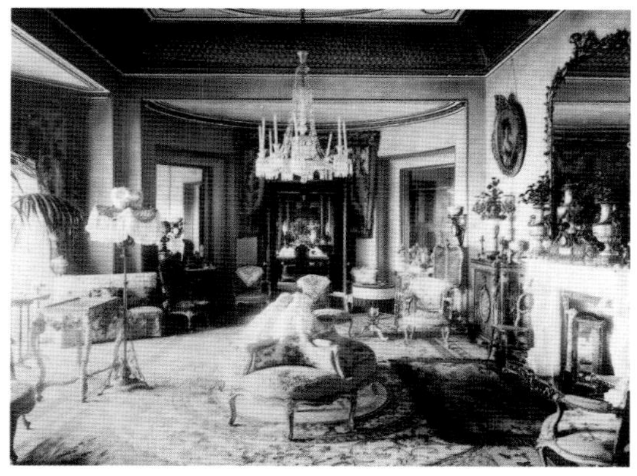

fig. 2
Unknown photographer
East Cowes Castle:
The North End of the Drawing Room,
***looking through into the Dining Room*,**
early 20th century

with the Turners at the National Gallery, rather than those at the Tate, and was twice toured in North America, appearing in a survey show of 'masterpieces' of British Art at the New York Museum of Modern Art in 1956 (ten years before Lawrence Gowing's presentation of Turner at the same venue).

In the early 1970s, as attention began to focus on the content of Turner's images, the perceived significance of the picture was further enhanced by David Thomas's suggestion that Turner's scene is a lamentation prompted by Lord Egremont's death in 1837.[12] No one seems to have remarked that this idea was at odds with the date of 1830 or 1831 given to the picture when it first came to light. Building on Thomas's thesis, however, Patrick Youngblood identified the setting as the Marble Hall at Petworth House, in which the earl's coffin had rested before his funeral.[13] He and John Gage both resolved that the picture should actually be titled 'The Apotheosis of Lord Egremont (Interior at Petworth)'.[14]

Looking at the picture in the wider context of the related interior scenes, Andrew Wilton expressed reservations about its by-then traditional association with Petworth as early as 1979, when he proposed a link with the architecture of Sir John Soane. A decade later he considered the *Interior* more likely to be a historical genre subject of the kind painted for the popular annual publications known as *Keepsakes*, which Bonington had helped to popularize.[15] He speculated it could be an incident from *The Merchant of Venice* or a scene showing the 'Sack of a Great House'. Others have since adapted these proposals, though the familiar link with Petworth has persisted in Simon Schama's recent suggestion that the image is one reflecting the ideas of reform in the wake of the crumbling of the 'old Protestant-Tory ascendancy', and that Turner, the working-class revolutionary, chose to revisit Petworth 'one last time, to smash it up'.[16]

Yet, if we return to the pencil study of 1827 (fig. 1), it is clear that the underlying design and structure of Turner's painting are derived from the drawing room at John Nash's Neo-Gothic home on the Isle of Wight.[17] The deep window bay on the right closely approximates to that which opened onto the castle's terrace, while the arched opening at the centre of the picture is a dramatic adaptation of the doorway that led through to the south-west facing conservatory. This viewpoint would help to explain the sharp contrast between the subdued fall of light in the main body of Turner's room and the exultant sunburst in the space beyond. The room also had mirrors in each corner, as can be seen in an old photograph showing the opposite end of the drawing room, which had semi-circular bays at either end (fig. 2). A link with East Cowes Castle should not be a great surprise, for another of the unfinished oil paintings formerly linked with Petworth has already been shown to be a reminiscence of Nash's octagon room.[18]

But the associations with Petworth and its collection of Old Masters are not easily dismissed. Turner's interior scenes were evidently conceived as a kind of homage to Rembrandt, some of whose works could be found there. And whatever the architectural starting point for these images, Turner subsequently began to invest them with historical details, which were most probably derived from his visits to Petworth. The confusion over the depicted locations (on our part, and perhaps his too) may arise from the coincidence of his visiting both country houses during the summer of 1827, and of Petworth subsequently becoming his regular bolt-hole from London, with the result that his experiences of both places fused. As a relatively new building, East Cowes Castle offered a fantasy version of the past but simply did not have the rich association with history that Turner found so stimulating at Petworth. So it remains a possibility that the incidents Turner invokes in his pictures are in some way connected with that house and its former inhabitants (see fig. 3).[19] But the imagery he uses could just as easily stem from more widely available sources, such as those novels by Sir Walter Scott set in the sixteenth and seventeenth century.[20] There is, too, a reasonable chance that the interiors do resonate with an awareness on Turner's part of the significance of changes to the constitution around 1829-30, which improved the civic and social status of British Catholics, and revoked the legally binding prejudice against them.[21] In the context of Turner's *Interior of a Great House*, the inclusion of objects that may refer to Catholic and Jewish religious practices could be seen as a plea to extend still further the scope of the newly available tolerance. For the moment, at least, these must remain unanswered speculations, as this elusive picture continues to deflect us with its captivating surface.

---

1. Hind 1910, p. 276; Strzygowski 1908, p. 341.
2. Wilton 1989, p. 27.
3. See Butlin and Joll 1984, nos. 445-50; Townsend and Warrell 1991.
4. Wilton 1990, p. 56, fig. 2; the X-radiograph was taken by Joyce Townsend.
5. I am grateful to Frances Collard of the Victoria and Albert Museum Furniture Department for shedding light on this feature.
6. Wilton 1990, p. 55; Butlin and Joll 1984, no. 332 (Tate, London) and no. 333 (Petworth House).
7. See, *Lucy, Countess of Carlisle, and Dorothy Percy's Visit to their Father, Lord Percy, when under Attainder* (Butlin and Joll 1984, no. 338; Tate, London); *Watteau Study by Fresnoy's Rules* (Butlin and Joll 1984, no. 340; Tate, London).
8. 5 February 1906; see also Hind 1910, p. 277.
9. Herrmann 1975, p. 37.
10. Strzygowski 1908, p. 341.
11. Clark 1949, p. 103; Clark 1973, p. 256.
12. London 1974, p. 111, no. 339; and Butlin and Joll 1984, no. 449.
13. Youngblood 1983b.
14. Gage 1987, pp. 166-67; Youngblood 1990.
15. See Wilton 1979, p. 210; Wilton 1989; Wilton 1990.
16. Schama 2006, p. 276; see also Rowell, Warrell and Brown 2002, p. 76, for David Brown's suggestion that the picture relates to *Pilate Washing his Hands* and perhaps shows the Sacking of the Temple in Jerusalem.
17. A more developed view of this, painted in watercolour and gouache is also in the Turner Bequest: TB CCXLIV 32 (Tate, London).
18. Youngblood 1983a.
19. Three of the pictures could relate to the 3rd Earl's sixteenth- and seventeenth-century ancestors, one of whom Turner depicted in 1831 (see above n. 7). *Dinner in a Great Room with Figures in Costume* (Butlin and Joll 1984, no. 445) could perhaps have been suggested by the visit of Elizabeth I to Petworth in 1563; *Figures in a Building* (Butlin and Joll 1984, no. 446) shows a prison or cellar, and could relate to the discovery of the Gunpowder Plot explosives under the Houses of Parliament, which led to the arrest of the 9th Earl of Northumberland; and the *Interior* itself may be intended to evoke the house during the turbulent period of the Civil Wars. Such a sequence would be comparable with the historical projects Turner undertook for his friend Walter Fawkes earlier in the 1820s.
20. Turner had already worked with Scott, and during 1830 he visited Peveril Castle in Derbyshire and Kenilworth, both of which provided settings for the novelist.
21. See Barry Venning, 'Turner, Catholicism and the Constitution' (forthcoming), based on a paper he gave at the Turner conference in Birmingham in 2004.

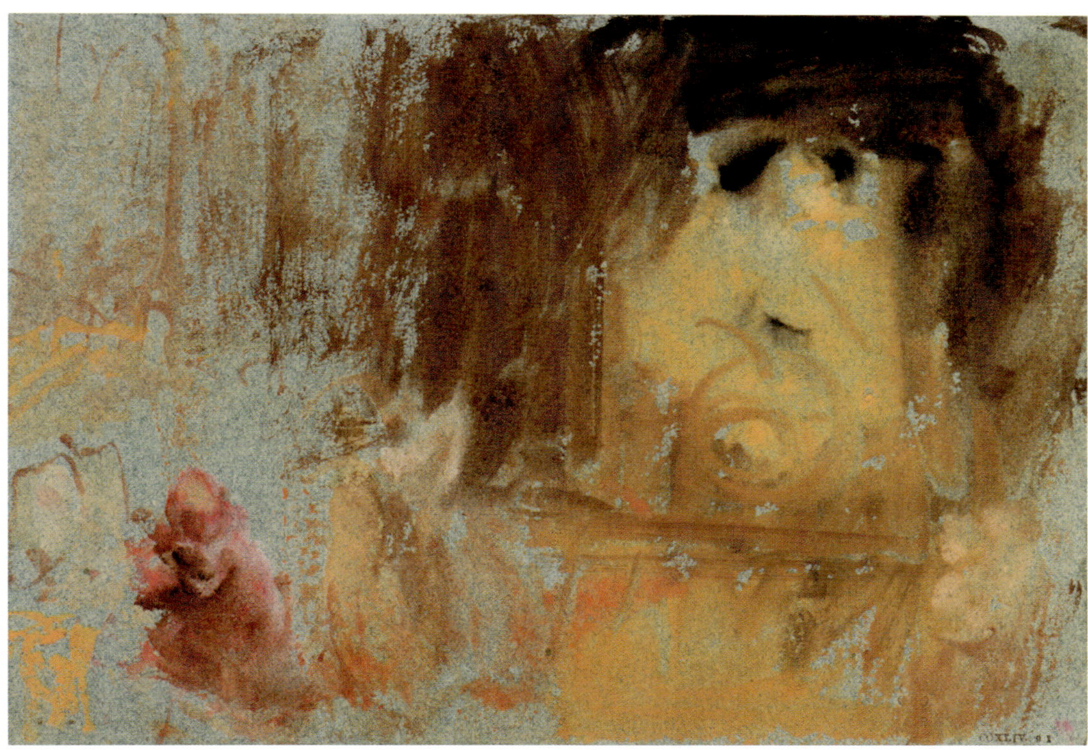

fig. 3
J.M.W. Turner, ***An Imaginative Historical Subject, apparently connected with Petworth***, 1827
Gouache and watercolour on paper, 13.6 x 19 cm; Tate, London

This image includes a globe, which could relate to the terrestrial globe traditionally assumed to have been acquired from Sir Walter Ralegh by Henry Percy, 9th Earl of Northumberland, when incarcerated in the Tower of London for his supposed part in the Gunpowder Plot.

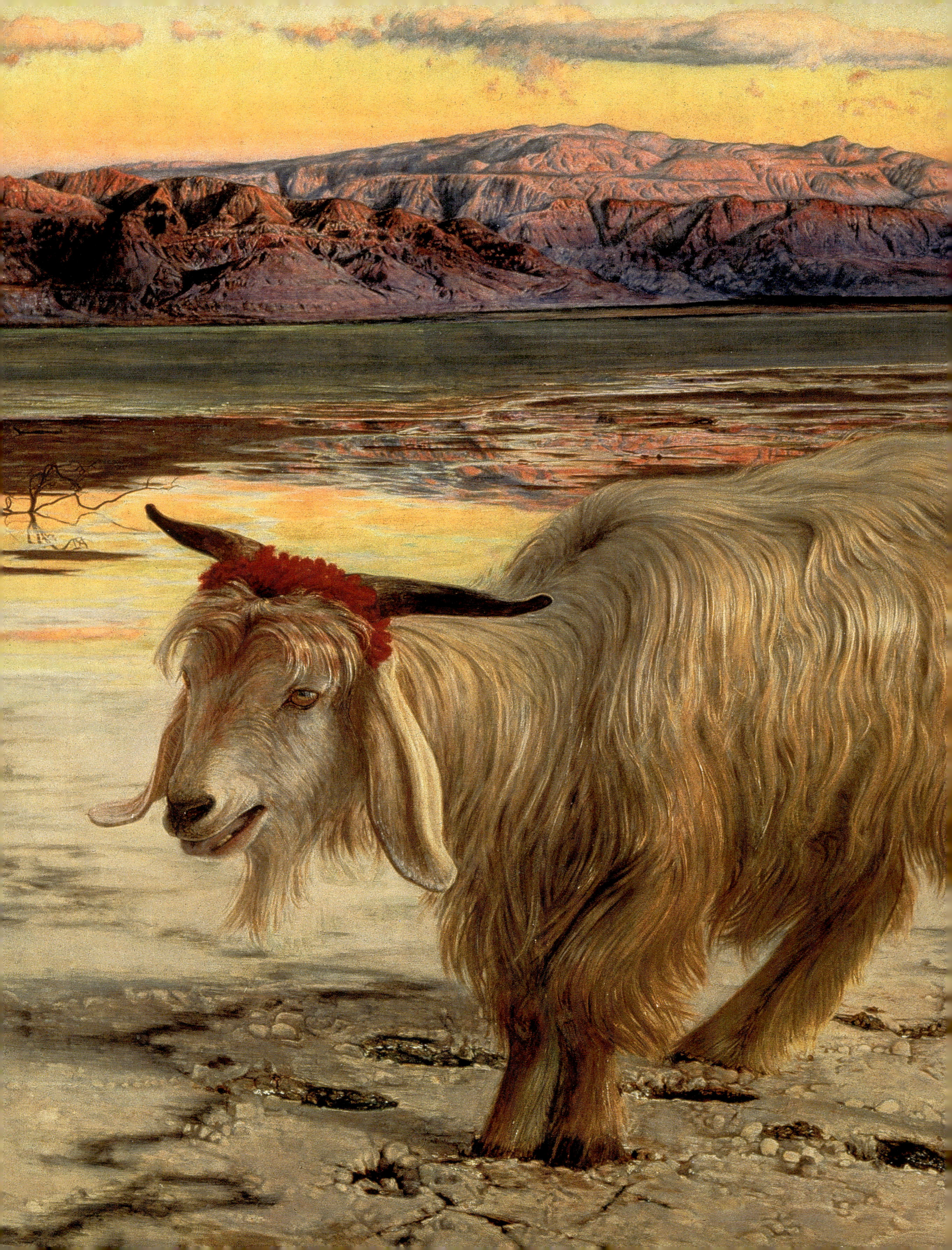

WILLIAM HOLMAN HUNT

The Scapegoat, 1854-55, 1856

CHRISTOPHER NEWALL

This is one of the strangest and most obsessive works of the nineteenth century: a painting of extraordinary pictorial power and bizarre beauty, and one into which are layered complex and interwoven didactic messages; an invention of febrile imagination that at the same time depends upon the mimetic representation of an actual physical setting, which caused the artist untold agonies. It shows a wild goat stumbling across a salt-encrusted shore, with a wide expanse of shallow water beyond – lying in which are skeletal remains of animals that had perished in this unwelcoming place – and a distant range of starkly eroded mountains, luridly lit by the evening sun.

Holman Hunt went to the Holy Land in 1854 because he believed that the way things looked in modern Palestine would provide evidence about the physical appearance of people and places in the ancient Kingdom of Judah, or in Palestine at the time of the life of Christ. He wanted to incorporate such anthropological, archaeological and geographical data into his paintings so that they might be regarded as reliable accounts of the appearance of people and landscapes in biblical times. This was to be a type of Protestant religious art suitable to an age hungry for information about distant lands and historical period, and questioning of the literal truth of the Bible.

Once in Jerusalem, Hunt embarked on *The Finding of the Saviour in the Temple* (Birmingham Museum and Art Gallery), in connection with which he made careful readings of the Talmud (probably from translations in John Lightfoot's *The Temple Service as it Stood in the Dayes of Our Saviour*, 1649), Josephus, and the Bible. In addition, he familiarized himself with Jewish religious practices, visiting synagogues and attending Passover services. Difficulties occurred when Hunt sought to recruit Semitic models for the seventeen figures. There was then a movement led by European Jews to improve the living conditions and establish the political identity of the expanding Jewish community in Palestine. A particular resentment was felt on the part of Jews towards the various Christian missions established to attempt to make converts. Prohibitions were made on Jews working for Christians or even communicating with them, and, as Hunt reported, 'a special curse' was placed upon him for having 'spoken to some [Jews] about sitting to him'.[1] Hunt denied that his work as an artist was connected with the Christian missions, although friends of his in Palestine were involved, and in a broad sense his work must be seen in the context of such proselytizing.

A second painting, likewise dependent on his researches into Jewish religious practices and texts but not requiring human models, was sufficiently formed in the artist's imagination to allow him to explain the subject, which he believed had 'never been done before', in a letter to Thomas Combe in mid-July: 'It is so full of meaning (one reason however against it) and it is so simple – The scapegoat in the Wilderness by the Dead Sea somewhere, with the mark of the bloody hands on the head.'[2] In late October Hunt made an expedition to the shores of the Dead Sea to find a suitable landscape setting for *The Scapegoat*. Following recommendations in Felicien de Sauley's *Narrative of a Journey Round the Dead Sea*, at the sea's narrow southern tip at Oosdoom he found a place 'which few travellers visit and none revisit [and which, he had been told, was] the wretchedest place in the whole world'.[3] A further attraction to Hunt, since he intended the painting to be imbued with baleful associations, was that he believed that this was the site of the ancient city of Sodom, 'the very name of which has become a proverb of God's judgment,'[4] as he wrote to Millais. Hunt set up a camp on the shore for some days in November, taking with him a billy-goat, which was to be the model. Apart from the place being a 'beautifully arranged horrible wilderness',[5] there was the threat of attack by Arab tribesmen; furthermore, the goat sickened and died. Parts of the landscape setting were actually painted in the open air at Oosdoom. However, after nine days he returned to Jerusalem, taking with him mud and salt so as to be able to recreate the scene in an improvised studio. The distant mountains and sky were painted from the roof of a house in the city which allowed distant views of the landscape on the eastern side of the Dead Sea.

The Scapegoat derives from Hunt's knowledge of Jewish sacrificial religion. According to the Talmud and as described in chapter XVI of Leviticus, on the Day of Atonement two goats were to be brought to the Temple; the first was to be ritually slaughtered so that its blood would splash the priest and the altar; the second was to be driven out into the wilderness to die as a symbolic expiation of sin. Around its horns was to be dressed a fillet of wool, which, if it turned from red to white, would be taken as a sign that God had accepted the sacrifice and thus offered forgiveness to the community. Hunt shows the miserable animal as it takes its last few footsteps before expiring from thirst and exhaustion; on its forehead remains the bloody handprint of the priest who had forced it from the Temple. Littered about are animal remains (with the goat's own shadow pointing forward to a skull), making clear the inevitability of the event. In his commentary to the painting when it was shown at the Royal Academy in 1856, Hunt emphasized the horror of the place and elaborated on the particular cruelty of the Jews (he describes how the goat was 'hooted at and driven away by every "Israelite who met it, until it reached a land not inhabited"'). This was principally a subject of Hunt's own invention,[6] and one that was intended for Christian spectators who might regard themselves as culturally and spiritually far removed from the barbarities of blood sacrifice. It was also intended as a missionary appeal to the Jews. Hunt explained in a letter to Millais written in November 1854 that 'any reflecting Jews' who might see it were to recognize 'the Messiah, as he was, and not as they understand – a temporal King'.[7]

In the same letter Hunt stated that the scapegoat was 'instituted as a type of Christ'; furthermore, as the inscriptions and decorative motifs on the painting's frame make clear,[8] there is a deliberate linking of the sacrifice of a goat with the Passion and death of Christ on earth. Describing the painting, Hunt quoted from Isaiah 1:18: 'Though your sins be as scarlet, they shall be as white as snow; though they shall be red like crimson, they shall be as wool,' a text that is interpreted as linking the Old Testament with the Advent and Crucifixion of Christ. The mocked and tormented goat is therefore to die as a consequence of the cruelty or indifference of mankind (and, according to the reading of the subject as a document of anti-Semitism, specifically of the Jews). Seen as a type of the Passion and Crucifixion of Christ, the red fillet tied to the goat's horns stands for the Crown of Thorns; furthermore, the goat dies agonizingly and slowly, as Christ died on the Cross, while the ibex skull and camel skeleton on each side are emblematic of the two thieves who died with Christ. Alternatively, the goat's death may have been associated in Hunt's mind with a gradual but inevitable demise of Judaism, with its exhausted body and the skeletal remains symbolizing what he saw as the redundant Jewish dispensation.

Responses to the painting when exhibited in 1856 were both confused and hostile; Hunt came to admit that he had 'over-counted on the picture's intelligibility'.[9] Various critics took issue with Hunt's choice of a goat – an animal which is emblematic of lubricity and as an avatar of the Devil – as a religious symbol. While the representation of the physical setting was occasionally admired, Ruskin considered the picture, 'regarded merely as a landscape … a total failure';[10] nonetheless, he conceded that 'of all the scenes in the Holy Land, there are none whose present aspect tends so distinctly to confirm the statements of Scripture as this condemned shore'.[11] Ford Madox Brown made the most straightforward and enthusiastic response, writing in his diary that it was something that 'requires to be seen to be believed in & only then can it be understood how by the might of genius out of an old goat & some saline incrustations can be made one of the most tragic & impressive works in the annals of art'.[12]

Aged twenty-seven when he painted *The Scapegoat*, Hunt was both radical and confused in his view of the world. The painting was extremely personal to him, perhaps more so than anything else he ever did. While working on it he kept a journal,[13] which conveys something of the neurotic guilt that he felt about his own personality and sexual desires. 'The Sea is heaven's own blue, like a diamond more lovely in a king's diadem than in the mines of the Indes,' he wrote, 'but as it gushes up through the broken ice like salt on the beach, it is black, full of asphalt scum – and in the hand slimy, and smarting as a sting .... If in all there are sensible figures of men's secret deeds and thoughts then is this the horrible figure of Sin – a varnished deceit – earth joys at hand but Hell gaping behind, a stealthy, terrible enemy for ever.'[14] Even in his encampment at Oosdoom, he was haunted by thoughts of Annie Miller, the girl in London he had attempted to educate and protect, and who he still hoped might become his wife.

In artistic terms the painting represents a pursuance of Pre-Raphaelite principles of rigorous observation and celebration of the beauty of the physical world, but incorporated into a subject that is both disturbing to the eye and that has alarming symbolical implications. In some sense Hunt seems himself to have been identifying with the fated animal. By 1854 the intimate circle of the Pre-Raphaelite Brotherhood, which had once provided companionship and mutual encouragement, was breaking up. Within the wider London art world, his exhibited paintings met with derision, hence Alan Bowness's description of the painting as 'a symbol of the artist, scorned and neglected by a philistine public'.[15] Hunt's decision to travel to the Holy Land, and even more so his undertaking the exercise in self-mortification that the *Scapegoat* became for him, may be seen as a self-enforced exile from the world and a departure from artistic and social convention so as to free himself to create a new and most original type of painting.

I am grateful to Judith Bronkhurst, author of the recently published Holman Hunt *Catalogue Raisonné*, for advice on the text of this essay.

1. Seddon 1858, p. 108.
2. Cited in Bronkhurst 2006, vol. 1, p. 180.
3. Hunt 1905, vol. 1, p. 469.
4. Cited in Staley and Newall 2004, p. 114.
5. Ibid.
6. An illustration showing the Jewish scapegoat appeared in the *Pictorial Bible* (1836-38), of which Hunt had a copy. Edwin Landseer's painting of stags in the Scottish Highlands, *Coming Events Cast their Shadow Before Them (The Challenge)* (Royal Collection) seems also to have been in Hunt's thoughts when creating *The Scapegoat*.
7. Cited in Bendiner 1979, pp. 282-303.
8. On one side is an emblem of the dove returning to the ark with the olive branch, a symbol of God's kindness to the Jews; on the other is a stylized pansy or heartsease, symbol of the Trinity. At the bottom edge is the seven-branched candlestick (the menorah); while above the seven stars are included as an attribute of Christ in Heaven.
9. Hunt 1905, vol. 1, p. 108.
10. Cook and Wedderburn 1903-12, vol. 14, p. 64.
11. Ibid., p. 63.
12. Surtees 1981, p. 174.
13. Published in part in Bronkhurst 1984, pp. 111-25.
14. Cited in Bronkhurst 2006, vol. 1, p. 180.
15. Bowness 1975, p. 264.

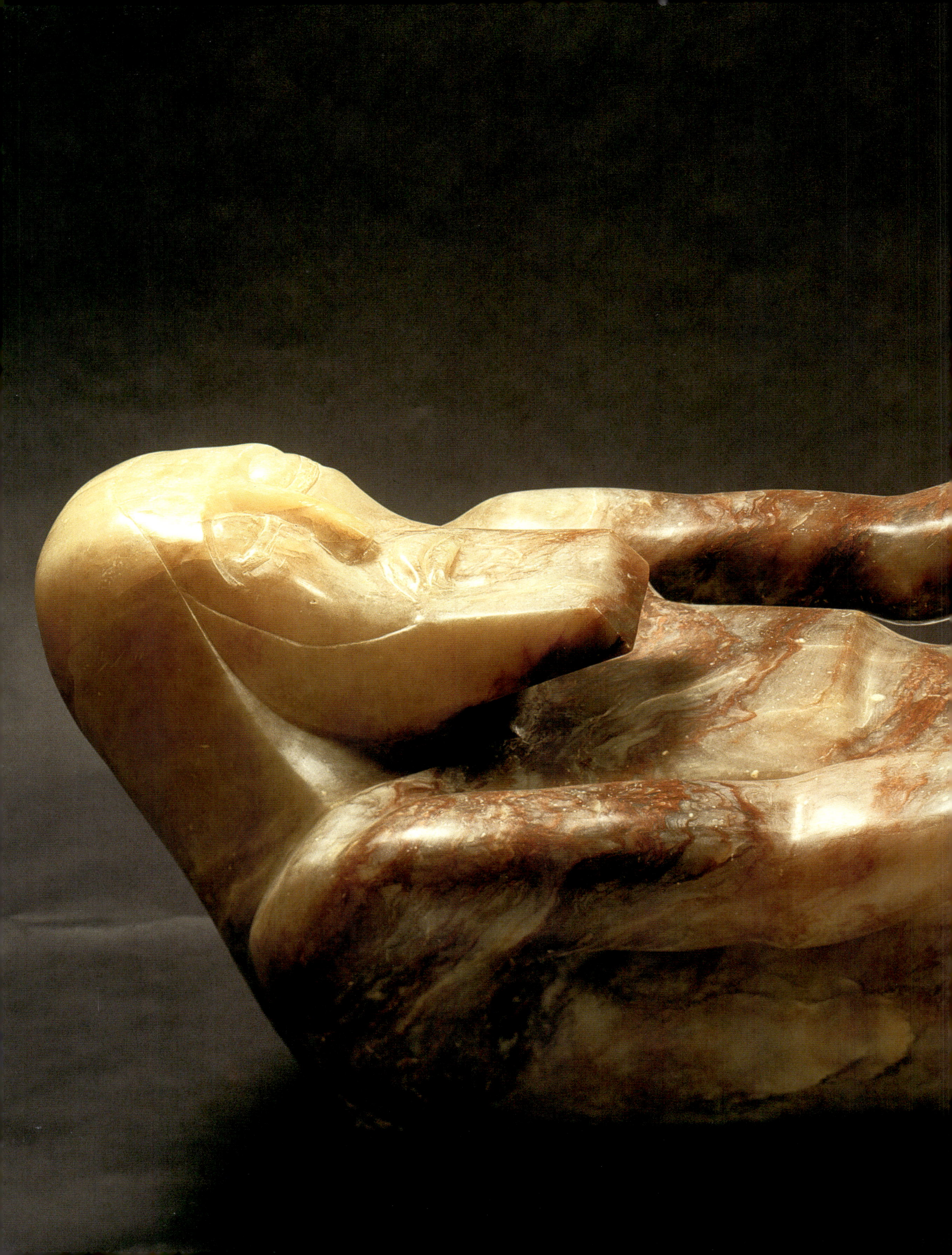

JACOB EPSTEIN

Consummatum Est, 1936-37

ROBERT UPSTONE

Face impassive, Christ holds out his hands, palms up, to show us the nail wounds of his Crucifixion. This is not a conventional illustration from the story of Christ's agony, nor is it a deposition. Instead, Epstein depicts a moment after his death as he returns to life. The prone saviour raises his head and shoulders from the ground and offers his hands as evidence both of mankind's evil and the reality of his Resurrection. 'Consummatum Est' – It is Finished – were Christ's last words before his death on the cross. But in Epstein's vision it becomes a description of the miraculous completion of the story of the Resurrection, the fulfilment of Christ's promise of redemption for mankind.

The title also suits Epstein's sense of achievement at summoning Christ out of the massive, life-size block of alabaster which had sat in his Epping Forest studio for a year before he decided what form it should take. Epstein described the origin of the sculpture in greater detail than that of any other, remembering how it came into his mind in 1936 by the stillness he felt while listening to Bach: 'While I work at other things I look at it from time to time. The block lies prone in its length, and I consider whether I should raise it, but decide to leave it where it is. I can conceive any number of works in it. I have been listening to Bach's B Minor Mass. In the section, Crucifix, I have a feeling of tremendous quiet, of awe. The music comes from a great distance and in this mood I conceive my *Consummatum Est*. I see the figure complete as a whole. I see immediately the upturned hands, with the wound in the feet, stark, crude, with the stigmata. I even imagine the setting for the finished figure, a dim crypt, with a subdued light on the semi-transparent alabaster.'[1]

Like other modern sculptors working at this time, such as Henry Moore and Barbara Hepworth, Epstein wanted his carvings to reflect the individual character, qualities and form of the original block of stone. Unlike bronze casts, 'direct carving' brought the sculptor into a very close relationship with the materiality of the sculpture, and enabled him, like Pygmalion, to form an intense bond with it. With direct carving went the idea of 'truth to materials' – preserving the feeling of the original block of stone or wood and creating simple uncluttered surfaces, or otherwise working the material so as to present its colour and texture or markings as aesthetic elements in themselves. Preserving the block, in particular, gives such early modern carved sculpture a quality of elemental force and weight, which was central to the aims of its creators. Epstein wrote in great detail about the process of carving *Consummatum Est* and the tenderness with which it emerged from the stone: 'The sculptor with his vision, planning, working, laying loving hands upon the willing and love-returning stone, the creation of a work, the form embodying the idea, strange copulation of spirit and matter, the intellect dominating hammer and chisel – the conception that at last becomes a piece of sculpture ... *Consummatum Est* – It is finished.'[2]

Epstein's mention of the 'copulation of spirit and matter' highlights his sense that carving a form out of a block of stone echoed the idea of sexual creation itself. For him, direct carving was inextricably bound up with the idea of free sexual expression, and it marks him as an artist engaged in a struggle against moral as well as aesthetic convention. Indeed, *Cosummatum Est* has an interesting formal connection with a bronze of 1931, *Sunita Reclining (Reclining Goddess)* (fig.3).[3] Here his model pushes her shoulders from the ground; her hands are laid flat rather than raised

Jacob Epstein, ***Consummatum Est*** (detail), cat. 301

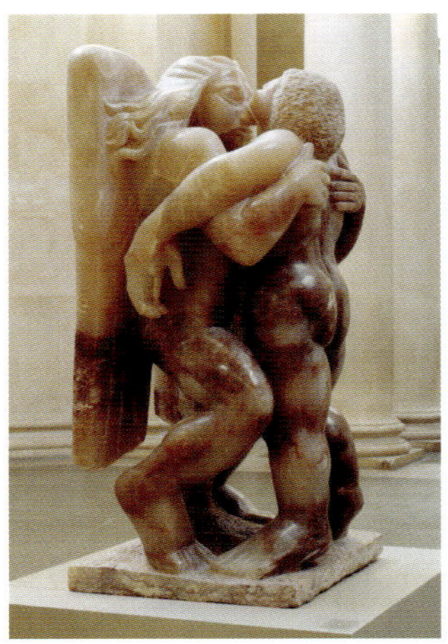

fig. 1
Jacob Epstein
***Jacob and the Angel*, 1940-41**
Alabaster, 214 x 110 x 92 cm
Tate, London

but there is a close correspondence with the format and pose of Epstein's rising Christ. Epstein was entranced by Sunita, believing her the most beautiful woman he had ever seen, and he persuaded her and her sister to move in and live with him and his wife. Whether they became lovers is unknown,[4] but there is a sizzling sensuality to Epstein's many drawings of Sunita that suggests a deep physical attraction. There are, then, in *Consummatum Est* complex parallels in Epstein's mind between carving, religion, sex and reproduction.

While organized religion in itself held no interest for Epstein. He was particularly fascinated by the stories and imagery of the Old Testament. In 1931 he conceived the idea of producing an extensive series of Old Testament drawings: 'I became so absorbed in the text,' Epstein wrote, 'and in the countless images evoked by my readings a whole new world passed in vision before me.'[5] Throughout the 1930s Epstein worked on a sequence of alabaster carvings that had Christian themes. *Consummatum Est* was exhibited for the first time at the Leicester Galleries in October 1937; *Adam*[6] was shown in June 1939 and *Jacob and the Angel*[7] (fig. 1) in February 1942. Alabaster was the material of choice for medieval religious carvings, and, as Epstein was aware, works made by English craftsmen were exported across Europe. The material therefore held an innate association with Christian tradition, practice and display. In making *Consummatum Est*, Epstein was returning to a subject that had brought him enormous hostility. His *Risen Christ* (1917-19)[8] was shown at the Leicester Galleries in 1920 and immediately stirred violent controversy. It was condemned as blasphemous, partly because Epstein utilized a portrait of his friend Bernard van Dieren and partly because of a perception that it made connection with non-Christian, non-European traditions of sculpture. The *Evening Standard* headlined the exhibition as 'Chambers of Horrors by Epstein',[9] and the racist Father Vaughan wrote in the *Weekly Graphic* of 'a Christ which suggested to me some degraded Chaldean or African, which wore the appearance of an Asiatic-American or Hun-Jew'.[10] Epstein was one of the first modern sculptors to take an interest in African tribal carvings, as well as early Greek sculpture. He formed an outstanding collection of African, Asian and Greek carvings, which profoundly influenced the direction of his own work. Abandoning any interest in continuing the established classical tradition of sculpture, Epstein developed instead a more vital style, which drew freely upon the energy and raw emotion of tribal art and appealed directly to the senses, unencumbered by traditional western motifs. By 1920 he was probably the most notorious modern artist working in Britain, condemned for the stylized treatment of form of some works and for the brazen nudity of others, notably the British Medical Association figures in the Strand. He was subjected to undisguised anti-Semitism, and one of the principal objections behind the furore of his *Risen Christ* was that as a Jew he should not conern himself with the Resurrection: 'The idea of a Jew and Christ,' Epstein wrote, 'seems, illogically enough, totally unrelated to many people.'[11]

When *Consummatum Est* was exhibited for the first time a wholly expected tirade of abuse followed. By 1937 there was a vigorous Fascist press in Britain, and many of its newspapers poured racist scorn on Epstein and his work. Epstein's sculpture was linked in the public mind to the polar struggle between Fascism and avant-garde art's perceived connection with progressive Socialism or Communism. 'Leave Epstein alone and your children will bless you,' wrote William

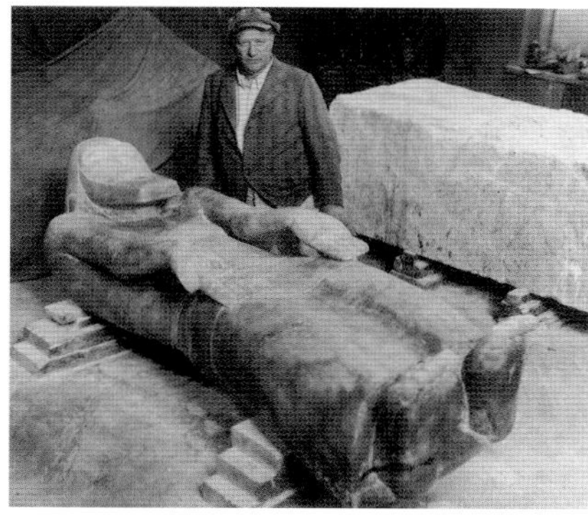

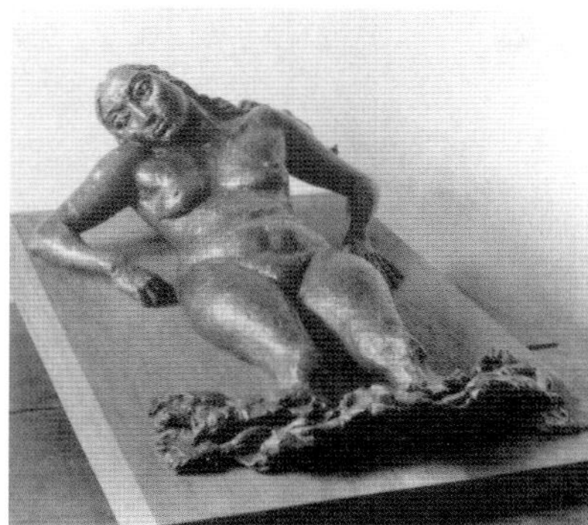

fig. 2
Epstein in his studio with ***Consummatum Est***, around 21 October 1937
Photograph

fig. 3
Jacob Epstein
Sunita Reclining (Reclining Goddess), 1931
Bronze, length 76 cm
Private Collection

McChance in the *News Chronicle* defence of *Consummatum Est*. 'Strangle him with abuse and receive the immediate blessings of Dr Goebbels and his band of tenth-rate reporters who are leading a nation to cultural suicide.'[12]

Although unsold at the Leicester Galleries, Epstein would not allow *Consummatum Est* to go on tour, mindful of the derision it would face. However, it was acquired shortly afterwards by an entrepreneur, Charles Stafford. Realizing the commerical potential of Epstein's notoriety, Stafford showed *Consummatum Est*, *Adam*, *Jacob and the Angel* and *Genesis* in a drapery shop surrounded by red velvet curtains; crowds were ushered in at the cost of a shilling by a barker on the street. Stafford then toured the works through American fun fairs during the war. Dismayed, Epstein was powerless to intervene, but worse was to follow when Stafford sold the works to Louis Tussaud's Waxworks in Blackpool. The *Evening Standard* reported: 'In between dance tunes, a recorded barker yelled an appeal to walk up and see "the strangest thing you have ever seen ... Come in to see whether you find it beautiful or shocking." What is the show? It is Jacob Epstein's *Consummatum Est* ... It rests on a sprinkling of sand with a background of "Middle East" houses. Near the foot of the figure lies Esptein's nude *Eve*. The figure is surrounded by human heads shrunk ... by head-hunters, moving marionettes and the embalmed body of Siamese twins.'[13] Placing Epstein within the context of freakish curiosity, especially after his experience of such anti-Semitic hostility, contributed to Epstein's decision not to create further large-scale sculpture.

1. Epstein 1955, p. 152.
2. Ibid.
3. Silber 1986, no. 206.
4. See Gardiner 1992, p. 262.
5. Epstein 1955, p.143.
6. Silber 1986, no. 288.
7. Ibid.
8. Ibid., no. 97.
9. *Evening Standard*, 8 February 1920.
10. *Weekly Graphic*, 14 February 1920.
11. Haskell 1931, p. 37.
12. *News Chronicle*, 28 October 1937.
13. *Evening Standard*, 3 October 1953.

225. **George Romney**

Dalton-in-Furness, Lancashire, 1734 - Kendal, Cumbria, 1802

John Howard Visiting a Prison, c. 1790-94

Pen and black ink with watercolour, wash over pencil, on paper

35.9 x 53.3 cm

Yale Center for British Art, Paul Mellon Collection, New Haven

In 1777 the philanthropist and humanitarian John Howard published his *State of the Prisons in England and Wales*, based upon first-hand inspections of the appalling conditions in hundreds of British gaols. Over the ensuing decade, Howard's tireless campaign for penal reform transformed him into a national hero, culminating in the erection of a statue to his memory in St Paul's Cathedral in 1796. George Romney was one of a number of British artists who, since the 1780s, had chosen to visualize Howard's prison work. He was unusual, however, in the intensity of his approach, producing a huge number of drawings, but no finished picture, relating to Howard visiting a lazaretto. At the same time, Romney made him the focal point for a sustained political allegory, where Howard - a prominent Dissenter - was envisaged as the embodiment of Liberty, engaged in a titanic struggle with the Satanic forces of darkness in the form of the gaoler, while the Michelangelesque bodies of the prisoners take on the aura of tortured souls. (MP)

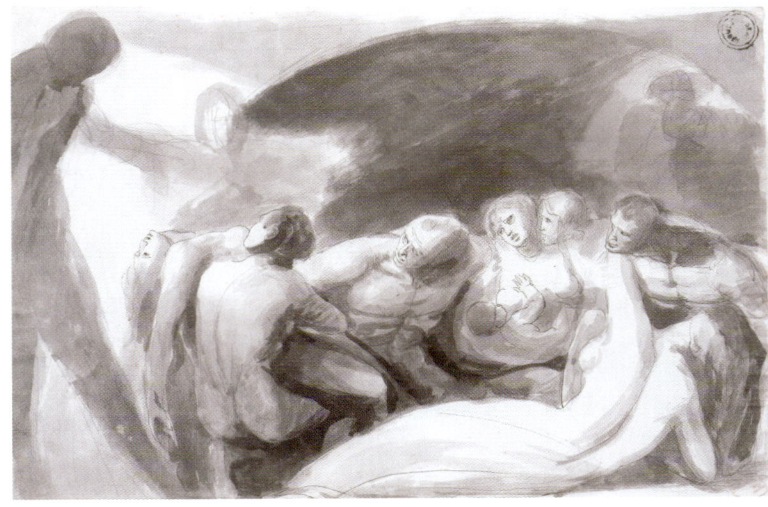

225

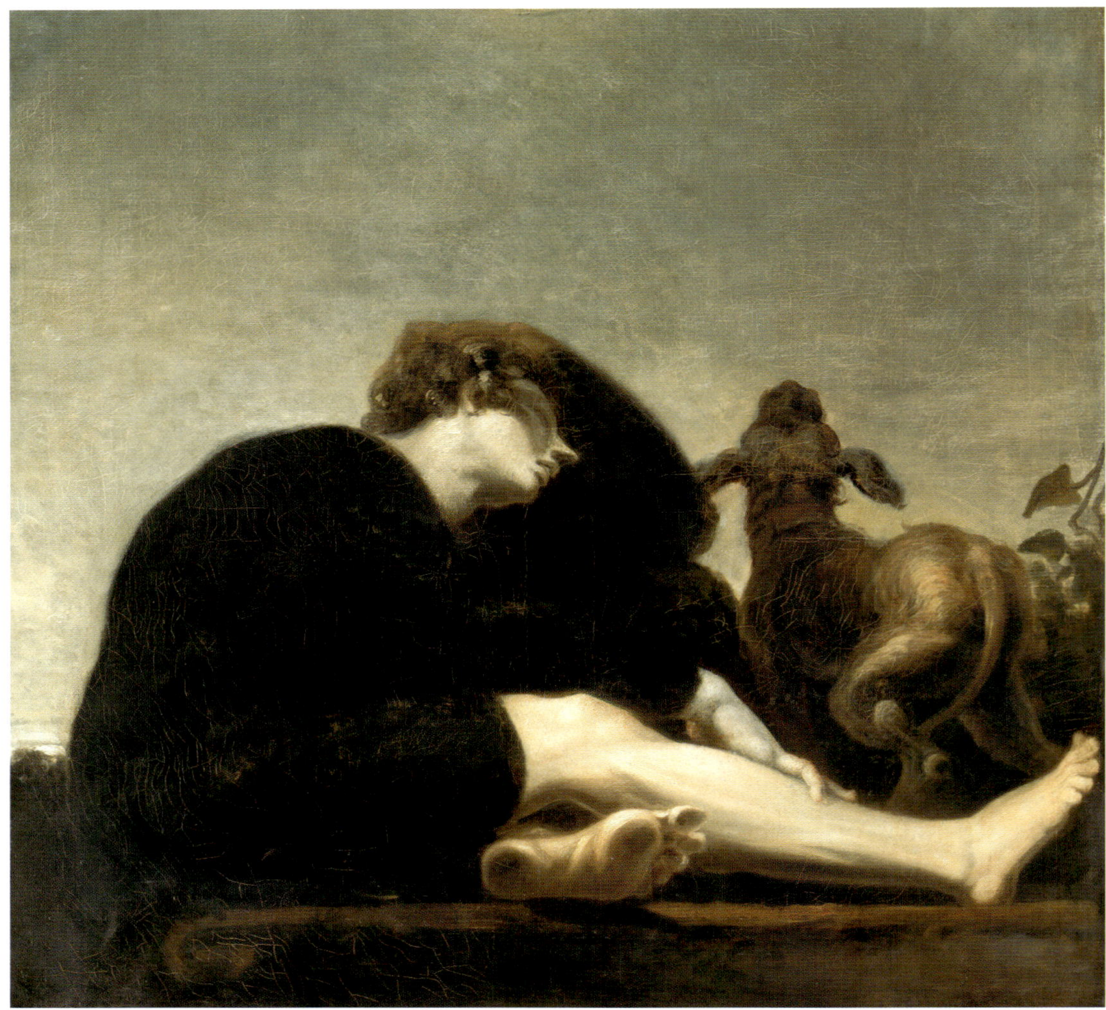

226

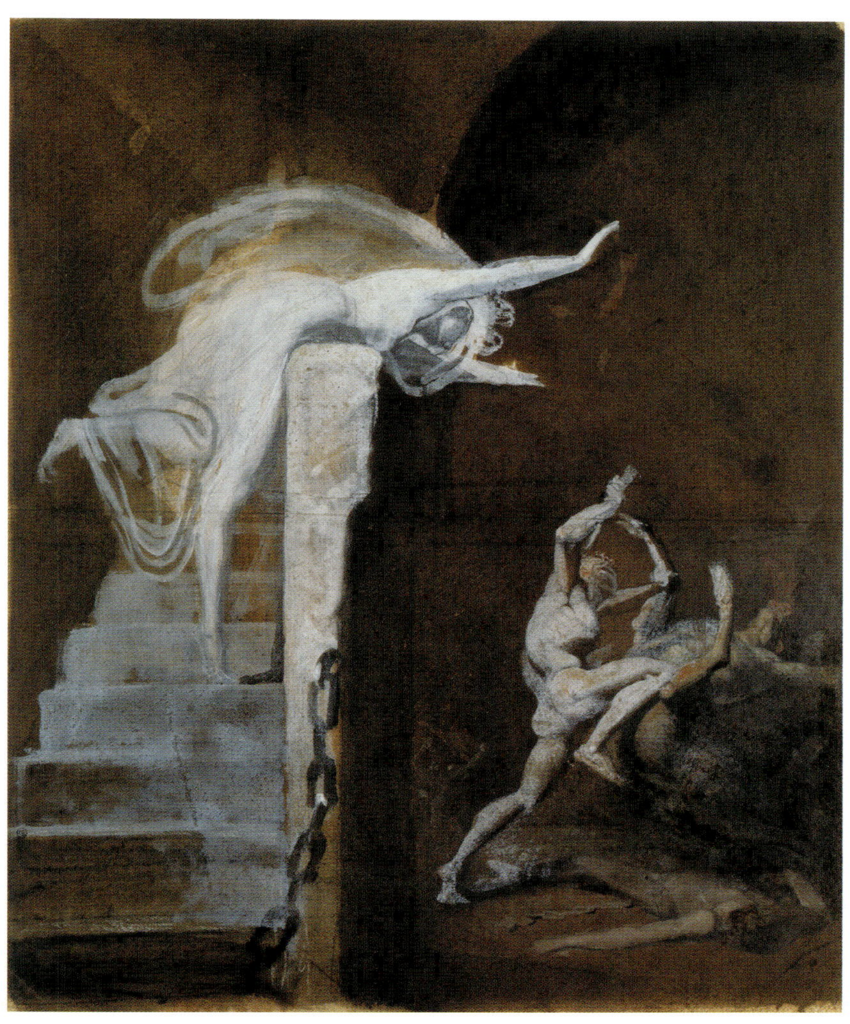

227

226. **John Henry Fuseli**
Zurich, 1741 - Putney Hill, near London, 1825
Solitude at Dawn (after Lycidas by John Milton), 1794-96
Oil on canvas, 95 x 102 cm
Kunsthaus, Zurich

This slumbering figure had originated as the central figure in a drawing of 1785 entitled *The Shepherd's Dream* (Albertina, Vienna), which Fuseli used subsequently as the basis for a large painting of the same title (Tate, London) for display at his Milton Gallery; a project which engrossed the artist's attention throughout the 1790s. Between May 1794 and August 1796 Fuseli adapted the sleeping figure as an illustration to lines from Milton's poem *Lycidas*, which also formed part of the Milton Gallery. In all, he produced three separate versions, of which the present one, it has been suggested, is the earliest, since it corresponds most closely to the figure in *The Shepherd's Dream*. Fuseli's Milton Gallery, which opened at James Christie's auction rooms in Pall Mall in 1799, comprised forty paintings. And although it proved to be a commercial disaster, the venture succeeded in forging a vital link between the nation's literary and visual traditions, encompassing epic poetry and high art. (MP)

227. **John Henry Fuseli**
Zurich, 1741 - Putney Hill, near London, 1825
Ariadne Watching the Struggle of Theseus with the Minotaur, c. 1815-20
Brown wash, oil, white bodycolor, with touches of white chalk and some gum over pencil on paper, 61.8 x 50.2 cm
Yale Center for British Art, Paul Mellon Collection, New Haven

This oil sketch was made towards the end of Fuseli's career, probably between 1815 and 1820, in preparation for the finished painting (Private Collection, Basel) exhibited at the Royal Academy in 1820. Fuseli had contemplated the subject as early as 1794, when he wrote to his patron, William Roscoe, about a possible painting of 'Ariadne Looking from a higher part of the Labyrinth on Theseus whilst he is combating the Minotaur below' (Weinglass 1982, p. 122). The picture was intended to be the pendant to his painting *Theseus Receiving the Thread from Ariadne*, which he had exhibited at the Royal Academy in 1788 (Kunsthaus Zürich). Fuseli's inspiration for the present work derived from the story of Theseus and the Minotaur, as recounted by Virgil and Ovid. Ariadne's voyeuristic presence at the sight of the struggle is, however, Fuseli's own invention, designed to add a hint of sexual frisson. (MP)

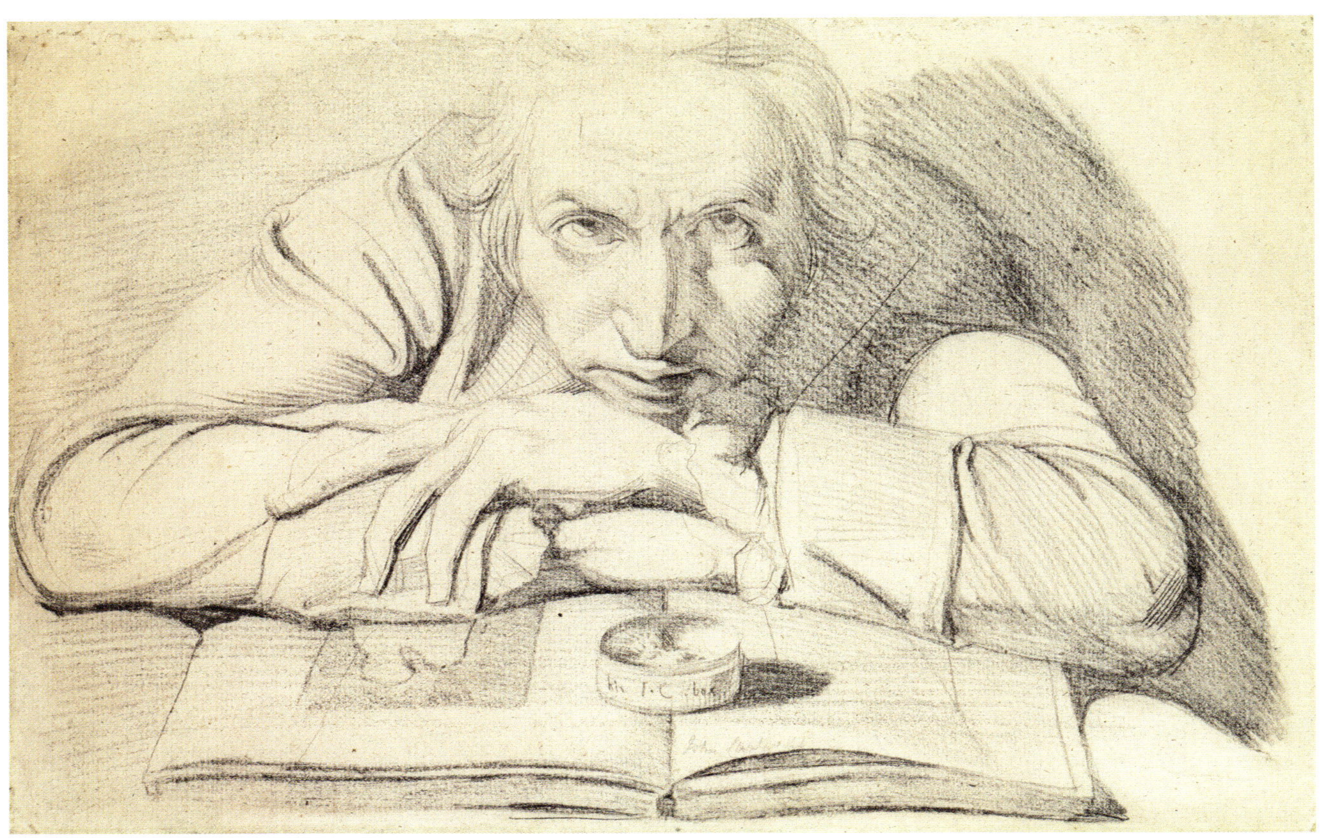

228

228. **John Henry Fuseli**
Zurich, 1741 - Putney Hill, near London, 1825
Probably John Cartwright, c. 1779
Black chalk on paper, 32.4 x 50.2 cm
Bottom centre on the book: John Cartwright
National Portrait Gallery, London

This study of artistic intensity was for long supposed to be a self-portrait by Henry Fuseli, whose features are, indeed, similar to those of the present subject. However, the inscription on the snuff box, 'IC his box', suggests that the sitter was in fact Fuseli's friend, the artist John Cartwright. A somewhat shadowy figure, Cartwright was a founder member of the Free Society of Artists in the early 1760s, before travelling to Italy in 1770 under the patronage of the 3rd Duke of Dorset, who commissioned him to paint several landscapes. According to one contemporary, Cartwright was 'very slow & shewed more inclination than genius' (Ingamells 1997, p. 188). It was in Rome, however, that Fuseli met Cartwright, appearing to have acted in the capacity of mentor, correcting his drawings and even appropriating one of his sketchbooks. On his return from Italy in 1779, Fuseli lodged for a number of years with Cartwright in St Martin's Lane, London, an indication of the closeness of their friendship, which is borne out by the intimacy of the present drawing. (MP)

229. **James Barry**
Cork, 1741 - London, 1806
Self Portrait, c. 1802
Reed pen and brown ink on paper, 29.3 x 24.2 cm
Royal Society of Arts, London

An Irish Catholic from Cork, Barry became a protégé of Edmund Burke. (A fascinating early self-portrait shows him together with Burke as Ulysses, fleeing a 'Polyphemus' usually interpreted as the British Government; both men opposed British policy in the American War.) Barry's lifelong sympathies were with the radical left, from Joseph Priestley to Godwin and Mary Wollstonecraft. Returning from Rome in 1771, he soon became an Academician, and from 1777 to 1783 worked on a vast mural cycle, *The Progress of Human Culture* (see p. 18, fig. 1), which can still be viewed at the Society of Arts. It left him broken in health, though he continued to produce history paintings on a heroic scale, such as the twelve-foot *Lear and Cordelia* (Tate, London). His polemical writings made enemies: in 1799 he was expelled from the Royal Academy. Already reclusive, he disappeared into his dilapidated, filthy house. Barry became a legend for the generation of Blake, and this late self-portrait shows him in the character of 'Melancholy Genius': 'weary, pensive and disillusioned' (Pressly 1983, p. 153). (TH)

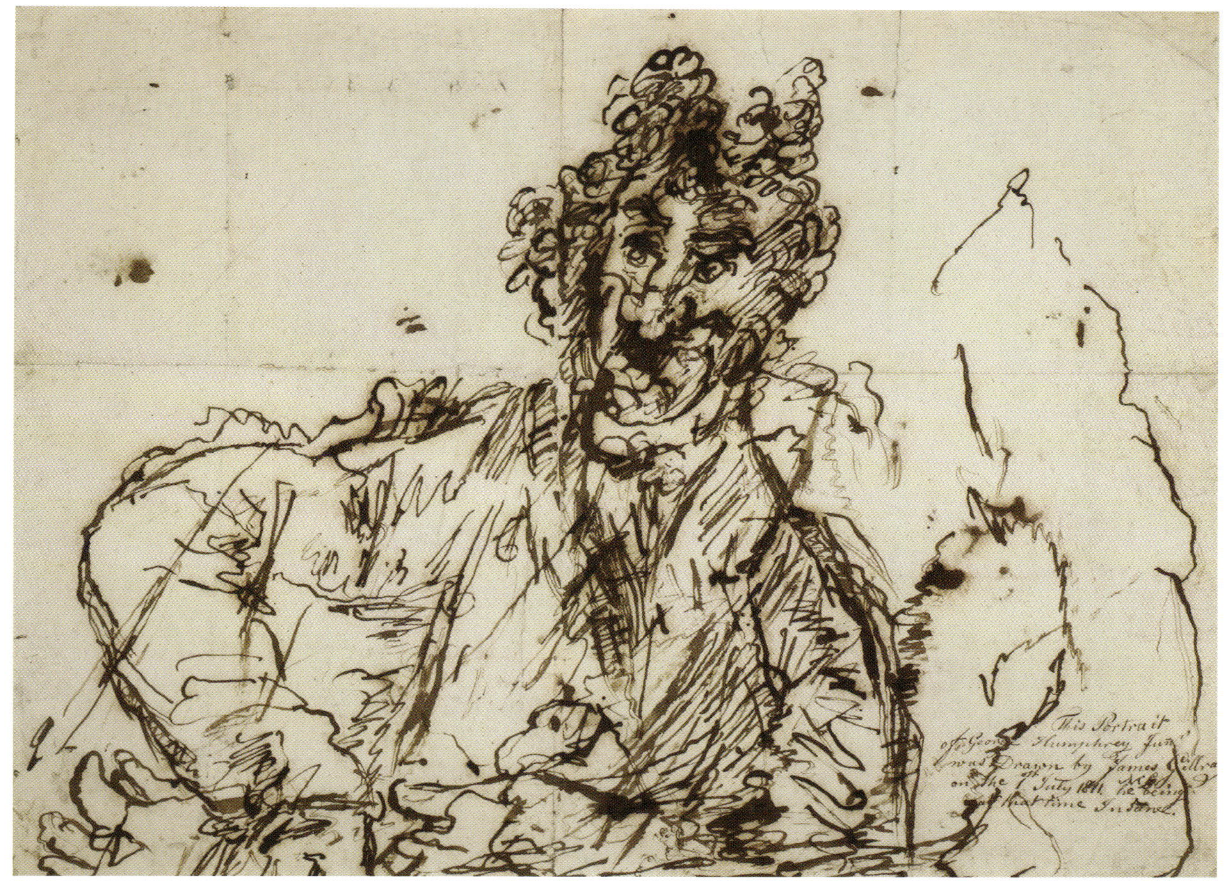

230

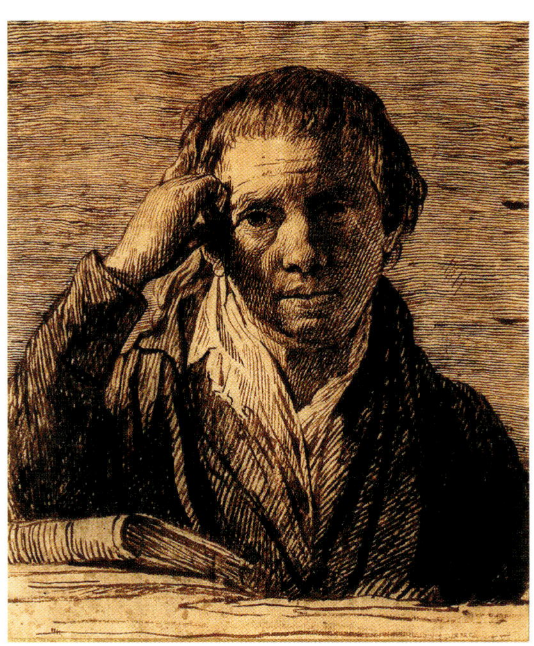

229

230. **James Gillray**

London, 1756 - London, 1815

George Humphrey II, 1811

Pen and and brown ink on grey paper, 37.2 x 49.2 cm

Bottom right: This Portrait / of George Humphrey Junr /

was Drawn by James Gillray / on the 1st July 1811.

he being / at that time Insane. [by George Humphrey II}

British Museum, London

One of the artist's largest, and certainly his wildest drawing, this extraordinary image was 'rediscovered' in the late twentieth century, to become widely exhibited and reproduced. Drawings by the insane (notably those of Antonin Artaud while confined at Rodez) have come to command a new recognition; Gillray's sense of the person sitting opposite him may now appear more psychologically 'true' than any Neo-Classical convention. The puckered dark orifice of the mouth is especially powerful and suggestive. (This drawing is also discussed on p. 102.) (TH)

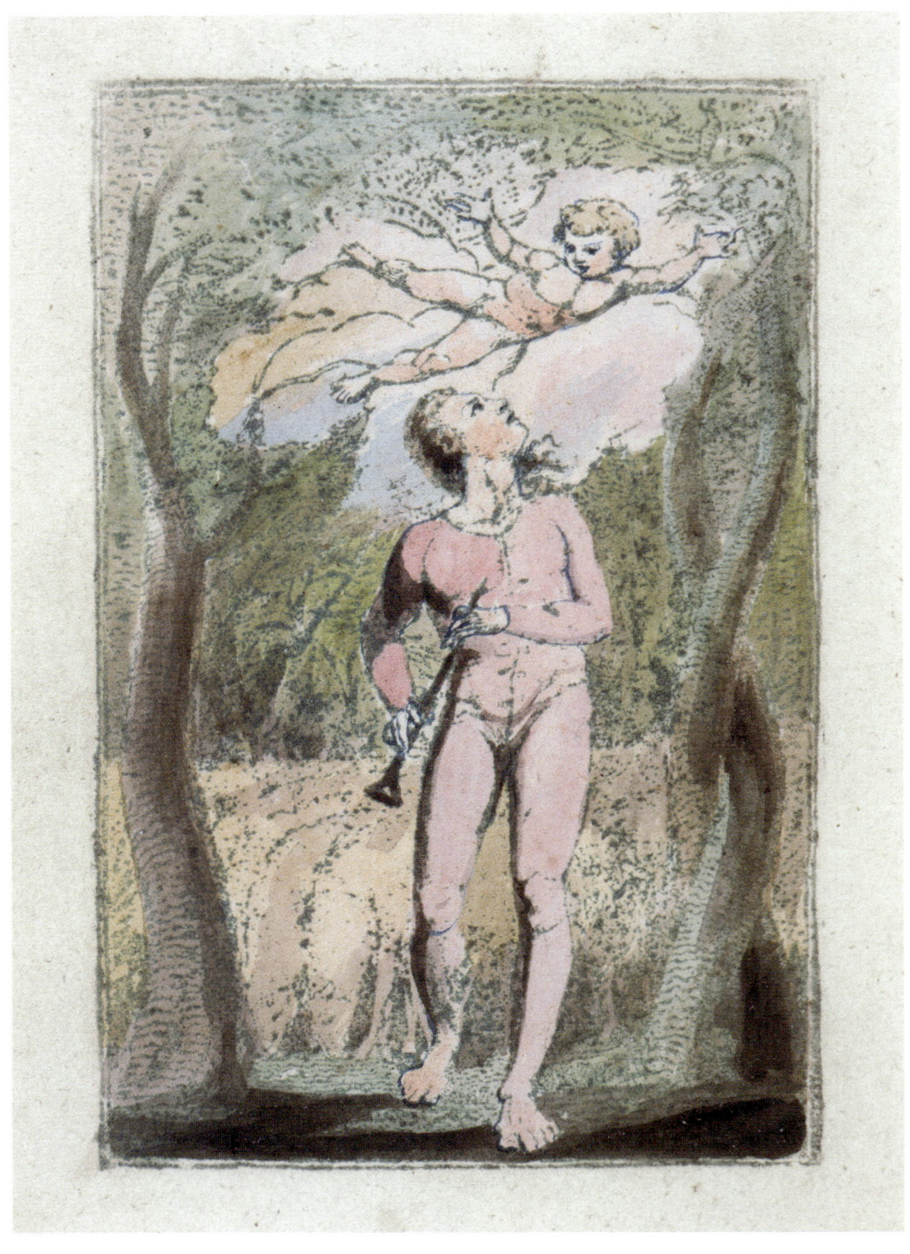

231

231. **William Blake**
London, 1757 – London, 1827
Songs of Innocence: Innocence (frontispiece, plate 1), 1789
Handcoloured relief etching with watercolour,
18,4 x 12,1 cm [paper size]
Yale Center for British Art, Paul Mellon Collection, New Haven

The frontispiece to *Songs of Innocence* sets a pastoral and sunny note to the series of poems. It illustrates the Introduction, which describes the poet, 'Piping down the valleys wild / Piping songs of pleasant glee', when he encounters a child in a cloud, who urges him to 'sit thee down and write / In a book that all may read.' The piper is thus the poet describing his inspiration for the poems that follow. It needs also to be seen against its counterpart in the frontispiece to *Songs of Experience*, first published five years later, in 1794. Though the scene is still pastoral, the shepherd poet no longer plays his rural pipe but carries, as if in distress, the winged child on his head; the idyll is over. (DB)

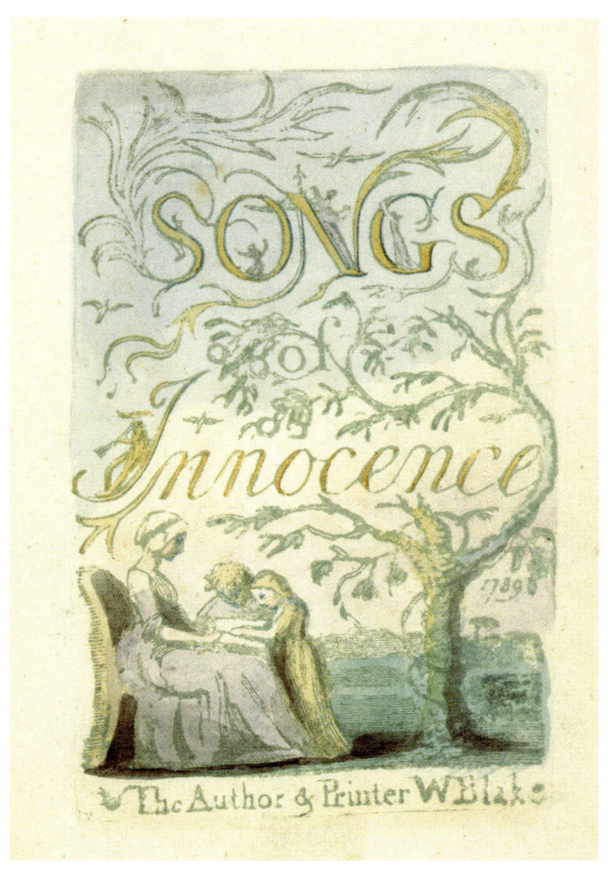

232

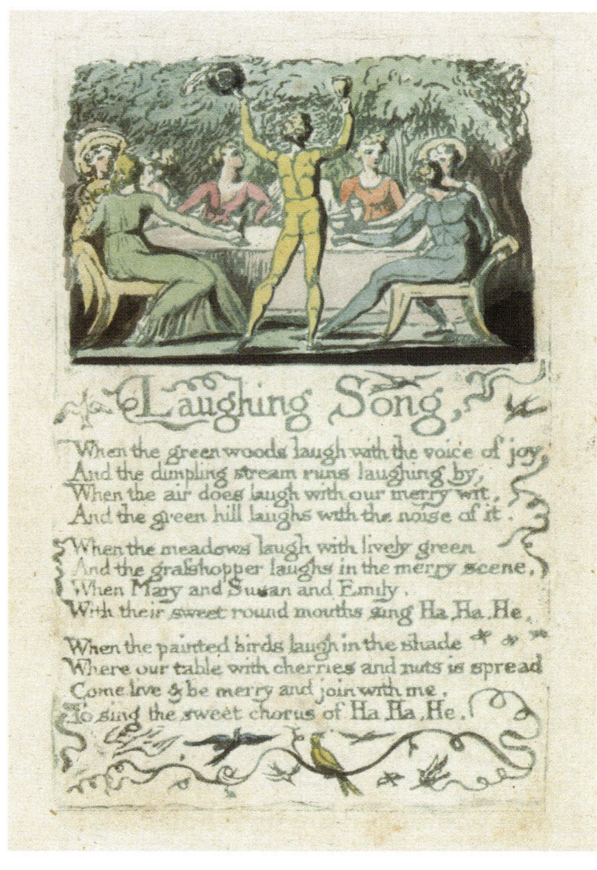

233

232. **William Blake**
London, 1757 - London, 1827
Songs of Innocence: Innocence (title page, plate 2), 1789
Handcoloured relief etching with watercolour,
18.4 x 12.1 cm [paper size]
Yale Center for British Art, Paul Mellon Collection, New Haven

The title-page image shows the *Songs of Innocence* as they might be experienced, read by a nurse to small children who are able to see the images at the same time. The joyful note is carried through the sheltering tree, where the words of the title are integrated with its branches and nature spirits clamber joyfully among the letters. Again the image needs to be set against the title page to *Songs of Experience*, where presumably the same children, now adolescent, mourn over the corpses of their parents in a strongly rectilinear and oppressive setting.

The image is one of the first in which Blake has exploited the full possibilities of his recently invented relief etching method, which enabled him to integrate text and design on the copper plate. The letters in the tree register clearly as letters yet are fully pictorial, an effect virtually unknown since the invention of letterpress printing in the fifteenth century. (DB)

233. **William Blake**
London, 1757 - London, 1827
Songs of Innocence: Laughing Song (recto, plate 13), 1789
Handcoloured relief etching with watercolour,
18.4 x 12.1 cm [paper size]
Yale Center for British Art, Paul Mellon Collection, New Haven

A poem and a scene of rustic innocence and delight, where nature and man are in perfect joyful harmony as in the Garden of Eden. The joyful note is emphasized by the decorative elements in the text area, the birds and the flourishes made possible by Blake's new relief etching method. Yet there is a slight dissociation between the childish note of the poem and the more grown-up adolescents drinking wine in the illustration. (DB)

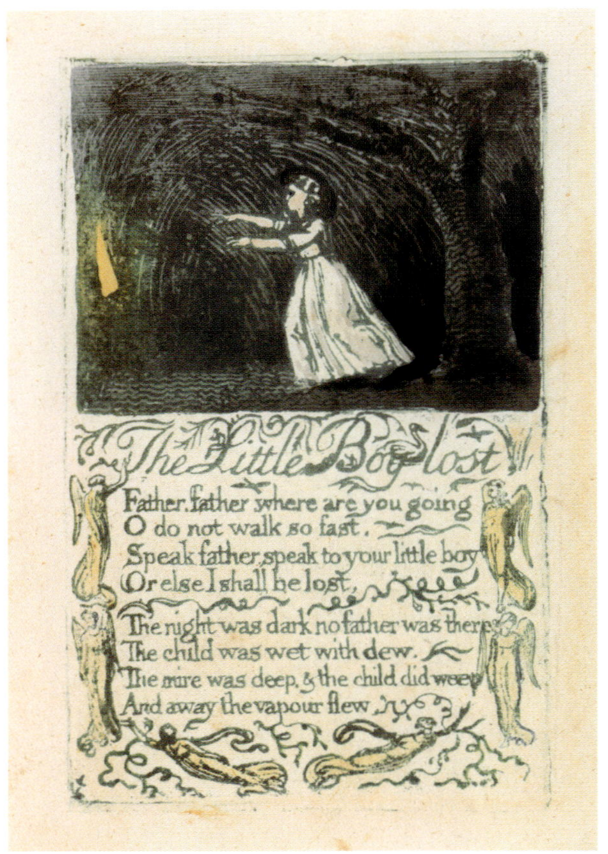

234

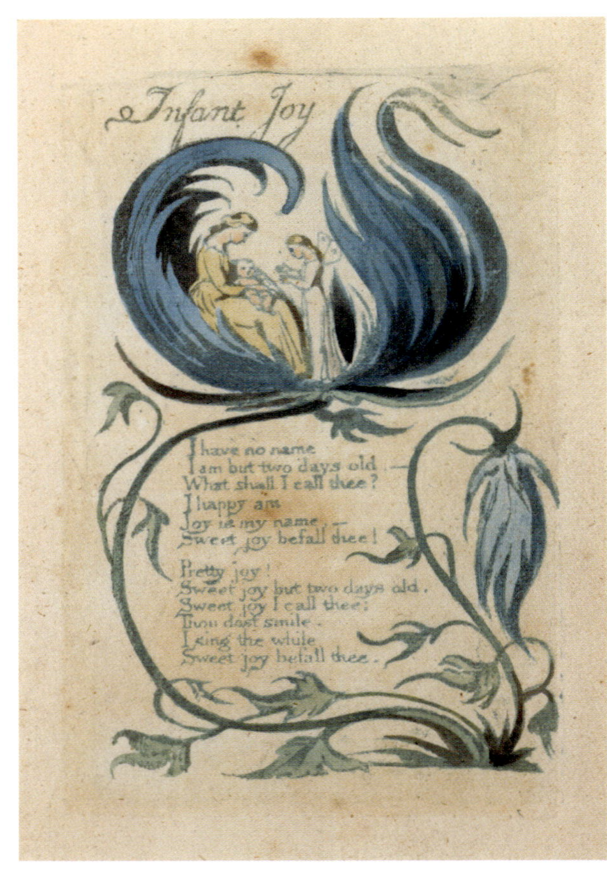

235

234. **William Blake**
London, 1757 - London, 1827
Songs of Innocence: The Little Boy Lost (recto, plate 15), 1789
Handcoloured relief etching with watercolour,
18.4 x 12.1 cm [paper size]
Yale Center for British Art, Paul Mellon Collection, New Haven

This poem brings a darker and more mysterious note to the *Songs of Innocence*, though there are protective angels in the margins of the text, and all is put right in the following poem, 'The Little Boy Found', where he is found by 'God ever nigh [who] Appeared like his father in white'. The nature of the 'vapour' or the light that the boy follows in the design is not explained, nor whether the father is dead or not. (DB)

235. **William Blake**
London, 1757 - London, 1827
Songs of Innocence: Infant Joy (recto, plate 27), 1789
Handcoloured relief etching with watercolour,
18.4 x 12.1 cm [paper size]
Yale Center for British Art, Paul Mellon Collection, New Haven

An extraordinary image of a mother and child with a nature spirit within the petals of a flower: the joys of childhood are shown as enacted throughout all levels of nature, and there are obvious hints of a Madonna and Child with St John from early Italian painting. It needs also to be set against the drooping flower that comes from the same root and its counterpart in *Experience:* 'Infant Sorrow'. Here birth is seen as a disturbing entry into the real world:

> My mother groand! My father wept,
> Into the dangerous world I leapt:
> Helpless, naked, piping loud:
> Like a fiend hid in a cloud. (DB)

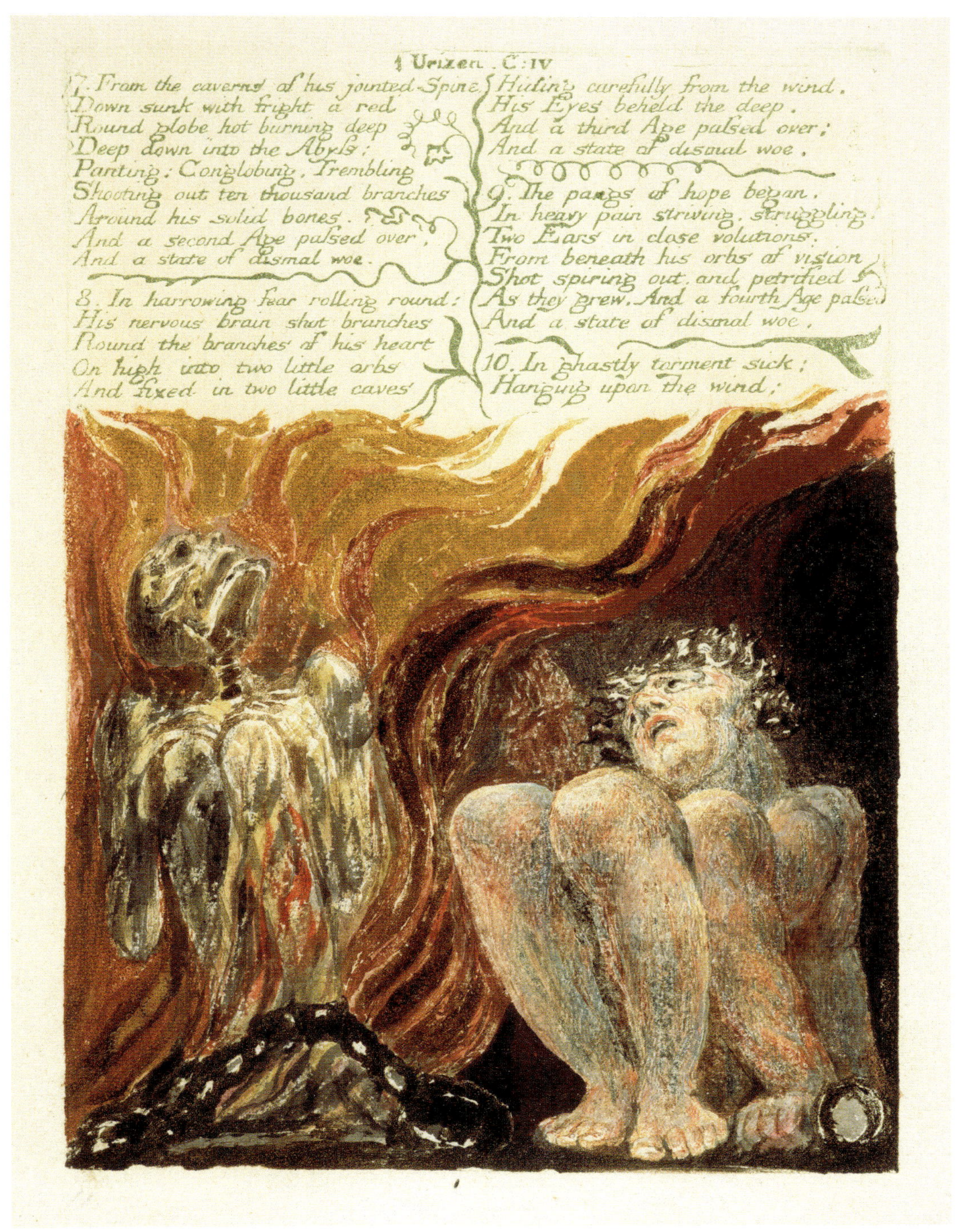

236

236. **William Blake**
London, 1757 – London, 1827
The First Book of Urizen: From the caverns of his jointed Spine … (plate 10), 1794
Colour-printed relief etching with watercolour,
30.2 x 24.4 cm [paper size]
Yale Center for British Art, Paul Mellon Collection, New Haven

The First Book of Urizen represents the myth of origins in Blake's revolutionary spiritual history of the world devised in the 1790s. It tells of the formation of the world out of chaos and of the image of the powers of the world. Los as the eternal poet has the task of giving form to the creator of the material world, whom Blake calls Urizen. Blake depicts him as a bearded old man, like the Jehovah of Raphael and Michelangelo, but he is in no way benign. Los is shown here in the process of forming Urizen's body, seen as a skeleton being forged into a still incomplete living being, held down by manacles. The use of colour printing here and in the other plates has the effect of suggesting the primeval world before the creation of man. (DB)

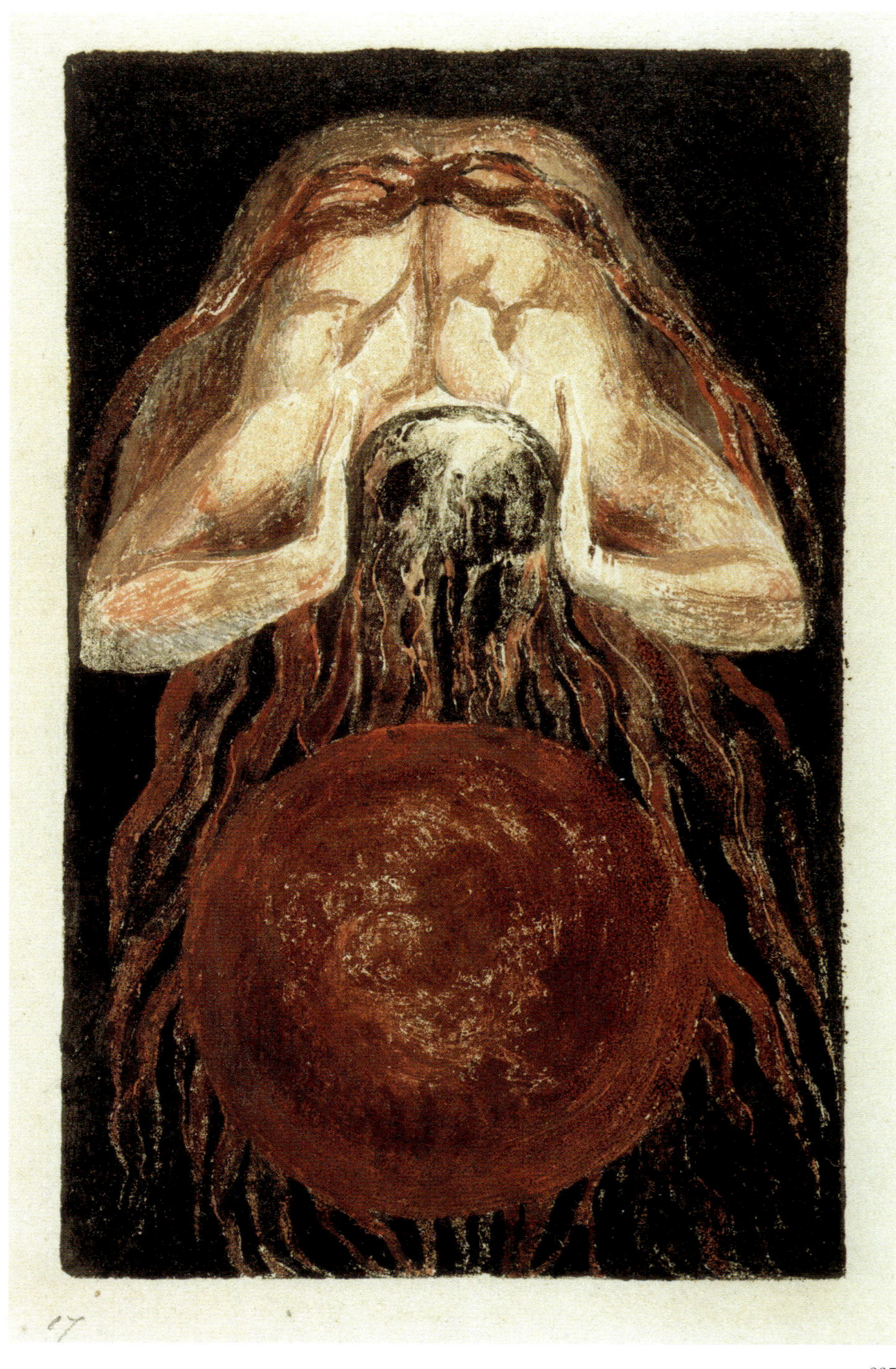

237

237. **William Blake**
London, 1757 - London, 1827
The First Book of Urizen (plate 16), 1794
Colour-printed relief etching with watercolour,
30.2 x 24.4 cm [paper size]
Yale Center for British Art, Paul Mellon Collection, New Haven

One of Blake's most mysterious and suggestive images, it belongs to an account of the formation of matter out of eternal chaos. It clearly shows 'the globe of life blood trembling' mentioned in the previous plate, which appears to represent the birth of 'the first female now separate'. It may also represent the formation of the world out of the head of Los, whose mythological role is to create form from the inchoate, though the figure has often been seen as female. (DB)

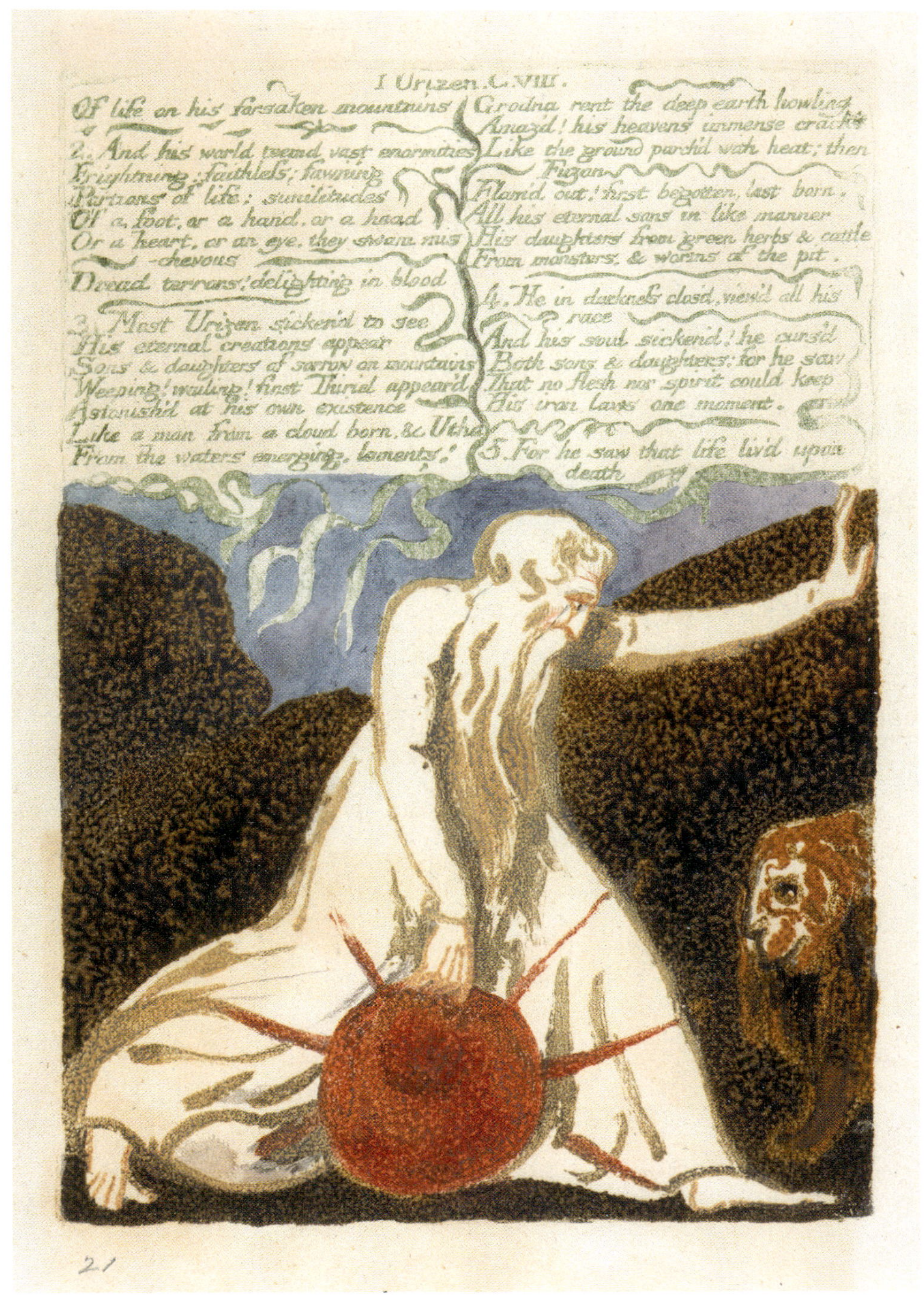

238

238. **William Blake**
London, 1757 – London, 1827
The First Book of Urizen: Of life on his forsaken mountains … (plate 20), 1794
Colour-printed relief etching with watercolour,
30.2 x 24.4 cm [paper size]
Yale Center for British Art, Paul Mellon Collection, New Haven

This shows the now completed Urizen looking about the created world, according to Chapter VIII of *The First Book of Urizen*:

Urizen explor'd his dens
Mountain, moor, & wilderness,
With a globe of fire lighting his journey
A fearful journey, annoy'd
By cruel enormities …

It is a horrifying vision that confronts him, of fragmentation, terror, sorrow and agony. It is a dystopian world based on 'The Net of Religion' that he has created, and it is also the world of the present day, which he still dominates despite the challenge of revolution. (DB)

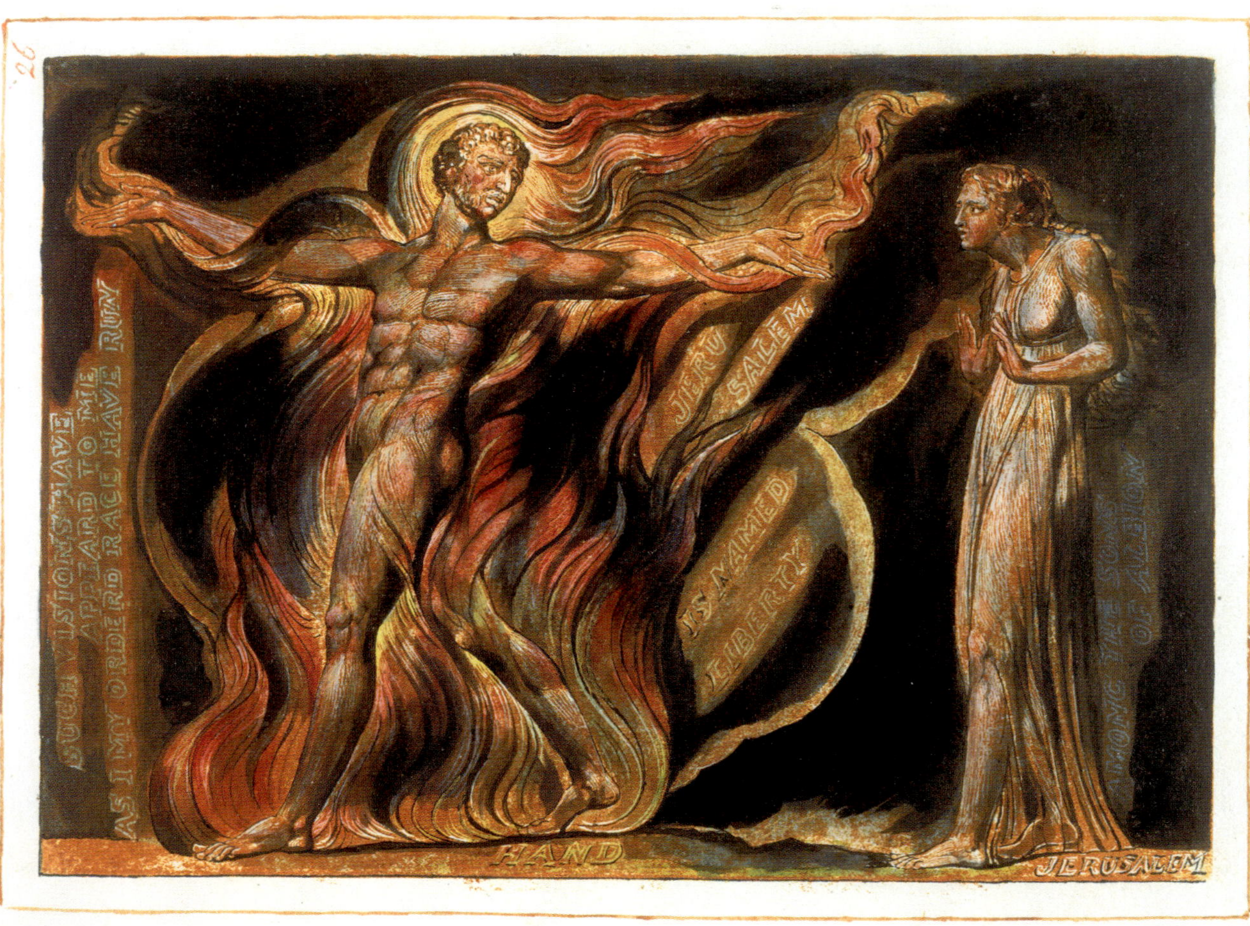

239

239. **William Blake**
London, 1757 - London, 1827
Jerusalem, the Emanation of the Great Albion (plate 26), c. 1804-20
Relief etching, printed in orange, with pen and ink and watercolour, 34.3 x 26.4 cm [paper size]
Yale Center for British Art, Paul Mellon Collection, New Haven

Blake's last prophetic book, *Jerusalem*, is concerned with national as well as personal redemption, embodied in the figure of Albion, who is both a universal man and Britain. It tells in a complex way the story of Albion in his divisions, and his longed-for redemption in the book's final vision. Albion's division embodies a conflict of his own faculties, his separation from and quest for his emanation, Jerusalem, and the alienation of his children, the people of Britain. He appears as an agonized figure, at war with himself and others. The particular copy of *Jerusalem* from which this and the following plates are extracted is a unique complete coloured copy, made in Blake's last years.

In this plate Jerusalem is confronted by the figure of Hand (possibly a reference to Robert Hunt, who wrote a scathing review of Blake's art), who appears as a false Christ, mimicking the form of Christ on the Cross surrounded by flames, but the serpent around his arm reveals him to be Satanic. Such false prophets flourish in Albion's divided state, threatening to lead astray Jerusalem, who is identified here as liberty. (DB)

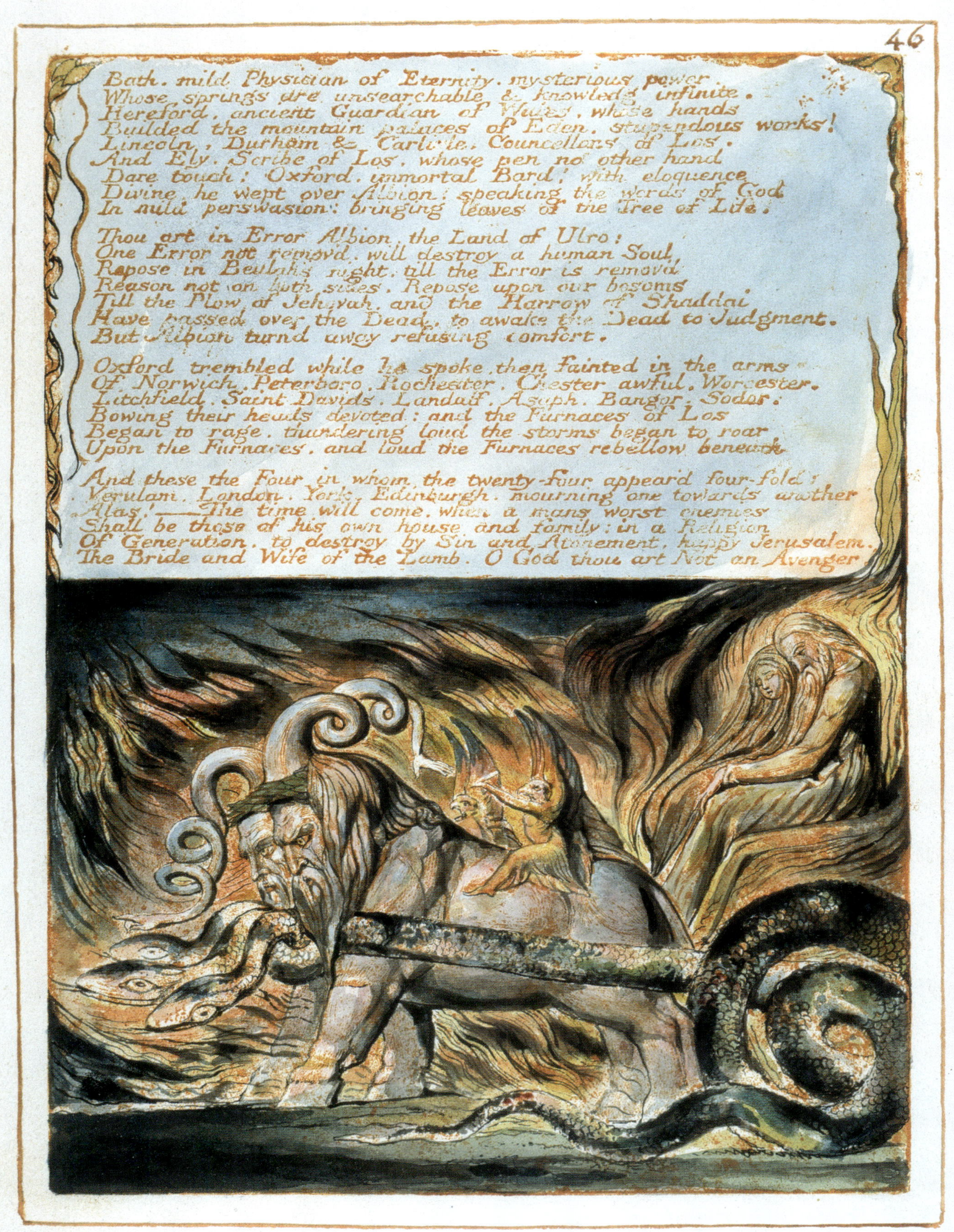

46

Bath. mild Physician of Eternity. mysterious power
Whose springs are unsearchable & knowledg infinite.
Hereford. ancient Guardian of Wales. whose hands
Builded the mountain palaces of Eden. stupendous works!
Lincoln, Durham & Carlisle. Councellors of Los.
And Ely. Scribe of Los. whose pen no other hand
Dare touch: Oxford. immortal Bard! with eloquence
Divine. he wept over Albion: speaking the words of God
In mild perswasion: bringing leaves of the Tree of Life.

Thou art in Error Albion. the Land of Ulro:
One Error not removd. will destroy a human Soul
Repose in Beulahs night. till the Error is removd
Reason not on both sides. Repose upon our bosoms
Till the Plow of Jehovah. and the Harrow of Shaddai
Have passed over the Dead. to awake the Dead to Judgment.
But Albion turnd away refusing comfort.

Oxford trembled while he spoke. then fainted in the arms
Of Norwich. Peterboro. Rochester. Chester awful. Worcester.
Litchfield. Saint Davids. Landaff. Asaph. Bangor. Sodor.
Bowing their heads devoted: and the Furnaces of Los
Began to rage. thundering loud the storms began to roar
Upon the Furnaces. and loud the Furnaces rebellow beneath

And these the Four in whom the twenty-four appeard four-fold:
Verulam. London. York. Edinburgh. mourning one towards another
Alas!—The time will come. when a mans worst enemies
Shall be those of his own house and family: in a Religion
Of Generation. to destroy by Sin and Atonement. happy Jerusalem.
The Bride and Wife of the Lamb. O God thou art Not an Avenger

240

241

240. **William Blake**
London, 1757 - London, 1827
Jerusalem, the Emanation of the Great Albion (plate 46), c. 1804-20
Relief etching, printed in orange, with pen and ink and watercolour, 34.3 x 26.4 cm [paper size]
Yale Center for British Art, Paul Mellon Collection, New Haven

One of the most mysterious, compelling and inexplicable images in *Jerusalem*, indeed in the whole of Blake. There is no consensus at all as to who the seated figures might be, nor what the extraordinary serpent wheels might signify. What is clear, however, is the variety of pictorial sources, from Assyrian reliefs, which lie behind the bizarrely horned creatures pulling the chariot, to the Bosch-like creatures on their backs. (DB)

241. **William Blake**
London, 1757 - London, 1827
Jerusalem, the Emanation of the Great Albion (plate 51), c. 1804-20
Relief etching, printed in black, with pen and ink and watercolour, 26.4 x 34.3 cm [paper size]
Yale Center for British Art, Paul Mellon Collection, New Haven

Thanks to a proof of this design (Fitzwilliam Museum, Cambridge), we know that those represented are identified by Blake as Vala, Hyle and Skofeld, all malign powers governing the Britain of Blake's own time. Vala is Blake's goddess of nature; Hyle, based on the poet whom Blake despised, William Hayley, stands here for abject despair; and Skofeld is based on the ignorant soldier Scofield, who caused Blake to be arrested as a spy. He stands for war and those who live in mental chains, what Blake called in the poem 'London' in *Songs of Experience* 'Mind-forg'd Manacles'. The image acts as a frontispiece to the section dedicated 'To the Deists' or

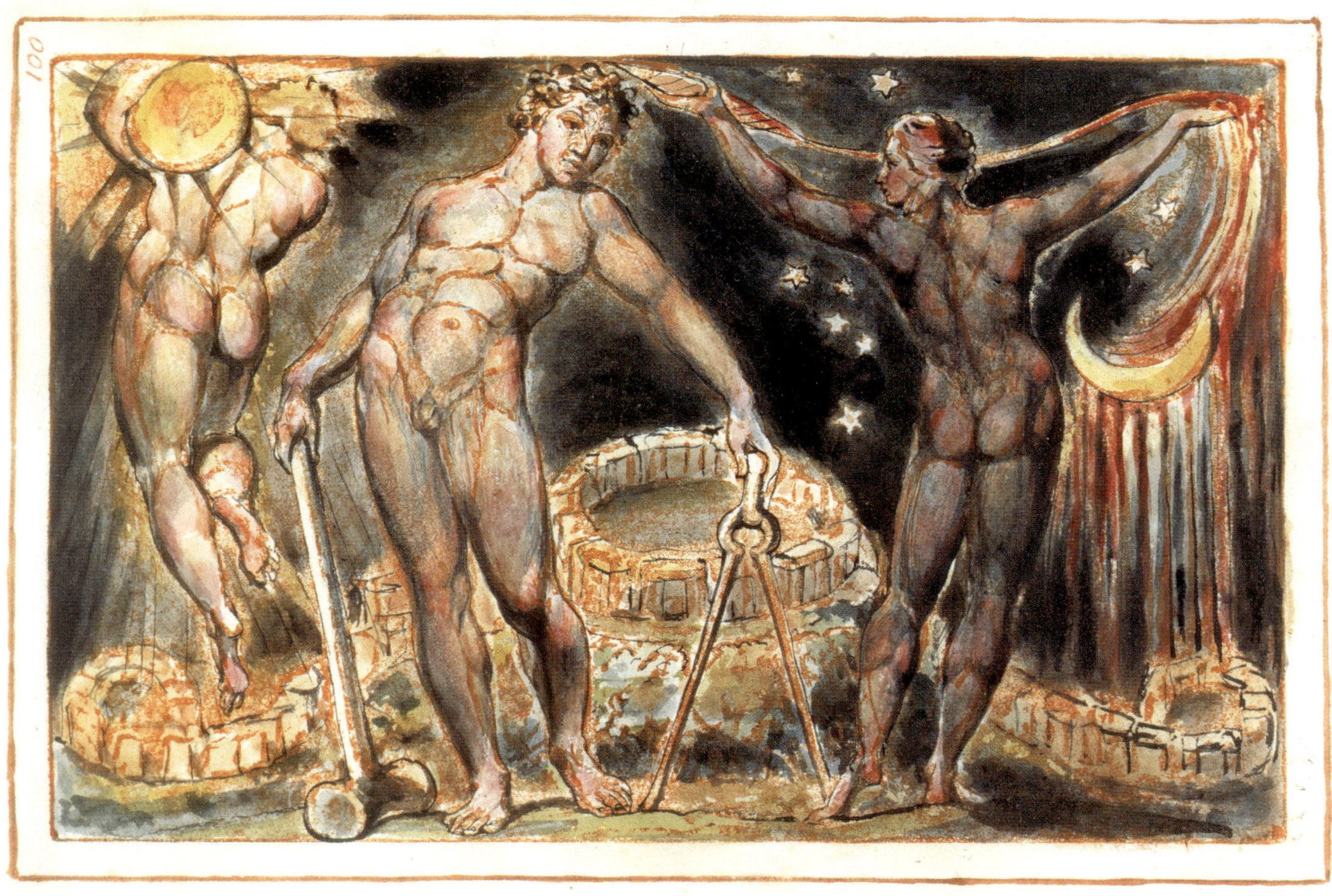

242

practitioners of the dominant 'Natural Religion' of the Church of England. The plate then perhaps acts as a critique of the consequences of such a belief on a Britain involved in the Napoleonic wars and governed by the 'Fiends of Commerce'. (DB)

242. **William Blake**
London, 1757 - London, 1827
Jerusalem, the Emanation of the Great Albion (plate 100), c. 1804-20
Relief etching, printed in orange, with pen, ink, watercolour and gold, 26.4 x 34.3 cm [paper size]
Yale Center for British Art, Paul Mellon Collection, New Haven

A positive counterpart to plate 51 (cat. 241), this is the final plate of *Jerusalem*, following the prophetic vision of Albion's awakening and the unification of all things. It brings the vision from apocalyptic time literally back to earth, showing Los, the eternal poet, continuing his daily work of building Jerusalem, while the figure on the left carries the sun on its diurnal round, and Enitharmon weaves the fabric of the world. Behind them is the serpent-temple that covers the island of Britain, making a connection between the country's ancient history as the site of the events of the Bible and the present daily task of making a Christian Britain. (DB)

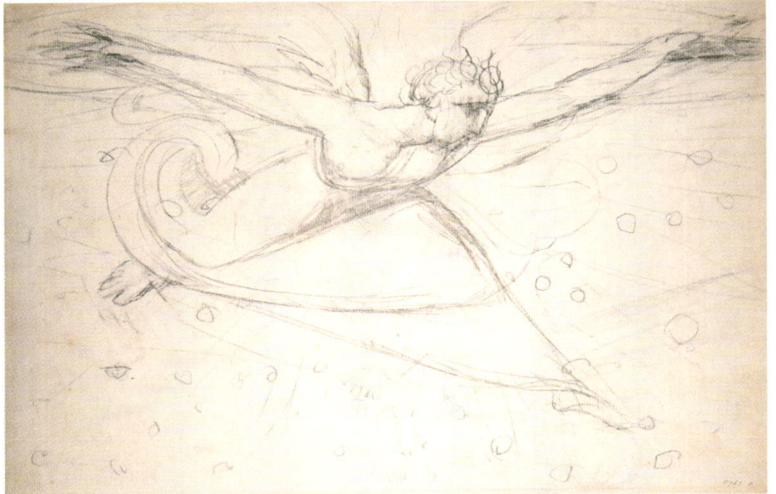

243

243. **William Blake**
London, 1757 – London, 1827
An Angel Striding Among the Stars, c. 1824-27
Pencil on paper, 27.5 x 40.4 cm
Victoria and Albert Museum, London

This extraordinarily expressive and economical drawing almost certainly belongs to the watercolour series for Dante's Divine Comedy, which dates from Blake's last years. It must be a study for the angel in the illustration to Purgatory canto XII (Butlin 1981, no. 812 82) descending at the close of the Circle of the Proud: 'Towards us came the beauteous creature, robed in white, and in his countenance he resembled a tremulous star at dawn. He opened his arms, then spread his wings, and said: "Come, nigh are the steps, and henceforth the way is easy."' (DB)

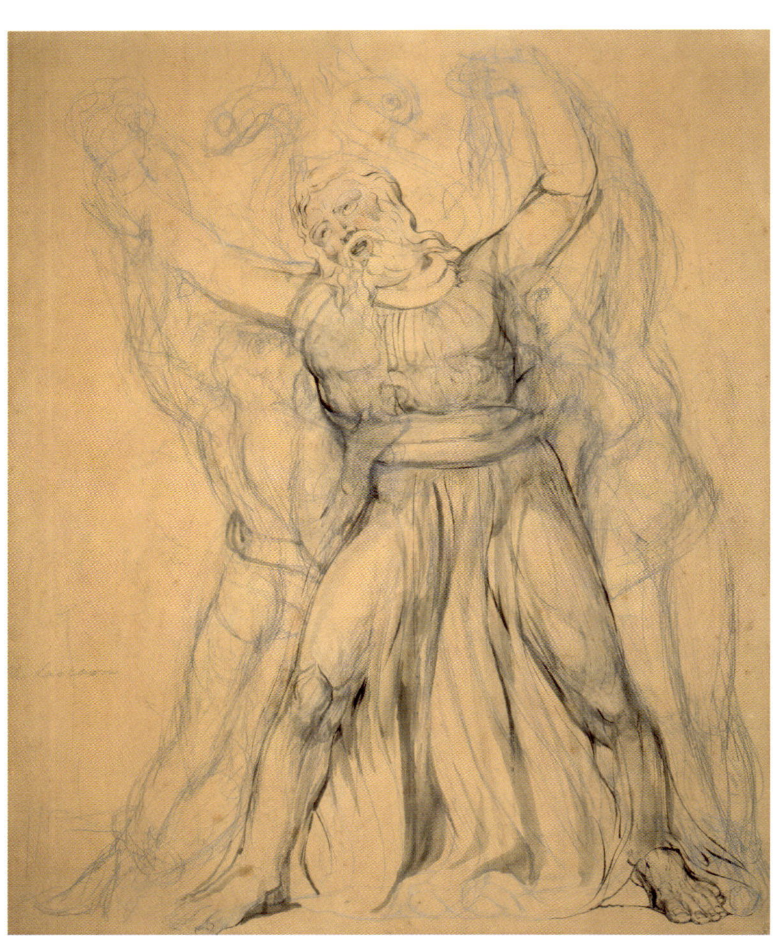

244

244. **William Blake**
London, 1757 – London, 1827
Free Version of the Laocoön, c. 1825
Pencil, pen and watercolour on paper, 54.7 x 44.7 cm
Left: The Laocoon
Verso: The Laocoon / Laocoonta petunt
Keynes Family Trust, on loan to the
Fitzwilliam Museum, Cambridge

This is related to two different treatments by Blake of the canonical Hellenistic sculpture *Laocoön*, then as now in the Cortile del Belvedere in the Vatican. The first was a commercial engraving for an encyclopaedia, published in 1820, the other is a very rare engraving of 1826-27, heavily annotated by Blake, in which he demonstrates his theory that the Greek antiquities were merely copies of the great Hebraic originals on the Temple of Solomon, claiming the *Laocoön* to be a memory of a lost original representing Jehovah with his two sons Satan and Adam. The present drawing is a more dramatic version of the sculpture, showing a more energetic response to the attack of the serpents than the restrained original. It is perhaps as an attempt to capture the vigour of the Hebraic original. Certainly it is an exceptionally powerful example of Blake's late style, where he employs much looser and more painterly handling than in his earlier work. (DB)

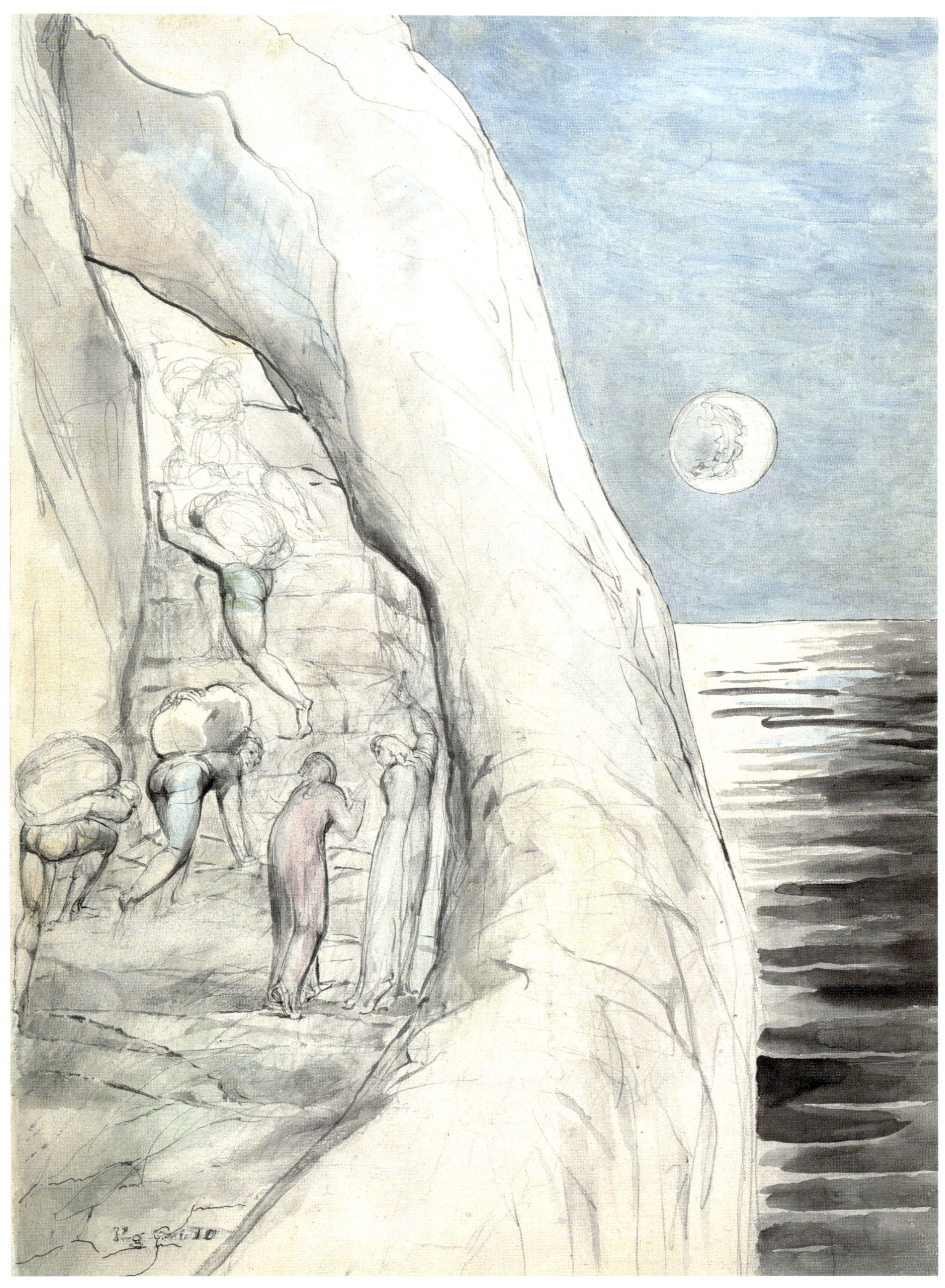

245

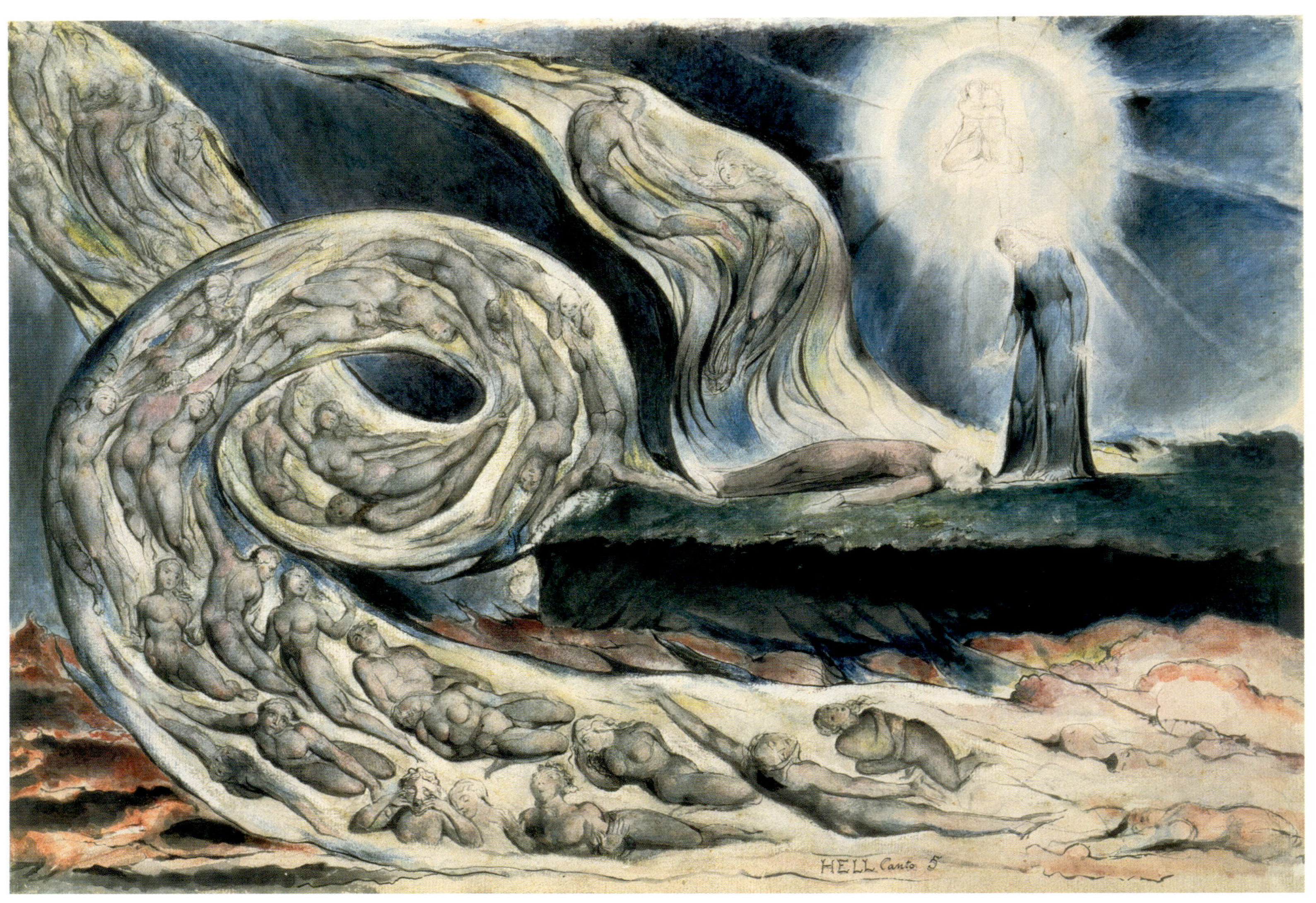

246

245. **William Blake**
London, 1757 - London, 1827
The Proud under their Enormous Loads, from Dante's ***Divine Comedy*** (Purgatory X and XI), 1824-27
Watercolour with pen and ink over pencil on paper, 51.7 x 36.5 cm
Bottom left: P–g Canto 10
Birmingham Museum & Art Gallery

A scene from *Purgatory*, when Dante and Virgil, near to the top of the mountain of Purgatory, meet a group of the Proud bearing enormous burdens. The figure who turns to Dante is probably Oderisi of Gubbio, a celebrated illuminator of manuscripts who, in a famous passage, tells Dante - as a warning to him - of the temporary nature of fame by noting how Giotto had surpassed Cimabue as the poet Guido Cavalcanti had surpassed Guido Guinicelli. Blake has carefully calibrated the view of the sea in each of the Purgatory images to suggest the passage through night and day and the emotional tenor of each scene. (DB)

246. **William Blake**
London, 1757 - London, 1827
The Circle of the Lustful:
Francesca da Rimini (The Whirlwind of Lovers),
from Dante's ***Divine Comedy*** (Inferno V), 1824-27
Pen and ink and watercolour over pencil on paper, 37.5 x 52 cm
Bottom centre to right: HELL Canto 5
Birmingham Museum & Art Gallery

Most artists who tackled the *Divine Comedy* chose to depict the story of Paolo and Francesca through the scene of their fatal transgression on earth, their interrupted kiss, but Blake characteristically depicts their dreadful punishment, to be caught up eternally in a whirlwind. The result is a design of consummate originality and imaginative power. Dante's collapse under the two figures of Paolo and Francesca is perhaps a recognition of his own lustful tendencies. (DB)

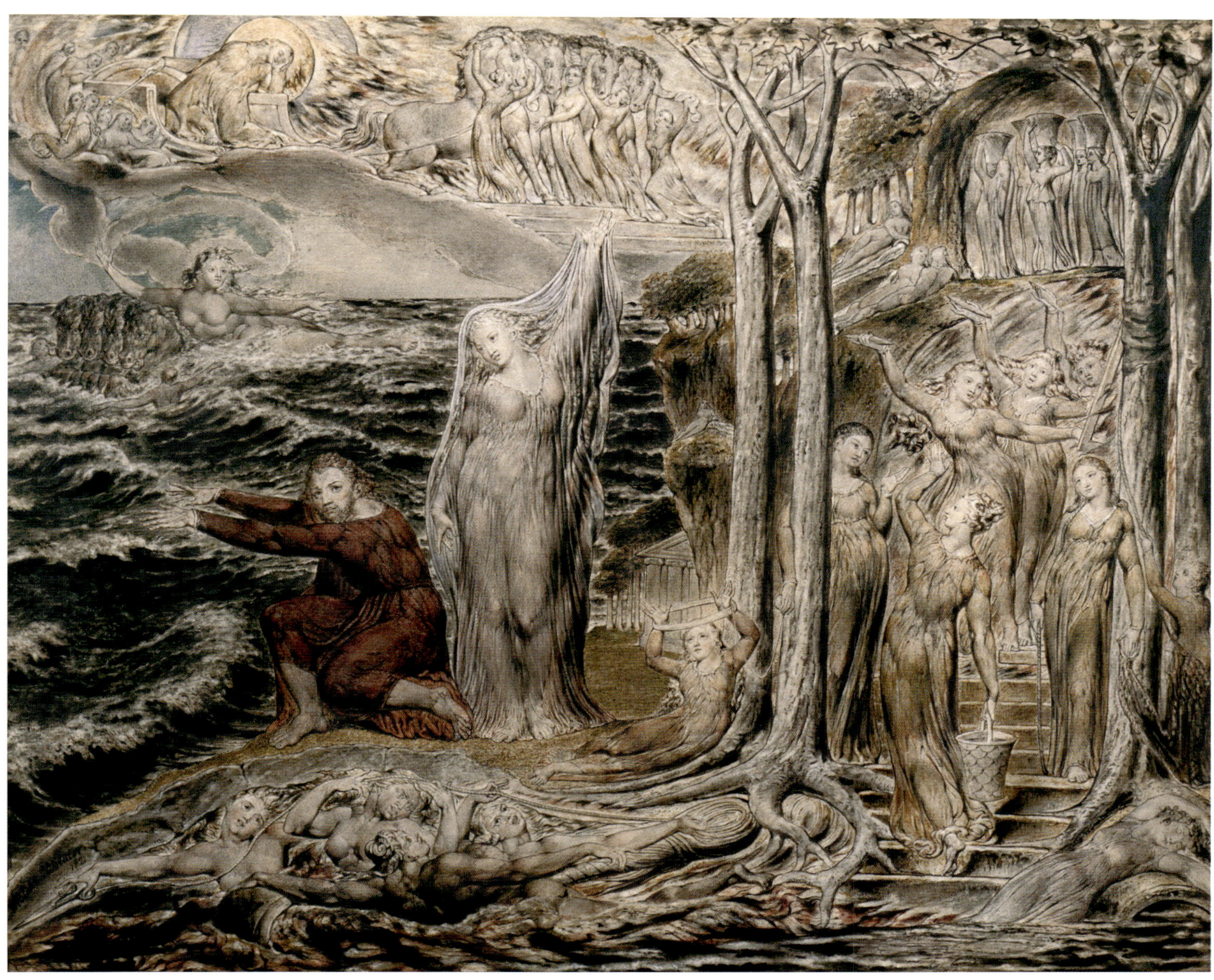

247

247. **William Blake**
London, 1757 - London, 1827
The Sea of Time and Space, 1821
Pen and ink, watercolour and gouache
on gesso ground on paper, 40 x 49.5 cm
Bottom left: W Blake inventor / 1821
Arlington Court, The Chichester Collection (The National Trust)

Since its discovery in 1947, *The Sea of Time and Space* has attracted much interest, although there has been no agreement on its subject or meaning. Blake's paintings generally have their origin in his own mythology, in the Bible or in literature, and the main figure has been variously identified as Christ, Blake himself, or Isaiah. However, the most convincing explanation of the iconography is that the picture shows a scene based on Homer, with Odysseus and Athena on the shore of the sea, which allows Blake to express his rejection of the nature-based religion of the classical world. (DB)

See essay pp. 315-17.

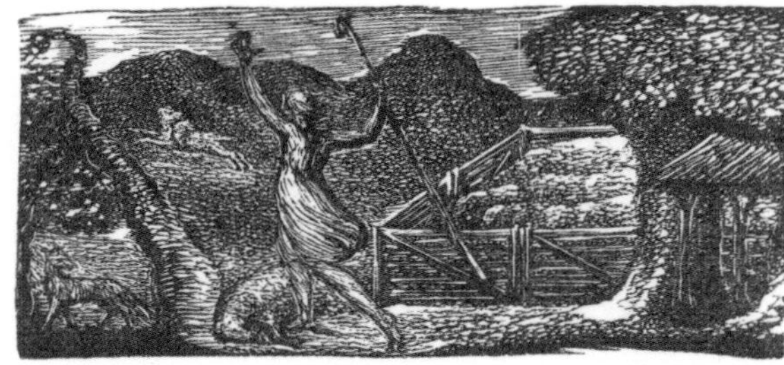

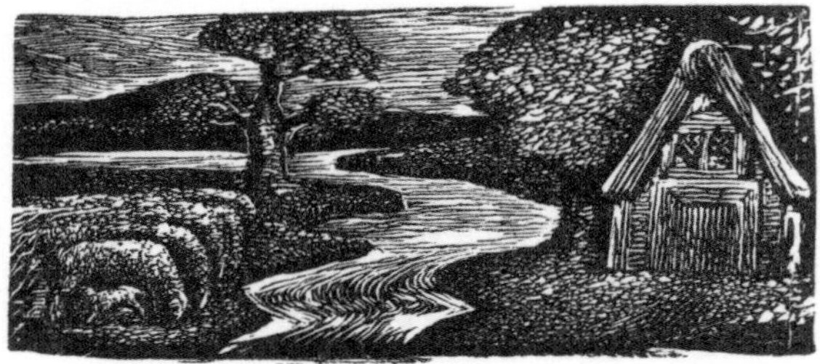

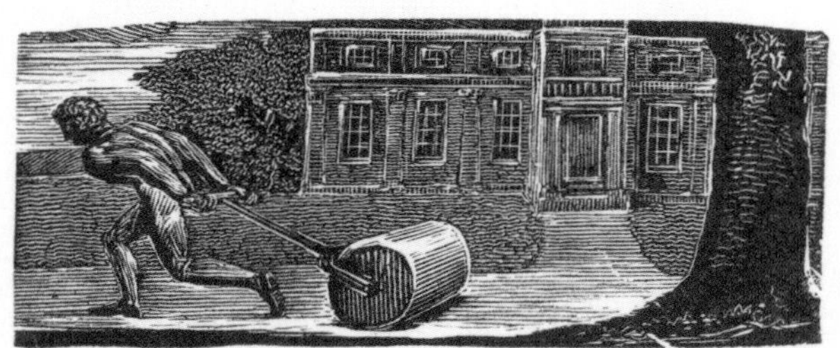

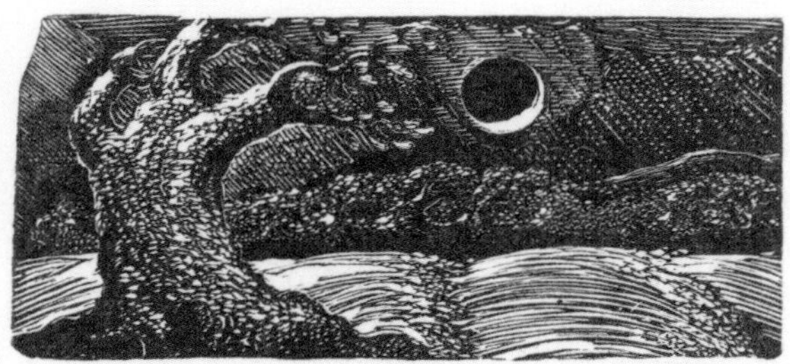

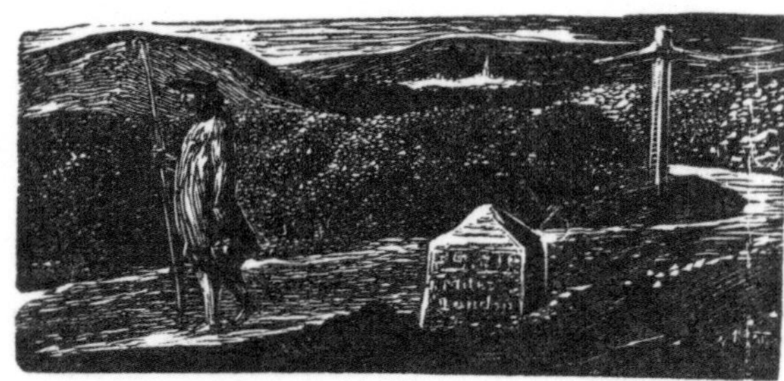

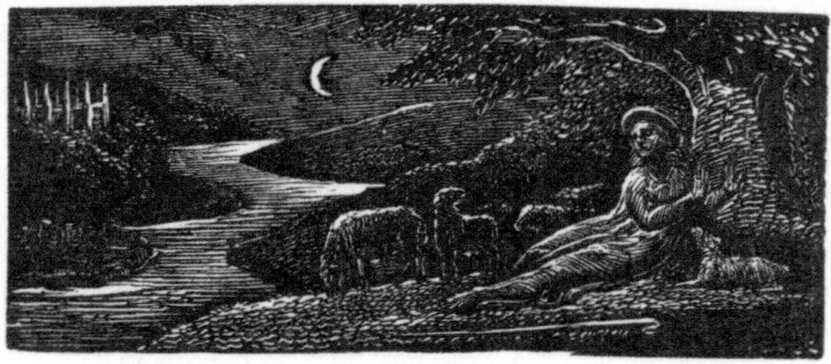

248

248. **William Blake**

London, 1757 - London, 1827
Illustrations for ***The Pastorals of Virgil,***
Edited by Dr. Robert J. Thornton, 1821

a. ***Shepherd Chases away Wolf***
b. ***Sabrina's Silvery Flood***
c. ***A Rolling Stone is ever Bare of Moss***
d. ***Blasted Tree and Flattened Crops***
e. ***Colinets' Journey***
f. ***Colinet Resting by Night***

Wood engravings from a series of seventeen
each approx. 3.2 x 7.5 cm
Reprinted in 1977 by Iain Bain and David Chambers from the original blocks in the British Museum
Private Collection

These wood engravings are from a series unique in Blake's work, in technique and in their intermediate position between his commercial and his imaginative work. They were designed for an 1821 school edition of Virgil's Eclogues in the translation by Ambrose Phillips edited by Robert Thornton, who described them as 'display[ing] less of art than genius'. They are notable for their power of poetic suggestion, and they had an enormous impact on Samuel Palmer, who famously described their 'mystic and dreamy glimmer', claiming that, 'They are visions of little dells, and nooks, and corners of Paradise; models of the exquisitest pitch of intense poetry.'(Bentley 1969, pp. 271-72). In reality, Blake's vision is less positive, for the wood engravings tells the story of the shepherd Colinet's need to escape the stultifying pastoral paradise to enter into the world of experience. (DB)

249. **Edward Calvert**

Appledore, Devon, 1799 - London, 1883
The Bride, from the portfolio ***The Early Engravings of Edward Calvert***, designed in 1828, printed in 1904
Line engraving, 10.5 x 15.7 cm
Published by the Carfax Gallery, London
Victoria and Albert Museum, London

Edward Calvert, Samuel Palmer and George Richmond were the three principal members of the 'Ancients', the little group who became disciples of William Blake in the few years before his death in 1827. They were all guided in a general way by his advocacy of a spiritual and visionary manner of working, but they were specifically influenced by his series of seventeen tiny woodblocks engraved as illustrations for Robert Thornton's

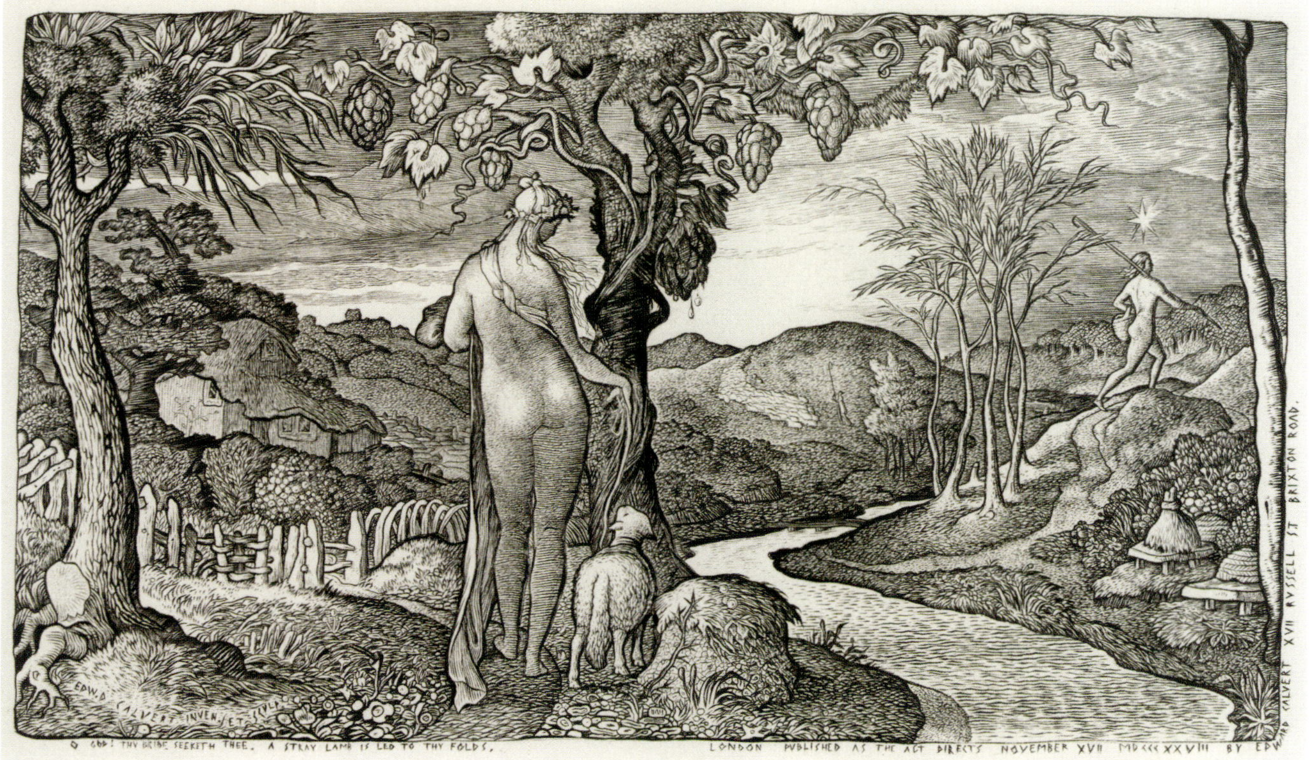

249

schoolbook edition of *The Pastorals of Virgil*, 1821 (cat. 248). Calvert, who was largely self-taught, made his first hesitant attempts at printmaking around 1824, but thereafter made extraordinarily rapid progress, mastering the two very different, but equally exacting, processes of line-engraving on copper and wood-engraving. *The Bride*, the largest and most important of his engravings, shows Blake's influence but also reveals Calvert's developing artistic confidence. The alluring and poised figure of the bride (based on an ancient engraved gemstone) standing in a luscious landscape suggests the sensuous mood of the *Song of Solomon*. Indeed, in the first known state of the print an inscription read 'The waters of this brook shall never fail to the married wife of the Lord God'; in later impressions (such as this from the third state) the lettering is erased as a reflection of Calvert's turning away from Christianity towards an idiosyncratic classically-inspired paganism. (SC)

250. **Edward Calvert**
Appledore, Devon, 1799 - London, 1883
The Chamber Idyll, from the portfolio ***The Early Engravings of Edward Calvert***, designed in 1831, printed in 1904
Wood engraving, 5.5 x 9 cm
Published by the Carfax Gallery, London
Victoria and Albert Museum, London

The Chamber Idyll is unique in English art of the era for its mood of exquisite but quite explicit eroticism. It is the last of Calvert's prints and generally held to be the very finest. Perhaps finding the minute technique of his wood- and copper-engravings too exacting, he ceased making prints and thereafter painted in watercolour or in oils on small panels. His subject matter became yet more limited - almost entirely small, dreamy visions of Arcadian shepherds - and, supported by private means and so lacking any compulsion to work, he seems to have passed much of his time in philosophical speculation and the elaboration of a complex theory of colour. Although he differed with the intensely religious Palmer over his 'pagan' ideals, the two remained friends for more than fifty years. Throughout his life, Samuel Palmer treasured a portfolio of all Calvert's prints. He described the *Chamber Idyll* as 'doubly condensed poetry' (Palmer 1892, p. 30, where A.H. Palmer recalls his father's opinion on Calvert's prints), but because of its subject matter kept it always in an envelope. (SC)

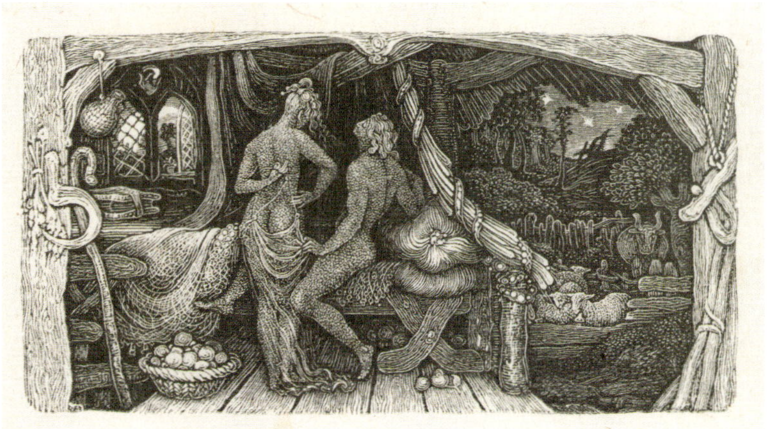

250

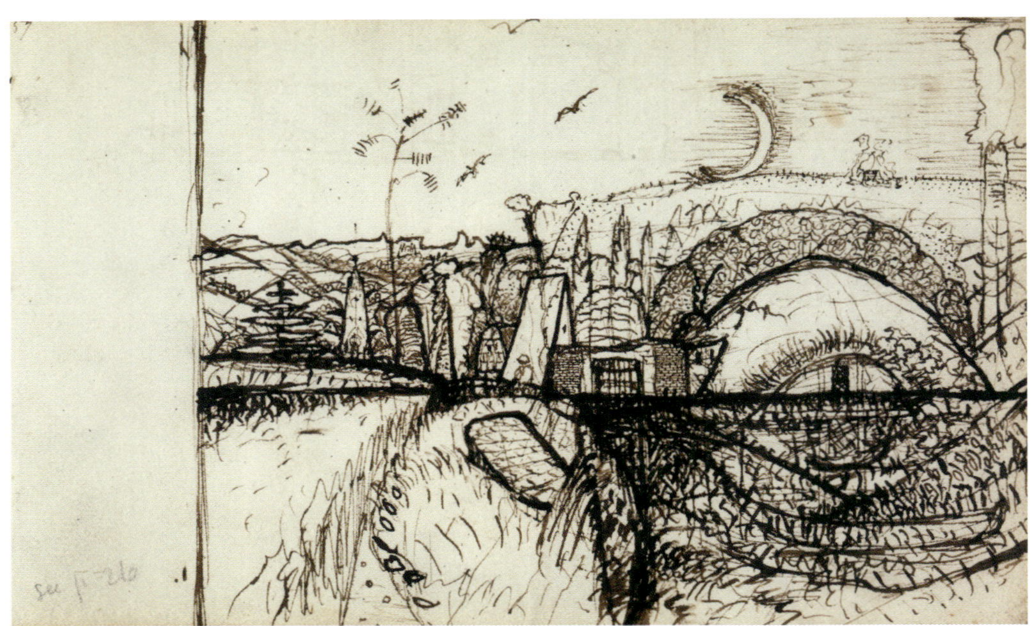

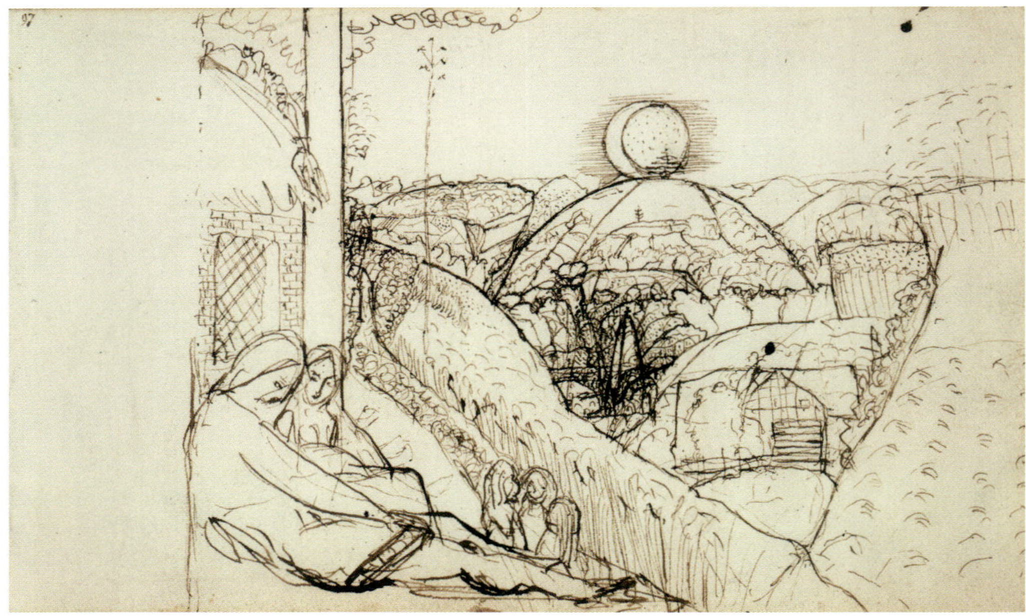

251 – 252

251. **Samuel Palmer**
London, 1805 - Redhill, Surrey, 1881
Hilly Landscape with Buildings including a Church and a House, page from a sketchbook, c. 1824
Pencil, indian ink and touches of watercolour on paper, 11.6 x 18.9 cm
British Museum, London

252. **Samuel Palmer**
London, 1805 - Redhill, Surrey, 1881
Hilly and Wooded Landscape with Domed Hill in Centre Distance, page from a sketchbook, c. 1824
Pen and brown ink on paper, 11.6 x 18.9 cm
British Museum, London

Before emigrating in 1910, Samuel Palmer's surviving son, A.H. Palmer, in a tragically misguided act of filial piety burned 'more than twenty' of his father's early sketchbooks, along with other papers which, as he saw it, revealed 'a mental condition which, in many respects, is uninviting ... a condition full of danger, and neither sufficiently masculine nor sufficiently reticent.' (Palmer 1892, p. 18) Fortunately, he saved from the flames one small book of drawings, which had originally been given by the artist during the Shoreham years to his friend and fellow 'Ancient' George Richmond. Richmond preserved it for sixty years until his death in 1896 and bequeathed it to A.H. Palmer.

This crucial sketchbook, now disbound, was begun by the nineteen-year-old Palmer in the summer of 1824, shortly before he was taken by his mentor John Linnell to meet William Blake. Its pages reveal the unmistakable genesis of the sensibility which Palmer would develop during his most fruitful period in Shoreham. The drawings were mostly made during rambles in the then still wooded hills and fields around Dulwich (close to the family's south London home at Walworth). They are interspersed with numerous written comments, revealing Palmer's constant struggle to find a manner of drawing that would express his overwhelming and spiritual response to nature. The designs include idealized landscapes beneath vast crescent moons; intense and minutely particularized studies from nature, especially of textured tree trunks and foliage; sketches of gothick towers and steeples, and some often awkward, but curiously expressive figure drawings. Mostly executed in a nervous, tight, linear manner with pen and brown ink, only occasionally varied with freer touches drawn with the brush or ink washes, the pages of the sketchbook reveal clearly the influence of Linnell's advice to the young artist to study the prints of Dürer, Lucas van Leyden and other sixteenth-century engravers such as Bonasone. This combination of a 'northern' or even 'Gothic' graphic mannerism with his more idiosyncratic and visionary feeling for the rich fecundity of nature made these works of Palmer's early years a key influence for the generation of Neo-Romantics who rediscovered his art in the twentieth century. (SC)

253. **Samuel Palmer**
London, 1805 - Redhill, Surrey, 1881
The Primitive Cottage, c. 1828-29
Pen and brown ink, grey and brown wash heightened with white, and traces of pencil on paper, 22.5 x 27.7 cm
Victoria and Albert Museum, London

In one of the exhortations to himself inscribed in the pages of his 1824 sketchbook Palmer wrote: 'Whatever you do, guard against bleakness and grandeur, and try for the primitive cottage feeling.' As his son, A.H. Palmer noted on the back of the drawing, this remained 'a subject dearly loved by SP throughout life'. Indeed, among the drawings of the 1824 sketchbook and in a great many of the works of the Shoreham period, Palmer constantly explores aspects of this cherished ideal. For him, the secluded cottage nestling in a fold of the landscape represented the charm of the simple life lived close to nature and a symbolic refuge from the more unpleasant aspects of modern life. In later years, living first in London and then in a new house in increasingly built-up Surrey, he seems to have suffered from a feeling of exile from the rural idyll of his early years. (SC)

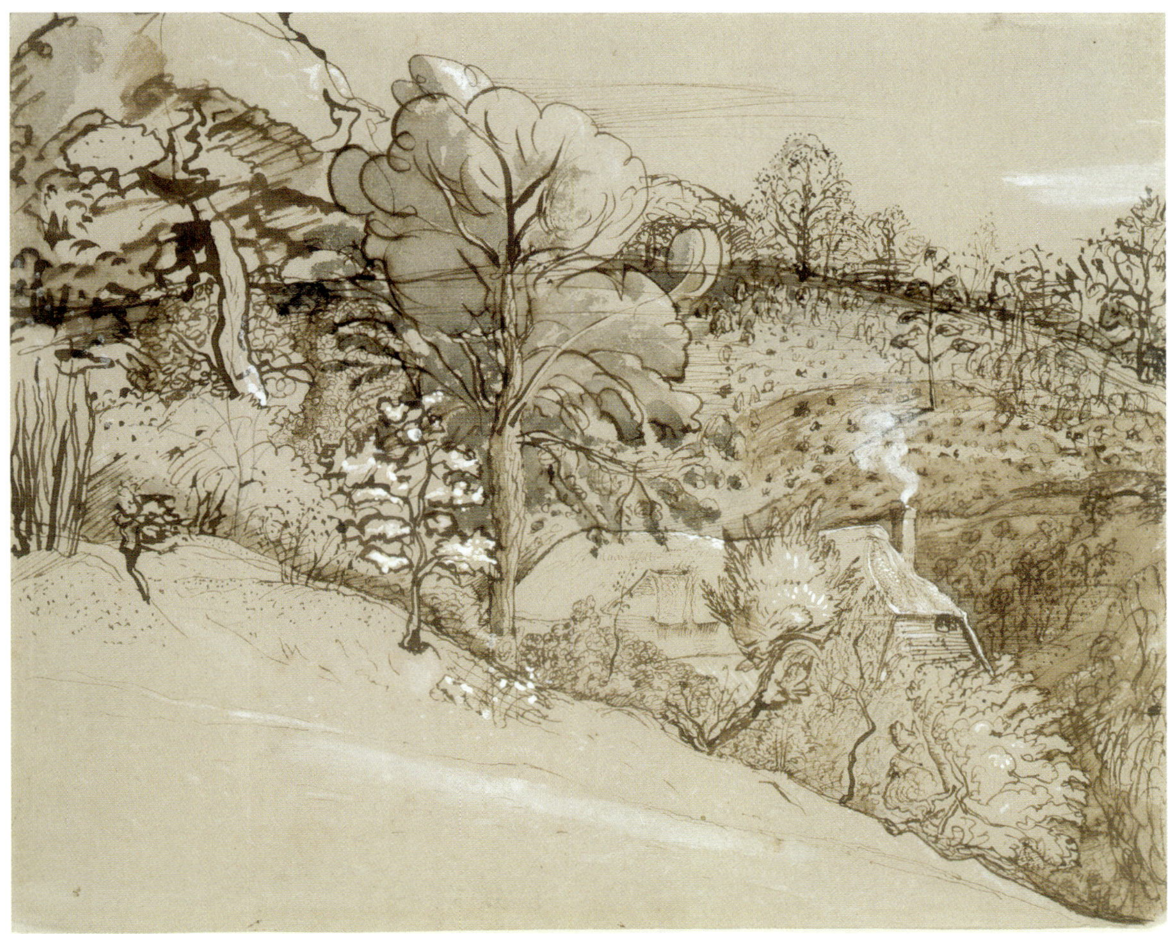

253

254. **Samuel Palmer**
London, 1805 – Redhill, Surrey, 1881
Landscape with Full Moon and Deer, c. 1829-30
Watercolour wash and point of brush on card, 13.5 x 9.4 cm
Victoria and Albert Museum, London

Palmer called the group of dark, almost monochromatic, watercolour drawings that he made during his Shoreham period his 'Blacks'. A number of motifs, including powerful full or crescent moons; brilliantly lit billowing clouds; high ruined towers and solitary, pensive figures of women or herdsmen, all recur throughout the series. Here the rich and freely handled foliage, painted with a rapid, blotty technique, is silhouetted against the full moon, thereby serving to increase its apparent brightness. (SC)

255. **Samuel Palmer**
London, 1805 – Redhill, Surrey, 1881
A Cornfield by Moonlight with the Evening Star, c. 1830
Watercolour and bodycolour with pen and ink, varnished, on paper, 19.7 x 29.8 cm
British Museum, London

Though not intended specifically as an illustration, this little picture – one of the greatest masterpieces of Palmer's Shoreham Period – can be convincingly linked to the mood of the opening lines of Virgil's *Georgics,* one of the artist's favourite poems and a text with which he was intimately familiar: 'What makes the Field of Corn joyous; under what Sign, Maecenas, it is proper to turn the Earth and join the Vines to Elms ... Ye brightest Luminaries of the World, that lead the Year sliding along the Sky ... Your bounteous Gifts I sing.' (Translated by Joseph Davidson, 1790)

In his consummate handling of the darkly silhouetted hill and contrasting heavy heads of corn brilliantly illuminated by the light of the waxing crescent moon and Hesperus, the evening star, Palmer achieves the 'glimmering' effect which was one of his principal aims in the depiction of landscape. William Vaughan has drawn attention to the remarkable similarity of sensibility in Palmer's *Cornfield* and the roughly contemporary moonlight scenes painted by Caspar David Friedrich (London & New York 2005, p.125). (SC)

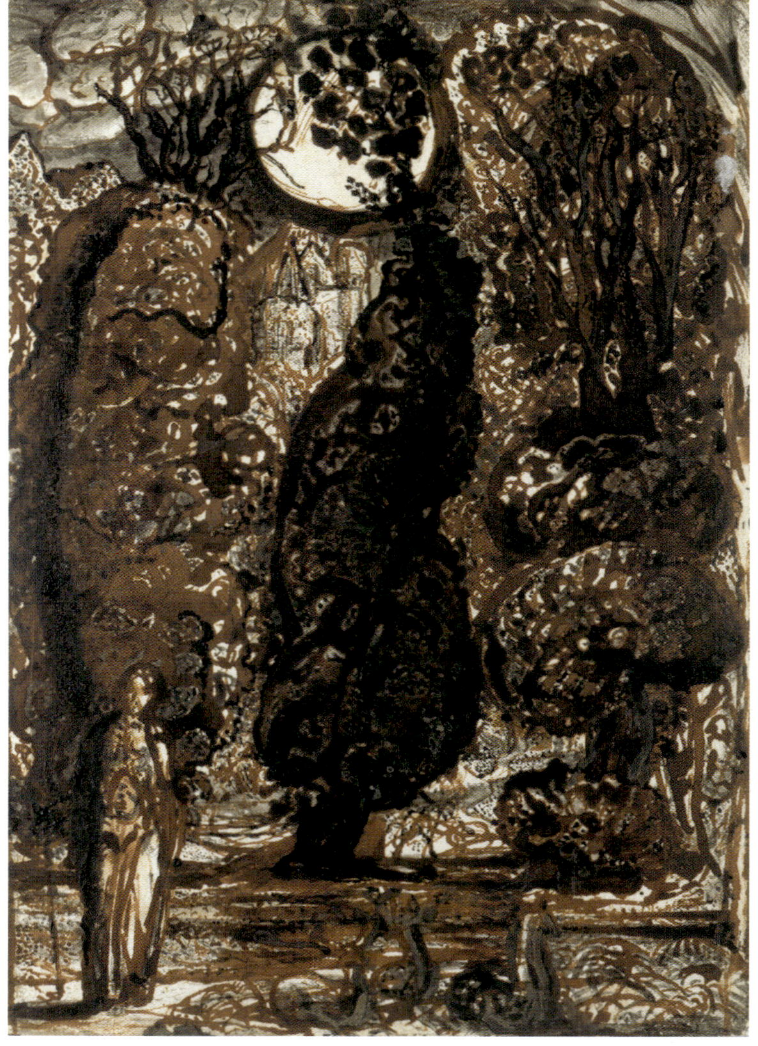

254

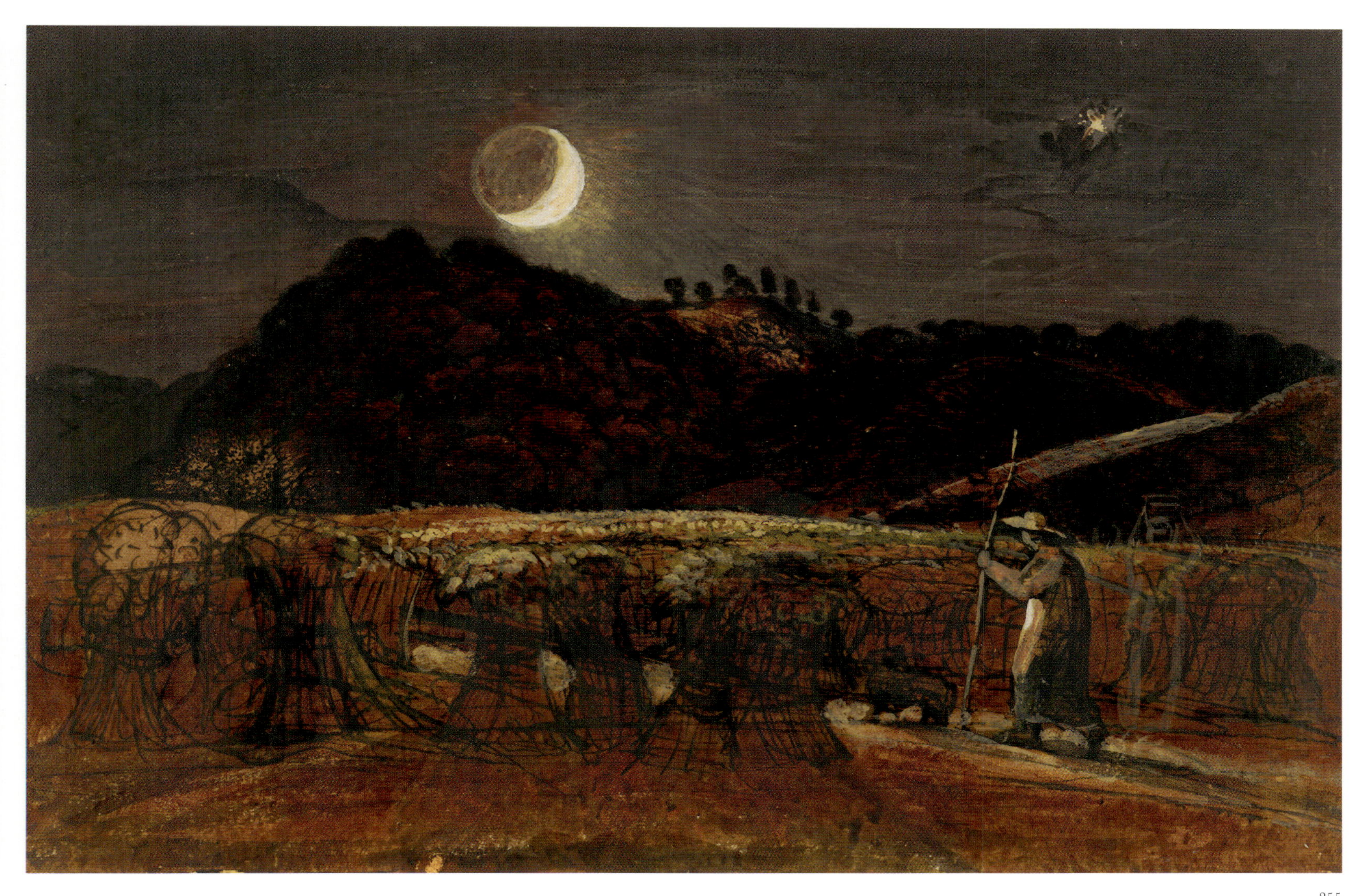

255

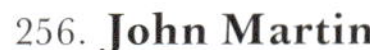

256. **John Martin**

Haydon Bridge, Northumberland, 1789 – Douglas, Isle of Man, 1854

The Deluge, 1834

Oil on canvas, 168.3 x 258.4 cm

Bottom right: J. Martin. / 1834

Yale Center for British Art, Paul Mellon Collection, New Haven

The first version (1826) of John Martin's *The Deluge* is known only through the artist's brilliant mezzotint engraving, published in 1828. That picture, which earned Martin a gold medal at the Paris Salon of 1835, appears to have been damaged, lost or destroyed relatively soon after that date, and the present, much larger, canvas reflects a number of changes Martin envisaged in about 1834, above all a distinct elongation of the composition and something of a diffusion of the remarkable effects of light that were initially concentrated into a tunnel-like, centrifugal spatial void, said by him to represent the supernatural conjunction of sun, moon and comet. (Halley's Comet was seen in England in October and November 1835.) This second picture was later described by Martin as his 'favourite', and in 1839, when he was visited in his studio by Prince Albert, Martin was commissioned first to produce a new picture (on a smaller scale), *The Eve of the Deluge* (Royal Collection), and then by Harriet, Duchess of Sutherland, a third and final canvas, *The Assuaging of the Waters* (Fine Arts Museums of San Francisco). Both new pictures, for which the present, earlier, significantly larger, *Deluge* painting was the conceptual keystone, were completed and first exhibited at the Royal Academy in 1840. *The Deluge* was sold in about 1845 to Martin's most important patron, Charles Scarisbeck of Leicestershire. (AT)

See essay pp. 319-23.

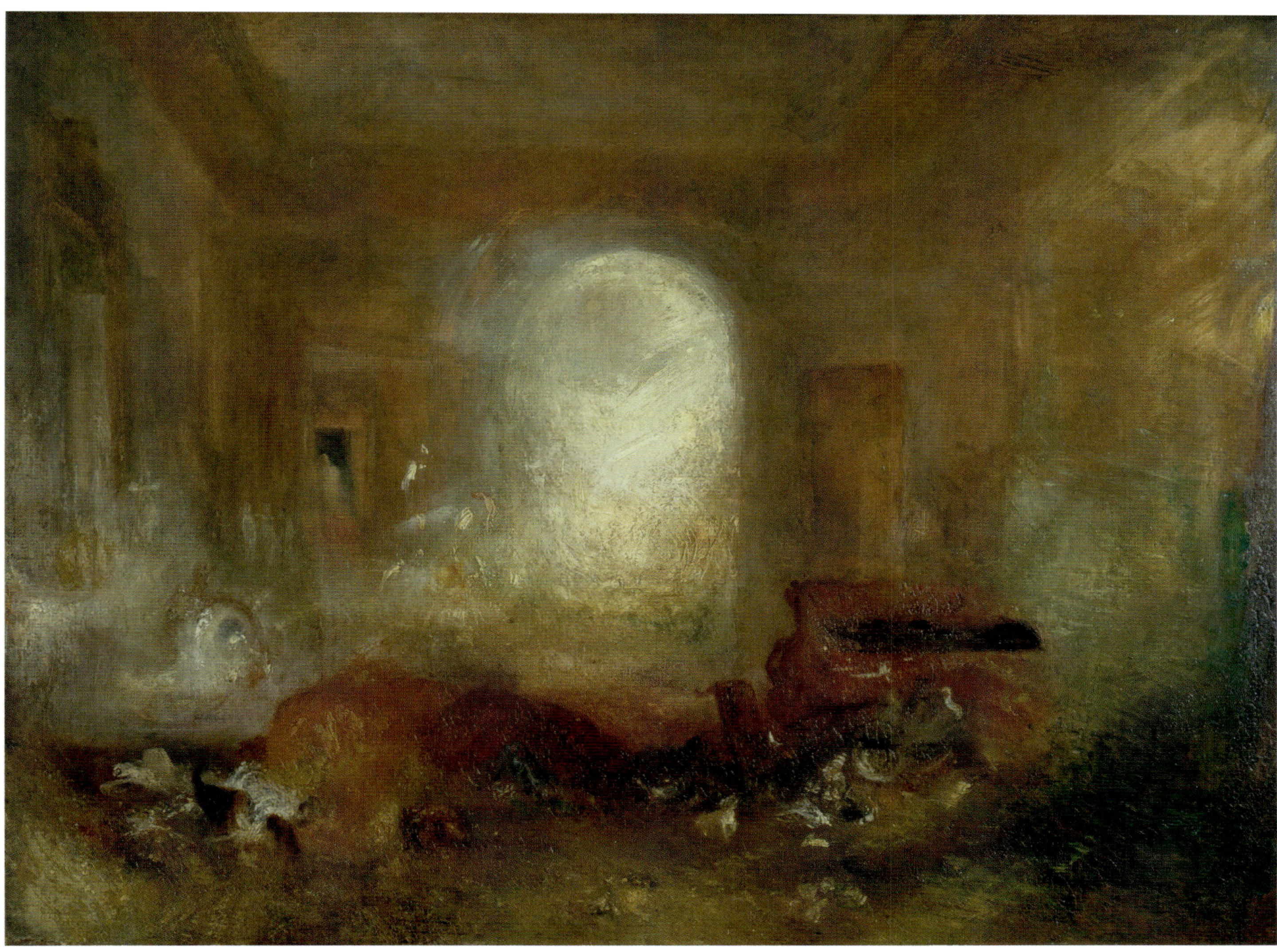

257

257. **Joseph Mallord William Turner**
London, 1775 - London, 1851
Interior of a Great House: the Drawing Room, East Cowes Castle, c. 1830
Oil on canvas, 90.8 x 121.9 cm
Tate, London, Bequeathed by the artist 1856

The painting is one of a group of atypical interior scenes and figure subjects that Turner painted in the late 1820s but later abandoned, so that the painting remained completely unknown until it was exhibited at the Tate Gallery in February 1906, as the centrepiece of the first cache of unfinished pictures from the Turner Bequest to be made available since the collection became national property in the mid-1850s. The vibrant brushwork led several writers at the time to claim Turner as a forerunner of the Impressionists, or even Expressionism. The identification of the interior as Petworth House, home of Turner's patron Lord Egremont, has been put into question recently, and the significance of this remarkable work remains enigmatic, although it seems clear that the architectural setting is derived from the drawing room in Cowes Castle, John Nash's Neo-Gothic home on the Isle of Wight. (IW)

See essay pp. 325-29.

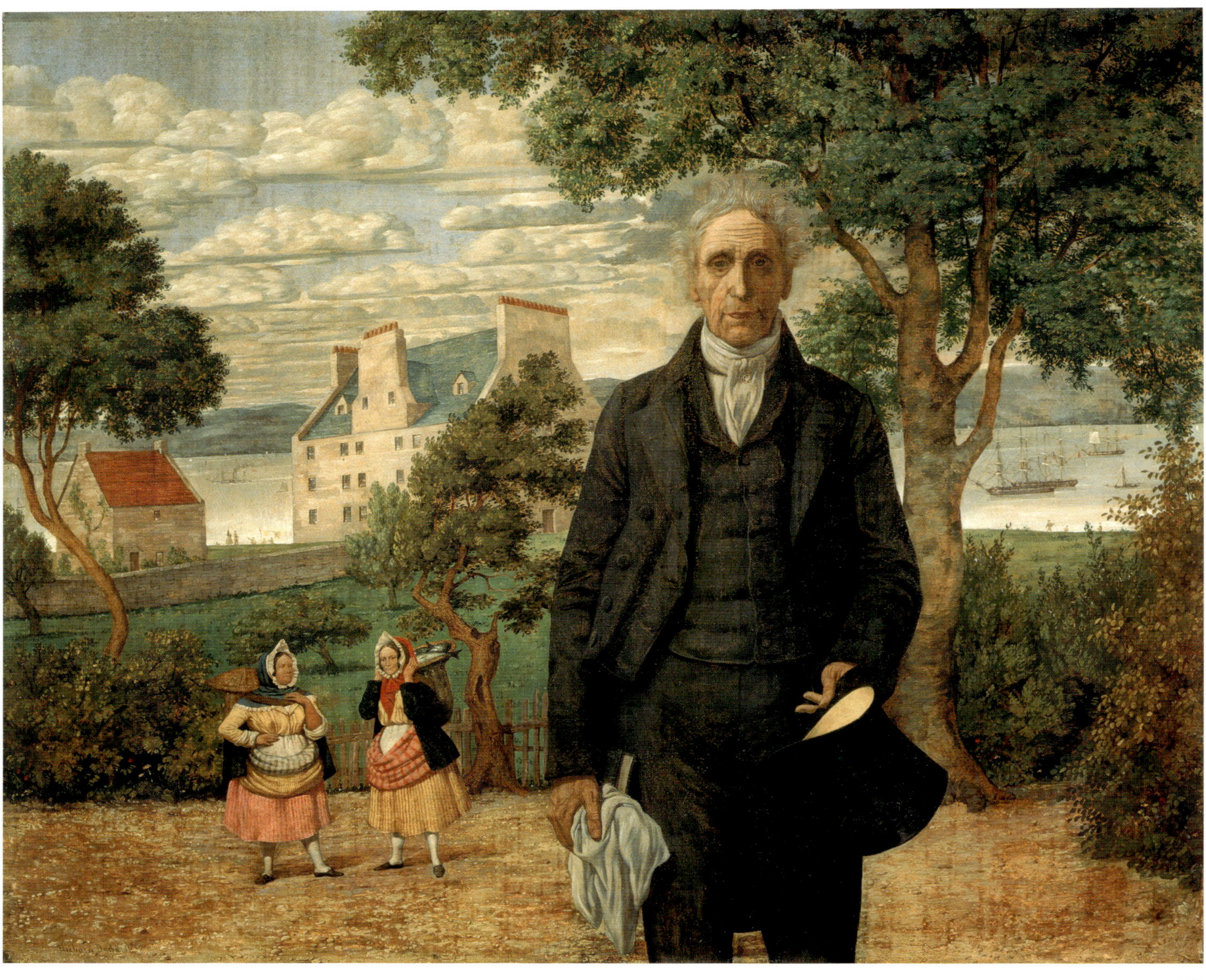

258

258. **Richard Dadd**
Chatham, Kent, 1817 – Broadmoor Hospital, Berkshire, 1886
Sir Alexander Morison, 1852
Oil on canvas, 51.1 x 61.3 cm
Bottom left: Richard Dadd 1852
Scottish National Portrait Gallery, Edinburgh

After murdering his father in August 1843, the promising young painter Richard Dadd was confined in Bethlem Hospital, where he caught the attention of the celebrated physician Sir Alexander Morison. It may have been Morison who encouraged Dadd to start painting again in 1845, despite the brutal conditions of the ward for the criminally insane. Did Morison actually pose, or did Dadd work from a photograph? Either way, 'the old man is depicted with painful exactitude, his face ravaged by time and ... by resignation, perhaps even exhaustion' (MacGregor 1989, p. 132). A note by Dadd on the back of the portrait explains that the setting is based on a drawing by Morison's daughter of Anchorfield, the family seat on the Firth of Forth. But the dark figure of the seventy-three-year-old is dropped into this innocent sunlit landscape like a Nosferatu; and the two incongruous, miniaturized fisherwomen seem like '"little people" ... escaped from Dadd's fairy world' (ibid.). Morison was the first of a succession of Bethlem stewards and visitors to collect Dadd's works; they were being resold on the market even within the artist's lifetime. (TH)

259. **Richard Dadd**
Chatham, Kent, 1817 - Broadmoor Hospital, Berkshire, 1886
The Child's Problem, 1857
Pencil and watercolour, heightened with white, on paper, 17.1 x 25.4 cm
Top left: The Child's Problem. A Fancy Sketch. by Richard Dadd. Decr. 18th. 1857. Bethlehem Hospital. London. St. George's in the Fields.
Tate, London, Presented by Dr R.C. Neville 1954

While his guardian sleeps, the fearful, intense boy peers over the table and stretches forth his bare arm in a gesture that seems momentous, charged with mystery and significance. The 'problem' surely goes much deeper than the simple arrangement of chess pieces; it may have some connection with slavery. To the left, a black slave raises his chained hands, the image inscribed: 'AM I NOT A MAN AND A BROTHER'. At right angles, a slave ship plies the seas. Is the child - pampered in ruff and frills - in some sense himself a captive, confined within the cluttered, windowless room? We seem close to fairy tales of luxurious enchantments that must be broken; and also to Alice's chessboard-nightmare in Lewis Carroll's *Through the Looking-Glass*. Is the walnut-cracking still life related to the acorn-splitting action at the centre of *The Fairy Feller's Masterstroke* (see cat. 261), Dadd's chief work of the later 1850s? Painted with an extraordinary refinement, *The Child's Problem* is one of several Dadd watercolours that develop a pale, almost bleached colour-world. It was owned by the Bethlem head attendant, Charles Neville. (TH)

260. **Richard Dadd**
Chatham, Kent, 1817 - Broadmoor Hospital, Berkshire, 1886
General View of Part of Port Stragglin, the Rock and Castle of Seclusion and the Blinker Lighthouse in the Distance, 1861
Pen and brown ink, and brown wash, with watercolour, on paper, 19.2 x 14.3 cm
Verso: General View of Part of Port Stragglin - / The Rock & Castle of Seclusion. / and the / Blinker Lighthouse in the Distance. / not sketched from Nature. / by R^{d}. Dadd. 1861, / Jany. Finit / Not a bit like it / [...] style sit [?]. very / What a while you are! / Of course it is!! / I don't like it. No
British Museum, London

This imaginary view of a bustling seaport overshadowed by a grim castle perched atop a vertiginous cliff is generally accounted the most sublime of Dadd's landscape *capricci*. Dadd's precision of technique, drawing minutely with the point of the brush and applying subtly modulated washes, serves to highlight the sense of unreality, whilst the overall pale tonality and muted colour scheme enhance the dream-like effect created by the scene. The subject matter of the drawing - and in particular the precipitous rock face, a motif that Dadd often employs, and the seemingly impregnable castle - may derive distantly from scenes observed during his travels. There may, however, also be some connection with the highly popular imaginative landscapes of John Martin, with their nightmarish distortions of scale. Based in part on the seemingly mad and inconsequential, but actually

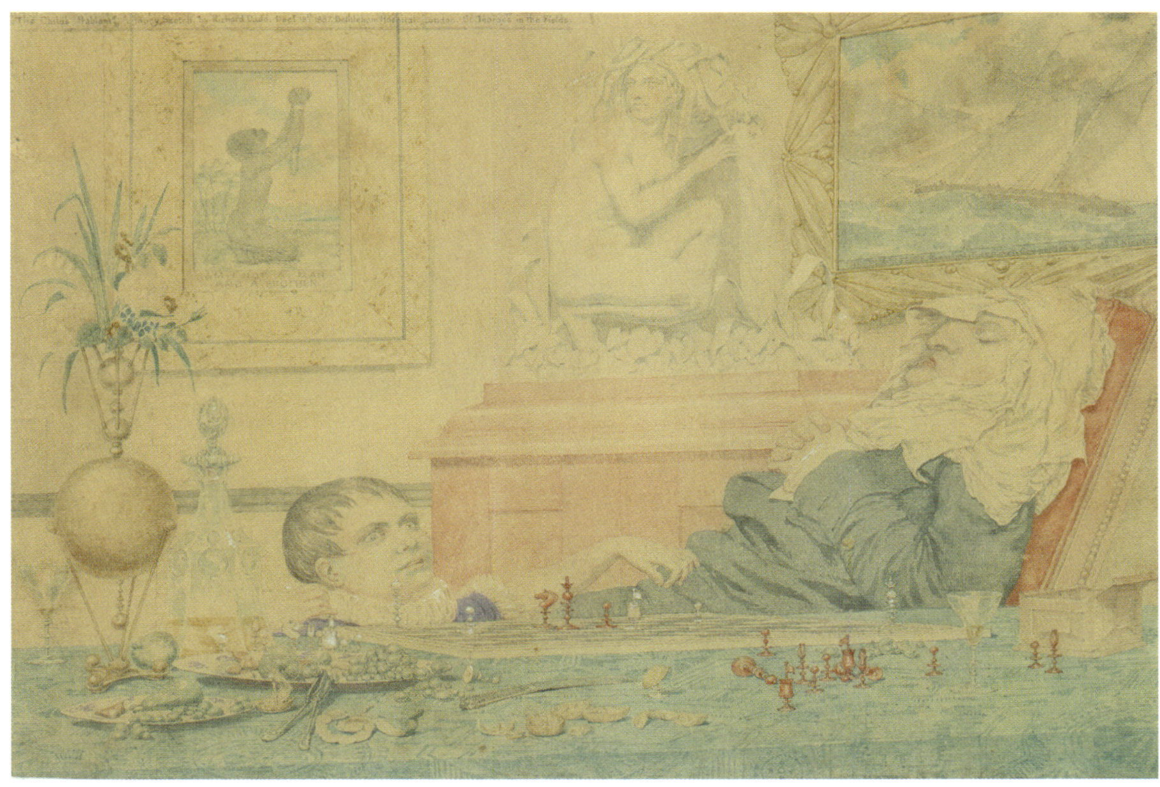

259

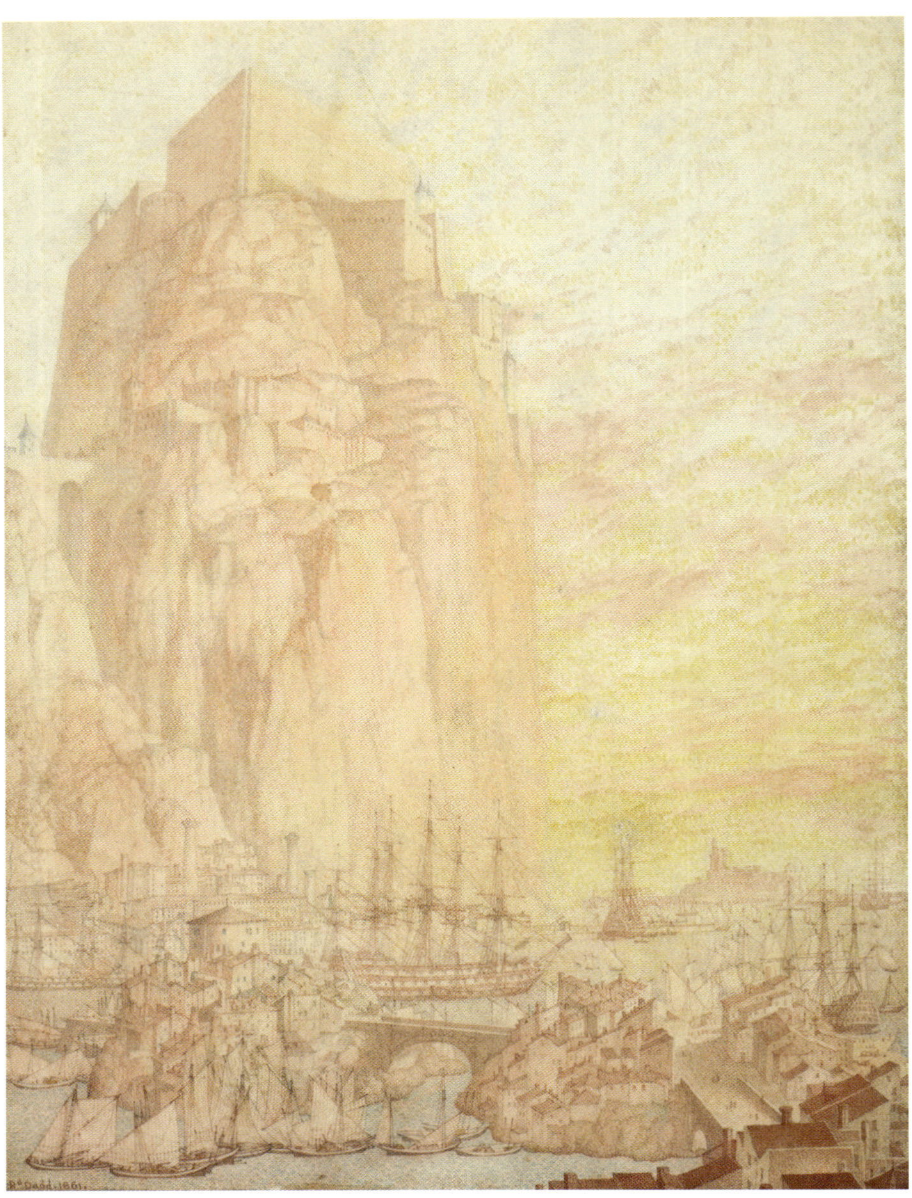

260

telling, inscriptions on the sheet, it has also been convincingly suggested by Patricia Allderidge that this 'Rock and Castle of Seclusion' should be identified as symbolic to Dadd of his isolation in the asylum (Allderidge 1974, p. 119). (SC)

261. **Richard Dadd**

Chatham, Kent, 1817 – Broadmoor Hospital, Berkshire, 1886

Songe de la Fantasie, 1864

Watercolour on ivory board, 38.3 x 31.4 cm

Top left: Songe de la Fantasie. / R^d^. Dadd Novr. 1864.

Lent by the Syndics of the Fitzwilliam Museum, Cambridge

When Dadd was moved in 1864 from Bethlem to the more remote asylum of Broadmoor, he left behind his almost completed oil painting *The Fairy Feller's Masterstroke* (Tate, London, see p. 26, fig. 11). But he may have brought with him a photograph, and in his first months in the new setting he completed this smaller, paler variant of his masterpiece. Dadd's earliest reputation was as a 'fairy-painter' in two scenes from *A Midsummer Night's Dream*. But the world of the *Fairy Feller* is far more impenetrable. In his doggerel *Elimination*, Dadd explains how the imagery appeared before him as he stared at the blank canvas; and then, very knowingly, suggests how the grasses and tendrils signify 'vagary wild and mental aberration styled' (Allderidge 1974, p. 125). In the *Songe*, those curving tendrils are even more emphasized, so that the figures recede. The central woodman ('Feller'), who raises his axe to cleave a hazelnut for Queen Mab's chariot, no longer dominates. At Broadmoor Dadd later painted a ten-foot mural of *Flora*; sadly no record of it survives. 'Flower Power' and hallucinogenic substances were the context for the popular rediscovery of Dadd in the 1960s. (TH)

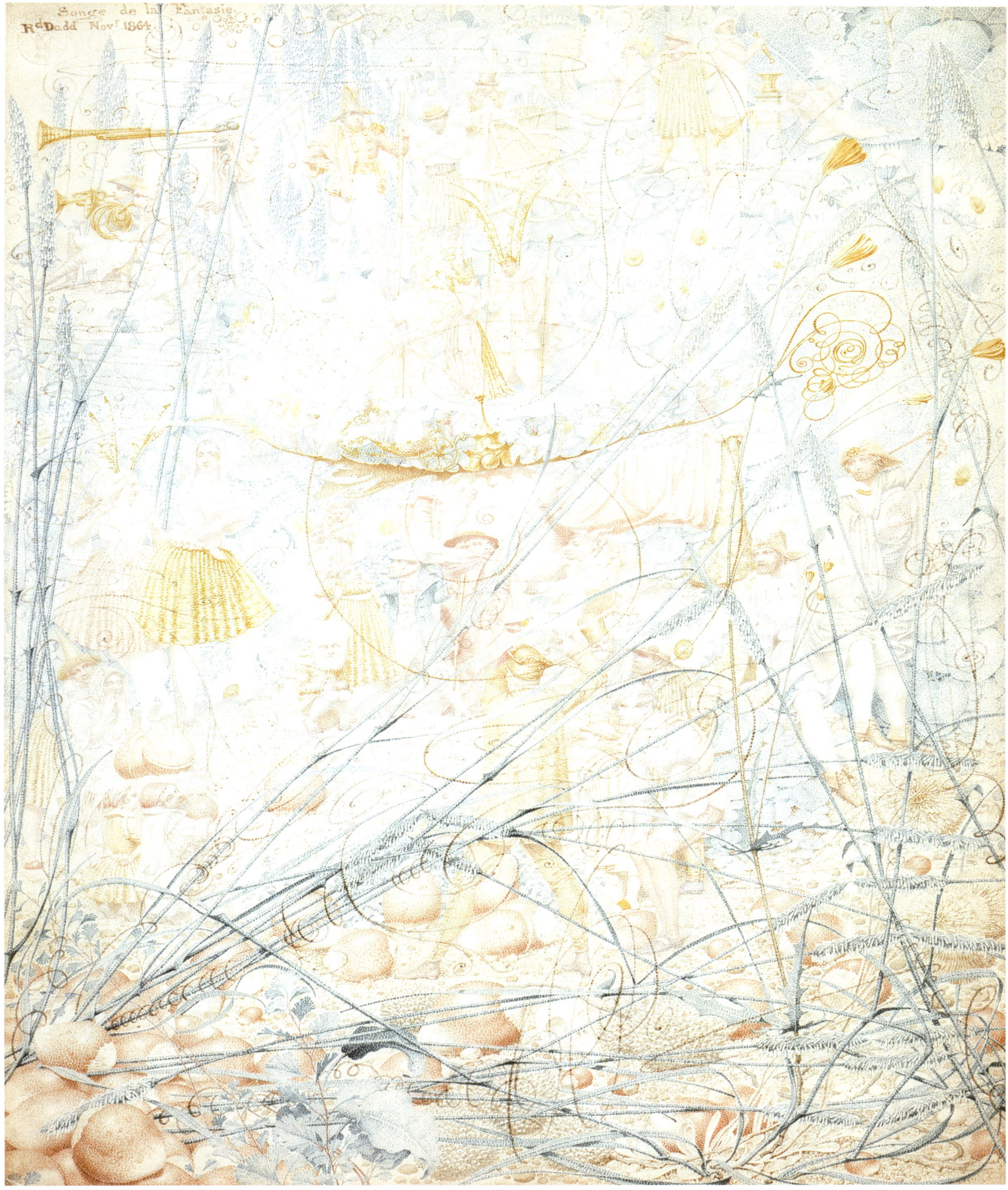

261

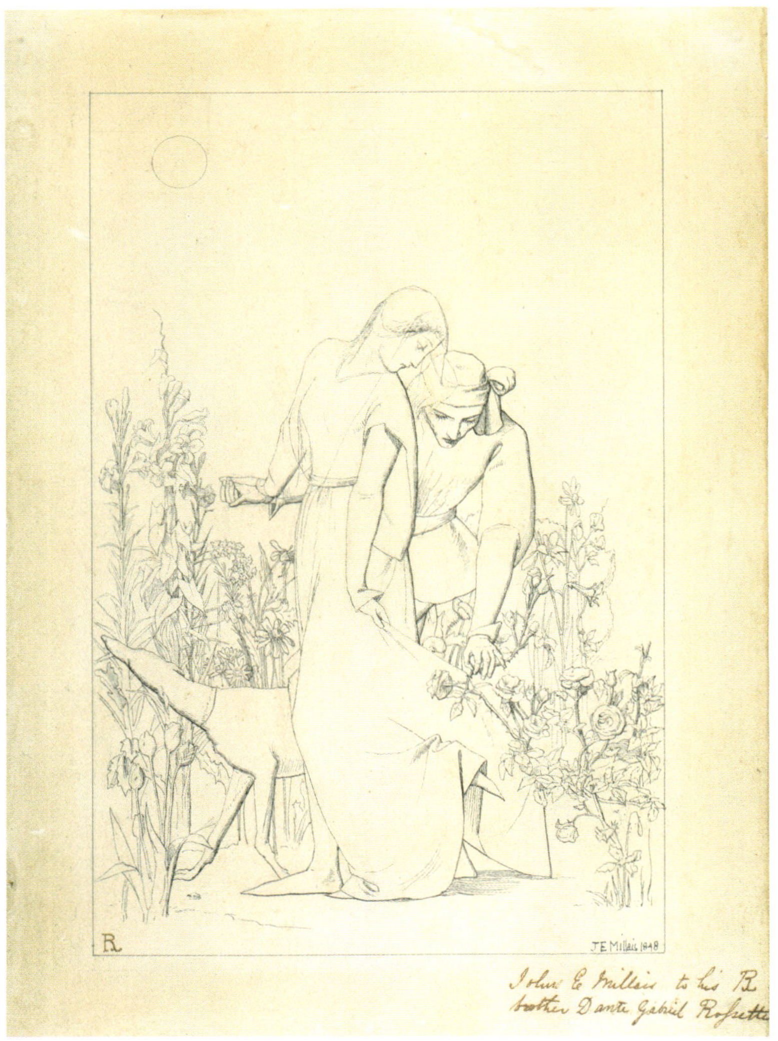

262

262. **John Everett Millais**
Southampton, 1829 - London, 1896
Lovers by a Rosebush (My Beautiful Lady), 1848
Pen and black ink, within a drawn border, over traces of pencil on paper, 25.4 x 16.5 cm
Bottom right: J E Millais 1848
Bottom left: PRB [monogram]
Bottom right, below image: John E Millais to his PRB [monogram] / brother Dante Gabriel Rossetti
Birmingham Museum & Art Gallery

This early drawing by Millais shares its subject - a long robe entangled in a rosebush - with the poem *My Beautiful Lady* (1850) by Thomas Woolner. Millais and Woolner belonged, together with William Holman Hunt and others, to the original Pre-Raphaelite Brotherhood, which was established in 1848. The drawing was Millais's gift to another member of the Brotherhood: Dante Gabriel Rossetti. This group of young, rebellious artists sought to breathe new life into British art, which in their opinion had become trivial and inauthentic.

Lovers by a Rosebush is one of the first works in the new drawing style developed by the members of the Brotherhood. The execution of the roses is the result of close observation from life. The human figures and the dog are linear, flat, angular and deliberately a bit awkward as a reminder of the pure innocence of the early Renaissance and art *before* Raphael as Millais and his friends imagined it. These two components, fidelity to nature and simplicity, also lend the first Pre-Raphaelite drawings of Rossetti and Holman Hunt an air of freshness and honesty (see cat. 263). (NP)

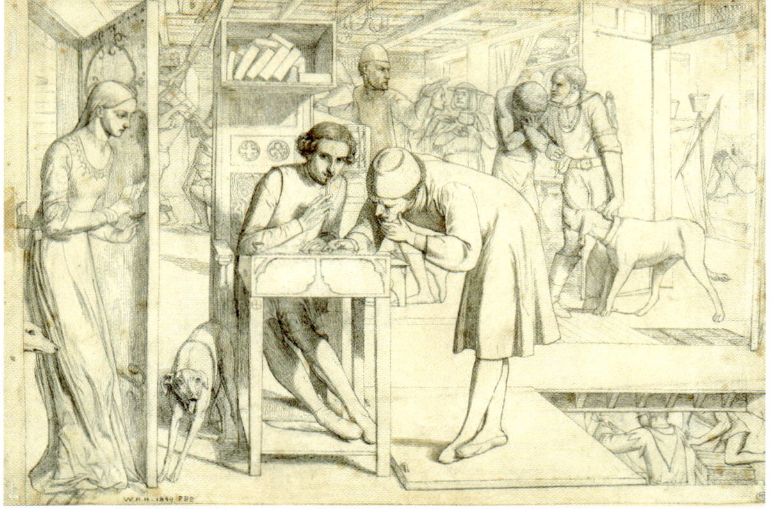

263

263. **William Holman Hunt**
London, 1827 - London, 1910
A Mediaeval Warehouse
(Lorenzo at his Desk in the Warehouse), c. 1848-50
Pen and grey ink, brush and grey ink, with traces of pencil on paper, 22.2 x 33.3 cm
Bottom left: W.H.H. 1849 PRB [monogram, unidentified hand]
Musée d'Orsay, Paris, deposited at the Département des Arts graphiques du musée du Louvre, donated by Edmond Davis, 1912

Like Hunt's well-known painting *Isabella and the Pot of Basil* (1866-68), this drawing illustrates the poem *Isabella; or, The Pot of Basil* (1820) by the then still relatively unknown poet John Keats, who was inspired by an episode in Boccaccio's *Decameron*. The work is executed in the same refreshing, early Pre-Raphaelite style as Millais's *Lovers by a Rosebush* (cat. 262). It also shows the same romanticized medieval world, but on another level it is a commentary on Victorian society. In the central scene and the various subsidiary scenes that take

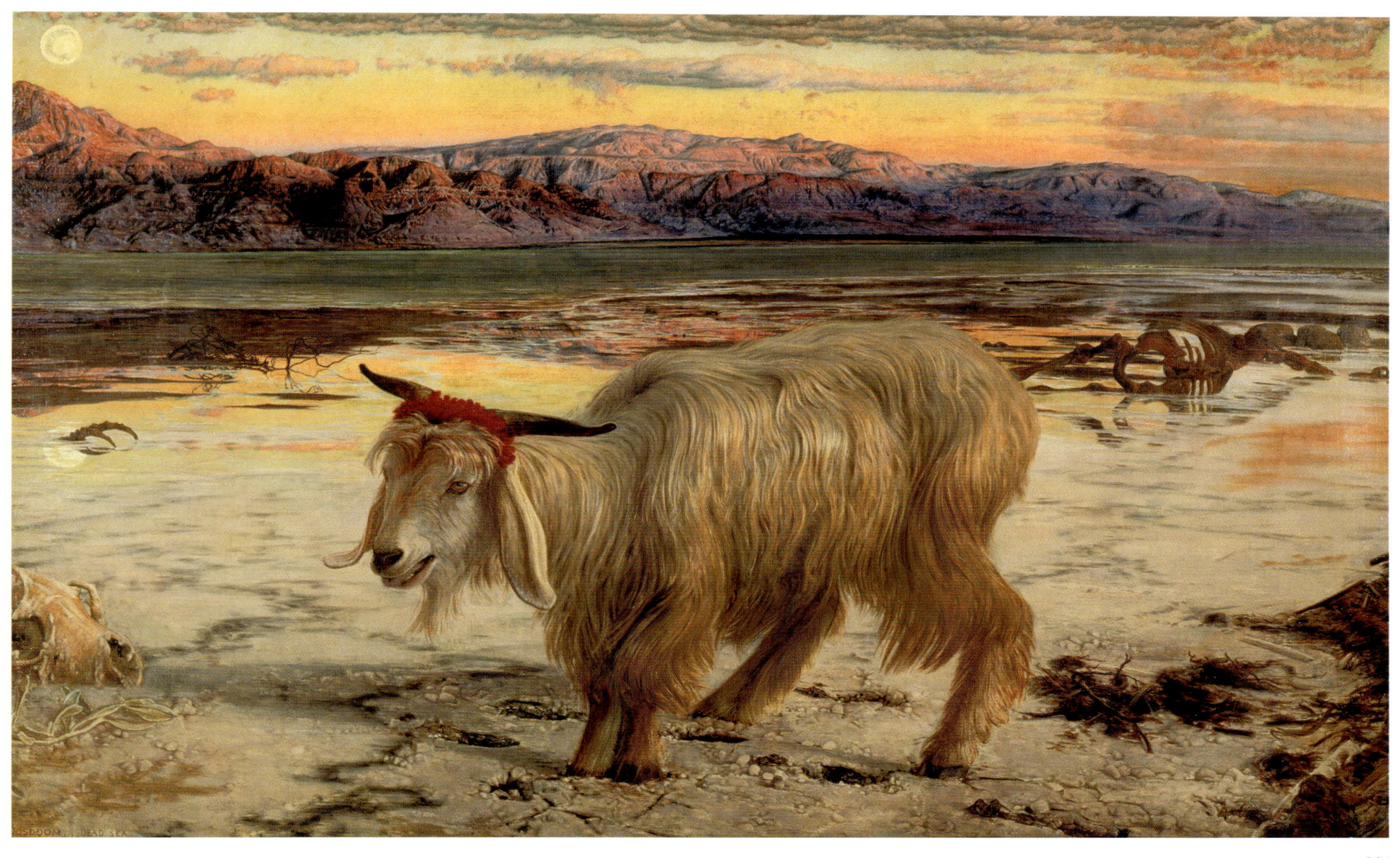

264

place around the principal figures, Hunt alludes to the difficult circumstances in which the less affluent classes earned their scanty wages.

In terms of technique, Prettejohn has remarked that the use of ink applied with a pen or fine brush reveals a labour-intensive approach and a high level of confidence. This technique enabled the Pre-Raphaelites to develop their clear, angular drawing style (Prettejohn 2000, pp. 139-40). (NP)

264. **William Holman Hunt**
London, 1827 - London, 1910
The Scapegoat, 1854-55, 1856
Oil on canvas, 87 x 139.8 cm
Bottom left: OOSDOOM. DEAD SEA / 18 Whh [monogram] 54
National Museums Liverpool, The Lady Lever Art Gallery

Holman Hunt set out for the Holy Land in January 1854, wanting to paint religious subjects in their actual geographical setting, and seeking to incorporate physiognomic types and styles of dress, as well as landscape forms, on the basis of close study in the places described in the Old and New Testaments. A man of devout Christian faith, Hunt believed that the Anglican Church needed a new and refreshed religious imagery that was not dependent on iconography and artistic conventions fostered by Roman Catholicism, but that would instead offer an archaeologically and anthropologically informed representation, which would aim at utmost authenticity and intensity of expression.

In Jerusalem Hunt commenced his multi-figured composition *The Finding of the Saviour in the Temple* (Birmingham Museum & Art Gallery), but found himself held up by the unwillingness of Jews to serve as models. He then embarked on *The Scapegoat*, the subject of which was drawn from the Old Testament book of Leviticus, and which represented the sacrifice of a goat in expiation of sin. He found the painting's extraordinary landscape setting on the shores of the Dead Sea at Oosdoom, and at least in the early stages worked in the open air to achieve a veracity of lighting effect. *The Scapegoat* draws both on the artist's highly individual oil technique, which captures the textures of the crusted surfaces of the foreground and the ravines of the mountainous backdrop as well as the silkiness of the animal's fur, and his distinctive colour sense, seen in the jaundiced yellows of sky and reflections in the static water, and weird pinks and purples of the vespertine distance. (CSN)

See essay pp. 331-33.

265. **Dante Gabriel Rossetti**
London, 1828 - Birchington on Sea, Kent, 1882
Fair Rosamund, 1861
Oil on canvas, 51.9 x 41.7 cm
Bottom right: D.G.R.[monogram] 1861
Amgueddfa Cymrueu - National Museum Wales, Cardiff

This work depicts a subject that was extremely popular with the second Pre-Raphaelite movement, which formed around Dante Gabriel Rossetti after the decline of the Pre-Raphaelite Brotherhood: Rosamund Clifford, mistress of the medieval King Henry II, in the labyrinth in which he hid her from his wife, Queen Eleanor. The rose as symbol of love is not only present in the name of the protagonist but also throughout the painting. In her hand, Rosamund holds the red thread that enabled Henry to find her in the labyrinth. According to the legend, Eleanor eventually used this thread to find and murder her rival.

Around 1860, Rossetti changed his style: he looked less to the early Renaissance, which the original Brotherhood had so much favoured, and more to the Venetian High Renaissance. From this period on, Rossetti painted his famous close-ups of seductive women, which are clearly influenced by Titian. (NP)

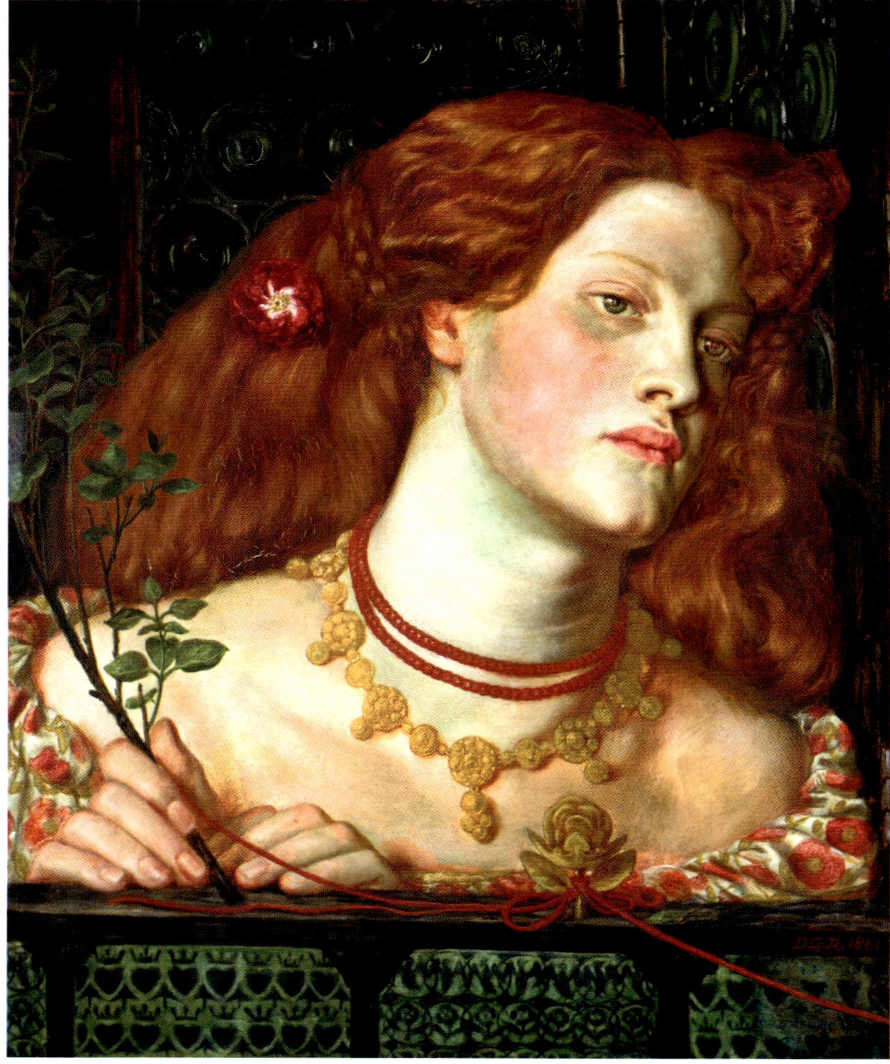

265

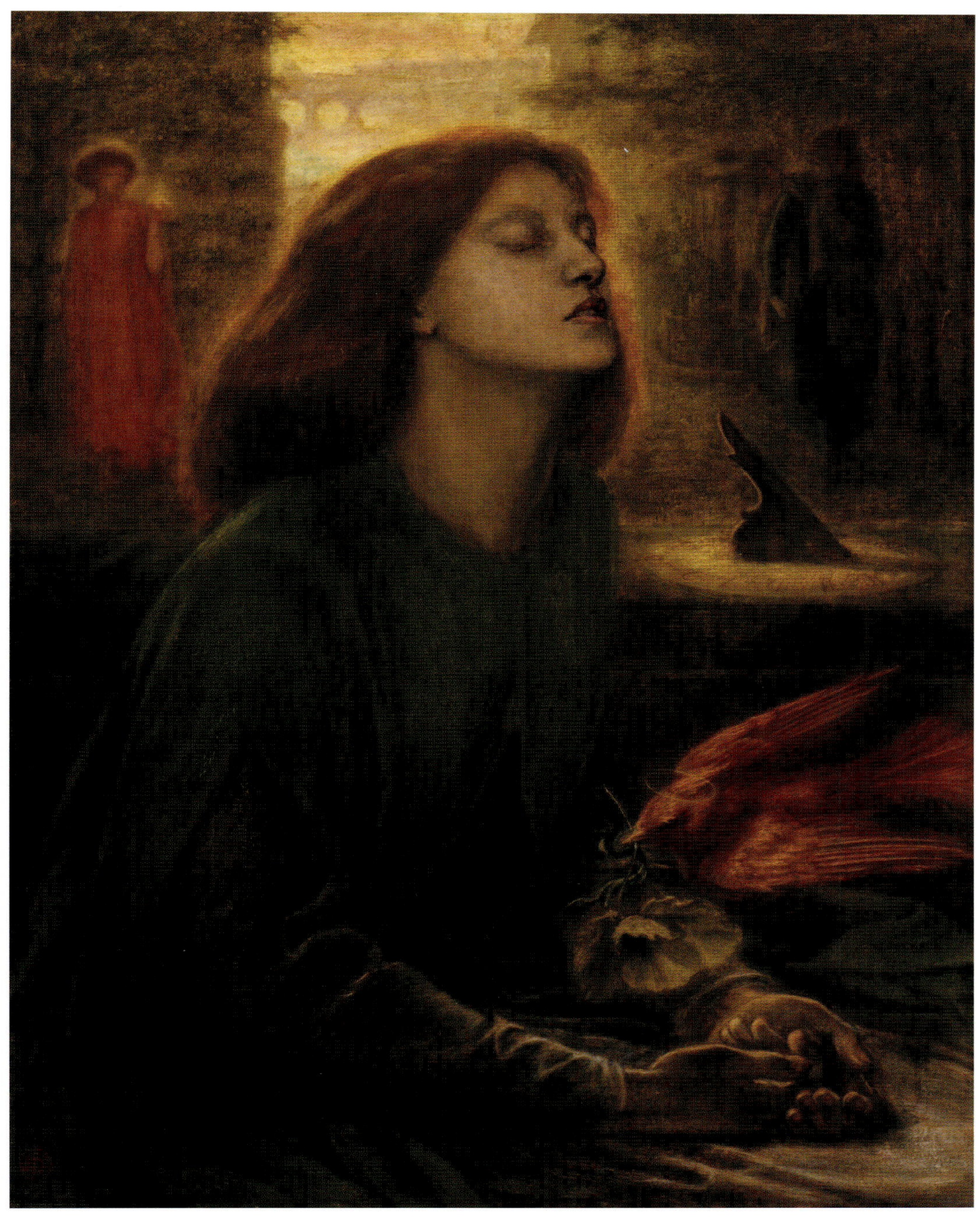

266

266. **Dante Gabriel Rossetti**
London, 1828 - Birchington on Sea, Kent, 1882
Beata Beatrix, c. 1863-70
Oil on canvas, 86.4 x 66 cm
Bottom left: DGR. [monogram]
Tate, London, Presented by Georgiana, Baroness Mount-Temple in memory of her husband, Francis, Baron Mount-Temple 1889

This painting alludes to Dante's *Vita Nuova* and the death of his beloved, Beatrice. In the foreground, a dove brings Beatrice a white poppy, a symbol of sleep and death. In the background, Dante watches the personification of Love carry her heart towards Purgatory. Rossetti wanted this work to be understood as the representation of a trance in which Beatrice is suddenly transported to Paradise: through her closed eyelids she already sees this new world (Wilton and Upstone 1997, no. 44)

However, the painting works on several levels. Although Dante is not explicitly mentioned, the Anglo-Italian Rossetti identified quite strongly with his medieval namesake. This appears in the countless references to his wife Elizabeth Siddal, who died of a laudanum overdose in 1862. Most striking in this respect are Beatrice's facial features and hair colour, which are clearly borrowed from Siddal. In this painting Rossetti seems to evoke the spirit of his departed wife (as he did literally through spiritualism). Alastair Grieve has remarked (in London 1984, no. 131) that the hazy style of *Beata Beatrix* recalls the soft-focus images of the photographer Julia Margaret Cameron, whom Rossetti admired (see cat. 272-273). In all likelihood, *Beata Beatrix* itself influenced the late, dreamlike drawings of Rossetti's friend Simeon Solomon. (NP)

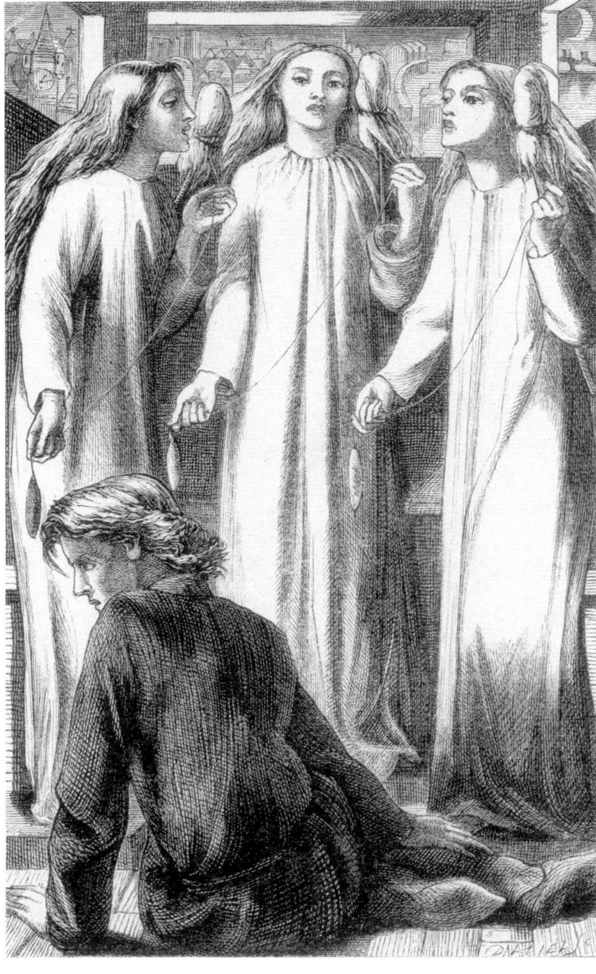

267

267. **Dante Gabriel Rossetti**
London, 1828 – Birchington on Sea, Kent, 1882
The Maids of Elfen-Mere, engraving for the ***Music Master*** by William Allingham, 1855
Wood engraving, proof, 12.8 x 7.8 cm
Engraved by the Dalziel Brothers
Victoria and Albert Museum, London, Given by Mr E Dalziel

This woodcut, after a design that Rossetti created as an illustration to a ballad by William Allingham, was made by the famous Dalziel brothers, who also worked with Simeon Solomon, among others. Once again, Rossetti enters the realm of the supernatural. The ballad concerns a village where three female apparitions come every night to sing and spin. They always disappear again at the strike of eleven. A lovesick young man hopes to make them stay longer and so turns back the village clock. The apparitions do indeed sing and spin longer than usual that night, but they are never seen again. As is common in such ballads, the young man soon dies of a broken heart.

In this depiction of the subject, skilful use is made of light and dark contrasts, which are characteristic of the medium, in order to create a spectral atmosphere. Rossetti's close framing reinforces this atmosphere and lends a certain monumentality to the three women.

According to J.W. Mackail (Mackail 1995, p. 87), this illustration played an important role in stimulating the young William Morris and Edward Burne-Jones to make woodcuts of their own (see cat. 276-277). (NP)

268. **Dante Gabriel Rossetti**
London, 1828 – Birchington on Sea, Kent, 1882
The First Madness of Ophelia, after ***Hamlet*** by William Shakespeare, 1864
Watercolour on paper, 39.4 x 29.2 cm
Bottom left: DGR [monogram] April 1864
Gallery Oldham, The Charles Edward Lees Collection

The young Pre-Raphaelites often took inspiration from Shakespeare. This watercolour illustrates scene five of the fourth act of Hamlet, in which Ophelia goes mad after being rejected by her beloved and learning of her father's sudden death. The radiant colours, detailed finish of the fabrics and expressive faces betray Rossetti's knowledge of late-medieval Flemish painting. The painting also recalls the medieval scenes created in the late 1850s by Rossetti and his future wife, Elizabeth Siddal, who died of an overdose of laudanum in 1862 (Ophelia, appropriately, has Siddal's features). In comparison to these earlier works, however, its composition is more simplified and therefore all the more poignant. (NP)

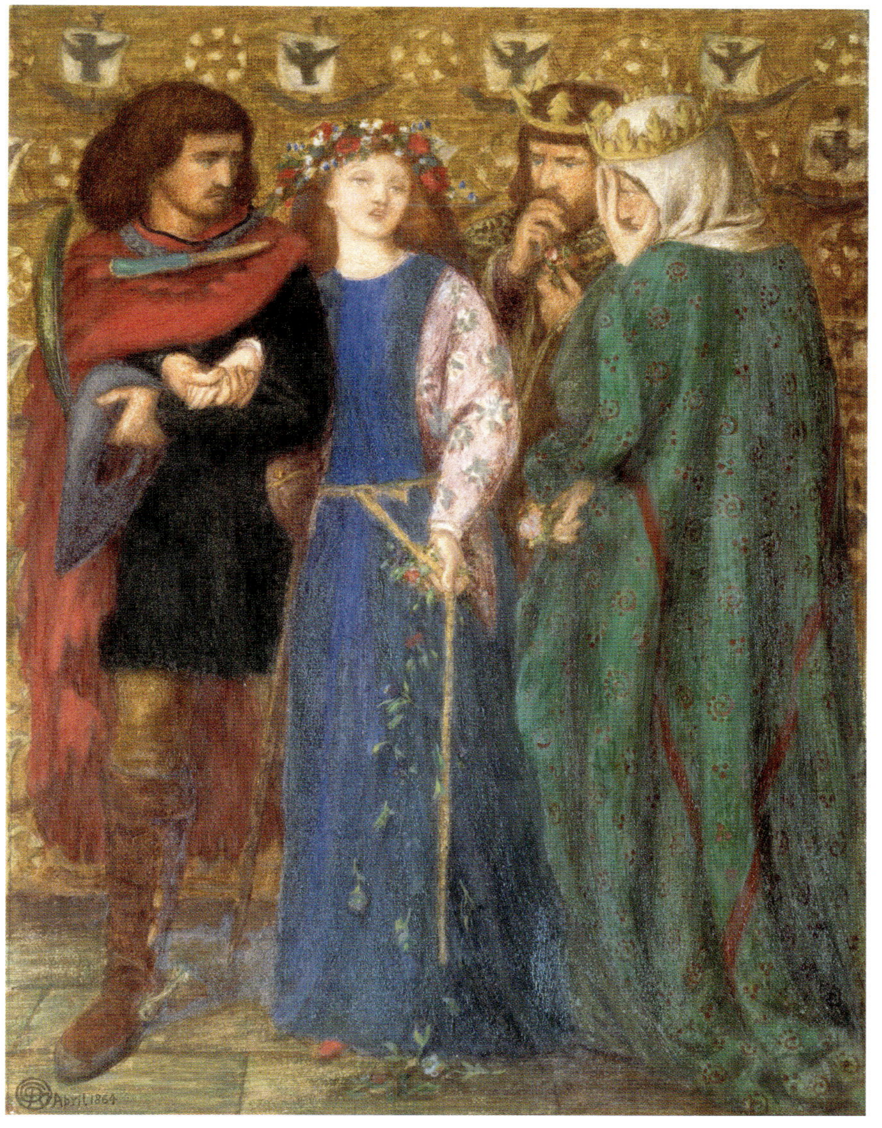

268

269. **Simeon Solomon**
London, 1840 - London, 1905
Until the Day Break and the Shadows Flee Away, 1869
Pencil and black chalk, with bodycolour and red chalk on paper, 12.9 x 15.4 cm
Bottom left: SS [monogram] / 1869
Bottom centre: UNTIL THE DAY BREAK / AND THE SHADOWS FLEE AWAY
British Museum, London

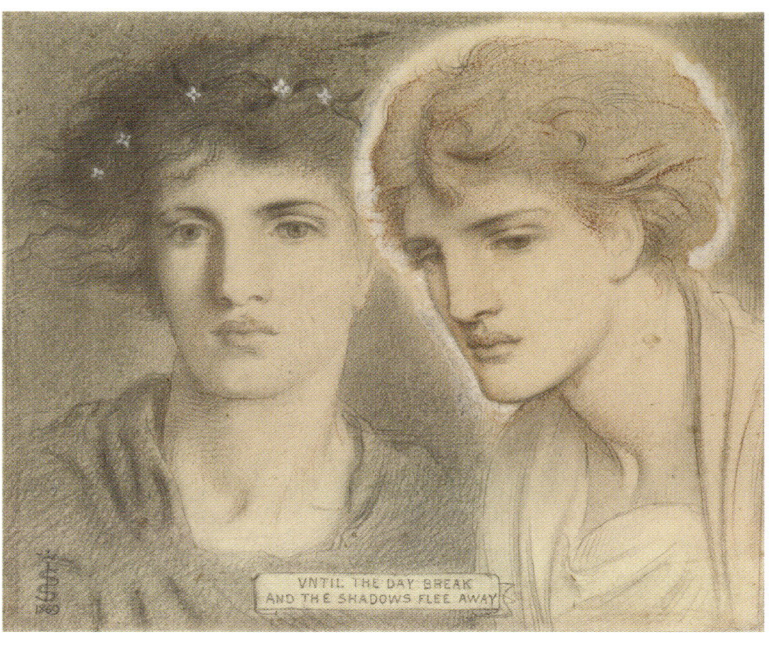

269

The title is borrowed from the *Song of Solomon* 2:17, but for the rest there is no clear connection between the drawing and the biblical book. Solomon later used the compositional technique seen here - the confrontation of two heads - in many of his Symbolist drawings. Although many of these drawings allude to night, sleep and death, they have no real narrative subject; they seek primarily to convey a mood to the viewer.

Solomon's early work borrowed from the realism of the original Pre-Raphaelite Brotherhood, but his later creations exhibit a flight from reality, characteristic of the second generation of Pre-Raphaelites, who gathered around the artists Dante Gabriel Rossetti and Edward Burne-Jones, of whom Solomon was for a time a close friend. (NP)

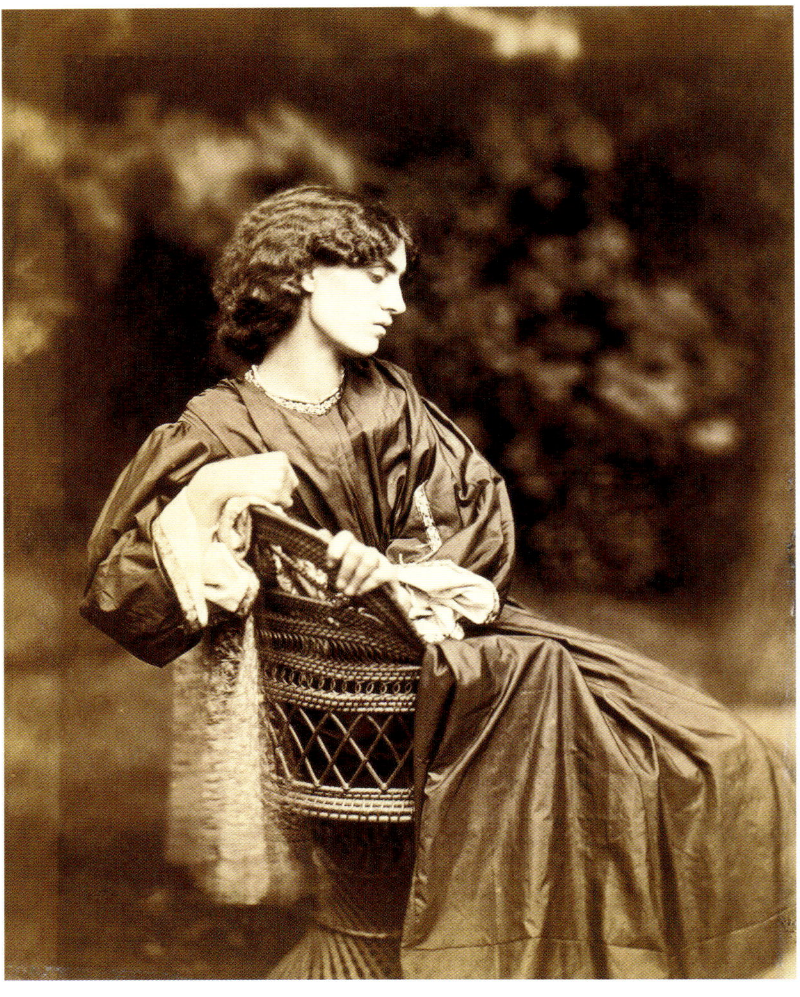

270

270. **Dante Gabriel Rossetti**
London, 1828 - Birchington on Sea, Kent, 1882
and **John Robert Parsons**
British, active 1850s - 1909
Jane Morris, from the ***Dante Gabriel Rossetti / Jane Morris Album***, 1865
Albumen silver print from wet collodion negative, 21.3 x 16.8 cm
Victoria and Albert Museum, London

Rossetti commissioned the photographer and painter J.R. Parsons to make a series of photographic studies of Jane Morris. The session took place in the garden of Rossetti's London house in Cheyne Walk on 5 July 1865. Eighteen photographs from the session were assembled in an album for Jane Morris's daughter May in 1933. In notes accompanying the album, its compiler, Gordon Bottomley, wrote that the photographs are 'in essence original compositions by Rossetti, and the proportion of figure to space is an expressive part of his intent'. The props used include chairs, a painted screen and the marquee that was a feature of the artist's garden. The sitter's dress is of interest, in that Jane Morris anticipated the loose, flowing garments typical of the Aesthetic Movement by dispensing with the hoops of the customary crinoline. The photographs informed a number of Rossetti's drawings and paintings from the later 1860s and early 1870s (Ford 2004). (MHB)

271. **Dante Gabriel Rossetti**
London, 1828 - Birchington on Sea, Kent, 1882
Elisabeth Siddal Standing at a Window, 1854
Pen and black ink on paper, 23.8 x 11.2 cm
Top left: Hastings May 1854
Victoria and Albert Museum, London

At the beginning and middle of the 1850s, Rossetti drew an extensive series of sensitive portraits of Elizabeth Siddal, a woman with whom he had an intense relationship but only married in 1860. She was his muse and model, but also his pupil: with Rossetti's support, Siddal began to paint and write poetry herself. In Rossetti's drawings, however, she is seldom seen as an active artist. As in this work, he frequently presents her as passive, dreamy - even pale and sickly.

Although Rossetti portrays her in everyday clothes and a domestic context, in this and other early drawings she already has something of a spiritual apparition, as in *Beata Beatrix* (cat. 266). (NP)

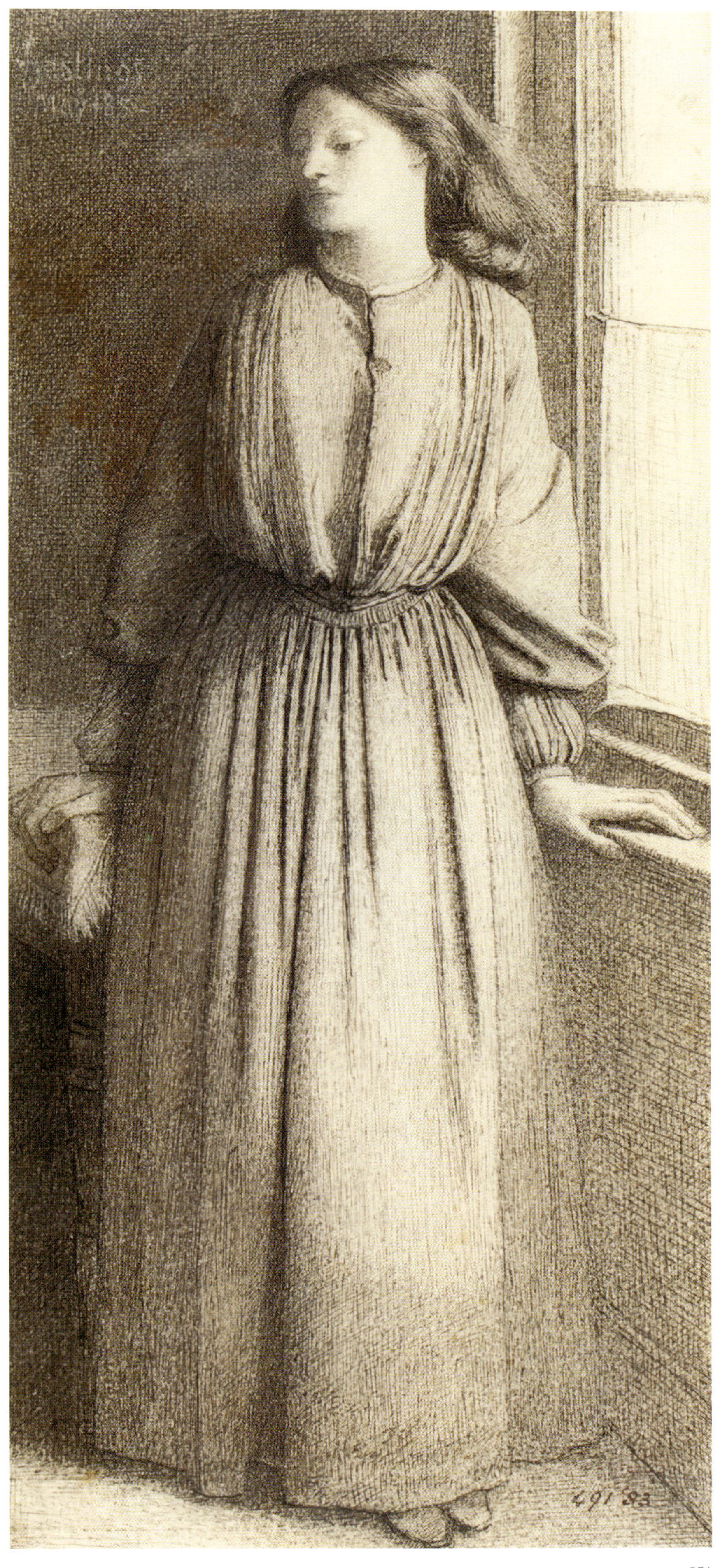

271

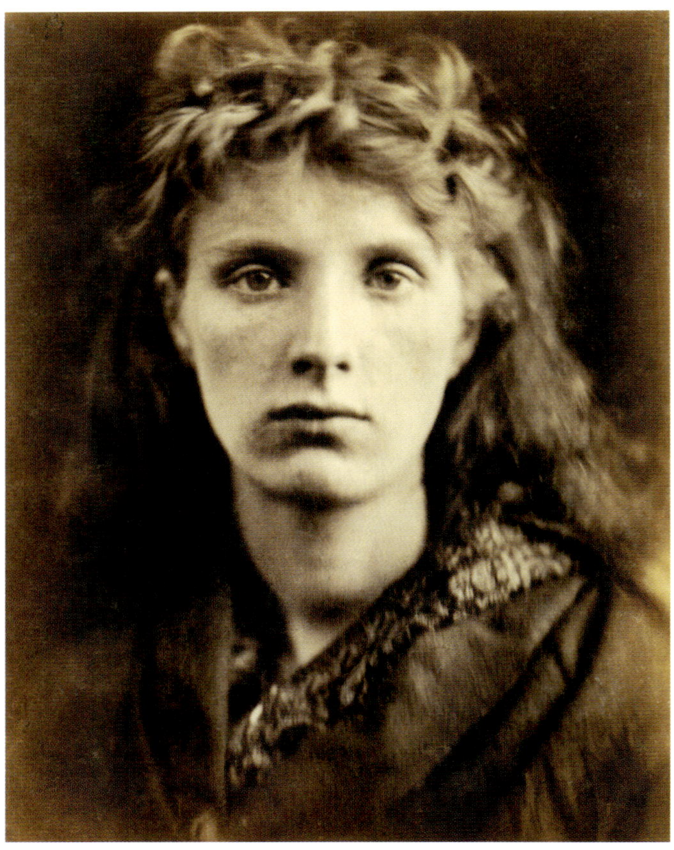

272

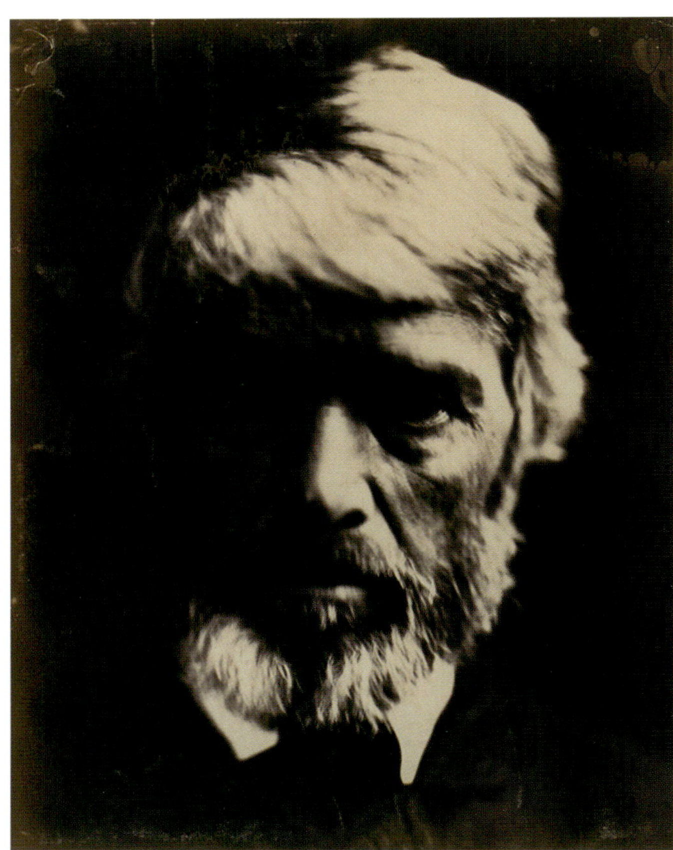

273

272. **Julia Margaret Cameron**
Calcutta, 1815 – Dikoya Valley, Sri Lanka, 1879
The Mountain Nymph, Sweet Liberty, June 1866, Mrs Keene, 1866
Carbon print, 34.1 x 26.5 cm
National Media Museum, Bradford

This photograph exemplifies Cameron's ambition of elevating the medium of photography from the commercial plane to a fine art. Instead of rendering the human subject as a bourgeois mannequin, Cameron strove for grander effects, with greater breadth of photographic draughtsmanship, and aimed at symbolic truth. The title is from John Milton's poem *L'Allegro* (1632). The photograph is one of at least six taken of Mrs Keene in June 1866. The qualities of this photograph were quickly recognized by Sir John Herschel, who described it as 'really a most *astonishing* piece of high relief – She is absolutely alive and thrusting out her head from the paper into the air. This is your own Special Style' (Cox 2003, p. 64). (MHB)

273. **Julia Margaret Cameron**
Calcutta, 1815 – Dikoya Valley, Sri Lanka, 1879
Thomas Carlyle, 1867
Carbon print, 35.4 x 27.6 cm
National Media Museum, Bradford

Cameron photographed the Scottish essayist, biographer and historian Thomas Carlyle at her sister's London home, Little Holland House. Later she inscribed one print of this famous portrait with the words, 'Carlyle like a rough block of Michael Angelo's sculpture'. The portrait is almost life-size, the lighting audacious, the effect visionary. As Julian Cox has observed, the writer's eyes 'bear only the slightest trace of illumination, and with an all-consuming gaze he peers right through the camera and seems intently fixed on the world beyond' (Cox 2006, p. 56). The portrait embodies not only Cameron's view of the role of 'Great men' in society, but that of Carlyle himself, who wrote: 'Portraits are the candle by which we read history.' (MHB)

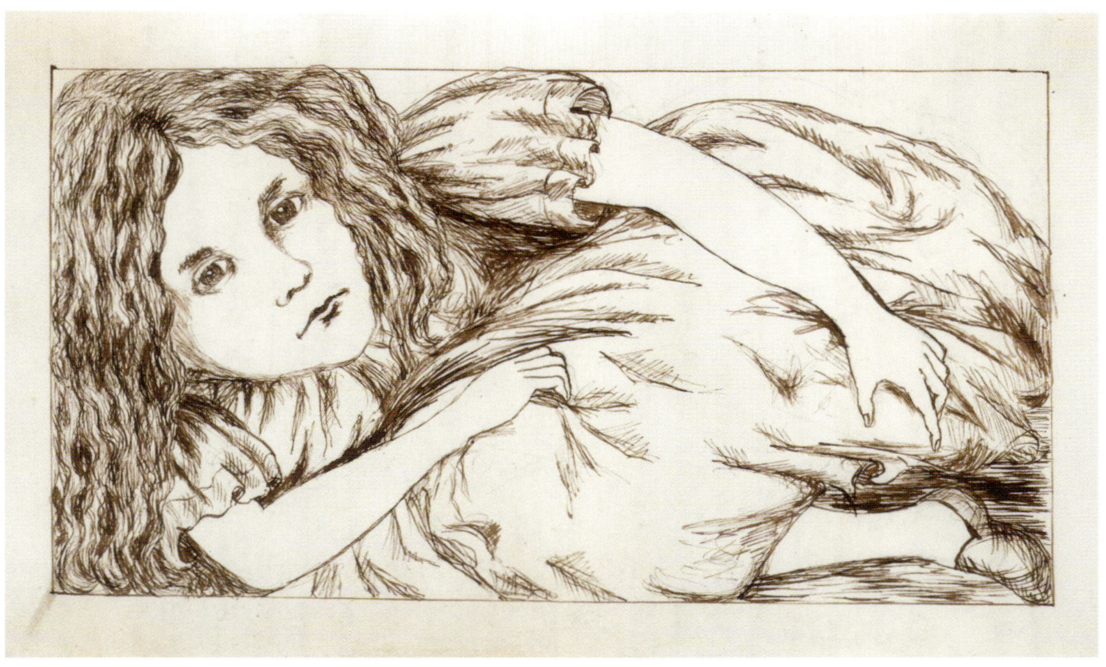

274

274. **Lewis Carroll** [ps. of Charles Lutwidge Dodgson]
Daresbury, Cheshire, 1832 - Oxford, 1898
Alice Grows and Grows in the White Rabbit's House,
from the autograph manuscript of ***Alice's Adventures Under Ground***, 1862-64
Pen and ink on paper, 12.3 x 19 cm
British Library, London

In its legendary origin, *Alice* was improvised on a summer afternoon in 1862, while its author was rowing the ten-year-old Alice Liddell down the Isis. Dodgson was only just into his thirties, a northerner who had become an Oxford mathematics don and an accomplished photographer. This unique manuscript was made for Alice, at her request. (When the fictional 'Alice' has grown to about nine foot tall, she reflects: 'There ought to be a book written about me ... and when I grow up I'll write one - but I'm grown up now ... at least there's no room to grow up anymore...') In the pages exhibited here, we are in mid-narrative. Alice, having been shrunk to three inches, has found a bottle in the White Rabbit's house. '"I know something interesting is sure to happen whenever I eat or drink anything so I'll see what this bottle does."' But the consequences are drastic: 'Before she had drunk half the bottle, she found her head pressing against the ceiling, and she stooped to save her neck being broken.'

The model for this confined, large-headed girl staring out at us lies mainly in a picture by Arthur Hughes, purchased by Dodgson from the studio just as he was making his *Alice* illustrations (see p.22, fig. 6). *The Lady with the Lilacs* has been described as 'emblematic', and is made so by 'the shallowness of the space she occupies' and 'the claustrophobic nature of her presentation as a whole', so that she becomes 'an icon of Victorian attitudes towards child-woman' (Finlay 1988). Dodgson's *Alice* drawing reinforces that claustrophobia with a dreamlike intensity; her head is based on an archetypal Rossetti 'stunner' photographed by Dodgson (the original Rossetti drawing, *Annie Miller*, would eventually belong to L.S. Lowry; see cat. 104). But *Alice's Adventures Under Ground* is also an illuminated manuscript, a work of the same revived medieval taste that inspired Blake's *Songs of Innocence* (cat. 231-235) and Morris's *Kelmscott Chaucer* (cat. 280).

One of the most rewarding territories of British art takes shape where childhood and comedy and dream converge. Something of Dodgson's disturbing strangeness is lost in Tenniel's published illustrations (cat. 58), although this leading *Punch* satirist does fulfil the parodic elements in both the *Alice* texts. Dodgson's own sensibility, however, often runs parallel to the weirdness of Richard Dadd, whose drawing *The Child's Problem* (1852, cat. 259) can be viewed through the more familiar chessboard of *Through the Looking Glass* (1867). *Alice* has cast a long shadow on both British and European artists. Writing in 1937 ('A New Poetry', *News Chronicle*, 7 June), Paul Nash linked Lewis Carroll back to Blake, Cruikshank and Edward Lear, but also forward to Nash's jazz-age contemporary Edward Burra (see cat. 81). The wonderful cross-hatched drawings by Balthus to *Wuthering Heights* (1932-35) were his youthful homage to Carroll and Tenniel, while the finest late twentieth-century British painter of the inner imagination, Ken Kiff, began his central work, *The Sequence*, in 1971 with an image entitled 'Something Unknown needs to be Eaten or Drunk'. (TH)

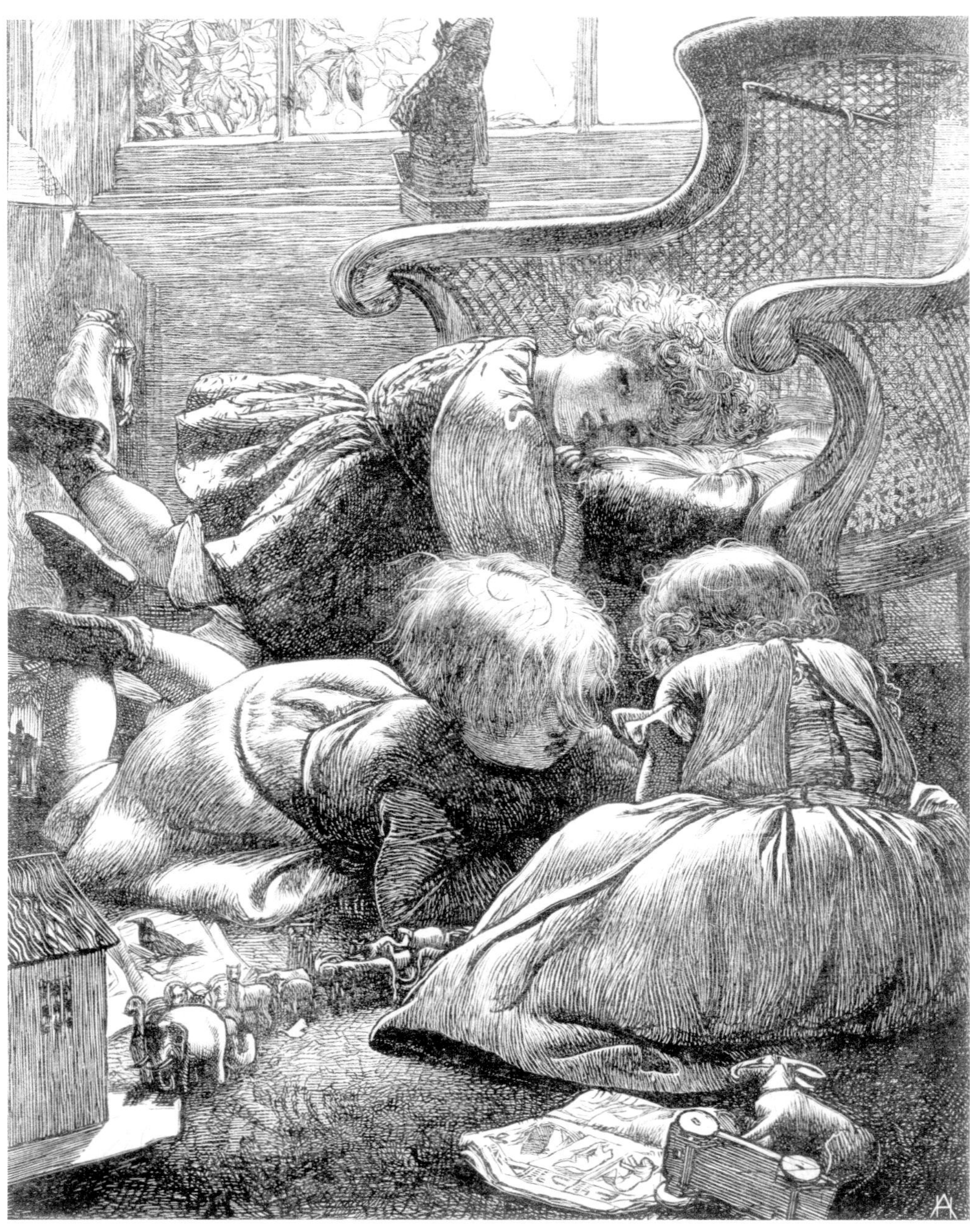

275

275. **Arthur Boyd Houghton**
Kotagiri, Madras, 1836 – London, 1875
Illustration for ***Noah's Ark*** by Dora Greenwell in ***Home Thoughts and Home Scenes***, 1865
Wood engraving, proof on paper, 17.5 x 13.5 cm
Bottom right: AH [monogram]
Engraved by the Dalziel Brothers
Published by Routledge, London
Victoria and Albert Museum, London, Given by the Dalziel Brothers

Houghton belonged to the brilliant generation of artists who came of age during the golden era of wood-engraved book illustration in the 1860s. A favourite with the Dalziel Brothers, the most important firm of engravers, he was similar in his facility as a draughtsman to Charles Keene, with whom he is sometimes compared, and certainly the equal of the more highly regarded John Everett Millais in range of subject matter and prolific output. Houghton originally had aspirations to be a painter, but the loss of the sight of one eye in a childhood accident had left him with an impaired colour sense and a tendency to severe and debilitating migraine attacks following sustained periods of work. As a result, the making of drawings for black-and-white reproduction in gift-books and magazines (*Noah's Ark* was made for an anthology of popular verse) suited him well, for he could, as he told Dante Gabriel Rossetti, complete such designs from initial sketch to finished drawing on the woodblock in just two or three hours. Houghton was a natural Bohemian and a popular and convivial figure at the Langham Art Club and in St John's Wood, where he had his studio. Ultimately dissatisfied with his lack of success as a painter, he took to drink and died at the early age of thirty-nine. (SC)

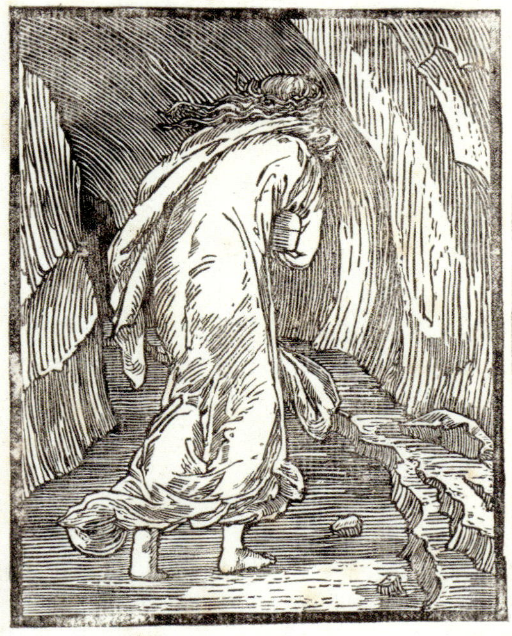

276

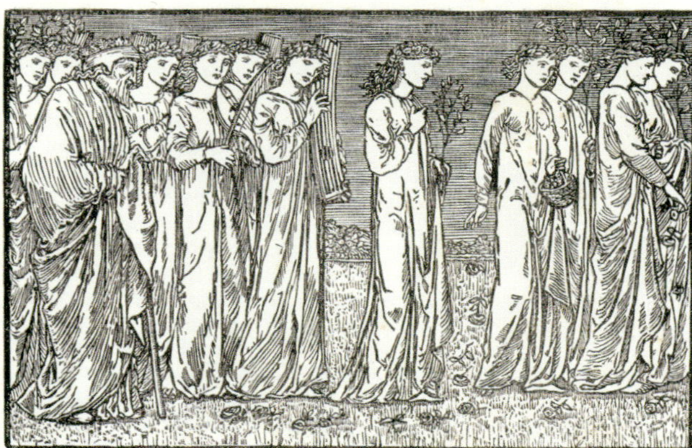

So then was Psyche taken to the hill,
And through the town the streets were void and still;
For in their houses all the people stayed,
Of that most mournful music sore afraid.
But on the way a marvel did they see,
For, passing by, where wrought of ivory,
There stood the Goddess of the flowery isle,
All folk could see the carven image smile.
But when anigh the hill's bare top they came,
Where Psyche must be left to meet her shame,
They set the litter down, and drew aside
The golden curtains from the wretched bride,
Who at their bidding rose and with them went
Afoot amidst her maids with head down-bent,
Until they came unto the drear rock's brow;
And there she stood apart, not weeping now,

277

276. **Edward Burne-Jones**
Birmingham, 1833 - London, 1898
and **William Morris**
London, 1834 - London, 1896
Psyche Entering Hades, from ***The Earthly Paradise***,
c. 1866-68
Woodcut, 10.5 x 8.2 cm
William Morris Gallery, London

277. **Edward Burne-Jones**
Birmingham, 1833 - London, 1898
and **William Morris**
London, 1834 - London, 1896
Cupid and Psyche, from the album ***Cupid and Psyche Proofs of Woodcuts***, c. 1897
Woodcut, 10.5 x 15.7 cm
William Morris Gallery, London

As students at Oxford in 1853 Burne-Jones and Morris became creative partners for life. Together with Dante Gabriel Rossetti, co-founder of the original Pre-Raphaelite Brotherhood, they formed the core of a second Pre-Raphaelite movement, which placed more emphasis on the visionary than on the detailed depiction of nature.

In the beginning, both had chosen careers in the church, but the young idealists soon realized that they wanted to change the world through art. Burne-Jones became a painter and Morris a designer, poet and, in 1861, head of his own firm, Morris & Co. (originally established as Morris, Marshall, Faulkner & Co.), which produced objects in the applied arts – textiles, wallpaper, furniture, stained glass and tapestry. One of Morris's lifelong goals was to elevate the quality of the applied arts by combining functionality with beauty and using traditional methods of production. He was also an important inspiration for the Arts and Crafts Movement. Burne-Jones and Morris worked together on countless projects for Morris's firm.

Morris wrote 'Cupid and Psyche' as one of twenty-four stories in verse for his longest work, *The Earthly Paradise* (1868-70). This encompasses Morris's vision of a more harmonious, pre-industrial world, an idea that animates his entire oeuvre – in literature as well as in the decorative arts.

Because he was an admirer of early printed books, Morris wanted to publish *The Earthly Paradise* with five hundred woodcuts after drawings by Burne-Jones. In the summer of 1866, Burne-Jones began sketching more than a hundred designs, seventy of which were destined for 'Cupid and Psyche'. Morris himself cut fifty woodblocks. In 1867, the project was called to a halt, probably because of typographical problems. One of those problems was finding a good balance between the blocks of text and the powerful lines of the illustrations and ornamental motifs. Cat. 280 is a proof sheet from *The Earthly Paradise* using a typeface that Morris designed based on medieval typography. It dates from around 1897 and was made by the Kelmscott Press, a press Morris established to keep the whole production process, including typography, in his own hands. However, *The Earthly Paradise* was never completed; 'Cupid and Psyche' was only published, with original woodcuts after drawings by Burne-Jones, in 1974. (NP)

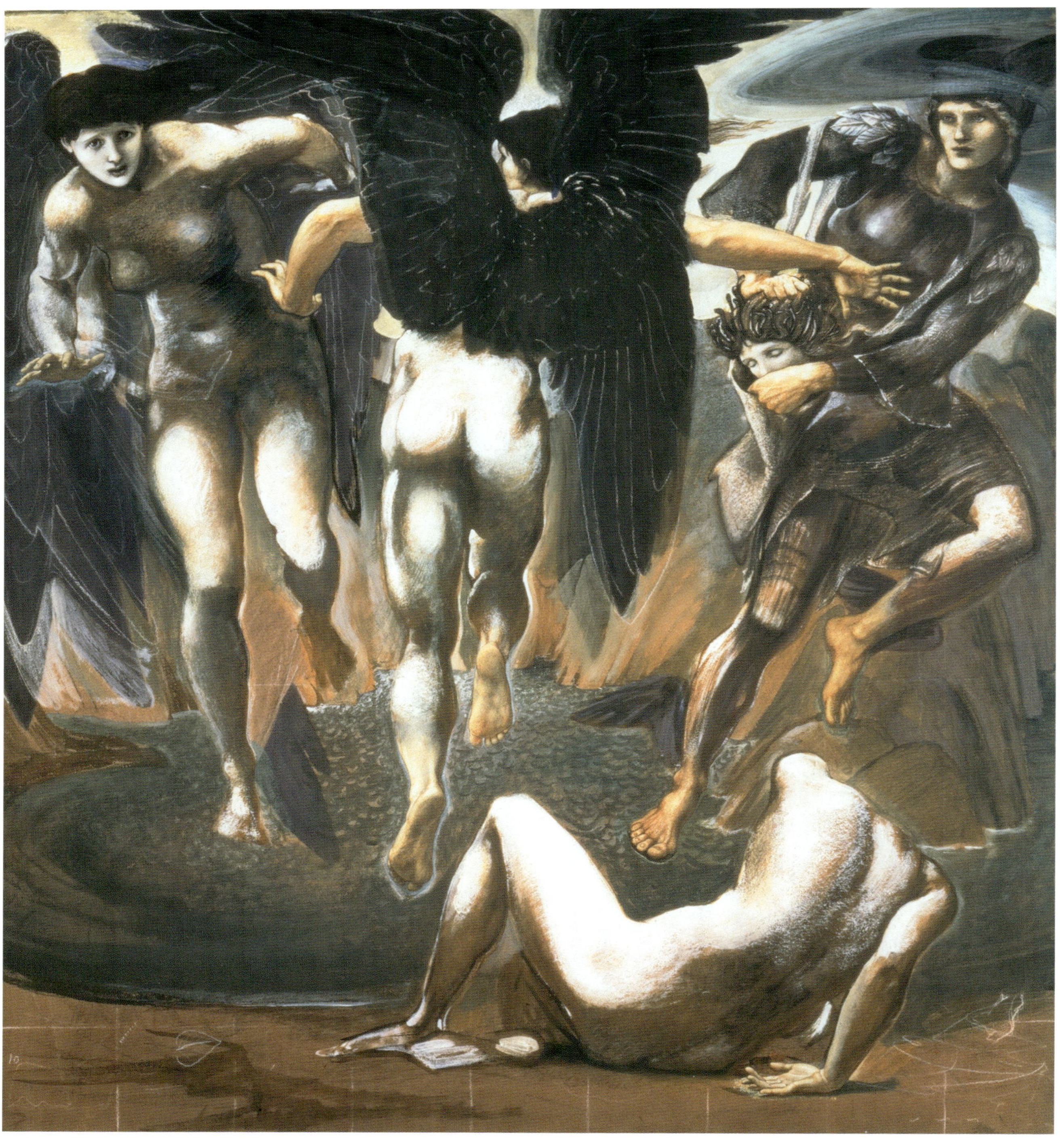

278

278. **Edward Burne-Jones**
Birmingham, 1833 – London, 1898
The Perseus Series: The Death of Medusa II, c. 1881-82
Gouache on canvas, 152.5 x 136.5 cm
Southampton City Art Gallery

279. **Edward Burne-Jones**
Birmingham, 1833 – London, 1898
The Perseus Series: The Baleful Head, 1885
Oil on canvas, 155 x 130 cm
Staatsgalerie, Stuttgart

The *Perseus Series* was commissioned from Burne-Jones in 1875 by future prime minister Arthur Balfour as decoration for his London home. However, Burne-Jones never completed the cycle. In addition to many studies, there is a series of cartoons in gouache (Southampton) and four compositions executed in oil (Stuttgart).

In *The Perseus Series* Burne-Jones relates the Greek myth of the hero Perseus, who was commanded by King Polydectes to fetch the head of the Gorgon Medusa, which had live snakes for hair. The head had the magical ability to transform all those who looked upon it into stone. Burne-Jones was familiar with the story from the work of classical

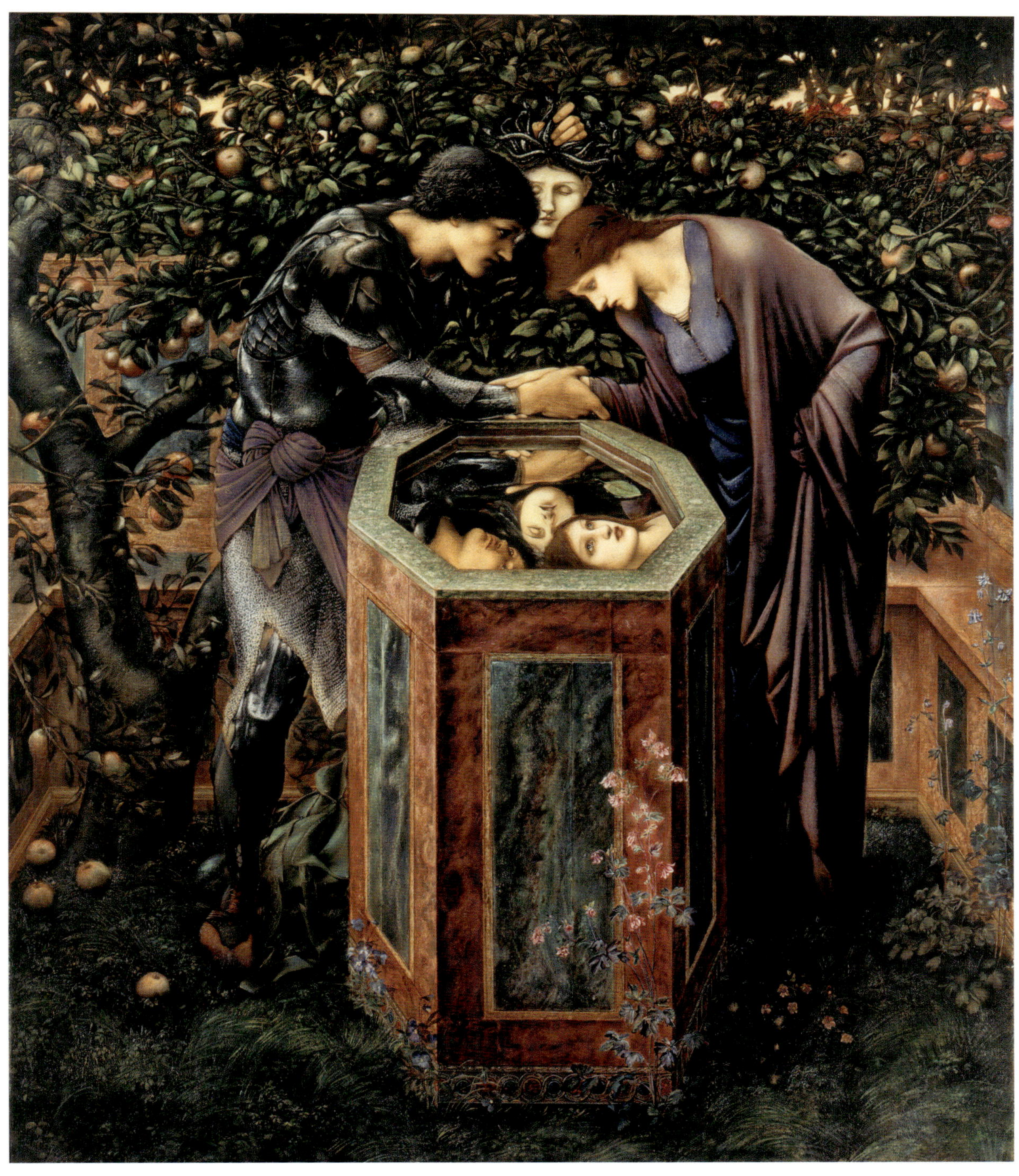

279

authors, but particularly from 'The Doom of King Acrisius' in *The Earthly Paradise* (1868-70) by his associate William Morris. It is this version that Burne-Jones follows in his paintings.

In *The Death of Medusa II* (cat. 278), Perseus has just decapitated Medusa and escapes from her sisters thanks to his winged sandals and a helmet that makes him invisible. This is an unusually dynamic composition for Burne-Jones. *The Baleful Head* (cat. 279), by contrast, is static and introspective. Perseus has rescued the princess Andromeda from a sea-monster and now wishes to marry her. In order to demonstrate his divine origins, he shows her the serpent-covered head of Medusa – safely, with the help of a reflection in a well. This allowed Burne-Jones the opportunity to design an intriguing play of faces and their reflections.

In the *Perseus Series* the narrative aspect is subordinate; Burne-Jones does not attempt to describe, as the Pre-Raphaelite Brotherhood would have done, but to evoke an imaginary, often frightening, world. (NP)

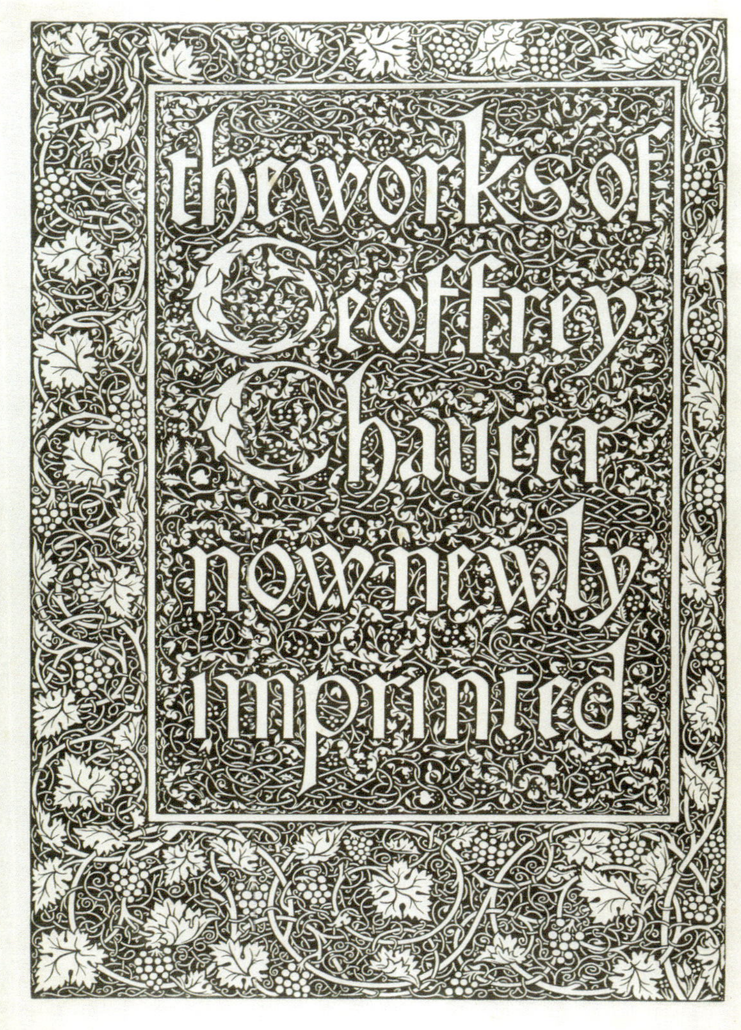

the works of Geoffrey Chaucer now newly imprinted

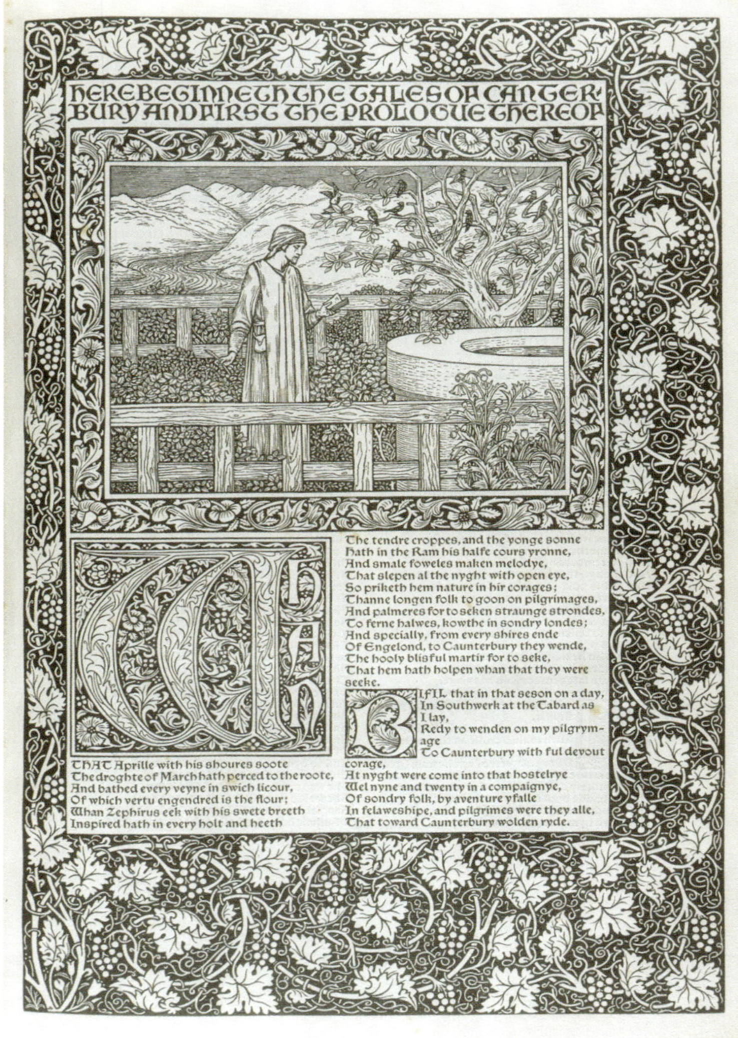

HERE BEGINNETH THE TALES OF CANTERBURY AND FIRST THE PROLOGUE THEREOF

WHAN THAT Aprille with his shoures soote
The droghte of March hath perced to the roote,
And bathed every veyne in swich licour,
Of which vertu engendred is the flour;
Whan Zephirus eek with his swete breeth
Inspired hath in every holt and heeth
The tendre croppes, and the yonge sonne
Hath in the Ram his halfe cours yronne,
And smale foweles maken melodye,
That slepen al the nyght with open eye,
So priketh hem nature in hir corages;
Thanne longen folk to goon on pilgrimages,
And palmeres for to seken straunge strondes,
To ferne halwes, kowthe in sondry londes;
And specially, from every shires ende
Of Engelond, to Caunterbury they wende,
The hooly blisful martir for to seke,
That hem hath holpen whan that they were seeke.
BIFIL that in that seson on a day,
In Southwerk at the Tabard as I lay,
Redy to wenden on my pilgrymage
To Caunterbury with ful devout corage,
At nyght were come into that hostelrye
Wel nyne and twenty in a compaignye,
Of sondry folk, by aventure yfalle
In felaweshipe, and pilgrimes were they alle,
That toward Caunterbury wolden ryde.

280

280. **Edward Burne-Jones**
Birmingham, 1833 - London, 1898
and **William Morris**
London, 1834 - London, 1896
The Works of Geoffrey Chaucer now newly imprinted,
1890-1896 (printed in 1896)
Woodcuts by W.H. Hooper after drawings by
Edward Burne-Jones
Book, printed by William Morris at the Kelmscott Press,
43.4 x 30.4 cm
Yale Center for British Art, Paul Mellon Collection, New Haven

Ever since their student days in Oxford, Edward Burne-Jones and William Morris had been great admirers of medieval illuminated manuscripts and Renaissance printed books. In the 1860s they worked together – one as an illustrator, the other as a typographer and designer of ornaments – on an edition of *The Earthly Paradise* (see cat. 276-277). However, they never succeeded in producing the book of their dreams, which they saw as a total work of art and compared to a medieval cathedral. It was not until the 1890s, when Morris established the Kelmscott Press, that the two artists could work intensively on the design of books. They then created a number of works in which Burne-Jones's drawings and Morris's typefaces and rich floriated border decorations form a harmonious whole. After many years of preparation, the 'Kelmscott Chaucer' appeared in 1896, only months before Morris's death. This book was considered the crowning achievement of their many years of collaboration, as well as one of the most significant expressions of nineteenth-century book design. (RH)

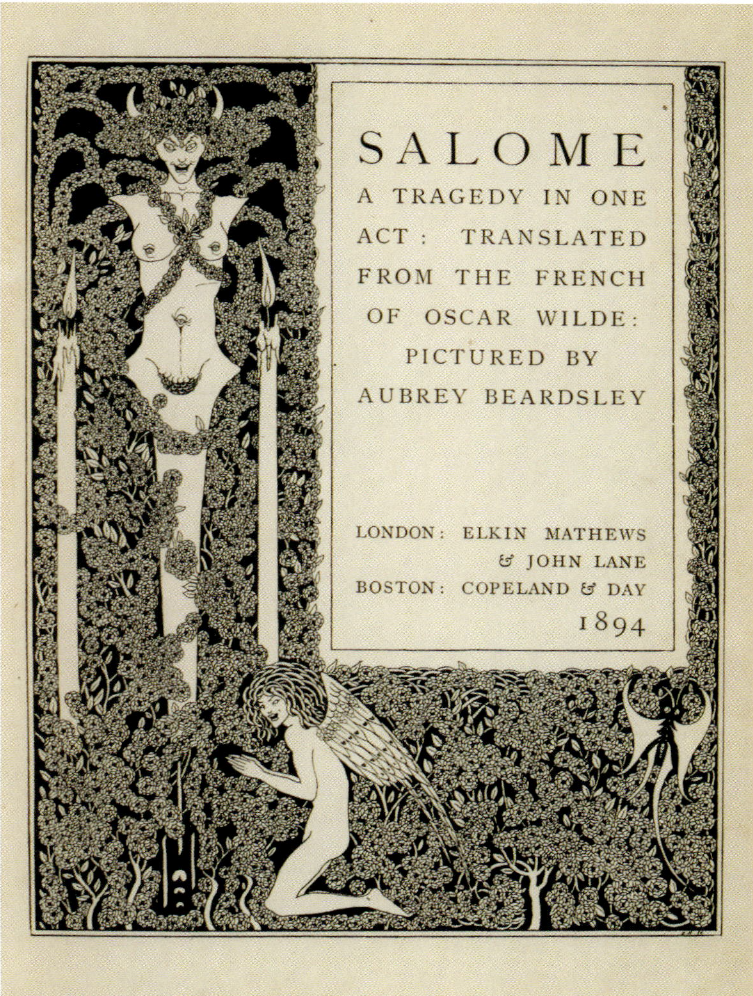

SALOME
A TRAGEDY IN ONE
ACT: TRANSLATED
FROM THE FRENCH
OF OSCAR WILDE:
PICTURED BY
AUBREY BEARDSLEY

LONDON: ELKIN MATHEWS
& JOHN LANE
BOSTON: COPELAND & DAY
1894

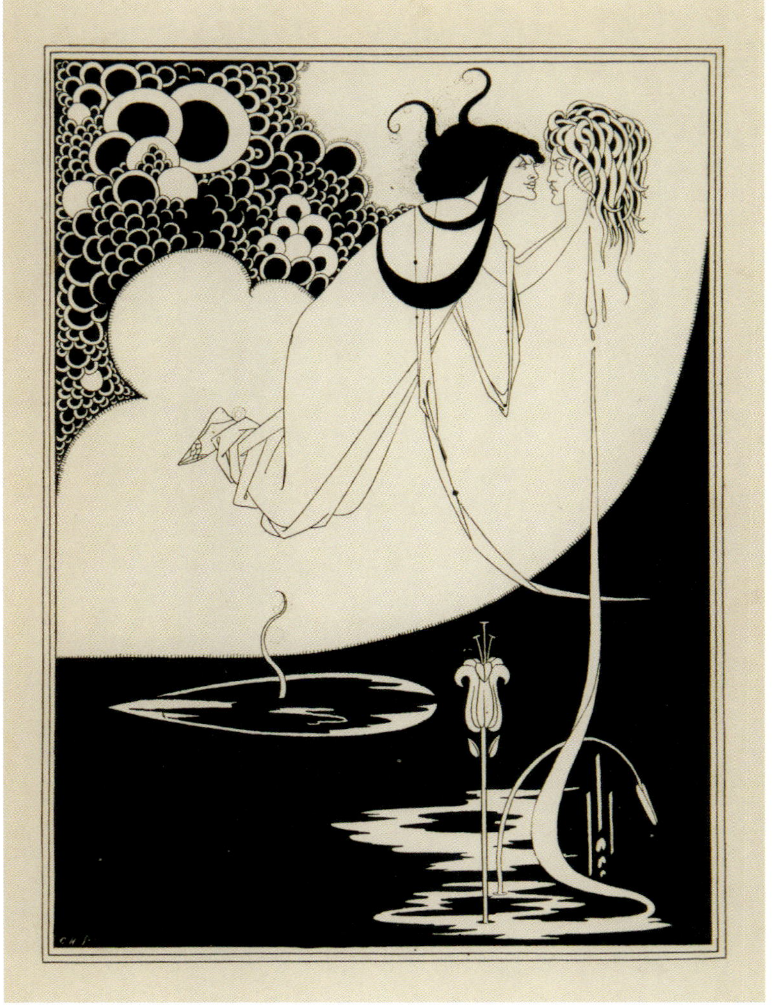

281

281. **Aubrey Beardsley**
Brighton, 1872 – Menton, 1898
The Climax, from ***Salome. A tragedy in one act: Translated from the French of Oscar Wilde: Pictured by Aubrey Beardsley***, 1894
Line block reproduction
Book published by Elkin Mathews and John Lane, London, and Copeland and Day, Boston, 21.6 x 15.8 cm
Private Collection

This is one of the illustrations Beardsley made for the English translation of Oscar Wilde's play *Salome* (1893), originally written in French. (The original drawing has been lost, but reproductions from a portfolio published in 1906 still survive.) In Wilde's version, Salomé harbours erotic feelings for John the Baptist. These remain unfulfilled until she has him beheaded and can finally kiss his – dead – mouth. Beardsley shows us the moment just after the kiss. With all its sexual connotations, the illustration is a gift for Freudians, who have written on it extensively, but the actual, phenomenal, graphic aspects also demand attention. Beardsley was a master of abstract decorative design and one of the first truly modern British artists. (NP)

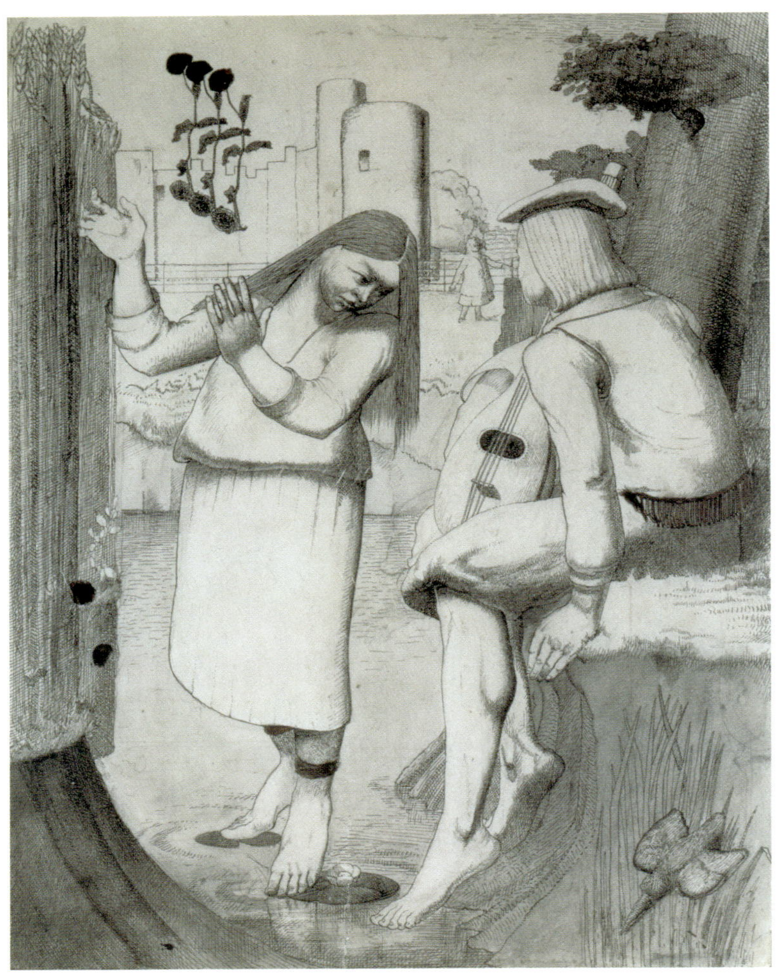

282

282. **Stanley Spencer**
Cookham, Berkshire, 1891 - Cliveden, Buckinghamshire, 1959
The Fairy of the Waterlily Leaf, c. 1909
Pen and ink on paper, 41.5 x 32 cm
Stanley Spencer Gallery, Cookham

The sixteen works by Spencer in *British Vision* cover only part of the range of this extraordinarily various artist. Brought up in the Thameside village of Cookham, Spencer began to emerge as a teenage prodigy while still a student at the Slade School of Fine Art. He was divided: by day, practising the cool forensic life-drawing prescribed by his teacher, Henry Tonks; but back in Cookham, exploring a more fanciful imagination. In this commissioned illustration for a local children's writer, a minstrel sits on the riverbank, while a very large-boned fairy conjures roses, grouped like musical notes, out of his lute. A hard, 'primitive' or medievalizing line, transmitted by the German Nazarenes to Millais and Rossetti (see cat. 262-263), as well as to Tenniel's Alice books (cat. 58) is part of Spencer's earliest underpinning. (TH)

283. **Stanley Spencer**
Cookham, Berkshire, 1891 - Cliveden, Buckinghamshire, 1959
Study for Apple Gatherers, c. 1912
Pencil, pen and ink and wash on paper, 27.6 x 32.1 cm
Tate, London, Bequeathed by Sir Edward Marsh through the Contemporary Art Society 1954

In Spencer's next ambitious composition after *The Nativity* (cat. 286), the Earthly Paradise or Golden Age seems again invoked, but with male and female oddly separate. He may have considered this drawing (another Slade prize-winner) too 'classical' or distanced. In the oil painting completed the following year, those decorous boys and girls will be transformed under the influence of Gauguin's Tahitians into heavy-featured primitives, whose huge muscular limbs can barely contain their gigantic fruits. The painting (now in the Tate, London) was first bought by Henry Lamb (see cat. 63). (TH)

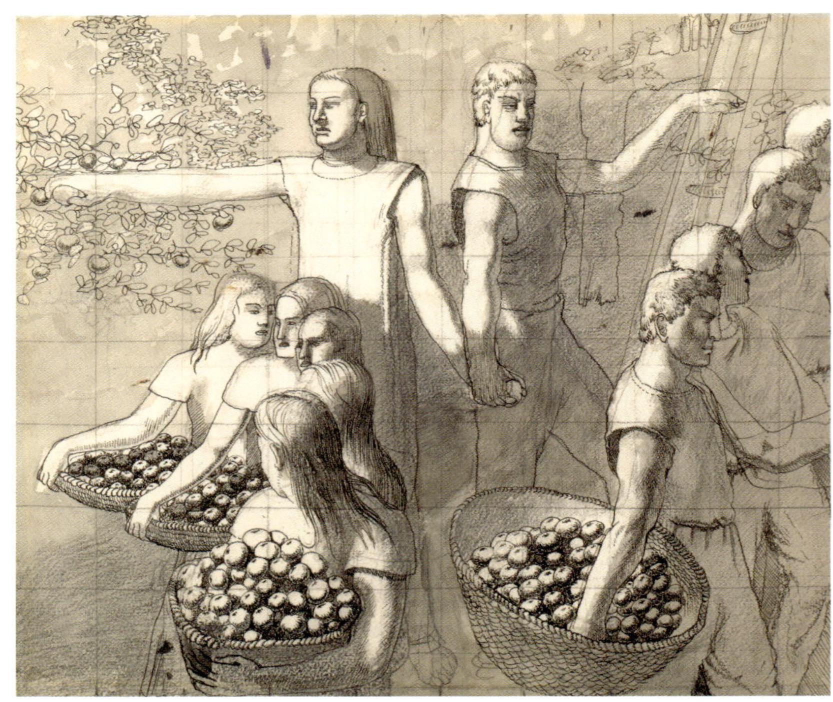

283

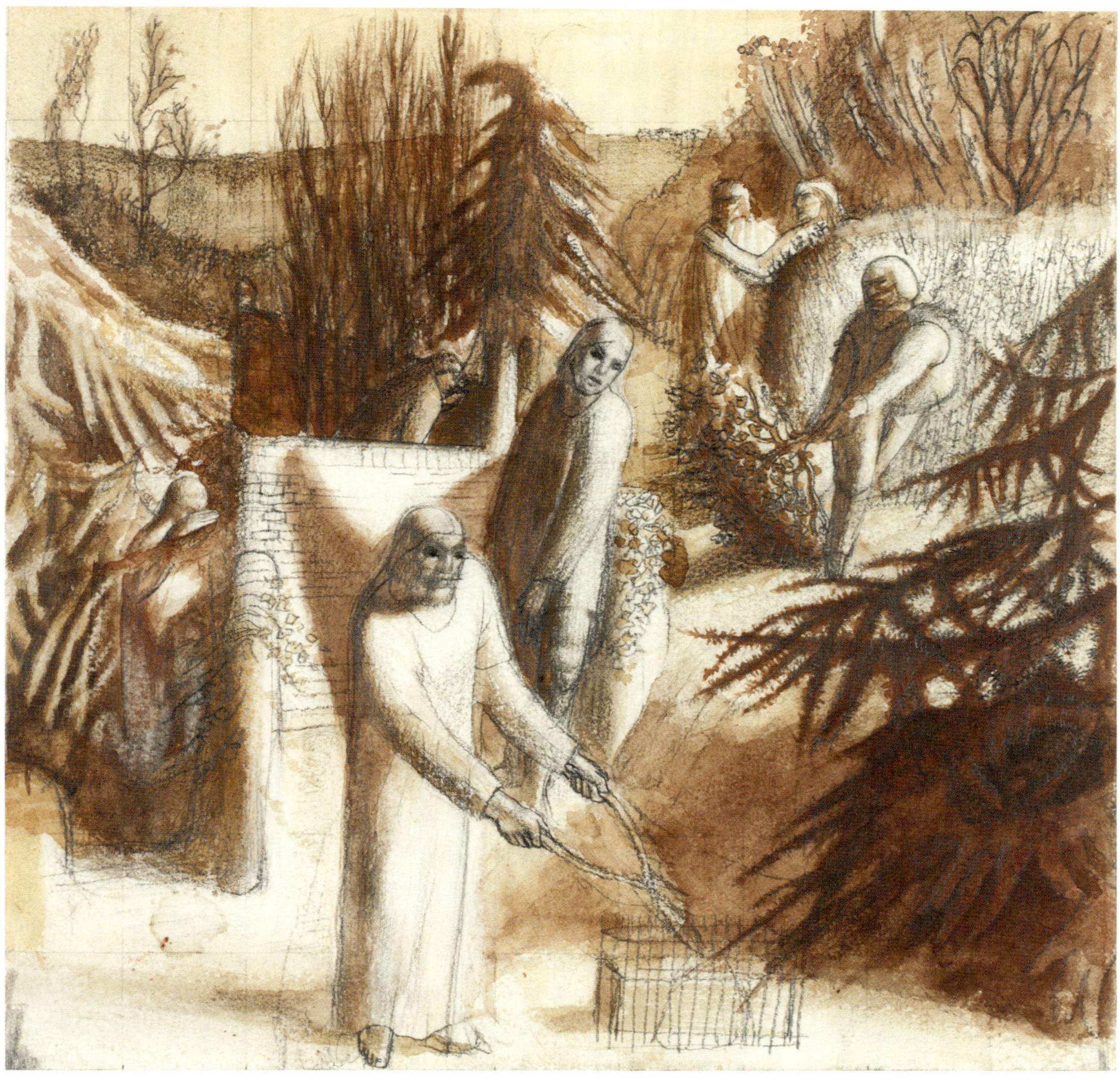

284

284. **Stanley Spencer**
Cookham, Berkshire, 1891 - Cliveden, Buckinghamshire, 1959
Study for Zacharias and Elizabeth, c. 1913-14
Pencil and brown wash on paper, 26.7 x 22 cm
Victoria and Albert Museum, London

This squared-up preliminary drawing for Spencer's greatest single early painting (now owned jointly by Sheffield and Tate) shows his close affinity with the young Samuel Palmer, whose Shoreham works he had probably seen at the Tate in 1913: a fusion of landscape and religion, of close local observation together with the recovery of childhood biblical associations. At the opening of St Luke's Gospel, the angel announces to Zacharias that his aged wife Elizabeth will bear a child - the future John the Baptist. Zacharias is shown at sacrifice, placing a coal on the altar, but with the gesture of a dowser; Gabriel comes behind him like some strange sleepwalker. The mystery occurs in winter in a specific Cookham walled garden. 'I wanted,' Spencer wrote in 1937, 'to absorb and finally express the atmosphere and meaning the place had for me.' In the eventual painting (see p.27, fig. 12) the zigzag brick wall will be transformed into a smooth whitewashed curve. (TH)

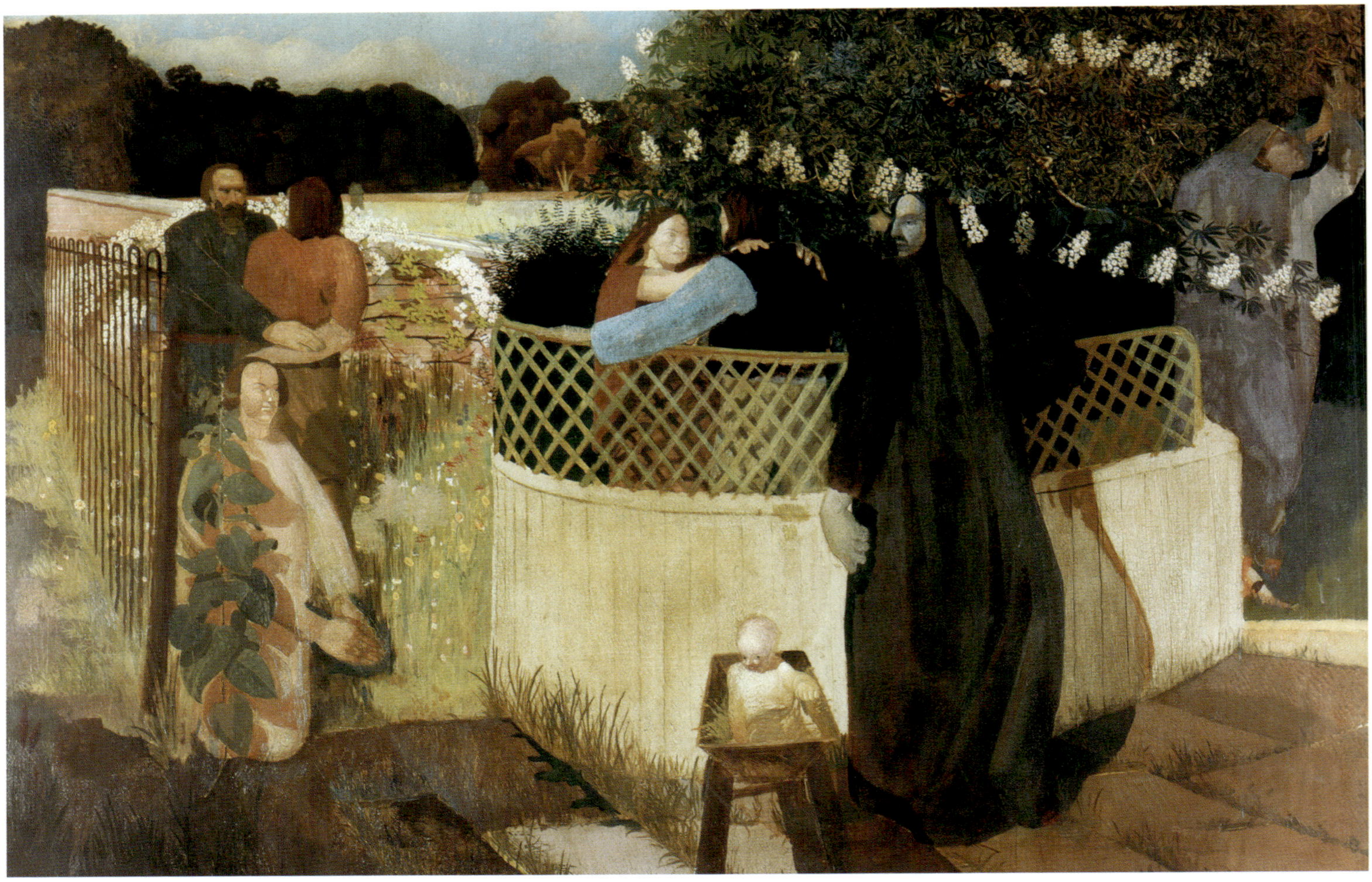

286

285. **Stanley Spencer**
Cookham, Berkshire, 1891 – Cliveden, Buckinghamshire, 1959
John Donne Arriving in Heaven, 1911
Oil on canvas, 38 x 40.5 cm
Private Collection
(on loan to the Fitzwilliam Museum, Cambridge)

Painted at home in Cookham, while the twenty-year-old Spencer was in his fourth year at the Slade, *John Donne* won him immediate recognition. His closest Slade friendship was with a couple six years older, Gwen Darwin and Jacques Raverat, who gave Spencer two key books: Donne's *Sermons*, and Ruskin's writings on Giotto. (They would also purchase the newly completed picture.) The poet-pilgrim is skirting heaven's high plateau, a schematized essence of the Berkshire chalk downs; the white figures stand like the shining menhirs of Avebury, casting their late-afternoon shadows along the turf. White forms on a steep green ground will recur in Spencer's work: gravestones, sheep, angels. The stark flattened simplicity fuses Giotto with recent French painting (especially Maurice Denis) – both transmitted through Roger Fry. In 1912 *John Donne* would hang in Fry's 'Second Post-Impressionist Exhibition'. (TH)

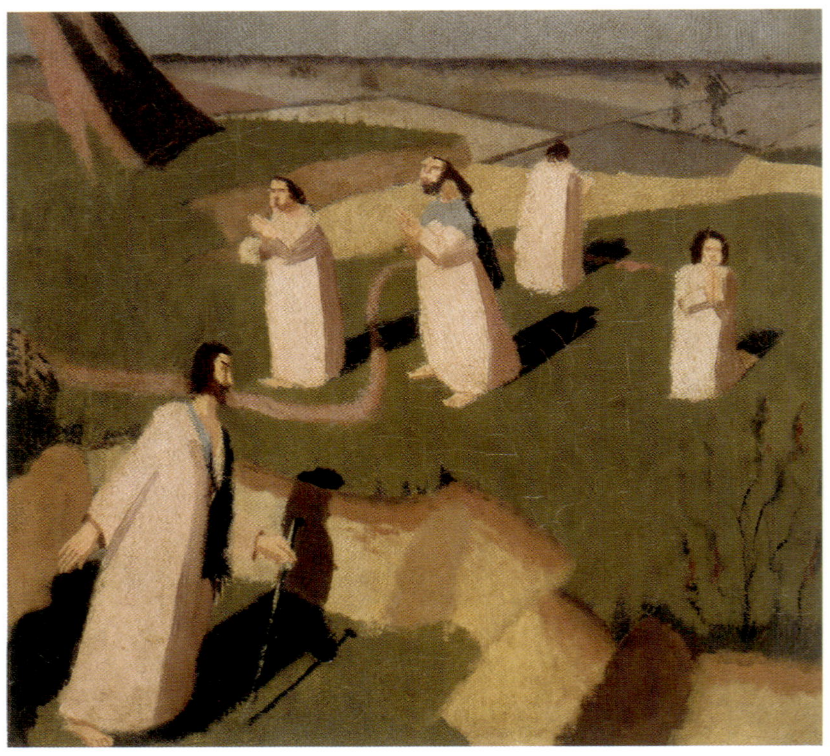

285

286. **Stanley Spencer**

Cookham, Berkshire, 1891 - Cliveden, Buckinghamshire, 1959

The Nativity, 1912

Oil on canvas, mounted on panel, 102.9 x 152.4 cm

UCL Art Collections, University College London

In his first large-scale picture, Spencer created his first great 'altarpiece of place', where the ostensible subject - the infant in the food trough - is secondary to the encompassing Cookham landscape setting. The centre is dominated by the enfolding trellis-fence; two embracing couples, magi or shepherds, seem extensions of this weather-beaten rustic construction. Mary is a dark Giottesque figure (close to *trecento* representations of Dante); on the right margin, Joseph is partly a reminiscence of Botticelli's *Primavera*, but also of the 'Joachim' figure from Rossetti's early *Childhood of Mary Virgin*. Echoes of Gaugin's *Bonjour Monsieur Gauguin* have also been identified. A newborn world, a second Eden, is unified within a lyrical and painterly handling - especially in the delicate grasses and blossoms and chestnut tree 'candles'. *The Nativity* won Spencer the coveted prize for the Slade's 'summer composition', in both the landscape and figure categories. (TH)

287. **William Roberts**

London, 1895 - London, 1980

The Return of Ulysses, c. 1913-14

Oil on canvas, 30.5 x 45.7 cm

Nottingham City Museums & Galleries

This image, which is hard to read, presents a roomful of Penelope's doomed suitors around the red void of the floor. Its stylization comes out of Roberts's involvement in Wyndham Lewis's Rebel Art Centre, working alongside David Bomberg (cat. 288). As their own figures moved towards the mechanistic, all three rejected the decorative aesthetic of Roger Fry's Omega workshop, aspiring to the wiry, tough contours of Pollaiuolo's engraving *The Battle of Nude Men*. Roberts had already made a remarkable transition since entering the Slade as a fifteen-year-old and coming into the orbit of Stanley Spencer at the moment of his *John Donne* (cat. 287). Brought up in Hackney, the son of a carpenter, and first trained as a commercial designer, Roberts did not share Spencer's pastoral Christianity. 'Neo-Primitivism' was soon superseded by 'English Cubism', and although still a teenager, he found himself painting some of the most drastically 'modernist' works of his era. An anonymous reviewer, probably Middleton Murry, wrote that Roberts 'had managed to compress the development of a lifetime into six months ... but one instance of the general insolvency which has followed an overdose of modernism' (*Westminster Gazette*, 21 May 1914). (TH)

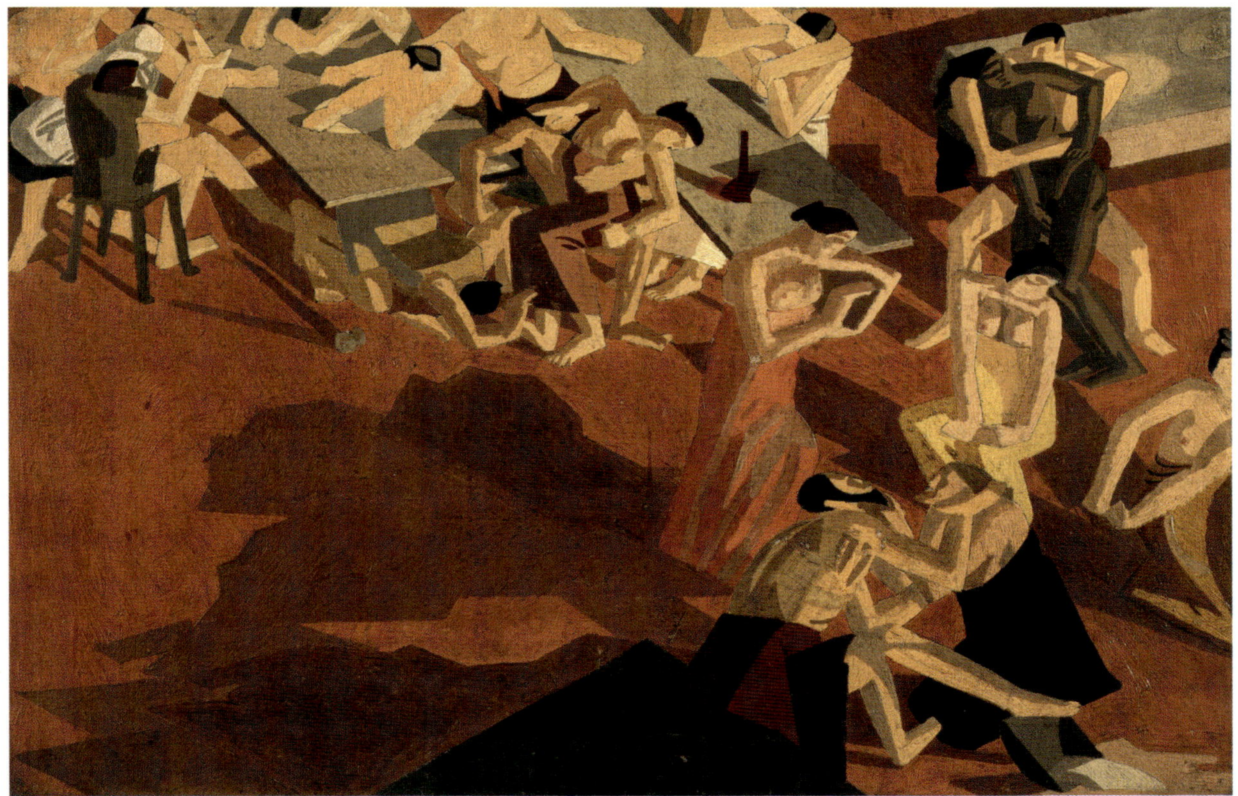

287

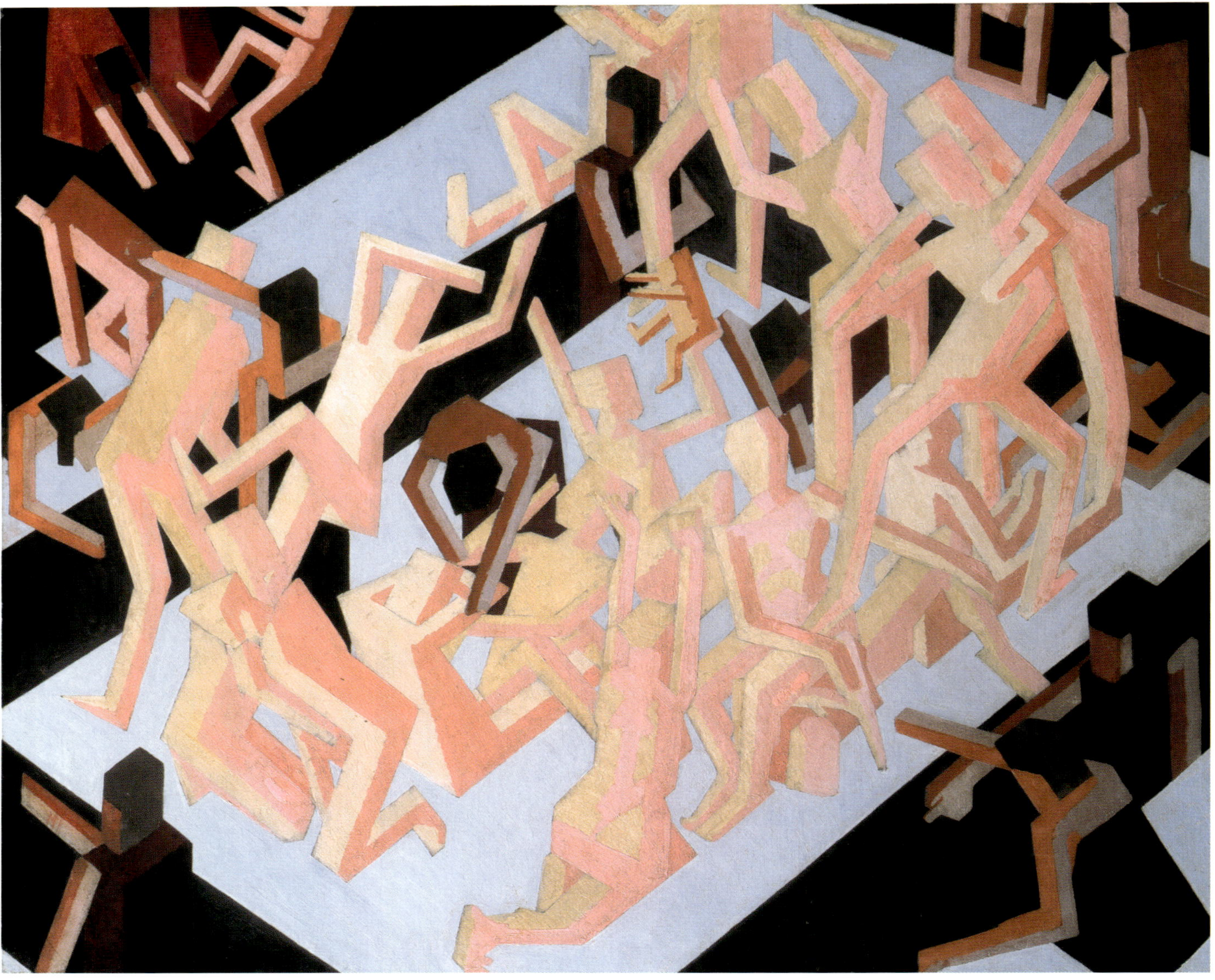

288

288. **David Bomberg**
Birmingham, 1890 – London, 1957
Vision of Ezekiel, 1912
Oil on canvas, 114.3 x 137.2 cm
Bottom right: Bomberg 12
Tate, London, Purchased with assistance from the Morton Bequest through the Contemporary Art Society 1970

Although neglected during his own lifetime, Bomberg was an active force in the development of British modernism. In this ambitious painting of 1912 he became one of the first British arts to reflect the European languages of Cubism and Futurism in his work. Across a series of preliminary drawings he evolved a composition dominated by angular, stylized figural forms. The title refers to a subject from the Old Testament, a deliberate reflection of Bomberg's Jewish background. The painting seems to illustrate a passage in the book of Ezekiel where the prophet is transported by God to a valley strewn with skeletons, 'and the breath came into them and they lived, and stood up upon their feet, an exceeding great army'. Even without knowledge of these verses, it is easy to interpret the joyful, animated nature of the surging mass of figures. Bomberg may have chosen the theme of resurrection and hope in response to the recent death of his mother. (NM)

289. **Percy Wyndham Lewis**
Amherst, Nova Scotia, 1882 – London, 1957
Study in Blue, 1912
Pen and ink, watercolour, wash, on paper, 25.5 x 20.5 cm
Bottom left: P Wyndham Lewis / 1912
Peter Simon Family Trust

Lewis's art contained a strong visionary element, which was integral to the expression of the totalitarian philosophy he had developed. He applied the fractured planes of Cubism and the energetic lines of Futurism to imaginary figurative fantasies as a means through which to develop his theoretical exploration of modernist human existence. In *Study in Blue*, two primitive

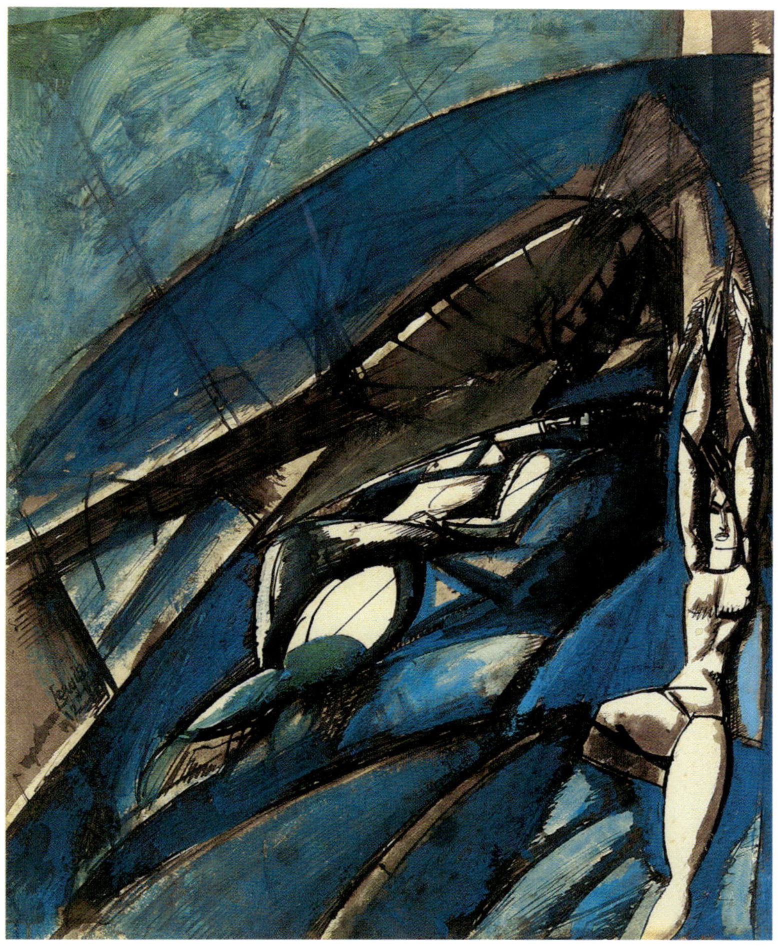

289

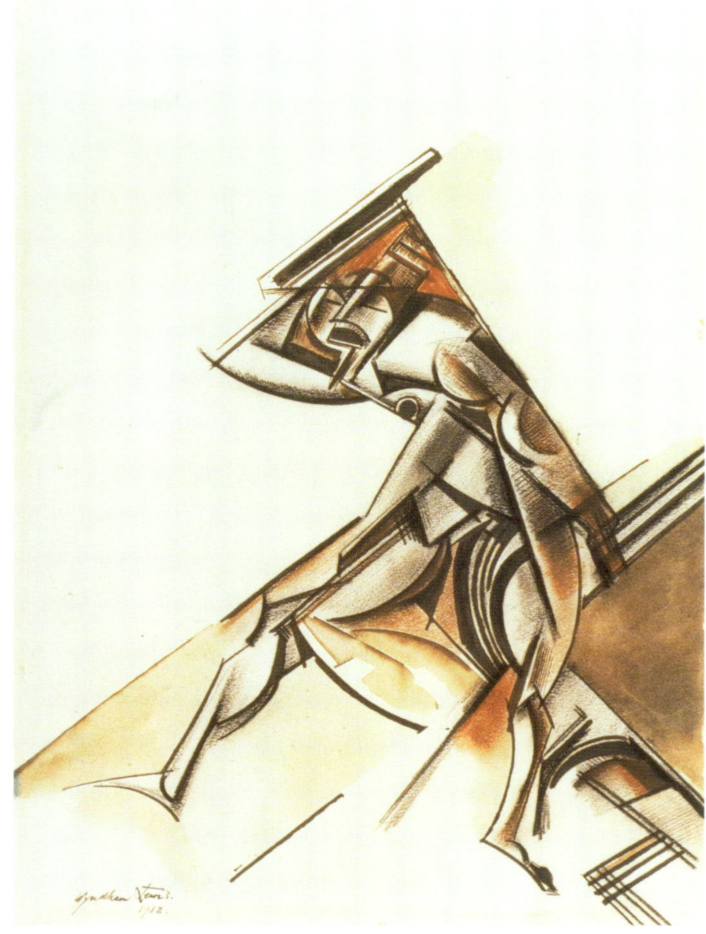

290

figures appear to heave themselves forcefully clear of the rolling, surging planes of an intense monochromatic landscape. The idea of creation emerging from energetic struggle was one outlined by the philosopher, Henri Bergson in his book *Creative Evolution* (1907). As a young man Lewis had attended Bergson's lectures at the Collège de France in Madrid, and the Frenchman's theories were extremely influential in the development of Lewis's own philosophies. (NM)

290. **Percy Wyndham Lewis**
Amherst, Nova Scotia, 1882 - London, 1957
The Vorticist, 1912
Watercolour on paper, 42.2 x 32.2 cm
Bottom left: Wyndham Lewis. / 1912.
Southampton City Art Gallery

Lewis's avant-garde ideas crystallized in the years before the First World War with the formation of 'Vorticism' and the establishment of an active group of like-minded artists and writers. The concept of the vortex, an all-encompassing swirl of energy with a still, reflective core, was adopted by the group as a metaphor for their shared intellectual programme. Vorticist artists, led by Lewis, adopted geometric and mechanistic forms as a suitable visual language through which to describe and explore the experience of modern life.

Lewis's watercolour *The Vorticist* is a prophetic visualization of the spirit of the group's principles, combining dynamism and aggression with aesthetic control and style. The pose, colouring and facial expression of the aggressively advancing figure is reminiscent of the martial warriors of traditional Japanese woodcuts and reveals Lewis's interest in the art of the Far East. (NM)

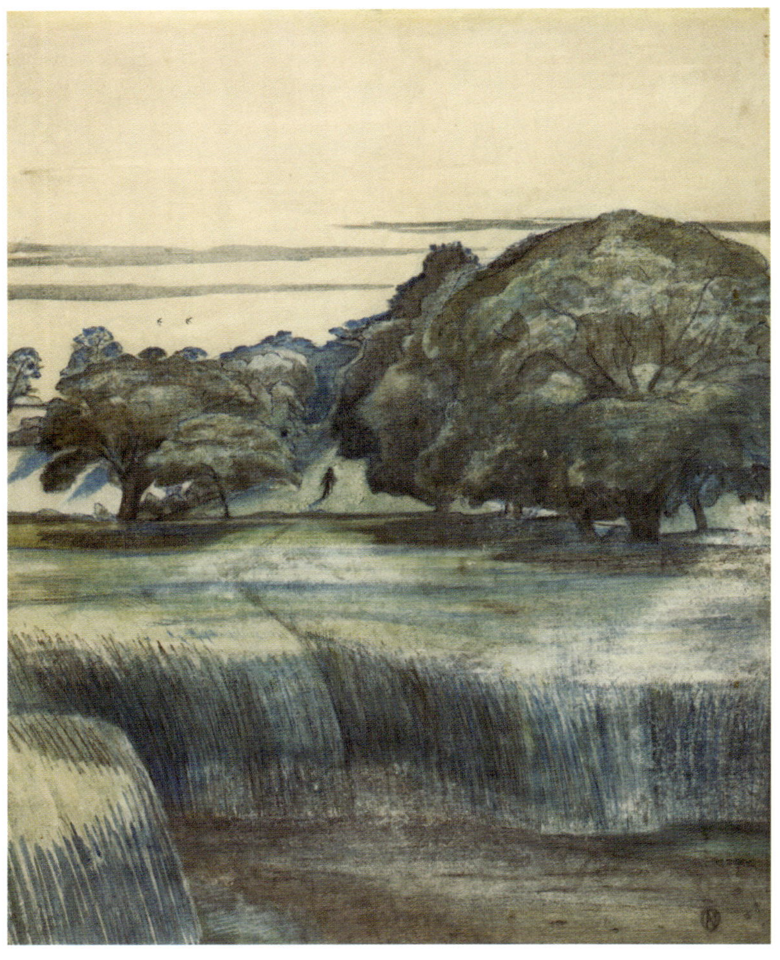

291

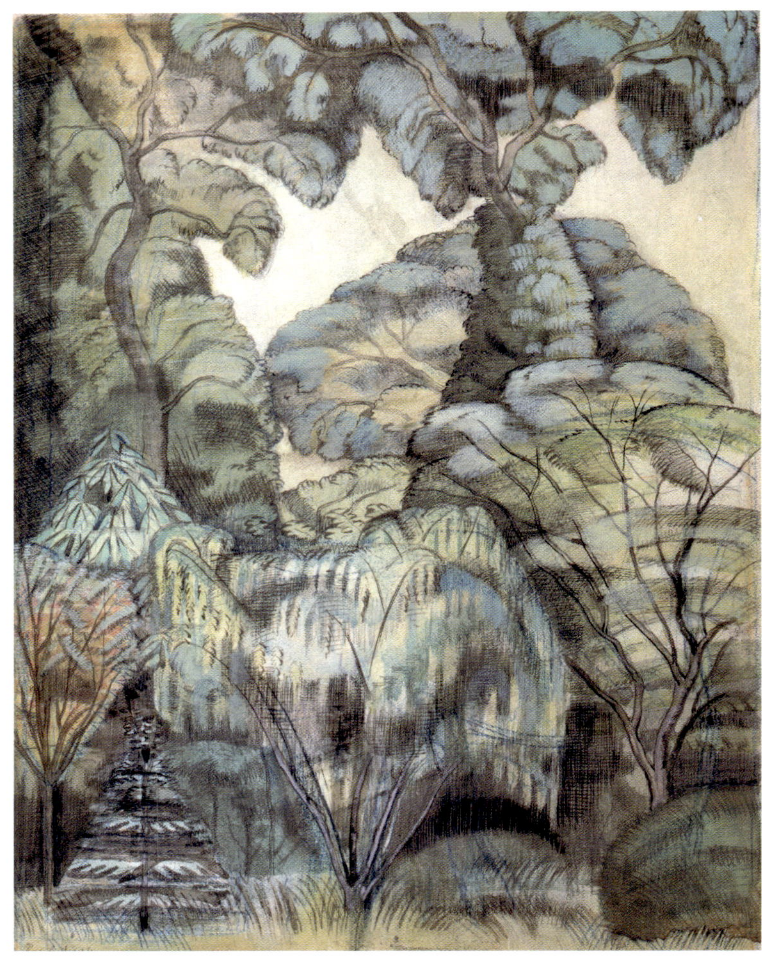

292

291. **Paul Nash**
London, 1889 – Boscombe, Hampshire, 1946
The Wanderer, 1911 [?]
Watercolour, with blue chalk, heightened with pencil on paper, 48.2 x 37.8 cm
Bottom right: PN [monogram]
British Museum, London

292. **Paul Nash**
London, 1889 – Boscombe, Hampshire, 1946
Trees in Bird Garden, Iver Heath, 1913
Watercolour, pen and chalk on paper, 40.6 x 31.1 cm
Bottom left: Paul Nash
Birmingham Museum & Art Gallery

In his early years as an artist, Nash worked exclusively with pencil, chalk, pen and ink and watercolour on paper. The works from this period, therefore, are intimate and delicately coloured drawings, which suited the subtle, dreamlike mood of his approach to landscape. The places he depicted were often ordinary native scenes imbued with a heightened sense of reality, such as the soft, dusky mystery of the wooded field in *The Wanderer*. The first significant location to inspire him was the 'Bird Garden', the view from the morning room in his family home at Iver Heath. According to Nash, this familiar and beloved site possessed an innate, unreal 'startling beauty', which he was able to explore through stylistic arrangement of the alluring forms of the trees. In his autobiography, *Outline*, he wrote that the garden's 'magic lay within itself, implicated in its own design and its relationship to its surroundings' (Nash 1949, pp. 106-7). (NM)

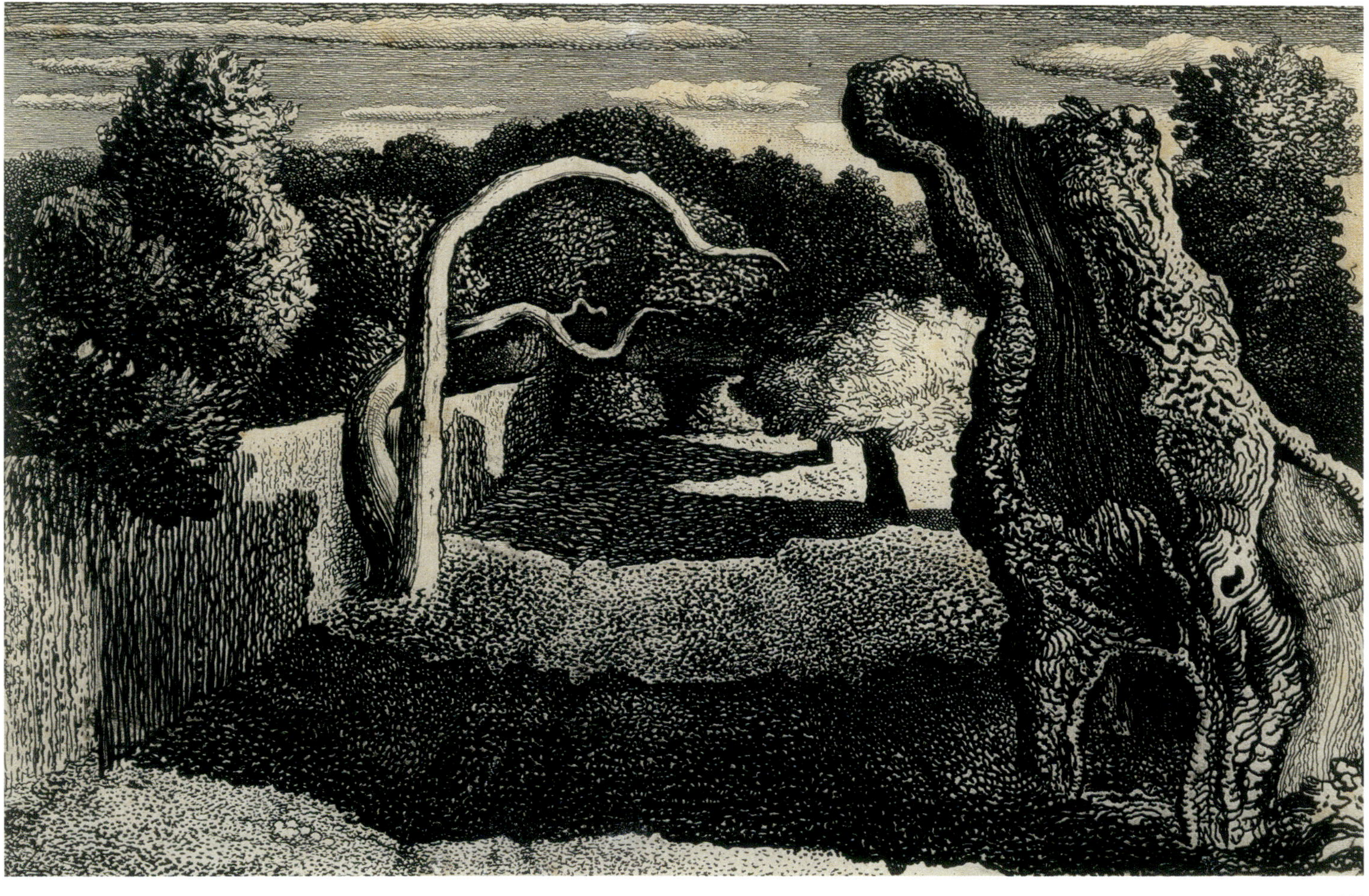

293

293. **Graham Sutherland**
London, 1903 - London, 1980
Pastoral Scene with Chestnut Tree, 1930
Etching, 13 x 19.5 cm
Bottom right: Graham Sutherland
Private Collection

Sutherland's etching illustrates the conflicting associations manifest within depictions of the British landscape between the wars. On the one hand, the visual language employed by the artist recalls the Arcadian vision of the prints of Samuel Palmer. The dense detail and tonal contrasts with which Sutherland has described the sylvan scene is reminiscent of the style of Palmer's rural idylls. The revival of interest in a romanticized pastoral Britain reflected the conscious national desire for a return to an earlier tranquil innocence in the years following the First World War. On the other hand, the central focus of the image is not a vital, fertile countryside but the twisted, impotent forms of two dead trees. Sinister, elongated shadows pattern the ground, and any sign of human activity is entirely absent. The pastoral landscape therefore has assumed a modern sense of foreboding and is ultimately a site of anxiety and tension. (NM)

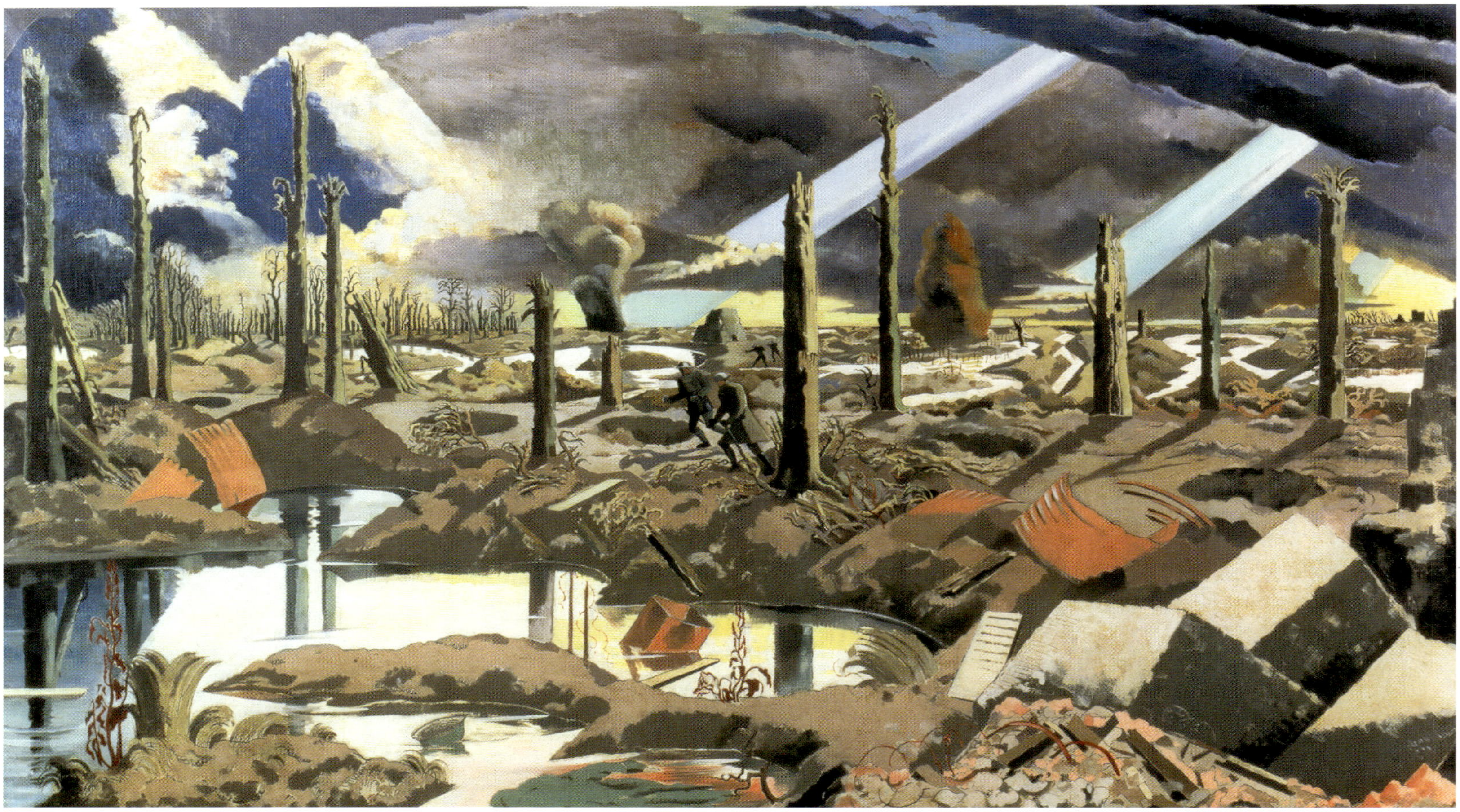

294. **Paul Nash**
London, 1889 – Boscombe, Hampshire, 1946
The Menin Road, 1919
Oil on canvas, 182.8 x 317.5 cm
Bottom left: Paul Nash / 1919
Imperial War Museum, London

Nash was commissioned by the British Ministry of Information in April 1918 to make a work for a proposed Hall of Remembrance. He began working in a barn studio near Chalfont St Peter in Buckinghamshire: 'How difficult it is ... to put [the luxuriant green country] aside and brood on those wasted in Flanders, the torments, the cruelty & terror of this war. Well it is on these I brood for it seems the only justification of what I do now – if I can rob the war of the last shred of glory, the last shine of glamour' (Paul Nash to Gordon Bottomley, 16 July 1918; Abbot and Bertram 1955, p. 99). Although Andrew Causey (Causey 1980, p. 81) argues that the composition appears too studiously arranged and that it lacks the intensity of works such as *Void,* 1918 (Ottawa, National Gallery of Canada), the constructed maze-like quality of the landscape, transcribed by the erratic patterns of flooded trenches, creates a sense of deliberate disorder and chaotic immorality, in which perceptions and expectations are upturned and the rules of the game unknowable. The road itself is devastated beyond recognition; explosions replace natural forms; bursts of sunlight become gun barrels and the reflections of trees, iron columns. (RT)

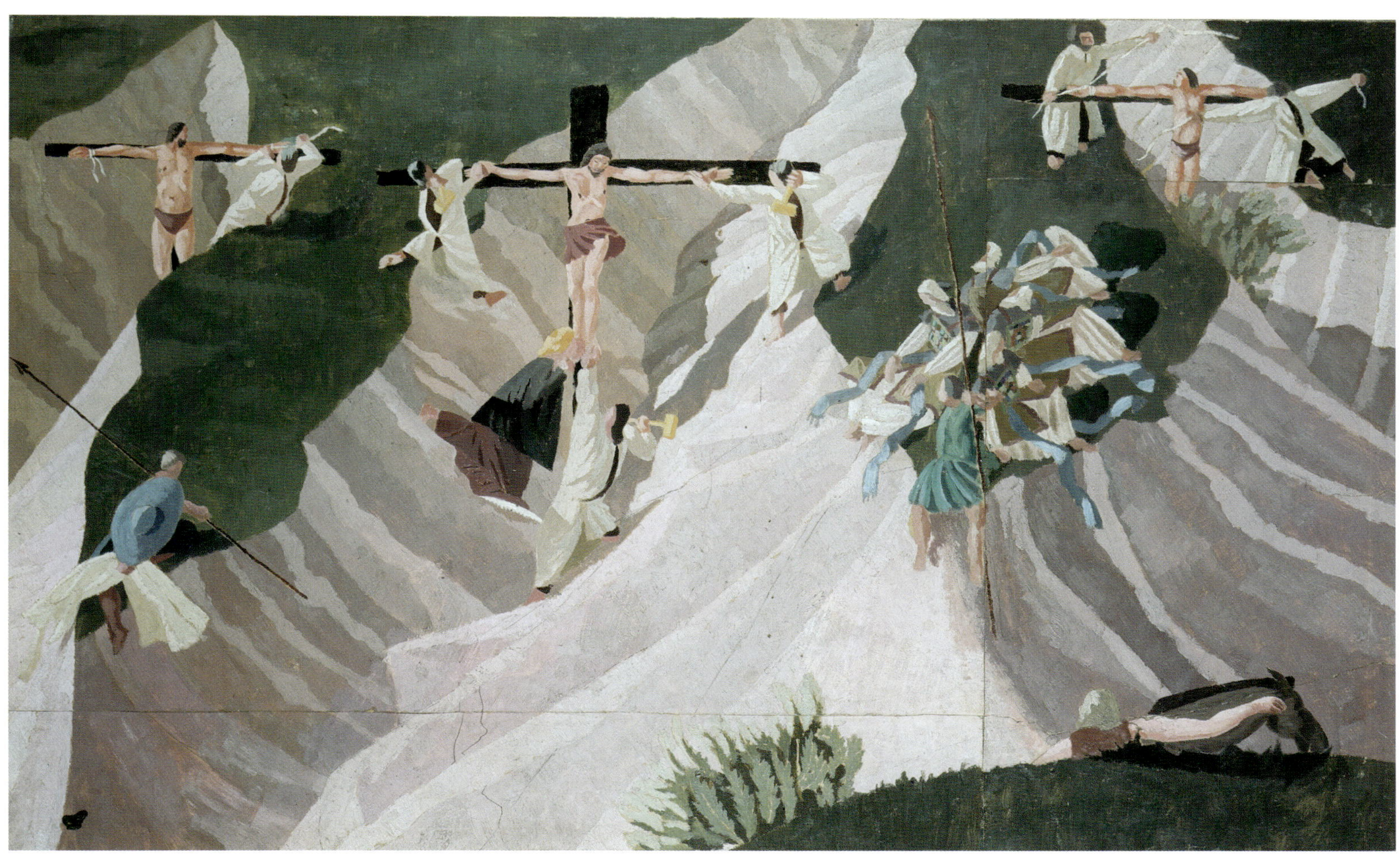

295

295. **Stanley Spencer**
Cookham, Berkshire, 1891 – Cliveden, Buckinghamshire, 1959
The Crucifixion, 1921
Oil on paper, mounted on canvas, 70.7 x 111.6 cm
Aberdeen Art Gallery & Museums Collections

Spencer spent almost four years away at war, first as an orderly in a Bristol hospital, then in the Macedonian campaign. Returning to Cookham at the end of 1918, he experienced a 'loss of Eden', as well as what he called 'war depression'. His ambitious mural schemes mostly failed to develop beyond sketch stage, while his work exhibits a new coolness of colour and handling and a formalized flat design. This *Crucifixion* was a preliminary study for the Village Memorial Hall at Steep, Hampshire, where Spencer was the guest of an older painter, Muirhead Bone. It starts out from a memory of a specific Macedonian chalk landscape, with 'three long gashes'. In this distant Golgotha, the thieves to either side of Christ are being roped to their crosses; but at the centre, three men are swinging their yellow hammers. (TH)

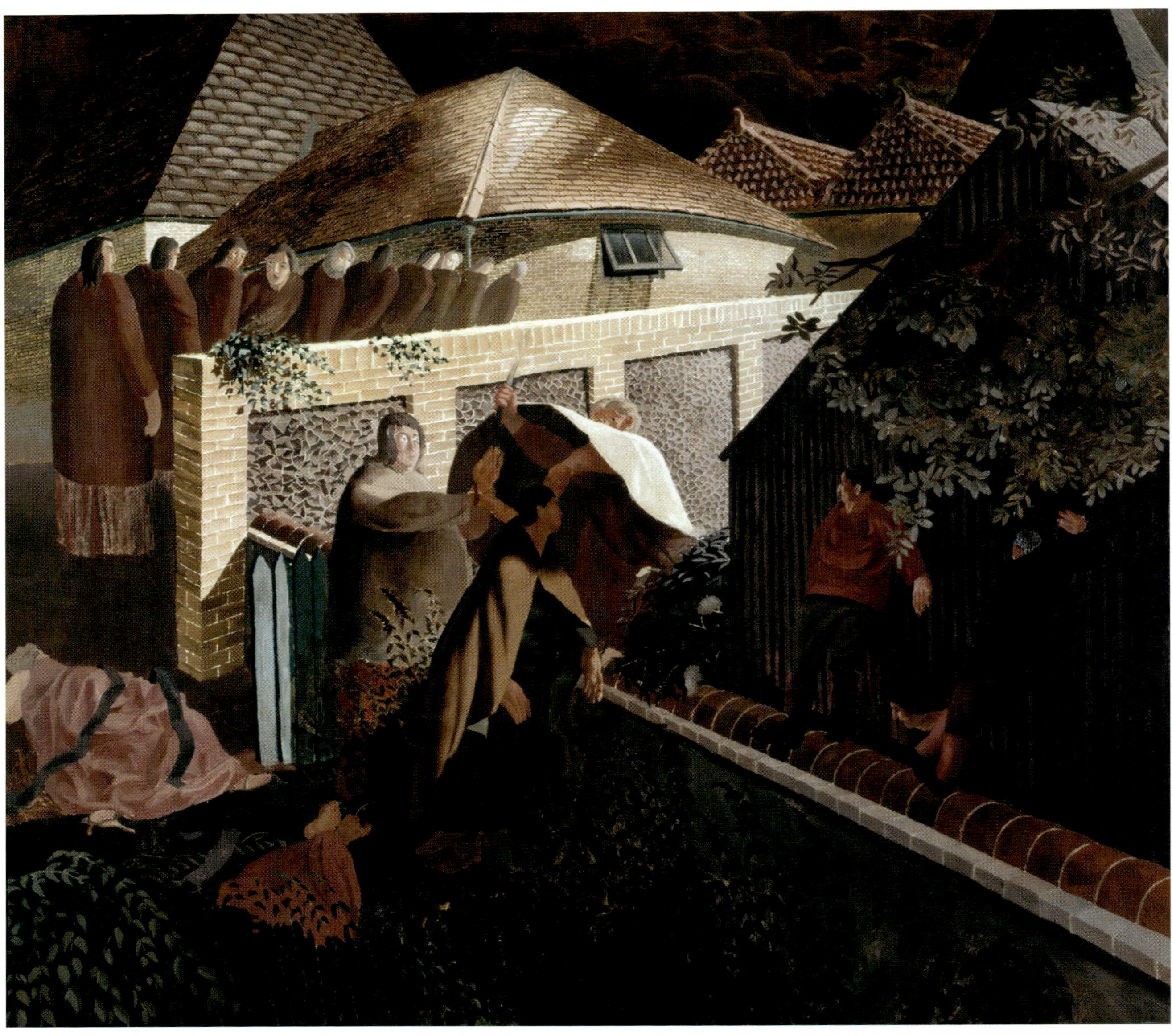

296

296. **Stanley Spencer**
Cookham, Berkshire, 1891 – Cliveden, Buckinghamshire, 1959
The Betrayal, 1922-23
Oil on canvas, 123 x 137 cm
Ulster Museum, Belfast

Spencer is one of the few British artists to have painted biblical subjects with any conviction. In 1914 he had painted a small *Betrayal*, set within the high Cookham walls and oast houses. Eight years later, he embarked on a much larger night scene, whose dramatic action is set in the back garden of the Spencer family home, Fernlea. He wrote to his patron Michael Sadler (the leading collector of the international avant-garde in Britain), 'I have been harking after it since 1912 ... I don't mind how long I spend on it.' In the Garden of Gethsemane, the scuffle around Jesus' arrest is observed by a row of ten very schematized brown-robed disciples; and, in the dark foreground, by two schoolboys in modern dress. The childhood of Stanley and his brother Gilbert is thereby memorialized; they lean against the corrugated iron shed which served as the Spencer schoolroom. His work on *The Betrayal* was interrupted, first by his engagement to Hilda Carline, then, in December 1922, by his move to Hampstead to live with her family. (TH)

297. **Stanley Spencer**
Cookham, Berkshire, 1891 – Cliveden, Buckinghamshire, 1959
Elsie Chopping Wood in the Coal Cellar, c. 1944-45
Pencil on paper, 40.6 x 28 cm
Collection of Mr and Mrs Thomas Gibson

This is one of a large group of pencil drawings made in scrapbooks, functioning partly as illustrations to the *Autobiography* Spencer was attempting to write throughout the later war years. But they are also squared-up for transfer to canvas, preparations for the sequence of 'chapels' in Spencer's imaginary 'Church of Me', each dedicated to a significant woman in his life. Elsie was the cherished maid-of-all-work within the Spencer household; here she toils beside the child-like Stanley. But in the foreground we see a Giotto-like 'disciple' or 'emissary' (transferred from Spencer's 'Last Day' mythology). He is shown squatting, and, as Spencer explains, 'looking up Elsie's skirt and spreading his own thighs in excitement'. This is the latest in date of Spencer's sixteen works in 'British Vision'; he continued to produce interesting pictures until his death in 1959. (TH)

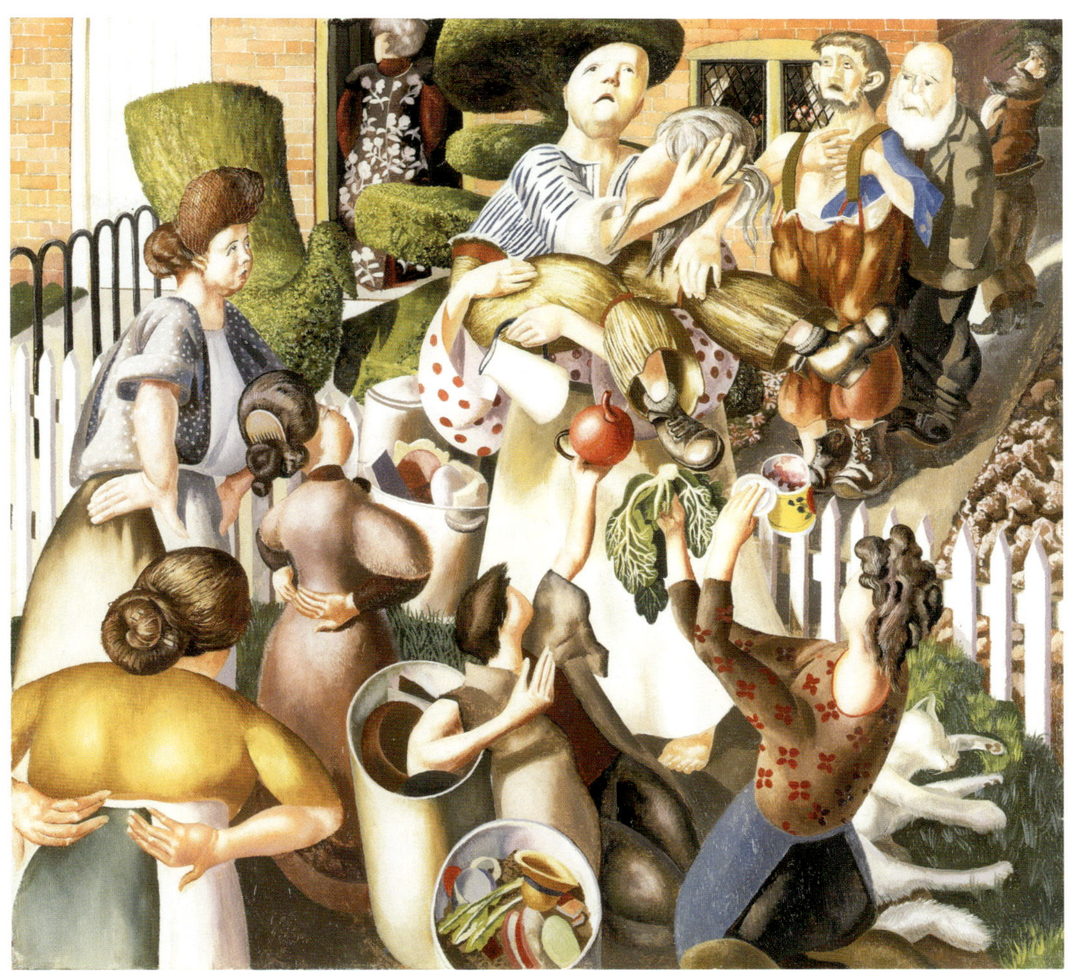

298

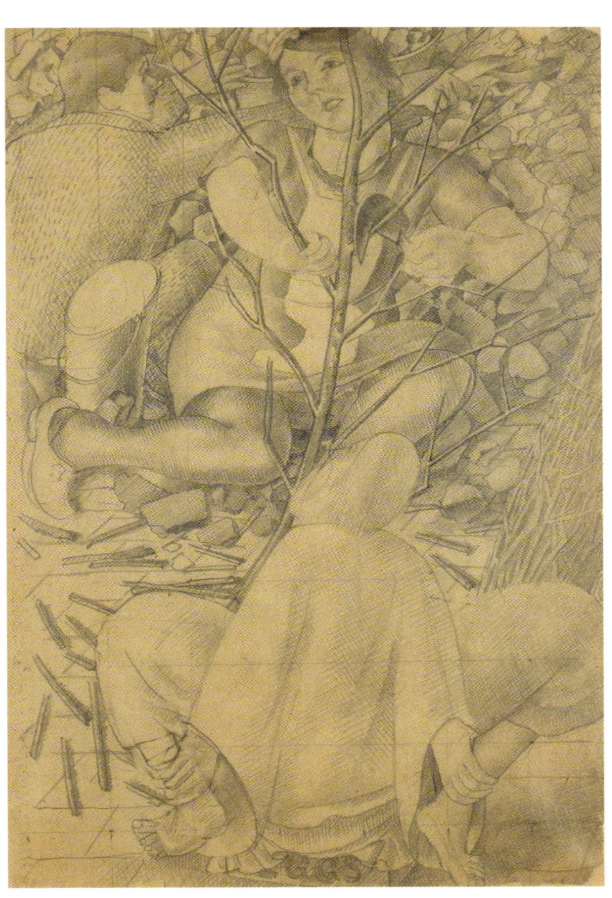

297

298. **Stanley Spencer**
Cookham, Berkshire, 1891 – Cliveden, Buckinghamshire, 1959
The Dustman or ***The Lovers***, 1932-34
Oil on canvas, 114.9 x 123.5 cm
Laing Art Gallery (Tyne and Wear Museums),
Newcastle upon Tyne

The first of Spencer's many 1930s compositions that might be described as 'preposterous', *The Dustman* is part of a sequence intended for his 'Church/House': imagery of a 'Last Day' of universal love, which Spencer imagines being enacted in Cookham. The dustman himself is being raised up, and the picture centres on 'all the signs and tokens of homelife, such as the cabbage leaves and the teapot, which I have so much loved that I have had them resurrected from the dustbin'. (Hyman and Wright 2001, p. 183) Spencer described the scene to Gwen Raverat in 1932: 'I got a big sort of wife to pick him up in her arms, while children in a state of ecstasy hold up towards him an empty jam-tin, a tea-pot and a cabbage stalk … This is all very nice in its way, but some sort of terrible quality has crept in …'. (ibid.) An uneasy, half-humorous, half-earnest tone permeates all Spencer's 'Last Day' compositions; they were mostly unsaleable, funded by his landscape practice (see cat. 209-210). *The Dustman* was rejected from the Royal Academy's Summer Exhibition, and Spencer's resignation followed. Sickert and Augustus John were among the fellow painters who protested in support of Spencer. (TH)

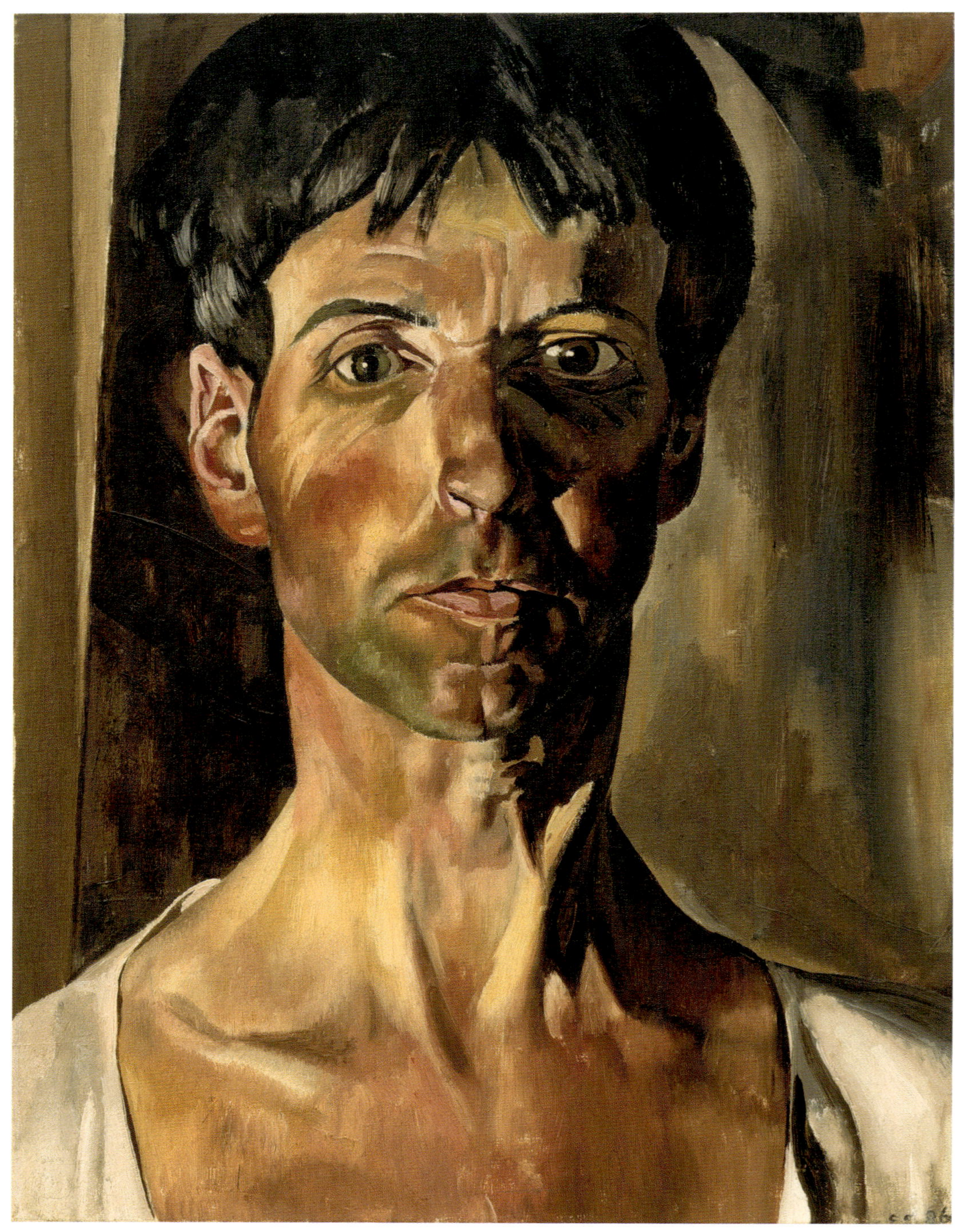

299

299. **Stanley Spencer**
Cookham, Berkshire, 1891 – Cliveden, Buckinghamshire, 1959
Self-Portrait, 1936
Oil on canvas, 61.6 x 45.7 cm
Bottom right: SS36 [monogram]
Stedelijk Museum, Amsterdam

This vigorous image was painted in the midst of Spencer's sequence of 'Naked Portraits' (see cat. 87) – a genre that implies the individual stripped bare and confronted close to, without defences. It was his first *Self-Portrait* painted direct from life since 1914; its frontality and dramatically divided lighting suggest Spencer may consciously be reprising his earlier (far more vulnerable) self-representation, as though to assert his transition away from Innocence into the harsher reality of Experience. In Spencer's 1936 exhibition at Tooth's, it would have stood out from both the 'Last Day' compositions and the Cookham landscapes, and it was almost immediately reserved by the Amsterdam museum – the first European public gallery to purchase Spencer's work. (TH)

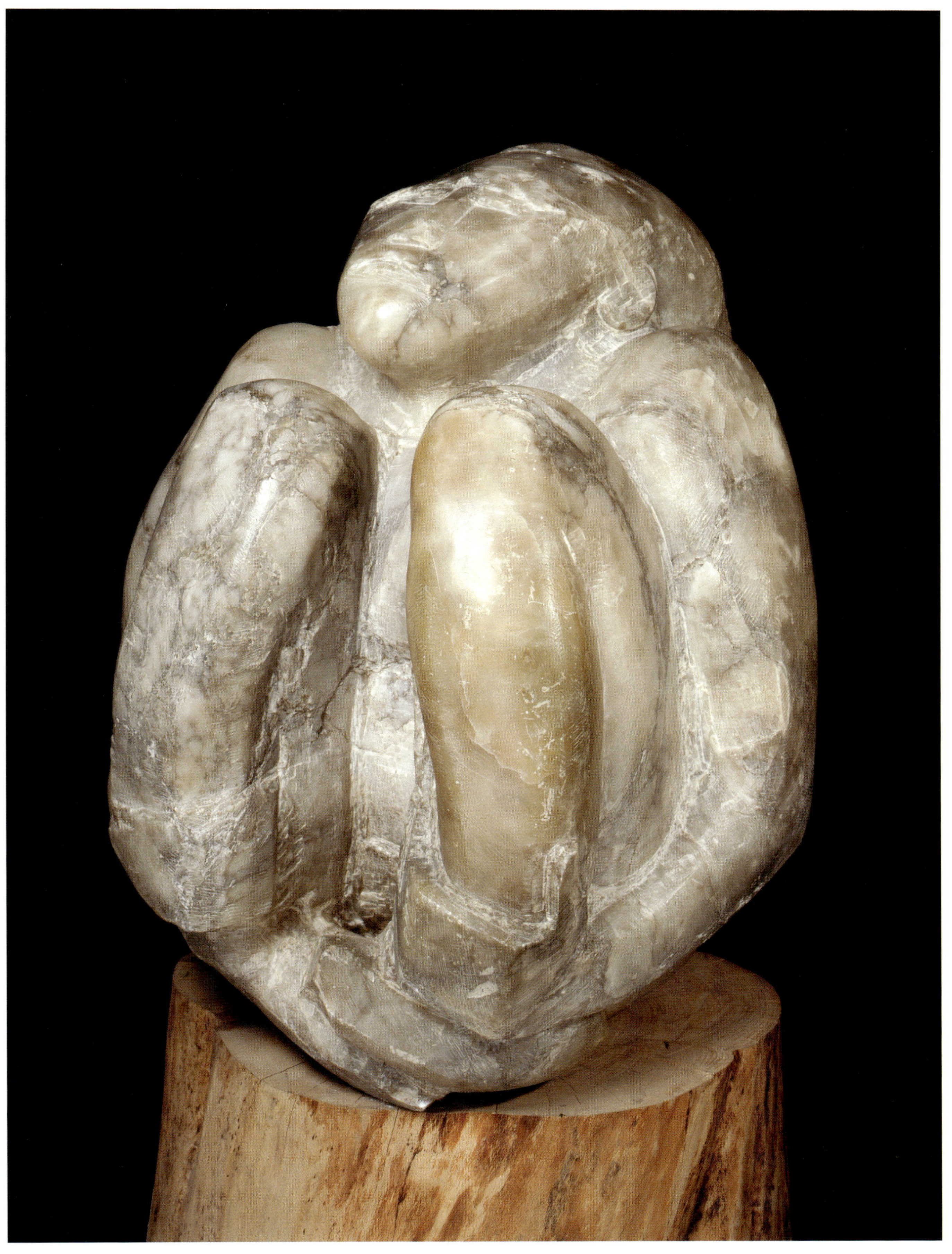

300

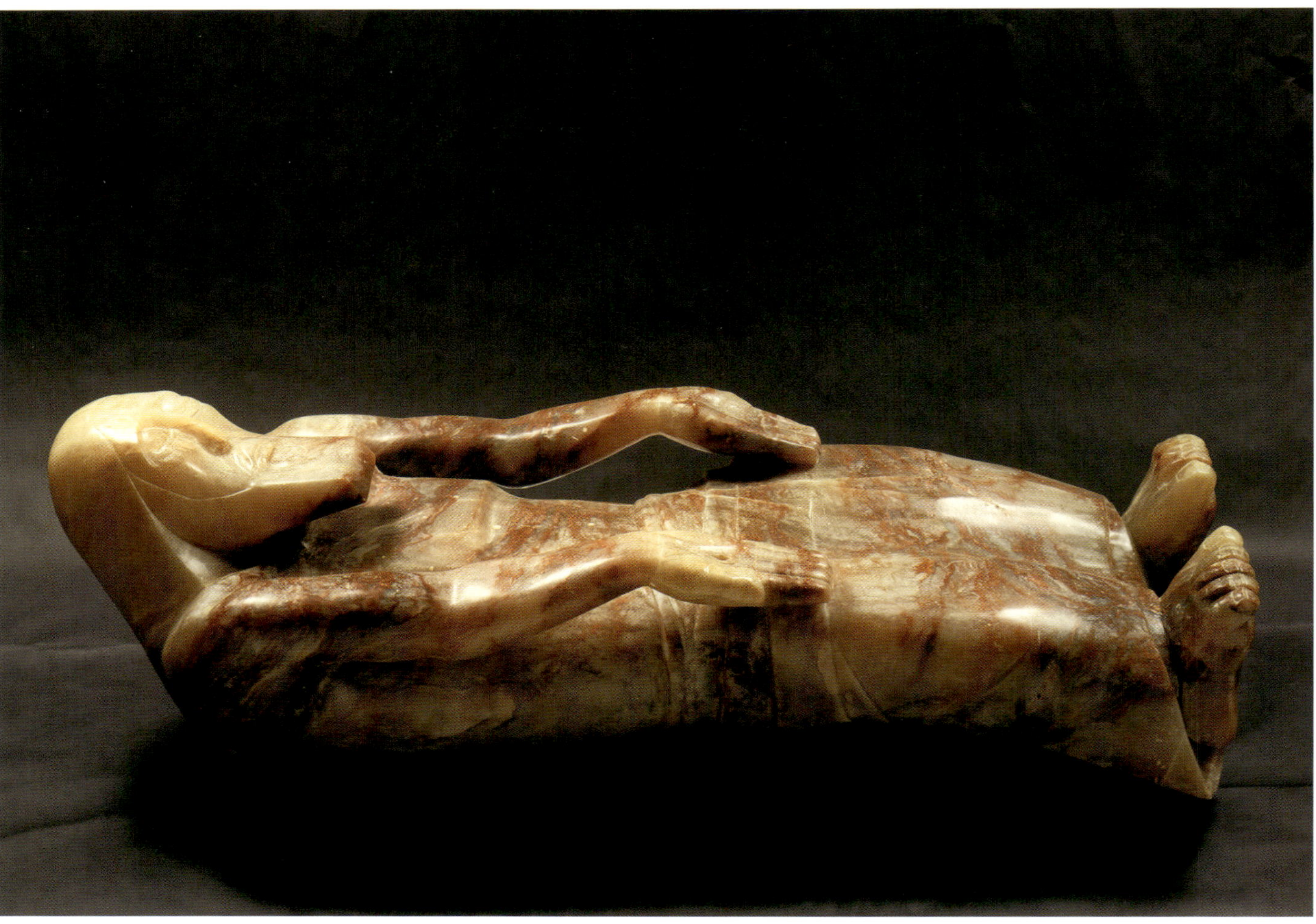

301

300. **Jacob Epstein**
New York, 1880 - London, 1959
Elemental, 1932
Alabaster, 81.3 x 58.4 x 66 cm
Private Collection

By the end of his life, Epstein, who had been subjected to as much prejudice and abuse as any modern artist, was described as 'the most traditional of the handful of major sculptors of his time' (John Rothenstein in London 1961). Nevertheless - as much as, say, Stanley Spencer - he exemplifies the visionary and the unorthodox in twentieth-century British art, most especially in the series of alabasters made during the 1930s, which included *Consummatum Est* (cat. 301) and this compact and powerful figure, made earlier in the decade, at the time of the equally striking alabaster figure of *Genesis* (The Whitworth Art Gallery, University of Manchester). It might be relevant to add that Epstein was also a highly successful portrait sculptor, and these two aspects of his work, carving and modelling (for bronze), represent the dichotomy of our exhibition, imagination and observation. (AD)

301. **Jacob Epstein**
New York, 1880 - London, 1959
Consummatum Est, 1936-37
Alabaster, 61 x 223.5 x 81 cm
Scottish National Gallery of Modern Art, Edinburgh

Epstein envisaged the form of the sculpture in detail while listening to Bach's B minor Mass, as he contemplated a block of alabaster that he had already had in his studio for a year. The process of carving it almost meant allowing the already envisaged form to emerge from the stone, which still retained its original integrity. The work was first exhibited in October 1937 and was subjected to the critical abuse that had become usual for Epstein's work, particularly his sculptures on Christian themes.

It was purchased for the collections of the Scottish National Gallery of Modern Art in 1981. (RU)

See essay pp. 335-37.

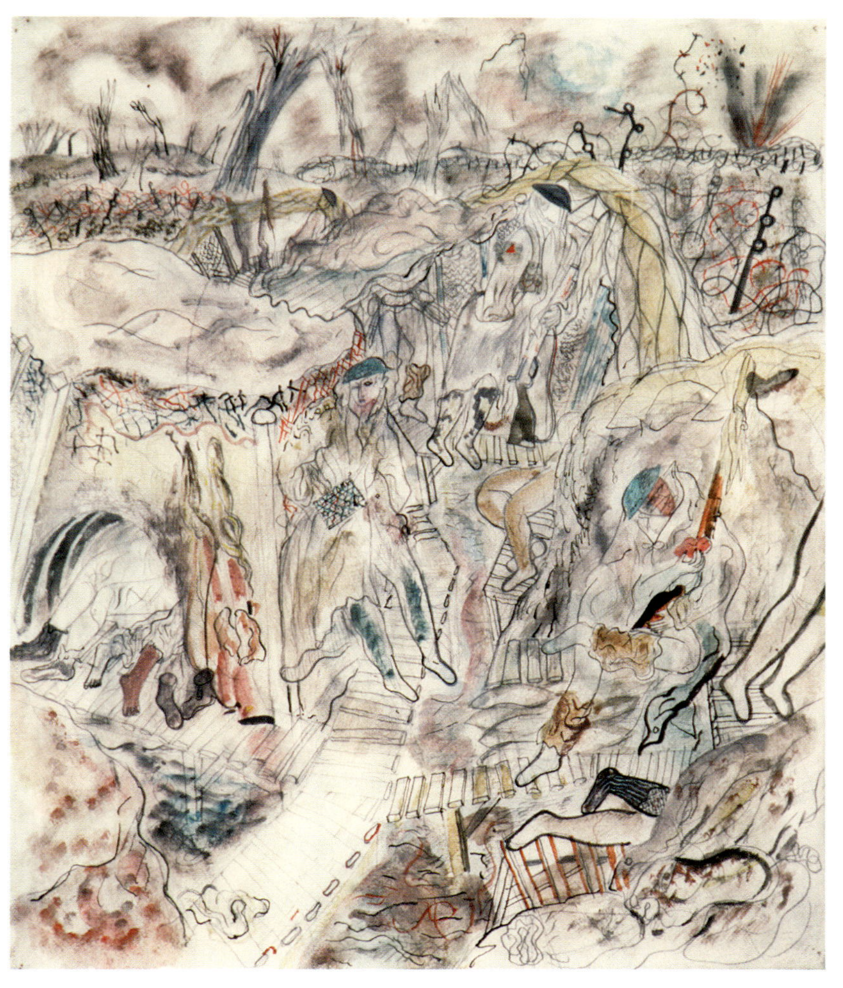

302

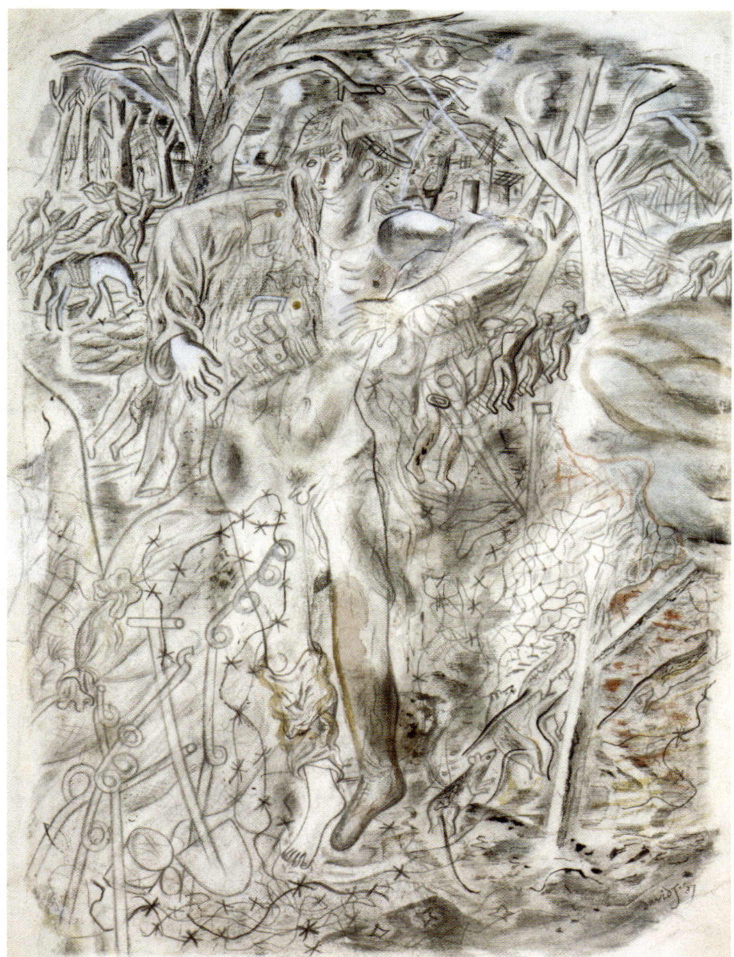

303

302. **David Jones**
Brockley, Kent, 1895 - Harrow, near London, 1974
Llys Ceimiad: La Baissée Front 1916, c. 1937
Pencil, ink and watercolour on paper, 38.7 x 32.3 cm
National Library of Wales, Aberystwyth

303. **David Jones**
Brockley, Kent, 1895 - Harrow, near London, 1974
Frontispiece for ***In Parenthesis***, 1937
Pencil, ink and watercolour on paper, 37.7 x 28 cm
Bottom right: david J. '37
Amgueddfa Cymru - National Museum Wales, Cardiff

304. **David Jones**
Brockley, Kent, 1895 - Harrow, near London, 1974
Vexilla Regis, 1947-48
Pencil, watercolour and bodycolour on paper, 75 x 55 cm
Bottom left: DAVID JONES 48.
Kettle's Yard University of Cambridge

David Jones's experience as an ordinary soldier in the First World War (he served with the Royal Welsh Fusiliers from 1915 to 1918) was of crucial importance for his art and his writing. In 1921 he converted to Catholicism, and he later worked as an illustrator for the semi-religious crafts guild run by Eric Gill, sculptor, engraver and typographer, at Ditchling, Surrey. Jones's copper engravings for Coleridge's 'The Rime of the Ancient Mariner' (1929) are a high point of British book illustration.

Jones was both a painter and a poet and is perhaps a more established figure in the history of English literature than in that of English art. *In Parenthesis*, with the war as its subject, was published in 1937 and *The Anathemata* in 1952. Both have become literary classics. W.H. Auden thought the latter the finest long poem in English of the twentieth century. But Jones was first an artist, and his sometimes weird but always beautifully realized watercolours and drawings have survived a period on the margins of acclaim, like the work of so many of the artists celebrated in this section of the exhibition. What could be stranger than the half unclothed soldier in the battlescape of trenches and stunted trees in the frontispiece to *In Parenthesis*.

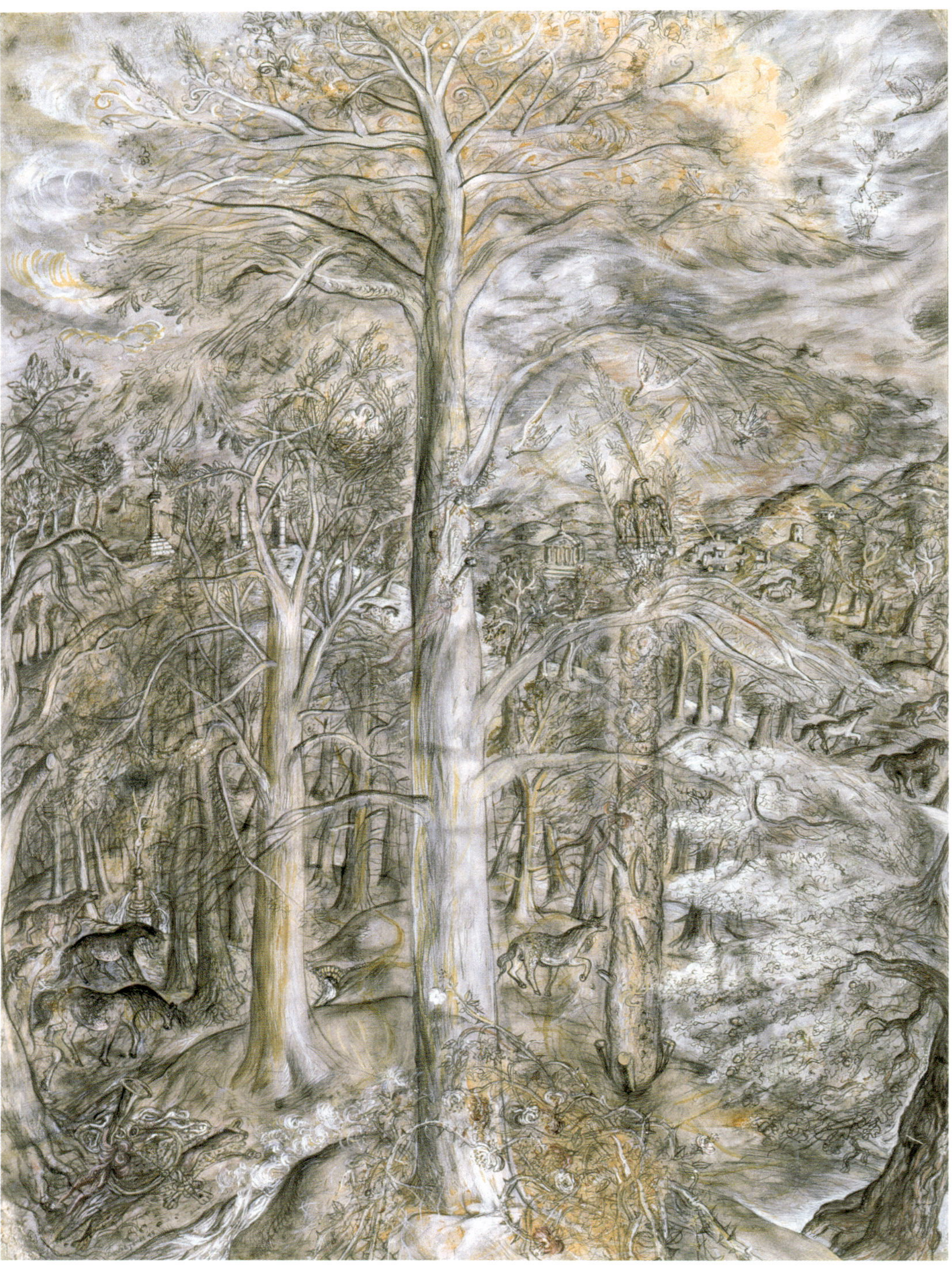

304

Llys Ceimiad: La Baissée Front 1917, with its plethora of socks and bootless legs, continues the theme of life in the trenches. Jones explained that Llys Ceimiad was meant as a hero's place or court. The scene is depicted with a delicacy and lightness which seems at odds with the subject but which is the more moving for this originality of treatment.

Vexilla Regis (the title derives from part of the Good Friday litany) was painted in 1947, when Jones was recovering from a nervous breakdown and had been encouraged to draw by his doctors. It makes allusion to the Cross and the tree of life but is more complex in its references. 'The general idea of the picture,' Jones said, 'was also associated in my mind, with the collapse of the Roman world. The three trees as it were left standing on Calvary...' (letter to Mrs Ede, October 1947, reprinted in Hague 1980, pp. 149-52). (AD)

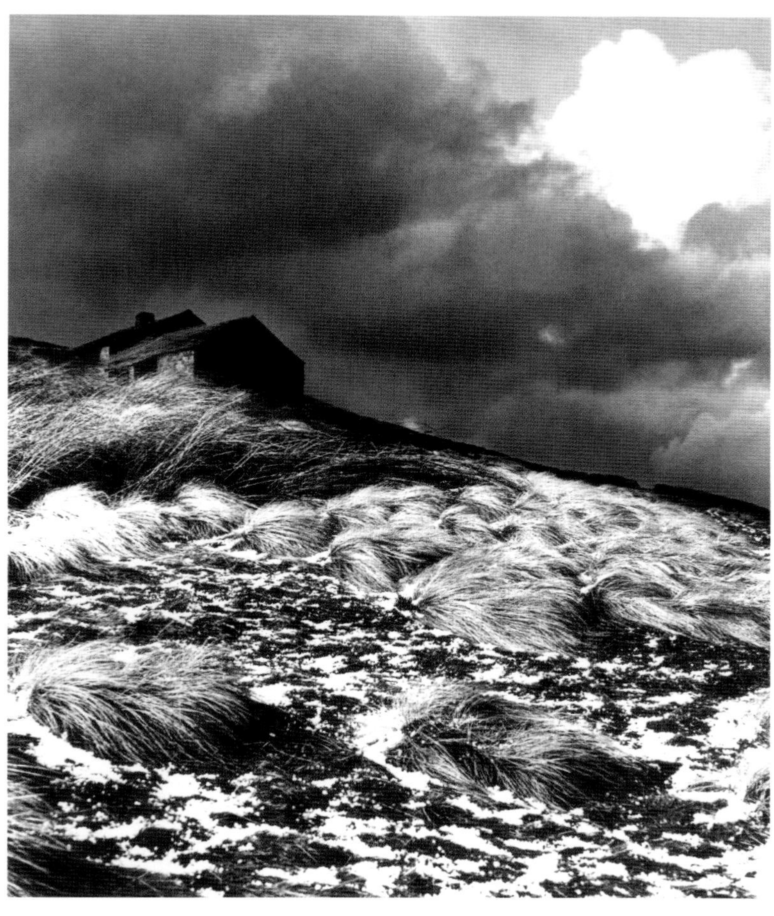

305

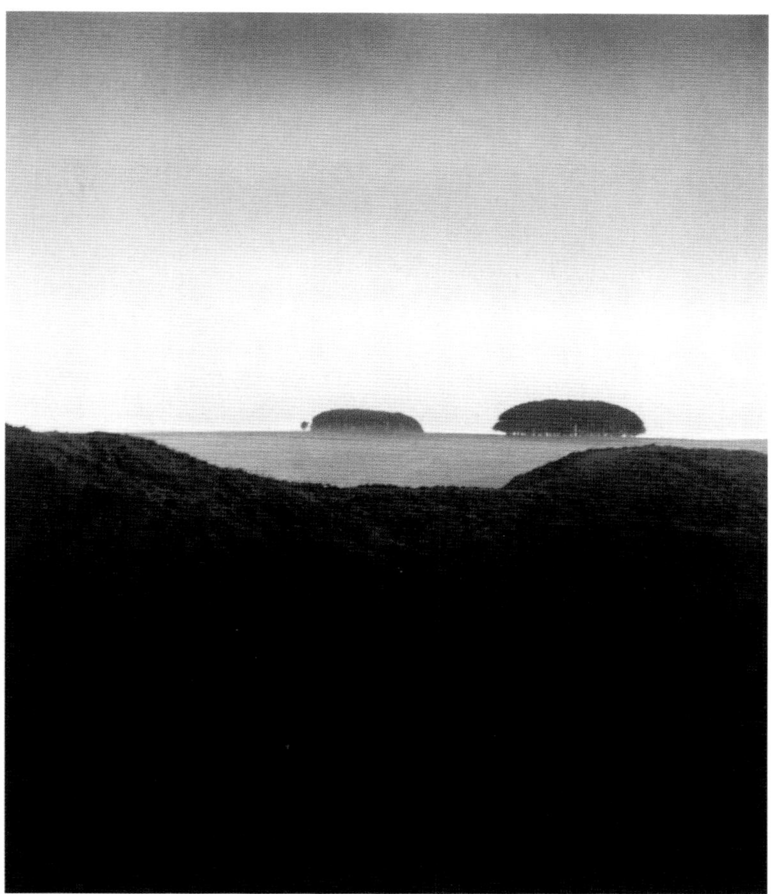

306

305. **Bill Brandt**
Hamburg, 1904 - London, 1983
Top Withens, West Riding, Yorkshire,
after Emily Brontë, 1944 (printed in 1975)
Gelatin silver print, 33.5 x 29 cm
Bottom right: Top Withins, West Riding, Yorkshire
Victoria and Albert Museum, London

An arresting quotation accompanied this photograph when it was first published in *Lilliput* (May 1945) and afterwards in Brandt's book *Literary Britain* in 1951:

'Wuthering Heights is the name of Mr Heathcliff's dwelling, "Wuthering" being a significant provincial adjective, descriptive of the atmospheric tumult to which its station is exposed in stormy weather. Pure, bracing ventilation they must have up there at all times, indeed...' - Emily Brontë, *Wuthering Heights* (1847).

Brandt's ability to abstract compositions - and to wait, for years if necessary, for the climatic conditions he wanted - helped him to achieve this remarkable photograph. It seems that he enhanced the drama of the scene by printing in a louring sky from a separate negative. The group of isolated buildings, whose actual name is Top Withens, still stands - now roofless - on the moors not far from the Brontë's home, Haworth Parsonage. (MHB)

306. **Bill Brandt**
Hamburg, 1904 - London, 1983
Barbary Castle, Marlborough Downs,
Wiltshire, 1948 (printed in 1975)
Gelatin silver print, 34.4 x 29 cm
Victoria and Albert Museum, London

Brandt's great period as a landscape photographer was the 1940s. His forte was 'Literary Britain', the title of his book of landscape photographs, first published in 1951, in which each photograph was faced by a literary text. The formula of landscape photograph and quotation was established in *Lilliput* magazine, for which Brandt photographed prolifically at this time. Such photographs answered a need during the war to celebrate national identity, which in turn involved a return to English literary classics. This photograph echoes the many paintings by Paul Nash of Wittenham Clumps near Oxford (see cat. 214). However, Brandt's composition could be regarded as even more radical, giving over about half of the space to the black tone that indicates an iron-age rampart - and thus the deep past. The accompanying quotation was from *Wild Life in a Southern County* (1879) by Richard Jefferies, which evoked the dreamlike qualities of this landscape. (MHB)

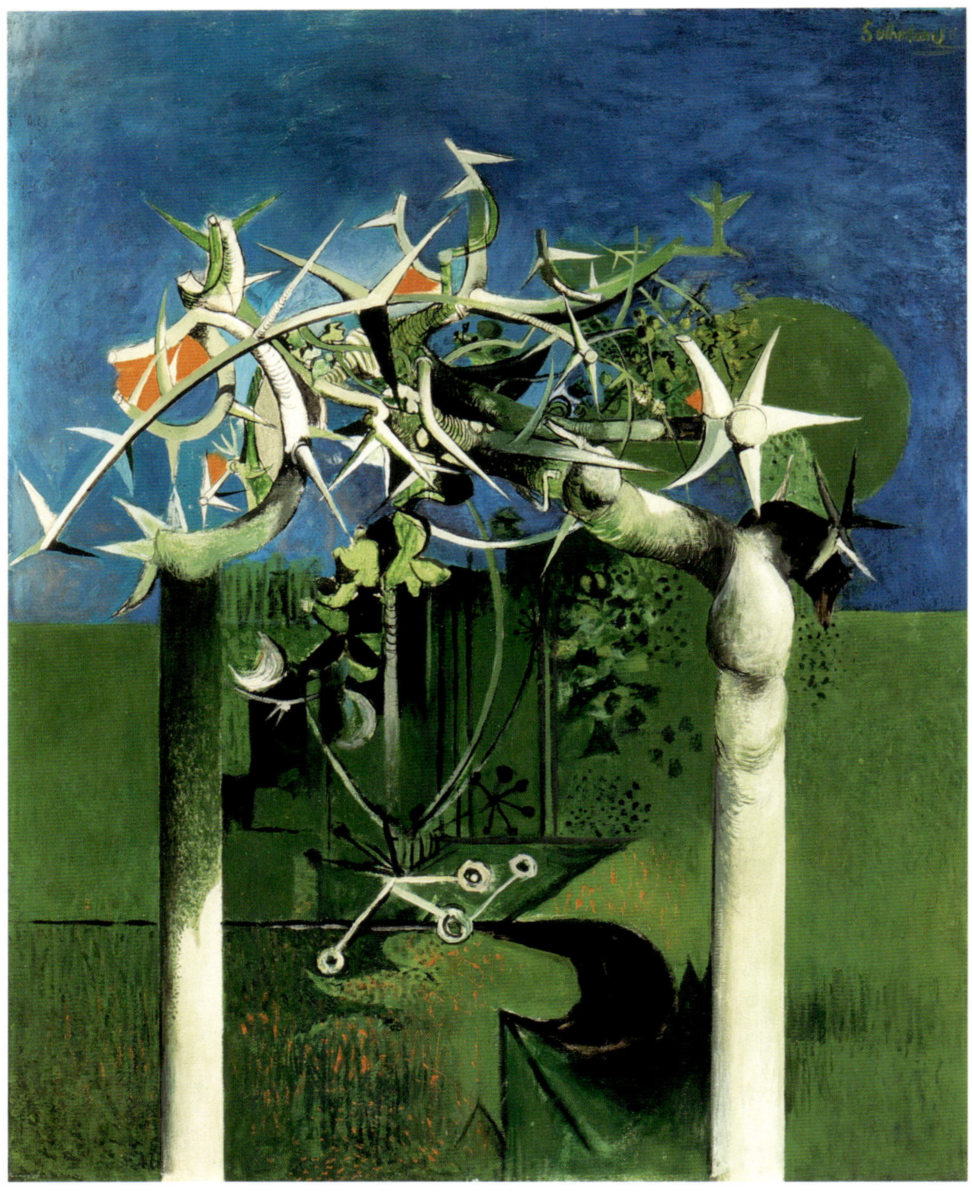

307

307. **Graham Sutherland**
London, 1903 - London, 1980
Thorn Tree, 1945-46
Oil on canvas, 127 x 101.5 cm
Top right: Sutherland.
British Council, London

In 1945 Sutherland was commissioned to paint an altarpiece of the Crucifixion for St Matthew's church in Northampton. As an artist more disposed to depicting organic forms than the human figure, he sought inspiration from the natural world and became preoccupied with 'the structure of thorns as they pierced the air' (Sutherland 1951). The commission was duly completed, but the drawings he made gave rise to a separate series of paintings in which the image of the thorn tree became a visual metaphor for the Crucifixion itself. In this version, the physical and spiritual agony of Christ's suffering is suggested by the wild mass of thorns inextricably tangled around the smooth twisting branches of the solid, straight, supporting trunks. The dramatic emotive impact is intensified by the purity of the clear blue sky and lush green earth, disturbed by the skeletal white of the thorns and the occasional violent patch of scarlet. (NM)

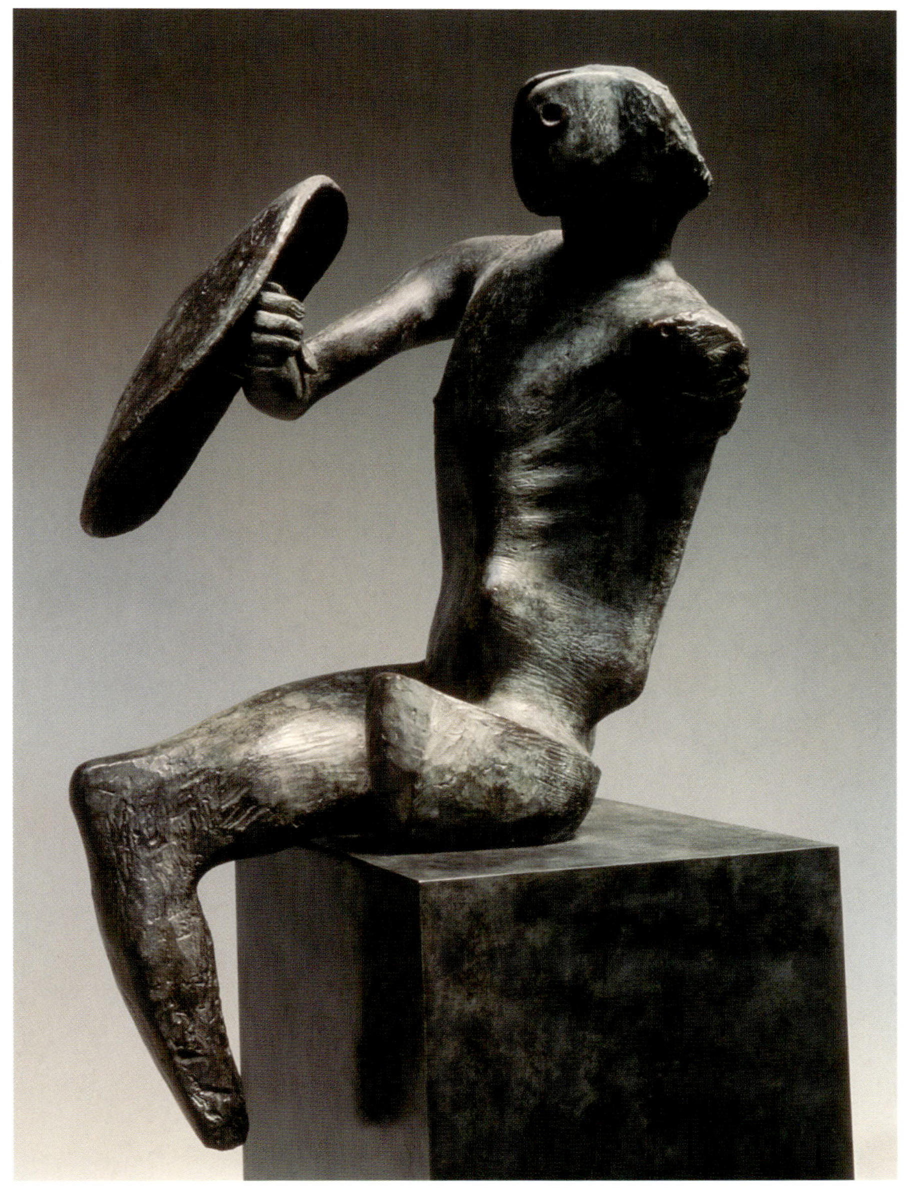

308

308. **Henry Moore**
Castleford, West Yorkshire, 1898 – Perry Green,
Much Hadham, Hertfordshire, 1986
Warrior with Shield, 1953-54
Bronze, 152.5 x 113 x 93 cm
Henry Moore Family Collection

This is a rare example of the large-scale male figure in Moore's work. He wrote: 'The idea for the warrior . . . evolved from a pebble I found on the seashore in the summer of 1952, and which reminded me of the stump of a leg, amputated at the hip.' (Letter to unknown recipient; cit. James 1966, p. 250) To this, Moore added body, limbs and finally a shield. The upright, seated pose creates a sense of defiance even in its 'dumb animal acceptance and forbearance of pain' (ibid.). As such the figure combines themes from two sets of wartime drawings: the deathly stillness and forbearance depicted in the Blitz shelterers (cat. 97); and the coalminers, robustly fighting against their underground environment. The figure appears to draw on classical forms, but its contemporary significance was immediately registered: the acquisition of a cast of *Warrior with Shield* by the city of Arnhem was specifically to commemorate the failed Allied attempt to secure the town in 1944, when German Panzers destroyed the houses sheltering British parachutists. (RT)

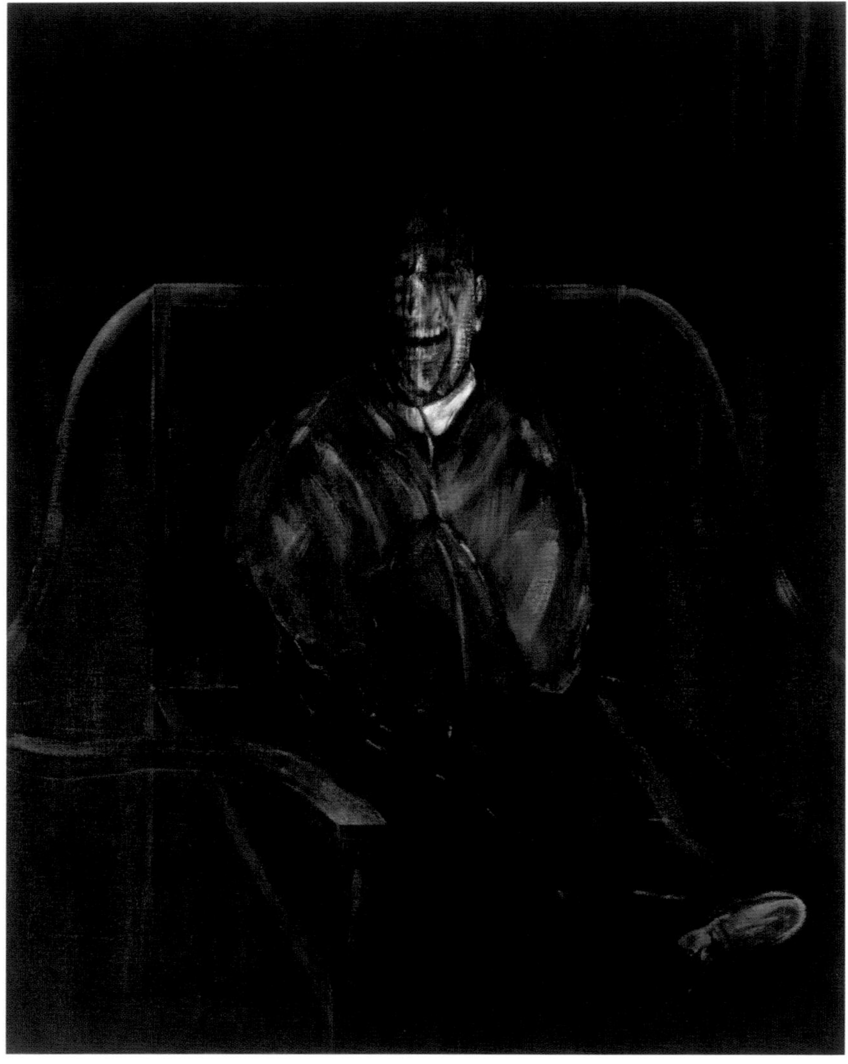

309

309. **Francis Bacon**
Dublin, 1909 - Madrid, 1992
Figure Sitting (The Cardinal), 1955
Oil on canvas, 152 x 117 cm
Stedelijk Museum voor Actuele Kunst, Ghent

Bacon's 'Popes', loosely based on the Velázquez portrait of Pope Innocent X, which the artist did not know at first hand, have become his most celebrated paintings. The series was begun in 1949. The Ghent painting relates to the series in subject and treatment, though it has attracted the title 'Cardinal'. The head has the threatening aspect of *Man in Blue I* (cat. 90) and is similar in composition to another early suited figure, *Study for a Portrait* (1953; Kunsthalle Hamburg). The menace of this cardinal seems at odds with the Church's teaching, but perhaps not with its actions, though, as ever, one should beware of reading too much specific sentiment into Bacon's figures. The painting by Velázquez was a portrait of one of the most powerful people in the known world at that time, but for Bacon its interest lay in the miracle that Velázquez had achieved, 'to keep it so near to what we call illustration and at the same time so deeply unlock the greatest and deepest things that man can feel' (Sylvester 1975, p. 28). (AD)

310. **Francis Bacon**
Dublin, 1909 - Madrid, 1992
Study for Portrait III
(after the Life Mask of William Blake), 1955
Oil on canvas, 60 x 51 cm
Private Collection

Alley records that the idea for this series (there are five surviving paintings after J.S. Deville's 1823 life mask of Blake) originated in a request from a young composer, Gerard Schurmann, to provide an illustration for the cover of his song cycle of Blake poems (Alley 1964, no. 94). Bacon apparently saw the National Portrait Gallery's cast of the life mask (which is in itself a striking object) but worked from photographs, or rather used the photographs as an *aide-mémoire*. Martin Harrison recounts that Lawrence Gowing subsequently gave Bacon a cast he had bought from the National Portrait Gallery in 'what he confessed was a misguided attempt to persuade Bacon to paint from the actual object' (Harrison 2005, pp. 133-34). But the special psychological power and insights of Bacon's work come as much from within himself, from his own personality and circumstances, as from the observed world. He may not have painted from life, but he made some of the most penetrating portraits of individuals in twentieth-century art. (AD)

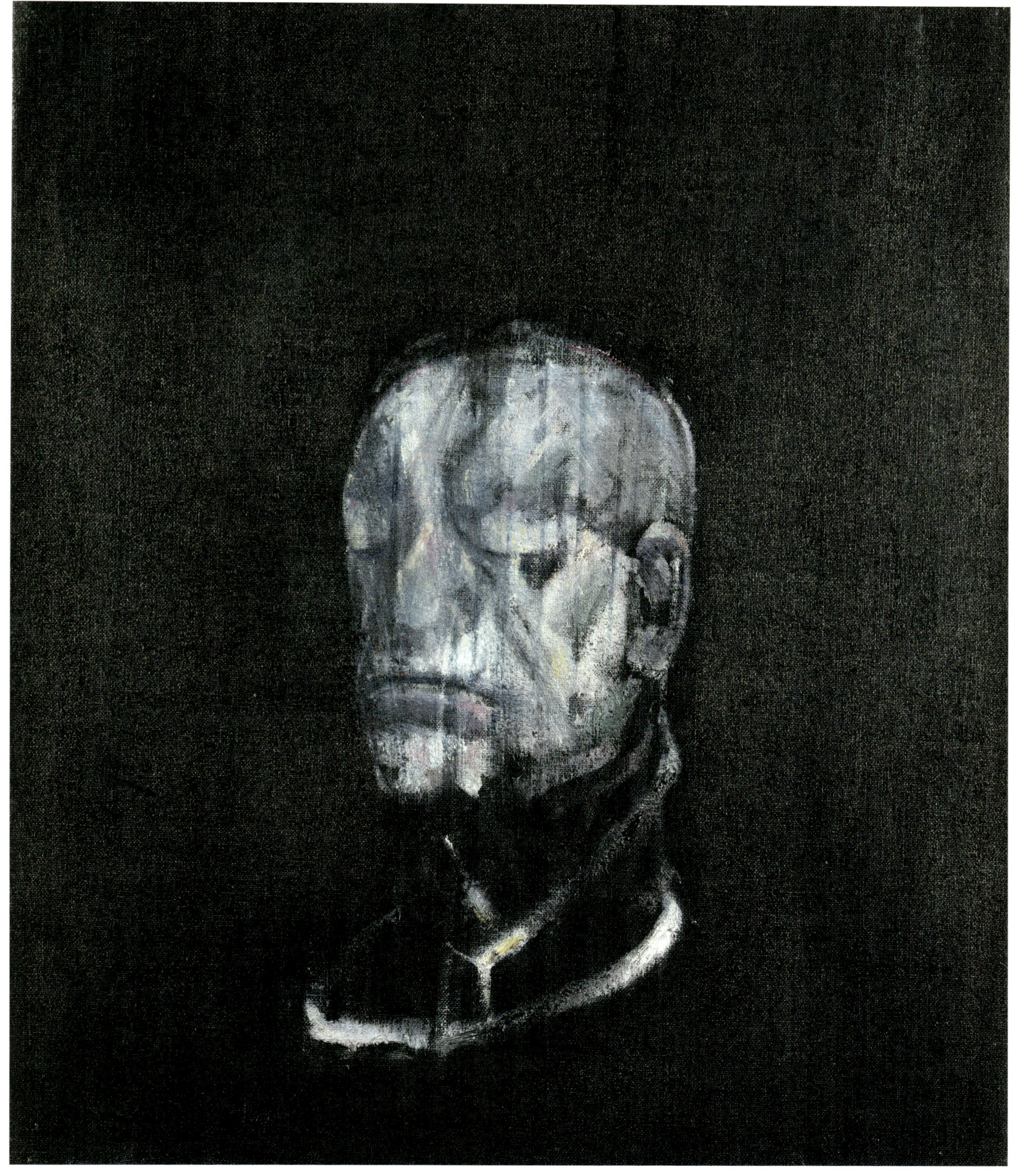

310

SHORT TITLES

Abbot and Bertram 1955
Abbot, Claude Colleer, and Anthony Bertram (eds.), *Poet and Painter: Being the correspondence between Gordon Bottomley and Paul Nash, 1910-1946,* London (Oxford University Press) 1955

Allderidge 1974
Allderidge, Patricia, *Richard Dadd*, London (Academy Editions) 1974

Allen 1991
Allen, Brian, *et al.*, *The British Portrait 1660-1960*, Woodbridge (Antique Collectors' Club) 1991

Alley 1964
Alley, Ronald, *Francis Bacon: Catalogue raisonné*, intro. John Rothenstein, London (Thames and Hudson) 1964

Alter and Kermode 1987
Alter, Robert, and Frank Kermode (eds.), *The Literary Guide to the Bible*, London (Collins) & Cambridge, Mass. (Belknap Press of Harvard University Press) 1987

Altick 1978
Altick, Richard D., *The Shows of London*, Cambridge, Mass. & London (Belknap Press of Harvard University Press) 1978

Andrews 1989
Andrews, Malcolm, *The Search for the Picturesque: Landscape Aesthetics and Tourism in Britain, 1760-1800,* Aldershot (Scolar) 1989

Andrews 2002
Andrews, Julian, *London's War: The Shelter Drawings of Henry Moore*, Aldershot (Lund Humphries) 2002

Antal 1949
Antal, Frederick, 'Mr. Oldham and His Guests by Highmore', *Burlington Magazine* 91, no. 554 (May 1949), pp. 128-32

Backhouse 1989
Backhouse, Janet, *The Luttrell Psalter*, London (British Library) 1989

Baker 1982
Baker, T. F. T. (ed.), *A History of the County of Middlesex, volume VIII: Acton, Chiswick, Ealing and Willesden Parishes*, London (Oxford University Press, for the Institute of Historical Research) 1982

Baldwin 2006
Baldwin, Gordon, 'The Valley of the Shadow of Death, 1855', in Haworth-Booth 2006, p. 30

Balston 1934
Balston, Thomas, *John Martin, 1789-1854: Illustrator and Pamphleteer*, Oxford (Oxford University Press) 1934: *Transactions of the Bibliographical Society* ser. 4, 14, no. 4 (1934)

Balston 1947
Balston, Thomas, *John Martin, 1789-1854: His Life and Works*, London (Duckworth) 1947

Baron 1973
Baron, Wendy, *Sickert*, London (Phaidon) 1973

Baron 1998
Baron, Wendy, 'Walter Sickert', in exh. cat. *James McNeill Whistler, Walter Richard Sickert*, Madrid (Fundación 'la Caixa') & Bilbao (Museo de Bellas Artes) 1998, pp. 77-88, 244-49

Baron and Shone 1992
Baron, Wendy, and Richard Shone (eds.), exh. cat. *Sickert: Paintings*, London (Royal Academy) & Amsterdam (Van Gogh Museum) 1992-93

Barrell 1980
Barrell, John, *The Dark Side of the Landscape: The Rural Poor in English Paintings, 1730-1840*, Cambridge (Cambridge University Press) 1980

Barringer 2005
Barringer, Tim, *Men at Work: Art and Labour in Victorian Britain*, New Haven, Conn. & London (Yale University Press, for the Paul Mellon Centre for Studies in British Art) 2005

Barry 1809
Barry, James, *The Works of James Barry*, 2 vols., London (T. Cadell & W. Davies) 1809

Beckett 1962-68
Beckett, R.B. (ed.), *John Constable's Correspondence*, 6 vols., Ipswich (Suffolk Records Society) 1962-68

Beckett 1970
Beckett, R.B. (ed.), *John Constable's discourses*, Ipswich (Suffolk Records Society) 1970

Bell 1945
Bell, Clive, *Victor Pasmore*, Harmondsworth (Penguin Books) 1945

Bemrose 1885
Bemrose, William, *The Life and Works of Joseph Wright, A.R.A., commonly called "Wright of Derby"*, preface C. Monkhouse, London (Bemrose) 1885

Bendiner 1979
Bendiner, Kenneth, *The Portrayal of the Middle East in British Painting, 1835-1860* (PhD diss., Columbia University, New York) 1979

Bendiner 1998
Bendiner, Kenneth, *The Art of Ford Madox Brown*, University Park, Pa. (Pennsylvania State University Press) 1998

Bennett 1984
Bennett, Mary, 'The Price of *Work*', in Parris 1984, pp. 143-52

Bentley 1969
Bentley, Gerald Eades, *Blake records*, Oxford (Clarendon Press) 1969

Bermingham 1986
Bermingham, Ann, *Landscape and Ideology: The English Rustic Tradition, 1740-1860*, Berkeley (University of California Press) 1986 & London (Thames and Hudson) 1987

Bindman, Ogée and Wagner 2001
Bindman, David, Frédéric Ogée and Peter Wagner (eds.), *Hogarth: Representing Nature's Machine*, Manchester (Manchester University Press) 2001

Binyon 1931
Binyon, Laurence, *Landscape in English Art and Poetry*, [London] (Cobden Sanderson) 1931

Black 1999
Black, Jonathan, 'A Curious, Cold Intensity', in Ingleby, Richard, *et al.*, exh. cat. *C. R.W. Nevinson: The Twentieth Century*, London (Imperial War Museum) & New Haven, Conn. (Yale Center for British Art) 1999-2000, pp. 27-37

Blake 1966
Blake, William, *The Complete Writings*, ed. Geoffrey Keynes, London (Oxford University Press) 1966

Blanche 1939
Blanche, Jacques-Emile, *More Portraits of a Lifetime 1918-1938*, trans. and ed. Walter Clement, London (J.M. Dent) 1939

Blayney Brown 2000
Blayney Brown, David, 'Nationalising Norwich: The "School" in a wider context', in London 2000, pp. 24-36

Bowness 1965
Bowness, Alan (ed.), *Henry Moore: Volume 3, Sculpture 1955-64*, intro. Herbert Read, London (Lund Humphries & Zwemmer) 1965

Bowness 1971
Bowness, Alan (ed.), *The Complete Sculpture of Barbara Hepworth 1960-69*, London (Lund Humphries) 1971

Bowness 1975
Bowness, Alan, 'The Victorians', in David Piper (ed.), *The Genius of British Painting*, London (Weidenfeld and Nicolson) 1975, pp. 249-290

Brandt 1948
Brandt, Bill, *Camera in London*, commentary by Norah Wilson, London & New York (Focal Press) 1948

Brandt 1966
Brandt, Bill, *Shadow of Light: A Collection of Photographs from 1931 to the Present*, intro. Cyril Connolly, notes Marjorie Beckett, London (Bodley Head) 1966

Bromberg 2000
Bromberg, Ruth, *Walter Sickert: Prints, A Catalogue Raisonné*, New Haven, Conn. & London (Yale University Press, for the Paul Mellon Centre for Studies in British Art) 2000

Bromfield and Robertson 1979
Bromfield, David, and Alexander W. Robertson, exh. cat. *Atkinson Grimshaw 1836-1893*, Leeds (City Art Gallery), Southampton (Art Gallery) & Liverpool (Walker Art Gallery) 1979-80

Bronkhurst 1984
Bronkhurst, Judith, '"An interesting series of adventures to look back upon": William Holman Hunt's visit to the Dead Sea in November 1854', in Parris 1984, pp. 111-25

Bronkhurst 2006
Bronkhurst, Judith, *William Holman Hunt: A Catalogue Raisonné*, 2 vols., New Haven, Conn. & London (Yale University Press, for the Paul Mellon Centre for Studies in British Art) 2006

Brooks and Glasspoole 1928
Brooks, Charles Ernest Pelham, and John Glasspoole, *British Floods and Droughts*, London (Benn) 1928

Brooks and James
Brooks, Lindsay, and Merlin James, exh. cat. *Lowry's People*, Salford Quays (The Lowry) 2000

Brown 1996
Brown, Christopher, *Rubens's Landscapes: Making & Meaning*, London (National Gallery), 1996

Bryant 1997
Bryant, Julius, 'Madox Brown's *English Autumn Afternoon* revisited: Pre-Raphaelitism and the environment', *Apollo* 146, no. 425 (July 1997), pp. 41-43

Burke 1998
Burke, Edmund, *A Philosophical Enquiry into the Origin of Our Ideas of the Sublime and Beautiful* (1757), ed. David Womersley, London (Penguin) 1998

Butlin 1981
Butlin, Martin, *The Paintings and Drawings of William Blake*, 2 vols., New Haven, Conn. & London (Yale University Press, for the Paul Mellon Centre for Studies in British Art) 1981

Butlin and Joll 1984
Butlin, Martin, and Evelyn Joll, *The Paintings of J.M.W. Turner*, rev. ed., 2 vols., New Haven, Conn. & London (Yale University Press, for the Paul Mellon Centre for Studies in British Art and the Tate Gallery 1984

Byron 1847
Byron, George Gordon, *The Poetical Works of Lord Byron*, ed. Thomas Moore *et al.*, London (John Murray) 1847

Carlyle 1912
Carlyle, Thomas, *Past and Present*, London (J.M. Dent: Everyman's Library) 1912

Causey 1980
Causey, Andrew, *Paul Nash*, Oxford (Clarendon Press) 1980

Clark 1949
Clark, Kenneth, *Landscape into Art*, London (John Murray) 1949

Clark 1973
Clark, Kenneth, *The Romantic Rebellion: Romantic Versus Classic Art*, London (John Murray) 1973

Clark 1974
Clark, Kenneth, *Another Part of the Wood: A Self-Portrait*, London (John Murray) 1974

Clarke 1981
Clarke, Michael, *The Tempting Prospect: A Social History of English Watercolours*, London (British Museum) 1981

Clifford and Clifford 1968
Clifford, Derek, and Timothy Clifford, *John Crome*, London (Faber & Faber) 1968

Conisbee 1979
Conisbee, Philip, 'Pre-Romantic *plein-air* painting', *Art History* 2, no. 4 (Dec. 1979), pp. 413-28

Cook and Wedderburn 1903-12
Cook, E.T., and Alexander Wedderburn (eds.), *The Works of Ruskin*, 39 vols., London (George Allen) & New York (Longmans, Green) 1903-12

Corbett 2001
Corbett, David Peters, *Walter Sickert*, London (Tate Gallery Publications) 2001

Cork 1974
Cork, Richard, exh. cat. *Vorticism and its Allies*, London (Hayward Gallery; Arts Council of Great Britain) 1974

Cosgrove and Daniels 1988
Cosgrove, Denis, and Stephen Daniels (eds.), *The Iconography of Landscape: Essays on the Symbolic Representation, Design and Use of Past Environments*, Cambridge (Cambridge University Press) 1988

Cox 2003
Cox, Julian, '"To…startle the eye with wonder & delight": The Photographs of Julia Margaret Cameron', in Cox, Julian, and Colin Ford, *Julia Margaret Cameron. The Complete Photographs*, London (Thames and Hudson) 2003, pp. 41-79

Cox 2006
Cox, Julian, 'Thomas Carlyle, 1867', in Haworth-Booth 2006, p. 56

Crouan 1982
Crouan, Katharine, exh. cat. *John Linnell: A Centennial Exhibition*, Cambridge (Fitzwilliam Museum) & New Haven, Conn. (Yale Center for British Art) 1982-83

Cunningham 1843
Cunningham, Allan, *The Life of Sir David Wilkie; with his Journals, Tours and Critical Remarks on Works of Art; and a Selection from his Correspondence*, ed. Peter Cunningham, 3 vols., London (John Murray) 1843

Cuvier 1827
Cuvier, Georges Léopold, Baron, *The Animal Kingdom*, 16 vols., London (Whittaker) 1827-35

Dalrymple 2002
Dalrymple, William, *White Mughals: Love and Betrayal in Eighteenth-Century India*, London (HarperCollins) 2002

Daniel 2004
Daniel, Malcolm, 'On Nature's Invitation Do I Come': Roger Fenton's Landscapes', in Baldwin, Gordon, Malcolm Daniel and Sarah Greenough, exh. cat. *All the Mighty World: The Photographs of Roger Fenton*, Washington (National Gallery of Art), Los Angeles (J. Paul Getty Museum), New York (Metropolitan Museum of Art) & London (Tate Britain) 2004-6, pp. 33-53

Daniels 1988
Daniels, Stephen, 'The political iconography of woodland in later Georgian England', in Cosgrove and Daniels 1988, pp. 43-82

Daniels 1992
Daniels, Stephen, 'Loutherbourg's Chemical theatre: *Coalbrookdale by Night*', in Barrell, John (ed.), *Painting and the Politics of Culture: New Essays on British Art, 1700-1850*, Oxford (Oxford University Press) 1992, pp. 195-230

Dayes 1805
[Dayes, Edward], *The Works of the late Edward Dayes: Containing and Excursion through the Principal Parts of Derbyshire and Yorkshire*, ed. Edward W. Brayley, London (Mrs Dayes) 1805

Delany 2004
Delany, Paul, *Bill Brandt: A Life*, London (Jonathan Cape) 2004

Deuchar 1988
Deuchar, Stephen, *Sporting Art in Eighteenth-Century England: A Social and Political History*, New Haven, Conn. & London (Yale University Press, for the Paul Mellon Centre for Studies in British Art) 1988

Donald 1996
Donald, Diana, *The Age of Caricature: Satirical Prints in the Reign of George III*, New Haven, Conn. & London (Yale University Press, for the Paul Mellon Centre for Studies in British Art) 1996

Donald 2001
Donald, Diana, '"This truly natural and faithful painter": Hogarth's depiction of modern life', in Bindman, Ogée and Wagner 2001, pp. 163-91

Eaves 2003
Eaves, Morris (ed.), *The Cambridge Companion to William Blake*, Cambridge (Cambridge University Press) 2003

Egerton 1978
Egerton, Judy, *British Sporting and Animal Paintings, 1655-1867: A Catalogue*, London (Tate Gallery) & New Haven, Conn. (Yale Center for British Art) 1978

Egerton 1984
Egerton, Judy, exh. cat. *George Stubbs, 1724-1806*, London (Tate Gallery) & New Haven, Conn. (Yale Center for British Art) 1984-85

Egerton 1990
Egerton, Judy, exh. cat. *Wright of Derby*, London (Tate Gallery), Paris (Grand Palais) & New York (Metropolitan Museum of Art) 1990

Einberg and Egerton 1988
Einberg, Elizabeth, and Judy Egerton, *The Age of Hogarth: British Painters born 1675-1709 (Tate Gallery Collections, vol. 2)*, London (Tate Gallery) 1988

Eitner 1971
Eitner, Lorenz, *Neoclassicism and Romanticism, 1750-1850: Sources and Documents*, vol. 1: *Enlightenment/Revolution*, London (Prentice-Hall) 1971

Eitner 1987
Eitner, Lorenz, *An Outline of 19th Century European Painting*, 2 vols., New York (Harper & Row) 1987

Epstein 1955
Epstein, Jacob, *[Let There be Sculpture] Epstein: An Autobiography*, London (Hulton Press) 1955

Erdman 1965
Erdman, David V. (ed.), *The Poetry and Prose of William Blake,* commentary by Harold Bloom, Garden City, NY (Doubleday) 1965

Erffa and Staley 1986
Erffa, Helmut von, and Allen Staley, *The Paintings of Benjamin West,* New Haven, Conn. & London (Yale University Press) 1986

Evans 2002
Evans, Mark, '"A more lasting remembrance": Constable's paintings of *Dedham Vale from the* Coombs and Claude's *Landscape with Hagar and the Angel*', *The British Art Journal* 3, no. 3 (autumn 2002), pp. 43-47

Farington 1978-84
Farington, Joseph, *The Diary of Joseph Farington*, 16 vols., ed. Kathryn Cave *et al.*, New Haven, Conn. (Yale University Press, for the Paul Mellon Centre for Studies in British Art) 1978-84

Feaver 1975
Feaver, William, *The Art of John Martin*, Oxford (Clarendon Press) 1975

Finlay 1988
Finlay, Karen, *Arthur Hughes: The Lady with the Lilacs*, Toronto (National Gallery of Ontario) 1988

Finley 1988
Finley, Gerald, 'Turner and the Steam Revolution', *Gazette des Beaux-Arts* 112 (ser. 6), no. 7/8 (1988), pp. 19-30

Fitzgerald 1975
Fitzgerald, Penelope, *Edward Burne-Jones: A Biography*, London (Michael Joseph) 1975

Fleming-Williams 1990
Fleming-Williams, Ian, *Constable and his Drawings*, London (Philip Wilson) 1990

Ford 1960
Ford, Brinsley (ed.), 'The Letters of Jonathan Skelton written from Rome and Tivoli in 1759', in *The Thirty-Sixth Volume of the Walpole Society 1956-1958*, London 1960 (Walpole Society, vol. 36), pp. 23-82

Ford 2004
Ford, Colin, 'A Pre-Raphaelite partnership: Dante Gabriel Rossetti and John Robert Parsons', *Burlington Magazine* 146, no. 1214 (May 2004), pp. 308-18

Fraser 1990
Fraser, David, 'Joseph Wright of Derby and the Lunar Society', in Egerton 1990, pp. 15-24

Freud 2003
Freud, Lucian, with William Feaver, *Lucian Freud on John Constable*, London (British Council) 2003

Fry and Creswell 1847
Fry, Katherine, and Rachel E. Creswell (eds.), *Memoirs of the Life of Elizabeth Fry,* 2 vols., London (Charles Gilpin) 1847

Fulcher 1856
Fulcher, G. W., *Life of Thomas Gainsborough, R.A.*, London 1856

Gage 1965
Gage, John, 'Turner and the Picturesque', *Burlington Magazine* 107, nos. 742-43 (Jan.-Feb. 1965), pp. 16-25; 75-81

Gage 1969a
Gage, John, *Colour in Turner: Poetry and Truth,* London (Studio Vista) 1969

Gage 1969b
Gage, John, 'Documents of Crome and Cotman', *Burlington Magazine* 111, no. 793 (Apr. 1969), pp. 215-16

Gage 1969c
Gage, John, exh. cat. *A Decade of English Naturalism 1810-1820*, Norwich (Castle Museum) & London (Victoria and Albert Museum) 1969-70

Gage 1979
Gage, John, 'Der englische Garten: ein sichtbare Exportartikel', in exh. cat. *Zwei Jahrhunderte englische Malerei: Britische Kunst und Europa 1680-1880,* Munich (Haus der Kunst) 1979-80, pp. 117-29

Gage 1987
Gage, John, *J.M.W.Turner. 'A Wonderful Range of Mind'*, New Haven, Conn. & London (Yale University Press) 1987

Gage 1996
Gage, John, 'Turner: a Watershed in Watercolour', in Lord, Michael (ed.), exh. cat. *Turner,* Canberra (National Gallery of Australia) & Melbourne (National Gallery of Victoria) 1996, pp. 101-27

Gage 2002
Gage, John, 'Le Paysage est ma maitresse', in Paris 2002, pp. 35-45

Gage 2006
Gage, John, 'Constable: the Lessons of Landscape', in exh. cat. *Constable: Impressions of Land, Sea and Sky,* ed. Anne Gray and John Gage, Canberra (National Gallery of Australia) & Wellington, Te Papa (National Museum of New Zealand) 2006, pp. 21-43

Galassi 1981
Galassi, Peter, exh. cat, *Before Photography: Painting and the Invention of Photography,* New York (Museum of Modern Art) etc. 1981-82

Galassi 1991
Galassi, Peter, *Corot in Italy: Open-Air Painting and the Classical-Landscape Tradition*, New Haven, Conn. & London (Yale University Press) 1991

Gardiner 1992
Gardiner, Stephen, *Epstein: Artist Against the Establishment*, London (Michael Joseph) 1992

Garlick and Macintyre 1978-84
Garlick, Kenneth, and Angus Macintyre (eds.), *The Diary of Joseph Farington*, 16 vols., New Haven, Conn. (Yale University Press) 1978-84

Gatrell 2006
Gatrell, Vic, *City of Laughter: Sex and Satire in Eighteenth-Century London*, London (Atlantic) 2006

Gilfillan 1858
Gilfillan, George, *The Poetical Works of Armstrong, Dyer and Green*, Edinburgh (James Nichol) 1858

Godfrey 2001
Godfrey, Richard T., *James Gillray: The Art of Caricature*, London (Tate Publishing) 2001

Goodway 2006
Goodway, David, *Anarchist Seeds Beneath the Snow: Left-Libertarian Thought and British Writers from William Morris to Colin Ward*, Liverpool (Liverpool University Press) 2006

Gowing 1971
Gowing, Lawrence, exh. cat. *Hogarth*, essay by Ronald Paulson, London (Tate Gallery) 1971-72

Gowing 1985
Gowing, Lawrence, *The Originality of Thomas Jones*, London (Thames and Hudson) 1985

Gowing 1988
Gowing, Lawrence, 'Here comes the Diesel', in exh. cat. *Leon Kossoff*, London (Anthony d'Offay Gallery) 1988, nos. 13-16

Green 1990
Green, Nicholas, *The Spectacle of Nature: Landscape and Bourgeois Culture in Nineteenth-Century France,* Manchester (Manchester University Press) 1990

Greenacre 1988
Greenacre, Francis, exh. cat. *Francis Danby, 1793-1861*, Bristol (City Museum and Art Gallery) & London (Tate Gallery) 1988

Greenacre 2005
Greenacre, Francis, *From Bristol to the Sea: Artists, the Avon Gorge and Bristol Harbour*, Bristol (Redcliffe Press) 2005

Grieve 2005
Grieve, Alastair Ian, *Constructed Abstract Art in England after the Second World War: A Neglected Avant-Garde*, New Haven, Conn. & London (Yale University Press, for the Paul Mellon Centre for Studies in British Art) 2005

Grigson 1947
Grigson, Geoffrey, *Samuel Palmer: The Visionary Years*, London (Kegan Paul) 1947

Grigson 1960
Grigson, Geoffrey, *Samuel Palmer's Valley of Vision,* London (Phoenix House) 1960

Hague 1980
Hague, René (ed.), *Dai Greatcoat: A Self-Portrait of David Jones in his Letters*, London (Faber & Faber) 1980

Hallett and Riding 2006
Hallett, Mark, and Christine Riding (eds.), *Hogarth*, Paris (Musée du Louvre), London (Tate Britain) & Madrid (La Caixa) 2006-7; London (Tate Publishing) 2006

Hamilton 2002
Hamilton, Richard, *Imaging James Joyce's Ulysses*, intro. and commentaries Stephen Coppel, London (The British Council) 2002

Hammer 2005
Hammer, Martin, *Bacon and Sutherland*, New Haven, Conn. & London (Yale University Press, for the Paul Mellon Centre for Studies in British Art) 2005

Hardie 1966-68
Hardie, Martin, *Water-Colour Painting in Britain*, ed. Dudley Snelgrove, 3 vols, London (Batsford) 1966-68 (vol.1: *The Eighteenth Century,* 1966, rev. 1967; vol. 2: *The Romantic Period*, 1967; vol. 3: *The Victorian Period*, 1968)

Hare 1895
Hare, Augustus J. C., *The Gurneys of Earlham,* 2 vols., London (George Allen) 1895

Harrison 1994
Harrison, Charles, *English Art and Modernism, 1900-1939*, 2nd ed., New Haven, Conn. & London (Yale University Press, for the Paul Mellon Centre for Studies in British Art) 1994

Harrison 2005
Harrison, Martin, *In Camera: Francis Bacon: Photography, Film and the Practice of Painting*, London (Thames and Hudson) 2005

Haskell 1931
Haskell, Arnold L., *The Sculptor Speaks: Jacob Epstein to Arnold L. Haskell: A Series of Conversations on Art*, London (William Heinemann) 1931

Haworth-Booth 2006
Haworth-Booth, Mark (ed.), *The Folio Society Book of the 100 Greatest Photographs*, London (Folio Society) 2006

Haworth-Booth and Mellor 1985
Haworth-Booth, Mark, and David Mellor, exh. cat. *Bill Brandt: Behind the Camera: Photographs 1928-1983*, Philadelphia (Museum of Art); New York (Aperture) & Oxford (Phaidon) 1985

Hayes 1970
Hayes, John, *The Drawings of Thomas Gainsborough*, London (Zwemmer) 1970

Hayes 1982
Hayes, John, *The Landscape Paintings of Thomas Gainsborough: A Critical Text and Catalogue Raisonné*, 2 vols., London (Sotheby Publications) & Munich (Prestel) 1982

Hemingway 2000
Hemingway, Andrew, '"Norwich School": Myth and reality', in London 2000, pp. 9-23

Heppner 1995
Heppner, Christopher, *Reading Blake's Designs,* Cambridge (Cambridge University Press) 1995

Herrmann 1975
Herrmann, Luke, *Turner: Paintings, Watercolours, Prints & Drawings*, London (Phaidon) 1975

Hill 1965
Hill, Draper, *Mr. Gillray, the Caricaturist: A Biography*, London (Phaidon) 1965

Hill 1999
Hill, David, exh. cat. *Thomas Girtin: Genius in the North*, intro. Susan Morris, Harewood House, Yorkshire, 1999

Hilton 1988
Hilton, Boyd, *The Age of Atonement: The Influence of Evangelicalism on Social and Economic Thought, 1795-1865*, Oxford (Clarendon Press) 1988

Hind 1910
Hind, Charles Lewis, *Turner's Golden Visions*, London & Edinburgh (T.C. & E.C. Jack) 1910

Hipple 1957
Hipple, Walter John Jr., *The Beautiful, The Sublime, & The Picturesque in Eighteenth-Century British Aesthetic Theory*, Carbondale (Southern Illinois University Press) 1957

Hoock 2003
Hoock, Holger, *The King's Artists: The Royal Academy of Arts and the Politics of British Culture, 1760-1840,* Oxford (Clarendon Press) 2003

House, Storey and Tillotson 1997
House, Madeline, Graham Storey and Kathleen Tillotson (eds.), *The Letters of Charles Dickens, vol. 9, 1859-1861*, Oxford (Clarendon Press) 1997

Howard 1969
Howard, Deborah, 'Some Eighteenth-Century English Followers of Claude', *Burlington Magazine* 111, no. 801 (Dec. 1969), pp. 726-33

Howard 2000
Howard, Michael, *Lowry: A Visionary Artist*, Salford Quays (Lowry Press) 2000

Hudson 1972
Hudson, Derek (ed.), *Munby: Man of Two Worlds: The Life and Diaries of Arthur J. Munby, 1828-1910*, London (John Murray) 1972

Hueffer 1896
Hueffer, Ford Madox [later called Ford Madox Ford], *Ford Madox Brown: A Record of his Life and Works*, London (Longmans Green) 1896

Hull, Glasgow & Plymouth 1977
Exh. cat. *Sickert: Paintings, Drawings and Prints of Walter Richard Sickert, 1860-1942*, Hull (Ferens Art Gallery), Glasgow (Art Gallery) & Plymouth (City Museum & Art Gallery) 1977-78

Hunt 1905
Hunt, William Holman, *Pre-Raphaelitism and the Pre-Raphaelite Brotherhood*, 2 vols., London (Macmillan) 1905

Hyman and Wright 2001
Hyman, Timothy, and Patrick Wright, exh. cat. *Stanley Spencer*, London (Tate Britain), Toronto (Art Gallery of Ontario) & Belfast (Ulster Museum) 2001

Ingamells 1997
Ingamells, John, *A Dictionary of British and Irish Travellers in Italy, 1701-1800*, New Haven, Conn. & London (Yale University Press, for the Paul Mellon Centre for Studies in British Art) 1997

Ingamells and Edgcumbe 2000
Ingamells, John, and John Edgcumbe (eds.), *The Letters of Sir Joshua Reynolds,* New Haven, Conn. & London (Yale University Press, for the Paul Mellon Centre for Studies in British Art) 2000

Jackson 2004
Jackson, Kevin, *Humphrey Jennings*, London (Picador) 2004

James 1966
James, Philip (ed.), *Henry Moore on Sculpture: A Collection of the Sculptor's Writings and Spoken Words*, London (Macdonald) 1966

Jennings 1982
Jennings, Mary-Lou (ed.), *Humphrey Jennings: Film-Maker, Painter, Poet*, intro. Roland Penrose, London (Riverside Studios); London (British Film Institute) 1982

Jones 1990
Jones, Rica, 'Wright of Derby's techniques of painting', in Egerton 1990, pp. 263-71

Keynes 1971
Keynes, Geoffrey, *Blake Studies: Essays on his Life and Work*, 2nd ed., Oxford (Clarendon Press) 1971

Keynes 1980
Keynes, Geoffrey (ed.) *The Letters of William Blake: With Related Documents,* 3rd rev. ed., Oxford (Clarendon Press) 1980

Khoroche 1990
Khoroche, Peter, *Ivon Hitchens*, London (André Deutsch) 1990

Klonk 1996
Klonk, Charlotte, *Science and the Perception of Nature: British Landscape Art in the Late Eighteenth and Early Nineteenth Centuries*, New Haven, Conn. & London (Yale University Press, for the Paul Mellon Centre for Studies in British Art) 1996

Lamb 1811
Lamb, Charles, 'On the Genius and Character of Hogarth', *The Reflector* 2, no. 3 (1811), pp. 61-77

Lampert 1978
Lampert, Catherine, 'A conversation with Frank Auerbach', in exh. cat. *Frank Auerbach*, London (Hayward Gallery) & Edinburgh (Fruit Market Gallery); London (Arts Council of Great Britain) 1978, pp. 10-23

Laughton 2004
Laughton, Bruce, *William Coldstream*, New Haven, Conn. & London (Yale University Press, for the Paul Mellon Centre for Studies in British Art) 2004

Leeds etc. 1978
Exh. cat. *Great Victorian Pictures: Their Paths to Fame*, text by Rosemary Treble, Leeds (City Art Gallery etc.; London (Arts Council of Great Britain) 1978

Leeds & London 1987
Exh. cat. *Jacob Epstein: Sculpture and Drawings*, texts by Evelyn Silber, Terry Friedman, Richard Cork *et al.*, Leeds (Henry Moore Centre for the Study of Sculpture, City Art Galleries) & London (Whitechapel Art Gallery) 1987

Leslie 1951
Leslie, Charles Robert, *Memoirs of the Life of John Constable, Composed Chiefly of his Letters* [1843/45], ed. Jonathan Mayne, London (Phaidon) 1951

Lindsay 1966
Lindsay, Jack (ed.), *The Sunset Ship: The Poems of J. M. W. Turner,* Lowestoft (Scorpion Press) 1966

Linnell 1994
Linnell, David, *Blake, Palmer, Linnell and Co.: The Life of John Linnell,* Lewes (The Book Guild) 1994

Lister 1974a
Lister, Raymond (ed.), *The Letters of Samuel Palmer,* 2 vols., Oxford (Clarendon Press) 1974

Lister 1974b
Lister, Raymond, *Samuel Palmer: A Biography*, London (Faber & Faber) 1974

Löcher 1973
Löcher, Kurt, *Der Perseus-Zyklus von Edward Burne-Jones*, Stuttgart (Staatsgalerie) 1973

Lochnan 2004
Lochnan, Katharine, exh. cat. *Turner, Whistler, Monet: Impressionist Visions*, Toronto (Art Gallery of Ontario), Paris (Grand Palais) & London (Tate Britain) 2004-5

London 1921
Exh. cat. *Tyros and Portraits: Catalogue of an exhibition of paintings and drawings by Wyndham Lewis*, London (Ernest Brown & Phillips, The Leicester Galleries) 1921

London 1961
Exh. cat. *Epstein: Arts Council Memorial Exhibition*, London (Arts Council of Great Britain) 1961

London 1974
Exh. cat. *Turner 1775-1851*, texts by Martin Butlin, Andrew Wilton and John Gage, London (Royal Academy of Arts) 1974-75

London 1976
Exh. cat. *Constable: Paintings, watercolours & drawings*, texts by Leslie Parris, Ian Fleming-Williams and Conal Shields, London (Tate Gallery) 1976

London etc. 1979
Exh. cat. *Ivon Hitchens: A Retrospective Exhibition*, intro. Andrew Causey, London (Royal Academy of Arts), Cambridge (Fitzwilliam Museum), Penzance (Newlyn Art Gallery), Hull (Ferens Art Gallery) & Nottingham (Castle Museum) 1979

London 1980
Exh. cat. *Gaspard Dughet, called Gaspard Poussin 1615–75: A French Landscape Painter in Seventeenth Century Rome and his Influence on British Art*, text by Anne French, London (Iveagh Bequest, Kenwood) 1980

London 1984
Exh. cat. *The Pre-Raphaelites*, ed. Alan Bowness and Leslie Parris, London (Tate Gallery and Penguin Books) 1984

London 1991
Exh. cat. *Constable*, texts by Leslie Parris and Ian Fleming-Williams, London (Tate Gallery) 1991

London 2000
Exh. cat. *Romantic Landscape: The Norwich School of Painters,* texts by David Blayney Brown, Andrew Hemingway and Anne Lyles, London (Tate Britain) 2000

London & New York 2005
Exh. cat. *Samuel Palmer, 1805-1881: Vision and Landscape,* ed. William Vaughan, Elizabeth E. Barker and Colin Harrison, London (British Museum) & New York (Metropolitan Museum of Art) 2005-6; London (Lund Humphries) 2005

London, Washington & San Marino 2006
Exh. cat. *Constable: The Great Landscapes*, ed. Anne Lyles, London (Tate Britain), Washington (National Gallery of Art) & San Marino, Calif. (Huntington Art Gallery) 2006-7

Lowry 2003
Lowry, Kate, 'Thomas Jones: A Technical Study of his Oil Paintings', in Sumner and Smith 2003, pp. 89-99

Lyles 2000
Lyles, Anne, '"That Immense Canopy": Studies of sky and cloud by British artists c.1770-1860', in Morris 2000, pp. 135-50

Lyles 2006
Lyles, Anne, 'Soliciting Attention: Constable, the Royal Academy and the Critics', in London, Washington & San Marino 2006-7, pp. 32-39

Lyles and Hamlyn 1997
Lyles, Anne, and Robin Hamlyn, exh. cat. *British Watercolours from the Oppé Collection*, London (Tate Gallery) etc. 1997-99

Maas 1975
Maas, Jeremy, *Gambart: Prince of the Victorian Art World*, London (Barrie and Jenkins) 1975

McCoubrey 1986
McCoubrey, John, 'Time's Railway: Turner and the Great Western', *Turner Studies* 6, no. 1 (Summer 1986), pp. 33-39

MacGregor 1989
MacGregor, John M., *The Discovery of the Art of the Insane*, Princeton (Princeton University Press) 1989

Mackail 1995
Mackail, John William, *The Life of William Morris* (1899), New York (Dover Publications) & London (Constable) 1995

Marks 1896
Marks, John George, *Life and Letters of Frederick Walker, A.RA*, London (Macmillan) 1896

Marsh and Nunn 1989
Marsh, Jan, and Pamela Gerrish Nunn, *Women Artists and the Pre-Raphaelite Movement*, London (Virago) 1989

Marsh and Nunn 1997
Marsh, Jan, and Pamela Gerrish Nunn, exh. cat. *Pre-Raphaelite Women Artists*, Manchester (Manchester City Art Galleries), Birmingham (Museum and Art Gallery) & Southampton (City Art Gallery), 1997-98

Matteson 1981
Matteson, Lynn R., 'John Martin's "The Deluge": A Study in Romantic Catastrophe', *Pantheon* 39, no. 3 (July-Sept. 1981), pp. 220-28

Mayhew 1968
Mayhew, Henry, *London Labour and the London Poor*, facsimile of 1861 ed., 4 vols., New York (Dover) 1968

Mayhew 1985
Mayhew, Henry, *London Labour and the London Poor: Selections made and introduced by Victor Neuburg*, Harmondsworth (Penguin) 1985

Miller 1995
Miller, Michele L., 'J. M. W. Turner's *Ploughing up Turnips, near Slough:* The Cultivation of Cultural Dissent', *Art Bulletin* 77, no. 4 (Dec. 1995), pp. 572-83

Moir 1964
Moir, Esther, *The Discovery of Britain: The English Tourists, 1540 to 1840,* London (Routledge & Kegan Paul) 1964

Moorman 1973
Moorman, John Richard Humpidge, *A History of the Church in England*, 3rd ed., London (A. and C. Black) 1973

Morris 2000
Morris, Edward (ed.), exh. cat. *Constable's Clouds: Paintings and Cloud Studies by John Constable,* texts by John Gage, Anne Lyles, Martin Suggett, John E. Thornes and Timothy Wilcox, Liverpool (Walker Art Gallery) & Edinburgh (National Gallery of Scotland) 2000

Nash 1949
Nash, Paul, *Outline: An Autobiography and Other Writings*, preface by Herbert Read, London (Faber & Faber) 1949

Nasmyth 1885
Nasmyth, James, *James Nasmyth, Engineer: an Autobiography*, ed. Samuel Smiles, London (John Murray) 1885

Newall 2004a
Newall, Christopher, 'Understanding the Landscape', in Staley and Newall 2004, pp. 133-43

Newall 2004b
Newall, Christopher, '"Impression of the Effect"', in Staley and Newall 2004, pp. 209-17

Nicholson 1948
Nicholson, Ben, *Ben Nicholson: Paintings Reliefs Drawings*, intro. Herbert Read, London (Lund Humphries) 1948 [reprinted 1955 as vol. 1, 1911-1948]

Nicolson 1968
Nicolson, Benedict, *Joseph Wright of Derby: Painter of Light*, 2 vols., London (Paul Mellon Foundation for British Art, Routledge & Kegan Paul) & New York (Pantheon Books) 1968

Olson and Pasachoff 1986
Olson, Roberta J. M., and Jay M. Pasachoff, 'New Information on Comet Halley as Depicted by Giotto di Bondone and Other Western Artists', *Proceedings of the 20th ESLAB Symposium on the Exploration of Halley's Comet*, Heidelberg 1986, pp. 201-13

Oppé 1934
Oppé, A. Paul, 'Art', in Young, G. M. (ed.), *Early Victorian England*, 1934, vol. 2, pp. 101-76

Oppé 1942
Oppé, [A.] Paul, 'Cotman and his Public', *Burlington Magazine* 81, no. 472 (July 1942), pp. 163-71

Oppé 1951
Oppé, [A.] Paul (ed.), *Memoirs of Thomas Jones, Penkerrig, Radnorshire, 1803*, London 1951 (Walpole Society, vol. 32)

Paley 1986
Paley, Morton D., *The Apocalyptic Sublime*, New Haven, Conn. & London (Yale University Press) 1986

Palmer 1892
Palmer, Alfred Herbert, *The Life and Letters of Samuel Palmer, Painter and Etcher,* London (Seeley) 1892

Paris 2002
Exh. cat. *Constable: Le choix de Lucian Freud*, Paris (Grand Palais) 2002-3

Parris 1973
Parris, Leslie, exh. cat. *Landscape in Britain, c. 1750-1850*, London (Tate Gallery) 1973

Parris 1984
Parris, Leslie (ed.) *Pre-Raphaelite Papers,* London (Tate Gallery) 1984

Parris, Shields and Fleming-Williams 1975
Parris, Leslie, Conal Shields and Ian Fleming-Williams (eds.), *John Constable: Further Documents and Correspondence,* London (Tate Gallery) & Ipswich (Suffolk Records Society) 1975

Pasmore 1951
Pasmore, Victor, 'The Artist Speaks', *Art News and Review*, 24 February1951, p. 3 [transcript of talk at the ICA, 9 January 1951]

Payne 1993
Payne, Christiana, exh. cat. *Toil and Plenty: Images of the Agricultural Landscape in England, 1780-1890*, Nottingham (University Art Gallery) & New Haven, Conn. (Yale Center for British Art) 1993-94; New Haven - London (Yale University Press) 1993

Pearce 2003
Pearce, Edward, *Reform! The Fight for the 1832 Reform Act*, London (Jonathan Cape) 2003

Pendered 1923
Pendered, Mary Lucy, *John Martin, Painter: His Life and Times*, London (Hurst & Blackett) 1923

Peppiatt 2006
Peppiatt, Michael, *Francis Bacon in the 1950s*, New Haven, Conn. & London (Yale University Press, Sainsbury Centre for Visual Arts) 2006

Pevsner 1956
Pevsner, Nikolaus, *The Englishness of English Art*, London (Architectural Press) 1956

Pidgley 1972
Pidgley, Michael, 'Cornelius Varley, Cotman, and the Graphic Telescope', *Burlington Magazine* 114, no. 836 (Nov. 1972), pp. 780-86

Pointon 1972
Pointon, Marcia, 'The Italian Tour of William Hilton, R.A. in 1825', *Journal of the Warburg and Courtauld Institutes* 35 (1972), pp. 339-58

Pointon 1979
Pointon, Marcia, *William Dyce, 1806-1864: A Critical Biography,* Oxford (Clarendon Press) 1979

Pressly 1983
Pressly, William L., exh. cat. *James Barry: The Artist as Hero*, London (Tate Gallery) 1983

Prettejohn 2000
Prettejohn, Elizabeth, *The Art of the Pre-Raphaelites*, London (Tate Publishing) 2000

Price 1810
Price, Uvedale, *Essays on the Picturesque, as Compared with the Sublime and the Beautiful…*, 3 vols., London (Mawman) 1810

Priestley 1804
Priestley, Joseph, *The Doctrines of Heathen Philosophy, Compared with those of Revelation*, Northumberland, Pa. (John Binns) 1804

Priestley 1934
Priestley, J.B., *English Journey: Being a Rambling but Truthful Account of what One Man Saw and Heard and Felt and Thought during a Journey through England during the Autumn of the Year 1933*, London (Heinemann and Gollancz) 1934

Prince 1988
Prince, Hugh, 'Art and Agrarian Change, 1710-1815', in Cosgrove and Daniels 1988, pp. 98-118

Rad 1956
Rad, Gerhard von, *Das erste Buch Mose, Genesis*, Göttingen (Vandenhoek und Ruprecht) 1956

Raine 1968
Raine, Kathleen, *Blake and Tradition*, 2 vols., Princeton (Princeton University Press) 1968

Rajnai and Allthorpe-Guyton 1979
Rajnai, Miklós, and Marjorie Allthorpe-Guyton, *John Sell Cotman 1782-1842: Early Drawings (1798-1812) in Norwich Castle Museum*, Norwich (Norfollk Museums Service) 1979

Reade 1987
Reade, Brian, *Aubrey Beardsley*, rev. ed., Woodbridge (Antique Collectors' Club), 1987

Reynolds 1909
Reynolds, Myra, *The Treatment of Nature in English Poetry between Pope and Wordsworth,* Chicago (Chicago University Press) 1909

Reynolds 1973
Reynolds, Graham, *Catalogue of the Constable Collection in the Victoria and Albert Museum*, 2nd ed. London (HMSO) 1973

Reynolds 1975
Reynolds, Joshua, *Discourses on Art,* ed. Robert R. Wark, New Haven, Conn. & London (Yale University Press, for the Paul Mellon Centre for Studies in British Art) 1975

Reynolds 1984
Reynolds, Graham, *The Later Paintings and Drawings of John Constable*, 2 vols., New Haven, Conn. & London (Yale University Press, for the Paul Mellon Centre for Studies in British Art) 1984

Reynolds 1996
Reynolds, Graham, *The Early Paintings and Drawings of John Constable,* 2 vols., New Haven, Conn. & London (Yale University Press, for the Paul Mellon Centre for Studies in British Art) 1996

Rhyne 1990
Rhyne, Charles, *John Constable: Toward a Complete Chronology*, Portland, Oreg. (author) 1990 (people.reed.edu/~crhyne/papers/jc_chronology.pdf)

Riopelle 2003
Riopelle, Christopher, 'Thomas Jones in Italy', in Sumner and Smith 2003, pp. 47-67

Roberts 1976
Roberts, William, 'Commentary' in exh. cat. *Paintings and Drawings by William Roberts RA*, London (Parkin Gallery) 1976

Robertson 1897
Robertson, Emily (ed.) *Letters and Papers of Andrew Robertson, A.M., Miniature Painter …*, London (Eyre & Spottiswoode) 1897

Robins and Thomson 2005
Robins, Anna Gruetzner, and Richard Thomson, exh. cat. *Degas, Sickert and Toulouse-Lautrec: London and Paris, 1870-1910*, London (Tate Britain) & Washington (Phillips Collection) 2005-6

Rodner 1997
Rodner, William S., *J. M .W. Turner: Romantic Painter of the Industrial Revolution,* Berkeley (University of California Press) 1997

Roget 1891
Roget, John Lewis, *A History of the 'Old Water-Colour' Society now the Royal Society of Painters in Water Colour*, 2 vols,, London (Longmans) 1891

Rose 1977
Rose, Andrea, *The Pre-Raphaelites*, Oxford (Phaidon) 1977)

Rosenthal 1982
Rosenthal, Michael, *British Landscape Painting*, Oxford (Phaidon) 1982

Rosenthal 1983
Rosenthal, Michael, *Constable: The Painter and his Landscape*, New Haven, Conn. & London (Yale University Press) 1983

Rosenthal and Myrone 2002
Rosenthal, Michael, and Martin Myrone (eds.), exh. cat. *Gainsborough*, London (Tate Britain), Washington (National Gallery of Art) & Boston (Museum of Fine Arts) 2002-3

Rothenstein 1973
Rothenstein, John, exh. cat. *Edward Burra*, London (Tate Gallery) 1973

Röthlisberger 1961
Röthlisberger, Marcel, *Claude Lorrain: The Paintings*, 2 vols., New Haven, Conn. (Yale University Press) & London (Zwemmer) 1961

Rowan 1982
Rowan, Eric, exh. cat. *Some Miraculous Promised Land: J.D.Innes, Augustus John and Derwent Lees in North Wales 1910-13 (Gwyrthiol wlad yr addewid: J.D. Innes, Augustus John a Derwent Lees yng Ngogledd Cymru 1910-13)*, Llandudno (Mostyn Art Gallery), Cardiff & Sheffield 1982

Rowell, Warrell and Brown 2002
Rowell, Christopher, Ian Warrell and David Blayney Brown, *Turner at Petworth*, London (Tate Publishing) 2002

Russell 1906
Russell, Archibald G.B. (ed.), *The Letters of William Blake: Together with a Life by Frederick. Tatham*, London (Methuen) 1906

Russell 1971
Russell, John, *Francis Bacon*, rev. ed., London (Thames and Hudson) 1971

Sadrin 1995
Sadrin, Anny, 'John Martin - *The Deluge*', *Interfaces* 7 (1995), pp. 11-26

Schaaf 2000
Schaaf, Larry J., *The Photographic Art of William Henry Fox Talbot*, Princeton & Oxford (Princeton University Press) 2000

Schama 1995
Schama, Simon, *Landscape and Memory*, London (HarperCollins) 1995

Schama 2006
Schama, Simon, *Simon Schama's Power of Art*, London (BBC) 2006

Schneede 1979
Schneede, Uwe M., exh. cat. *Der Zeichner und Grafiker Max Beckmann*, Hamburg (Kunstverein) 1979

Schneider 2002
Schneider, Pierre, *Matisse*, rev. ed., London (Thames and Hudson) 2002

Schwartz 1990
Schwartz, Sanford, *Artists and Writers*, New York (Yarrow Press), 1990,

Seddon 1858
[Seddon, John Pollard], *Memoir and Letters of the late Thomas Seddon, Artist. By his Brother*, London (James Nisbet) 1858

Seymour 1979
Seymour, Anne (intro.), exh. cat. *Richard Hamilton Drawings, Prints and Paintings 1941-55*, London (Anthony d'Offay) 1979

Seznec 1964
Seznec, Jean, *John Martin en France*, London (Faber & Faber) 1964

Shanes 1979
Shanes, Eric, *Turner's Picturesque Views in England and Wales, 1825-1838*, intro. Andrew Wilton, London (Chatto and Windus) 1979

Shanes 2001
Shanes, Eric, exh. cat. *The Golden Age of Watercolours: The Hickman Bacon Collection*, London (Dulwich Picture Gallery) & New Haven, Conn. (Yale Center for British Art), 2001-3

Shesgreen 2001
Shesgreen, Sean, 'William Hogarth's *Enraged Musician* and the Cries of London', in Bindman, Ogée and Wagner 2001, pp. 125-45

Shone 1988
Shone, Richard, *Walter Sickert*, Oxford (Phaidon) 1988

Short 2000
Short, Brian, 'Forests and Wood-Pasture in Lowland England', in Thirsk, Joan (ed.), *Rural England: An illustrated history of the landscape,* Oxford (Oxford University Press) 2000, pp. 122-49

Silber 1986
Silber, Evelyn, *The Sculpture of Epstein: With a Complete Catalogue*, Oxford (Phaidon) 1986

Smith 1828
Smith, John Thomas, *Nollekens and his Times: Comprehending a Life of that Celebrated Sculptor; and Memoirs of Several Contemporary Artists, from the Time of Roubiliac, Hogarth, and Reynolds, to that of Fuseli, Flaxman, and Blake*, 2 vols, London 1828

Smith 1983
Smith, Bernard, 'William Hodges and English *plein-air* Painting', *Art History* 6, no. 2, June 1983, pp. 143-52

Smith 2002
Smith, Greg (ed.), exh. cat. *Thomas Girtin: The Art of Watercolour*, texts by Peter Bower, Anne Lyles and Susan M. Morris, London (Tate Britain) 2002

Solkin 1982
Solkin, David H., exh. cat. *Richard Wilson: The Landscape of Reaction*, London (Tate Gallery) 1982-83

Spencer 1987
Spencer, Robin, 'The Aesthetics of Change: London as seen by James McNeill Whistler', in Warner, Malcolm, exh. cat. *The Image of London: Views by Travellers and Emigrés, 1550-1920*, London (Barbican Art Gallery; Trefoil Publications) 1987, pp. 49-72

Spicer and Orr 1997
Spicer, Joaneath A., and Lynn Federle Orr, exh. cat. *Masters of Light: Dutch Painters in Utrecht during the Golden Age*, San Francisco (Fine Arts Museums), Baltimore (Walters Art Gallery), London (National Gallery) 1997-98

Stainton 2003
Stainton, Lindsay, 'Before Italy: The Making of an Artist', in Sumner and Smith 2003, pp. 23-45

Staley 1973
Staley, Allen *The Pre-Raphaelite Landscape*, Oxford (Clarendon Press) 1973

Staley 2001
Staley, Allen, *The Pre-Raphaelite Landscape*, 2nd ed., New Haven, Conn. & London (Yale University Press, for the Paul Mellon Centre for Studies in British Art) 2001

Staley and Newall 2004
Staley, Allen, and Christopher Newall, exh. cat. *Pre-Raphaelite Vision: Truth to Nature*, London (Tate Gallery), Berlin (Alte Nationalgalerie) & Madrid (Fundación 'la Caixa') 2004

Stevenson 1991
Stevenson, Sara, exh. cat. *Hill and Adamson's 'The Fishermen and Women of the Firth of Forth'*, Edinburgh (Scottish National Portrait Gallery) 1991

Story 1892
Story, Alfred T., *The Life of John Linnell*, 2 vols., London (Richard Bentley and Son) 1892

Strzygowski 1908
Strzygowski, Josef, 'Turner's Path from Nature to Art', *Burlington Magazine* 12, no. 60 (March 1908), pp. 335-42

Sturgis 2005
Sturgis, Matthew, *Walter Sickert: A Life*, London (HarperCollins) 2005

Sumner 2003
Sumner, Ann, 'Who was Thomas Jones? The life, death and posthumous reputation of Thomas Jones of Pencerrig', in Sumner and Smith 2003, pp. 1-21

Sumner and Smith 2003
Sumner, Ann, and Greg Smith (eds.), exh. cat. *Thomas Jones (1742-1803): An Artist Rediscovered*, Cardiff (National Museums & Gallery), Manchester (Whitworth Art Gallery) & London (National Gallery), 2003-4; New Haven, Conn. & London (Yale University Press) 2003

Surtees 1981
Surtees, Virginia (ed.), *The Diary of Ford Madox Brown*, New Haven, Conn. & London (Yale University Press, for the Paul Mellon Centre for Studies in British Art) 1981

Sutherland 1942
Sutherland, Graham, 'Welsh Sketch Book', *Horizon* 5, no. 28 (April 1942), pp. 225-26, 230, 234-35

Sutherland 1951
Sutherland, Graham, 'Thoughts on Painting', *The Listener* 46, no. 1175 (6 Sept. 1951), p. 376

Sylvester 1975
Sylvester, David, *Interviews with Francis Bacon*, London (Thames and Hudson) 1975

Sylvester 1991
Sylvester, David, exh. cat. *Richard Hamilton*, London (Anthony d'Offay Gallery) 1991

Taylor 1853
Tom Taylor (ed.), *Life of Benjamin Robert Haydon, Historical Painter, from his Autobiography and Journals*, 3 vols., London (Longman, Brown, Green and Longmans) 1853

Thompson 1977
Thompson, E.P., *William Morris: Romantic to Revolutionary*, London (Merlin Press) 1977

Thornbury 1877
Thornbury, G. Walter, *The Life of J.M.W. Turner, R.A.: Founded on Letters and Papers Furnished by his Friends and Fellow-Academicians*, rev. ed., London (Chatto and Windus) 1877

Townsend and Warrell 1991
Townsend, Joyce H., and Ian Warrell, '*Figures in a Building*, c.1830: *Martello Towers, near Bexhill*, c.1810; Picture Note', *Turner Studies* 11, no. 1 (Summer 1991), pp. 54-57

Trumble 2006
Trumble, Angus, '1727 in Retrospect', *Esopus* 7 (Fall 2006)

Turner 1980
Turner, J.M.W., *Collected Correspondence*, ed. John Gage, Oxford (Clarendon Press) 1980

Uglow 2002
Uglow, Jenny, *The Lunar Men: The Friends who Made the Future, 1730-1810*, London (Faber & Faber) 2002

Uwins 1978
Uwins, Sarah, *A Memoir of Thomas Uwins, R.A.* (1858), Wakefield (EP Publishing) 1978

Vaughan 1996
Vaughan, William, 'Constable's Englishness' , *Oxford Art Journal* 19, no. 2 (1996), pp. 17-27

Wagner 1979
Wagner, Monika, *Die Industrielandschaft in der englischen Malerei und Grafik, 1770-1830*, Frankfurt am Main (Lang) 1979

Warner and Blake 2004
Warner, Malcolm, and Robin Blake, exh. cat. *Stubbs and the Horse*, Fort Worth (Kimbell Art Museum), Baltimore (Walters Art Museum) & London (National Gallery) 2004-5; New Haven – London (Yale University Press) 2004

Weinglass 1982
Weinglass David H., (ed.), *The Collected English Letters of Henry Fuseli*, Millwood, NY (Kraus International) 1982

Whitley 1928
Whitley, William Thomas, *Artists and their Friends in England, 1700-1799*, 2 vols., London & Boston (Medici Society) 1928

Wilton 1979
Wilton, Andrew, *The Life and Work of J.M.W. Turner*, London (Academy Editions) 1979

Wilton 1989
Wilton, Andrew, 'The "Keepsake" Convention: *Jessica* and some Related Pictures', *Turner Studies* 9, no. 2 (Winter 1989), pp. 14-33

Wilton 1990
Wilton, Andrew, '*Study for the Sack of a Great House? (Interior at Petworth)*: Picture Note', *Turner Studies* 10, no. 2 (Winter 1990), pp. 55-59

Wilton and Upstone 1997
Wilton, Andrew, and Robert Upstone (eds.), exh. cat. *The Age of Rossetti, Burne-Jones and Watts: Symbolism in Britain, 1860-1910*, London (Tate Gallery), Munich (Haus der Kunst) & Amsterdam (Van Gogh Museum) 1997-98; London (Tate Gallery Publishing) 1997

Woodall 1963
Woodall, Mary (ed.), *The Letters of Thomas Gainsborough*, rev. ed., Ipswich (Cupid Press) 1963

Woolf 1934
Woolf, Virginia, *Walter Sickert: A Conversation* (1934), reprinted, London, n.d.

Woolf 1940
Woolf, Virginia, *Roger Fry: A Biography*, London (Hogarth Press) 1940

Wordsworth 1974
Wordsworth, William, *Prose Works*, ed. W.J.B. Owen and Jane Worthington Smyser, 3 vols., Oxford (Clarendon Press) 1974

Wornum 1848
Wornum, Ralph Nicholson (ed.), *Lectures on Painting: By the Royal Academicians, Barry, Opie and Fuseli*, London (H.G. Bohn) 1848

Wright 1997
Wright, Alastair Ian, 'Suburban prospects: vision and possession in Ford Madox Brown's *An English Autumn Afternoon*', in Watson, Margaretta Frederick (ed.), *Collecting the Pre-Raphaelites: The Anglo-American Enchantment*, Brookfield, Vt. & London (Ashgate) 1997, pp. 185-97

Wyndham Lewis 1915
Wyndham Lewis, Percy, 'the European War and Great Communities', *Blast*, 2 July 1915

Youngblood 1983a
Youngblood, Patrick, 'Three Mis-Identified Works by J.M.W. Turner', *Burlington Magazine* 125, no. 967 (Oct. 1983), pp.615-16, 618-19

Youngblood 1983b
Youngblood, Patrick, "That house of art": Turner at Petworth', *Turner Studies* 2, no. 2 (Winter 1983), pp. 16-33

Youngblood 1990
Youngblood, Patrick, 'Letter to the Editor', *Turner Studies* 10, no. 1 (Summer 1990), p. 51

BIBLIOGRAPHY

GENERAL BIBLIOGRAPHY

Abadie, Daniel (ed.), exh. cat. *Un siècle de sculpture anglaise*, Paris (Jeu de Paume; Réunion des Musées Nationaux) 1996

Alfrey, Nicholas, Stephen Daniels and Martin Postle (eds.), exh. cat. *Art of the Garden: The Garden in British Art, 1800 to the Present Day*, London (Tate Britain), Belfast (Ulster Museum) & Manchester (City Art Gallery), 2004-5; London (Tate Publishing) 2004

Altick, Richard D., *The Shows of London*, Cambridge, Mass. & London (Belknap Press of Harvard University Press) 1978

Baron, Wendy, *The Camden Town Group*, London (Scolar) 1979

Baron, Wendy, *Perfect Moderns: A History of the Camden Town Group*, Aldershot & Brookfield, Vt. (Ashgate) 2000

Barrell, John, *The Dark Side of the Landscape: The Rural Poor in English Painting 1730-1840*, Cambridge (Cambridge University Press) 1980

Barringer, Tim, *Reading the Pre-Raphaelites*, New Haven, Conn. & London (Yale University Press) 1999

Barringer, Tim, *Men at Work: Art and Labour in Victorian Britain*, New Haven, Conn. & London (Yale University Press, for the Paul Mellon Centre for Studies in British Art) 2005

Bermingham, Ann, *Landscape and Ideology: The English Rustic Tradition 1740-1860*, Berkeley (University of California Press) 1986 & London (Thames and Hudson) 1987

Black, Jonathan, Christopher Adams, Michael J.K. Walsh and Jonathan Wood, exh. cat. *Blasting the Future! Vorticism in Britain 1910-1920*, London (Estorick Collection of Modern Italian Art) & Manchester (Whitworth Art Gallery); London (Philip Wilson) 2004

Blayney Brown, David, *Oil Sketches from Nature: Turner and his Contemporaries*, London (Tate Gallery), 1991

Blayney Brown, David, Andrew Hemingway and Anne Lyles, exh. cat. *Romantic Landscape: The Norwich School of Painters*, London (Tate Britain) 2000

Bowness, Alan, and Leslie Parris (eds.), exh. cat. *The Pre-Raphaelites*, London (Tate Gallery; Penguin Books) 1984

Burke, Joseph, *English Art, 1714-1800, The Oxford History of English Art (vol. 9)*, Oxford (Clarendon Press) 1976

Calvocoressi, Richard (ed.), exh. cat. *From London: Bacon, Freud, Kossoff, Andrews, Auerbach, Kitaj*, Edinburgh (Scottish National Gallery of Modern Art), Luxembourg (Musée National d'Histoire et d'Art), Lausanne (Musée Cantonal des Beaux-Arts) & Barcelona (Fundació Caixa de Catalunya); London (British Council) 1995

Clark, Kenneth, Alan Bowness, John Gage, Michael Kitson, Ellis Waterhouse *et al.*, exh. cat. *La Peinture romantique anglaise et les préraphaélites*, Paris (Petit Palais) 1972

Compton, Susan (ed.), exh. cat. *British Art in the 20th Century: The Modern Movement*, London (Royal Academy of Arts) & Stuttgart (Staatsgalerie); Munich (Prestel), 1987

Cooper, Suzanne Fagence, *Pre-Raphaelite Art in the Victoria and Albert Museum*, London (V&A Publications) 2003

Corbett, David Peters, *The Modernity of English Art 1914-30*, Manchester & New York (Manchester University Press) 1997

Corbett, David Peters, and Lara Perry (eds.), *English Art 1860-1914: Modern Artists and Identity*, Manchester (Manchester University Press) 2000

Corbett, David Peters, Ysanne Holt and Fiona Russell (eds.), *The Geographies of Englishness: Landscape and the National Past 1880-1940*, New Haven, Conn. & London (Yale University Press, for the Paul Mellon Centre for Studies in British Art) 2002

Corbett, David Peters, *The World in Paint: Modern Art and Visuality in England, 1848-1914*, Manchester & New York (Manchester University Press) 2004

Cork, Richard, exh. cat. *Vorticism and its Allies*, London (Hayward Gallery); London (Arts Council of Great Britain) 1974

Cork, Richard, *Vorticism and Abstract Art in the First Machine Age*, 2 vols., London (Gordon Fraser) 1976

Cork, Richard, *Art Beyond The Gallery in Early 20th Century England*, New Haven, Conn. & London (Yale University Press) 1985

Cork, Richard, exh. cat. *A Bitter Truth: Avant-Garde Art and the Great War*, Berlin (Altes Museum) & London (Barbican Art Gallery); New Haven, Conn. & London (Yale University Press) 1994

Deuchar, Stephen, *Sporting Art in Eighteenth-Century England: A Social and Political History*, New Haven, Conn. & London (Yale University Press, for the Paul Mellon Centre for Studies in British Art) 1988

Donald, Diana, *The Age of Caricature: Satirical Prints in the Reign of George III*, New Haven, Conn. & London (Yale University Press, for the Paul Mellon Centre for Studies in British Art) 1996

Edwards, Paul (ed.), *Blast: Vorticism 1914-1918*, Aldershot (Ashgate) 2000

Egerton, Judy, *The British School (National Gallery Catalogues)*, London (National Gallery) 2000

Einberg, Elizabeth, and Judy Egerton, *The Age of Hogarth: British Painters born 1675-1709 1709 (Tate Gallery Collections, vol. 2)*, London (Tate Gallery) 1988

Engen, Rodney, *Pre-Raphaelite Prints: The Graphic Art of Millais, Holman Hunt, Rossetti and their Followers*, London (Lund Humphries) 1995

Farr, Dennis, *English Art 1870-1940, The Oxford History of English Art (vol. 11)*, Oxford (Clarendon Press) 1978

Foss, Brian, *War Paint: Art, War, State and Identity in Britain 1939-1945*, New Haven, Conn. & London (Yale University Press, for the Paul Mellon Centre for Studies in British Art) 2007

Galassi, Peter, exh. cat. *Before Photography, Painting and the Invention of Photography*, New York, (Museum of Mondern Art) 1981

Gatrell, Vic, *City of Laughter: Sex and Satire in Eighteenth-Century London*, London (Atlantic) 2006

Gere, John A., *Pre-Raphaelite Drawings in the British Museum*, London (British Museum Press) 1994

Gowing, Lawrence exh. cat. *Painting from Nature, The Tradition of Open-Air Oil Sketching from the 17th to 19th Centuries*, Cambridge (Fitzwilliam Museum) & London (Royal Academy of Arts); London (Arts Council of Great Britain) 1981

Grieve, Alastair Ian, *Constructed Abstract Art in England after the Second World War: A Neglected Avant-Garde*, New Haven, Conn. & London (Yale University Press, for the Paul Mellon Centre for Studies in British Art) 2005

Grigson, Geoffrey, *English Drawing from Samuel Cooper to Gwen John*, London (Thames and Hudson) 1955

Hallett, Mark, *The Spectacle of Difference: Graphic Satire in the Age of Hogarth*, New Haven, Conn. & London (Yale University Press, for the Paul Mellon Centre for Studies in British Art) 1999

Harrison, Charles, *English Art and Modernism 1900-1939*, 2nd ed., New Haven, Conn. & London (Yale University Press, for the Paul Mellon Centre for Studies in British Art) 1994

Harrison, Martin, exh. cat. *Transition: The London Art Scene in the Fifties*, London (Barbican Art Gallery; Merrell) 2002

Haworth-Booth, Mark (ed.), exh. cat. *The Golden Age of British Photography 1839-1900*, London (Victoria and Albert Museum), Philadelphia (Museum of Art), Houston (Museum of Fine Arts), Minneapolis (Institute of Arts), New York (Pierpont Morgan Library) & Boston (Museum of Fine Arts) 1984-86; London (Aperture) 1984

Haworth-Booth, Mark, *Photography: An Independent Art. Photographs from the Victoria and Albert Museum, 1839-1996*, London (V&A Publications) 1997

Hedinger, Bärbel, Inés Richter-Musso and Ortrud Westheider (eds.), exh. cat. *Wolkenbilder. Die Entdeckung des Himmels*, Hamburg (Bucerius Kunst Forum, Jenisch Haus, Altonaer Museum), Berlin (Nationalgalerie) & Aarau (Aarauer Kunsthaus); Munich (Hirmer Verlag) 2004

Herrmann, Luke, *British Landscape Painting of the Eighteenth Century*, London (Faber & Faber) 1973 & New York (Oxford University Press) 1974

Herrmann, Luke, *Nineteenth Century British Painting*, London (Giles de la Mare) 2000

Hewison, Robert, Ian Warrell and Stephen Wildman, exh. cat. *Ruskin, Turner and the Pre-Raphaelites*, London (Tate Britain) 2000

Hilton, Tim, *The Pre-Raphaelites*, London (Thames and Hudson) 1970

Hipple, Walter John Jr., *The Beautiful, The Sublime, & The Picturesque in Eighteenth-Century British Aesthetic Theory*, Carbondale (Southern Illinois University Press) 1957

Hodnett, Edward, *Five Centuries of English Book Illustration*, Aldershot (Scolar) 1988

Hofmann, Werner (ed.), exh. cat. *William Turner und die Landschaft seiner Zeit*, Hamburg (Kunsthalle); Munich (Prestel) 1976

Holt, Ysanne, *British Artists and the Modernist Landscape*, Aldershot (Ashgate) 2003

Hughes, Henry Meyric, and Gijs van Tuyl (eds.), exh. cat. *Blast to Freeze: British Art in the 20th Century*, Wolfsburg (Kunstmuseum) & Toulouse (Les Abattoirs) 2002-3; Ostfildern-Ruit (Hatje Cantz) 2002

Humphreys, Richard, *The Tate Companion Guide to British Art*, London (Tate Publishing) 2001

Hyman, James, *The Battle for Realism: Figurative Art in Britain During the Cold War 1945-1960*, New Haven, Conn. & London (Yale University Press, for the Paul Mellon Centre for Studies in British Art) 2001

Kitson, Michael, John Gage, William Vaughan and Christopher White, exh. cat. *Zwei Jahrhunderte englische Malerei: Britische Kunst und Europa 1680-1880*, Munich (Haus der Kunst) 1979-80

Klonk, Charlotte, *Science and the Perception of Nature: British Landscape Art in the Late Eighteenth and Early Nineteenth Centuries*, New Haven, Conn. & London (Yale University Press, for the Paul Mellon Centre for Studies in British Art) 1996

Lyles, Anne, and Robin Hamlyn, exh. cat. *British Watercolours from the Oppé Collection*, London (Tate Gallery) etc. 1997-99

MacMillan, Duncan, *Scottish Art 1460-2000*, Edinburgh (Mainstream) 1990

Malvern, Sue, *Modern Art, Britain and the Great War: Witnessing, Testimony and Remembrance*, New Haven, Conn. & London (Yale University Press, for the Paul Mellon Centre for Studies in British Art) 2004

Mellor, David, *Modern British Photography, 1919-1939*, London (Arts Council of Great Britain) 1980

Monrad, Kasper (ed.), exh. cat. *Turner and Romantic Nature*, Copenhagen (Statens Museum for Kunst) 2004-5

Moore, Jerrold Northrop *The Green Fuse, Pastoral Vision in English Art 1820-2000*, Suffolk (Antique Collectors' Club) 2007

Morphet, Richard, exh. cat. *The Hard-Won Image: Traditional Method and Subject in Recent British Art*, London (Tate Gallery) 1984

Myrone, Martin (ed.), exh. cat. *Gothic Nightmares: Fuseli, Blake and the Romantic Imagination*, London (Tate Britain) 2006

Nairne, Sandy, and Nicholas Serota (eds.), exh. cat. *British Sculpture in the Twentieth Century*, London (Whitechapel Art Gallery) 1981

Newall, Christopher, *Victorian Watercolours*, London & New York (Phaidon) 2001

Noon, Patrick (ed.), exh. cat. *Constable to Delacroix: British Art and the French Romantics*, London (Tate Britain), Minneapolis (Institute of Arts) & New York (Metropolitan Museum of Art) 2003-4; London (Tate Publishing) 2003

Orchard, Karin (ed.), exh. cat. *BLAST: Vortizismus - Die erste Avantgarde in England 1914-1918*, Hannover (Sprengel Museum) & Munich (Haus der Kunst) 1996-97; Berlin (Ars Nicolai) 1996

Parris, Leslie, exh. cat. *Landscape in Britain c. 1750-1850*, London (Tate Gallery) 1973

Payne, Christiana, exh. cat. *Toil and Plenty: Images of the Agricultural Landscape in England, 1780-1890*, Nottingham (University Art Gallery) & New Haven, Conn. (Yale Center for British Art) 1993-94; New Haven & London (Yale University Press) 1993

Pevsner, Nikolaus, *The Englishness of English Art*, London (Architectural Press) 1956

Pointon, Marcia, *Hanging the Head: Portraiture and Social Formation in Eighteenth-century England*, New Haven, Conn. & London (Yale University Press, for the Paul Mellon Centre for Studies in British Art) 1993

Prettejohn, Elizabeth, *The Art of the Pre-Raphaelites*, London (Tate Publishing) 2000

Rosenthal, Michael, *British Landscape Painting*, Oxford (Phaidon) 1982

Rosenthal, Michael, Christiana Payne and Scott B. Wilcox (eds.), *Prospects for the Nation: Recent Essays in British Landscape, 1750-1880*, New Haven, Conn. & London (Yale University Press, for the Paul Mellon Centre for Studies in British Art) 1997

Simon, Robin *Hogarth, France & British Art, The Rise of the Arts in 18th-century Britain*, London (Paul Holberton) 2007

Smiles, Sam, *Eye Witness: Artists and Visual Documentation in Britain 1770-1830*, Aldershot & Brookfield, Vt. (Ashgate) 2000

Solkin, David H., *Painting for Money: The Visual Arts and the Public Sphere in Eighteenth-Century England*, New Haven, Conn. & London (Yale University Press, for the Paul Mellon Centre for Studies in British Art) 1992

Solkin, David H. (ed.), exh. cat. *Art on the Line: The Royal Academy Exhibitions at Somerset House 1780-1836*, London (Courtauld Institute Gallery); New Haven, Conn. & London (Yale University Press, for the Paul Mellon Centre for Studies in British Art and the Courtauld Institute Gallery) 2001

Spalding, Frances, *British Art since 1900*, London (Thames and Hudson) 1987

Spalding, Frances and Ian Jeffrey, exh. cat. *Landscape in Britain 1850-1950*, London (Hayward Gallery), Bristol (City Museum and Art Gallery), Stoke-on-Trent (City Museum and Art Gallery) & Sheffield (Mappin Art Gallery); London (Arts Council of Great Britain) 1983

Stainton, Lindsay, *British Landscape Watercolours 1600-1860*, London (British Museum Publications) 1985

Staley, Allen, *The Pre-Raphaelite Landscape*, 2nd ed., New Haven, Conn. & London (Yale University Press, for the Paul Mellon Centre for Studies in British Art) 2001

Staley, Allen, and Christopher Newall, exh. cat. *Pre-Raphaelite Vision: Truth to Nature*, London (Tate Gallery), Berlin (Alte Nationalgalerie) & Madrid (Fundación 'la Caixa') 2004

Tickner, Lisa, *Modern Life and Modern Subjects: British Art in the Early Twentieth Century*, New Haven, Conn. & London (Yale University Press) 2000

Treuherz, Julian, *Victorian Painting*, London (Thames and Hudson) 1993

Vaughan, William, *British Painting: The Golden Age*, London (Thames and Hudson) 1999

Warner, Malcolm, exh. cat. *The Image of London: Views by Travellers and Emigrés 1550-1920*, London (Barbican Art Gallery; Trefoil Publications) 1987

Waterhouse, Ellis, *Painting in Britain 1530-1790*, new ed., New Haven, Conn. & London (Yale University Press) 1994

Werner, Marcia, *Pre-Raphaelite Painting and Nineteenth-Century Realism*, Cambridge (Cambridge University Press) 2005

Wilcox, Tim, exh. cat., *The Pursuit of the Real*, Manchester (City Art Galleries), 1990

Wilcox, Scott, and Newall, Chrisopher, exh. cat. *Victorian Landscape Watercolours*, New Haven, Conn. (Yale Center for British Art), Cleveland (Museum of Art) & Birmingham (Museums & Art Gallery) 1992-93; New York (Hudson Hills Press) 1992

Wilton, Andrew, and Anne Lyles, exh. cat. *The Great Age of British Watercolours 1750-1880*, London (Royal Academy of Arts) & Washington (National Gallery of Art); Munich (Prestel) 1993

Wilton, Andrew, and Robert Upstone, (eds.), exh. cat. *The Age of Rossetti, Burne-Jones and Watts: Symbolism in Britain, 1860-1910*, London (Tate Gallery), Munich (Haus der Kunst) & Amsterdam (Van Gogh Museum) 1997-98; London (Tate Gallery Publishing) 1997

Yorke, Malcolm, *The Spirit of Place: Nine Neo-Romantic Artists and Their Times*, London & New York (Tauris Parke) 2000

MONOGRAPHS

Francis Bacon

Alley, Ronald, *Francis Bacon: Catalogue raisonné*, intro. John Rothenstein, London (Thames and Hudson) 1964

Sylvester, David, *Interviews with Francis Bacon*, London (Thames and Hudson) 1975

Russell, John, *Francis Bacon*, rev. ed., London (Thames and Hudson) 1993

Martin, Hammer, *Bacon and Sutherland*, New Haven, Conn. & London (Yale University Press, for the Paul Mellon Centre for Studies in British Art) 2005

Rose, Andrea, Richard Calvocoressi, Martin Hammer and Philip Long, exh. cat. *Francis Bacon: Portraits and Heads*, Edinburgh (National Galleries of Scotland) & Hamburg (Hamburger Kunsthalle) 2005-6

Aubrey Beardsley

Reade, Brian, *Aubrey Beardsley*, rev. ed., Woodbridge (Antique Collectors' Club), 1987

Stephen, Calloway, *Aubrey Beardsley*, London (V&A Publications) 1998

William Blake

Gilchrist, Alexander, *Life of William Blake*, London (Dent) 1945

Bindman, David, *Blake as an Artist*, Oxford (Phaidon) 1977

Bindman, David, *William Blake: The Complete Illuminated Books*, London (Thames and Hudson) 2000

Bindman, David, *William Blake: The Divine Comedy*, Paris (Bibliothèque de L'Image) 2000

Hamlyn, Robin, and Michael Phillips (eds.), exh. cat. *William Blake*, London (Tate Britain) & New York (Metropolitan Museum of Art) 2000-1; London (Tate Publishing) 2000

DAVID BOMBERG

Richard, Cork, *David Bomberg*, New Haven, Conn. & London (Yale University Press) 1987

BILL BRANDT

Brandt, Bill, *Shadow of Light: A Collection of Photographs from 1931 to the Present*, intro. Cyril Connolly, notes Marjorie Beckett, London (Bodley Head) 1966

Haworth-Booth, Mark, and David Mellor, exh. cat. *Bill Brandt: Behind the Camera: Photographs 1928-1983*, Philadelphia (Museum of Art); New York (Aperture) & Oxford (Phaidon) 1985

FORD MADOX BROWN

Surtees, Virginia (ed.), *The Diary of Ford Madox Brown*, New Haven, Conn. & London (Yale University Press, for the Paul Mellon Centre for Studies in British Art) 1981

Bendiner, Kenneth, *The Art of Ford Madox Brown*, University Park, Pa. (Pennsylvania State University Press) 1998

EDWARD BURNE-JONES

Fitzgerald, Penelope, *Edward Burne-Jones: A Biography*, London (Michael Joseph) 1975

Wildman, Stephen, and John Christian (eds.), exh. cat. *Edward Burne-Jones: Victorian Artist-Dreamer*, New York (Metropolitan Museum of Art) , Birmingham (Museums & Art Gallery) & Paris (Musée d'Orsay) 1998-99

JULIA MARGARET CAMERON

Cox, Julian, and Colin Ford, *Julia Margaret Cameron. The Complete Photographs*, London (Thames and Hudson) 2003

WILLIAM COLDSTREAM

Laughton, Bruce, *William Coldstream*, New Haven, Conn. & London (Yale University Press, for the Paul Mellon Centre for Studies in British Art) 2004

JOHN CONSTABLE

Leslie, Charles Robert, *Memoirs of the Life of John Constable, Composed Chiefly of his Letters* [1843/45], ed. Jonathan Mayne, London (Phaidon) 1951

Parris, Leslie, and Ian Fleming-Williams, exh. cat. *Constable*, London (Tate Gallery) 1991

Lyles, Anne (ed.), exh. cat. *Constable: The Great Landscapes*, London (Tate Britain), Washington (National Gallery of Art) & San Marino, Calif. (Huntington Art Gallery) 2006-7; London (Tate Publishing) 2006

Morris, Edward (ed.), exh. cat. *Constable's Clouds*, Liverpool (Walker Art Gallery) & Edinburgh (National Gallery of Scotland) 2000

ALEXANDER AND JOHN ROBERT COZENS

Sloan, Kim, exh. cat. *Alexander and John Robert Cozens: The Poetry of Landscape*, London (Victoria and Albert Museum) & Toronto (Art Gallery of Ontario) 1986-87; New Haven, Conn. & London (Yale University Press) 1986

RICHARD DADD

Allderidge, Patricia, exh. cat. *The Late Richard Dadd*, London (Tate Publishing) 1974

ARTHUR DEVIS

D'Oench, Ellen, exh. cat. *The Conversation Piece: Arthur Devis and his Contemporaries*, New Haven, Conn. (Yale Center for British Art) 1980

JACOB EPSTEIN

Epstein, Jacob, *Epstein: An Autobiography*, 2nd ed., intro. Richard Buckle, London (Vista Books) 1963

Silber, Evelyn, and Terry Friedman (eds.), exh. cat. *Jacob Epstein: Sculpture and Drawings*, Leeds (Henry Moore Centre for the Study of Sculpture, City Art Galleries) & London (Whitechapel Art Gallery) 1987

ROGER FENTON

Baldwin, Gordon , Malcolm Daniel and Sarah Greenough, exh. cat. *All the Mighty World: The Photographs of Roger Fenton*, Washington (National Gallery of Art), Los Angeles (J. Paul Getty Museum), New York (Metropolitan Museum of Art) & London (Tate Britain) 2004-6

HENRY FUSELI

Mason, Eudo C. (ed.), *The Mind of Henry Fuseli: Selections from his Writings*, London (Routledge and Paul) 1951

Becker, Christoph (ed.), exh. cat. *Johann Heinrich Füssli: Das Verlorene Paradies*, Stuttgart (Staatsgalerie; Gerd Hatje) 1997

Lentzsch, Franziska (ed.), exh. cat. *Fuseli: The Wild Swiss*, Zurich (Kunsthaus; Scheidegger & Spiess) 2005-6

THOMAS GAINSBOROUGH

Rosenthal, Michael, *The Art of Thomas Gainsborough: 'A Little Business for the Eye'*, New Haven, Conn. & London (Yale University Press, for the Paul Mellon Centre for Studies in British Art) 1999

Rosenthal, Michael, and Martin Myrone (eds.), exh. cat. *Gainsborough*, London (Tate) 2002

JAMES GILLRAY

Godfrey, Richard T., *James Gillray: The Art of Caricature*, London (Tate Publishing) 2001

THOMAS GIRTIN

Smith, Greg (ed.), exh. cat. *Thomas Girtin: The Art of Watercolour*, texts by Peter Bower, Anne Lyles and Susan M. Morris, London (Tate Britain) 2002

DAVID OCTAVIUS HILL

Stevenson, Sara, *The Personal Art of David Octavius Hill*, New Haven, Conn. & London (Yale University Press, for the Paul Mellon Centre for Studies in British Art) 2002

DAVID HOCKNEY

Tuchman, Maurice, and Stephanie Barron (eds.), exh. cat. *David Hockney: A Retrospective*, Los Angeles (County Museum of Art), New York (Metropolitan Museum of Art) & London (Tate Gallery) 1988-89; Los Angeles (County Museum of Art) & London (Thames and Hudson) 1988

WILLIAM HOGARTH

Bindman, David, *Hogarth*, London (Thames and Hudson) 1981

Hallett, Mark, and Christine Riding (eds.), exh. cat. *Hogarth*, Paris (Musée du Louvre), London (Tate Britain) & Madrid (La Caixa) 2006-7; London (Tate Publishing) 2006

ALFRED WILLIAM HUNT

Newall, Christopher (ed.), exh. cat. *The Poetry of Truth: Alfred William Hunt and the Art of Landscape*, New Haven, Conn. (Yale Center for British Art) & Oxford (Ashmolean Museum) 2004-5

WILLIAM HOLMAN HUNT

Bronkhurst, Judith, *William Holman Hunt: A Catalogue Raisonné*, 2 vols., New Haven, Conn. & London (Yale University Press, for the Paul Mellon Centre for Studies in British Art) 2006

Jacobi, Carol, *William Holman Hunt: Painter, Painting, Paint*, Manchester & New York (Manchester University Press) 2006

GWEN JOHN AND AUGUSTUS JOHN

Fraser Jenkins, David, and Chris Stephens (eds.), exh. cat. *Gwen John and Augustus John*, London (Tate Britain) & Cardiff (National Museum & Gallery) 2004-5

THOMAS JONES

Gowing, Lawrence, *The Originality of Thomas Jones*, London (Thames and Hudson) 1985

Sumner, Ann, and Greg Smith (eds.), exh. cat. *Thomas Jones (1742-1803): An Artist Rediscovered*, Cardiff (National Museum & Gallery), Manchester (Whitworth Art Gallery) & London (National Gallery) 2003-4; New Haven, Conn. & London (Yale University Press) 2003

EDWARD LEAR

Noakes, Vivian (ed.), exh. cat. *Edward Lear 1812-1888*, London (Royal Academy of Arts; Weidenfeld and Nicolson) 1985

PERCY WYNDHAM LEWIS

Edwards, Paul, *Wyndham Lewis: Painter and Writer*, New Haven, Conn. & London (Yale University Press, for the Paul Mellon Centre for Studies in British Art) 2000

Laurence Stephen Lowry

Howard, Michael, *Lowry: A Visionary Artist*, Salford Quays (Lowry Press) 2000

John Martin

Feaver, William, *The Art of John Martin*, Oxford (Clarendon Press) 1975

Henry Mayhew

Mayhew, Henry, *London Labour and the London Poor: Selections made and introduced by Victor Neuburg*, Harmondsworth (Penguin) 1985

John Everett Millais

Barlow, Paul, *Time Present and Time Past: The Art of John Everett Millais*, Aldershot & Burlington, Vt. (Ashgate) 2005

Rosenfeld, Jason, and Alison Smith, exh. cat. *Millais*, London (Tate Gallery) 2007

Henry Moore

Sylvester, David, exh. cat. *Henry Moore*, London (Tate Gallery; Arts Council of Great Britain) 1968

Mitchinson, David, and Roger Tolson, exh. cat. *Henry Moore: War and Utility*, London (Imperial War Museum) 2006-7

William Morris

Thompson, E.P., *William Morris: Romantic to Revolutionary*, London (Merlin Press) 1977

Banham, Joanna, and Jennifer Harris (eds.), exh. cat. *William Morris and the Middle Ages*, Manchester (Whitworth Art Gallery; Manchester University Press) 1984

Parry, Linda (ed.), exh. cat. *William Morris, 1834-1896*, London (Victoria and Albert Museum) 1996

Paul Nash

Nash, Paul, *Outline: An Autobiography and Other Writings*, preface by Herbert Read, London (Faber & Faber) 1949

Eates, Margot, *Paul Nash: The Master of the Image 1889-1946*, London (John Murray) 1973

Causey, Andrew, *Paul Nash*, Oxford (Clarendon Press) 1980

Montagu, Jemima (ed.), exh. cat. *Paul Nash: Modern Artist, Ancient Landscape*, Liverpool (Tate Liverpool); London (Tate Publishing) 2003

Ben Nicholson

Lynton, Norbert, *Ben Nicholson*, London (Phaidon) 1993

William Nicholson

Campbell, Colin, Merlin James, Patricia Reed and Sanford Schwartz, exh. cat. *The Art of William Nicholson*, London (Royal Academy of Arts) 2004-5

Samuel Palmer

Grigson, Geoffrey, *Samuel Palmer's Valley of Vision*, London (Phoenix House) 1960

Vaughan, William, Elizabeth E. Barker and Colin Harrison (eds.), exh. cat. *Samuel Palmer 1805-1881: Vision and Landscape*, London (British Museum) & New York (Metropolitan Museum of Art) 2005-6; London (Lund Humphries) 2005

Dante Gabriel Rossetti

Marsh, Jan, *Dante Gabriel Rossetti, Painter and Poet*, London (Weidenfeld and Nicolson) 1999

Treuherz, Julian, Elizabeth Prettejohn and Edwin Becker, exh. cat. *Dante Gabriel Rossetti*, Liverpool (Walker Art Gallery) & Amsterdam (Van Gogh Museum) 2003-4; Zwolle (Waanders) & London (Thames and Hudson) 2003

Thomas Rowlandson

Hayes, John, *Rowlandson: Watercolours and Drawings*, London (Phaidon) 1972

John Ruskin

Hilton, Tim, *John Ruskin*, New Haven, Conn. & London (Yale University Press) 2002

Walter Sickert

Robins, Anna Greutzner, (ed.), *Walter Sickert: The Complete Writings on Art*, Oxford (Oxford University Press) 2000

Baron, Wendy, *Sickert Paintings & Drawings*, New Haven, Conn. & London (Yale University Press, for the Paul Mellon Centre for Studies in British Art) 2006

Stanley Spencer

Bell, Keith, *Stanley Spencer: A Complete Catalogue of the Paintings*, London (Phaidon, with Christie's and the Henry Moore Foundation) 1992

Glew, Adrian (ed.), *Stanley Spencer: Letters and Writings*, London (Tate Publishing) 2001

Hyman, Timothy, and Patrick Wright, exh. cat. *Stanley Spencer*, London (Tate Britain), Toronto (Art Gallery of Ontario) & Belfast (Ulster Museum) 2001

George Stubbs

Egerton, Judy, exh. cat. *George Stubbs, 1724-1806*, London (Tate Gallery) & New Haven, Conn. (Yale Center for British Art) 1984-85

Warner, Malcolm, and Robin Blake, exh. cat. *Stubbs and the Horse*, Fort Worth (Kimbell Art Museum), Baltimore (Walters Art Museum) & London (National Gallery) 2004-5; New Haven, Conn. & London (Yale University Press) 2004

William Henry Fox Talbot

Hedtmann, Sophie, and Philippe Poncet, *William Henry Fox Talbot*, Paris (Les Editions de l'Amateur) 2003

John Tenniel

Morris, Frankie, *Artist of Wonderland: The Life, Political Cartoons, and Illustrations of Tenniel*, Cambridge (Lutterworth Press) 2005

Joseph Mallord William Turner

Gage, John, *J.M.W. Turner. 'A Wonderful Range of Mind'*, New Haven, Conn. & London (Yale University Press) 1987

Wilton, Andrew, *Turner in his Time*, London (Thames and Hudson) 1987

Shanes, Eric (ed.), exh. cat. *Turner: The Great Watercolours*, London (Royal Academy of Arts) 2000-1

James McNeill Whistler

Dorment, Richard, and Margaret F. MacDonald (eds.), exh. cat. *James McNeill Whistler*, London (Tate Gallery), Paris (Musée d'Orsay) & Washington (National Gallery of Art) 1994-95

David Wilkie

Tromans, Nicholas, exh. cat. *David Wilkie: Painter of Everyday Life*, London (Dulwich Picture Gallery) 2002

Richard Wilson

Solkin, David H., exh. cat. *Richard Wilson: The Landscape of Reaction*, London (Tate Gallery) 1982-83

Joseph Wright of Derby

Egerton, Judy, exh. cat. *Wright of Derby*, London (Tate Gallery), Paris (Grand Palais) & New York (Metropolitan Museum of Art) 1990

LENDING INSTITUTIONS / PRIVATE COLLECTIONS / SPECIAL THANKS

LENDING INSTITUTIONS

Aberdeen Art Gallery & Museums Collections: 201, 204, 208, 295

Aberystwyth, National Library of Wales: 302

Amsterdam, Stedelijk Museum: 299

Bath, Holburne Museum (on loan from a private collection): 160

Bedburg Hau, Stiftung Museum Schloss Moyland: 32

Bedford, Cecil Higgins Art Gallery: 100, 192

Belfast, Ulster Museum: 48, 109, 296

Birkenhead, Williamson Art Gallery and Museum: 197

Birmingham, Barber Institute of Fine Arts, University of Birmingham: 148

Birmingham Museum & Art Gallery: 22, 142, 196, 245, 246, 262, 292

Bradford, National Media Museum: 186, 187, 272, 273

Bradford, Royal Photographic Society at the National Media Museum: 143, 188

Brighton, Royal Pavilion, Libraries and Museum: 68, 211

Brussels, Koninklijke Sterrenwacht van België: 171(b)

Cambridge, Fitzwilliam Museum: 23, 181, 261

Cambridge, Fitzwilliam Museum (on loan from the Keynes Family Trust): 244

Cambridge, Fitzwilliam Museum (on loan from a private collection): 285

Cambridge, Kettle's Yard, University of Cambridge: 304

Cardiff, Amgueddfa Cymru - National Museum Wales: 121, 195, 265, 303

Carlisle,Tullie House Museum & Art Gallery: 207

Cookham, Stanley Spencer Gallery: 282

Derby Museums and Art Gallery: 6

Derby Museums and Art Gallery (on loan from a private collection): 7

Edinburgh, City of Edinburgh Museums and Galleries: 67

Edinburgh, National Gallery of Scotland: 1, 15, 125

Edinburgh, Scottish National Gallery of Modern Art: 78, 213, 214, 301

Edinburgh, Scottish National Portrait Gallery: 258

Edinburgh, Scottish National Photography Collection, National Galleries of Scotland: 16, 17

Ghent, Museum voor Schone Kunsten: 59, 75

Ghent, Stedelijk Museum voor Actuele Kunst: 110, 309

The Hague, Gemeentemuseum (on long term loan from the Museum Boijmans Van Beuningen, Rotterdam): 90

Hamburg, Departmentbibliothek Physik, Universität Hamburg / MIN-Fakultät: 170

Ipswich Borough Council Museums and Galleries: 147, 153, 154

Kendal, Abbot Hall Art Gallery: 189

Leeds Museums & Galleries (City Art Gallery): 88, 200, 206

Leicester Arts and Museums Service: 101

Leuven, K. U. Leuven, Centrale Bibliotheek: 18

Lille, Palais des Beaux-Arts: 155

Liverpool, National Museums Liverpool, The Lady Lever Art Gallery: 264

Liverpool, National Museums Liverpool, Walker Art Gallery: 2, 64, 114, 198

London, Arts Council Collection, South Bank Centre: 95, 216, 218

London, Ben Uri Gallery, The London Jewish Museum of Art: 77

London, British Council: 89, 97, 212, 307

London, British Library: 4, 274

London, British Museum: 46, 117, 118, 168, 182, 230, 251, 252, 255, 260, 269, 291

London, The Samuel Courtauld Trust, Courtauld Institute of Art Gallery: 71

London, Guildhall Art Gallery, City of London: 19, 193

London, Imperial War Museum: 72, 73, 74, 98, 99, 294

London, Museum of London: 12

London, National Portrait Gallery: 85, 86, 228

London, The National Trust (Arlington Court, The Chichester Collection): 247

London, Palestine Exploration Fund: 144

London, Royal Academy of Arts: 163, 164, 165, 175, 184

London, Royal College of Art Collection: 111

London, Royal Society of Arts: 229

London, Science Museum: 169

London, Tate: 3, 10, 11, 20, 63, 76, 87, 120, 123, 130, 131, 149, 151, 152, 157, 162, 166, 173, 178, 179, 194, 257, 259, 266, 283, 288

London, UCL Art Collections, University College London: 53, 286

London, Victoria and Albert Museum: 25, 26, 27, 28, 29, 30, 33, 34, 35, 41, 56, 58, 60, 82, 83, 84, 91, 92, 93, 96, 124, 140, 145, 146, 156, 159, 161, 176, 177, 183, 185, 190, 243, 249, 250, 253, 254, 267, 270, 271, 275, 284, 305, 306

London, William Morris Gallery: 276, 277

Manchester Art Gallery: 21

Manchester, Whitworth Art Gallery, University of Manchester: 126, 129, 136, 138, 167, 172

Much Hadham, The Henry Moore Foundation: 221, 222

New Haven, Yale Center for British Art, Paul Mellon Collection: 5, 8, 14, 37, 50, 51, 52, 119, 122, 134, 135, 171(a) , 225, 227, 231, 232, 233, 234, 235, 236, 237, 238, 239, 240, 241, 242, 256, 280

New York, New York Public Library: 47

Newcastle-upon-Tyne, Laing Art Gallery: 199, 219, 298

Norwich, Norfolk Museums and Archaeology Service: 132, 158

Nottingham City Museums & Galleries: 112, 287

Nottingham, University of Nottingham, Manuscripts and Special Collections: 116

Oldham, Gallery Oldham: 215, 268

Oxford, Ashmolean Museum: 24, 62, 174

Paris, Musée d'Orsay: 263

Paris, Museé du Louvre: 180

Preston, Harris Museum & Art Gallery: 141

Rotterdam , Museum Boijmans Van Beuningen, (on long term loan to the Gemeentemuseum, The Hague): 90

Salford, The LS Lowry Collection: 102, 103, 104

Southampton City Art Gallery: 65, 66, 80, 115, 278, 290

Southport, Atkinson Art Gallery: 70

Stuttgart, Staatsgalerie: 279

Sudbury, Gainsborough's House Society: 13

Swansea, Glynn Vivian Art Gallery: 202, 203, 205

York, National Railway Museum: 69

Zurich, Kunsthaus: 49, 226

PRIVATE COLLECTIONS

Leeds, The Earl and Countess of Harewood and the Trustees of the Harewood House Trust Ltd.: 61

London, Mr and Mrs David Dallas: 191

London, Andrew Edmunds: 36 (a-h), 38, 39, 40, 42, 43, 44, 54, 55

London, Mr and Mrs Thomas Gibson: 297

London, The Estate of Barbara Hepworth: 220

London, Leon Kossoff courtesy of LA Louver, Venice, California: 223

London, Lefevre Fine Art Ltd: 81

London, The Henry Moore Family collection: 308

London, Peter Simon Family Trust: 289

Newmarket, Jockey Club Estates Limited: 150

Orkney, The Robertson Collection: 139

Oxford, Richard Hamilton: 105, 106, 107, 108

and the private collectors who wish to remain anonymous

WITH SPECIAL THANKS TO:

Alan Cristea, London

The Fine Art Society, London

Richard Green, London

Lefevre Fine Art, London

ON THE AUTHORS

Tim Barringer is Paul Mellon Professor in the Department of the History of Art at Yale University, following appointments at the Universities of Birmingham and London and at the Victoria and Albert Museum. His books include *Reading the Pre-Raphaelites* (1998) and *Men at Work: Art and Labour in Victorian Britain* (2005). He was curator, with Andrew Wilton, of *American Sublime* (2002) and co-author of the catalogue, and has recently curated *Opulence and Anxiety: Landscape Paintings from the Royal Academy* (2007). He is co-editor of several volumes, most recently *Art and the British Empire* (2007).

David Bindman is Emeritus Professor of the History of Art at University College London. He has written on William Blake, William Hogarth, Louis-François Roubiliac, and on the English response to the French Revolution. In recent years he has been working on the representation of race. His latest book is *Ape to Apollo: Aesthetics and the Idea of Race, 1700-1800* (2002).

Stephen Calloway is Curator of Prints in the Word & Image Department of the Victoria and Albert Museum. He has made a particular study of the cultures of romanticism, decadence and dandyism. He has curated many exhibitions, including the *Aubrey Beardsley* centenary show (1998) and *Corners of Paradise: William Blake, Samuel Palmer and the Ancients* (2005) at the V&A, and *Rex Whistler: The Triumph of Fancy* at Brighton Museum and Art Gallery (2006). His books include *Twentieth Century Decoration*, *Baroque, Baroque: The Culture of Excess* and *Aubrey Beardsley*.

Andrew Dempsey was Assistant Director in charge of the Hayward Gallery, first with the Arts Council of Great Britain and then with the South Bank Centre, from 1975 to 1992. He has organized exhibitions for the British Council, *Stanley Spencer* (USA & Mexico 1997-98) and *Constable* (Paris 2002), and among other exhibitions he has curated are *Whistler and Sickert* (Madrid & Bilbao 1998) and *La mirada fuerte: pintura figurativa de Londres* (Mexico City 2000).

Mark Evans is Senior Curator of Paintings at the Victoria and Albert Museum. He previously worked as a curator at the National Museum of Wales and the Walker Art Gallery, Liverpool, and taught at the University of St Andrews. He has written extensively on painting from the Renaissance to the early twentieth century. His publications include *Impressions of Venice from Turner to Monet* (1992), *Princes as Patrons* (1998) and *The Painted World: From Illumination to Abstraction* (2005).

David Fraser Jenkins was a curator at Tate Britain and the National Museum of Wales. He has contributed to exhibitions, as curator or catalogue author, on Gwen and Augustus John, John Piper, John Singer Sargent, Stanley Spencer, Jacques Lipchitz and James Pryde. He is preparing an exhibition of Paul Nash and a monograph on John Piper.

John Gage is a Fellow of the British Academy, Visiting Research Fellow at the University of New South Wales, Sydney, and former Reader, Cambridge University. He is the author of *J.M.W. Turner: a Wonderful Range of Mind* (1987). He was curator/co-curator of *A Decade of English Naturalism* (Norwich & London 1969), *La Peinture Romantique Anglaise et les Pré-Raphaélites* (Paris 1972), *Turner 1775-1851* (London 1974), *Zwei Jahrhunderte der englischen Malerei* (Munich 1979), *Turner* (Paris 1983), *George Field and his Circle, from Romanticism to the Pre-Raphaelite Brotherhood* (Cambridge 1989), *Constable: Le Choix de Lucian Freud* (Paris 2002) and *Constable: Impressions of Land, Sea and Sky* (Canberra 2006).

Mark Haworth-Booth is Visiting Professor of Photography at University of the Arts London and Honorary Research Fellow at the Victoria and Albert Museum. He worked at the V&A from 1970 to 2004, serving as Senior Curator of Photographs 1977 to 2004. His books include *Photography: An Independent Art* (1997) and *The Art of Lee Miller* (2007).

Robert Hoozee is director of the Museum voor Schone Kunsten. In 1979, he published the first catalogue raisonné of Constable's paintings. He is a specialist on Belgian art of the 19th century, with publications and exhibitions on the themes of Belgian landscape painting, Flemish expressionism, George Minne and James Ensor. In 1997 he was co-curator (with Anne Pingeot of the Musée d'Orsay) of the exhibition 'Paris-Brussels/Brussels-Paris' at the Grand Palais, Paris, and in Ghent; in 2000 he curated the exhibition 'Brussel kruispunt van culturen' (Brussels, Crossroads of cultures) at the Palais des Beaux-Arts, Brussels; and in 2001 he was selector of the James Ensor exhibition at the Drawing Center, New York.

Timothy Hyman is a painter and writer on art. As well as eight solo shows in London, he has exhibited widely in Britain and internationally, and his work is in many public collections. He has published frequently in *The Times Literary Supplement*, *London Magazine*, and elsewhere. He has published monographs on *Bonnard* (1998) and *Sienese Painting* (2003). In 2001 he curated the Tate retrospective of *Stanley Spencer*.

Anne Lyles is a curator at Tate Britain specializing in late eighteenth- and early nineteenth-century landscape painting. She has researched the art of J.M.W. Turner and the British watercolour school, but now concentrates chiefly on the work of John Constable. She has helped curate and contributed to the catalogues of a number of exhibitions, including *The Great Age of British Watercolours 1750-1880* (London & Washington 1993), *British Watercolours from the Oppé Collection* (1997), *Romantic Landscape: the Norwich School of Painters* (2000), *Thomas Girtin: the Art of Watercolour* (2002), all at Tate, *Constable: le Choix de Lucian Freud* (Paris 2002) and *Constable: the Great Landscapes* (London, Washington & San Marino 2006-7).

Nicola Moorby currently works in the Curatorial Department at Tate Britain. She was previously the Collections Registrar for Prints and Drawings and managed Tate's two Print Rooms. She is a co-author of a forthcoming catalogue on the Camden Town Group and has also published on Walter Richard Sickert and J.M.W. Turner.

Christopher Newall is an independent writer and historian specializing in nineteenth-century British art. Among the exhibitions he has helped to organize have been *Leighton* (Royal Academy 1996) and *The Age of Rossetti, Burne-Jones & Watts* (Tate Gallery 1997). In 2004 he was the co-curator of *Pre-Raphaelite Vision: Truth to Nature* (Tate Britain 2004). His books include *Victorian Watercolours* (1987), *The Art of Lord Leighton* (1982) and *The Grosvenor Gallery Exhibitions* (1995).

Nic Peeters is an independent art historian. He has published extensively on the art of the Pre-Raphaelites and their followers. His main research interests are Victorian feminism and spiritualism and their impact on art. He is currently working on a PhD dissertation for the University of Brussels (VUB) about the witch images in late Victorian painting and the innovative influence on these of the artist Evelyn De Morgan.

David Peters Corbett is Professor of History of Art at the University of York, where he has also been involved in the Research School in British Art and the Centre for Modern Studies. He has written widely on British painting between 1848 and the 1930s and is currently working on American city and landscape art 1850-1913.

Martin Postle is Assistant Director for Academic Activities at the Paul Mellon Center for Studies in British Art. He was previously curator and Head of British Art to 1900 at Tate Britain, and adjunct Associate Professor of Art History at the University of Delaware. His exhibitions include *Joshua Reynolds: The Creation of Celebrity* (Tate Britain 1995), *The Art of the Garden* (Tate Britain 1994) and *The Artist's Model from Etty to Spencer* (London, York & Nottingham 1999). His publications include *Sir Joshua Reynolds: The Subject Pictures* (1995) and *Thomas Gainsborough* (2002).

Roger Tolson is Head of Art at the Imperial War Museum. Recent catalogue essays include 'Henry Moore and the Machinery of War' in *Henry Moore: War and Utility* (IWM 2006), 'A Common Cause' in *Shared Experience* (Australian War Memorial, Canberra, 2005) and the introduction to *Art of the Second World War* (IWM 2007), and he was co-curator of these exhibitions. He also wrote the introduction to the catalogue of the Imperial War Museum's oil paintings (London 2006).

CREDITS

Julian Treuherz is a freelance art historian and curator, and an expert on Victorian art. From 1989 until 2007 he was Keeper of Art Galleries at National Museums Liverpool, responsible for the Walker Art Gallery, the Lady Lever Art Gallery and Sudley House. Before that he was at Manchester City Art Gallery (1971-1988). He has curated many exhibitions, including *Hard Times: Social Realism in Victorian Art* (1987), *Alma-Tadema* (1997) and *Dante Gabriel Rossetti* (2003), and he is currently working on *Art in the Age of Steam* to be shown in Liverpool during European Capital of Culture year 2008. He is also writing a book on the art and architecture of Sicily.

Angus Trumble is Curator of Paintings and Sculpture at the Yale Center for British Art. He was previously Curator of European Art at the Art Gallery of South Australia, Adelaide. He curated the touring exhibition *Love and Death: Art in the Age of Queen Victoria* (2001-2), and he is the author of *A Brief History of the Smile* (2003).

Robert Upstone is Curator of Modern British Art at Tate Britain. He has published and broadcast widely on nineteenth- and twentieth-century art and culture. He is the author of *William Orpen: Politics, Sex and Death*, published to accompany the exhibition at the Imperial War Museum and the National Gallery of Ireland, Dublin. He is currently preparing a survey of the Camden Town Group, which will open at Tate Britain in 2008.

Ian Warrell is a curator at Tate Britain, specializing in eighteenth- and nineteenth-century British art. He is responsible for the Turner Collection and has curated numerous exhibitions, at Tate and elsewhere, about the artist, including those examining the connection with Claude Lorrain (Nancy 2002), as well as Turner's views of the River Loire (1997), the River Seine (1999), and Venice (2003). He is the curator of the first full exhibition survey of Turner's work in the United States (National Gallery of Art, Washington, and touring, 2007-8). He has also worked on Victorian artists, particularly Ruskin and the Pre-Raphaelites, and aspects of nineteenth-century British photography.

Photographic credits for catalogued works:

Thanks are due to all those individuals and institutions who provided photographic material for the catalogue, or gave permission for its use. Copyright in the photograph and permission to reproduce is as given in the lender credit.

References below are to catalogue numbers, with figure illustrations denoted by page number (p.).

Additional credits:

Bill Brandt Archive Ltd: 82, 83, 84, 96, 305, 306, p.132

Bridgeman Art Library, London: Millais (19), Gertler (65), John (66), Burra (79), Spencer (88), Wright of Derby (115), Holman Hunt (141), Dyce (193), Nicholson (206), Bomberg (216), Grimshaw (200), Burne-Jones (278), Spencer (282), Wyndham Lewis (290), Nash (294), p.31

British Museum, London: Blake (248, a-f)

Christies Images: Wyndham Lewis (289)

Fine Art Society: Sutherland (293)

Marcus Leith: Wilson (112), Spencer (210), Auerbach (224), Epstein (300)

Duncan McNeill: Coldstream (94)

National Trust Photo Library/Derrick E Witty: Blake (247)

Réunion des Musées Nationaux, Paris/Hervé Lewandowski: Constable (155), Turner (180)

Réunion des Musées Nationaux, Paris/Gérard Blot: Holman Hunt (263)

Science and Society Picture Library: Gore (69), Russell (169), Cameron (272, 273), Fenton (143, 145, 188), Fox Talbot (186, 187)

Copyright credits for catalogued works and figure illustrations:

INDEX – *Numbers between square brackets refer to the catalogue entries and illustrations.*